**Amateur Fencing Association**
**West Midlands Region**

# British Age Group Championships

----------------------------------

## Winner of the
## Under 16 Boys Foil
### 17th Oct 1993

*The Swordsman's shop*
**GLADIATORS**
101, High Street, Evesham, Worcestershire, WR11 4DN
Tel: 0386 421296   Fax: 0386 421298

# MODERN BRITISH FENCING
1964–1981

Charles de Beaumont: an oil portrait by A. D. Craig (1958).

# MODERN BRITISH FENCING

*A history of the
Amateur Fencing Association*

# 1964–1981

EDMUND GRAY

A Memorial Volume to
Charles de Beaumont
including a short biography
by Richard Cohen

Amateur Fencing Association: London

First published by the
Amateur Fencing Association
The de Beaumont Centre
83 Perham Road, London W14
1984
ISBN 0 9509216 0 2
Biography © Richard Cohen 1984
Remainder of the text copyright © Edmund Gray 1984

Designed by Ian McLeish

Photoset in Great Britain by
Rowland Phototypesetting Limited
Bury St Edmunds, Suffolk
Printed in Great Britain by
The Thetford Press Ltd
Thetford, Norfolk

# Contents

| | |
|---|---|
| Foreword *Mary Glen Haig, C.B.E., President of AFA* | 7 |
| Preface | 10 |
| Charles-Louis de Beaumont | 13 |
|     I  The family background | 15 |
|     II  Cambridge and after | 23 |
|     III  The Olympic athlete | 31 |
|     IV  The dangerous thirties | 43 |
|     V  The ring-master | 53 |
|     VI  The curious case of the Chippendale commode | 70 |
| The AFA – Growth and change, 1964–81 | 76 |
| Sections and associated bodies | 129 |
| Competitions chronicle | 173 |
| AFA officers, honours and statistics | 474 |
| Competition results | 481 |
|   Outstanding international results | 481 |
|   Headquarters events: Men's Foil | 490 |
|                           Ladies' Foil | 498 |
|                           Epee | 509 |
|                           Sabre | 518 |
|   University Championships | 525 |
|   Public Schools Championships | 527 |
|   Inter-Services Championships | 530 |
|   Scottish Championships | 534 |
|   Provincial tournaments | 536 |
|   Granville Cup | 542 |
|   London v. Rest of Britain | 543 |
|   Winton Cup | 544 |
|   Quadrangular Match | 544 |
|   Commonwealth Games and Championships | 545 |
|   World and Olympic Championships | 547 |
|   World Youth Championships | 556 |
| Indexes | 559 |

# Foreword

Mary Glen Haig, *President of the Amateur Fencing Association*

The three volumes produced by Charles de Beaumont cover the period up to and including the 1964 Olympic Games. The fourth volume should have been produced following the 1972 Olympic Games. His books not only give the history of the AFA and the development of fencing in this country, but also provide valuable reference to fencing achievements. Charles was, I know, collecting material for his fourth volume and it is a source of sorrow that his notes have never been found either in his office in Brompton Road or at his home. There are many fencers who are aware of the little black book in which he noted the results of all competitions. In his day, with no joint weapon committee (until the early sixties) and no qualification system for selection to international teams, many a selection could not have taken place without the black book. This present volume, which also gives competition results, would not have been possible but for the diligence of Margaret Somerville, who has undertaken the research in this field.

Charles would, I know, have approved and appreciated the AFA decision to produce this book. For without him modern British fencing would not exist today. As a young man not long down from Cambridge he was anxious to serve on the AFA Committee and in 1930 joined it as an elected member at the age of 28. In 1936 he became Honorary Secretary of the AFA. But it was from 1946 until he died in 1972 that he really was 'Mr Fencing'. Before the war, the numbers involved in fencing were so small that Ted Morten, who as Secretary to the Committee assisted Charles with AFA clerical work, could out of his head give the address of any member you wished to name. There were only three centres which had overseas masters: Birmingham, Edinburgh (where the Crosniers taught) and London – where there were such clubs as Bertrand's, Tassart-Parkins', Paul's, Behmber's and Gauthier at the London Fencing Club. After the war a number of these did not re-open, finding their old masters retired. It was at this point that Charles produced his National Training Scheme and brought young Roger Crosnier over to England to get it off the ground. The country had been divided up into thirteen regions by the Central Council of Physical Recreation, and Charles, who served on the Executive Committee of this body, followed their demarcation lines when he produced the AFA Sections. The Central Council's organisers round the country were responsible for setting up agencies locally for the development of fencing and many of the CCPR Technical Officers were among the first Leaders produced by the National Training Scheme. Charles was also responsible for persuading the Royal Marines to release Sgt R. G. J. Anderson, so that he could travel around the country with Roger Crosnier to be trained not only for his personal performance but also to become a first class coach at all three weapons. Eventually, as most fencers know, this turned out very fortunately for the AFA. When Roger, for family reasons, decided to return to France, Bob Anderson was available to take Crosnier's place. Very many fencing masters and coaches now teaching have gained their initial expertise from this training scheme. I always understood that Roger Crosnier regarded the scheme solely as a first step, to be followed by a scheme for training masters; that this did not happen may be due to the re-forming of the British Academy. Charles's influence was again to be seen in this connection, encouraging and assisting and attending meetings in his usual dynamic fashion. When one works closely with someone like Charles, there are bound to be many ups and downs, but on looking back over these years, one of the highlights was for us both the BAF annual general meeting, delightfully presided over either by Professor Leon Bertrand or Professor Leon Paul. If they could not compare with the present day on correct procedure, they more than made up in the delightful and amusing incidents which took place.

From the time that Charles became involved with fencing administration he was living in London and had his own business as an antique dealer, which it was possible for him to combine with his work for fencing. He travelled about the country in search of antiques and at the same time was able to visit and meet those helping to develop fencing in the Sections. Someone with a professional commitment could not have given the time to undertake this development work.

Back in 1933 he had founded the All England Club, the qualification for membership being to have fenced for Great Britain. He organised many pleasant social gatherings for this club, but its main contribution to fencing was in the field of public relations, taking the form of what came to be known as Charles's Circus, usually consisting of two fencers at each weapon. The props – still used – were some fine old court swords, epees and broad swords. Charles delivered a potted history of sword play. He spoke at the rate of 240 words a minute, and old hands never listened intently, but were attuned to certain words. Thus at the phrase 'under the dripping tree' the two ladies would prepare to demonstrate the stance. The Circuses would be called upon to perform in village halls, school class rooms, for mothers' unions, boy scouts – no request for Charles to talk or demonstrate fencing ever went unheeded.

He assisted in the development of fencing in what was then the British Empire, now the Commonwealth, as well as in this country. He not only helped with the development of the organising committee in New Zealand but

# Foreword

also in the setting up, at the 1950 Auckland Games, of the British Empire Fencing Federation, of which he was elected the first President, a position he held till his death. As AFA delegate to the FIE he kept the Commonwealth informed by sending reports on FIE Congresses and World Championships and by translating the French FIE competition rules. And on all trips abroad he would take time and trouble to visit fencers, wherever they lived. He also offered endless hospitality to fencers passing through London.

One last strand of Charles's manifold services to fencing deserves mention here. It was he, in 1946, who negotiated the move by the London Fencing Club (whose office was also that of the AFA) from Cleveland Row to the premises of Salle Bertrand off Hanover Square. (It was sad that this merger sounded the death knell of that old-established Salle.) When the lease of these premises in turn expired and a new home for the AFA and the LFC had to be found, Terry Beddard, one of Charles's greatest fencing friends, suggested Charles should consider approaching Queen's Club, and the fifty-year lease of the present de Beaumont Centre was negotiated. The LFC contributed part of the capital and the AFA share was provided by a large loan for which Charles stood as a guarantor. I well remember being concerned about what seemed then a vast debt and the problems of repayment for the AFA. Charles's reaction was that he had never been afraid of taking a chance.

Perhaps Charles did too much himself, but it is always easy to see other people's faults. His energy and enthusiasm are without question, and there can be no doubt that he did more for fencing than any one individual will ever be able to do again.

# Preface

This book is both a memorial to Charles de Beaumont and a sequel to his three earlier volumes of *Modern British Fencing*, which told the story of the Amateur Fencing Association up to 1964. The first section is a biography of the remarkable man himself. The rest of the book continues his coverage of the various aspects of the sport and its organisation. It is a volume of record, like its predecessors, but I have tried to make it a readable narrative as well. In particular, I have gone much further than the earlier volumes in giving descriptive accounts of competitions. Originally I intended these to be hardly more than an anthology of passages from reports in *The Sword*, but this proved unsatisfactory and the end result is more of a rounded survey. I must stress, however, that I am almost entirely dependent on the coverage in *The Sword* (and to some extent also *Fencing* and the Scottish *Newsletter*); I cannot claim to be entirely balanced or consistent. If the reader's own finest performance is ignored, this is almost certainly because it was never written up. My personal knowledge is inevitably limited, and getting assistance from other fencers is usually about as rewarding as searching for grub-screws in a flowerbed.

To help offset the extensions I have made in the coverage of this volume I have tried to reduce to a minimum the duplication inevitable in a work of this kind. In the Competitions Chronicle, for instance, I avoid repeating information provided in the lists of results at the back of the book unless I can significantly enlarge on it. So too, in the chapter on Sections and clubs, fencers are for the most part merely listed, since their achievements will be found elsewhere. I have also avoided a stultifying consistency; so, for instance, provincial events are sometimes treated as Combined Events and sometimes separately under the different weapons. (The Quadrangular and World Youth, Olympic, Commonwealth and World Championships are, however, invariably dealt with as Combined Events.) In all these cases, and whenever information cannot be found where it is expected, readers should use the index, for which I am indebted to Julian Tyson (who also helped with many of the drafts of the text). I should add that I am very aware of the unevenness of the coverage of clubs. For the consequent injustices I can only plead ignorance.

In its lists of competition results, this volume, like its predecessors, covers not just the recent past but the whole course of modern British fencing. In this volume, however, they have been extended in three ways. A selection of provincial tournaments has been added; all six finalists are listed for the major

# Preface

headquarters events over the period since 1964, and a select list of international British results has been introduced. It seemed unbalanced to record every winner of the Public School Championship back to 1896, for instance, and yet not to list Olympic finalists and winners of major foreign tournaments. I hope I will be forgiven the necessarily arbitrary character of this list.

The responsibility for the final form of the lists of results and any remaining mistakes is mine, but the credit for almost all the laborious work involved must go to Miss Margaret Somerville, who was also prompt beyond compare.

A word on conventions adopted. Accents have been dispensed with for words which have become naturalised such as epee, fleche and even the place-name Duren, but retained where required for clarity (e.g. coupé). Captions to illustrations list the people shown from left to right. When finalists are listed they are given in the (descending) order in which they were placed.

One addendum to the first volume of Modern British Fencing should be noted here. Britain was represented at the European Championships of 1921 by E. Amphlett and R. A. Hay.

In acknowledging help, I would like to thank, first and foremost, Ian McLeish, who, although not a fencer, rashly and generously volunteered to undertake the design of the book and to see it through the press, 'for fun' as he said. His labours have been heroic. The design of the jacket I owe to my mother, Nicolete Gray.

Many other people helped in different ways. Section Secretaries and others round the country looked at drafts on their areas and in some cases most usefully produced wholly new texts: I am particularly grateful to Arthur Banks, Leslie Jones, Bob Southcombe, Leslie Veale, John Cotton and Graham Ayliffe. On the Scottish narrative Alex Rae, John Fleck, Neil L'Amie and Hugh Kernohan were especially prompt and helpful. Sandy Maggs deserves warm thanks for the financial table, however scrambled by me. Hilary Cawthorne, Jack Magill and Steve Fox kindly provided narratives for their own weapons covering the years 1978–80; I remain grateful even if they will not recognise the text that is printed. I can only mention a few of the people who were good enough to read drafts of different parts of this book or supply information: Mary Glen Haig, Joyce Pearce, Bob Anderson, Bobby Winton, Peter Hobson, Bill Hoskyns, Allan Jay, Ralph Cooperman, Clare and Nick Halsted, Mildred Durne, Janet Cooksey, Ian Spofforth, Graham Paul, Andrew Cornford, Joe Eden, John Pelling, Mary Hawksworth, Richard Oldcorn and Richard Cohen.

I can also only make a general acknowledgement to the authors of all the competition reports I have plundered. Many of these are unsigned and foremost among the others is the indefatigable Charles de Beaumont himself; but I should mention Richard Oldcorn, Peter Jacobs and Peter Hobson; also Mildred Durne, Nick Halsted, Teddy Bourne, Kristin Payne; Eve Davies, Vic Lagnado, Steve Boston, Malcolm Fare, Clare Halsted and Shiela Arup. For my notes on Salle Paul, Salle Boston and the Poly I am indebted to the club histories by Harry Cooke, Richard Cohen and Derek Evered respectively.

For photographs I owe thanks especially to Gabor Scott (who took those on pp. 117l, 367, 381, 437, 460), Peter Hobson (pp. 177, 314, 323, 326, 332), Rosemary Seligman (pp. 107, 121, 302, 339), Korin Evans (p. 143r), to my sister Cecilia Metternich for the frontispiece and to Dorrien Belson (p. 396), Ralph Evans (p. 356l), Derek Holt (p. 155), Nino Moscardini (p. 468), Raymond Paul (p. 309) and Mike Riggall (pp. 90, 446a); also to Roy Goodall who loaned six items from the archive of *Fencing*; also to the following who lent precious prints: Bob Turner, Steve Boston, Peter Jacobs, Ralph Johnson, Graham Mackay, Richard Cohen, Sue Wrigglesworth, Leslie Jones, Bill Hoskyns, Brian Hill, Teddy Bourne and John Pelling. Most of the photos, however, are drawn from *The Sword* archive and are of unknown authorship; for the use of these I hope copyright owners will accept this general acknowledgement, given that this is a non-commercial memorial volume prepared entirely by voluntary effort.

I would also like to thank those who typed the book from my tangled handwriting, especially Helen Widdess, Yvonne Strong (who did the greater part), and Caroline Wright (who did whole tracts out of pure kindness).

Finally, I must thank those who have been good enough to read the proofs, particularly Ralph Evans, but also Graham Watts, Hilary Cawthorne, Richard Cohen, Wendy Grant and Mark Slade (who also did much copy-editing).

ELG

## Biographer's note

I would like to thank the large number of people who over a number of years have given their time and their help to me in writing the memoir of Charles de Beaumont: his own family, particularly Robin and Marguerite de Beaumont; John Berry; the late 'Punch' Bertrand; Herr Willie Blumenthal; Cdr Frank Booth; Sir Robin Brook; Fr Francis Edward; Mrs Mary Glen Haig; Nick Halsted; Rex and Renée Henry; Peter Jacobs; the late Sir Oswald Mosley; Lady Norman; Gordon Pilbrow; and Mrs Pat Taylor.

For their valuable help in reading the script and pointing out its many errors I am very grateful to Edmund Gray; Emrys Lloyd; James Noel; Ion Trewin; and Bobby Winton.

Finally, I owe a particular debt of thanks to Mrs Sarah Barratt, who pointed out to me the important matter of cycling round Norfolk on a radish.

RAC

# Charles-Louis de Beaumont
*A short biography by Richard Cohen*

For almost forty years Charles de Beaumont was at the centre of British fencing. He came to embody the sport. Four times British epee Champion (on the fourth occasion when he was past fifty), he captained the British team from 1933 until his death in 1972. The British Olympic fencing team he captained from 1936 on, himself fencing in those Games, as well as in 1948, 1952 and 1956. In 1933 he missed the final of the epee individual of the European Championships by one hit, most probably as a result of a pre-arranged bout between two of his opponents. While he specialised as an epeeist, at sabre he was a regular finalist in the British Championships – indeed, he could boast a sabre team bronze medal from the European Championships, won in 1933 – while he also was a keen if infrequent foilist.

The major part of his involvement in fencing, however, was as an administrator. Secretary of the Amateur Fencing Association for twenty years, President from 1956 until his death, he only narrowly missed election as the first British President of the world governing body of fencing, the Fédération Internationale d'Escrime. No one in the history of fencing can have done so much in organising so many events as Charles de Beaumont, while he also translated into English the rules of the sport for use throughout the Commonwealth. He built the present headquarters of British fencing, the de Beaumont Centre in West Kensington, wrote or contributed to over twenty books on the sport, and was tireless in publicising and promoting fencing throughout most of his life.

Yet there was much besides fencing to take up his time. To dominate any sport or activity for such a long period, be it British fencing or British fretwork, inevitably involves the person concerned in any number of associated activities. So, for instance, it is no surprise to find that Charles was in 1964 Commandant of the entire British team at the Tokyo Olympics; later became Deputy Chairman of the British Olympic Association; was Deputy Chairman of the Council for England for the Commonwealth Games; and also was on the executive committee of the Central Council of Physical Recreation, forerunner of the Sports Council, most influential of all amateur representative bodies that represent British sport.

In his chosen career of selling antiques Charles ran a highly successful business for nearly fifty years. He was also elected President of the British

Antique Dealers Association, and then re-elected, most unusually, for a second term. Shortly before his death he was elected President of the World Antique Federation. He dealt in real estate, founded a wine company, wrote treatises on his family's history – which with some justice he believed could be traced back to the French crown. He was twice married, while his family background was full of character and incident. His social world ranged from the Hon. Christabel Russell – the wife of the famous 'Ampthill Case' – to Sir Oswald Mosley, himself an international fencer, whom Charles knew well and for whom he worked assiduously when Mosley's New Party was formed. Charles had so many interests in so many different areas that one wonders how he found the time for fencing at all! This memoir is naturally mainly concerned with Charles's life in so far as it affected fencing, but I have also attempted to say something of his other interests, as well as drawing on people's memories to portray his character.

Finally, a personal note. I met Charles – or at least, first saw him – when in the early 1960s he brought a group of leading fencing internationals down to my school in Somerset to introduce the sport to a crowd of star-struck schoolboys. This was one of Charles's famous 'circuses' – promotion exercises which he carried out throughout the length and breadth of the country. After that I met him often, first while I was at University, then later when I made the national team. I got to know him better after I had taken over *The Sword*, the national magazine for fencing, and from being a gruff, rather detached elder statesman, as he had at first appeared, he revealed himself in something of his true colours, not least in the many kindnesses he showed me and the interest he took in what I did.

While researching his life I came across a short motto inscribed in one of the books in Charles's library. For me it is a perfect clue to the man. It is a quotation from the main doorway of the chateau at Pellouaille, near Marignac in South West France, and is the family motto of a seventeenth-century de Beaumont. 'Il faut que le vouloir soit egal au pouvoir', it runs, 'One's will must be equal to one's powers'. In everything he did, Charles's was.

# I  The family background

One little known fact about Charles de Beaumont is that his surname for his first twelve years was Klein. His father, Leopold Martial Klein, although French on both sides, was one of those, like the Battenbergs (who became Mountbattens) who chose to change their name to a less Teutonic one amid the anti-German fervour just before the outbreak of the first World War. On Leopold's mother's side – the de Beaumonts – the family was one of the most illustrious in France, and dates back to one Humbert I, who died about 1050; another early de Beaumont appears, red-bearded, on the Bayeux tapestry. Well into the nineteenth century the family possessed the impressive Chateau de Gibeau, the large family home built during the Hundred Years War at Marignac, near Pons in the south-west of France. Leopold's great-grandfather Leon was made Mayor of Marignac in 1809. The last Comte died as recently as 1861, at the family's later home at Saintes.

It was there that the family was living when on 19 July 1870 France declared war on Prussia. Leopold Klein was 21, of good family and in good health – ideal material for the army. However, he had already been bought out of the service by his parents and had qualified as a doctor. Yet within a few days he chose to enlist as an 'engagé volontaire' in the French cavalry, and was given the rank of lieutenant. He was following an honourable family tradition; on his father's side a Klein relative had served as one of Napoleon's marshals.

The Franco-Prussian war proved particularly bitter. The French suffered a resounding defeat, and Leopold Klein was to recall eating rats for food when, towards the war's end, Paris was besieged and starving. On the battlefield he acquitted himself well, on one occasion saving the French flag, and for his bravery being awarded the Medaille Militaire, although he never chose to wear it since it was a Republican honour and he was a monarchist. On another occasion, following the battle of Buzainville, he was escorting a gun carriage over a bridge when his horse shied, crushing his leg against the moving vehicle. That scar he was to bear for life. Eventually he escaped from the Paris siege and fled to his parents at Cherbourg, their home during the war. He arrived critically ill with pneumonia, and was thought to be dying.

His mother, Marie-Antoinette Klein, a highly religious woman, made him promise that, should he recover, he would become a priest. His father was a confirmed freethinker, who hated the idea of his son disappearing into the Church, but after Leopold had made his recovery it was his mother who won the day. Leopold was happy enough with the decision, but he had no wish to become a simple country parish priest, and chose instead to study for the Jesuits, the most intellectually rigorous of all religious orders, and the one to which his own academic leanings most inclined him. During his early medical training, following his initial studies in Paris, he had been sent to England for further medical experience; and it was decided that he should be sent across the Channel again, to Stonyhurst College outside Preston, to study for his Doctor's degree in philosophy and divinity. Admitted to the Society of Jesus on 30 May 1878, he stayed at Stonyhurst until 1881, before being sent to St Beuno's, near Tremeirchion in North Wales, to study theology. It was the same college at which the poet, Gerard Manley Hopkins, was also studying.

Four years later Leopold was sent to the Jesuit Province in Dublin. It was here that he came into contact with the O'Hagans, one of the most powerful Catholic families in Britain. Lord O'Hagan had for many years been a leading QC at the Dublin bar, from 1860 to 1861 had been Solicitor General for Ireland, and was from 1861 to 1865 the Irish Attorney General. For three years he was MP for Tralee before being appointed Lord Chancellor of Ireland by Gladstone, of whom he was a friend and great admirer until he broke with him over Irish Home Rule. At the same time as his appointment he was raised to the peerage, as Baron O'Hagan of Tullahogue, Co. Tyrone, and in fact served two terms as Chancellor, from 1868 to 1874, and from 1880 to 1882. He and his wife had two sons and two daughters, the younger daughter, Mary Caroline, marrying General Sir Charles Carmichael Munro, later to be one of those commanding the British Army at Gallipoli.

The O'Hagan family were thus socially most influential. Leopold had already during his studies won for himself a reputation as a scholar, and Lord O'Hagan and his friend Lord Emly decided to enlist his services in the task of organizing and equipping the biology and botany sections of the Royal University of Ireland, sited in Dublin, which both men were anxious to see established, and indeed became successive Vice-Chancellors after its establishment in 1880. In 1885 Leopold was appointed Professor of Physiology at the University.

Very quickly – certainly by the end of 1895 – Leopold became a regular visitor at the various O'Hagan homes: at Hereford House in Park Street, at their thirteenth-century family seat, Towneley, near Burnley, and at their Irish home in Rutland Square, Dublin. It was at Towneley that he first met Kathleen O'Hagan, the elder daughter, who had been born in 1876. In her memoirs she records that it was not long before the earnest French Jesuit took an interest in her work, and by 1890 he had got to know her well. It soon became obvious that, despite the great disparity in their ages (at the time of their marriage he was 47, she 20), his interest in her was not merely that of teacher to pupil. As for her, almost from their first meeting she admired his

# The family background

intelligence, and admiration soon blossomed into devotion. Her memoirs record:

> As a child he showed exceptional intellectual promise and he was given a very comprehensive education, both classical and scientific. I might describe his knowledge as encyclopaedic, and to the end of his life he was a student in many fields; Latin, Greek and Hebrew held no secrets for him. He was as familiar with Italian and English as he was with his own French language. He was an ardent student of Dante. He was a doctor of science and a doctor of medicine, a biologist, botanist, anthropologist, geologist. But before all else, as he frequently has said to me, he hoped he was a philosopher . . . to me, who knew him so well from my earliest youth, his life appeared as one of constant and uninterrupted religious quest and devotion wherein intellectual achievement was subordinate to spiritual insight and inspiration.

Throughout the period of Leopold's stay in England his father had maintained his disapproval of his son's actions and totally ignored him. However, after the death of Leopold's mother, they did meet once again, in about 1895. They talked together,* and as Leopold was about to leave his father commented casually: 'By the way, your old nurse Marie died not long ago. I went to see her because she sent me an urgent message. She told me she had something on her conscience which she dared not die without revealing. This was that, owing to her fault, you had never been baptised. At the time of your birth your mother was very ill and Marie was entrusted with the arrangements for your baptism in church. However, at the instigation of the *facteur*, the family "homme d'affaires", whom you may remember and who turned out to be such an evil man, his own illegitimate child was baptised instead of you. Marie felt she could not die without confessing the truth. She thought she had committed a mortal sin. I felt you might like to know this, although, as far as I am concerned, I don't think it matters whether you were baptised or not.'

To Leopold it mattered intensely. According to Catholic doctrine none of the other seven sacraments, of which priestly ordination is one, was valid unless preceded by the initial sacrament of baptism. What then became of his vows as a priest? Immediately Leopold took his story to the Jesuit superior at Farm Street, Mayfair, then as now the centre for the Jesuit Order in England, and from there to Cardinal Vaughan. The Cardinal pushed the matter aside, saying that where there was 'invincible ignorance' no sin could be committed. He told Leopold that the matter could easily be put to rights, and that he would baptise him as soon as he wished, reordain him and all would be well. Leopold

---

\* This account is taken from Kathleen de Beaumont's memoirs. Their reliability is questionable; but the main events of Leopold's leaving the priesthood and the Catholic Church have been corroborated by the Jesuit authorities at Farm Street.

would have none of that and on 8 November 1887 he was formally dismissed from the Jesuits.

His disaffection was shared and probably exacerbated by the O'Hagan family, who one by one announced they were leaving the Church of Rome. Lord O'Hagan was a man of highly independent mind and when, in July 1870, the announcement had come that it was a basic doctrine of the Church that the Pope was infallible he had refused to accept it. He did not openly repudiate the Faith, but by the time he died in 1885 he was a Catholic in name only.

Throughout these years his family discussed whether they too should not make a stand. Darwin's latest theories were being eagerly debated; progressive thinkers such as James Martineau, a famous figure in the Unitarian Church, and Thomas Huxley came on several occasions to stay at Towneley; while the O'Hagan's local priest was telling them to their disgust that to believe in Darwin's views on evolution was a sin.

In some confusion of mind Lady O'Hagan went to visit Cardinal Newman, the leading Catholic luminary of the time, to ask his advice. He heard out her story and then said, 'If you cannot stay in the Church through your own belief, then please will you do it for the Church's sake?' Her reply was brief and final: 'If that is all you, as a leading light of the Church, can say, then I don't wish to remain.' The dyke walls had cracked open, and later that year, 1895, a London evening paper placarded the streets of London: LADY O'HAGAN LEAVES THE CHURCH OF ROME.

Leopold Klein had taken an even more firm step away from the Church, the previous year becoming a Unitarian. It caused no rift with the O'Hagan family: on the contrary, he was joining them in their stand. The same year as Lady O'Hagan's defection he and Kathleen O'Hagan became engaged, and two years later they married. The ceremony took place at the Unitarian Church in Marylebone: for they had shifted rather than abandoned their religious convictions and indeed Leopold became a part-time Unitarian Minister in Liverpool, where they set up home. Here, in Devonshire Road, their two daughters, Elizabeth and Marguerite, were born. Towards the end of 1901 Kathleen announced that she was again pregnant, and the family moved to a larger house in Alexandra Drive. On 5 May 1902 she was delivered of her third child, Charles-Louis.

That Charles's father was nearly thirty years older than his wife soon led to his adopting the role of an elderly patriarch; but Kathleen de Beaumont was a strong character in her own right. After her husband's death in 1934 she became a friend of Sir Francis Younghusband, with whom she helped found the World Congress of Faiths, a religious society which could claim to be one of the first modern ecumenical organisations; and this became the major interest of her life. She was one of the first people to discover the writings of the Jesuit theologian Teilhard de Chardin, and she continued lecturing and

The young Charles

A studio silhouette

Charles and Elouise during their time at Clermont House, in Norfolk.

writing about his work well into her eighties. Almost until her death she organised regular soirees at her home, attended on occasion by such figures as Harold Macmillan and Lord Hailsham. Well into her nineties, she wrote her memoirs, some 25,000 words, which, both lively and informative, provide the best source available for both her parents' and her children's lives.

She was fond of both Charles and his sisters but had little directly to do with their upbringing. Immediately after Charles was born his father gave up his work at the Unitarian Church in Liverpool and the whole family, together with two nurses, left to spend the winter in Athens, travelling via Italy. On their return they stayed with Lady O'Hagan for a time, first at Prygo Park in Essex and later at her London home in Chesham Place in Knightsbridge. Finally they acquired the lease of a house in Gloucester Terrace, Regents Park, and it was here that they lived from 1904 to 1913. Charles's early years were punctuated by regular visits to the Regents Park Zoo of which his father was a Fellow; the whole family became well known to keepers and animals alike.

Besides the two nurses there was a governess, a Miss Greenaway, as well as a young French-Swiss girl. The children were accompanied by their parents, however, on regular trips to the continent, mainly to France but also to Italy.

The family was soon to move to Clermont House, a small estate near Methwold in Norfolk. Leopold had bought the land when still living in London, and at first they lived in a farmhouse while the main building was erected. In her memoirs Kathleen de Beaumont wrote:

> It was a very comfortable, well-planned house. Water was pumped up daily into a tank in the roof by a horse going round and round the machinery of the well. . . . Our heating was by coal fires. Our children enjoyed tremendously their carefree life in the country, which was so excellent for their health.

For Charles it was the house in which he spent in many ways an idyllic childhood. He took a great interest in birds, and gained their trust sufficiently for them to eat happily from his hand. He was put in charge of rearing a batch of Rhode Island Red chickens. He also bred mice. With his sister Marguerite, just one year his senior, he used to roam through the countryside on natural history jaunts, scrambling in hedges for specimens to take home. Marguerite was indeed his constant companion, and throughout their lives the two remained close. More than a friend to Charles, she was frequently a vital prop. During his early years he came to rely constantly on her not only to cover up for him but to complete tasks he was not strong enough to do himself. For although in his later life he was well known for his good health and stamina, Charles was not a strong child, and that he turned himself into an outstanding athlete was due almost wholly to his own efforts.

Leopold was not keen on his children going to school too young, and until Charles was in his ninth year he was educated at home; while his two sisters

# The family background

never went to a formal school. When Charles was finally sent away it was to a school in Cambridge, the town to which the family moved in 1915, to live first at Selwyn Gardens, then at No. 4 St Paul's Road. Although a fee-paying establishment, 'The Perse' was not strictly a public school, and would approximate to a top-level grammar school. Even then this was a social distinction Charles felt keenly, once going to his doctor to ask for a certificate to say that it was bad for his head to wear the school cap. School life itself was neither particularly memorable nor happy. It provided a sharp contrast to the freedoms he enjoyed at home, and academically Charles did not excel, seeming bored with the curriculum and anxious to move on.

At home Charles's father was becoming mildly eccentric. Their house in Norfolk was twelve miles from the nearest railway station, and generally they would use a pony trap for getting about. Leopold Klein, however, also bought a tricycle, on which he would cycle around the neighbourhood with his wife. He became interested in astronomy and would travel regularly into Cambridge, where he was allowed to work with Professor Eddington at the Madingley Road laboratory. He also insisted on cutting down the trees near the house so that he could peer at the moon through his telescope, and his wife often remonstrated with him over the many windows left open all night long with various pieces of equipment sticking out of them and Leopold, flat on his back, peering at the stars. He also tried to grow tobacco commercially, but it went straight back into the ground again. Many other of his ventures met a similar fate. In 1909, during one of the family excursions to France, noticing the popularity of Le Touquet, he decided that the fashion could become more popular, and promptly bought three separate plots of fenced-in sand dunes further along the north coast, at Hardelot. The enterprise did not flourish: the sands remained just that, sands, and it was not until many years after his death that the area duly became the popular watering place he had imagined, complete with luxury holiday flats and lido.

Just before the outbreak of the first World War Charles's father was prevailed upon by his mother to change his name. He had been known as 'Doctor Klein' until his marriage, when he took up his mother's name and the family were called 'de Beaumont-Klein'. His family was from Alsace, and the German sound of their name was unmistakable. In 1913 he duly became a naturalised British subject and took the name 'de Beaumont' by deed poll. Of course he was not alone in taking such an action. Besides the Battenburgs, Lowensteins became Lowes, Schmidts became Smiths, and so on. Yet in her memoirs Kathleen de Beaumont wrote of his action: 'I am the only person who can know what it cost him to take such a step.'

About this time Leopold, already in his sixties, decided to take up yet another interest: he started to study Russian, and was soon almost fluent. It was his seventh language, and the ease with which he picked up other tongues was of all his abilities the one most clearly inherited by his son. Yet Leopold longed for Charles to share his interest in the world of ideas, and he was severely disappointed when his son showed instead a far more practical intelligence. It was thus with pride but with few expectations that in October 1920 he watched Charles go up to Trinity College, Cambridge, to read natural sciences.

## II  Cambridge and after

> 'Dear de Beaumont, I am sorry not to have replied sooner to your kind telegram of greeting, but as you will see I was away from home when it reached me. Please give my very best wishes to the Cambridge University Rovers and many thanks for the Scouty message.'
> Letter to Charles de Beaumont from Sir Robert Baden-Powell, 22 May 1923

Cambridge was a revelation to Charles. The natural sciences course, made up in his case of zoology, botany and biology, was sufficiently close to the hobbies he had pursued at home to engage his interest and he emerged with a respectable second-class degree. He was always to find it easy to make friends, and at Cambridge this was particularly true. He learned to play the banjo, took up sport seriously for the first time, rode regularly, went stag and fox hunting, and became a highly proficient dancer. But, above all, there were the Boy Scouts.

He had become interested in the Scout movement some years before, following the enthusiasm of his two sisters and of his mother and actually became a Scout when eleven. Kathleen de Beaumont wrote of how, in 1909, she and her two daughters, the girls complete with broomsticks which they had in lieu of scout poles, had illegally attended the first Scout Rally at the Crystal Palace. They smuggled themselves in wearing scout hats they had borrowed, and with the broomsticks marked off in inches to look like the real thing. It was not long before they fell under the eye of Sir Robert Baden-Powell, who inquired who they were. Elizabeth de Beaumont cried out: 'Please sir, we're the *girl* scouts': Baden-Powell rejoined: 'I've never heard of you, but you can join in.' Convinced of their enthusiasm for the Scout movement, he added that something would have to be done for them. Sure enough, as Kathleen de Beaumont records, some time later a conference was held near Bath to discuss the possibility of organising a Guide movement. 'Subsequently Sir Robert asked me if I would accept the position of County Commissioner for Guides, and gave me the choice of the counties of Norfolk or Cambridgeshire. As we were then about to move to Cambridge, I chose that county and for thirty years held the position of County Commissioner for Guides for Cambridgeshire and the Isle of Ely, where I and my daughters organised the Movement.'

The de Beaumont family was thus instrumental in the setting up of the Girl Guide movement. They also became friends of Robert Baden-Powell and of his sister Agnes. Marguerite later wrote an official biography of Lord Baden-Powell, *The Wolf That Never Sleeps*. It became a minor best-seller and was translated for foreign editions.

In the summer of 1920, just before he went up to Trinity, Charles and a number of undergraduates attended a special meeting at which it was decided to found a Cambridge section of the Scout movement, and just over a year later, on 30 November 1921, the 'Cambridge University Rover Scout Troop' was born. By the Easter of 1923 Charles had become Troop Leader. It was probably the Scouts which gave him the greatest pleasure and took up most of his time at University; certainly it was his time in the Scouts that first gave Charles the chance to organise others and provides the first signs of his basic competitiveness and wish to excel.

Charles also founded and rowed for a Boy Scouts crew in the 1923 'bumping races'. There were two separate sets of races, the 'Mays', held by and for the colleges, and a 'Town' equivalent. The separate league organised by the Town consisted of such teams as the YMCA first and second boats and two crews from the 'University and College servants'. There were two Scouts crews, and Charles rowed for the first team at number 5, a position in the middle of the boat where most of the hard work is needed. The crew 'bumped' – that is, caught up with and touched – the crew in front three times out of the four days' racing, and only failed to win their oars – the reward for catching your opponent on all four days – because of a pile-up in front of them when three boats all caught up on one another. 'Well rowed, Scouts!' commented the local Cambridge paper.

Charles was filling out. His figure at this time took on the compact and muscular form he was to maintain throughout his life: far more a boxer's figure than a fencer's. Photographs show him with well-developed shoulder and stomach muscles, solid rather than graceful, but undeniably powerful. His father disapproved of games, but in 1921 Charles became a member of the University boxing club* and also started to swim seriously, at which he became so good that he only narrowly missed gaining a Blue at water polo. Marguerite, who used to go regularly to see Charles play, remembers: 'The art of the sport seemed to rest on your ability to kick your opponent in the stomach and push

---

* Charles took up the sport through a friend, a Singhalese named Paul Deraniyagala, who was also at Trinity, and who was to captain the University team. The son of the Governor of Ceylon, he was a first-class scientist who went on to become Curator of the Singhalese Museum. In his final year the Cambridge boxing team visited the United States; but Deraniyagala was denied a visa because of his colour. When one thinks of Charles's later championing of the right of South Africa to remain part of the international fencing community it is interesting to recall this important early friendship.

# Cambridge and after

his head under the water. Charles's strength was a great help here, and he seemed to drown everyone.' He also became an adept dancer, though without ever taking formal lessons. Marguerite was nearly always his partner, both at dances given at home and at the Cambridge May Balls. 'This even caused some scandal at the time,' Marguerite recalls, 'and people couldn't help asking me the name of my dancing partner.' They both played up to this, Marguerite once pointedly sitting on Charles's lap in a public conservatory, and only after the gossip-mongers had got to work did she take Charles up to the ringleaders and introduce him as her brother. 'We were like *that*,' says Marguerite, holding up her two fingers intertwined.

The picture of Charles's time at Cambridge, then, is of one filled with activity, but with little academic work, of hearty companionship on the playing fields but few women friends. And, of course, it was at Cambridge that he first took up fencing.

The Cambridge Boxing and Fencing Clubs had been united late in the nineteenth century, and perhaps in consequence of the two sports taking place side by side Charles found himself taking an interest in swordplay. That he took it up so energetically may simply have been due to his rapidly proving himself so well suited to it; equally, one suspects that his father's dislike of body-contact sports must have influenced his decision and, of course, his father would have associated fencing with France, an automatic recommendation. Anyway, by the beginning of 1922 one finds Charles coming fifth in the epee at the University Trials, while his first mention in the press was for his abilities as a sabreur. A report in *New Cambridge* of 24 January 1923 on a University match against 'past members of the Club' reads: 'The best exhibition of sabre play was given by Mr. de Beaumont who, showing good style and judgement, won all his fights in a most distinctive manner.' Under the instruction of a Mr Fordham, 'membre de l'Academie d'Armes, Paris, instructor in boxing, fencing, physical culture, etc.', Charles's fencing improved rapidly, and he duly represented Cambridge against Oxford only one month later, on 23 February, at sabre. Cambridge won 7–6, a strange score explained by the two facts that the teams had only two members in the sabre event rather than the now customary three, and that the University match was divided into two, foil and sabre at the February meeting and an epee encounter in the summer. Charles won one fight and in the other was, to quote *New Cambridge* again, 'somewhat unlucky to lose the decision against the Oxford captain, Mr Trevis.' That same year he came third equal in the British Junior Epee Championships, his first result of consequence at national level. He was on his way. Well before he left Cambridge he told Marguerite: 'I am going to be an international fencing champion.'

When in the summer of 1923 Charles went down from University he had no immediate idea what to do next, or what career he would follow. There was, however, a brief interlude before any decision about his future became necessary. Charles had joined no political club while at Cambridge, but he had spoken regularly at the Cambridge Union in the days when its debates had greater public standing than now, and his contributions were usually well thought out and appreciatively received. In his last year both as secretary of the Fencing Club and head of the Scout Troop he had become well known round the University. At any rate, he and one other Cambridge student were chosen, with two Oxford undergraduates, to make a tour of Eastern Europe as part of a joint university mission to inspect student relief for the Imperial War Relief Fund. This was financed by the universities and was principally a goodwill trip, with little political significance. How much understanding there was between the four undergraduates and the people they visited is doubtful, since it is recorded that many of the conversations were held in dog-Latin, the only language which they and their East European hosts are said to have had in common.

Typically Charles took his fencing bag along. It proved the passport to at least one interesting experience. While in Prague he and two others in the group visited one of the student fencing clubs where the students were secretly practising with the heavy basket-hilted *Schlager* (somewhat akin to a Scottish claymore and used for serious duelling). The doors of the salle were locked before fencing commenced, and only Charles was allowed in, due to his fencing background – his two Oxford companions, 'mere oarsmen', being resolutely excluded.

Charles returned home looking for work. No one from either side of his family had previously worked in trade, but he now allied himself to the Linen Thread Company, a small but prosperous concern with good connections overseas. When one of their subsidiaries, based in Milan, found itself in difficulties Charles was sent as right-hand man to the owner of the factory. He arrived at the local station to be met by a young Italian who spoke neither English nor French, Charles's only languages at that point, but who managed to explain that the head of the factory was ill and could not meet his new English colleague. It soon looked as if 'Signore' would be running the factory on his own for some time to come. Promising his informant, who was looking round anxiously for means to escape, that unless he received all possible help he would beat the boy personally, Charles managed to be taken to the factory and to find lodgings, and for the next two years, picking up Italian as he went – even taking the office boy home with him at night to give him lessons – he ran the factory single-handed. And, of course, there was fencing. Possibly he only joined the firm in the expectation of being posted to Milan. Certainly he was determined to study fencing under the best masters of the day, and perhaps the best epee teacher in the world at that time was Professor Giuseppe Mangiarotti, whose salle was in Milan. Under his tutelage Charles won a first-class epee competition in Milan and was grounded in the classic Italian style.

The old London Fencing Club, with Charles, eyes shut, demonstrating the sabre with Col R. E. Cole.

Before fencing took its hold – Charles the boxer, during his first year at Cambridge.

In almost the only autobiographical writing that he left – part of a series of short stories about fencing that he contributed to *The Sword* at the end of the fifties – Charles gives something of the flavour of his time in Italy:

> When I was a member of the Salle Mangiarotti in Milan in the twenties it was quite common for people to turn up for a couple of weeks to train for a duel. In these early days of the Mussolini regime duelling, although illegal, was unofficially encouraged as a virile pursuit.
>
> One summer, when few members frequented the salle because of the heat and the absence of the Master, who had gone to Sicily for the Italian championships, the editor of a local paper arrived to train for a duel ten days later. He had done very little fencing, and was somewhat perturbed to find the master absent. Having seen the drill a number of times I volunteered to train him.
>
> The method used was to fence stripped to the waist, without masks and wearing an ordinary glove which buttoned at the wrist.
>
> The triple point was exposed as much as possible. I can recommend this exercise to anyone who fosters the illusion that fencing epee in the normal way, with jacket, mask and glove, bears any resemblance to a duel.
>
> In the short time available I concentrated on teaching my pupil to remain on guard well covered, keeping his head well back – the pricks I inflicted on his bare arm whenever he departed from this basic position at least taught him caution. When our sessions drew to a close he invited me, a considerable honour, to witness his duel, which was against another journalist about some article my friend had written.
>
> On the appointed morning we arrived early at a sports stadium on the outskirts of Milan which was deserted at that hour. The gates were locked when the duellists, their seconds, the President (an army officer in full uniform), a doctor and two or three friends had arrived. A piste was marked out on the running track, the doctor unpacked an impressive array of instruments and bowls and the seconds produced and measured the epees.
>
> The two contestants stripped to the waist, wearing their ordinary trousers and shoes, and the President, holding a cane in one hand and a stopwatch in the other, called them on guard. The doctor then carefully wiped the blades with disinfectant, and the President called 'Play'.
>
> The duellists were extremely cautious and moved up and down the piste, well out of range of each other, until time was called. If I remember aright, they fenced for one minute and then had a minute's rest before starting again. Whenever a blade touched the ground or the President's clothing (he stood very close to them) the bout was stopped and the doctor again disinfected the blades.
>
> After two or three 'rounds' like this the strain was visibly affecting the contestants, especially my friend's opponent, who was a tubby little man with an even more rudimentary knowledge of fencing than my 'pupil'.
>
> Eventually the fat man decided that he must do something to finish it off and started to try to reach his opponent's forearm by bent-arm thrusts over his coquille. The result was a foregone conclusion, if only my 'pupil'

# Cambridge and after

remained in the covered position I had taken such pains to impress on him to maintain. Fortunately he did, and at a more vigorous thrust out of line, the fat man impaled himself on my friend's point, which penetrated his forearm by several inches.

The President immediately called 'halt' and struck up the blades with his cane. A surprising amount of blood flowed from the wound, which the doctor bound up, declaring that the recipient was in an inferior physical condition. So the duel was over but no reconciliation took place.

Something else happened while Charles was in Milan: he fell in love. He was a paying guest of an impoverished old lady who rented out a number of rooms in her house, and it was there that he met another of the guests, a young French girl, Renée Chanchet, who had come to Milan to act in her first film, *The Fan of Venice*. She was strikingly beautiful, intelligent and vivacious, and Charles was captivated. It was not long before she made it plain that his feelings were returned, and they discussed marriage. At this point Charles told his family of his intentions. Whether his father's view that it was an undesirable match put an end to his plans is not clear, but he now returned to England. In any case, he felt himself bound by a promise he had made to a girl he had known in Cambridge. Close to the de Beaumont home lived a wealthy Irish family, the Grove-Crofts, and the daughter of the family, Guinevere, had been a member of the Guide movement at the time Charles had first joined the Scouts. The two had got on well at first, although Charles had little contact with her after he had left for Italy, at which point she had been studying the violin at the Royal College of Music. Before leaving for Milan, however, Charles had made a promise that the two of them should marry, so that not long after his return to England they became formally engaged. By 1924 they were married.*

On Charles's return from Italy he found Guinevere much changed. Her father had died when she was very young and her mother remarried. She spent much of her time travelling the world, leaving Guinevere from the age of five in the care of expensive boarding schools. While Guinevere was studying in London her mother died, leaving her a considerable fortune and Charles recorded in the extensive diary he kept at this period that whereas before she had been sweet, thoughtful and kind, he now found her hard, modern and selfish. His sense of 'scout's duty' and his real feeling for her made him hope that she would become more loving, less self-centred and less harsh towards him. However, this was not to be and within four years the marriage had foundered.

In September 1926, while they were living in Scotland, Guinevere gave

---

* For her part Renée soon met another Englishman, Rex Henry, and in November 1928 they were married. Typically, Charles agreed to be a witness at their marriage, and remained a friend of the Henrys for the next 45 years, often helping Rex Henry financially, and after the war starting up with him a wine company, 'Rex and Charles', which flourished briefly before being disbanded.

birth to Charles's only son, Robin. Before he was two years old she had left their new house in Beaufort Gardens, next door to Harrods, to settle in Paris. By this stage, Charles had left his job in the Irish Linen Thread Company and had set up as an antique dealer in the Brompton Road. After the separation he acquired a house in Montpelier Street and arrangements were made for Robin's upbringing and education. For the next ten years Guinevere lived a somewhat unhappy life in Paris. During this time she saw Robin only on annual visits to England, sometimes not even then. He was looked after by a succession of governesses until, at the age of eight, he went to Cheam and subsequently, at the beginning of the War, to Marlborough College where Lord O'Hagan, Charles's uncle, had been.

In 1938, amid the growing turmoil in Europe, Guinevere left France and bought a large Edwardian shooting lodge near Stirling which a friend, Charlie January, ran as a hotel while she had her own private suite in a wing.

While Guinevere was in Paris and even more when in Scotland Charles saw her rarely; and in the end it was she who was reluctant to see him. For the first fifteen years there was no question of either wanting a divorce but, although her friends advised her to agree and financially it would have been to her advantage, it was to be many years before the stigma she felt to be attached to such action was finally overcome. However, by the end of 1927 Charles was again in effect single, with friends and relatives enough to look after Robin. He was freer than he had ever been in his life before. And that meant, to a large degree, being free to fence.

# III  The Olympic athlete

> 'There has always been a difference of taste between the purist of the point and the enthusiast for the sabre. It has almost been as sharply drawn as that between the lovers of brass music and those who care only for the music of the reed.... The French have always associated Scotland with the point.'
> W. G. Burn Murdoch, writing in 1927 in *The Scotsman*

After his sojourn in Italy Charles did not immediately settle in London, but went instead to work in Glasgow, the headquarters of the Linen Thread Company, for which he was still working. It was during the two years that he was to remain there that he established himself as one of Britain's leading epeeists.

Two years previously, at Cambridge, his teaching had been first at the hands of Professor Fordham; then, in his last year, under Professor Dap, a tall, rangy Frenchman, who used to live by the dictum 'Before you can do a difficult thing well you must learn to do the easy things perfectly.' Charles duly did.

Further improved by the lessons he had received in Italy, Charles had become a formidable opponent, and his entry into Scottish competition brought him immediate results. In 1926 he came second in the Scottish sabre Championship to Roger Crosnier, the Anglo-Frenchman whom after the war Charles was to appoint Britain's first national fencing coach. He also came second in the epee Championship, and the following year represented Scotland at both weapons against the North of England. In 1927 he went one better, winning both the sabre and the epee titles, whilst also winning one of the main foil tournaments, the Seton Trophy in Edinburgh.

About this time Charles made two important decisions about his fencing. First, despite his earlier connections with Scotland, he opted firmly to represent England on any occasion where he had to choose between the five home countries, and in November 1928 refused to fence for Scotland in the first of their annual matches against England, arguing that he was not of strict Scottish parentage, despite being over half Scottish on the O'Hagan side. Instead he was nominated epee reserve for the English team. The Scots were furious; it was bad enough losing one of their most promising young

Winning the Scottish Epee Cup, 1927. That year Charles also won the sabre, as well as Scotland's leading foil tournament. Looking on is Charles Hope, who was to be Scottish Champion a total of nine times, at all weapons.


fencers, but Charles had already captained the Scottish team in an earlier fixture, and their selectors were well aware that they were losing too a powerful personality.

Charles's second decision was to make epee his main weapon. It was a choice that brought him almost immediate rewards. Towards the end of 1927 he won his first national title, the Junior Epee. Writing in the *Sunday Times*, Leon Bertrand, one of the leading fencing Masters in the country, commented:

> I find it very difficult to criticise the victor, and it is with mixed feelings that I confess that the major part of his success was due to the fleche movement. In truth, de Beaumont affords us the least conception of the duellist in a 'cold grey dawn'. But he is extremely combative, gets to work at once and keeps his adversary on the move throughout.

Later that year, when Charles came seventh in the Junior Foil, *The Times* noted that 'his methods were successful but far from academic'. Charles could afford not to worry; he was now on the brink of the national team, and all within four years of serious competition.

His rise to prominence should be seen against the particularly conservative and traditional world of 1920s fencing. The clubs in London seem now from another time, salles being named either after long-forgotten masters like Tassart and Stempel or with titles that have since disappeared, like the

'Artists' Rifles Fencing Club' or the 'Inns of Court School of Arms'. When in 1923 a display was held at the Hotel Cecil in aid of Earl Haig's appeal for ex-servicemen and of the British League of Help for the Devastated Regions of France the *Morning Post*, later to be absorbed into the *Daily Telegraph*, commented:

> From the beginning the audience was keenly interested. They knew to a man and a woman, probably, hunting ballads like John Peel, but to most of them the ballad of the foil, the sabre, and the epee was unfamiliar, and they read its refrain in the programme with quickened anticipation. The song runs with a lilt of its own that catches the rapture of the fencing enthusiast:
> 'Oh! there's never a joy by field or flood
> That a strong man's heart can feel,
> Like the supple wrist and the flashing eye,
> And the stamping foot and the sudden cry,
> And the ring of the glittering steel! Hola! Touché!'

At the premier club in London, the London Fencing Club, the atmosphere was similarly old-fashioned. The club occupied the penthouse floor of a luxury block of flats at 7 Cleveland Row, close to what was to become Prunier's famous fish restaurant, off Little St James's Street and opposite St James's Palace. The club – the first of its kind to exist in Britain – as distinct from a salle belonging to a Master – had been founded in July 1848 for use by the Guards Regiment at the Palace. It soon gained a number of distinguished members, while those who wished to join were rigorously scrutinised. Fencing was seen as an art, and the club records include a note that should a member during the course of a bout hit his opponent with a remise he should remove his mask and apologise. Women who came as private pupils were required to have left the club by 4.00 pm: it was not until after the 1939–45 War that women were allowed to become actual members. Baths were available on the premises and there was a steward to look after members' needs, supplying a refreshing glass of sherry and laying out members' clothes.

On leaving Scotland Charles had joined Felix Bertrand's Club, Salle Bertrand, but soon found that Bertrand was not primarily an epee master but a specialist in foil and sabre. At the London Fencing Club, however, the French Master André Gauthier gave lessons, and he was a specialist at epee, possibly the best Master of that weapon the club was ever to have. A captain in the French army, he had come to London in 1929, and in fact was rarely referred to as 'Maitre' but simply as 'Le Capitaine'. By 1933 Charles had become his pupil. Gordon Pilbrow, only a fortnight younger than Charles and for many years his colleague in the British team, recalls: 'The old school thought of Charles as precocious, someone who, forty years younger than they, wanted to reform everything. In the early twenties fencing was all good manners: Charles wanted to *win*.'

Foreign fields: a sabre outing in Dieppe.

The typical de Beaumont stance (note the epee, held by the pommel). Contesting the Miller-Hallett in Lincoln's Inn Fields.

And win he did. In 1929 he came tenth in the National Epee Championships and second in the new international Miller-Hallett competition, only the second time it had been held. The following year he won the Miller-Hallett outright and was chosen to fence for Britain at both epee and sabre at the European Championships at Liege. At that first European Championships he fenced once, during the epee team event, and is described in the official report as being there only as 'a delegate of the Association' to the FIE Congress. His marginal place in the team, however, did not prevent him recording some unusual highlights:

> The fencing took place in a long room on the ground floor of a large building. Those were the halcyon days before the electrical apparatus brought serenity to the foil and epee events and 'temperaments' were the order of the day.
> In one bout a well-known Belgian fencer became increasingly exasperated at the decisions of the jury. When the penultimate hit in a needle bout was given against him he threw his mask on the ground and jumped on it with both feet. Another mask was procured and the match continued. When the last hit also went against him this fencer threw his weapon, mask and glove out of the window and took a flying leap after it – the eight-foot drop was fortunately into a well-dug flower bed.

The next year, when the European Championships were held in Vienna, events were less dramatic, while Charles fenced at two weapons for his country.

It is worth a word of explanation here on the relative importance of the Miller-Hallett competition that Charles won and of the European championships he was now attending. Britain has, besides four national championships at foil, epee, sabre and women's foil, four international competitions, one for each weapon, open to both professionals and fencers from abroad. By custom the National Championships have a special kudos since their winner is thus 'National Champion' at the weapon concerned, and few people outside fencing have any particular interest in one's winning the Miller-Hallett (epee), Corble (sabre), Coronation (foil, and since retitled the 'Leon Paul International'), or Hutton (women's foil, and since retitled the 'de Beaumont Cup'), the importance of which is less easy to explain. However, it is usually the international competitions which have had the higher standard, and, although foreign participation during the thirties was slight compared with recent years, Charles's winning of the Miller-Hallett, as he was to do in 1932, 1933 and 1934, and on three other occasions besides, remains a fine achievement.

As for the European Championships, they were the forerunners of the World Championships, which in turn, every four years, were subsumed into the Olympic Games. Whatever their title, they are of relatively recent origin. A European individual tournament, at epee, the first weapon to have such a championship, was first held in Paris in 1921. A sabre championship was added the following year, whilst 1924 saw the Olympics, at which fencing had been one of the original sports in 1896. The first European Championships with a complete programme of team and individual events for men at all weapons – but with still only an individual championship for ladies – took place at Liege in 1930 and continued after that in each non-Olympic year. A European ladies' team event was held for the first time in 1932, and became part of the Olympics in 1960.

No one had really thought of calling these championships anything other than European, since the main fencing nations were all covered by that term; but in 1937 the championships were re-christened 'World Championships' for a curious reason. At that time Italy, under the Fascist regime, was giving tremendous encouragement to sport for national prestige. Anyone who won an Olympic or world title received medals, decorations and considerable privileges from the state, such as free travel, free seats for state theatres, and so on. The Italian fencers found that the European titles they won were not considered for these privileges, and mainly to oblige them the FIE, of which Italy was one of the most powerful members, altered the title of these championships to give them 'world' status. One aspect of this, incidentally, was that when Gwen Nelligan took all before her to win the women's foil title for Britain at the 1933 championships she could only call herself 'European Champion', though in real terms she had won the world title.

Charles, then, had to wait until after the Berlin Olympics before competing in an actual World Championship; but already his fencing career was advancing on other fronts. In 1931 the British team Captain, Robert Montgomerie, a pre-1914 foilist and epeeist, had given notice that he intended to retire. The following year saw the Olympics in Los Angeles, and only one men's foilist and two women foilists were sent. (They were particularly successful: Emrys Lloyd came fifth, Peggy Butler eighth and Judy Guinness took the Silver Medal.) The next year, when a full fencing team again turned out for the European Championships, the issue of who should be the new Captain came up in earnest. Charles's only possible rival for the position was a banker, Michael Babington-Smith, a fellow international – he had captained the foil team in Vienna – but a man neither as active nor as interested in fencing as his ambitious young colleague. Charles was now not only on the AFA Committee but in 1930 had become the British representative at FIE Congresses abroad. In 1931, when the FIE published a complete set of rules for fencing, Charles had quickly and efficiently translated them. On top of all this he was at the height of his powers as a fencer, having won the Miller-Hallett title three years running and having gained the best results abroad of any of the British epeeists. Not surprisingly, he was duly elected overall Captain.

So to the Championships at Budapest. Charles had his best result ever, while the team were also highly successful. The Championships were held in the open air on the island of St Margit. Not only did Gwen Neligan win the women's title, but of the four women teams competing the British ladies took the Silver Medal. Emrys Lloyd (christened '*wespen taille*' or 'wasp-waist' at the 1931 Vienna Championships) came third in the foil. There was no British foil team entry, but the epee team came fourth. In the team sabre event Hungary won the Gold – from 1904 until 1960 they won the Gold 21 times out of 24 attempts – Italy took the Silver and Britain beat Poland 9–3 to take the Bronze, arguably her best sabre result of all time.

Charles's personal epee results were outstanding. He won 14 of his 24 fights in the team competition, and in the individual failed by only one hit to reach the final. Three members of the epee team reached the semi-final stage, a result all the more interesting as these were the first European Championships at which electric epee was used and only the second year at which fights were the best of three hits rather than sudden-death, one-hit affairs. Charles, to judge from the score sheet, might fairly have claimed to have been eliminated by a 'combine' or arranged fight: in the last bout of the pool the weaker man earned a draw and, by so doing, a place in the final. Charles, as if to underline this injustice, recorded in his team Captain's report to the AFA following the championships that he had personally suggested to the FIE that where 'two fencers favouring each other were playing out time ... time expiring, a defeat be recorded against each player'. Besides making this suggestion for both epee and sabre, he also put forward the view that a minimum expectation for each British team member at a European Championships should be two wins per match.

Charles's appointment as team Captain was an immediate success, off as well as on the piste. After the Championships a team member wrote anonymously to the AFA pointing out how useful the new young Captain's proficiency as a linguist had proved and adding: 'Mr. de Beaumont showed himself to be a most energetic and painstaking captain, and in my opinion the gratifying results obtained were in no small measure due to his efficiency, quite apart from his popularity with our opponents.' Charles personally received letters from most of the team warmly thanking him for all he had done. It was not by accident that when he and Gwen Nelligan organised a 'Fencing Ball' at the Savoy Hotel in April of the following year it should be an immense success, more than £400 being raised for charity: a considerable sum at the time.

Charles was equally popular with the majority of fencers from foreign nations, and continued to be, even when no longer an active participant. There was his flair for languages, of course; but Charles was also the person to whom people from France or Italy (perennially at each other's throats), from America or from Eastern Europe turned for an impartial opinion, for *fairness*. He was not always treated in similar fashion. In one of his infrequent autobiographical articles he wrote:

I remember fencing the famous French epeeist Philippe Cattiau in the epee event (in 1930) when he gave me my first lesson in 'jurymanship'. We came on guard after he had saluted me with a kindly if rather patronising smile, indicating to the jury how pleased he was to meet an aspiring beginner. At half lunge an *Eh la dessus!* brought his point to within a good six inches short of my coquille. Off came his mask with a beaming and knowing smile – and the judges duly gave the hit. Once again we came on guard, the same stroke with an even more assured shout and he rushed across slapping me on the shoulder, wringing my hand and thanking me effusively for the bout before the President had even called halt. The score registered 2–0 against me although I had not been hit.

The curious thing was that of course he could have beaten me as he liked – but he preferred to be an artist with the jury.

For Charles's own career as a fencer the 1930s continued to be the high-water mark. In 1934 he came only seventh in the National Epee Championship but again won the Miller-Hallett title, then later in May travelled with the rest of the British team to New York for what was then a regular quadrennial fixture with the Americans. He also designed a 'long blue coat' as part of the official dress for British internationals. Of his fourth consecutive Miller-Hallett victory *The Times* commented: 'His play was spirited without being unduly reckless. Most of his hits were delivered with the light crispness that characterises his play at his best.' A less sympathetic critic, noting that the competition lasted throughout one long day, commented that it was really an endurance event for those involved, and that Charles was simply fitter than anyone else.

So what was Charles like as a fencer? He *was* very fit, certainly, and had been trained by the best masters of his time – Mangiarotti, Felix Bertrand, Delzi and Gauthier. He did not, however, have a truly classical style – though it might be termed classical compared with the posturings of many of today's epeeists. His timing was good, and that, allied to a good sense of distance and his obvious fitness, made him a difficult opponent. He was an opportunist. His sister Marguerite accurately used to call him 'spring-heels', for he was always an aggressive fencer, and as soon as any bout had begun he would rise on to the balls of his feet and make rapid darting attacks at his opponent's arm. Such attacks were often successful: his regular lessons had given him an accurate point. The criticisms made of his frequent fleching were part and parcel of the fact that Charles was such a mobile fencer, and indeed brought into his fighting many moves – stop-hits with a turned body, crossing over his legs – which today are commonplace but which were then innovations.

Leon 'Punch' Bertrand,* son of Felix, and who was for many years to be the Master at the LFC, was to write privately after Charles's death:

* The origin of the late Punch Bertrand's nickname has been much debated, but he himself told me he earned the name the day he was born when his father, looking at him, exclaimed, 'Good Lord, what a Punch and Judy show!'

What amazed me is that without possessing an ounce of technique in his whole body he should show such a profound theoretical knowledge of our art, a talent which commands my fullest admiration. . . . I do not know, but I suspect his complete lack of technique was due to his having boxed at Cambridge. This would be fatal to the acquisition of technique. The excess of mobility, destroying any subtlety in the choice of time in the attack, the incessant onslaught beyond the bounds of reason and finally the footwork: when you are on the balls of your feet stability vanishes.

'Complete lack of technique' is unkind, the over-reaction of one of the great teachers of classic fencing; but the points about boxing are well made. In the end Emrys Lloyd's appraisal of Charles is probably as accurate as anyone's: 'His fencing reflected his nature: it was not blessed with genius, but he was a very good fencer, competitive, energetic, quick and accurate.' It was enough.

The aggressiveness Charles brought to his epee came in equally useful at sabre. At international level, however, Charles was only a makeweight member of the sabre team; in his day sabre was always the last event of the World Championships, so he could happily stay on to compete without any danger of his doing so affecting his epee performance. But when the British team won their World Championship Bronze Medal in 1933 Charles was only the number six in the team and did not himself fence, although he was awarded a medal. Gordon Pilbrow commented 'The only thing I can say about his sabre was that it was robust – and very painful', but perhaps this was the biased view of a leading sabreur who on occasion found himself trailing behind the interloping epeeist. Charles clearly possessed very considerable flair even at sabre to achieve the results he did. It was generally acknowledged, however, that if you fenced sabre with Charles you could expect to be nursing the weals for days afterwards. His opponents used to compare bruises.

Charles did little foil, and although he did once reach the semi-finals of the National Championships he kept his weapon for when he fenced the ladies. They in turn found him not only a more useful opponent but one of their earliest supporters within the AFA. Indeed as soon as he was elected to the AFA Committee in 1930 he proceeded to take a particular interest in their affairs. He did not always win battles on their behalf, however, and when in 1933 he founded the All England Fencing Club, based at Hurlingham and meeting each fortnight for practice matches, he was initially unable to accept women members. They were eventually admitted in 1937. Before that, in April 1935, Charles travelled to Brussels for the annual congress of the FIE. The Hungarians proposed that skirts for women fencers should be outlawed and that instead 'lady fencers must wear large (slack) trousers closed below the knee'. Charles fought for skirts to be allowed as well, but 'after considerable discussion' the Hungarian proposal was accepted by 25 to 14. One wonders how many women sat in on these debates.

That same year Charles came fourth in the National sabre, third in the epee; but his main advance was as an administrator. He helped form the Irish Fencing Union, and in 1935 was awarded their Vice-Presidency. In the spring of 1936 Charles H. Biscoe had retired as Honorary Secretary of the AFA, a post he had held since 1928. Charles was appointed in his place. The Secretaryship was at this period the key office in the Association, the Presidency being honorific rather than executive: Lord Howard de Walden, President from 1926 till 1946, probably never attended meetings of the AFA Committee, and possibly not even AGMs. Charles immediately began to make changes, starting a regular system of sub-committees that was to mark the first step in getting the AFA better organised. He set up a committee to promote the sport, and on 9 May 1936 himself did a commentary on the National sabre final for the BBC, the first time fencing had ever had a programme to itself transmitted on the radio in Britain.

It is worth making the point how recent any organisation to help amateur fencing in Britain has been. Originally an 'Association of Fencing Clubs' had been founded in 1896 as the Fencing Branch of the Amateur Gymnastic and Fencing Association. On 1 February 1900 this branch decided on autonomy, and on 3 December 1901 the decision to make them so was finally taken, to be effective from the beginning of 1902. By the time Charles became Secretary the AFA, which in 1902 had comprised sixteen clubs and 36 individual members, had grown to 67 clubs and 476 members. He was to preside over fencing's expansion into one of the most popular of all minority sports, and a census taken in December 1948, only three years after the war (when there had been practically no fencing), revealed 155 'associated bodies and clubs' and 589 members throughout the United Kingdom.

Charles's competitive career, however, was now to become involved in a political controversy: the Berlin Olympics. At the beginning of 1936 he won the Miller-Hallett again, despite having his sword arm heavily strapped to offset a tennis elbow. He also at last won the National epee title, losing only one fight in the final pool of twelve to the runner-up, Terry Beddard. As the 1936 Olympics approached, Charles found himself also a member of the sabre squad, although he eventually was sent to Berlin only for epee.

He had been too young to make the 1928 Olympics and at the tenth Olympiad at Los Angeles in 1932 only three fencers had been sent. Now at last he had his chance, and to captain the fencing team on his first appearance. The 'Nazi Olympics', as they were later dubbed, were for their part probably the most interesting and notorious of all the fencing championships which Charles attended. As early as 1932, even as the German Olympic team had travelled across the States, the Reichstag elections of 31 July had returned Hitler's candidates to power with their first-ever majority. By 1936 Hitler's anti-semitic policies were well under way. There were those who advocated a boycott of the Berlin Games, but they had little influence among athletes. This was partly because the famous runner Harold Abrahams, although as a Jew he might have been specially sensitive to Nazi anti-semitism, strongly supported participation. He had been on the post-university tour of Eastern Europe with Charles, who agreed with his attitude, in spite of the case of the famous German fencing champion, Helene Meyer. Olympic Gold Medallist in 1928 and World Champion in 1929 and 1931, in 1933 she was expelled from her club in Offenbach for being half Jewish. Nevertheless, she was eventually invited to take her place in the 1936 German team.

The British team travelled to Berlin in August to make up the 11,148 participants in the Games, which in the event were well organised, highly efficient, and remarkable for the many superb athletic performances achieved. The Nazi presence was obvious, but generally kept itself on a short lead. Charles – along with leading French and American fencers – was eliminated in the first round of the epee, although another Briton, Ian Campbell-Gray, reached the final, to come eighth. There were three hundred contestants in the fencing from 31 nations, with thirty pistes, including eight laid down on some hard clay tennis courts outside the main stadium. Hitler made a personal visit to the fencing, and public interest in the sport was high throughout, with fights going on far into the night, the outside pistes splendidly floodlit. The tournament was dominated by the Italians, Hungarians, French and Germans, approximately in that order, and had as their obvious climax the performance of Helene Meyer. She finally won the Silver Medal – and gave a Heil Hitler salute on receiving it.

After the completion of the Games Charles returned to England to suggest that a competing captain and a non-competing manager should in future both be sent with the British team to any world or Olympic Championship: the job of manager was too much for one man.

In March 1937 Charles travelled to France for the FIE Congress, where he was present at the first demonstration of electric foil. The Congress also noted the decision of the Olympic Committee to hold the 1940 Olympics in Tokyo. Back home again Charles won the National epee title for the second time and came sixth in the National sabre. He also competed in Scotland, becoming Scottish sabre Champion again, pushing Gordon Pilbrow, at that time Britain's leading sabreur, into second place. He went to the World Championships in Paris, where he fenced sabre as well as epee. Altogether it was a crowded year. Charles's official newsletter for the 1937 Championships included this stern advice:

> Daily exercises on the lines of the enclosed pamphlet issued by the Central Council for Recreative Physical Training [sic] should be carried out for at least three weeks before the championships. The playing of open-air games and walking will improve condition and help to avoid staleness.

Fencing was still very much an amateur sport, and it evidently did not do to train too vigorously.

Charles began 1938 by joining up as a member of the Auxiliary Air Force, the Territorial arm of the RAF, but the worsening international situation did not prevent him fencing, and he had one of his best years. The National Epee Championship and the Miller-Hallett were fenced for the first time with electrical equipment and again, as in 1933, Charles proved that he was ready for the change. He won both titles outright, the Miller-Hallett for the sixth time in nine years. He was also second in the sabre Championships. That summer the World Championships were held in Piestany in Czechoslovakia. No British team was sent; it was already too dangerous. Instead, two 'non-international' epee teams participated in a competition in Le Touquet. The next World Championships were given to the Italians, to be held in Murano, and a British team was selected and was soon busy training for the event. The Championships never took place.

# IV  The dangerous thirties

> Great Britain's team are captained by a young man whose good looks have made him the favourite of pretty Parisian girls, who have flocked to watch the sport. Tall, agile, indefatigably energetic, he has that sleek type of good looks and 'guardee' type of moustache that Continental women admire as being typically English.
>
> *Daily Mail,* July 1937

From the end of the 1920s to the outbreak of war Charles may have spent much of his time fencing, but he was also making his mark on society. As the nephew of Lord O'Hagan he could be sure of notices such as that given to him in the *Daily Mail*, and he proceeded to cut an elegant figure in the ballrooms and partyland of London society.

Meanwhile at home there was Robin to educate. On his birth Charles had cabled to his friends the Henrys, 'UN ATHLETE COMPLET', but just as his own father's expectations had been dashed in him so Charles's hopes that Robin would become an outstanding athlete were never met. Robin did take up fencing, and in 1942 came third in the Public Schools senior foil, but he was never really good at the sport and soon gave it up. Charles did not try to persuade him otherwise.

After school Robin entered the RAFVR and was accepted for pilot training. First he went on a six-month RAF short course to Cambridge, to Charles's old college, Trinity, to study economics, but by the time he had completed his first solo flight the war in Japan was over, and rather than sign on for another three years to complete his training he decided to relinquish his commission, like many of his contemporaries. For the next three years he toured the Middle East with the Vocational Advice Service, then returned to Trinity to study architecture. After a three-year degree course he completed his training at the Architectural Association in London before entering a West End practice. In the early sixties he left to join a precast concrete manufacturer but this business was eventually taken over in 1977 and he moved on again. Always interested in collecting books and, having written occasional articles on the subject, he changed direction completely and in September 1978 started an antiquarian book department for Stanley Gibbons.

Marguerite on her farm in Shalbourne, near Hungerford.

Robin's progress, then, though Charles was always to show an interest in it, caused his father few problems; Charles instead had his own life to consider. His first rooms in London were at 9 Beaufort Gardens, SW3, and it was here that he lived until 1929, when he bought the house at 44 Montpelier Street which was to become his main home. It was a hotchpotch of styles, with some unusual decorative effects. The dining room contained a bottle of dissected sea-mice left over from Charles's Cambridge days, while Robin's room boasted a bell from the 1936 Olympics, and also a photo of the insides of an ostrich. One of the living rooms contained a portrait of an early de Beaumont, with a slash in the painting made at the time of the Revolution. The main phone was in the form of a candlestick. For a while Charles employed a butler, and at various other times there was an old cook, Rose, a maid, Flora, and an Italian couple. During the war the house was also the home for a lively black-and-tan dachshund, given to Charles to look after by a girlfriend, who in turn had been given the dog by Charles's mother, who herself had won it in a raffle during a ball at the Dorchester Hotel.

Before leaving for Italy Charles had purchased a small antique shop at Bentley, in Hampshire. He also rented two showrooms above Universal Aunts at 37 Wilton Place. On selling up his Hampshire concern he purchased a second London shop, at 194 Brompton Road, then a third, at 170 Brompton Road, and it was this that was to become his main workplace, the home of 'Gloria Antica', just two minutes' walk from his house in Montpelier Street.

If Charles's working and living conditions were changing, so too were the lives of his immediate family. In 1934 his father died. Charles's mother was already immersed in the Guides and in her religious activities, in which she was aided by her elder daughter, Elizabeth. 'Elise', as she was often called, had gone in 1928 to the Royal College of Music to study the violin, and for a long time lived in that world, with such friends as Malcolm Sargent and Chavehavadze, a well-known concert pianist of the time. She also knew Sir Francis Younghusband, and it was from her friendship with him that her mother became involved in his religious ventures. In 1932 Elizabeth married Major The Hon. Richard Coke, a younger son of the Earl of Leicester, by whom she had a son and two daughters. When he died in the early 1960s she moved to Walsingham, close to the Anglican shrine of Our Lady of Walsingham.

Marguerite's life was very different. She continued her work in the Guides, at one time also becoming Commissioner for Home Office Schools and Borstal Institutions for England. But her main occupation, which she began in 1935, was to breed prize-winning horses. One of her ancestors on the Towneley side had at one point bought a horse at a fair. The horse, Kettledrum, went on to win the Derby in 1861. For her part Marguerite only occasionally bred racehorses, concentrating instead on show hacks and Welsh ponies, and in her own field she soon became one of the leading breeders in the country. She wrote two books on the subject which sold well and twice, in

1952 and 1954, with Honeysuckle and her brother, Juniper, she won the 'Hack of the Year' award at Harringay, the annual prize given to the owner of the best riding horse in England: to win such an event twice with horses from the same family is highly unusual. She lived with her partner, Doris Mason – who was to remain her companion until the latter died in the late 1960s – in a beautiful Elizabethan manor house in Shalbourne, outside Hungerford, and it was here that Charles used to go for brief moments of rest and tranquillity.

For he remained close to his sister, and on his visits to Shalbourne would help in the garden and enjoy with Marguerite the pleasures of the countryside. For a while after the war he even discussed buying a cottage close by. Robin was to stay with Marguerite throughout the war years, so there was more than one reason for his father's visits. But these interludes, though frequent, were always squeezed into a schedule full of other commitments.

Charles always exercised an acute sense of responsibility as regards his family. He did not expect any such consideration in return. But if he was sensible of his duties to those closest to him there were areas where he could be almost dangerously single-minded.

Charles had hardly any political sense in the conventional meaning of the term: by background, upbringing and disposition he belonged to the upper class, and was infrequently in contact with those less fortunate than himself. When in the 1960s South Africa first became internationally notorious for its position on apartheid and was attacked vigorously within the sporting arena Charles was one of its most staunch defenders, frequently speaking out on South Africa's behalf when her banning from international competitions was mooted, more often than not succeeding by his logic and good sense in preventing hasty and ill-considered moves by other countries. He won a reputation for always examining questions on their merits, acting with care and with a strong practical streak that those more emotionally committed to the cause in question usually lacked. But, equally, he could be blind to the overall political implications of a situation; and this was particularly the case over Sir Oswald Mosley.

Mosley had taken up fencing at school at Winchester, and in 1912, aged sixteen, had won the Public Schoolboys Championships at both foil and sabre. Fencing became his obsession. In 1931 he was joint runner-up with C. B. Notley in the epee Championships and the following year was third behind Notley and I. D. Campbell-Gray; he was thus one of the leading epeeists of the time, and for two years at least a member of the British team.

By 1930 Mosley was at the height of his parliamentary career, and when, earlier, in 1924, he had left the Tory party for the Labour side, commentators had simply said he was a future Labour Prime Minister rather than a Tory one. But he decided that the normal party alignment held no future for him, and that he would start a 'New Party', which he did on 28 February 1931. Many illustrious names followed him, drawn by his personal magnetism and intellectual brilliance. The economist Maynard Keynes assured Mosley of his vote; Harold Nicolson, too, a Tory MP and a leading literary figure of the day, rallied to his support, filled with thoughts of the exciting future the new adventure promised. The 12-year-old nephew of Winston Churchill, Esmond Romilly, campaigned for Mosley at his preparatory school. The Sitwell family, scions of the London literary world, were keen supporters; while in another world Peter Howard, captain of the Oxford Rugby XV and soon to captain England, joined the pack. Leading Labour intellectuals such as John Strachey and Alan Young added weight to Mosley's group, but after the latter fought and lost a by-election for the New Party Mosley's ambitions took on a new tinge. Strachey for instance claimed that it was at this moment that Mosley's fascism was born.

Mosley had early on expressed himself keen that his followers should be 'fit' and 'in training' and for this reason he took up fencing again. On 30 September 1931 he set up a nation-wide network of athletic clubs to attract young men, and the development of this 'active force' was put under the direction of Edward 'Kid' Lewis, one-time welter-weight boxing champion of the world. 'From that moment onwards,' comments Mosley's biographer, Robert Skidelsky, 'the New Party started to have the dual character associated with its successor, the British Union of Fascists.' The National Government had been formed on 24 August 1931; on Tuesday 27 October a general election followed. Although Mosley was slow to realise it, the fear caused by the financial crisis earlier that year, which had made people flee from the liberal centre of politics to causes such as Mosley's own, had abated; the majority were returning to parties that were tried and trusted. Yet the New Party still had the glamour to attract leading figures: the novelist Peter Cheyney – who was also a fencer at Salle Paul – joined, as did Brendan Bracken and Randolph Churchill, while Christopher Isherwood wrote for the New Party's magazine *Action*. Malcolm Campbell carried the fascist colours on his car 'Bluebird' when it broke the land speed record. It was half-way through 1931 that Charles rallied to the cause.

Whatever other reasons there were behind the relationship Charles had with Mosley, one motive is certain: Charles felt that he could use Mosley to promote fencing, and it was for this reason that he urged the political leader to practise the sport. When in 1931 Mosley joined the London Fencing Club, however, he found that he was not popular with older members, most of them Tories, who felt he had been a traitor to their party. Charles was somewhat out on a limb in supporting him. Gordon Pilbrow recalls: 'He was very enthusiastic about Mosley at first and tried to get other fencers to go with him to Mosley's meetings. Yet I never heard Charles discussing politics at all.' In fact, Charles was never a paid-up member of either the New Party or its successor, the BUF. Yet he not only went along to the meetings but spoke at them, being an effective and accomplished orator. And politics, Charles must have felt, could be fun. Years later he was to tell of one occasion in Birmingham, when young Communists tried to break up a New Party meeting. They succeeded: almost every chair in the hall was broken. Afterwards Mosley, Charles and Kid Lewis were walking down a nearby street when a gang of thugs, who had earlier broken into the meeting, caught up with them. Mosley was an imposing figure of over six feet and Charles was also a formidable sight. The diminutive Lewis, the collar of his coat almost meeting the brim of his hat, was unrecognisable. The leader of the gang, as he thought sizing up the situation correctly, chose Lewis as his victim. The boxer, turning round in a single movement, sent his attacker sprawling on to the pavement with a blow.

In the October General Election the New Party did disastrously. Whereas the Communists, their bitter enemies, gained 70,844 votes from the 26 constituencies in which they fought, Mosley and his supporters could manage only 36,377 from 24 constituencies. Kid Lewis, who was standing in Whitechapel, received the grand total of 154 votes: a Jew, christened 'Gershon Mendeloff', he was frozen out of the Party by the end of the year. Skidelsky comments: 'Following its electoral debacle, the New Party virtually ceased to exist.' Charles remembers a party held in Maldon following this debacle where he and others urged Mosley not to change the name of the party to something declaredly Fascist. The plea failed. In April 1932 Mosley adopted the fasces as his party's symbol, the bundle of sticks symbolising unity, the axe the power of the State as carried by the lictors of ancient Rome. On 1 October 1932 the British Union of Fascists was formed; in 1936 Mosley introduced a new emblem, a flash of lightning within a circle. He also brought in the famous blackshirts, the uniform modelled on a fencing jacket.

But Mosley's involvement in fencing was serious: Skidelsky mentions that, early in 1931, Strachey and Young had complained that 'it was impossible to get Mosley to transact important New Party business because he was so busy fencing.' He goes on: 'To have returned with a gammy leg from a twenty-year lay-off to become runner-up in the British Epee Championship in 1932 was a formidable achievement. It also took up a formidable amount of time. Throughout 1932 he was fencing all over England.'

After 1932, with political pressures reduced, Mosley had plenty of time on his hands, and he used much of it to fence. A programme for a 'Blackshirt Ball' dated 12 October 1934 advertises a display of epee fencing between Mosley and Charles, Charles being described simply as 'Scottish sabre and epee Champion'.

The next year Mosley was a member of the British epee team that came fifth at the European Championships at Lausanne. However, he was not chosen for the Olympic team the following year and after 1937, when he was again a team member, he drifted away from the sport. As for the British Union of Fascists, it reached its peak in 1934, with 10,000 'active' members, 30,000 'non-active'; by 1940 the figures were just over 1000 and 7–8000 respectively.

A British team group at the European Championships in Lausanne, 1935. *Back:* O. G. Trinder, Sir O. Mosley, A. D. Pearce, Miss P. Etheridge, E. Morten, L. Mowlam, A. Pelling, D. Paterson, J. Tait. *Front:* D. Dexter, J. E. Lloyd, C-L. de Beaumont, Gwendoline Neligan.

Charles and Mosley at practice. Note Mosley's injured right foot.

In retrospect it is easy to be critical of Charles's connection with a movement which only subsequently reached the more extreme and brutal phase which has chiefly earned it condemnation. Even now, Mosley is admired for his brilliant gifts and personality which attracted Charles, who for his part wanted to use Mosley for the benefit of fencing. Interestingly, when Mosley was asked for his memories of Charles, he picked out a quality that had little to do with fencing or politics: that his comrade in arms had an unfailing sense of direction, the skill to find his way about in whatever strange country he visited. Charles, one likes to think, would have appreciated the irony of the comment coming from such a source.

When war came Charles was already a member of the Auxiliary Air Force, and desperately wanted to fly; but his eyesight, which had never been good, and which had led to his having special metal-rimmed glasses to wear under his mask when fencing, let him down. Accordingly Charles found himself grounded as 'unfit for flying duties'. Still in his thirties he found the restriction an intense disappointment. When a posting finally came it was in Balloon Command; and after a short spell with a Balloon Squadron he became Training Officer with responsibility for the efficiency of all men who worked in barrage balloons within the London Area. He soon realised that balloons were very much more than a dainty afterthought: on the very morning that Chamberlain announced over the radio that Britain was at war with Germany there were already 624 balloons in the air. Within two years the number had grown to some 2400. The object was not so much to bring down enemy aircraft (with 600 pieces of fabric needed to make one balloon, it could be a laborious deterrent) but to force enemy aircraft to fly at a height at which they could not bomb accurately, and at which they could be most effectively dealt with by the heavy anti-aircraft guns below.

Throughout the whole country there were at first just ten squadrons, each consisting of 800 men – 'balloonatics', they were called. Charles soon buckled to and quickly moved from the rank of Flying Officer to that of Squadron Leader (the equivalent to an army Captain). His main responsibility was the physical fitness of his men, and his principal problem, he discovered, was that they spent much of their time simply waiting till their balloons were hit, and were consequently without anything except repetitive duties to occupy their time. Charles determined to find them some hobby. He asked Marguerite's advice, then issued a command that in every park in London where his balloons operated the men should keep – geese. The order was carried out, though some people questioned the point of the exercise. Charles had a ready answer: not only was it a useful hobby for the men but he intended that each goose, come Christmas, would make a handsome dinner. In the event, matters worked out differently: when Christmas came the geese had become firm favourites with the men, and hardly a single one was killed.

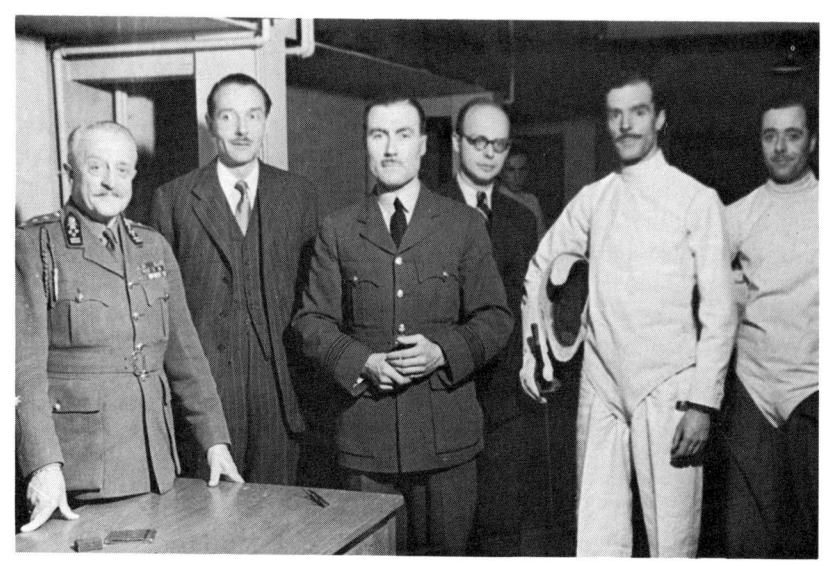

19 December 1941. Squadron Leader de Beaumont presides over a foil match between a BBC team and the Belgian army. On the far left is Gen Chevalier van Strydonck de Burkel, Inspector-General of the Belgian forces in Britain.

In 1943 Charles was posted to the Air Ministry (Planning Division) off Berkeley Square. From there he was sent to the Staff College in Gerrards Cross to train as a staff officer: he was to be promoted to Wing Commander. However, he was still unhappy fighting the war from London, and at the end of 1943 volunteered for the Allied invasion of Sicily. His request to see action was again refused and instead he was co-opted to work for Combined Operations, planning first for D Day and other major initiatives, then for the post-war planning departments on 'how to make Europe whole again'. Again, his judgement and energy quickly won him the respect of the people with whom he worked.

During the 1930s Charles also found time to deal in property. His method was to buy property quickly, occasionally renovate it and sell it almost at once; but although he had the touch for it he never involved himself in this world to any great degree, and at any one time never had more than six properties under his control. One such, a three-storey block, consisting of a garage and a couple of flats, was sited at the back of 170 Brompton Road, in Cheval Place. The top of this building he turned into a roof garden, bringing earth for it from Marguerite's country home. Later, during the war, on a narrow strip of concrete, with bricks taken from blitzed buildings nearby, he grew chives, lettuce and tomatoes, which he either used himself or gave away. He also returned to his boyhood hobby of keeping hens, some of them disappearing to the kitchen when occasion demanded. One friend recalls vividly the games of rummy they would play – this in the summer of 1944, at the time of the flying-bombs, or V1s, which would clatter like taxis down nearby mews. They would listen for each bomb to stop, knowing that they had then some fourteen seconds before the bomb exploded. Charles was lucky: next door to his shop a building belonging to United Dairies was blitzed, but 170 remained untouched. Just in case, Charles had the basement of his shop shored up with beams, and also stored away a thermos and a torch, as well as a wooden mallet to tap with should he get covered with rubble. The V1s continued during the day; on one occasion Charles rescued an old lady who was hanging on to the edge of a bombed building. He also went on organised shoots in the park to bring down the pigeons. On one occasion he blasted a pigeon with a twelve-bore from his bedroom window – accidentally also blasting the window of the actor, Gordon Harker, who lived opposite.

Outside these hazards Charles found plenty of time to enjoy wartime London. Before the V1s started, and while Charles was still part of Balloon Command, his job entailed that he should travel round the city and its outskirts visiting the balloon sites. This he did, in his old grey Ford – at the same time scouring the area for suitable antiques. If it was not quite 'business as usual' Charles still managed to survive the war with very little stock being either broken or destroyed.

Towards the end of the war, in the period Charles was involved in the post-hostilities planning in Whitehall, there was a girl working in Combined Operations in the same building, Paula Holdsworth. She was a Wren at the time, and, aware that she would soon need a peace-time job, began to look round for suitable occupation. It was not long before Charles had her polishing furniture in his basement at thirty shillings a week, and was telling her how lucky she was. Nor was that necessarily exaggeration: girls who worked for Charles before the war were only on ten shillings a week. As it was, Paula's father, a timber importer, had died in 1929, and her Scottish mother died in November 1945, leaving Paula anxious to strike out on her own. By the summer of 1946 she and Charles had fallen in love. They were married, and had one daughter, Carolyn, now Mrs Richard Peel, with two sons of her own, James and Christopher.

# V  The ring-master

> This is the story of a continued effort by a truly amateur Association which, among nations where sport is increasingly subsidized and sponsored by governments, has, by the work of its headquarters, sections and county union staffs, the section coaches and leaders of its masters brought fencing to the youth of this country and has reached the highest position in the international field.
>
> From *Modern British Fencing, 1948–56*, by C-L. de Beaumont

The war saw the almost complete extinction of fencing in Britain. All AFA competitions stopped from 1940 until 1945. However, Charles did all he could to make sure that at least some fencing was done. He egged on Leon Paul, the firm that before the war had made only fencing clothing, and they agreed to start making blades, financed from their own savings. To help pay for the effort Charles urged any emigrés based in London to continue fencing, and soon found there were enough old hands at the London Fencing Club for it to function. The fencing, however, was mainly continued through a small group of epeeists, Luke Fildes, Terry Beddard, Major R. M. P. Willoughby and Col Hay being among the stalwarts. Charles also arranged displays for the forces, for schools and such new clubs as there were, and even provided presidents for any matches that took place. There is evidence that he rescued an Italian, Fortunato Delzi, then in his late forties and in his prime as the sabre Master at the London Fencing Club, from being sent to an internment camp. Charles worked through unofficial channels, but his action was enough to free Delzi, and to provide fencing at the LFC sufficient to give the Italian a living throughout the war years and after. And this was not the only occasion during these years that Charles was to combine genuine compassion and his own interests; he also enabled the famed Leone, who before the war ran the Quo Vadis restaurant in Soho, to escape internment, arranging with Lord Granville, a cousin of the Queen and briefly a sabre international, to take him on as his chef in Ireland. When peace came Leone returned to Soho and held a celebration dinner for Charles and his friends.

Early in 1945 Charles was demobilised and by the beginning of 1946 Gloria Antica was open for business. By the autumn of 1945 official fencing activities had been resumed. The first post-war fencing gala was held in Brussels that October, and Charles travelled over, to beat the Belgium champion, de Beur, 10-6.

All the same, fencing both in Britain and abroad had to be put together again. During the war the headquarters of the FIE had been in Belgium, and as part of their plan for the reconstruction of Europe, the Germans, assisted by the Italian and Hungarian federations, attempted to found a European Fencing Federation to replace the FIE. As Charles himself was to record, 'Great pressure, including a term of imprisonment, was brought to bear on the president of the FIE, M. Paul Anspach, to induce him to approve these plans, but with great courage and devotion he resisted every effort to liquidate the FIE.' In addition, all the records of the FIE were seized by the Gestapo and removed to Berlin, to the main sports stadium, and were later accidentally burned by American troops at the fall of Berlin in the course of disinfecting the premises.

Another kind of disinfecting, a 'commission for purging', was set up by the FIE, and by 1947 eighteen people were excluded from fencing by their federations for 'acts against the FIE' as they were called. Three Czechs were named, four Austrians, five Norwegians, a Pole, two Dutch and three Belgians. Surprisingly, no Germans were included. With these slight hiccups the international fencing community duly got under way again, and it was not long before the sport was running smoothly. The first post-war congress of the FIE was held in Brussels on 8 November 1946, with Charles there as British representative.

The first post-war World Championships were in 1947, in Lisbon. A small British team went, paying their own expenses. The following year saw the Olympics in London, with Charles as ever heavily committed. The fencing events were held in the Hall of Engineering at Wembley, and passed off without a hitch. Emrys Lloyd came fourth in the foil, remarking afterwards to his team Captain, 'I'm terribly sorry, Charles'; Ron Parfitt reached the epee final, Charles himself the quarter-final; and Mary Glen Haig, present President of the AFA, came eighth in the ladies' foil, after topping her semi-final pool, including a victory over the eventual Gold Medallist, Ilona Elek of Hungary. Trained by such top masters as Morel and Parkins, Mary had been 21 in 1939, and thus saw what were probably her best competitive years eaten up by the war.

Elsewhere the Games passed by with high British efficiency. The ceremonial was precise and much admired, the general atmosphere one of an amateurism determined to see the Olympic Spirit triumph over memories of Hitler's Olympics of twelve years before. Monique Berlioux, a swimmer at the 1948 Games and now a Director of the IOC, has called them the 'last real Olympics'. Perhaps they were. Although Luke Fildes – known colloquially as 'Val', but whom Charles still addressed as 'Sir' – was on the main organising

1948, and the London Olympics: Charles takes on Asfar of Egypt in the first round of the epee individual.

committee's Technical Committee it was Charles who was chiefly responsible for the fencing, and the official FIE report on the Games reads: 'The man to whom we are indebted for the work and success is Charles de Beaumont: never will you be able sufficiently to express your indebtedness to him.'

In the January of 1949 Charles appointed the first national coach for fencing, Roger Crosnier, and together that year they revived the British Academy of Fencing, the professional body for fencing in the country, originally founded by Henry VIII. Crosnier, a Frenchman brought up in Edinburgh, fenced as an amateur in Britain in his early days, then turned professional to become Master to the French Army and to the University of Paris, as well as having his own salle in Paris. He was twice second in the French professional championships at both foil and sabre, and represented the French professional teams at international level at all three weapons. He had also been an active member of the Resistance during the war. The year before coming to England he had trained with and advised the French Olympic team, and was largely responsible for their great success during the Olympics. His stay in London provided Charles with the chance to use his persuasive powers, and Crosnier made his decision. He was to be among the most notable of a number of leading fencing masters from abroad who came to live in Britain. Crosnier duly reported to Vine Street Police Station on his arrival and the desk sergeant in all seriousness marked on his passport, 'duel nationality'. Before long, however, Crosnier and his French wife decided they found England unbearable, and they returned to France; but another Frenchman, Pierre Cottard, three Hungarians – Bela Imregi, John Erdelyi and Akos Moldovanyi – a Bulgarian – George Ganchev – as well as many others, came over to London to work in the decades after the war.

Charles next started up the system of Sections, by which the country was divided into manageable groups of counties with Section Championships, Section Coaches and a general devolution of power from London. In 1937 he had organised the first AFA Annual Dinner; this was now revived with success. The old Alfred Hutton Memorial Challenge Cup, first presented in 1913 as the trophy for the ladies' international tournament, had been melted down during the war; Charles promptly put up his own trophy, the de Beaumont Cup, to replace it.

It was at about this time that he also engaged himself energetically in a system of fencing 'circuses' by which he would arrange for established British internationals to give demonstrations of the four weapons. Charles had in fact organised such exercises before the war – soon after the All-England Fencing Club had been founded – but now he promoted them in earnest. He himself would start off the show with a brief run-down of how fencing had developed through the ages, antique swords readily to hand. Over the years he conducted literally hundreds of these occasions not only throughout Britain but in many other parts of the world, at health clubs, Girl Guides' meetings, University openings, RAF bases, schools, polytechnics and colleges. The best of all memoirs of these outings was that written by Ossie Reynolds, a British foil international, in an article in *The Sword* in the spring of 1955.

After an international had performed at a certain number of circuses he or she would be awarded a special badge, a white oblong framing a black seal balancing a Tudor rose on its nose. Accordingly Reynolds wrote under the pseudonym of 'Sea Lyon', and entitled his gentle satire 'The all-egal fencing club-circus'. It reads in full:

> Every now and then Mr. Charles de Be–u–o–t takes what he pleases to call his 'circus' to some far away place in order to demonstrate to the local inhabitants the joys of fencing.
>
> We are usually received at the hall by a local dignitary (who on one recent occasion thought he was going to see archery) and a string of excuses to explain the inadequacy of the audience: 'Bad time of year this, y'know, everybody got 'flu', dry rot, death watch beetle,' etc., etc.
>
> Charles is then introduced to the audience. To us, the members of his circus, various scraps of the introduction are audible through noises of hysteria, which, by this time, Miss Margaret Spofford is almost certainly producing. 'Ladies and gentlemen', says the introducer, 'We are all highly honoured . . . distinguished guests . . . , survival from the past . . . , junior epee champion 1897 . . . , Charles de Beau–––t.' Amid cheers Charles takes the stage, wearing a benevolent smile and as many Union Jacks as he can muster. He then begins his short history of fencing. 'Ladies and

One of the famous circuses in promotion of fencing, this time in front of an RAF audience in Surrey. The other combatant is the international sabre fencer, John Rayden.

gentlemen, we are here to tell you something about this ancient and unnatural sport of fencing ... shown to have been carried out in Egypt in 4,000 BC ... Tablets discovered in the basement of a Kensington antique dealer's shop, etc.' While all this is going on the members of the circus are either dozing quietly or looking at the programme to see what it says about them. Spelling mistakes are always interesting. Who, for instance, are Mrs. Mary Grim-Hate, Miss Gillian Spleen, and Messrs. A. G. Ibrow, Raymond Boil, and Bill Beastley?

Charles has by now probably passed the bit about chess being like a game of fencing played at lightning speed and has gone on to duels in the dim early morning light, under dripping trees, with sharp epees. (Bob [Anderson] says if he was challenged to a duel he'd pick wet lettuce leaves.) So we begin the demonstration.

'Ladies and Gentlemen, we are very fortunate to have with us Miss J–r–e–s–n, who has come all the way from Denmark in order to be with us in Shacclesdump tonight. She will be opposed by Mrs. Grim-Hate, who has been for many years one of our most promising young fencers.

'Now suppose Mrs. G.-H. wishes to hit Miss J.: she will straighten her arm, and with a rapid extension of the arms, legs and trunk which we call the plunge, carry her point on to the target. (No dear, target.) Now, these are lady champions and if you were to thrust at them directly like that you would be parried 99 times out of 100.' This always causes a subdued explosion in the participants' corner. And so on, to the advance and retire. The two demonstrators, agonisingly immobilised in the on-guard position, are suddenly awakened by the command 'Advance'. Now, unless there has been some previous arrangement, this poses a problem. Usually both, on the assumption that their opponent is stupid, retire simultaneously. The error is rectified immediately and both advance smartly, the movement coinciding exactly with Charles's command 'Retire'. This puzzles the audience.

Charles then goes on to say that foil is a weapon for girls, and men who are not strong enough to do epee and sabre.

Any information that the spectators may have gleaned from the demonstration of judging and presiding is quickly dispelled by the matches. What layman, or novice, could be expected to cope with such masterpieces as: 'Halt. The attack from my right? No? No?? Ha, ha, ha. Against my left. Six-five. On guard! Ready? Play! Halt! Parried? Parried? Riposte? Leg. Mask. Against my right! and now, ladies and gentlemen, they are at seven-all, match point'?

After one or two matches Charles potters up to us and says: 'Now boys, who is going to do sabre with me?' There is a sudden silence, faces pale, and a voice is heard murmuring, 'Rather fence with a combine harvester.'

After bringing the house down with the sabre we depart contentedly for home, suitably filled with beer, jam butties and toasted tea cakes. We have to be fairly quiet because of the gentleman on the stretcher, but one of the members may usually be heard describing how his prof. caught him skipping with a length of small intestine.

On 1 January 1949 Charles appeared on the popular BBC Television show, 'In Town Tonight', fencing against Brian Johnston, the programme's main commentator. He also wrote his first book, *Modern British Fencing: A History of the Amateur Fencing Association of Great Britain*, tracing the history of fencing from its earliest days until 1946. The year ended with his being invited to the 1949 World Championships in Cairo as a member of the Directoire Technique.

Charles was not just involved in the administration and publicising of fencing, however; he was still an active and eager competitor himself. In 1950 fencing was included for the first time in the Commonwealth Games, which that year took place in early February, in Auckland, New Zealand. Charles headed the English team and duly made the epee final. There he lost to a young member of the Australian team, one Allan Jay, but his opponents also lost fights and by the end of the six-man final he found himself in a triple barrage with another Australian, Lund, and his British colleague, Bob Anderson. In the first bout of the fight-off Charles beat Anderson in a close encounter and then went on to beat the Australian 3–2 – an extremely impressive performance for a man of 48. From New Zealand he travelled with Mary Glen Haig to Monaco for the 1950 World Championships, where the British girl took fourth place, and the ladies' team the Bronze Medal. Next year the Championships were in Stockholm, followed by the Olympics in Helsinki with a re-Anglicised Allan Jay, now resident in London, narrowly missing the epee final on his first full international appearance. Charles was not only continuing as a member of the British team; he was the driving force behind that band of fencers that was to make Britain one of the half-dozen best fencing nations in the world throughout the 1950s and early 1960s.

In 1953, a few days after his fifty-first birthday, Charles appeared at the AFA to contest the National Epee Championship. His last win in the competition had been in 1938 and now, fifteen years later, he triumphantly brought off a fourth victory, beating fellow-international Eddie Knott in yet another barrage. Allan Jay was third. *The Sword* commented: 'How often does it happen – in epee particularly – that fencers that just scrape through the early rounds do well in the final pool? . . . Charles de Beaumont tied for the last place in his first round pool both in victories and in hits received, and went up to the semi-final on one hit scored at the expense of John Pelling [a future international]. In the semi-final he was in the barrage for the last place and at the end of the barrage hits had to be counted again and once more he tied on hits received and was promoted on hits given.' It was an amazing performance, and in case the result was not enough to show he was well worth his place in the national team that year he also came sixth in the Miller-Hallett. As for his second weapon, he was no longer included among sabreurs at international level, yet in 1948, when 46, he was one of only three Englishmen in a nine-man Corble Cup final composed mainly of Frenchmen or Hungarians of the calibre of Gerevich and Kovacs, both ex-World and Olympic Champions.

In 1954 Charles again travelled to the Commonwealth Games as member and Captain of the British team, and although he failed to make the individual epee final he gained a gold medal in the team event. He was also granted the honour of being standard-bearer for the English team at the opening ceremony to the Games. His competitive days, however, were drawing to a close, and the next year he travelled to the Rome World Championships still as Captain, but only as reserve for the team itself. He did not fence. He was to continue fencing at club level into his seventies and presided at major events for almost as long; but now it was administration of the sport that was to take up his time.

It was in 1955 that Charles accomplished one of his most far-reaching reforms. The rules of fencing required a fresh translation from French into English, and he offered to do the job in partnership with Val Fildes. By the end of the year the work was done – although in fact Charles was to continue translating amendments to the rules for the rest of his life. The joint Fildes–de Beaumont translation was immediately taken up throughout America and the Commonwealth as the official version. It was a gruelling task, the various amendments – made by the French themselves, the Hungarians and Italians – often making contradictory reading and requiring Charles and his collaborator in effect often to interpret what they were trying to say.

The following year Charles was awarded the OBE 'for services to fencing'. Recognition of all he had done for the sport had started to come to him before this, however. In the summer of 1949 the French elected him a Membre d'Honneur of the FIE, something which had only been given thirteen times since the foundation of the FIE and never before to an Englishman. In the winter of 1951 he received a further award, again from the French, the gold medal of the Physical Education Order of France; this too was the first time an Englishman had been so honoured. Then, in the spring of 1956, he was given the Challenge Feyerick, a trophy awarded every two years to the person, team or nation who 'during the previous two years is considered to have done most to further fencing and maintain the ideals of selflessness and sportsmanship so as to provide an example to the future and the fencers of the world'. Such recognition was pleasant enough, but in 1956 a more important appointment was at hand, for Luke Fildes announced he wished to retire from the Presidency of the AFA. Charles was his obvious successor, and on 14 August was elected to the post.

It was to be a crowded year. Britain staged her first World Championship – for the ladies' individual and team events, which that year were held separated from the men. Charles presided at the Championships, which went off without mishap, amid a hazy English summer. Next came the Olympics in Melbourne, and a major triumph: Gillian Sheen, a young trainee dentist, won the Gold Medal in the individual women's foil. It was Britain's first-ever Olympic fencing title but was soon followed by Bill Hoskyns's epee world title win – in 1958 – and Allay Jay's foil win in 1959. After Melbourne Britain was officially recognised as No. 3 among fencing nations, only France and Italy being placed ahead.

Charles rounded off 1956 by writing the official history of the London Fencing Club and began 1957 by formally announcing his retirement from competitive fencing. The July World Championship in Paris saw the introduction of five-hit epee – which Charles had long recommended – and the continued success of the British teams abroad. In 1958 Charles published the second volume of British fencing history, leading up to and including the events of 1956. He also wrote *Fencing Technique in Pictures*, the second of his many introductory books on fencing and one which quickly ran through two editions. That same year his publishers told him that an earlier book, *Know the Game – Fencing*, on which he had collaborated with Roger Crosnier and which had been published in 1951, had sold over 20,000 copies. He did not lay claim to great merits as a stylist, but he was a scrupulous researcher and his work is still a valuable source of material on all aspects of British fencing which no one else would have been in a position to attempt to achieve.

As in most areas of his life, he seemed indefatigable: history books, technical books, essays for magazines and papers, contributions to part-works and encyclopaedias all flowed easily from his pen. In 1960, the year that Charles published one of his fluent works, *Fencing: Ancient Art and Modern Sport*, he received yet another award: as a Cavaliere Ufficiale al Merito della Republica Italiana. However, none of these honours was enough to offset the

Charles and his two most famous male champions: Bill Hoskyns (*centre*) and Allan Jay.

greatest disappointment of his entire career. He tried for the Presidency of the FIE and lost.

The FIE had been founded in 1913 and had never left the continent of Europe. Twice Belgium had won the presidency, and once each Italy, Holland and Switzerland had done so. The other three presidencies had belonged to France. The headquarters of international fencing was in Paris. It had always been in Paris. The officers of the organisation, the leading competitors, all hailed from France. The very language of the sport was French. However, Charles's command of languages, his energy, enthusiasm and general high standing, not least his freedom from financial worries and the nature of his antiques business, both of which allowed him to attend most international congresses and competitions, meant that he had a hold on the way international fencing was conducted that no other contender could command.

By 1960 he was sufficiently obvious a choice for the presidency that he was already busy planning the way in which he would run the FIE once it became based in London. (It was a tradition that whichever country won the presidency had the right to transfer the entire FIE office to that country; although no previous President from outside France had taken up this option.) He had purposely kept all dealings with the Federation very much in his own hands, most of the correspondence going straight to his home address, and other people in Britain had little or no idea what was actually happening on the international scene. Pierre Turquet, the then captain of the British foil and sabre teams, would often travel with Charles to major congresses, but he had little or no idea of what was involved in the day-to-day running of the organisation. Yet Charles told Pierre that he would be his nomination as Secretary of the FIE. He told Robin Brook that he would like him to become the Federation's treasurer. His mind was also full of ideas for the reform of the FIE – then as now hardly an efficient body. Charles, too, lobbied vigorously, and received enough promises of votes cast in his favour to feel assured of the presidency.

It was not to be. He was duly nominated, but the French, seeing the danger of his candidature, put up the Belgian, Charles de Beur, against him. They then organised as many non-aligned countries as possible to vote for their candidate. Even so, when it came to a vote the two factions were in deadlock, with neither able to command a sufficient majority. One of the most powerful characters within the FIE at that time, Commandant Bontemps, a singularly inappropriately-named French official, now set about improving his side's chances behind the scenes. A further candidate, Miguel A. de Capriles, a member of the American Olympic team, was put forward, and despite the backing given to Charles from the emerging Iron Curtain countries, and from France's deepest rivals, the Italians, it was Capriles who was elected.

A year later, in the summer of 1961, a *Sword* columnist, 'Total Abstainer', wrote:

> There have been doubts on how efficiently America will be able to run the Federation, bearing in mind their geographical separation from the leading fencing nations, and the fact that experience on the international scene has been somewhat limited . . . It will be interesting, however, to see how they get on, and in particular what headway they make against the voting power of the leading European nations should they decide to try and introduce changes . . .

Mr Capriles introduced no changes – no notable ones, at least. The presidency was remarkable only for the fact that viewed from a distance it could have been mistaken for the presidency of a Frenchman. 'Total Abstainer' in that same article also put in correct perspective something of what the loss of the presidency meant to Charles:

> Charles de Beaumont has suffered many defeats in the long and arduous years he has devoted to fencing, but none could possibly have been as bitter as losing the presidency of the FIE to Miguel de Capriles of America a year ago, on, as it were, the last hit of a barrage . . .

Charles did stand a second time, but he never had so good a chance of the presidency again, and while he continued to be a leading member of the FIE he ended his career without winning the one prize he coveted probably above all others.

On the home front the story was one of continued and rapid progress. Gillian Sheen's Olympic win meant a sudden upsurge of interest in fencing, and also gave Charles acute pleasure. Probably of all the women Charles met through fencing Gillian meant most to him: pressed within one of his

# The ring-master 63

seventeen scrapbooks on the sport is a flower taken from her Melbourne winner's bouquet. The continued progress of the rest of the team meant that the British press gave regular coverage to fencing's major figures and Sheen, Hoskyns and Jay became household names.

This prestige brought some unexpected benefits. In 1959, when Allan Jay and Bill Hoskyns were fencing in a large foil competition in Paris sponsored by Martini and Rossi, they asked why a similar competition sponsored by Martini should not be held in London. When they returned home they told Charles of their plan and he approached the publicity department of Martini and Rossi in London. So was born the international Martini Competition for epee, now the premier competition in Britain.

Fencing was becoming, in its small way, one of the post-war boom sports, and Charles realised that it was now in need of a proper centre. The Association had first acquired an office in the same year of 1936 that Charles became Honorary Secretary, most probably as a result of his influence. This was at 12 Berkeley Square. It was transferred to 15 Bruton Street, nearby, in February 1937, but in August of the same year this building was demolished, so the AFA moved again, this time to the LFC premises at 7 Cleveland Row, where they paid a nominal rent to the club for the offices they used. In 1948 both moved once more to 1a Tenterden Street, off Hanover Square, close to Oxford Circus.

The lease of these premises was due to expire in June 1962 and in June 1961 the Oriental Club, their landlords, gave notice that it would not be renewed, as the whole site was to be redeveloped. In the event the premises were destroyed by fire in May 1962, together with most of the Association's records, but Charles had begun to hunt for a new headquarters two years before. This proved fruitless; so Charles turned to the idea of a completely new building, one that had been in his mind for many years – the creation of a totally new and up-to-date centre for fencing, and a permanent home for both the LFC and the AFA.

Where was such a centre to be built? One of Charles's closest friends in fencing, Terry Beddard, had contacts at Queen's Club in West Kensington: ever since the war Charles had coveted the empty ground behind the tennis courts.... Approaches were made, there were numerous confidential discussions and planning sessions, until at last on 21 December 1962, at a cost of some £45,000, the new centre opened. Charles personally underwrote much of the AFA's payment. A lease was granted for fifty years, while within the year £23,000 was raised in reimbursement to him. The bank loan and interest of some £8,000 was subsequently raised and the fixed loan of £15,000 remaining was secured by the AFA taking out a life policy on Charles's family – the interest on which was to be paid by the Association.

At the time the centre was the only hall in the world to have been built especially for fencing. Among its special features were the underground

Britain's premier competition, with the final held en gala at the Seymour Hall in London – the International Martini Epee. Charles was organiser, travel agent, committee d'arbitrage, host and compere.

wiring system for electric foil and epee, with the special non-flickering lights for the central illumination which Charles himself had found in Belgium and which he had installed to avoid fencers being put off during bouts. Unfortunately the centre also had weaknesses; but perfection was hardly possible at the remarkably low cost involved. The ceiling was uncomfortably high, being open to the roof; the kitchen was not ideally sited; and a room that was meant to be an office for the Women's Association was so small that it soon became used simply as a security closet. But all-in-all the building was a major achievement, the focus of fencing in Britain, and another contribution to the solid foundations which Charles had given his sport. At the suggest of others the centre was given his name.

The 1960s continued to see an increase not only in the numbers practising the sport but in Charles's hold over it. He was still winning both appointments and awards outside the world of the AFA. He was already Deputy Chairman of the Council of the British Olympic Association; in 1964 he was appointed Team Commandant at the Tokyo Olympics, in effect in command of the entire British team; and in June of that year the French awarded him yet another honour, this time coming from the entire French sporting fraternity and not just the FIE: he became a Commandant de Merite Sportife. Next, in December 1966, the Italian government appointed him a *Commendatore*.

The continuing committee work, of innovations large and small, the growth of a system of diplomas to reward aspiring amateurs and the crucial development under Bob Anderson – Robert Crosnier's successor as National Coach – of a system of 'Leaders', or amateur coaches, all belong to these years. They are thoroughly charted in Charles's own books on the history of British fencing.

Charles's character is not. What kind of person had he become over the years, as he grew from the schoolboy with bad eyesight who loved countryside rambles into the tough, capable boy scout, and then on into successful businessman, Olympic fencer, a national celebrity, figurehead of his chosen world? Some eccentricities – seemingly so much of his family background – came to flourish. He took to wearing a red carnation, if not daily then certainly to any major fencing event. Only in France did the style change: then it was white. 'I am a royalist,' he would explain. Care over dress – always stylish, never gaudy – extended even to his fencing socks, which he made sure were topped in red, white and blue. And, as Emrys Lloyd noted in his tribute at Charles's Memorial Service, anyone in fencing administration for any length of time soon became used to

> those tatty envelopes we received from him through the post. They were used envelopes with an economy label stuck on them to save the AFA the cost of a new envelope. Addressed in Charles's own scrawling hand, they would contain some letter or memorandum, typed (and not well typed) by Charles himself on a typewriter that might have qualified as an antique, but clearly expressed and outlining some plan or some scheme he had carefully

thought out and which must have meant for him the burning of much midnight oil.

This practice did not change on Charles's becoming President of the AFA. On the contrary, right up to his last days he could be seen scurrying about the de Beaumont centre, picking up cigarette butts, opening or closing windows, smoothing down the edges of the metal pistes, collecting empty glasses left in the salle and returning them to the bar. 'That was his trouble,' commented Bobby Winton, who knew him from the days when the LFC and Bertrand's were amalgamated just after the war. 'He didn't know when to let go. He was never a person who could see someone else do a job which he thought he could do better.' On the weekend of the London Martini Charles would be up at the crack of dawn to sign in the arriving competitors. 'You can't trust the young crowd to do it,' he would say.

Yet strangely Charles always remained a very private person. 'He was never the sort of man about whom anecdotes were told,' Emrys Lloyd remembers. 'Not that he was a dull chap; just not a caricaturable one, so to speak.' He had a hearty appetite, was especially fond of foods like fruit, cream and butter, and was knowledgeable about wine, with a particular knowledge of the Bordeaux area. His reading was largely limited to the worlds of fencing and antiques, but for relaxation he would turn with pleasure to blood-and-thunder American detective stories. A less obvious trait is mentioned in the letter about him alluded to earlier, written by Sir Oswald Mosley:

> My most vivid recollection of him is during the world championship in Paris in 1937, when we were both members of the British Epee team. He had among other gifts the extraordinary sense of direction which you usually find only in birds. We were billeted somewhere in the suburbs, and with unerring instinct he would find his way to our appointment in the centre of Paris and back again to the suburbs without any knowledge of the city and without any inquiries.

Mosley goes on: 'His invariable gaiety and extraordinary capacity for endurance were noteworthy, and rendered him the best of companions either in happiness or adversity.' Charles also had a dry wit which was never far from the surface. One typical foray was printed in the Spring 1954 issue of *The Sword*:

> Sir,
> My heart has been wrung, as have doubtless the hearts of all those concerned with the organisation of fencing events, by the cri de coeur from 'Wedded to a sword' in your last issue. The debt which fencing owes to the forebearance of fencing widows cannot be estimated or exaggerated but they have an advantage over their ancestresses of the age of chivalry when knights were wont
> 'To battle with giant and wizard breed

or conquer realms at the doubtful need
of ladies weeping by wells'.
I can assure them that judging at LAFU competitions should not be regarded as the modern equivalent.
Perhaps fencing widows might more often grace our competitions with their presence, but for those who have been too long wedded to the sword to be lured by swordplay I am willing to organise an AFA 'Solace for Widows Service'. Selected foilists would be available during epee or sabre competitions and vice versa so that no fencing widow need languish for want of consolation.
Sir, the age of chivalry is not dead.
                                   Yours,
                                   C-L. de Beaumont
P.S. – My telephone number is (censored by Editor).

Again, in his team report following the 1965 World Championships, held in Paris, he wrote: 'We found comfortable and pleasant quarters at a surprisingly reasonable cost within a stone's throw of the Folies Bergères in Montmartre. This was not allowed to interfere with the training and, if the venue of the competitions was some way away, at least our fencers had the distinction of "going to work" in a Rolls Royce.'

The Rolls, like the Bentley that preceded it, commanded attention. Yet for years Charles owned a succession of battered Fords, then after the war a Sunbeam. It was not until the mid sixties that he decided to acquire something more noticeable, and his Rolls – more often than not stuffed full of antiques – became an inseparable part of the fencing scene.

Charles was not one to wear his heart on his sleeve, but he was a kind man. Bobby Winton recalls: 'He was always someone who had time to speak to you, and while he did so would make you feel that it was *you* he wanted to talk to at that particular moment, rather than anyone else.' A mixture of thoughtfulness and good management, perhaps. Another memory is of Luke Fildes, in his eighties, blind and living in a nursing home in Kensington, regularly visited by Charles on Sunday evenings. Even more moving was Charles's action when, himself very ill, he learned in 1972 that Gwen Nelligan was in hospital and about to die from cancer. An enormous bunch of red roses arrived at her bedside. With it was a message: 'Remember, you always get the last hit – Charles.' She never lived to see it.

As was inevitable with anybody who personally transacted so much of the work of the Association, who came to hold so many of the leading offices and wielded such great influence, Charles attracted criticism, especially as younger generations of fencers, more disposed to question authority, appeared on the scene. A few were to attribute to him the failure to produce a growing number of masters of top calibre, on whom the future success and growth of British fencing would depend; but this was not a matter easily remedied (and

Charles at home with his family. To his left are Robin's wife, Joy, Paula, Carolyn, Robin and (*below*) Robin's two children, Lys and Dominic.

did not improve after his death); and Charles had at least helped to found the British Academy of Fencing and to produce a small army of coaches to nurture the sport around the country through the National Coaching Scheme. Some criticised him for favouring epee and epeeists, sabreurs particularly feeling it hard to gain his attention. His answer might well have been that, as offering much the best hopes of success, epee best rewarded his attention and correspondingly the sabreurs could claim the least. Some thought he was antisemitic. This was untrue. Others thought he had favourites among team members and that there were occasions when he was biased as a selector. But, though directly concerned with epee selection as chairman of the selectors and indirectly with all selection as Chairman of the Joint Weapon Sub-Committee (which vetted all World Championship and Olympic selections), he was always one among several who made the decisions. Possibly he was over-inclined to stick to the tried and tested, though equally on occasions he certainly sometimes favoured fresh blood and young contenders. He is also said to have stated that qualification for the epee team included the fencer being 'the sort of person who was going to make a harmonious side', an arguable criterion but one which could obviously open the door to favouritism. On the other hand, one of his surviving fellow epee selectors, John Pelling, feels that this was not Charles's point of view. He also recalls that Charles did not attempt to impose his views on fellow selectors and that indeed decisions were often reached after closely-contested argument. His father, Bert Pelling, has given a similar account of the long period over which he too had been an epee selector.

There was a tendency, likewise, to exaggerate Charles's monopoly of power on committees and his insistence on having his way. He certainly exercised great influence. As President he chaired the main Committee, as he did the Epee Sub Committee (from 1962), the National Training Sub-Committee (from 1952), the England Teams Sub-Committee (from 1951) and the less formally constituted Joint Weapon Sub-Committee. And although he did not chair the numerous other sub-committees his influence was pervasive if only because he directly shouldered so much of the work and was willing to give his time and money to travelling to almost every World Championship, every FIE Congress, every World Youth Games, Commonwealth Games, every home Quadrangular. He personally carried on nearly all correspondence over participation in foreign events. He not only master-minded the Martini Epee Tournament but personally did most of the work. He was to be seen at practically every national competition and until his last years he commonly presided the finals.

In committee he was an extremely experienced and efficient chairman, who pushed on rapidly with the business of the meeting without losing sight of the principles at stake. He held strong views and was seldom neutral, and if things were going against him was capable of saying 'Oh well, you *can* do it that way . . .' and threaten to withdraw from the project under discussion. Colleagues may frequently have felt that they could not afford to risk losing his enormous contribution to the fencing world or even in some cases that they would suffer from his personal disfavour, a natural response to a strong character doing so much of the work; but actually, as one committee member recalls, he bore no grudge against those who opposed his views. On the contrary, he warmed to those who made positive contributions to committee work, even if at variance with himself. His scorn was reserved for those who sat on the fence.

There was, however, a definite adverse side to Charles's supremacy, which was the dearth of fencers a generation younger than himself contributing to running the Association. This can mainly be attributed to people's reluctance to come forward to take a share in the work when there was a willing hand doing it already, but the strength of Charles's leadership was also a factor and the situation naturally tended to compound itself. Its bad effect was felt at its keenest when Charles died and there were few practised hands to take up the reins of power.

# VI The curious case of the Chippendale commode

'Ringing' you already know about I'm sure, is where dealers get together and do not bid for a choice item, say a lovely French commode. When it goes to Dealer A for a paltry sum – i.e. when it's been successfully 'ringed' – he'll collect his cronies and they'll auction it again privately in a pub nearby, only on this occasion Dealer A is the auctioneer and his mates are the congregation, so to speak.
You'll probably think this is against the law. Correct, it is.

From *The Judas Pair*, by Jonathan Gash

Antiques, and the selling of them, were Charles's main interest. He may have given more time to fencing, derived greater pleasure from it, but it was essential to his financial well-being that his venture into selling antiques should work; and he conducted his business life with the same flair, hard work and single-mindedness that he employed for fencing. The antique business was not often to take him into the national headlines; but its importance in his life was considerable.

He had set up 'Gloria Antica' in 1929 in the Brompton Road, on the Knightsbridge side of Brompton Square. He came to specialise in English porcelain, and to a lesser degree in eighteenth-century and early nineteenth-century furniture, but he never ceased to be a general dealer, with a sharp eye for anything that would sell, and with a good idea of its value. He did most of his buying at weekends, often combining it with either a fencing competition or some other appearance connected with fencing, and at World or Olympic Championships would often take a day off, wherever the venue, to go round looking for possible purchases. Not surprisingly, he also possessed an outstanding collection of fencing prints and books on the sport.

The shop itself had a main room some thirty feet by twenty in size, with a small enclosed office towards the back where Charles kept his books, and there was a second storeroom downstairs. A large white china cat sat in the window.

It was said by a friend that if a customer came into his shop asking for a picture of a family ancestor (and come they did, for even when selling antiques Charles was a great individualist), Charles would readily supply something suitable, and that he was also as eager as anyone to see that any American visitor with money to burn did not go away empty-handed. He also did all his own 'books', although a fellow epeeist, Wilfred Evill, would be consulted on legal questions. It was clear, however, that Charles was scrupulously honest, and for this reason never got involved in the 'ring' of antique dealers which came to light in the early 1960s, and which caused a major scandal in the antique world. When Charles did get drawn into the affair it was very much against his wishes.

The story broke in a long article in the *Sunday Times* on 8 November 1964, written by the famous 'Insight' team who were to make such a speciality of extensive investigations for the paper. At a sale in Leamington Spa in November 1962 the household effects of the late Sir Wathen Waller and Lady Waller were put up to auction. The sale was particularly interesting because it involved one of the finest pieces of English antique furniture to come on the market for many years – a mahogany *bombé* commode by Chippendale, which was later to become a star exhibit at that year's Antique Dealers' Fair. The *Sunday Times* argued that in a room packed with dealers at least five people knew the true value of the commode, but the bidding was surprisingly sluggish, and the commode fetched only £750. Within hours it was resold for £4,350, a handful of knowledgeable dealers meeting at a private room in a local hotel, and this time bidding against each other in earnest. The commode's real value was later put at £10,000. The difference between the public auction price and the private price, some £3,600, was distributed among the expert 'rivals'. Besides the two men who had put up the separate bids there were four other dealers present, and they each took a share-out of £600. It was their reward for not bidding in the showroom. The entire two-day sale of the Waller collection yielded just over £7,500: an independent valuer later estimated that nearly £20,000 might have been realized if the bidding had been genuinely competitive.

The *Sunday Times* article, followed by extensive correspondence in the paper and a lengthy sequel the following week, created a storm. In a Commons debate on rigged bidding, the Ulster Unionist MP and Tory whip, Mr Robert Chichester-Clark, put the matter plainly: the 'knockout', as it was called, was a criminal offence, and 'those who practised it were crooks' – whether they liked it or not, and whether they knew it or not. The Commons debate acknowledged that there was some doubt about what constituted a knockout, but as another Conservative MP said, voicing the general feeling of the house, rings 'were corrupt and corrupting practices – corrupting because they brought in on the edges of these deals men who otherwise had excellent reputations for probity and integrity.'

The British Antique Dealers' Association found itself at the centre of the controversy, and reacted not a little uneasily. For from time to time since 1927, when an Act of Parliament had made auction rings illegal, they had raised the issue among themselves but had in effect allowed the practice to continue. They could turn a blind eye no longer. Now, as a result of the *Sunday Times* publicity, two former presidents and nine other members of the 32-man council of BADA resigned – not necessarily through a guilty conscience. A number felt the Association had not acted quickly or effectively enough.

At an extraordinary general meeting of the Association held at Church House, Westminster at the beginning of December, a resolution against participation in knockouts at auction sales was carried unanimously by the 262 members present. It was here that Charles's involvement came to the public eye. As Vice-President of the Association he was required to present to the public at large the views of British dealers as a whole. Typically, he not only did much to re-establish the integrity of their image but also pointed to the double standard underlying the issue. Referring to the 'great crisis in our affairs', he declared:

> Britain is being recognized as a centre of the fine arts of the world because of the integrity which we have built up. Last year £29,500,000 in foreign currency came into Britain to buy works of art, an advance of £10,000,000 on the previous year. Antiques are not an unimportant contribution to the tourist trade.
> The picture built up over the last forty-six years depends on public confidence, but this is shaken by virulent attacks on us on the subject of the 'knockout' and this, I fear, at the present time has given rise to very grave public concern, not only in this country but in America.

He was on the defensive, but it was not long before he went on the attack. A year later he spoke at length about the question, pointing out that the 'knockout' was illegal only in Britain; he added that not only had it long existed in other public sales – such as those for cattle and for metal – but that the Act of 1927 had anyway always proved unenforceable. (The *Sunday Times* had called the Act 'one of the most ineffectual in legal history'.) At the end of his speech he said:

> All our members have signed a declaration that they will not take part in rings and after-auction knockouts. I cannot say that these practices have entirely stopped, but they used to be blatant and now they are not apparent. The example of the Antique Dealers' Association has had some effect.
> The answer really lies in the hands of the seller. If they were not so mean and had a proper evaluation done, you would not get these things happening. Some of these county auctioneers only know about auctioning cattle. If you walked into a shop and saw a diamond valued the same price as a piece of cut glass, wouldn't you buy it at the price stated?

That really was the nub. Charles realised that, although auction rings had to be watched for carefully and could often do harm, the small, elite world of antique dealers often acted as the final arbiter of taste and value, and there was no practical way of altering that authority or monitoring the way those experts did their business. Most often they acted for the good. As with so much else, the dividing line between accepted practice and illegality was a fine one.

That same year, 1966, saw him elected for a one-year term as President of BADA, an association whose council he had only been persuaded to join in 1963. (Yet before the sixties were out he had also taken on the presidency of the Kensington and Chelsea Chamber of Commerce.) On his election he set about rationalising the Council's administration, extending the work of its executive branch and cutting out the duplication of work that took place among its numerous committees. Under him the Council inaugurated a series of well-attended specialist lectures for younger members of the trade, and he was also instrumental in setting up the prestigious Grosvenor House Fair. When his term of office ended he was elected to a second term, which was without precedent since the thirties and which coincided with the fiftieth anniversary of the founding of BADA. Charles arranged special exhibitions at the Victoria and Albert Museum, a series of 'star' lectures, and finally a grand banquet at the Guildhall, which five hundred people attended. In 1971, he was awarded the Association's gold medal for distinguished service, an honour rarely given throughout the Association's history.

Charles's gift for languages meant that he did not rest satisfied with streamlining the organisation of BADA alone, but became involved in the international trade in antiques. Often in conjunction with fencing trips abroad he would attend trade conferences, and it was not surprising that, also in 1971, he was elected to the Presidency of the International Confederation of Art Dealers, CINOA, an organisation that co-ordinated the activities of all the major European antique dealers associations and those of the United States and South Africa. Immediately he started on plans to revitalise its administration, one of these ambitions being to have every antique of note photographed in standardised form, and the photograph kept in central record bureaux as a protection against art thefts. It was a highly ambitious scheme, but Charles was already very ill. In the summer of 1972 his sister Marguerite called on him at his shop. He turned to her and said, 'Not very long, darling.'

The late sixties and early seventies found Charles still occupied in fencing affairs. In 1965 came the first year of government financial assistance for British teams travelling abroad, and this gave a new lease of life to fencers wanting to take part in foreign competitions, the administration of which tended to fall on Charles. The following year saw the publication of the third volume of his history of British fencing, covering the period 1957–64. There were new battles to be fought, and Charles was one of the first people to try to get teams to include competent presidents at World Championships as a matter of course. Always quick to notice new trends in fencing, in his report following the World Championships in Moscow in 1966 he was one of the first to put on record the deterioration he saw in sabre fencing and the constant 'double attacking' in that weapon. And of course he was still Captain of the British team.

Despite his other preoccupations, Charles managed to give as much time and attention to running British fencing in the late sixties and the start of the seventies as he had ever done, but in some respects the emphasis changed. For instance, partly because at World Championships, in addition to his overall captaincy, he was a constant member of the Jury d'Appel and involved in the higher councils of the FIE, he was not always able to give the epee team the concentrated leadership which he had devoted to it so successfully as Captain continuously from 1935 and which had helped it to its Olympic and World Championship medals in 1956, 1957, 1960 and 1965. With his ready assent, the Epee Committee therefore elected Peter Jacobs Captain in 1971 to revivify a team then somewhat in the doldrums. Charles remained an epee selector and Chairman of the Epee Committee, as well as overall Team Captain.

His hitherto robust health, however, began to give him trouble at about this time. Early in the new year of 1971, while holidaying up in Yorkshire at Pateley Bridge, at the small farm he had recently bought for himself and Paula, he fell badly on the winter ice, knocking his head, but thought nothing of it. However, a little later he complained of an unpleasant taste in his mouth, and was persuaded to visit his doctor. A series of x-rays followed, but nothing seemed to be fractured, and Charles carried on as before. But the knock had left him ill and uncertain; he started taking tablets, fearing he might have dyspepsia, and almost for the first time in his life began to bother about his health. He travelled to Genoa for the World Youth Championships that Easter, then on to South Africa and to Vienna for the World Championships that July. It seemed as if he had recovered something of his old self, and that October, as young girl fencers from all over the country poured into the de Beaumont Centre for the ladies' Team Foil Championship, Charles was there as usual straightening the edges of the pistes and hoeing the garden outside. During the Saturday's fencing Mary Glen Haig told him she would keep a place for him for the final the following afternoon. To her surprise he failed to turn up.

He had suffered a heavy stomach haemorrhage, and was rushed into Westminster Hospital. An operation followed, during which he nearly died from loss of blood. He would only say of his ordeal: 'I think they found rather more than they thought they would.' He recovered, and travelled back home, where a nurse was installed to look after him. His return to health continued slowly, and by Easter the following year he was well enough to travel to Madrid for a further Under-20 Championships, where he had the pleasure of seeing two young British fencers reach the finals. Mary Glen Haig, by this time closest to him of all those in the fencing world, accompanied him. 'Throughout our time in Madrid I had to support Charles; sometimes he was very depressed, at others back to his usual form. For instance, we went to a private art museum there, and he was thrilled by what he saw.'

He returned to London, to be confronted by Gwen Nelligan's terminal cancer. He immediately went to visit her, and reported back, 'She says she feels like death, but she's determined not to die, as she doesn't want me to write her obituary.' Meanwhile the fencing season was in full swing, and he travelled to the Quadrangular match in Cardiff, while the Antique Dealers' Fair was scheduled for June.

A few friends both in and beyond the fencing world knew he was very ill, but to most people he seemed to have recovered. Everyone knew how much he was looking forward to captaining the British fencing team at the Olympic Games in Munich, which were to be held that July, and discussions took place as to whether Charles might be given special accommodation outside the Olympic village. One night in the first week of July Charles retired to bed in the normal way; by 7 July he was dead.

Fencers were stunned by the news. Despite his protracted sickness the end had come quickly and before any proper provision had been made for his successor. The positions he held required some half-dozen people to fill them; some tasks found no successor at all.

The obituaries and messages of condolence ran into hundreds and spanned the full range of his interests. When the memorial service was held – a service specially arranged by Charles's widow and mother – over eight hundred people crowded into Holy Trinity, Brompton, next to the Oratory. At either side of the altar were set two enormous displays of dark red carnations. Meanwhile he had been buried at the ancient chapel of rest at Bewerly, near the hillside farm he loved at Pateley Bridge.

'*Son vouloir était egal au pouvoir.*'

# The AFA – Growth and change, 1964–81

This account opens at a time when a number of important developments had recently taken place under the presidency of Charles de Beaumont. In October 1963, the new W. Kensington headquarters of British fencing, named the de Beaumont Centre in 1965, was opened. This replaced the antiquated and cramped headquarters in the former stables of the Oriental Club off Hanover Square, and was likewise shared with the London Fencing Club. Also in 1963, government money for administration was forthcoming for the first time, in the form of a grant of £3,250. This made possible the appointment on a full-time basis of Mrs Goddard to manage the new headquarters and to take the place of Edward Morten, who had retired as part-time Secretary to the Committee in 1961 after serving since 1933. In 1964 Lady Simmons retired as President of the Ladies Amateur Fencing Union, subsequently being awarded the Gold Medal in tribute to her sixteen years' service. She was succeeded by Mrs Glen Haig, who briefly also carried on the work she had done as Honorary Secretary to the AFA since 1956. In April 1965 it became possible to appoint a full-time Secretary on increased government grant. Lt Cdr R. T. Forsdick was the first holder of this office.

Finally, it was in 1963 once more that some members of the Wandsworth School Parents' Association, led by Joseph Eden, offered to run the Men's Under-20 Championships and largely to finance the sending of the British team to the World Youth Championships. Thus was set up the Men's Under-20 Sub-Committee, whose work was to culminate in 1976 in the first British winner of the World Youth Championship.

As well as providing advantages, the new headquarters posed a financial challenge: how to defray overheads by letting the hall during the daytime. The building had cost the modest sum of £44,939, but only £26,056 of this was received in grants and donations, so a debt of £18,883 had to be serviced. (Of this, £3,883 was a bank loan and £15,000 was loaned by Charles de Beaumont.) In addition there was the ground rent of £200 p.a. on the fifty-year lease from the Queen's Club. Initially two thirds of these costs were met by the Association, one third by the LFC (though the debt was finally cleared by the AFA alone).

At the AGM held in July 1964 Pierre Turquet, Treasurer of the Association since he succeeded Robin Brook in 1961, was able to report very satisfactory

# Growth and change, 1964-81

lettings of the hall to the BBC for television rehearsals. These continued for several years, which was fortunate, as it was not easy to find tenants for premises in which no permanent furnishing could be installed – the hall had to be clear for fencing each evening as well as at the weekend.

There was the further good financial news in July 1964 that the Department of Education and Science would for the first time give grants for travel to selected first class events abroad, including World Championships. These amounted to £1,000 over the following season, augmented by £274 from the Association's International Matches Fund.

To keep pace with the increased state aid as well as with inflation and the growth of fencing, in April 1966 the Finance and General Purposes Committee brought to the AGM a proposal to increase the individual subscription to 30s from 10s, the level at which it had stood since 1950. It was suggested that the Sports Council, as dispensers of state aid – £5,106 in 1965–6, out of a total expenditure of £9,247 – might look askance at the subscription rates, which were low compared with other sports. Much thought, it was claimed, had been given to differential rates of subscription according to the degree of involvement in the sport, but they had been found impracticable.

There was strong opposition from non-London Sections to the rise, as a result of which the rate was set at £1 instead of 30s, while club subscriptions, which it had not been intended to touch, were instead increased from £2 2s to £4 4s (£1 1s to be retained by the Sections, as before). At the Annual Conference, held in October, it was strongly argued that in the case of school clubs this too was unduly onerous. So, at the Extraordinary General Meeting at the end of the month, school clubs, for the first time, were given a concessionary rate of £1 1s. At the same time it was decided that in future entrants to AFA Schools Championships must be members of the AFA or of an affiliated club.

Under the new subscription, which came into force at the start of the 1966–7 season, all members automatically received the Association's magazine, *The Sword*, for which previously a separate annual subscription of 15s 6d had been payable. This had been urged over the years by Dr Roger Tredgold, the first editor (in 1948) and his successors, Arthur Smith, Harry Cooke and Geoffrey King, the last of whom, an art teacher and member of Latista, took over from the start of 1963 and edited eight issues. Charles Rentoul, son of the fencer Feré Rentoul and freshly down from Oxford, took over the Winter 1965 issue.

For its wider audience (enlarged by about a third) *The Sword* donned a shiny cover. It even began to have a few photographs, including vivid shots of foreign events taken by Peter Hobson, though only two of British fencers in action appeared before the 1969–70 season.

The Sports Council, which had been set up in 1964 to advise the government and to which Mrs Glen Haig was appointed in 1966, had requested a plan for future growth. This was the work of Charles de Beaumont and Mary Glen Haig. It was deliberately pitched optimistically. An assistant secretary was envisaged, partly to travel round to Sections, which were themselves to get clerical aid, grants for travel to meetings and judging apparatus. *The Sword* was to have four issues per year instead of three. There were to be travel grants for provincial fencers entering national events, for foreign entrants to provincial tournaments and for more British fencers to compete abroad, as well as for delegates to the International Fencing Federation. There was to be more training of all kinds and loans to masters starting up in the provinces. Perhaps most important of all, there were to be bursaries for masters to train on the continent. Nearly all of this remained in the realm of aspiration.

At the end of 1966 Pierre Turquet resigned as Treasurer because of his professional commitments. He was succeeded by Joyce Pearce, who had been Assistant Treasurer since 1959. On the suggestion of Robin Brook, committee-man of long standing, the AFA now arranged that the £15,000 advanced towards the cost of the HQ building by Charles de Beaumont should be repaid through an endowment policy on a reducing premium (initially of £862 10s p.a.). It was due to mature in 1986 (i.e. by then the debt would have been paid off). The remaining costs of the building for 1965–6 had been £3,479, after deduction of rental income, compared with £4,230 for the previous year, indicating a great improvement in lettings.

In June 1967 Major O. C. Weeks, MBE, took over as Secretary of the AFA from Lt Cdr Forsdick, under whose administration improvements had included the taking over of the handling of entries for national events from the Weapon Sub-Committees. Later that year Mildred Durne retired after ten years hard work as advertising and distribution manager of *The Sword*.

During the year Elizabeth Carnegy Arbuthnott, a Vice-President of the AFA, received the OBE for Red Cross work and Bill Hoskyns the OBE for his World Championship and Olympic achievements. Recognition was given to the special services of the late Professor Leon Paul when a memorial plaque was unveiled at the de Beaumont Centre in April.

In 1968 Margaret Somerville was awarded the Gold Medal of the Association after serving as secretary of the LAFU with outstanding success from 1962 (having previously held the same office from 1949 to 1954). She was succeeded by Mrs Henrietta Davies-Cooke. Eileen Jones, Treasurer since 1963, was succeeded by Elizabeth Wilcox. Theresa Offredy then took over, from 1969 to 1974.

Several notable figures died in these years. As a reminder of another epoch came the news of the death in 1965 of Count de Lavradio, a Portuguese who came to England as a member of the court of the exiled Manoel II in 1910 and remained till after the Second World War. An expert horseman, and a handsome, immaculate figure, he sported monocle, carnation, long cigarette

# Growth and change, 1964-81

holder and velvet-collared fencing jacket. He was in the Champion 1925 Bertrand epee team and in 1932 captained a victorious team of foreign residents of five countries against the Epee Club (to whom he later donated a cup).

A contrasting personality was that of Betty Puddefoot, who died in August 1965 after many months' illness. She had won the Junior Championship in 1929, reached the National final five times and was many times a member of the British team, always modest and good humoured, in the finest tradition of sportsmanship. After the war, in which she served in the Red Cross HQ, she gave without stint as team manager and, until deafness supervened, as an excellent president.

Terry Beddard died in 1966. He took up fencing on a visit to France after leaving Eton (where he later did much to foster the sport) and was fencing for Britain at epee by 1925. After some years in Marseilles he returned and was a regular member of the team from 1933 to 1948 and a member of the AFA Committee from 1936-9. He took a great interest in the Epee Club, of which he became Vice-President. During the war, he was a Squadron Leader in the RAAF. At the end of his life he was responsible for setting in train the negotiations which led to the AFA's lease from the Queen's Club. A charming companion and a witty writer and after-dinner speaker, he had a host of friends.

One area of fencing that leapt ahead was that of the Under-20s. The new Men's Sub-Committee raised the money to send the team to the World Youth Championships (in team track suits, what is more). One change was made. The Wandsworth Parents' Association had taken on their task on condition that the first three in the National Under-20 Championship at each weapon would automatically form the World Youth team. This lent excitement to the Championships; it was also free from selectors' vagaries. On the other hand, the form of fencers varies so much that selection on a single competition risks being arbitrary. 'Total Abstainer', the independent columnist in *The Sword* from 1948 to 1967, instanced Tony Power as a victim of the system in its very first year, having shown his high quality in other events.

Now it was agreed that the third place should be discretionary, to be selected by the three nominees of the weapon sub-committees who had sat on the Under-20 Committee from the outset, together with three other fencing members of the Committee (who had to be members of the AFA).

In December 1966, it was decided that Britain should stage the 1968 World Youth Championships and a committee was set up to prepare for the first world event staged in this country since the 1948 Olympics (with the exception of the Ladies' World Team Championship in 1956). It consisted of Charles de Beaumont, Mary Glen Haig, Joyce Pearce, Prof. R. G. Anderson (National Coach), Dr Arthur Banks of the NW Section, Joseph Eden, Raymond Paul (the foilist and director of Leon Paul Ltd), Bobby Winton and Robert Kilvert.

The estimated cost of the Championships was £7,500. £3,000 was donated by Messrs Brown & Poulson, who were assigned all publicity rights. An appeal fund sponsored by the AFA Coaches' Club and organised by Mrs Rachel Thompson raised over £1,600. Judging apparatus was donated by Leon Paul Ltd, metal pistes by Bowater and clocks by Omega.

The mid-sixties were also years of great activity in the field of schools fencing. The Proficiency Scheme, launched in 1966, was a measure of growth and stimulus to it. There were three levels – Bronze, Silver and Gold – and Awards were earned in tests showing ability to carry out progressively more complex movements. The fee was 5s, with cloth badges available at 5s 6d. Meanwhile an improved and more extended framework for schools fencing was being urged. In October 1966 Bill Hoskyns advocated at the Annual Conference the division of the school championships into several age-groups. That autumn a working party was set up to work out the best organisation for schools (and Universities) under Peter Upton of Dane Court School, who turned professional, however, and was therefore succeeded as convenor in February 1967 by David Martin of Mill Hill School.

In the Winter 1967 issue of *The Sword*, Bill Thompson, Secretary of the NW Section and a man of reforming zeal, wrote urging the formation of a School Fencing Association. In the Spring 1968 issue a similar plea was made for a national organisation from Peter Upton himself, who illustrated by developments in his own Kent County Union. Here, as elsewhere, fencing had been spreading in state schools in addition to the traditional bases in independent schools. The first County Championships for Senior and Junior schoolboys had been held in 1955, with 36 entries from five schools. In 1967 there were 150 entrants from 22 schools and clubs. In 1962, epee and sabre were added (possibly before any other county). An event for schoolgirls was started the same year and by 1967 there were a hundred entries from fifteen schools and clubs. Likewise in 1967, a Kent Schools Fencing Association was formed to place organisation in the hands of teachers. This, Peter Upton subsequently argued, should be the model for the rest of the country since it would correspond to Education Authority Areas (unlike Sections) and more schools would be attracted than at Section level.

All these voices had their way when the Schools Fencing Union was instituted in February 1969, with a constitution written by Charles de Beaumont. The Chairman was Tom Norcross, who had also contributed to the debate in *The Sword*, Bill Thompson was Secretary, John Ramsay Treasurer and May Davies, Peter Hobson and Peter Upton the other members.

As far as the training of school coaches was concerned, an important step had already been taken in the 1964–5 season, when the first Leaders' Course for teachers was arranged at Leicester under the auspices of the Local Education Authority, and other experiments were launched in Sheffield and

# Growth and change, 1964-81

the Manchester area, thus helping to fill a need which most amateur coaches could not meet because of the time of day. They were immediately successful.

On the wider training front there was continuous progress in the mid sixties. The main element was the National Training Scheme, started in 1949 when Prof. Roger Crosnier was appointed, with the first government aid, to the newly created post of National Coach to run it. His pupil, Prof. R. J. G. Anderson, who had been a member of the British sabre team from 1950 to 1954, succeeded him in 1954. The main object of the scheme was to train an ever increasing number of amateur coaches (or Leaders, as they were known till 1966), who would in turn instruct a swelling army of fencers in clubs throughout the country. Under the supervision of the National Coach, courses were organised by Section Coaches and Leaders' Clubs or Coaching Panels. An Advanced Coaching Certificate had been introduced in 1959 for those who already had coaching qualifications at all three weapons and were Grade II Presidents. Its holders were automatically entitled to a Provost's Diploma if they turned professional.

Personal performance courses for schoolchildren, Leaders' refresher courses and judging and presiding courses were also given by Prof. Anderson, as well as lecture-demonstrations in schools and colleges under arrangements with the Central Council for Physical Recreation. In addition he ran a special (Olympic) training course. This initially comprised four fencers aged under 25 selected by each weapon sub-committee, meeting on average one weekend each month at the Army School of Physical Training at Aldershot. There were also sessions for larger groups at each weapon about once a month for competition practice and matches at Headquarters.

The LAFU started in 1965 a weekend training course for young fencers recommended by the Sections. From April to July they ran a monthly training course under Prof. Pat Pearson on Saturday afternoons. Other training enterprises of these years were tactics sessions given by internationals and, in 1967, two weekends on epee and sabre tactics for schoolboys given by Profs Boston, Simmonds, Harmer-Brown, and Imregi for the London Section.

In October 1967 Leon Hill was appointed as second National Coach. A 31-year-old science teacher from Lancashire and joint founder of Hydra Club, he was himself a product of the National Training Scheme, getting his Advanced Coach's award in 1963. He turned professional in 1964 and only the statutory waiting period between Provost and Diploma exams held back his professor's status till 1968. His main task was to be the course for coaching awards and the Personal Performance and Presidents' courses – and tours of clubs. Prof. Anderson, now designated Senior National Coach, was thus freed to concentrate on national team training, Advanced Coaching courses and the booming schoolteachers' courses (for which there was a new syllabus). They staffed all national courses together.

It was also in 1967 that Bob Anderson organised the first Amateur Coaches

An Advanced Leaders' course, 1963. *Back:* P. Pearson, K. Rowlands, R. Tiller, A. Banks, M. Steele, C. Anderson, L. Grosfils, N. Heads. *Front:* Anita Maguire, Val Matheson, Beryl Wrigley, Beryl Banks, Prof. J. Fethers, Prof. R. Anderson, Jenny Loyd, Frankie Mooney, Hazel Rogerson.

Conference, held near Nottingham, largely to discuss teaching methods. There was a shift away from the prohibition of any fighting in the early stages of learning (for fear of bad habits) towards the development of technique and fighting practice hand in hand, both as better training and as more likely to retain fencers through the early rigours of the sport. The conference became an annual event.

Following a letter from Tom Norcross in *The Sword*, attributing the continuing shortage of active amateur coaches to the rule whereby they lost their amateur status if they claimed any reimbursement beyond their expenses, the status of Registered Coach was introduced in 1968, allowing receipt of half the fees paid (over and above the expenses element), provided these were paid through the AFA Section or a body appointed by the latter, without loss of amateur status except in respect of the national championships (senior and junior, individual and team) and international events.

Other rule changes concerned the national team championships. From 1966, largely because so many teams were being entered from Salle Boston, clubs were allowed a maximum of two teams per event. In 1969 it was agreed that incomplete teams could compete, but fights of absentees must be recorded as defeats.

A much more sweeping change was made in the whole range of ladies' individual national events when the Category System was approved in March 1968. Fencers were to be assigned to one of three categories according to the points won in nominated British and foreign events during the previous season. Entry to each of six national competitions was restricted to members of appropriate categories. The advantages of this system, which had largely been devised by Herietta Davies-Cooke and her husband David, were that it served as an incentive for fencers to earn promotion, that it encouraged them to compete abroad and that it helped control the number of entries to competitions. At the end of a three year trial period a poll of women fencers confirmed the system by a two to one majority.

At the end of 1968 Prof. Hill resigned as National Coach. Ken Pearson was his successor. After 22 years in the Navy he had retired as Chief Petty Officer. He took his first course under Bob Anderson in 1947 and qualified as a Services instructor after three months under Roger Crosnier. Navy Champion at all three weapons a total of seventeen times, he had also been AFA Junior Champion, at both foil (1964) and sabre (1962), and had only missed the 1964 Leamington foil title in a close final bout with Hoskyns. He had been coach to the Irish team at the Mexico Olympics as well as to the British Under-20 team at Genoa in 1969. Before starting on his new job, he took an intensive master's course at the Institut de Sport in Paris.

Following various negotiations, the President reported to the AGM of June 1969 that about £800 government grant would be available for group training in the form of fourteen sessions of seven periods for each weapon. In addition to the fifty per cent travel grants to top foreign events, the government would pay 75 per cent of the cost of obtaining the services of a foreign coach for a month each year.

The foreign coach chosen to visit Britain the following three summers was Dr Zbigniew Czaikowski, who had once studied at Edinburgh University, spoke fluent English, had risen to be Polish National Coach and was a dynamic and articulate teacher. He did much to popularise the practice whereby the master, instead of exercising pupils in set movements or sequences, would offer a mixture of alternative openings, to which the pupil had to respond with appropriate alternative reactions. Technical tuition was thus combined with something approximating to fighting conditions.

During his stays, Dr Czaikowski visited various Sections on a week's tour organised by Prof. Anderson, concluding at the Fencing Coaches Conference at Loughborough. He also attended the Advanced Course at Loughborough and ran courses for the British Academy of Fencing (BAF).

Under the overall supervision of Prof. Anderson, who also co-ordinated physical training and tests, specialist team coaches were for the first time appointed for each weapon: Ken Pearson for ladies' foil; Vic Lagnado for men's foil; Bill Harmer-Brown for epee and George Ganchev for sabre.

A further sign of the growing rigour of national team training was the introduction for the four-year cycle of a Qualifying Standard for selection to the 1972 Olympic team. The rules were as follows: 'Each weapon sub-

committee will select each year a list of four to six top class continental competitions at their weapon. By agreement with the Joint Weapon Sub-Committee, events of comparable calibre to qualify for selection may be added, even retrospectively, to these lists. Fencers must reach the last sixteen by direct elimination, or the semi-finals under the pool system, at least three times (one of which at least must be in the last full season before the Games) during the four years concerned to be considered for selection for the 1972 Olympic team. Selection Committees reserve the right (subject to approval by the Joint-Weapon Sub-Committee):
(a) To consider a fencer who achieves outstanding performances in the finals of international competitions abroad during the last full session prior to the Games, but who has not fulfilled the above requirements, as eligible for selection;
(b) Where only four competitors achieve the standard at any weapon, to select a fifth who has not so qualified to make up a team;
(c) To take into account outstanding results in international competitions in this country when deciding if a fencer is eligible for selection.'

Only eight fencers at each weapon were eligible for government travel grants (though other possibles joined them for the training sessions). In 1970 grants became available each season for half the travel costs of sending five fencers and an official to four events at each weapon plus the Under-20s (including the World Championships, but not the Olympics, for which funds were raised by the British Olympic Association). Officials were thus assisted for the first time.

Some private aid was also forthcoming in 1969. Robinson's Barley Water awarded a £1,000 scholarship, mainly for the expense of competing abroad, to Terry Wishart, a promising Under-20 sabreur. Robin Brook, himself a former sabre international, gave £150 towards a junior training scheme at sabre organised by Peter Hobson under the auspices of the CCPR.

At the end of the decade, the Association suffered changes of Secretary at somewhat frequent intervals. In September 1969 Major Weeks retired, having served two years. After two retired officers came two fencers. John Creek was a long-standing member of the London Fencing Club and of the Epee Club who had recently retired as Company Secretary to British Condensers Ltd. He served till 1970 when he was succeeded by Len Mowlam, a member of the British epee team in 1931 and 1935, and another Epee Club enthusiast, who had been a bank manager. He retired at the end of 1972.

In 1969 the Award of Merit was instituted for the recognition of outstanding services to British fencing. A Torch Trophy covering many sports went to Rachel Thompson for her devoted work for fencing in the NW over many years.

School fencing continued to develop. Following the pioneering work by Bill Hoskyns in the SW, the National Schoolboys Championships were extended in 1969 to epee and sabre under his organisation. Peter Hobson, then a deputy headmaster in London, who had been very successful in experiments with introducing pupils directly to sabre instead of the traditional foil, argued forcefully for the extension of Proficiency Awards to sabre and epee. With the support of Arthur Banks, this was approved by the AFA Committee in 1970, to apply from October 1970.

A threat to schools fencing was posed in 1969 when the Department of Education, at the behest of the NUT, decreed the gradual elimination of all 'unqualified' school teachers. Paradoxically this would have meant barring the most qualified fencing masters – the full-time professionals, normally holding the full Diploma of the BAF – who naturally tended not to have qualifications as general school teachers. Charles de Beaumont wrote to Denis Howell, Minister of Sport, and he and Mary Glen Haig argued the case at London County Hall. As a result of this and parallel representations, an exception was made for such cases, though not in Scotland.

The Association as a whole was equally alert to get fencing included at an early planning stage among the sports provided for at the sports centres that were beginning to be built by the larger local authorities, funnelling information collated by the Sections through the Sports Council.

Under-20 fencing received in 1970 the considerable boost of two new international events. Millfield School, in Somerset, had run a men's International Foil Competition since 1967, organised by Peter Turner. It was now possible to extend this, thanks to the sponsorship of Irving Allen, a theatrical entrepreneur. Meanwhile in London, Joe Eden, long active in fund-raising as Chairman of the Men's Under-20 Sub-Committee, had secured Nescafé as sponsors of events at all three weapons, teams from seven countries being paid for. Nescafé continued to back the competitions for the next three years.

1970 also saw considerable changes in men's Under-20 selection procedure. The AFA Committee asserted that the Under-20 Coach, a member of the Sub-Committee from 1968, must not take part in selection. The Under-20 Committee itself adopted a points system for selection. Jack Berry, who had been Treasurer of the Committee from the start and Manager at seven World Youth Championships, considered that this would detract from the status of the Under-20 Championships. In June he resigned. The LAFU had operated a points system for the Ladies' Under-20 team since 1965 but the system now devised by Teddy Bourne was more sophisticated and was to be the model for those adopted by both the epee selectors and the foil selectors in 1974. Points were gained on each fencer's best foreign results and five best home results, though participation in the Under-20 Championship was still required. The object was to ensure evident fairness and to encourage fencers to gain foreign experience. In the following year the system was refined by introducing a qualifying standard and giving more weight to foreign events.

Bobby Winton                    J. L. Hope

1970 was notable for two major events staged in Britain. The Commonwealth Games took place in Edinburgh. On this occasion Gold Medals of the Association were awarded to Dr L. G. Morrison and J. L. Hope, respectively President and Secretary-Treasurer of the Scottish Fencing Union. The Award of Merit, inaugurated in 1969, was conferred on Christine Tolland, especially for her organisation at the Games. The World Professional Championships were held in London (at Crystal Palace), the chief organiser for the BAF being Akos Moldovanyi.

Seven other Awards of Merit were made in 1970: to Mrs Doris Allwork, secretary of the LAFU 1955–61 and thereafter of the Public Schools Sub-Committe; to Alec Kaye, secretary of the Foil Sub-Committee (1961–73); to Teddy Fuller, an elected Committee member (1961–72), who helped launch the Schoolboys' Championships in 1961 and was indefatigable at competition paperwork, Derek Holt, Secretary of the SW Section (1962–71), Les Johnson, coach, competition organiser and W. Midlands Chairman (1969–73), Ray Parsons, another coaching stalwart and about to become E. Section Chairman, Arthur Banks, a key figure in the NW and in the world of coaching, and Colin Tyson, E. Midlands Chairman (1961–72).

In the Birthday Honours Mary Glen Haig was awarded the MBE for her services to fencing. She was also becoming a figure of importance in the wider world of sport. Since 1952 she had been a member of what became the Sports Council and in 1966 had joined the Central Council of Physical Recreation, the mouthpiece and co-ordinating body for different sports and outdoor recreations. She remained on both bodies after their reconstitution in 1971 and 1972 respectively. She served as Deputy Chairman of the CCPR from 1973 and as Chairman from 1974 to 1981. Robin Brook, a member of the

CCPR from 1949, was Treasurer from 1962 to 1977. He was also a member of the Sports Council from 1971 and was Chairman from 1975–8.

Sadly the new decade witnessed the deaths of four who had played varying roles in fencing at the national level. In April the Association's previous President, Val Fildes, died at the age of ninety. Son of the Victorian painter, he had risen to be Company Secretary to Unilever. He had two quite separate fencing careers. Starting at the sport in Paris in 1902 under the legendary Kirchoffer, he was subsequently taught in London by Volland and Tassart and in 1908 competed in the Olympic Games at epee. In 1909, with Robert Montgomerie and Major R. M. P. Willoughby, he drafted the AFA Articles, which remained substantially unchanged till 1973. He was frequently a 'captain-selector' and organiser up to the First World War, in which he served in the Grenadier Guards. Thereafter until 1925 business kept him in Liverpool and he ceased fencing. He then made a remarkable comeback, winning both the Epee Championship and Miller-Hallett at the age of 52. After Tassart's death in 1930 he continued with Tassart's pupil, Prof. Alfred Parkins, whom he was instrumental in establishing after the war at the Lansdowne Club, of which he was Chairman.

Val Fildes regarded himself primarily as an administrator. He was President of the AFA from 1953 to 1956, joint organiser of the fencing at the 1948 Olympics and President of the Epee Club from 1927 till his death. Though a formidable personality, he was a man of invariable charm and courtesy.

Almost the same age, Lt Colonel A. Ridley Martin OBE died in May 1970 at 89. As a sabreur, he fenced in British teams from 1911 till 1931. He competed in the Olympics of 1912 and 1920 and won the British Championship in 1910 and 1913, as well as many Services events. He was Treasurer of the AFA from 1946 to 1948.

In November 1971 Captain Cecil Kershaw, RN died. Once described as 'the finest athlete in the world', he held, among many fencing honours, the national sabre titles in 1920, 1925 and 1926. He fenced in the Olympics in 1920, 1924 and 1928. But he was also the oustanding English scrum-half in the years after 1918, winning sixteen international caps – and he excelled at cricket, hockey and squash. His speed, accuracy and brilliance of footwork were matched by the vitality and enthusiasm of his personality. His daughter, Mrs Maxwell Davies, presented the cup which he had won outright in 1926 to the AFA.

Also a man of abounding vitality, Vincent Bonfil died in May 1971 at the tragically early age of 25 from a fencing accident in South Africa, where he had recently gone as a mining engineer. During a simultaneous attack in a club foil bout, his opponent's blade broke and penetrated beneath the armpit. He died within five minutes. At London University and at Thames Club he had been a pupil of Prof. Harmer-Brown. By natural flair, hard work and determination he reached the British team in 1969. His character was warmhearted,

England Quadrangular team 1966. *Back:* M. Breckin, J. Moore, V. Bonfil, J. Shaw, C. Purchase, I. Single, R. Ford, D. Acfield. *Front:* Eileen Jones, Sue Brick, Mrs M. Glen Haig, René Paul, Charles de Beaumont, Margaret Paul, Sheila Ward.

generous and loyal. Fittingly, he captained London University in their fourth year without a match defeat and also led them to victory in the foil Team Championship.

His mother donated a trophy named after him, which was awarded to the foilist with the most points gained from the best six results in a nominated list of graded events. (To give scope for provincial results not more than two of these could be foreign, nor more than two be drawn from the Doyne Cup, the Coronation Cup and the Championship.)

Financial matters dominated the annual Conference of the AFA in October 1970. Joyce Pearce reported that AFA revenue was proving inadequate and warned of a possible deficit of £4,000 by the end of 1969–70, largely due to the BBC no longer renting the hall at Headquarters. *The Sword* alone accounted for 10s of the £1.00 subscription and the Annual Report, the Fixture List and postage for the remaining 10s. There was therefore nothing to cover the third main item which did not attract government grant – the Association's two-thirds share of the costs of the de Beaumont building, amounting in 1970–71 to £1563 (against which competition proceeds of £730 could be set). As was pointed out at the subsequent AGM by Ian Spofforth, Secretary of the Epee Club, but speaking now as AFA auditor, the Association was thus making a loss on each extra member recruited.

One economy approved at the Conference, on the suggestion of Charles Rentoul, was for *The Sword* no longer to be sent to affiliated clubs (where it seldom reached many fresh readers), though, on the advice of Eric Mount-Haes, it was still to go to school clubs. This was reckoned to save about £200 per annum. Circulation to clubs was resumed later, on whose decision is unclear. Various fees were also raised. Entry fees for national events had already been put up for the 1970–71 season (the main rate rising from 10s to 75p). In 1971 the fees for the services of the National Coaches went up from £10 to £15 per week and from £5 2s to £8 for a weekend.

These measures were not enough, however, and in the summer of 1971 the Finance and General Purposes Committee therefore proposed increases in subscription rates. Although the loss for the previous year had only been £471, subscription income had amounted to no more than £3,950, compared with government grant of £12,864 – and the new rates were intended to hold for a number of years. The individual rate was to rise from £1 to £3, but for the first time there was to be a concessionary rate of £1 for schoolchildren, provided it was paid through affiliated school clubs. Club subscriptions were not to be touched.

The new rates were accepted, but only after much debate both in the Committee and at the AGM (though with the required two-thirds majority at the latter). It was the tripling of the main rate in one step which was particularly deplored by those like Derek Parham, organiser of the Leamington Tournament over many years, who warned that the AFA seemed remote and to offer little to the provincial fencer. Charles de Beaumont pointed out in a circular on the increases that had organisers of provincial tournaments insisted on the rule that all entrants must be AFA members, a lesser increase would have been required.

The question of the increases came up again at the 1971 Conference, for according to Les Veale, Chairman of the Northern (Yorkshire) Section, the entry for the Novices Foil in the Section had fallen from forty to fourteen as a result of the increase. This, however, was only one aspect of the poor relationship between London and the rest of the AFA, as he saw it. Out of some fifty places on the Committee, only twelve were for Section representatives. Communication was also bad and the Articles of the Association did not specify the role of Sections.

Mary Glen Haig, chairing the meeting, as Charles de Beaumont was ill, responded by proposing a committee to consider these issues, to be convened by Peter Kirby. It reported in June 1972. Recommendations immediately implemented included the holding of alternate meetings of the Committee at weekends, the encouragement of recruitment by giving the Sections a discount on copies of *The Sword* sold to non-members and, most significantly, the setting up of a Sections Sub-Committee, with representatives from each. Later, the recommendation that club subscriptions should be paid direct to

Leslie Veale and Gordon Wiles

HQ (and the Section quota then remitted) was also implemented (the professionally staffed HQ being more efficient than the frequently changing Sections officers).

Meanwhile in February 1972, at the instance of Gordon Wiles of the East Midlands, the inter-Section Winton Cup, instead of being confined in its final series to six teams, the rest being eliminated in earlier knockout matches, was henceforth to comprise all twelve Sections in two divisions over one weekend (the bottom and top two teams of each group changing places each year). The second division were to compete for a trophy presented by Robert Southcombe. For reasons of space the event was transferred from the Lillieshall Sports Centre to Loughborough College.

# Growth and change, 1964-81

At the instance of Richard Cohen, an economy adopted (unusually, against the advice of the President) was the excision from the Annual Report of the lists of affiliated clubs, of individual members of the AFA and of AFA Champions since 1898, which took up 54 pages.

In the following years both the Report and Fixture List were reformed, mainly by Edmund Gray, to economise and to remedy the previous illogical order, duplication and prolixity. The Fixture Notice was reduced to about half its length in 1973 and the Report was reshaped in 1973 and 1974 to revitalise it as well as improve it as a vehicle of information. So, included for the first time were reports by the weapon captains, the Treasurer and the President (the last taking the place of the anonymous Committee one) and an international survey, from the fluent, encyclopaedic pen of Andrew Cornford. Yet the rest of the Report was so much condensed that the number of pages was no greater.

Richard Cohen, involved with the ideas for the Report, had already taken on the larger task of reshaping *The Sword*, as from the summer issue of 1971. A Cambridge graduate, he worked on the staff of the Catholic weekly *The Tablet* from 1969 to 1971. He joined Collins, the publishers, as an editor in 1973. He was thus able to impart high professional standards of journalism to *The Sword* – even if the amount of trouble he put in sometimes resulted in delay. He enlarged the format, for the sake of printing economy and larger photographs, and had the cover redesigned. The contents of the first issue give an idea of *The Sword*'s new character: 'The Scandal of the Combines', 'Profile of the Paul Brothers', 'Leamington's 30 Years' and 'Views of a World-Class President'. The number of photographs inside went up from three to ten; the layout was transformed. In all it became a model for rivals round the world.

The changes were widely welcomed, though there was criticism that *The Sword* became too concerned with the sport at the international level, at the expense of the humbler news about fencers round the country; and also that the tone was occasionally unduly scurrilous, particularly in the 'Backstabber' column, introduced in 1976. The improvements meant a rise in costs from £848 in 1969-70 to £1,761 in 1971-2. (The parallel rise in AFA administrative costs was from £4,910 to £6,316.)

In mid 1972 came a major turning-point in the history of the Association. On 7 July the Committee was convened, chiefly to receive selectors' recommendations for the Olympic Team. It was greeted with the bombshell from Emrys Lloyd, as a Vice-President, that the President, Charles de Beaumont, had died that very morning, and moreover that the foil Captain, Dr Gordon Signy, had also died only two weeks before.

An account of the life and work of Charles de Beaumont has been given earlier. Gordon Signy (photo p. 241) was a very different man, though his death struck equally prematurely. Of international distinction as a pathologist, he was also a person of very human qualities. He was founder-editor of the

*British Journal of Pathology* from its inception in 1944 to his death, shortly before which he declined the presidency of the World Association of Pathological Societies in favour of a younger man. The war deprived him of his best years as a fencer. He was fifth in the Epee Championship of 1939 and third in 1951. His towel, clearly borrowed from the hospital mortuary, could be seen at most epee and foil competitions. Captain of LFC for a period and often president at ladies' competitions, he was an elected member of the AFA Committee from 1952 till his death and a member of the F & GP from 1968. In 1960 he became foil Captain, accompanying his team to Olympics, World Championships and untold numbers of international events, largely at his own expense. He had a happy knack of being able to mix with all ages and background, playing football at training sessions, joining in horseplay abroad and blessed with an infectious sense of humour. Over five hundred people attended the memorial meeting at the British Medical Association.

In April 1972 the death had also occurred of Gwendoline Neligan at the age of 66 (photo p. 49). The outstanding British woman fencer before the war, she was sometimes known as the Greta Garbo of fencing. In 1933 she became Britain's first World Champion (then termed European Champion). A pupil of Prof. Leon Bertrand from the late twenties, she said herself that he was the only master who could have 'turned a carthorse into a racehorse'. Though possessing a magnificent physique, she was ungainly and so slow to learn it seemed she would never get more than good exercise out of fencing. But on adopting the Italian foil she was suddenly transformed. She won the Hutton International Cup in 1932 and 1934 against very strong foreign opposition, was Ladies' Champion in 1934, 1935, 1936 and 1937, and was European finalist in 1934 and 1935. But for appendicitis, she might have won the Gold Medal at the 1936 Olympics. Tall, classic in style and of limitless determination, she was famous for attacks en marchant (she never stooped to a fleche). Witty and forthright, her brusqueness hid a kindness of heart ever-ready to help anyone in need.

After paying an immediate tribute to the late President at the Committee assembled on 7 July, Emrys Lloyd invited it to elect itself a chairman (there being no provision for a deputy in the Articles). Bobby Winton was elected. Knowing of a problem arising from the rules of the Olympic Qualifying System, he took the Committee through these meticulously (see p. 83). It was agreed without dissent that the rules laid down that an unqualified fencer could only be selected for fifth place 'where only four competitors achieve the standard', and that the rules must be upheld. The names for three of the weapons were then presented and approved, but Peter Kirby, representing the foil selectors, did not submit names, as he said the decision of the Committee would clearly not admit the team selected. Instead he asked if he could consult Michel Kallipetis, his surviving fellow-selector. (Gordon Signy had died after the selection.)

# Growth and change, 1964-81

The meeting was therefore adjourned to the following day, immediately before the AGM, when, however, decision was further deferred on the request of the foil selectors to enable them to consult the Joint Weapon Sub-Committee. On 27 July the Committee was hard-pressed by a very heavy agenda and such procedural issues as whether members who attended under more than one entitlement had multiple votes. (It was decided that they had.) The foil selectors contended that the Joint Weapon Sub-Committee had in practice modified some of the Qualifying Rules and the Committee should therefore accept the breach of them involved in their proposed selection. It was pointed out that only the Committee had power to alter the Rules and it had not done so. Nevertheless, after much discussion, the Committee ignored its own decision to uphold the Rules and approved the team, with the fifth man unqualified and the qualified fencer named as reserve.

Charles de Beaumont was intended to go as Captain of the team as he had at every Olympic Games since 1936. Peter Hobson, the sabre Captain, was elected to take his place. The late President's role had been so wide ranging that his death left the Association in some disarray and the ensuing period was one of considerable reconstruction. At the AGM, for which Bobby Winton was again elected chairman, Raymond Paul, seconded by Colonel Hay, proposed an ad hoc committee to consider the role and responsibilities of the President and the future of the AFA. It consisted of Bobby Winton, Mary Glen Haig, Peter Hobson, Joyce Pearce, Peter Jacobs (epee Captain), Peter Kirby, Sandy Leckie, Richard Cohen and Alec Kaye. It was convened by Raymond Paul. It recommended that future Presidents should not be asked to bear the burden of the comprehensive functions which Charles de Beaumont had exercised – indeed should be deterred from doing so. The President should be chairman of the Committee, but not chairman of any standing sub-committees (except, it was subsequently agreed, the Honours Sub-Committee), not automatically the delegate to the FIE or any other body, nor captain of a British team unless appointed by the Committee for a specific event. Expenses incurred at the behest of the Association should be reimbursed to the President. Finally, it was recommended that the President should not be eligible to serve for more than two terms of three years each.

At the Conference in October, 1972 the AFA Committee approved all these proposals and added the further one that the President should be elected by postal ballot of all members, not at the AGM. Meanwhile the Committee followed the normal procedure for a casual vacancy of the Presidency and elected Emrys Lloyd (photo p. 49), a solicitor who had been helping to run the AFA since 1933, who had been one of the finest foilists Britain had ever produced and whose outstanding sportsmanship was recognised through the award in 1948 of the FIE's highest accolade, the Challenge Feyerick.

With the advice of Allan Jay, now Honorary Legal Adviser, the relevant amendments to the Articles of the Association were drafted and put to the

Extraordinary General Meeting on 4 March 1973. Together with minor technical amendments (such as deleting the requirement for a two-thirds majority of the Committee to affiliate a club), all were passed by the two-thirds majority required for changes to the Articles – with one exception. Edmund Gray opposed the limitation of the President's term of office to two periods of three years, on the ground that the Association might not be so well endowed with good candidates that it could afford to preclude the continuance in office of an outstanding President. The voting was 47 in favour of the limitation, 32 against – five short of two-thirds.

A further group of amendments to the Articles, which could not be voted on for lack of due notice, was proposed at this EGM by Leslie Veale. To alter the preponderance of London votes he proposed each Section should have one representative (or proxy vote) for every fifteen clubs and one for every twenty members. He also wished to abolish the right of an affiliated club (or set of several) with twenty or more AFA members to nominate a member to the Committee, since the clubs exercising this right were in practice nearly all London-based (partly because they were the largest but also because others did not trouble to make nominations).

To consider these proposals and the general question of the composition of the AFA Committee and related provisions of the Articles, Raymond Paul suggested yet another working party (it had been notable that the one on the role of the President had comprised Londoners only). This one was chaired by Bobby Winton. After many meetings and drafts it put a set of amendments to the AGM in February 1974. This time Leslie Veale's views largely took effect. A stiff rearguard action to save club representatives was led by Peter Jacobs, Peter Hobson and Raymond Paul, who feared that those who carried on most of the central work of the AFA would be outvoted on the Committee by those with less involvement or experience from the provinces. Others, such as Bobby Winton, thought these fears groundless and wished to satisfy the aspirations of non-London Sections.

Ironically for both sides of the dispute, the provinces already had good scope for imposing their views on London, as was illustrated at this AGM, through Article 23, which allowed each affiliated club a proxy vote. On this occasion, Jim Pilkington of the SW thus had 24 votes, Leslie Veale 22, Robert Dye of Hertfordshire 17, Peter Hobson 12, Jim Hamments of the SE 5 and Sandy Leckie of London 3. Not surprisingly, therefore, club representatives were abolished and the counter-proposal to abolish proxy votes at General Meetings, though it had been included in the working party's amendments, was defeated. But instead of either change the number of elected members to the Committee was increased from nine to twelve. Vice-Presidents – senior members of the Association who were elected en bloc from year to year – were no longer to be ex-officio members, though as positions of honour they were subsequently re-instituted. These changes had less practical effect than might

# Growth and change, 1964-81

be thought. For instance, four of the ten people representing London clubs immediately resurfaced as elected members.

At the proposal of the Working Party there were numerous other revisions, a few of significance. The Committee was henceforth to elect a Vice-Chairman. (Peter Hobson was to fill the position to the end of our period.) The immediate Past President was given a seat on the Committee. Sub-committees could be represented by a substitute if the Chairman was unavailable. Subscription rates were no longer specified in the Articles, though changes still required a two-thirds majority at an AGM. Disqualification by other amateur sports bodies would not, as previously, be binding on the AFA. Greater notice was to be required for nominations, requisition or notification of a general meeting and proposed alterations to the Articles.

The Single Transferable Vote was adopted. But on this occasion there was only one candidate. Mary Glen Haig was nominated by three separate groups and duly took up office, as the first woman President, at the end of the AGM of July 1973. She had been National Champion in 1948 and 1950 and won Gold Medals at the Commonwealth Games of 1950 and 1954 and a Bronze Medal in 1958. She was a finalist in the 1948 Olympic Games and fenced in the team from 1948 to 1960. She captained the ladies' team from 1950 to 1957. Having been head of Medical Records at the Royal National Orthopaedic Hospital, in 1974 she became Administrator (Hospitals) of the S. Hammersmith District. An admirably brisk chairman and a forceful personality, she devoted an enormous amount of time to her work for amateur sport.

Some of her ideas for the future of fencing were revealed in an interview published in *The Sword* in Autumn 1972. There she insisted that many people must run the Association and initiative come from many quarters. She instanced the need for weapon sub-committees to raise their own money and attract audiences. She also considered – more controversially – that they should look after Under-20 training. She wanted to see some half dozen regional coaches, as well as part-time paid secretaries, in the Sections. She agreed that to meet the great need for masters there were three means: paying to train masters abroad, bringing foreign masters to Britain and setting up a college of instruction like the Paris INS (as advocated by Prof. Anderson and Prof. Moldovanyi). She also wished to see the end of the distinction between amateurs and professionals (and indeed a single organisation and magazine). Finally she wanted a great recruitment drive, maybe getting the estimated 18,000 fencers who were not members of the AFA to subscribe merely 10s a head.

At the AGM in February 1974, she described her role as one of guiding, not dictating. At the same meeting she paid tribute to Cdr Frank Booth, RN, who had taken over as Secretary in January 1973, at first on an almost-full-time basis for a trial six months. He and his staff had the issue of membership cards and Proficiency Badges fully up-to-date for the first time since the move to the new Headquarters, in spite of the burden of extra business arising from the reconstruction after Charles de Beaumont's death. Moreover they had had to produce the Report and accounts in record time to permit the holding of the AGM so much sooner after the close of the season. Emrys Lloyd, who had himself put in much hard work, had thanked Mary Glen Haig at the previous AGM, together with Joyce Pearce and Bobby Winton, for much voluntary labour during the transitional period.

The new President strongly supported one decentralising move, the holding of national events away from London. During the 1973-4 season the de Beaumont Cup was successfully staged at the Thornaby Pavilion, Cleveland. Les Veale reported that the holding of the 1973 Corble Cup on Teesside had encouraged recruitment in the area.

At Headquarters, competition equipment proved a chronic minor headache. The last official Armourer, Liam Flynn, retired in 1970. Thereafter John Hall, with the help of Brian Hill, put in many hours of work at various times, but the running of competitions by a large number of barely co-ordinated volunteers with many other preoccupations meant poor control in setting aside and listing defective items and avoidance of damage to the metal pistes, the edges of which rapidly creased and split. Fortunately new sets of pistes were periodically donated by Messrs Bowater after use in paper mills. Leon Paul took over the repairs from September 1973.

Allan Jay and others produced new rules on disciplinary action in November 1973. Any case arising, under FIE rules or otherwise, was to be referred to a tribunal of five appointed by a Disciplinary Sub-Committee consisting of the President, the Secretary and the Chairman of the Rules and International Committee. The accused was to have the right to answer the case, call witnesses and cross-examine, but the decision of the five was to be final.

Three rule changes were made for the 1973-4 season, as a by-product of the reform of the Fixture Notice. Foreign entrants were to be regarded as 'residents' after six months, the lower age limit of fourteen for Under-20 events was abolished and the concessionary entry fee of 35p for schoolboys to the Junior Championships was withdrawn. As from 1975, pool sheets were only issued to competitors who sent stamped addressed envelopes.

As suggested by the President, some weapon sub-committees obtained sponsorship, publicity and a sizeable audience for certain events. Thus in 1973 the foilists staged a GB v. Europe match with the support of the Egg Marketing Board, which attracted four hundred spectators to HQ, and in 1974 they held the Coronation Cup at the Sobell Sports Centre, N. London, which had recently been opened.

On the other hand, a major setback to fencing was its exclusion from the events included in the Commonwealth Games by the cities sponsoring them – Auckland in 1974 and Edmonton in 1978. As a second-best, separate Commonwealth Championships were held in Ottawa in 1974 and Glasgow in

1978. At the meeting of the Commonwealth Fencing Federation at Ottawa it was agreed that the case for fencing in the Games should be collated by the Secretary, Mary Glen Haig, from Scottish and New Zealand reports, but little was heard of any results at the next meeting, in 1976. Emrys Lloyd was elected in 1974 to succeed Charles de Beaumont as President and the subscription of member countries, then numbering twelve, was raised from £2.10 to £5 p.a. In 1978 Emrys Lloyd retired and was succeeded by Mary Glen Haig. It was agreed to persist with Commonwealth Championships as long as fencing was excluded from the Games.

Seven awards were made for services to fencing at national level in the summer of 1973. Foremost was the Gold Medal for Joyce Pearce for her outstanding and continuing services on the financial side. Silver Medals were awarded to Gordon Signy (posthumously); to René Paul, in recognition of his distinguished career as a fencer, his sportsmanship and his loyal service to the Association; to Bert Pelling, three times epee Champion, a member of the AFA Committee from 1935 to 1972 and an epee selector for many years; and to Colonel Hay for his long and devoted services to fencing, particularly in the Services and in Scotland and in recognition of his career as an active fencer for over sixty years. W. C. Burgess received the Award of Merit for long and devoted service to fencing in the Civil Service.

In the New Year Honours of 1974 Robin Brook, as Chairman of the British Chamber of Commerce, received a knighthood for his services to exports and Sgt Jim Fox the MBE for his sustained achievements in the pentathlon: he had been a bright hope at Tokyo in 1964, he came eighth at the Mexico Olympics and fourth at Munich in 1972.

There were various competition innovations in the early seventies. Edmund Gray proposed that the three-weapon Granville team event, which had become somewhat lack-lustre, should include ladies' foil and that the scoring should be cumulative up to 28 hits, each successive bout starting at the score of the previous one, instead of being by majority of fights won (which frequently meant that the third weapon was not fought at all). After being at first adopted only for an extra experimental event, this format was eventually accepted in 1978. On the proposal of Bobby Winton, the rules for the team championships were changed in February 1972 to allow three reserves to a club's weakest team.

Another innovation was the introduction of ladies' epee and sabre. In 1973 the latter was rejected by the Committee; but pressure increased, views changed and by December 1975 approval in principle for both weapons was forthcoming following consideration by a LAFU party headed by Danuta Joyce, though entries by ladies for men's events were still rejected. Events were organised for 1976–7 at Sheffield for epee and Bristol for sabre.

The international rules for competitors had been completely revised in 1972 by a committee of the FIE which included Charles de Beaumont. The major task of producing an English translation in 1974 was carried out by

Steve Higginson (assisted by Peter Jacobs). Leon Paul supplied the attractive cover, put up the capital and retailed it jointly with the Association. James Noel produced an extremely useful (and impeccably accurate) digest as a special foldout supplement to *The Sword*.

The FIE, pressed for information about rule changes, was slow to reply, as on other queries. It was felt that the elderly Frenchmen positioned in key offices and with the advantage of the use of their own language overdominated business and held back change at the Annual Congresses. These were attended by Peter Hobson, Peter Jacobs and René Paul in 1972 (at Munich), by Emrys Lloyd, Peter Jacobs and Steve Higginson in 1973, and by one or both of the latter two in subsequent years, as well as by Mary Glen Haig after she became President of the AFA.

In view of the weak British influence on the Congress, the Finance and General Purposes Sub-Committee queried the rate of subscriptions to the FIE, which was linked to the number of votes allotted. Together with France, Italy, Russia, Poland, Hungary and W. Germany, Britain had four votes and paid 7,175 francs p.a. Three votes were to be had for 3,010 frs, two for 2,000 and one for 665 frs. These rates increased by ten per cent in 1974. Each country's quota of FIE licences (necessary for all international competitions) was linked to these rates, but the British quota of 4,100 licences was vastly in excess of needs. The negligible return on this expenditure was illustrated by the fact that Britain had only one member on any FIE committee – Ron Parfitt on the Technical Committee, and he served only as a correspondent. In this context the F & GP wrote to the FIE warning that the AFA might cease paying £645 for its three extra votes. In 1977 the AFA began to recover its representation. Peter Jacobs was appointed to the Commission des Statuts (i.e. rules of FIE organisation) and Martin Joyce to the Commission d'Arbitrage. In 1979 Mary Glen Haig became a member of the Committee for the Scale of Votes and Peter Jacobs that for the Rules of World Championships. (He also served on the Directoire Technique at the 1979 World Championships and at the 1980 Olympics.)

On the domestic front, the AFA was able to hold its own surprisingly well financially in the mid-seventies, years of high inflation (11% in '73, 19% in '74, 25% in '75, 15% in '76) despite the excessive building up of stocks of Proficiency Badges to the value of £4,139 in 1972 and poor hirings of HQ in the same bad year. When Value Added Tax was introduced in 1972 and sports bodies were not exempted, the F & GP agreed to absorb the burden in view of the undertaking to hold subscriptions for a number of years. £1,085 was paid in the first full year. Only the rate for Life Membership was raised – from £30 to £50, in 1975. Meanwhile, further heavy additions to costs flowed from increases in salaries for the National Coaches, and for HQ staff, who were assimilated to Sports Council scales from 1975. The two coaches' salaries and expenses amounted to £5,505 in 1970–72 and £15,304 in 1975–6 (though

£1,163 and £5,550 respectively were recovered in fees). The salaries of HQ staff came to £3,285 in 1971–2 (including audit fee) and £9,611 in 1975–6. Apart from the Secretary, there were two to three part-timers from the mid sixties onwards. Mrs Jean Rathbone joined in 1969. Lesley Hamments did a stint in the sixties and rejoined in the late seventies. Both still sustained the office in 1981. Fortunately government grant covered 75 per cent of both coaching and administration, as it did almost the whole of the largest item of all: training and travel grants, up from £6,169 in 1971–2 to £23,288 in 1975–6.

Total expenditure almost trebled between 1971–2 and 1975–6 from £18,850 to £55,233 (while the value of money fell 64%). But after deduction of government grant, there was actually a slight reduction, from £6,161 to £6,146, in costs falling on the Association. This was largely due to three items. On the revenue side, the profit on the Proficiency Scheme increased from £431 to £1,547, after the fees were raised. On the expenditure side, the cost of *The Sword* and the share in that of the HQ building doubled rather than trebled. *The Sword* was restricted to a budget of £1,000 p.a. in 1973 (and there were only two issues in 1973–4). As for the costs of the HQ building, the premiums payable on the endowment policy tapered off from £863 in 1970–71 to extinction in 1975–6, the interest on the £15,000 loan remained constant at £750 and fuel bills only rose from £1,312 in 1971–2 to £1,830 in 1975–6. Hiring revenue, however, was volatile and after rising from £1,557 in 1970–71 to £3,575 in 1973–4 (mainly from Hill House School) was still only £1,471 in 1975–6. In 1975 the Association accepted that its share of the cost of the premises should rise from two-thirds to three-quarters, as more fairly reflecting its share in the use of the building (now extending to two evenings a week as well as weekends).

Two sources of income were less than buoyant. Competition fees, which rose to a peak of £822 in 1968–9, dwindled to £728 in 1969–70. When the main rate of fee was doubled the following season the yield was much less than double – £1,176. In other words, the number of entrants at national events – which had been rising steadily in the 1960s – had declined substantially. This relates to the other, more important, element that sagged, subscription income, since AFA membership was chiefly required for national events (as it was also for the open provincial events whose entries mainly boomed in these years, but for which AFA membership was less consistently ensured). Subscription income stood at £2,945 in 1970–71, rose to £6,174 with the increased rates of the next season and virtually stuck at this level (£6,847 in 1975–6).

Individual membership was already declining before the increases of 1971. It then sank from 2,315 to 1,455. By 1976 (with various reminder campaigns by Commander Booth) it had risen to 2,237, although in real terms the £3 adult rate was only half what it had been in 1971.

Proposals put to the F & GP for widening and reforming the subscription structure fell on stony ground, but a more limited scheme put forward by John Pilkington, SW Section Secretary, had the political push to make a breakthrough at the AGM of February 1974. An Associate Membership at £1 per head paid through club secretaries via Sections was to be offered to fencers who wished to give modest support to fencing and be able to enter County and Section events. It was agreed in March 1975 to apply this system experimentally from the beginning of the following season in two Sections, the SW and the NW.

The results were disappointing. Although it appeared there was barely any switch from full to Associate Membership, there were only 236 Associates in the SW and 63 in the NW by the end of 1975-6. However, the principle of more than one type of membership was gaining acceptance and in 1978 Associate Membership was extended to all Sections.

Fencing was very lucky that at a time of deepening economic gloom on the national level, there was a great increase in government grants in the mid seventies – both in the budget for national coaches and, especially, in the funds for travel by the national training squads. The travel and training budget had risen from nil in 1964 to £1,760 in 1967-8, bumping down to £935 the next (Olympic) season, but then rising steeply in successive years – £3,869, £5,969, £8,653, £8,011, £10,753. Then came a jump to £21,307 for 1974-5 (and £23,288 for 1975-6). This was partly accounted for by a rise from two-thirds to three-quarters in the proportion of travel costs covered. It also coincided with a change in the system. Because the Sports Council regarded the AFA as outstandingly well-controlled by the Treasurer, it was willing to make the experiment of providing a block grant to be distributed between training and travel needs of the squads at the discretion of the Association, which delegated it to the weapon sub-committees and their selectors. This made possible greater flexibility and a shift towards travel subsidies. The cost of training varied considerably since the Senior National Coach (with his own budget and on AFA premises) sometimes trained a squad himself; sometimes a squad could constitute an Adult Institute Class (subsidised by the local authority) – and sometimes, regrettably, a squad trained without professional supervision – the men's foil squad had no master between the resignation of Leon Hill and 1979, for instance.

The scale of grant-aided travel is indicated by the figure of eighty for the number of foilists sent to competitions abroad in 1974-5, compared with twenty the previous season (excluding World Championships). The new flexibility did not permit the extension of travel subsidies to cover accommodation at foreign events. Nor did it provide for subsidy of the travel or accommodation of visiting teams from abroad; this was met from AFA funds, including sums sometimes contributed to general funds by competitions abroad which subsidised British participants.

Although it was partly to satisfy the British Olympic Association of adequate standards of performance by those selected it was also to encourage fencers to go abroad more that the Olympic Qualifying System had been instituted. The scale of financial help was beginning to make the encouragement superfluous, but the BOA still needed satisfying, since they bore the cost, not the Sports Council.

In June 1973, revised Olympic Qualifying Rules worked out by the Joint Weapon Committee under the chairmanship of Peter Hobson were enacted. Instead of having to reach the last sixteen in 4–6 nominated top class events to gain a qualifying point, fencers had to reach the last twelve in one of a list of events per season, or gain a result equivalent to the quarter-final of a World Championship. The fifth place could go to an unqualified fencer, however many were qualified. And the Joint Weapon Committee could consider as qualified 'one fencer per weapon whom exceptional circumstances (e.g. illness) have prevented from gaining a necessary qualification in the final year'.

In February 1976, the Rules were amended to meet a limit of thirteen set for the combined number of the men's weapons by the International Olympic Committee, as follows: 'The Joint Weapon Sub-Committee may consider as qualified (to the extent necessary for the purpose of reducing the size of the men's team to thirteen) not more than two additional men (whether qualified in any weapon or not) to fence in two or more weapons.' Fortunately the rather absurd limitation was removed after the 1980 Olympics.

There was a separate set of new rules on the procedure of selection which was included in the committee's new terms of reference. These provided, in particular, that the results of all possible candidates should be available to members of the Joint Weapon Sub-Committee (as well as to the candidates themselves), so that they could scrutinise the selectors' choice thoroughly and subsequently vouch to the AFA Committee that they had done so (partly to avoid debate on the merits of particular fencers in an inappropriate forum).

Terms of reference were also drafted for the Joint Weapon Sub-Committee, which hitherto had been entirely ad hoc. The only points of contention were the claims of the Under-20 Committee that their representatives should sit on the Joint Weapon Committee and that the training of under-twenty fencers should be under the control of themselves, not the respective weapon sub-committees. In the end, it was agreed that representatives of the Under-20 Committee should attend when anything relevant was on the agenda, and in particular at the ad hoc meeting of weapon representatives for the annual drafting of the competition calendar. On the score of training, after some discussion on joint arrangements, Joe Eden went it alone on a scheme sponsored by the Inner London Education Authority in the form of a Youth Group initially with Prof. Boston as overall coach, to which sixty fencers were invited. The Joint Weapon Committee accepted the fait accompli.

The terms of reference of the Joint Weapon Sub-Committee were approved by the AFA Committee in September 1973. On the proposal of Peter Kirby, the Senior National Coach was included as a non-voting member. At his own wish, Prof. Anderson's role in Olympic training for the 1972–6 cycle was to give extended lessons at HQ to an elite of one or two fencers at each weapon. The main squads tended to concentrate, partly on Prof. Anderson's advice after the 1976 World Championships, on fitness, in which the British teams compared poorly with more successful countries.

Joe Eden continued to be active in fund raising. In 1972 he presented HQ with a photo-copier and 150 chairs on behalf of the Under-20 Men's Sub-Committee. In 1975 the committee bought a minibus to help with the many journeys by Under-20 parties to foreign events.

As with the seniors, there was some dispersion of Under-20 activity in the middle seventies. Prof. Leon Hill started an Under-20 team championship in September 1974. The following year this was recognised as a national event. Junior regional training was also developing with the foundation of a squad in the SW with Prof. Mike Webster as coach.

Perhaps somewhat surprisingly, the organisation for schools fencing remained quite separate from the Men's Under-20 Committee, though in 1975 they accepted mutual representatives. The Schools Fencing Union was reconstituted in 1975 to include a representative from each Section. It was given revised terms of reference and allowed to nominate a representative to the LAFU and to the Coaching Sub-Committee, as well as the Under-20s. Competition rules were also rewritten and in particular the top age group was now opened to all fencers under the age of nineteen, whether or not at school. This put an end to the difficulties of defining a school amidst proliferating sixth-form colleges and the like and brought them into line with other sports, as advocated by Peter Hobson.

In a renewed effort to boost fencing in schools, a letter drafted by the President and Secretary was sent out during the 1974–5 season to fourteen Area PE organisers. The well-attended and well-organised Under-14 Championships in the excellent Barnstable Sports Centre was just one event that demonstrated the thriving state of schools fencing in the mid seventies.

National training was another area under reconstruction at this time, following papers by Prof. Anderson and by Derek Parham, amongst others. The latter considered that the chief requirement was the raising of the standard of coaches, to staunch the wastage of fencers after the initial stage of low-level tuition. The retention of medium-level fencers would also strengthen the finances of the AFA by increasing the entry to competitions for which AFA membership was required. To attain this, it was particularly worthwhile for the AFA to subsidise the training scheme; indeed this was the chief service the AFA could offer the Sections.

Prof. Anderson, on the other hand, reported a decline in the demand for coaching courses, attributable to the successful build-up of a network of coaches in most areas of the country. In his view the next stage should be the appointment of Regional Coaches. This was the policy adopted.

As part of the rethinking, a fresh brochure was published in cooperation with the Sports Council on what was renamed the National Coaching Scheme (to avoid possible confusion with national team training). The sub-committee was likewise renamed and given fresh terms of reference. It was to comprise the National Coach and a nominee of each of the following: the AFA Committee, the Coaches Club, the Schools Fencing Union, the Men's Under-20 Sub-Committee, each weapon sub-committee, each Section and the Combined Services. Observers from the Sports Council, the Department of Education and the BAF were to be invited. It was to have power to co-opt, partly to retain the membership of at least three amateur coaches.

A development plan for regional coaches was drawn up by Arthur Banks, Chairman of the Coaching Sub-Committee. While the Senior National Coach increasingly stayed in London, concerned with Olympic training and such ventures as the class for schoolgirls on Tuesday evenings at HQ (sponsored by the ILEA), Prof. K. Pearson tested the ground in the NE for an experimental three months. Proving successful, this was followed by the permanent appointment there of his brother, Prof. Pat Pearson, as the first Regional Coach in 1974.

At this point, financial stringency became an obstacle. At the same time as the general economic crisis following the huge rise in oil prices and the confrontation between the miners and the Heath Government, the Houghton Award gave to National Coaches, now paid on the Pelham Scale, substantial rises backdated to May 1974, with a further increase for April 1975. As a result, instead of appointing an extra coach, it was planned that from September 1975 Prof. Ken Pearson should cease his roving engagements as second National Coach and operate from a fixed base as Regional National Coach for the E. and W. Midland Sections. That summer, however, he resigned to take up a non-fencing post and at very short notice the Coaching Committee and the two Sections appointed Tom Norcross instead. Previously a W. Midlands Section Coach, he had been in charge of fencing for three years at Millfield School. As a sabreur, he had been in the Junior final and also a member of the Welsh team at the 1974 Commonwealth Championships.

The dispersal of National Coaches showed its advantages in increased net income for 1975–6. Travel time and expenses were reduced and more courses were staged. Ladies were this season allowed to take Coaching Awards in sabre and epee. The exam for the Advanced Coaching Award was also modified to cover all weapons and to include a written paper. One motive for this change was the worryingly low standard of sabre and epee and the low number of young fencers at those weapons.

Another concern of the Coaching Committee was the adequate provision of presidents in the Sections. To this end a new examination structure was drawn up in 1973 and the existing list of AFA Presidents was revised by the Weapon Sub-Committees. Partly as a result of FIE requirements for more presidents to accompany teams and partly through the advocacy of Bobby Winton and the energy of Jackie Erwteman, the Rules and Presidents Sub-Committee (renamed the Rules and International Sub-Committee) was strengthened in 1976 to raise standards in this area. In 1977 the Junior Administrator's Award was introduced mainly to encourage young fencers to learn to preside.

Amateur–professional issues were also under consideration. In January 1975, at the Annual Conference held this year on the same day as the AGM, Prof. Anderson reported that the International Fencing Academy was proposing that those who taught fencing for gain should be treated as amateurs and only those who competed for gain be ineligible. Already, he claimed, at least in effect, fencing masters ranked as amateurs both in Eastern Europe and in France (where they could give group but not individual lessons). The British Academy did not ask for this but it did believe that its members should be able to serve on AFA committees. Section representatives deplored the loss of useful officers when they turned professional. At the subsequent discussion at the Coaches' Conference, Emrys Lloyd gave his view as a lawyer that the French were infringing FIE rules (possibly stricter than those of the AFA).

Actually, as Allan Jay confirmed, there was already no bar in the Articles to exclude professionals from any AFA body, except the Committee. Some – such as the Under-20 Sub-Committee – had included them for many years. However, pending a complete amalgamation between the AFA and the BAF, which the latter did not want, a joint working party was set up in December 1973, to investigate closer links. It consisted of Mary Glen Haig, Bobby Winton and Peter Hobson for the AFA and Profs Anderson, Hill and Moldovanyi for the BAF. To test amateur opinion, in the spring of 1975 Bobby Winton drafted a questionnaire on such issues as whether professionals should sit on committees and if so on what terms. The response was broadly favourable but on the grounds that many did not reply, no action was taken for the time being, though Arthur Banks (Chairman of the National Training Sub-Committee since 1972) and the Coaches Conference were both pushing hard in 1976, and in June 1977 one small advance was made: professionals were declared eligible to preside at competitions (though not normally over pools containing pupils) and to be included in the AFA lists of presidents on the same terms as amateurs.

Certainly the general inclination was towards relaxing rules in this area, partly as the degree of subsidisation of amateurs in many countries made nonsense of the distinction. In September 1974, the Joint Weapon Committee approved the IOC rule permitting payment for loss of earnings for up to 45 days p.a. while engaged in training and competition. In 1976 the F & GP was scrutinising the AFA rules on amateurism to ensure that they were no stricter than was necessary to conform with IOC and FIE rules – which were far from identical and in the latter case seemed to be internally contradictory.

An important competition rule change agreed by the FIE in 1975 was that henceforth the reserve could substitute for a team member on request of the captain whether or not injury had occurred. Soon afterwards the bane of simultaneous attacks at sabre was met by the rule that after three such attacks a coin should be tossed to decide which fencer should have priority for the next hit landed.

A calmer period followed the surge of activity of 1972–4. The AGMs of 1975 and 1976 were short and saw no major changes and there were fewer meetings of the Committee. There were some new departures, however. Press coverage, when it occurred (such as an article on fencing in the *Sunday Telegraph* colour magazine) had a definite effect on recruitment. But the decline in coverage of fencing events in the national press since the early fifties could not be reversed despite the efforts of Raymond Paul, for long the Publicity Officer (and from 1974 Chairman of the more or less one-man Publicity and Promotion Sub-Committee) and of the agency journalist John Gillon, or even the remarkable achievement of Marjorie Pollock-Smith in consistently reporting major events in the *Daily Telegraph* even when her health confined her to her flat.

The AFA's own journal, *The Sword*, enlarged its format yet further in 1976 and adopted more economical and versatile photo-litho methods. James Noel was now doing the paste-up and organising production as well as acting as deputy editor (as he had since mid-1974). On some issues, such as the one on the Montreal Games, he spent several weeks' labour. Clare Halsted edited the tournament reports. For a while broadsheet bulletins, with photographs, were put out in association with Leon Paul in addition to the regular issues.

In 1975 British fencing lost two major figures who had been active until a few years before. They died within a few days of one another in December. Both were distinguished psychiatrists and both only in their early sixties.

Roger Tredgold was born in 1911, began fencing at Winchester and fenced for Britain (at foil) while still at Trinity College, Cambridge. Between 1937 and 1955 he won the Sabre Championship six times, in spite of the seven year gap of the war. He also competed in every one of 23 national championships between 1934 and 1963 and reached the final on every occasion. And he continued to excel at foil – he fenced both weapons in the 1936 Olympics and only lost the 1947 Championship in a barrage with René Paul. He was a genial but formidable competitor with surprising lightness and speed of movement for his 6ft 4ins, which he used to achieve the astonishing reach on which much of his success was based.

Following an eminent father in his speciality, in 1948 he was appointed Consultant at University College Hospital and thenceforth had little time to fence. He pioneered the study of the stresses of industry and by his inspiring teaching and organisation made his department one of the most highly respected in the country. He had deep concern for others, based on unobtrusive religious convictions, an easy informality and humour, and he won the trust of colleagues and patients alike. He was married and had two children. He had many recreations from a strenuous job, especially foreign travel and bird-watching, but he found time to write extensively, both on psychiatry and as editor of *The Sword* from 1948 to 1952, turning the 8 a.m. train from Tunbridge Wells to London into a mobile office. He was a member of the AFA Committee from 1938 to 1950 and from 1959 to 1972 and also contributed much to the Sabre Sub-Committee.

Pierre Turquet was born in 1913 and went to Westminster School (where he started fencing) and Trinity College, Cambridge (where he gained his half blue). He qualified just before the war and reached the rank of Major in the RAMC. He served for 24 years at the Tavistock Clinic, becoming senior consultant.

He won the sabre Championship in 1951 and fenced in the Olympics of 1948, 1952 and 1956 and in the intervening World Championships. He was Treasurer of the AFA from 1961 to 1966 and sabre Captain on numerous occasions in the fifties. Though sometimes impatient with those he judged were not destined for the team, he was untiring in his efforts to meet every fencer's special needs at foreign events. In those days of no government grants he even gave financial assistance to enable the less well-off to compete abroad. A lover of good food and good wine, he and his charming wife would entertain visiting and home teams at a restaurant or their elegant Kensington home.

Donald Paterson (photo p. 49) also died in 1975, attempting to save a drowning boy. Also educated at Westminster School, he won the Doyne at the age of 26 in 1934 and was four times in the final of the Foil Championship. In 1935 he fenced for Britain in the European Championships. A quiet, unassuming man with a warm smile, he had many friends in the Epee Club and elsewhere. After periods of dentistry (at which he qualified with honours) and at the bar, he found a gift as a very successful inventor of photographic equipment.

1976 was a good year for fencing. The high point in the British calendar – the Challenge Martini – was perhaps the strongest ever, thanks to the organisational energy of Peter Jacobs and to the generous sponsorship of Martini-Rossi, whose budget of £3,000 for the event they had sponsored since 1960 made them the most important private patron of British fencing over the period covered by this book. Major John Coventon, who as head of Martini Publicity, had supported the tournament since its inception, retired this year. The AFA had presented him with a Gold Medal in 1971, in appreciation for his services to fencing. To celebrate Robert Bruniges' victory in the World Youth Championship and as a send-off for the Montreal team, Martini gave a

Kate Hurford and Henrietta Davies-Cooke

party in their New Zealand House 'terrace' at which Sir Robin Brook presented Mary Glen Haig with a silver Tudor rose as a tribute to her work and achievements.

At the AGM in February 1976, Joyce Pearce and Margaret Somerville were made Vice-Presidents in recognition of their many years' unstinting and continuing labour for the Association. The Silver Medal went to Captain Eric Mount Haes, who till 1973 was for 25 years Secretary of the National Training Sub-Committee and who had chaired the Public Schools Championship Sub-Committee from 1954. Leslie Veale was awarded the Silver Medal for his work with the disabled and for the Northern (Yorkshire) Section.

At this meeting Mary Glen Haig was nominated unopposed to her second three-year term of office as President. In the next New Year Honours List she was made Commander of the Order of the British Empire, for her work as Chairman of the CCPR. This was the more marked as a tribute to her work for sport as it came only six years after her MBE. In the LAFU there was a change of President. Eve Davies moved to Winchester and was succeeded by Mrs Henrietta Davies-Cooke, a former member of the British team, a member of the LAFU Committee since 1967 and Hon. Secretary from 1968 to 1970. Sally Kennealy took over from Jackie Erwteman, who had been Treasurer since 1974, and Ann Tetlow succeeded Kristin Payne, who had been Hon. Secretary since 1969.

In Spring 1977 *The Sword* announced the death of Paul Gallico, the writer, who was taking lessons from Prof. Parkins until a few months before although almost eighty and who fenced epee ambidexterously. Later in 1977 came the death of Lord Adrian, the Nobel Prize winner who had also been Public Schools runner-up in 1908. Another death was that of Prof. Ken Russell, Treasurer of the BAF 1964-75 and former Captain in the Army Physical Training Corps. In addition to his capabilities as a fencing master, he was the holder of a Lonsdale Belt for boxing and numerous trophies for rugby, football, gymnastics, cycling, swimming and shooting. Another master who died, sadly prematurely, was Prof. Harry Porter who trained under Prof. Wren and after a success as a competitor left a promising career in industry to teach, at which he combined patience, humour and technical skill.

There also died two men who made notable contributions to fencing administration. Bert Pelling (photo p. 49) was one of the outstanding fencers of his generation. Trained as an epeeist by McPherson and Morel, he attained international rank in 1928 and later fenced in the Olympics of 1936 and 1948. Each time he went to the European or World Championships he helped the team to excellent results: to fifth place in 1930 and to the semi-finals in 1935 and 1937. From 1935 he served on the AFA Committee and for many years acted as epee selector. He was always ready to encourage young fencers, especially at Grosvenor and the Poly. In 1965 he suffered a heart attack after a bout. He nearly died and was advised to stop fencing; but he could not be kept from the piste for long and even resumed coaching, which he continued after his retirement in 1968 at the Bournemouth Espada Club. There once again his geniality and enthusiasm quickly won him admiration and affection.

Captain Eric Mount Haes died in autumn 1976, at the age of 79. Going to sea in the First World War, and witnessing the surrender of the German fleet in 1919, he ended his naval career as training officer of HMCS Cornwallis, going on to be HM Inspector of Schools in 1947. He regularly represented Scotland at both sabre and epee, and was three times Captain. He came third in the Junior Sabre in 1954. He captained the RN athletic and cross-country teams. From 1949 to 1972 he was Secretary of the National Training Sub-Committee and in 1954 began a twenty year stint as Chairman of the Public Schools Championship Sub-Committee. Unfailingly friendly to all he met, he was always willing to put himself out for any cause in which he believed.

In July 1977 A. W. Fagan also died. He had competed in the 1912 Olympics and continued to enjoy his weekly lesson at LTFC almost to the end.

The late seventies were a world away from 1912. Now, to have any hope of competing on equal terms with the virtual professionals of many other countries, it was vital to secure financial aid for promising British fencers. To this end Mary Glen Haig had been engaged in discussions with Wilkinson Sword. There resulted a ceremony televised as part of the Grandstand programme in 1977, four fencing scholarships of £2,000 each for Elizabeth Wood, Mark Slade, John Llewellyn and David Seaman to meet all types of expenditure involved in training for the 1980 Olympics (with a further £2,000 as a reserve fund). This was only the latest and most generous of Wilkinson's contributions to fencing. For three years they had been giving bursaries to school fencers towards the cost of competing abroad: 35 had been awarded so far. They also sponsored the men's Under-20 invitation foil event.

Another source of help was the Sports Aid Foundation, formed by a group of businessmen, which this year awarded Robert Bruniges £500 p.a. to prepare for the Olympics. Martini awarded Ralph Johnson a bursary for the same purpose. Linda Martin meanwhile benefited from the Churchill Travelling Fellowship, going to Germany to improve her technique for three months in 1978. Leon Paul did their bit when they sponsored the Coronation Cup at Leatherhead Leisure Centre. From 1976 they also gave the provincial circuit of competitions a substantial boost by providing electrical equipment.

At the 1977 AGM Joyce Pearce warned that subscriptions would have to go up the following year after being held since 1971 in spite of a rise in the retail price index of 125 per cent. Government grant had accounted for nearly two thirds of expenditure in 1971; now it had risen to 83 per cent. In the event, Joyce Pearce felt that immediate increases were required, so an Extraordinary General Meeting was called. Adult subscriptions were increased from £3 to £7, Adult Clubs from £4.20 to £7.50, school clubs £1.05 to £5. At the instance of the LAFU Under-20 Sub-Committee, a new Under-18 rate of £1 was introduced alongside the Under-20 rate, which was raised from £1 to £3. An over-65 rate of £3 was also introduced.

Several rule changes were made in 1977. The qualifying standard for the Olympics was to be by varying numbers of points for varying results, instead of a single inflexible point per result. Calibration was to be by position reached – from the last 32 upwards – and by strength of event. Events attracting nearly all leading fencing nations were to be classed A; those including at least fifteen foreign fencers who had reached the second round of the World Championships were to be classed B and those including at least six fencers of this calibre were to be classed C. Scores were to be doubled in the third year of the Olympic cycle and quadrupled for the fourth year. Complete teams could only be entered at each weapon for the Olympics if at least three members were qualified, but the fourth and fifth members did not need to be qualified and in 'exceptional circumstances, e.g. illness', the Joint Weapon Sub-Committee could deem an unqualified fencer to be qualified. If there were no qualified fencers a single person could be entered.

Entries to events abroad, always subject to AFA control at the behest of the FIE, were henceforth to be checked by captains and selectors for each weapon, partly to meet the new FIE requirement for Grade A events of one president for every seven fencers entered by a country and partly because some popular major tournaments were limiting national entries and partly because the exemption from the first round usually given to foreigners imposed some obligation on national federations to ensure their entrants were of a minimum standard.

A significant change in FIE competition rules was that making it illegal to turn one's back while fencing. At foil this was justified as a safety measure; at epee there was no discernible reason, only the impoverishment to the repertoire through the outlawing of the pirouette – a surprise move at close quarters with which Bill Hoskyns had often delighted audiences.

Back at home, the Sports Council agreed to make a two-thirds grant to non-Londoners towards the cost of attending the AFA Committee or the Coaching Sub-Committee up to three times each year. And during the summer break of 1977 AFA Headquarters underwent considerable renovation. Roof and external woodwork were repaired, the cork floor surface inside was patched and sanded. Credit for the fact that the whole work cost only £2,500 was largely due to Commander Booth, who had only recently recovered from serious illness but who expended great effort, even if he did not personally ascend ladders with paint brush in hand as he had in the past. A complete new set of judging apparatus was also purchased, together with six copper pistes of more durable gauge than the ex-paper mill ones.

At the 1978 AGM ten AFA awards were made. The Silver Medal was given to Marjorie Pollock-Smith, above all for her unfailing persistence as fencing correspondent for the *Daily Telegraph*. Silver Medals also went to Robert Bruniges for his magnificent performance as the first British winner of the World Youth Championships and to Harry Cooke for his many years of past service to British fencing.

Awards of Merit were presented to the following: to Bernard Piddington as Secretary of the SE Section, adviser to the London and SE Regional Sports Council, organiser of successful courses on a large scale and especially for a very fruitful liaison over Butlins Sports Weeks; to John Lewis of the King's School, Rochester, for over 25 years of organising and teaching fencing in Kent; to Lesley Hamments for long service to the SE Section, as organiser of LAFU events, as architect of improvements to the Categories System and on behalf of the Sections Sub-Committee; to Lesley's husband Jim for voluntary labour at HQ in addition to wide-ranging services to the SE Section; to Mrs Joan Scrivenor for her many years of effort for the Middlesex County Union in organising events and administrating; to Mrs Jackie Tyson, who had coached regularly for twenty years in the E. Midlands, untiringly served on its committee and made massive contributions to fencing tournaments, especially the Leicester Open; and finally to Gordon Wiles, likewise a coaching and committee stalwart in the E. Midlands, as well as Winton Cup strategist.

In February the AFA Committee appointed Jack Magill to succeed Richard Cohen as editor of the *Sword*. Magill was educated at the Royal Belfast Academical Institution, the focus of N. Ireland fencing. He was first Champion of the province in 1968, at epee, his least favourite weapon. He was already team Captain at the 1970 Edinburgh Games at the age of only nineteen. By a pleasingly Irish arrangement, he fenced at World Championships for the Republic (and in the 1975 team event beat two of the French Gold Medal foilists). After reading English at Cambridge, and post-graduate work on the modern novel, he had started a teaching career at Bedford. He was aided by two current Cambridge students; Ann Brannon, reading Anthropology, who became competitions editor and Mark Slade, reading Natural Sciences, who took over the production side.

At the latter end of 1977 there were further deaths of prominent figures in the fencing world. Prof. Paddy Power died at the age of 67. An ebullient character of great strength and energy, he did an enormous amount for fencing in the York area. After a career as an army physical training instructor he started teaching boxing and fencing at St Peter's School, York in 1945. He soon became widely known as an enthusiastic coach of young fencers. He ran several evening classes as well as developing fencing at the Mount, at Bootham's and at York University. He inculcated fitness and aggression and his pupils achieved much success, especially his son Anthony and Sue Wrigglesworth, who began with him. One who enjoyed controversy, he was also a Samaritan who helped many in trouble.

Bill Burgess was 68 when he died. He took up fencing alongside gymnastics in the thirties. From 1952 till 1975 he was secretary of the Civil Service Fencing Union, and Chairman thereafter. A colourful competitor, capable of using either hand, he was Civil Service Champion in 1952 at both foil and sabre and third in epee, and came fourth at sabre as late as 1976. He was also Kent foil and sabre Champion. Despite a bad heart attack in 1961 and three hernias and other medical handicaps, he remained extremely active, fencing three nights a week up to his death.

Alan Askew had died in May 1977 at the early age of 54. While studying medicine at Sheffield from 1946 to 1952 and as a pupil of 'Sarge' Cofield, he became possibly the best-known provincial foilist, with a flamboyant, unpredictable style and devastating speed and strength. Several times Section champion and a regular finalist in the University Championships, he fenced for England in the Quadrangular of 1953. Such was his enjoyment of the game, he laughed and shouted in approval of any good move by his opponent – or by himself; but as time went on he became increasingly taken up with his career as a leading exponent of homeopathic medicine.

Even more tragically premature was the death in a car accident in early 1978 of Caroline Parham. Following the involvement of both her parents in fencing, she represented University College, Swansea and then the University of Wales. Doing doctoral research at Liverpool, she gained a further group of fencing friends and achieved fourth place in the University Championships.

The starting point for discussion at the 1978 Conference was the review of the AFA carried out by Jeremy Booth, son of the Secretary, and the written responses to this from committees round the country. His recommendation for all committees to have terms of reference was gradually implemented in the following couple of years. The Sections, in so far as they had criticisms of the AFA, complained of slowness of communication and lack of contact with central officers; they were by no means unfavourable to great efforts to achieve international success, which they saw as one means of boosting fencing at the grass roots. Demonstrations at schools were seen as another means, though Prof. Anderson considered that the courses given at Butlins Camps, initially by himself and Ken Pearson, did more to recruit new fencers: 20,000 children between eight and fifteen had received basic tuition that season. He suggested leaflets to distribute at these courses suggesting clubs children could join back at home.

The Conference ended by setting up a working party to pursue all the ideas thrown up, consisting of Mary Glen Haig, Joyce Pearce, Bobby Winton, Nick Halsted, Lesley Hamments, Laurie Scott of the Eastern Section and B. P. Wheelhouse, an advocate of greater democracy; but their deliberations threw up little more than the proposal, in 1979, to abolish the Conference. Henceforth its functions were taken over by the AGM of the Sections Sub-Committee, held during the Winton Cup weekend at Loughborough, to which members of the AFA Committee were invited.

Further rule changes were made. Late entries to competitions on payment of a surcharge were introduced at foil in 1976 and at epee in 1977. In 1978 they applied to all weapons. At the discretion of the organiser they could be accepted up to fifteen minutes before the start of an event on payment of £4. (£2.50 was retained by the weapon committee.) The following year the same principle was applied to team events: clubs could add fresh names to teams on payment of £2.50 per head. This had also been pioneered by the Foil Committee, as was another team rule adopted in December 1979. If no reserve was named, one member of the 'B' team could transfer to the 'A' team provided he or she had not yet fenced. Moreover, up to eight names could be included on the entry in the case of a single team and up to thirteen names in the case of two teams (*either* four plus reserve for the 'A' team and eight for the 'B' team *or* four for the 'A' team and nine for the 'B' team).

The AGM of 1979 saw the relaxation of the rules of amateurism brought to a conclusion, largely through the preparatory work and cogent persuasion of Nick Halsted. The opposition was led by Allan Jay, who deplored the growing professionalism of sport. AFA Article 25 now read as follows: 'An amateur is a person who (a) in all respects complies with the rules of amateurism laid down in the Statutes of the FIE, (b) having forfeited his amateur status is reinstated as an amateur persuant to Article 32 or (c) has received financial remuneration for practising a sport other than fencing but who in all other respects complies with the rules of amateurism in force for the time being and laid down in the

BAF-AFA dinner dance 1978: Cdr Booth, Mrs Lloyd, Prof. Hill, Sir R. Brook, J. E. Lloyd, Lady Brook, Prof. Moldovanyi, Prof. Pitman.

Statutes of the FIE.' A note was added pointing out that fencers qualifying under (b) and (c) were amateurs for AFA events only.

The crucial FIE statute was no. 92 which stated that amateurs must not profit from fencing, though grants for specified expenses were allowable to Olympic and certain other fencers (c.f. p. 104) and payment for costs involved in fencing was allowable to all fencers; the AFA proposed to interpret 'profit' as income less expenses. In addition, Statute 93 B2 (a) allowed payment to supervisors of fencing courses whose *duties* did not include giving lessons even if they did *in fact* give lessons (a somewhat casuistic distinction). It was this last provision that had for some time permitted amateurs in France, for instance, to give lessons and even qualify as Maitres d'Armes provided they postponed taking up their diplomas.

The object of this more elastic concept of the amateur was one aspect of putting British fencers on a more equal footing with their foreign rivals; the complementary aspect was the commercial sponsorship which would enable fencers to train and compete far more fully than would be achieved in the spare time and on the spare cash available from an ordinary full time job. During the 1978–9 season the Sports Aid Foundation gave grants totalling £6,370 to seventeen fencers, most of them instalments towards Olympic or World Youth Championship preparation. State Express made a large contribution to sending two coaches with the British Team to the 1979 World Championships in Melbourne. As part of their continuing support, especially to young fencers, Wilkinson Sword presented a number of their trophies during the same season; recipients included the Public Schools Championships, the W. Midlands and NE Sections and the Quadrangular Match, now rechristened the Home International Match.

Two fresh sources of aid were gained in the 1979–80 season. Alka Seltzer sponsored the US-GB-Belgium match at the Birmingham Tournament, which attracted a good deal of publicity, including television coverage. The Mars Health Education Fund met the cost of an Olympic training weekend (as well as supplying large numbers of Mars Bars!).

Mary Glen Haig, who played the principal role in securing sponsorship for the AFA, was elected unopposed to a third three years' office at the time of the 1979 AGM.

There were also two external awards to AFA members. Emrys Lloyd was presented with the International Olympic Committee's Silver Medal in tribute to his fencing achievements and to his forty years' service as honorary Legal Adviser to the British Olympic Association and member of the IOC Juridical Council from 1974. Mrs Doris Allwork was awarded a Torch Trophy, for her dedicated voluntary work, as a member of Poly from 1936 to 1973, of the LAFU Committee from 1949 to 1962 and above all as Secretary of the Public Schools Sub-Committee from 1962 to 1979, contributing non-stop work, including correspondence, duplicating, telephoning, accounting and catering, for an event having over five hundred entrants a year.

In April 1978 Mrs Joan Pienne became Assistant Secretary of the Association. As Miss Shipston, she fenced for Britain in the 1952 Ladies' World Team Championship (then excluded from the Olympics). She married the distinguished epeeist Arnold Pienne and although she came second in the 1953 Desprez Cup, family life in Kent effectively removed her from the fencing scene and meant also that she only took on incidental employment such as being Secretary to Folkestone Grammar School.

Prominent fencers of three different generations died in 1979. Major G. L. G. Harry was 82. From the ranks of the Grenadiers he was commissioned in the E. Surrey Regiment and fought in the First World War. After leaving the army he became managing director of a wine firm. He was sabre Champion in 1928 and was runner-up no less than four times (1927, 1930, 1931 and 1936). He fenced in the British team in 1928, 1930, 1934 and 1936, starting and finishing with the Olympic Games, and being sabre Captain in 1930 and 1936. He outlived most of his fencing contemporaries but his later years were marred by arthritis.

Eddie Knott died suddenly of a heart attack in November. From Birmingham University he went on to Frankfurt University and gained a DPhil in organic chemistry. In 1937 he joined Kodak, becoming Research Director in 1968. He published many papers and patents and was awarded the Fellowship of the Royal Photographic Society for his scientific contributions. He joined Polytechnic FC before the war. In 1949 he was second in the Junior Championship and was repeatedly a senior finalist in the fifties, gaining second place four times. Very tall, left-handed, slender and long-limbed, he was spiderlike in stance and subtlety. He nearly always won the epee for Poly in the Granville and was in their winning team in 1963. In the Savage he twice

# Growth and change, 1964–81   115

helped Poly to second place and was in Grosvenor's winning team in 1953. In 1953 and 1954 he fenced in the British World Championship team. For several years he was a selector.

He also won far more Epee Club Competitions than anyone else. He won the Berlian Cup for best overall performance five years running from its inception in 1957 and last won it in 1973 when he was almost sixty, his youthful fitness belying his age. He was survived by his second wife Pat, and three children. He was a man of quiet friendliness, with a gift for rapport and humorous anecdote. A good skier, a keen gardener and fluent linguist, he was usually the centre of interest and always good company. He left a prize for the Martini Qualifying Cup.

The third death of 1979 was that of Paul Rogers. At the age of only 37 he was shot by an IRA gunman while in the back of a Landrover after taking a cadet to visit an injured soldier. He was master in charge of fencing at St Paul's from 1968–74 and was also involved with schools fencing throughout the country as Secretary of the Schools Fencing Union from its inception till 1973. It was as an officer in the cadet force of St Edmund's School, Ware, that he met his death. Of high personal standards, he often seemed a lonely man, but those who knew him saw that he was sincere and courageous, more concerned with his pupils' welfare than their esteem.

As the new season opened in September 1979 the foil selectors introduced a new system for the awarding of travel grants to eight foreign events and for membership of all but four of the sixteen places on the squad, tied to results in five tournaments: the previous Championship, Leicester, the Welsh Open, the Leon Paul and Birmingham. The result, as intended, was further to strengthen the provincial tournaments, as well as inducing team hopefuls to compete yet more.

Two new Vice-Presidents were appointed at the AGM: Arthur Banks, in recognition of his many years service in the NW and as Chairman of the Coaching Sub-Committee for seven years, and Peter Hobson, who was Chairman of both Joint Weapon and Sabre Sub-Committees and Vice-Chairman of the AFA Committee since the inception of that office. The following were presented with Awards of Merit: Joe Eden, for his services as Chairman of the Men's Under-20 Sub-Committee since its creation in 1963; Mrs Anne van Beukelen, for many years Match Secretary and County Secretary in Surrey, on the SE Committee and as competition organiser; David Littlejohn (husband of Hazel, née Twomey), who restored Kent as a well-run County Union and was Vice-Chairman in the SE; Sheila Briggs as Treasurer and team stalwart in the Northern (Yorkshire) Section; Dr Gillian Thorne for her activity in all aspects of fencing in Hertfordshire and the E. Section for over 25 years; Mrs Joan Mason for wide and long service to the S. Section. Awards of Merit also went to John Ramsay for his devoted service to the Schools Fencing Union, of which he was Chairman from 1969–77 and whose meetings he rarely missed despite the problem of travel from Ipswich, where he ran fencing at Woolverstone School; to Mrs Kate Hurford, for many years the driving force of the SFU and generally one of those few always willing to lend a hand whenever it was needed; to Dorothy Mellor for her many years ensuring salle and equipment were ready for LAFU competitors and for her unobtrusive but effective work on the AFA and LAFU Technical Sub-Committees, and finally to Nigel Watkins, Chairman of the W. Midlands, for his organisation of the Centre of Excellence at Birmingham and the famous Easter Tournament since 1970.

In February 1979, after thirty years service to the AFA, Prof. Anderson retired to take up a job in film making (having already done much fight arranging in his career). Not long after, he became Technical Director to the Canadian Fencing Federation. In August of the same year Prof. Norcross also retired, in his case to become Hong Kong National Coach. In paying tribute to Bob Anderson's all-important role in expanding British fencing over all those years, Arthur Banks recalled in particular his many-sided leadership of the week-long annual meeting of the Coaches Club for advanced coaching training, followed by the club championship and AGM. During warm-up sessions he was (simultaneously) coach, player and referee at basket ball; in the evenings he was liar dice champion; during lunch breaks he was film director, cameraman, script-writer and performer (practically simultaneously). They were splendid weeks, always fun, but above all ending with far better coaches than they started with. A farewell party and presentation took place at the Winton Cup.

Bob Anderson had straddled two roles which had become increasingly difficult to combine. On the one hand he was chief itinerant coach for the National Training Scheme, above all nurturing amateur coaches who were the lifeblood of grassroots fencing. On the other hand, he was coach to the national team. At the start of his career this meant sometimes giving training before the World Championships (and for more substantial periods before Olympic Games) mainly to promote fitness, and always travelling with the team to give warm-up lessons. As time went on team training became very serious. Individual weapon coaches were brought in, but Prof. Anderson still bore the overall responsibility. Latterly, partly as deputies and Regional Coaches took on some of the work and also because demand seemed to be declining, he went on his circuit less. The Coaching Sub-Committee under Arthur Banks now recommended that any future National Coach should be relieved of national team functions; moreover that the keynote on the Training Scheme side should be flexibility, ideally to be financed by a block grant which could be varied in its distribution as need changed, to pay both a part-time National Coach and other part-time coaches, all to be on at most five years contracts. Negotiations were initiated with the Sports Council towards these ends.

Leon Paul winner: Ziemowit Wojciechowski.

Prof. Tamas Mendelenyi.

Meanwhile, fortuitously, the gap on the national team side could largely be filled due to an earlier approach to the Sports Council for aid towards the employment of two part-time weapon coaches, both of whom were world-class fencers from abroad. Tamas Mendelenyi, who took over the sabre squad, had been Hungarian national sabre coach from 1972 as well as the 1955 World Youth Champion, third in the World Championships of 1957 and second in 1959 and three times team Gold Medallist. He was a doctor who was retraining in order to practice in Britain. Ziemowit Wojciechowski, who became foil coach for both ladies and men, had been a qualified coach to two top Warsaw clubs. He had twice been World Youth Silver Medallist and in the World Championships had come fourth in 1974 and seventh in 1975. He had come to Britain in 1977, taking up a post which Leon Paul Ltd provided and teaching in the evenings, while retaining, albeit controversially, his amateur status until his present appointment.

The reformed National Coaching Scheme was approved by the Sports Council in July 1980. Grant aid was to cover 75 per cent of the salary of the National Coach, who was to work sixty per cent of full time. Prof. Brian Pitman was appointed to the new post in April 1981. He was made personally responsible for Advanced Coaching Award courses and acted as guide and co-ordinator of standards for other Coaching and Proficiency Awards.

Born in 1932, Brian Pitman served in the Navy till 1957. He became an amateur coach active in the Sussex area in 1952, while training at Salle Paul under Prof. Zabielski and at Thames under Prof. Harmer-Brown. In 1954 he gained his Leader's Certificate. Competitively, he reached the final of the Junior Sabre and in 1962 was in the Thames team which came second in the Foil Team Championship, but he was always chiefly interested in coaching and turned professional when the firm for which he was Sales Manager wished to promote him but also to move him to the north in 1962, the year he married Eileen Nicholls, who herself helped develop fencing in Sussex. It says much for the wide respect and popularity which he commanded that he was almost immediately the Provost and Associate Representative member of the BAF Committee. He also became organiser of the BAF summer courses coached by Revenu, Lukovitch and Perone. He gained his Diploma in 1971. Douai School and the Universities of Cambridge and Sussex were among his teaching commitments, as well as St Paul's and Thames, at both of which he continued on becoming National Coach. He had also been Under-20 coach, both on the men's side and then the ladies', and ran the BAF Sunday training sessions for the South of England (Pat Pearson running the ones in the North). He intended continuing these but opening them to amateur coaches.

Under the new scheme grant aid was also to cover 75 per cent of the fees of Area Coaches up to £1,000 p.a. per Section. By means of fee-paid part-time coaches the object was to spread the coaching network and thus to improve the ratio of coaching time to travelling time. It was furthermore expected to reduce the cost of courses to participants, which was causing a decline. A generous offer by the Army to include civilians at Aldershot Coaching Award courses at minimal cost was a further contribution to solving this problem, as was the amalgamation of the summer school at Loughborough with the one at Lilleshall. The general objective remained that of producing enough amateur coaches to maintain, and expand, the sport at grass roots level.

There was a setback in one sector: the four Centres of Excellence, in Newcastle, Birmingham, Leicester and Bristol (the last initiated in 1979 by Colin Hillier). Staffed by the Regional Coaches, these lost their main source of grants – from the Sports Council, which was forced to make cuts. They continued, but with much reduced programmes. However, the broad advance now provided for was already beginning to take effect in 1981.

Associate membership, intended to broaden the base of AFA membership, was hardly succeeding in this objective, with only 492 subscribers in 1978–9. For the following season the system was simplified so that Sections, Counties, clubs and competition organisers could all buy blank membership cards in bulk and claim refund on unused blanks at the end of the season.

In terms of the overall members involved in the sport, fencing was probably holding its own in the later seventies, but it was subject to keen competition from the boom in squash, which had the advantage of attracting television coverage and had special appeal to city workers for its high fitness input for low time consumption. The growth of such combat sports as judo and karate, stimulated by Brian Jacks' Bronze Medal at the 1972 Olympics, and probably also by the increase in muggings, likewise tended to draw away potential fencers.

Fencing has always had the disadvantage that coaching has to be on a largely individual basis, which is expensive. Because after the Second World War most clubs operated as adult education classes, usually in schools during the evenings, they were vulnerable to the squeeze on public expenditure resulting from Britain's economic problems. In London, for instance, from 1976 physical education instructors were limited to three hours tuition on any one evening and but for strong representations it would have been two hours. In 1980 classes were restricted to the periods of school terms. The exclusion of students below the age of fifteen was a long-standing drawback which everywhere tended to be more rigorously enforced. Youth clubs offered an alternative, but were usually not adapted to operate as fencing clubs, and in turn excluded adults. Mary Glen Haig strove as Chairman of the CCPR to overcome such obstacles to children's participation in sport, while as early as 1977 Gillian Thorne in vain approached the Sports Council in an attempt to get amended the high charges and other restrictions on the use of schools for fencing. The pressure on grass roots fencing persisted, however, as witnessed by the decline in the number of affiliated adult clubs from 277 in 1978 to 193 in 1981.

Affiliated school clubs were declining in number even more drastically, from 288 in 1978 to 162 in 1981, also mainly due to education authority cuts, it would seem. Other indications of school fencing activity were less gloomy, however. The number of Proficiency Awards won climbed to a peak of 4,590 in 1976–7 and after sinking to 3,740 the following year recovered to 4,139 in 1979–80, and the Under-18 category of individual membership rose from 657 when it was introduced in 1977–8 to 1,057 in 1981, partly due to the efforts of John Hall, master in charge of fencing at St Pauls, who chaired the Schools Fencing Union from 1978 to 1980, but partly also because in 1979 individual membership was made a condition for Gold and Silver Proficiency Awards (on the recommendation of the Coaching Sub-Committee but against the advice of Prof. Anderson). Meanwhile, the number of entrants to the National Age Group Championships bounded ahead to over 3,000 by 1981.

At the AGM of February 1980 the AFA–BAF working party at last saw its work concluded after overcoming various obstacles such as the FIE statute barring professionals from the national 'bureau' (agreed to mean the officers of the AFA, not the Committee). The Articles of the AFA were amended to provide for up to three professionals to be elected to the AFA Committee, the total number of elected members being increased from twelve to fifteen. There would also be one non-voting representative of the BAF, but not two as hitherto. Under a further amendment the limitations on professional participation in all committees (including those of Sections) were to be determined at a General Meeting. The limitations now adopted were as follows: the number of professionals on a committee was not to exceed four or 25 per cent, whichever was the less, at the start of any season; nor could any vote be taken if professionals with votes exceeded half the number of amateurs with votes. Professionals were not to be chairmen, treasurers, selectors or team captains, nor, in compliance with FIE rules, were they to take part in questions of international policy. In order to avoid practical difficulties with the numerical limits, professionals were not to act as representatives for one committee on any other (and thus could not represent a Section on the main Committee). Finally, professionals were not normally to be eligible for expenses for service on a committee unless amateurs were similarly paid. Professional candidates for the Committee were to be on a common list with other candidates. If the election of a professional would cause the number on the Committee to exceed three, the amateur with the next largest number of votes would be elected instead.

March 1980 saw the death of Prof. Leon Bertrand, who must rank as the outstanding teacher of fencing in this country so far this century. His grandfather Baptiste emigrated from France and set up a fencing academy in Warwick Square – off Regent Street – his father Felix took over when he died in 1898 and Leon – always known as Punch – succeeded in turn in 1930, after training in Paris under Georges and Adolphus Ronleau and in Italy at sabre. A measure of the club's dominance was its seven wins of the Ladies' Foil Team Championship between 1928 and 1938 and its three of the Sabre Team Championship. Several times his pupils took all three top places in the Ladies' Championship. It also drew the rich, the aristocratic and the theatrically brilliant. Many national competitions were held there in the thirties. In 1933 Gwen Nelligan won the European Championships; in 1956 Bertrand again secured the ultimate victory when Gillian Sheen was Olympic Champion. For him fencing was an art and he was a technical perfectionist. He deplored the athleticism and heavy training of modern fencing which he contrasted with the 'poetry in motion' of a Lucien Gaudin; but fencing for him was more than a recreation. He passed on a philosophy, not just a technique, to his pupils, and it is no coincidence that many continued as fencing administrators after they had retired.

He was himself active as a competitor in the twenties and continued for many years to visit Italy annually both to compete and to train under Prof. Nadi. He also regularly wrote on fencing for the *Daily Telegraph* and elsewhere. He was the author of *Cut and Thrust* in 1927 and of the popular *Fencer's Companion* in 1935. During the Second World War he served in the Air Force, as he had in the First World War. After the war he was one of the founders of the British Academy of Fencing, of which he was President from 1949 to 1955. In 1946 he re-started his salle in a school in Stanhope Street, aided by such fencers as Bobby Winton and Robin Brook. From 1946 they shared the

Prof. Leon Bertrand

premises of the LFC, to which he also became joint coach with Fortunato Delzi, renewing a connection started by his grandfather 95 years before. But in 1953 when the LFC asked Salle Bertrand to leave, alternative premises could not be found and to Punch's sadness the club closed. He continued to teach at LFC, however, including among his pupils Elizabeth Arbuthnott, Tredgold, Porebski, A. R. Smith, D. A. and E. B. Hopkin, E. B. Christie, Feré Rentoul, Signy, de Beaumont and Mildred Durne. 'I regret everything, every succeeding year', he declared; but he weathered the move to W. Kensington and an illness which would have killed most men and continued to teach till 1977, when he was over eighty, still spurring on such pupils as Kate Hurford, Sally Littlejohns, Sue Olley and, for a time, Janet Wardell-Yerburgh with his unique mixture of old-world deference and a tongue of Cockney roughness.

An even longer career was that of Ted Morten, who died in September

1980 at the age of ninety (photo p. 49). He joined Ellerman's, the shipping firm, at the age of eighteen and finally retired from its service *seventy* years later, being re-engaged after first retiring because no one else was so skilled at assessing the logistics of loading and turn-round. During the First World War he served in the Guards Field Artillery. He only took up fencing in 1928, at the Poly as an extension to drama classes there. He favoured epee. In addition to lessons from Alfred Parkins and Lucien Morel he joined Prof. Leon Paul's Saturday training and fenced for Poly under the captaincy of Bert Pelling.

In 1935 he was included in the British team in the European Championships. He became Assistant Secretary to the Epee Sub-Committee in 1933 and the same year Secretary to the AFA Committee, the first paid officer of the AFA, albeit part-time, assisting Charles Biscoe, the Hon. Secretary, at whose office in the City he would call on most mornings. Until 1936 a spare room at the Mowlams, with whom he then lodged, was virtually the first AFA headquarters. When de Beaumont succeeded Biscoe in 1936 he agreed to see through the transition. He stayed another thirty years. He was an official with the British team in 1936, 1937, 1948, 1950, 1952, 1953 and 1955, usually as Manager. During the Second World War he used to travel from Cobham to the LFC, which along with de Beaumont he largely kept going; after the war he continued as the club's ever-zealous Secretary, upholding from his own small office the traditions of the gentleman's club till he retired in 1977 after forty years in the post.

The question of whether the Moscow Olympics ought to be boycotted dominated the 1979–80 season. It had first been discussed on the AFA Committee in December 1978 in terms of the general evils of the Soviet state, but then seemed unlikely to gain sufficient support to be a feasible measure. In December 1979 Russian forces invaded Afghanistan. The USA responded by calling for an Olympic boycott. Mary Glen Haig sent a questionnaire to all members of the AFA; there was a majority against a boycott, but by a margin of less than ten of the 330 or so replies (a result in any case complicated by the inclusion of clubs as well as individuals) and the Committee considered this too narrow to be binding. On 16 February 1980, having heard the views of weapon sub-committees and the national squad, and after long discussion, it decided to instruct its representative on the British Olympic Committee (Mary Glen Haig) to vote against sending a national team. The chief proponents of boycott were Nick Halsted and Ted Bourne, mainly on the ground that to participate in the Games would be to condone the invasion. They were opposed by Edmund Gray and Les Veale, who argued that a boycott would do no good and that the wrongfulness of introducing politics into the Olympics was not justified by the Russians doing so. The voting was 17–5 in favour of boycott, but it was agreed that in the event of the BOC

# Growth and change, 1964–81

deciding not to boycott, the Committee should consider whether the AFA should send a team.

On March 25 the BOC decided to send a British team, eighteen sports voting in favour and four, including fencing, voting to defer the decision. After further sounding of opinion, including the Sections, sub-committees and potential team members, the AFA Committee met again, on 9 April, and passed the following resolution by 26–1: 'The AFA maintains its view that the BOA should not send a national team to Moscow, but, in the light of the decision of the BOC to send a national team, the AFA resolves to send a fencing team, any selected fencers remaining free not to go if their conscience so dictates.' Both Halsted and Bourne favoured this decision as they considered that if the bulk of the British team was going it would be an ineffective gesture to exclude a fencing team.

In the event, Nick Bell (foil), Richard Cohen, Jim Philbin, John Deanfield and Terry Etherton (sabre) and Ralph Johnson and Tim Belson (epee) declined selection on grounds of principle.

In the Birthday Honours of June 1980 Joyce Pearce received the MBE for services to fencing which included twenty years of meticulous stewardship as Assistant Treasurer and Treasurer of the Association.

From the start of 1981 Joan Pienne, after deputising for two and a half years, took over as Secretary from Frank Booth, who had reached retirement age, but was now so committed to his adopted world of fencing that he continued to assist part-time.

At the 1981 AGM Eve Davies was elected as Vice-President of the Association, following her retirement as Chairman of the LAFU and her many years as ladies' Captain. The Silver Medal of the Association was presented to Mildred Durne, who had fenced for Britain for a number of years and was subsequently ladies' Captain and selector. The following received Awards of Merit: Gerald Earl, who for many years taught without fee and served as president, armourer, committee member and Treasurer to Kent County Union; Wilhelm van Beukelen, who performed similar services in Surrey, for which he was a team member from 1961 to 1976, when he ceased active fencing; Winifred Pass, who was a mainstay in the organisation of the Birmingham Tournament, after helping at Leamington from the early sixties; Jeff Featherstone, who had been master in charge of fencing at Brentwood for the formidable span of 28 years as well as organising the London Schools Epee Championship; Mrs Barbara Hillier, who had worked for the SW Section since the 1950s, was currently Section Coach and had largely been responsible for recruiting Norman Golding as professional coach and for keeping the section Under-20 training scheme going; her husband Colin Hillier, who had likewise served the SW over many years, including as Chairman; Peter Bird who for many years had been Chairman of the Hereford and Worcester County Union where the growth in fencing owed much to his coaching and leadership; Hilary Hammond, who had been helping to organise Midlands fencing since the mid fifties and who for many years until forced to retire by ill-health a year before had been Hereford and Worcester Secretary and had done much to raise the County Open event to national standing; and Derrick Cawthorne who, apart from his achievements as a fencer, had served on many AFA committees, had provided valuable expertise and practical help with headquarters equipment and had given his services as a senior president at countless competitions all over the country.

On the recommendation of the F & GP the 1981 AGM decided to increase subscriptions for the first time since 1977, although inflation had risen 42 per cent in the three years to January 1980. The individual rate was to go up from £7 to £10 (£1 to £2 for under-18s, £3 to £5 for under-20s and over-65s). The club rate was to go up from £7.50 to £15 (schools from £5 to £7). The Associate rate was to rise from £1.50 to £2.50. Since VAT, previously included, was now to be extra, 15 per cent had to be added to all the new figures.

These rates had only been approved by the Committee earlier on the same day after a good deal of opposition and the setting up of a working party on the subscription structure of the AFA (consisting of Dr John Purkiss, Chairman of the W. Midlands Section, Nick Norcliffe, Chairman of London Section, Patricia Casey, Hon. Secretary of the LAFU since 1979, Robert Dye, new Chairman of the Coaching Sub-Committee, and Bobby Winton, with Edmund Gray as chairman). Although the new rates secured an ample majority at the AGM, this followed an assurance that the working party would aim to produce any proposals for revised subscriptions in time for an EGM, so as to apply to the 1981–2 season, if desired.

After the AGM, Mary Glen Haig circularised all affiliated clubs, asking for the numbers of their members in different categories of AFA membership but also for suggestions on the subscription structure. Rather over forty replied. A number enrolled extra Associates, but the total for these at the end of the season was only 475 and many clubs commented that fencers did not perceive benefits in either level of AFA membership commensurate with the fees, especially since only two issues of *The Sword* had appeared since Winter 1979 and many parts of the country had not seen a national coach for a long time (none had visited Wales, for instance, since Ken Pearson last came in 1970). Many clubs were themselves struggling for existence, sometimes gamely surviving with less than a dozen members, though the average size was 29. Schools likewise reported that fencing was only just holding its own against competition from other sports. The expense of fencing made it a natural victim, especially in the state sector coping with Mrs Thatcher's onslaught on public expenditure. The feedback from the Sections Sub-Committee at its annual meeting at the Winton Cup was broadly similar.

As ever, the problem confronting the working party was seen as one of how to curb the main subscription rates by recruiting the broader mass of fencers at low rates, especially school fencers and adult 'social' fencers who ended the evening's lesson and free play with a convivial visit to the pub, and who never competed at all, as like as not. New inducements for such fencers which suggested themselves were a passport-type membership booklet, with pages for Proficiency Certificates etc. (as recently introduced by the French federation) which it was claimed would attract schoolchildren, and an accident insurance policy, which should appeal to prudent club fencers and which could be obtained cheaply on a block basis by the AFA. At £2 p.a. it was hoped to recruit some 2,000 schoolchildren – indeed the Schools Fencing Union predicted at least 3,000 if compulsory membership were introduced for all entrants to the National Age Group Championship, which was one change in membership requirements recommended by the working party. There were tentatively estimated to be 20,000 fencers in the country, of whom perhaps three-quarters were schoolchildren. At £4 p.a. it was hoped to recruit about a fifth of the 5,000 or so adults.

The working party also grappled with the problem of open tournaments round the country. There had been some half dozen of these in 1964; now there were about thirty. They had also grown in size and now attracted an estimated 4,000 at all weapons. This growth should have resulted in more members for the AFA, but organisers were reluctant to drive away entrants by enforcing full membership and probably at least a quarter of entrants were evading subscription. The working party proposed a more easily enforceable and equitable system whereby an AFA Levy of 50p was made on every entry, but only Associate membership (now renamed Ordinary membership) was required.

The Levy and the reformed Associate membership were estimated to produce nearly an extra £10,000 income, against which would be set insurance and booklets costing up to £5,000 in the first year (booklets would only require stickers for renewals of membership). There could therefore be an easing of the rates for affiliated clubs, the numbers of which fell by a third in the two years from 1979 in both adult and school sectors; so it was proposed that the adult rates should be reduced from the AGM figure of £17.25 to £11.50 and the school rate from £8.05 to £5.75 (all inclusive of VAT). Individual full rates were left untouched, but they would be less onerous since the benefits were to be increased and full membership was no longer to be required for entry to open tournaments or for the final series of the Novices' Foil or Gold and Silver Proficiency Awards (in view of this last, and for simplicity, Full Under-18 membership was to be abolished).

These recommendations were broadly accepted by the Finance and General Purposes Sub-Committee and by the AFA Committee, though the requirement of Ordinary membership for Proficiency Awards was dropped, in view of the competition now offered by the BAF's rival three star system of awards, and doubt was cast on the attraction of a membership booklet for adults. At the EGM in September 1981 the proposed rates were carried, but unexpectedly the booklet was deferred even for schoolchildren (to whom, if feasible, *The Sword* was to be issued instead). The Tournament Levy, on which opinion was divided, was also held over, because in equity, it needed to apply from before the printing of the notices of the earliest tournaments in the season, a date already passed. The EGM also adjusted the rates to give round sums inclusive of VAT as follows: Full Adult £11.50, Full Under-20 £5.75; Ordinary Adult £4, Ordinary Under-18 £2.30; Adult Club £11.50, School Club £5.75.

Early in 1981 Geoffrey Trinder died. He won the Sabre Championship in 1930, 1931, 1933 and 1934 and was in the first three on four other occasions (photo p. 49). He was runner-up to de Beaumont in the 1934 Miller-Hallett. He fenced in the World Championships for Britain in 1930, 1931, 1933, 1935 and 1947 (and at foil 1930 and 1935). He reached the semi-finals of the 1936 Olympics. He was remembered for his unfailing good humour and complete dedication to fencing. His analytical mind and remarkable memory enabled him to advise on any opponent he had previously tackled, though his own skill and unorthodox methods were not easily imitated. He represented his club, RAC, on the AFA Committee for many years. The death also occurred of Dr T. Miller, a much-liked, idiosyncratic character who used to come to Bristol FC in his later years still clad in spats and wing collar.

Fittingly, early in 1981, the Year of the Disabled, the Committee set up a working party on the problems of fencing for the handicapped. Its convenor was Les Veale, long active in this field, which had developed steadily in the post-war years. Sport in general was recognised increasingly as a vital means of improving the quality of life for the handicapped, and fencing was one of the first sports to be included in experiments for the war-disabled.

AFA and BAF members subsequently became involved as coaches and administrators. Brian and Bunty Western organised the national events. They were succeeded by Norman Heads. From 1973 Les Veale ran national and international events, and was chairman of the International Fencing Sub-Committee for Wheelchair Fencing (responsible for rule-writing) and acted as national coach for paraplegic fencers. Irene Addison, also of Sheffield, coached British teams at international events and was Secretary of the Association of Wheelchair Fencing, which organised coaching sessions and disseminated information.

By this time paraplegic fencers numbered perhaps a hundred in Britain, divided into two categories, depending on whether paralysis affected most of the body or only the legs to a greater or lesser extent. For both, fencing helped balanced co-ordination and physical and mental well-being. Their technique could be as highly developed as the able-bodied within the limits of their restrictions; indeed even very competent ordinary fencers were likely to lose in combat from a chair with a paraplegic.

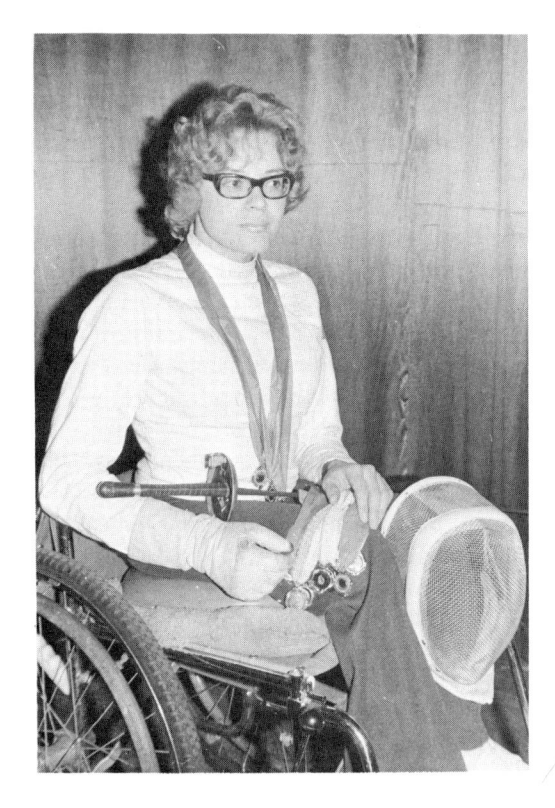

Caz Bryant, winner of five Bronze Medals at 1976 Paraplegic Olympics, including two for fencing.

Paraplegics tended to practise several sports, but fencing ranked high. An ordinary coach could teach them, but, as they were scattered, competition was difficult to arrange and many fencing clubs had problems of access. The main centre in Britain was Yorkshire. This was reflected, for instance, in the 1974 British team Gold Medal for sabre at the International Paraplegic Games, won by Cyril Thomas, Terry Willett and Ron Parkin, all from Yorkshire. Cyril Thomas also won the epee individual.

As time went on, fencing was taken up by people suffering from all kinds of disabilities including deafness, amputation, and mental handicap. Rules were adapted from those of the FIE under the aegis of the International Stoke Mandeville Games Committee (which controlled all wheelchair sport). A well-established structure of local, national, international and Olympic events developed, the latter contested by some fifteen nations. Britain was a regular medal winner in both team and individual events.

The working party of 1981 was slow to get to work because of the sheer volume of activity during the year, including demonstrations, try-it-out sessions and the designing and making of special equipment as well as a heavy programme of national and international events, such as the first European Wheelchair Championship, in Bremen. Bill Tomlinson and Les Veale put on a training session at the Coaches' Conference. There was also a proliferation of organisations to be contended with, including the British Sports Association for the Disabled, of which Mary Glen Haig became President at the beginning of the year.

An English version of the latest edition of the FIE competition rules appeared in 1981 after considerable gestation. Steve Higginson, again assisted by Peter Jacobs, once more bore the brunt of translation, while James Noel masterminded the production, this time in loose-leaf form in a ring binder, facilitating the insertion of the ever-frequent revisions. Among the changes in the new edition was a consolidation of the penalty provisions, which came into force on 1 January 1981. There were now three categories of offence. A 'minor' warning applied to the first category (mainly equipment faults) and was valid for the bout only, the penalty itself being a negative hit, i.e. one subtracted from the offender's score, the application of which, however, could not lose him the bout. A 'severe' warning, likewise valid for the bout, but relating to more serious offences, was also followed by negative hits, which *could* result in the loss of the fight. A 'special' warning, for the most serious offences, was valid for the whole pool and entailed the fencer's exclusion from the competition on the first or second repetition.

1981 also saw a change in the editorial team at *The Sword*. Richard Hill, the Salle Paul foilist, took over as editor. He was just down from Oxford, where he had read Philosophy, Psychology and Physiology, but not yet in a job. He was abetted by John Franck and Graham Watts, the latter on the production side.

If the start of the eighties presented presented difficulties for fencing, as for so many fields of activity in Britain, it also offered good auguries for the future. In addition to the revitalisation of the grassroots through the resurgence of the National Coaching Scheme, there was a series of outstanding international results. Robert Bruniges won the Duval foil tournament, Richard Cohen won the Touzard sabre event, and Steven Paul was the first British winner of the London Martini since 1962. The outlook was challenging, but hopeful.

# Sections and associated bodies

The number of adult affiliated clubs is given at the head of each entry (with school clubs in brackets).

*NORTH EAST 1966 17, 1970 26, 1975 24(11), 1980 16(4)*

Founded in 1949, the Section covers Cumbria, Northumberland, Tyne and Wear, Durham and Cleveland.

At the outset of the period the Tyneside Tournament, which had been started by Bunty and Brian Western in 1956, was organised by Northumbria Sword Club. Inter-Section matches were held with the N. (Yorks), the NW, and E. and W. Scotland and there was also a club league. Notable interest by young people was observed in 1966, and the Section had two representatives (F. Davison and D. Russell) in the British Under-20 team. Following a visit by a team from Bergen in 1967, a return match took place in Norway later in the year. 1968 saw the retirement from professional coaching of Mrs Bunty Western. She and her husband were emigrating after doing so much for fencing in the NE. 1969 saw a further boost to activity especially among the young, many of whom travelled to London events. The section was represented internationally by Jane Swanson and Celia Whitehurst. In 1970 Julia Raine and Jane Swanson represented Britain in the World Youth Championships. In 1971, for the first time in some years, a Section team entered the Winton Cup. In 1972 a Schools Association was founded and a Ladies' Aggregate Competition was introduced. In 1973 the Section took over the running of the Tyneside Tournament, under the leadership of John Charney, who was still in charge in 1981. In 1974 the de Beaumont Cup and GB v. Poland match were successfully staged on Teeside.

Prof. Pat Pearson was appointed Regional Coach in 1974, following a three months' pilot scheme by his brother Prof. Ken Pearson, which demonstrated the need for a full-time coach in addition to the only qualified professional, Prof. Mervyn Dinsdale. Initial progress was disappointing, but after two years the income for work done began to exceed expenses. The formation in 1977 of a Centre of Excellence in Newcastle boosted standards, producing, for instance, an Under-14 and Under-18 finalist and two girls in the Category list. In 1979 and 1980 Penny Whitehead won the Under-16 Championships; in 1981 she won the Under-18 and Chris Brockbanks was third in the sabre; she was in the British Under-20 team for two events abroad; and Newcastle won the Universities Athletic Union Championships in 1980. In 1981 the Junior League flourished, as did the Tyneside Tournament, which now gained generous sponsorship from Vaux Breweries.

*Northumbria Sword Club* was probably one of the first clubs in the area. It owed much to the Westerns and included many of the leading fencers, particularly ladies.

*Newcastle Fencing School* was founded by Prof. van Oeveren, a former member of the Dutch epee team, who had taught in Amsterdam and in 1965 spent a year as National Coach in Israel and came to Newcastle in 1967 at the invitation of Bunty Western. He was probably the first full-time coach in the NE. His rented salle, comprising two full-length pistes, was unusually elegant, with seventeeth-century prints on the walls. Among his pupils were Celia Whitehurst, Jane Swanson and Julia Raine. He returned to Holland in 1971.

OFFICERS
*Presidents:* 1979– J. Stansfield and J. Torday (joint).
*Chairman:* 1965–8 D. Redhead; 1968–73 Mrs B. Almond; 1973–4 J. Crouch; 1974–6 J. Torday; 1976–9 J. Stansfield; 1979–80 G. Whitehead.
*Secretary:* 1964–8 Miss D. Stobbs; 1968–70 J. Stansfield; 1970–1 R. Howard; 1971–3 J. Crouch; 1973–6 J. Stansfield; 1977–9 Miss D. Kerr; 1979–80 M. Leigh; 1980– Mrs E. Howard.

CHAMPIONS
*Ladies:* 1965 F. Grainger; 1966, 1967 and 1968 A. McGuire; 1969 C. Bishop; 1970 C. Whitehurst; 1971 J. Swanson; 1972 and 1973 C. Whitehurst; 1974 B. Pearson; 1975 D. Foster-Smith; 1976 S. Smith; 1977, 1978 J. Fraser-Smith; 1979 P. Whitehead; 1980 P. Nixon; 1981 B. Pearson.
*Foil:* 1965 R. Griffin; 1966 D. Russell; 1967 D. Redhead; 1968 D. Russell; 1969, 1970 and 1971 J. Crouch; 1972 J. Gibson; 1973 C. Garner; 1974 S. Hannah; 1975 R. Kirby; 1976 I. Gaff; 1977 R. Howard; 1978 A. Leece; 1979 E. Zakreszewski; 1980 B. Nesbitt; 1981 K. Hawkins.
*Epee:* 1965 D. Redhead; 1966 J. Stansfield; 1967 I. Campbell; 1968 J. Crouch; 1969 K. Gordon; 1970 J. Crouch; 1971 and 1972 I. Campbell; 1973 J. Stansfield; 1974 C. Dodds; 1975 B. Diaz; 1976 J. Clark; 1977 and 1978 C. Gardner; 1979 K. Pearman; 1980 W. Bialosky; 1981 C. Garner.
*Sabre:* 1965 R. Griffin; 1966, 1967 and 1968 B. Western; 1969 J. Zapasnik; 1970 C. Walker; 1971, 1972 and 1973 I. Campbell; 1974 and 1975 M. Tooley; 1976 C. Dodds; 1977 C. Hannah; 1978 R. Butler; 1979 C. Dodds; 1980 and 1981 C. Brockbanks.

## YORKSHIRE AND HUMBERSIDE 1966 26, 1970 32(9), 1975 39(13), 1980 36(11)

The Northern Section, hived off from the North and Midlands Section in 1949 (under the chairmanship of Dr Dorothy Knowles), originally extended from coast to coast. It immediately split with the formation of the Yorkshire County Union in 1950 and the crystallisation of the Lancashire and Cheshire County Unions the other side of the then quite formidable barrier of the Pennines. There were about a dozen affiliated clubs in each union. The Section won the first Winton Cup in 1950, eleven of the fifteen team members coming from Yorkshire. Yorkshire also founded the first ever coaching panel that year; four of its members were selected for the England team. Frank Luckman (of Huddersfield) was the Chairman and Laurie Wood (of Manchester) was the Secretary.

In 1955 the division from the NW took place, though the rather absurd title of 'Northern (Yorkshire)' had to be borne until 1979. The new Section immediately organised the first international match to be held in the provinces – Great Britain v. France at Harrogate, together with the first tournament at the same place (from 1965 transferred to Halifax). Since then fortunes have fluctuated. Growth was fairly static in the early sixties, though York Fencing Association, for instance, flourished greatly. Difficulty was found in responding to the many requests for coaching from small or isolated centres. Following visits by Charles de Beaumont and Prof. Anderson in 1964–5 the number of leaders and presidents increased, but epee and sabre waned.

In 1967–8 an Inter-Club League was inaugurated and one-day training sessions proved popular. The following season saw a notable upsurge in activity. There was a record entry in all championships (e.g. 120 in the Junior event). The Yorkshire Mixed Pairs attracted nineteen teams and was very successful, being doubled in the next session (foil/epee and foil/sabre). In 1969–70 an open competition was organised in Leeds. By 1971 there were more clubs but slightly fewer fencers.

Of the three dozen affiliated clubs in 1972 most were in the valleys of the Pennines from Leeds to Sheffield, with outlying centres in York and Hull; more peripheral clubs tended to have transient lives. As elsewhere, there was a dearth of professionals, but the improvement in communications produced by the M1 helped recruitment, matches, competitions, even administration. The support of the CCPR was also invaluable in arranging courses, backing a newsletter and giving clerical help.

In 1973 the staging of the Corble Cup and a GB v. Poland match were outstanding successes. Numbers of affiliated clubs continued to rise. In 1974–5 a marked improvement in the standard of school fencing was achieved through regular training sessions in York and Sheffield. The Kirklees Tournament in Huddersfield was launched in 1978. At the turn of the decade both epee and sabre were weak – for instance, in 1979 the Sabre Championship was cancelled for lack of entries. To help remedy the situation, the national sabre squad held a training weekend in York in 1981. However, at foil, the Under-14 and Under-16 events reached new peaks, both for numbers and quality, and in 1981 there were two national Under-14 finalists, including the winner, Peter Kay.

*York Fencing Association* was founded by Paddy Power c.1960 in the disused barn and outbuildings put at his disposal by the University, where he also taught. Rowing and cycling machines and weights were used to promote fitness and speed, and pupils took lessons on an inclined piste wearing weighted waistcoats. Among notable members were Prof. Power's son Tony, Susan Wrigglesworth, Lucienne Bleasdale and Caroline Hall. The club ended with Paddy Power's death in 1977, but Norman Millar, who had already taught a club at York College of Art and Technology, took over with his new *York FC*, established coincidentally at a recreation centre managed by Tony Power. Peter Kay was one of several enthusiastic young fencers he launched before he had to give up in 1980. The club was then reformed, with Mark Chetwood as Chairman, Francesca Lightowler and Greg Kay as Captains and Prof. Pat Pearson coaching once a fortnight.

OFFICERS
*Chairman:* 1964–7 P. Haigh; 1967–70 J. Stangroom; 1970–76 L. Veale; 1976–7 W. E. Rotchell; 1977–81 L. Veale; 1981– M. Chetwood.
*Secretary:* 1964–6 L. Veale; 1966–8 S. Beverley; 1968–71 Miss S. Tuck; 1971–2 Mrs S. Isherwood; 1973–4 Miss J. Whitaker; 1974–81 Mrs. B. Rotchell; 1981– Miss C. Hudson.

CHAMPIONS
*Ladies:* 1965 F. Dunn; 1966 Mrs M. Hawdon; 1967 Mrs S. Isherwood; 1968 and 1969 P. Phillips; 1970 S. Wrigglesworth; 1971 S. Isherwood; 1972, 1973 and 1974 S. Briggs; 1975 G. Bloor; 1976 S. Briggs; 1977 C. Beagrie; 1978 Mrs A. Parker; 1979 C. Wilson; 1980 B. Wallace; 1981 F. Lightowler.
*Foil:* 1965 and 1966 J. Stangroom; 1967 L. Wall; 1968, 1969 and 1970 A. Power; 1971 A. Daglish; 1972 M. Beevers; 1973 A. Daglish; 1974 D. Nicholls; 1975 S. Graham; 1976 A. Daglish; 1977 A. Tait; 1978 N. Norcliffe; 1979, 1980 and 1981 M. Chetwood.
*Epee:* 1965 and 1966 J. Stangroom; 1967 E. Bird; 1968 J. Ratcliffe; 1969 W. E. Rotchell; 1970 and 1971 L. Wall; 1972 A. Hazel; 1973 A. Daglish; 1974 D. Nicholls; 1975 and 1976 B. Matless; 1977 J. Tomlinson; 1978 B. Matless; 1979 W. Payne; 1980 M. Chetwood; 1981 A. Pinder.
*Sabre:* 1965 M. Eiserfey; 1966 L. Wall; 1967 S. Beverley; 1968 L. Wall; 1969 J. Stangroom; 1970 L. Wall; 1971 A. Daglish; 1972 M. Pearce; 1973 A.

Daglish; 1974 D. Nicholls; 1975 and 1976 A. Daglish; 1977, 1978 and 1980 P. Myers; 1981 F. Hardwick.

*NORTH WEST* 1967 20, 1971 24(9), 1976 41(22), 1980 24(8)

Fencing thrived in the mid sixties, with large entries at events in the Section. Team training and Presiding courses were organised in addition to the services of the Coaching Panels, of which by 1956 there were four, covering N. Lancashire and Westmorland, E. Lancashire, W. Lancashire and S. Lancashire and Cheshire.

The death in 1966 of J. D. Aylward, who had chaired the Section's inaugural meeting in 1955, was a loss not only to the Section but to the whole fencing world. He was a man of courtly charm and an outstanding writer on fencing. Both *L'Escrime Française* and *The Sword* were graced with many witty and learned articles from his pen. His books *The Small Sword in England*, *The English Master of Arms* and *The House of Angelo* became collectors' pieces. Born in London in 1871, he began fencing with a second-hand foil and mask and a shilling book of instructions at the age of fourteen. The next year he was introduced to German duelling in Bonn. At 22 he fenced in Paris and on return to London became a pupil of Tassart.

His job in banking put a stop to his fencing. *Fifty* years later, when he retired at over seventy and settled in Cheshire, he started fencing again under Prof. Zaaloff of Liverpool, who became a close friend. The club held a party in the

Dr D. Knowles and Prof Zaaloff

salle to celebrate the ninetieth birthday of this remarkable man who was still to take his last lesson! From 1885 he amassed many rare and beautiful swords and an unrivalled collection of fencing books. Such was the respect he earned that he became one of the few Associate Vice-Presidents of the AFA and was the first Honorary Member of the BAF.

Prof. Zaaloff died two years later in February 1968. He came to Britain in the Tsarist Diplomatic Service. When he was made redundant by the Revolution he continued on a professional basis the concert party he had previously run as an amateur venture. Then he turned to fencing as a career and was invited to move to Liverpool by Dr Dorothy Knowles of Liverpool University, who in 1936 also started the Liverpool Open Foil Tournament, which is thus one of the oldest tournaments in the country. Besides his own salle Prof. Zaaloff taught at both Liverpool and Manchester Universities. As a side line he ran a successful bridge school. Although he had given up music professionally, his good bass voice and balalaika playing were much appreciated at parties.

In 1968 the three northern Sections joined in holding the North of England Championships. The winners – Mary-Anne Watts-Tobin and A. Russell – were both from the NW. Dr. Czajkowski paid a short but useful visit in 1970. In 1971 the Section won the Winton Cup for the first time. The Polytechnic National Fencing Championships were inaugurated in Liverpool in 1972: Liverpool Polytechnic dominated all events in subsequent years. Liverpool University won the UAU Championships in 1973, their outstanding fencer being Steve Lavington, who was a member of the Rest of Britain team from 1974 to 1977, in addition to winning both the UAU and the BUSF epee championships in the 1976–7 season.

In 1968 Sue Green became the first NW Section fencer to gain a place in the British team; Philbin, Taylor and Glaister followed. Wedge was Under-20 Foil Champion in 1973 and 1974 and in the latter year was Junior Foil Champion and fenced in the Commonwealth Championships.

1975 was another golden year. Glaister won both the Under-20 and the Junior Foil and with Wedge, Lynne Taylor and Brenda Hewitt went to the World Youth Championships; and Hydra Under-20 Club won the Under-20 Foil Team Championship (retained in 1976).

The Section was also active in the organisation of fencing, especially through a standing committee of the Coaches Club, led by Dr Arthur Banks, with Mrs Beryl Wrigley as Secretary, which established the annual coaches Conference at Loughborough as a major event, following the first conference organised by Prof. Anderson. The proposal that the club should sponsor the 1968 World Youth Championships at Crystal Palace was made by Mrs Rachel Thompson, who (together with the Chairman, the Secretary, Elizabeth Hamm and Mrs Beryl Banks) put in a remarkable effort at fund-raising and deservedly won the Torch Trophy in 1969.

In 1976 the Section broke new ground by organising a successful Section Conference at Warrington, but the end of the decade saw falling numbers both in competitions and club membership.

*Ashton Tameside Fencing Club* was formed in 1951 from a fencing section started two years earlier at a local engineering works. Until he emigrated to Canada in 1957 the Hungarian-born Latsi Salamon set the standard of excellence. Les and Win Jones, husband and wife, were founder Secretary and Social Treasurer respectively. Les was elected Chairman in 1961 and President in 1966; Win became a Vice-President.

For the first ten years success was mainly confined to the Section. In 1957 Les Jones became the only fencer ever to win the foil, epee and sabre Championships in one season. He also fenced in the Quadrangular that year and became Captain of Lancashire and the NW. In 1955 de Beaumont had appointed him founder Secretary of the Section and in 1957 he became a member of the National Training Sub-Committee. On the management of a Manchester electrical engineering company, he had become Section Coach after gaining his Leaders' Certificate at all weapons under Prof. Crosnier. His fellow coaches at the club were Frank Lord, Tom Echells and John Siddall, who took sabre (and was a BAF member, like Les Jones). By 1976 Bernard Hallam looked after epee. The Club met three times a week, with a membership of between thirty and forty.

In the early sixties the rules were altered and fencers under sixteen recruited. One of the first of these was Marilyn Holmes, who started fencing at the age of eleven and by 1964 had won the Junior Schoolgirls Championship, an event won by the Club nine years running. Next year she added the Senior title, became Under-20 Champion, fenced in the Quadrangular and went to the World Youth Championships – all by the age of fifteen. Individual coaching several nights a week and special training sessions including fitness training at weekends made the Ashton ladies the most successful in the country. In 1968 Colette Bailey won the Junior Schoolgirls and Andrea Hill the Senior, Marilyn Holmes won the Universities title and Sue Green won the Under-20 and National Championships and began her long period in the British team by going to the 1968 Olympics. The club reached the semi-finals of the Ladies Team Championship in 1969 and in 1970 became the first provincial team ever to win the event, an achievement repeated in 1973. In 1972 it became the only club in Britain to have won every national ladies' event, and by 1975 it had captured the three British international events as well. Janice Deakin, Janet Yates, Brenda Hewitt, Jane Popland and Susan Blanchard were among the notable performers. In the early seventies Caroline Hall and Celia Whitehurst moved to the club.

In 1960 Ashton had been the first club to take members to continental Under-20 events by minibus. Annual visits to Duisburg and Gelsenkirchen ensued, and coaches gathered up to fifty fencers from all parts of Britain. In every year but two between 1964 and 1976 the club figured in the World Youth Championship team. Les Jones went three times as coach, having been invited by the LAFU in 1970 to take on the Under-20 Squad and being appointed in 1973 as joint Coach with Prof. Anderson to a combined senior and Under-20 squad. In 1976 his eldest daughter, Janet, reached the last sixteen at Poznan. His second daughter, Hilary, opened her career in 1975 when she won the NW Junior Championship at the age of sixteen.

In 1973 the open tournament organised by the club celebrated its 21st anniversary with a gala match between France, England, Scotland and Wales. At the end of the decade Louise Meeks, Gary Fletcher and Richard Sage were notable members of the club and Les Jones was nurturing yet another generation of young girls, mainly from the school where his daughter Janet taught.

*Chester FC* under Basil Thompson was the training ground of his own sons Mark and John and of Ann and Andrew Brannon. Mrs Rosemary Castle was especially important as coach to the club.

*Hydra Club* was founded by Geoff Hawksworth and Leon Hill in 1961. Both had started fencing at Ashton under Latsi Salamon. Geoff Hawksworth, a toolmaker by trade, had played professional football in the Cheshire League, and run for Sale Harriers and was a keen highjumper before he started fencing in 1952. Leon Hill was a senior science master at West Hill. Having learnt to coach through the National Training Scheme, they jointly purchased and with assistance from club members, converted a Nissen hut, previously used by a church football team, into a fencing salle. Later they had a new hall some 70 by 22 ft built, complete with changing rooms. Hydra was thus one of the very few clubs outside London with its own premises – and it was independent of any LEA. Foil and sabre were the predominant weapons. Membership varied between thirty and fifty.

The two founders continued to train together and together passed their AFA Advanced Coaching Award and in 1967 their BAF Diploma. Around them they built up a strong coaching group including Hazel Rogerson, Frank Hindle and Jim Philbin. They also both taught at a number of schools. Fencing pupils from West Hill included Paul Wedge, Steve Glaister, Greg and Glenn Jones and Graham Kay. Tom Etchells came to teach at the club in 1970, when he turned professional.

Geoff Hawksworth's wife Mary was also a notable fencer: three times a member of the England Quadrangular team, a member and captain of the NW Section team which won the Winton Cup in 1971, nine times a member of the Rest of Britain team and then manager. She was also an AFA coach, and Chairman of the Section for six years. Janet Varley, Eric Bradbury, Alan and Lynne Taylor (not related), Jane Law and Pauline Tovey were other key members.

# West Midlands

OFFICERS

*Presidents:* 1955-80 Viscount Leverhulme; 1980- Dr A. Banks, Prof. L. Hill and Prof. G. Hawksworth.
*Chairman:* 1965-6 J. Lunt; 1966-72 Mrs M. Hawksworth; 1972-5 B. Hallam; 1975-6 P. Bruce; 1976-80 M. Tilling; 1980-81 I. Hall; 1981- R. Merry.
*Secretary:* 1965-70 W. Thompson; 1970-3 Miss M. Kibbly; 1973-5 F. Hindle; 1975-6 Miss I. Steen; 1976-7 J. Littlehales; 1977- R. Courtenay.

CHAMPIONS

*Ladies:* 1965 M. Hawksworth; 1966 J. Varley; 1967 M. Holmes; 1968 S. Green; 1969 J. Yates; 1970, 1971, 1972, 1973, 1974 and 1975 S. Green; 1976 J. Law; 1977 L. Taylor; 1978 B. Hewitt; 1979 J. Law; 1980 J. Roberts; 1981 L. Meeks.
*Foil:* 1965 L. Hill; 1966 B. Hallam; 1967 F. Hindle; 1968 E. Goodall; 1969 and 1970 F. Hindle; 1971 A. Hughes; 1972 A. Taylor; 1973, 1974 and 1975 J. Philbin; 1976 and 1977 G. Jones; 1978 D. Carlisle; 1979 S. Glaister; 1980 A. Banks; 1981 R. Sage.
*Epee:* 1965 A. Banks; 1966 and 1967 P. Lees; 1968 A. Banks; 1970 A. Taylor; 1971 R. Dennis; 1972 D. Partridge; 1973 S. Lavington; 1974 R. Dennis; 1975 S. Lavington; 1976 B. Green; 1977 S. Lavington; 1978 not held; 1979 A. Brannon; 1980 D. Carlisle; 1981 J. Whitworth.
*Sabre:* 1965 B. Hallam; 1966 R. Oldcorn; 1967 T. Etchells; 1968 B. Hallam; 1970 E. Bradbury; 1971 A. Taylor; 1972 B. Hallam; 1973 and 1974 J. Philbin; 1975 G. Kay; 1976 J. Philbin; 1977 G. Kay; 1978 J. Philbin; 1979 T. Briscoe; 1980 and 1981 G. Fletcher.

*WEST MIDLANDS 1965 35, 1970 38, 1975 34(10), 1980 24(11)*

This is the oldest of all the Sections, having been founded in 1937 as the North and Midlands Section, with Col Cole (photo p. 27) as Hon. Secretary. It shrank to its present size in 1949.

In 1964-5 Stratford-on-Avon FC visited Germany and Holland and Portland FC visited Luxembourg. In 1965-6 the Section pioneered very successful leaders' courses for teachers in Warwickshire and other areas. A schoolboy team competition was also inaugurated and a schoolgirls' match against Londoners took place at Rugby. There was marked increase in young competition entries. A match against Bonn University was held and Portland FC toured Germany. Clive Purchase won all three Section Championships for the third year running.

A county union was formed in Worcestershire in 1969. In 1972 growth in the number of clubs put new life into the Section. Courses by Prof. K. Pearson and Jan Mottel of Poland in 1973 were very successful. That year Gerry Harding was ladies Champion for the ninth successive year. The massive entry which Leamington Tournament had continued to attract over the years somewhat diminished in 1974, and in 1975 it was transferred to Birmingham University. Tom Norcross was appointed National Coach for the Midlands Region in 1975 and in 1978 launched a Centre of Excellence in Birmingham which was already producing national results from fencers such as Mark Hall, Steve Henshall, Chris Ward and Margaret Browning before he left in 1978 to become National Coach in Hong Kong. Peter Northam, Section Coach, took over, but in 1980 the Regional Sports Council terminated the scheme.

It was also in Birmingham that the education authority, having resisted fencing for twenty years, introduced it to three schools, using the mini-epee method developed by Bill Hammond. At the end of the period the Area Coaching Scheme was doing very well under Prof. Northam, who also started a full Under-20 training squad.

*Birmingham Fencing Club* is one of the oldest in the country, having its origins in the Birmingham Athletic Club, which was founded in 1866. In the early days, the military defensive section of the athletic club indulged in a rather robust type of fencing, using single-stick, quarterstaff and bayonet as well as foil. It was only in 1927 that the fencing section formed a separate club of its own as the Birmingham Fencing Club, its first President being Col. R. B. Campbell. Club members, particularly Col. R. E. Cole, played an important part in the development of fencing in the country as a whole as well as in the Midlands. Dennis Pearce won the Foil Championship in 1927 and in 1928 V. Clayton-Morris won the first Miller-Hallett Tournament. Sir Oswald Mosley was a member of the club when he was MP for Smethwick. Those who fenced in Quadrangular and Rest of Britain events included Muriel Chesney, P. Fletcher, D. Parham, G. Ayliffe, P. Beard, C. Purchase, C. Kovanda, R. Evans and N. Milligan. Dennis Pearce was a member of the 1928 and 1936 Olympic teams. Clive Purchase was in the 1966 British team and Geoffrey Grimmett in those of 1975–7.

OFFICERS

*Chairman:* (till 1968 President): 1954–67 B. Sapcote; 1967–9 D. Parham; 1969–73 L. Johnson; 1973–5 J. Thorn; 1975–80 N. Watkins; 1980 Dr J. Purkiss.

*Secretary:* 1964–7 Mrs C. Parham; 1967–9 D. la Touche; 1969–70 Miss C. Faux; 1970–2 Miss W. Pass; 1972–5 Mrs E. Thorn; 1975–6 Miss Y. Southern; 1976–80 Mrs M. Butler; 1980– Miss D. Walker.

CHAMPIONS

Ladies: 1965, 1966, 1967, 1968, 1969, 1970, 1971, 1972 and 1973 Mrs G. Harding; 1974 M. Browning; 1975 G. Harding; 1976 and 1977 E. Thorn; 1978 M. Browning; 1979 J. Whitehouse; 1980 J. Morris; 1981 M. Browning.
*Foil:* 1965 and 1966 C. Purchase; 1967 A. Morrish; 1968 C. Purchase; 1969

G. Grimmett; 1970 and 1971 N. Watkins; 1972 and 1973 N. Milligan; 1974 D. Tilles; 1975 N. Watkins; 1976 and 1977 C. Giles; 1978 P. Carson; 1979 M. Allen; 1980 and 1981 S. Higginson.
*Epee:* 1965 and 1966 C. Purchase; 1967 D. Parham; 1968 B. Yates; 1969 A. Morrish; 1970 L. Johnson; 1971 R. Evans; 1972 M. Lock; 1973 R. Evans; 1974 B. Henshall; 1975 R. Sanders; 1976, 1977, 1978, 1979 and 1980 B. Henshall; 1981 S. Higginson.
*Sabre:* 1965, 1966, 1967 and 1968 C. Purchase; 1969 C. Kovanda; 1970 C. Purchase; 1971 G. Kovanda; 1972 and 1973 N. Milligan; 1974 and 1975 C. Kovanda; 1976 and 1977 M. Hall; 1978 N. Milligan; 1979, 1980 and 1981 C. Morris.

*EAST MIDLANDS* 1965 *33*, 1971 *33(13)*, 1975 *67(29)*, 1980 *47(17)*

The Section was created in 1949, with County Unions in Leicestershire and Nottinghamshire. The open tournaments founded in the two counties, in 1956 and 1959 respectively, continued to flourish throughout our period. The 1966–7 season saw a revival of interest in Lincolnshire and among the young. An event for senior schoolgirls was started in 1968. The Section twice beat a strong RAF team in 1968–9. By 1971 there were many events at County Union level. Arthur Gundle, who had represented the Section at epee for many years, died that season. Largely through the efforts of Colin Tyson and David Green, in January 1975 Tom Norcross started to work in the Section as Regional National Coach, with immediate success. Among his undertakings was the creation of an Under-20 scheme and in 1978 of a Centre of Excellence, with Prof. Cassapi, who took over when he left later that year. In 1977 Gordon Wiles won his sixteenth Section Championship and in 1978 the Section won the Winton Cup for the eighth time, equalling the SW's record. In 1980 Julian Tyson organised a junior training squad.

*Leicester YMCA (Salle Cassapi)* had its origins in a club which was founded by L. G. Cotton in 1949 as a branch of a youth club which he ran. In 1952 when the local Education Authority demanded a higher fee for the hall of St Matthew's Church where they met, Colin Tyson and Len Cotton arranged the club's incorporation in Leicester YMCA.

The club set great store on high technical standards: Colin and his wife Jackie and Ken Dilkes became qualified coaches early on and then trained others, so that at one time the club boasted nine coaches. Fencing in those days continued from 8 to 11 p.m. Whenever possible professional teaching was also obtained. Prof. Imregi taught soon after his arrival in Britain, as did Tom Norcross in the later seventies. In 1979 Prof. Cassapi took over and the club adopted his name.

For a decade from the mid sixties the club held all Leicestershire and East Midlands team and individual trophies. It provided, in Jackie Tyson, Gordon

Wiles and others, the nucleus of the East Midlands team. Alan Painter became Services Champion and Andy Eames Commonwealth foil Champion. John Cotton and Paul Tyson carried the traditions of the founders into the second generation.

The development of the club was closely linked with the Leicester Tournament, first organised by the Tysons and Ken Dilkes, backed by Charles de Beaumont. It gradually grew to be one of the foremost provincial events in the calendar, attracting ever growing entries. Eric Mount Haes arranged the use of the Polytechnic gymnasium for the tournament, being then a Ministry of Education Inspector as well as a member of the club. It was he too who persuaded Colin Tyson as Section Coach to put on the first ever school teachers' course. For his part, Colin Tyson, with Bill Courtney-Lewis and Charles de Beaumont, launched the Rest of Britain match.

OFFICERS
*President:* 1964–7 C. Courtney-Lewis; 1976–72 M. Amberg; 1972– C. Tyson.
*Chairman:* 1961–72 C. Tyson; 1972–6 G. Wiles; 1976–81 G. Rudge; 1981– G. H. Smith.
*Secretary:* 1964–78 W. Mann; 1978– Mrs J. Allton.

CHAMPIONS
*Ladies:* 1965 and 1966 Mrs P. Courtney-Lewis; 1967 Mrs J. Tyson; 1968 E. Hart; 1969 Mrs A. Palker; 1970 Mrs G. Smith; 1971 Mrs K. Smith; 1972 M. Browning; 1973 Mrs J. Harris; 1974 Mrs S. Merrill; 1975 A. Lambert; 1976 Mrs J. Lambert; 1977 S. Glover; 1979 D. Dove; 1980 D. Hall; 1981 A. Randle.
*Foil:* 1965 A. Painter; 1966 R. Turner; 1967, 1968, 1969 and 1970 G. Wiles; 1971 A. Eames; 1972 A. Painter; 1973 A. Eames; 1974 R. Berry; 1975, 1976 and 1977 G. Wiles; 1979 R. Sedols; 1980 J. Tyson; 1981 D. Eames.
*Epee:* 1965 R. Greenfield; 1966 A. Gundle; 1967 G. Wiles; 1968 D. Partridge; 1969 G. Wiles; 1972 M. Allton; 1973 G. H. Smith; 1974 D. Brooks; 1975 M. Allton; 1976 D. Brooks; 1977 P. Brown; 1979 M. Cawton; 1980 P. Brown.
*Sabre:* 1965 W. Manners; 1966 J. Sanderson; 1967 A. Painter; 1968, 1969, 1970, 1971, 1972 and 1973 G. Wiles; 1974 A. Painter; 1975 G. Wiles; 1976 R. Berry; 1977 G. Wiles; 1979 and 1980 R. Berry; 1981 S. Walker.

*EASTERN* 1965 46, 1971 50(23), 1975

Founded in 1951, by 1964 the Section was well established. County Unions had been functioning for several years in Essex and Hertfordshire. They were formed in Bedfordshire in 1964–5 and in Suffolk and Cambridgeshire two years later. A committee reported on methods of improving facilities and boosting the sport in 1968, but shortage of money and people prevented the adoption of many of the recommendations.

The Section varies greatly in character, from rural Norfolk to London boroughs on the edge of Essex. Transport across the Section is difficult; wherever the Section championships are held some competitors will have travelled for several hours. Transport into London is generally easier than across the Section. Because of this, and because many of the clubs in the Section are within easy reach of London, most of the best fencers bred in the Section migrate to the metropolis. Examples in the seventies were Elizabeth Wood and Linda Martin. Towards the end of the decade County Championships lapsed in the East Anglian counties and even faltered in Bedfordshire, Cambridgeshire and Hertfordshire; but several open competitions were organised by clubs such as Redbridge, Ilford, Wickford and the Norfolk Open. The Cyrano competition flourished for many years. Several schools also organised open competitions for different age groups, and entries for Section junior events were good, contrasting with those of senior events. Among the leading clubs was *Chase*, founded in 1967 by a group headed by John MacGowan and Ken Foreman, who taught there till he injured his back, shortly before Kim Cecil, Louise Dale, Gillian Stanley and Fiona Wilson won the Under-20 Team Championship for the club. Prof. Boston was master from 1979.

OFFICERS
*President:* 1968–79 J. Fitzmaurice.
*Chairman:* 1957–68 J. Fitzmaurice; 1968–71 R. Parsons; 1971–4 R. Dye; 1974–5 R. Rand; 1975–6 I. Barrow; 1976–7 T. Wood; 1977–9 J. Dennett; 1979– T. George.
*Secretary:* 1965–6 E. Dains; 1966–9 D. Coverdale; 1969–74 D. Ainley; 1974–5 I. Barrow; 1975–6 C. G. Wrzesien; 1976–7 Dr G. Thorne; 1978–9 L. Scott; 1979– R. Bales.

CHAMPIONS
*Ladies:* 1965 Mrs E. Davies; 1967 Mrs M. Annavedder; 1968 S. Olley; 1970 Dr G. Thorne; 1971 E. Joyce; 1972 D. Joyce; 1973 Mrs A. Parker; 1974 L. Martin; 1974 C. Arup; 1975, 1976 and 1977 Mrs C. Hamilton; 1978 K. Cecil; 1979 Mrs A. McKechnie; 1980 Mrs D. Powell.
*Foil:* 1965 A. Gilbert; 1967 R. Jones; 1968 J. Meares; 1969 R. Cohen; 1970 I. Keddie; 1971 and 1972 J. Magill; 1973 J. MacGowan; 1974 R. Dye; 1975 R. Turner; 1976 and 1977 R. Rand; 1978 M. Harris; 1979, 1980 and 1981 D. Dale.
*Epee:* 1965 and 1967 J. Fairhall; 1968 M. Walker; 1970 W. Calvert; 1971 M. West; 1972 Kasponis; 1973 and 1974 I. Hodges; 1975 M. West; 1976 and

1977 I. Storey; 1978 P. Brittain; 1979 I. Hodges; 1980 D. Lamothe; 1981 A. Downing.
*Sabre:* 1965 D. Royall; 1967 and 1968 J. Hopson; 1970 S. Parkhurst; 1971 J. Zarno; 1972, 1973, 1974 and 1975 D. Riddle; 1976 and 1977 D. Nash; 1978 N. Carr; 1979 B. Bertrand; 1980 D. Ip; 1981 T. Yassir.

*LONDON* 1965 70, 1970 91(41), 1975 67(39), 1979 32(25)

London is so bound up with fencing at the national level and contains so many major clubs that little need be said about it as a Section. In late 1964, a founder member of the Section Committee in 1953, Keith Paddle, died. When London became the first Section to hold junior and senior schoolboys' championships — in 1954 — he was the mainstay of the organisation and remained so for nine seasons, until overtaken by illness, unsurpassed for reliability in all he undertook. In 1966 there died Prof. Ernest Froeschlen, a pupil of Felix Gravé. It was said that he never raised his voice or lost his temper. In 1980 a London League was re-started by John Larner and Graham Watts and the Section was admitted to the Winton Cup, in which it headed the second division.

OFFICERS
*President:* 1966– R. Winton.
*Chairman:* 1953–72 R. Winton; 1972–4 L. Linger; 1974–9 S. Fox; 1979–80 B. P. Wheelhouse; 1980– N. Norcliffe.
*Secretary:* 1957–69 N. Waddleton; 1969–75 V. Cawthorne; 1975–6 J. Macleod; 1976–8 Mrs C. Mealing; 1979–80 N. Norcliffe; 1981– Mrs J. Norcliffe.

*Salle Behmber.* It was a great sadness to all who knew him when Prof. Reggie Behmber died in 1969 at the age of 63. He started his fencing in the late twenties as a Provost under the great Felix Gravé, whose salle he continued, with his fellow pupil Madame Perigal, a sparkling personality who also gave lessons in her home and at various girls' public schools and who died in 1968. He opened his own Salle at St Augustine's Church Hall, Queen's Gate, around 1951, with his lifelong friend and colleague Prof. Suzanne Ridley. Later it moved to Our Lady of Victories School, Clareville Street (also in S. Kensington), as part of an Adult Institute.

His whole life was dedicated to fencing; at the same time he was remarkably free from professional jealousy or ambition. At his Salle and at the Poly – his other principal club – he was the classic master of many outstanding fencers – Theresa Offredy, Osmund Reynolds, Claudia Gentili, Angus McKenzie, Shirley Parker and Julia Barkley among them – but he gave equal encouragement to the less brilliant. A purist in all he did, he worked for precision: if a pupil's point was flat or passé he would chuckle and scratch the spot on his

*My fencing masters. M. Ellis* ✓

Prof. Behmber                Prof. Harmer-Brown (see p. 151)

plastron; if the pupil missed altogether he would turn and peer in the direction the point had gone. Always coaxing the best from pupils and with never an unkind word, he continually earned their loyalty and affection. The absence of showers, the smallness of the gym and the furnishing built for 5-year-olds counted for nothing against these personal qualities.

He also trained many well known masters, including Profs Nicklen, Boston, Sullivan, Pat Pearson and Goodall. He was particularly successful with school fencers, at the Lycée and at Dulwich and St Paul's. The last two between them took twenty of the senior Public Schools titles between 1949 and 1968, and St Paul's won the overall trophy seven times between 1949 and 1958.

Not least important, he contributed to the re-foundation of the British Academy of Fencing in 1949, was its guiding light and from 1969 its President. He valiantly concealed a long illness and continued to work as long as he was physically able. His last assistant, David Austin, joined Prof. Ridley in carrying on the club when he died. Among their notable pupils were Jackie Erwteman, Lindy Prys-Roberts and Wendy Grant.

*Salle Boston.* Steve Boston was born in London in 1920. In his youth he had successes at cross-country running (N. Counties 3-mile champion), weight-lifting and cycling; but his chief love was boxing. Known as Speedy Boston for his footwork, he won 240 out of 266 contests between 1932 and 1956. He started fencing in the army. His best result was the semi-final of the Corble in 1954. After the war he taught fencing as well as boxing in boys' clubs. For fourteen years he was an insurance salesman, which fitted in well with sport, but among other varied occupations he was one half of a comedy act – 'The Boston Brothers – the Party without the Tea' – which appeared on television and in two films.

He founded Leyton Fencing Club in 1946 and Ilford FC in 1950. He served his apprenticeship as a master under Prof. Behmber, whom he also assisted at Poly and St Paul's School (where he started in 1956). In 1957 he took on Brentwood. In partnership with Jeff Featherstone, master-in-charge, he very rapidly made it dominant among schools and boys such as Green, Acfield, Russell, Underwood and Floyer formed the nucleus of his Salle when it opened in 1961, together with Alyth Hughes, whose national possibilities were ended by marriage. In 1961 Jean Read (trained jointly with Prof. Behmber) was third at Leamington, and fifth in the Desprez; but she emigrated next year. There followed successes, both great and small, from such as John Fairhall, Jean Fitch, Angela Herbert and Julia Bullmore and from the Pauline sabreurs Richard Ford, Brian Fisher, Barsby and Brearley. In the mid-sixties D. C. Martin, E. Gray and J. Payne transferred to the club. The breakthrough came with the winning of the Epee Championship by Bourne in 1966 and of the Epee Team Championship in 1967. Other Brentwood recruits in the sixties were Fairburn, Mark West and Mather.

Steve Boston also taught at St Dunstan's (whence came Lennox, Johnson and the younger Price), at Forest (whence came Waldman and Lambourn) and at Cambridge University from 1968 (whence arrived Loveland, Cohen, Deighton, Magill, Etherton and Ann Brannon). Other notable members were Davenport, Burr, Wishart, Fox, Tyson, Stanbury, Zarno, Osbaldeston, Sue Youngs, Hazel Twomey and Sue Olley. Noel, Rouxel, Scotland (of Jamaica), Wasley (of Australia) and Dr Knowles were members for a while at the end of the sixties. Later arrivals from Brentwood included Steventon, Slade, the Li brothers and Dale. From elsewhere in the seventies came Bruniges, Gosbee, Eames, Leopold, Zitcer, Carr, Jonathan Lewis, Michael Price the elder, Mark Hall, Hilary Cawthorne, Clare Montgomery, Sue Hoad and Kim Cecil. The club won the Epee Team Championship eight times between 1967 and 1981, the sabre likewise, the men's foil three times, but never the ladies' (though four times runners-up).

Assistants during these years included Roy Goodall, Zolt Vadaszffy (from 1964 till he moved to Poly in 1971), John Fairhall and Ray Emery, who was already a trained master when he arrived in 1967 as an ex-army PTI. He became national epee coach in 1977 and by the end of the seventies was taking the top epeeists at the club, while Steve Boston concentrated on sabreurs.

*Brownhill Club* was formed in 1972 by Prof. Fairhall as the evening institute offshoot of the flourishing fencing sessions of Catford comprehensive school, which he had been coaching since 1968. John Fairhall was born in 1930 and was in banking from the age of seventeen until he gained his Diploma and became a full-time master in 1968. He started fencing in the RNVR, but his real training was in Lloyds Bank FC, which met in the premises of the LFC, where he was taught the flowing French style by Len Mowlam and from 1957 a more staccato style by Prof. Moldovanyi. He also had lessons from Prof. Delzi and was a member of Wanstead FC.

He joined Steve Boston's Ilford FC in 1958 and soon began coaching, while achieving considerable success as an epeeist; subsequently he took over the club, where Valerie Windram was amongst his pupils. In 1966 he began regular teaching at Salle Boston and Park Lane FC. He started Streatham FC (which produced Chris White) in 1967 and also taught from 1976–81 at Grosvenor and at St Paul's. For two seasons he took the epee side of the under-20 squad.

Catford and Brownhill pupils included Bruniges, Llewellyn, Emberson, Knell, Sigrist, Lovejoy, Cooper, Ingleson, Tourmentin, Shaban, Ally Smith, Chris Brown, John Ford and his own son David. In the later seventies, when Brownhill moved to the Crofton Leisure Centre, the Gobey sisters were members. In the earlier years the Catford Parents' Association had given much support and help, especially for trips abroad. Later, in the face of pressures on maintained schools, and perhaps because the idea of excellence was not so highly prized, fencing became a low priority and in 1981 Prof. Fairhall left for more favourable pastures.

*Salle Ganchev*, noteworthy for ploughing a new furrow at the end of our period, was started by the Bulgarian George Ganchev as an Adult Institute class in Fulham, exclusively for sabreurs, when he left the LFC in 1973. He emigrated to America the same year on a film scholarship, though he kept in touch and returned for a short period each year till 1979. Paul Romang, an assistant at the outset, took over. Born in 1951, he had trained as a drama teacher and had taught economics, but he now settled down as a fencing master, succeeding Prof. Ganchev at Kenwall Manor School in the SE outskirts of London, whence were to come West, Branscombe, Booton and Wade. From 1976 he also taught at City of London (which produced Klenerman and Bovill), at Haileybury (whence Yassir) and at King's College School, Wimbledon. Bryant and Moscardini were amongst those recruited from elsewhere.

Ganchev and Romang started with the concept of taking talented eleven-year-olds and training them in a rigid, disciplined, almost E. European way. A group of about a dozen new members was selected each year, discussions were held with parents on the financial implications of fencing abroad three or four times a season from the outset and all the boys were offered three lessons a week, required to attend at least twice a week and expected to fence almost every weekend at the height of the season. The commitment demanded was matched by that of Paul Romang, who continuously sustained each pupil's progress. Fully supporting the club's approach was Prof. Mendelenyi, who became principal master in 1979 (as he did likewise at City of London), providing technical tuition of the highest standard from which Romang himself also benefited, his main training up to that point having been watching and questioning coaches on self-financed visits to Hungary and Bulgaria.

The club began to achieve results in 1977; by 1981 it furnished the entire Under-20 team, the top five Under-20 finalists, both Public School Champions and the winners of four provincial tournaments; and still greater achievements were clearly just around the corner.

*Salle Goodall* was founded in 1969 as a Youth Club in Clerkenwell and was then called Fleet FC. Born in 1928, Roy Goodall started fencing in Peterborough in 1944, intensified in the Army, began coaching back in Peterborough and won the E. Midlands foil. He moved to London in 1953 solely to take lessons from Prof. Bertrand, and fenced foil for LFC 'A', but then left fencing to be Assistant Manager of Queen's Ice Club for five years. In 1963 he began to train and coach at Salle Boston, where he met his wife and colleague Angela, and founded Edmonton Club, where he taught John Hall and was to launch his foremost pupil, Pierre Harper, on his career. By 1968 he was teaching at Combined Circles in Surrey, where Wendy Ager started. At Salle Goodall, which moved to Islington in 1978, John Titchmarsh, Alan Morgan, Neil Calder, Graham Watts, Tim Smith, Adrian Collins, Diane and Susan Freeman and Paul and Mark Chetwood were amongst pupils. Prof. Angela Goodall also taught at Morley College, James Allen's and City of London Girls' School. Roy taught at Carshalton HS (whence came Seaman) and at Dulwich (whence came Rhodes). He also became a stage fight arranger and teacher.

*Grosvenor* began, and for long remained, a company club, founded within the famous civil engineers John Mowlem & Co. by its director Sir George Burt in 1922 after an enthusiastic group of employees had watched him win the Epee Championship at Lincoln's Inn Fields. According to Bert Pelling, one of its outstanding members, it was very much a working men's club. Only a few outsiders were allowed, as the club was limited to about thirty members. It says something for its reputation that for much of its history there was a waiting list.

It started in the company offices in Millbank. Later it met in the top of an air raid shelter and then in the head office off Chelsea Bridge Road. The first master was Prof. Fred McPherson, then Prof. Morel, who remained till he died after the war. There followed a succession of distinguished professors, including Bertrand, Cottard, Erdelyi, Chipola, Imregi, Pat Pearson, Boston and Fairhall.

The club met only once a week and restricted itself to epee. (Sir George believed this would be the easiest for the first members to learn.) Many members also fenced at other clubs. After the war a ladies' section was started but soon failed – they all got married! A continuing strand in the club's history was formed by the Pellings, father and son. Bert fenced in the British team over a formidable span, from the Olympic Games of 1928 to those of 1948. John's record was equally impressive; he was a member of the team every year from 1957 to 1967, except when no epee team was sent, and participated in the Silver Medal places won in 1960 and 1965, as well as being National Champion in 1961 and 1965 and individual Silver Medallist in the 1962 Commonwealth Games. Sadly, his job took him away from London and from fencing in 1972. Pre-war members included B. Childs, J. James, C. and J. Ellis and F. Kent; while among post-war members, who carried it to further victories in the Team Championship (won for the thirteenth time in 1963) were E. Knott, J. Glasswell, P. Jacobs, D. Giles, D. Pomeroy and W. Romp.

In 1968, while maintaining links with Mowlem, the club moved to modern accommodation at Hurlington School as part of an Adult Institute. In 1972 its Golden Jubilee was celebrated by a splendid party, with gala match, in Belgrave Square. Notable members in the later seventies included David Fairhall, Howard West and David Brooks.

*The London Fencing Club* was founded in 1848. Its earlier history is outlined in the first volume of *Modern British Fencing*. The AFA moved its office to the club premises in Cleveland Row in 1936. In 1946 Salle Bertrand and the LFC agreed to share Cleveland Row, with Prof. Leon (Punch) Bertrand and Prof. Delzi as masters to both clubs. The same year women were admitted for the first time. Notable members before and after the war included Elizabeth Carnegy Arbuthnott, Dorothy Breese, Mrs Gytte Minton, Emrys Lloyd, de Beaumont, A. R. Smith, Oscar Trinder, Lord Leveson, Turquet and Tredgold. In 1948 the two clubs, together with the AFA, moved to 1a Tenderden Street, off Hanover Square, where all AFA national events soon came to be held (having previously been staged at the Duke of York's Headquarters, the Poly and elsewhere). The clubs merged in 1953. Gillian Sheen, Mary Glen Haig, Joyce Pearce, Dorothy Knowles, Mildred Durne, Feré Rentoul, Beatley, Pienne, Porebski and the Amberg brothers were prominent members in the fifties.

In 1957 Prof. Bela Imregi joined Prof. Bertrand. Born in 1908 in N. Hungary, he did two years' national service in the army and then trained at the Institute of Sport and Gymnastics. From 1935 to 1940 he taught at the Military Grammar School, but only became a full-time fencing master in 1940 (foil and epee being his preferred weapons). From 1941–4 he was on the staff of the Ludovic Academy, the equivalent of Sandhurst. After the war, he taught at Csepel, the leading Budapest club. Gerevich and Berseli were among his pupils. He also coached the national ladies team, including the famous Eleks. From 1948 he taught at the military Honved Club and from 1951 at the Vasas Club. Exile followed his service on the 1956 revolutionary committee of the fencing association. He soon taught at Westminster School and Oxford University. Although he regarded himself primarily as an epee master and numbered such top-flight epeeists at Halsted and Higginson, Michael Alexander and Netburn for periods among his pupils, he also gathered round him a galaxy of sabreurs such as Straus, Oldcorn, Rayden, Leckie and Graham Wilson.

After the move to W. Kensington there was a severe decline in membership. In 1967 Prof. Imregi transferred to Poly. Some of his pupils migrated before his departure, some after, the latter meanwhile being taught by the tall, handsome George Ganchev, a Bulgarian pop star and man of many talents, who taught at the club from January 1968 to June 1973. He introduced such fencers as Hutt, Wasilewski, Lankshear and Edroy Poole, all of whom came from the far from affluent context of Christopher Wren School, Shepherd's Bush. John Simpson, an Australian and 1959 winner of the Miller-Hallett, who trained as a professional in Paris, taught from January 1973 till mid-1977: Sally Littlejohns was among his pupils. Barry More, pupil of Prof. Simmonds and former assistant of Prof. Harmer-Brown, taught from 1974 to 1977. Punch Bertrand finally retired, aged over eighty, early in 1977. The epeeist Brian Hill was his last notable pupil.

Later in 1977 the club merged with Thames Club. LFC provided the premises and many members. Thames provided Prof. Harmer-Brown, Prof. Pitman and Frank Charnock as masters and most of those who had belonged to it in Pimlico. It proved a happy and successful union, attracting a large membership. Recruits at the turn of the decade included Olivia Pontefract, Elizabeth Whitfield, Gillian Wood, Linda Strachan, Sandy Maggs, Sue Rochard, Ann Fraser-Smith, Pat Casey (and her husband Peter, who became Chairman), Lesley Calver (who married fellow-member Don Macrae), Howard West, Melville, Moscardini, Troiano, Cocker, Carpenter, Hudson, Shepherd, Hiam, Woodall, Greenhalgh, Fancourt and Lavington. Up to 1977, LFC had won the Team Championship at men's foil twice, at ladies' foil fourteen times, at epee nine times and at sabre fourteen times – a total of 39, only rivalled by Salle Paul's 36.

*Salle Paul* was formed by Prof. Leon Paul, a Frenchman, in 1931, in the premises in Monmouth Street where he also made and sold fencing (and angling) equipment. In early years there were only some dozen active members, but they had about the same number of matches every season. The most successful members before the war were Cooke, Seruya, Parfitt and 'Papa' Paul's teenage son, René. Bombed out in 1941, the club continued through the war as guests elsewhere. In 1946 it joined an Adult Institute in Buckingham Gate in school buildings. Its strength by 1952 is shown by the team in its 21st celebration match against a Bolivian team: René and Raymond Paul and Harry Cooke (foil); Parfitt, Jay and Greenhalgh (epee), and Wendon, Cooperman and Pringle (sabre).

Suzanne Fleming was the driving force behind the ladies' side of the club, known as 'Pauleans'. Eve Berry, Margaret Stafford and Judith Bain all fenced for Britain; Eileen Jones, Susan Fisher, Therese Cousins and Jeanne McCombie (née Paul) were other leading members.

In the sixties René's sons Graham and Barry rose to prominence, together with Kirby, Fisher, Single, Pearman, Partridge, Ortt, Craig, Scott and Murch. David Eden and Sandy Leckie were members in the middle of the decade.

The enormous success of the club can be traced in the results of its members in the Appendix. Suffice it to say that between them from 1947 to 1981 they supplied just over a quarter of all winners of the National Championships. Notable for their tremendous team spirit, up to 1981 they won the men's foil Team Championship 23 times, the ladies' three times, the sabre four times and the epee six times (coming second eight times), even though little epee was fenced in the salle. Members of the club fenced in every World Championship and Olympic team from 1947 to 1981, except for 1951, when only ladies went, and 1958, when it was a team of two. One special achievement was that of contributing Jay, René Paul and Cooke to the foil team which defeated France to gain third place at the 1955 World Championships, the best result ever by that team.

Prof. Paul continued to teach until his death in 1963 at the age of 82. In 1959 the AFA presented its Diploma when his pupil Allan Jay won the World Championship. He was assisted by Major George Zabielsky, a Polish refugee who also taught at Westminster School. He was succeeded on his death in 1957 by Prof. Akos Moldovanyi, who was born in Hungary in 1918 and was educated at a grammar school, where he began to fence at the age of about fourteen. From the Military Academy, Budapest, he was commissioned into the army in 1939. His competitive career was cut short by the war, in which he received a leg wound. Now married and with a son, he studied economics at the university and in 1950 started teaching fencing again. He won his diploma shortly before going into exile in 1956. In London he taught at Lloyds Bank FC and in about 1958 began not only at Salle Paul but also at King's College and Imperial College, and at Merchant Taylors', Alleyn's, and Highgate Schools. Among his pupils were Clive Fisher, Judith Bain, Sue Lomax, Penny Johnson, Pearman, Partridge, Craig, Scott and Campion.

Prof. Vic Lagnado became joint master after 'Papa' Paul's death. He was born in 1924 in Egypt of a Gibraltarian father and Italian mother. He spoke Italian and French at home, went to a German school (where he learnt English) and also mastered Arabic. After five years in the British forces in the Second World War, he came to England in 1947 and trained as a teacher, becoming a modern languages specialist at Bexley Heath School till he turned full-time as a fencing master in 1972. Trained by Prof. Bertrand, he taught from 1961 at Whitgift and from 1958 at Poly, from which Ken Staines accompanied him to Salle Paul. Among other pupils were Allan Jay, Peter

Kirby, Graham and Barry Paul, Ian Single (from the age of 11), the Grimmett brothers, Susan Wrigglesworth and Liz Wood, Richard Hill, Hiam, Franck and Lawrence. He suffered a severe stroke in 1977, but, from being in a wheelchair, in due course he was giving fencing lessons again.

In addition to its own members, Salle Paul welcomed other fencers as visitors. Bruniges, Bell and Harper were only three of those who thus added to its magnetism as a centre of foil.

*The Polytechnic FC* was founded in 1883. A stalwart in the tens and twenties was Capt W. C. James, the father of Mary Glen Haig, who (though she later fenced for Lansdowne as a pupil of Prof. A. Parkins) was herself a member under Prof. Morel in the early post-war years when Charles Stenholm as Hon. Secretary was putting the club back on its feet. Prominent members then included A. Pelling, E. Watts, A. Payne, E. Knott and W. Burgess (who was left-handed at foil, right-handed at sabre!). By 1952–3, with over 110 members, the club was the largest in Britain. Waddleton, the Match Secretary, arranged 45 matches that season.

The club enjoyed the services of a long list of distinguished masters, including Erdelyi, Nicklen, Sullivan, Lagnado and Moldovanyi. Competition achievements reached a peak in 1952 when Birks, Hobson, Stringer and Trent beat Salle Paul 9–3 at sabre and L. Cook, Nicol, Price and Trent took the national foil Team Championship for the second time. Jolly, Howes and Mann (who also represented New Zealand) were other prominent members. In the sixties Ken and Pat Pearson and Ken Staines moved into the world of coaching.

Until 1973 the ladies formed a separate club with a formidably strong membership, including Margaret Somerville, Barbara Screech and Mrs Louise Copping and, in the sixties, Theresa Offredy, Jeanette Bailey, Shirley Netherway, Julia Davis, Janet Bewley-Cathie and Jennifer Dorling.

From 1951 till his death Prof. Behmber was principal master, with Prof. Suzanne Ridley, who stayed on till the mid seventies, as his colleague and David Austin as assistant. In 1967 Prof. Imregi arrived, in due course attracting, as at the LFC, most of the top sabreurs: Deanfield (his pupil at Westminster), Oldcorn, Philbin, D. Eden, B. Lewis (pupil at Oxford), Gryf Lowczowski, Kubiena, Roberts, Wasilewski and finally, in 1976, Cohen and in 1977 Zarno. His epeeists were also strong: Netburn, Beevers, Evans, Edwards, Jaron, Tatrallyay and Desmond Turner and the Oxonians Forward and Bird; prominent at various periods in the seventies on the ladies' side were Sue Lewis and Linda Martin, while the latter's brother Andy was of note among male foilists.

Poly twice won the Team Championship at men's foil, eleven times at ladies' foil, once at epee and eight times at sabre, all since the war – an enviable all-round record.

*Thames Club*. It was typical of the unassuming character of Professor Bill Harmer-Brown that he should not apply his own name to the club whose members were bound together by respect and affection for him. Born in 1917, he pursued fencing in his youth alongside swimming, middle-distance running and football and other sports. During the war he served in France in 1940 and again in 1944 (as a parachutist). He began to train as a master after the war but while still in the army, taking lessons from Roger Crosnier, and was soon running Londack Club, with John Sanders as his assistant.

He opened Thames Club as a part of the Chelsea–Westminster Adult Institute in 1952 after some two years at Beaufoy Institute. Among his assistants were Gomer Williams, Barry More, Frank Charnock and above all from 1967 Brian Pitman, who was also an early member.

Prof. Harmer-Brown also taught from 1953 to 1968 at Cambridge, where pupils such as John Glasswell, Michael Alexander and Peter Jacobs were good enough to reach the World Championship team (at epee) while barely down from the university, the latter two both gaining team Silver Medals. He also taught at London University from c.1953, at Westminster School (from 1952) and at Worth School.

Thames won the men's foil Team Championship in 1973 (and was second five times), the Ladies' Foil Team in 1965 and 1974, and the epee in 1969 (again being second five times). Among the more notable members of the club were Mary-Ann Pritchard (Mrs Watts-Tobin), Kate Hawkins, Justin Kelly, Lionel Martin, Miranda Cobb, Elspeth Earle, Anna Savva, Shiel Toller, Jill Dudley, Wendy Ager, Alda Milner-Barry, Clare Henley, Glasswell, Ben-Nathan, Breckin, Steele, Tomlinson, Blomquist, Hudson, Halsted, Higginson, Fare, Bonfil, Wooding, Noel, Bell, Belson and Eames (for a couple of years). The club amalgamated with LFC in 1977.

*SOUTH EAST* 1965 *84(37)*, 1970 *109*, 1975 *114(65)*, 1980 *88(42)*

The Section was formed in 1951, as were the County Unions of Surrey, Kent and Middlesex. Sussex followed in 1953. A team championship was introduced in 1969. School fencing had a particularly good year in 1970: six fencers were included in the England Schools Team and the schoolgirls won a triangular match against Southern and London Sections. In the following year they won the Inter-Section Schoolgirls' Foil, both senior and junior. 1972 saw 180 fencers at the one-day personal performance course organised by MEL Club. In 1975 there was a plan for appointing a Regional National Coach in conjunction with Southern Section; but government cuts nipped this in the bud. Every year from 1973 fencing was a major part of Butlin's Sports Holiday Camp at Bognor, largely through the efforts of Bernard Piddington. In the late seventies and early eighties there was concern at falling entries to Section events and at the cost of hiring venues.

The two main professionals were Prof. Russell, active north of the Medway, and Prof. Mallard, in south Kent. Alf Mallard was introduced to bayonet fencing in 1932 as a Marine and to foil on a PE course in 1938. He was at the naval PT School alongside Bob Anderson for two years after the war and then he was three years in Plymouth, teaching at the Naval College but also at Plymstock FC and elsewhere, earning the gratitude of Joyce Pearce amongst others. During his two years at Greenwich Naval College he taught at King's Cross and founded Welwyn FC. In 1952 he both gained the Diploma and retired from the Navy. Thenceforth he worked from his home in Deal, mainly as PE and fencing master at Dover College Junior School, but also at King's Canterbury, several evening institutes and at his own *Folkestone FC*. Among his pupils were Deighton, Burr, Bird, Olympitis, Ogley, Mallett, Gavin Brown, Gilbert Thompson and his daughter Gillian. His wife Irene also taught, chiefly in schools, and both played important roles in developing the County Union, along with Prof. Russell and Peter Upton, and with crucial backing from the local education authorities, especially Ann Readman, PE adviser.

OFFICERS
*Chairman:* 1962–6 M. Patient; 1966–8 G. Squires; 1968–73 C. Freedman; 1973–5 W. Allen; 1975–9 Mrs L. Hamments; 1979– D. Littlejohn.
*Secretary:* 1961–8 Miss J. Avis; 1968–9 Mrs D. Woodfine; 1969– B. Piddington.

CHAMPIONS
*Ladies:* 1965 Mrs E. Jones; 1966 G. Mallard; 1968 H. Twomey; 1969 J. Erwteman; 1970 T. Thompson; 1971 Mrs H. Davenport; 1972 Mrs J. Madeley; 1973 Mrs Y. Grammer; 1974 V. Windram; 1975 G. Sharp; 1976 J. Erwteman; 1977 P. Johnson; 1978 N. Jacobson; 1979 J. Hall; 1980 and 1981 J. Ertweman.
*Foil:* 1965 J. Hamments; 1966 D. Mabey; 1968 J. Hamments; 1969 J. Tyson; 1970 F. Mills; 1971 B. Wasley; 1972 J. Shackwell; 1973 J. Hamments; 1974 J. Ford; 1975 I. Hodges; 1976 J. Hamments; 1977 and 1978 M. Ward; 1979 J. Calvert; 1980 J. Pitman; 1981 J. Calvert.
*Epee:* 1965 J. Payne; 1966 D. Foster; 1968 N. Bell; 1969 T. Flood; 1970 J. Stanbury; 1971 G. Tomlinson; 1972 J. Hall; 1973 P. Huggins; 1974 R. Davenport; 1975 and 1976 H. West; 1977 A. Archibald; 1978 R. Bird; 1979; 1980 C. Periera.
*Sabre:* 1965 W. van Beukelen; 1966 J. Rayden; 1968 and 1969 W. van Beukelen; 1970 J. Hamments; 1972 and 1973 W. van Beukelen; 1974 J. Shackell; 1975 and 1976 J. Gryf-Lowczowski; 1977 D. Riddle; 1978 R. Pye; 1979 D. Duvallon-Lonan; 1980 and 1981 R. Pye.

*SOUTHERN* 1967 35, 1971 67(23), 1975 63(35), 1980 46(25)

The Section was established in 1951 by representatives of clubs in Reading, Pangbourne, Bournemouth and Portsmouth, which had already taken part in the formation of two County Unions – Hampshire and the triad Berks–Bucks –Oxon. The Wiltshire union was formed later. The Army at Aldershot and the Navy at Portsmouth were mainstays for the Section. Portsmouth and Southsea FC played an important role in organising body of the Portsmouth Foil Tournament.

In the early sixties activity was growing especially in schools and colleges. County Unions were very active in the early seventies. At the end of the decade there were encouragingly strong entries for boys' and girls' Under-14 events. In 1978 the Section ran the first Ladies Open Epee very successfully. From the same year there were regular matches with Normandy. Simon Routh-Jones was Foil Champion for the eleventh time running in 1981. After a gap of twenty years the Section won the Winton Cup in 1981 for the seventh time.

Long notable for its harmony and the willingness of members to undertake voluntary work, at the end of the period the Section was in a very healthy state, in terms of well-supported championships, excellent results in national and open events and a full coaching programme.

*Reading FC* was formed by John Savill in about 1947. He was a part-time professional who later gained his BAF diploma. Pam Patient started with him; Tony Finch was also a member. Frank Tanner joined in 1948, obtained his first coaching award in 1950 when he also started at Reading University, where Marilyn Holmes was a pupil. Remaining an amateur, he took over from Prof. Savill, who moved to Harlow at the end of the fifties. The club was originally an evening institute, but under pressure of spending cuts it became a private body with accommodation at a concessionary rate at Bullmershe College, meeting three times a week at different levels, with a membership of about thirty. Strongest at epee, Llewellyn, Greenhalgh, Patman and Tayler were among notable members; Davenport joined at the end of the period. Despite his full-time job on the signals and telegraph stores side of British Rail, Frank Tanner was assiduous in accompanying his pupils to competitions and his classic teaching, especially in fine bladework, obtained excellent results.

Among other clubs of note were *Espada*, in Bournemouth, home base of John Payne, and *Wellesbourne FC*, High Wycombe, run by Prof. Ken Pearson after his retirement as National Coach until 1980, when he left for S. Africa.

OFFICERS
*President:* 1958–66 N. Winton; 1966–78 G. MacLochlan; 1978– F. Tanner.
*Chairman:* 1962–6 D. Mabey; 1966–71 J. Townsend; 1971–5 D. Parry; 1975–9 A. Horton; 1979– T. Finch.
*Secretary:* 1964– Mrs J. Mason.

CHAMPIONS
*Ladies:* 1965 and 1966 M. Paul; 1967, 1968 and 1969 P. Patient; 1970 F. Alexander; 1971 and 1972 P. Patient; 1973 B. Williams; 1974 and 1975 P. Patient; 1976 P. Monk; 1977 P. Patient; 1978 B. Williams; 1979 B. Mitchell.
*Foil:* 1965 L. Edmonds; 1966 D. Mabey; 1967 N. Heads; 1968, 1969 and 1970 A. Loveland; 1971, 1972, 1973, 1974, 1975, 1976, 1977, 1978, 1979, 1980 and 1981 S. Routh-Jones.
*Epee:* 1965 F. Tanner; 1966 D. Foster; 1967 D. Johnson; 1968 J. Fox; 1969 T. Harrison; 1970 and 1971 J. Fox; 1972 and 1973 J. Payne; 1974 J. Llewellyn; 1975 S. Routh-Jones; 1976 J. Llewellyn; 1977 S. Routh-Jones; 1978 B. Patman; 1979 M. Gilbert; 1980 J. Hall; 1981 R. Greenhalgh.
*Sabre:* 1965 D. Simpson; 1966 K. Pearson; 1967 T. Walsh; 1968 R. Tiller; 1969 T. Finch; 1970 R. Tiller; 1971, 1972 and 1973 T. Finch; 1974 J. Clark; 1975 T. Finch; 1976, 1977, 1978, 1979 and 1980 S. Routh-Jones; 1981 D. Allen-Williams.

## SOUTH WEST 1966 *50*, 1971 *75(37)*, 1975 *95(56)*, 1980 *49(31)*

The Section was founded in Exeter in 1948 by Bill Park, his CCPR team and Bob Southcombe of Yeovil Club. In the 1952–3 season the Excalibur competition for county teams of one fencer per weapon was started, organised by Bath Sword Club. (Surrey led the field up to 1981 with 17 victories.) In the mid sixties Downside School, led and taught by Dom Philip Jebb, 'the Fighting Monk', shone in the Public Schools, producing, amongst others, James Noel and Richard Cohen, whose father Leslie did much to set up the Cornwall County Union in 1965–6.

Arthur Bishop of the Admiralty in Bath (a non-fencing father of a fencer) took over as Secretary from Bill Park and was succeeded first by Derek Holt of RAF and Devon and latter by Jim Pilkington, architect of the AFA subscription revision in 1975.

The indefatigable Peter Turner of Millfield School was Chairman and entrepreneur-in-chief for several years. He took endless parties of schoolchildren on charter flights to foreign events and got the all-electric 6-piste salle built at Millfield, where in 1968 he founded the Under-20 international men's and ladies' competitions. The same season Plymouth FC started their open mixed doubles Mayflower Cup. New competitions next season included a ladies' sabre within the Section followed by two years of running the 'National Ladies' Open Sabre'. In 1969 the number of clubs in Cornwall doubled.

All this time the Section Coach, Prof. John Sanders, applied enormous patience and set the highest standards. Somerset born and bred, he had returned to the SW in 1954 as the youngest member of the BAF, to clock up 36,000 miles a year, at first on a motor cycle, starting clubs, running courses and fostering competitions. Downside and Millfield were only two of the clubs that benefited from his teaching.

Prof. J. Sanders

The 25th anniversary was celebrated in 1974 in Yeovil, with Mary Glen Haig, Joyce Pearce and John Sanders as guests of honour. Serious training under the chairmanship of Jim Putz of Devon was extended and a special committee chaired by Colin Hillier, with Bill Hoskyns as secretary, was set up to supervise and develop under-20 training schemes with regular sessions under the ex-Marine Prof. Mike Webster, formerly of Birmingham FC. He was Section Coach from 1975, following the retirement of John Sanders, who was suffering from ill-health, particularly to his sword-arm, and whose fencing equipment firm, Jasco, was making inroads on his time. By 1977 there were 27 coaches. Mrs Tanya Houkes was the first woman to qualify as a coach in all three weapons.

The Section stretches two hundred miles from Cheltenham to Penzance. Venues ranged from an old cheese hall in Somerset to an aircraft-sized gym at RAF Locking. Nevertheless up to 1980 it won the Winton Cup eight times, only equalled by the E. Midlands. A Centre of Excellence ran successfully from 1978 under Mike Webster, but increased travel costs put a dip in entries to Section events in the late seventies and in 1980 Prof. Webster became disenchanted with fencing and retired to run a croft in the Orkneys. Barbara Hillier was appointed Director of Coaching to help fill the gap and Norman Golding took over as Section Coach, with encouraging results. He ran courses throughout the Section, including remote localities, and, with Pauline Carter, he trained the Centre of Excellence squad.

*Bath Sword Club*, founded in 1948, grew to over forty members. By 1970 it had nurtured such fencers as John Buffery and Ted Hudson. It celebrated its twenty-first anniversary in the Georgian splendour of the Assembly Rooms with sponsorship from the Avon Rubber Co.

*Bristol Fencing Club*, supported by Colin and Barbara Hillier, and *Phoenix FC (Bristol)* sustained by Dennis and Audrey Hunt, among others, benefited in the early days from the expertise of Prof. Joe Field (ex-Royal Marines), who gave much help in the formative period of the Section. Prof. Reynolds also came over from Cardiff for a number of years. In 1979 Phoenix became Salle Roeder, when the young French coach of that name took over, although he left in 1981.

*Yeovil Club* was founded in 1947 by Bill Park and Bob Southcombe (who later served variously as Section Treasurer, Chairman, Team Captain and President). Pam Hodson was a mainstay of the club from almost as early. The Section Coaches were the successive masters – mainly John Sanders, a perfectionist with a great capacity to understand and inspire his pupils. Bill Hoskyns fenced there as a schoolboy and from 1960 it was his sole club, from which he went forth to conquer the world.

*Taunton Club*, also founded after the war, was where John Sanders fenced as an amateur and Dr Tommy Pitts gave much help in early years. *Exeter*, *Plymouth* and *Plymstock* Clubs were notable for Ivor Jackett, Phil Redhead and Joyce Pearce.

OFFICERS
*President:* 1962–72 H. W. Hoskyns; 1972– R. Southcombe.
*Chairman:* 1962–7 D. Pedder; 1967–9 C. Hillier; 1969–70 P. Redhead; 1970–5 P. Turner; 1975–9 J. Putz; 1979– D. Holt.
*Secretary:* 1962–71 D. Holt; 1971–2 M. Bellamy; 1972–5 J. Pilkington; 1975–6 A. Molloy; 1976–7 A. Houkes; 1977–9 J. Pilkington; 1979– Mrs P. Spink.

CHAMPIONS
*Ladies:* 1965 M. Green; 1966 P. Hodson; 1967 Mrs A. Hunt; 1968 M. Green; 1969 D. Joyce; 1970 M. Ecob; 1971 S. Williams; 1972 Mrs A. Hunt; 1973 E. Joyce; 1974 and 1975 F. Alexander; 1976 J. Regulski; 1977 S. Holman; 1978 S. Benney; 1979 Mrs S. Lewis; 1980 C. Fray; 1981 S. Davis.
*Foil:* 1965, 1966 and 1967 H. W. Hoskyns; 1968 P. Redhead; 1969 E. Hudson; 1970 D. Hill; 1971 P. Michaeledes; 1972 G. Evans; 1973 P. Redhead; 1974 and 1975 G. Evans; 1976 J. Lawrence; 1977 J. Harrington; 1978 H. W. Hoskyns; 1979 R. Hillier; 1980 G. Evans; 1981 M. Evans.
*Epee:* 1965 P. Redhead; 1966 M. Hewitt; 1967 E. Hudson; 1968 H. W. Hoskyns; 1969 E. Hudson; 1970 P. Redhead; 1971 D. Cambridge; 1972 M. Walker; 1973 E. Henniker-Heaton; 1974 P. Redhead; 1975 R. Phelps; 1976 J. Harrison; 1977 R. Phelps; 1978 and 1979 B. Lewis; 1980 H. W. Hoskyns; 1981 P. Nicholson.
*Sabre:* 1965 H. W. Hoskyns; 1966 C. Hillier; 1967 and 1968 H. W. Hoskyns;

# Welsh Amateur Fencing Union

1969, 1970, 1971 and 1972 D. Hunt; 1973 E. Hudson; 1974 H. W. Hoskyns; 1975 and 1976 D. Hunt; 1977 E. Hudson; 1978 and 1979 M. Hunt; 1980 D. Hunt; 1981 M. Hunt.

*WELSH AMATEUR FENCING UNION 1965 13, 1970 25, 1975 21(2), 1980 17(1)*

A Section was formed in the principality in 1947, only preceded by the North and Midlands Section, and Glynne Reynolds and H. L. Birch (Vice-Chairman) were the first to gain Leaders' Certificates when this qualification was inaugurated in 1949. That year Wales joined Scotland and England in the Triangular Match (Quadrangular from 1950). Glynne Reynolds and his salle became the focus of Welsh fencing. A full professor from 1952, he was awarded the BEM in 1965 for his work in physical rehabilitation. He was tireless in his efforts to promote fencing, acting as a very hard-working unpaid National Coach. His children Frances, Andy and Robert, all fenced for Wales and the last achieved the distinction of a Bronze Medal at epee at the 1966 Commonwealth Games. Mrs Reynolds, a member of the Ladies' team from 1951 to 1956, was Chairman of the Welsh Fencing Union in 1959 and again from 1962 to 1970. A young training squad formed the nucleus of the team, which engaged in regular matches against each of the three Services.

Welsh fencing always tended to be concentrated in the south, where the mass of the population was to be found. This was reinforced by the topography which makes the journey to North Wales from Cardiff considerably longer than to London. In 1968, when a club subscription was introduced, the Union consisted of seven clubs in Cardiff, two in Penarth, two in Swansea and one each in Chepstow, RAF St Athans and Brecon. Under three hundred people were involved. Nevertheless there was plenty of activity. An invitation event, initially for ladies as well as epee (part of the Welsh Games for various sports) was founded in 1964. Teams were sent to Belgium and Holland and later to Ireland, Italy and Denmark (twice).

Prominent fencers in the early sixties included John Evans, John Williams, Roger Maunder, John McCombe, Ted Lucas (who sadly died in 1975), Julia Davis, Meg Walters, Jenny King and Marilyn Edwards (who married Peter Lennon, the England sabreur). In the later sixties Linda Brown, Ian Edwards, Derek Lucas and John McGrath came to the fore. Howard West flashed briefly across the scene. Spanning almost the entire period was the timeless Bob Turner, Captain in 1964 and still Captain in 1978, tending, if anything, to improve as he got older. In 1977 he became Hon. Secretary of the Commonwealth Games Council for Wales.

Glynne Reynolds suffered a severe heart attack in 1968 and by 1970 was forced to retire.

New members frequently in the team in the seventies were Sharon Williams, Margaret Riley, Audrey Bennett, Lyndy Prys-Roberts, Colin

Welsh team 1966. *Back*: M. Hope, A. Reynolds, J. McGrath, R. Reynolds, M. Edwards, Prof. G. Reynolds. *Front*: Mrs J. Reynolds, F. Reynolds, A. Julian, D. R. Turner, J. Davis, S. Turner.

Hyndman, Edmund Gray, Lyndon Martin, Anthony Garrington, Bryan and Christine Lewis and Gareth and Marvin Evans. Gradually filling the much-felt coaching gap was Peter Stewart, who began fencing at school in Blackburn, started again under Glynne Reynolds in the mid-fifties, then sidetracked into cycling and National Service, rose in the amateur ranks to team level, taught increasingly and became Provost in 1976. By 1980, when he obtained his Diploma, though still part-time, he was vigorously attacking the problem area of schools, of which none had been affiliated clubs in 1976, and he was even running courses in far-flung spots in mid, west and north Wales. He was appointed National Coach in 1981. Financial help from the Welsh Sports Council had been forthcoming from the early seventies, for administration as well as team travel.

    The Welsh Open, held in the Cardiff National Sports Centre from its opening in 1972, continued to expand and attracted four hundred contestants in 1975. Though without medals in 1970 and 1978, in the 1974 Commonwealth Championships Wales secured a Silver at team epee. In 1977 Wales won the Quadrangular and in 1980 the Winton Cup, both for the first time.

# N. Ireland Amateur Fencing Union

OFFICERS
*President:* 1953–J. E. Lloyd.
*Chairman:* 1962–70 Mrs J. Reynolds; 1970–80 D. Mort; 1980– R. Lawson.
*Secretary:* 1962–6 B. Turner; 1966–9 C. Davies; 1969–70 Mrs N. Whyte 1970–71 Mrs J. Ferris; 1971–2 Mrs P. Diamond; 1972–3 Mrs V. Ellis; 1973–9 Mrs L. Perry; 1979– Mrs N. Melvin.

CHAMPIONS
*Ladies:* 1965 and 1966 A. Julian; 1967 L. Brown; 1968 J. Davis; 1969 and 1970 J. Barkley; 1971 C. Whitehurst; 1972 L. Brown; 1973 A. Bennett; 1974 L. Brown; 1975 A. Bennett; 1976 M. Riley; 1977 Mrs L. Norrie; 1978 L. Prys-Roberts; 1979 C. Lewis; 1980 Mrs M. Myers; 1981 C. Lewis.
*Foil:* 1965, 1966, 1967, 1968 and 1969 R. Reynolds; 1970 J. McGrath; 1971 R. Reynolds; 1972 I. Edwards; 1973, 1974 and 1975 G. Evans; 1976 I. Edwards; 1977 C. Hyndman; 1978 G. Evans; 1979 M. Evans; 1980 B. Heder; 1981 G. Evans.
*Epee:* 1965 J. McGrath; 1966 R. Reynolds; 1967 D. Gillett; 1968 and 1969 R. Reynolds; 1970 and 1971 D. Lucas; 1972, 1973 and 1974 E. Gray; 1975 and 1976 D. Brooks; 1977 B. Lewis; 1978 and 1979 D. Brooks; 1980 and 1981 M. Wood.
*Sabre:* 1965, 1966, 1967, 1968 and 1969 A. Reynolds; 1970 R. Reynolds; 1971 and 1972 I. Edwards; 1973 B. Lewis; 1974, 1975, 1976, 1977, 1978 and 1979 I. Edwards; 1980 M. Evans; 1981 I. Edwards.

*N. IRELAND AMATEUR FENCING UNION* 1966 9, 1970 13, 1975 18(12), 1980 21(15)

Established as a Section in 1952, it adopted the designation Union in 1963. In 1965 the Schoolboy and Schoolgirl Championships attracted a record entry of 130. Although drawn from only seven schools the number was 150 by 1968, when a Torch Trophy was awarded to Brenda Kenyon, who as Section Coach was assisted only by four amateur coaches. The same season a very active Schools Association was set up. There was, however, a shortage both of more advanced fencers and of competitions. Visits were made to events in the Republic, but even there fencers found themselves continually opposite the same opponents. Among the schools the Royal Belfast Academical Institution was the strongest. Coached by Charles Gault, in 1970 it won the overall team trophy in the Public Schools Championship, a remarkable feat in competition with the strongest London schools with their professional masters and many other advantages.

Most seasons, at least in the earlier years, saw matches against Scotland, sometimes with additional engagements at school and student levels. By the early seventies a professional coach was being sought and progress was made in spite of the background of violence. In 1974 even a preparatory school joined the ranks of affiliated clubs, its oldest pupil being eleven! Several fencers at this period were making regular visits to mainland events. The rising cost of travel was offset with the help of the N. Ireland Sports Council.

In the foil at the Commonwealth Championships of 1974 the Leicester-based Andy Eames won the individual Gold Medal, while the team beat England and was unlucky enough only to achieve Bronze. The cancellation of the Coleraine venue for the 1975 Quandrangular, when planning was already advanced, was felt as a major setback. At this date there was a serious dearth of coaches, so that a four-day course in 1976, sponsored by the Old Bushmills Distillery and superbly run by Prof. Emery, was especially welcome: it resulted in eleven Coaches' Awards. Earlier visits by the National Coach and later by Prof. Boston were consolidated by the appointment in 1976 of Prof. Hans Mater as National Coach – who, however, promptly departed to Scotland. Mike Westgate coached the team from the 1978 Commonwealth Championships onwards and regularly visited the province; in 1979 he was appointed part-time National Coach. In 1980 Royal Belfast again did well in the Public Schools, chalking up four finalists, including Mark Wilson, who won the epee.

OFFICERS
*President:* 1961–78 Brig R. Broadhurst; 1978– C. Gault.
*Chairman:* 1965–7 J. Prentice; 1967–71 G. Beamish; 1971– W. Cumming.
*Secretary:* 1965–8 Mrs S. Martin; 1968–9 Miss J. Ewing; 1969–71 C. Grey; 1971–5 I. McConaghy; 1975–8 J. Ferguson; 1978 J. Pearson; 1979– B. Robinson.

CHAMPIONS
*Ladies:* 1965 and 1966 B. Mackay; 1967 and 1968 F. Davison; 1969 N. Parker; 1970 V. Byrne; 1971 and 1972 C. Convill; 1973 K. Thompson; 1974 C. Convill; 1975 I. Dumigan; 1977 and 1978 C. Convill; 1979, 1980 and 1981 P. Stonehouse.
*Foil:* 1965 B. Gubbins; 1966 B. Gregory; 1967 B. Herron; 1968 R. Grey; 1969 J. Bouchier-Hayes; 1970 J. Magill; 1971 D. Carlisle; 1972 I. McConaghy; 1973 and 1974 J. Magill; 1974 R. Pearson; 1975 J. Magill; 1977 A. Horne; 1978 J. Davis; 1979 W. Hamilton; 1980 and 1981 R. Pearson.
*Epee:* 1968 J. Magill; 1969 G. Jones; 1970 J. Bouchier-Hayes; 1971 L. Gubbins; 1972 I. McConaghy; 1973 D. Carlisle; 1974 R. Pearson; 1975 A. Horne; 1977 J. Davis; 1978 and 1979 W. Hamilton; 1980 J. Ferguson; 1981 S. Mann.
*Sabre:* 1965 B. Gregory; 1966 and 1967 G. Beamish; 1968 K. Balnave; 1970 C. O'Brien; 1971 D. Carlisle; 1972 S. Carson; 1973, 1974 and 1975 J. Magill; 1977 B. Robinson; 1978 S. Carson; 1979 J. Davis; 1980 and 1981 S. Carson.

## SCOTTISH AMATEUR FENCING UNION 1965 26, 1970 45, 1975 25(39), 1980 24(43)

Modern fencing had begun in Scotland in 1909 when the Scottish Fencing Club was formed, with Professor Leon Crosnier as master, assisted in due course by his son Roger. The Union was set up in 1923, with the Duke of Atholl as President and Captain C. M. Usher as Honorary Secretary and Treasurer. From 1924 an annual match was held between Scotland and N. England. This became an Anglo-Scottish match in 1928, a Triangular Match with the inclusion of Eire in 1939 and a full Quandrangular in 1950 after the inclusion of Wales. The King Edward VII Cup, a handsome bronze vase assigned to the match from its inception, was contested by England and Scotland alone and was first won by Scotland in 1938. Captain of the winning team was J. L. Hope, President of the Union from 1949 and kinsman of Sir William Hope, the seventeenth century founder of the Society of Scottish Swordsmen. Also in the team was Dr L. G. Morrison, President from 1959 to 1973.

The Second World War caught Prof. Crosnier in his native France and fencing would have been totally halted but for the indefatigable Col Ronald Campbell, who became President when the Union was revived in 1948. Prof. Crosnier gallantly returned in 1946 to teach for two winters, not in his own Salle but in a gym provided by Charles Usher, now a Colonel, who succeeded Campbell as head of Physical Education at Edinburgh University and who encouraged the Polish Major W. Segda to teach at both Edinburgh and Glasgow. Early post-war fencing was indeed concentrated in the four universities, Adele Mackinnon at Aberdeen being another key figure. The outstanding competitor was also a Pole, Zbigniew Czaikowski, who later returned to Poland and represented it at foil and sabre. Other notable fencers were Neil L'Amie from Edinburgh, who became the prime mover in schools fencing, and from Glasgow Christine Tolland, John Fleck and Alex Rae. It was Alex Rae who in 1959 started the *Newsletter* in whose compactly-printed pages the full spectrum of Scottish fencing activity was reported.

By 1950, when fencing was first included in the Commonwealth Games, there were twenty clubs. In 1951 Scotland was divided into two Sections: E. and W. In 1961 N. and Central Sections were added. In 1959 the Australian-born John Fethers, a pupil of Roger Crosnier in Paris, was appointed Maitre d'Armes to SAFU, a minimum salary being guaranteed personally by Committee members and others, whose pledges fortunately did not need to be redeemed. An outstanding foilist, he had been British Champion and twice Commonwealth Silver Medallist. He fostered a gradual expansion of schools fencing and his work for the team was reflected in Scotland's victories in the Quadrangular in 1966 and 1967, although he resigned in 1966 to be Australian National Coach.

He was succeeded by Bert Bracewell, who became by arrangement with the Scottish Education Department, the first National Coach, running a National Coaching Scheme, partly financed by government grant. He was thirty and had been a fencer for some seventeen years, trained by Prof. Alf Simmonds. He won the RAF junior foil title during his National Service and later reached the national Junior final and captained Latista when it reached the final of the Team Championship. As an amateur, he started the well-known Cyrano Club in Essex. An assistant to Prof. Simmonds he had been a professional for five years. He was runner-up to Prof. Fethers in the BAF Championships. A circular to directors of education offering his services in schools soon had a widespread response and in his very first season there was an impressive growth in schools fencing in the Edinburgh area, thanks to his talent and energy.

Before the Second World War only a few schools in Edinburgh practised fencing, the oldest surviving club being that of Merchiston Castle School (1933). After 1954 when fencing was started at Glasgow High School for Girls by the Principal, Frances Barker, it rapidly fllourished, especially from 1956 when Mrs Moya Barrie, the former Scottish international, took over the coaching. The club soon had 150 members, probably making it the largest of any British school. It produced Judith Herriot, Sue Youngs, Gillian Ritchie, Sandra Robertson, Barbara Williams and Cath Wotherspoon. Moya Barrie's own club was Caledonian. The only other Scottish professional apart from the National Coach was Mrs Jane Macnair, whose Glasgow FC boasted Tony Mitchell, Joe Rorke, Judith Herriott and Margaret and Ian Duthie. Aberdeen, however, was another significant centre of fencing in these years, Dr Peter Hobson teaching at Bon Accord Club, which boasted the epeeist John King, while Pat Cormack, another international, taught at Aberdeen Academy.

In 1965 Janet Little and Alexandra Wilson of Glasgow and George Sandor of Edinburgh were the first Scots to fence in the World Student Games. A Scottish team entered the British Team Championships for the first time since before the war. The Usher-Vaux scheme continued to provide financial support this season, giving grants to eight younger fencers for training and travel. Sandra Robertson, Sue Youngs and Judith Herriott regularly commuted south.

In 1966 Judith Herriot was fourth in the British Championship, the best position of a home-trained Scot for thirty years. After moving south, she fenced for Britain in the 1968 Olympics. J. Innes Macnair (husband of Jane Macnair) retired in 1966 from business and from eighteen years active work for fencing in the west of Scotland, especially as organiser for the Inverclyde Tournament at Largs from its inception in 1959.

In 1969 the Scottish Schools Fencing Committee was set up. By then there were nineteen school clubs in Edinburgh, but only the one in Glasgow. That year all the Schools Championships were fenced together over one week in the

Easter holidays. This was an idea of Bert Bracewell's (a full Professor from 1967), successfully organised by Neil L'Amie, Convenor of the SSFC. By now there were also eight university clubs. A trophy for the best individual results in the Inter-University Team League had been presented by Col Hay, veteran of Scottish fencing, who had fought in the historic Scottish-US match of 1923. He had also donated a team trophy for the British Universities Championship, which in 1981 he had the satisfaction of presenting to Edinburgh, the first Scottish university to win.

In 1970 SAFU staged the fencing events of the Edinburgh Commonwealth Games with an efficiency unsurpassed, in de Beaumont's view, at any World Championship or Olympic Games. AFA Gold Medals were awarded to Leslie Morrison and to J. L. (Tommy) Hope and the Award of Merit was made to Christine Tolland. Scotland won an impressive total of five medals in the Games, three more than in 1966. In 1971 Leslie Morrison became Vice-Chairman of the Commonwealth Games Council for Scotland; in 1974 he became Chairman.

In 1970 Prof. Hans Mater was appointed Assistant National Coach. Born in 1938 in Utrecht, he had done varied fencing work including a stint in Israel. He proved indeed rather a rolling stone and only stayed in Scotland a couple of years. To develop the teaching of fencing a Basic Coaching Certificate was introduced in 1967. The Scottish Coaches Association was set up in 1969 and in 1970 the Intermediate Coaches Exam was introduced. In 1971 an Awards Scheme was started, primarily for schools. The brain-child of Prof. Bracewell, it was organised by Neil Melville and comprised six levels and a judging award. By 1975, 1,550 Awards at the lowest level (green) had been issued and 1,237 at the other levels.

In 1971 Barbara Williams became the first home-based Scot to gain British colours and the Aviemore Tournament was started by Dr Peter Hobson. It ran till 1974 and was followed, in 1976, by the Highland Open at RAF Kinloss, organised by Dave Jerry. Also in 1971, Mark Maclagan died; aged only 25, while playing squash. A recent recruit to the Committee, he was the founder of Lothian Club and an enthusiastic coach at Napier College and elsewhere. He had been the admirable Armourer at the 1970 Games. The death also occurred, in 1971, of Hannah Gunn, who won the Scottish Open at the wide interval of 1929 and 1949 and who did much to keep Scottish fencing going before and after the war. In 1972 came the death of Prof. Leon Crosnier, who more than anyone had sustained Scottish fencing for two generations. Prof. Roger Crosnier could not attend SAFU's jubilee dinner, held in 1973, but sent a recorded message. The dinner was attended by most of the leading figures in Scottish fencing from Col Usher onwards, though Alex Rae could not be present to receive the trophy marking his exceptional services as Editor of the *Newsletter*, which continued in spite of his move to Leeds in 1967.

In 1972 Tommy Hope retired as Secretary and Treasurer after nearly fifty years' service to Scottish fencing. He was Scottish Champion at sabre in 1934, 1936 and 1952 and at epee in 1930, 1939 and 1946. He was drawn into administration when he succeeded his brother Arthur as Secretary of the Scottish Fencing Club in 1929. In the war he rose to the rank of Lieutenant-Colonel. His devotion to the Union was shown in his willingness in 1958 to step down as President to take on the lesser but no less onerous posts. He lavished incalculable time, care and energy as well as the knowledge and training of a professional lawyer. He was the motive force behind many of the developments in Scottish fencing, including the National Coaching Scheme and the establishment in 1967 of the Scottish Fencing Trust, which was aimed at raising funds to obtain a permanent headquarters. He received a Torch Trophy for his work in 1975.

He was succeeded as Secretary by Christine Tolland and as Treasurer by the 25-year-old accountant Sandy McDougall. Under their auspices, in the same year, an individual subscription to SAFU was introduced for the first time. Henceforth a SAFU Licence was required for all Scottish and senior Section events. (Issued through clubs, up to seven licences initially cost £3.50 and every additional one 50p, schools being charged only £2, without limit of numbers.)

Tony Mitchell won the Sabre Championship for the seventh time in 1972 (giving him a total of eight titles). And in 1973 Derek Russell won the foil for the second time and the epee for the fifth successive time. Both thus equalled records set by Arthur Hope (photo p. 32). He, however, gained his nine titles in all three weapons, including five successive foil wins.

A major blow in 1972 was the exclusion from all teaching posts in state schools of anyone without specific teacher-training qualifications. This meant that precisely the most highly qualified fencing masters, the fully professional National Coaches, could not continue what had been, up to this point, their most fruitful work. The exceptions which prevented the parallel English measure from inflicting its most objectionable consequences were never introduced, even by such professed opponents of restrictive practices as the government of 1979.

In 1973 Leslie Morrison retired after serving as President for fourteen years. He was succeeded by Neil L'Amie. Following the example of the schools, a universities week was now established, combining all their mutual matches. SAFU officers were somewhat galled to learn of the choice of Ottawa for the Commonwealth Games Championships only six months before the event, having been unrepresented at the Commonwealth Federation meeting which made the decision at the 1972 Olympics. There was some movement in favour of trying to obtain full national status, if not at the Olympic Games, at least as a separate member of the FIE and as a participant in the mooted European Championships.

Having in 1972 decided that resident Scots should be given preference over

The Scottish team and other Commonwealth fencers, at the 1958 Games. *Back*: J. Tapley, Col Hay, I. Lund (Aus.), A. Watson, R. Richardson, J. King, D. Doyle (Aus.). *Front*: T. Broadhurst, Dr L. Morrison, Miss D. Pleurs, Miss C. Tolland, A. Martonffy (Aus.), R. Thompson (NI), V. Chalwyn (Aus.), Miss M. Maries (Can.).

those south of the border in team selection, the Committee decided in January 1974 on a further tightening of selection rules in favour of resident Scots in these terms: 'As far as possible, only Scottish based fencers will be included in teams for major events.' Non-residents were required to take part in the main Scottish events and in squad training. Only rare exceptions would be made, such as cases of those obtaining more than one result of a very high order in a non-Scottish event.

Derek Titheradge was appointed Assistant National Coach at the end of 1973. Born in Rutland, he had been fencing for seventeen years, starting with Prof. Simmonds at Wandsworth School and Latista. He reached the last eighteen at sabre in the 1963 World Youth Championships. A Mechanical Engineering apprenticeship restricted competitive fencing but led eventually to a job designing wirework. He turned part-time professional in 1967 and by 1969 had three evening classes of his own, worked at Latista another two nights and was at competitions with pupils most weekends. Although in 1970 he withdrew from fencing for a year for the sake of his family life, he was soon re-absorbed and in 1973 he decided to go full time. He travelled seven hundred miles a week in Scotland, based first in Ayrshire and later in centrally placed Stirling.

It was slightly disappointing after 1970 only to win two (Bronze) medals at the 1974 Commonwealth Championships. In October of that year Adele Mackinnon, mainstay of fencing not only for Aberdeen but for universities generally over many years, received the first of SAFU's Swords of Merit. Sadly, the same month Frances Barker died. A teacher of wide interests who had been instrumental in founding the Scottish Schoolgirls Athletic Association, she played a key role in post-war Scottish fencing, always active, helpful and calming and bringing to bear her administrative tact and expertise. After her retirement Glasgow High School had become Clevedon Comprehensive School; fencing was gradually squeezed out.

In 1975 the number of Sections was increased from four to six: E., N., W., Central, Border (later re-christened S.) and Fife-Tayside. 1975 also saw the introduction of a points system. Although it did not bind the selectors, it was critcised by Hugh Kernohan (an aspirant junior) and Gordon Wiles (the seasoned multi-national) for under-rating the strength of non-Scottish competitions which both believed Scots ought to enter if they were to succeed in the Quadrangular and internationally. The same year the Sword of Merit was awarded to John Fleck, who fenced in the Triangular Match in 1949, and the same year took a teaching post at Dingwall Academy, where he had been coaching fencers ever since, amongst them Zawalynski, Mackay, Urquhart and Hossack. He also contributed more generally to schools fencing, which continued to flourish in the seventies. In 1975, for instance, an Under-13 Championship was added to the calendar and an Under-12 one in 1980. Elizabeth Wright succeeded Neil L'Amie as Convenor of the SSFC. In 1976 Dr Frank Riddell took over as Match Secretary from Tony Mitchell, who had held the post since 1966. That year Scotland again won the Quadrangular, a success repeated in 1978.

Glasgow was host to the Commonwealth Championships only eight years after the Edinburgh Games. Once again Christine Tolland took on a great deal of the organisation. It was disappointing that Scotland only won two medals, more so to learn that the Commonwealth Games Council for Scotland was not to offer fencing as one of the sports to be included if the 1986 Games were in Edinburgh.

In 1979 there occurred the untoward death of Jock Russell, aged 53. He ran fencing (and the history department) at Kingussie High School in the middle of the Highlands and was Team Manager at the Commonwealth Championships in 1974 and again in 1978. He was a kindly and likable man of many talents, whose kilted figure moved determinedly among the pistes of competitions patiently coaching the weak fencer with as much care as the international. A model organiser at Ottawa, he smoothly sorted out the snags, obtained training facilities even before the Canadians, ran a branch of the Bank of Scotland out of his own pocket and master-minded an inexhaustible supply of soft drinks, so necessary in the heat.

In 1980 Christine Tolland, who had been resolutely fighting off cancer for some years, finally succumbed, also prematurely. She had had a distinguished career as a fencer, having been Scottish Champion four times running from 1959 to 1962 and Ford Cup Winner no less than seven times. In 1961 she became the first Scottish lady fencer, at least since the war, to reach the final of the British Championship. Already in those years she was prominent on the administrative side. She was largely responsible for keeping the Jard Club going by her coaching and enthusiasm and was very much the organiser of the Jard Trophy, an event for clubs of the W. Section. She was secretary and treasurer of the Section from 1955, responsible for ten competitions. In 1965 she was awarded a Torch Trophy for her cheerful and selfless work, which increasingly extended to the national level. As Secretary from 1972 she carried most of the administrative burden of SAFU.

A degree of reconstruction followed her death. Already the constitution of SAFU had been revised under the leadership of Dr John Ross, a university administrator, who was Treasurer in 1980 and Secretary from 1980 to 1981. For the first time, there was provision for representation on the Committee as sections of non-geographical areas of activity. Initially, schools fencing was the only such area to be represented. To reduce the Committee to a more manageable size, the number of representatives per Section was reduced from four to three, thus also making it easier for the more remote Sections to be as strongly represented as the nearby ones. The Fife-Tayside Section, which had not enjoyed much vigorous life, was merged with Central Section. For the office of Vice-President the title of Honorary Life Member was substituted, formalising what had in practice already occurred.

At the same time working parties were set up to study coaching and team management and selection. New Instructor Certificates (Grades 1 and 2) were set up for those unable to take the Basic Coaching Certificate. A permanent team manager and team captains holding office for at least a complete season were instituted, together with an enlarged training squad with firm discipline and a tightening up of the points system.

The Sports Council provided funds for equipment to develop fencing in remote areas and also video equipment which could be loaned round clubs, but pressed SAFU to spend less of its grant on the *Newsletter*, which henceforth became an annual, while *The Point*, a newssheet produced speedily by modern methods was started under the editorship of Karen Kernohan (whose husband Hugh had become the Match Secretary in 1980).

The change of era after Christine Tolland's death was emphasised by the unusually sweeping change of officers at the end of the seventies. Dr David Mends of Edinburgh, Scottish Champion at foil in 1951 and 1952 and at epee in 1953, took over as Secretary and Piers Jones of Stirling succeeded John Ross as Treasurer. A mainstay of the N. Section over many years, Dr Peter Hobson, had retired in 1978. John Fleck took over from him and then became President of SAFU on the retirement of Neil L'Amie in 1981. Another watershed came with the death of Col Usher in January 1981, at the age of 89. Educated at Merchiston and Sandhurst, he was commissioned into the Gordon Highlanders in 1911. The army and sport were his life. In the First War he was unlucky to be a prisoner for over four years. In the Second War he won the DSO at Dunkirk. A well-known rugby international, at the age of fifty he only missed the 1950 Commonwealth Games epee final by one hit. He was made Honorary President of SAFU in 1964.

During the seventies there was a change in the pattern of clubs, especially due to the opening of sports centres, where the two national coaches now concentrated their efforts. Thus in 1972 Bert Bracewell moved from the Scottish Fencing Club (which henceforth tended to be a residual label), first to Lothian (a notable paraplegic club which opened its doors to other fencers but later also became to a large extent a label) and then to the Meadowbank Sports Centre. Later he also taught at Craiglockhart Sports Centre, where he was able to apply his talents in the teaching of schoolchildren. Derek Titheradge served the Stirling and Glenrothe Sports Centres. Bellahouston Sports Centre became the main centre of fencing in Glasgow (Jard FC had discontinued by 1981). Moray House College of Education in Edinburgh, where Norman Miller taught, was another institution which admitted outsiders.

A continuing feature was the concentration of activity in the central belt of the country. Elsewhere fencing depended vitally on individual amateur coaches. In the south the main centres were provided by Mr and Mrs John Wilson at Annan and by Fred Green and Colin Scott at Hawick (where the Under-13 Championships were held). In the north, though Bon Accord closed at the end of the decade, Aberdeen University Club continued, other clubs were opening and Dingwall Academy and Club continued to flourish under John Fleck's care.

Overall, fencing was in good heart. It was estimated that there were over a thousand active fencers in 1981. Being very little centred on evening institutes, Scotland did not suffer from the same squeeze as England, and there was a broader base than might have been expected, given the small population and the huge distances between centres (250 miles, for instance, within the N. Section between its furthest venue and its centre in Inverness). The quality at the top was also of the highest, with Fiona McIntosh and Donnie McKenzie in the British team (the former after moving south but the latter while still at Edinburgh University), and many fine fencers not far behind – except perhaps in sabre. (It spoke of a sparsity of talent as well as for Bob Elliott's prowess and persistance that he was able in 1981 to win the sabre Championship for the seventh time and the sixth time running.) For all this the chief credit must go to Prof. Bert Bracewell and his enthusiasm, skill and persistence over nearly two decades, recognised in 1980 by the award of the BAF's Gauthier Trophy.

OFFICERS
*Hon. President:* 1964–81 Col C. M. Usher.
*President:* 1958–73 L. G. Morrison; 1973–81 N. St C. L'Amie; 1981– J. M. M. Fleck.
*Secretary:* 1958–72 J. L. Hope; 1972–80 Miss C. J. Tolland; 1980–81 J. Ross; 1981– D. R. B. Mends.

British Academy of Fencing 169

CHAMPIONS
Listed on p. 534.

*BRITISH ACADEMY OF FENCING*

Reformed in 1949, the BAF had been growing steadily since then. In 1965 three members attended a course at Coburg, Germany, and Prof. Pearson trained in Hungary. In September at the Congress of the Academie d'Armes Internationale Prof. Moldovanyi was elected to the Technical Commission; in 1968 he was elected Vice-President of the AAI. Courses were held in London, Manchester, Nottingham and London. Prof. Czaijkowski on his visits from Poland gave courses in 1969–70 and 1970–71. In the 1970–71 season a match was held against Dutch masters in Amsterdam.

To celebrate the 25th anniversary of the Academy in 1974 a riverboat fancy dress party was held on the Thames. A major revision of the syllabuses and procedure for the BAF exams was also started in 1974 and Prof. Revenu gave the first of the residential courses held annually by the Academy ever since. The BAF magazine *The Fencing Master*, edited by Roy Goodall and now in its fifteenth year since it started as a newsletter edited by Gomer Williams, was retitled *Fencing*. On retiring from the Presidency in 1975, Prof. Ganchev was elected an Honorary Life Member in recognition of his twice winning the World Professional sabre title. Masters' courses were taken by Prof. Luka-

A BAF group. *Standing:* Roy and Angela Goodall, Pat Pearson, David Austin. *Seated:* John Fairhall, Mike Joseph, Chris Norden, Maestro Perone, Tom Norcross, Brian Pitman.

vitch of Hungary in 1976 and by Maestro Perone of Italy in 1977, when it was also decided that women could take their exams in all three weapons.

In 1977 the Gauthier Trophy, newly donated by Emrys Lloyd, was presented to Prof. Anderson. Prof. K. Pearson gave a course for Associates and Provosts, culminating in a week's residence, which remained an annual event till Prof. Pearson left for S. Africa in 1980. The Championships were suspended from 1978 for lack of support, as was the BAF-Coaches Club Conference. In 1979 Prof. Pitman was elected to the Technical Commission of the AAI. In 1980 a personal accident and public liability insurance scheme on favourable terms was negotiated for members and a BAF Proficiency Scheme was introduced which was foreseen as a useful source of income.

MEMBERSHIP

|      | Full | Provosts | Associates |
|------|------|----------|------------|
| 1965 | 26   | 12       | 36         |
| 1970 | 29   | 15       | 96         |
| 1975 | 37   | 16       | 102        |
| 1980 | 36   | 19       | 66         |

OFFICERS

*President:* 1961–9 Prof. Anderson; 1969–70 Prof. Behmber; 1970–5 Prof. Anderson; 1975– Prof. Hill.
*Vice-President:* 1964–7 Prof. Behmber; 1965–70 Prof. Harmer-Brown; 1970 Prof. Mallard; 1959– Prof. Moldovanyi; 1972–4 Prof. Boston; 1974–5 Prof. Hill; 1975– Prof. Sanders; 1976– Prof. Pitman.
*Secretary:* 1963–9 Prof. Behmber; 1969–71 Prof. Boston; 1971–2 Prof. Ridley; 1972–4 Prof. Emery; 1974– Prof. R. Goodall
*Treasurer:* 1964–75 Prof. Russell; 1975– Prof. Ridley.

DIPLOMAS

1965 Mrs Miszewska, H. Porter, K. Wren; 1967 G. Williams, H. Bracewell; 1968 L. Hill, G. Hawksworth, G. Ganchev; 1971 R. Emery, R. Goodall, B. Pitman; 1974 J. Fairhall; 1975 R. Tiller, Mrs R. Castle, D. Austin, M. Webster; 1976 Mrs A. Goodall, V. Cassapi; 1977 T. Norcross; 1980 M. Joseph, M. Law, P. Stewart; 1981 P. Northam.

CHAMPIONS

*Foil:* 1965 J. Fethers; 1966 R. Anderson; 1967 and 1968 D. Mabey; 1969 J. Fairhall; 1973 T. Burch; 1974 J. Fairhall; 1976 S. Lennox; 1977 R. Tiller.
*Epee:* 1965 J. Fethers; 1966 Z. Vadaszffy; 1969, 1970, 1973 and 1974 J. Fairhall; 1976 S. Lennox; 1977 J. Fairhall.
*Sabre:* 1965 J. Fethers; 1966 R. Anderson; 1968, 1969 and 1973 G. Ganchev; 1974 and 1976 M. Webster; 1977 R. Tiller.
*Ladies:* 1976 Mrs S. Parker.

## COMBINED SERVICES FENCING ASSOCIATION

Founded in 1936 and reconstituted in 1951, the Association was largely revitalised after the war by Col George Gelder, whose son, Major George Gelder, was a leading competitor in the fifties and early sixties, was concerned with running the fencing events at the Royal Tournament from 1949 onwards, became Secretary of the Army Fencing Union and generally played a central role in Services fencing.

The Services continued to provide support for fencing throughout the period. Scorers and timekeepers were invaluable at the Martini from its inception as well as at events such as the 1968 World Youth Championships and Services instructors often gave helpful tuition at civilian clubs in their spare time.

There was a considerable upsurge in fencing among junior soldiers in the later sixties and early seventies – among other ranks as well as officer cadets. A combined services team regularly took part in the Luxembourg epee tournament, and in 1978 Lt Belson was runner-up to Bessemans. From 1973 the annual match against an AFA team under the flag of the All-England Club became a feature of the Royal Tournament and was sponsored by Wilkinson Sword from 1975. By the mid-seventies there were also regular fixtures with Dutch officers and entries to the Dutch NCOs tournament – in which QSMI J. Larkham came second in 1978 and CPO Brierley was the winner and Sub Lt Kenealy third in 1979.

Lt Col John Moore, RA won the Champion at Arms, three-weapon title for the third successive year in 1976, following in the footsteps of his father, Major G. Moore, APTC, who achieved the same feat. In 1978 the RAF scored one of their rare victories in the Inter-Services Triangular, and won all three weapons the next year, but the Army was far ahead in total wins up to 1981, with 24, compared with the Navy's seven and the RAF's six since the event started in 1939.

In 1979 2nd Officer Barbara Williams won the Combined Services Ladies Foil and SSI Peter Brierley won the epee – both for a record fifth time. At both foil and sabre, Col Sgt Bob Anderson's post-1914 record of five wins remained intact, as did his similar tally at sabre, which had also been attained by SMI G. Wyatt and Col John Moore – but in both weapons he was surpassed by the great Lt J. Betts, who won the sabre six times, the foil seven times and epee three times, excluding his nine wins as a sergeant in the Other Ranks events (separate from the Officers' events until 1905, and probably of a higher standard). In total wins Sgt Anderson's twelve was the nearest to his sixteen.

## MODERN PENTATHLON ASSOCIATION OF GREAT BRITAIN

In the mid sixties pentathletes who also did well in AFA events were Howard and Bright, the latter of whom went on to be coach to the senior squad.

Amongst others there followed Finnis, Howe, Fox, Lillywhite, Darby, Flood, Rob Phelps, and Brierley. Major Monty Mortimer played a key role as Manager in the later sixties in gaining sponsorship and taking the team abroad. Mike Proudfoot took over in 1970.

From being almost exclusively military, pentathlon progressively broadened, so that by 1975, for instance, the junior and senior Championships comprised 11 entrants from the Army, 8 from the Navy, 3 from the RAF and 42 civilians; and only Fox of the team which won the Olympic Gold Medal in 1976 was in the Services. Parker came fifth and Nightingale tenth in those Games.

In the later seventies, although pentathletes were not making the same impact at the top end of British fencing, there were many more competing in events round the country and there was a flourishing junior squad (managed for a time by Andy Archibald), which was gaining results both in pentathlon and at fencing. Richard Phelps, for instance, won both junior and senior MPAGB titles at the age of eighteen in 1979 and went to the World Youth Championships for the AFA in 1981. Baldry, Brodie and Tayler were other juniors of note.

The rise of ladies' pentathlon was another feature of the late seventies, culminating in the first Ladies' World Championship at Crystal Palace in 1981, in which Wendy Norman came third and shared the team Gold Medal with Sarah Parker and Cathy Tayler, both sisters of epeeists.

# Competitions chronicle
# 1964-5
*MEN'S FOIL*

Allan Jay and Bill Hoskyns were still the dominating figures of British foil in 1964, as they had been since the earlier 1950s. Both born in 1931, they were both left handed and both Oxford graduates. Jay entered the British team for the Helsinki Olympics of 1952. Hoskyns did not follow, at foil, till 1955, but he immediately affirmed his world class by playing a major part in getting the team its Bronze Medal that year. (He beat all four members of the French team.) By 1965 he had been six times in the first three of the Championship or the Coronation Cup. The equivalent figure for Jay was fourteen; neither, however, could approach the brothers René and Raymond Paul. Between 1939 and 1962 René reached the first three of these two major championships 21 times and between 1949 and 1960 Raymond did so fifteen times. On the loftier international plane the younger men were supreme. Jay had been fourth in the 1956 Olympics, third in the 1957 World Championships, winner in 1959. Hoskyns was seventh in 1960, sixth in 1961 and seventh again both in 1963 and 1964. (Amazingly, Britain entered no team in 1962.) The Paul brothers had achieved less, but still more than any British foilist over the period 1964 to 1981. René was three times a semi-finalist and seventh in 1957 and Raymond was eighth in 1956 and a semi-finalist in 1957.

It was Allan Jay, now aged 33, who duly won the *Coronation Cup* for the fourth time, a record equalled only by René Paul since the inception of the event in 1937. After Cheltenham College, where in 1947 he came fourth in the Junior Public Schools Championship, he emigrated with his parents to Australia, which he represented in the 1950 Commonwealth Games. He returned to go up to St Edmund's Hall, Oxford, to read Law. He also joined Salle Paul, where he was taught by Prof. Leon Paul (and after his death in 1963 by Prof. Vic Lagnado). Now practising as a solicitor, he reached world class at foil in 1952, when he won nine out of ten fights against French 'A' and 'B' teams, including the famed d'Oriola. In 1959 he married. He also won the World Foil Championship and came second in the epee, a double feat only ever equalled by four others and henceforth unlikely to be repeated by anyone.

He considered retirement after the 1960 Olympics (where cramp sabotaged him in the foil individual but he won all twelve of his fights in the team event). He couldn't bear to stop, however, though he carried on at reduced intensity. He had reached the third round direct elimination in the 1964 Olympics, losing to Revenu of France. He was very fast and very strong, with superb timing and very good reactions, although his parries tended to be wide. He was particularly formidable in fleches and broken-time attacks, both unleashed at tremendous speed.

One other long-established fencer joined Jay in the final of the 1965 Coronation Cup: Prof. John Fethers, Scottish National Coach, who had first reached third place eleven years before, when he had also won the Championship. He now came fourth (2v). All the other finalists were much younger, aged around twenty. Second was Peter Kirby of the London Fencing Club (3v). Third was Tony Power, who was taught by his father at York FC and was very strong, fit and fast. In fifth place was the rapidly improving Graham Paul (S. Paul), taking up the baton from his father René and his uncle Raymond (2v). He had started fencing at the age of ten and had his first win in 1963 in the Junior Schoolboys Championship and was still only a seventeen-year-old at City of Westminster School. Already tall and strong, he was notable for aggression and confidence and specialised in double coupé fleches and duck stop-hits. In sixth place was 23-year-old Nick Halsted, from Westminster School and Oxford, who had won the Junior title and fenced in the World Student Games of 1963 at both foil and epee, and reached this final in spite of concentrating on epee since then (1v). He was an intelligent fencer with a strong physique, fast bladework and great determination, qualities that took him to this final in spite of a strong entry which included fencers from France, Italy, Germany, Sweden, Finland and Australia.

The *Championship* saw yet another Oxford man supreme. Taught there and at the London Fencing Club by Prof. Bela Imregi, the 27-year-old Sandy Leckie reached the top of British fencing as a three-weapon man. He fenced foil and epee in the World Championship of 1959 and had since figured in the team at foil or sabre (and often both). He had won the Championship in 1961 and the Commonwealth Games Gold Medal in 1962 and barraged with Jay and Hoskyns for the national title in 1964. Now, as in the Games, he pushed Jay into second place, being able to use his skills as a sabreur to penetrate his lateral blade movements. Hoskyns, the reigning Champion, was absent this time, doing little foil this year. Leckie also won the premier provincial tournament, at *Leamington*, where he successively beat Kirby and Trost (Austria) in the last stages of the direct elimination.

It was Peter Kirby of LFC, a Cambridge graduate for a change, and a lightly-built left-hander with small hands and a delicate technique, who came third in this Championship, an impressive follow-up to his Coronation performance. Derrick Cawthorne, of Salle Froeschlen, who had won the title in 1960, came fourth. Fifth was the neat left-hander Bob Peters of the RAF, and sixth was Mike Breckin, now a pupil of Prof. Harmer-Brown at Thames and London University, who as a pupil of Bert Bracewell at Cyrano had been Under-20 Champion and runner-up in the Junior the previous season, and was a strong, stocky left-hander, with good, fast technique if a limited game at this stage.

The coming younger fencers showed their form in the provincial and junior events. Power was *Under-20 Champion*, winner at *Ashton* and sixth in the *Junior* as well as third in the *Emrys Lloyd Cup*. Breckin was second in both the Under-20 and the Emrys Lloyd. Peters was *Inter-Services* Champion, ahead of Alan Painter and George Gelder, and fourth in the Junior. Barry Paul, a year younger than his brother Graham, and taught, like him, by their grandfather, was third in the Under-20, a notable second in the Junior and winner at *Portsmouth*.

David Eden, who had started fencing under Prof. Alf Simmonds at Wandsworth School at the age of eleven and continued under him at Latista Club, was the flamboyant but complex Junior Champion. His brother Laurie, a year younger and still at Wandsworth, was *Schoolboys* Champion. David Acfield, a pupil of Prof. Boston at Brentwood School, won the *Public Schools Championship*. He was also *Novices* Champion, followed by Richard Cohen of Downside, like him to be better known as a sabreur. Graham Tomlinson won at *Leicester* and Gunter Hanselman for the second year running at *Nottingham*. The Hungarian-born George Sandor won the *Scottish* title and Charles Rentoul of Oxford the *Universities Championship*.

The *Team Championship* was won for the fifteenth time since its inception in 1948 by Salle Paul – only the London Fencing Club and the Polytechnic interrupting this triumphal progress (each twice). As Champion club, Salle Paul competed in the *Paris Coupe d'Europe*, where they reached the quarter-finals and lost by only one hit at 8–all to the French champion club, Salle Leblond. In the associated individual *Challenge Rommel* Jay reached the quarter-finals. He also came eighth in the *Coppa Giovannini* in Bologna, a very strong event. Halsted did excellently in reaching the semi-finals in *Warsaw*.

The team for the World Championships consisted of Jay, Hoskyns and Leckie, together with the new colours Kirby and Power, in place of Cawthorne and Ralph Cooperman, both of whom had been in the team since 1960. Gordon Signy was captain, as he had been in 1961 and was to be each year till his death in 1972 except 1969 (when there was no weapon captain) and 1970, when Charles de Beaumont acted as captain.

## LADIES' FOIL

The *Championship* was won for the first time by the forceful, self-possessed Janet Bewley-Cathie, who was undefeated. Taught at Cheltenham College by

Madame Perigal, she won the Under-21 Championship and came third in the Junior Championship at the age of sixteen. After being out of fencing from the age of eighteen to 22, she resumed at the LFC and then under Prof. Nicklen at Poly, entered the Championship 'for fun' and came second. She joined the team the following year, 1963, and was runner-up in the Championship both that season and the next. A left-hander, she was not especially remarkable for technique, for intensity of training or for athleticism, but she was a natural fencer, with good timing, a steely wrist and, above all, concentration and will to win. She was now at the start of a long supremacy.

All three top places in the Championship went to Poly. Shirley Netherway, a pupil of Prof. Reggie Behmber, was second, having been third in 1961 and winner in 1964 (as well as winner of the de Beaumont Cup in 1960 and 1962). Third was Julia Davis (aged 24), Schoolgirls Champion in 1959 and second to the Junior in 1963, who had started fencing under Prof. Glynne Reynolds in Cardiff in 1953 and moved to the Poly under Prof. Behmber in 1962. Mildred Durne of Salle Pearson, herself third as far back as 1957 and four times in the top three of the Silver Jubilee Trophy, was fourth. Fifth was the Champion of 1961 and 1962, Theresa Offredy; and sixth Mrs Davies, erstwhile Eve Berry, Junior Champion of 1962 and winner of the Desprez Cup in 1955 and 1958. A notable eighth was Marilyn Holmes of Ashton FC, aged only fifteen, who also won the *Under-20 Championship* and both *Junior* and *Senior Schoolgirls Championships* this season.

The *de Beaumont Cup* had some fifty British entries and a score of foreigners from France, Germany, Hungary, Holland, Belgium, Luxembourg and Australia. Four Britons reached the last sixteen: Janet Cathie, Eve Davies, Sue Fisher and Shirley Netherway. None unfortunately reached the final, of which Gapais (France) was the undefeated winner, and the equally vocal Marosi (Italy) second.

Janet Cathie won the *Desprez Cup*. Runner-up here was Joyce Pearce of LFC, formidable in her reach, and third was Shirley Netherway, unrivalled for lunges.

The *Team Championship* comprised 24 teams from eighteen different clubs, including three universities. In the direct elimination Pauleons beat Thames to reach the final, but Thames also got to the final through the repechage after a tense 8-all win over Poly, the champions for the previous three years, who were now without three of their leading fencers, including Janet Cathie. (Instead the team consisted of Jeanette Bailey, Louise Cuppage, Shirley Netherway, Margaret Paul and Gillian Mallard.) In the final, in front of a large audience, Mary-Anne Watts-Tobin, Mrs Henrietta Davies-Cooke, Christine Duront and K. Olhof, for Thames, avenged themselves 9–5 on the Pauleons Eileen Jones, Eve Davies, Sue Fisher, Sue Brick and Vicky Lengyel-Rheinfuss.

Two of the major provincial events were won by national fencers: *Notting-*

Janet Wardell-Yerburgh

*ham* by Janet Cathie and *Inverclyde* by Mildred Durne. Mrs Pauline Courtney-Lewis capped a distinguished competitive career (begun when she won the Felix Cup in 1956) by winning at *Leicester*. Pam Patient, often formidable on the piste, won both the *Portsmouth* Tournament and the biggest of them all, at *Leamington*, where she excelled herself to beat Niermann of W. Germany 7–6 in the title bout. Janet Cathie won the fight-off for third place against Janet Little of Glasgow University, who put up a remarkable performance to get so far.

The winner at *Ashton* was Mrs Gerry Harding (née Evans) of Birmingham School of Arms. She went on to win the *Junior Championship* with a thoughtful mixture of attack and defence. She was undefeated and only hit thirteen times in the final of eight. A healthy sign of the distribution of talent was that five of the others were also non-London fencers. Angela Julian of Salle Reynolds, Cardiff, was second, displaying a solid defence. Just behind on hits was Mrs Mary Hawdon of Halifax, with a good line in staccato attacks. Marilyn Holmes was fourth, suffering from knee injury, again separated only on hits from Alex Wilson of Glasgow, who had showed a lively preference for an attacking game until she too suffered knee injury and was rendered static. Gillian Mallard was sixth with two wins, just one hit ahead of the tall, partly W. Indian Benny Pitman of Salle Boston, a forceful but classical fencer. Audrey Hunt of Phoenix, Bristol (wife of Dennis), though eighth with only one victory, was by no means outclassed, her good technique forcing her opponents to work hard to overcome her.

Abroad, Gerry Harding also did well. She was sixth at *Noordwijk* and again in *Amsterdam* and won the open-air tournament at *Dieppe*. Here the quiet but effective Shiela Toller of Thames was fifth and Mrs Eileen Pitman (wife of Brian) was sixth. In *Brussels* Miranda Cobb was sixth. On the formidable level of *Como* Janet Cathie reached the third round. She and Shirley Netherway reached the semi-finals at *Warsaw*, where a team which also included Julia Davis and Theresa Offredy beat a Polish team by two hits at 8–all.

Back at home, Britain had three training matches in April. Against Hungary they lost 10–6 (Netherway 3, Cathie 2, Bailey 1, Offredy 0). Against W. Germany they drew 8–all, but lost by seven hits (Netherway 3, Pearce 3, Cathie 2, Davis 0). And against France they lost 12–4 (Davies 2, Pearce 1, Watts-Tobin 1, Patient 0).

Those selected for the World Championships had all been in the team before: Eve Davies (1954, 1957, 1959; Captain), Jeanette Bailey (1957–1963), Janet Cathie (1963, 1964), Theresa Offredy (1959 and 1961–4), Shirley Netherway (1960–64) and Joyce Pearce (1961–3). It should be added that only Gillian Sheen went in 1958 and no team was sent in 1962.

## EPEE

At epee, as at foil, the two commanding figures in 1964 were Allan Jay and Bill

Hoskyns. Jay had reached the World semi-final the very first year he joined the British team in 1952. Hoskyns also reached the semi-final as soon as he joined the epee team, in 1955. In 1957 Jay was fifth in the World Championships (as well as third in the foil). In 1958 Hoskyns was World Champion. In 1959 Jay only missed adding an incredible double to his World foil title when he lost the epee barrage on the last hit. He followed this in 1960 by winning the Silver Medal in the Rome Olympics, again only missing the Gold in the barrage. Hoskyns came eighth in 1961 and then in his turn was Silver Medallist at the 1964 Tokyo Olympics after barraging for the Gold (as well as being seventh in the foil).

Over the period from 1958 to 1964 Hoskyns must be reckoned as having been the world's foremost epeeist, just as probably only Delfino and Khabarov could dispute the number two position with Jay.

Born into a farming family in Somerset, Bill Hoskyns took up fencing at Eton, encouraged by his mother, who had also fenced, and taught by Capt Len Laxton. He did a bit of boxing too and coxed at rowing, but was a slow developer and was handicapped by his diminutive size. He only grew to 6ft 1in during his eighteen months' National Service. He then went up to Magdalen, Oxford, to read agriculture, at which he collected a fourth (distinguished for its rarity) and was coached by Prof. Cromarty-Dickson. In 1952, in his second year he won the British Junior Championship at both foil and epee and came third in the sabre – the nearest anyone has got to winning all three titles in one season. (B. P. Cazaly won all three titles, but in different years – 1929, 1930 and 1932.)

A leg broken skiing shortly after this took a year to recover. The temporary loss of mobility, according to Hoskyns himself, 'did wonders for my parry-riposte'. Certainly his ability to pick up his opponent's blade at the very last moment was one of his great strengths, together with his way of foxing opponents not so much by spectacularly varied tactics as by subtle variations of distance and speed. On top of this he fully made up for lack of extreme speed, by his ability to put his opponents under continuous pressure so as to induce them to attack at the moment of *his* choosing.

In 1954 he fenced sabre in the World Championships; in 1955 at all three weapons. Later sabre took a back seat, but in 1958 as well as winning the World Epee Championship, he won the Sabre Gold Medal at the Commonwealth Games (as a last-minute replacement) and missed the World Final at sabre by a single, disputed hit. From the beginning he was taught at Yeovil by Prof. John Sanders, who gave very technical lessons, with emphasis on blade control and finger control. But from his Oxford days till 1958 he also fenced at Lansdowne Club in London, under Prof. Alfred Parkins, and competed under the colours of that club.

By 1964 he was much less able to train in London. He had married in 1960, started a family of five and become more engaged in farming his 600 acres.

Gone were the carefree days of piloting his own plane to competitions as far afield as Budapest (as well as his part-time soldiering in the N. Somerset Yeomanry). 1964 was the last year of regular lessons. It was, however, far from being the last year of the presence in the British team of a man equally renowned for his sportsmanship and unruffled demeanour on all occasions and for the buffoonery and practical jokes that made the youngest newcomers feel him to be almost a contemporary.

Hoskyns and Jay had been supported by other epeeists to the extent that in the World Championship team event Britain had been fourth in 1956 (for the first time since 1933), third in 1957 and Silver Medallists in 1960. John Pelling had been in the team since 1957. He had come sixth in the Championship in 1952 when he was barely sixteen and had only just started fencing. He came third in 1955 and was the winner in 1961, ten years after the trophy was last won by his father Bert Pelling, who was his constant teacher, though he had lessons from many other distinguished masters who successively taught at Grosvenor Club. He was 5ft 10ins, lean and muscular and for some years was the only right-hander in the epee team. He was an instrumentation scientist in Shell Research and pursued no other sports.

Only recruited to the team in 1961 but very much in the ascendent was Peter Jacobs, who was some three years younger, and one of the galaxy of talent nurtured by Prof. Nicklen at Merchant Taylors School. From Cambridge University he had won the World Student title in 1962. There and at Thames Club he was taught by Prof. Harmer-Brown. He won the Championship in 1961 and 1964 and the Paris Picon in 1963. His job was in marketing with Ford. As well as giving an edge to his dynamic style by doing a lot of gymnastics at school, he competed at cross-country skiing and running. Shortish for an epeeist at 5ft 9ins, he made up for it not only by speed but by fencing with a straight arm and constantly bouncing on his rear foot. He was even leaner than Pelling, and left-handed.

The fifth place in the team was now rather open, since Captain Mike Howard of the Army, a member continuously since 1956, was now retiring, though he had won the Miller-Hallett only the previous season. One contender was John Glasswell of Thames Club, a Cambridge graduate who taught chemistry at St Pauls and had been epee Champion in 1963 and a member of the team in 1961 and 1963. Another obvious candidate was Nick Halsted, born in 1942, who had fenced at Westminster and at Oxford where he read Law at Wadham. There and at the LFC he was taught by Prof. Imregi. As a schoolboy he had reached the final at Leamington and in 1963 he was Universities Champion. His leap to national class was achieved when he came third in the 1964 Miller-Hallett.

This year the *Miller-Hallett* was won by Lagerwall of Sweden, who had been second in the World Championships of 1961 and was temporarily working in England. In the final of twelve (including five foreigners) he was defeated only by the Finn Czarnecki, but didn't fight Charles Llewellyn of the Royal Navy, who retired hurt, and had to barrage for first place with Halsted, who had lost 5–3 to Glasswell. Third place went to Jacobs, after a fight-off with Zampini, of Italy and Salle Paul. Robert Rhodes of Oxford hit a streak of form to come sixth (5v). Glasswell tied on hits with Chris Green of Salle Boston (7th=; 4v). Following J. Puissesseau (France) and P. Schmidt (W. Germany) came John Shaw of Mayfield (11th; 2v).

The epee sub-committee had decided that the final of the *Championship* should be a poule unique of 24, which required over nine hours of combat, a strain on both competitors and officials. The most remarkable feature of the event was the second place of Teddy Bourne of Brentwood School, a pupil of Prof. Steve Boston. At one bound this tall gangly schoolboy of sixteen joined the front rank of British epeeists, where he was to remain very firmly almost to the end of the period covered by this book. Fencing with elan and considerable abandon, he long led the field, energetically probing his opponents' defences preparatory to unleashing devastating fleches, often initiated with an upward tweak of the wrist. It has to be added that neither Jay nor Hoskyns took part in the event, as often happened in the early sixties.

The winner was Pelling, currently taught by Prof. Pat Pearson at Grosvenor. He got eighteen wins, one more than Bourne. After his usual shaky start, he fenced with polish and consistency, maintaining the improvement in technique and determination which had been evident in the previous season. Halsted was third, only three hits behind. Jacobs, the holder, had a somewhat patchy day but still achieved fourth place (14v, 32 hits received). His bout with Pelling, including four double hits in the last minute, was a classic. Consistent and courageous fencing deservedly gained Shaw fifth place (14/40). Sixth was Steve Higginson of LFC (13v). From Merchant Taylors and Oxford, and now a modern languages teacher, he had won the Junior Foil Championship in 1962 and achieved the very impressive feat of winning the Miller-Hallett while still a student in 1963. The other places were as follows: 7. Glasswell (Thames) 12/22; 8. Clive Purchase (Birmingham) 12/26; 9. Bill Romp (Grosvenor) 12/31; 10. John Anderson (Behmber) 11/21; 11. Graham Paul (Paul) 11/27; 12. John MacGrath (Cardiff) 11/35; 13. David Pomeroy (Grosvenor) 10/20; 14. Don Giles (Grosvenor) 10/22; 15. Clive Layton (Thames) 10/27; 16. M. Roberts (Cambridge) 19/21; 17. Chris Green (Boston) 9/24; 18. Derek Parham (Birmingham) 9/26; 19. Mervyn Vickery (LFC) 8/25/36; 20. John Fairhall (Boston) 8/25/35; 21. Ron Bright (Army) 7/22; 22. John Payne (Boston) 6/22; 23. Roland Griffin (Newcastle) 3. Mike Howard retired injured.

The *Martini International*, the high point of the season, had taken place earlier. It followed the pattern established since its inception in 1960. Fifteen British epeeists qualified from a preliminary event headed by the unorthodox but talented Chris Green, ahead of Loetscher (visiting from Switzerland) and

Graham Paul. The 1964 British team was exempt from this and joined the foreigners direct. These included the Hungarian Gold Medal team and the champions of seven other countries.

The second round comprised five fencers each from Britain, Hungary and Sweden, two each from Poland, France and Belgium, one Dutchman and one German. In the direct elimination from sixteen, Allan Jay, in his best form and heading the match plan, defeated Kausz, Hungarian 1962 World Champion, 5–4. Bill Hoskyns beat Mouyal, the French 1957 World Champion, 8–5. And John Pelling narrowly lost to Larsson (Sweden) 10–9 in an epic bout. Nielaba (Poland) beat Lindwall (Sweden) 8–3; Lagerwall (Sweden) beat Nemere (Hungary), the holder, 7–5; von Essen (Sweden) beat Kulcsar (Hungary), 10–9; Gabor (Hungary) beat Kurczab (Poland), 8–5; and Nagy (Hungary) beat Andrzejewski (Poland) 8–4.

The standard of the gala final (as usual in the Seymour Hall) was claimed as higher than that of the Olympic final in Tokyo, with considerable contrast in styles and much excitement. In the first bout Jay beat the young von Essen 8–1, showing a form which he had not reproduced since the 1960 Olympics, some of his compound attacks en fleche being devastating and a delight to watch. Hoskyns, suffering from a heavy cold, could not quite get to terms with Nielaba, and lost a protracted bout 8–6 on a final double-hit, after having pulled up from 3–7 down. The aggressive Gabor had a surprisingly easy 8–3 win over the impeccable Lagerwall, while Nagy defeated the twenty-year-old Larsson 8–5.

Jay, rather more subdued, beat Nielaba 8–6 in the first semi-final, thus reaching the final bout of this event for the first time. In the other semi-final Nagy, 28-year-old railway technician and relative newcomer to his team, foreshadowed later members with his crouching stance and a somewhat forward position of head. He beat Gabor 10–9, showing a remarkable gift for attacks at hand, as well as an effective hit to foot at close quarters (as Jay was to discover).

In the final bout Jay, who favoured active defensive tactics and an upright stance with trunk and head kept out of range, scored at once with a determined attack at arm. Nagy immediately replied with a similar movement. Two double hits brought the score to four–all. Nagy then went ahead with an attack at wrist on preparation. Jay replied with a counter-time with fleche to level the score once more. Nagy then scored with a stop hit at wrist, went to match point 7–5 with a splendid quarte-riposte and finally ran out the winner at 8–6 with a double hit on Jay's fleche.

Jay lost only three bouts throughout the day. He perhaps suffered from having fenced little epee this season and he certainly tired during the final bout. Nevertheless in coming second he gave a performance noteworthy even in his distinguished career.

Abroad, Jacobs scored a notable success when he came sixth in the *Paris Monal* out of an entry of 260. At *Duren* Howard reached the last eight. In the

European Team Championships at *Heidenheim* LFC beat Luxembourg 9–6 and Denmark 10–6 to reach the direct elimination, where they lost 9–7 to Budapest, the ultimate winners. In the individual event Pelling reached the direct elimination stage, where he beat Nemere of Hungary. In the *Coupe des Trentes, Brussels*, Pelling was 14th, Jacobs 18th and Halsted 19th. In July, again in *Brussels*, Jacobs reached the last eight.

Unsurprisingly, it was Halsted who took the fifth place in the World Championship team, alongside Hoskyns, Jay, Jacobs and Pelling.

At the junior end of the spectrum, there was reason to be hopeful for the future. In the *Under-20 Championship* Barry More of Latista (1st) and Rhodes (2nd) were good enough to push Bourne into third place. David Floyer of Brentwood, fourth in this event, won the *Public Schools*. He started by losing to his school-mate Derek Russell 4–1, had a double defeat and then met Ken Pearman of Highgate, who fenced well till he did an ill-advised direct fleche. In the end these two barraged. Floyer twice scored with stop-hits on attacks at leg, then got a hit on foot during a clash and finally a counter-sixte direct riposte to win 4–0. He thus became the first boy to win this event twice, after seeing the title apparently beyond his grasp. Russell was third, Jeremy Lawday of City of London fourth. Ralph Johnson of St Dunstans was sixth.

The *Junior Championship* attracted a record entry of a hundred, necessitating sixteen first round pools. The average age of the twelve finalists was lower than in earlier years – around twenty. Clive Layton (taught by Prof. Bill Harmer-Brown at London University) led the field up to the last round, with Purchase of Birmingham, the enthusiastic Graham Tomlinson (London University) and Rhodes only one victory behind him. In his last bout Layton went down by the odd hit to Bob Turner of Cardiff. Purchase then had a chance of a barrage if he could overcome the tall, lanky Llewellyn, against whose reach, however, he made no impression – leaving Layton the winner. Barry More fell, injured his back and had to retire just as he was finding his touch.

The *Universities* title went to George Sandor of Edinburgh. At *Leamington* Jacobs won the final bout of direct elimination over John Anderson of Salle Behmber (1963 Junior Champion). Tony Mitchell of Glasgow, principally a sabreur, won at *Inverclyde*, showing manoeuvrability and opportunism. John Payne of Bournemouth (his home base where he had started fencing in 1950 just before National Service), won the barrage for second place over Bob Wilson, another Glaswegian – a triumph of the terrier over the bulldog. He was an indefatigable competitor who had been working and training in London since 1954 and had won Inverclyde in 1960. Joe Rorke, yet another member of Glasgow FC, was fourth on hits over Gougnoux of France. David Hunter of Bon Accord, Aberdeen, and a stalwart of Scottish epee, was sixth. His club-mate John King, however, was winner of the *Scottish Championship*, for the fifth time since 1955, ahead of Mitchell and Rorke.

There were 22 teams in the *Team Championship*. In the quarter-finals Salle Paul beat Grosvenor 'B' 9–4, LFC beat Boston 'B' 9–3, Grosvenor 'A' beat Salle Paul 'B' 9–1 and Boston 'A' beat Thames 9–1. In the semi-finals Grosvenor had little difficulty in beating Boston 8–4, whereas Salle Paul had a protracted struggle before they overcame LFC, the holders, 8–7. The final was something of an anti-climax. Grosvenor, three times winners in the early sixties, fell prey to Salle Paul surprisingly easily at 9–3. For Salle Paul, Jay (3/3) was in devastating form, while Graham Paul (3/3), who had already been sixth in the 1964 Championship, showed what a formidable team fencer he was. They were backed by Zampini (2/3) and Kai Czarnecki (1/2 + d.d.). For Grosvenor, Jacobs, Glasswell and Romp each got one win, Pelling none, but one double defeat.

*SABRE*

Since the retirement of Mike Amberg (prominent throughout the fifties and early sixties) the two leading figures of British sabre had been Ralph Cooperman and Sandy Leckie. The former started fencing in 1947 in the RAF. When he left, he joined the Polytechnic Club and then Salle Paul, where he had lessons at foil from Prof. Leon Paul, but no regular sabre lessons at first. A left-hander, and by profession an accountant, he won the Sabre Championship in 1954 (on a barrage from Hoskyns), but he had already been runner-up at foil the previous year. For the next decade he was nearly always in the sabre team and sometimes in the foil team as well. He reached the semi-final of the World Championships at sabre in 1957, probably equal to any previous British performance, and better than any since. He also collected eight Commonwealth Gold Medals (at the two weapons).

For the two previous seasons it had been the much younger Leckie who had won the British Championship. Born in 1938, he began fencing at Merchant Taylors under Prof. Nicklen, who imparted tactical training as well as a stylish technique (including a classic stance, with legs well bent and trunk held upright). At Oxford, Leckie read Modern Languages and trained hard, becoming perhaps the most athletically complete fencer of his generation, beautifully controlled and very fast, with a fleche that was formidable at all weapons. In 1959 he reached the semi-final of the World Under-20 Championship at sabre, and won the Junior, but went to the World Championships at foil and epee! From 1961–3 he worked for EMI in Paris and was taught by Cottard at the Racing Club (for whom he got three wins in the final of the French Foil Team Championship, alongside Magnan, Cazaban and Foulon). Back in London, he resumed under his Oxford coach Prof. Imregi at LFC (Prof. Nicklen had left the profession).

With Cooperman absent from the 1965 *Championship*, Leckie was clear favourite, but at the end of the second phase of the final of twelve, with only three fights per fencer to go, Leckie, John Rayden and Graham Wilson had two defeats each, whereas the very tall 27-year-old Richard Oldcorn, a member of LFC like the other three, only had one and looked set to win. He had started sabre at Tonbridge and, although not a precocious developer, had already, in 1963, won the Ystad Tournament. In spite of thus being the only British winner of a substantial international sabre event between 1959 and 1981, he never won the British Championship. Perhaps he was better endowed with the psychological qualities to excel competitively in the toughest international events than with the slightly different qualities required to *win*, even at a somewhat lower level. Leckie, with his outstanding home results but somewhat disappointing performances abroad, was perhaps the opposite in his psychology. In this case, from a winning position Oldcorn let slip two of the last three fights when he was expected to win them, and ended third. Wilson also lost a further fight off for first place. Leckie duly got his hat trick, his only predecessors in the feat being C. A. Wilson in 1904–6, Amberg in 1957–9 and Tredgold in 1947–9. Rayden's second place brought him to new heights. New faces in the final were Rodney Craig (8th), John Moore (9th), Edward Ben-Nathan (10th) and John Shewring (11th); all were under twenty, except Capt Moore (who was second to Petty-Officer Ken Pearson in the *Combined Services Championship* this season).

Twelve clubs took part in the *Team Championships*. The only early surprise was the elimination of Boston 'A' 9–7 by Reading and 9–1 by Combined Services in the first round. The LFC 'A' team of Leckie, David Martin, Oldcorn and Rayden was far too strong for any of the opposition, trouncing Combined Services, LFC 'B' and Poly, who took places in the final pool in that order.

In February a *match against Belgium* had been won 11–5 (by Cooperman, Leckie, Oldcorn and Rayden). The Belgians defeated a 'B' team by the same score. There followed the *Amateur-Professors Cole Cup* which was won by Brasseur, followed by Oldcorn and Leckie.

On the eve of the Corble Cup in mid June, *two matches against West Germany* were held. In the first match, the British 'B' team fenced extremely well to hold the Germans to 7–9. (David Eden 2, Martin 2, Wilson 2, George Birks 1; Theuerkauff 4, Woehler 2, Roeth 2, Jantsen 0.)

For the main en gala match, the Germans dropped Jantsen and brought in Borucki, thus considerably strengthening their team. Nevertheless Britain achieved a convincing 10–6 victory, Leckie and Oldcorn fencing well to gain three victories each and Cooperman and Rayden scoring two apiece.

Those of the 38 British entrants who had qualified joined the five Germans in the *Corble Cup* next day. Cooperman was surprisingly beaten in the first round of direct elimination by Martin, and in the second round Theuerkauff was beaten by Oldcorn. However, by virtue of the repechage, both Cooperman and Theuerkauff reached the final six, where they joined Leckie, Oldcorn, Borucki and Martin. Borucki emerged winner with four victories over Leckie, Oldcorn and Theuerkauff, all with three victories, in that order. Cooperman with two victories was fifth. Martin had no wins.

The 20-year-old, 5ft 11ins David Eden won the *Junior Championship*, thus being the only person ever to win foil and sabre junior events the same season. The runner-up, as he had been the previous year, was Derek Titheradge, likewise a pupil at Prof. Alf Simmonds' Latista Club, which produced numerous good subreurs in these years. He was also the winner at *Ashton* and third after a barrage at *Inverclyde* (Vausell of France was first and Fethers second). Third in the Junior was Bob Brearley of St Paul's and Salle Boston.

The *Under-20 Championship* went to Rodney Craig of Sandhurst (who had won the Public Schools title for Merchant Taylors in 1963). In a barrage he beat David Acfield of Brentwood 5-1. They were followed by Edward Ben-Nathan of Cambridge (3v), Bob Brearley (2v) and Rocco Forte of Oxford (0v).

Abroad, Michael Straus of LFC reached the last 32 in the first strongly attended *Brussels Martini*. He was notable, despite being now in early middle age, for the speed and fluency of his long compound movements en fleche. At *Amsterdam* Martin gained eighth place and Rayden eleventh. At *Padua* Leckie and Oldcorn reached the last 32. A *match against Italy* the same weekend was lost 10-6 (Cooperman 3, Oldcorn 2, Rayden 1, Leckie 0).

For the World Championships, Cooperman, Leckie and Oldcorn were joined by Rayden and Martin (in place of Hoskyns and Mike Howard, who had doubled sabre with epee at Tokyo).

## COMBINED EVENTS

The British team at the *World Youth Championships* in Rotterdam was this year very strongly backed. Charles de Beaumont was Chef de Mission, as he continued to be each year till his death. Jack Berry and Mary Glen Haig were team managers, the former to continue till 1969, the latter till 1970 (and several times thereafter). Prof. Anderson was coach, as he was to be for the next three years. Brian Wigzell went as armourer. Among those who travelled out at their own expense to assist were Mrs Holmes, Paddy Power of York Club, Prof. Boston and Prof. Moldovanyi, and Mr and Mrs Western. The championships attracted a large entry and were well organised in the spacious Energie-Halle, though the accommodation on boats moored in the harbour was unluxurious.

If the Britons were technically below the high standard prevailing in the later stages, they all fenced to the top of their ability, a few excellent results were achieved and extra experience was gained through the record number of extra-curricular matches.

In the 61-strong foil Barry Paul was ousted in round one, but Breckin and Power went through two rounds to the direct elimination of 32. Here Power had a 10–4 win over van Hollebecke (Belgium). In the last sixteen he lost a good bout to Tiu of Rumania by 10–6. Breckin, whose performance had got him a bye, fenced decisively to beat Giger (Switzerland) 10–2 and reach the last eight. He then lost to an experienced Frenchman, Dimont, 10–5, and was placed equal fifth, a very good result achieved in spite of a sprained ankle.

In the ladies' foil Sue Brick, Marilyn Holmes and Felicity Davison lacked experience of the big event and failed to survive the first round, the last-named – from Northumbria FC – only after a barrage.

The epee, with an entry of 56, was of a high standard. The finalists included Donin and Zajitski of USSR, Francesconi of Italy and Losert, the title-holder who was also World Champion (and who had to be content with fourth place). After three barrages the first place was shared between the frail-looking seventeen-year-old Jacobson (Sweden) and Brodin (France), who had won the event in 1962 at the age of fifteen.

Bourne and More, lacking experience, went out in the first round, but Rhodes, after a shaky start, got through by beating Prat (Monaco) 5–3 in a barrage. Thus encouraged, he produced decisive epee play and topped his second round pool. In the direct elimination stage he defeated Aron (USA) 10–3 to reach the last sixteen, a good performance on his first time out. He finally lost to Zajitski 10–3.

There were 41 entries for the sabre event, in which the standard was also good. The final was won undefeated by the 18-year-old Marot of Hungary. Craig gained promotion from the first round with three victories and Acfield had the remarkable experience of surviving with only one victory, while Ben-Nathan, with a similar score in his pool, lost a barrage to Gyorgy Gerevich (son of the fomer Olympic champion) 5–2. Thereafter they were somewhat outclassed.

England staged the *Quadrangular Match* in 1965, in the new AFA Headquarters. It lived up to its reputation as one of the most friendly and enjoyable fixtures in the calendar. Mainly due to the men's foil team, comprising Kirby, Power, Rentoul and Barry Paul (who lost only 4 out of 23 bouts) England were again the winners. They beat Scotland 21–15, Wales 24–11 and Ireland 30–6. Scotland took second place by defeating Wales 22–14 and Ireland 25–11 – one of their best results achieved under their genial captain, Tom Broadhurst. In the crucial match with England they started well with a 6–3 victory at ladies' foil (Alex Wilson 3, Janet Little 2, Judith Herriot 1). They also only lost at sabre 4–5 (Sandy Leckie 3, Tony Mitchell 1, John Harris 0), but went down 7–2 in the men's foil to opponents in dazzling form (Rentoul 3, Kirby 2, Power 2). Epee, however, was the Scots' consistent weakness. They lost to England 3–6, to Wales 4–5 and to Ireland 2–7. Overall, Alex Wilson only lost one fight, Leckie only two (both at foil) and Mitchell and Sandor

England team 1965. *Back:* R. Craig, A. Power, R. Bright, G. Paul, C. Layton, B. Paul, D. Eden, C, Purchase, P. Kirby, C. Rentoul. *Front:* Marilyn Holmes, Geraldine Harding, J. Pelling (Captain), W. J. Rayden, Gillian Mallard, Benny Pitman.

likewise, at sabre and foil respectively. Wales and Ireland hotly disputed their match for third place. Both teams suffered from being too small. Under the manful leadership of Bob Turner, the Welsh comprised only seven: Linda Brown, Sue Turner (the captain's sister), Angela Julian, John McGrath and Frances, Robert and Andrew Reynolds, children of Prof. Reynolds, their coach. The Irish, under the irrepressible Vincent Duffy, also had seven: Noreen Bligh, Hazel Murphy, Nuala Parker, John Bouchier-Hayes, Colm O'Brien, Ray Cooke and Jean Fouere. They finished 18–all, with Wales just ahead by 124 to 127 hits received.

Twenty-four universities were represented in the biggest *Universities Championships* yet held, competition being sharpened by the bait of selection for the World Universiade. At epee, Rhodes of Oxford was surprisingly ousted in the semi-final, as was Tony Alexander of Cambridge from the same pool, almost eliminating Oxbridge from the final. This ended with a fight for the title in which Sandor (Edinburgh) fenced with great caution and concentration to win 5–3 over a rather tired Layton. The rest were very closely bunched together, with M. Reid (Durham) doing well to emerge in third place.

In the foil final, Rentoul (Oxford), and Ben-Nathan (Cambridge) barraged for first place. Rentoul, tempted into his quarte defence, was twice caught with ripostes as well as a stop-hit, but learnt rapidly from his mistakes, and in his turn deceived Ben-Nathan's quarte parry three times and made two attacks over the stop hit to win without being hit again.

Ben-Nathan was also in the sabre final. In his first fight he found himself 4–1 down to Jake Gordon of Strathclyde, but struggled through to win that fight and then forged steadily ahead. He beat Roger Burt (London), easily and Forte (Oxford) on the last hit. Malcolm Dobson of London (and previously City of London School) drew equal third with Forte, winning a furious barrage 5–4.

# Competitions chronicle 1964–5

This year, for the first time, a men's team event was organised for which points were awarded for all semi-final and final placings. London won with 35 points and Cambridge were second over Oxford.

At the Budapest *Universiade* in August, it was a pity that Halsted, the most experienced fencer, never found his form. In the foil he could not win a bout. However, Power did very well to reach the last sixteen by beating Cavin (Switzerland) before losing to Kamuti, fourth-time winner, and to Pirone (Italy) in the repechage. Rentoul, also going well, lost at the same stage to Revenu (France) and to Drimba (Rumania). In de Beaumont's view the final was higher in standard than the World Championships.

The foil team lost to Poland 11–5, Power fencing really well to win three and Halsted and Layton contributing one each. They were eliminated when they lost to Germany 9–4, each winning one fight.

None of the ladies survived the first round, although Janet Little won three bouts in her pool. (Miranda Cobb and Alex Wilson got one each, but Gillian Mallard none.) The finalists were 1. Gapais, 2. Cymermann, 3. Schmid, 4. Galacsy, 5. Palm and 6. Level.

The ladies' team at least got plenty of practice because their pool went a complete round. They lost to Germany 15–1, to Hungary 14–2, and to Rumania 13–3.

Things seemed to be going better at epee. In the first round of the individual Halsted at last hit form and won his pool undefeated and Rhodes also qualified with three victories, though Sandor, with two victories, was eliminated. However, in the second round Halsted and Rhodes each scored only two victories. The team event was disappointing. The British should have survived a pool with Holland, Czechoslovakia and USSR. After a lethargic start, they beat Holland 9–7, Sandor fencing well to win three bouts and Green, Halsted and Rhodes two each. But against Czechoslovakia, who were really a team of foilists, they lost 8–7. Sandor again won three bouts, Green two and Halsted and Rhodes one each. At 7–6 down they had an advantage of five hits, but Halsted could not win the last bout. Against the Russians Layton came in for Halsted, but they lost 12–4 (Layton winning two and Rhodes and Sandor one each).

Also in August, a two-a-side four-weapon *match against Belgium* was held at Crystal Palace. Britain won 11–5 (Bewley-Cathie 2, Davies 1, Jay 2, Kirby 1, Pelling 1, Hoskyns 0, Cooperman 2, Leckie 2).

The *Public Schools Championships*, held at Sarah Siddons School, Paddington, in April, attracted a record entry of 615 – 118 up on 1964, so the length of the events was particularly gruelling, though bouts were only for four hits as usual. Coached by Prof. Steve Boston, Brentwood confirmed the position of dominance from which they were never long to be dislodged in the period covered by this book. They had first won the overall Graham-Bartlett Cup in 1962, when they also first took a title. (Chris Green won both foil and epee.)

They had retained the Cup ever since and now made a clean sweep of the first places, junior and senior.

After five rounds, Acfield was the undisputed winner of the foil (the final being electric for the first time); but only after being 3–1 down to Floyer (runner-up) and 2–0 to Russell (5th), both also from Brentwood. Cohen (Downside) unexpectely did not improve on his fourth place of the previous year. The junior foil title went to Mark West, who had only recently recovered from polio, but whose patience made up for his lack of aggression.

The sabre was totally dominated by Acfield, showing far greater maturity and versatility than the other finalists. He was only hit four times in the final, three of these being from his school-mate David Royall, whom he beat at assault point with a direct fleche on his advance. If he had appeared hesitant in this early fight, he made no mistakes when confronted by the runner-up, Francis Coulson of Westminster, likewise three wins up at this stage. He produced a parry riposte, a broken-time attack, a stop-hit and a direct fleche on Coulson's preparation, and that was 4–0.

There was also a record entry for the *World Championships* in Paris; 335 fencers from 28 countries. Repechage was added to the direct elimination stage, comprising, as before, the last 32 fencers. In this stage, fights were of three bouts, each of five hits, instead of eight or ten hit bouts, with a deciding bout if required, as previously. Moreover, the final was of six instead of four fencers.

Charles de Beaumont was overall Captain, as ever. Prof. Anderson was also with the team, as he was regularly to be till his retirement at the end of 1979; and there was the much appreciated support of a number of British fencers. If the results both at foil and sabre were somewhat disappointing, the day was saved by the epeeists, who put up a marvellous performance in particularly difficult conditions.

The men's foil started well, everyone except Power surviving the first round and Kirby showing excellent form in beating such eminent foilists as Rodocanachi (France) and Geresheim (W. Germany). He and Leckie did not survive the second round, however. In the direct elimination Hoskyns beat Lisewski, an awkward Pole, in three bouts, but lost to Revenu (France) in the next round. He then had to fence Lisewski again in the repechage and lost this time by the odd hit in the third bout. Meanwhile Jay had lost his first match by one hit to Czipler (Rumania), but bounced back to beat Shimizu (Japan) and revenge himself on Czipler before being eliminated by Rodocanachi in the penultimate repechage round. It was one of the disadvantages of the repechage system, as it then operated, that a fencer was liable to meet the same opponent at every other fight.

In the team event Britain drew Poland and Denmark, being seeded sixth of the fourteen teams on the results of the individual. Denmark was comfortably beaten 11–5, Hoskyns being undefeated, Leckie winning three and Jay and

Power two apiece. This put the team in the last eight, where it lost disppointingly 9–5 to Poland (who were to take second place), Hoskyns winning three, Leckie and Power one each and Jay surprisingly none. There was still a chance of fifth or sixth place, but the team was eliminated by Japan 9–5. Kirby, who came in for Jay, won two and Hoskyns, Leckie and Power only one each. This meant a place of seventh equal.

All the ladies started well, but only Shirley Netherway (now Mrs Parker) could gain promotion from the second round. In the direct elimination she lost to Samusenko (USSR, World Champion in 1966) and was eliminated in the repechage by Becker of Germany, to whom she lost in three bouts. In the team event the ladies were drawn with Russia, Poland and Ireland. They kept abreast with Poland for three-quarters of the match. Eve Davies, Jeanette Bailey and Janet Cathie each won two bouts but Shirley Parker struck a bad patch and got only one. Nevertheless, at the last bout, with the score 7–8 against them, they were sufficiently ahead on hits to win if they could get to 8–all. However, Janet Cathie could not quite cope with the forceful Cymermann, who was undefeated, and they lost 9–7, still with the advantage of 44–45 hits. They then had to meet the might of Russia, the ultimate winners, and were eliminated 9–2, only Eve Davies and Janet Cathie scoring.

So to the epee. In the individual, all five survived the first round, Halsted, the new colour, topping his pool. Hoskyns, Pelling and Halsted gained promotion from the second round, but Jacobs went down by two hits in a pool containing three of the eventual finalists and Jay could not yet find his touch.

At the direct elimination stage Pelling lost to Paolucci, the tall Italian, by the odd hit in three bouts and Halsted lost to the redoubtable Kostava (USSR). In the repechage Pelling went out to Kriss (USSR), the Olympic champion, and Halsted was eliminated by the experienced Bourquard (France), albeit in three bouts. Kriss was himself eliminated by Paolucci.

Hoskyns continued serenely on his way. Clear wins over Dreyfus (France) 5–1, 5–3, Baranyi (Hungary) 5–3, 5–4 and Khabarov (USSR), the 1959 World Champion, 5–3, 5–4, secured his place undefeated in the final pool of six. The others undefeated were Nemere (Hungary) Kostova and Brodin (France). They were joined by Breda und Paolucci from the repechage.

The final was easily the best and most exciting of these Championships. Bill Hoskyns was once again in superb form and it was soon apparent that the title lay between him and Zoltan Nemere, who won the London Martini in 1964, and who was fencing with care and aggression. Hoskyns had an early defeat by Brodin, but gained a notable 5–2 victory over Nemere himself, during which he executed a magnificent second counter-riposte by disengagement all in the course of a fleche attack. He went on to beat Breda and Paolucci.

At the last round there was the probability of a quadruple barrage if Breda beat Nemere or a win outright for Hoskyns if he beat Kostava. However, neither happened. Kostava produced five electrifying fleche attacks into

Hoskyns' preparations to beat him 5–1. According to Hoskyns' own account he was unable to find an answer to the greater mobility and length of fleche of the Russian. Nemere made no mistake and by defeating Breda 5–3 ran out a worthy winner. Hoskyns had an advantage of no less than six hits over Kostava for second place and Brodin was fourth two further hits behind. With Kostava, Hoskyns was the only survivor of the Olympic final of the previous year. Silver Medallist then, he showed a rare consistency in gaining second place again.

The epee team event began none too auspiciously. Hoskyns appeared that morning with a broken rib, the result of one of Kostava's violent fleche attacks the previous night, which made it difficult for him to parry quarte. He had to be rested all that day so that he could have intensive treatment. A compensating factor was the way the team knit together in an unprecedented way, until it was almost unstoppable.

Thanks to the good results in the individual, they were seeded fifth of the nineteen countries entered and found themselves in a pool with Italy, Denmark and Finland. They started with Finland and had little difficulty in disposing of them 9–5, Jacobs winning all four fights, Pelling and Halsted taking two each and Jay, who was only gradually getting into rhythm, winning one. They then met Denmark and had a still more decisive victory 8–3 to gain promotion. Here Pelling won three, Jay and Jacobs two each and Halsted one. This good performance earned the team a rest that afternoon, as they had a bye through the next round to the last eight.

Unluckily, that evening Pelling went down with a severe attack of enteritis. So when the direct elimination started next day the team found itself with only four men available, amongst whom Hoskyns was so disabled by his injury that he could not parry and so had to restrict himself to fleches. In the quarter-finals they met the Hungarians, the reigning Olympic Champions, with a team containing both Nemere, the new individual Champion, and Kulcsar, hero of the team event in Tokyo.

Undaunted, the team fenced with such spirit as to be leading 7–5 when Jay met Nagy (who had beaten him in the final bout of the Martini earlier in the year). Cautious fencing brought them to 3–all when a minute was called. With only seconds to go, Jay scored with a desperate fleche at wrist. This was the sort of situation which he relished. He started running back with loud shouts and threats to demoralise his opponent and waste precious seconds and, as Nagy was pursuing him also with loud shouts, the president never heard the time-keeper call halt (no bell was provided) and awarded Nagy an equalising hit which arrived well thereafter. The mistake was pointed out to him and supported by the timekeeper, who averred that no hit was registered until well after he had called 'Halt', and the president then annulled the hit, thus giving Jay the victory. The Hungarian, Sakovits, would have none of this and protested that the president only could decide whether a hit arrived before or after the halt. The president said frankly that as he never heard the 'Halt' he had no opinion at all. The Directoire Technique decided that as it was the timekeeper's 'Halt' which stopped the bout the hit should be annulled.

The Hungarians then demanded a jury d'appel. De Beaumont, as team captain, pointed out that in any case the hit could not be awarded because it was doubtful, so that all the president could do would be to put the fencers on guard again. This was impossible because there was no doubt that time had run out. The only possible result was that Jay had won the bout. This view prevailed by a unanimous vote, only Russia abstaining.

All this took a considerable time and certainly worried their opponents more than the British. On the resumption, Hoskyns, impeded by his injury from executing other movements, simply produced five sizzling fleche attacks in a row and the match was won 9–5. Jacobs did outstandingly, winning two out of three bouts. Jay and Hoskyns each won three and Halsted one.

In the semi-finals the team had to meet the formidable Russians, who were hot favourites for the title and who had just had an easy 8–1 win over Sweden. This was an epic match. The British established a lead in the first two rounds which they never lost. Jay and Hoskyns, in superb form, won three victories each; both Jacobs and Halsted defeated Kriss, the reigning Olympic Gold Medallist; Jacobs also beat Kostava, the reigning Olympic Bronze Medallist – in what he later rated as the best fight of his life, ending with a stop-hit on the knuckles as Kostava was in mid-air, fleching. In the light of subsequent events it is interesting to note that the most formidable of the Russians in this match was a comparative newcomer, Nikanchikov.

Although it was well after lunch-time, a large crowd followed the match, among whom not the least fervent supporters of the British were the French team, who were as relieved as they were astonished by the 9–5 victory over their most feared opponents. They had themselves defeated Switzerland 8–7 and W. Germany by 58 to 62 hits at 8–all.

After their tremendous efforts the British could not hold the French in the final in front of a home crowd. Dreyfus, in superb form, was undefeated. Jay and Jacobs fenced extremely well to score two wins each, while the injured Hoskyns scored one, to leave the final score at 9–5.

So the epeeists regained the Silver Medal position they had gained at the Rome Olympics in 1960. With their fourth place at Melbourne in 1956, third place in Paris in 1957 and second place in the 1960 Rome Olympics, it added up to a distinguished record, largely due to the performance of Jay and Hoskyns.

The sabreurs gave a better showing than for some time but still some way behind world class. Oldcorn and Rayden went out in the first round but Martin, the new colour, who showed particular promise, as well as Cooperman and Leckie, survived.

Only Leckie reached the direct elimination, where he had a hard draw. He lost to Calarese, the Italian Champion, and then went down in the repechage to Mavlikhanov, an Olympic medallist. The event was won by Pawlowski, who repeated the triumph he had previously won in the same hall in 1957.

The sabre team lost disappointingly to Germany 11–5, Richard Oldcorn winning three but Cooperman and Leckie only one each and Martin none. To go up they then had to beat USSR, the eventual winners. They lost 9–5, Oldcorn again contributing three excellent victories and Martin the other two.

The Coupe des Nations was won by the USSR, with France second, Hungary third, Poland fourth, Britain and Rumania equal fifth and Italy seventh.

## 1965–6

### MEN'S FOIL

The *Team Championship* had an unexampled 47 entries. The London Fencing Club only emerged from the quarter-finals after a win on hits over Latista (conspicuous in their yellow tracksuits at a time when tracksuits were something of a novelty in the fencing world). After another tight struggle in the semi-final, with London University, in the final they could not match the youth and enthusiasm of Salle Paul, who had beaten Thames 9–2 in the semi-final. The 18-year-old Ian Single, in the team for the first time, rose to the occasion flamboyantly, for instance beating Halsted from 4–1 down. Cool and accurate, Graham Paul confirmed his quality, his improved footwork enabling him to be more relaxed and less reliant on fleches. The Italian Roberto Zampini was making his last appearance at the end of a period of residence. Jay contributed ebullience as well as experience to the 9–1 victory. Peter Kirby got the sole win for the LFC team, which also included Leckie.

The decisive encounter in the *Junior Championship* was between the short and slight Vincent Bonfil and the larger, more solidly built Ian Single, both seen as future team possibles. Bonfil won 5–2, scoring twice with good attacks on the blade, in a fight in which no fewer than eighteen off-target hits had been registered by 2–all. A pupil of Prof. Bill Harmer-Brown at London University and at Thames Club, Bonfil clinched his victory when Single lost a scrappy fight 2–5 to Gordon Wiles of Bedford. He ended with a clean slate when, on assault point, he beat Edward Ben-Nathan (5th, 1v), who was now a club-mate of Bonfil's at London University and Thames – a slight but stylish and intelligent fencer, who, as a pupil of Prof. Behmber at St Paul's, had been Public Schools Champion at both foil and sabre in 1964. There were three non-London fencers in the final: Wiles, who was two hits behind Single; Derek Russell of Newcastle University but also of Salle Boston (4th, 3v); and Bob Richardson of Glasgow (6th, 0v). The semi-finals ousted Barry Paul.

# Competitions chronicle 1965–6

On the Saturday of the Coronation Cup, a four-a-side match against Italy was held (but billed as '*London v. Rome*', thus not entitling participants to the Tudor Rose awarded for full internationals). The team possibles Paul and Breckin were chosen along with Jay and Hoskyns. The Italians also fielded their two best, plus two less experienced. The score reached 2–all, 4–all and then 6–all. In the last round, in spite of Jay's precise yet lightning parries, Granieri got home 5–2. Paul next let off half a dozen of his very fast and difficult-to-see-coming fleche attacks to beat La Ragione, the Italian champion, 5–3 and so levelled to 7–all. Breckin then lost to Celentano; but Hoskyns beat Del Francia to take the match by seven hits, the two British possibles having each two wins like their seniors.

Granieri took the *Coronation Cup*, but Leckie was second and only Vaselli of the other Italians was ahead of Hoskyns, Jay and Paul.

Twelve pools opened the *Championship*. Shewring and Robin Humphreys were amongst those who did well in the early rounds. In the quarter-finals Rentoul, Cohen and Raymond Paul were noteworthy eliminations. Kirby and Single went out in one semi-final, and in the other Cawthorne (who had ceased training seriously after the death of Prof. Froeschlen) and Eden (who lost the barrage to a stabler Peters in spite of a dogged recovery from 0–4).

A long final began with Graham Paul's youthful forcefulness and mobility giving him victory over his father René. He continued to fence positively to take three more, including one against Jay, but lost to a more compact and accurate Breckin. Leckie had a lucky hit on the mask to win against Breckin and he followed this with two more victories before he lapsed completely against Hoskyns. Graham Paul, despite the weight of encouragement from Salle Paul, then lost to Leckie, and they both now had four apiece.

Hoskyns had lost his first fight to Ben-Nathan, but recovered to take three quick victories before he met Graham Paul, against whom he could only salvage one hit. Jay defeated René Paul, and then lost two rather torpid bouts before recovering to beat Ben-Nathan. Against Leckie he reached 4–all just as six minutes was called and then obtained victory with a characteristic riposte. René Paul yielded a fifth win to a punishingly accurate Leckie, and a barrage with Graham Paul ensued after Hoskyns was prevented from making it triple by a now decidedly alert Jay. Leckie took the first three hits, but Paul levelled the score. His next hit was something of a prod, but having scented victory and with the Salle Paul pack roaring encouragement, nothing could stop his final attack. Still barely nineteen, he thus won the National title for Salle Paul and his master Prof. Vic Lagnado, a very popular result. Though less noisily acclaimed, the effective fencing of two pupils of Prof. Harmer-Brown was additional proof that the gap between the generations had been closed. Ben-Nathan was fourth (two hits ahead of Jay) and Breckin (3v) sixth, uttering squeaky shouts as he landed his hits. The 44-year-old René Paul was seventh with two wins and Peters brought up the rear with one.

Breckin overtook Paul in the *Under-20 Championship*, with Bonfil in third place. He also won the *Universities Championship* and was third in the *Universities Tournament* in Holland. At *Leamington* the Scots scored a great success. Four of them reached the last sixteen. Here Broadhurst lost 5–8 to Jacobs and Wilson by one hit after a long fight with Rosner of W. Germany, but Sandor and Rorke beat other Germans and in the last eight Sandor successively beat Eden and René Paul (both 7–6), while Rorke had a walk-over against Kirby and beat Rosner 7–6. Sandor won the all-Scottish final bout. Rorke, however, was the winner both at *Inverclyde* and in the *Scottish Championship*. Bob Wilson was the runner-up in each case.

Abroad, Hoskyns reached the quarter-finals of the Paris *Martini*, being eliminated 10–2 by Magnan of France. Jay was fifth in the *Rommel*. Leckie won the Toronto Exhibition Tournament and Graham Paul was second.

Graham Paul and Breckin joined the team for the World Championships, alongside Hoskyns, Leckie and René Paul.

*LADIES' FOIL*

Janet Cathie managed to win the *Desprez Cup*, although still recovering from an operation, after a barrage with Joyce Pearce. It was a good day for Poly, for besides the winner they claimed third, fourth and fifth places in the persons of Shirley Parker, Jeanette Bailey and Eve Davies. Janet Cathie also won the invitation *Silver Jubilee Bowl*, ahead of Eve Davies and Joyce Pearce.

In the *Championship*, Shirley Parker was the winner, recapturing from Janet Cathie the cup she had won in 1964. The lively, emotional Julia Davis (a PE teacher) was again third, but fourth was a Scottish newcomer, Judith Herriot (winner of the *Inverclyde Tournament*), while fifth was the spirited Margaret Paul of Poly (no relation of Leon Paul). Joyce Pearce was sixth.

Taking advantage of the fact that four Italians had entered for the de Beaumont Cup, the LAFU staged an *Anglo-Italian* match. Those with long memories were delighted that Maestro Athos Perone, who had taught fencing under Professor Bertrand at Tenterden Street before the Second World War, should be accompanying them. Shirley Parker, who lost only to Lorenzoni, was the most attractive fencer to watch. Janet Cathie, just married to the Olympic oarsman Hugh Wardell-Yerburgh, also won three fights and fenced with determination and excellent timing. Both Julia Davis and Alex Wilson fenced aggressively, if lacking in adaptability. The score level-pegged until the Italians produced reserves of skill and energy at the end to win 10–6.

There were thirteen foreigners and 64 British in the *de Beaumont Cup*. Seven British and nine foreigners went into the direct elimination stage. Only one of the British girls was victorious in the first series of matches, but things went better in the repechage. Janet Little, the *Scottish* Champion, did especially well to beat Lorenzoni, but it was Shirley Parker by defeating Tarzoni (Italy), who went through to the final with Janet W-Y and Flesch (Luxembourg), Gapais (France), Mees (W. Germany) and the voluble Masciotta (Italy) – who won. Shirley Parker could not repeat the fine accuracy and speed of the previous match and ended sixth. Janet W-Y fought, as always, with determination, but, with only two victories, was placed fourth.

Jeanette Bailey, Julia Davis, Jennifer Dorling and Janet W-Y won the *Team Championship* for Poly for the seventh time (over Pauleons) by 9–5. Poly also won the team event at *Leamington* for a record sixteenth time.

The *Junior Championship* brought success to the Celtic fringe. It was won by Angela Julian, a pupil of Prof. Reynolds and runner-up the year before, while Judith Herriot of Glasgow FC was fourth. Sue Brick (Pauleons) was second, as she also was in the Under-20 Championship. Louise Cuppage (Poly) was third, Sheila Ward (Pearson) fifth and Mary Hawdon (Halifax) sixth.

The *Under-20 Championship* was won by Anna Savva (Tottenham Technical College), a fiery fencer, who beat the holder, Marilyn Holmes (Manchester GS), in a barrage, after losing to the sixteen-year-old Clare Henley (taught by Steve Seager at Southside FC), still at Croydon High School but already stylish and precociously launching herself on a distinguished career. She came third (and was again third in the *Schoolgirls Championship*). The event was also notable for three fourteen-year-olds: Georgina Netherwood of York, who was sixth, and Susan Green and Andrea Hill of Flixton GS, Manchester, who reached the semi-finals, the latter being the *Junior Schoolgirls* Champion and both pupils of the able and hard-working Les Jones. Marilyn Holmes had her triumph for Ashton when she won the invitation *Felix Cup* (ahead of Judith Herriott and Georgina Netherwood).

The *Universities Championship* was won by Elspeth Earle of London, a pupil of Prof. Harmer-Brown who used her intelligence to good effect.

Abroad, the controlled Mildred Durne (winner at *Ashton*) came third at *Melun* and Sheila Ward was sixth in *Brussels*. Jeanette Bailey, who had one of the fastest ripostes known, reached the quarter-finals at *Como*. She went on to an outstanding equal third place in the *Paris Jeanty*, where Eve Davies was ninth and Julia Davis thirteenth. In the lesser event at *Dieppe* Gerry Harding was second and Clare Henley fifth. In August Janet W-Y won the *Toronto Exhibition Tournament* and Julia Davis came tenth. In the Turin *Coupe d'Europe* for champion clubs, Thames reached the last eight. In the *Amsterdam Inter-Cities Tournament* the London team comprising Eileen Jones (winner at *Leicester*), Marilyn Holmes, Pam Patient and Alex Wilson came a commendable second.

The same team was selected for the World Championships as the previous year, less Theresa Offredy.

## EPEE

This year junior and senior ends of the spectrum almost joined up. Bourne won the *Public Schools* and was second to Graham Paul – long to be his bogeyman – in the *Under-20 Championship*, followed by Russell, a fast, aggressive fencer. Rhodes, who won the *Universities Championship*, was another epeeist who had already won his seniority and was therefore ineligible for the *Junior Championship*, which was captured by a senior of a different kind, Sgt Mick Finnis, who was an Olympic Pentathlete, current *Services* Champion and an experienced epeeist. A left-hander with a determined fleche attack and good judgement of distance, he asserted his superiority throughout the competition.

The next three fencers each had seven victories. Second place went to Bob Wilson from Glasgow, an ebullient fencer with a rugby player's physique, by three hits over A. H. Jones from Ruislip FC. Barry More, still only seventeen and at Wandsworth School, looked a likely winner for three-quarters of the pool, but tired towards the end and had to be content with fourth place. The other places were as follows: 5. Payne (Boston) 6/10; 6. Johnson (St Dunstan's) 6/17; 7. Robert Reynolds (Reynolds) 5v; 8. Tomlinson (Thames) 4/9/39; 9. Ian Single (Paul) 4/9/38; 10. Eric Wilson (Behmber) 4/11; 11. David Johnson (Reading Univ.) 4/14; 12. Barry Lillywhite (Sandhurst) 2v.

Bob Wilson was the winner at *Inverclyde*, ahead of Mike Steele of London University. His fellow Scot, Joe Rorke, did very well at *Leamington*, successively beating Purchase, Rosner of W. Germany and (by 7–5) Jacobs, against whose fleches his timing was brilliant. In the final his form was affected by having just fenced in the foil final, and he lost to Steve Netburn. The team event was won for the ninth successive time by Grosvenor. Pelling had been in the team each time, usually accompanied by Jacobs, Glasswell and often by Giles, Romp or Pomeroy, as he was in the national Team Championship.

It was Netburn who led the final of the *Martini Qualifying* competition, a poule unique of sixteen. A much-liked American at Southampton University, he commuted to the LFC, where he was taught by Prof. Imregi. Graham Paul was second, followed by Glasswell, Bourne, Single, Dan Nathanson (Cambridge Univ.), Rorke, Roberts, Breckin, Romp, Giles, Rhodes and Wilson.

For the *Martini* itself there was a record foreign entry of 68 from eleven countries, including no less than 28 from W. Germany. The twelve first round pools started at a grisly 8.30 a.m., normal abroad but in Britain traditional only in this event. Many well-known epeeists failed at this first test, including the Polish Gonsior and the French Boissier, Bourquard and Boulot (their Champion). The first round of direct elimination also produced some surprising results. The top seed, Barburski of Poland, was beaten 8–4 by Tapprogge, an unknown German. At the other end of the match plan, Saccaro, the eminent Italian champion who had easily topped his pool, went out 8–1 to Jung of Germany, who had only survived his pool after a barrage. Both the remaining French epeeists, from an entry of eleven, were defeated, and of the five British fencers who had reached this stage only Jacobs and Hoskyns reached the last sixteen, which included eight Germans, and here Tapprogge beat Jacobs 8–5 and Lagerwall of Sweden beat Hoskyns 8–6.

There were still five Germans in the final of eight; and having previously eliminated Lagerwall and Engdahl of Sweden, Jung and Kilbert met in an all-German fight for first place. Jung won decisively, 8–4.

On the Sunday there were the customary *post-Martini matches*, on this occasion between the Swedes, the Germans, the British and a composite team of two Americans, Godhelp of Holland and some British fencers. There was even a junior practice pool. The Swedes proved impressive, beating a British team composed of Glasswell, Jacobs, Pelling and Higginson by 13–3, only the last three scoring. They then beat the Mixed Team by a similar score and the German team 9–7. The British team in turn lost to the Germans 9–7, Purchase coming in for Pelling and scoring three good victories. Finally the Mixed Team beat the Germans by the same score. There were no other international matches this season.

The *Miller-Hallett* in February had an entry of 68 and a hotly-contested final of twelve of high standard. At the three-quarters stage Pelling led the field, closely followed by Hoskyns, with Glasswell and Jacobs coming up fast. Meanwhile Netburn lost his first three bouts, found a fault in his epee, changed it for a more reliable instrument and proceeded to beat Hoskyns 5–3 and thereafter went from strength to strength. Eventually Hoskyns, rather less decisive than usual, missed the chance of an all-out victory when he lost his last bout to Glasswell and found himself with eight victories in a barrage with Netburn. Probably short of practice, he proved vulnerable to aggressive attacks, with which he usually coped so well but which over the coming years a number of opponents were to find a means of penetrating his mastery. Netburn won 5–2, scoring with attacks on preparation and counter-sixteripostes of the best quality.

Glasswell (7v) earned his third place with greater decision and control than during the previous two seasons. Pelling (6v; 4th) lost concentration in the later stages, while Jacobs, three hits behind, could not overcome his shaky start. In sixth place and also with six wins was Ralph Johnson of St Dunstan's and Salle Boston, who fenced consistently well throughout the competition and thus became a senior epeeist while still at school. There followed: 7. Higginson 6v; 8. David Shapland (London Univ.) 5v; 9. Reynolds 4v; 10. Purchase 4v; 11. Parham 2v; 12. Mike Steele 2v.

The *Championship* produced a sensational result. The winner was Teddy Bourne, aged seventeen. The nearest comparable win of either the Championship or the Miller-Hallett was Allan Jay's Championship win at the age of 21 in 1952, and there is all the difference in the world between seventeen and

21. The achievement was underlined by Bourne's clear lead of two wins and by the presence of all the previous year's World Championship Silver Medallists except Jay and Halsted. As if Bourne's record was not enough, Graham Paul celebrated his nineteenth birthday by following up his first place in the Foil Championship three weeks earlier with a second place at epee.

Third place went to the steadily improving Purchase, whose success showed what could be done by diligent application and eagerness to take every opportunity to fence in London and abroad. Hoskyns took fourth place by two hits scored over Pelling, the holder, who had a disastrous start. Mike Howard, making a reappearance on the epee scene, and short of practice, was sixth. The other results in the final of sixteen were: 7. Jacobs (Thames) 9v; 8. Fairhall (Boston) 8/15; 9. Higginson (LFC) 8/20; 10. Glasswell (Thames) 6/13; 11. Bob Turner (Reynolds) 6/15; 12. W. Greaves (Thames and USA) 6/17; 13. Steele (London Univ.) 6/20; 14. Knott (Poly) 3v; 15. Julian Gray (ex-Cambridge Univ.) 2v; 16. John McGrath (Reynolds) 1v. Eddie Knott was considerably older than almost anybody else in the competition – a selector collecting his data at first hand.

In the semi-finals of the *Team Championship* Salle Paul beat Salle Boston 9–2, and LFC beat Grosvenor 9–4. The final match was an entertaining spectacle between closely matched teams. The holders, Salle Paul, led by Allan Jay, who had not lost a bout in the competition up to that point, were the more homogenous team. Graham Paul and Ian Single joined their captain in getting two victories apiece, while René Paul brought up the rear with one victory – one better than his opposite number, Nigel Creagh-Snell.

However, the LFC had the advantage of the thoughtful fencing of Netburn and the return to the scene of Ian Spofforth, both of whom were undefeated, while Leckie, although he could only contribute one victory, ran his first three bouts to 4–all, and in his last clinched victory by beating René Paul 5–0. LFC thus regained the Shield they won in 1964.

There was an outstanding tally of results abroad. In October Jacobs, with Ben-Nathan as the Under-20 foilist, reached the last eight of the tandem event in *Chaux des Fonds*. At *Nancy* Steve Higginson came second. At *Louviers* Jacobs was the winner. Pelling reached the last eight in *Lyons*. In *Beirut* he also came eighth and fourth in two events. Jacobs excelled again by coming third in the *Picon* and in the *Monal* reaching the last eight after beating Allemand of France and Romza of Germany in successive stages of this wholly direct elimination event. He lost to Baranyi, runner-up to Kulcsar, and so was classified sixth.

In February a British team comprising Hoskyns, Pelling, Glasswell, Higginson and Purchase took part in the *Coppa Ferrania*, an account of which provides a sample view of the many trips abroad by British fencers in these years. Stretching the taxpayer's contribution as far as possible, the five chose three different routes and suffered missed trains, unintended de luxe hotels

C. Purchase, S. Higginson, H. W. Hoskyns, J. Glasswell, J. Pelling.

and undelivered telegrams before they managed to rendezvous half an hour before the event. From its start on ten raised pistes to its conclusion in the handing out of numerous cameras as prizes, this was admirably organised by the famous Maestro Mangiarotti and his son Eduardo.

In the first round of 31 teams they beat their opponents 9–0 without Hoskyns and earned a bye to the third round, where they beat the Carabinieri 8–3, Glasswell resting this time. Next morning they got an early lead over Vercelli (who included Tassinari and Cipriani) and finished them off 9–1, only Glasswell dropping a fight (and Purchase sitting out). The other foreign teams were eliminated at this stage.

So to the final of three teams beneath the chandeliers of the Societa Giardino. Against Cassa, led by Saccaro, the British were always in the lead and won 9–5 (Pelling 4–0; Hoskyns 2–1; Purchase 2–2; Glasswell 1–2). They then met the holders, Giardino, who had beaten Cassa 10–6. The first round was level, Glasswell lost to Breda, Hoskyns beat Pellegrino, Higginson beat Albanese 5–3 after being led 3–0 – seven of the eight hits being on the wrist – and Pelling lost to a very promising Francesconi. The second round was disastrous, Glasswell, Higginson and Hoskyns losing in turn to Pellegrino, Breda and Francesconi. At 5–2 down things looked bad, but Pelling started rescue operations by beating Albanese. Higginson then beat Pellegrino, Glasswell had a fine 5–1 victory over Francesconi and Pelling, in tremendous form, overcame Breda, who up till then was looking unbeatable. This put the British in the lead at 6–5. But Hoskyns now slipped up and lost to Albanese after leading 3–0. In the last round, Higginson beat Francesconi and Pelling made it 8–6 by beating Pellegrino. Glasswell after being 4–0 down to Albanese, nearly pulled it off but lost 5–4. Hoskyns then went on against Breda thinking that four hits would give them victory. So at 4–3 down and one minute to go he played out time. Only afterwards did he discover that the British had won before the fight started.

Pelling, vulnerable to depression in individual events, gained and transmitted confidence in team events such as this, in which his fencing was of the highest class. Glasswell, though luck sometimes tended to go against him for the very reason that he felt it was doing so, got some notable wins. Higginson had an extremely good weekend, losing only one fight. Many of his hits were all the more spectacular because his style was so very keen and foil-like. Purchase was only in his second competition abroad, but looked good, especially beating Saccaro. As for Hoskyns, he found it a pleasant change to be carried by the rest of the team (i.e. he won seven and lost four fights).

The same weekend Jacobs topped up an outstanding foreign season when he came sixth in the *New York Athletic Club Tournament*. In March Mike Steele of Thames was eighth at *Huy*. At *Poitiers* Higginson did extremely well to come sixth. In May he was seventh in the *Coupe des Trentes*. Finally, Pelling came fourth at the *Toronto Exhibition Tournament*.

Jay having temporarily retired from the team and Halsted having been out of fencing altogether with jaundice since January, there were two vacancies in the team, which went to Higginson and Purchase.


## SABRE

At the junior end of the spectrum, Prof. Boston's pupils carried all before them. Brian Fisher of St Paul's won the *Public Schools Championship*. The eighteen-year-old 5ft 9ins David Acfield, now at Cambridge (where Prof.

# Competitions chronicle 1965–6

Harmer-Brown was master), won both the *Universities* and the *Under-20 Championships*. In the *Junior Championship* Boston made a clean sweep of the top three places, with Richard Ford, Bob Barsby and Acfield – followed by Dennis Hunt of Bristol, the left-handed Peter Lennon of the Army and Brearley of Boston.

Under-20 runner-up (after a barrage), and one place better than the previous year, was Ben-Nathan (still at Cambridge). Another pupil of Bill Harmer-Brown, Mike Breckin, showed his versatility by taking third place, while Richard Cohen of Downside opened a notable sabre career in fourth place, ahead of Duncan Wherrett of Thames and Latista and Antony Preiskel.

The *Cole Cup* was won a record fourth time by Cooperman, with excellent sense of timing and one deadly hit, particularly against right-handers – a stop cut to the outside of the arm – delivered with great accuracy, always as a counter-attack. Oldcorn was second, as he had been the year before. Hoskyns was third. Oldcorn did well to come second again on a barrage in the *Championship* (after an indifferent semi-final). The established leaders here were somewhat lack-lustre. Cooperman, Leckie and Martin were third, fourth and fifth, separated on hits. Rayden, looking slower and less fit than usual, was sixth (3v). Bob Wilson, having a very good season as a three-weapon man, was seventh (2v). Craig (1v, 8th) had good patches but lacked consistency. Perhaps the general lack of speed and aggression was partly due to the magic skill with which the winner was accustomed to beguile his opponents into fencing at a tempo to suit himself. For the Champion was none other than the ubiquitous Bill Hoskyns, chalking up another victory for Yeovil FC and his master, Prof. John Sanders. He had fenced himself in during the earlier rounds and was much the steadiest finalist. His strengths at sabre were his excellent hand and superb sense of timing, particularly with counter stop-hits. His legs were a weakness and his fleche virtually non-existent at sabre. Oldcorn matched him hit for hit to four–all in the barrage, but it was Hoskyns who got the last one. He was thus only the second fencer ever to be British Champion at all three weapons (Edgar Seligman won the foil in 1906 and 1907, the epee in 1904 and 1906 and the sabre in 1923 and 1924).

Notable among those eliminated in the semi-final were Hunt, Eden, Acfield and Straus. Although the entry of about forty was up on the previous few years, the number of spectators at the final was low.

The *Corble Cup* came close to a repeat performance of the previous year. Borucki was again first and Leckie second. Third place went to Rayden, not Oldcorn this time, while Cooperman moved up one to fourth. Gral and Luxardo were fifth and sixth.

In the provinces Gordon Wiles put victories at *Ashton* and *Inverclyde* towards the unrivalled 26 major provincial wins he was to gain by 1979; while Oldcorn showed he *could* come first by wins at *Nottingham* and *Leamington* (ahead of Rabe of W. Germany in the last).

For the third year running, LFC won the *Team Championship*. Leckie, Rayden, Oldcorn and Martin beat Salle Paul 9–7.

Abroad, Leckie, Craig, Rayden and Wilson lost a *match against W. Germany* 9–7 at Kaub. Rayden reached the last eight at *Duren*. A British team again lost a *match against W. Germany* by 9–7 in *Munich*, but Leckie did well to gain sixth place in the individual event. Oldcorn, Rayden, Craig and Martin drew a *match against Padua* (61–61 hits), Oldcorn saving defeat by winning his last two fights 5–0, 5–0. Finally, in the French provincial event at *Dieppe* Roger Burt was second and Brian Waddelow of Wandsworth School was in the semi-final.

The World Championship team was the same as the previous year: Cooperman, Leckie, Oldcorn, Rayden and Martin.

## COMBINED EVENTS

The *Oxford and Cambridge* match is always difficult to predict. Even the combined presence of Jay and Hoskyns at Oxford in the early fifties was not enough always to ensure victory. This year Cambridge looked far the stronger team, but they were beaten by Oxford at Hurlingham in February by 15–12. Oxford began well by winning the foil 6–3 against a team including Ben-Nathan and Acfield. Forte was undefeated, using his fleches only where they worked. Backing him were the stylish Reuben Lynn, a promising Hong Kong Chinese who had been coached there by Christopher Grose-Hodge before going to Sutton Valence School, and Bernard Rix, a Pauline, who made up for his immobility with laser-like ripostes. They won the epee 7–2, Rhodes being undefeated, and Delvaque and Lynn each winning two fights. Alexander and Roberts got Cambridge their two victories, but their captain Dan Nathanson was off-form.

The task of winning the sabre 9–0 not surprisingly proved too much for Cambridge, though they won 7–2, Ben-Nathan being undefeated and Acfield and Cohen winning two each. Dick Eiser and Forte scored Oxford's wins.

There was a total entry of one hundred for the *Liverpool Open Foil*, well stage-managed by Derek Master. The ladies final was exciting and technically good. It produced a five-way barrage. Janet Varley (Hydra, Manchester) won; second was Gerry Harding (Birmingham Sch. of Arms) and third Mrs Hazel Rogerson (Hydra). Dr Dorothy Knowles, several times winner of the cup, started well in the final and might have won with a metallic piste, as she often failed to score by touching the floor in the course of a fast attack.

The men's final was a bit rough and there were too many double attacks. Persistent absence of blade resulted in a lack of sentiment du fer in the view of Prof. Zaaloff, who had been organising the tournament for twenty years and who, like many observers of the foil scene in these years, deplored the tendency for athleticism to supplant technique. The winner was Alan Hughes

(Manchester Univ.), ahead of Eric Wilson (LFC) and Leslie Jones of Ashton Fencing Club, in which he was already becoming a successful master.

The *World Youth Championships* were this year held in Vienna. As usual, the men's team was sponsored by the Under-20 Men's Championship Committee, while the ladies' team were sponsored by the LAFU who had raised funds through a football pool, selling omelettes at competitions and holding a bring and buy sale (organised by Mary Glen Haig). Eve Davies and Jack Berry were the untiring team managers. Prof. Pat Pearson and Prof. Boston augmented the coaching.

The men foilists did exceedingly well. All three survived both rounds of pools to reach the direct elimination. Here Graham Paul's good results earned him a bye. He then lost to Tiu (Rumania), but was only eliminated in a good match with Verbrugge (Holland) 5–4, 3–5, 5–4. Bonfil lost to another finalist, Olexa (Czechoslovakia) and took Terqueux (France) to three bouts in the repechage. Breckin fenced extremely well, with strength and assurance. In the direct elimination, clear victories over Filipkowski (Poland) and Reichert (Germany) brought him to the last eight where he lost by one hit to Berkovits (Hungary) who was to be second overall. In the repechage he beat Celentano (Italy) and only failed to reach the final at the last hurdle against Grigorian, a determined Russian. He thus had the distinction of being placed equal seventh for the second year. He got further than any other W. European foilist.

Clare Henley, Marilyn Holmes and Anna Savva were all extremely young and did as well as could be expected. Anna Savva, who alone survived the first round, showed temperament and strength. The strength of the event was indicated by the exit of two World Championship finalists (including the Champion) in the direct elimination.

The epeeists had a satisfactory championship. Russell survived the first round and both Graham Paul and Bourne reached the direct elimination stage. Indeed, Graham topped both his pools, to gain second seed.

In the direct elimination Bourne lost to Pongracz, an experienced Rumanian, but in the repechage he fenced very well to beat Midling (Norway) and Friis (Denmark). He then had to meet the joint holder, Jacobson of Sweden, to whom he narrowly lost, 5–4, 5–4. Charles de Beaumont continued to criticise Bourne for his 'almost non-existent technique', noting that his foot normally moved ahead of his hand, that he was rarely covered on guard and that he did not use his considerable reach to advantage.

By contrast, in de Beaumont's view, Graham Paul fenced extremely well and had great potentialities, but as an epeeist rather than as a foilist. Graham continued to prefer foil. It is difficult, even in retrospect, to see who was right. After a bye in the first round of the direct elimination, he beat Giger (Switzerland) clearly and was within one hit of qualifying for the final in his bout with Zajitsky (USSR). He then beat Jansen (Denmark) in the repechage to reach the last eight. Like Bourne, he came unstuck against Jacobson. He

Scottish Quadrangular winners 1966. *Back:* J. Rorke, A. Leckie, G. Sandor, J. Gordon, J. Harris, A. Mitchell, R. Wilson. *Front:* M. Joyce, P. Roberts, A. Wilson, R. Richardson, J. Herriot, J. Little, T. Broadhurst.

was thus placed equal seventh. The epee was won by Brodin – incredibly, his fourth victory in this event. He was only hit ten times in his five fights in the final.

At sabre Ben-Nathan came out in the first round, but both Acfield and Breckin survived, and the former went on to the direct elimination stage. Here, Acfield had the misfortune to draw Nagy (Hungary), the ultimate winner, in his first bout. In the repechage he fenced particularly well to eliminate Prikhodko (USSR) 5–2, 4–5, 5–3. In the last twelve he found Gos (Poland) too fast and experienced for him, although he went to three bouts. Charles de Beaumont considered Acfield the best potential sabreur for some time, with an admirable temperament for the big occasion. The sabre final was monopolised by Eastern Europe – three Hungarians, two Poles and a Russian.

The three-weapon *Granville Cup* produced some surprise results. In the quarter-finals Paul 'A' were overcome by a mere LFC 'B', while their 'B' team lost to Boston 'A'; and in the semi-final LFC 'B' was in turn overthrown by their own 'C' team, while their 'A' team failed to survive the onslaught of Boston 'A'. In the final, Acfield of Salle Boston, fencing very well, beat David Martin of LFC. At epee Johnson failed to outclass the admittedly more experienced Rhodes. It was thus open to Rentoul of LFC to rise to the occasion and defeat Russell.

This year the *Quadrangular* was reduced to a triangular owing to the much regretted absence of the Irish. It was notable for the first Scottish win since 1938 and took place on their home ground at Largs. They owed much to

Leckie, who only lost one bout out of twelve; but all fenced well. Sandor, especially, was impressive at both foil and epee. Wales again suffered from too small a team, though their ladies, especially Julia Davis, were in very good form. They lost to Scotland 24–12.

In their crucial match with England, Scotland drew first blood with a 6–3 victory at men's foil (Leckie 2, Sandor 2, Rorke 2). They also won the ladies' foil 5–4; but England won the sabre by the same score. All therefore depended on the epee (in which England was handicapped by the unexplained non-arrival of the number one). In spite of three sterling wins by John Shaw, the Scots trio, Rorke, Sandor and Wilson, won 5–4 to take the match 20–16. Scotland now had 44 victories; England needed a formidable 28 fights in their match against Wales to draw level. The latter can rarely have had more vociferous support than they now got from the Scots. English hopes rose when they took the men's foil 7–2 and the epee 6–3 and still more when the strong Welsh ladies could make no initial headway against them and the simultaneous sabre also looked a possible clean sweep; but the tide turned and they ended three short of the target with a 25–11 victory. Building on the work of John Fethers, Sgt Martin Joyce had provided the immediate training for this signal victory.

As the Irish Amateur Fencing Federation had decided no longer to participate in the joint Irish team, it was unanimously decided to invite the Northern Ireland Union to take part on its own in future and to include IAFF fencers in the team when desired.

In the *Rest of Britain Match* the ladies beat London by a small margin, with two victories apiece for Pam Patient and Shirley George (Northampton FC; sister of Pauline Courtney-Lewis); but the London men's foil team comprising Breckin (3v), Bonfil (3v) and G. Paul (1v) had better timing and won 7–2. In the epee the score was reversed. The Rest were better able to fence for the wrist against opponents too prone to fleche. Purchase and Reynolds both scored three victories, even though their opponents included Bourne and Johnson.

All thus depended on the sabre. When Craig, Hunt and Wiles went to a 3–1 lead London supporters became noticeably quiet; that was their limit, however, and a 6–3 win by D. Eden (3v), Breckin (2v) and Ford (1v) gave probably the youngest London team yet overall victory by 19–17.

Five Sections were represented in the *Winton Cup* and the competition was keen. The SW Section and the E. Midlands entered their final match undefeated. The latter started well, winning the ladies' foil 7–2 and the men's foil 5–4. The SW then took the epee and the sabre and the match 19–17, Hoskyns being in splendid form, losing only one fight during the weekend.

The *World Championships* were held in Moscow for the first time. Long negotiations produced some Government aid towards the fares of competitors, but it still cost each of them, and still more the officials, a considerable sum of money. Russian bureaucracy almost failed to produce visas and denied the party advance information about any of the arrangements. On arrival, however, the team was well cared for and the organisation proved excellent. Fencing took place in a sports palace seating 20,000. The finals were televised and attracted nearly three thousand spectators, who were interested, vociferous and partisan.

After the successes of the two previous years, results were disappointing, for no readily apparent reason. Each team had trained carefully and morale was good.

Graham Paul, understandably nervous in his first championship, went out in the first round. René Paul, Breckin and Leckie fell in the next. Only the staunch Hoskyns once again reached the direct elimination stage. He never, however, struck true form and lost to Okawa (Japan) 1–5, 5–3, 5–3, and was eliminated in the repechage by the aggressive Woyda of Poland 5–4, 5–4 in a good fight. Woyda had been second in the 1962 World Championship and was to be Gold Medallist in 1972.

The foil team should have beaten Italy, but from a bad start went on to lose 11–5. Hoskyns and a tenacious Breckin won two each and Graham Paul one, while Leckie, quite out of touch, failed to win a bout. They then had to beat USSR to go up. Graham Paul fenced courageously to win a couple and Breckin, Hoskyns and René Paul won one each.

In the sabre, Cooperman and Leckie alone survived to the second round of pools. In the team event the team was drawn with E. Germany and USSR, which appeared favourable. However, they lost 10–6 to E. Germany, Leckie winning three and Oldcorn, Cooperman and Martin one each, and went down to USSR 9–0.

At ladies' foil the sad tale continued. In the individual, only Joyce Pearce and Janet Wardell-Yerburgh survived to the second round. In the team event a draw with Sweden and Hungary again seemed to provide a chance, but inexplicably the Swedish team, which had only one top-class fencer in Kirstin Palm, built up a lead and won 13–3, Shirley Parker, Janet Wardell-Yerburgh and Jeanette Bailey each scoring one. Hungary completed the tale at 13–3, Shirley Parker winning two and Jeanette Bailey one.

The epeeists, Silver Medallists the previous year, might have redressed the balance – but it was not to be. In the individual, Hoskyns, Jacobs and Pelling survived the first round of pools quite easily. Hoskyns had an injury to his hand during this round which aggravated his lack of form. He failed to survive the second round, as did Jacobs, who could not get his distance right. Pelling, fencing very well, alone reached the direct elimination stage. Here, he was drawn with Dreyfus, the French star, and lost 5–0, 4–5, 5–3. In the repechage he beat Sepsin (Rumania) 5–4, 5–3, but once again found himself opposed to Dreyfus and went out 5–2, 5–3.

The epee team was the most disappointing of all. They were drawn with

Holland and USSR. The Dutch fielded a tall and forceful team which had admittedly scored a sensational win over Hungary the previous year in Paris. Nevertheless, to beat them or at least run them close should have been well within British capabilities. To lose 13–3 seemed inexplicable. Higginson fulfilled his contract with two victories and Hoskyns won the other one, but neither Jacobs nor Pelling scored. The team then lost 8–2 to Russia, only Hoskyns scoring.

The Russians won five of the eight events. At sabre Pawlowski reached his thirteenth world final and won for the third time.

Shortly after the World Championships came the *Commonwealth Games*, staged by Jamaica, the smallest country ever to do so. In the fencing there were 58 competitors from seven countries and 21 entries for each men's event. Two pistes were in a school which had a gallery for spectators; a further two pistes were in a kind of dutch barn at some distance. The programme was arranged to avoid the hottest part of the day.

Prof. Anderson coached both English and Scottish teams. He complained that the former had their own ideas to such an extent that he felt like the only fencer with eleven coaches. The five Scots trained particularly enthusiastically but were very unlucky when Joe Rorke strained his leg badly before the foil began and in the first round pools Leckie, the holder, received a cut on the knee from his opponent's coquille which necessitated several stitches and his withdrawal until the sabre events.

The Welsh team included Robert, Andrew and Frances Reynolds, backed by Prof. G. Reynolds and by Mrs Reynolds, so it was more of a family party than ever.

Heat affected an otherwise good foil final. Jay was in excellent form and long led the field until, progressively handicapped by cramp in his thighs, he lost to Henderson and Pickworth, both of New Zealand. Graham Paul remained in close attendance, losing only to Jay and Hobby (Australia), but in his last fight he too got cramp (in the stomach) and lost 5–3 to Brian Pickworth, to leave Jay a clear winner, his first individual title after competing in five Commonwealth Games.

Hoskyns, after losing to both his team mates, achieved second place on hits scored over Paul. Pickworth defeated all three England fencers, but came fifth by two hits to Hobby, who was handicapped by an injured finger. Henderson was sixth with three wins. Seventh was McCowage (Australia) by only one hit over Sandor of Scotland.

In the semi-final of the men's foil team England beat Scotland 5–0 and Australia beat New Zealand 5–3. In the final Australia conceded a 5–1 victory, only Hobby scoring by the odd hit, over Jay. Scotland, despite the absence of Leckie, took third place with a resounding 5–1 victory over New Zealand, all fencing with elan. Tubby Wilson in particular (fortified by endless lemon meringue pie) was an inspiring sight in full cry.

The fifteen entries for the ladies' individual necessitated two semi-final pools, in one of which there was a four-way barrage. The final pool, which was of fair standard, was dominated by Janet Wardell-Yerburgh and Shirley Parker of England, who eventually tied for the title, the former winning the barrage by the odd hit. Third place went to Gaye McDermitt (New Zealand) who had a nice style and great determination, by four hits over Jeanette Beauchamp (Australia) a left-hander of much promise. Fifth was M. Coleman (Australia) with three wins by a single hit gained, over Julia Davis (Wales). Angela Julian (Wales) was seventh, with two victories; Joyce Pearce (England) was eighth (ov).

A ladies' team event was held for the first time, but was contested by only four teams in a single pool over two days. England beat New Zealand 6–3, but only overcame Angela Julian, Julia Davis and Frances Reynolds of Wales by the last hit of the last bout. They then faced a formidable Australia, who had beaten Wales 7–2 and New Zealand 6–3. However, the morale of the Australians collapsed and England won 5–0 in under half an hour. New Zealand were third after a convincing 5–2 win over Wales.

The epee events provided the best fencing of the meeting. In the exciting individual final Pelling (England) fenced extremely well, beat both his team mates – Hoskyns and Jacobs – and led the field until he lost to Reynolds (Wales) 5–0 and, in his last bout, to John Humphreys (Australia) by the odd hit. This bout illustrates the element of chance in sport. At 4–all Pelling executed a perfect parry in the course of which the heel of his plastic orthopaedic grip snapped off, so that his riposte went wide and he was hit with a remise which was to cost him the title.

Meanwhile, Hoskyns, after an initial defeat from Pelling, won all his bouts until he met Reynolds, at which point, if the latter won, there was a prospect of a quadruple barrage. However, at 4–all time ran out and a double defeat extinguished Reynolds' chance of the title. Similarly Humphreys, fencing with great aggression, kept among the leaders, with only one loss (to Hoskyns) until beaten in the later stages by Peter Bakonyi (Canada) 5–3 in an unsatisfactory bout. Once again a 5–2 defeat at the hands of Jacobs in his last fight removed his chance of tying for the title. In the resultant barrage Hoskyns beat Pelling 5–1 to regain the title which he had won in 1958. Reynolds well deserved his third place for his excellent speed and control. The other finalists were: Bakonyi (4v–27), Humphreys (4v–28), Jacobs (3v), Sandor (2v), Wiedmaier (Canada, ov).

In the team epee the England trio were the 1965 World Silver Medallists and they dominated the event. In the semi-finals they beat Scotland 5–2, while Canada annihilated Australia 5–1. In the final England beat Canada 5–0. Australia took the bronze by beating Scotland 5–3 in a good match.

The sabre events appeared to be the most open and if initially the standard was poor it certainly improved in the finals. In the semi-finals of the pools of

England Commonwealth Games team 1966. *Back:* P. Jacobs, W. J. Rayden, G. Paul, Prof. R. Anderson (Coach), R. Oldcorn, H. W. Hoskyns, J. Pelling. *Front:* Janet Wardell-Yerburgh, Shirley Parker, R. Cooperman, de Beaumont (Captain), Joyce Pearce, Mary Glen Haig (Ladies' Official), A. Jay.

the individual event Oldcorn (England) and Bob Foxcroft (Canada), both of whom had won their first round pools, were surprisingly eliminated. In the final Cooperman (England), fencing really well, retained his 1962 title undefeated and was never taken to the last hit. Second place went to Leckie, despite his injury, while the Bronze Medal was deservedly won by the very fast Gavin Arato, an Australian naval officer. Other finalists were: John Andru (Canada, 3v–29), Brian Pickworth (NZ, 3v–30), R. Binning (NZ, 3v–31), W. Rayden (England, 2v) and Raymond Jackson (Jamaica, 1v).

The sabre team event appeared open and was hotly contested. In the semi-final matches England beat Canada 5–4 and Australia beat New Zealand 5–3. The final should have been close, but only Arato scored for Australia and England ran out easy winners at 5–2. Canada beat New Zealand 5–3 in a good match for third place.

Thus England won all eight Gold Medals, which was a record for any sport at these Games, though they had achieved the same result at the previous Games. They also won three Silver Medals and a Bronze. New Zealand got two Bronzes; Wales and Canada one apiece. Hoskyns with three Gold Medals and a Silver was the most successful individual fencer. At the meeting of the British Commonwealth and Empire Fencing Federation, Charles de Beaumont was re-elected President and Mary Glen Haig Secretary-Treasurer. Fifteen countries now belonged.

# 1966–7

## MEN'S FOIL

An event that boded well for the future was a *match against Germany* in Cologne in November followed by an individual event. If the British started slowly, losing the first two bouts, thereafter they drew steadily ahead, and at 8–5 were in the happy position of only needing to score three hits in the remaining three bouts to win. In fact, they clinched a fine victory 10–6. The German team was not full-strength, but nor, in the absence of Jay and Leckie, was the British.

The hero was Breckin, who fought like a tiger, imposing his game with a fine disregard for reputations. He only surrendered five hits in his four victories and impressed the experts as both a thoughtful and a forceful foilist. He was ably seconded by Halsted, who had been rather press-ganged into the party, but contributed three sterling victories. Better known as an epeeist, he was outstanding for his tenacity at both weapons.

Graham Paul started badly, but once he managed to curb his too-obvious fleche attacks, he secured two victories. Hoskyns was short of practice and though his first bout, which he only lost by the odd hit to Brecht, produced foil play of the highest class, thereafter he could not find his touch and only scored once – most unusually for him in a match.

The *Cologne individual* was a marathon event. By the third round exhaustion began to set in and Paul and Halsted, prone to take a great deal out of themselves, could do no more. Hoskyns, however, pacing his effort, topped his pool and Breckin, in spite of fatigue, qualified too. In the last sixteen Hoskyns defeated von Kriegstein (W. Germany) 5–1, 5–2 and Breckin, ever resilient, beat Hein (W. Germany) 5–0, 5–2. In the last eight Hoskyns drew Noel (France), who had recently won the pre-Olympic meeting in Mexico, and in a very good fight, lost 2–5, 5–4, 2–5. Breckin met Brecht, the German Champion, who took the first bout 5–0. Breckin now showed his quality by correcting the fault which had brought disaster and, fencing with great confidence, won the next two bouts 5–3, 5–2 to reach the last four. In the first semi-final match Berolatti (France) defeated Noel in three bouts. In the other, Breckin started to get cramp in his sword hand and could not cope with the experience of Jacques Dimont (France), losing 5–1, 5–1. Berolatti beat Dimont for the title.

For three years LFC had been runners-up to Salle Paul in the *Team Championships*. Now they couldn't even scrape together a team. The champions – by two hits – were London University; but then Graham Paul (undefeated, only hit eight times) and his brother Barry (2v) contributed quite a Pauline tinge to the team, alongside the Thames-derived pair, Breckin (2v)

A Salle Paul group: B. Waddelow, Prof. V. Lagnado, P. Kirby, H. Maslin, M. Eden, I. Single, G. Paul, B. Paul, L. Eden, A. Leckie, P. Harden, D. Eden, R. Craig, René Paul.

and Bonfil (ov). Both Jay and Kirby won three fights for Salle Paul, but Single and David Eden could only manage one each.

104 boys competed in the *Under-20 Championships* for the three places of the World Youth Games team assigned to the top three finalists. Even Graham Paul had to struggle for promotion after losing to the small 14-year-old Kevin McCollum, who attacked with tremendous courage. He was one of a nine-strong team from Millfield to London with their master, Peter Turner, who had built up a team in only two years, after making Beverly one of Surrey's leading fencing schools. Two of his boys, Steven Frith and Michael Hewitt, reached the quarter-final and the latter narrowly missed the final in a close fight with Acfield. They contributed to the geographical spread of the last 24. Along with six from Salle Paul and Prof. Boston's four from Cambridge University, two from Brentwood School and three from Salle Boston, there were individual representatives from Worth School, from King's Canterbury, from LFC, from St Paul's and from Newcastle University.

In the final, Graham Paul was undefeated, although Barry Paul took him to the last hit and he was within an ace of losing to Cohen, who got second place in a 5–3 barrage with Barry.

In the final of the *Junior*, Stuart Wooding (Risinghill) beat the spidery, awkward Chris Green (Boston) 5–2 with fast, determined, simple actions in his penultimate fight and looked a clear winner. However, Ralph Johnson, who had lost his first four fights, found his touch in this last bout and won 5–1. And in the barrage a cool and dominating Green came back with a 5–1 victory against an over-anxious Wooding. Single, losing to Green 5–4 and Wooding 5–3, had more in him than his third place suggested. Jim Hamments (Mayfield) was fourth on two wins and Wiles, now at Leicester, was fifth, ahead of Johnson on hits.

Leckie was the winner at *Leamington*, but only on the last hit over René Paul, the winner on nine previous occasions. Wiles won third place over Koch of Copenhagen.

In the quarter-finals of the *Championship*, Ben-Nathan was eliminated on hits, with the young Martin Murch, in a barrage with Breckin and Eden. In the semi-finals, Raymond Paul had to retire with a pulled leg muscle resulting from his leap of delight at scoring the fifth hit against Graham Paul. In consequence, Breckin had to barrage with Graham (who was already assured promotion) and then, when he lost, with Hoskyns, to whom he went out on the last hit.

The atmosphere of the final was enlivened by the many people who had come for the unveiling of the memorial to Prof. Leon Paul beforehand. Graham Paul lacked his usual edge and ended fifth. Bonfil showed excellent footwork and was undefeated till he lost to Leckie in his fourth fight and then 5–1 to Single and had to be content with third place. Single came fourth in his first national final, fencing with determination and scoring a masterly victory over Hoskyns, with a broken time attack, a remise, a redoublement, a disengagement and a direct riposte. Jay fenced brilliantly in patches and was unlucky to lose to both Leckie and Bonfil on the last hit. But it was Leckie's day. Now at Salle Paul, taught by Prof. Lagnado, he brought great coolness as well as his technical and athletic prowess to a series of victories broken only by a thumping 5–0 loss to Hoskyns (who ended last). He was thus the sixth person to win the Championship three times.

In the *Coronation Cup*, Cawthorne and Klette of Norway were notable casualties of the second round, while Koch and Kestler of the USA were disposed of in the repechage by Breckin and Leckie (the latter, unwontedly inaccurate, in turn succumbing to the fierce aggression of Bonfil). Barry Paul and Power (who had reached the last eight by beating Single and René Paul) were both eliminated by Hoskyns.

Breckin, in London University colours, opened the final with a swift 5–4 win over Bonfil, then added comparatively easy victories over Jay and Halsted. The latter had started with a quick win over Hoskyns, and after losing to Jay as

Competitions chronicle 1966–7

well as Breckin, was spurred into a restrained fury that Bonfil was unable to stem. Graham Paul beat Jay in a bout where physical forcefulness produced a series of avuncular embraces, and then Bonfil and Hoskyns. Thus he and Breckin met with three wins apiece. In this crucial fight, marked by simultaneous attacks, Breckin proved to be the less hurried fencer, and won on the last hit. By contrast, Hoskyns beat Jay in a fight of craft, even gamesmanship, rather than speed. Graham secured second place from Halsted, while Breckin bid for the title in his last fight, with Hoskyns. This had more of the qualities of epee than of foil, but that didn't prevent Breckin at 4–3 taking the title with a very positive riposte. Hoskyns was fourth, three hits behind Halsted.

Making a last attempt to score against Bonfil in the final bout, Jay tried all his tricks unavailingly, ending desperately attempting to drive him into the ground, only to find himself impaled. This gave Bonfil fifth place, with one win but three hits ahead.

Among notable foreign results was Breckin's win of the *Chaux-de-Fonds* two-man team event (as the under-20 foilist in partnership with Halsted as the epeeist), an excellent performance. At *Melun* in February, he reached the last eight and Graham Paul the last sixteen. Halsted was fifth in *New York* and fourth in *Toronto* in April, winning the overall prize for the latter (being also second at epee).

The World Championship team remained unchanged but for the return of Jay, taking the place of René Paul.

*LADIES' FOIL*

In October, the LAFU invited a German team to take part in a specially arranged *Under-20 match* and individual competition. Sadly, the three British teams made very little impact on Pulch, Giesselmann and Gnaier – admittedly a strong trio – in spite of the encouraging number of spectators. Marilyn Holmes won two bouts and Georgina Netherwood and Angela Herbert (Boston) made valiant efforts, but the other six girls offered little resistance.

In the *German–British Under-20 individual*, Monika Pulch reached the final by beating Sandra Maggs (of Bristol Phoenix) and Susan Green (in three bouts); Karin Giesselmann beat Lorna Croft and Andrea Hill; Clare Henley beat Janet Yates (Flixton GS) and Hella Gnaier; Marilyn Holmes beat Kate Whitcomb and Georgina Netherwood. Susan Green and Hella Gnaier also reached the final via the repechage. It was success for the Ashton girls all the way. Marilyn Holmes, who showed both determination and constructive thinking, beat Pulch and only missed an outright win when she lost to Giesselmann. In the ensuing barrage, she beat Pulch again with her powerful attacks to win 4–2 and gain the prize donated specially by Lady Simmons.

Susan Green was fifth, contesting every hit with vigour and determination.

In the *Junior*, the previous year's second and third – Sue Brick and Louise Cuppage – were defeated in the repechage and only one of the finalists reappeared – Sheila Ward, who came third. The undefeated winner was the determined Jennifer Dorling, a pupil of Prof. Behmber at Poly (and previously of Glasgow FC). Clare Henley was second, Hazel Rogerson fifth and Elspeth Earle sixth.

In the *Junior Schoolgirls' Championship* the NW showed its future strength again. Andrea Hill and Janet Yates, both of Flixton, took first and second places. Danuta Joyce, of La Sainte Union Convent, Bath, was one hit behind, followed by her schoolmate Rosemary Staples. Judith Young (Bexley) and Colette Bailey (Harrytown HS, NW) completed the final.

There were thirty entries from 23 clubs for the *Team Championships*. The quarter-finals were notable for the very brave fight against LCF put up by Ashton, all of whose members were still at school. In addition to great team spirit, they showed a high technical standard, especially Susan Green, for whom a bright future was already predicted.

In the semi-finals Poly avenged their defeat by Thames the previous year (by 9–5), while Pauleons beat LFC. And in a final of intense excitement, Poly beat Pauleons at 8–all by 42 hits to 50, with Julia Davis undefeated.

The final of the *Desprez* produced a record for the shortest fight (Wardell-Yerburgh v. Rogerson: 4 hits, 30 seconds) and the longest (Dorling v. Herriot: 5 hits, 7 minutes), and a dramatic last fight. For a few moments Janet W-Y was a defeated champion and Marilyn Holmes had a sight of glory. Perhaps the three-times holder was surprised by the confidence and accuracy of her opponent. A direct riposte put Marilyn 2–0 in the lead. Janet made it 2–1, but Marilyn went on to 3–1, then 4–1, fighting beyond her years as a schoolgirl taking her A levels. In the barrage the spectators asked for a repeat performance; but this was under-estimating Janet. She made no mistake now and won very efficiently 4–1. The last hit was a direct attack into the low line, which had confidence, timing, distance and accuracy. No one else displayed all these qualities. Jennifer Dorling was third (3v), Pam Patient (Reading) fourth (2v), Judith Herriot (Glasgow) fifth (2v) and the small but energetic Hazel Rogerson (Hydra) sixth (0v).

In the *Championship*, Julia Davis started the final at a cracking pace, beating Jennifer Dorling 4–0 in an aggressive fight; but thereafter she lost her accuracy and worried her supporters by stopping to look at the box and thus getting hit (3v; 5th). Joyce Pearce, with her strong remising point, took the last hit from Janet W-Y, but only got two wins (7th). Clare Henley (now at Bristol University) produced some delightful spirited bursts (3v, 6th). But in the end it was a matter of whether anyone could sustain the aggressive attacks necessary to break through Janet W-Y's watchful concentration. The result

## Competitions chronicle 1966–7

was decided towards the end when Judith Herriott was beaten 4–0, thus losing the chance of a barrage. She had fenced very steadily and intelligently, and earned her second place with five victories. Marilyn Holmes was third, one hit behind. Mildred Durne (Pearson) was fourth with three wins.

The *de Beaumont Cup* had one of the largest entries ever, including a strong young team of three from France, two from Holland, and one each from W. Germany, Ireland and the USA. Jennifer Dorling and Clare Henley missed the final in the repechages. Janet W-Y lost the first fight of the final to Judith Herriot of Glasgow, who seemed to have the cup within her grasp until her last fight, when she lost 4–1 to Herbster of France. In the barrage Judith met Janet W-Y again, but tired as Janet smashed her way 4–0 to victory, yet again making sure of her second chance. The two British girls for once showed better sense of timing and distance than the Continentals, and made good use of stop hits. So, for the first time since 1962, the cup was retained in Britain.

The two invitation events in June each had twelve contestants. The invitation *Felix Cup* for trainees was won by Janet Varley, who lost only one bout. Vicky Lengyel-Rheinfuss was second, Gerry Harding third, Hazel Rogerson fourth, Shiel Toller fifth and Mrs Sue Yeomans (née Brick) sixth. The senior *Silver Jubilee Bowl* was won by Janet W-Y after yet another barrage, this time with Mildred Durne. Among the younger fencers, the performance of Anna Savva in coming third was outstanding. Margaret Paul (now Mrs Fentum) was fourth, Julia Davis fifth and Clare Henley sixth.

In the provincial events Elspeth Earle, now a medical student, won a striking double at *Leicester* and *Nottingham*. At *Leamington* Janet W-Y was the winner, ahead of Gerry Harding, Hazel Rogerson and Mielke of Cologne. At *Inverclyde* the holder, Judith Herriot, was unbeaten in the entire competition. Runner-up was Fay Shields of Glasgow FC (who won the *Scottish Championship* ahead of Paula Robinson of Scottish FC), Mrs Margaret Duthie (Glasgow FC), Sue Youngs (Glasgow HS), Cath Wotherspoon (Caledonian), Pat Roberts (Bon Accord, Aberdeen), Barbara Williams (Caledonian) and Sandra Robertson (Glasgow HS), a line-up replete with future talent.

There was considerable activity abroad during the season. In October, a London team consisting of Joyce Pearce (Captain), Louise Cuppage, Elspeth Earle and Sheila Ward was third in the *Amsterdam Inter-Cities Tournament*. Mildred Durne reached the last eight at *Melun* in February. A notable and exciting triumph was Julia Davis's win of the large *Duren* Tournament, directing her natural exuberance to excellent effect. Jeanette Bailey again got to the quarter-finals of *Como*.

Janet W-Y, winner of every major British event, also showed her form in reaching the last twelve *Goppingen* in April, coming third at *Amsterdam* and reaching the last eight of the *Jeanty* in Paris, all in successive weekends. Anna Savva and Shiel Toller also reached the last eight at *Amsterdam* and Julia

Davis got to the last 24 of the Jeanty. Sue Green reached the last eight at the *Duisburg Under-20 Tournament* in October, while at the tail end of the season Julia Bullmore (Boston), another stylist, was second and Elizabeth MacKenna (Edmonton and Scotland) third at *Dieppe*.

Clare Henley and Marilyn Holmes joined Janet W-Y, Julia Davis and Jeanette Bailey from the previous year as new and youthful members of the British team.

## EPEE

In the *Junior Epee* the average age continued to sink. The winner, Ken Pearman of Salle Paul, was nineteen and Barry Paul, second, taught by Prof. Lagnado at the same club, was only seventeen. In the barrage between them Paul got a 4–2 lead, but with great resilience Pearman drew level and snatched the title with a final time thrust. He was a pupil of Prof. Akos Moldovanyi, as he had been at Highgate School. Mike Steele, now at Cambridge University, was third, ahead of Floyer, who was disappointed with his performance and, like many others, was to be drawn out of fencing by the demands of a career in medicine. M. Roberts (Cambridge Univ.) and Ian Single (S. Paul) were the other two finalists.

At this period the *Under-20 Championship* was tougher than the Junior. Pearman did well to come third and Russell even better to win, Bourne being runner-up and Graham Paul fourth – followed by the steadily improving Ralph Johnson and by David Exeter (Danecourt School). Mark West of Brentwood was *Public Schools* Champion.

The premier provincial event, at *Leamington*, was won by Graham Ayliffe, a pathologist, formerly at Behmber, now at Birmingham FC. The *Inverclyde Tournament* was won for the second time by Tony Mitchell, a shipbuilding engineer of Glasgow. Wiles was runner-up in both events.

For the 1967 *Martini* it was decided to have one round of pools rather than two, in view of the crowded schedule of the previous year. Those who thus passed to the direct elimination included ten British, four French, three Swedes, two each from Poland and Italy and one each from Belgium, Germany, USA, Austria and Switzerland. Jay had a spectacular bout against the French champion Allemand, the top seed. With Jay 8–7 down, the president thought the bout over, forgetting that there had to be a difference of two hits to win. This error corrected, there ensued an argument as to whether time had expired. It was finally established that half of one second remained. As soon as 'Play' was called, Jay hurled himself at this opponent and levelled the score. Thus encouraged, he snatched victory by a riposte en fleche to win a place in the final. Kulcsar, the famous Hungarian, came almost as close to elimination when he only beat a Belgian opponent 3–2 on time.

There was another British finalist: Halsted, who had won the qualifying competition. He had fenced consistently well all day and in the direct elimination beat the redoubtable Italian champion Saccaro 8–6, with characteristic patience and determination – scoring hit after hit by parry-riposting at well-chosen moments and with extreme vigour.

Unfortunately, the first bout of the final opposed Jay and Halsted. Halsted won 8–6. Kulcsar beat Boms (Sweden) 8–4. The gangling Netburn then put up a remarkable performance in beating the much fancied Losert (1963 World Champion) in a desperately close match 10–9. Barany (Hungary) beat Skogh (Sweden) 8–5.

The interlude, a constant feature of the Martini Gala, this year took the form of an 18th-century prize fight. It was performed by Bob Anderson (frequent protagonist) and Martin Joyce, who both showed such nerve, split-second timing and contagious sense of fun, that they brought the house down.

The semi-final bouts were a triumph for the Hungarians. Kulcsar, Gold Medallist of Tokyo and winner of the Paris Monal for the second successive year only a few weeks previously, was in wonderful form, displaying well-nigh perfect sense of distance and point control. Probably no fencer in the world could have withstood him. Halsted lost 8–3. Barany, using all his guile and mobility, defeated Netburn 8–5.

After a final bout of exhibition epee in which Kulcsar got the last three hits with one of his lightning attacks at the forearm from apparent immobility, a delightful stop at wrist and a forceful reprise, he collected his prize from Denis Howell, Minister for Sport.

The chief of the *post-Martini training matches* was labelled London v. Stockholm. At one point the Swedes led 7–2, but the British team fought back and only finally succumbed at 9–7 in a hard fought contest (Engdahl 3, Skogh 3, Broms 2, Jacobson 1; Pelling 2, Halsted 2, Higginson 2, Jacobs 1).

In another match three Dutch fencers and Jung of Germany, winner of the 1966 Martini, were defeated 10–6 by a team of three British fencers, ably supported by Major Sundfelt, captain of the Swedish team (Purchase 3, Johnson 3, Sundfelt 3, Steele 1; Feith 3, Langeweg 0, Godhelp 1, Jung 2).

There were 74 entries for the *Miller-Hallett*, which ended with a poule unique of sixteen. After losing his first bout in the final to Spofforth, Halsted won all the others, only twice being taken to the last hit, thus winning impressively his first major title. Second was Jacobs (12v) by ten hits over Pelling (Grosvenor). Hoskyns (11v) took fourth place.

Ian Single (Paul) was fifth, a very good result for a fencer who was primarily a foilist, which would have been even better if he hadn't lapsed in the last quarter. Spofforth (9v), fencing in his first major event after several years in Iran, took sixth place on hits over Johnson. The other places were as follows: 8. Bourne (7v); 9. Bob Wilson (now at Salle Paul after moving south; 6v); 10. Jim

Fox (Army, 5–10); 11. Townsend (Latista and Sussex Univ., 5–11); 12. Fairhall (Boston, 5–17); 13. Julian Ogley (Oxford Univ., 4–9–47); 14. Pearman (4–9–45); 15. Bill Romp (Grosvenor, 4–12); 16. Terry Burch (Risinghill, 2v).

The order in the *Championship* final of sixteen only three weeks later was very different. Hoskyns demonstrated his knack of running into form just at the right time by winning for the fourth time, with twelve victories. In the two preliminary rounds he was undefeated and only surrendered nine hits in eleven bouts. He had last won the event in 1958.

Runner-up was Bourne (11v), recovering the form which had so far eluded him this season. Third place went to Graham Paul (10v) by three hits over Higginson. Halsted (9v) in turn was fifth by one hit over Jacobs, who was plagued by double defeats. Barry Paul (9v), fighting with great elan, was seventh. He was followed by: Johnson (9–12); Martin Murch (Paul, 8–20); Single (Paul, 7–15); Purchase (Birmingham, 6–15); Green (Boston, 4–10 –45); Edmund Gray (Boston, 4–10–48); Pelling (Grosvenor, 4–15); Bob Peters (Behmber 4–16); Ogley (0v).

There were twenty entries for the *Team Championship* in June. In the semi-finals, Thames crushed Salle Paul 9–1 and Salle Boston (victors over the holders LFC by 9–5 in the quarter-finals) beat Grosvenor 9–5. The final provided a sensational reversal of form. The Thames team of four current internationals should have been unbeatable. But their young opponents were obviously quite unimpressed and proceeded to inflict on them a devastating 8–2 defeat to win this event for the first time.

For the winners, Bourne was in splendid form throughout and unbeaten in the final, fencing with greater calm and thoughtfulness. His team-mates backed him with brio and determination, Fairhall and Green securing two wins apiece and Russell one. For Thames, Halsted and Jacobs got a win each, Purchase a double-defeat and Higginson no wins.

It was a sparse year for foreign results. Halsted was second in the *Toronto Tournament*. Johnson started his international career by reaching the last sixteen at *Eupen*, but did not quite attain the British team, the fifth place being retained by Pelling.

## SABRE

The *Championship* final of eight was so closely fought that the result remained in doubt almost until the end, and Rayden in second place had only one more victory than Hoskyns, who was seventh. Sandy Leckie (now at S. Paul) won, even though he showed only occasional glimpses of his immense natural ability in brilliantly executed hits. He thus won both sabre and foil national titles, repeating the double he achieved in 1965. Montgomerie was the only other fencer to win two national titles in one season. (He also did it twice, at foil and epee, in 1905 and 1909).

In second place was Rayden, showing improved footwork and a more offensive approach. Acfield jumped up a whole class in coming third. He was a real fencing natural, who now also possessed an excellent technique. Eden (4th) did not always control the exuberance which admittedly gave him speed. Breckin (5th) had a limited repertoire, but his footwork was considered a lesson to sabreurs. Martin's good technique was sometimes jeopardised by his variable temperament, but in sixth place he was ahead of Hoskyns, the holder. Oldcorn (8th) seemed temporarily to be in something of an impasse, with a need to improve his lunge and add to his repertoire.

LFC's grip on the *Team Championship* was broken by Salle Paul, which at this juncture was able to field a team consisting of Cooperman, Leckie, Eden and Jay. They beat LFC by a handsome 9–2.

Acfield again won both the *Universities* and *Under-20* titles. As a Senior, he was now ineligible for the *Junior*. This was won by Brian Fisher, quite an achievement for a schoolboy still at St Paul's. He was also runner-up in the Under-20s, ahead of Brian Waddelow (S. Paul), Cohen, Geoff Parsons (ex-Brentwood) and Laurie Eden, the middle of the three brothers. The other finalists in the Junior were Lennon, Eiser (now at London University), Titheradge, E. Nyiri (Poly) and Cohen (now at Cambridge). Wiles was the winner at *Inverclyde*, ahead of Broadhurst (Ardeer) and Mitchell. *Leamington* was won by Wischeidt of Dormagen, W. Germany, over David Eden, Kubbeler (Cologne) and Rayden.

John Rayden, now taught by Prof. Pat Pearson at LFC, was the winner of the *Corble*. Nearly always in the top three or so of the National or the Corble from 1964 to 1971, this was his moment of supremacy, well-earned by his outstanding technical ability, his hard work and his persistence in competitions at home and abroad. Oldcorn, his chief sparring partner and fellow traveller to foreign events, was second. Like him, Hoskyns in third place, was improving on his Championship result. By contrast, Leckie had to be content with fourth place. Acfield and Martin were missing from the top six, but Craig was fifth, ahead of Borucki, who was relegated to bottom place in the pool.

Hoskyns and Oldcorn both again did better in the *Cole Cup*. Hoskyns won, twelve years after doing so previously, while Oldcorn was second for the third year running. Leckie was third.

Abroad the only notable result was the good sixth place achieved by Oldcorn at *Hamburg*. At home he won at *Nottingham* for the third time running.

Leckie, Oldcorn and Rayden remained in the World Championship team from the previous year. Taking the places of Martin and the retired Cooperman were Breckin, selected for the first time, and Hoskyns, who had not been included since 1964. Both had the advantage of doubling at another weapon and thus saving costs on the expensive trip to Montreal. In the absence of foreign results comparable to those achieved at other weapons, sabre continued to be given second-class status. Acfield had to wait for his place in the team.

## COMBINED EVENTS

At the *Ashton Tournament* electric foil was now used from the second round onwards, thanks to fencers who brought equipment with them, but there was a shortage of non-competing presidents with the exception of Martin Joyce, who was invaluable – as he was to be in so many events during this period.

Victory in the ladies team event went to the AFA Leaders 'A' Team over their own 'B' team 5–2. In the individual event, there were surprises. Mary Hawdon (Huddersfield) and Susan Green, seeded fourth and fifth respectively, went out in the repechage. The winner was Gerry Harding. Having lost to Marilyn Holmes (3rd), she won the barrage with Anita Maguire of Netherwell.

In the men's foil, fencers of the calibre of Vince Bonfil, Michel Kallipetis and Barry Paul went out in the repechage. The average age of the finalists was about nineteen, younger than ever. At just past the halfway stage only Wooding, with three wins, was undefeated. Graham Paul, having lost to the very determined 18-year-old American Junior Champion, Kestler, who was fencing at Poly, beat Wooding 5–3 to stay in the running. He then beat Power, while in the last fight Eden made sure of Paul's victory by beating Wooding and put himself into second place on hits. Power with two victories was fourth on hits, Single taking fifth place above Kestler.

Victory in the epee went to Bonfil, who only lost to Barry Patman of British European Airways FC, after the result was certain. Although a foilist, he mastered the epeeists by greater mobility. In second position was John Anderson of Behmber (3v, 17). Third was Patman (3v, 19), followed by Purchase (2v), Payne (1v) and Kallipetis (1v).

Oldcorn sailed through the sabre final undefeated. Only Eden, runner-up with four wins, took him to the last hit. Third place went to Lynn Wall of Leeds University with three wins.

The tenth *Leicester* Tournament was a triumph for the home club, YMCA, who provided four foil and two sabre finalists from an entry of over 150 fencers from all parts of the country.

Despite the absence of big names from the foil events, the standard was good. Elspeth Earle (London Univ.) won undefeated. Second was Pam Patient (3v), third was the large and cheerful Janet Jones (Pauleons and no relation of the Joneses of Ashton; 3v), fourth the left-handed American, Mrs Mary Annavedder (2v), fifth Hazel Rogerson (Hydra, 2v), and sixth Mary Hawdon (0v).

In the men's foil, Alan Painter (YMCA) became the first person to win the event twice running when he beat Kestler 5–4 in the barrage. The other finalists were Alan Hughes (YMCA, 3v), Malcolm Priestley (YMCA, 2v), Ken Staines (BAF, 1v) and Gordon Wiles (YMCA, 1v).

The sabre final lacked passion. It was won by Oldcorn (fencing for Portland), with Rayden second and Wiles third. Epee was not yet included in the tournament.

The 25th *Liverpool Tournament* was held in February in the magnificent new University gymnasium. The men's foil was won by Charles Rentoul of LFC over Bob Kilvert and Eric Wilson, both of Behmber. The ladies' title, fought for with verve, good humour and much noise, was claimed by Hazel Rogerson over Fay Shields of Glasgow, by 4–2 in a barrage.

In the *Sandhurst Tournament* in February, Pam Patient won the ladies' Foil over the stylish, long-lunging, quite sabreur-like Jo Moir (S. Pearson) and Shiel Toller (Thames). At men's foil Kestler was the victor, followed by Eric Wilson and Alan Morgan (Goldsmiths).

The *Wanstead Tournament* had a good year. Chris Green beat Ralph Johnson in a barrage for the foil title, followed by Kestler and Staines. Boston beat London University in the team event. Jennifer Dorling won the ladies' in another barrage, with Gerry Harding and Shiel Toller, with Muriel Wilson (Cambridge) fourth.

Poly won the *Granville Cup* for the second time – with an all-American 'B' team consisting of Kestler, Netburn and Eliot Mills.

For the second year running Scotland won the *Quadrangular*, which this year included N. Ireland for the first time. Leckie, Sandor and Wilson led off with a remarkable 8–1 victory over the English foilists Single, Bonfil and Peters (who got the solo win). They followed this by holding Elspeth Earle, Clare Henley and Hazel Rogerson 5–4 – Judith Herriott being undefeated. Tubby Wilson beat Bourne, Pearman and Russell in the epee, supported by Sandor and David Hunter to win that weapon 5–3. The Scottish sabreurs (Leckie, Joyce and Mitchell) won 5–4, in spite of 3 wins by Acfield.

The Scottish success continued in the other matches. They beat N. Ireland 9–0 at men's foil, 6–3 at ladies' foil, 7–1 at epee and 9–0 at sabre. Against Wales they again won 9–0 at foil, 5–4 at epee and 9–0 at sabre, but lost the ladies' foil 6–3 to Frances Reynolds, Angela Julian and Linda Brown.

Scotland's captain, Leckie, was the mainstay of their effort – he won seventeen out of eighteen fights at foil and sabre; Wilson and Sandor, doubling at foil and epee, each had only one more loss (a double defeat in Sandor's case). Judith Herriott and Martin Joyce both won eight out of nine fights.

The English retained second place by defeating Wales 28–8 and N. Ireland 35–2. Wales beat N. Ireland 26–10.

The government had promised a grant towards the expense of the *World*

*Youth Championships* which were in Tehran, but this was not forthcoming as late as five days before departure. Only an hour before an emergency meeting was to be held to consider cutting down the team, the glad tidings came through, thanks to the intervention of the Minister for Sport, Denis Howell. To help Prof. Anderson and sustain his three pupils in the team, Prof. Boston travelled out at his own expense.

In the men's foil the second round of pools proved too hot for Barry Paul and Richard Cohen, but Graham Paul excelled himself to earn first place on the match plan for the last sixteen direct elimination. Here he beat Bergonzelli (Italy) 3–5, 5–1, 5–3; but in the last eight he lost to Talvard 5–3, 1–5, 3–5, in a good fight in which the more classic Frenchman gradually asserted his class. Meeting Bergonzelli again, Paul won a long and exhausting match 5–1, 4–5, 5–4. Finally a decisive 5–4, 5–1 victory over Czakkel (Hungary) got him a place in the final pool. Here he was too tired to produce his best. He had been fencing on and off for nine hours and his perpetual motion style had taken a great deal out of him. Nevertheless he sprang a considerable surprise in his last fight of the pool, when he defeated the winner, Romanov (USSR), 5–3 in an excellent bout during which he imposed his game on his much more experienced opponent, thus earning a good fourth place – a fine performance.

At epee, neither Pearman nor Russell could survive the first round pools. Bourne went up third and, gaining confidence, topped his second round pool, to reach the last sixteen. In the direct elimination against Veanes (USSR) he won his first bout comfortably 5–3. The Russian then tightened up his game and by parries and ripostes against Bourne's fleche attacks took the second bout 5–1. Bourne persisted in the same approach and lost the deciding bout 5–3. In the repechage he was eliminated by Kozejowski (Poland) in a very similar match 5–3, 4–5, 1–5.

There were only 24 in the ladies' event. Marilyn Holmes gained promotion by two hits over Gneier (W. Germany), while Susan Green went out by one hit. Clare Henley had to fight a barrage with Aredondo (Mexico) and won decisively 4–2.

The direct elimination proved lethal: Marilyn Holmes lost to Antropova (USSR) 4–1, 4–2 and Clare Henley went down to Nemeth (Hungary) 4–1, 4–1. In the repechage Marilyn lost to Giesselman (Germany) 4–2, 1–4, 1–4 and Clare lost to Urbanska (Poland) 4–1, 4–2.

The sabreurs did rather better. Acfield confidently topped his first round pool. Fisher and Waddelow also survived but could not win a bout in the second round. Here Acfield was promoted third. In the direct elimination of sixteen he lost to Frolich (Hungary) 5–3, 5–3 in an unconstructive bout. Both were imbued with the necessity to attack, which they did simultaneously with monotonous regularity. Frolich was the faster, so eventually won. In the repechage Acfield fenced much better to beat Popescu (Rumania) 5–3, 5–4, which got him into the last twelve. Here once again he found himself up against Frolich and the match followed much the same course as their previous encounter, 5–4, 3–5, 5–2. He thus retained his placing of the previous year.

At the *World Championships* at Montreal, the British team were, somewhat surprisingly, housed by charming nuns (for whom a fencing 'circus' was put on). The team received a government grant of fifty per cent of the fare only, together with a small grant from the International Matches Fund, but the trip still required a considerable financial effort. The officials got no assistance. The expense reduced entries from lesser teams and thus raised the standard of early rounds. Nevertheless, British results were rather better than the previous year.

In the men's foil Leckie went out in the first round and Hoskyns on hits in the second. In the last 32, Graham Paul lost in three bouts to Kamuti, who was to be second in the final, Allan Jay lost to Szabo (Hungary) and Breckin to Romanov, who was to gain fourth place. In the repechage, Paul lost to Midler (USSR, often a finalist and this year 6th), Jay to Pinelli (Italy) and Breckin to Lisewski (Poland).

In the first round pool of the team event Britain, as so often, made a slow start against Germany and never caught up. Hoskyns won two bouts and Jay, Paul and Breckin one apiece. And so to the USSR, Champions for the previous eight years. Contrary to all expectations, there ensued a remarkable match, reckoned by cognoscenti to be the best for many years for excitement and quality. The team got its second wind with a vengeance and soon established a 5–1 lead. The Russians fought back and scores were level at 5–all, then 6–all and 7–all. By that time a large crowd had collected and vociferously applauded the remarkable British spirit. Amid great excitement, Breckin defeated Charov to give an 8–7 lead and Paul faced the new world champion Poutiatin in the final bout. Hits ran level to 4–all and Britain was within one hit of a sensational victory. Paul made a last desperate fleche which landed off target: but the President judged Poutiatin's counter movement a riposte, which levelled the match score at 8–all and the match was lost by 64–66. Hoskyns, Jay, Breckin and Paul each scored two victories, so this was a real team effort which gave much hope for the future. The Russians beat Germany 9–6 when they met later in the direct elimination stage.

In the sabre individual, Hoskyns, Rayden and Oldcorn survived the first round but Leckie once again was unable to score. Only Oldcorn gained promotion from the second round and in the direct elimination he lost to Nazlimov (USSR) and to Theuerkauff (Germany).

In the team event Britain drew USSR and USA. USA should not really have won 9–7, Leckie and Hoskyns winning three bouts each but Rayden only one and Oldcorn none. The Russians, eventual champions, won 13–3, Leckie, Hoskyns and Oldcorn winning one each.

The ladies did better than the previous year. In the individual all except

Clare Henley gained promotion from the first round. The pace in the second round pools, however, was too hot for all except Janet Wardell-Yerburgh, although Julia Davis was only eliminated on a count of hits. In the direct elimination Janet lost 4–0, 4–2 to Gapais (France), who was in tremendous form but tore a muscle on the last hit and had to retire.

In the repechage Janet beat Oggero (Italy) 4–3, 2–4, 4–2 and thus qualified to meet Gapais once again and so had a walk-over into the next stage, in which she met Lydia Sakovits (Hungary), the former world champion. Fencing splendidly and with great concentration, she won an epic match 3–4, 4–2, 4–3. A sterling 4–3, 4–3 victory over Lorenzoni (Italy) then put her in the last eight which, in circumstances other than those of the prevailing rules, would have been accounted the final. However, she then had to meet Heidi Schmidt (Germany), the former Olympic and World Champion, for a place in the final six. She lost, but only 3–4, 4–3, 3–4; on the last hit there were two lights, and Schmidt had right of way.

Thanks largely to this effort, the ladies' team found themselves with the fortunate draw of Canada and Italy in the first round of the team event. They had little difficulty with the weak Canadian team, whom they beat 11–5. Janet W-Y won four, Julia Davis and Jeanette Bailey three each and Marilyn Holmes one. The match with Italy, for seeding only, was a most curious one, during which the Italians argued fiercely among themselves as to whether it would not be better to lose in order to avoid meeting Russia during the direct elimination stage. They finally won 9–5. Marilyn Holmes and Clare Henley won two each, Julia Davis one and Jeanette Bailey none (while Janet W-Y rested).

Under current rules the British had to meet Italy again in the direct elimination. This was a disappointing match, lost 9–5 in spite of another fine display by Janet, who was undefeated, beating Ragno, the runner-up in the individual, 4–2. Clare Henley won one, but neither Jeanette Bailey nor Julia Davis could score. There followed a match against France in the repechage to decide fifth and sixth placings. Janet was out with a pulled muscle and the match was lost 9–3, Jeanette Bailey, Clare Henley and Marilyn Holmes alone winning one apiece.

In the epee individual only Hoskyns and Halsted survived the first round, though Jacobs and Pelling went out on hits. Hoskyns got through to the direct elimination, but then lost to Boissier (France) and to Nemere (Hungary), both in three bouts.

This poor showing put Britain in the hardest pool in the team event, with Italy, Sweden and the Argentine. Against the powerful Swedish team nothing went right. Bourne fenced splendidly to win three bouts, but Hoskyns and Pelling could only win one each and Halsted none, so it was 11–5. Against Italy it was the same score. Hoskyns and Pelling won two each and Jacobs one, but Bourne, disappointingly after his previous good showing, had four defeats.

The Russians won six of the eight events at Montreal, but lost the team foil in a brilliant final to a very fit and enthusiastic Rumanian team, who gained their first world title, under the leadership of the lissome left-hander Drimba. In the ladies' team they were also pushed out of the top position, this time by Hungary.

The British team for the fencing events at the *Universiade* held in Tokyo in late August was one of the strongest yet fielded. It had trained vigorously under its manager Sandy Leckie, but its performance was patchy in spite of weakened opposition due to the withdrawal of the Soviet bloc in a protest over the nomenclature of N. Korea.

In the men's foil first round Bonfil was outclassed. In the direct elimination Paul beat Bois (Switzerland) 5–0, 5–0 but then lost to Tsuruta (Japan) 5–4, 5–0. In the repechage he won a very good match with Berolatti, 5–2, 2–5, 5–3 and only failed to reach the final when he lost to Rodocanachi 5–1, 2–5, 5–2. He fenced really well, but once again was beaten, mostly by exhaustion, partly through inability to adapt his game to different opponents. Breckin, after an initial 5–1, 5–2 win over Kauter (Switzerland), came up against Pinelli (Italy) the ultimate winner, and lost a very good match 5–4, 2–5, 5–1. In the repechage he beat Kim (S. Korea) 5–1, 5–0 and reached the final by a good 5–4, 1–5, 5–3 win over Yogi (Japan). In the final, an initial victory over Tsuruta (Japan) assured him fifth place and he had the distinction of alone running Pinelli to the last hit. Had he too been better able to vary his game (and avoided dropping his hand in his attacks) he might have exceeded even this excellent performance.

In the poule unique of five teams the British lost to Japan, the winners, 10–6 (G. Paul 3v, Breckin 2v, Power 1v, Bonfil 0v), to Italy (in a good match) 8–8, 54–50 hits (Breckin, the Pauls and Power each getting two victories), and to France 9–4 (G. Paul 1v, M. Breckin 1v, A. Power 2v, B. Paul 0v). A 9–7 victory over Switzerland (G. Paul 3v, Breckin 2v, Power 3v, B. Paul 1v), however, gained a fourth place. Graham Paul virtually carried the team, Breckin fenced adequately and Power, short of competition practice, improved markedly as he went along.

The epee individual was of a much higher general standard than the foil. Johnson alone survived the first round. Graham Paul was unlucky to be eliminated only on hits, but Bourne was not up to his usual form. In the direct elimination Johnson put up a very good performance, on virtually his first big international occasion. He was cool and resourceful under pressure and his ability to apply advice given him during a match, won praise from de Beaumont, the adviser. In the first round, he defeated the very experienced Swedish von Essen 3–5, 5–3, 5–4, but then lost to Granieri (Italy) again in three bouts. In the repechage he defeated the best French epeeist, Ladegaillerie, 4–5, 6–5, 5–4 and reached the final with another desperate 6–5, 0–5, 5–3 victory over Brocherie (Italy).

In the final, lack of experience and sluggish footwork were his only handicaps. He had sterling victories over the two best epeeists in the pool, Losert and Kauter (Switzerland) and was unlucky to have to be content with sixth place when level on victories with four other members of the pool.

In the team event the epeeists were disappointing, losing to Italy 12–3 (G. Paul 2, B. Paul 1, E. Bourne 0, R. Johnson 0) and to Switzerland 10–5 (G. Paul 2, B. Paul 1, E. Bourne 1, R. Johnson 1), thus being eliminated in the first round.

There were no sabreurs, as such. Breckin entered the individual mainly for fun and survived the first round. A scratch team was placed fourth by beating a weak Thailand 15–1, and losing to Italy 15–1, to France 12–4 and Japan 9–3.

# 1967–8

## MEN'S FOIL

In the *Team Championship* it was a question of under whose name the cup should appear on Doreen Paul's mantelpiece, as once again Salle Paul's main rivals were a London University team with two members of the Paul family. However, Salle Paul had a hard time from Thames in the semi-final. With Ben-Nathan fencing extremely well and Jacobs' devastating epee technique, at 5–1 down they faced defeat. Hit by hit they fought back, most fights going to assault point except for Ben-Nathan's decisive wins for Thames, and Leckie's consistent if cautious game on the Paul side. They emerged winners by two hits. In the other semi-final, Salle Paul 'B' went down to London University 9–2, in spite of Eden beating Breckin 5–1 and Bonfil 5–4.

In the final, youth and confidence was on the side of London University, while Salle Paul were exhausted. Jay put Raymond Paul in his place to face his two bloodthirsty nephews. Graham lost to Leckie, who by now looked invincible, but Breckin was on form, raining hits from every possible angle. Bonfil lacked drive and accuracy – exerting himself unnecessarily. Single tended to miss and to parry wide. Kirby was brilliant, but fleetingly. Uncle Raymond was almost his young self again, humorous, full of vitality, the accomplished showman. The result was 9–6 to the students.

Barry Paul, now aged 21 and a student of mechanical engineering at Queen Mary's College, London, won the *Junior Championship*, but only after scrambling out of a triple barrage in the quarter-finals against Alan Loveland (Cambridge Univ.), and Don Anderson (S. Boston). He raised his game considerably in the final, which was of high standard, presided by Michel Kallipetis and watched by an audience of 46. Paul won his first fight against Gordon Wiles 5–1 and then went from strength to strength, displaying a sound sense of timing and distance, combined with turn of speed. Abroad, he reached the last twelve in the Under-20 event at *Weinheim*.

Wiles of Leicester used his experience to good purpose to come second. Third place went to Bourne, the only one to defeat Paul (in the last bout of the final). Terry Burch (4th) showed technique and accuracy. Although Richard Cohen (5th) pulled out some brilliant strokes, he was too impetuous. Ralph Johnson (6th) fenced steadily but no more.

Sponsored by Clarkes of Street and organised by Peter Turner, the first *Millfield Under-20 Invitation International Tournament* had over ninety entries. Alan Loveland impressed with his classic style, although more aggression would have brought him an easier victory. Millfield's Steven Frith and Michael Allen came second and third after a count of hits. James Noel of Downside was fourth (2v).

In the *Under-20 Championship* Johnson bested Barry Paul and the 17-year-old Mark West (Boston). Simon Routh-Jones of S. Section won both the *National Schoolboys* and *Novices Championships*, while Geoff Grimmett of King Edward's School, Birmingham, was *Public Schools* Champion.

Apart from the absence of Breckin and of the title holder, Leckie, the *Championship* final witnessed little more than a re-shuffling of the top fencers. Graham Paul won, as he had in 1966; Hoskyns was second (6th in 1967 and 3rd in 1966); Halsted was third (not in the two previous finals, but third in the 1967 Coronation Cup); Barry Paul was fourth (the one newcomer); Jay was fifth (second in 1967 and fifth in 1966); Bonfil was sixth (third in 1967).

The first three places of the *Coronation Cup* were taken by Germans: Hein, Wolfgarten and Gerresheim. Halsted was fourth (though concentrating on epee this season). Cawthorne, who had persuaded Derek Allen to take over the former Salle Froeschlen and was making a bit of a comeback, was fifth. Bonfil was sixth. Graham Paul was absent taking his finals. During the weekend, Breckin, Halsted, Hoskyns and Leckie failed by 11–5 to repeat their earlier success against *W. Germany*, but a 'B' team comprising Ben-Nathan, Bonfil, Jacobs and Single beat *Denmark* 8–all on hits. The month before, in a *match against France* in Montpelier for which colours were awarded, Jay, Hoskyns, Breckin and Graham Paul lost 9–7, Graham winning three.

Graham Paul did very well to gain second place in the individual event at *Montpelier*, defeating Magnan in the last four. He and Halsted won the *Chaux de Fonds* two-weapon event, Britain's second successive win. To complete a very impressive run, Graham came equal ninth at *Bad Durkheim* and again ninth in the very strong *Martini*. Here Breckin did even better, with eighth place. Barry Paul and Halsted reached the last 32 of the *Rommel*. Jay was ninth at *Melun*.

Unsurprisingly, though disappointingly for Bonfil, the World Championship team consisted of Jay, Hoskyns, Halsted, Breckin and Graham Paul.

## LADIES' FOIL

This was the year that Sue Green of Ashton took wing. It began with the *Under-20 Championships* in which she consigned Marilyn Holmes – twice a winner – to third place and Clare Henley to fourth. She only lost to Sally Littlejohns, a pupil of Prof. Imregi at Oxford University, with an effective, if original, technique, who came second. Janet Yates (5th) delighted spectators with her neat, controlled style. Sue Youngs (Caledonian) had her moment of triumph getting into the final: equal on hits with the fast-riposting Angela Herbert (Boston), she won the barrage 4–0. Georgina Netherway and Susan Olley were snarled in the semi-finals – as in the Junior.

Susan Green went on to gain considerable international success. In *Duren* she reached the last sixteen and in the *Turin Martini* the last 32. In *Remich* (Luxembourg), she came fifth and at *Saarbrucken* she reached the semi-finals along with Julia Davis and Jeanette Bailey. Other successes include Marilyn Holmes' fifth place in the Under-20 event at *Duisburg*, final places in the junior event at *Gelsenkirchen* for Angela Herbert (Boston) and Sue Olley (Cyrano and Latista), and fifth place for Julia Bullmore (Boston) in the Under-20 event at *Weinheim*. Janet W-Y reached the last four at *Melun*, was fourth at *Duren* and was in the last 32 at *Como*.

Meanwhile, in the *Junior* Sue Green only came sixth. The winner was the very promising Anna Savva, who unfortunately soon gave up the sport. She was now a pupil of Prof. Harmer-Brown, who also taught Shiel Toller, the runner-up. Janet Yates of Ashton was third, followed by Janet Varley and Sally Littlejohns.

Elspeth Earle, yet another Harmer-Brown pupil, was the winner of the Scottish open *Ford Cup*, ahead of Fay Shields (Jard), Paula Robinson (Scottish FC), Sue Youngs (Caledonian) and Margaret Duthie (Glasgow FC). Sue Youngs overhauled Fay Shields when she beat her 4–0 in the barrage of the *Scottish Championship*. They were followed by Pat Roberts (Bon Accord, Aberdeen) and Sandra Robertson (Caledonian).

Perhaps due to the fine weather, 38 per cent of the 98 entrants failed to appear for the *Championship*, the final of which witnessed the completion of Sue Green's triumph, Janet W-Y having departed in the third round (first round proper), recovering from pneumonia. Judy Herriot (now Mrs Bain and in London with Pauleons) found success in fencing with absence of point and, although this led to numerous double hits, she reached second place, with three wins, on hits scored over the more conventional Julia Davis (Poly). Clare Henley put Jeanette Bailey into fifth place by two hits scored. Marilyn Holmes seemed to lose her usual precision and timing after her first defeat and only got one victory. After much trouble with her equipment prior to the final, Susan Green, still only seventeen, fenced exceedingly well to win, being only defeated by Jeanette Bailey. Among younger aspiring fencers, Sally Littlejohns and Angela Herbert reached the semi-finals.

At the schoolgirl level it was convents to the fore. Andrea Hill, with typical, attractive Ashton style, won the *Senior Schoolgirls*, followed by Sue Olley (St Bernard's Convent) and Susan O'Connell (Oaklands Convent), while Colette Bailey (Harrington Convent and Ashton) won the *Junior Schoolgirls Championship*, from an entry of four from each Section (except N. Ireland). Second after a barrage was Janet Pollock (Glasgow HS); her school-mate Heather Grant was third.

Marilyn Holmes' win of the *Universities Championship* completed the remarkable run of wins by Les Jones's Ashton pupils. She was now at Reading.

There was a strong foreign entry of eighteen for the *de Beaumont Cup*. Only four Britons remained in the direct elimination – Janet W-Y, Julia Davis, Pam Patient and Marilyn Holmes. Janet reached the final and came fourth after beating the winner, Rejto of Hungary. Mees (W. Germany) was second after a barrage. Schmid (W. Germany) was third and the last two places were taken by Bobis and Sakovits of Hungary. As all the other finalists had been in the top three of the World Championships and three of them World Champions, this was no mean performance by Janet.

At the end of the season came a notable triumph for Judith Bain when she won a triple barrage for the invitation *Jubilee Bowl* by defeating Janet W-Y and Julia Davis – a reversal of her results in the pool, and achieved in spite of her limited repertoire. Janet had conceded only sixteen hits in eleven fights in the pool, losing to Julia and Sheil Toller. In the barrage she made no mistakes against Julia, but seemed quite out of touch against Judith, her concentration perhaps impaired by the absence of continental tempo in the pool. The 'reservists' Mildred Durne and Eve Davies, called in to fill vacancies at the last minute, achieved fourth and sixth place respectively.

Preparatory to the division of competitions into three categories of strength for the 1968-9 season, fencers were awarded points on the three senior British competitions of 1967-8. The lists give an idea of the relative standing of the fencers of this date (and those of earlier and later vintages).

*Category A*

| | | | |
|---|---|---|---|
| J. Bain | 49 | E. Earle | 28 |
| J. Wardell-Yerburgh | 46 | M. Durne | 23 |
| J. Davis | 45 | A. Herbert | 22 |
| C. Henley | 42 | J. Yates | 22 |
| M. Holmes | 42 | S. Fisher | 21 |
| P. Patient | 42 | E. Davies | 20 |
| S. Green | 39 | J. Pearce | 20 |
| J. Bailey | 38 | S. Toller | 17 |
| J. Beauchamp | 32 | J. Varley | 17 |

*Category B*

| | | | |
|---|---|---|---|
| D. Knowles | 17 | V. Bond | 11 |
| S. Littlejohns | 17 | J. Bullmore | 11 |
| L. Hamments | 16 | J. Dudley | 11 |
| G. Harding | 16 | C. Kendrick | 11 |
| J. Lockyer | 16 | G. Netherwood | 11 |
| D. Austin | 15 | A. Savva | 11 |
| J. Dorling | 15 | L. Ruffe | 10 |
| K. Storry | 15 | D. Mellor | 9 |
| H. Davies-Cooke | 14 | P. Phillips | 9 |
| E. Jones | 14 | S. Youngs | 9 |
| S. Yeomans | 14 | I. Foulkes | 8 |
| S. Ward | 13 | S. Olley | 8 |

*Category C*

| | | | |
|---|---|---|---|
| V. Matheson | 7 | E. Peppercorn | 7 |
| C. Matthews | 7 | M. A. Watts-Tobin | 7 |
| J. Moir | 7 | A. Hill | 6 |
| S. O'Connell | 7 | | |

During the season there were a number of international matches. Elspeth Earle, Julia Bullmore, Anna Savva and Shiel Toller came second for London at *Amsterdam*. Janet W-Y, Julia Davis, Marilyn Holmes and Judith Bain lost to a German team 10-6. And at *Como* the same team, with Jeanette Bailey instead of Marilyn Holmes, beat an Italian team 11-5.

For the Olympic Games only four were chosen: Janet W-Y, Julia Davis, Judith Bain and Susan Green.

*EPEE*

The standard of the *Junior* was up, even if there was more courage and aggression than variation of timing and distance. In the very even final of nine, five fencers tied, with five victories apiece, and it might well have been six had Burch of Risinghill, handicapped by cramp, not lost his last two bouts. In the barrage, fitness favoured Jim Fox (Army), Britain's leading pentathlete. His only defeat was against Julian Ogley of Oxford, who achieved a remarkable performance: 1-4 down at five minutes he scored with a succession of well timed fleche attacks to win by the odd hit at 5-all within the time limit. The lower barrage positions were very level again. Murch, D. Johnson and Ogley were placed in that order on hits with two wins each. They were followed by John Henniker-Heaton (Cambridge) 5v; Burch, 4v; Jonathan Haile (Oxford) 3v; Nick Bell (Worth School) 1/36; Robin Davenport (Ealing Tech. Coll.) 1/38 – the last a promising 21-year-old left-hander who had started fencing at Tonbridge, continued it at Southampton University and was now at Salle Boston.

True to form, but for the first time, Bourne won the *Under-20 Championship*. Equally predictably, Johnson was second, but making their mark for

Winton Cup 1968. *Back:* M. Fare*, E. Hudson*, P. Redhead*, A. Russell, W. Osbaldeston, R. Southcombe*, R. Dennis. *Middle:* D. Holt*, J. Noel*, H. W. Hoskyns*, R. Turner†, A. Gundle†, M. Rainbow†, G. Wiles†, E. Bradbury, J. Haile, A. Loveland, D. Partridge†, F. Lord, A. Hughes. *Front:* J. Buffery*, D. Hunt*, R. Cohen*, C. Hillier*, P. Patient, J. Varley, M. Hawksworth, R. Castle, A. Taylor, E. Goodall, F. Hindle, P. Lewis. (*S.W., winners; †E. Midlands, runners-up).

the first time were James Noel, aged seventeen and taught at Downside by Prof. Sanders (3rd), Emanuel Olympitis (ex-King's Canterbury; 4th) and the nineteen-year-old Brian Hill (LFC), who had decided his long, lanky physique might be more suited to epee than the family sport of rugby. Sixth was Barry Paul. Bourne, however, could not stop Graham Paul winning the *Universities Championship* for the second year running.

Johnson topped the eighteen-strong final of the *Martini Qualifying Competition*, with Gray and Fox exactly equal second, followed by: Olympitis (London Univ.) 11/26; Pearman (S. Paul) 11/30; B. Paul (Paul) 10/30; Purchase (Birmingham) 10/33; Barry Lillywhite (Army) 9v; Bill Osbaldeston (Northampton) 8v; and Barry Patman (BEA) 7v.

There were 37 foreign entries in the *Martini* itself, from fourteen countries. The thirty fencers in the direct elimination included eight British, six French, four Poles, three each from Italy and Hungary, two each from Austria and USA, a German and a Mexican. Ladegaillerie (France) and Fenyvesi (Hungary) had byes through the first stage, but neither reached the final.

Hoskyns, Graham Paul and Pearman reached the second round of elimination, unfortunately at the expense of Lillywhite, Jacobs and Halsted respectively. Jay went out to Allemand (winner of this year's Monal) and Johnson to Birnbaum (Austria).

The next round, which produced the eight finalists, saw Paul defeat the French international Jeanne 8–6 and Pearman, in splendid form, beat the formidable Fenyvesi by the same score. Hoskyns had the misfortune to meet the 1965 World Champion Nemere (Hungary) on top form.

The final evinced some beautifully controlled, entertaining and very fast fencing. Nemere beat Nielaba 8–3 and Birnbaum beat Andrzejewski 10–9. Graham Paul could not cope with the speed of foot and accuracy of measure of the effervescent Francesconi and lost 8–5, but Ken Pearman continued to produce the form which delighted while it surprised his supporters and won a good bout with the difficult ex-Hungarian Keresu 8–6.

In the semi-final bouts Nemere almost disdainfully liquidated Birnbaum 8–2 and Pearman found Francesconi too fast, though he held on to 8–6. The final bout was one-sided – no one could live with Nemere in the form he produced that day. With devastating attacks, mostly with a beat on preparation, and accurate stop hits which seemed to have all the time in the world even against Francesconi's remarkable speed of fleche, he recaptured by 8–3 the cup he had won in 1964.

One gratifying result in the *post-Martini matches* was the 6–3 defeat of the redoubtable Poles, Nielaba, Gonsior and Andrzejewski, by Hoskyns, Jay and Jacobs.

The *Championship* saw Ralph Johnson of Salle Boston reach the top, at nineteen the second youngest ever to do so. The final was a poule unique of 24, which suited his capacity for sustained care with occasional peaks of great effort, but he certainly did well to lose only three bouts in this marathon, containing every leading epeeist except Jay. Technically stylish, with a strong parry and an ability to put his point on the target from difficult positions at close-quarters or in a melee, he compensated for his comparatively short stature for an epeeist by a long and elastic lunge, sustained by powerful thighs, and a penchant for balestra and redoubled attacks.

Hoskyns the runner-up, was only twice taken to the last hit in his eighteen victories, but appeared to tire towards the end. Ten hits behind, but eight hits ahead of Bourne, was Fox, whose repertoire may have been limited but was applied athletically and with determination. Along with familiar old-stagers, there followed some new, young fencers: 5. Halsted 17v; 6. Pelling 15/35; 7. Lillywhite 15/39; 8. Glasswell 15/40; 9. Higginson 13/30; 10. Jacobs 12v; 11. Noel 11/33; 12. Payne 11/34; 13. Ted Hudson (ex-Bath Sword Club, now at Birmingham FC while training as a teacher) 10/28/83; 14. R. Bright (Army) 10/28/78; 15. Purchase 9/24; 16. Pearman 9/27; 17. Hill 9/28; 18. Burch 9/29; 19. Single 8/17; 20. Brian Wigzell (Thames) 8/23; 21. Gray 5/13; 22. J. Anderson (Hanwell) 5/19; 23. Nick Mylne (Army) 5/20; 24. Patman 4v.

Johnson was absent (sitting exams) from the final of sixteen of the *Miller-Hallett* – for which there were no foreign entrants. Bourne here reasserted his predominance. He shared a double defeat with Hoskyns and lost to Jay and George Ganchev (the Bulgarian fencing master), but otherwise was never taken to the last hit, and ended a full four victories ahead of the field. Once again, Hoskyns looked a possible winner, but tired towards the end and came second, by a hit over Halsted, with Higginson, showing a return to form, two hits behind. Fifth place went to the tall, spindly, 21-year-old David Partridge, a pupil of Prof. Moldovanyi at Salle Paul, who had a poor lunge but aggressive bladework and flexed arm movements which made him difficult to stop-hit and who thus appeared in the upper ranks of British epee in one bound. The other places were: 6. Jacobs 8/47; 7. Jay 9/51; 8. Glasswell 8/56; 9. Purchase 7/57; 10. Fox 7/60; 11. Lillywhite 7/61; 12. Pearman 6/58; 13. Mike Howe (Army) 5/65/56; 14. Ganchev 5/65/54; 15. Fairhall (now BAF) 5/67; 16. Turner (Reynolds) 4v.

The *Team Championship* attracted an entry of 29 including the 'Scottish Club', who came down in a caravan and got to the quarter-final round by defeating Thames 'B' by three hits at 8–all. Thames decisively reversed the previous year's final by beating Boston 9–3 in the semi-final, but in the final by 9–6 could not hold London University, who combined three Salle Paul stalwarts with Bourne from Salle Boston (Pearman 3, Bourne 2, G. Paul 2, B. Paul 2; Jacobs 3, Halsted 2, Glasswell 1, Higginson 0).

In the first half of the season Bourne gained a resounding foreign success by winning the *Under-20 Challenge Schmetz* in Paris, foremost event at this level, after a barrage with Behr and Ghezzi. Johnson also excelled to gain fourth place. Bourne then came fourth both in the 'Champions' Pool' and in the open event at the *Tauberbischofsheim* Under-20 meeting. He also reached the last eight in the Under-20 invitation event at *Stolberg*, and, along with Jacobs, the last 32 in the *Paris Monal*. As well as winning again at *Chaux*, Halsted came eighth at *Poitiers*, one of the strongest events in the world. Hoskyns was third in the *Bad Durkheim* Tournament between the champions of eight countries. A team consisting of Purchase, Fox, Johnson and Pearman came third at the tournament at *Bergamo*. Johnson was fifth in *Amsterdam* in October and tenth at *Soest* in June. In the competition between the champion teams of European countries at *Heidenheim*, Salle Boston reached the second round on a pool-deciding 8–all win over the Austrians, Bourne, Johnson, Glasswell and Gray each getting two wins.

It was in the *Heidenheim* individual event – the biggest and strongest apart from the World Championships – that Bourne scored the most signal success of the later part of the season by coming sixth.

The top four – Bourne, Halsted, Johnson and Hoskyns – picked themselves for the Olympic team. Jacobs, no doubt partly on his Monal result, gained the fifth place over Pelling, who was four places ahead of him in the National, but did not reach the last sixteen in the Miller-Hallett and had no notable result abroad. Which of the top four should fence in the individual at Mexico was a difficult choice, but on his results it was surprising that Bourne should be dropped.

## SABRE

This was a promising season. To start with there was a greater depth of good sabreurs in the *Junior Championship* than had been seen for a long time. Although it was difficult to predict who would make the final, it was surprising that 19-year-old Richard Fairburn (Boston) was eliminated. The very first fight of the final proved crucial for David Scott (S. Paul), as he conceded his only defeat in the pool to his club-mate Brian Waddelow after leading 4-0. Paul Rizzuto (LFC), a member of the 1964 Australian Olympic Team, though clearly out of practice, gained third place with three wins. Waddelow fought below his best and only managed to beat Charles Kovanda (Birmingham) and Nyiry, who finished fifth and sixth. His control did not match his speed.

Richard Cohen fought soundly throughout, his only defeat being 5-0 to Scott; so these two met again to barrage for first place. Cohen trailed 1-4 and 3-4 before squaring at 4-all and taking the final hit by drawing Scott onto his extended point, showing the gritty determination that was so important an element in his success.

A different cast of rising sabreurs was to be found in the *Under-20* final. Jeremy Lawday, a pupil of Prof. Sanders at Bristol University, was the winner, ahead of Melvyn, youngest of the Eden brothers (S. Paul) and still only sixteen, Fisher (now at Cambridge), Jake Gordon (of Scotland and Cambridge), Terence Etherton (St Paul's School) and Michael Mazowiecki (Lilia).

The *Championship* was won for the fifth time by Leckie (now back at LFC, taught by the recently arrived Bulgarian coach, Prof. George Ganchev). Only Roger Tredgold equalled or surpassed this record with his six wins between 1937 and 1955. Craig (Army FU) shot up to second place, pushing Rayden one place down. Oldcorn, Hoskyns and Acfield followed.

The *Corble Cup* had an entry of 41, including four foreigners. In the second round Cohen, Fairburn, Robert, Viscount Jocelyn (LFC) and Alain Alexandre (Belgium) were among those eliminated who might have gone further.

John Moore, who had fought consistently well to become fourth seed, lost first to David Martin and then to George Ganchev in the repechage – lacking the necessary versatility. David Martin also went out, while the much improved Peter Lennon went under to Acfield. The holder, Rayden, lost twice to Hoskyns, who always did well against him. Ganchev also lost to Hoskyns, making the mistake of fighting him at his own game – Hoskyns was always at his best against simple attacks. Victor in the final was Brasseur, defeated only by Acfield (5-1), whose nerves prevented him from unleashing his splendid natural speed and timing until this, his last fight (so that he finished sixth). Hoskyns was second by four hits over Craig, while Leckie's 5-0 victory over Oldcorn gave him fourth place by one hit.

*Inverclyde* and *Nottingham* provided Wiles with this season's double wins, while in the third *Birmingham FC's Invitation Tournament* Rayden beat Oldcorn in a barrage to win for the second year running with nine victories. The other fencers in the poule unique of twelve were in this order: G. B. Wilson (8v), Wiles (8v), Craig (7v), Clive Purchase (7v), Derek Parham (5v), D. Eden (4v), Bob Turner (3v), A. Painter (3v) and Martin Warner (2v) and Tony Morrish (1v), both of Birmingham.

Although back at LFC, Leckie was not in the team which reclaimed the *Magrini Cup*. Runners-up were not, however, Salle Paul, the holders, nor Poly or the Services, the only other finalists of the previous ten years, but the rising force of Salle Boston, reaching the final for the first time. What is more, Oldcorn, Rayden, Rizzuto and Straus only beat the younger team on hits, by 62-57.

Finally, there was a rich haul of foreign successes. Oldcorn went one better than the previous year with fifth place in *Hamburg*. He and Acfield reached the last 32 at *Montreuil* in France and he and Hoskyns did the same in the *Brussels Martini*, where the entry of 156 was very strong in spite of the absence of the Russians and Hungarians. No less than fourteen British sabreurs participated, of whom ten survived the first round. After gaining promotion from the second round, Oldcorn lost to Maffei (Italy) in three bouts and Hoskyns to Majewski (Poland). In the repechage Hoskyns was eliminated by Borucki; Oldcorn, after beating Minnen (Belgium) in three bouts, lost to Maffei once again.

The packed gala final was graced with flowers for the ladies, and a pop star to present the prizes (which were as lavish as the hospitality). It was refreshingly free of double attacks. The great Pawlowski of Poland and the 1964 Silver Medallist Arabo of France met undefeated in the last bout, one of the best of the decade, fought at speed but with complete control, phrases going to the second and third movement. Amid intense excitement, Arabo won the title with a counter-riposte en fleche.

A *quadrangular match* back in London was won by W. Germany, with Switzerland second, followed by two British teams. This result concealed the notable feat by the British 'B' team of defeating the Germans. The *Cole Cup* next day was won by Alisaat. Second was Duschner (also of Germany) with Leckie the best British performer, in third place.

A month later, in April, Leckie, Oldcorn, Acfield and Craig lost to W. Germany 12-4 in *Munich*, where Oldcorn reached the last sixteen. He capped his good run by reaching the last 32 at *Padua*, and the season ended with a second *Hamburg* tournament in which Craig came eighth.

Only four sabreurs were entered for the Mexico Olympic Games: the now veteran Leckie and Oldcorn, plus Craig and Acfield (in place of Rayden, Hoskyns and Breckin from the 1967 team).

## COMBINED EVENTS

*Ashton* had a strong entry this year, attested by the following results. Ladies' individual: (after barrage) 1. G. Harding (Warley); 2. H. Rogerson (Hydra); 3. S. Green (Ashton). Men's foil: 1. A. Power (York); 2. D. Russell (Newcastle); 3. D. Eden (Salle Paul). Epee: 1. C. Purchase (Birmingham); 2. J. Fox (Mod. Pentathlon); 3. B. Lillywhite (Mod. Pentathlon). Sabre: 1. G. Wiles (Leicester); 2. D. Eden (Salle Paul); 3. L. Wall (Leeds). Ladies' Teams: 1. Ashton (Susan Green, Andrea Hill, Janet Yates); 2. AFA Coaches Club.

The *Quadrangular* was organised by N. Ireland for the first time, at the premier fencing school, the Royal Belfast Institution. England resumed its dominance, beating Scotland 26–10, Wales 30–6 and N. Ireland 27–9, Halsted at foil and Scott at sabre being undefeated. The Scots lacked Leckie, but their ladies, led by Judith Bain, beat England 5–4, Wales 7–2 and N. Ireland 8–1. Overall, they beat Wales 25–11 and N. Ireland 27–9. Wales, led by Bob Turner, had only five men – and no members of the Reynolds family. They beat N. Ireland 23–13 for third place, though N. Ireland won the sabre. The dinner was chaired with histrionic talent by Brigadier Broadhurst.

Great attention focussed on the *World Youth Championships* this year, as they were promoted by Britain, at Crystal Palace Sports Centre. But although the team included in Teddy Bourne and Ralph Johnson members who were already of international calibre, Britain scored no signal success.

In the first round of the men's foil Mark West, though scoring two victories, was eliminated. In the second round Barry Paul came top of his pool with five victories, including a 5–2 win over Delukin (USSR). Ralph Johnson with two victories was eliminated by a single hit.

Barry Paul's good score earned him a bye in the direct elimination. He then met Delukin again and, after winning the first bout 5–3 was gradually worn down by the stamina of the Russian as much as by his own persistence in attempting to take the blade against an opponent who had learned to cede it, and went down 3–5, 2–5. In the repechage he beat the Swiss epeeist Stricker 5–2, 5–0, but that brought him up against Delukin once more. He started confidently and took the first bout 5–1. Delukin exactly reversed the score 1–5 in the second. The decider alternated to 4–all, when Paul, who had continually come from behind with good attacks, made the error of taking a rest and lost the deciding hit.

The ladies started well; in the first round only Marilyn Holmes with two victories was eliminated by three hits and she at least beat Kozlenko (USSR), the ultimate winner. In the second round Clare Henley could only notch one victory. Susan Green reached the direct elimination, but there Pulch of West Germany (who was to win third place) proved too strong by 4–0, 4–2. In the repechage she found Reynolds (USA) too big and too tough, but she was only eliminated in three bouts, each of which went to the last hit. Her lack of reach was not compensated for by sufficient mobility or security in taking the blade.

The epee followed a similar pattern. Noel scored two wins in the first round and went out by two hits. In the second round Johnson with the same score went out by four hits scored.

The direct elimination was once again disappointing. After an initial victory 5–4, 3–5, 5–1 over Jonsson (Sweden), Bourne had the misfortune to draw the ultimate winner Samochkin (USSR) and was annihilated 5–3, 5–0. In the repechage he once again met Jonsson, who this time proved the winner 5–4, 5–2.

The sabreurs had no great pretensions. In the first round Lawday went up with one victory in a pool of five. Fisher's one victory earned him a barrage with Puff (W. Germany), which he lost 5–3, while Melvyn Eden could not win a bout. Lawday failed to score at all in the second round.

Of the 24 finalists, nine were Russian, followed by the Poles with four, the Germans with three and the Hungarians and Italians with two each. The French had only one, a sabre Silver Medallist. Three of the Gold Medals went to Russia.

113 kind people helped with the Championships, in addition to nineteen NCOs from the Army Physical Training Corps and thirty Sea Cadets. Charles de Beaumont, ubiquitous as ever, was Chairman of the Organising Committee. Among others in what proved a very efficient team were Margaret Somerville, Mary Glen Haig, Joyce Pearce, Bobby Winton and Brian Wigzell (who constructed the scoreboards). The staff of Leon Paul worked till midnight on successive nights installing the equipment which the firm provided free.

As the *Olympic Games* took place at high altitude in Mexico, the team flew out a month in advance. They were lucky to be almost a full complement in view of the limits imposed on other sports with quantifiable standards of performance. In the foil all three men survived the first two rounds to reach the direct elimination stage of 32. Here Breckin lost successively to Parulski (Poland).5–2, 5–1 and to Wellman (Germany) 5–3, 4–5, 5–2. Hoskyns – in his thirteenth and final successive appearance in the team at foil – lost to Pinelli (Italy) 2–5, 5–4, 5–4, beat Birnbaum (Austria) 5–3, 5–3 and then once again met Pinelli, to whom he lost 5–3, 5–4. Graham Paul went the farthest. He lost initially to Wessel (W. Germany) 5–4, 5–2, but in the repechage he beat Abunza (Mexico) 5–3, 5–3 and came back on Wessel 5–2, 2–5, 5–2, eventually being eliminated by the experienced Muresan (Rumania) 5–2, 2–5, 5–1.

In the team event the foilists were seeded ninth of the seventeen teams. In the first match, with USA, they started well and after a sticky patch won 9–7 (Paul 3, Jay 3, Halsted 2, Hoskyns 1). This ensured promotion, but a crushing defeat 9–0 by the USSR in the second match of the pool meant a poor

Olympic team 1968. *Back:* R. Craig, D. Acfield, M. Breckin, G. Paul, R. Oldcorn, E. Bourne, W. R. Johnson, N. Halsted, P. Jacobs. *Middle:* J. Bain, J. Wardell-Yerburgh, J. Davis, S. Green. *Front:* A. Jay, A. Leckie, A. G. Signy, C-L. de Beaumont, E. Davies, Prof. R. Anderson, H. W. Hoskyns.

seeding. They thus met Japan in the bye-round to reach the last eight teams for direct elimination. After a slow start they recovered to 8–all, but lost 64–66 on hits. Paul and Jay again won three each, but Halsted and Breckin could only win one each. Hoskyns, for so long the sheet anchor in team events, was affected both by flu and a blister. Graham Paul was the most successful foilist, but had not yet learned to pace himself during a long competition.

The ladies had a disappointing time. Judith Bain and Susan Green were eliminated in the first round without much resistance and Janet Wardell-Yerburgh, on whom great hopes were set, only survived the first round on hits and was eliminated in the second round without reaching her true form (though it has to be remembered that with an entry of only 37 the standard was scorching from the start). As a result, the ladies' team was seeded ninth of the ten teams. This faced them with Rumania, who won 13–3 (Wardell-Yerburgh 2, Davis 1, Bain 0, Green 0) and then USSR who won by the same score (Bain 2, Wardell-Yerburgh 1, Davis 0, Green 0).

Less was expected of the sabreurs. Leckie, Oldcorn and Craig each scored three victories in the first round. Oldcorn went out on hits. The other two departed in the second round.

The team was seeded ninth of the twelve teams. They defeated Mexico 11–5 (Leckie 4, Craig 3, Oldcorn 2, Acfield 2) to reach the last eight. In the pool classification match they lost to the USSR 9–1, Oldcorn scoring the one victory. In the consequent direct elimination plan they met USSR again and repeated the score, Leckie being the sole victor this time. They then fenced Poland to decide the fifth and sixth places and lost 9–2. Craig, fighting with elan, scored both wins.

In the epee individual, Hoskyns, Halsted and Johnson all survived both rounds of pools. In the direct elimination Hoskyns still had not regained his usual form and lost to Saccaro 5–3, 5–4 and to Dumke (East Germany) 5–4, 1–5, 5–2. Halsted lost to Gonsior (Poland) 5–3, 5–1. He then beat Haukler (Rumania) 5–2, 5–2 in the repechage, but this brought him up against Gonsior once more and he lost 5–1, 5–1. Ralph Johnson fenced very well to beat Loetscher (Switzerland) 1–5, 5–4, 5–4 to reach the last sixteen. He then lost to Kulcsar (Hungary), the eventual winner, 5–3, 5–4. In the repechage he again met Loetscher and this time lost 5–1, 5–2.

These efforts ensured a seeding of sixth of the 21 teams. Brazil was beaten 10–6 (Halsted 4, Bourne 3, Hoskyns 2, Johnson 1) and Cuba annihilated 14–2 (Halsted 4, Hoskyns 4, Bourne 4, Jacobs 2). The team then met France in the pool classification match and rose to the occasion to the tune of 9–4 (Hoskyns 3, Johnson 3, Bourne 2, Halsted 1) a result not achieved against the French before.

Having thus improved their seeding to fifth in the last eight, they drew W. Germany and had they continued the same day would probably have overcome a less powerful team than the French. Alas, the next morning the steady Germans notched a 7–0 lead. The British fought back, but could only make it 9–5 (Hoskyns 2, Johnson 1, Halsted 1, Bourne 1). In the matches for lower places they lost, probably unnecessarily, to Italy 9–4 (Johnson 2, Hoskyns 1, Halsted 1, Bourne 0) and had to be content with equal seventh placing.

In Mexico Russia won three titles in contrast to the six in the previous World Championships. The Hungarians won both epee events. The French, in a brilliant display of technique, won the team foil for the first time since 1958. Drimba took the foil individual for Rumania and the 35-year-old Pawlowski took the sabre for Poland.

# 1968–9

*MEN'S FOIL*

With the absence of the former winners Alan Jay, Sandy Leckie (now retired) and Graham Paul, the *Championship* was more open than in previous years. Other potential finalists, such as Bonfil, Halsted, Bourne, Peters and Russell, were eliminated. The final was not notable for technical display, but was exciting and hard fought. Sandor, fencing in his first senior final, gave a good account of himself and came fifth. Single (6th) fenced with determination if still lacking finish. Fourth place was taken by the 47-year-old René Paul, exactly thirty years after first reaching the top three of the Championship!

Barry Paul was third and with a little more controlled footwork might have won. The imperturbable Hoskyns came second, showing more than once how easy it was to win with a minimum of effort. It was a calm, controlled Breckin, however, who claimed the title.

Prof. Ganchev, Harald Hein of Germany and two Israeli boys gave the *Coronation Cup* international flavour. Apart from Geoff Grimmett, now at Oxford, there were no younger fencers challenging the established leaders, while the absence of Breckin, Halsted and Barry Paul was not fully balanced by the return of Power to national fencing.

The five foot five Hein showed endless vitality, and concentration to retain the title. An opportunist par excellence, he did much to pioneer the style that became so widespread, of closing distance to just short of corps-à-corps and jumping and twisting in that position till landing a hit, while inhibiting the opponent's response. It could be viewed as a development or a destruction of classic technique; at this stage British fencers found it hard to cope with. The exception was Bonfil, who rose to the occasion and gained a barrage. Here he started on the defensive, as he had in his first encounter with Hein, but then pressed with attacks, often out of time, giving Hein the chance to put in his multi-directional stop hits.

Despite obvious lack of training, Jay came third with three wins, by one hit over Tony Power, who showed more confidence, accuracy and adaptability than before. Graham Paul (5th) lacked coherence, fleching repeatedly and often missing. He only beat Peters, who fenced well but failed to win.

For the third year running the London University combination of the Paul brothers, Breckin and Bonfil snatched the *Team Championship* from Salle Paul, this time by 9–3, the best margin yet.

In the *Junior Championship* Gordon Wiles of Leicester at last put himself on the top of the heap, having been runner-up as long ago as 1963, three times in the top three and eight times in the final. Born 'on the site of the fast lane of the M80' in 1939 (and therefore eligible to fence for Scotland), he moved to Bedford at the age of six, and there, at the age of eleven, started to fence under Jeff Featherstone and John Fitzmaurice, who taught him never to stop till he had landed a hit at least twice. Later he went on many fencing courses. From Bedford School he went on to Loughborough College, at which he had the distinction in 1962 of winning the University Championship at all three weapons (a feat only equalled in the history of the event by Leckie in 1959), but missing the Universiade on a redefinition of universities. He was a possible for the 1964 Olympics, but was side-tracked by exams and apart from once going to Holland with the Rest of Britain team (and in 1974 with Scotland to Ottawa) he never fenced abroad – odd for such a constant competitor in home events. Now in production engineering, teaching and research, this season he won *Nottingham* tournament for the third successive time at foil, and his burly, bearded figure, aggressive on the piste, jovial off it, was familiar in endless provincial finals. (At Leamington, for instance, though never a winner, he was twice in the last four at all three weapons.)

In winning the *Leicester* tournament, the even more seasoned campaigner René Paul concluded a tally of at least a dozen major provincial foil wins since the Second World War, about double the achievement of either Wiles or Hoskyns, his nearest rivals at this weapon. Sandor was the *Inverclyde* winner (on the last hit of a barrage with Flt-Lt Alan Painter of Leicester YMCA, who was also 1969 *Inter-Services* Champion). Julian Tyson of Aberdeen University was third, followed by Harvey Smith (Leicester), Wiles and Martin Joyce (Glasgow FC).

Runner-up in the Junior was Bourne, with fellow-Bostonians Loveland and Cohen in fifth and sixth places and David Scott of Salle Paul third. Fourth and a rising star amongst Under-20s was Simon Routh-Jones, who was also fourth in the senior event at *Amsterdam* in February and again in the *Under-20 Weinheim* tournament in March, though he was only fourth (yet again) in the home *Under-20 Championship*. This was won by the 19-year-old, left-handed Nick Bell of Thames, a pupil of Prof. Harmer-Brown there and previously at Worth School, where he started fencing in 1963 (he had been second in the National Schoolboys the previous season). He was followed by James Noel (Downside) and Terry Etherton (St Paul's). An Under-20 team composed of Bell, Etherton and John Deanfield (5th in the Under-20 Championship) was fifth out of seven nations at *Huy*. Bell was seventh out of 21 in individual placings.

At senior level there was only one notable foreign result this season, albeit a good one: Halsted reached the last sixteen of the top-ranking *Paris Martini*. Nevertheless a full five foilists were included in the tiny British team at the World Championships. For the first time since 1955 neither Jay nor Hoskyns took part (Jay confining himself to epee after thirteen appearances in the foil team at the World Championships or Olympic Games since 1952). Their places, and that of Breckin, were taken by Bonfil, Power and Barry Paul, alongside Halsted and Graham Paul.

*LADIES' FOIL*

This season saw the inauguration of the Categories system. The first of the five events was the *Toupie Lowther*, open to unclassified fencers only. It attracted 44 entrants. The winner was Jackie Tyson of Leicester YMCA (wife of Colin), followed by Mary Hawksworth of Hydra (wife of Geoff) and Mrs Rosemary Castle of Chester FC.

The second category event was the new *Parker Trophy*, for which Shirley Parker had donated a magnificent engraved silver tray. This was open to unclassified and Category C fencers. The final was cautious in mood and became frigid in temperature when the noisy heater was switched off, leaving an unnatural silence, broken only occasionally by the clash of blades, and the cheers of a thin, largely male audience. With the sole Londoner – Valerie Matheson, Pauleons – in bottom place, this was a triumph for the Rest. Moreover, of the other five, all but the winner, Hilary Gardner of Risinghill, had started the season unclassified. Mary Hawksworth was second. Third was Paula Robinson (Scottish FC) four hits behind, with Jackie Tyson another two hits back. Margaret Duthie (Glasgow) was fifth with one win on one hit given.

The third category event was the old Junior, the *Bertrand Cup*, now restricted to Category C and B fencers. It was won by the accurate and intelligent Sally Littlejohns of Oxford University, ahead of Mrs Lesley Hamments of Salle Pearson (2nd), Dr Dorothy Knowles, temporarily at Salle Boston (3rd), Kate Storry of LFC (4th), Julia Bullmore (5th) and in her third final, Mary Hawksworth.

The younger fencers were not an overlapping group this season. The *Under-20 Championship* was won by Hazel Twomey, aggressive and persistent on the piste as she was mild and amiable off it. She was taught by Prof. K. Wren at Blackfriars. Runner-up was Sue Olley of Latista and Cyrano, who was the winner of the *Felix Cup*. Janet Yates of Ashton was third.

In the *Universities Championship* better known fencers had to submit to the undefeated supremacy of Marion Ecob of Bristol. Her accuracy, carefully-timed ripostes and long lunges were exemplary. Marilyn Holmes of Reading had to work very hard for her second place. Clare Henley (3rd), though the fastest and most technically advanced finalist, tended under pressure to adapt an uncommitted, low on-guard position and to lead with her feet.

There were no fewer than 26 teams fencing in the *Team Championships*. In the second round Ashton unexpectedly went out after leading 6–2 over Pearson, who went on to beat Excalibur and LFC in the quarter and semi-finals. Boston, having beaten Thames on hits in the quarter-finals, lost to Poly in the semi-finals. Poly won for the third successive time, by 9–5, in spite of an early lead by Pearson – for whom Mildred Durne in particular earned admiration for beautifully exact low-line parries.

As Team Champion, Poly represented Britain in the Turin *Coppa Europa* in March. Jeanette Bailey, Julia Barkley (née Davis) and Janet W-Y from the first team were joined by Dianne Austin, captain of the Polytechnic's second team. Maureen Kennedy went as non-fencing captain.

Geneva were the first opponents and should not have caused undue worry. After half an hour London were 3–0 down, and though Jeanette Bailey (reminded that her captain held all the meal tickets) improved the situation with a 1–4 win, the Swiss soon led by 6–2. At this point Dianne Austin produced a clear win, Julia Barkley followed suit, Jeanette fought back to win from 3–0 down, and Janet levelled the score at 6–all. Finally it was a 9–7 victory.

The second match was against Prague, who had already lost 7–9 to Turin, but who fought with such fire that their first fencer was three hits up before Janet took command of the situation. They continued to press hard all the way through, but the British team were always ahead. Unfortunately, in the next round Turin lost to Geneva and Poly had to fence Turin on two pistes simultaneously with one scorer. They were now determined that nothing would stop them from getting through: Julia and Janet, at the top of their form, competed for the speediest win; Dianne again scored at a crucial point in the match; and Jeanette, less happy with this off-one-piste-and-on-the-other-situation, nevertheless finished up with a clear victory which gave them a lead on hits even before their ninth win.

On their return from a very late and hurried lunch, the British were astounded to find themselves seeded seventh out of eight teams – to meet the Russians! The organiser blandly informed them that only Moscow and Bucharest had been seeded; the rest had been drawn by lot. Maureen Kennedy's rage at seeing the team effectively robbed of the chance they had fought so hard for was all the greater because she was unable to argue their case effectively in Italian or French; fortunately Mildred Durne, who had just arrived, murmured something about a jury d'appel. Maureen shot back to the table where pool sheets were being written out, bellowed in Mangiarotti's ear 'Nous demandons un jury d'appel' and retired to a safe distance with a dramatic flourish. Mangiarotti redrew the teams, seeding Moscow first, Bucharest second, Budapest third and Poly fourth. The remaining four were drawn by lot, giving Moscow the Poles and London the Czechs. Thereupon the Polish team withdrew in protest.

The second match against Prague was fenced in the friendliest of atmospheres; up to 4–all the score was even, then Dianne Austin started a run of four successive wins and Janet completed the match at 9–6 to put Poly into the final of four.

Their first opponents here were Dinamo Moscow and for a few delirious moments it seemed possible that another victory was in sight. Janet beat Gorochova and Samussenko, and Julia took both Gorochova and Zabellina to the last hit – the Czech team enthusiastically applauding every move of the British girls – but the power and experience of the Russians proved too much. Poly lost 2–9 and, in the sixth match of the day, lost to the Hungarians as well, in the fight-off for third place. The Russians beat the Rumanians 9–7 for first place.

The *Martini* individual competition, next day, always huge, had an entry of 168. Julia Barkley and Jeanette Bailey (still complaining bitterly about all this violent exercise so early in the morning) topped their first round pools. Together with Janet W-Y and Kate Storry of LFC, they were eliminated in third round pools that seemed to have at least one World Champion apiece. The final was won by the Rumanian Drimba over the three Russians, Palm and Lorenzoni.

The Martini hospitality was lavish, complete with car service and a dinner lasting into the small hours.

The *Desprez Cup* was now Competition IV, restricted to Categories A and B. The top three were no surprise: Janet W-Y, Jeanette Bailey and Marilyn Holmes.

The *Championship* itself was now Competition V in the new system. It was likewise restricted to Categories A and B and there were only 36 entries. Eliminated from the semi-finals only on hits were Hazel Twomey and Gerry Harding. The audience for the final was larger than usual but passive even in the penultimate bout when Marilyn Holmes and Janet W-Y, each with four wins, met for the deciding fight. Marilyn Holmes showed fine style and combined superb timing in simple attacks with a complete use of her long reach: but she was unable to stop Janet W-Y (still at Poly but taught now by Prof. Suzanne Ridley), who fenced calmly, even cautiously, but came out with sudden devastating attacks when least expected. Only five hits were scored against her in the final. Third and fourth places also went to Poly fencers: Julia Barkley and Jeanette Bailey; while a perennial finalist of more than a decade – Mildred Durne – was matched by a new and determined face, that of Sue Youngs (Caledonian), who had fought her way up from the qualifying round to sixth place.

Contrary to hopes, there were no Hungarian entries for the *de Beaumont* and only one French, but there proved to be five Germans, three Dutch girls, two Belgians, one Irish girl and one New Zealander.

The British lost the *match against the Germans* on the Saturday by 9–7 (Julia Barkley 3, Janet W-Y 2, Janet Varley 2, Marilyn Holmes 0). Janet W-Y had to scratch from the individual event. (Next day she read in *The Times* that she had retired from fencing as she was having a baby, a fact she was unaware of, though her doctor then found it to be true.) Mrs Green (Exeter) did well to reach the quarter-finals, where the left-handed Kate Storry was unlucky to go out on hits. The semi-finals saw the exit of the last four Britons. In one of them Marilyn Holmes went down by one hit and Mildred Durne by two. In the other, Kristin Payne, who fenced very well to reach this stage, was fourth with two victories, while Julia Barkley had only one win, although she had headed her quarter-final over the eventual winner, Giesselmann of W. Germany.

This season was something of an annus mirabilis for Gerry Harding. Not content with winning at *Ashton* for the fourth consecutive time, she was also the winner at both *Leicester* and *Portsmouth*. The stylish Gerda McGechan of Thames and New Zealand won the *Inverclyde Tournament*, ahead of Sue Youngs, Margaret Duthie and Sue Yeomans, Barbara Goodall and Jackie Tyson. Janet Varley won at *Tyneside* for the third year running.

Sue Youngs also did well to come second in the Under-20 event at *Remich* and, along with Sue Olley, Janet Yates and Hazel Twomey, to beat W. Germany in a *triangular match at Duren*, even if they had to accept third place after losing to France.

On the other hand there were no notable results among the seniors to add to those at Turin, apart from the quarter-final place at *Como* in June by the 23-year-old Kate Storry. This may have contributed to the decision not to send any fencers to the World Championship.

*EPEE*

The *Junior Championship* was carried off by a cool and confident John Henniker-Heaton, after a barrage with James Noel, of Downside and now also Boston, who showed more talent but less nerve, coming within one hit of the title no less than five times, but each time missing the kill. Peters of Behmber was third, ahead of Burch, Davenport and Stuart Wooding (Thames).

Noel was favourite for the *Under-20 Championship*, but it was a first-time finalist who took the cup: Richard Deighton of Cambridge, shrugging off the loss of his first fight, fencing with seriousness and concentration, mainly from absence of blade, drawing counter-attacks and stop-hits and hitting with a fast counter-time. Julian Tyson of Aberdeen University (2v, 4th), the only finalist to beat him – and the most classical – lacked nothing but fire. Steven Frith (5th), fencing for Old Millfieldians, beat both Tyson and Noel, using prises-de-fer on the latter's long, searching advances. Noel thus had to barrage for second place with Mark West of Boston, whose neat, accurate hits to arm he overcame 5–1. John Hall of Edmonton (1v) gave promise of future prowess in sixth place.

This season was the high point in the career of Derek Russell, now resident in Scotland where he was champion at both epee and foil (in both followed by Sandor). He would make the overnight train journey to London events sleeping in the luggage rack. Much practice at sprint starts lent speed and surprise to his fleches. He won the *Martini Qualifying* with thirteen victories in the final of eighteen. Other places were: 2. Richard Deighton (Cambridge University) 12v; 3. Robert Reynolds (Reynolds) 11v; 4. Sgt Terry Harrison (RM) 10/33; 5. Fairhall 10/32; 6. Hill 10/34; 7. Richard Bird (Oxford Univ.) 9/19; 8. M. West 9/20; 9. Partridge, 9/29; 10. Higginson, 8/20; eq 11. Noel Boston, Bill Osbaldeston (Northampton) 8/23; 13. Jim Patterson (LFC) 8/25; 14. Howe (Army) 7/18; 15. Payne (now at London University) 6/18; 16. Gray 5/11; 17. Steve Lennox (Boston) 5/17; 18. Richard Sharp (Salle 64) 3v.

There were thirteen nations and four of the six Mexico finalists in the *Martini* itself. Bourne was among the eight fencers who earned a bye on the results of the first round of the four other British survivors went out at this point. Graham Paul lost to von Essen 8–3, Hoskyns lost to Barburski (Poland) 8–6 and Jacobs lost to Allemand 8–3. Only Halsted triumphed, beating Saccaro 8–3, even more decisively than in the 1967 Martini. In the second series of sudden deaths Bourne was overcome by the tall Trost (Austria) 8–4, while Halsted was eliminated 8–4 by Reant (France).

In the gala Reant beat Andrzejewski and Nielaba, to meet in the final bout his compatriot Varille, who for his part had narrowly beaten Trost and despatched the still taller Gonsior, bouncing in and out and shooting hits from every angle. At first Reant's actions, always on the direct line, were the complete answer to Varille's activity and out of line tactics. He quickly led 5–0. Then he relaxed while Varille completely altered his tactics. At 6–2 he started a series of rapid false attacks, continually altered the measure and hitting with devastating accuracy to recover to 7–all. He finally won with two scorching ripostes at wrist.

The interlude this year was provided by a demonstration bout between Magnan and Berolatti, classic foilists of the French Mexico Gold Medal team. The evening ended as usual with a splendid supper for the foreign visitors on the Martini Terrace of New Zealand House.

Hoskyns, Halsted and Jacobs were all absent from the *Championship*, which was won by Graham Paul, the most consistent fencer in the final of twelve. He lost one bout early on to Noel but otherwise was only twice taken to the last hit in his ten victories. To complement his very fast fleche, his qualities as a foilist ensured a sounder defence than most of his rivals in this pool. Second place went to the holder Johnson by two hits over Bourne. They and Paul were a class above the rest of the pool. Noel jumped a class in gaining fourth place even if his technique did not altogether match his formidable length.

The surprise of the pool was Martin Clarke, who although in his mid thirties achieved his seniority in seventh place, beating both Johnson and Bourne and running Paul to the last hit. His skill in advancing en marchant with his sword arm withdrawn practically round his back blossomed quite suddenly at this juncture and was to disconcert other opponents with more obvious athletic and technical endowments.

The *Miller-Hallett* final of twelve was dominated by Hoskyns, who fenced steadily to victory and ended with two fights in hand, only surrendering one bout by the odd hit to Blomquist of Norway (temporarily at Thames). His two previous victories in this event were fifteen and eleven years before. Second place went to Jacobs by six hits over Blomquist. Returning to form, he had the same number of hits received as the winner, though he was two victories behind! Ganchev, the first fencing master for a long time also to be a notable competition fencer, showed his versatility once again by coming fourth.

Partridge repeated his fifth place of the previous year, while Davenport of Boston reached the last six of a senior event for the first time. The lower places were evenly divided between Thames (Noel 7th, Hudson 10th – both new members), Grosvenor (Clarke 11th, John Simpson 12th) and Salle Paul (Pearman 8th, Zampini 9th – evidently on a visit).

The *Team Championship* was one of the closest and most exciting on record. In the semi-finals London University, the holders, beat Salle Paul in a good match 9–7. For the winners Bourne and Pearman were in particularly good form, while for the other side, Jay, after a long absence from epee, showed much of his old guile. Thames had an easier passage in beating Salle Boston 9–5.

So, as in the previous year, London University faced Thames for the trophy. First one, then the other took the lead, Bourne, Pearman and Graham Paul gaining two victories each for London University and Bonfil one; while Jacobs gained two and Hudson, fencing splendidly, beat Bonfil by the odd hit to give Thames the lead with two hits in hand. In the final bout, Higginson, who had contributed three sterling victories, faced Bourne. After a grim struggle Bourne won 5–2. This exactly levelled the scores to 8–8, 63/63 hits.

Peter Jacobs and Teddy Bourne, the two captains, were then appointed to fence the deciding bout. Hits alternated in a very lively manner, with Jacobs generally just ahead and imposing his tactics. At 4–all he won the match with a perfect riposte en fleche.

Johnson got the only outstanding foreign result of the season when he won the *Bad Durkheim* pool of European champions. He also came fourth in the *Catania* Under-20 event. Pelling was second at Dieppe. Noel put himself on the map by reaching the semi-finals of the Under-20 *Schmetz*, coming seventh in the *Tauberbischofsceim* Under-20 event and fifth in the senior *Amsterdam* tournament.

After their Silver Medal in 1965, the epeeists had fallen far. This year they sent a strange and incomplete team to the Cuba World Championships. Of the six top fencers with good results, three were unavailable: Hoskyns, Bourne and Jacobs. Instead, alongside Johnson and Halsted (the latter also fencing foil) was Jay who had declined to fence foil because of work commitments, but was then prevailed upon by Charles de Beaumont to fence epee. Power was borrowed from the foilists for the team event.

## SABRE

There were 67 entrants for the *Junior*, the final of which was judged the best for many years. Fairburn and Jocelyn looked out of practice when they went out of the quarter-finals, but the semi-final was well contested. Nyiry, Carruthers and Tony Wall of the RAF (betrayed by inconsistency) were among the unlucky victims.

Having so nearly won the year before, David Scott of Salle Paul made no mistakes this time. What he lacked in flair he more than made up for in determination and in technique, especially a very strong defence. His only defeat was to the very promising runner-up, the part West Indian, part British Terry Wishart (Wandsworth School), taught by Prof. Simmonds, who was Scott's antithesis – prone to the odd mistake but with excellent timing and a deep fleche made without preparation. Kovanda was there as ever – third this time – the best technician in the final but not always able to adapt himself quickly enough to the unexpected. Waddelow, fourth, as in the previous year, looked as if he should do better but somehow didn't care to; he was also handicapped by too much of a foilist's technical background. John Buffery (Bath Sword Club) was five hits behind. Mazowiecki, though last, fenced well, with good counter-time.

The slight but flamboyant Wishart went on to win both the *Schoolboys* and the *Under-20 Championships*, in the latter followed by Frith, Terry Etherton, Michael Allen (Cambridge, ex-Millfield), David Hughes (Oxford) and Humphrey Tizard (Oxford).

Once again, largely due to the efforts of John Seymour, Secretary and later Chairman of the Sabre Sub-Committee, a *quadrangular match between Germany, Switzerland and Britain 'A' and 'B'* was combined with the Cole Cup. In the 'B' team, Wishart showed his potential, though his almost reflex counter-time movements made him vulnerable to compound counter-attacks. Scott won two of their three victories against the German team, which included Duschner and Wischeidt. Waddelow and Martin made amends by winning two fights apiece against Switzerland. The 'A' team beat the 'B' team 9–1, the Swiss 9–7 (Rayden gaining three) and kept level with Germany up to seven-all but then lost the two fights. Acfield, Oldcorn and Craig were the other members of the 'A' team. Technically both British teams were sound but lacked the ability to go all out on an attack – too often the fastest part of the attack being in the middle and not at the end. In general the Continental fencers were not so compound in their actions and thus less open to counter-attacks and stop hits.

For the *Cole Cup* four Poles and ten Dutchmen (from the University Team Championship) were added to the foreign tally. The standard was such that eight of the Dutch went out in the first round, along with Rayden and Craig.

For the first time in Britain a Hungarian system was used: semi-finals and final were all eight-strong, but fights between finalists who had met in the semi-final were not repeated, the scores being carried forward. Oldcorn, Martin and Eden departed from the last sixteen. Martin was unlucky with four wins to go out in a barrage to Leckie.

The standard of the final was high, Witzak and Pregowski being in the top eight in Poland and Mohoss (Swiss, but ex-Hungarian) fencing very well to get fourth place. Leckie and Acfield were not at all disgraced in seventh and eighth positions, with Wischeidt only five hits ahead and the rest of the Germans already eliminated. Undefeated until the last bout were Witzak and

Ganchev, who combined 6ft 5ins with a remarkable turn of speed and an excellent technique – his parries always beautifully controlled and his attacks devastatingly long. Witzak, however, had studied his opponent and beat him with intelligently calculated aggression and quinte parries to carry off the cup – in spite of having spent three days in a train and fenced from 8.30 a.m. in the Universities Quadrangular on the Saturday, followed by a trip round Soho until 3.30 a.m.

The *Brussels Martini* was another demonstration of the firm's impressive hospitality. Among the 139 contestants Acfield, Leckie and Oldcorn and Rayden were invited by Martini and Gordon, Fisher, Cohen and Mazowiecki went under their own steam. Of top sabre nations only the Russians were absent. All the British except Mazowiecki survived the first round, but only Acfield and Oldcorn the second. In the direct eliminations, Acfield lost to Pawlowski and Oldcorn to Kawecki, both of Poland. Oldcorn survived one round of the repechage before losing to Kawecki again, Acfield losing immediately to Panella of Italy, both in three matches.

The final comprised the entire Hungarian team of five and Pawlowski, the idol of the Brussels spectators. Kalmar won, followed by Atila Kovacs and Pawlowski.

The *Championship* was marked by two innovations: it took place on the Sunday alone and the forty contestants were drawn into the pools just before the start, thus avoiding difficulties caused by late scratchings.

The fencing even in the semi-finals was of a high standard and here David Eden and Richard Cohen, both of whom had been fencing very well, made their exits, together with Michael Price the elder (Poly).

The final consisted of the three members of the 1968 Olympic team, together with their reserve (Rayden) and two members of the foil team. The first fight between Leckie and Rayden went to the last hit, as did half of the remaining fourteen contests. It was a final of fine recoveries from adverse situations. Three times Acfield was substantially led, first by Craig, whom he beat 5–3, having been 3–1 down, then by Hoskyns, whom he defeated 5–4 and, finally, in the last fight of the afternoon, by Rayden, who having established a 4–1 lead had it eroded into a 5–4 loss. Acfield thus added the national title to his Under-20 and university triumphs. His stirring fight-backs were interspersed with interesting bouts in which Hoskyns (3rd) produced some splendid hits and Breckin – three hits behind him – some extraordinary ones (including an angulated point riposte on the back of Craig). After losing to Acfield, Craig only conceded nine hits in his next four fights.

Presided by David Eden, it was a final notable for the equanimity of the contestants, and for the size of the audience of some fifty people. It marked the beginning of the Acfield era of dominance over the domestic field, just as it marked the end of the era of Leckie, who retired from serious training after the Olympics on domestic and career grounds and who took sixth place on hits below his LFC club-made Rayden. Hoskyns too was making his last serious sabre appearance, in the fifteenth season since he barraged for the title in 1954.

Acfield and Leckie were both absent from the *Corble* (the former playing cricket for Essex, the latter moving house), as was Eden (suffering from teeth extraction); and there was only one foreigner. Wishart went out in the first round, underestimating his opponents, and Breckin tumbled in the quarter-final, with only one win. The semi-finals provided some excellent fencing. Dennis Hunt was unlucky to miss his first senior final on hits. Purchase and the incredibly fit John Moore also departed at this stage.

In the very hot weather, the final was entertaining but also tame. The most improved fencer was Cohen. His footwork had come on considerably and he was a lot faster on the piste. Beaten only by Brasseur and (5–4) by Ganchev, he well deserved third place in this, his first Senior final. Oldcorn followed three hits behind. Craig (5th), who had been tied up with exams, was less aggressive than usual but, as ever, seemed to enjoy his fencing. Brasseur, the previous year's winner and reigning Belgian champion, again demonstrated his fluent technique, though he lost 4–5 to Rayden (6th). But for this, his 5–2 defeat of Ganchev would have given him the title with no defeats. As it was, he was forced to barrage with the giant once again. Both fights were well worth watching – in the second Ganchev kept his distance just a bit better and kept his attacks very direct. At 4–4 he made a direct fleche on which Brasseur counter-attacked out of time to give Ganchev his first major British title.

For the first time in this country the competition was fenced using an 18 metre piste (and not 24 metres as previously). There appeared to be little difference – the more aggressive fencers like Ganchev possibly finding life a little easier.

Seventeen teams took part in the *Team Championship* in April. The semi-finalists were the four top seeds. LFC (again lacking Leckie, who was fencing in South Africa) beat Salle Paul 9–7 in a hard match and Boston annihilated Poly 9–0. The finalists were thus the same as the previous year.

Boston soon established a 4–1 lead and looked set to run LFC off their feet as they had Polytechnic, but now the cliff-hanging started. Rayden, Oldcorn and Straus each won their second fights and LFC levelled at 4–all. Martin beat Straus to give them an 8–7 lead and what would have been a victory on hits even had Acfield lost to Oldcorn in the last fight (which he didn't). Thus Salle Boston, a young, fast, balanced and well trained side, justified their promise of the previous year. Acfield and Martin both got three wins, Cohen two and Fisher one. For LFC, John Rayden played the captain's part with four wins, three of them from 4–all. Oldcorn had two wins, Straus one and Rizutto nil.

This season Craig was *Inter-Services Champion* for the third time running and Wiles scored his provincial double at *Nottingham* and *Inverclyde*, winning the latter for the fourth time running (ahead of Titheradge, Painter, Mitchell, Lewis Smith of Heriot-Watt and Mike Dee of Edinburgh University).

Abroad as at home, it was Cohen who improved dramatically, gaining a very good fourth place at *Hamburg*. His fencing was an excellent combination of intelligence and determination. Oldcorn was sixth. At the *Maccabiah* Games, open to Jews throughout the world, Cooperman came fourth in the sabre, and with David and Melvyn Eden, Mike Price the elder and Terry Wishart, won the team event. Prof. Ganchev won the *Amsterdam* Tournament. At Under-20 level, Melvin Eden, Wishart and John Deanfield of Westminster School all reached the quarter-final at *Goppingen*; Eden was sixth in *Ghent*.

No sabreurs accepted the invitation to fence in the World Championships in Cuba, for which they would have had to pay £200 each.

## COMBINED EVENTS

At the *Ashton Tournament* Les Jones and his club colleagues managed to complete a seven-event competition at four weapons in a weekend, although the number of entries was double that of the previous year. In the men's foil final, Wiles remained unbeaten till he succumbed to cramp and lost his last fight to Eden, some of whose fights had looked like the long-awaited electric sabre (especially against Ganchev, 5th). Eden then won the barrage. Malcolm Priestley (Leicester) was fifth and Alan Hughes (Manchester Univ.) sixth.

The ladies' foil final, with no fencers from the south of England, was an affair of refreshingly continental ferocity (as was the ladies' foil team final), and it was easy to see how Sue Green (still in Mexico) had proved herself so quickly, surrounded by this sort of opposition. Gerry Harding (Warley) retained her title after a barrage with Jackie Varley (Hydra). Janet Yates (Ashton, 3rd), who won her first two fights easily, but thereafter seemed unable to attack, was followed by Mary Hawksworth (Hydra), Rosemary Castle (Chester) and Jackie Tyson (Leicester).

The epee provided a surprise in the descent of the holder, Purchase, into third place. Instead, victory went to the young and mobile foilist Geoff Grimmett (third at his own weapon), ahead of Robin Davenport (Boston), Bill Osbaldeston (Leicester), Martin Clarke (Victoria, S. Paul's tandem club) and Bob Turner (S. Reynolds).

The sabre final was the best. Everyone assumed – with justification – that Ganchev would win, so every hit against him was applauded as a master stroke. He provided an object lesson in sabre and only David Scott (3rd) took him to the last hit in a very exciting fight, although Wiles (2nd) still suffering from cramp and relying on considerable tactical ingenuity, seemed to worry him most. Prof. McNeil was fourth, Eric Bird (RAF) fifth and Andrew Reynolds (S. Reynolds) sixth.

The 38th *Leamington Tournament* comprised 380 competitors and 600 entries in the four weapons. Eight countries were represented. The team events followed the Mayor's evening reception, as usual. In the ladies' foil, Sue Youngs, Sandra Robertson and Catherine Wotherspoon of Caledonian beat Salle Boston. The sabre was won by London FC against Rhineland. The epee was won by Thames against Birmingham. Saturday and Sunday were spent fencing off the individual preliminary rounds. On Saturday evening the traditional dance was held. On Monday the finals were held en gala in the Town Hall. Pam Patient of Reading won the ladies' foil, ahead of Hage (Holland) and Mildred Durne. Derek Russell of Scottish FC won both foil and epee, having already scored the same double in the Scottish Championships. He was followed in the foil by Fairhall and René Paul and in the epee by Davenport and Wiles. At sabre the winner was Wischeidt (Germany), ahead of Acfield and Ganchev.

After the Universities Championships a British team fenced in a *universities quadrangular*. At the bleak hour of 8.30 a.m. the British got off to the familiar infamous start, against Poland. Of the sixteen wins (to the Poles' 48) Breckin and Graham Paul accounted for the five foil victories and Bourne and Rouxel the four at epee, while the sabreurs were very hard put to it against their refined opponents.

The British then beat the Dutch, and the French – almost as good as their Mexico finalists – defeated the Poles 34–29 in the most exciting series of fights of the day. If only the British had risen to the Poles as they now did to the over-relaxed French! From 7–3 down the foilists rallied to 7–8 and were actually ahead on hits, only to have Berolatti snatch the last fight from Graham Paul. The ladies similarly lost 9–7; a very fine effort against Level, Ceretti and Josland, Celia Whitehurst of S. van Oeveren going especially well, after only fencing for eighteen months. Unfortunately the epeeists went down 5–11 to Varille and his colleagues; on average they hit their opponents a bare twice. The sabreurs, with fine aggression, won 8–all, each winning two fights. Overall, the British came third.

In its tenth year, the *Nottingham Tournament* continued to rise in popularity and in standard. In the ladies' final Gerry Harding, the holder, was not on form, although most of her fights were only lost by the last hit. Janet Varley, the winner, fought consistently and with determination. She was followed by Rosemary Castle, Mrs Inga Foulkes (Portland) and Maria Ecob (Bristol Univ.). Wiles got his third successive win of the men's foil when he beat Frank Hindle in a barrage. Third and fourth places went to the young and energetic Chris Brown (Catford) and Andy Eames (Leicester City Boys). Sabre had a poor entry and was won, predictably, by Wiles, over Brian Price-Thomas (Poly).

In the *Quadrangular Match*, held at the de Beaumont Centre, England and Scotland ran neck and neck for the title. Thanks to three sterling victories from Wiles (not yet claimed by his country of birth and prematurely described as 'veteran'), England just captured the men's foil 5–4 (Rorke saving two fights); but the Scots girls reversed this result 5–4 in spite of three victories from Janet Varley. (Sue Youngs and Janette Stewart only dropped two fights each throughout the weekend.) In the epee, Scotland forged ahead to 5–0, but the English made a surprising recovery and won the next four fights. All therefore depended on the sabre match. Sandy Leckie, the captain, stepped in to replace Jake Gordon, who had torn his ankle in the Irish match although winning all three fights. Nevertheless, largely due to three victories from David Eden, England won 6–3 and took the whole match by 19–17. A Welsh team led by Robert Reynolds beat N. Ireland 25–11 for third place.

At *Halifax* there was a record entry of fourteen for the Ladies' Team Cup. Ashton were the winners, with Cromwell second. The individual, with an entry of over fifty, was won by Hazel Rogerson. Mary Hawdon was second and Sue Green third. The men's foil was won by Ian Bissitt, from Leeds SC. Peter Lees (Ashton) was second, Lynn Wall (Leeds Univ.) third. Out of 25 sabreurs Alan Taylor (Hydra) was the winner. Wall was second and Rob Kilvert third. At epee there was a single pool, won by Kevin Bayliss of Hydra.

The *World Youth Championships* were held in Genoa. Eve Davies added to the backing on the ladies' side, while Prof. K. Pearson and Prof. Boston replaced Prof. Anderson as coaches. The male foilists had a disappointing time. Bell and Routh-Jones could only win one bout each in their first round pools. Etherton won a couple but could not survive the next round. The ladies fared little better. In the first round Susan Olley and Janet Yates were eliminated. Hazel Twomey fenced well and with four victories went up second, but in the second round only won one bout. In de Beaumont's opinion the foilists lacked technique, having learnt to run before they could walk. The epeeists were more successful. In the second round Deighton and Noel were easily eliminated, but Mark West fenced very well to take third place in his pool and reach the last 24. In the direct elimination he drew Bena, a difficult and determined French left-hander, and won the first bout 5–3. Even in the second bout he led 4–1, but then erred by attacking and lost 5–4. By the third bout Bena's experience took charge and he won 5–3. In the repechage West met Jaretzky of Austria and only lost the first bout by the odd hit. In the second he fenced extremely well to win 5–2, but then tired and went out 5–1.

At sabre, though Steven Frith was eliminated in the first round, David Hughes got to the second and Terry Wishart had four excellent victories in the second round to reach the last sixteen – no mean performance at his age. Unfortunately, he could not maintain this form in the direct elimination and lost to Popescu (Rumania) 5–3, 5–2 and, in a better bout, to Quivrin (France) 5–2, 1–5, 5–0.

World Youth team 1969. *Back:* J. Deanfield, J. Noel, M. West, S. Frith, T. Etherton. *Middle:* J. Berry, (Men's Manager), R. Deighton, Hazel Twomey, Janet Yates, K. Pearson (Coach), Sue Olley, Prof. S. Boston (Coach), D. Hughes, N. Bell. *Front:* Mrs May Davies (Ladies' Manager), T. Wishart, S. Routh-Jones.

In a post-Olympic year, the October *World Championships* in Cuba provided to be too inconveniently timed and too expensive (even with a fifty per cent travel grant) for a complete team to be mustered.

Though there were endless breakdowns of equipment (personal as well as official), the organisation was good and the fencing halls and hospitality excellent. The intense, humid heat was an exhausting drawback.

In the first round of the men's foil Graham Paul started badly, eventually got three wins, but was eliminated on hits, as was Barry Paul with two wins, while Bonfil could only manage one.

In the second round, Power was in the curious position of tying with Kamuti on three wins and a hits ratio of one. He did very well to win the barrage 5–4. In the quarter-finals he fenced as a man inspired and beat La Ragione (Italy), Dimont (France), Romanov (5–0) and Gil (Cuba) in record time, only surrendering four hits in these four victories. He topped the pool with only one defeat, from Parulski (Poland). To reach the last twelve in the world in this fashion was a remarkable performance and, while the fitness training in which he specialised helped, his technical fencing was of the highest order.

Meanwhile, Halsted, promoted to the third round on hits, found that exhaustion had caught up with him and he failed to score. Fencing had now been going on almost continuously for close on twelve hours.

It was too much to hope that Tony Power could reproduce quite such magnificent form in the semi-finals next morning, but he had the distinction of beating Drimba, the Olympic Champion, 5–4 and Berolatti 5–2 and only lost to Parulski and Romanov 4–5 and to Wessel, the eventual winner (5–1). He was thus placed fourth and missed promotion to the final by one bout.

In the team foil Britain drew Italy and USSR. Against Italy they started badly and never caught up. Graham Paul was in good form and won two bouts, but Halsted, Power and Bonfil could only win one apiece. For the Russian match Barry Paul replaced Tony Power. He and Graham both beat Poutiatin, but that was the extent of success against this champion team.

In the epee individual Jay topped his first round pool with four victories, Johnson with three victories was second and Graham Paul, also with three victories, was fourth and also promoted. Halsted was completely out of touch and could only record one win. As at foil, the second round with only three promoted out of six was a severe test. Paul with two victories and Johnson with one were eliminated. Jay, fencing with his wonted elan, scored two good wins and went up to the quarter-finals (last 24) on hits. He thus went a long way to justify his participation. In the quarter-final he got two wins, tying with four others on victories for the last place for promotion. However, this time his hits ratio was not good enough and he was eliminated. This proved to be Jay's last appearance at a World Championship or Olympic Games after participating fifteen times. It was the tenth time he had reached the quarter-final or better at foil or epee.

The epee team drew Italy and Poland, perhaps harder than at foil but still not an impossible task. The match with Italy was disappointing. Johnson scored three victories to show what could be done, Jay had two wins and Graham Paul one, while Halsted could not score. Against Poland, strong at any time, the team again trailed. Graham came back to form with three victories and Halsted and Johnson got one apiece. This time Jay failed to score.

# 1969–70

*MEN'S FOIL*

At the junior end of the scale, the 13-year-old Robert Bruniges first made a significant impact with second place in the *Junior National Schoolboys* and second again in the *Under-20 Championship*, to Mick Knell. From the beginning, he had a remarkably mature defence, partly due to his excellent balance, which it is tempting to relate to the asymmetrical adjustments he made for the congenital loss of his non-fencing right hand. This disability was clearly in more general terms a challenge which only served to evince a triumphant response.

Like Knell, Bruniges was at Catford School, where he had started to fence two years before. Here John Fairhall had been teaching since January 1968 and rapidly produced a whole generation of successful pupils.

The *Senior National Schoolboys* and *Public Schools Championships* were both won by the talented Gavin Brown of Dover College, taught by Prof. Mallard.

In the first *Under-20 Nescafé Tournament*, the British could not match the continentals' footwork or blade control and were obsessed with broken-time attacks. In the team event, GB 'C' (Peter Michaeledes of Millfield, Waldman and Etherton) did best, coming fourth. The Italians won, beating France and Belgium into second and third places and swamping GB 'A' 8–1 (Hall scoring the sole win). Noel, not included in any of the teams, did best in the individual events, missing the final by one hit. Grimmett, Etherton, Routh-Jones and Deanfield also reached the semi-finals. Bernkopf (Italy) was the winner, while the strength of the opposition is shown by the other finalists: Flament, Dutripon, Pezza, Reant and Montano.

The *Junior Champion* was 27-year-old Malcolm Fare of Thames, a tall lanky fencer whose tactical skill and intelligent reading of his opponent's game would have taken him even further but for lack of athletic prowess. Before a spell in Australia from 1964 to 1967 he had been taught by Prof. Sanders of Taunton for six years. Runner-up was Waddelow, who went on to come fourth in the *National*. An even more impressive rise was achieved by Stuart Wooding (now at Thames), who had narrowly failed to win the Junior as far back as 1967 and now only came third, but went on to win *Leicester*, to come second in the *Emrys Lloyd* and third in the *Coronation*. It was Mike Breckin, however, who was supreme on the home front, winning both the Emrys Lloyd and the Coronation and coming third in the Championship. Barry Paul was second in the Championship and third in the Emrys Lloyd, while Graham Paul, absent from the National final, was second in the Coronation. Bill Hoskyns doesn't figure in the records for this season – with one exception. He won the Championship (on a barrage)! He was only the seventh foilist thus to win three times, the first occasion being in 1959.

With Graham and Barry back in the fold, alongside Jay and Single, Salle Paul resumed its accustomed grip on the *Team Championship*, winning the final 9–1 against Boston, who were runners-up for the first time.

Abroad, Graham, Barry, Breckin and Waddelow all reached the last 24 of the *Rommel*, a very solid impact on an event of the highest standard. Salle Paul in the associated *European Team Championship* beat Austria 10-6 in the first round, but then lost to the USSR, the ultimate winners, 9-3.

At *Bad Durkheim* Breckin, Halsted, G. Paul and Single lost a match against Germany 9-7. Graham Paul did outstandingly well to win the individual event. Halsted also excelled in third place and Breckin reached the semi-finals. At *Cologne* Graham reached the semi-finals and sixth place was taken by Geoff Grimmett, who also notched himself up to a higher level by coming fifth in the Championship and second in the *Under-20 Luxembourg Tournament*. Tall and talented, he was a thinking fencer who kept his movements as simple as possible.

To confuse the picture, Jay, who didn't figure in the home results, came second in the *Flanders Golden Foil*, out of an entry of 88. Power reached the last 64 of the *Paris Martini*, to add to his fourth place in the Coronation.

Breckin and the Pauls were selected for the English Commonwealth team. Added for the World Championships were Tony Power and Ian Single – the latter a surprise choice as he had not been in the final of the Championship or Coronation or the top three of the Emrys Lloyd and had obtained no notable foreign result. This was a major disappointment for Wooding.

## *LADIES' FOIL*

In the Under-20 *Perigal* Catherine Wotherspoon of Edinburgh University fenced with spirit up to the semi-finals, as did the rising star Susan Wrigglesworth, who had started training under Paddy Power at York two years before and was now, still aged only fifteen, at Salle Paul under Prof. Lagnardo. The final was won by van Eyck of Belgium after a barrage with Picard and Eckert of France. Three home fencers each had two wins. Sixth on hits was the inexperienced but skilfully riposting Danuta Joyce, of Bath Convent. Fifth was Janet Yates (Ashton), controlled but not at her best. Susan Green did not add enough in the way of tactics and accuracy to her long lunge, so effective against the British, to beat the high-speed foreigners.

Britain provided the largest foreign contingent at the *Duisburg Under-20* competition, with ten girls from Ashton, two from Newcastle and one from London. Five girls went through to the second round, where Janice Deakin of Ashton came unstuck, and the diminutive Susan Wrigglesworth, fencing in her first foreign competition, surprised her opponents with her speed and aggressiveness but went down on hits. Susan Blanchard (Ashton) did outstandingly to reach the quarter-finals. Here Janet Yates did well to beat Zeh, but went out with three wins on hits, as did Susan Green from a very tough pool in spite of beating Armbrust 4-2. Van Eyck won the event.

In the *Under-20 Championship* Janice Deakin, Jane Swanson (S. van Oeveren) and Catherine Wotherspoon got no further than the quarter-finals.

Lorna Andrews (Poly), who showed potential, was unlucky to go out in the semi-finals on hits. Susan Green, making her last appearance in the event, was undefeated victor – only being extended by Julia Raine (S. van Oeveren), who was second with three wins and might have won if she had used her full length in attacks. Janet Yates followed on hits but looked at the box too often. Susan Wrigglesworth was fourth, also on three wins. Celia Whitehurst, yet another pupil of Maitre van Oeveren, fenced with gusto to fifth place on one win. Colette Bailey (Ashton) was sixth.

In the match before the *Under-20 Nescafé Tournament*, Susan Green (undefeated), Janet Yates and Danuta Joyce beat Belgium 8–4, Germany 5–4, GB 'B' 6–3 and GB 'C' 9–0, but had to be content with third place, equal on match victories with France and Germany. The individual event was won by Muzio (France), ahead of Van Eyck. Susan Green beat Muzio and Oertel and ended fifth. One critic thought she could have done even better if she hadn't tended to close distance at the end of her attacks, leaping around trying to hit her opponent's back. Next on hits was Janet Yates. Susan Wrigglesworth, Jane Swanson, Danuta Joyce and Julia Raine reached the semi-finals.

Non-Londoners were again to the fore in the first three Category competitions. Hazel Rogerson won the *Toupie Lowther* and then went on to claim the *Bertrand Cup* for Hydra as well. Olivia Drummond of Latista was second in the Lowther and then fourth in the *Parker Cup*, which was won by Mrs E. Cook (née McKenna) of Warley FC. The other places in the Lowther were Rosemary Castle (Chester FC, 3rd), Lesley Wheeler (Pauleons, 4th), Sharon Williams (Cardiff, 5th) and Margaret Young (Blackfriars, 6th). There were two more Cardiff fencers in the Parker, both from Prof. Reynolds' own salle: Linda Brown (2nd) and Frances Reynolds (5th). Alda Milner-Barry of Thames was the only London fencer in this final (3rd).

Barbara Williams of Glasgow FC was runner-up in the Bertrand, followed by Hazel Twomey, now at Boston, Catherine Wotherspoon (who also won the *Universities Championship*), Mrs Ingrid Foulkes of Warley and Mrs Jill Dudley of Thames.

The most notable feature of the provincial events was Mildred Durne's victory at *Ashton*, an event she had won three times before, the first occasion being in 1956.

115 fencers entered *de Beaumont Cup*, even more than the previous year. Belgium, France, West Germany, Australia, Ireland, New Zealand and South Africa were represented. Susan Green and Janet Yates suffered from 'knee trouble' and went out in the quarter-finals, along with Susan Wrigglesworth. Julia Raine did exceptionally well to be one of the seven British fencers in the semi-finals. A touch of unwonted formality was given to the final by Michel Kellipetis's introductions of the fencers. The standard was higher than for some time. The president was Charles de Beaumont himself. Judith Bain started well with a 4–1 victory over Janet Wardell-Yerburgh (Poly), but then

lost her next three bouts, only recovering to defeat Nicolet (France) in her last. Lecomte (Belgium) got through three bouts with only Pulch taking her to the last hit. Clare Henley (now at Thames) raised British hopes by beating her by the odd hit, for this gave Janet W-Y the chance of snatching the title in the last fight of all. But Lecomte regained top form to win 4–2. On a recent FIE ruling the places of the remaining four fencers who each had two wins were decided by ratio of hits from the second round onwards. This favoured the British, Clare Henley coming third and Judith Bain fourth.

The *Championship* marked something of a changing of the guard. Jeanette Bailey, Judith Bain, Julia Barkley and Mildred Durne, who had reigned in many finals up to the previous year, were displaced and three young fencers reached their first national final: Hazel Rogerson of Hydra (2nd), Kate Storry (LFC), a very strong fencer who used her length, (3rd; 3v) and Hazel Twomey with her forward-leaning, angular style, who grew in confidence (2v; 4th). Clare Henley (5th) had some beautiful forward parry-ripostes. Marilyn Holmes (still at Reading University) had one win.

Janet Wardell-Yerburgh (now taught by Prof. Bertrand and sporting joint Poly-LFC colours) retained the title with her usual concentration and simple but well-timed, fast and accurate attacks. She lost to Clare Henley 4–2, but had only two other hits scored against her.

The *Jubilee Bowl* was also awarded to Janet W-Y (fencing for Poly) when she was undefeated in an invitation pool of twelve, devised as a training event prior to the World Championships. She fenced so consistently she was only hit twelve times. Hazel Davenport of Boston (née Twomey, now married to Robin the epeeist) got one of her best results in coming second with seven wins, showing pertinacity if not the most organised of styles. Susan Green, Julia Bullmore, Julia Barkley (victim of tennis elbow) and Liz Cook were separated in that order on hits with six wins. Kate Storry had five wins, Janet Yates, Mrs Jill Dudley (Thames), Gerry Harding, and Jeanette Bailey had four wins, and Hazel Rogerson three.

The *Team Championship* was captured at last by the classical training and physical fitness of the young Ashton quartet. Poly, the holders, had suffered the loss of Prof. Behmber the previous summer and Janet Wardell-Yerburgh was fencing in spite of the tragic death of her husband only days before. They lost in the semi-finals to the northern team, who went on to defeat Thames, although they trailed almost to the end, Susan Green scoring her only victory to bring them to 8–7 and Janet Yates her fourth to complete the job.

In the *Coppa Europa* eleven teams were entered. Ashton drew three very strong opponents in their first round. Against Warsaw, Susan Green, Janet Yates, Janice Deakin and Susan Blanchard soon led 4–2 but unfortunately only one more victory was scored. Janet Yates had two victories and her team-mates one apiece. Next was the formidable Dinamo Moscow with three former World Champions. With Susan Blanchard replaced by Dorothy

Ashton team Champions. *Back:* Colette Bailey, Janice Deakin, Janet Yates. *Front:* Sue Green, Les Jones.

Skidmore, they lost 16–0, Susan Green being injured in her first fight. They then met the hard-fencing Germans: Janet Yates scored three magnificent victories and lost the fourth by one hit. Dorothy Skidmore registered one victory. That was that. (In the final, Hungary beat Russia by one hit in a fight-off.)

In the *Turin individual* the best performance of the ten British came from Kate Storry. She never gave up fighting, pulling through three rounds to the quarter-finals and within touching distance of the semi-finals: a notable performance in a world class tournament that lacked only the Rumanians. The order in the final was: Gorokhova, Palm, Novikova, Masciotta, Rejto and Ceretti.

The month before, Mildred Durne and Julia Raine had reached the last 16 at *Duren*. The following weekend, Janet W-Y reached the last 24 of the *Jeanty*. In April, Susan Green reached the semi-final at *Goppingen* and, in June, Julia Bullmore reached the same stage at *Eupen*. The fast, balanced Clare Henley was third in the *Decade Sportive* in Brussels. Finally, in July, Susan Wrigglesworth came second at *Dieppe*, a good end to a good season.

For the Commonwealth Games English team, Janet W-Y, Clare Henley and Susan Green were selected. For the World Championships Julia Barkley and Kate Storry were added (the former fencing for Wales in the Games).

## EPEE

The *Junior* title went to the fast-improving Ted Hudson, who had also been the winner at *Leicester*. He was fencing for Thames, to which he now travelled from Oxford. After an initial double defeat with his club-mate Tim Belson, he fenced with concentration to win all his remaining bouts. Well placed on guard, he showed a good sense of distance and a fast attack on riposte taking the blade, and now and then brought off a very accurate hit on the wrist. Second place in the pool of eight went to Gray of Boston, who long led the field, only losing to the winner and Belson. Norman Rouxel of Scottish FC and Hill of LFC, who showed great improvement, tied exactly on hits. Rouxel won the barrage 5–3. Russell started well, but lost concentration. Belson showed his potential, but lacked tightness and accuracy. Bernard Ortt (Paul) was in eighth place at the age of 45, behind John Hall (now at St Paul's College, Cheltenham).

Russell retained his *Scottish* title, ahead of Rouxel, Tyson, David Hunter (Bon Accord, 1960 Champion), Ian Hunter (Scottish FC) and Brian McMicken (Dollar Academy).

Mark West of Boston won the *Under-20 Championship*, ahead of Deanfield and Bird, both pupils of Prof. Imregi. Jonathan Stanbury, previously taught by David Martin at Mill Hill and now at Boston, was fifth. Robert Jamieson of Scotland was sixth. James Noel, who came fourth, was the only British finalist in the first *Nescafé Under-20 International*, displaying a rather straightlegged and often bouncy style. He lost 5–4 after apparently having the beating of Opgenorth (Germany). The latter won his first three fights, but was unable to recover after being thrashed 5–1 by the winner, Debiard of France. Noel took second place on indicators. Ivanoff and Evequoz of Switzerland and Condoumi of France occupied the other places.

Hudson confirmed his success by winning the *Martini Qualifying* competition, after a 5–2 barrage with Partridge, the *Universities Champion* of this season. Both had eight wins in the final of twelve. The other places were as follows: 3. Pearman, 7/14; 4. Jacobs, 7/17; 5. Hall, 5v; 6. Higginson, 5v; 7. Clarke, 4v; 8. Belson, 3/8/38; 9. Payne (London Univ.), 3/8/31; 10. B. Bollobas (Cambridge Univ.), 2/6; 11. M. West, 2/8; 12. B. More (now BAF) retired injured.

Nineteen British fencers were included in the *Martini* itself and Chris Green did extremely well to head the first round with Larsson, the Swedish Champion, and so win a bye through the first stage of direct elimination. Of nine other British fencers only two won through. Pearman lost to Ladegaillerie 8–3, G. Paul lost to Trost 8–3, Jacobs lost to Netburn 8–6, Higginson lost to Fenyvesi 8–2, Johnson lost to Melcher (USA) 8–6 and Jay lost to Nielaba 8–5. From an internecine conflict Clarke emerged victor by 8–5 over Hudson, while Hoskyns beat Caraes (France) 8–6.

In the last sixteen, Netburn was too much for Green (8–2). Clarke excelled to put six hits on Larsson, while Hoskyns had a hard match with Testoni, the Italian Champion, but beat him 10–8.

In the first bout of the excellent final it was a delight to see how the 38-year-old Hoskyns slowed the fast, athletic Trost – a regular finalist in world events – pressing him insistently, and hitting him with fleches that seemed to float onto his chest. Unfortunately in the semi-final bout Hoskyns met Netburn, who had just beaten Fenyvesi and who was now on one of those streaks when everything he tried came off. With hits on the hand, the knee and the forearm either in attack of counter-attack he so demoralised his opponent that the last three hits came from simple attacks – and he triumphed 8–1.

Meanwhile Varille had beaten Melcher 8–3. In the final bout he took the lead alternately with Netburn, with never more than a hit between them. Varille, aggressive, confident and extremely mobile, was determined to retain the title. Netburn, deceptively indolent, fenced extremely well, mixing stop-hits and counter-time with excellent point control. But at 7–all Varille brought off one of his spectacular shots at the inside of the hand from a seemingly impossible angle, and clinched the bout with a very fast attack on preparation.

A *match against Germany* on the eve of the Miller-Hallett was lost 10–3, though Britain took the last three bouts to make the final score 10–6. Geuter and Jung, both accomplished left-handers, collected three victories apiece, while Kilbert and Hauk each won a couple. Bourne fenced well to win three victories. Johnson only scored one victory, but ran Jung to 5–all and Hauk to the odd hit. Hoskyns and Graham Paul also managed only one win each.

The *Miller-Hallett* itself devastated leading British fencers. Jacobs and Partridge went out in the first round; Johnson, G. Paul and Higginson fell by the wayside in the second, to which had been added the teams plus four extra Germans and Pesthy (US Champion). Bourne, Hudson and More reached their ceiling in the quarters.

The final consisted of the German team and two Britons. Jung, winner of the 1966 Martini, won in splendid form. But the revelation of the tournament was James Noel of Thames who fenced consistently to reach the final and there fought with controlled aggression and accuracy of point. After losing his first bout to Hoskyns 5–3, he went from strength to strength and beat both Kilbert and Hauk 5–0, and Geuter 5–1, so that had he not lost his last bout to Jung by the odd hit he would have tied for the title (and he was actually hit four times less than Jung). Fourth place went to Hoskyns, behind Kilbert, but ahead of Geuter on hits with two wins. Hauk won no fights.

Jacobs made a storming come-back in the *Championship*, repeating his victories of 1962 and 1965, having been out of the final since 1967 (though he'd retained a place in the top six of the generally tougher Miller-Hallett continuously till 1969). He looked easily the most relaxed and freshest finalist. His fleches were as devastating as ever and his positive blade work and timing got him clear victories. Only Bourne came within a hit of beating him – but for him, nothing went right: he ended fifth with one win and four defeats on the last hit. Graham Paul (3v) was not as accurate as sometimes, but took second place on indicators over Hoskyns. Johnson was fourth on wins over Paul and Fox was sixth with one victory – and could have done better if he hadn't suffered from too much respect for his blue-chip rivals.

In the *Team Championship* the epeeists who had made London University so strong had returned to their normal clubs; the interloper among the top teams this time was the Army, who beat Lansdowne 9–1, Grosvenor 9–3 in the quarters and Boston 7–6 in the semis. In the final, however, they slumped. Jim Fox, Tony Flood and Jim Darby each got one win and Belson nil. They were up against the esprit de corps of Salle Paul. Partridge, so unphysical and seemingly lackadaisical in comparison with his muscular opponents, took three wins off them, while Paul, Pearman and Single each took two.

Abroad this season, Graham Paul came fourth in the *Bad Durkheim* pool of champions. Bourne and Jacobs both did well to reach the semi-finals of the *Monal*. Hoskyns was fifth at *Laupheim* after a British team also containing Johnson, Noel and Hudson had lost to a German team 10–5.

In the Coupe d'Europe Team event at *Heidenheim* Thames was represented by Jacobs, Halsted, Higginson, Hudson and Noel. To face, at 8.00 a.m., teams from eighteen countries did nothing to warm their spirits, already depressed by the inch of snow lying all over the town so unseasonably. The first round draw placed Thames with Dynamo Minsk, Ankara and Bonn. The stark fact that a loss against Germany would require a victory against Russia (led by Nikanchikov and Smoliakov, first and second in the 1966 World Championships) so stimulated Thames that in very un-British fashion they started flat-out and soon led 5–1, to win ultimately 9–6. After being reassured by Nikanchikov that Turkey were 'very bad fencers' they only beat them 9–7; even this largely by the efforts of Halsted, holding an epee for the first time since Cuba, who won his last fight from 4–1 down.

The direct elimination draw gave Heidenheim. At 7–all, in the last two fights, fenced simultaneously on adjacent pistes in the centre of the hall, two Thames fencers and two supporters were overcome by two Heidenheim fencers and about two thousand local fans.

Revitalised by an official dinner, a late night story-swapping session with the Czech team in four languages and a fast spinning drive down the ice-clad hill in the morning, the British – reinforced by Bourne – set about the individual competition of 260 fencers (including 140 non-Germans), without doubt the strongest Western European event of the year at any weapon. Three of them reached the direct elimination (last 64). Here their efforts seemed largely concentrated on mounting a revenge on Heidenheim team members. Higginson eliminated the international Wurz (Heidenheim) before losing in the last 32. Bourne succumbed at the same stage to Miesse of the German team, whilst Jacobs, having a very good weekend, beat Fenyvesi of Hungary and Muck of Heidenheim before losing on the last hit to Rohlin of Sweden in the last sixteen.

The event demonstrated the breadth of epee fencing across Europe by this date. There were eighteen countries in the last 64 and five in the last eight, and the standard was of the highest – a banquet of epee, the high point being the fight in which the great Nikanchikov was 3–8 down against Schmitt of Germany, was still 8–6 down with one minute to go, but equalised two seconds before time was called with a forward reprise en fleche and finally won – going on to win the competition.

Higginson came third in the *Brussels Decade Sportive*, but his outstanding achievement was at *Poitiers*, the only event apart from Heidenheim attracting the Russians at this period. The first two rounds of pools eliminated all but two of the British entrants, along with several notable epeeists from elsewhere. In the knockout Lawrence Burr (Boston) lost to Coutard 5–1, 5–4. Higginson was seeded only 23rd out of the top 32, but promptly beat the tenth seed, Duchene of France, 5–4, 3–5, 5–2, and went on the beat Livak, a leading Russian, 5–3, 3–5, 5–2, thus putting himself in the gala of the last eight in the medieval Hall of Justice. He lost the first fight against Fenyvesi 5–2, but fought back in the second and even led 3–2 before the Hungarian emerged the winner at 5–3. Of the Russians, Nikanchikov was eliminated at the same stage, while Kriss beat Zagitski for the title in a barrage.

Bourne and Hoskyns were clear candidates for the World Championship, but it was not so easy to sort out Paul, Higginson, Johnson and Noel. In the event, it was the last who was the disappointed contender. Jacobs was persuaded to emerge from retirement to fence for England in the Commonwealth Games, along with Hoskyns and Johnson (rather than Bourne). Halsted missed the whole latter part of the season through a torn cartilage.

*SABRE*

The *Junior* was rich in future internationals, the high standard proved by the quality of the sabreurs who fell by the wayside: Kovanda and Arato, the Australian Commonwealth Games finalist, were both eliminated in the semi-finals and Mazowiecki in the quarters.

With four fencers under the age of twenty, the final was marked by speed and mobility rather than thought and decision. John Deanfield was the exception; he wasted less energy and was more incisive than the others. He won with four victories. Only seventeen, left-handed and rising six foot tall, he had previously gained success as a schoolboy at foil rather than sabre. Now, at one bound, without, for instance, having previously reached the final of the Under-20 Championship, he put himself within striking distance of the

British team. He had been taught at Westminster by Prof. Imregi and was now his pupil at Poly. He had also spent part of 1968 in Koblenz and training there under another Hungarian, Prof. Somos, contributed to his being the most stylish sabreur to emerge since Leckie.

David Hughes (3v) was second. He relied upon a good defence interspersed with well-timed and well-executed stop-cuts. In a final of broken time attacks he was in his element. Etherton, one hit behind, showed himself a very neat all-round sabreur but as yet lacked determination and also betrayed his foil provenance. Peter Lennon (2v, 4th) was out of practice after a year in the Persian Gulf; he was often hit by counter-actions.

The speed and panache of Wishart's strokes sometimes outdistanced the thinking behind them. Peter Mather (Brentwood) having topped his semi-final, failed to find form in the final and ended sixth: still only sixteen, it was predicted that he would go far if experience were added to his enthusiasm.

Deanfield was again the winner of the *Under-20* Championship. Fencing confidently, he lost to Mather (5th) in the final, but his German-style fleche to head, his fitness and his accuracy saw him to victory in the barrage against a tenacious, stylish Melvyn Eden. Wishart (3rd), Etherton (4th) and John Zarno (6th) monopolised the lower places for Salle Boston.

As in the other weapons, 1970 saw the inauguration of the *Nescafé Under-20 Team and Individual Tournament*. In the former the French were never fully extended. Britain 'A' lost to them 6–3 (Deanfield winning two), a better score than that of the Germans, to whom, however, the 'A' team then succumbed 7–2. Victory over Holland by the same score put them in third place.

Deanfield also did best of the British in the individual event, in sixth place. He might have done even better but for too many mistimed counter-attacks. Hamm of Holland won, ahead of Quivrin and Bena of France.

An *international triangular match* preceded the Cole Cup. Against a German team with only one of their Olympians, the British looked nervous and never got going. They lost the first two fights 4–5, improved to lead 3–2, but trailed 4–5 again, faded and finally lost 9–4, though Acfield, very fast and using a nice mixture of disengage point counter-attacks and very direct attacks, won three fights 5–2 and was unlucky to lose 4–5 to Wischeidt.

The match with Poland went better. Fencing for the first time for Britain, Deanfield had a splendid match, winning two fights, including one in which, having trailed 2–4, he took the last hit against a very determined Kosciel-niakowski with a beautifully direct fleche. Craig, having flown in that morning from his army posting in Germany, only got going in the second match. Very fit and powerful and using his broken time beat attacks to great effect, he also won two fights, as did Oldcorn, with his usual mixture of good and indifferent. Unfortunately, Acfield had injured his foot in his first fight against the Germans and only won one fight; but Britain led at 5–2 and right up to the last fight victory was possible.

In the *Cole Cup* itself, the British did well. Hoskyns and Cooperman were absent and Leckie went out in the second round; but Acfield, Craig and Oldcorn all survived semi-finals in which Witzac, the holder, the volatile Ganchev (2nd in 1969), Koscielniakowski, Stroka (3rd in 1969), Wierzbicki and Mardzoko went out. Czernicki, a typically mobile and aggressive fencer from Poland, was the winner. Only Oldcorn, with a splendid quinte flank riposte for last hit, defeated him. Acfield, though slowed by his injured foot, was still on excellent form and should have won. But he lost 4–5 to his arch-rival Craig, as well as to Czernicki. Convents (W. Germany), aged only twenty, came third on two wins. Only the brave, like Acfield (whose point stop hits gave him a 5–1 victory), could deal with his deep compound attacks. Oldcorn, Wischeidt and Craig also all had two wins and finished in that order on hits.

In the *Championship* five non-Londoners reached the quarter-finals, where surprisingly Deanfield, still a shade temperamental, faded out. Scott went very strongly till the semi-finals, where the elimination of Leckie and Rayden, on the other hand, confirmed the change of generations at the top of sabre fencing, of which the medal winners were also evidence. Acfield, for the second year, was undefeated throughout the competition. Craig (2nd) lost only two bouts – both in the final – and Cohen (3rd), also with three wins, using controlled and varied strokes, lost only four – three of them to the other two. Nevertheless the final was closely fought (eight bouts went to 5–4). It was also pleasantly free from simultaneous attacks. Indeed, counter-riposte and counter-time played as great a part as direct attack. Martin was fourth with two wins and Oldcorn and Purchase were fifth and sixth, each with a single victory.

Acfield was absent from the *Corble*, playing cricket, as were Leckie and Martin, the former sure of his place in the Scottish team for the Commonwealth Games, the latter perhaps not hopeful of his chances of getting into the English one. The only foreign entrant, Dellocque, of the French team, came third. The surprise elimination was that of Scott in the quarter-finals, fencing fast but without his usual control.

Ganchev, making effective use of the stop-point, was the winner of the spirited final. In a barrage, he kept his edge over Craig, who also had four wins. Cohen (4th; 2v), while certainly not afraid to attack, tended to do so without always knowing why. Oldcorn was again fifth on one win on hits, this time over Rayden.

Ganchev had been asserting himself in provincial events for some years. This season he carried off the trophies at *Ashton* for the second year running and at *Leicester* for the third time running. Wiles won the hat trick both at *Nottingham* and in the *Scottish Championship*, but his run at *Inverclyde* was broken by Martin Joyce. Mitchell won for the fifth time (and the fourth time running) at *Tyneside*.

Only fourteen of the 21 entries appeared for the *Team Championship*, which was not of vintage standard. The Army fielded a weak team, lacking John Moore, Mike Howard or George Gelder. With Craig conceding a 5–1 defeat to Brian Waddelow, they lost 9–5 to Salle Paul. In the semi-finals, Boston, even without Acfield, beat Salle Paul 9–4. LFC, however, had a hard struggle against Poly, for which George Birks, brought in from the stud pastures, had some beautiful hits, though he was limited by an old Achilles tendon injury and could only win one fight, and Rocco Forte attacked with great verve and deserved more than his two victories. So, at the last fight, LFC only led 8–7, but then Oldcorn made no mistake, beating Michael Price 5–2.

In the final, LFC made surprisingly easy work of the holders, Salle Boston. From a 3–0 lead they quickly went on to 8–3, Leckie fighting at his best, accounting for three of these, though it was left to Gabby Arato to put the final nail into Salle Boston's coffin. With a long compound fleche he beat Etherton 5–2 and won the match 9–5.

Abroad, Craig was fourth at *Duren* and third at *Hamburg*. Oldcorn was seventh at Hamburg, reached the last sixteen of the *New York Martini* and the last twelve in *Munich*. Ganchev won the *Amsterdam Tournament* for the second year running. Cohen was second and Craig fifth. In the *Brussels Decade* Deanfield was third and Cohen fifth. Deanfield also reached the semi-finals of the Under-20 event at *Goppingen*, where Wishart gained fourth place.

The *Brussels Martini*, always top-class, this year attracted five Russians (two world Champions and three world finalists). Cohen and Scott went out in the first round, while Acfield, Oldcorn and Fairburn gained promotion, but only Acfield, who was fencing splendidly, survived to the third round – where, alas, he had to compete for the three promotions with Rakita, Meszena and Pawlowski, who came second, fourth and fifth respectively in the dazzling final, of which Sidiak was the victor. A feature of sabre fencing conspicuous here, and becoming widespread, was the advance at a run, with the feet crossing, in place of the traditional steps, balestras and limited fleches.

The English Commonwealth team places went to the three who topped the Championship – Acfield, Craig and Cohen. For the World Championships, the selectors put their faith in promise, choosing the nineteen-year-old Deanfield along with Oldcorn and the other three, even though he had never been in a senior home final. The old-stagers Leckie and Rayden must have been his rivals, if available, together with Martin.

*COMBINED EVENTS*

The *Portsmouth Tournament*, held for the third time at the Royal Naval School of PT, had a record entry. In the ladies' event Julia Barkley (Poly) took the title, receiving only one defeat in the final, from Frances Alexander of Reading

(3rd, 3v). Julia Bullmore (Boston) was second (3v), followed by Jill Dudley (Thames, 2v), Arlette Bowen (Pearson, 2v) and Alda Milner-Barry (Thames, 1v).

In the men's event, the young Simon Routh-Jones of Salisbury lost only one bout throughout the contest (in the semi-finals to Geoffrey Elder of Salle Boston, who came third), and suffered only six hits in the final. Alan Loveland (Boston) had no wins after very good results in early rounds. Fare was second with four wins, Barrs (Blackfriars) fourth with two wins and Kilvert (Behmber) fifth with one win.

In the *Public Schools Championships* Bryan Lewis of King's School Rochester, where he was taught by his father, John Lewis, won both sabre and epee titles, the only boy ever to do so apart from C. T. J. Cripps of Eton, who won all three weapons in 1934 (a unique feat, though 16 others won two weapons in a single year and M. Waddington of Eton won all weapons over two years).

The *Quadrangular* was held at Largs. The English team was captained by Hoskyns, whose great popularity was shown by the warmth of his reception at the customary dinner speeches. It had three clear wins: 25–11 over Scotland, 20–16 over Wales and 33–3 over N. Ireland. Interest centred on the close battle for second place. At men's foil the Scots, led by Tony Mitchell, beat Wales 5–4. Then the Welsh ladies reversed this score. The Scots won the sabre 6–3, but three bouts from the end of the epee were still not home and dry when Sandor levelled with Turner in the last seconds of this bout to gain a double defeat, which proved vital, as Wales got the last two fights. Captained by Gerald Beamish, N. Ireland lost to Scotland 32–4, but only 23–13 to Wales.

The Easter Tournament at *Leamington* required even greater feats of organisation by Birmingham Fencing Club than usual. The favourite for the ladies' foil, a nervous Herbster of France, was beaten by Susan Youngs (Caledonian), who seemed to do much of her fencing sitting on the piste. Her previous fight, with Gerry Harding, had been a marathon in which one-all had been reached at six minutes, 2–all at seven minutes and the deciding hit two minutes later still.

The men's foil was heavily dominated by Salle Paul, but Loveland of Boston ensured they did not take all three prizes. Graham Paul defeated Single for the trophy. The holder of both foil and epee, Derek Russell, reached the last eight of the foil and the very final bout of the epee; there he was beaten by Hudson, continuing with the seasons's triumphant progress and relying mainly on fast and well-timed fleches to body.

Some surprising defeats in the last sixteen of the sabre gave a final of eight with four British in one half and three Germans and an Austrian (Prause) in the other. In the last bout Wischeidt of Germany beat Acfield, as he had done the previous year, their display of fast and fluid sabre fencing delighting the audience.

# Competitions chronicle 1969-70

At the Minsk *World Youth Championships* Charles de Beaumont and Joe Eden headed the British officials with Jack Berry (for the last time) as manager for the men and Mary Glen Haig for the women. Prof. Boston and Prof. Ken Pearson were the coaches.

In the men's foil Stanbury was ousted in the second round with one victory and Etherton with none. Grimmett went a round further, to the last 24, but there failed to score. He showed a determination and courage but was not so good in his stance, his lunge or his co-ordination of hand and foot, and he tended to squander his energy.

The girls (all 18-year-olds) did better in their first round. Janet Yates and Julia Raine, who used her length and good bladework, did well to head their pools undefeated. Jane Swanson fenced intelligently if not with great mobility to a second place and beat Nikonova (USSR), the ultimate winner, 4-2. Both the latter were pupils of Maitre van Oeveren, who, like Prof. Ganchev, had come to Minsk at his own expense. All the girls, sadly, went out in the next round, the last 24.

The sabre was disappointing. In the not especially difficult first round Deanfield (relying too much on stop-hits) scored only two victories, Wishart one and Melvyn Eden none.

At epee, Noel and West went out in the second round, but Bird showed himself strong, aggressive and intelligent and topped both first and second rounds undefeated, in the latter repeating Noel's 5-3 victory over the finalist Ioffe (USSR). His reactions were remarkably quick for his considerable height, which he exploited to the full. In the last 24, after winning two bouts, he ran out of steam and tantalisingly lost all the others on the last hit.

The *Fencing Masters World Championships* were held in Britain (at Crystal Palace) thanks mainly to the tenacity and organisational ability of Prof. Akos Moldovanyi, the BAF International Secretary, but aided by many others. The Friends of the BAF provided funds, Leon Paul Ltd provided equipment and clothed the British team and Les Jones's children charmingly handed out the prizes. Even the weather smiled.

The format at each weapon was that of a poule unique of six or seven teams (some unavoidably of mixed nationality). Individual scores were derived from the matches.

In the foil, the 'A' team, consisting of Ganchev, Hawksworth and Hill, had mixed fortunes. They beat Holland 6-3, Germany 8-1, and GB 'B' 5-4, but lost to USA 8-1, to Italy 9-0, to Greece 7-2 and to Switzerland 5-4. The 'B' team, consisting of Ken Pearson, Pat Pearson and Gomer Williams, fought very hard and beat Greece 5-4 and Switzerland 5-4, but lost to Germany 5-4, USA 7-2, Italy 8-1 and Holland 5-4.

The USA gained both team and individual trophies, the calm, lean Richards being only twice defeated. Britain 'A' won the bronze medal on the basis of the top three scorers (regardless of team): Ganchev (6th), K. Pearson

BAF team 1970: L. Hill, K. Pearson, G. Hawksworth, G. Williams, K. Wren, R. Anderson (Coach), D. Sullivan, G. Ganchev, A. Mallard, A. Moldovanyi.

(11th) and Williams (16th); (Hill 17th, P. Pearson 20th and Hawksworth 21st).

The intended 'A' team for the epee scratched because of injury to two members and to save them for the sabre. The 'B' team beat Greece 5–4 but lost to Germany 5–3, USA 7–2, Holland 8–1, Switzerland 9–0, and Italy 9–0. Mallard (14th) had the best individual place in the field of 21 (Wren 19th, Sullivan 20th). Maestri and the Italians were the winners.

In the sabre, the British hope was George Ganchev, whose progress was watched by a large and enthusiastic crowd. He lost only two fights out of 22, but still had to barrage with Monshouwer of Holland. At first it looked as though he was too keyed-up and was forcing his attacks, for he was soon 2–1 down, but he recovered and won 5–2. The Americans won the team event. In the individual placings Ken Pearson was 11th, Hill 15th, Hawksworth 18th, Williams 19th and Pat Pearson 20th.

The organisation of the fencing events of the Edinburgh *Commonwealth Games* at Meadowbank was of high standard, due perhaps above all to Christine Tolland.

There were 77 competitors from twelve countries, including Ronnie Theseira leading a team for Malaysia, where he had done much to establish fencing, Barry Scotland from Dominica, Raymond Jackson at the head of the

Jamaican team and David Redhead representing Guernsey (where he was furthering fencing in schools).

The general standard was higher than at previous Games and it was gratifying that the many seats were sold out every day and even the competitors' seats had to be sold for the finals.

There were 32 in the men's foil. In the final Barry Paul created something of a surprise by beating both Graham Paul and Breckin 5–3 and appeared a certain winner until he surrendered the last hit in his bout with Benko (Australia). Meanwhile Breckin made no further mistakes. In the resulting barrage he imposed his game on Barry, winning the title 5–3. Graham, who only lost to his team mates, took the bronze medal.

The left-handed 17-year-old Gregory Benko – well placed on guard and with a very powerful, fast attack, albeit limited in repertoire – was fourth with three wins. Brian Pickworth of New Zealand was fifth. Fighting with his usual elan, he was in his fourth Commonwealth foil final, no mean feat at 41, and without his left arm. M. Conyd of Canada was sixth on hits.

The ten teams entered at men's foil formed three pools, followed by two semi-finals and a final pool of four teams, the pattern of all weapons. There were no surprises except perhaps the defeat of Wales 6–3 by the young N. Ireland team.

The finalists were Australia, Canada, England and Scotland. In the first matches the Scottish foilists, Sandor, Russell and Wiles, all of whom had reached the semi-finals of the individual event, lost unexpectedly to Canada by 8–1. They recovered to beat Australia 5–4, but had to be content with fourth place. Sandor conceded only five fights in the final pool; Russell lost and won eight and Wiles won eight and lost seven.

The England team, much more experienced, had little difficulty in securing the gold medal, with victories over Australia 5–4, Scotland 6–3 and Canada 8–1. Graham Paul was unbeaten, Breckin lost only three and Barry Paul five fights in the final pool. The young Australians beat Canada 6–3 and got the silver. Canada took the bronze.

There were eighteen entries of the ladies' individual event. Out in the semi-finals were Judith Bain, representing Scotland, Clare Henley of England and Gaye McDermitt of New Zealand, third in Jamaica. Janet Wardell-Yerburgh, unbeaten throughout the competition, seemed certain of the title by winning four fights in the final with only six hits surrendered. However, she was surprised by the forceful attacks of the 18-year-old Marion Exelby (Australia), made the tactical error of retiring in the face of these attacks and lost the deciding hit in their bout. After this success, Marion Exelby in her turn headed the pool until she met Susan Youngs. The Scottish girl, in great form, attacked without respite and quickly beat the Australian 4–1, making up in energy and courage what she lacked in inches and deservedly winning the Bronze Medal on indicators with three wins. In the barrage with Marion

Commonwealth team Silver Medallists for Scotland: Paula Robinson, Barbara Williams, Judith Bain, Sue Youngs.

Exelby, Janet W-Y imposed her game to retain her title by 4-0. Susan Green was fourth on hits, Julia Barkley (Wales) being fifth with one win and Barbara Williams (Scotland) sixth, without a win.

Only six teams contested the ladies' team event, and in the semi-finals England and Canada qualified at the expense of New Zealand, while Scotland and Australia eliminated Wales. In the final, England beat Canada 8-1, Scotland 7-2 and Australia 5-4. Janet W-Y was unbeaten in the pool, Susan Green lost three and Clare Henley five. Second place went to Scotland with victories over Australia 5-4 and Canada 6-3. Judith Bain recovered her form and joined Susan Youngs in winning eight out of twelve fights. Paula Robinson and Barbara Williams each got one win.

Bill Hoskyns was on his best form in the epee final, undefeated except against Peter Bakonyi of Canada when the title was already assured. He was thus the first fencer to win the Commonwealth title at any weapon three times. Second was the wrist-hitting Lester Wong (Canada) with three wins, on indicators over Peter Jacobs. Bakonyi was followed by Russell with two wins and Johnson, well below form, with one win.

In the team final England beat Canada 7-2 and New Zealand 5-0, but had a splendid match with Scotland which they only won 5-4 when Jacobs defeated Sandor 5-2 in the last bout. Hoskyns lost only two fights in the final team pool, Johnson three and Jacobs four. Scotland fully deserved the Silver Medal, beating New Zealand 5–4 and Canada 5–2. Russell beat all the English and was only once defeated in the final team pool; Sandor won five out of eight and Ian Hunter two out of nine. Canada beat New Zealand 5–3 for third place.

In the sabre, a major upset was the elimination in the semi-finals of Acfield, fencing too casually. The final was dominated by an undefeated Sandy Leckie, who produced outstanding technical quality with a nice balance of caution and aggression. This was a very popular victory. With his competitive career drawing to a close, perhaps largely through a fading of his appetite for victory (never very strong), Leckie made up his mind on one last triumph when carrying the Scottish flag in the opening parade. Second place went to Craig, with only one loss; while Cohen fenced well in his first major event to beat Wiles for the Bronze Medal. Samek and Foxcroft of Canada got one and nil wins respectively.

Nine sabre teams formed three preliminary pools in which the major surprise was the defeat of the experienced Welsh team, again to the young Northern Irish (7–2). England were clear winners, defeating Scotland 6–3, Canada 7–2 and Australia 9–0. Craig was undefeated in the final pool, Acfield had only one loss and Cohen four. Scotland beat Australia 8–1 and Canada 5–3 to take their third Silver Medal, Leckie winning seven out of nine fights, Mitchell five out of eight and Wiles four out of nine. The young Australians unexpectedly beat Canada 6–3 for the Bronze.

The young trio from N. Ireland attempted everything and gave a good account of themselves. Their captain, Jack Magill, reached the foil semi-final and Richard Gray only failed to do so at epee on indicators. They reached the semi-finals in both foil and epee team events, Magill getting six wins out of fifteen, Gray nine out of sixteen and Richardson six out of sixteen. They might have achieved even more success had they not overslept and been scratched from the epee!

The Welsh team were all seasoned competitors, but were out of touch and out of luck. No one got out of the first round of the individual events except Julia Barkley and Robert Reynolds – who reached the sabre semi-final. In the team events they didn't win a match, though the ladies lost both theirs 5–4, Julia Barkley and Linda Brown each scoring four out of six but Frances Reynolds drawing a blank. In the men's foil Ian Edwards won three out of five fights, Robert Reynolds none and his brother Andrew Reynolds one. In the sabre out the same trio only Andrew Reynolds scored, with two wins. In the epee Bob Turner had three wins out of five, Derek Lucas one out of six, while John McGrath and Robert Reynolds drew a blank in the match each fought. Robert Reynolds was captain as well as fencing all three weapons, too great a burden for any individual. Professor Glynne Reynolds' severe illness had also handicapped the training of the team.

Overall, once again, England took the lion's share of the honours with seven Gold, two Silver and two Bronze medals. Scotland obtained their best ever result with one Gold, three Silver and a Bronze medal, and they only missed the epee team Gold by three hits. Australia scored two Silver and a Bronze Medal and Canada gained one Silver and three Bronze Medals.

Whereas epee had traditionally been regarded as the least technical of the weapons and the last interesting to watch, it was indicative of a reversed situation that at the Ankara *World Championships* the standard of the epee was judged the highest, with Nikanchikov displaying his remarkably complete game to win for the third time (only the third epeeist ever to do so). By contrast, foil and sabre were characterised by endless double attacks alternating with lightning retreats the length of the piste. In the case of sabre, Charles de Beaumont had no doubt that there were also pre-arranged results in the final in repayment for previous favours. But this was nothing to the riot by the Italians enraged at Montano's defeat in the last fight of the sabre.

British participation was less dramatic. In the foil Single and Breckin were eliminated on hits in the first round. In the second round Graham and Barry Paul both topped their pools with four victories, but Power found the pace too hot. The last 24 saw Barry out on indicators and Graham with one victory over Woyda, the Polish finalist. Wessel won the event, the first German ever to do so.

In the team event Britain was seeded with Italy and USSR. Graham Paul was in splendid form against Italy and won his first three fights with the loss of only three hits. Barry scored two victories and Power and Breckin one apiece. All turned on Graham's last fight, against Granieri. Sadly, he lost this on the final hit, and Italy went on to fourth place. Against Russia, Barry scored the only two victories.

Kate Storry, Janet Wardell-Yerburgh and Susan Green all went out in round one, the last two on ratio of hits. Clare Henley fenced with great determination to get through the tough second round with three victories. She succumbed in the last 24, in spite of beating Pulch 4–2.

In the team event the ladies had a good match with the strong Polish team and held them up to halfway. Clare Henley ended with two wins (and one lost by the odd hit) and Janet Wardell-Yerburgh, Susan Green and Julia Barkley one each. Against France, Kate Storry replaced Julia Barkley (whose elbow injury trouble intensified). Janet W-Y and Susan Green each scored twice and Clare Henley once. Although eliminated, they then took on Turkey, which was fourth in the pool, and won 15–1, Janet, Susan and Kate being unbeaten.

Higginson, Johnson and Graham Paul went out in the first round of the epee, the last on hits. Hoskyns went out in the second round. Bourne went on another round. Showing much improved control, he beat the former World Champions Kriss and Nemere in the quarter-final, as well as Jacobson (Sweden), and was only eliminated on indicators.

The team was drawn with France, Switzerland and Turkey. They held the Swiss up to 5–all. Paul and Bourne won two apiece, but Hoskyns and Johnson only one each. The Swiss went on to a Bronze Medal. The French prevailed too, though the score was only 9–7 – not bad against a team which included two individual finalists. Paul and Bourne did well to win three victories each. Higginson in place of Johnson won one, but Hoskyns could not score. In the purely friendly match with Turkey, Johnson and Bourne won four each, Paul three and Higginson two.

The sabreurs started inauspiciously: Acfield, Cohen and Deanfield departed in the first round. Oldcorn topped his pool but got only one victory in the second round. The team event, however, provided the best British performance at Ankara. The first match with Rumania was remarkable. After losing the first five bouts, the team came to life to such effect that they ran out winners at 9–7. Acfield and Oldcorn won three splendid bouts each, Craig scored two and Richard Cohen one. The next match, with Iran, was little more than a formality (Craig 4, Oldcorn 4, Cohen 3, Acfield 2). Unfortunately Craig tripped over the lethal straining bars at the end of the piste and had to withdraw. Now certain of promotion, the team lost 9–1 to the strong Hungarians.

In the direct elimination, being seeded eighth, they met USSR, the eventual winners, and lost 9–2. Cohen solidified his new place in the team by scoring both victories. In the subsidiary elimination for fifth place, they lost to France in a good match 9–7. (Acfield 3, Cohen 2, Oldcorn 1, Deanfield 1). They thus had to be content with equal seventh place (out of fifteen), the best performance of the sabre team for many years.

31 countries were entered for the *World Student Games* in Turin in August. The standard was as high as ever. Graham Paul and Breckin did well to reach the foil semi-finals, considering that all the French, German and Austrians had already been eliminated; but otherwise nothing substantial was achieved in the individual events. In the team event the foilists got through a qualifying direct elimination by beating Switzerland 9–4, but in the quarter-finals were ousted by Hungary 9–3. At epee the first round of matches by direct elimination saw W. Germany beat Britain 9–3. At sabre Cohen excelled himself by beating all four of the French, at least three of whom were national team members.

# 1970-1

*MEN'S FOIL*

Graham Paul won the *National* after a barrage and on the last hit from his brother. When on form he was truly devastating, both his direct fleche and his coupé coupé fleche being unbeatable. But he could perhaps have resorted more to defensive tactics, thus also reserving energy, for he had a good defence, and his parry-ripostes were top class. He came third in the *Coronation* and was the winner of the *Leicester Tournament*. He came second both at *Groningen* and at *Bad Durkheim*.

Barry Paul was a very different fencer and was by now a joy to watch. He was a more complete foilist than his brother, if not so outstandingly endowed with confidence, and had a good blend of attack and defence, always attacking on the blade, and often with deliberate second intention collecting the stop hit en marche. He moved so well and fenced so fluently and with such determination that he looked set to go even further than he had so far. He was fourth in the Coronation and was the winner at *Ashton*. More importantly, abroad he reached the quarter-finals in *Bologna*.

Mike Breckin won the *Coronation Cup*, in which the German team competed. He was beaten by Graham Paul and taken to the last hit by Barry, but was not taken beyond two hits by any other finalist. In the National he was third. He had developed a very individual style, fencing rather front-on and coming in from around the corner with an exceptionally fast remise, flicked onto the chest, which made any delay in the riposte against him fatal. However, he was a somewhat moody fencer and if he had a bad patch tended to accept the situation too easily. On the other hand he was of invariably good temper – even when he put on a facade of anger. Many considered he had the potential to be world-class.

Ian Single had a good season and consolidated his prospects. He won the *Leamington Tournament*, came second in the Coronation Cup, and reached the semi-finals in *Bad Durkheim*; he did better than other team members in the *match at Bad Durkheim*, and confirmed this by gaining the best result in the *match against W. Germany* which preceded the Coronation Cup. Coached by Prof. Lagnado, he had developed a technically composed game with fast handwork and in general a surprising turn of speed given his size. It looked as though he had shaken off his insecurity against foreigners and novices. His best result of all was at *Bologna*, one of the very strongest events in the calendar, with over a hundred competitors, including strong contingents of Russians, Poles, Rumanians, French, Germans and, of course, Italians, where five Britons happily survived the first two rounds. Otherwise only the Russians were able to boast a hundred per cent record at that stage, in the almost World

Championship conditions. In the third round (last 36) Graham Paul, Breckin and Halsted succumbed to the fury of the opposition, but Ian Single and Barry Paul fought their way through to the last 24. Doing so, Single was a rousing sight as he trounced Magnan (France), Stankovich (USSR) and Lisewski (Poland) in successive fights.

Fifth place in the team would normally have gone to Tony Power, who was sixth in the National. However, just at the very worst time, he suffered an injury whilst fighting with an epee and was out of action for the German match, the Coronation, Bologna and also for inclusion in the World Championship team.

Nick Halsted, having been out with a torn cartilage, hardly fenced in the early part of the year, started a little foil under pressure and managed to be selected almost in spite of himself. An excellent team member as well as a consistent individual performer, he reached the third round of Bologna and did very well to reach the last sixteen in the *Paris Martini*.

Knocking on the door were a number of fencers who showed various degrees of promise but not yet much fulfilment. Geoffrey Grimmett had not been able to fence much because of his Oxford finals, in which he got a First in maths, but he did attend many training evenings. Still rather limited in range, and with a tendency to become stereotyped early in his career, he nevertheless had great fighting qualities and appeared always to have a chance in almost any fight.

Stuart Wooding certainly tried hard, although perhaps this year he did not devote quite as much time to fencing as in the past. He got very near and yet never managed to clinch a place, though he was fourth in the National. Tall and strong, he had few weak points and was nearly always difficult to beat, but his performances abroad did not quite match up to his gifts.

Brian Waddelow was another foilist with potential. His technique was good, and several senior fencers found him almost the most difficult to defeat in club fencing, but he didn't reach the final of the National or the Coronation.

The newest recruit to the squad was Tony Barrs (S. Paul). He had already made his mark as a junior, but this year reached the final of the Coronation, disposing in the process of Reichert of Germany (fifth in the world). He was not afraid to attack, and was so thin that he offered little target. He was keen enough to miss his brother's wedding to fight in Cologne (where unfortunately he went out in the first round). A criticism was that he was obsessed with the high prime-riposte on the back.

John Grimmett, brother of Geoffrey, won the *Portsmouth Tournament* but was otherwise not much in evidence. He had shed some weight and was leaving to work on the Continent, so he was hopeful for the future.

Bill Hoskyns was absent from the scene this season. Allan Jay was sporadic, but he pulled off fifth place in the National and narrowly missed the final of the Coronation, even without training hard, losing weight more than inter-

Catford School (Sept. 1970): A. Smith, P. Emberson, E. Dyer, M. Knell, C. Brown, R. Bruniges, John Fairhall.

mittently or ceasing to smoke. But no one's fitness was as good as it should have been, even that of the Paul brothers.

A temporary resident was the popular Australian Barry Wasley (of S. Boston), who did well to come fifth in the Coronation. Earlier in the season he had been in the *Junior*, in which there were also interlopers from the epee world. After twice gaining sixth place (in 1967 and 1968), Ralph Johnson here attained undefeated victory. Barrs was second, with four wins, followed by three Bostonians with two wins apiece: Bourne being third and Loveland fifth. Laurie Edmonds of Salle Paul also made the final, but one place down on the previous year. He did well to gain sixth place at Groningen.

The *Under-20 Championship* was won by Carl Waldman of Cambridge University without a loss. Bruniges was second after a barrage with Charles Ackle of Thames. The lower places went to the Boston fencers Stanbury (2v), Wishart (1v) and Christopher Brown (1v). The last was sixth in the Under-20 event at *Huy*. Bruniges was second again in the *National Schoolboys*, won by Andy Eames of Leicester. Waldman and Bruniges also took successive places at *Nottingham*, following Wiles in first position. Breckin was *Inverclyde* victor, ahead of Painter and Wiles of Leicester and the Brownhill trio, Mick Knell, John Fairhall and Alistair Smith.

The *Team Championship* was a repeat of the previous season, a 9–4 victory by Salle Paul over Thames. The two Pauls, Jay and Single each suffered only one defeat, though only Single reached his last fight. On the other side, Breckin, who should have led the way, had no wins. Halsted and Geoff

Grimmett each got one win, while Jacobs, though very much a part-time foilist, was, as so often, the most determined and consistent fencer in these encounters and got two wins (though he was the only one to reach his last fight).

The semi-finalists were Boston and Salle Paul 'B'.

The World Championships saw Breckin and Single back in the team, together with Halsted and the Pauls. (Bonfil had taken a job in South Africa.) Gordon Signy was Captain for the eighth and what was to prove the last time.

*LADIES' FOIL*

The scene was still dominated by Janet Wardell-Yerburgh (now fencing at LFC under Prof. Ganchev). She won the Championship, the de Beaumont Cup and the *Jubilee Bowl*. Her strengths continued to be excellent timing, concentration and above all tremendous will to win which were combined with a lively and dominating personality; her weakness was her footwork, apparent against faster-moving foreign competitors. She fenced very well to reach the fourth round in *Turin*. Here, as at Como, were all the competitors to be met with at the World Championships, plus extra Russians, Rumanians, Hungarians, and so on, who were almost as good.

Janet won the *de Beaumont* with a typical display of controlled tenacity, storming through the other five finalists as though by predestined right. Nobody put more than two hits on her. There was quite an array of foreign entrants – from France, Germany, Switzerland, Belgium, South Africa, Australia, New Zealand, even the United States – headed by Muzio, with three wins in the final. Fractionally behind were her compatriot Hoyau and Sally Littlejohns of LFC. Gaye McDermitt of New Zealand and Scottish FC was fifth, with one win, and Marilyn Holmes, newly enlisted in the WRAF, showed much of her old quality in coming sixth.

Susan Green, another fencer with great self-possession, was the sole finalist to beat Janet W-Y in the *Championship*, although she only ended fourth. She had a consistent season. She was third in the *Desprez Cup*. At *Duren*, against a large entry including the best French and Italian fencers, as well as a strong German contingent, she came sixth. Her knee injury, which had caused her such disappointments in previous seasons, seemed to be a thing of the past. Her technical ability and attack could be devastating; her problem was adjusting her tactics to her opponents. Still under twenty, she also came second in the *Under-20 Tournament* at *Ashton*, and, more significantly, at *Gelsenkirchen*.

Clare Henley of Thames was third in the Championship and second in the Desprez Cup, but failed to get outstanding overseas results. Her fencing was at its best when she was aggressive; she was vulnerable when she lost confidence and retreated, and she was short on stamina, as were many of the training squad.

Barbara Williams of Glasgow, a promising challenger, was second in the *Championship* and went to her first foreign competition in *Goppingen*, where she reached the second round. In *Como* she was in excellent form and reached the quarter-final, beating Drimba and Demaille (who later won the World title in Vienna). An athletic fencer with a good match temperament, on home ground she came third in the *Inverclyde Tournament*, which this year had a distinct antipodean flavour. Gaye McDermitt was runner-up and the stylish Gerda McGechan of New Zealand and Thames was fifth. Barbara Goodall of Scottish FC was the winner.

Hazel Davenport's best result was to reach the semi-final in the *Jeanty* in Paris. She made good use of her length of arm to achieve her hits and had good timing, even if she was somewhat static. She came sixth in the Desprez.

Kate Storry (who became Mrs Hurford in 1971) had a rather disappointing season, her best result being to reach the third round in Turin, her speed and fitness not matching her other qualities.

Sally Littlejohns, still at Oxford but also fencing under Prof. Ganchev at LFC, started the season very well, winning the *Desprez Cup* with a most efficient accuracy of point. But her results were erratic and her fencing sometimes uncontrolled. She was third in the Parker and only a semi-finalist in the Bertrand, though she bounced back with fourth place in the de Beaumont.

Hazel Rogerson showed a good knowledge of tactics, and was a good team fencer who never gave up until she was well and truly beaten. Her best foreign result was at *Eupen*, where she came third. At home she was the winner both at *Leicester* and at *Nottingham*.

Early in the season a London team of Julia Bullmore, Hazel Davenport, Kristin Payne and Kate Storry came second by 9–3 to the host city in the *Amsterdam Inter-City Tournament*, having successfully defeated Bosch (10–6), Rotterdam (10–6), Dusseldorf (9–3) and the Hague (9–5).

Britain sent seventeen fencers to *Duisberg* in a coach with fourteen supporters, including Les Jones and Liam Flynn as armourer. Thirteen were promoted from the first round this time, though only four got beyond the second round. By then it was 11.00 p.m. in spite of German efficiency. Next morning was chaos. The hotel had forgotten the morning call and, with fencing due to start at 8.30 a.m., at 8 o'clock those who had managed to wake were still frantically trying to locate those who hadn't. As it turned out, the start was again delayed. The fast and determined Elizabeth Simpson of Hydra now found herself outclassed, but Janet Yates topped her pool, both in this round and the quarter-final. Susan Green and Susan Wrigglesworth also passed both rounds well, the former beating the eventual winner, Popken (Germany)

4–2, the latter beating Trachez (France), who came fifth in the final, by a splendid 4–0.

Thus for the first time there were three British girls in the semi-final. Susan Wrigglesworth remained determined, calm and good-humoured, but lacked the length and the experience to get through a very difficult pool. Janet Yates was unconfident and plagued by faulty equipment and doubtful decisions, though at the end she got a good victory over Picard of France. Susan Green, however, continued her excellent run to join a final in which only Muzio had not been a finalist in the 1970 World Youth Championships. She started badly with two defeats (4–2, 4–1), but did not lose her nerve and went on to a 4–2 win over Muzio, to whom she had lost twice in previous rounds. She had a somewhat lucky win over Oertel by 4–0. Then she met Popken, who was fighting for the title. Susan attempted to dominate with speed, but Popken showed superior point control and made it a convincing 4–1 victory. She thus won the trophy. Armbrust was second and Muzio third. Susan Green was fourth, ahead of Trachez and Oertel, a very pleasing result.

An *Under-Twenty Quadrangular* match between three British teams and a German one was held before the Perigal Cup. Surprises came early, for the 'A' team consisting of J. Yates, J. Raine, and S. Blanchard lost 5–4 to the 'B' team consisting of J. Deakin, E. Simpson and S. Wrigglesworth – the last of whom went undefeated throughout the afternoon. Later 'A' showed more determination against Armbrust, Schaffner and Villing of Germany, whom they beat 5–4. As both 'A' and 'B' overcame 'C', there were three teams with two victories. Both 'A' and Germany won sixteen fights and both scored 82 hits, but Germany had one less hit received.

The *Bertrand Cup* culminated in a barrage of four, in which Jane Swanson won no fights and each of the others, with two victories, had to be separated on ratio of hits. Barbara Goodall (Scottish FC) was the winner, Susan Wrigglesworth second and Judy Young (now at Liverpool Univ.) third. The last had a good season, winning the *Toupie Lowther*, coming third in the *Ashton Under-20* and reaching the semi-final at *Gelsenkirchen*.

Relative outsiders were Shiel Toller (Thames), sixth in the Bertrand, and Celia Whitehurst, Prof. Van Oeveren's pupil, with speedy and often deceptive fleches. She was fifth in the Bertrand and winner of the Parker Cup, where Muriel Wilson of Cambridge was sixth. Here a welcome variety and depth of talent showed itself – the twelve semi-finalists came from as many different clubs.

Susan Wrigglesworth, now at Salle Paul under Prof. Lagnardo, was the outstanding Under-20 fencer. Aged seventeen, her light build and youthful appearance belied her speed and determination. She was tremendously fit and had an ideal temperament, unruffled and never overawed. She rarely had a bad day. Her technique was steadily improving, even if she still had a rather limited repertoire, especially in defence. She was sixth in the National, reached the semi-final at Gelsenkirchen, fourth in the Ashton Under-20 and fifth in the *Perigal*. The last was won by Villing in a barrage over Janet Yates, now aged twenty, whose technical merit was sometimes let down by her nerves. Her game tended to be defensive, and her speciality was a well-timed stop-hit. However, she was working on offensive moves and at Ashton demonstrated that she could come out with a devastatingly long lunge. She fenced here with courage, confidence and determination.

Janice Deakin, aged eighteen, came fifth in this event and third in the Perigal. She always looked good and had seemed promising for several years. Given a little more aggression, she was expected to do even better.

Liz Simpson, of Hydra, aged eighteen, was doing well. She was third in the *Felix Cup* (which was won by Susan Blanchard of Ashton), second in the Parker and at Nottingham, a quarter-finalist at Gelsenkirchen and a semi-finalist in the Bertrand. Her best performance was fourth place in the Desprez. She had a surprising turn of speed, great determination and good point control, and thought about what she was doing.

Lorna Andrews of Poly, now seventeen, was sixth in the Perigal, fifth in the Parker and reached the third round at Gelsenkirchen. She gave the impression of being a rather casual fencer, but could be extremely effective with a long, fast attack, taking opponents by surprise, and a good parry-riposte.

This year the *Team Championship* was wrested from Ashton 9–7 by an LFC team which combined Janet W-Y, Kate Hurford, Sally Littlejohns and Sue Wrigglesworth. In the *Coppa Europa* LFC got through the first round by beating the Poles 10–6 (though losing to France 9–7). In the direct elimination they lost to the Russians 9–1.

In a *triangular match at Eupen* a mere scratch team beat Luxembourg 13–3 (Hazel Rogerson being undefeated). They then fenced extremely well against a tough Belgian team including the wily (and undefeated) Wallet. Amid rising excitement, they won 9–7 (Harding 3, Herbert 3, Olley 2, Rogerson 1).

The *World Championship* team consisted of three previous members, Janet W-Y, Susan Green and Clare Henley, together with two new ones, Hazel Davenport and Barbara Williams. (Julia Barkley had retired in 1970, expecting her first child.)

## *EPEE*

In the final of the *Junior*, Tim Belson, pupil of Prof. Harmer-Brown at Worth School and now at Thames, was undefeated and only once taken to the last hit. A tall left-hander in the Army but still under twenty, he now showed good point control and sense of distance. Aggressive and particularly determined when most in danger, he could at this stage be criticised for unco-ordinated footwork, insufficiently effacing his target and placing too much weight on the rear foot.

Second place went deservedly to Bill Osbaldeston (now at S. Boston), the most experienced finalist, who only lost to Belson (5–3). Next came the mobile left-hander Peter Brierley (Army) – a little too reliant on opportunism. In fourth place Brian Hill of LFC used his length but lacked calm and the ability to adapt his game to his opponent. Chris Hallett, in fifth place, was another Bostonian, while Chris White in last position was a pupil of John Fairhall at Streatham FC.

Belson, naturally favourite to win the *Under-20 Championship*, was beaten into second place by the undefeated Jonathan Stanbury of Boston, advancing aimlessly into four of his stop-hits, delivered, like his direct attacks, from preparations consisting solely of bouncing up and down with absence of blade. Perhaps suffering from lesson-deprivation in the Army, Belson achieved less than his potential, though he used his reach and changes of tempo to effect. The barrage of three for third place was won by White, who generally gained his hits by Ali-style rassemblement counter-punches while retreating with his guard down. Peter Keuls, from Worth School and Thames, was third, showing good blade work but poor use of his height, hardly straightening his rear leg on the lunge. Bruniges, in fourth place, still only fourteen, had good control of footwork and weapon, but was very negative, haunting the back line and constantly going to full time, though his rare attacks were fast and effective. (Later in the season he reached the semi-finals of the National.) Bryan Lewis of Oxford University as a three-weapon man tended to rely on pseudo-sabre movements, which like his elastic, rather simple preparations, could only carry him to a certain level. He only beat White.

Belson did much better in the *Nescafé International*. Although there were five Britons in the semi-finals, he was the only finalist. Using all his length and speed, he beat the winner, Van der Voodt of Holland and only weakness in defence lost him the fight against Guy Evequoz (Switzerland) by 5–4. His confidence then ebbed a little and he added a second 5–4 loss (to Duchene of France); so he did not join the barrage with the Dutchman and the Swiss, but had to be content with third place.

Pip Emberson of Catford was *Schoolboys Champion* at the age of only fourteen. He was also sixth in the *Inverclyde Tournament*, which was won for the second year running by Ian Hunter. In between were Fairhall (2nd), Herwig Steiner (an Austrian resident in London), Rouxel and Wiles.

Early in the season there were two exciting international matches. At Speyer a surprisingly large audience watched a *German–British match* run neck-and-neck all the way: till at 7–all Britain (seven hits behind) had to take both remaining fights. Graham Paul's fleches were too much for Hauk, but unfortunately Zimmerman was at his very best in a tight corner and, despite Higginson's valiant resistance, won on the last hit, thus giving his team victory by five hits. Hudson fenced with great tenacity, winning three fights from behind, and Paul and Higginson each got two, but Noel could find no way of beating the Germans or even be miserly with hits.

The tension in the *match against Belgium* at Duren was different. Everybody except an assured Johnson kept losing till the score stood at 7–3. Then the tide turned – 7–4, 7–5, 8–5, 8–6; at this point a lead on hits assured victory if the British could achieve 8-all. Goose stonewalled for a double defeat against Johnson, who nevertheless gained the deciding hit with three seconds to go. Graham Paul then rampaged home to the eighth victory. A marvellous second half for the many and vociferous British supporters, but not a minute too early (Johnson 4, Paul 2, Bourne 1, Higginson 0).

Hoskyns was absent from these matches, as from much else this season, because he was Deputy High Sheriff of Somerset for the year.

Nick Halsted came storming back onto the epee scene by winning the *Martini Qualifying* final of twelve, only surrendering twenty-four hits in his nine victories. Second and third places went to Barry More (8v) and Jonathan Stanbury (7v), who beat the winner 5–2. Close behind was the maverick beanpole Howard West (7v) who had started fencing with Wynford Seymour at Swansea FC in 1966 at the age of seventeen and come to Kingston Poly in 1968. He had uncanny skill in deceiving his opponents with attacks accelerating from en marchant to fleche. Fox was next with six wins.

Fifteen countries were represented at the *Martini* itself, including the French, Belgian, Polish and Swiss national teams. It was again Halsted, along with Guy Evequoz, who topped the first round to gain byes in the first round of the direct elimination, in which the winners were Hoskyns, Bourne, Hudson and Johnson for Britain, together with Allemand, Ladegaillerie and Jeanne (France), Bretholz and Giger (Switzerland), Gonsior and Andrzejewski (Poland), Pesthy (USA), Fernandez (Venezuela) and Cipriani (Italy).

In the next round Hoskyns beat Evequoz in a desperate match 11–10, Bretholz beat Allemand 8–5, the towering, phlegmatic Gonsior beat Teddy Bourne 8–3, Fernandez beat Hudson 10–8, Andrzejewski beat Ladegaillerie 8–1, Johnson beat Giger 10–9, Jeanne beat Cipriani 8–4 and Halsted beat Pesthy 8–5.

Thus for the first time there were three British epeeists in the gala final. But in the quarter-final bouts Bretholz, the young Swiss Champion, proved too fast for Hoskyns and by determined attacks and counter-attacks in the low line won 8–5. Gonsior beat Fernandez 8–4. Andrzejewski, the 1969 World Champion, had an excellent match with Johnson, which he won at 8–6, and Jeanne, the French Champion, beat Halsted 8–4, sadly extinguishing British hopes.

The semi-finals produced the best fencing. Jeanne led Andrzejewski 5–1, but the latter then changed his tactics and by some remarkable second intention attacks and stop-hits to wrist won a dramatic bout 8–5. In the other bout the score of 8–2 was a mark of Gonsior's superiority over Bretholz. Gonsior, who had so often reached the final, used his reach and accuracy of point with deadly effect, to win the title 8–3 from his fellow-Pole by controlled aggression.

In April the British team had its revenge in a *match against Germany* en gala in the Pump Room at Leamington as part of the Easter tournament. This time they got off to a first class start by winning all the vital opening bouts. The World Bronze Medallists put in a big effort and pulled back. But, to the delight of the dense crowd, the British under the enthusiastic captaincy of Peter Jacobs showed great resilience. In a truly magnificent fight, Teddy Bourne secured the vital ninth victory. The team went on to make the score 10–6. Bourne, Johnson and Graham Paul got three victories apiece; Hudson got one, showing determination, if not his best level of accuracy.

In the *Championship* it was soon apparent that the title rested between Paul, who had fenced consistently well throughout the competition, and Bourne, back in his best form. When Paul beat Bourne 5–4 (after leading 4–3), all seemed to be settled, but in his next fight he could do nothing right against Davenport, to whom he lost 5–2. The resulting barrage between Paul and Bourne ran exactly the same course as their previous bout. By forceful attacks Paul led 3–1; Bourne pulled back to 3–all, but a fine riposte gave Paul the lead at 4–3 when time was called. A good stop-hit at wrist once again levelled the score, but finally Paul clinched the bout with a reprise just a few seconds before time. In combination with the foil Championship, he thus achieved a double unequalled since Robert Montgomerie in 1909. Jacobs, the holder, beat Johnson, who was in the run-up to his law finals, into fourth place. He was in his usual ebullient form which diminished the credibility of his retirement. It was the twelfth successive year in which he was in the top six of the Championship or Miller-Hallett. Davenport and Hudson (Thames), each with one win in that order, were both in their first National final.

During the Miller-Hallett *match against Austria*, Britain again got off to a flying start, Paul, Bourne and Hudson taking the first three fights in fine style, whilst Hoskyns only lost the fourth on the last hit. But when the Austrians dug in, Bourne was unprepared and Graham Paul was 4–1 down to Muller before he settled down to pick his moments, though he climbed back to 4–all before losing. Bourne and Hudson (nicely combining caution and aggression) each won a second fight, and Hoskyns chalked up a victory; but the Austrian dominated the last quarter, to win 10–6.

The foreign entry raised the standard of the *Miller-Hallett* to the point where Bretholz of Switzerland succumbed in the second round. Hoskyns, Hudson and Losert were eliminated in the quarter-finals (third round) – the latter two in pools topped by Ken Pearman and Brian Hill, both fencing excellently.

Cramer of Brazil did well to reach the final, albeit in last place. Halsted was fifth, having bettered Polzuber, a Mexico finalist, by .011 in the semi-finals.

Normann, of Norway, 1970 World semi-finalist and a fast but rather impetuous 19-year-old, slackened concentration and came fourth, likewise on two wins. Trost of Austria, third in the 1967 World Championship, was in third place by two hits. Bourne, unbeatable in the semi-final, still had a chance of a barrage when, in the last fight, he faced Muller – a very tall Austrian with an exceedingly fast hand and excellent use of variations of straight and bent-arm fencing, who had only been hit six times thus far in the final. Now somewhat off the boil, Bourne put four hits on the Austrian, but could not stop him taking the title.

There were only twelve entries for the *Team Championship*. In the semi-finals Salle Paul inflicted a severe defeat on Thames while Salle Boston more narrowly beat the Army. The final was entertaining. For a confident Salle Paul, Graham and Barry Paul won three apiece and Partridge impressed with his two victories; indeed, the turning point was probably his good 5–3 win over Bourne. Pearman added one win. For Boston, Bourne, Davenport and Johnson each got two wins, Stanbury nil.

Foreign results were patchy. There was nothing notable from the Under-20s. On the other hand, at *Duren* (now 250 strong) Johnson was second, Graham Paul fourth and Hudson sixth and at the *Monal* James Noel achieved the best British result since Jacobs came sixth in 1966, missing the final by only one hit – and that to Saccaro, the ultimate winner. Unfortunately only one other Briton reached the last 48, out of 22 entered.

At *Heidenheim* Salle Paul beat Belgrade 12–4, lost to Heidenheim on hits at 8–all and went through to the last 15. In the direct elimination they lost to Warsaw 9–2.

At *Gothenberg* Bourne was fifth in the individual event, after a *quadrangular match* with the three Scandinavian countries, none of which was quite overcome.

The core of the team remained Bourne, Johnson and Paul. With Hoskyns out of the running, the remaining places went to an oldstager who showed in the Martini and in the Miller-Hallett that he still had skill and tenacity – Nick Halsted – and to a newcomer who up to this point did not live in London – Ted Hudson. Close to the team must have been James Noel, who could beat world-class opponents but still lacked consistency, and Robin Davenport, who had worked hard and improved his results abroad, but not quite to the level of the team.

## *SABRE*

This was another season of great talent at the junior level, which was sometimes more abreast of continental technique than the senior level, according to Sandy Leckie, the team captain. It was a particularly good performance by Wishart of Salle Boston to win the *Under-20 Championship* against rivals like Deanfield (3rd), Mather (4th) and Etherton (5th). He went on to win the *Inverclyde* trophy, ahead of Zarno, Mitchell, Wiles, Bob Elliott (of Lothian FC and half Chinese) and David Carruthers (of Glasgow FC). Abroad, Wishart was sixth in the Under-20 event at *Koblenz* in which Deanfield came fifth. In the home international, the *Nescafé*, Mather was the top Briton, in third place after Grosser and Weissgerber of W. Germany. (Britain came second, between Germany and Belgium, in the team event.)

For the second year running, missing the Under-20 title only in the barrage and undefeated winner of the *Junior Championship*, was Melvyn Eden of Salle Paul, where he was taught by Prof. Moldovanyi. He was unlucky to miss the World Youth Championships, only taking fourth place under the new points system, such was the competition. Second in the Junior was Mather, followed by Lawday, Wishart, Fairburn and David Hughes (Oxford). All but the last were pupils of Prof. Boston, who still had the lion's share of younger sabreurs: seven of the twelve finalists of the Junior and Under-20 championships as well as the winner of the *Public Schools* – Mather – and of the *Universities Championships* – Etherton (Cambridge). But there were welcome signs of new blood from other quarters, such as Brooke House School, where boys learnt sabre as a first weapon at first directly from Peter Hobson, master in charge, and then from Prof. Imregi. David Keal, winner of the *National Schoolboys'*, was a noteworthy product of the system.

There were also promising fencers emerging from beyond the London area. In the Junior, Norman Milligan, a pupil of Ted Beverley at Cromwell, only just missed the semi-final, while Jim Philbin and Alan Taylor, pupils of Prof. Hawksworth at Hydra, were within .04 of an indicator of the final (at which stage Jan Gryf-Lowczowski (Lilia) and John Zarno (Boston) also failed). Also from Hydra, Eric Bradbury came third at *Nottingham*, where Kovanda of Birmingham was second and Wiles was winner for the fourth time running.

Wishart again did well in the *Championship*. He was a finalist for the first time (4th; 2v), as indeed was Deanfield (3rd). The winner once again was a relaxed David Acfield, looking for all the world as if this were his annual benefit match. The pity was that he didn't fence more and develop his great natural talents to the highest international level. His concurrent pursuit of a cricket career – in which his relatively more modest achievements as off-spin bowler for Essex still meant more in the world of British sport (unlike Hungary, for instance, where fencing was a major national sport).

Craig was third-time runner-up, but could be well satisfied with this position, as he was not on best form and was handicapped by knee trouble. Cohen, in fifth place this time, showed a very balanced mental approach, combined with energetic and robust tactics, if his technique still called for more polishing. In sixth place, also on one win, was David Eden, despite the little training he had done.

At the *Brussels Martini* only Zarno of the eight British entrants fell in the first round – and indeed Mather defeated Meszena and topped his pool. Along with Acfield, Cohen, Deanfield, Eden and Fairburn, he went out in round two. Only Oldcorn reached the last 48. Here, in the eighth-finals, he too made his exit, along with all the French and Germans. The final was composed of three Russians, two Hungarians and Pawlowski, and was won by Kovacs.

Oldcorn was again the best performer at *Hamburg*, in March, when he reached the last twelve.

Pawlowski led the Polish in the five-a-side match before the *Cole Cup*, which the guests won 15–9. Oldcorn had three wins, Acfield two and Mather, doing extremely well in his first senior international, also two, while Cohen and Deanfield gained one each. In the Cup itself Pawlowski duly won, but Ganchev (4v), Oldcorn (2v) and Deanfield (2v) managed to interpose themselves amongst the five Poles, in fourth, fifth and seventh places.

The *Corble*, supposed to be the premier home international, attracted only one foreign entry this year and the selectors felt no compunction in sending five top fencers to a Polish event the same weekend. Partly because of exams, there were only four British entries on the closing date, though 23 were ultimately persuaded to appear. The twelve who survived a preliminary round formed a poule unique. The result was as follows:

1. G. Ganchev (BAF, 11v); 2. P. Hobson (Poly, 9v); 3. J. Rayden (LFC, 7v); 4. D. Scott (S. Paul, 7v); 5. A. Leckie (S. Paul, 6v); 6. J. Lawday (Boston, 5v); 7. J. Zarno (Boston, 5v); 8. Kucziewicz (Belgium, 4v); 9. J. Hamments (Pearson, 4v); 10. Gryf-Lowczowski (Lilia, 4v); 11. J. Murray (S. Paul, 3v); 12. C. Kovanda (Birmingham, 1v).

Ganchev thus won for the third time running – a double record, no-one having previously won more than twice. For the rest, both the superannuated and the newly-arrived got their chance. In particular it was a triumph for Peter Hobson, who had been out of fencing with serious elbow trouble for several years.

Meanwhile the chosen five were at the return fixture with the hospitable Poles, romantically staged in the courtyard of the thirteenth-century *Golub Castle*. It was a *quadrangular*, with two teams from Poland and one from Rumania, preceded by an individual event in which Deanfield and Oldcorn both narrowly missed promotion to the final. The winner was Budahazy of Rumania.

The first match, against Rumania, was lost 9–2, Craig and Oldcorn gaining a fight each, but not Cohen or Deanfield (who had a damaged foot). Against Poland 'A' the same quartet managed 9–5 (Cohen two, the others one each). The Poland 'B' match proved very exciting. Cohen, though he started slowly and was rather static, won three fights. Craig was not at his best, while Wishart, coming in for Deanfield, was understandably nervous on his first major outing at senior level, but Oldcorn was steady throughout, finishing strongly to win a vociferous last fight and secure the match by one hit.

The trip included a banquet, a visit to the opera, free shopping in a blizzard, with a secret agent 'Blotto Otto' in attendance, and ended with a carriage drive.

Although only contested by fifteen teams, the *Team Championship* was given interest by some surprise results. Brooke House reached the quarter-finals by beating LFC 'B' and the outsiders Hydra got to the semi-finals by downing the Army, though they in turn succumbed 9–4 to Boston. Salle Paul overcame LFC in the semi-finals only in a fight-off after equality on hits as well as bouts. In the final Boston moved from 3–all into a devastating top gear and finished 9–4 – John Zarno, much improved this season, being the hero of the hour, with four victories, followed by Cohen with three, Mather with two and Wishart with none. (For S. Paul, Murray got two, the Edens one each and Scott none.)

Due to his cricketing commitments, Acfield was unavailable for the World Championships; so Craig, Oldcorn, Cohen and Deanfield were augmented by Sandy Leckie, whose experience was reckoned to lend more solid strength to the team than the still unproven Wishart or Mather.

## COMBINED EVENTS

At the beginning of the season came a splendid success in the admittedly slightly light-hearted four weapon four-a-side event at *Alassio*, at which a single performer at each weapon takes up the score of the previous pair. It was contested this year by Sweden, W. Germany and Italy. Against the Germans, Janet Wardell-Yerburgh gave an excellent start for Graham Paul, Oldcorn and Johnson, who each gained clear wins. Janet W-Y again gave a good lead against Sweden, which was maintained at foil and sabre. A large and excited crowd came to see the celebrated and immensely tall Edling repeat against the much smaller Johnson the success he had had in scoring eighteen times before his Italian opponent could score seven. This time he only had to score fifteen hits in twelve minutes before Johnson could score ten. In a thrilling bout Johnson fenced most intelligently. Though the Swede, fencing extremely well, led at 3–1, Johnson recovered to 6–4. Then, to his team's dismay, he was 10–5 down. Repeatedly pushed to the back line, he became ragged. But suddenly he found inspiration and made five consecutive attacks on the long upper arm of Edling, all arriving within about ninety seconds of play. He got home at 10–10, thus giving Britain its second victory at 38–32.

Meanwhile, the Italians had beaten the Germans. In the final match they had to beat Britain 38–35 or better. The match was a beauty. Janet Wardell-

Yerburgh led 5–1, dropped to 5–2, 6–2, then suddenly completely lost her touch when the Italian girl – cheered on by the crowd – made four coupé ripostes to reach 6–6. Just in time, Janet came to life, launched two tremendous counter-attacks on preparation and won 8–6.

Oldcorn was in his most aggressive and vocal form, demoralising the judges, as well as his technically elegant opponent, Maffei, who only happened to be the season's World Champion. Down 3–4, he regained the lead at 5–4, was down again at 6–7 and then 7–9, only to win in a dash at 10–9 – a splendidly fought match, appreciated by the shaken Italians. The score now stood at 18–16.

Paul then had to meet his old rival, Granieri, to whom he had recently lost in Ankara in a survival bout. He started well, leading 2–1, then 5–1. 6–3 up, he lost three consecutive hits to make the scores level. It looked as though he was tiring, and was mastered again. But then he found hidden resources and launched four consecutive beautifully balanced coupé fleche attacks from an awkward angle. They left Granieri standing flat-footed, and the crowd speechless. Britain led 28–22.

And so to the last fight: Johnson against Testoni. Once again an early lead was converted into a hair-raising situation, but again Johnson achieved a second burst of energy and the final score of 10–all won the match 38–32 – a fine performance by all four fencers, who could retire to savour the delights of this best of Riviera resorts with light hearts.

The *World Youth Championships* were held at Notre Dame University, Indiana, a hundred miles south of Chicago. The entry was thinner than usual and there were no teams from Poland or Rumania, but the standard of the finals was as high as ever.

The British party was led by Charles de Beaumont, with Joe Eden and Prof. Boston looking after the men and Kristin Payne, Maitre van Oeveren and Leslie Jones the girls.

The tale of the foilists is soon told. Christopher Brown and Michael Knell won one bout each in the first round, the former gaining promotion on indicators, while Carl Waldman was out with two wins. One victory in his quarter-final was insufficient for Brown to go further.

The girls were a different matter. Though Julia Raine, a prey to nerves, went in the first round, Janet Yates and Susan Wrigglesworth passed serenely through the quarter finals, while such previous finalists as Burochina, Oertel and Popken fell by the wayside. By hazard of indicators, both were in the same semi-final. Susan Wrigglesworth, with four sterling victories, was equal top, thus having the distinction of being the first British girl to reach the final in these championships. Unfortunately Janet Yates could never find her touch, although she beat the Russian Kostrakova 4–3.

It was too much to expect Susan Wrigglesworth with her limited experience to make much showing in the final. But she never gave up and her charming

World Youth team 1971. *Front:* Maitre van Oeveren, L. Jones, J. Eden, C-L. de Beaumont, K. Payne, Prof. Boston. *Middle:* J. Raine, J. Yates, J. Deanfield, P. Mather, C. White, M. Knell. *Top:* C. Brown, J. Stanbury, S. Wrigglesworth, T. Belson, C. Waldman.

smile in triumph or adversity delighted the crowd. With more technical ability than many of her elders and still only sixteen, a considerable future was predicted for her by Charles de Beaumont. She lost 4–3 to Schwarzenberger, the winner, and three other bouts at 4–2, but by beating Armhurst 4–2 achieved fifth place.

The epee brought good news too, though White was eliminated in the first round and Belson in the second. Stanbury was promoted through this round with four victories, and in the semi-final started well by beating Karagian (USSR), a classical epeeist. Two other 5–2 wins gave him promotion on indicators over Vandervoort, winner of the Nescafé and the Schmetz.

In the final he gained three victories and had two losses at the last hit, either of which would have given him the title. He also provided the climax of the final when he met Abushakhmetov (USSR) who then only needed this bout to win the title. Hits alternated until the Russian led 4–3 and the warning for time was called. Stanbury, unperturbed, then placed two of his shots at the hand, won the fight and forced a quadruple barrage. His game was unusual: bouncing rhythmically with absence of blade he could unleash stop hits or attacks as occasion demanded, with appropriate disengages. But he was now getting tired and his opponents were getting wise to him. He lost by the odd hit to Lofficiel (France) and then went down 5–3 to the winner, Karagian, and 5–2 to Abushakhmetov in a poor bout in which he submitted to the same stop hit four times! He thus had to be content with fourth place. This still left him the first British epee finalist since 1967.

Disappointment with the sabreurs was in proportion to the high hopes for them. All three passed the first round without difficulty, Deanfield topping his pool undefeated, including a 5–3 victory over Komar (USSR) the eventual champion. But disaster struck in the not especially difficult quarter finals. Wishart and Mather could only win one bout each and John Deanfield, who seemed overawed, failed to win a fight.

At *Leamington* Angela Herbert disconcerted her opponents by constant aggression to reach the ladies' final, but there Geraldine Harding found the answer by using her reach and timing to counter-attack when she came within distance. The runners-up were Clare Henley (Thames) and Pam Patience (Reading). Of the three Pauls in the last eight of the men's foil, Barry beat Graham, while Raymond vainly tried to break Barry More's concentration by changes of tactics. Single, who had eliminated Geoff Grimmett of Birmingham FC, won the final bout by a series of well-judged time attacks on Barry Paul.

In the epee, the piquancy of Noel (top seed) losing to Hudson (16th) was followed by Graham Paul's excellent win over Hehn (prospective Olympic Silver Medallist) in the last four, where his time-mate Jung beat Hudson. In splendid form, Paul went on to dominate his fight for first place with long and fast attacks, against which Jung had no successful defence.

In the sabre, after the elimination of Cohen and Zarno, the deciding bout was once again between Wischeidt and David Acfield, both displaying admirable speed and mobility. Acfield was in the lead at 7–6, but could not get the decider to give him the required 8–6, and at 9–all Wischeidt won, as twice before, by the odd hit. There followed a sporting gesture by Wischeidt which caused a standing ovation: he gave Acfield the Cole Memorial Sabre just awarded to himself.

At the end of the first day of the *Winton Cup* in its 21st year, the NW (the only Section never to have won the cup) led slightly over the SW (most frequent winners). Towards the end of the next day the SE could snatch away the victory if they won their last match 9–0 and the SW beat the NW. But it was not to be. The SW continued to slip, while the SE fell short of their ambitious target by 8–1.

The outstanding performance was by the NW ladies, who lost only four out of 45 fights. The NW sabreurs and SE men's foil and epee were also unbeaten.

Bob Southcombe's retirement as captain of the *Rest of Britain* team was marked by their third successive and best ever win over London, by 40 to 24. The match was four-a-side for the first time and there was the usual unpredictability as to which side many of the fencers might belong. The unbeaten stars were Alan Hughes (foil) and Osbaldeston (epee) for the Rest, Zarno (sabre) for London.

The *Quadrangular Match* would normally have been held in Wales this year.

# Competitions chronicle 1970-1

However, by general consent it was transferred to Belfast so that it could be held within the framework of the celebrations for the fiftieth anniversary of the founding of Ulster, somewhat unhappy in their timing though these proved to be. Owing to concern over the supposed risks of violence, England fielded a weaker team than usual, but still beat Scotland 23-13, Wales 27-8 and N. Ireland 31-5. Malcolm Fare at foil and Richard Fairburn at sabre were unbeaten throughout.

Scotland were without most of their Commonwealth Games stars but under Tony Mitchell they took second place by beating N. Ireland 26-10 and Wales in a good match 19-15. The latter, led by Bob Turner, fielded a team without a single Reynolds. They took a creditable third place by beating N. Ireland 26-10. Gerry Beamish added to his duties as admirable organiser the captaincy of the N. Irish: all they lacked was greater training and experience.

The *World Championships* were in Vienna. The team mostly arrived by car and were put up in a parkland youth hostel. Prof. Boston came as coach, in addition to Prof. Anderson.

In the first round of the men's foil Halsted and Single were eliminated, the former on indicators. The second round proved disastrous: Breckin and the two Pauls came out. The team, for once, seemed to be favoured with a reasonable draw – with E. Germany, Poland and Yugoslavia. Against E. Germany Graham Paul won all his four bouts, surrendering only six hits, and Barry won two. However, Breckin could only win one bout by the odd hit and Single failed to score, so Britain lost 9-7. If Barry could have won the last bout from 4-all then they would have won on hits. Against the Polish team, who were destined to reach the final, Halsted replaced Single, but the score was 13-3, Barry Paul winning two and Graham the other one.

The ladies fared a little better. In the first round Barbara Williams with two victories was eliminated on hits. Susan Green beat Belova (reigning World Champion) in her first round but lost confidence and won no fights in the second. Janet Wardell-Yerburgh got three victories in the second round but went out on indicators when Chirkova (USSR), undefeated till her last fight, seemed to make little effort against Szeja of Poland. Hazel Davenport went out with two victories and Clare Henley who had got three wins, after topping her first pool, was also nevertheless eliminated.

In the team event the ladies had a hard draw with France and Poland. They lost to Poland (who were eventually third) 12-4 after being 9-0 down. Janet W-Y achieved two victories and Clare Henley and Barbara Williams one apiece, but Sue Green could not score. This was another example of a British team waking up too late – underlined by the 6-10 score against the strong French team in the next match. Janet, her form regained, won three, Sue two and Clare one, though Hazel Davenport, lacking in experience, met with no success.

The best results came at epee. Halsted withdrew from the individual to save an injured shoulder for the team competition and in the first round Hudson was eliminated, and Johnson in the second. But Graham Paul fenced very well to reach the quarter-finals (fourth round) where he beat Andrzejewski (1969 World Champion) and Fenyvesi (1972 Olympic Champion) and only missed the semi-final in his last fight. And Teddy Bourne, fencing with just the right mixture of tactical thoughtfulness and inspired flair, topped his pool in each round up to the quarter-finals, where he excelled himself in a particularly difficult pool, beating Nikanchikov, the holder, 5–2 and Kulcsar, the Olympic Champion, 5–1.

After this gruelling round the semi-finals were as much a test of stamina as anything else. Bourne beat Kriss, the eventual winner, 5–2 (for the second time in the event) and Floquet (France) 5–4, but in his last bout, with the difficult E. German Melzig, he ran out of steam and after leading 4–1 was gradually worn down and lost 5–4. One tantalising hit from a World Final! This was the best result in the World Championships since Hoskyns in 1965. Bourne's technique had improved greatly and this gave him increased confidence. A fault that remained, in Charles de Beaumont's view, was that he wore himself out with constant violent movement. Peter Jacobs saw the problem more in terms of volatility and his reaching his peak a round too soon.

Thanks to the good results, the team got a reasonable draw with Poland and Luxembourg. They beat the latter 10–6, Johnson, Bourne and Halsted winning three each and Graham Paul (tired after three events) one. They were thus sure of promotion, but still had to meet Poland for seeding. It was a curious match. The Poles openly declared that they did not want to win so they would not have to meet USSR or Hungary before the semi-finals. In the event they were beaten straightaway by W. Germany. Johnson won all four bouts, Hudson, who replaced Halsted, three and Bourne one, but Graham Paul could not score, though losing three of his bouts by the odd hit. This added up to a 69–56 hits win, a hollow victory. In the direct elimination from sixteen they drew E. Germany, much tougher than expected. Hudson came in for Paul, but each fencer got only one win.

Hopes for the sabreurs were high after their encouraging showing in 1970, but Acfield was absent and Craig's injured knee kept him out of the individual event, in which Leckie went out of a difficult first round pool with an indifferent jury. In the second round Deanfield and Cohen could only achieve one victory each. Oldcorn, however, got three victories and for the first time reached a World Championship quarter-finals, although he failed to get any wins there. Maffei won the event, the first Italian to do so since 1949.

In the team event a draw with USSR and Austria seemed a reasonable proposition. Austria had only beaten a British 'B' team 10–6 and the Russians could be depended on to do the rest.

Against Austria, Craig fought with great determination despite his injury and won three victories, only losing the fourth by the odd hit. Cohen and

Deanfield 'fulfilled their contract' with two victories each, but Oldcorn, though largely responsible for the favourable draw, could only achieve one 5–4 victory. At the end it was a tie – 8–8, 64–64 hits. So whichever team did best against the Russians would gain promotion.

The British team met the USSR first. Cohen surpassed himself to win three bouts and Oldcorn redeemed himself somewhat and won one. 12–4 was not bad and normally Austria could not have expected to do better, but unfortunately there was no reason why the strong Russian team should exert themselves unduly (and Rakita lost all his fights, irritated, it seemed, at being made to fence in this match). The Austrians fenced well and only lost 9–7. So that was that.

# 1971–2

*MEN'S FOIL*

The season began well with a striking foreign result. Graham Paul came sixth in the *Trial Olympics* in Munich in August in a distinguished field, including Reichart, Haerter and Romanov (the Russian who was second in the 1970 World Championships and third in 1971). In January it was Barry Paul's turn to gain an outstanding result when he won the *Warsaw Open Tournament*. This led to an immediate invitation to train for a fortnight with the Poles, followed by a second fortnight in April, along with Graham. Thus both missed the *Championship*, which proved a close-run thing. If Single, leading Power 4–1, had won that fight, there would have been a four-way barrage (though he wouldn't have been included in it and had to be content with last place on one hit below his club-mate Tony Barrs on hits).

As it was, Power had his moment of triumph, well-timed in an Olympic year, after his second withdrawal from national fencing. Although three times in the final of the Coronation, he had never previously been in that of the Championship. Now he was defeated only by Breckin (5–4), who came third on three wins, ahead of Jay by a tiny difference of ratio but by a clearer one behind Geoff Grimmett, now doing post-graduate maths at Oxford, who thus reaffirmed his challenge to the top foilists.

Eden and Cohen missed the final on indicators and the latter was invited onto the foil squad, along with Bruniges, winner of his quarter-final and beginning to make his mark in senior fencing. Notable casualties of earlier rounds were Wooding and Hoskyns (who found lack of frequent lessons more hampering at foil than at epee).

The *Coronation Cup* was held in early June, preceded by *Matches against Austria* (beaten 10–6) and *Canada* (beaten 13–3). Breckin won in an exciting barrage with Graham Paul, after being 4–2 down. He thus gained the title three years running, a record equalled before or since only by René Paul; the record of a total of four wins is also held jointly by these two. The next three were all on two victories, but Single was better on hits than Bruniges and Power. Nonna in last place was the only foreigner. Graham Paul too claimed a double record when he won the *University Championship* for the third successive time and for the fifth time altogether.

Meanwhile some further useful results were being chalked up abroad. Alan Jay and Graham Paul (out of the eight entered) reached the last 32 of the *Paris Martini*. The latter, as the selectors testified, was determined to show that his fitness belied his years both in competitions and in enthusiastic membership of the training squad. In March he and Single reached the last 32 of the *Duval*, while Barry Paul went on to gain an excellent sixth place. In April a British team lost to W. Germany 10–5 at *Bad Durkheim*. In the individual event Power reached the quarter-final and Graham Paul reached the semi-final. Jay got an Olympic qualifying point by coming sixth. This was his 27th major international tournament result (as reckoned in the table on p. 481, and not including World Championships). It was to be his last, as he retired after this season; but in May he re-emphasised that his tremendous capabilities were by no means extinguished when he gained ninth place in the *Brussels* poule unique of 32, in which Breckin came eleventh.

For the Olympic Games the selectors chose Graham and Barry Paul, Breckin, Power and Single, with Jay as reserve. René Paul went as captain.

Salle Paul won the *Team Championship* once again, defeating Thames 9–3 in the final (Single 3/4, G. Paul 3/4, Jay 2/4, B. Paul 1/4). Peter Jacobs was again the most tenacious of the losers, with two wins. Breckin only managed one, Geoff Grimmett and Wooding none (again, each with one to go).

Grimmett showed his true mettle when he won the *Birmingham Tournament*. Barry Paul won at *Ashton* and *Leicester*. At *Portsmouth* the victor was Malcolm Fare, who beat Barrs 5–2 in the fight-off. Barry Wasley won the *Welsh Open* and Wiles won at Nottingham. Ian Campbell of Lothian won the *Inverclyde* ahead of Bruniges, Bartlett, Loveland, Painter and Tyson. Jim Philbin, Frank Hindle and Bernie Hallam of Hydra beat Bruniges, Knell and Smith of Brownhill to win the team event. Flt-Lt Alan Painter was *Combined Services Champion* for the fourth time.

Early in the season the *Junior Championship* had fallen to John Grimmett, fencing for Salle Paul, though he was very lucky, as well as pertinacious, to overhaul Alan Loveland (Boston), who was hit only four times in the final, apart from a 5–4 defeat by Philbin, but who let slip a 4–2 lead over Grimmett in the barrage. In fourth place behind Philbin came another northerner, 25-year-old, left-handed Martin Beevers, beginning to make a national impact, although he'd only started fencing three years before at the late age of 22, in Nottingham, and got individual tuition from Prof. Imregi when he arrived at the Poly in 1970. Carl Waldman (Cambridge Univ.) was fifth on one win, ahead of Jim Hamments (S. Pearson) on hits.

Bruniges dominated the Under-20 scene. In December he was undefeated victor of the *Gelsenkirchen* tournament. Having risen through four earlier rounds safely but unspectacularly, he so raised his game in the final that he beat Vatter and Fischer of W. Germany by 5–2 and 5–3 respectively, although he had earlier lost to both. He also beat the best of the Germans – Telm – by 5–3. His tally was completed with a 5–1 victory over J. B. Evequoz of Switzerland and 5–0 over a fifth German, Puschel. Partly because of his quiet, unassuming manner, the audience gave him a tremendous ovation.

The British generally did well at Gelsenkirchen: Mick Knell, Jonathan Stanbury and Andy Eames reached the semi-final, where the last only went out on indicators. Gilbert Thompson, David Wade and P. Michaeledes fell in the quarter-finals, all on indicators.

Knell beat Bruniges at Gelsenkirchen (quarter finals) and in the *Under-20 Championship*, where he held him 5–4 in a barrage after both had won four fights in the final. Knell had now left Catford, but continued under John Fairhall at Brownhill FC. Third was Gilbert Thompson who came from Folkestone, fourth Wade, who was at Millfield (which had contributed twelve entrants to the event, more than any other club). Philip Murray of Leicester and Ian Campbell of Lothian held the last two places.

In February, Bruniges won another tournament, this time at *Basel*. In March Eames was second and Knell third in the Under-20 event at *Luxembourg*. In the *Millfield* Tournament Bruniges was the best-placed British fencer, being runner-up to Bach of W. Germany.

The Under-20 points scheme gave the following order prior to the World Youth Championship: Bruniges 414, Knell 263, Eames 255, Thompson 125, Murray 119, D. Tilles 90, Wade 86, Michaeledes 73, Tony Bartlett (taught by Bill Wilson at Beaufoy School, Lambeth) 67, Bryan Lewis 38, Ian Paretti of King's Taunton 36.

*LADIES' FOIL*

The early part of the season was dense with Under-20 events and dominated by Sue Wrigglesworth, Salle Paul, still only seventeen, who won at *Arlon*, in the Perigal and at Duisberg.

The foreign teams invited to the *Perigal Cup* unfortunately failed to materialise, but the final was invested with a sense of occasion by the presence of Mrs C. Miszewska, daughter of Madame Perigal, and some thirty guests of hers. Wendy Ager showed her potential by defeating Sue Wrigglesworth in an early fight and then winning her next three bouts. She first learnt to fence at Wilhelm van Beukelen's Saturday morning classes in Surrey. She was now aged eighteen and taught by Roy Goodall at Combined Circles. She only missed immediate victory by losing the final fight of the pool to Caroline Hall (16, of York Club) – who thus gained her second 4–1 win, to come fourth on indicators. In the barrage that followed, Sue did not repeat her unsuccessful counter-attacks and won the cup convincingly. Jocelyn Hurst (16, of Boston) was third with three wins.

A coach party to *Duisberg* of 23 fencers (including boys) was ably organised by Les Jones. Only one girl slipped in the first round, and three reached the quarter-finals, where Liz Simpson and Wendy Ager came unstuck. Sue Wrigglesworth, however, went on to the final. Here she made a shaky start – 2–3 down to Barry of France before pulling round – but then got three excellent wins (4–2 over Oertel, 4–2 over Oreste of Italy and 4–3 over Kercheis of W. Germany) and as it turned out, she could afford to lose 4–1 to Mochi of Italy in her last fight. She was thus the winner of an event ranked only after the World Youth Championship among junior events of Western Europe.

In the *Ashton Under-20* tournament on home ground, it was the turn of Janet Yates to triumph after a barrage with Jocelyn Hurst, who exploited her already considerable height in launching stop-hits, her favourite move in an invariably defensive game. (She was the winner of the *Invicta* tournament.) Liz Simpson, now at Kent University and suffering from lack of lessons, was third with three wins. Caroline Hall was fourth on indicators over the 19-year-old Hilary Cawthorne of Allen F.C., daughter of Derrick Cawthorne, who had started fencing in 1969 at the Henrietta Barnett School and was launching herself into a notable career. Janet Jones, daughter of Les Jones, aged only fifteen, but forging ahead, and fencing in the attractive style of Ashton, took up the last place as she had also in the Perigal.

At *Gelsenkirchen*, in December, Susan Wrigglesworth disappointed her supporters by going out in the quarter-finals. Lorna Andrews reached the semi-finals, but failed to adapt to the pace there, while Janet Yates, who had topped her quarter-final, suffered from a loss of accuracy.

In January 1972 the *Nescafé Tournament* was preceded by a five-sided match. GB 'A' only beat GB 'B' 5–4 and ended third, after France and W. Germany, although it overcame Italy and Switzerland. In the individual event nineteen from Britain competed with seventeen foreigners. Only three of the British were semi-finalists (though Sally Mitton of S. Paul was unlucky to go out on hits in the previous round after an exciting win over Cob of Italy). Sue Wrigglesworth and Jane Popland failed to reach the final, but Wendy Ager gained sixth place after Appert, Oertel, Ducamp, Beck and Armbrust – a strong field. Michel Kallipetis turned his gifts as a barrister to fluent use in providing a commentary over the loud-speaker system, as he did at numerous other Under-20 events in these years.

The *Under-20 Championship* a week later fell to Caroline Hall, who lost to

Sue Wrigglesworth, but was otherwise taken beyond two hits only by Wendy Ager, who came second. Third on hits was Sue Wrigglesworth, who lost to both Wendy Ager (4–3) and 4–0 to Lorna Andrews (4th). Fifth was Lynne O'Keefe, ahead of Valerie Windram (Boston).

Janet Jones did very well to come third at *Leicester*. A little like Susan Green, she had good footwork, mobility and a long, elastic lunge. She was improving in skill and confidence all the time and not only took the *Junior Schoolgirls* title but also carried off the *Parker Trophy*. Pursuing her here in second place with fearsome Scottish war-cries was Alex Parker (S. Darnell, Grimsby). Next, on indicators, was Linda Brown of Salle Reynolds, showing good timing, control and backwards speed. Sue Rochard (now at LFC) didn't exploit her length, but got her nose ahead of Valerie Windram. Frances Alexander was the only one to disconcert the winner, but couldn't maintain a positive approach against the others.

In the *Bertrand Cup*, Wendy Ager and Caroline Hall, true to form, were each undefeated in the semi-finals and barraged for the title. Wendy Ager of Salle Goodall was the very convincing victor. Strong, fit and aggressive, her favourite move was a fleche attack, often preceded by a beat. Julia Bullmore of Boston, on an upward trend, took third place. Pam Patient of Reading was fourth and fifth was Valerie Windram (whose bout with the winner was a demonstration that fencing is a combat sport). Helen Whicher of Thames and the Antipodes did well to reach the final from a five-way tie in which Janet Jones, Sue Olley (now at Boston) and Alda Milner-Barry (Thames) were the unlucky contestants.

Barbara Rae (ex-Goodall) won *Inverclyde* again. For the fifth year the team event was won by Caledonian, whose team generally comprised Sue Youngs, Catherine Wotherspoon and Sandra Robertson. At *Portsmouth* Rosemary Castle won the title from Gerry Harding on the last hit in a barrage, while Hazel Rogerson won at *Nottingham*; but the dominant figure in the provincial tournaments was Sue Green, who won at *Ashton*, at *Leicester* and at *Birmingham*.

In the senior headquarters events, however, Janet Wardell-Yerburgh's supremacy was more comprehensive than ever. She made a clean sweep of the Championship, the Desprez and the de Beaumont. She took the *Championship* crown for the fourth successive time, equalled only by the famous Gwendoline Neligan and exceeded only by Gillian Sheen's staggering eight successive wins (from 1951 to 1958). It was also the sixth time she had won, only bettered by Gillian Sheen's ten times. Not content with this, she won the *Desprez* Cup for the sixth time as well, in this case breaking *all* records. Here mini-pools of four were tried in the quarter and semi-finals, making for greater tension and some surprise upsets, such as the elimination in the quarters of Janet Jones, Sue Green and Valerie Windram and in the semis of Sally Littlejohns, the holder, and Angela Herbert (Boston), who had fenced well till her barrage for

1972 Championship: Janet Wardell-Yerburgh v Sue Wrigglesworth (Sally Littlejohns seated in front of Prof Lagnado; Barbara Williams in front of Prof. Emery and Kristin Payne; Mildred Durne in front of René Paul).

the final. This was taken by Martin Joyce, whose sure and unruffled presiding benefited so many events till he left to take up a job at the European Parliament. Janet W-Y (LFC) did not have it all her own way, because she lost to an aggressive Hazel Davenport, who ended fourth, and only won on the last hit in the barrage (as she had in the pool) against Clare Henley, who was fencing with precision and good timing. Wendy Ager continued her youthful run of successes by coming third, while Mildred Durne showed how experience allied with determination could still succeed by surmounting two barrages and claiming fifth place on hits over Sue Olley.

Janet W-Y had to barrage again for the *de Beaumont Cup*, this time with her LFC club-mate Sally Littlejohns, who thus won through to the top rank. There were no foreigners in the final, but it was still a notable achievement for Paddy Power's pupil Caroline Hall to gain fifth place. This was Janet W-Y's second successive win, which Gillian Sheen had curiously enough never achieved, though she and Karen Lachmann both won six times in all, double Janet's score.

In the *Championship*, Janet W-Y (still taught by Prof. Ganchev) did not have to barrage, but three of her wins were on the last hit – with Sue Green (5th) and with Clare Henley and the fast improving Sue Wrigglesworth, who shared second place on identical hits, both given and received. Hazel Davenport also got three victories (albeit this time scoring only one hit against Janet), but had to be content with fourth place again. Julia Bullmore of Salle Boston gained sixth place; probably her friendly and easy-going approach prevented her doing better on this and other occasions.

On this occasion, Wendy Ager, along with Janet Yates, had faltered in the semi-finals. In the quarters Sue Youngs, Angela Herbert and Kate Hurford had been notable victims. Janet W-Y also claimed the *Silver Jubilee Bowl* – for the third year running and the seventh time in all. (Gillian Sheen won it five times.) She barraged with Sally Littlejohns this time.

In the second round of the *Team Championship*, early in the season, Salle Pearson succumbed to Salle van Oeveren only on hits, as likewise Poly did to Thames, while Salle Goodall dented the impregnability of LFC the holders. In the semi-finals the Ashton–Boston match proved both boisterous and technically good. From 2–4 the London club crept up to 6–7 (Sue Olley scoring a good 4–1 win against Janice Deakin); but there they stuck. Meanwhile LFC extinguished Thames by a surprising 9–0.

The final was an anti-climax. LFC had become unstoppable and overran Ashton 9–2, though by common consent the match was carried on to a final score of 12–4. Sue Green and Janet Yates each got two wins. Janet Jones and Janice Deakin could not score. For LFC Janet W-Y was undefeated, Sue Wrigglesworth and Sally Littlejohns got three wins each and Kate Hurford, although she was ceasing to train or travel, two wins.

It was almost the same team (with Clare Henley instead of Sally Littlejohns) that fenced for Britain in an invitation tournament in *Brussels*, where they achieved joint third place with the Belgians, behind France and Germany. Janet W-Y took third place in the individual classification.

A London team came second to the hosts in the *Amsterdam Inter-Cities Tournament*. At Duren Britain got third place in a *5-sided match* in which Belgium and Scandinavia were defeated but two German teams prevailed. Janet W-Y reached the semi-final of the *Duren* individual event and Clare Henley the quarter-final. In *Turin*, LFC (as Champion team) reached the quarter-finals (where they were eliminated by the USSR). Sue Wrigglesworth showed that form had by no means deserted her by doing best of the fourteen British in the individual, reaching the last 24.

The British entered the tournament at *Minsk* for the first time, most of them almost missing the start after a disastrous journey. Clare Henley again notched up a creditable quarter-final. In matches of varying status here Leningrad and USA were defeated (though not Russian, French or Cuban teams). At *Goppingen* Janet W-Y came sixth, Clare Henley reached the semi-finals and Sue Green the quarter-finals.

In May Britain beat the USA 8–all and Canada 9–7 in London, and a week later came third yet again at *Eupen*, where Sally Littlejohns gained third place in the individual event, underlining this performance by reaching the last sixteen of the Paris *Jeanty*. She was rated the most improved fencer of the season by Eve Davies, the Captain, adding better footwork to her already excellent timing and point control, aided perhaps by living close to the LFC.

The Olympic team contained the existing members Janet W-Y, Clare Henley and Sue Green, together with Sue Wrigglesworth and Sally Littlejohns, who took the places of Hazel Davenport (this season without the foreign results to match her home performances) and of Barbara Williams (who had joined the WRNS in 1971, but did not gain the anticipated training opportunities and had had a disappointing season, hampered by a knee injury).

## EPEE

The standard of phrasing and bladework in the *Junior Championship* compared favourably with the 'fishing' prevalent in earlier years. Stanbury and Osbaldeston were the most notable casualties prior to the final of nine. In this lengthy pool the 19-year-old Chris White of Streatham led undefeated until the last quarter, fencing calmly and defensively throughout. But then John Hall (Goodall; 4th) and Desmond Turner (Poly; 6th) overcame him with hustling tactics, taking advantage of his poor footwork. Meanwhile, Brian Hill, pupil of Prof. Bertrand at LFC, having started badly with two defeats, got into his stride, exploiting his height to marry a new speed and aggression with deceptively wide arm movements. He narrowly secured his last two fights and then chased Chris White out of the title in the barrage. Richard Bird of Poly, a tall straight-arm fencer, was third with five victories. Adrian Silvey of Combined Circles was fifth.

Medals were awarded for the first time in the *Martini Qualifying Competitions*, and even bottles of Champagne from Martini. The order of the final poule unique of eighteen was as follows: 1. D. Partridge, 13v; 2. eq. J. Stanbury and R. Davenport, 12v; 4. C. Green, 11v; 5. S. Higginson, 11v; 6. J. Hall, 10v; 7. J. Noel, 10v; 8. B. Hill, 10v; 9. K. Pearman, 10v; 10. P. Emberson, 9v; 11. W. Osbaldeston, 8v; 12. B. Paul, 7v; 13. A. Silvey, 7v; 14. C. Hallett, 6v. None of these managed to get through the preliminary round to the 36 in the direct elimination of the *Martini* itself – which could mainly be attributed to the strength of the entry in an Olympic year. In the bottom eight, who fenced first, Hoskyns lost to Gonsior 8–6, Jacobs lost to Marchand 8–5, but Ted Hudson did well to beat Levasseur 8–6. Then, in the match plan of 32, Hudson went on to beat Delhem (Belgium), 11–10, while Johnson, the only Briton in the top 28, beat Varille, winner in 1969 and 1970. By ill chance the two survivors met in the last sixteen. Johnson dispatched a tired Hudson 8–2.

At the Seymour Hall, Ralph Johnson at his most dominating and incisive gratified the audience with an 8–2 destruction of Zawadski of Poland, who had previously beaten the world medallist von Essen of Sweden. Maybe this success and an early 3–0 lead over the little fancied Sennecka of Monaco induced him to continue in the same vein too easily when Sennecka changed his tactics, widening the distance so that Johnson fell short in his favourite low-line attacks and then scoring with a counter-attack and occasional fleche. A good bout ended with a 9–7 defeat.

In the last bout, Muck of W. Germany was also nearly overcome by the outsider, being 5–2 down at the last minute and only winning by the odd hit after the expiry of time.

From the most senior to the most junior. The *Schoolboys Championship* registered the dominance of Catford School, London, where John Fairhall was supported by a parents' association which subsidised numerous trips to foreign events. Bruniges, Emberson and Colin Sigrist, the qualifiers for the SE, made a clean sweep of the top places in that order. White was sixth at *Leicester*, fourth at *Ashton*, a semi-finalist both at *Goppingen* and in the *Schmetz* and fourth in the Under-20 poule unique of 24 at *Tauberbischofsheim*. He had, however, to be content with fourth place in the *Under-20 Championship*, where he proved somewhat negative and vulnerable to reprises while steadying himself on the retreat. Pip Emberson was the winner, after a 5–4 barrage against Keuls of Thames, who could have done much better if he'd been less lackadaisical and used his considerable length more. Emberson (who also came sixth at Inverclyde), was relaxed, mobile and deep in attack – and only fifteen years old.

Bruniges was a semi-finalist at Goppingen, fifth at Tauberbischofsheim and winner at Inverclyde and Ashton; he was alone of the British in reaching the semi-final of the *Nescafé*, but didn't get to the Under-20 final. Neither did Ally Smith of Catford, who had showed promise in reaching the Goppingen semi-final. Three other promising epeeists were the 15-year-old Paul Tarran (Newport, Essex, pupil of Chris Green), David Brooks (Corby) and M. Allton (Gateway), who were third, fifth and sixth respectively in the Under-20 Championship.

It was one of the disappointing features of epee over the following years that of all these fencers only Bruniges and Brooks were to persist in training and competition (and foil soon monopolised the former).

The *Championship* produced a final without surprises, except perhaps that Hoskyns came so close to winning the title he had first claimed eighteen years before. He was undefeated until his last fight, against Johnson, which he lost on a disputed decision. In the barrage Teddy Bourne applied the tactics that were to become the standard recipe for aspirants to victory over the old master: simple attacks delivered at top speed. Timing and distance had to be just right; but this they were in Bourne's five fleches.

Third was Davenport, now in the top ranks of British epeeists. Johnson, as so often, had taken time off for solicitors' exams, but got fourth place on hits over Halsted, who in turn had missed most of the season, first recovering from a shoulder operation to prevent recurrent dislocation and then from breaking a leg skiing. Hudson reached the final but won no fights.

Up to the semi-finals, the *Miller-Hallett* (innocent of foreigners, except for the Irish) also ran true to form. In one of these, however, Johnson, hitherto undefeated, only won two fights, as did three others: Graham Paul (absent from the Championship), Higginson and Howard West – and it was West who had the hits, along with Hoskyns and Osbaldeston. West and Osbaldeston were both thus Senior finalists for the first time. In the other semi-final, Bourne and Noel were joined by Hudson, who was two hits ahead of Davenport and Hill.

Aptly enough, James Noel's family motto is 'All or Nothing'. This final was an occasion for 'all'. After a 5–4 victory over his Thames club-mate Hudson he steadily gained in confidence, using his length devastatingly. He ended by winning 5–1 over Bourne, who was otherwise only once taken even to the second hit. Hudson was third, Hoskyns fourth, West fifth and Osbaldeston sixth, each being beaten by all those above them.

In the *Savage*, Salle Paul were after the hat-trick. This time, however, they failed to demoralise Thames. In a hard semi-final match they lost 9–7; while Boston beat the Army 9–6 in spite of Belson defeating both Bourne and Johnson. It was a see-saw final. Thames climbed to 3–1, including a win by Hudson over Johnson. Then Boston won seven fights in a row, including two by Bourne, but also one by Gray over Noel, the tail-ender against Thames's hitherto top scorer. Prof. Boston was puffing his cigar with visible contentment. But then the pendulum swung hard over – until there were only two fights to go and Boston needed four hits to win. Gray got three of them off Hudson, oblivious in the excitement of a wound received in his fierce encounter with Higginson (which had to be stitched up afterwards). This left Jacobs with the unenviable task of beating Johnson 5–0 to force a barrage. 1–0, 2–0 ... everybody on the edges of their seats ... 2–1; Boston had made it! Bourne had got three wins, Johnson and Davenport two each and Gray one, while Thames got two apiece.

Back in November a *Scottish–Norwegian epee match* had been arranged by Bergen Club. Russell did well to win three fights; Hunter also got one win against strong opponents; Jamieson and McMicken were unable to do so. (Krogh 4, Normann 3, O. Morch 3, C. Morch 2). In the individual event next day during close fighting the epee of one of Hunter's opponents slipped under his mask and penetrated his eye (and he also hit his head on falling). Fortunately he made a good recovery from this serious injury. The Norwegians were as generously helpful after the accident as they had been hospitable before it.

*Inverclyde* saw Hunter already back in action. It was won by Bruniges in an all-Brownhill barrage with Fairhall and Smith. Ralph Evans of Birmingham University won at *Nottingham*. *Leamington* was extremely high in standard owing to the presence of the German team. Two Welsh fencers, Bob Turner and Howard West, did very well to reach the last eight along with Johnson and Gille. Noel came fourth and Jacobs showed in the final bout against Bohnen, the winner, that though he might be past his peak he could still fight harder than anyone in the country.

The crowded, festive Pump Room at Leamington had provided the ideal setting for a *match against Germany* during the Easter Tournament. Bourne was on top form and undefeated, Hudson had regained some of his verve and won two, but Noel, troubled by a knee injury, was less happy. After reaching 6–all amidst growing excitement, against Bohnen, Behr, Gille and Peter, the team lost three of the last four bouts.

Previously a weaker team had fenced a *match against Belgium* in the Officers' Mess of the Belgian army camp at Duren in NW Germany (where fencers were accommodated in spartan conditions). The British were 6–1 down, then 8–all – a tremendous recovery but a loss on hits.

The first match against France for twelve years, in the *post-Martini* series, started similarly: 6–2 down, then take-off with five of the next six fights. Hoskyns manipulated a highly advantageous double defeat to make up a hits leeway; then Johnson beat Ladegaillerie, twice a world finalist. A fine victory, with Bourne and Noel each winning three fights. There followed an 11–5 revenge on Belgium and an 8–all win over Poland which went neck-and-neck till at 7–8 Noel met Bartecki: 3–1 up, 3–all, then two excellently judged hits to arm to win the match and give Noel seven out of eight fights over the weekend.

At Bern the team lost a *match against Austria* 8–7. In December in yet another *match against Germany* Davenport got the best result of his numerous team appearances by beating Maier, Behr and Hehn (Bourne 2, Hudson 0, Noel 0).

In individual events abroad Bourne had an even better run than in 1968. In November he won the *Bad Durkheim* pool of Champions. In February despite two months' exam work he was in the last twelve in the *Monal* (and Jacobs, Partridge and G. Paul were in the last 36). In April came a climax, with fifth place at the toughest event of all, the *Heidenheim* tournament, with 304 epeeists from 24 countries, including twelve Russians. He beat Paramanov and Fenyvesi in the direct elimination before losing to the eventual winner, Behr of W. Germany by only 10–9. At the end of that month he reached the quarter-finals at *Bern*, along with Johnson and G. Paul. Finally in May he was third in *Berlin*. No British epeeist except Jay and Hoskyns in their great days had put up such a series of performances. It earned him equal eleventh place in the world ranking. Johnson was equal thirtieth.

Hoskyns himself came second at *Duren*. Noel was fourth, fading after an excellent start. At *Poitiers* in May both reached the last 32, together with Davenport. Andrew Cornford of Thames accompanied them to the second round. Olympic hopes for Halsted were extinguished in the first round. The winner here was the veteran Nielaba. Hudson, though out in the first round at Poitiers, secured second place in a more modest event, at *Le Havre*, and thereby a somewhat marginal Olympic qualification and a place in the team, along with Bourne, Johnson, Hoskyns and Paul.

*SABRE*

At the junior end of the spectrum, success went to the sabre-first Brooke House School. In the *Schoolboys Championships* Frank Gardiner, Michael Streater and Robert Neal took first, second and fourth places in the senior event, while John Bailey won the junior one. In the *Public Schools*, talent was distributed more evenly. Jonathan Lewis was undefeated champion for St Paul's, Steve Pankhurst of Brentwood and Boston was second, Shahin Sanjar of Cheltenham (already an international for Iran) third, Ross Campion of Merchant Taylors fourth, while Gavin Brown and Gilbert Thompson secured the last two places for Dover College and Prof. Mallard.

Pankhurst scored a greater success in the *Under-20 Championships*, in which he came fourth – after a five-way barrage produced two wins all round. The winner on indicators was Bryan Lewis of Oxford University, whose thoughtfulness, careful timing and determination triumphed over the greater dash and technique of such fancied opponents as Mather, who was second, or the younger Mike Price of Boston (3rd) – no relation to his Poly namesake – who showed his eagerness by starting his attack before the word 'play' no fewer than 23 times! Dennis Hutt (LFC) ran out of steam in the barrage, while Chris Grzesik (Lilia) was well off out of it. Deanfield was absent from the event, but maintained his leading position in the Under-20 circuit. He missed the *Koblenz* final by a mere hit and was third at *Goppingen*, behind Quivrin and Weissgerber and ahead of Grosser, Bena and Romano. Peter Stafford did well to reach the quarter-final. In the *Nescafé* Deanfield and Price reached the semi-final. (Quivrin won, ahead of Bena and Romano.)

In the *Junior*, Price chalked up a new high by coming sixth and Mather did himself better justice in second place; but it was older fencers who filled the other places. Charles Kovanda of Birmingham FC, where he was taught by Prof. Faubert, at last captured the trophy, having started to fence at the age of sixteen. He used his experience to avoid over-exertion, and brought off many excellent second-intention attacks and ripostes. Philbin (3rd) was the only one to take him to the last hit. Tom Norcross, also of Birmingham, was fourth. Fairburn having topped his semi-final, tended to bring his arm back at the start of attacks and ended fifth. Milligan was unlucky not to reach the final.

The five foot seven Kovanda was winner at *Nottingham* too, displacing Wiles, who got the *Inverclyde* trophy instead. David Scott triumphed in the

1971 Junior: Tom Norcross and Charles Kovanda.

invitation event put on by Salle Pearson, in which he beat Cohen and Eden in the barrage. Tony Mitchell was *Scottish* champion for a record eighth time.

Poles and Germans lent strength to the *Cole Cup*. Ganchev and Oldcorn went out in the same quarter-final; Acfield, Eden and Deanfield succumbed in the semi-finals. Cohen carried the flag in the final, securing fifth place by beating Malmurowicz of Poland. Convents of W. Germany was undefeated; Wischeidt (who was to miss the 1972 Olympic final only on hits) was second.

In the associated *matches* Britain could perhaps have done better than 7–9 against an under-strength Polish team (Deanfield saving three). But an 8–all win on hits against a German team lacking only Hohne from its full strength was an excellent result. Oldcorn won three here.

Earlier, Cohen, Deanfield, Oldcorn and Zarno had been invited to a training weekend at *Bonn*, where they lost 5–10 to W. Germany (6 bouts being lost on the last hit), and 7–9 to Switzerland (Deanfield winning three), but beat Belgium 8–8 on hits, Oldcorn and Cohen getting three apiece.

The *Brussels Martini* saw twelve of the fourteen Britons survive the first round of the 196 from twelve nations: a new strength in depth. Fourteen out of eighteen of the second round pools were topped by Iron Curtain fencers – the other four by two Frenchmen, an Italian and Deanfield. Ten Britons were among the casualties (Mather missing promotion on hits). 21 of the original 24 E. European fencers went through the next round to the last 36. The last Britons, Deanfield and Cohen, didn't make it among the fifteen westerners (one of whom, Maffei, was the winner).

The following weekend, at the *Paris Touzard*, which drew entries from Belgium, Czechoslovakia and Italy, Oldcorn and Cohen missed the final by a fight each, but Deanfield took a good sixth place behind five members of the French team.

In *Hamburg* Britain lost to Austria, Holland and Poland and in the individual only Alan Taylor distinguished himself, reaching the quarter-final. At *Montreuil*, it was Cohen's turn to make sixth place, amongst entries from six countries including W. Germany and Bulgaria. (Oldcorn was in the quarter-finals.) At *Munich* nothing was achieved. Deanfield's outstanding result in the World Youth Championship is recounted later.

Rodney Craig had a cartilage operation in March, and though he reached the quarter-final at *Cracow* in May, he missed the *Championship* back in April. Acfield left the cricket field to win his customary crown for the fourth successive time. Oldcorn (5th) occasionally looked deprived of his rightful dues; Cohen (4th) gave only sparingly of his heart-rending impressions of injured innocence, while Deanfield (2nd), leapt triumphantly now and again with outstretched arms to consolidate a doubtful hit; but there was little acrimony. Mather did well to come third, though with two wins he was only divided on hits from David Eden (fencing for Latista) in last position. The average fencing time per bout was fifteen seconds.

Philbin and Zarno were in the semi-finals, as was the veteran George Birks, in spite of finishing off his Achilles tendon and all but chopping off his thumb within the previous year. Rayden and Porebski (on a visit from Canada) represented different generations of past Champions.

In *pre-Corble matches* Britain beat Canada 10–6 (Mather 3, Deanfield 3, Oldcorn 2, Craig 2), and Holland 9–6 (Mather 0, Oldcorn 3, Cohen 3, Craig 3). A very satisfying result.

For the *Corble* itself there were also Austrians, Swedes and Mexicans. Nevertheless, four Britons were in the final alongside Kalmar (1969 World Silver Medallist), who won, and Hamm of Holland, who was third. It was Mather who shone. Although the youngest of the British, technically he was the best. He gained second place. Oldcorn, Cohen and Craig were fourth, fifth and sixth.

The Olympic team consisted of these last three, together with Acfield and Deanfield. Mather was a hot candidate, but was not selected.

The *Team Championship* saw a provincial team – Hydra – rise to the final, the first ever to do so (unless the Army answers the description). Taylor, Philbin, Bradbury and Hallam disposed first of Boston 'B' (9–4) and then of Birmingham (9–7, Taylor being unbeaten). Boston 'A', though favourites, were below form, and mistakenly resting Zarno in favour of their number five, they were beaten 9–7 by LFC, for whom Hutt scored three victories. In the final, LFC overcame Hydra 9–2 (Oldcorn 3/3, Wasilewski 2/3, Hutt 2/3, John Lankshear 2/2). Philbin and Taylor got the Hydra victories.

An account of the season would be incomplete without recording the first ladies' sabre tournament in Britain (at least for many years). This open event, held at Plymouth, was won by Frances Blackmore of the home club.

## COMBINED EVENTS

Britain again did well at the relay event at *Alassio*, even if a win was beyond reach this time. Janet Wardell-Yerburgh beat the ebullient Masciotta of Italy 5–4. Graham Paul beat Simoncelli 10–9. Cohen did well to stem M. T. Montano 10–12. Bourne held the Vienna Silver Medallist, Granieri, 8–10. Against the French, Janet Wardell-Yerburgh again gave an excellent lead by beating Gapais 8–7. Paul lost to Leseur 11–7, but Cohen fought desperately to overcome Quivrin 11–10. Bourne thus met his fellow world semi-finalist Floquet at 28–26 down. He proved a tower of strength, winning 12–9 to save the match by one hit. So Britain contended for the title with Sweden (who had beaten France 38–28 and Italy 38–34). Janet succumbed to the formidable Palm 8–4. Paul beat Abrahamson 13–10, but Kalmar moved ahead by a 10–5 win over Cohen. From 18–22 Bourne lost 10–6 to Edling, the third world-class Swede.

All this was to a background of royal entertainment provided by ever-munificent Martini and bathing in the azure Mediterranean.

At *Leicester* Colin Tyson and his band of organisers marshalled 250 fencers punctually as ever through a close and enjoyable tournament. Salle Paul fought a private barrage in the foil, Barry Paul being the victor and Tony Barrs taking second place from Ian Single. Andy Eames of Leicester YMCA moved up a rank by gaining fourth place. Geoff Grimmett, fifth, was below form, while Jim Philbin made up for absence from the sabre final by coming sixth.

In the ladies' final Sue Green met Mary Hawksworth with level wins and won 4–0. Janet Jones took third place for Ashton and Rosemary Castle sixth

Alassio 1971: a characteristic Bourne reverse hit against Floquet.

for Hydra. The intervening places went to Mrs Anne-Marie Krimke of Garrick F.C., Stratford-on-Avon, and Alex Parker (Darnell).

At epee, Partridge won the title, but not without a battle from Turner of Cardiff, already described as evergreen, and Beevers (3rd), who had only been fencing epee for a year but also reached the final at *Ashton*. There followed Pearman (4th), Osbaldeston (5th) and White (6th).

Competition in the sabre was severe. Hobson and Mather went out in a second round and Keal, Kovanda, Scott and Hunt in the semi-final. In the final the result was settled when Cohen met Ganchev, both undefeated throughout. Ganchev led 4–2, but Cohen won.

Some 240 competitors from 33 countries took part in the lavishly mounted *World Youth Championships* in Madrid. The British officials were Charles de Beaumont, Mary Glen Haig, Kristin Payne and Joe Eden. Assisted by John Fairhall, Prof. Boston coached the men, Leslie Jones the women.

The men's foil started badly when Bruniges was eliminated in the first round, with two victories. In the second round Eames went out with one win and Knell with none. The standard of the final was high. The order was: Godel (Poland), Rodionov (USSR), Pietruszka (France), Ruziev (USSR), Benko (Australia) and M. Behr (W. Germany).

Five were promoted from pools of six in the ladies' first round and all three of the British survived. Sue Wrigglesworth and Wendy Ager went out with a win apiece in the second round, but Caroline Hall survived to the last 24 (where she got one win). After a very good final, Filatova (USSR) beat Makowski (Poland).

At epee, Emberson went under in the first round, with two wins, and White in the second round with none. Bruniges fenced well in the second round, obtaining three wins, but completely lost his way in the quarter-finals. The winner was G. Evequoz (Switzerland) over Janikowski (Poland).

An over-impetuous Price failed in the first round of the sabre. Two wins was not enough for Mather in the second round. But Deanfield forged steadily ahead, with two wins in the first round, three wins in the second, three again in the quarter-finals (including 5–2 against Komar of Russia). In the semi-finals he was in stiff company. With two wins under his belt, he was 3–all in the last fight. There were ten successive simultaneous attacks. Then his opponent missed; he was 4–3 up. There followed eleven successive simultaneous attacks. On the twelfth Deanfield happily extended his arm, so that his opponent fell on the point.

In the final he lost form. Although he beat de la Torre of Cuba, he had to accept sixth place. Nevertheless, this was one of the best British performances either in the World Youth Championships or on the part of any British sabreur for many years. The first four were: Pavlenko (USSR), Quivrin (France), T. Montano (Italy) and Gulacsi (Hungary).

The *Quadrangular* took place in the new Cardiff Sports Centre. The

English team swept the board. At foil Bell and the Grimmett brothers beat Scotland 7–2, N. Ireland 8–1 and Wales 9–0, John Grimmett being undefeated. Caroline Hall, Wendy Ager and Janet Jones beat Scotland 5–4, N. Ireland 6–3 and Wales 8–1. At sabre John Moore was undefeated. With Philbin and Kovanda, he beat Scotland 6–3 and both N. Ireland and Wales 8–1.

The Scots comprised Barbara Goodall, Gillian Ritchie, Sue Youngs; Mitchell (Captain), Campbell, Wiles, Russell, Tyson and Robert Elliott – with much doubling of weapons. The ladies beat N. Ireland 5–4 and Wales 6–3. The male foilists beat N. Ireland 5–4, but lost 7–2 to Wales. The epeeists beat N. Ireland 6–3 and Wales 5–4; while the sabreurs swept over N. Ireland 9–0 and Wales 7–2.

For once the N. Ireland team were out of fourth position. Under Jack Magill, they fielded Christine and Olive Convill, Pamela Lewis, Kate Thompson, David Carlisle, Steve Carson, James Ferguson, Ian McConaghy, Colin Nelson and William Richardson. They beat Wales on eighteen victories with a margin of five hits.

Wales was represented by Bob Turner (Captain), Linda Brown, Yvonne McCombe, Sharon Williams, Derek Lucas, Ian Edwards, Gerry Poote, Edmund Gray, Peter Stewart and Colin Hyndman. Their best achievement was to come within four fights of beating Scotland.

411 fencers from nearly forty schools entered the *Public Schools Championships*. The outstanding result was by Gilbert Thompson (Dover; Prof. A. Mallard). He won the foil, was second in the epee and sixth in the sabre. Nevertheless, Brentwood once more won the overall Graham Bartlett cup.

The *Granville Cup* was won for the third year running by Salle Boston. Second was LFC for whom Hill beat Bourne 5–4, 5–4. Wasilewski, however, went under to Johnson 5–0, 5–0 at foil, while Oldcorn lost to Cohen 5–4, 1–5, 5–3.

Training for the *Olympic Games* was probably more thorough than for any previous event. It culminated in a session for the whole team at Aldershot two weeks before departure. The Olympic village in Munich was new housing three miles from the converted exhibition halls where the fencing took place. The facilities were outstanding, with 42 training pistes (22 of which had electrical equipment) and so was the organisation.

The Captain, elected to fill the place left vacant only weeks before by Charles de Beaumont's death, was Peter Hobson, who doubled as sabre captain (with Rodney Craig as deputy). Mildred Durne, René Paul and Peter Jacobs were the other weapon captains. Team coaches were Prof. Anderson and Prof. Boston. Mary Glen Haig accompanied the party as delegate to the FIE.

As usual, only three contestants were allowed in each individual event. Breckin and the two Pauls survived the first round. Mike Breckin was

1972 Olympic team: *Back:* R. Craig, B. Paul, J. Deanfield, I. Single, G. Paul, H. W. Hoskyns, E. Hudson, D. Acfield. *Middle:* W. R. Johnson, M. Breckin, R. Cohen, S. Wrigglesworth, S. Littlejohns, S. Green, A. Power, E. Bourne, R. Oldcorn. *Seated:* C. Henley, René Paul, Prof. Anderson, P. Hobson, P. Jacobs, E. Davies, J. Wardell-Yerbergh.

eliminated in the second round by one hit given, behind Wessel (1969 and 1970 World Champion). Barry and Graham Paul reached the quarter-finals (third round).

These results gave a seventh seeding for the team event, and France and Cuba as opponents. Cuba streaked to a lead of 5–1, held a challenge at 7–4, then bounded off again to 9–4 and 11–5. The Pauls each got two wins, but Tony Power could only get one and Mike Breckin got none.

As so often, an initial match which ought to have been won was followed by a good performance against a world class team. Single replaced Breckin and got one win (against Revenu, who failed to score). Power also beat Magnan, as did Barry Paul. Graham got one. The score was 5–all before dipping to 10–6, Talvard and Berolatti being undefeated.

In the ladies' individual it was a great disappointment that Janet Wardell-Yerburgh, whose prowess gave hopes of great things, should go out in the first round. She and Clare Henley both got two wins but inadequate hits. Susan Green fenced with decision and confidence, varying her attacks and riposting very efficiently. Having thus earned herself twelfth seed in the quarter-final, she sadly lost her confidence and did not win a fight.

Seeded sixth in the team event, the ladies drew Rumania (7th) and France (1st). Janet W-Y now showed her true form by winning three against Rumania, while Sally Littlejohns, in her first international, won two. One win apiece from Clare Henley and Sue Green still left a defeat at 7–9.

As with the men, the team had thus to attempt the Himalayas. Janet, in champion form, beat Demaille, Josland and Gapais (-Dumont). Susan Wrigglesworth, a second new colour, came in for Clare, whose form had probably been upset by back injury. In calm, controlled style, she thrilled British supporters by beating Josland 4–2 and devastating Demaille (1971 World Champion) 4–1. Sadly, Sue Green only got one win and Sally Littlejohns none.

In the sabre, Cohen surprisingly failed to win a bout in the first round. He had perhaps reached a peak too soon, and gone stale. Deanfield and Oldcorn each got two wins in the second round and were eliminated on hits (Deanfield being classified 25th, with an indicator better than two quarter-finalists).

In the team event the sabreurs were bronze medallists of a kind, since they drew Italy, the eventual winners, and USSR, the runners-up, and were by no means pulverised. Although Acfield did not score against the Russians, Oldcorn beat Vinokurov, Craig beat Rakita and Sidiak (who happened to be newly crowned Gold Medallist) and Cohen beat all three illustrious opponents. 10–6 was a very creditable score. Against Italy they had a smaller impact, with Craig and Deanfield never going beyond four hits, but Oldcorn beat T. Montano and Cohen, still fencing brilliantly, overcoming Salvadori as well. The Italians won the event for the first time since 1950.

Highest hopes were set on epee, given the individual results over recent years, particularly those of Teddy Bourne, who perhaps suffered from these very hopes. In the first round he started with two decisive victories, but an unexpected defeat by Istrate of Rumania punctured his confidence, though he gained promotion. Johnson went up third more safely in a pool which eliminated von Essen, ranked first in Europe. Graham Paul topped his pool.

The second round was disastrous. Johnson got no wins, relying on strokes which left him vulnerable when they failed. Graham Paul's chances were dashed on losing 5–all to Semecka, while Bourne for his third win had to beat Trost, thrice world finalist, and lost 5–3.

In the team event both Norway and Britain protested against the misseeding of W. Germany in the latter's pool, along with France and Lebanon. Both were pleased when Norway was swapped with Germany, confident of victory in the match between them. Unfortunately the Norwegians had more justification. The trouble was not the usual slow start: scores were level all through; rather it was lack of sparkle – four of the nine defeats were on the last hit. Paul's zest and energy were sapped by a heavy cold on top of a stomach upset, while Johnson, troubled by a bruised hand, seemed unable to expand beyond attacks underneath the wrist and counter-attacks to upper arm, neither successful. He got one win; each of the others got two.

So yet again it was the French who had to be beaten. Here Hoskyns, who had only missed skewering all four Norwegians by the couple of odd hits, really came into his own. Aged 42 and doubtful of inclusion in the team only months before, he accounted for half the British score, beating Marchand 5–4 and both Jeanne and Brodin (6th in the individual) 5–2. Hudson came in for Johnson. Like Paul and Bourne, he had to remain content with beating Marchand. So it was 10–6 and a sad departure.

# 1972–3

## MEN'S FOIL

Among the 28 clubs in the *Team Championship*, Brownhill did well to reach the quarter-finals. Here Poly only narrowly lost to Thames. In the semi-finals Boston 'B' only got three wins against Paul (Carl Waldman beating Single and G. Paul and Julian Tyson beating B. Paul), but an energetic Boston 'A', led by Bourne with three wins, overcame Thames 9–4 (Breckin stemming the flood with two wins out of three).

Salle Paul faltered at first in the final, when David Eden beat Barry Paul and Johnson beat Geoff Grimmett (who had recently migrated from Thames), but then took control, conceding only one more bout, by Single to Eden, and with Graham Paul undefeated.

In the *Junior* Knell was unlucky to go out in the harder semi-final; Chetwood and Llewellyn were other Under-20 foilists who went out, on the opposite side. John Higgins (unattached) fought his way all the way from the first qualifying round to sixth place in the final (where he defeated Beevers). Jim Hamments (S. Pearson) achieved fifth place on experience and skill in spite of unfitness. Loveland could not cope with Beevers at all and had to accept fourth place even though his unflurried accuracy defeated the high-speed tactics of the man in third place. This was Fox, whose performance was remarkable, for he had lost a finger two years before and been forced to relearn fencing as a left-hander. His speed and aggressive penetration defeated Beevers, whose mixed run nevertheless secured him second place on hits over Fox and Loveland when he decisively defeated the winner – Nick Bell of Thames. Bell misapplied his nervous, jerky style in this fight. He was equally active but more thoughtful in the last deciding bout with Loveland. He won 5–0. Now training as a doctor in London, but not having exams this season, he made very rapid progress, going on to claim the *Universities* title and that of *Leamington* and then to rise to yet greater heights when he came fourth in the *Championship*.

Loveland also had a good season. He was the winner both at *Ashton* and *Portsmouth* and came sixth in the Championship. The top of the field was still dominated by the same trio, however. Graham Paul won the Championship for the fourth time. Barry Paul won the *Coronation* (for the first time). And in

# Competitions chronicle 1972-3

what was to prove his last season of serious fencing, Breckin showed his continued quality by securing second place in the Championship and third in the Coronation. This was the fourth year running that he'd been in the first three in both events: a record of impressive consistency.

With a mirror image second in the Coronation and third in the Championship, the man who looked as if he might take up Breckin's torch was Grimmett. Single hung on to his team place with a fourth in the Coronation, in which he was followed by youth in the person of Tony Bartlett and by Cawthorne, showing what the veteran could achieve. Cohen showed what a sabreur could do by taking fifth place in the Championship.

Among the Under-20s, Bruniges was now in a class of his own, if not particularly on the basis of home results. He won the *Ashton Under-20* event (over Campbell, Knell, Paul Wedge of Hydra, David Wade and John Ford of Brownhill); likewise in a barrage he came second to Andy Eames (Leicester) in the *Under-20 Championship* (followed by Campbell, 3v; Knell, 2v; Wedge, 2v; and Bartlett, 0v). With an injured sword-hand, he again came second to Eames at *Leicester* on hits after a stalemate barrage of four, in which Frank Hindle and Jim Philbin, both of Hydra, were third and fourth. Eames scored with a simple but deceptive technique of blitz fleches. It was in international events that Bruniges showed his true maturity, with major results. Before Christmas he won both the *Gelsenkirchen* and *Millfield Under-20* Tournaments, the former for the second year running. In January he reached the last sixteen in the *Paris Martini*. (Single was in the last 32.) Third in the World Youth Championship at Easter, he got to the semi-final of the very strong *Giovanini* at *Bologna*, where Graham Paul also reached the quarter-final. He also won the *Spitzer* (combined with a training camp on the coast of Israel). His winning hit, from 4–all against Offlager of the host country, was a typical Bruniges stroke (probably first developed by Sveshnikov): a riposte at close quarters delivered round his back and over the opposite shoulder. All this was achieved against a background of equal activity and nearly equal success at epee. Robert Bruniges thus won for himself and his master John Fairhall the distinction of inclusion in the British team without needing to reach the final of either the Coronation or the Championship. He took the place of Tony Power, who bowed out of the foil scene after Munich. René Paul was Captain again.

The order for the *Bonfil Trophy*, with its emphasis on provincial results, provides a somewhat different perspective from national and international rankings. Here are the top fifty names:

| | | | | | |
|---|---|---|---|---|---|
| 1755 | R. Bruniges | 990 | N. Bell | 674 | G. Wiles |
| 1467 | A. Loveland | 918 | F. Hindle | 622 | J. Cooper |
| 1460 | G. Grimmett | 846 | B. Green | 620 | M. Fare |
| 1154 | S. Fox | 830 | J. Grimmett | 615 | T. Harrison |
| 1153 | G. Paul | 820 | C. Waldman | 608 | M. Beevers |
| 1148 | D. Cawthorne | 780 | J. Ford | 604 | M. Breckin |
| 1057 | J. Philbin | 716 | B. Paul | 604 | R. Cohen |

| | | | | | |
|---|---|---|---|---|---|
| 571 | A. Eames | 448 | J. Gay | 336 | D. Harris |
| 534 | G. Evans | 440 | P. McLachlan | 330 | E. Bradbury |
| 534 | J. Tyson | 416 | R. Tiller | 330 | K. Lovejoy |
| 530 | M. Cullen | 414 | M. Knell | 330 | L. Taylor |
| 530 | J. Llewellyn | 398 | C. Hyndman | 322 | I. Edwards |
| 504 | R. Green | 390 | R. Paul | 320 | D. Poole |
| 495 | I. Single | 390 | S. Wooding | 304 | J. Bulinski |
| 468 | G. Silverman | 360 | T. Bouchier-Hayes | 300 | J. Hall |
| 466 | R. Elliott | 352 | J. Higgins | 300 | I. May |
| 460 | A. Bartlett | 348 | I. Campbell | 300 | A. Mitchell |
| 450 | M. Chetwood | | | | |

*LADIES' FOIL*

After her long years of dominance, Janet Wardell-Yerburgh had retired. There was no revolution amongst the other leading fencers, however.

Sue Green took both the *de Beaumont* and the *Desprez*, and was fifth in the *Championship*. Clare Henley was now married to Nick Halsted and with him in Brussels and was therefore absent from the Desprez and Silver Jubilee, but won the Championship at last after first reaching the final in 1967 and was fourth in the de Beaumont. Susan Wrigglesworth won the *Silver Jubilee Cup* for Salle Paul, ahead of Sue Green, was third in the Desprez, fourth in the Championship and sixth in the de Beaumont. Sally Littlejohns, now John Simpson's pupil at LFC, was runner-up in the de Beaumont for the second year running, but slipped to third place in the Silver Jubilee and was sixth in the Desprez.

Wendy Ager, now fencing for Salle Pearson, was the main newcomer at the very top. She was runner-up in the Championship, and third in the de Beaumont, in each case fencing in the final for the first time. Also moving upwards was Hilary Cawthorne, now fencing at Boston, above all in gaining second place in the Desprez. She lost (on the last hit) only to Mildred Durne (5th), losing the barrage with Susan Green 1-4, after beating her 4-3 in the pool. She was also fifth in the de Beaumont.

The de Beaumont contained only a sprinkling of foreigners; Lecomte reached the last 24 and Petrus (Holland) the last twelve, but it was an all-British final. Sally Littlejohns got off to a cracking start by beating Susan Green, but thereafter the latter's determination gradually told and she scored some delightful counter-ripostes with angulation on the shoulder in close quarter fighting. Clare Halsted, fencing for Ixeloise, faltered, as did Susan Wrigglesworth, who seemed to tire.

Not content with her national victories, Sue Green also won both at *Ashton* and at *Leicester*, though at the latter she had to barrage with Hilary Cawthorne after losing to Jill Dudley (Thames), who ended fourth behind Janet Yates but ahead of Mary Hawksworth. Sue Olley had a signal triumph in winning in the final at *Leamington* against Sue Green, while Wendy Ager added to her successes by winning at *Redbridge* and *Portsmouth*. Gillian Ritchie won the *Universities Championship* for Oxford, was fourth in the Bertrand, and was *Scottish* Champion for the third year running (leaving Christine Tolland's four successive wins still the record). *Inverclyde* went to her compatriot Sue Youngs. The *Welsh Open* was also won by a member of the home team, Linda Brown. The very effective, if technically unremarkable, Celia Whitehurst, the previous season's winner of the Welsh, who was now at Ashton, won the *Bertrand* (though only after having to barrage in the mini quarter-finals with Jane Court). Valerie Windram went out in the semi-final of the Bertrand, suffering from a knee injury, and so, surprisingly, did Alda Milner-Barry. Second place went to Inga Foulkes of Bath FC on hits over Caroline Arup of Boston. Lynne Taylor of Hydra was fifth, followed by Yvonne Grammar of Edmonton.

Celia Whitehurst was only second in the *Parker Trophy*, which she had won in 1970. She was followed by Sheila O'Connell (Dublin), Danuta Joyce (Poly) and Eva Joyce (Bath) – twins who were aptly fourth equal – and Judy Madeley (Boston). The winner was Lucienne Bleasdale, a pupil of Paddy Power at York, who at the age of fifteen produced a remarkable display of economical and precise fencing, only being hit three times. She also won the *Toupie Lowther Cup*.

The winner of the *Felix* was Linda Martin, who had been given a good technical grounding by her father Dick at Manchester YM since 1968 and had now moved south and was taught by Prof Imregi at Poly. Second was Sue Rochard of Millfield, who was the *Senior Schoolgirls* Champion, showing the potential that was never quite realised. Valerie Windram was third. Jane Popland of Macclesfield HS and Ashton was winner of the *Junior Schoolgirls*. She was also third in the *Under-Twenty Championship*, beating Caroline Hall of York FC, who nevertheless retained her title. Caroline Hall in her turn came third in the Senior Schoolgirls, on hits behind Christine Convill who flew over from N. Ireland for the day.

The Under-20 *Perigal Cup* was another triumph for Sue Wrigglesworth, who was only hit six times in the final and became the only fencer to win three times (successively, what's more). Ann Tulloch of Scotland was second (and fourth in the Under-20 Championship), one place behind (on hits). Janet Jones of Ashton came third (her high point being fourth place in the Desprez). Jane Popland and Caroline Hall followed closely, also on two wins.

Susan Wrigglesworth was the top scorer in three other junior events. In a match against a French team, staged to open Bletchley Leisure Centre, she won two fights, Wendy Ager and Janet Jones scoring one each. San Miguel, Barrey and Appert took first, second and seventh places for France in the subsequent poule unique. Sally Mitton of Salle Paul (sixth in the Under-20 Championship) did well to come third equal with Jane Popland. Anne Tulloch (5th), also on six wins, was ahead of Wendy Ager on hits. Lynne Taylor (8th) pipped Sue Rochard on four wins, followed by Caroline Hall (2v, 10th) and Olivia Meyrick (Thames; IV). Janet Jones scratched with an injured heel.

The *Nescafé* was also preceded by a team event, with Italians, Swiss and Canadians. Wendy Ager and Sue Wrigglesworth were the best of the 'A' team and Janet Jones of the 'B' team. In the individual, as in the teams, the Italians led. Grande was first, Batazzi third, Guercia fifth and Riccardo sixth, but Sue Wrigglesworth came second with three wins and Caroline Hall fourth with two, both fencing tenaciously and intelligently against noisy and ferocious opponents. Anne Tulloch, Janet Jones and Sue Rochard were semi-finalists.

Yet again a match was coupled with the *Millfield Tournament*, sponsored by Irving Allen. Against a formidable German team, Sue Wrigglesworth got two wins (with one each to Wendy Ager and Anne Tulloch). She went on to win the individual, losing to Oertel, but overcoming Kircheis in the barrage with an onslaught of fleches. Wendy Ager (4th) was two wins ahead of Lotter, while sixth place went to the tall Linda Martin.

Abroad, Susan Wrigglesworth excelled herself in December by winning the Under-20 *Gelsenkirchen* event after a barrage with Hickenbusch. Among the other 39 British girls organised by Les Jones, Jane Court did very well to come sixth in the final, which Caroline Hall only missed by one hit. Sue Wrigglesworth also reached the quarter-finals at *Goppingen*, along with Sue Olley. Jane Popland was fourth in the *André Spitzer*.

Sally Littlejohns had opened the senior season abroad with a victory in *Beirut*. At *Duren* Clare Halsted, Caroline Hall, Janet Yates and Jill Dudley all reached the quarter-finals. In the *Coppa Europa* LFC reached the quarter-finals likewise. In *Berlin* in May, Clare Halsted was a semi-finalist. The same weekend Wendy Ager did well to reach the quarter-final of the *Jeanty*. So did Caryl Holland of Latista to get to the semi-final at *Eupen*.

The successes continued. Janet Yates reached the quarter-final at *Como* and Hilary Cawthorne the last 32 at *Balaton*. Jane Popland came second in the Under-20 event at *Arlon*, where Janet Jones reached the quarter-finals. They both reached the quarter-finals of the senior event. Finally, at *Dornbirn* in Austria in September, Jane Court was in the quarter-finals and Linda Martin in the semi-finals.

Under the captaincy of Mildred Durne the team for the World Championship remained unchanged except that Wendy Ager came in to fill the gap left by Janet W-Y – who had come out of retirement to help LFC to victory in the *Team Championship*, alongside Susan Wrigglesworth, Kate Hurford and Sally Littlejohns. Boston went down with five wins (Julia Bullmore – now married to Ian Single – 2, Susan Youngs 2, Susan Olley 1). The losers in the semis had been Salle Pearson and Ashton – the latter only after a dead heat and a fight-off in which Sue Olley used her long reach to beat Sue Green.

## EPEE

The *Junior* was won by Mark West of Salle Boston. Unspectacular but relaxed and consistent, he outstayed such fancied names as White and Fare and in the final took four victories, two of them on the last hit. Martin Murch of Salle Paul was second. Equally assured, had he used his height more explosively he would have swept the board, since he got three convincing wins and lost both the others on the last hit. Emberson also nearly won the cup with three victories and an unlucky loss to West. Fourth, likewise on three wins, was a two-weapon Scot, the mobile, improving Ian Campbell. Vigorous and controlled, if somewhat short for an epeeist, he had topped his semi-final and was the only person to beat the winner. Hall, now at Thames, started very strongly, but after two wins lost his edge, to his obvious annoyance, and ended fifth. Adrian Silvey of LFC did well to reach the final, but was also handicapped by temperament, which in his case made him too negative to win a fight.

Beevers of Poly was the rising star at senior level. He won the *Martini Qualifying* ahead of Partridge and Hall and, with Partridge, was among the ten Britons to survive a first round of the *Martini* itself that was probably the strongest ever, thanks to the presence of the Russians for the first time since 1961. Szlichcinsky of Cambridge University did well to reach this stage, at which Higginson, Pearman, Ganchev and Hoskyns were eliminated (together with such as Edling and Testoni). It was not bad going for four Britons to remain in the last 24. Hill excelled himself to do so, getting through perhaps the hardest first round and a tough second round. Now he led the Russian twice-world-finalist Modzolevski before succumbing 10–7. Bourne, often unlucky in this event, lost to von Essen on the last hit. Graham Paul, however, stormed onwards, with a 10–8 win over Pezza of Italy (fresh from the Monal final and destined to be third in the 1973 World Championships). Much matured and now varying his game skilfully to suit his opponent, Paul followed this with an impressive 10–7 victory over Rutecki of Poland to put himself in the gala final. Also in the last sixteen was Ralph Johnson, who was top seed and had earned a bye. In common with all but one of the byes, this seemed to be to his disadvantage. He tumbled 10–2 to Normann of Norway, persistently falling short, while his opponent got everything right, ignoring with blunt skill the web of feints he was offered.

The final was a Russian triumph. Valetov beat Normann 10–5. Lukomsky beat von Essen 10–6. Only Modzolevsky went under, to Giger, Swiss victor of the Spreafico. Graham Paul was unlucky to meet Paramanov, the top Russian, who only lost one fight throughout the event. With his coupé fleches and long lunges, Graham established a 3–1 lead, but by 5–all the tall expressionless Paramanov had altered tempo and distance and his stop-hits were devastating. He won 10–6.

The semi-finals were won by Valetov over Lukomsky, 10–8, and by

Paramanov over Giger by one hit after expiry of time. More easily, Paramanov took the title 10–5.

On the Sunday after the Martini a gala *match against the USSR* was held at the de Beaumont Centre (briefly interrupted by demonstrators against Soviet anti-semitism). Bourne had a notable personal success by defeating Valetov, Zagitsky and Modzalevsky, and indeed midway the British were in the lead, but Hoskyns was unable to score and Paul's win over Valetov and Johnson's over Lukomsky were not enough to make up.

There were no foreigners in the *Miller-Hallett*, Bourne and Paul were absent and two team contenders, Davenport and Noel, went out in the quarter-finals and semi-finals respectively, leaving a final of six left-handers. Bruniges showed his versatility of stroke but ended last. Beevers consolidated his position with fourth place. Belson fenced with speed and determination but lost his chance of a barrage when he was beaten by Jacobs, who, in third place, was celebrating the thirteenth time he had been third or better in the Championship or Miller-Hallett.

Johnson was the winner, as he ought to have been, but he and Bourne spoilt each other's chances of the *Championship* with a double defeat. Paul was again absent, along with Jacobs and Higginson, so this event too was more open than usual. It was Hudson who seized his chance. Only fifth in the Miller-Hallett, his declaration of non-availability for the World Championship unleashed his confidence and he clinched his victory by narrowly beating Partridge after a good win over Johnson, who thus came third, after Bourne. Hoskyns, below his best except for a remarkable one-two-three in his victory over Bourne, came fourth. Bruniges was again sixth, behind Partridge.

The quarter-finals had been distinguished by Colonel Hay's victories over Hall and Beevers – at the age of 75. Fare of Thames was unlucky to miss the final by 20/21 to 21/22 after a barrage deadlock with Hoskyns and Bryan Lewis of Oxford University. The latter showed his class in his first full year of national fencing by defeating Hoskyns with an excellent sense of distance and in the timing of his fleches (though by moving on the balls of his feet he inhibited his lunges). The other semi-finals saw Noel and Davenport again frustrated, along with the Poly fencers Beevers and Tatrallyay (a tall, aggressive Canadian-Hungarian).

In the *Team Championship* the four semi-finalists would perhaps have been the same as in the previous three years if the Army had fielded a full team. As it was, Poly took their place, though Richard Bird's three wins were unsupported by his team-mates against Boston. On the opposite side, Salle Paul beat Thames by 9–6, deploying their customary heckling as well as some vigorous and skilful fencing. Although all but Partridge were very much part-time epeeists, all had many years of competitive experience, including their victories of 1970 and 1971.

Allan Jay, who had transferred his allegiance to Boston and fenced for them

Savage Shield 1973: R. Davenport v B. Paul (J. J. Lewis and B. Hill between them; Prof. and Mrs Imregi to right).

up to the semi-finals, did not wish to fight his old club, which won by the same score as in 1971: 9–6. Graham Paul got three wins (with one to go), Barry two, Partridge three and Single one. Bourne got three wins, Johnson two (with one to go), Gray one and Davenport none. Lothian, the young Scots team, was the only non-London club to make the last eight.

In the provincial events John Fairhall was the winner at *Ashton*, over Gray and two of his own Brownhill pupils, Bruniges and Cooper in that order. At *Leicester* Beevers opened his season of successes, showing a steely domination of the final, in which he was never hit more than twice except by Howard West, now at Grosvenor (6th). Gray was again second, on hits over Fare. There followed two Brownhill boys, Lovejoy and the 15-year-old Cooper, who did well to reach two provincial finals.

Beevers, along with Keuls, Lillywhite, Fare and Bird, was among those who did not reach the final at *Sandhurst*, a strong epee event run over several seasons by QMS Peter Lennon. The winner, on home ground, was Jim Fox, who otherwise was hardly seen on the epee circuit. Terry Harrison of the Marines was second and Gray third. Silvey showed his form in fourth place, while David Brooks of Corby, scoring one of his first noteworthy results, was fifth, ahead of Hall. Bob Turner was the winner of the *tournament at Edinburgh*, which – with a gala Scottish–Welsh foil match (won by the Scots) – formed part of the celebrations of Britain's entry into the EEC.

Bill Osbaldeston (Boston), steadily overcoming his tendency to lose his edge on first being defeated, was the winner of the *Welsh Open* for the second time running, enticing opponents into the jaws of his endless tight counter movements. Lewis won at Nottingham. Derek Russell, though no longer seen in the south, won the *Scottish Championship* for the third time running, while Malcolm Allton of Leicester YMCA was top of the heap at *Inverclyde*. The leading provincial event remained *Leamington*, however, and here David Partridge triumphed, beating Jonathan Stanbury (Boston) 8–3. John Higgins reached a peak in securing third place by 8–6 over Osbaldeston. The others in the last eight were Graham Paul, Mark West, Davenport and Nettingsmeyer. Boston won the Friday evening team event after the mayoral sherry party by beating Salle Paul in the last fight. In June the *Cyrano* tournament was held in Southend for the last time. Davenport was the winner with four wins, followed by Gray, H. West, Peter Huggins, Ian Worthington of Boston and Richard Edwards of Poly.

The *Universities* Champion was Bryan Lewis (Oxford) after a barrage with Mike Mayo (Stirling and Lothian FC, Edinburgh), who also came third in the foil. There followed James Noel (Goldsmiths, London), Andrew Wickham (Cambridge), John Higgins (Surrey) and Mike Hawthorne (Oxford).

At the junior end of the spectrum there was judged to be little promise beyond the top half-dozen or so. There were no British finalists in the *Nescafé* and at the *Under-20 Championship* most fencers seemed to know no movements and in consequence, usually did nothing. If they attacked, it was with bent arms. The winner was Bruniges, who prevented Pip Emberson from retaining his title largely by his superior concentration, which remained intense even when he was winning. He was undefeated and taken to the last hit only by Tarran, who took third place for the second year running. Campbell of Lothian was second, with an impressive sense of timing and good use of simple prises-de-fer.

A more important win in Bruniges' extraordinarily rich season was in the Under-20 tournament in *Genoa*. He followed this up at senior level with a quarter-final place in *Berlin* and then a major performance in reaching the last eight at *Poitiers* (eliminating Jeanne). Not many post-war fencers could rival his achievements at two weapons simultaneously. Partridge was in the last sixteen (losing to Brodin).

It was in general a good foreign season, if there were no great peaks. Johnson was sixth at *Catania* and reached the fourth round at *Bern* ($\frac{1}{8}$th-final), along with Hudson. Davenport reached the third round (last 48) in the *Spreafico*. At *Duren*, a British team lost the *match against Belgium* 12–4, but Hoskyns was the winner of the individual event. Davenport was fourth and both Beevers and Hudson reached the last twelve. In the *Monal* Bourne reached the last 24, Noel and Stanbury round five and Hoskyns and Hill round four. At the smaller event at *Huy*, Hall and Hill reached the quarter-finals and Gray the semi-finals. Nielaba won. At *Heidenheim* Bourne was in the last sixteen, beating Friis in the first round of direct delimination and Giger in the second, but losing to Edling in the third round. Johnson lost to Szepesi in the first direct elimination. At the end of the season Bourne was sixteenth in the World Rankings. In the *Coupe d'Europe* Boston lost 8–7 to the Austrians (Bourne 3, Johnson 3, Davenport 1, M. West 1), 9–7 to the Czechs (Bourne 3, Gray 2, Johnson 1, Davenport 1) and 12–4 to the eventual winners, the Hungarians Fenyvesi, Pap and the Erdos brothers (Bourne 1, Johnson 1, Gray 1, West 1). In *Berlin* Hoskyns again stalked his incredulous opponents on a victorious progress to the semi-final. Bruniges was a quarter-finalist. At more modest level, Fare won at *Dieppe*. In August, in *Luxembourg*, Bruniges was the winner, Johnson third and Jacobs a semi-finalist.

For once, the team remained unchanged: Bourne, Johnson, Hoskyns, Paul and Hudson, who was persuaded to go after all. Halsted had this season retired from serious competition, 'giving up in despair and bandages'.

## *SABRE*

The season opened with a win at *Ashton* by Jim Philbin. His Mancunian sparring-partner, Alan Taylor (taught at Hydra by Tom Etchells) won at *Leicester*, to his third place and Wiles's second. Zarno of Boston was fourth, followed by Jack Magill (now at Cambridge University) and Norman Milligan (Birmingham). The cast in the *Junior* was much the same. Taylor, who had not reached the final the year before, was only taken to the last hit by Michael Price the younger (Boston, 3rd), until after he had secured the title. Then he lost to Milligan (5th) who impressed with balanced movement and repertoire of strokes – as did Gryf-Lowczowski (Poly, 6th), albeit over-predictable and with too many composed attacks. Philbin in second place and Magill in fourth completed a final of high standard, from which Fairburn and Jeremy Thorn were only excluded on hits.

In January, Peter Mather of Cambridge won a not very strong *Under-20 Championship* undefeated in the final. The next three places also went to pupils of Prof. Boston: Price (3v), Jonathan Lewis (3v) and Pankhurst (2v). Lankshear (2v) was fifth and the foilist Tony Bartlett (ov; S. Pearson) sixth. Mather was also the only British finalist in the *Nescafé*, in third place, thinking more and double-attacking less than his German and French rivals, though it was Kohler of the latter whose speed and precision won first place. Jonathan Lewis went on to be *Public Schools* Champion for the second year running.

Staging the Corble and a match with Poland in Sheffield showed the problems as well as the advantages in organising competitions away from Headquarters. Peter Hobson put the idea to Les Veale, Chairman of the Northern (Yorkshire) Section – who was agitating against neglect of the Sections – who sent out six hundred letters to local firms appealing for funds. He got £30. Yorkshire Clubs ran jumble sales. Demonstrations, competitions and coaching courses were made to yield more cash. Local fencers, students'

1972 Junior: J. Philbin (2nd), A. Taylor (1st) and M. Price (3rd).

unions and friends round the country all chipped in. When the media had been alerted, further help came. The University offered a sherry reception as well as two gyms for the Corble. Ellis Pearson, the glass firm, footed the bills for posters, tickets and programmes. The City promised a civic reception. Alan Daglish and Mike McDonald devised large extensions for the stage of the City Hall; Dave Nicholls visited local firms, cadging prizes; Janet Turton – a Polish speaker – took on hospitality and diplomacy; Malcolm Pearce and his university union did much organising; and that is to mention only a few of the helpers.

The double event was a great success. Little local problems like the hotel being locked up were solved (in that case through the house-breaking skill of Pawlowski). Goodwill blossomed at the parties. Above all, over *a thousand spectators* watched the match in the Town Hall. David Eden presided with style and a microphone. Yorkshire Television publicised fencing. Both teams were presented with hand-forged daggers by the Master Cutler; all Corble entrants received paper knives from BSC. It all cost £500 – and was judged by the Section to have been well worth while, particularly in boosting fencing.

As for the results, the *match against Poland* was lost 13–3. The captain, Oldcorn, largely blamed himself for the severity of the defeat. Cohen got two of the wins. The Poles also took the top five places in the *Corble Cup*, led by Pawlowski. Eden was the one British finalist.

The *Cole Cup* was only graced by a single foreigner, for the first time for several years; but he proved the winner. It was Convents' second successive triumph. Cohen was second and Ganchev third.

Germany was also represented at *Leamington*, but the triumph went to Hydra. After beating Boston on the last hit of the last fight in the semi-final, they defeated Rhineland. Taylor and Philbin each got two wins, the latter beating Wischeidt, current German Champion, while Eric Bradbury rose to the occasion to take the last deciding fight. Wischeidt had his revenge in the individual, beating his team-mate von Aspern in the final bout. This was his sixth successive victory and his last appearance. Philbin beat Eden for third place by 10–9.

The *Universities Championship* was won by Breckin (London), ahead of Magill (Cambridge), Milligan (Birmingham), Malcolm Pearce (Sheffield), Lewis Smith (Edinburgh) and Chris Latter (Cambridge).

With the retirement of Craig and of Acfield (who became a professional at cricket after the Olympics), the *Championship* presented opportunities, though only forty entered for it. After the loss of Jay (making his second sabre appearance of the year) in the first round and of Scott in the second, there were semi-finals with the following results: A: Cohen (4v), Oldcorn (3v), Philbin (3v), Milligan (2v), Eden (1v, his bout with Oldcorn unfought), Hutt (1v). B: Mather (5v), Deanfield (4v), Zarno (3v), Gryf-Lowczowski (2v), Leckie (1v), Taylor (0v). Milligan lacked experience at this level; Eden lost form; Gryf lost control.

Oldcorn retired from the final injured. In the inter-Boston preliminaries Mather beat Zarno, who beat Cohen, who beat Mather. Meanwhile Deanfield destroyed three opponents. To barrage between themselves, Cohen and Mather both had to beat him, which they did, 5–2 and 5–3. Mather then annihilated Cohen 5–0. Like Acfield, he was Prof. Boston's pupil at Cambridge and before that at Brentwood. At nineteen, he was the youngest ever sabre Champion. Zarno and Philbin (Hydra) shared fourth place.

In the last eight of the *Team Championship* LFC 'A' struggled to a 9–7 win over Birmingham in spite of the highly-developed defence of Kovanda and Milligan. Boston 'A' beat Cardiff (avenging Cardiff's earlier defeat of Stanhope, alias Boston 'C'). Hydra never got going against Salle Paul, although Taylor won three of the four wins. Poly 'A', like Boston 'A', had a bye to this stage and, being cold as well as lacking the injured Oldcorn, had a disastrous loss to a determined Boston 'B' in spite of Deanfield's three easy wins.

In the semi-finals Boston 'A' beat LFC, with Zarno trampling to four victories, Mather undefeated and Jay for his new club contributing far more in aggressive spirit than his lack of wins suggests. Leckie won two of the young LFC team's five victories (the 17-year-old Edroy Poole showed particular promise). But the real excitement was in the other semi-final: S. Paul against Boston 'B'. Scott showed great determination and won three; two Mexican

Leamington 1973: Cohen in full cry. Derek Parham, veteran tournament organiser, is judging.

transients, Gomez and Chapella, each won two; while for Boston Price did very well to win all four. The result was an 8–8, 60–60 draw, so the champions of each side met in homeric combat that kept up the suspense to the last hit – gained by Price.

Inevitably the all-Boston final was an anti-climax, though the standard was high for all that the score was uneven: 9–1. (Melvyn Eden beat his brother David.)

It was Mather's year internationally as well as at home, in the few outings he allowed himself in the intervals of pentathlon, rowing, canoeing, hockey and other Cambridge pursuits. Apart from narrowly missing a World Youth medal, he reached the last 24 in the *Brussels Martini*.

Deanfield, who was in the previous Brussels round, as a medical student found time a problem too. His tendency to fence for stylish effect rather than to win was another reason why he seldom quite got the results his great ability promised. By contrast, Cohen through hard work, intelligence and aggression continued to get excellent results in spite of unpolished technique. He reached the quarter-final in *Hamburg*, the last twelve in *Munich* and got the best British result at *Padua*.

No one else got notable foreign results, and indeed the lack of sabreurs at all levels continued to place Britain at a disadvantage at a weapon at which technical practice is supremely important. The national training squad under Prof. Anderson averaged only five attenders and by the end of the season was reduced to a warming-up and a few individual lessons, though it was supplemented by weekends at Aldershot and the AFA under Prof. Boston.

The full Olympic squad consisted of the following, in the selectors' ranking which corresponded to the World Championship selection: 1. Mather, 2. Cohen, 3. Deanfield, 4. Oldcorn (who also captained the team), 5. Philbin, 6. Taylor, 7. D. Eden, 8. Zarno, followed by C. Grzesik (Poly), Gryf-Lowczowski, Lankshear, Milligan and Price, all ranked equal.

Before leaving the Army for IBM Craig won the *Inter-Services* sabre a fourth time. He had risen to the rank of Major and had the remarkable record of being undefeated in over forty bouts in Inter-Services sabre matches over a period of seven years, a feat paralleled by his unbroken run of over forty wins for Dortmund FC in the German team championships of 1972, including victories over every member of the German Olympic team.

## COMBINED EVENTS

The *Public Schools Championships* saw both future prospects and outsider schools in the finals. Neal Mallett of Dover College, a pupil of Prof. Mallard, won the junior foil over Mark Slade and John Steventon of Brentwood. An unruffled and stylish Mark Thompson of King's Chester won the senior foil in a barrage from Gilbert Thompson of Dover College. Steve Carson (Royal Belfast) was third and Mark Chetwood (Dulwich) fourth. Mike O'Shea of Downside won the epee. Carson achieved his hat trick by getting fifth place both in this and the sabre, while Mallett and Slade precociously appeared in each final respectively. Sanjar of Cheltenham, displaying magnificent technique, was the only sabreur to beat Jonathan Lewis, whose speed of attack stampeded others, but second place went to Ross Campion of Merchant Taylors.

In addition to sending a universities team to Holland this season, the Welsh joined other sports in a *match against Denmark*. They won the sabre 10–6 (Lewis 4, Edwards 3, Norcross 2, John Norrie 1), but lost the epee against a strong team, including Kemnitz and Munster (Gray 3, Turner 2, Lewis 1, Martin 0), as well as both foil events (Evans 3, Edwards 2, Gray 1, Georgiou 0; M. Riley 3, L. Brown 2, A. Bennett 1, J. Stewart 0). However, the team much enjoyed the trip, which included giving a display match in Tivoli Gardens.

The *World Youth Championships* were in Buenos Aires. Prof. Boston, now a permanent fixture as coach, was this year assisted by Steve Lennox. For the first time Joe Eden was on his own as official, without Charles de Beaumont as Chef d'Equipe and without a ladies' official (there being only one lady fencer). In the foil Bartlett did well to get three wins in the first round, with limited technique and experience, but fell to the indicators. Andy Eames got to the semi-finals of four fencers (third round), where he beat Koutcher (USSR). But Robert Bruniges was the star. He topped both quarter-final and semi-final pools. In the final he began by losing 5–4 to Widera of Poland, who continually forced him to his metre line, but he came back well to defeat Poffet and Bellone. He then lost to Behr (for the first time in the competition). This left him to face the undefeated Pietruszka of France. If he beat him he would get the Silver Medal, if he took two hits he'd get the Bronze. He lost 5–3. At the age of only seventeen, this was a notable triumph for Bruniges, and for his master John Fairhall. It was the first medal gained for Britain at any world level since Hoskyns and the epeeists won Silver Medals at the 1965 World Championship.

It was largely due to the high travelling expense that there was only one entrant apiece for the ladies' foil and sabre. Caroline Hall fenced with distinction, if limited footwork and defence, and reached the second round. At sabre, Mather topped his first round, then went up third in the second. In the mini semi-final he excelled himself by beating Levevasseur (top French seed) 5–0, as well as Danosi (USA) 5–2, to go into the final undefeated. Here he began by beating Jablonowski (Poland) 5–4, but then disappointingly lost to Gulacsi (Hungary) 5–1, the reverse of the first round score. He came back magnificently to beat the eventual winner, Tomaso Montano (Italy) 5–3. All the leaders now had one defeat; but thereafter Mather narrowly lost to

England team 1973. *Back:* J. Gryf Lowczowski, C. Grzesik, M. Price, M. Beevers, M. West, W. Osbaldeston, A. Loveland, M. Murch. *Front:* L. Bleasdale, H. Cawthorne, Col. J. Moore, Mrs M. Glen Haig, P. Hobson (Captain), J. Bullmore, N. Bell.

Losonczy (USA) 5–4, suffering from some doubtful decisions, and then went down to Romano of Italy by the same score. This left him fifth. Nevertheless this was a fine performance. He was congratulated by both presidents as the best sabreur in the final, which was attested by the fact that of the 147 double attacks there and in the semi-finals he was involved in only three.

At epee, Campbell, despite his determination, was eliminated in the first round, and the second saw Emberson fall, too prone to bent-arm actions. Bruniges, however, almost made his second final, only being ousted in a semi-final comprising Wiech (Poland), Behr (W. Germany) and Mocchi (Italy) after two barrages.

Overall, Britain did better than ever before, being sixth, ahead of Hungary, with 17 points, to France's 20 and Italy's 37.

The *Quadrangular* was staged impeccably by the Army at Sandhurst. England won for the sixth successive year, beating Scotland 25–11, Wales 19–17 and N. Ireland 23–13. Scotland beat Wales 21–15 and N. Ireland 23–13. Wales beat N. Ireland 20–16.

The *Rest of Britain Match* was a closer affair. The ladies of the Rest won 9–7. Janet Yates was undefeated (only hit six times), while Sally Mitton won three out of four for London. The sabreurs followed up devastatingly by taking their first eleven fights, though London recovered to take four of the last five. (Wiles 4, Taylor 3, Dennis Hunt 3, Eric Bradbury 2; Steve Fox 2, Price 1, Lankshear 1, Grzesik 0). The men's foil looked similar when the Rest led 5–1, but the end was a win on hits for London. Eames got three wins, as Loveland and Waldman did for London, though, unusually for him, Fox scored a blank.

To save the match, London now had to win the epee 14–2: Noel romped calmly through all opponents to take London towards its target and Terry Harrison and Martin Beevers scored three each; but Bill Osbaldeston with three wins out of the Rest's five ensured a match victory.

For the *Granville*, the Alassio type of cumulative scoring was adopted for the first time. This did not prevent Salle Boston winning for the third year running. The strongest challenge came from Salle Paul in the quarter-final. Barry Paul beat Teddy Bourne 10–7 at foil after trailing 2–6, but Scott succumbed to Cohen 6–10 and Johnson just beat Partridge, after being 6–7 down. The final with LFC was more decisive. Oldcorn lost 8–10 at sabre and Leckie 5–10 at foil, leaving Hill with little hope.

In the fifth *Ilford Tournament* Sally Mitton (Paul) beat Pat Casey (Thames) in the barrage, followed by Linda Martin (Poly; 2v), Olivia Meyrick (Thames; 2v), Lorna Andrews (Wickford; 2v) and Jackie Erwteman (Poly; 1v). Poly narrowly won the team event from Thames. At epee, Bryan Lewis (Oxford), consistent throughout and undefeated in the final, was followed by Colin Sigrist (Brownhill; 4v), Richard Jones (Loughton; 3v), Chris Green (BAF; 2v), David Fairhall (pupil of his father John; 1v) and Steve Roose (Newham; 0v) – the last a fencer destined for higher things.

The *World Championships* in Goteborg began with an organisational blunder when the Directoire Technique only circulated notice of a change from four to three promoted from the first round of the men's foil near the end of the round. Graham Paul and Breckin were both eliminated in fourth place. Single also went out, scoring only eight hits in a pool of five, but Bruniges went through and Barry Paul did excellently, heading his pool. In the second round (last 48) Paul lost his touch, rushing at his opponents with little feel for the tempo and crossing his feet in his fleches. Bruniges was unlucky to have to cope with both the eventual winner (Noel of France) and the runner-up (Tschij of Russia), but put up a fine performance for a 16-year-old in his first World Championship. He already performed a limited range of strokes and tactics outstandingly; he had only to extend this and he could reach world class.

In the team, after a nervous start against Spain, Britain emerged victors by 14–2 (G. Paul 4, B. Paul 4, Bruniges 4, Breckin 2), but were crushed by France 9–1 (Barry Paul beating Talvard 5–4). In the second round a 4–2 lead over Poland was established, both Bruniges and Barry Paul hitting form; but the Poles raised their game and only one more win was achieved (B. Paul 2, Bruniges 2, G. Paul 1, Breckin 0).

Oldcorn and Philbin fell in the first round of the sabre. Cohen and Deanfield were seeded in the same second round; both got two wins and needed their last fight. Cohen lost to de la Torre (Cuba) and Deanfield to Nowara (Poland) from 4–2 up. Both opponents reached the semi-finals. Mather also came unstuck, after fencing excellently in the first round. Aldo

Montano was the winner over Sidiak and Nazlimov. Pawlowski was robbed by the president's mis-phrasing from being second and thus the most successful fencer ever, at least by one reckoning.

The team started hurriedly against Japan, but 0–2 and then 4–7 was followed by a run of wins to 9–7 (Mather and Deanfield 3, Oldcorn 2, Cohen 1). Against Hungary, Deanfield won two fights, but no one else any. In the second round, against Cuba, misfortune struck at 1–all when Deanfield strained his wrist in a collision. (Philbin came in after his second fight.) Only three wins were scored, two by Cohen, one by Oldcorn.

The ladies had one round more than the men. Clare Halsted, totally off form, went out in the first, but the others went on to the third. Sally Littlejohns, Sue Green and Sue Wrigglesworth succumbed here, the last after a barrage, but Wendy Ager, fencing with tremendous zest in her pool of four, beat Zolnowski of Hungary and Jahna of Austria to reach the quarter-final in her first World Championship. Sadly, she tensed up next morning and fell back on out-of-time counter-attacks, losing the first two fights 4–1, 4–0, though trouncing the third girl 4–0.

In the team event Britain got a good seed (7th), as it was one of the four countries to get four fencers to the third round. A good start was made with a 12–4 win over an admittedly inexperienced Spain (Ager 4, Green 4, Littlejohns 3, Halsted 1). The team recovered from 3–1 down against Italy, but only to 8–6. In the second round, against Japan, Sally Littlejohns had an excellent match, her long prise de fer attacks and ripostes overcoming her first three opponents. But from 7–5 up, two fights went to Japan, only one to Britain, and Noguchi overtook Sue Green in the last deciding fight from 2–3 down with two attacks on incautious preparations, and Britain went out on just one hit.

The epee first round saw off Hudson, whose lack of confidence made him look like a shadow boxer, and Hoskyns, who had a very nasty pool, compounded by a fight thrown to Szepesi (W. Germany); both got two wins. Johnson was eliminated in the second round. In the third round (last 48) Bourne hit top form, beating Muller (Austria) 5–2, von Essen (Sweden) 5–1 and Matwiejew (Poland) 5–4, while Graham Paul beat Modzolevski (USSR) 5–3, but could not handle the deceptive bladework of Munich finalist Pongratz (Rumania) and lost 5–4 in an excellent fight with Szepesi. Bourne could not retrieve his form next morning in the quarter-finals and lost to Pezza (Italy) 5–2 and Szepesi 5–4. The giant Edling won the event. Drakenberg in 1935 had been the only Swede to do so before.

In the team epee a good start was made with an 11–3 win over Belgium, with Bourne undefeated. A great effort was then made to beat Italy, so as to meet Denmark rather than Hungary in the second round. This failed 9–4, but the Poles turned out to be the next opponents since France had defeated Sweden. Graham Paul was the mainstay of this very exciting match, winning his third fight at the start of the last quarter to make Britain only 6–7 down after earlier being 2–5 and 4–7 (though Hoskyns had also left two opponents at a total loss with his fleches and pirouette ripostes). The two weaker Poles, Barburski and Wiech, were to follow and, with the hits running favourably, victory was in sight. It was not to be. Sadly, of Britain's nine losses four were on the last hit (two after recoveries from 4–1 down by Johnson).

The new overall captain, Jacobs, pointed out that only Bourne was ranked in the world's top twenty, and on current form only luck could take Britain to the last eight. He believed the only way to better results was the kind of intensive and sustained training which this year got the W. Germans a finalist and a team Gold.

Under the captaincy of Steve Higginson, the following fenced at the *World Student Games*: Clare Halsted, Beevers, Bell, Breckin, Deanfield, Grimmett, Partridge, G. Paul, Mather and Zarno. The Games were held in Moscow and the rigid policing and the organised heckling of the Israelis left a disagreeable impression. Deanfield fenced well to reach the semi-finals of the sabre.

# 1973–4

## MEN'S FOIL

Early in the season came an exciting – and novel – result in the *Team Championships*. Salle Paul was comfortably 5–1 up on Thames in the final when suddenly, perhaps because concentration slipped, the tide turned. Andy Eames, a newcomer to Thames, got a close win over Barrs. Breckin, fencing superbly throughout, dismissed Single. Wooding ended with a remarkable 5–0 over Barry Paul and Thames had won 9–6.

Provincial events saw a mixture of old and new faces. Derrick Cawthorne made a splendid comeback to win the *Leamington Tournament*, which he had previously won in 1957. (He came sixth in the *Coronation* for good measure.) Bruniges was the winner at *Leicester* and in the *Welsh Open*, where he was followed by Gareth Evans (Phoenix), John Hall, Richard Berry (Leicester), Steve Lennox (BAF) and Rob Collins (Millfield). The slight but fit Evans, who fenced fast and intelligently, registered himself on the scene both here and as second in the *Junior*, fifth in the *Under-20 Championship* and runner-up to Bruniges in the Under-20 points system. Paul Wedge, a few points behind, was both the Under-20 and Junior Champion. A pupil of Prof. Hill at Hydra and a fencer of great natural flair, he was making dramatic progress this season. His club-mate and another highly determined little fighter was Steve Glaister, who won the *Inverclyde* tournament and was fifth in Under-20 rankings in spite of missing the Under-20 final. Darryl Harris of Liverpool

University came out of the blue to take third place in the Junior, while in fifth place was Jim Hamments (Mayfield), finalist in the two previous years (and in 1967).

The *Public Schools* title was wrested from Mark Thompson (King's Chester) in a splendid final by Steve Carson (Royal Belfast), who thus made the top three in all weapons. Neal Mallett of Dover College was third.

For the second year running, Bruniges won the *Millfield Under-20 Tournament*, followed this time by Gaille of Switzerland. He was equally prominent at senior level, if lacking finishing power. The most impressive fencer in the *Coronation* final, he was hit *only once* in his first four fights; but the Pauls' experience, fitness and determination won the day. Barry's win enabled Graham to fight and win the barrage. Siffels, one of only two foreign entries, took fourth place.

In the *Championship* Bruniges was undefeated in his semi-final, followed by Graham Paul, behind Halsted, the team captain, and Wedge, in his first senior semi-final. In the second semi-final Bell had to barrage with Barrs (sixth in the Coronation) to join Barry Paul in the final. The third pool produced the unexpected Hoskyns and Bourne, over Single (fifth in the Coronation) and another newcomer, Ian Hodges (of Benfleet Blades but also now a pupil of Prof. Harmer-Brown).

Bruniges began the final by losing 5–4 to Bell (*Universities* Champion for the second year running), whose nervous but aggressive style was a curious amalgam of brio with seeming fragility. Later Bruniges beat Hoskyns 5–3 and Graham Paul 5–1, and ended fourth above Bell on hits. He nearly did much better, as he was alone in taking Barry Paul to the last hit. Hoskyns was making his first appearance in the final since 1970 (when he won), having since concentrated on epee. This time he had to be content with sixth place. This was to be his last serious competitive appearance at foil. Bourne, the other interloper, imposed himself with his boundless energy to take second place. His 5–1, 5–1, 5–3 wins put him well ahead of Graham Paul. He lost, perhaps significantly, to both Pauls.

So Barry Paul seized the crown at last, after first getting to the final six years before and twice being second (and twice absent). Although taken to assault point in two semi-final fights and not having to face Breckin or Geoff Grimmett (the one permanently, the other temporarily retired), there was no element of luck in his dominance of the final, which he started by crushing his most serious rival – his brother – 5–1.

Abroad, Barry also did well, though sometimes eliminated prematurely through exhaustion. He reached the last 32 (out of 92 entrants) in *Budapest* (G. Paul, Bell and Single were in the second round). In the poule unique *Brussels Debeur* won by Noel he was 13th out of 34 from France, W. Germany, Poland, Italy, Switzerland and Belgium. Paul Wedge did excellently in his first senior foreign event to come seventeenth. Twentieth was Bell and 26th Single, who, along with Graham Paul, reached the last 36 at *Bologna*, where Bell went out in the first round. Graham earned the only Olympic qualification at *Bonn* by reaching the last 24 of two hundred fencers from countries including France, Rumania, Poland – and Russia. One round behind in the last 28 were Bruniges and Barrs. In his first senior event abroad Mark Thompson of Ashton (and of Chester FC, where his father was coach) was in the second round, along with Bell, who sprained an ankle.

At the start of the season John Grimmett reached the last 32 in the *Paris Duval*, but then got married and faded from the scene. At the end of March the *Golden Foil of Flanders* offered an alternative to Budapest. Frank Hindle, Alan Loveland, Steve Fox and Dennis Barnes of Hydra were in the second round. At *Chalons* in France, against a strong entry of over a hundred, including Russians, Germans, Italians and Hungarians, Fox and Hindle reached the last 32, losing to Saffra and Szabo respectively. At the *Rommel* Bruniges reached the third round. Occasionally he was devastating but by his standards did not have a specially good season. He was now on a scholarship at Millfield where he was taught by Tom Norcross (and faced with exams). Perhaps the division of his attention between foil and epee and between senior and Under-20 foil was a disadvantage. In the pretty hopeless first round pool of the *Coupe d'Europe* preceding the Rommel he scored two wins against both Melun (the holders) and the Rome Fencing Club. Bell scored one against Rome and two against Melun. Eames and Wooding scored one apiece in their respective matches. Breckin, though mainly responsible for Thames being there, unfortunately failed to score.

Sponsored by the Egg Marketing Board, was an unusual *match against a star team* comprising Woyda (Olympic Gold Medallist), Noel (World Champion 1973), M. Behr and Hulin (Belgian Champion). Breckin, Bell, and Barry each won one victory, Graham none. In a *match against Holland*, Barrs and Graham scored one win; Single and Wedge each scored two.

In the World Championships Bell filled the gap left by Breckin. Barrs and Wedge were first and second reserves. Nick Halsted took over as Captain, a role he continued to fulfil till 1977.

*LADIES' FOIL*

At the most junior level, the *Under-16 Schoolgirls* Championship saw the start of Liz Wood's rise to fame: undefeated throughout, she was only hit three times in the final. She fenced for Loughton and Salle Boston and was followed by Ann Brannon, Cathy King and Clare Montgomery. She also won the *Perigal*, ahead of Caroline Hall (transferred to Ashton) and Janet Jones. Alison Simpson of Edinburgh, the winner of the *Under-19 Schoolgirls*, by contrast ascended from first round and quarter-finals only on indicators, though in the final she won all her fights with few mistakes. Next was Jane Popland; then Janet Jones and Brenda Hewitt (also of Ashton).

True to form, Sue Wrigglesworth won the *Under-20 Championship*. Sue Rochard fenced with determination to take second place. Anne Tulloch, Linda Martin and Barbara East were separated on indicators with three wins, with Caroline Hall sixth. In the *Millfield Tournament*, however, Sue Wrigglesworth went out in the semi-finals (losing to Ganser of Austria and Griekowski of Germany). It was Sue Rochard who travelled on to the final, when she won two fights and was unlucky to be sixth. In the team event Britain beat Switzerland but slumped against Germany.

Top places in the *Toupie Lowther* went to Spartan Club of Birmingham, in the persons of Marilyn Worster and Margaret Browning, the latter a good stylist with a penchant for counter-attacks. Both *Parker* and *Bertrand* were won by Hazel Davenport, now fencing at Brownhill, still a fencer who never stopped attacking till she scored. In the final of the Bertrand she had only four hits against her. Second place went to that other endogamous wife, Julia Single (Boston), followed a couple of hits behind by Lynne Taylor, who also got good Under-20 results abroad: second at *Duisburg* and sixth at *Gelsenkirchen*. Also still under twenty was Sue Rochard (now at Thames), who came third, and continued excellently by thrusting her way into sixth place in both the de Beaumont and the Championship. Jane Popland (5th) had already had notable success with her second place in the Under-20 event at *Arlon* (after barraging for first place). Lorna Andrews (Boston), who had been runner-up in the Parker, ahead of Christine Ord of Edmonton, was sixth. Linda Brown missed the final on a barrage.

The leader in provincial events was Sue Green, who got her hat trick at *Ashton* and won at *Birmingham*. She was third in the Desprez and fourth in the championship, reached the third round at *Turin* and rose triumphantly to retain the *de Beaumont*, after a 4-3 barrage over Hanisch of W. Germany, showing acute timing in attack and counter-attack and the ability to nerve herself for the big occasion. The new Teeside County were hosts of the event at the Thornaby Pavilion, providing food, lodging and transport, and the foreign entry was large and strong. Doing well as the third British finalist was Julia Single, in fifth place.

Three titles were all barraged for – to the last hit – by the same pair. Sue Wrigglesworth won the *Desprez* and *Silver Jubilee*, while Wendy Ager carried off the *Championship*. As a Surrey schoolgirl sprinter, the latter had surprising acceleration and strength of leg. She might not have completely adjusted to the disciplines of training, but she had great competitive spirit. This was something which Clare Halsted, who came third, had somewhat lost. Abroad she scored a third round at *Goppingen* along with Jill Dudley, Sue Harris of Behmber and Sally Littlejohns, but here again it was Sue Wrigglesworth to the fore: she reached the final (though she felt constrained to scratch to catch her plane). At *Duren* Caroline Hall and Jill Dudley reached the quarter-finals.

Other good results abroad were achieved by Sue Olley in the third round of *Como* and by Sally Littlejohns again, who got to the third round in *Minsk* and the last 24 of the *Jeanty*, thus earning an Olympic Qualification. Curiously, these two achieved nothing comparable at home. In the Championship, for instance, Sue Olley, like Hazel Davenport, succumbed in the quarter-finals and Sally Littlejohns (who perhaps found her job as Tax Inspector preoccupying) went out in the semi-finals, along with Sue Youngs, Jane Popland, Hilary Cawthorne and Celia Whitehurst (Ashton).

The last two were both included in matches at Minsk. Against *Azerbaijan* Hilary Cawthorne scored three, and Celia Whitehurst and Sally Littlejohns one each. After one win Wendy Ager retired with a leg injury. She wasn't to recover fitness until towards the end of the season. Sue Olley took over and got one win too. Against *Byelorussia* Celia Whitehurst failed to score; the others each got one. At Goppingen against *W. Germany* Clare Halsted was in Sue Olley's place and got one win; the others got two apiece. Finally at Thornaby there was a full-strength turn-out against the *Poles*, but still no victory. Susan Green and Susan Wrigglesworth scored two each, Sally Littlejohns and Hilary Cawthorne one each.

For the World Championships team the only change was the replacement of Clare Halsted by the newcomer Hilary Cawthorne, mainly on her match results (the winning of *Redbridge* being her domestic high note).

## EPEE

At the Under-20 end of the spectrum the Points System totals best illustrate the position: R. Bruniges 502, P. Tarran 267, J. Llewellyn 260, P. Emberson 64, J. Cooper 30, K. Lovejoy 30, P. Ayliffe 18. After the first two of these, only Lovejoy (3rd) and Ayliffe (5th) figured in the *Under-20 Championship*. Abroad, Bruniges took time off from foil to score two scorching Under-20 results. He won at *Budapest* in January and was second at *Genoa* in February. Tarran and Llewellyn were semi-finalists in each respectively. Keith Lovejoy gained a notable victory at *Ashton*. But he only reached the quarter-final of the *Junior*. Only John Llewellyn of the Under-20s got as far as the semi-finals, where he was eliminated along with Bill Forward of Poly, Murch, Pete Brierley, Barry Patman and Terry Harrison. The winner was an old hand, Malcolm Fare of Thames, with his club-mate John Hall second on a barrage. They were followed by two Bostonians, Stanbury and Worthington (the latter hitting unexpected form). David Brooks of Corby and John Higgins of Thames each had one victory.

At *Sandhurst* Hill was the undefeated winner, ahead of Belson, Brierley,

The mature Hoskyns fleche; Loetscher is the victim.

Hudson, Fare and More. Mark West won at *Nottingham*, over Brooks and Colin Sigrist (Brownhill), and at *Ilford*, over Gabor Scott (Paul) and Neal Mallett (Kent). Bruniges won the epee (as well as the foil) in the *Welsh Open*, followed by Partridge. At *Birmingham* the pentathletes Brierley, Fox and Phelps won the team event, over 'Neasden' (Hudson, Partridge, Pearman). Howard West was individual victor. The *Martini Qualifying* was won by Pearman. It was Bourne and Hoskyns, however, who were the only British to survive to the last 24 in the *Martini* itself. Hoskyns was one of the eight best who had byes to the last sixteen, but he failed to meet the reflexes and fitness of the Hungarian Schmitt by 10–2. Bourne did well to beat Osztrics, a younger Hungarian ace, by 10–8, but then lost 10–5 to Ladegaillerie, Olympic Silver Medallist. In the final, five out of the eight fights went to 10-all! Remarkably, the winner was the youngest competitor, sixteen-year-old Poffet of Switzerland, who bettered all the steely finesse and experience of Schmitt to win the last bout 11–10.

The *Championship* was gruelling: over eighty fencers, sticky weather, first round pools of eight. Ousted from one semi-final were H. West, Belson and Noel and from the other Davenport, Beevers and Gray. In the final Bourne overcame by 5–4 his bogeyman, Paul, for the first time in nearly a dozen encounters and was otherwise never taken beyond a second hit. Hudson got three solid wins, again benefiting from non-availability for the team. Bruniges, despite little epee this season, was up one place, to third, while the long, lanky, light-fingered Murch firmly established his seniority with fourth place. Hoskyns was a shade off-form and Paul just failed to get a win.

The *Miller-Hallett* was equally large, but was unbalanced by the absence of Paul, Beevers, Johnson and Bruniges, all either injured or abroad, and by the elimination of Belson and Hoskyns in the semi-finals. Higginson (5th) and Netburn, briefly in England again (6th), made reappearances on the scene. Claus Morch of Norway, likewise in England for a spell, was third on two decisive wins, over Davenport, who beat both foreigners and almost the winner. Noel, preoccupied with finals but perhaps gaining from the relief that gave him from the pressures of qualifying for the team, fenced with care to three wins. As for Bourne, his undefeated performance was described by Peter Jacobs as 'Teddy's afternoon stroll' – though this is not quite the way his opponents would have described the controlled whirlwind of his attacks.

Abroad, Bourne was also far in the ascendant. In the *Monal*, more star-studded than for many years, he got perhaps his best-ever result. He rose brilliantly through quarter and semi-finals (disposing for instance of Jacobson, reigning Silver Medallist) and in the final of six beat Hehn and Bertinetti to come fourth, behind Fenyvesi (1972 Olympic Champion), Erdos and Edling (reigning World Champion). He was the first British finalist since Jacobs in 1966. Not content with this, he reached the final of another 'A Category' competition when he came fifth at *Bern*. He was also in the last sixteen at *Poitiers*. At the end of the season he was sixteenth in the world rankings.

Hoskyns was usually close behind. He reached a semi-final of the Monal equivalent to many a World Championship final, a stunning performance at the age of 43 (which included a crushing win over Brodin, Silver Medallist at the end of the season). Like Bourne, he was in the last sixteen at *Innsbruck*, and was one round behind at Poitiers. At the start of the season he was the victor at *Duren* (his 43rd major international result). Noel, Osbaldeston and Belson were in quarter-finals. This was the season when Tim Belson romped into international class. On his first visit to *Heidenheim* he rose all the way to the last eight and missed the final of four only on the last hit of ten against von Essen. Of large build, with the muscle to exploit it, his technique was solid rather than brilliant, but his aggressive concentration could be formidable indeed, as he proved again when he won the middle-strength event at *Innsbruck*, with a hundred fencers from six countries.

Graham Paul's explosive speed was beginning to wear a bit uneven, but he was in the last 24 at Bern and again at *Berlin* and the last 32 at Heidenheim, as was David Partridge who gained the same level at Poitiers. In the 64 at Heidenheim and in the last 48 at Bern was Bill Forward, an ex-Oxford Poly fencer now working abroad, whose natural athleticism and confidence would undoubtedly have taken him to greater things had he fenced seriously. Less hypothetical contenders for the team were Davenport and Beevers, in the last 32 at Poitiers. At a more modest level, Bruniges was second at *Rheims*, losing a barrage with Wolinetz 5–3; Belson was in the last eight and Pearman in the last sixteen. At *Dieppe* Fare was third and Turner eleventh.

Johnson and Hudson both early declared themselves unavailable (the former being in Australia from March to July). The fifth place thus left open was filled by Partridge. As the points-table for the season shows, his results belied his unphysical, apparently languid style.

| Bourne    | 602 | Hudson   | 159 | Davenport | 94 |
| Belson    | 301 | Bruniges | 144 | Pearman   | 72 |
| Hoskyns   | 275 | Forward  | 129 | Higginson | 72 |
| G. Paul   | 200 | Beevers  | 112 | Jacobs    | 64 |
| Partridge | 174 | Murch    | 108 | H. West   | 60 |
|           |     | Noel     | 103 |           |    |

Team results did not compare with individual achievements. At Innsbruck in a *four-nation match* Britain won on hits at 8–all with Austria, with Bourne winning four fights, Belson and Paul two and Hoskyns none. Against Rumania, Belson got two wins, but Bourne and Beevers only got one and Paul none. In the last match, against Germany, the team recovered: Bourne, Belson and Hoskyns each got two and Paul one.

The domestic *Team Championship* was lent novelty by the ephemeral Excalibur Team comprising Hoskyns, Hudson, Noel and Bruniges, all SW Section team members, though in this event usually met with under the banner of a London club. They beat Paul 'B' 9–0 in the quarters and Boston 'A' 9–4 in the semis – a striking result even given Johnson's absence.

The other finalists – Polytechnic 'A' – had a tougher time of it, getting an 8–all win over Thames in the quarters and the same against Paul 'A' in the semis. Perhaps match-tight on this account, they leapt to a 3–1 lead on Excalibur. Netburn and a startlingly good Forward were undefeated with three wins apiece, Beevers had two wins, one loss and one to go, and Bryan Lewis (characteristically suffering from a crushed toe, inflicted at sabre by Jay the weekend before) had three losses but gained the clinching win. For Excalibur Bruniges scored two, Hoskyns and Noel one and Hudson nil (each except Hudson having one fight to go).

*SABRE*

There were few dramatic features to events for younger sabreurs. Mark Slade of Brentwood was young enough to win the *Under-16 Schoolboys Championship* and good enough to come second in both the *Under-20* and the *Public Schools* Championships, the former being won by Jonathan Lewis and the final of the latter containing three other Brentwood pupils (Stafford-Bull 3rd, Howgego 5th and Steventon 6th). The trophy however, went to Steve Carson of Royal Belfast as hors d'oeuvre to his foil win.

There were no notable under-20 results abroad, the thin tally of points-holders being headed by Carl Morris of Birmingham FC (160), Ross Campion, third in the home Championship (129) and Chris Grzesik, fifth in the Championship (112).

More established sabreurs dominated both the *Universities Championships*, won by Deanfield for London (though Morris was second) and the *Junior Championship*, which went to the doughty campaigner Bryan Lewis of Poly, over Price and Etherton, both of Boston, who showed more classic technique but less determination. Gryf-Lowczowski was fourth, ahead of Milligan and Streater (Boston). Only the fourth and sixth of these were newcomers to the final.

In the provincial events it was a season of hat-tricks: Kovanda at *Nottingham*, Ian Edwards in the *Welsh Open*, Philbin at *Ashton* and Wiles at *Inverclyde*.

In the *Cole Cup* too it was a hat-trick, for Convents, third place going to Deanfield and fifth to Taylor, but the rest to Germans and Austrians.

To lure over the Vasas Club of Budapest, including all the Goteborg Gold Medal team members, for five days was quite a coup. An individual event of 24 was held with a final of twelve. The five Hungarians took the top places, Taylor being the only Briton to beat one of them (T. Kovacs, by 5–3). He was followed by Deanfield and Cohen in seventh and eighth places. There followed a match in which the visitors beat a combined Poly-Boston team 10–6. Deanfield, Oldcorn and Eden each claimed two wins; Cohen apparently concentrated on fun and self-education.

The same team, fencing for Britain, beat Austria 9–7. This was a solid effort against no mean opponents. Each scored two, except Deanfield, who scored three. Against a young W. German team there was a less happy result: 2–9.

Richard Cohen won the home *Championship* for the first time, having trained as hard as any sabreur had ever done in Britain, with enhanced technique, if not yet total fluency, in his aggressive game. The standard of the final was high in spite of the absence of Deanfield (down with chickenpox) and Oldcorn (with injured back). Philbin matched Cohen's speed and attack and took him to a barrage. Having beaten him 5–4 in the pool, he even led 4–2 in this; but victory eluded him. In the first fight of the final he had got a 5–2 win over Eden, who was not on best form, and was also beaten 5–4 by Cohen in spite of tremendous efforts, though he only conceded two, three and three hits respectively to the other finalists. It was the first of these, David Scott (S. Paul), who, starting very fiercely, thwarted Philbin of outright victory, by 5–4, after being 0–4 down, going on to beat Taylor 5–2 but losing to Zarno by the same margin. Taylor beat Zarno 5–1 to come fifth on hits.

In a field of only 31, many younger fencers made spirited attempts to reach the semi-finals: first-timers who succeeded were Slade and Morris (now at Cambridge).

The *Corble* was won by David Eden, whose improvement was one of the striking features of the season. Having been close to the team for a number of years, he had not made the final breakthrough perhaps partly for temperamental reasons, but also because his work in the fashion business periodically monopolised his energies. After a period of residence in Holland he returned quite late in the season, but trained hard and evidently benefited from his new master, Prof. Imregi. When going badly, his skill and even more his will to win still tended to evaporate, but going well, as in a *match against Holland* when he got four wins and was only hit seven times, he was a veritable tiger.

He was followed in the Corble by Storme, Oldcorn, Cohen, de Wisscher and Gomez (who was also the winner at *Leamington*). Deanfield was absent.

At the end of the season the *Team Championship* saw a shift in the balance of clubs, only partly attributable to Poly having attracted Eden as well as Oldcorn. Poly 'B' reached the semi-final, and there only fell to the 'A' team. The other semi-final saw Boston 'A' beat Salle Paul by 9–5. In the final Boston swept to 5–0 and then 7–2. Victory drinks were firmly in view. But Poly wrenched the next four fights, and really reversed the odds when, by 5–4, Lewis overturned Mather, hitherto undefeated, and Eden beat Cohen 5–2. Zarno pulled the score back to 8–all by beating Deanfield 5–3, but too late: Poly had won by two hits, each fencer having won two victories. (For Boston, Etherton won one, Cohen and Zarno two each.) The president was Philbin, who won the rare accolade of praise from the losers.

It was Cohen again who led in achievements abroad. He gained a third Olympic qualification by reaching the last 24 in the tough *Hamburg* event. He reached the same stage at *Montreuil* in France, a medium-strength event with entries from Bulgaria, Switzerland and Belgium. Also quarter-finalists here were Philbin, Taylor and Deanfield. Eden and Oldcorn reached the last twelve, where Oldcorn won two fights in his pool of four but went out in the barrage. Zarno was in the last thirty. The winner was Hamm of Holland.

*Munich* was another typical W. European competition. Deanfield, whose season was already disrupted by ten weeks' midwifery in Stoke-on-Trent, had to scratch with a leg injury. Philbin and Taylor reached the last 36. In the last 24 Cohen lost to Wischeidt and the winner, Bonnissent, and Zarno scored one good win over Duschner.

*Budapest* was the big event: with approximately two hundred of the best sabreurs in the world. Eden and Philbin were ousted in the first round and Deanfield and Taylor in the second. At the other end of the scale of seriousness, Steve Fox – better known as a foilist – was winner at *Dieppe*.

Eden and Taylor were the newcomers to the World Championship team, taking the places of Mather (whose university preoccupations kept him out of competitive fencing) and Philbin.

*COMBINED EVENTS*

This year the *World Youth Championships* were held in the Istanbul Palace of Sports, cold and austere but with a magnificent view of the Bosphorus. The team was managed as usual by Joe Eden and coached by Prof. Boston. Richard Oldcorn was captain for the men and Jackie Erwteman for the ladies.

In the foil Gareth Evans went out in the first round, too nervous to do himself justice. Paul Wedge was perhaps unlucky to go out in the second round with two wins and a 5–4 loss to Lamon of Switzerland after two questionable decisions: he showed great determination if rather less technique. Robert Bruniges edged through the first three rounds. In the semi-final his formidable concentration sometimes faded and success narrowly eluded him. He lost 5–4 to Kuki (Rumania) the eventual winner and again, in an excellent fight, on the last hit to Smirnov of Russia, the future double World Champion. It was a very strong final: Behr (Germany, 2nd), Pietruszka (France, 3rd), Dal Zotto (Italy, 4th) Martewisz (Poland, 5th) and Bellone (Italy, 6th). Three of these were previous finalists and several were soon to be dominant as world finalists.

Suffering from a cold, Sue Wrigglesworth was ousted in a first round barrage in the ladies' event. Caroline Hall, though showing promise of real ability, lacked drive and lost her crucial fight with Moody of Australia 3–4, in a difficult pool. Lynne Taylor went through to the second round on wins over Grajczyk (Poland), Jahna (Austria), and by 4–1 over Verschraegen (Belgium) – Sue's victor. With true fencing intelligence, she knew when to attack and when to defend and did both well. She was unlucky to have in her quarter-final Sidorova, the eventual winner, as well as Batazzi (Italy), to whom she lost in a spirited 3–4 bout, her thrusts twice just failing to block the attack.

For the first time for ten years no sabreurs were entered, no one having achieved the qualifying points total. In the epee, the injury-prone John Llewellyn, fencing with his arm in plaster, got as far as the second round, where he twice fell and got one win. Things went well for Paul Tarran, however. Not just one of those left-handers who only sits and waits, he also had a fine range of attacks that could catch the best opponents unprepared. He went up top in his first pool, got four wins in the second round and succumbed to distinguished opponents in the quarter-final pools of four: Boisse (eventually 4th), Mochi and, by 5–4, Forgacs. Bruniges went even better and was undefeated in the quarter-finals, but then lost the initiative to Pezza (Italy, eventually 6th) at 4–2 up, which perhaps in turn led to a 5–3 loss to Krebs (France, eventually 5th). The final was again very strong, with Poffet first, Pusch second and Wiech of Poland third.

The championships ended with a banquet at the Hilton. Wine flowed freely and the fencers joined in the cabaret. The Russian chef d'equipe drew tears from Oldcorn with his song and dance act and Lynne Taylor brought the house down, with a dance that rivalled Salome's!

At Aberdeen England won the *Quadrangular* yet again, beating Scotland 19–17, Wales 21–13 and N. Ireland 22–14; but second place was taken, for the first time since 1963, by Wales, who beat Scotland by a handsome 21–15

Linda Martin v Caroline Hall in the 1974 Rest-of-Britain Match (Andy Martin and Julia Bullmore between them).

and N. Ireland by the same score. Scotland beat N. Ireland 25–11. A civic dinner was enjoyed out of endowments of Robert the Bruce.

Just before the World Championships came the *Commonwealth Championships*, staged in Ottawa (in the somewhat stifling University gym), fencing having been excluded from the Commonwealth Games in Christ Church. Andy Eames of N. Ireland was the surprise of the foil. His blitz fleche was unstoppable and he was only hit eight times in the final. The favourite, Benko of Australia (4th in the 1973 World Youth Championships), had to be content with the Silver Medal on one hit over Nick Bell (England), with Obst (Canada), also on three wins, just behind. For Scotland, Ian Campbell got one win and Tom Beattie none – a sad reversal for him after being undefeated in a semi-final in which Eames only went up on a tiny difference of hits over Wiles (Scotland). Mayo (Scotland) and Beevers (England) went out in Benko's semi-final.

The team events were run as poules uniques of seven, with the unusual feature that the host nation was allowed to field two sides. At foil it was at first again N. Ireland to the fore. They beat England 5–4, Wales 5–4 and Scotland 6–3 (Eames 1v, 3v, 2v; Magill 3v, 1v, 3v; R. Gray 1v, 1v, 1v). But they couldn't keep it up and lost to Australia (with one win each) and to Canada 'A' (Eames 2, Magill 0, Gray 1). This put paid to hopes of Gold, though they ensured Bronze by beating Canada 'B' (Eames 2, Gray 1 and Carson 2).

Rallying vociferous support, England recovered to beat Canada 'A' 5–4, Canada 'B' 7–2, Australia 5–4 and Wales 6–3. In the last decisive match against Scotland only Campbell withstood their attack (until they had already won). Out of 18 fights apiece their wins were: Wedge 15, Bell 13, Fox 7.

Scotland was disappointed after the individual successes. They beat Wales 6–3 (Campbell 3, Wiles 2, Mayo 1) but then dropped Wiles and lost 6–3 to Australia (Campbell 2, Beattie 1, Mayo 0). The new three each got only one win against N. Ireland and the last three matches were frustratingly all 5–4 defeats. Against Canada 'A' Campbell scored one win, Beattie two and Wiles one, while against both Canada 'B' and England it was Campbell three, Beattie one and Mayo nil.

The Welsh had a mixed time, beating both Canadian teams but slumping 8–1 to Australia at the end. Their totals were Evans 11, Hyndman 6 and Edwards 4 (with Stewart replacing Edwards against Australia without a win).

True to form, Sue Wrigglesworth won the ladies' foil, undefeated in the final. Marion Exelby, now married to Richard Gray, excelled to retain her 1970 Games Silver Medal for N. Ireland, on three wins and a few hits better than Sue Youngs, likewise regaining her 1970 Bronze Medal. Fourth was Hilary Cawthorne (England) and fifth Linda Brown (Wales) who with one win and three losses on the last hit bettered Helen Smith (Australia) on index. Janet Pollock and Diane Devlin of Scotland and Sue Olley of England came unstuck in the semi-finals.

In the ladies' team event England lost 5–4 both to Australia and to Scotland; in both, the scores were Wrigglesworth 2, Cawthorne 1, Olley 1. They beat the other teams convincingly. Of the twelve fights apiece Wrigglesworth won twelve, Cawthorne 8 and Olley 7. But they were lucky to get Silver Medals on a count of bouts over Scotland, who spoilt their chances by losing 5–4 to Canada 'A' as well as Australia. Their ratios of wins to fights were: Youngs 12/18, Devlin 9/15, Pollock 6/12, Linda Ramage 3/9.

The Australians Helen Smith, S. Pratt, C. McDougall and L. McLaren swept to victory, but only after an initial plummeting 7–2 loss to the Welsh (L. Brown 3, A. Bennett 3, M. Riley 1). Wales went on to 5–4 wins over Canada 'B' and N. Ireland, but then lost to the other teams. (Total wins: Brown 11, Bennett 9, Riley 6). N. Ireland beat Canada 'B' and almost beat Wales and Canada 'A', Marion Gray only dropping one fight in those three matches; but ended in sixth place. (Totals: M. Gray 12, C. Convill 6, I. Dumigan 0).

In the epee, to make up for his loss of the foil, Greg Benko's natural timing and lightning speed secured him the Gold Medal, only Campbell scoring more than two hits on him in the final. D. Partridge (England) was second with four wins, followed by three fencers with two wins: J. Noel (England) got the bronze with a 5–0 double, while J. Primeau (Canada) was ahead of B. Lewis (Wales) by a splinter. Campbell, who had defied extinction in each successive round, was thus a finalist a second time, albeit without wins.

Rollo (Scotland), Beevers (England) and Higginson (taking time off as England's non-playing captain), succumbed in the semi-finals, along with B. Turner and E. Gray of Wales.

In the epee team event the hopes of the undefeated Welsh team rose after a 5–4 win over England in the fifth round. In the sixth round Scotland nearly sealed England's fate, but in the seventh, Wales, although still undefeated, could not afford less than victory over Australia unless England slumped 7–2 against Canada 'A'. England *won* 7–2; while Wales suffered a 5–3 loss to opponents physically determined to secure bronze. So it was England 37, and the Gold Medal and Wales 32, with the Silver, half jubilant, half brokenhearted. The fight ratios were Noel 15/18, Beevers 10/18, Partridge 9/15, Higginson 3/3; Gray 12/18, Lewis 11/18 (and 2 double defeats), Turner 7/15 (and one double defeat) and Martin 2/3. Saying something about the heat and exhaustion of the event was Lewis's feat in falling asleep on the floor in mid-match—leaving a perfect image of himself in sweat when he got up.

Scotland was fifth, between the two Canadas, with wins over Canada 'B' and N. Ireland (and three 5–4 losses). John MacKenzie scored 11/15, Rollo 5/9, Mayo 5/15, Campbell 4/12. N. Ireland scored a blank (Carson 4, Richardson 3, Gray 1).

It was at sabre that the English were most dominant, sweeping the first three places. Eden won a barrage over Taylor by 5–4, while Philbin beat the three Canadians who completed the pool (M. Lavoie 4th, P. Samek 5th and B. Wither 6th). Wiles and Mitchell of Scotland were both fifth in the semis. Lewis (Wales) missed the final on a barrage with Wither after dead heat on hits. In the same pool Carson was just behind Mitchell on hits.

The team sabre followed the same pattern. England were undefeated in their six matches (Philbin 16, Eden 14, Taylor 13). Only Scotland got as many as three wins off them, but otherwise had a sad time, with a win only over N. Ireland by 6–3. (Wiles, never dropping more than one fight, got 13/18, McKenzie 5/15, Mitchell 3/15, Beattie 0/3.) The Canadians firmly took both Silver and Bronze; while Australia beat all three British fringe countries. Wales beat Scotland 5–4 and N. Ireland 8–1 and was thus fifth. (Lewis 12/18, Edwards 8/18, Norrie 2/9, Norcross 2/9.) N. Ireland beat only Canada 'B' (Totals: Magill 8, Richardson 5, Carson 4). Scotland were in sixth place by four wins.

The *World Championships* were held in the enormous Palais de Grace of the Winter Olympic complex at Grenoble, attracting a record entry of over five hundred from 43 countries, including China, an FIE member of only two months. Most unusually, two of the four individual titles were retained by the holders. Hungary went into decline; Russia revived. Peter Jacobs was again British captain, as he was to remain till 1976.

All the British foilists survived the first round. In the second, Graham Paul was off form, Bell was over-excited and Single went down in a pool with three who reached the last twelve; but Bruniges and Barry Paul (who beat Romankov, eventual winner, 5–2) sailed into the last 48, where Barry fenced outstandingly, varying overwhelming attacks with crisp ripostes and achieving third highest seed. Rob was unable to lift his game to the required aggressive level. In the quarter finals Barry lost his edge and went out, in company with Noel.

The foil team was seeded ninth out of 21. Brazil was rapidly beaten (promotion thus being ensured). Hungary asserted themselves 9–5. In the eighth-finals Japan led 5–2 and 6–3. The team then made a tremendous effort, got to 8–7 up, but lost the last fight and went down on hits. The Russians won a final of high technique from the Poles by 8–6.

In the sabre Cohen lacked fire and went out in the first round, as Eden and Taylor did in the second. Oldcorn was in command until the third round. Here Deanfield held his mature, steady form and was unlucky, with three wins, to miss the quarter-finals. The standard of the sabre was high. M. Montano won.

In the team event Britain disappointingly lagged 4–0 to the USA and lost 9–5, only Deanfield showing form. They then lost 13–3 to USSR, the eventual winners. (Rumania was disqualified from second place for drug-taking.)

The ladies did well. Hilary Cawthorne went out in the second round, not yet able to take on all-comers, but Sue Green, Sally Littlejohns and Wendy Ager fenced with drive and concentration and reached the third round. Susan Wrigglesworth (in spite of a combine) went on to the mini quarter-finals. Here she had an excellent win over Demaille, 1971 Champion and local heroine, but lost to Rejto, veteran Tokyo Champion, after being 0–3 and then 3–all, and also to the aggressive Bartos of Rumania.

The final consisted of three Russians and three Hungarians, the latter taking the top two places.

Britain was seeded sixth in the team event, thanks to the good individual results. In the first round Finland and Brazil were easily disposed of, but Italy reversed the seeding by 9–3, only Sally Littlejohns showing form. This resulted in a poorer seeding in round two, with Poland as opponents. After a bad slide to 2–4, the team made a tremendous come-back to 6–all, but technique and tactics frayed in the heat of battle and the Poles took the last three fights with careful fencing. In the final the Russians revenged themselves on the Hungarians.

The epee entry of 133 was, as usual, the largest. All the British got through the first round. In the second Partridge did not master the situation quickly enough, while Hoskyns went out with two wins in a very difficult pool. Belson, in outstanding form, now had the second highest indicator on both rounds. In the third round Paul went out with Jacobsen, 1973 runner-up, in an extremely tough pool. Belson, lagging on concentration, took two defeats before he settled down; he lost the deciding bout with Lukomsky 5–2. Bourne, sadly, was in uncertain form and lost a similar critical fight with von Essen 5–4.

Only Edling of the previous year's finalists could repeat the very exacting effort. He lost 5–0 to Brodin of France but was only hit five times thereafter. Only Cattiau, Mangiarotti and Nikanchikov had ever before won two years running. His characteristic time-thrust whipped over the top of the opponent's guard was eventually to be widely adopted, especially by the hard school of German epeeists at the end of the decade.

In the team epee, from a depressing 3–5 against a weak USA the British went on to 10–6, Partridge drooping the match point on to his opponent's wrist. The other opponents were the Swiss: it was excellent to achieve 7–all (with one double defeat), if sad to miss the last win. In the knock-out, the team, after being 1–4 down to Hungary, hauled back to 6–all. Hoskyns, in particular, was in top form, dumbfounding Osztrics and Erdos with his technique and timing. The Hungarians then reasserted themselves. The event was won by Sweden, for the first time.

# 1974–5

## MEN'S FOIL

The *Millfield Under-20* event sponsored by Irving Allen saw 130 entrants reduced to twelve foreigners and twelve British by the quarter-finals. Eliminated in the semi-finals were Mark Thompson, Glaister and Bartlett (now at Salle Pearson), along with Gaille (Switzerland) and Stemmerick (Holland), both finalists the previous year. In the final Siffels was undefeated when he met Bruniges, who had lost to van Hilten. The English fencer won and went on to take a 4–2 lead in the barrage and sit out time to take the title – the first person to do so three years running. Tonges was third and van Hilten fourth. Lamon was fifth on hits with one win, over Paul Wedge.

True to form, in the absence of Bruniges (out for the rest of the season with a torn cartilage), Wedge retained the *Under-20* title, the first to do so since the event started in 1964; but not without a struggle. He recovered from 4–0 down to Mark Chetwood (S. Paul) but lost 5–2 to Tom Beattie of Edinburgh in his last bout and had to barrage with these two opponents. He overcame Beattie 5–4 and Chetwood 5–1. Beattie then secured second place, likewise by 5–1. Glaister was fourth with two wins. Pierre Harper of Salle Goodall was beginning to make an impact, in fifth place with one win, at the age of seventeen. Mark Reynolds (son of Osie Reynolds) was sixth, with four 5–4 losses but no wins.

Reynolds went on to win for St Paul's School both the *Schoolboys' Cham-*

*pionship* and the *Public Schools* title (ahead of Mallett). He was also in the semi-final of the direct elimination stages of the 32-strong schoolboys invitation event sponsored by *Wilkinson Sword*. This was won by Mark Thompson, who beat Andrew Cashen of Wells in the final. The left-handed Bill Gosbee, taught by Geoff Tonks at St Clement Danes School, did well to reach the quarter-finals aged only thirteen. (Later he won the *Under-14* title.)

Abroad, the under-20s did well. At *Wentdorf* in August 1974, at the end of an international training camp run by a group of masters including Prof. Boston, the hard-training Glaister came second. At *Duisburg* Wedge achieved an excellent third place (with Beattie, Ford and Glaister in the quarter-finals). At *Gelsenkirchen* Glaister came fifth in star-studded company. Bartlett, Wedge and Harper reached the quarters, Thompson the semis. The *Budapest* event in January, usually formidably strong, was weakened by late arrival of the Swiss, Poles and Italians, but Gilbert Thompson's sixth place was still very creditable. The unrelated Mark Thompson was again a semi-finalist.

In the *Junior Championship* the 18-year-old Glaister succeeded Wedge in taking the title for their coach Leon Hill, leaving Evans in second place again. Among the 126 entrants early casualties included Fox, Tyson, Gilbert and Mark Thompson, Jim Hamments and Mike Cullen. Salle Paul lost its hopes in the semi-finals with Scott, Chetwood and John Franck, Thames with Hall. In the final Glaister faltered only against Ford, whom he beat from 1-4 down. Fast, aggressive and always under control, he timed his attacks well and consistently arrived with his ripostes.

In the provincial events Alan Loveland won at *Portsmouth* for the third time running. Carl Waldman was *Combined Services* champion for the second successive year. At *Leicester* Cawthorne was the winner at the age of 43. At *Nottingham* Chetwood did well to beat Eames into second place. At *Birmingham* – to which the Leamington tournament had transferred – Single was runner-up to the Belgian Soumagne.

At the senior end of things, Graham Paul won the invitation *Emrys Lloyd* pool of sixteen, with twelve wins. Geoff Grimmett was second with ten wins, ahead on hits of the promising Ian Hodges (Benfleet). In the *Coronation Cup* Graham was again to the fore – third after Pfeiffer and Haerter of E. Germany (the latter fifth in the 1973-4 world ranking). Loveland did very well to reach this final, in sixth place following Lossius of E. Germany and Englebracht of Holland.

Barry Paul retained the *Championship* despite fencing below his best. He lost to Single and won three of his other fights on the last hit, two from 4-2 down – a testimony to his ability to raise his game against the odds (with perhaps a little help from providence). Graham was denied the chance of a barrage by Eames who showed his Ottawan speed and accuracy to reach third place on his first appearance in the final. Another newcomer was Evans, now training at Salle Paul, who was very fast and light on his feet even if he didn't

# Competitions chronicle 1974–5

quite have the aggression to cope with more competitive opponents and only beat Eames. Bell, preoccupied with exams this season, had 5–0 and 5–1 wins and two 5–4 defeats and had to be content with fourth place, ahead of Single on hits.

On a one-man tour of the Middle East, Bell had opened the season with a third place in *Beirut*, fourth in *Istanbul* and second in *Ankara*. Spurred on by the introduction of a points system and a wider spread of grants, twenty British fencers went to the *Paris Martini* with 400 entrants from all the major countries. Grimmett, proving himself again a foilist of great natural ability who fully exploited his length, reached the last 32 along with Barry Paul.

23 fencers went to the *Duval*, likewise in Paris, which included Hungarians, Germans and Belgians. Graham Paul reached the last sixteen; in the last 32 were More, Grimmett and Ford, an excellent result in his first senior event abroad for Ford, who was a technically able, well-programmed fencer, short only perhaps on the killer instinct. A month later still at the *Rommel*, again in Paris, Fox reached the third round.

It was here in the strongest of all events, perhaps stronger than the World Championships, that Barry Paul achieved the best British foil result since the great days of Jay and Hoskyns. He fenced magnificently round after round. In the quarter-finals he beat the reigning World Champion Romankov 5–1, Kojejowski of Poland 5–4 and Kovacs of Hungary 5–4. In the semi-finals he walked through Isakov of Russia 5–2 and Czakkel of Hungary 5–1, losing only to Wojciechowski of Poland by 5–4.

In the final he won his first two bouts against Hein and Kovacs (again), both 5–4. An outright win seemed a real possibility. In his third fight against Boscherie of France he started by scoring the first four hits. Then exhaustion and nervousness combined suddenly to halt his relaxed, flowing movements. He lost this fight 5–4, could not regain composure and lost to Noel 5–1 and Wojciechowski 5–2, to take fifth place on hits behind Hein. Nevertheless this was a magnificent result.

In *Budapest*, which attracted all the leading countries except France, both British entrants, Graham Paul and Grimmett, reached the third round. In the *Golden Foil of Flanders* the same weekend Bell did well to come second and Harper showed great promise in coming sixth among a mixed entry from France, Germany and Holland. In the *Debeur* poule unique, of 29 from W. Germany, Italy, Poland and Switzerland, in Brussels, Graham got eighteen wins and was unlucky to be only ninth. Barry got twelve wins and was eighteenth. Grimmett retired with a cut sword hand. Again, the same weekend, at *Magdeburg* in E. Germany (along with Poles, Hungarians, Austrians and Czechs), Single reached the third round and Glaister and Fox the second. Single was fourth at *Ostend*.

Graham Paul got to the semi-final at *Bonn*, which even in the unaccustomed absence of Russia and Hungary was of a strength to earn him an Olympic

Qualification. Single and Bell were in the last 48 of this 150-strong event. Finally, in the top-level *Bologna* Tournament at the end of May it was Grimmett's turn to achieve a qualification by reaching the quarter-finals.

Team performances were less promising. Although Fox, Grimmett and G. Paul edged to a 5–4 win in a match with *Belgium* at the Birmingham Tournament, the E. Germans had a 12–4 walkover in a match combined with the Coronation (Grimmett 2, B. Paul 1, Glaister 1, G. Paul 0).

The domestic *Team Championship* saw an 8–7 win by Thames over Boston in one semi-final contrasted with Paul's easy win over Ashton in the other. In the final S. Paul avenged themselves on Thames by 9–4 (G. Paul 3/3, B. Paul 3/3, Single 2/4, Grimmett 1/3; Halsted 2/3, Eames 2/3, Bell 0/3, Wooding 0/4).

The World Championship team, with Bruniges off the scene, after his leg injury, and Single out through a sprained ankle, comprised the two Pauls, Grimmett and Bell.

*LADIES' FOIL*

This was a season of expansion, revival and occasional disappointment. The introduction of block grants combining both training and travel gave flexibility and allowed the awarding of 103 travel grants to 43 fencers, as well as training weekends for LAFU's training groups in Manchester, the SW and London and the sponsorship of Wendy Ager and Hilary Cawthorne to train at Melun under Revenu for a month.

In foreign Under-20 events Connie Beagrie was runner-up in the *Spitzer* in Israel, Caroline Hall narrowly missed the final at *Dornbirn* and did well to come second at *Duisberg*, and Elizabeth Wood reached the quarter-finals at *Gelsenkirchen*. At senior level Clare Halsted reached the quarter-finals at *Duren*, both she and Wendy Ager were in the third round in *Turin*, and she, Sally Littlejohns and Sue Harris were in the third round at *Goppingen*, and these two plus Sue Wrigglesworth and Sue Rochard got to the third round of the *Jeanty*. Wendy Ager, in a season of peaks and chasms, reached the semi-final at *Offenbach* (where Sue Green was a quarter-finalist) and got one of the few Olympic Qualifications of the season by reaching the quarter-finals at *Como* (where Hilary Cawthorne was in the third round). She was also the winner in *Brussels*, where Sue Olley came fourth. Linda Martin barraged for first place with Madsen at *Aarhus* in Denmark. Hilary Cawthorne travelled considerably. As far afield as *Iran* she came third and the same month she was in the other hemisphere, coming tenth in *Montreal* (where Linda Martin was 16th). Nearer home, the 27-year-old diminutive Maggie Riley of Cardiff won the *Irish Open*.

# Competitions chronicle 1974–5

The revival came in the *de Beaumont Cup*, the quality and number of the 23 foreign entrants creating an atmosphere of excitement that had not been seen for some years. Revived too was Clare Halsted, who was sixth. The other British finalist and the only one to beat Max Madsen of Denmark, was Susan Green, but she could not quite sustain the sureness of timing she had shown in earlier rounds and ended fifth on two wins. The Pole Skladanowska was third between the E. German Eltz and Dick. Clare Halsted was second in both the *Desprez* and the *Jubilee Bowl* (missing the Championship through illness); while Susan Green, though striking few sparks abroad, was the winner in both these events, beating Clare in the barrage of the former and snatching the decisive bout back from her at 3–1 down in the latter. She was also third in the Championship. Wendy Ager and Sue Wrigglesworth had both gone out in the semi-final of the Desprez. Hilary Cawthorne lost only to the two leaders. Jill Dudley (Thames, 2v), Angela Herbert (Boston, 1v) and Alda Milner-Barry (Thames, 0v) did well to gain final places.

Hilary Cawthorne repeated her third place in the Silver Jubilee and came second in the *Championship*. Here it was Susan Wrigglesworth who made it to the top of the slippery pole for the first time, nobody hitting her more than twice. Potential rivals such as Wendy Ager, Sally Littlejohns and Sue Olley came unstuck in the quarter-finals. Seizing their opportunity, Sue Lewis (née Youngs; 2v, 4th), Linda Martin (2v, 5th) and Valerie Windram, now of Brownhill, (1v, 6th) were all first-time finalists.

The premier provincial event, now at *Birmingham*, was won by Sue Lewis, who beat Linda Brown, Caryl Oliver and Val Windram in successive rounds of the knockout. The *Welsh Open* was won by Sue Harris after a barrage with Val Windram (2nd) and Audrey Bennett (Cardiff FC). Maggie Riley, already runner-up at *Leicester*, was fourth. Maggie Browning was the winner at *Portsmouth*. Linda Brown was second. Together with Maggie Riley and Karen Eyton, she won the team event for Cardiff by a decisive 5–1 over Boston.

Earlier in the season the cheerful, well-built Angela Herbert of Boston had returned to the scene to capture a fiercely but intelligently contested *Bertrand Cup* in a 4–3 barrage against the rising Ann Brannon of Chester. Janet Jones (3v) was third. Caryl Oliver (Boston, 2v), the winner at *Redbridge*, was fourth, ahead of Caryl Holland (Latista, 1v) and Shiel Toller (Thames, 1v).

Earlier still in the *Toupie Lowther* the position had been reversed, with Ann Brannon the winner and Angela Herbert the runner-up (ahead of Yvonne Grammar), and Angela was only sixth in the *Parker Trophy*, behind Barbara East on one win. Ann Brannon (3v) was third that time, between Pam Patient of Reading (3v) and Elizabeth Spires (2v), who sadly died later of leukaemia. The undefeated winner was Brenda Hewitt, yet another pupil of Les Jones at Ashton, who also came fifth in the *Perigal Cup* and again in the *Under-20 Championship* – both of which were won by the cool Elizabeth Wood of Boston in barrages, the latter with Janet Jones and the former with Caroline Hall,

Janet Jones and Kathy Keuls, who ended in that order. In the *Senior Schoolgirls Championship*, Janet Jones was the winner, followed by Clare Montgomery. Sophie Arup of Godolphin and Latymer, London, was the *Under-14* Champion.

Brenda Hewitt rose to her peak when she won the *Millfield Under-20 Tournament*, ahead of Astalosch of W. Germany, Connie Beagrie of York (the winner at *Nottingham*) and Elizabeth Wood (4th). Austrians took the other two places.

The not-quite-official *Under-20 Team Championship* was won by Salle Boston 5–2 over Ashton and ushered Caroline, another member of the Arup family, into prominence (Wood 3, Arup 2, East 0/3; Hewitt 1, Hall 1, Jones 0/3). In a quadrangular at *Dornbirn* Lynne Taylor, Caroline Hall, Brenda Hewitt, Liz Wood and Caroline Arup beat Austria, Switzerland and Czechoslovakia. The senior *Team Championship* had 22 entries. The semi-finalists were as expected, but not the results. Ashton lost to Boston and LFC to Thames. In the final Clare Halsted scored magnificently 4–0, 4–0, 4–1, 4–1 to take Thames to its first victory by 7 hits. Jill Dudley got two wins, Wendy Ager one and Alda Milner-Barry one. Caryl Oliver got three of Boston's wins, Hilary Cawthorne and Sue Lewis two each and Julia Single one.

Back in September a British team won a *Danish match* 9–7 (A. Milner-Barry 3, L. Martin 2, H. Cawthorne 2, J. Single 2). In April there was a 9–7 loss to W. Germany, which some thought might have been a win with different presiding (S. Wrigglesworth 2, S. Green 2, H. Cawthorne 2, W. Ager 1). The same weekend a 'B' team beat the Swiss 9–7 (L. Martin 3, A. Herbert 2, A. Milner-Barry 2, S. Littlejohns 2). In May Germany and Belgium were defeated in three-a-side matches in Brussels. Wendy Ager and Hilary Cawthorne picked up the five wins in each match, only Sue Olley failing to score.

The World Championship team was unchanged except that Clare Halsted returned, filling the place of Sally Littlejohns, who had retired.

*EPEE*

A delighted John Hall of Thames won the *Junior Championship* after being frustrated in the finals of the three previous years. He was master in charge of fencing at St Paul's and though heavily built and apparently more suited to rugby, one of several sports he pursued, he possessed great speed as well as a good technique. The rapidly improving John Llewellyn, now a pupil of Frank Tanner at Reading FC, was second. He lost to Hall on assault point, but also succumbed to Robbie Phelps, the experienced pentathlete from Gloucester (2v; 4th). Trailing on hits in third place was Jonathan Stanbury, who beat Hall when he had already secured the title, but lost to another improving epeeist,

David Brooks (2v, 5th), fencing for Corby FC but also a pupil of John Fairhall, of wispy build, who had a capacity for deceptive disengages. Brierley of the Army (ov) returned to the final after an absence of three years.

Llewellyn was evidently absent from the *Under-20 Championship* (along with Bruniges, whose injured leg precluded his chance of a hat-trick). It was won by Paul Tarran on a 5–3 barrage with Hugh Kernohan of Lothian, to whom he had lost in the pool. Martin Gilbert of Merchant Taylors (3v; 3rd) was followed by David Fairhall, Prof. Fairhall's son (2v), Pip Emberson (1v) and Peter Young of Millfield (1v), who produced the barrage by beating Kernohan 5–2.

Neal Mallett won the *Under-19 Championship* for Dover College after a barrage with Gilbert. N. Allen beat David Rapley for third place.

At *Zofingen* in Switzerland an Under-20 team did badly in a *quadrangular with Austria, Switzerland and Poland*, but Bruniges did excellently to win the individual event, ahead of Poffet. Llewellyn did very promisingly to come fifth. At *Wattenscheid* it was Emberson's turn to win – an outstanding performance in a final which included Pusch. George Jaron of Poly did well to get to the quarter-final. Llewellyn and Mallett reached the third round. In January at *Genoa* Tarran reached the third round and Llewellyn the semi-finals of a tough event. At the *Schmetz*, the premier Under-20 event, Emberson got to the third round, Bruniges reached the quarter-finals and Tarran the semi-finals.

In the provincial events Osbaldeston came top at *Inverclyde*, ahead of Bob Turner, Pip Emberson, John Fairhall, John Llewellyn and Julian Tyson. Howard West won at *Leicester*, ahead of Hall, Brooks (winner at *Nottingham*), Beevers, Lennox and Emberson. Reading, led by an undefeated Llewellyn, won the *Portsmouth* team event. At *Birmingham* Ralph Evans was the victor, on home ground, over Steve Lavington while Brooks gained the bronze medal in the fight-off with Bryan Lewis. The *Epee Club Cup*, which was now revived as a one-day event of two poule uniques for invited fencers from the provinces and from the national squad, was won by Beevers, followed by Paul and Belson. Fox was *Inter-Services* Champion for the third time and the *Martini Qualifying* event was headed by Johnson.

The *Martini* itself included 71 foreigners, five World Champions, two Junior World Champions and a galaxy of talent. The holder, Poffet, went out in the first round and Kulcsar, Fenyvesi, Hoskyns and Johnson in the second. In the direct elimination from 32 Bourne lost 10–8 to Loetscher and Davenport 11–10 to the 1972 winner Muck. Others lost more heavily: Belson 10–3 to Suchanecki, Paul 10–4 to Kauter, Bill Forward 10–5 to Matwiejew of Poland and Partridge 10–5 to Munster of Denmark.

The sole remaining Briton was Noel, who devastated Fischer of W. Germany 10–2. In the last sixteen he beat C. Morch of Norway 10–3, but couldn't carry over his good form to the Seymour Hall and find the answer to

1975 Martini: it takes the giant World Champion Edling to stem Bourne's whirlwind fleche.

Champion at Poitiers: Tim Belson on the shoulders of Bourne and Pearman.

the speed and accuracy of Jacobson of Sweden, the 1973 World Silver Medallist. He lost 10–1.

In the other quarter-final bouts the Swedes Flodstrom and Edling beat Loestscher and Munster 10–9 and 9–8 (on time) respectively, and the Polish Wiech beat the Swiss Suchanecki 10–5. In the semi-finals Flodstrom beat his club-mate Jacobson 10–9 and Edling beat Wiech 10–3. A slightly uncertain Edling then faced Flodstrom, who combined great speed with accuracy and acute timing to win 10–9.

The *Championship* possessed better drama and surprise. Eliminated in the quarters were Jacobs (along with Mark West and John Warburn) Noel (with Higginson and Stanbury), Davenport (with D. Fairhall and M. Fare) and Hill (with Lewis and Brierley). The seeding produced by the rule book in the semi-finals was very unbalanced. Partridge (ov), Hudson (iv) and Johnson (2v) were eliminated from the first, Tatrallyay (ov), Hall (2v) and Murch (2v) from the second; those promoted from the first won ten fights in all in the final, those from the second only five.

The title nearly went to Hoskyns: he beat Bourne, the holder, 5–3, and only lost to Belson 5–all, in the very first bout; but he also lost to Beevers on assault point. Alternatively Beevers could have barraged for it if Osbaldeston (2v; 5th) had not gained a surprise win over him in his last bout. As it was, the Championship fell to a jubilant Tim Belson in spite of his 5–2 loss to Bourne (who was third, on hits behind Hoskyns but ahead of Beevers). Evans (0v), with a delicate, elusive style was in his first national final.

There were four Austrians and five Norwegians in the *Miller-Hallett*. Only five of these survived as far as the quarter-final pools of four, from which were ousted Single and Stanbury; Davenport and Hill; Partridge and Gray; Tatrallyay and Tyson; Paul and Osbaldeston and Llewellyn and M. West. Belson, Noel and H. West were victims of the semis, with the Morch brothers and Niedermuller. Bourne was on better form this time but was beaten 5–2 in the final and just outreached again in the barrage by Muller of Austria (winner in 1971), whose casual manner disguised very fast reactions. It was the 17-year-old Koppang of Norway (3v; 3rd) who forced the fight-off. Hoskyns (4th) beat the two other Britons: Beevers (1v) and Hudson (1v), both now at Poly.

The same weekend there were *matches against Norway and Austria*. GB 'A' beat Norway 11–5 (Bourne 4, Paul 4, Hoskyns 2, Belson 2) and Austria 14–2 (Belson and Bourne dropping one each). The 'B' Team lost to Norway 10–6 (Davenport 3, Beevers 1, Johnson 1, Noel 1); but they beat Austria 12–4 (Noel 4, Davenport 3, Johnson 3, Beevers 2).

Back in February a scratch team had lost a *match against Belgium* at Duren. After the Martini there were *matches against five countries*. The 'A' team lost to the W. German Olympic Silver Medallists 11–5 (Bourne 2, Hoskyns 2, Paul 1, Belson 0); to Switzerland 8–7 (Bourne 2, Johnson 2, Noel 2, Paul 1) and to Poland 11–5 (Johnson 2, Bourne 1, Hoskyns 1, Paul 1). The 'B' Team beat a by no means weak Denmark 8–6 (Johnson 3, Hudson 3, Hall 2, Davenport 0) and against Brazil 12–4 (Hall 4, Beevers 3, Johnson 2, Hudson 2).

There were some extremely good individual results abroad this season (as well as poor patches). Very promisingly, Stanbury came sixth at *Duren* (Hoskyns, Hudson and Hill reaching the quarter-finals). The same month he got to the last 48 in the *Monal*, along with Hoskyns, Johnson and Belson. Thereafter dental training preoccupied him.

At *Bern* Graham Paul got his best ever result, spurred on by his brother's success in the Rommel. On the Saturday he scraped from round to round but on the Sunday he took fire. Undefeated in the third round pool of six, he was undefeated again in the quarter-final pool of four and yet again in the semi-final pool of four where he beat Hehn, S. Erdos and Cessac. Sadly, during the break before the final he lost his edge and had to be content with sixth place with one win, behind the Pusch brothers, Erdos and Giger. Beevers got to the quarter-finals; Bourne, Belson and Davenport to the fourth round.

At *Heidenheim* Bourne got to the last 32 by beating Torok (Hungary), but then lost to Duchene (France). At the same stage Belson beat the 1976 Silver Medallist, Hehn, and only lost 12–11 to Ladegaillerie, that of 1972. At *Catania* Noel reached the semi-finals and Johnson the quarter-finals.

In May at the medium-strength *Innsbruck* event Belson and Beevers were semi-finalists. Britain here won a *match against Austria* 10–6 (Beevers 3, Davenport 3, Belson 2, Johnson 2), but lost a *match against Switzerland* 9–7 (Belson 3, Johnson 3, Beevers 1, Davenport 0).

The bevy of matches came to a climax with the *Eight-Nations Tournament at Tauberbischofsheim*. Czechoslovakia was beaten 11–4 and Rumania 8–all, but Germany 'B' won on hits and less than full-strength Swedish and Italian teams by 9–7. Fencing in six of these matches, Belson got 14 wins, Bourne 13 and Noel 6. Fencing in five of them Beevers scored 11 and Hoskyns 5.

At a team event in *Genoa*, Evans, Lewis and Hudson – all residents of Oxford – reached the direct elimination stage, against strong Italian clubs and other foreign teams.

The greatest moment of the season was at *Poitiers*, a classic event if smaller and less strong than Heidenheim, and one of the very few to attract the Russians. Tim Belson and Ralph Johnson barraged for first place with Wiech of Poland – and Belson won. A great triumph for Belson and a much-needed result for Johnson, who otherwise would have been dropped from the team for the first time since he joined it. A superb 5–4, 5–3 win over Modzolevski to reach the last four was evidence of the form he could produce to reach a final when he needed to. Bourne reached the last sixteen.

At *Berlin*, among many world class epeeists, Johnson and Beevers did well to top up their results by reaching the semi-final. In the lesser event at *Toulon* Mike Mayo of Scotland was a creditable semi-finalist. Just before the referendum Bourne won the *Common Market Cup* in Brussels from representatives of the other eight. Finally in *Moulins* Graham Paul was the winner. Johnson was second and Belson sixth. In a *match against a French 'B' team* Britain won 11–5.

For the World Championships the team consisted of Bourne, Johnson, Belson and Paul, plus Beevers in place of Hoskyns.

In the home *Team Championship* Boston beat Paul in the semi-final, while Thames beat the army in a match that could have gone either way up to the end. The final was even closer. Thames included Hoskyns (in exchange for Excalibur having borrowed Noel the previous year) and he won three fights for them, but this wasn't quite enough. In the last fight Noel needed to beat Johnson 5–2 to force a tie: he managed 5–3, but left Boston winners by one hit. (Bourne 3, Morch – working in Newcastle – 2, Davenport 2, Johnson 1; Noel 2, Hall 2, Jacobs 1.)

## SABRE

The *Under-16* title was won by the Mauritius-born Collin Tourmentin, who was at Catford under Prof. Fairhall, one of several successes for the school at different weapons this season. Runner-up was Max Visholm of Hereford School, Grimsby, ahead of the jocular Kenric Li of Brentwood on hits. The *Senior Schoolboys* title, now re-styled Under-19, went to Slade, but only after being 4–all in a barrage with Andrew Cashen of the SW. Third was Chris Webb, of Brentwood, who was undefeated winner of the *Public Schools*, though Li ran him a close second, losing on the last hit.

Webb was fourth in the *Under-20 Championships*, exactly equal with Jonathan Lewis, the previous holder, now at Manchester University, and three hits given ahead of Cary Zitcer of Kings Cross. The winner was Ross Campion, now at Salle Paul, taught by Prof. Moldovanyi, who was taken to the last hit only by Slade (3rd). Streater was runner-up with four wins.

Moderate success was gained in two Under-20 internationals. At the very strong *Göppingen* event there were nine British among the 96 entrants. Slade and Lewis reached the quarter-finals (4th round). They and Campion reached the same stage at *Koblenz*.

The *Junior* was thirty strong. 23 spectators watched a good but temperamental final. Slade smoothly led the field at first, with four wins, including one over Price, who had been sixth, third and second in the three previous seasons. Then Slade lost 5–1 to Wasilewski (2v; 4th). So he faced a barrage with Price. Technically interesting, this alternated to 4–all; but Price got the last hit. Dennis Hutt of LFC impressed with his fencing and his equanimity, and came third. Robert Neal was fifth on one win, a few hits ahead of Gryf-Lowczowski.

Deanfield's technical superiority won him the *Cole Cup* in spite of his being in the run-up to medical finals. He lost only to Philbin, who, on three wins, was a few hits behind Cohen and ahead of David Eden. Zarno (2v) and Taylor (0v) followed.

Hutt rose to new heights in the *Championship*, knocking Mather out of the semi-finals (along with Wasilewski and Bradbury). Oldcorn and Eden were among the big names who had departed even earlier. The winner for the first time was Deanfield, whose technique, together with Hutt's enthusiasm, saved the final from lethargy. He lost only to Cohen, who in turn lost, from 4–1 up, to Hutt and by 5–2 to Taylor (3v, 3rd) and was thus second once again on hits. Bryan Lewis, fourth in his first senior final, got 5–1 wins over Hutt (2v; 5th) and Scott (1v; 6th).

In the *Corble*, Cohen finally came first, in the absence of Deanfield, but against formidable foreign opposition, including Brasseur (2v; 5th), the winner in 1968, and Gomez (0v; 6th), who again won at *Birmingham* (by 8–6 over Oustende, having beaten Wiles in the semi-final). Cohen beat Storme in the barrage by 5–4, in fine form. Philbin, fencing with his usual dash, but getting upset over decisions, was third on hits over Kaufman, the third Belgian.

Cohen also won *Leicester* for the second year running. Wiles was *Inverclyde* champion for the fourth successive time, and the eighth time in nine years.

The *Team Championship* made up in closeness what it lacked in novelty. Poly beat Boston 'B' and Boston 'A' beat Salle Paul in the semi-finals, both by 9–2. The final progressed by spasms of argument interspersed with fencing to the point where Poly led 8–3. They failed to deliver the coup de grace, however, and with Etherton beating Deanfield 5–3 in the final bout the match ended 8–8, 62–62. Deanfield won the fight-off with Cohen 5–4, so Poly retained the cup by the narrowest possible margin. (Deanfield 3, Philbin 2, Eden 2, Lewis 1; Cohen 3, Mather 2, Etherton 2, Zarno 1.)

The international season effectively started in February when Cohen and Philbin did well to reach the last twelve at *Graz*, which, though small, included Hungarians, Italians and Germans. At *Hamburg*, one of the strongest events, Oldcorn Price and Taylor reached the last 48, the latter missing the quarter-finals on hits. Here there were *matches against four countries* by various combinations of Cohen, Zarno, Philbin, Taylor and Eden. A 9–3 loss to W. Germany (Cohen 2v) was hardly bettered against Germany 'B', with two wins apiece. Against Hungary, Cohen and Philbin alone scored in a 14–2 walkover. The best result was 6–10 against Poland: Taylor, Philbin and Cohen each won two.

In *Budapest*, as strong as any event, Deanfield got to the last 48. And in *Munich*, which attracted French, Austrians and Rumanians, Cohen and Oldcorn got to the last 24. In the Brussels *Decade Sportive* Philbin gained second place. Mid-season he had been persuaded to move south and showed significant improvement under Prof. Imregi.

The team for the World Championships was Deanfield, Cohen, Philbin, Oldcorn and Taylor. Mather hardly fenced, though he reached two national semi-finals. Lewis, all but selected, was reserve.


*COMBINED EVENTS*

The *World Youth Championships* were held in the Olympic Stadium in Mexico City. For the sake of television, each weapon was compressed into one day; the heat, diet and altitude added to the strain on fencers.

At men's foil, Wedge was disappointingly ousted in the first round pools of four with one win. Glaister, however, reached the quarter-finals after topping his first two rounds. Bruniges also went out here with only one win, his knee injury still handicapping him. Kuki of Rumania was the winner for the second year running.

Lynne Taylor reached the second round, and only went out on hits. Liz Wood and Brenda Hewitt both got to the quarter-finals (third round). Trinquet of France won.

At epee Emberson came unstuck with one win in the first round and although Llewellyn did well by topping his first-round pool and beating Boisse, he went out in the second round, along with Bruniges, on two victories. The title was again retained by the holder Poffet.

Sabre proved no respite: a nervously indecisive Slade got only one first round win, while J. Lewis, after beating the Polish champion and Pinto (Brazil), lost his other two fights, the last one 5–4 to Sullivan of USA, apparently suffering from poor judging and presiding.

The gloom was assuaged by David Eden's successful sabre presiding from first round to final, combined with both captaincy and honeymoon!

The *Public Schools Championships* were won by St Paul's for the first time since 1958. Reynolds, showing something of his father's classical technique, snatched the foil title from Mallett on the last hit in a four-way barrage. Mallett was also runner-up in the epee, to Simon Webb, another Pauline, whose brother Andrew won the junior foil. Chris Webb of Brentwood, who won the sabre, was no relation, however.

At *Ashton*, in a gala triangular match, the French were the victors. More remarkably, the Welsh team comprising Maggie Riley, Turner, Lewis and Gareth Evans came within two hits of defeating the English team which comprised Sue Green, Johnson, Philbin and Grimmett. In the individual epee Turner came second to Teintenier.

The *Quadrangular* was held in Cardiff rather than in N. Ireland, owing to the troubles. England, combining the youthful and the experienced, won yet again, beating Scotland 20–16, Wales 21–15 and N. Ireland 30–6. Scotland beat Wales narrowly 19–17 for second place, Campbell, Elliott and Beattie winning the foil 9–0 and Wales taking the sabre 6–3 (Lewis 3, Edwards 2, Norrie 1) and the ladies' foil 7–2 (Riley 3, Brown 2, Bennett 2). Mike Mayo won three of the Scots' 5–4 wins at epee.

There was almost complete television coverage for the finals of the *World Championships* in Budapest. An exhibition of fencing history was mounted too, and a special stamp issued. Sadly, the hosts won no Gold Medals, for only the third time in fifty years.

The men's foil saw the exit of Glaister in round one, though with a good win over Isiakov of Russia. In round two Grimmett used his attacks to effect, only going down on hits to an eventual finalist and two semi-finalists. Bell and Graham Paul also went out at this stage. Barry Paul reached the next round, the last 48. Noel and Talvard took both Gold and Silver for France for the first time in ten years.

In the team event Spain was only overcome by a single hit, Bell winning three fights; but by contrast Hungary was taken to 7–8, Graham Paul winning three. Defeat came rapidly in the direct elimination at the hands of Italy, themselves narrow losers in the semis.

All five Britons survived the ladies' first round, Susan Wrigglesworth and Hilary Cawthorne topping their pools. The latter was in excellent form, making fine use of second intention. In the second round Clare Halsted fenced strongly and was promoted with two eventual finalists, as was Susan Wrigglesworth by the skin of her teeth; but the other three were knocked out.

In the last 48, Susan, over-reliant on her long attacks, could go no further; but Clare put up a tremendous fight in a pool with the eventual finalist Wysoczanska and Rejto, the twice World Champion and 1973 Bronze Medallist. She only went out from 3–all in a barrage.

The team event unfortunately put Britain in a pool with Italy, greatly under-seeded, as well as Poland. Both won 11–5. Clare Halsted continued on form, beating three Poles.

There were only 88 sabreurs. Deanfield, though fencing in a tough first round pool, denied himself hits through impatience and 'misdirected sportsmanship' and went out by one hit with three wins. Cohen was far below his high level of the early season and Taylor was also off form. In the second round of the last 48, Oldcorn's riposte and stop-hit, his main assets, did not quite have the needful edge. Philbin fenced on equal terms in select company and only just missed promotion to the quarter-finals.

In the team event, headlong onslaught by Spain (again) got the British 4–0 down before they climbed back to 9–7 (Deanfield and Philbin each winning three). After losing to Hungary, they were rather quickly dispatched in the knock-out by France. In the final, Nazlimov, winner of the individual, carried Russia to a 9–7 victory over Hungary with four wins and a loss of only six hits.

Disappointingly, Johnson, losing his end-of-season form, as well as an over-tense Beevers, went out of the first round of the epee. In by far the two hardest second round pools Bourne sailed through, but Paul came fifth, while Belson inexplicably went out by one hit in a weak pool. Bourne was in better form than all season until, in the last 48, and leading Osztrics of Hungary 4–2 in the last minute of his key fight he seemed suddenly to be hit by mental exhaustion and was unable to adapt tactically – forgivably in a temperature of 94°, high humidity and stale air, which probably accounted for the premature departure of other leading epeeists (including Edling in the semi-finals). 21-year-old Pusch won, ahead of Lukomsky and Osztrics – the first German ever to win.

After yet another bad start in the team event, the British beat Turkey 10–6, Bourne winning four. There ensued a tremendous match against Switzerland.

Paul replaced Beevers and Johnson recovered form. Britain led 8–4, the Swiss fought back to 7–8; then Belson took his fourth win, and the match, with a thundering counter-attack at 4–all. This was the first win over the Swiss over six matches. Unfortunately, the good form was fleeting and Rumania extinguished hopes in the next round. The Swiss went on to beat Russia 9–1, but lost to W. Germany, who in turn lost to Sweden, Edling now being undefeated.

After presiding half the individual sabre final, David Eden received the ultimate accolade when he took the whole team final, no-one else being acceptable to both sides.

# 1975–6

## MEN'S FOIL

The *National Schoolboys Under-14* Championship was won by Louis Skelton of London, undefeated, followed by Simon Baldry (Whitgift), Mark Wright (George Heriot's), Justin Pitman (11-year-old son and pupil of Prof. Pitman), Tim Spiers (St Paul's) and Lloyd Ingleson (Catford). A. Thompson of E. Section (4v) was the *Under-16* Champion, followed by Alan Tait (St Peter's, York, winner of the *Junior Public Schools*; 3v), Gosbee (3v), Andy Brannon (Chester; 2v) and David Lakey (2v) and David Brown (1v), both of Catford. Richard Hill of Whitgift won the *Under-19 Championships* (over Glenn Jones) as well as the *Public Schools Championship*. Matthew Chell of Brentwood (fourth in the Under-19s) won the *Wilkinson Trophy* by 10–1 over Andrew Webb of St Paul's.

For the *Under-20 Championship* there was a different and more seasoned cast. Glaister was the winner, only being hit eight times. Bruniges (now back in London and at Salle Boston), beat everybody else. Harper in turn beat the other three, who each had one win: the 18-year-old Duncan Paterson of Meadowbank (4th) and – equal on hits – Ford and Tim Smith (Wandsworth School). The *Under-20 Team Championship*, now official but in its final year, was won for the second time running by the Hydra team of Glaister, Kay and Jones, though they were hard-pressed by the Goodall team of Harper, David Seaman and Graham Watts. The event was contested by only six teams and was therefore arranged as a poule unique which also yielded an individual winner, but only in the very last fight when Glaister and Harper met, both undefeated. Harper easily took the first three hits, but Glaister fought back with skill and resilience to win 5–3. The lower places were taken by Seaman, Jones, Jervis Rhodes (Dulwich College) and Graham Kay.

Pierre Harper was the winner of the *Junior Championship*. Now eighteen, he was half French and had begun fencing in ILEA evening institute classes. A credit to his master, Roy Goodall, he was very fit and keen and developed an excellent technique. He only required more experience and confidence to reach a high level of performance. He achieved last-hit wins over the two Bostonians Tyson (3v, 2nd) and Fox (2v, 3rd). Frank Hindle (4th) and Mark Thompson (5th) each had two wins. Waldman only beat Tyson.

In the *Millfield Under-20 International* Bruniges lapsed into second place behind Robak of Poland, although once again ahead of Siffels. The *University Championship* was carried off by Wedge, now at Manchester. No one hit him more than once except Murray (4th), who took him to assault point. He was followed by Beattie (4v) and Ford (3v). Carson beat Chetwood to come fifth.

Abroad, the Under-20s had a good run, six of them qualifying for the World Youth Championships by mid-January, and no less than 36 scoring some result. Graham Kay was fifth at *Gelsenkirchen* and in the last eight at *Budapest* (which was headed by Lossius and Dal Zotto) and got five other qualifiers. John Ford was eighth at Gelsenkirchen and got four other qualifiers. Pierre Harper was sixth in the (senior) *Flanders Golden Foil*, in which Fox reached the last twelve, Single the last eight and Bell came fourth. Harper also made the semi-final at *Duisburg*. Rob Collins, though in no final, got three qualifiers. Duncan Paterson reached semi-finals at Gelsenkirchen (with Mike Peat of Edinburgh University) and barraged for third place at Budapest. Donald McKenzie of Trinity School, Edinburgh, was fifth in the *Brussels* Under-16 event. Gosbee scored a creditable win at *Le Havre*, albeit a lesser event; Howard Bailey was eighth and David Seaman and Graham Watts (both Goodall) were in the semi-final. Mark Thompson was in the semi-final at *Basel*. Bruniges kept a low profile until late on in the Under-20 season, when he burst forth to a win at *Heilbronn*.

Glaister, the leader in the Under-20 points scheme, scored his main successes in senior events. He reached the fourth round of the *Martini*, along with Fox and Evans. Graham Paul reached the last 32. In the *Duval*, Bruniges, starting his comeback, reached the last sixteen, as did Barry Paul and Grimmett. Graham came an excellent fifth. In the *Rommel*, the third Paris event, Glaister reached the third round and Barry the last 24.

If not showing quite the sparkle and dominance of the previous season, Barry Paul got at least one excellent result when he reached the last twelve in *Budapest* and collected an Olympic Qualification. Evans did well to reach the last sixteen at *Magdeburg* and Bell and Barry to get to the last eight. At *Bonn* Bell reached the third round and Graham the last 32. In *Brussels* Fox was 24th, Evans 23rd and Glaister 18th in a poule unique of 33. At *Bad Durkheim* Tony Bartlett was in the last 32. Finally, at *Bologna* Barry got to the last 24.

In *international matches* the British had a narrow five-a-side 13–12 loss to the Racing Club de France, which included Noel and Berolatti (both Pauls and Grimmett got three wins, Bruniges two and Glaister one). In the Coupe d'Europe, Salle Paul got a creditable 9–7 win over Bucharest to reach the last eight (G. Paul 3, Bell 3, B. Paul 2, Grimmett 1). In Magdeburg a half-strength team lost to *E. Germany* 'B' 9–7 and to *Hungary* 9–6.

Back at home the *Emrys Lloyd* Cup was won by Bell, now aged 25. Second was Teddy Bourne, ahead of Graham Paul.

The *Coronation Cup*, in February, showed that Bruniges had now fully got over the leg injury of the previous season, though lapses of concentration alternated with his flashes of brilliance. He yielded the cup to Graham Paul, fencing with characteristic determination from 4–1 down, and all his bouts were decided on the last hit, except with the stylish Soumagne, whom he relegated to third place by 5–0. Grimmett collected three competent wins well clear of the American Ashley. Barry Paul's unaccustomed nil wins were attributed to a sprained ankle.

The *Championship* was held in the recently-built Sobell Sports Centre in Islington, with a final by direct elimination, a divertissement and an audience of two hundred. Barry Paul was now back on top, gaining the hat trick after beating his brother 10–8 in the semi-final and Bruniges 10–6 in a final bout of outstanding quality in which he held back his attacks until precisely the right moment to avoid those devastating ripostes that Bruniges could produce from seemingly impossible positions. Derrick Cawthorne, sixteen years after winning the title, was fourth. Before losing 10–6 to Bruniges, he had beaten Bell, top seed of the last eight, by 10–7. He fenced with a crispness and control that made many of his younger opponents look clumsy. The others in the last eight were Fox (who lost 10–2 to Barry), Grimmett (who lost 10–6 to Graham) and Glaister (who lost 10–4 to Bruniges).

Barry Paul was the eighth person since the inception of the Championship in 1898 to win three times; more strikingly, he was only the fourth person ever to win three times in a row. J. Jenkinson did it in 1902–4, R. Montgomerie in 1908–10 and Emrys Lloyd in 1930–33. Since then, nobody.

In the *Spartan Tournament*, held in a newly-opened shopping mall in Birmingham, Bell was the winner, ahead of Loveland, Fox, Beevers, Graham Guenigault and Cawthorne. At *Nottingham* John Ford did well to win and the aggressive Scott to come second, both ahead of Glaister. At *Birmingham* there was direct elimination from the last eight. C. Noel beat B. Paul 10–4; G. Paul beat Soumagne 10–8; Leseur beat Crahay 10–4; Grimmett beat Menon 10–3. In the semi-finals C. Noel beat G. Paul 10–3 and Grimmett beat Leseur 10–9. Noel beat Grimmett for the title by 10–4. Leseur got third place from Graham Paul by 10–5. Tyson scored a notable double first at the *Inverclyde* and in the *Scottish Championship*. Barry Paul won for the third time running at *Tyneside*.

The *Team Championship* was a close repeat of the previous year. Salle Paul beat Thames 9–4. Once again the Pauls got two each with one to go; this time Grimmett did likewise, while Single got three wins. The Thames members reversed themselves: Bell got three, Halsted one and Fare none, each with one to go, while it was Eames's turn to score a blank.

The Olympic team was the same as the previous year, except that Bruniges was back and Single had retired.

## LADIES' FOIL

At the junior end of the scale Fiona McIntosh, taught by Prof. Bracewell at Lansdowne House, Edinburgh, and at Lothian FC, began her upward climb by winning the *Under-16 Championship* undefeated, ahead of Ann Charles and Kim Cecil. She was also runner-up in the *Felix Cup*, *Scottish* Champion and third in the *Spitzer* in July. In the *Under-18 Championship* Debbie Hall of Millfield lost only to Ann Brannon in the final and beat her in the barrage. Helen Griffiths and Pippa Bell also took third and sixth places for Millfield. The international event bearing the name of Millfield moved to London, however. In spite of 23 foreigners, including W. Germans, Swiss, Dutch and Austrians, Ann Brannon came third, Liz Wood fourth and Brenda Hewitt sixth in an excellent final which was dominated by Losert, Austrian World Youth finalist.

The stylish and intelligent Ann Brannon of Chester FC, who was noted for her flunge (half lunge, half fleche), won the Felix Cup, reached the last sixteen in the strong field at *Gelsenkirchen* and came fourth in the *Under-20 Championship* (on hits from the second and third). Under-20 Champion was Janet Jones, defeated only by Moira Dignan (another pupil of Bert Bracewell, at Meadowbank), and she did well to come fourth at Duisberg. Brenda Hewitt, also of Ashton, second in the Under-20, was winner of the *Bertrand* in a barrage with Lorna Andrews of Boston – followed by Sue Harris (now at Thames), Pat Casey, Jane Law and Margaret Riley.

But it was Liz Wood (now at Salle Paul), still only seventeen, who rose meteorically. Third in the Under-20, she reached the last sixteen at *Duren*, was second at *Duisburg*, winner at *Inverclyde*, and then astounded everyone by barraging for first place in the *Championship* and only losing 5–4 (ladies' bouts now being for the same score as men's). Her coolness on the piste almost amounted to indifference; her stop-hits and counter-attacks could be devastating.

There was a wide spread of finalists in the two lower Category competitions. Anne Tetlow of Poly was undefeated winner of the *Toupie Lowther*. Sheila Gallagher (a pupil of Geoff Tonks at Maria Fidelis School who was also fourth in the Under-18 Championship) was third and Lindy Prys-Roberts of Behmber sixth. The *Parker* final was an agreeable mixture of old and new faces, of the metropolitan and the far flung (including a stronger entry from

The Championship at the Sobell Centre: P. Harper v G. Grimmett (D. Eden and N. Halsted judging).

Spartan Tournament: Steve Fox's speed is too much for Martin Beevers.

the NE, attributed to Pat Pearson's coaching there). Till near the end it was very open, but then Lesley Hamments of Paladin Sword Club asserted her dominance and beat both Yvonne Grammar (2v, 6th) and Sue Holman of Avalon (3v, 2nd) by 5–1. Mavis Bragg of Brownhill was third, ahead of Moira Dignan on hits with two wins.

*Nottingham* was won by Marilyn Worster ahead of Maggie Browning and Lynne Taylor. The *Spartan Trophy* went to Hilary Cawthorne over Linda Martin. At *Birmingham* in the last eight Linda beat Debbie Hall 10–4, José Lambert beat Schlettweiss 10–6, Lorna Andrews beat Marilyn Worster 10–7 and Hilary Cawthorne beat Ann Brannon 10–4. In the last four Linda Martin beat José Lambert 10–2 and Hilary Cawthorne beat Lorna Andrews 10–6. For third place José Lambert beat Lorna Andrews 8–4. Linda Martin took the title 10–6. The *Meadowbank Open* fell to Lynne Taylor, ahead of Jackie Jamieson (Lothian), Fiona McIntosh, Moira Dignan, Alison Simpson (Meadowbank) and Catherine Robertson (Ainslie Park).

Linda Martin swelled her successes by winning the *Welsh Open*, and at *Redbridge* and *Leicester*. Her fine style, length and competitive sparkle also brought her the supreme triumph of winning the *Championship*. Here the final was almost a complete reversal of the previous year. Sue Wrigglesworth, the holder, was sixth, only beating Hilary Cawthorne, who was down to fifth from second. She in turn beat Wendy Ager, who had moved on to LFC (2v, 4th).

Clare Halsted was third with three wins, but as on other occasions, asserted her class in foreign company, being fourth and the only British finalist in the *de Beaumont Cup*, the others being Weniger, Palm, Dick, Madsen and Gosch, in that order. Now 27 and a medical student after gaining a doctorate in bio-chemistry, through hard work and application she was achieving mature results. She reached the last twelve at *Duren*, the last sixteen at *Magdeburg* and the last 24 of the *Jeanty*. She was the winner at *Salzburg*, with Linda Martin second, Wendy Ager third and Hilary Cawthorne sixth.

With admirable economy of effort, Sue Wrigglesworth, now 21, won the *Desprez Cup* undefeated. In a symmetrical manner, she was followed by Hilary Cawthorne, Wendy Ager, Sally Littlejohns, Linda Martin and Janet Jones, each losing to those above them.

Wendy Ager, now aged 22 and a cartographic draughtswoman, was the winner of the *Silver Jubilee* (followed by Linda Martin and Sue Wrigglesworth). She reached the last sixteen in the very strong event at *Goppingen*, the third round in *Turin*, and the last 32 in both the *Jeanty* and at *Como*. Linda Martin was in the last 32 at *Duren*, the last sixteen at Magdeburg and the third round at Como. Sue Wrigglesworth was in the last twelve at Duren and the last 32 at Goppingen. Hilary Cawthorne, now aged 24, did well to reach the last eight at Magdeburg. Sue Green was unable to train till Christmas through injury and apart from winning at *Ashton* was quiescent on the home front. But she reached the last sixteen at Duren, the last 32 in Turin and the last 32 in the

De Beaumont final: Weniger v Halsted.

Jeanty. Finally, at *Offenbach*, Angela Herbert reached the third round and Caryl Oliver the fourth.

There were two *international matches* of note. At Goppingen Clare Halsted, Sue Wrigglesworth, Linda Martin and Hilary Cawthorne lost to W. Germany by four hits after leading 4–1. And at Madgeburg they beat Czechoslovakia 9–5 and E. Germany on hits.

The home *Team Championship* was marked by the absence of Hydra and Ashton, while recent changes of allegiance made it difficult to know who was fencing for whom in the semi-finals, in which Salle Paul squeaked past Thames on hits, and LFC overcame Boston. The vociferously supported final was won 9–6 by LFC, who gained four wins from the Swiss Francoise Helbling's committed lunges. (LFC: Olley 3, Ager 2, Littlejohns 0/3; S. Paul: Wrigglesworth 3, Whitehurst 2, Wood 1, C. Arup 0/3.) This was LFC's fourteenth win of the event since 1949, a record only rivalled by Salle Bertrand which won it eleven times before merging with LFC.

The squad of Olympic possibles trained under Barry More at Headquarters. For the first time the principle of day release was agreed with some employers, which enabled sessions to be held on Tuesday afternoons for a period.

The team for the Olympic Games was the same as the previous year: Clare Halsted, Susan Wrigglesworth, Wendy Ager, Susan Green and Hilary Cawthorne. To the dismay of some, Linda Martin, although Champion, was only reserve.

## EPEE

John Llewellyn won both the *Under-20 Championship* and the *Junior*, where his grim determination was illustrated by his victory from 5-all over Martin Gilbert of Merchant Taylors (2v; 5th) and his refusal to concede a single hit to his rival John Steventon of Brentwood (3v; 3rd), who was technically his equal. Richard Edwards of Poly, whose drooping on-guard position concealed the length he utilised in counter-attacks, was second with three wins (including 5-3 over the winner), but had losses of 5-4 to Steventon and 5-3 to the flamboyant Steve Lavington of Liverpool University (2v; 4th), who was unlucky to lose two hits for faulty weapons and to suffer a double defeat with Peter Twine of REME (ov; 6th).

In the Under-20 final Llewellyn was only hit five times. Steventon gained three of these, but was again third, as he also lost 5-3 to David Fairhall, runner-up with four wins. Glenn Jones of the NW was fourth, with one win over D. Karlin (1v; 6th) who in turn beat Peter Young of Millfield (1v; 5th).

Llewellyn had already made his mark among the seniors at the outset of the season when he came sixth in the *Epee Club Cup*, which was won by Bourne after a barrage with Beevers, followed by Noel, Jacobs and Johnson. Steventon's turn to win came with the *Public Schools* and the *Under-18 Championship*. Internationally, the juniors had only the odd quarter-final to show, but Llewellyn made a big impact in British provincials by winning both the *Welsh Open* and *Inverclyde*. He also put himself within a stone's throw of the British team by winning the *Martini Qualifying*.

The *Martini* itself had an exceptionally large entry, and a very strong one, the absence of Russia, Hungary and Rumania making less of a gap than it would have a few years earlier. Many top-rank epeeists including Jeanne and two current French team members, as well as James Noel, came unstuck in the first round. Flodstrom, the holder, went out in the second round, along with Ladegaillerie as well as Belson, Johnson and Hoskyns (who was having lessons from Mike Webster, now that Prof. Sanders had retired).

Only three Britons reached the direct elimination. Beevers lost in the last 32 to Koppang of Norway, finalist in his teens. Steve Higginson, although several years retired from international contention and now teaching in Wiltshire, fenced with a rare assurance and was only eliminated in the last sixteen by Pusch, current World Champion. Bourne went out at the same stage, finding the Austrian Lindner's fleches too much for him.

Edling, Swedish World Champion in 1973 and 1974, lost to the Swiss Giger in the last eight. In the last four, Pusch beat Boisse of France 10-9 in a magnificent demonstration of coolness and adjustment of distance, and Giger beat the unranked Vino of Italy. The final again showed Pusch's ability to adapt and improve as he reached towards the prize. From 5-2 down to Giger he won 10-9.

The British were in good form in the *post-Martini matches*, beating Switzerland 10–6 and Poland, another strong team, 11–5, though losing to W. Germany 12–4. Johnson won seven out of eight fights. The 'B' team did less well, losing to Norway 10–6 and USA 11–5, though beating Iran 14–1.

In October the *Spartan Tournament* was headed by Howard West and Beevers. In January the *Welsh Games*, an invitation poule unique, was won for the sixth time by Johnson, followed by Hoskyns and Noel. At *Birmingham* Noel beat Osbaldeston 10–6 in the final bout. Andrew Brannon of Chester FC, at the age of only sixteen, did very well to come fourth, losing the fight-off for second place to Richard Edwards of Poly 10–6, having disposed of Beevers, no less, in the last eight. Brian Henshall of Birmingham FC, Mark West of Boston and Gough of W. Germany were the other quarter-finalists. Henshall did even better when he came second in *a one-hit training event* at Chelsea Barracks comprising almost all the top epeeists. Jim Fox, in his element as a pentathlete, was the winner.

Bill Osbaldeston had another good season, even though ski-bobbing had taken over as his main sport, winning at both *Ashton* and *Leicester* and coming second at *Nottingham*, where Tyson won and Roose was third.

Noel won the *University Championships* for the second year running, followed by Graham Mackay (Glasgow, 2nd), B. Diaz (Durham, 3rd), Stanbury (London, 4th), Sam Anderson (Sussex, 5th) and Mike Peat (Edinburgh, 6th).

In the *Championship* Llewellyn was unlucky to be narrowly eliminated in a tough quarter-final. Belson, out at the same stage after teetering on the brink in earlier rounds, was simply off form. Hill, now combining a rampaging style of en marchant advance with skilled and accurate blade-work, reached a personal high in getting to the final, though his form then somewhat evaporated. Paul (5th), Johnson (4th) and Noel (3rd) each had two wins, while Bourne and Beevers never looked in danger from any of them. Their own bout went to 4–all before Bourne got the title for the fourth time, at the age of 27.

The *Miller-Hallett* attracted a number of old acquaintances among the foreigners as well as epeeists from Luxembourg, Egypt, Brazil, and America. The two rounds of pools on the Sunday put paid to Koppang and to Krebs of France, as well as to Belson, Johnson and Paul. The direct elimination saw another promising performance by Llewellyn and the defeat of Noel. In the final, Bourne beat both Hoskyns and Muller (1971 and 1975 winner) and took the huge Riboud of France to the last hit, but became inhibited by tendon trouble; whereas Hoskyns beat Normann 5–4 and Ole Morch, another Norwegian, 5–2 and slipped into second place by beating Riboud when he was already assured of victory.

In *pre-Miller-Hallett matches* Luxembourg was beaten 10–5 and Norway 8–7, but France gained a 10–6 win. The next month in the Swiss ski resort of

*Flims* Britain did well to beat both France and Norway 12–4, though conceding 11–5 to Switzerland.

Back in the autumn, a Welsh Team had travelled through the night in a constricted minibus to take part in a *quadrangular match in Copenhagen*. Turner, Evans, Lewis and Gray lost to Norway 10–6 (the former pair winning two apiece), beat by 12–4 an Italian team, the fourth place in which was taken by their own Bob Lawson, then, collapsing with fatigue and lack of lunch, slumped 15–1 to Denmark 'B'. After re-fuelling, they lost only 8–7 to Denmark 'A' (Lewis being undefeated). In the individual event, recouped somewhat on sleep, Gray came sixth in the final, defeating Koppang, who lost the consequent barrage to Normann.

On the loftier plane of the *Spreafico* Beevers reached the fourth round and Bourne the third. At *Duren* Hoskyns was in the last 32 and Llewellyn in the last eight; and it was won by Johnson. In the *Monal* Beevers reached the last 32 and Belson the last eight. At *Bern* Johnson got up to the last sixteen and both Bourne and Belson were in the last eight, making a very solid impact on a very tough event. At *Heidenheim* Bourne, who was training with that wholeheartedness so characteristic of him, notched up a place in the last twelve.

In *Budapest* in April Graham Paul, who was rationing his commitment to epee this season, reached the last eight. At *Poitiers* Belson got to the last 32; and in the last sixteen were Beevers and Hoskyns, coming into form for the Olympic run-up. In the third round in *Berlin* were Beevers and Johnson (who otherwise had a bare patch towards the end of the season, in spite of strenuous training). Finally, at the seaside event in *Dieppe* Malcolm Fare achieved first place over Bob Turner, with Richard Edwards fourth.

The Olympic team consisted of Bourne, Johnson, Belson, Beevers and Hoskyns. Llewellyn consolidated his position at home, but his opportunities abroad were curtailed by injury (as were those of Hall, who had been runner-up in the Martini Qualifying). Noel was more consistent than in the past but at a slightly lower level than the team.

## SABRE

This was a year in which little impact was made on the levels above them by the Schoolboy Champions, Andrew Cashen of the SW (*Under-18*), Chris Webb of Brentwood (*Public Schools*) or, more naturally, Mark Hall of Sacred Heart College, Droitwich (*Under-16*). Indeed, the finalists of the *Under-20 Championship* and still more the *Junior* were largely sabreurs who had figured on the scene for several seasons. Mark Slade of Brentwood was undefeated Under-20 Champion (2nd in 1973/4, 3rd in 1974/5) and third in the Junior (2nd in 1974/5). Cary Zitcer (LFC), a solid fencer with a solid physique, was Under-20 runner-up (6th in 1974/5). Third was the interloping foilist,

Glaister, and fourth the very fast and capable Gary Li (2nd in the Public Schools 1974/5).

Winner of the Junior was Terry Etherton of Boston (3rd in 1973), who fenced with speed as well as intelligence and lost only to Wasilewski (1v; 6th; 4th in 1974/5). Runner-up was the neat Milligan of Birmingham (3v; 5th in 1972 and 1973). His 5–2 win over the more mobile Slade was notable for firm parries and clean ripostes into exactly the right line. It put him one hit ahead of Slade, who was below his best. Tony Roberts of Poly (2v; 4th), fencing determinedly but erratically, was a newcomer, as was Steve Fox of Boston, another interloping foilist.

In junior events abroad Slade did extremely well, reaching the last twelve in *Budapest* and coming second at *Arnsberg* in W. Germany; but there were no other noteworthy results.

The notable feature of the provincial events was the triumph of Robert Elliott not only in the *Scottish Championship* but also at *Inverclyde* and *Nottingham*. Cohen won the *Spartan Tournament*.

Nationally, it was the year of Jim Philbin's leap to the top rank. He won the *Championship* undefeated and looked a likely winner for most of the finals of both Corble and Cole Cup. A much improved Etherton was the only Championship finalist to put four hits on Philbin, but it was Cohen who was second (after losing the opening fight to Zarno, who indeed followed him on hits). Hutt was fifth for the second year running, his victory being over Zarno. The two newcomers to the final were Etherton (2v; 4th) and Slade (1v; 6th).

In the *Cole Cup*, Philbin beat Levavasseur 5–1, Peeters 5–3 and Bauer 5–4, but this time lost 5–2 to Cohen, the only other Briton in the final, as well as to Barbaud (5–4). It was these two who barraged for the cup and Cohen who won it by reversing their previous 5–4 score. Philbin was third with three wins.

In the *Corble*, Philbin beat Cohen 5–4, these two being again the only Britons in the final. Philbin also beat Brandstaetter (Austria) 5–3 and Fitting (W. Germany) 5–4; but he lost to Marik (Austria) 5–4 and Sekunda (Canada) 5–3. If in the penultimate bout he had beaten Sekunda, who had got no more than two hits on anybody else, Philbin would have gained a distinguished outright win. As it was, there was a four-way barrage, after Cohen beat Marik 6–5 in the last bout. Again Philbin beat Cohen 5–4; but Brandstaetter reversed his 5–4 loss in the pool and Marik beat him 5–2. Cohen then beat both Brandstaetter and Marik 5–4. Marik also had two wins in the barrage and better hits; but Cohen had enough hits in hand from the pool to carry him to victory. Brandstaetter, on the other hand, was clear of Philbin on hits and took third place.

In some ways foreign events presented a different picture. Peter Mather appeared as if nearly two years out of competition had made no difference. He came tenth in the *Paris Touzard* in January and got to the last sixteen in *Graz*, gaining him the vital qualifying point and a ticket to Montreal. Hutt reached the last sixteen in *Katowice* and came twelfth in the Touzard. He was also twelfth in the *Paris Taillandier* but this didn't quite add up to a qualification for Montreal.

David Eden retired, apparently definitively. More unexpectedly, Alan Taylor disappeared. Oldcorn was in the last 24 in *Graz* and the fourth round at *Padua* (where he chipped an ankle), but this wasn't sufficient to get him to his fourth Olympics. Rising towards the gaps they left were Etherton, who reached the last 36 in *Munich* and the last sixteen in the Taillandier, and Slade, who reached the last 48 in Hamburg.

Philbin reached the last sixteen in the Touzard, the last 24 in Graz and the last 48 in Hamburg, but this wasn't enough to qualify him. Cohen, on the other hand, excelled abroad as he had at home: eleventh in the Touzard, in the last sixteen in Graz and a very good last eight in Munich.

Deanfield, absent for most of the season after smashing a kneecap in the Granville in November, was selected as the third sabreur for Montreal on the basis of past form (under the rule covering injury).

There was a *match against Austria* in Graz, which was lost 9–4 and one in Munich *against W. Germany* which was won 11–5. At home the *Team Championship* was won by Boston (Cohen 4, Etherton 3, Zarno 2, Mather 0). Poly were runners-up, fielding Philbin, Deanfield, Eden and Bryan Lewis.

*COMBINED EVENTS*

In the *World Youth Championships* in Poznan, Poland, Britain won the first world Gold Medal at any level since Peter Jacobs won the Student Games in 1961. Robert Bruniges had competed four times before. After being eliminated in the first round in 1972 he achieved the best ever British junior result by gaining the Bronze Medal in 1973, but relapsed to the quarter-final in 1975.

This time he fenced through three rounds of pools to be seeded ninth in the last 32, but he was only promoted because a German retired hurt. He then comfortably defeated Lossius of E. Germany. This brought him against Robak of Poland in a bout that lasted two hours on four different pistes owing to electrical problems after he and Robak got a succession of off-target lights from apparently good hits. On a fresh piste the score reached 5–all. At first Robak and his team had been sceptical about the fault, but it was their turn to protest when it now recurred. The fencers were taken to a changing room and they and their equipment were dried off. In vain. Only at 8–all was it realised the batteries were running down. Bruniges' nerve held better than Robak's through all this (though he got through innumerable cigarettes) and on mains power he won the last two hits imperturbably. The third opponent on his route

Bruniges v Kuzma in World Youth final

World Youth Champion: Robert Bruniges.

to the final, the left-handed Capek of Czechoslovakia, gave him no trouble. He played a waiting game, made use of simple quarte ripostes on Capek's attacks and beat him 10–4.

Bruniges seemed a class ahead of the other finalists, with the possible exception of Dal Zotto of Italy, who was to be Olympic Champion four months later. Throughout he was both stylish and thoughtful. He beat Kuzma (Poland) 5–4, then lost to Dal Zotto 5–3. The next three fights he fenced with that rare mastery of the finalist's game which he possessed when he was on his true form, most of his hits being scored with only one light coming up. He beat Jolyot of France 5–4, his last hit being in counter-time. After beating Lemenage, also of France, he could face his last fight with the 14-year-old Borella of Italy in a relaxed frame of mind, since everyone but he had two losses. He constantly drew Borella onto his point and at 4–3 up against a direct attack he won the title with a lightning riposte in octave, his body averted.

The hit had hardly registered before the whole British team erupted to throw the new Champion in the air in the now customary manner. Acclaim arose on all sides. The German captain praised him as the best technician in the final, the Italian as the most intelligent and the Russian for his tactical sense. His triumph was a tribute to his masters, especially John Fairhall, who taught him from the beginning in 1968 till he was awarded a year's sporting scholarship at Millfield in 1975, and Steve Boston, who led him out of the doldrums to this achievement, and who was with him now as team coach (in tandem with Prof. Jones).

Jolyot was runner-up on hits over Dal Zotto. Kuzma in turn led Lemenage on hits, with Borella sixth.

The other two British were eclipsed. Glaister went out in the first round, perhaps penalised by the electrical faults, and Kay in the second. The girls, however, excelled. Brenda Hewitt and Liz Wood both reached the direct elimination and Janet Jones produced some very polished fencing to get to the last sixteen. There she lost 8–7 to Teranek of Poland.

There were hopes in the epee, but Steventon was ousted in the first round and Llewellyn in the second (after some rough presiding). Poffet was the winner for the third year running. (Llewellyn won the consolation event.)

Sabre offered the toughest competition, with many national team members present. Slade and Zitcer both won through to the second round and got victories there, Slade only being eliminated on hits, perhaps a shade too disposed to accept defeat by 'better' fencers.

The *Quadrangular*, in Huddersfield, saw the third win by Scotland since the inception of the full event in 1950. Sustained by Derek Titheradge, as coach, they beat England 19–17 and had a very exciting victory over Wales by a mere 129–136 hits when Tyson won the final epee bout on the last hit against Lawson. Having come so near to beating the winners, the Welsh were disappointed to lose to England 23–13 despite Bob Turner's captain's score at epee – only one fight dropped throughout the weekend (to N. Ireland), but then, for England, Loveland (at foil) and Etherton (at sabre) were undefeated throughout. N. Ireland lost to Scotland 30–6, to England 25–11 and to Wales 24–12.

The Scots also did well in the *Schools Quadrangular*, staged with generous hospitality in Edinburgh. England beat Scotland 66–62 on fights, but the Scots won 5–3 by weapons. N. Ireland unfortunately could not send a team.

By contrast with Budapest the previous year, the weather for the *Montreal Olympics* was unseasonably comfortable. Moreover, the accommodation was acceptable and the organisation good (except on the part of the FIE). Peter Jacobs was British captain for the last time.

The entry for the men's foil was down from 119 in 1975 to only 56, due to the limit of three per country, but the British all survived the first round. Graham Paul (20th) and Rob Bruniges (23rd) both fenced well to reach the last 24. The latter with sharper concentration and less discouragement from the president might have reached the last sixteen. The winner was the unconventional Dal Zotto, with his rush attacks from extended distance, his body twists to avoid being hit and his corps-a-corps. He was the seventeenth Italian winner of the foil in the World Championships or Olympic Games, but the first since 1958.

Rumania and Russia posed daunting obstacles in the first round pool of the team event. Grimmett lost all his fights to the Rumanians, who led 5–2 and then 7–4, but the others mounted a colossal comeback to win 8–all by seven hits, a fine achievement, Barry Paul and Bruniges winning three and Graham two.

Promotion was now assured, although spirited defence against Russia brought only three wins (B. Paul 2, Bell 1, G. Paul 0, Bruniges 0). In the quarter-finals came a similar defeat by a very sharp French team (B. Paul 1, G. Paul 1, Bruniges 1, Bell 0). This left the team to fight for fifth to eighth places. With their edge slightly blunted, they slid from 7–4 in the lead over USA to 7–all before Barry beat Makler 5–1 and thus won the match, the Americans being ten hits behind. Each of the unchanged team won two fights. Superior defensive technique and possibly the advantage of doubtful presiding won the day. The Poles left their claim to fifth place in no doubt, winning 9–1 (Barry getting the one). However, sixth was not only the best result for the foil team since the 1950s, but the best placing at any weapon since 1965. The W. Germans took the Gold Medal, for the first time.

All three sabreurs got through the first round of 46, Cohen fencing excellently to take thirteenth seed. Sadly, in the second round he needed one more hit against Mikhailov of Bulgaria from a Hungarian president with unhelpful convictions to get to the last 24, though he achieved 27th place. Deanfield went out in a singularly difficult pool, while Mather did not quite find his timing; his two-year absence from the team militated against fulfilment of his earlier promise. The Russians took all three medals for the first time.

Hoskyns joined the other three to make up a team. They lost 11–5 to Cuba (Deanfield 2, Cohen 2, Hoskyns 1, Mather 0) and 14–2 to Rumania (Deanfield and Cohen salvaging one each). Cuba was only just beaten by Hungary in the quarter-finals and Rumania almost beat the Russians in the semis, though Soviet mastery was so clear in the final against Italy as to still the anti-Russian partisanship shown by the crowds at all sports in these Olympics.

There were 48 entries for ladies' foil. Only Russia, France and Britain got all their fencers through to the last 24. Clare Halsted, Wendy Ager and Susan Wrigglesworth all fenced with tenacity and concentration. Susan, in top form, stormed to first place in her pool. And in the direct elimination she at first took the lead against Josland of France, who, however, began to find the answer to her (and was later to play a heroic part in gaining a team Silver Medal). The score levelled and then alternated up to 7–all. Finally Susan prepared an extended attack insufficiently and was hit by the riposte. In the repechage the task of beating Bobis, 1974 World Champion, proved too great. She achieved a laudable thirteenth place, however.

The excellent individual results – on aggregate the best since Gillian Sheen's 1956 Gold Medal – gave the team fifth seed out of an entry of thirteen. Against the USA, Clare Halsted pulled the team together from an uncertain start with forceful, intelligent fencing, contributing four wins to a 9–7 victory (Ager 2, Cawthorne 2, Wrigglesworth 1). Iran was defeated comfortably, 8–4 being reached with a massive hits lead. (Green 3, Ager 3, Halsted 2, Cawthorne 1.) This ensured promotion in spite of a 9–2 loss to Italy (Halsted 1, Ager 1, Wrigglesworth 0, Green 0). Unfortunately another 9–2 loss to Hungary prevented further advance, only Clare scoring of the same team.

In the fight-off for fifth to eighth places Britain met the Poles, who were always one or two fights ahead till 7–5. At 8–7 Clare had to beat Bebel 5–0 to win the match on hits, and almost did it! She got to 4–0 before winning 5–2 (Ager 3, Cawthorne 3, Halsted 2, Wrigglesworth/Green 0).

Hopes were highest at epee but were largely dashed. Belson, nervous and sluggish, went out in the first round. Bourne, in a hard second round, needed three hits on Granieri in his last fight; he was caught by stop-hits under his wrist and lost 5–2. Johnson, however, began his first round by beating Alex Pusch 5–1. The same brio carried him out of a tight corner in the second round when he had to win his last fight 5–1 to ensure his promotion over the Russian, Abushakmetov (a finalist) and again in the third, when at the end of a pool fenced at an outstandingly high technical level, he had to beat Janikowski (eventually fifth in the final) in order to ensure promotion over Lukomsky (medallist in 1974 and 1975). Determined to stretch his supporters' nerves to the limit, he took it to 5–all before winning with a full-blooded counter-attack.

Sadly, he had insufficient reserves left for the direct elimination, where he lost 10–5 both to Osztrics (eventual fourth) and to Hehn (who won the Silver Medal). He thus ranked thirteenth equal. Pusch was the Champion, for the second year running, an achievement perhaps exceeded by Kulcsar's win of the Bronze Medal after his Gold in 1968 and Bronze in 1972.

In the team event Britain beat Austria 11–5 after a sticky start (Hoskyns 3, Johnson 3, Belson 3, Bourne 2). W. Germany beat Austria too, thus ensuring promotion for Britain. W. Germany rapidly also led Britain, to the tune of 7–1, but the match then eased and ended 9–5 (Beevers 2, Bourne 1, Johnson 1, Belson 1).

Unfortunately the bluntness incurred in this easing-up could not be shaken off in the next round against Norway, the seventh seeds. Only Hoskyns looked sharp. Koppang and Normann were on form and after 3–all the match slipped away to 5–8 (Hoskyns 2, Johnson 1, Bourne 1, Belson/Beevers 1). So Britain came ninth. The Swedes won for the third year running, Hogstrom, Jacobson, von Essen and Edling each getting two wins. Overall, W. Germany caught up with Russia in top position, Italy waxed stronger, Hungary declined. Epee was admitted to be the weapon of highest quality. British results were slightly better than in Mexico and a great improvement on Munich. Hoskyns added to his other records a sixth Olympic appearance, unequalled by any other Briton – and he more than justified that appearance by being the top scorer in the epee team event.

The team could take some small pride in the Gold Medal won by the

The 1976 Pentathlon Gold Medallists with H.M. the Queen and Prince Edward: Michael Proudfoot (Team Manager), Jim Fox, Adrian Parker, Andy Archibald, Danny Nightingale and Ron Bright (Coach).

Pentathletes Jim Fox, Adrian Parker and Danny Nightingale, who over the years had competed and trained with other British epeeists and who received strategically marshalled support from fencers round the cross-country course.

# 1976–7

## MEN'S FOIL

Pierre Harper confirmed his promise with an excellent second place at *Kussnacht*. He was also second in the *Millfield*, after Tonges. At *Steinfurter Schloss* John Ford was in the last sixteen. At *Papendal* in June, at the other end of the season, Billy Gosbee was second, Andy Martin (brother of Linda and also at Poly) was fourth and John Troiano of Salle Ganchev was fifth.

True to form, Harper won the *Under-20 Championship*, but only after a barrage in which he beat Martin, Mike Peat (Nemo) and the promising David Seaman. The lower places went to John Ford (2v) and Marvin Evans (2v), younger brother of Gareth and also at Phoenix.

The *Wilkinson Sword Trophy* fell to Gosbee, who defeated Mike Harris of

Welwyn in the final bout. Max Visholm and Anthony Garrington were the other semi-finalists. The eliminated quarter-finalists had all been in the final of the *Under-18* (formerly Schoolboys) *Championship*; Donny McKenzie (1st), Tait (4th), Chris Ward (Birmingham; 5th) and John Troiano (6th). McKenzie (born in 1960) was at Trinity Academy, Edinburgh, where he was taught fencing by the classics master, Neil Melville, though he was now also taught at Meadowbank by Prof. Bracewell. Tait had also been second in the *Public Schools Championship*, between Julian Ferguson of Worth (5v) and Steve Meredith of Brentwood (2v).

John Lawrence won the *Junior Championship* for Salle Paul with four victories in an evenly balanced pool. Combining length and speed with some neat hand-work, he was only defeated by Mark Thompson, who made judicious use of the side-step and stop-hit but who missed a barrage as a result of a late spurt on the part of Gilbert Thompson. On hits, Guenigault was third, ahead of Gosbee. Tyson could repeat none of the defeats he'd inflicted on all but one finalist in earlier rounds.

Most of the people in the *Universities* final were familiar from the junior scene, but the winner was a 'mature' student from more senior levels, Stuart Wooding of Cambridge (enjoying himself several years after retiring from serious fencing). The others were: Beattie (Heriot-Watt; 3v), Chetwood, also the 1976 *Combined Services* Champion (Cambridge; 3v), Wedge, the holder (Manchester; 2v), Mark Thompson (Cambridge; 2v) and Ford (City University; 1v).

Bob Elliott was the *Inverclyde* winner, ahead of Brian Green (Pendle), Loveland, Lewis Smith (Lothian), Ford and Andy Webb. Elliott, Smith and Mike Mayo won the team event for Lothian 5–4 over Wiles, Tyson and Painter of Leicester.

Early in the season Eames put himself at the head of the senior pack. Though limited in style, he worked up his favourite moves to a speed and precision that could overcome almost any opposition. He won both at *Ashton* and *Leicester* and triumphed a third time in the *Emrys Lloyd*, ahead of Bruniges (11v), B. Paul (11v), Bell (10v), Loveland (10v) and Fox (10v), but he figured in neither of the other two major domestic finals. In the *Coronation Cup* Bruniges, after being second twice running to each of the Pauls, finally overcame his bogeymen to win his first major senior competition. Whether due to the quality of the eight finalists or to the splendid venue at the Leatherhead Leisure Centre, with a paying audience of over two hundred (and more watching from above), the fencing in the direct elimination bouts was noticeably better than during the earlier rounds.

In the first bouts, with one exception, youth bowed to experience. Gareth Evans lacked the confidence to combat Graham Paul's long-arm stop-hits (by 10–3). Glaister found Single's fast remises and broken-time attacks too much to handle (10–5); but Bruniges managed, not without difficulty at first, to cope with the speed and agility of the Belgian Crahay (10–6). Paul then put a stop to Single's progress by 10–6, whilst Bruniges gained a quick 4–0 lead over the other Belgian, Soumagne, lost it against some very fast prise-de-fer attacks and then won the last two hits with well-timed cut-over attacks to win 10–8.

In the final bout Bruniges again started well to lead 3–0, but relaxed and allowed Paul to level the score; stop-hits from one and attacks from the other made it 4–all, 5–all, 6–all before Bruniges clinched the title with a couple of ripostes pulled out of the air and a final double-cut-over.

This gala final owed much to the organisation of Roger Turner and Nick Halsted, the commentary by Michel Kallipetis and the support and publicity of Ranmore FC.

It was perhaps an indication of the depth and evenness of British foil this season that only the two Pauls and Evans were in the finals of both Coronation and National *Championship*. Running the latter on the direct elimination system for the first time for some years produced interesting results, including a straight run to his first senior final for Harper and a similar series of three victories for Fox. More predictably, the Pauls came through without too much trouble, while working their way through the repechage came Gareth Evans and Bell – who twice defeated Bruniges over ten hits, no mean feat.

Any hopes Barry Paul had of retaining his title vanished as he lost successively to Bell (after being 4–2 up) and Fox (from 4–all after being 4–0 down), though he salvaged the second place. Graham Paul forfeited his chances by losing to his brother as well as to Bell, and Evans put himself out of the running, and into fourth place, by losing his last three fights. Nick Bell fenced enthusiastically and accurately to gain the title even before he had won his last fight, in spite of the disadvantage of his heavy commitments as hospital houseman. As ever, he made good use of his long reach, which, like the Pauls, he often extended by holding the foil by the pommel. Fox got fifth place over Harper by four hits given (on one win).

By winning the *Team Championship*, Boston entered the select company of clubs who had wrested the trophy from Salle Paul. Direct elimination was applied after the 32 entrants had been halved. The most exciting second round match was between Poly and Thames 'B', who had only overcome a spirited Whitgift team by two hits the day before. Now they raced to a 7–0 lead; but Poly recovered admirably (though with much barracking of the president) until the score was 8–7 and they only needed 8–all to win on hits. The last bout between John Deanfield and Ian Broadley reached 4–all before the latter got the winning hit.

In the quarter-finals Salle Paul 'A' beat a strong Cambridge side 9–4, Hydra U-20 ended Thames 'B's run 9–3, Salle Paul 'B' trounced Thames 'A' 9–2 and Boston beat Salle Goodall by the same score. Paul 'A' overcame Hydra U-20 9–5 with some difficulty in the semis, while Boston beat Paul 'B'

9–2. Boston's victory in the final was unexpectedly decisive. (Eames 3/4, Bourne 3/3, Bruniges 2/3, Waldman 1/3; Grimmett 1/4, B. Paul 2/3, G. Paul 1/3, Single 0/3.)

Large numbers of British foilists continued to go abroad. Between January and April there were 54 entries to foreign events – but only twenty results better than first round. Bartlett, a gifted foilist with quick handwork who was now at Salle Paul, was one of the few newcomers among the seniors to make any mark; he reached the last eight in *Antwerp*. Existing team members were uncertain quantities. Barry Paul withdrew for half the season and came back fresh but not over-fit to confirm his top position by getting in the last sixteen at *Bonn* (as well as being in the last twelve in Antwerp). Graham Paul had, for him, a bleak season. Bell was in the last eight in Antwerp, but much engaged in medicine. Grimmett got more than adequate results: he reached the last 32 in both the *Martini* and the *Duval* and the third round of Bonn, but his job as mathematics don at New College, Oxford, may have partly accounted for his impression of indifference to fencing. Finally, Bruniges, for a wide range of reasons, including lost concentration and sense of staleness, withdrew from fencing for much of the season. It was Eames who supplied new enthusiasm. He got to the fifth round (last 48) of the Martini and was tenth in the *Brussels Debeur*.

Sporting Record 1976: A. Eames v G. Paul – both in characteristic action.

In *matches* reasonable credit was earned. In Antwerp, for instance, B. Paul, Bell and Bruniges beat Canada 5–0 and a German team 5–4, losing first place to France by 5–3.

On the strength of its sixth place in the Olympics, the British team was invited to the *Seven-Nations Tournament*. They lost to Hungary and Germany 'A' 11–5, but beat Poland and Germany 'B' and only just lost to France (8–8), to Italy (9–7) and to USSR (9–7) – an excellent performance against the world's top teams. All five members pulled their weight and it was the same five who were selected for the World Championships: the Pauls, Bell, Grimmett and (in place of Bruniges) Eames.

## LADIES' FOIL

The same juniors were to the fore as in the previous season, except that Janet Jones was now over twenty. Ann Brannon won the *Perigal* and the *Ashton Under-20* event and was the only British finalist in the *Millfield*, in fifth place between Viret of Switzerland (5th) and Drori of Israel (6th). She was also in the last 24 at *Etampes*. Liz Wood won the *Under-20 Championship* and was in the last eight at Etampes. Fiona McIntosh was winner of the *Under-18 Championship*, second in the Perigal and third in the Under-20 Championship, and was in the last twelve at *Dornbirn*. Brenda Hewitt was second in the Under-20 Championship and third in the Ashton Under-20. Debbie Hall, highly-strung and strong in counter-attacks, was second in the Ashton Under-20 and was in the last 24 at Etampes and the last twelve at Dornbirn. Sheila Gallagher was fourth in the Perigal and in the last twelve at Dornbirn.

Kim Cecil of Chase was the winner of the four-way barrage for the *Parker Trophy*, showing good sense of timing and successful attacks on the preparation. Pauline Tovey of Hydra was second. Third was Ann Charles from Mike Law's Presdales Club, Ware (who was also in the last 16 at Dornbirn). Fourth place went to the small but persistent Lesley Calver of Thames and New Zealand. Kate Elvin of Boston and N. Ireland and Sue Freeman of Goodall took the remaining places in the final.

The *Bertrand*, next step up the Category ladder, was won by Jane Law of Hydra, who was only forced to the last hit once in the final. Each of the other finalists got two wins. The determined, resourceful and technically polished Sue Hoad of Allen was second, ahead of Sue Youngs (now married to Bryan Lewis and fencing at Poly), and the diminutive but determined Ann Fraser-Smith of Northumbria FC (who was 5th in the Perigal). The spirited Maureen Hillier of Thames (sister of Tony Bartlett) was fifth and Caroline Arup sixth.

In *Liverpool* Cath Robertson (*Scottish* Champion) was beaten only by Jenny Hawcroft of Stockport (4th). Second was Rosemary Castle (also on four wins);

Olivia Drummond was third. At *Ilford* Sue Uff (née Harris), a strongly defensive fencer, emerged the winner, taken to the last hit only by Kim Cecil (5th). The other finalists were Liz Wood (4v, 2nd), the analytic Maureen Lloyd of Newham (3v, 3rd), Sue Hoad (2v, 4th) and Fiona Wilson of Chase (0v, 6th).

The *Universities Championship* went to Sue Rochard (London). Caroline Arup (Cambridge) was second. Both did well to get ahead of Sue Wrigglesworth, missing the two previous years, and José Lambert (Loughborough) also with three wins.

Sue Rochard also reached the final of the *Desprez* (2v, 5th); only her philosophy degree course was seen as an obstacle to her enthusiastic progress. Liz Wood was sixth in the *Championship*. The finals of the two events otherwise comprised the same people in much the same order. Both were won by Hilary Cawthorne, a notable feat surprisingly rarely achieved in the history of the two events. Now representing Allen F.C. again, she also achieved a triple victory at *Leicester, Redbridge* and *Birmingham*. Sue Wrigglesworth was second in the Championship and third in the Desprez. The mirror of these positions was gained by Wendy Ager, now Mrs Grant, who had reached Salle Behmber on her migration through the clubs. Linda Martin was fourth in both, and Ann Brannon, now seriously challenging her seniors, was fifth in the Championship and sixth in the Desprez.

In the Championship Hilary Cawthorne won all four of her wins in the final on the last hit and then beat Sue Wrigglesworth on the last hit again in the barrage. But she was again the leader in the *de Beaumont*: third with three wins, after Wolthius of Holland (4v, 1st) and Appert of France (3v, 2nd). If limited in repertoire, what she did was fast and effective. Wendy Grant was fourth (2v) and Linda Martin sixth (1v), separated by Skapska of Poland, in a very even final of high standard with a good sense of timing being the common factor to otherwise varying styles and a cautious game tending to result in simultaneous attacks.

The result of the *Silver Jubilee* didn't see a great change of names. Linda Martin won, in a barrage with Wendy Grant. Sue Wrigglesworth was third.

As these results suggest, Susan Green and Clare Halsted had retired; but the former had stayed to contribute two wins to Poly's victory in the *Team Championship*, along with Halina Balon, a top Polish fencer (2v), Linda Martin (3v) and Sue Lewis (2v). Salle Paul thus went down 9-7 (S. Wrigglesworth 3, C. Arup 3, E. Wood 2, S. Gallagher 0). They had narrowly beaten Thames in the semi-finals, in which Poly had convincingly beaten Boston. A Scottish school team, led by Fiona McIntosh, did well to reach the quarter-finals, losing to the Champions only 9-4.

Foreign results were slightly disappointing. Wendy Grant laudably reached the last sixteen at *Goppingen* (where Linda Martin was in the third round) and did even better to reach the last twelve at *Como*. She also reached the third round at *Minsk*. Sue Wrigglesworth got to the third round both in the *Jeanty* and in *Turin*. Liz Wood did likewise in Turin and was in the last sixteen at *Duren* as well. In the last 24 here were Linda Martin, Sue Rochard and Clare Montgomery (who was third in the Perigal). Hilary Cawthorne was unable to match her outstanding home results.

In *matches* the team lost respectably at Duren 9–6 to France but slumped 9–3 to Belgium. In Minsk, which they reached after an epic and hilarious journey, they succumbed to Moscow 9–4 but beat Georgia, Czechoslovakia and Cuba, all by 9–7 and came ninth out of seventeen teams.

Linda Martin now joined the World Championship team, as did Liz Wood, alongside Susan Wrigglesworth, Wendy Grant and Hilary Cawthorne.

## *EPEE*

John Steventon reversed the previous *Under-20 Championship* by pushing Llewellyn into second place, fencing coolly throughout; he beat him in his last fight even though Llewellyn himself was both confident and fast and had previously only conceded four hits. Jervis Rhodes of Dulwich College (who was also fifth in the Public Schools) and Mike Bernard of Worth School did well to reach third and fourth places respectively on two wins, ahead of the experienced Fairhall and Young (1v; 5th and 6th).

Steventon, Fairhall and Mallett were absent from the *Junior Championship*. Nevertheless, the standard was higher than the previous year. Raymond Paul's son Steven, aged 22, was the winner. First taught by Gordon Signy at Salle Paul, he had just returned from two years' training at the Institut Nationale des Sports in Paris. He showed himself capable of using his length in fast lunges and fleches as well as producing some good counter-attacks. It was reckoned that a certain tentativeness would soon go in the rough and tumble of international competition and that shortly he could rival Llewellyn as a contender for the team.

Edwards of Poly was runner-up again, fencing intelligently, followed by Tyson, now at Leicester YM, displaying controlled technique and continued youthfulness, Brierley, making his third appearance in the final since 1970, and another two Poly members, the large George Jaron, of Hungarian origin, given to advancing aggressively with circular movements and the comparatively short Desmond Turner, a scientist with a neat and deceptive technique whose patience and confidence had not always been so firm.

The *Under-18 Championship* was won by the undefeated Bernard, ahead of George Liston (George Heriot's; 4v), Matthew Wood (pupil of Tom Norcross at Birmingham; 3v), Gregor Henderson (George Watson's; 2v), the awkward left-handed J. Ferguson (Worth; 1v) and Julian Williams of Cardiff FC (0v). The *Under-Sixteen* was won by Alistair Carnie of Dingwall Academy and the *Public Schools* by Andy Brannon of King's Chester (brother of Ann). The

*Universities* Champion was Steve Lavington of Liverpool, ahead of Ewan Ferguson of Edinburgh (also 4v), Steventon of London (3v), Patrick Bentham of Oxford (2v), Mallett of London (1v) and A. Russ of Surrey (1v).

Osbaldeston won at *Ashton* for the second year running. Steve Roose was victor at *Ilford*, taken to the last hit only by Matthew Chell, the thoughtful Brentwoodian. Andy Archibald, the pentathlete, was third (2v), ahead of Llewellyn (2v) and Mark Carpenter, an improving 19-year-old pupil of Prof. Pitman (2v). Howard West (1v), was sixth. *Inverclyde* was won by the Glaswegian Gerry Toland on a barrage from Tyson. They were followed by Chell, David Rollo of Jard, William Ross (Scottish Coaches' Association) and Norman Rouxel (Lothian).

There were over five hundred entrants for *Birmingham*, where David Fairhall excelled (taking full advantage of the non-arrival of Belson, his first opponent in the last eight). He beat Prochotta to reach the final bout. There he was beaten by Frohwein of W. Germany's champion club team. Prochotta beat Steven Paul for third place. Brierley, Stanbury and West reached the last eight.

The *Martini Qualifying* was won by Davenport, but also on seventeen wins were Graham Paul and West, whose ceaseless but calculated dive-bomb attacks suitably economised on effort for a final of 24. There followed D. Brooks (16v), S. Paul (16v), B. Lewis (16v), B. Turner (14v) and J. Hall (14v).

The *Martini* itself was not a success for the British. Thirteen went out in the first round. Fifteen reached the second: the Scottish Kernohan and the Welsh Team members Turner, Lewis, Gray and Lawson, together with Fairhall, Mallett, Brooks, Stanbury, Paul and Bourne – the last of whom had now retired from the team and from competitive training. Johnson and Beevers reached the last 32. Robin Davenport scored a personal success, ousting Pusch in the second round and giving Jana, one of the W. German musclemen, a tough fight in the last sixteen.

The final, which was televised for the first time, made up in excitement what it lacked in local interest. Fenyvesi, the Hungarian 1972 Olympic Champion, was on his inimitable best form, bouncing high in the air between devastating attacks against Kauter of Switzerland, the runner-up (and eliminator of Johnson). Behr was third over Jana. Hehn, Kulcsar, Osztrics and Riboud were the other impressive finalists.

The *post-Martini matches* were less disastrous for Britain. W. Germany only won on hits and Poland by 9–8, though Switzerland came through 11–5.

Back in the autumn, Bourne had been an easy winner over Hoskyns and Belson in the *Epee Club Cup*. The 19-year-old Mallett, less rigid and more assured than before, was a promising sixth. Belying his retirement, Bourne won both the *Championship* and the *Miller-Hallett*. In the former, Hill, Turner and Roose (fencing with great assurance) reached one semi-final, Osbaldeston, Hall and Hoskyns the other. Johnson beat Bourne in the first bout of the final but then faded, ending fifth (2v). Thereafter Bourne steadily asserted himself, even if Belson (3v, 3rd) gave him some trouble. In the end it was Llewellyn who was his rival; but he dominated him in the pool and won the barrage 5–1. West (2v, 4th) was in his first Championship final; Davenport (ov, 6th) was in his third.

The *Miller-Hallett* was fought on the new FIE repechage system. Victors in the last sixteen were, in seed order, Steven Paul, Bourne, Pearman, Hoskyns, West (who beat Davenport 10–3), Stanbury, Johnson and Beevers (who beat Tyson, the fourth seed). In the next round of direct elimination (to yield four of the finalists) Johnson beat Paul 10–6, Beevers beat Hoskyns 10–2, Pearman beat West 10–9 and Bourne beat Stanbury 10–7. The losers of this round then met the re-shuffled winners from the initial losers' knockout. Paul beat Hall 10–5; Hoskyns beat Mallett 10–2, Stanbury beat Noel 10–8 and West beat Edwards 10–7. To produce the other two finalists from these, Hoskyns beat Paul 10–9 and Stanbury beat West even more narrowly 11–10.

Johnson again beat Bourne (5–2) in the final of six. He then beat Hoskyns, Stanbury and Pearman 5–0, 5–0, 5–0 – but lost 5–3 to Beevers. Bourne, meanwhile, won all his other fights, if less crushingly, and, come the barrage, raised his tempo to the scorching level which few in the world could sustain. Johnson lost 5–1. Hoskyns (4th) was in the final for at least the fourteenth time.

Unsurprisingly, Boston beat Thames – unwontedly without Jacobs – 9–5 in the *Team Championship* (Bourne 3/3, Bruniges 3, Johnson 2, Davenport 1/3; Hall 2, Hoskyns 1/3, Belson 1/3, West 0).

Abroad, Llewellyn did well to come fourth in the *Differdange* event. Steventon was ninth and Fairhall nineteenth. At *Duren*, Beevers, Lavington, Lewis, Llewellyn and Steven Paul reached the third round. David Brooks got to the last 32. Mike Peat and Neal Mallett did well to figure in the last 24. Stanbury went on to the last sixteen, Johnson to the last twelve. In a *triangular match* a British team lost 9–4 to a German 'B' team, but beat Belgium.

At the smaller event in *Rennes*, Hill and Edwards reached the last 24, Roose came ninth and Brooks excelled to come second. At the Grade 'A' *Bern* tournament Roose, Hoskyns, Hill, Davenport and Steven Paul reached the third round and Johnson got to round four. In the even tougher *Heidenheim* event Hoskyns and Steventon reached round three, Steven Paul got to the last 48 and Llewellyn and Johnson to the last 24 (the former beating Edling 10–5 to do so, an excellent achievement).

After a week's training in *Tauberbischofsheim* under Prof. Emery came some good matches. Though USSR won 9–3, Switzerland 9–3, Germany 'A' 9–4 and even Germany 'B' 9–6, Italy, Rumania and Hungary were all defeated 9–7. At Poitiers Belson, Steve Paul and Llewellyn reached the last 32 and in *Brussels* Beevers was sixth, Steve Paul fifth and Belson second.

The tally of results was affected by Belson's concentration on his Army

Rennes 1977: D. Brooks, B. Hill, R. Edwards, S. Roose.

commitments as well as the retirement of Bourne, Noel and Graham Paul, which left wide gaps in contenders for the team. So both Llewellyn and Steven Paul joined Hoskyns, Belson and Johnson for the World Championships.

## SABRE

Among the juniors, although Mark Slade was clear leader overall, he didn't win the *Under-20 Championship* – the standard of which was high throughout. He lost his second fight to Kenric Li of Brentwood (2v; 5th) – a loss of which Martin Hunt (Boston and Bristol Grammar School) took full advantage, eventually wresting the title from Slade 5–3 in a barrage from 3–0 down. He was the son of Dennis Hunt and had a posse of vociferous supporters from the SW. Mark Hall (Birmingham), aged only sixteen, recovered from a nervous start and narrowly missed joining the barrage when he lost 5–4 to Slade. Gary Li was fourth, ahead of his brother on hits. Sebastian Muir was sixth (ov).

There were other promising young sabreurs. Kris Kubiena (*Under-16 Champion*) reached the last twelve at *Dourdan* in October (together with K. Li). Here Gary Li came fifth and Slade second. The *Under-18 Championship* was won by G. Li, undefeated. His brother was second, ahead of Hall on hits. (The next two places went to epeeists: Chell and Brannon.) The top two places in the *Public Schools Championship* went exactly the same way. Third in this case was Jervis Rhodes of Dulwich (finalist at both the other weapons). Prof. Imregi's pupil Kris Kubiena was fourth and Gordon Drummond (Brentwood) – second in the Under-16 Championship – was fifth, clear of Steven Campbell (Brentwood).

Slade was *Universities Champion* (for Cambridge) followed by Tom Beattie (Heriot-Watt), Jonathan Lewis (Manchester), Steve Carson (Hull), Steve Lavington (Liverpool) and Howard Bailey (London). Abroad, Slade was second in the *Budapest Under-20* event, the only Briton, it was claimed, ever to fence in a sabre final in Hungary. He was also second at *Dourdan* in France.

The *Junior Championship* final comprised a mixture of old and new: the winner was Tony Roberts of Poly, who had gradually worked his way up the ranks (fourth the year before). Both the runner-up, Gryf-Lowczowski (also of Poly), and Magill (Boston), in third place, had first been finalists in 1972. The lower three were all newcomers, however: Richard Jandula (of Polish family), Morris and Lewis. In contrast to the two previous seasons, none of the finalists seriously impinged on the senior end of the British sabre.

On the home front Jim Philbin went from strength to strength. He had the remarkable achievement of winning everything he entered: *Bristol Phoenix, Ashton, Leicester, Brighton, Welsh Open, Birmingham, Corble* and *Championship*. Also clocking up a record was John Moore, now a Colonel, who won the *Inter-Services* title for the fifth time, a record only equalled by SMI G. Wyatt and Col-Sgt Bob Anderson and surpassed by Lt J. Betts' six wins.

The runner-up in the *Championship*, Deanfield, looked a likely winner till he lost a late bout to Etherton (2v, 4th); while Cohen (3v, 3rd) gave away his chance by the odd hit against Oldcorn (2v, 5th), who was in his first Championship final since 1973. Slade (1v) did well to slip into the last position over Hutt, while Zarno was a trifle unlucky not to make the final.

The *Corble* went to Philbin on the last hit of the barrage with Cohen, so narrowly preventing Cohen's hat-trick. The Canadian Lavoie was third. Etherton was again fourth, beating Lavoie and Deanfield – who only beat Zarno. In turn Zarno, who had eased into the final over Slade, beat Etherton 5–0, but was still just sixth on hits.

The *Cole Cup* was won by Fitting in a four-way barrage with Eden (2nd), Cohen (3rd) and Etherton (4th). A notable semi-finalist here, as he had been in the Championship, was Gary Li. Not far behind was Hall, in the last 24 of Cole Cup, Championship and Corble, showing himself to be a natural, if ungainly, sabreur, with much flair.

The *Team Championship* was won 9–6 by Poly over Boston, unsurprisingly since, to add to the strength of Deanfield, Eden, Philbin and Oldcorn, Cohen had transferred from the latter to the former.

Abroad it was again Cohen in the lead, with an excellent place in the last 24 in *Warsaw*, where he also won fourteen of his 28 bouts in the *7-Nations Team* event, with three wins against the young Russian squad and four against the Polish 'B' team. Still prone to the occasional lapse of concentration but improving in mobility, he was thought to have the potential to reach a yet higher rung of the international ladder.

Philbin was beginning to get the good foreign results to match his home ones. In *Munich* he got qualifying points for reaching the last twelve. (At the end of the season he was handicapped by an injured Achilles tendon.) Deanfield, in spite of his commitments as a doctor, had a good season. In the Warsaw matches he had eight wins (two each against Hungary and Poland 'A' and three against Russia). At *Budapest* he had a splendid second round before going out in the last 48.

Etherton continued to improve, especially as a team fencer. His eight wins in Warsaw included three against Cuba and two against W. Germany. In the *Paris Taillandier* he was seventh equal, almost earning a qualifying point. Oldcorn put himself back in the World Championship team by his third round at *Hamburg* and second round in *Budapest*. Zarno disproved the cynics who had regarded him as too limited in technique ever to produce good international results by picking up 1½ qualifying points in the last sixteen in Munich and reaching the last eight in the Taillandier. He was thus selected as a sixth team member for the World Championship. Hutt did much better abroad than at home, gaining 2½ points – in the last sixteen in *Vienna* and the last 24 in Munich; but seemed to run out of steam at the end of the season. Promisingly, Hall reached the last 48 in Munich and the last sixteen in the Taillandier.

## COMBINED EVENTS

The *World Youth Championships* were in Vienna, reducing travel costs for most participants. Further savings could have been made if the FIE had not insisted on 50 presidents for a maximum of twelve pistes. The five-day length of the event could also perhaps have been reduced.

Ford and Gosbee were eliminated in round one on two victories. Harper, however, fenced with maturity and impeccable control, only collecting seven hits in his first round (his victims including Abashidze of Russia) and beating Lossius (eventual sixth) and losing only to Jolyot (1976 runner-up). Sadly, he lost form in the third round, winning only two fights. Lapitski of Russia was the winner.

Clare Montgomery succumbed in her first round and Ann Brannon went out with one victory in a second round pool containing Fekete, the eventual winner. Liz Wood got three wins in the first round and four in the second, but then went off the boil.

Wales, Quadrangular winners 1977: *Back:* D. Brooks, R. Lawson, C. Hyndman, B. Lewis, P. Stewart (Coach), A. Pearce (Armourer). *Front:* G. Evans, I. Edwards, A. Bennett, L. Brown, M. Riley, E. Gray, M. Evans.

All the sabreurs got up from the first round, Kenrick Li beating Baianov of Russia, the eventual runner-up, but in the second round Gary Li got only two wins and Kenrick and Mark Slade only one. None raised their tempo sufficiently, most noticeably Slade, whose depth of technique would otherwise have got him further. The final was a Russo-Hungarian affair, the Pole Wodke (5th) being sole interloper. Ismailov won. John Zarno presided.

Steventon and Mallett faltered in the second round but Llewellyn got a confident four wins here and only lapsed somewhat in the third round. Enough, however, to get a low seed and have to face the tall, spindly Mojaev of Russia, who beat him 10–7. In the repechage Llewellyn had a very close fight with Bicher of E. Germany but emerged the winner by 10–9. Unfortunately even under the new system he then met Mojaev again. Afflicted with cramp (perhaps due to the almost vibrato tenseness which went with his considerable speed) Llewellyn only managed three hits this time. His twelfth place was nevertheless creditable, particularly as Mojaev went on to a Bronze Medal, behind Koppang of Norway and Beckmann of Germany but ahead of both Riboud and Poffet.

For the first time in its 28 years, the *Quadrangular*, held in Glasgow, was won by Wales. The experienced Linda Norrie (née Brown) together with Maggie

Riley and Audrey Bennett, laid excellent foundations by beating both English and Scots 5–4 and overwhelming N. Ireland 9–0. The sabreurs won all three matches 5–4. Lewis's undefeated run here was the lynch pin of victory. He wasn't so all-conquering at epee, but instead Lawson won three of the 7–2 victory over the Scots and two in the 5–4 victory over the Irish. Brooks, having scored two in each of these matches, was undefeated against the strong English trio, West, Edwards and Steve Paul (who suffered his sole two losses of the weekend in this match). Gray, replacing Lawson, got two more to make it 5–4. This left the Welsh foilists only three to gain in the last match against England. (They had previously outshone N. Ireland 7–2 but lost 6–3 to Scotland.) Fittingly, it was the captain, Ian Edwards, who clinched the whole event with a 5–3 win over Mark Thompson (though England won the foil 5–4).

Scotland had a patchy time and came third, though Cath Robertson won eight out of nine fights, and Wiles seven. For N. Ireland, Magill inflicted a personal 6–0 victory over England at foil and sabre. The English sabre team was notable for the inclusion of father and son: Dennis and Martin Hunt.

Prof. Tiller was the hero of the *BAF Championships* organised by Prof. Fairhill. At one point Prof. David Austin (4th) was only one hit from winning the foil and in the subsequent four-way barrage Prof. Roy Goodall (3rd) was in the same position; but in the end Ray Tiller won the title on indicators from John Fairhall.

In the sabre Tiller again won in a barrage, over the surprise performer Jes Smith – who was also third at epee, which was won by Fairhill over E. Kelman. Prof. Tiller won the master-at-arms trophy presented by Mrs Harry Porter in memory of her husband.

It was unclear why the fencers of the world had to assemble for the *World Championships*, mostly at great expense, in an unheated stone-floored shed in mid-winter Buenos Aires. The British team was accompanied by Nick Halsted as overall and foil captain, Mildred Durne as ladies' captain and James Noel, Derrick Cawthorne and John Zarno as presidents. There were 71 in the ladies' event. Everyone survived the first round, but Hilary Cawthorne went out in the second, along with Sue Wrigglesworth (despite three wins), Wendy Ager (too nervous to gain more than two wins in her tough pool) and Liz Wood (the newcomer, who fought coolly, lacking only a certain conviction).

Linda Martin, however, went from strength to strength, fencing magnificently in both second and third rounds, again and again devastating her opponents with a simple step forward and stop hit. She thus reached the direct elimination seeded thirteenth, against Trinquet of France (eventually fifth). A touch awestruck, she now froze and only got three hits. In the repechage she lost to Kniazeva of the USSR by the same score. Her final position was thirteenth, an excellent achievement for a new colour.

The final was an affair of screams, tears, wild jabbing and endless off-target hits; only Sidorova of Russia was more controlled. She won.

The British were seeded seventh in the team event. They beat Argentina 15–1, despite vigorous support for the home side. After promotion was assured, they started well against Rumania, but eventually had to concede 9–5 to aggressive, determined opponents.

In the next round they faced Russia, who were to win the Gold; brave fencing yielded three wins. Thereafter they met the toppled third seed, France, in the fight-off for the lower places. They lost 9–4.

British team, 1977. *Back:* T. Belson, H. W. Hoskyns; *4th row:* G. Grimmett, S. Paul, A. Eames, J. Deanfield, N. Bell, B. Paul; *3rd row:* W. R. Johnson, G. Paul, J. Llewellyn, D. Cawthorne; *2nd row:* E. Wood, J. Zarno, T. Etherton, W. Ager, J. Philbin, R. Cohen. *Front:* L. Martin, R. Oldcorn, H. Cawthorne, S. Wrigglesworth, N. Halsted.

In the 96-strong men's foil it was necessary to beat the inexperienced S. Americans to gain promotion from the first round. Grimmett neglected an Argentinian and Columbian to his cost. Graham Paul lost to a Venezuelan, but made up for it by beating Hein, prospective Silver Medallist. Hein got his revenge in the second round, where Graham got only one victory. Bell and Eames both got two wins here, but didn't look like getting a third. Barry Paul was just getting into his stride, but had an exceptionally tough pool and despite wins over Stankovitch, 1971 Champion, and Dal Zotto, that of 1976, was unlucky enough to be eliminated on three wins. Romankov was the winner for the second year running.

Hoping to equal or exceed their sixth place at Montreal, the team were seeded seventh and found themselves in a pool with France, Venezuela and Kuwait. The latter were defeated for a combined loss of only three fights. Bound to be promoted, the British now aspired to an improved seeding by beating France. There was an intensely exciting match. From 3–0 down they recovered to 5–4 up, but then lost the next three. Wins thereafter alternated to a 9–7 defeat. Eames and Barry Paul fenced superlatively, each winning three. The others, sadly, raised only one win between them.

To reach the last eight they faced the Americans – a much stronger team than the one they beat at Montreal. Barry, at his familiar best, again won three, as did Andy Eames, excelling at his first World Championships, combining variety of movement with both speed and accuracy, in both attack and defence. Again, however, the others could only raise one win between them.

The final proved extremely dramatic. Italy raced to a 7–1 lead over W. Germany – who then, unbelievably, recovered to 7–all. Hein got to 4–1 against Borella – one hit from the medal – but lost 5–4. Reichert then won the match from Coletti.

All the sabreurs did well in the 72-strong first round, including Zarno, replacing Oldcorn, who had back trouble. In the star-studded second round both new colours, Zarno and Etherton, though fencing with skill and confidence, could only get one win apiece. Philbin following his first round win over Montano now beat Kovacs, but could add only one more win. Cohen pulled out all the stops and fenced with a skill and determination that was a pleasure to watch. He beat a Venezuelan and ousted both Nilca of Rumania (5–3) and Hammang of Hungary (5–1). In the quarter-finals he was surrounded by two prospective finalists, two previous finalists, and a not inexperienced Russian. Four hits on the 1975 Silver Medallist Bierkowski was the best he could manage. A measure of his achievement is the fact that he was the only fencer outside the magic circle of the top five sabre nations to reach the last 24, apart from one W. German.

The final, ably co-presided by John Zarno, was of high quality. By 5–4 in the barrage, after 5–4 in the pool, Gerevich just prevented Nazlimov winning twice running.

The British were again seeded seventh in the team event. They beat Venezuela 14–2 and against Hungary Deanfield got two fine victories and Etherton a third. In the direct elimination Italy piled up 9–3, but Etherton got a magnificent two wins and Philbin a beauty against Arcidiacono (who had just won the Bronze). For a place in the last six they then fought Poland. Cohen got the only win, and the team retired to the warmer weather of Rio de Janeiro.

Epee results were extremely uneven. Both Hoskyns, burdened with the captaincy, and Steven Paul, in his first World Championship, went out in the first round. After three wins here, Llewellyn almost beat Riboud in the second round, but couldn't maintain the pressure. Both he and Belson, who lacked drive, went out with one win. Johnson gathered strength, however, winning three wins in both rounds (Pusch being eliminated with nil wins in the second). In the third round he began by losing to a Chilean, but then dramatically tightened up and dominated his four other opponents, including Edling, Boisse of France and Erdos.

In the direct elimination next day Johnson was seeded fifth, against Hogstrom. Showing no sign of nerves, he outplayed him in everything he did. In a virtually faultless display, he sapped Hogstrom of confidence both in attack and defence. At 9–2 down, in acknowledgement of his hopeless position, he proffered his open arm. So, just one bout to the final.

Kozejowski was unknown as an epeeist, but had long been a highly effective member of the Polish foil team. For the first eight minutes the two combatants eyed each other, moved cautiously and feinted tentatively. Kozejowski was clearly uncertain what tactics to adopt, while Johnson was unsure about the reaction his epee moves would provoke. Tension mounted. Johnson took his courage in both hands and scored once and then again. After a further double hit one minute was called. The Pole had to move to attack and with long broken-time attacks exasperatingly managed to pull back to 3–3. Time was called and just one hit now separated Ralph from the final. The tension was almost unbearable. Would Britain have a world finalist at last after all these years? Suddenly the tall, athletic Pole launched a flat-out fleche, Ralph took a solid parry and riposted as his opponent was passing. That riposte may have been parried, it may have missed, but one thing stood out clearly and that, heart-rendingly, was a light against Johnson. Into the repechage he went.

However upset Johnson was, it was not to be allowed to affect him in the next bout against the lanky Dunaev of the Soviet Union. He soon took charge and after a brief exchange of touches he built up a lead which he retained without ever looking really threatened to run out the winner 10–7. Once more he was fencing for a place in the final, his adversary being young Gaille from Switzerland, a neat, darting fencer with a foil background, who had already won world team medals but never been in an individual final. Johnson started with a few solid hits but was not quite as confident as before. With admirable control, speed and deceptive timing, Gaille turned the deficit into a 7–4 lead.

Ralph Johnson

Searching for ways to hit him and with relentless tenacity, Johnson brought the score back to 6–7. Then by a fraction of an inch he missed a well-timed stop-hit. What could have been a 7–all became an 8–6, and Gaille was not to be stopped from putting on the last two hits to win by 10–7.

In spite of the brilliance of his performance and the excellence of his seventh place, it was impossible for long afterwards to feel anything but anguish over what could so easily have been the best British result since 1965.

Gaille came third in the final, after a four-way barrage won by the super-fit Harmenberg of Sweden.

In the first round of the team event Britain hammered Mexico and in turn were hammered by Russia. In the last twelve they had a disastrous 9–1 to France, all but Belson looking out of their class, including Johnson.

The cast for the *World Student Games* in Sofia was not so very different, especially since perpetual student status suits eastern European pseudo-amateurism. The British team only included two national team members out of a party of ten, and unfortunately neither did well. Sue Wrigglesworth had a first round equal to a World Championship third round; on top of that the Russian girl inexplicably lost to Sue's rival for promotion in the last bout. So she got no further. Bell, in less than best form, got to the second round, as did Wedge and Magill (who had the eventual Silver and Bronze Medallists in his pool). Tom Beattie went out in the first round both in foil and sabre. Magill got to the second round in the sabre. Here Slade put up a remarkable display against some very tough opposition. Only in the third round did he succumb, fencing noticeably faster than in the World Youth, though still not so as to do himself full justice. Stanbury at epee also went well, looking as if he might go on to the direct elimination, but for tiredness and erratic concentration which led him to fall back on silly movements. Lavington and Noel, the latter retired and present mainly as captain, were first round victims.

For the team events the ten combined as best they could. At foil, after losing 12–4 to France, they did well to force seven bouts from the Poles, Wedge channelling his exuberance into three splendid wins for the loss of only seven hits, and Beattie's determination securing two, with one each to Bell and Magill. Switzerland they beat 10–6, admittedly after both teams had been eliminated. Beattie excelled to win four (Wedge 3, Bell 2, Magill 1).

Bell did better at epee than at his own weapon, whereas Noel took his epees from the loft without great effect. A loss of 13–3 was sustained against France (Stanbury 2, Bell 1, Lavington 0, Noel 0) and one of 11–5 against Hungary (Bell 2, Lavington 2, Stanbury 1, Noel 0). The sabreurs fared no better: 15–1 to Rumania (Slade 1, Beattie 0, Magill 0, Lavington 0); 11–5 to W. Germany (Lavington 2, Slade 1, Beattie 1, Magill 1).

# 1977-8

*MEN'S FOIL*

The season marked a considerable turning point, since three members retired from the team, at least for the time being. Geoff Grimmett's retirement was no surprise, but that of the Paul brothers came when both of them had the potential to remain for several more years, especially Barry. However, they had both put in many years service. Graham first went to the World Championships in 1966 and Barry in 1969. Both had remained solidly in the team ever since, a good deal longer than most foreign contemporaries as well as longer than any other British foilists since the retirement of Jay.

The spectacular star was Pierre Harper, still only twenty years old. Thanks to Prof. Roy Goodall, his technique was now exceptionally good. He was also fit and his attitude was wholesome and enthusiastic, not always the case with top British fencers. He began with a scintillating victory in the *Coronation Cup* and went on to win both *National* and the *Commonwealth Championship* and to gain a final place at *Bad Durkheim*. These results earned him sizeable competition grants, and support from the Sports Aid Foundation.

The Coronation attracted Japanese entrants – who took third and fourth places. Eames was the runner-up in the knock-out final, as he was in the *Emrys Lloyd* (with 9 wins). The winner here was Tony Bartlett, now rising fast despite not very strong legs and not much training (also on 9 wins). Harper was third (8v), followed by J. Ford, (8v), G. Paul (8v) and G. Evans (8v).

To show even more clearly that he hadn't retired altogether, Graham Paul was close on Harper's heels in the *Championship*. He took him to the last hit and dismissed all the other finalists, except Bell, 5–1. Bell in turn lost to Graham Kay of Hydra U-20 but was still one fight clear in third place. Bruniges re-entered the scene in fifth place, with one win, over Bartlett, who couldn't score on this occasion.

The top foilists were active too on the provincial circuit. Wojciechowski, visiting England with a view to possible future employment, was the winner of *Ashton* and also at *Leicester*, when he won the barrage with Eames 5–3, having lost to him 5–4 in the pool. They were followed by G. Paul (3v), Harper (3v), Gabor Scott of Salle Paul, who was also winner at *Portsmouth* (2v), and G. Evans (0v).

Bell, now in Paris practising medicine (and not very much fencing), reappeared to win the *Birmingham Tournament*, showing more accuracy and directness of purpose if less imagination than Bruniges, the runner-up. Glaister came fourth to a delighted (re-amateurised) Barry More. Carl Waldman, practising medicine in the RAF, won the *Inter-Services* foil for the third time. At *Liverpool* the surprise of the semi-finals was the elimination of

Wedge. Kay won, defeated only by David Carlisle (Instonians), who was fifth (2v). All on three wins and all from Hydra were Glenn Jones (2nd), Steve Glaister (3rd) and Ray Swinnerton (4th), who also was *Novices Champion*. Sixth was John Gay of the Navy.

Bill Gosbee of Salle Boston was the *Under-20* Champion, making up in sparkle what he lacked in reach. He was followed by Seaman, another fencer lacking the advantage of height, and John Troiano of Ganchev, by contrast tall and rangy, and by Glenn Jones, Visholm and McKenzie. The first three were generally the junior front runners. In good performances at *Kussnacht* Gosbee was fourth and Seaman sixth, Jones being placed ninth. At *Burgsteinfurt* Gosbee and Andrew Martin of Poly were in the last 48 and Troiano in the last 24. In the *Under-16 Brussels* event Justin Pitman (again the *Under-14* Champion) was in the last twelve and Paul Mitchell (S. Paul) in the last eight. Pitman, a fencer with excellent timing and spirit, was winner of the *Moers Under-16* event. Douglas Dale (Brentwood) was second and Ross Atkinson (Wandsworth) third. At *Papendal* in June McKenzie was second and Andrew Webb and Andrew Alderman (Boston) were in the last sixteen; in the team event they were second, losing 5–3 to Duisburg (McKenzie 2, Alderman 1, Webb 0).

Back at home, Gosbee, showing how well trained as well as how talented he was, won the *Eden International* trophy ahead of Vuille (Switzerland) and Troiano. Seaman got his reward for conscientious training when he won the *Millfield Tournament*, followed by Gosbee, Driessen (Holland), two Belgians and a W. German.

The invitation *Wilkinson Sword* trophy was won by McKenzie. Second was Chris Ward of Birmingham FC, who was also runner-up in the *Junior Championship*, losing the barrage 5–2 to Martin of Poly who made up for lack of aggression with an excellent technique. Mark Thompson of Cambridge was third on hits over Mike Thornton of Poly, in spite of losing to him in the last fight and forfeiting a share in the barrage. Jim Hamments made his fourth appearance in the final since 1967, in fifth place, followed by John Woods, a classical foilist with a strong defence, a crisp, fast quarte-riposte and effective angulated one-two, who came from the S. Section and was now at Oxford.

By contrast, there were a healthy 31 entrants for the *Team Championship*. The closest match of all was in the early rounds, between Boston 'B' and Cambridge, where a fight-off was won 5–4 by Mark Thompson over Loveland. In one semi-final Boston 'A' beat Elliott, Paterson, Smith and Beattie, fencing under the newly-devised banner of Ecosse, who had done very well to dispose of both Poly and Paul 'B'. In the other, Hydra Under-20 avenged their loss to Pauls the year before by racing to an 8–3 lead and then winning 9–6. Pauls were thus absent from the final for the first time since 1962 (apart from three years when leading members were fencing for London University).

In the final, Boston never allowed their young opponents to get on top, though Glaister was undefeated, with one to go. (Kay 1/3; Wedge 1/4; Jones 0/4). For the winners, Fox equalled Glaister (Bruniges 2/3; Eames 3/4; Waldman/Bourne 1/4).

Results abroad this season were good. At *Besançon* Harper was in the last sixteen and Bartlett in the last 32. Eames began a run of consistently good results with a place in the last sixteen of the *Martini*, where he only missed a yet more outstanding result when, at 9-all with Pietruszka of France, a French president gave what by all accounts was a stop-hit against his direct attack. Of the others, Bruniges, Fox and Glaister were in the last 48. Eames also reached the last sixteen in the *Duval*, came seventh in the *Debeur* (with Harper 13th) and was in the last 24 in *Venice* (where, to show that he too had not totally retired, Barry Paul was in the last 48). In *Warsaw* Harper and Glaister were in the last 24 and Bartlett in the last 32. In *Antwerp* Bartlett capped a good season with fourth place, followed by Fox in fifth place and Kay in the last sixteen. Finally, at *Bad Durkheim* Bell reached the last 24, and Bruniges the last sixteen. Bruniges continued to tantalise by the disparity between his quality, which had the potential to take him to the top of world fencing, and his drive, which was much more wavering. This season he showed what he had it in him to do by getting to the last twelve of the mighty *Rommel*.

The team for the World Championship consisted of Harper, Glaister and Bartlett – all new members – together with Bruniges, Eames and Bell (the last for the team event only). Ian Single took over from Nick Halsted, who had been captain since 1974.

*LADIES' FOIL*

Reporting on the Under-20s, Sheila Arup (mother of three fencers) expressed concern at the steep fall in the number of competitors. The Millfield tournament had to be abandoned for lack of British support, while the existing points system, she considered, induced top contenders to give precedence to senior events.

Liz Wood, now nineteen, won the *Perigal*, came third at *Dornbirn* and was in the team which won there, but otherwise fenced with the seniors now that she was a member of the British team. Ann Brannon (still fencing for Chester), in her last junior year was fifth at Dornbirn, in the last eight at *Etampes*, in the last 32 of *Gelsenkirchen* and second in the *Under-20 Championships*; she also won the *Universities Championship* for Cambridge. She displayed good technique and directed competitiveness. Clare Montgomery (Boston), in her last year too, was fifth at *Kussnacht*, in round three at Etampes, and won the Under-20 Championship. An attacker with wide movements, she used her intelligence to effect on the piste. Third both here and in the Perigal was Fiona McIntosh (Meadowbank and Fettes), still only seventeen and on a Lorimer Trust

Bursary. She got to the third round at Gelsenkirchen and again at Etampes and was the winner of the *Ashton Under-20*. Impairment of composure and technique under pressure prevented her getting the same excellent results abroad as she had already gained at home.

A remarkable season was achieved by Kim Cecil of Chase Club and Coopers Coburn School, who was only aged sixteen. She was second in the Perigal, won the *Felix Cup*, was in round three at Etampes, came sixth at Kussnacht and did best of all the British as runner-up at Dornbirn. On top of all that she was the winner of the *Tyneside* and the *Welsh Open*. Clare Gobey of Brownhill, also aged sixteen, did well at home, being fifth in the Perigal and third in the Ashton Under-20; later on she was second in the *Arnhem Under-20*. Julia Verne of Saint Paul's School was Under-18 Champion (having been third in the Felix the year before) while Kate Arup (14) was Under-16 Champion, in the last eight of the Perigal, sixth in the *Brussels European Under-14* event, ninth in the *Zurich Under-20* and winner of the *Dorothy Knowles Liverpool Under-20*.

The *Team Championship* was won for the first time by Salle Paul, who had been runners-up the two previous seasons. After beating Poly only in the last fight of the semi-final, they made short work of a rather sluggish London –Thames, by 9–4 (C. Arup, S. Gallagher, E. Wood, S. Wrigglesworth; S. Uff, Mrs S. Kenealy, née Littlejohns, A. Milner-Barry, S. Rochard).

Among the Category events, the *Lowther Cup* for the unclassified was won by Jo Millott of Allen F.C., ahead of Mrs Janet Hall (Elmbridge), Diane Freeman (Goodall), Pauline Stonehouse (taught by Mike Westgate at Sondes Place; 2v), Muriel Wilson (2v) and Mavis Bragg (Poly; 1v). The *Parker* was won undefeated by Janet Jones of Ashton, followed by Penny Johnson of Salle Paul, aged only seventeen (3v), Olivia Pontefract, née Meyrick (London –Thames, 3rd, 3v), Julia Verne (2v), Nicky Jacobsen (5th, 1v) and Louise Dale of Chase (1v). Penny Johnson (5th, 2v) and Olivia Pontefract (6th, 1v) also made it to the final of the *Bertrand*, in which the top four fought a barrage, won undefeated by Jacky Erwteman of Salle Behmber over Fiona McIntosh (2nd), Janet Jones (3rd) and Maureen Lloyd (4th), who was married to Jes Smith of the BAF.

The final of the *Desprez* had two surprise entrants from Scotland: Cath Wotherspoon, now wife of Lewis Smith, in sixth place (0v), and in fifth place Janet Wardell-Yerburgh (1v), now Mrs Cooksey and living in St Andrews, who had been *Scottish* Champion for the second year running this season. The other places were more predictable: Liz Wood (4th, 2v), Hilary Cawthorne (3rd, 3v), Wendy Grant (2nd, 4v) and Linda Martin undefeated for Poly in first place. Sue Wrigglesworth was missing here; in the *Championship* it was Linda Martin who lost her way in the repechages. Wendy Grant, fencing skilfully and relaxed by her decision not to fence in international events this season, narrowly missed the crown when she lost to Liz Wood, whose competitive talent no one could match, in spite of patchy fencing before she scented victory. Ann Brannon (2v, 3rd) moved up two places on the previous year, while Hilary Cawthorne (2v, 4th) and Susan Wrigglesworth (2v, 5th) both moved down three places. Brenda Hewitt (1v) took the last place.

Back in February, the *de Beaumont* was of truly international standard, with Danish, Dutch, Swiss and French entries and the world Silver Medallist team from E. Germany. The main British hope in the final lay with Linda Martin, who was only seeded seventeenth after three rounds of pools, but then showed her best form to brush aside first the top-seeded Schubert and then the Danish Max Madsen on her straight path to the last six. Susan Wrigglesworth had more of a struggle. She lost to Janke 8–6 and then had to beat Hertrampf (also of E. Germany) and Hilary Cawthorne, which she did, 8–1 and 8–4.

Janke got an early lead in the final by beating her two compatriots, but seemed to under-estimate Linda Martin and lost 5–3. This shook her confidence and she lost her next fight to Sue Wrigglesworth, who had collected one defeat. Hanisch, the W. German Olympic finalist, was also one down; even if, as seemed possible, she beat Janke, Sue Wrigglesworth would have the opportunity of a barrage. In fact Janke panicked her into a quick 5–1 defeat and Sue Wrigglesworth was the outright winner with four victories, in very distinguished company.

Sue went on to collect the best British results abroad, along with Linda Martin and Hilary Cawthorne, although they had all been outdistanced in the Championship, perhaps because the others had more to prove. In *Amsterdam* Linda Martin was the winner and Hilary Cawthorne was in the last eight. Sue Hoad was in the last twelve. At Katowice Liz Wood excelled to gain eighth place. Hilary Cawthorne was in the last sixteen, Linda Martin in the last 24. Sue Wrigglesworth only reached the last 32, but got an outstanding third place in *E. Berlin* amongst the Russians, with Hilary Cawthorne not far behind in the last sixteen.

At *Duren* twelve Britons reached the last 48, Kim Cecil did well to gain the last 24, Sue Wrigglesworth was in the last sixteen and Hilary Cawthorne got to the last twelve. In the *Challenge Chabine* in Paris Maureen Hillier was in the last 24. At *Goppengen* Sue Wrigglesworth was in the last 24 and in *Turin* again did excellently, only missing the final by one fight. Linda Martin was in the last 32 there, and reached twelve at *Offenbach*, where Hilary Cawthorne got to the last 32. In the *Jeanty* Linda Martin reached the third round, as she did at *Como*, along with Hilary Cawthorne and Liz Wood.

There were three *matches* at Katowice. Linda Martin, Liz Wood, Hilary Cawthorne and Sue Wrigglesworth beat Leipzig 9–1 but lost to Katowice 9–4 and to Warsaw 9–7. In the *Seven Nations Tournament* in Frankfurt the same team, reinforced by Ann Brannon, did very well to beat Poland and W. Germany, both by 10–6. With Ann Brannon taking the place of Wendy Grant (who had retired) it was again the same team at the World Championships.

Mildred Durne was captain for the sixth time. Linda Martin was able to train at Tauberbischofsheim for several weeks beforehand, thanks to a Churchill Scholarship.

## EPEE

The first national event, the *Epee Club Cup*, was fittingly a triumph for Beevers on the eve of his departure to work as a civil engineer in the Persian Gulf. Delivering needle-sharp hits from an implacably statuesque position, he was undefeated in the final, ahead of Bourne (3v), Llewellyn (3v), Steven Paul (2v), Edwards (1v) and Lavington (0v). Hill, Fairhall and Ewan Ferguson narrowly missed promotion from one of the preliminary pools of eighteen; Roose, Stanbury and Higginson from the other.

Before he left, Beevers also won at *Brighton*, followed by Edwards, David Rapley, Mark Carpenter, John Payne and Robert Brooks, twin brother of David, fencing for Leicester YM.

The *Under-20 Championship* lost several leading contenders before the final. Wood and Roger Greenhalgh (Reading), both too worried to fence at their best, were knocked out in the repechage by David Commander of Latista and Mike Thornton of Sondes Place; Kernohan, off his normal aggressive form, was knocked out 10-7 by Matthew Chell, now at Cambridge. Steventon, compact, somewhat staccato and with a sense of counter-time, was outright winner, showing considerable promise. Storming straight into second place (and taking Steventon to the last hit) was the large, slightly heavy-footed but also distinctly promising 17-year-old George Liston of Meadowbank, Edinburgh (3v). Fairhall of Grosvenor (2v; 3rd) possessed great ability in terms of speed, accuracy and timing, but was handicapped by his footwork, rushed tactics and volatile temperament; great things were predicted for him if these were rectified. The gangling Thornton (2v; 4th) was a little lacking in aggression, but showed intelligence; as did Chell (2v; 5th), who was also beginning to get some needful mobility. Young (1v) set up a new record by coming sixth for the third year out of the previous four. Like Edling, he had a long reach, and he seemed set on being like Edling in using the minimum repertoire of moves, but, as yet, not quite so successfully.

Liston went on to win both *Under-18* and *Public Schools* titles for George Heriot's. His school-fellow Mark Wright was sixth in the latter. Alexander Foss of Eton was second, ahead of Andy Brannon and Ian Manley, both of King's Chester. Abroad, Chell reached the last 32 at *Differdange*; at *Laupheim* he and Fairhall reached the third round and Young got to the last 24.

None of the under-twenties got to the *Junior* final, won by Steve Roose, now at Bath, who had been steadily improving over the previous two years, with a classic stance and patient, accurate tactics. Runner-up was David Brooks, now in London, taught by Prof. Fairhall at Grosvenor. Edwards, thwarted of the title yet again, was third, followed by the interloping foilist Bell (London –Thames), who entered many epee events this season. Lewis, now a master at Millfield, was fifth, followed by Nigel Clark, a pentathlete strong on length and aggression.

Bell did even better to come third at *Birmingham*, still the top provincial event. The winner was Weglinski of Gornoczy Club, Katowice, which won the Friday evening team event over the Modern Pentathletes, and provided the runner-up, Drozdzowski. Fourth was Graham Paul and fifth Roose, who, though seeded second, faced the winner in the last eight. Davenport and Stanbury were sixth and seventh, ahead of the Dutch Kuperus.

The most widely successful fencer in the provincial events was Steven Paul, who won *Ashton*, *Leicester* and the *Welsh Open* – the last after a barrage with Graham Paul and Howard West. David Brooks, with his slippery disengage counter-attack and darting hit to foot, was fourth here, but was the winner at *Bristol*, where Turner fenced steadily into second place, ahead of fellow Cardiff member Lyndon Martin, who produced surprising mobility from a heavy-weight physique. Third was the emerging Jerry Melville, RAF technician and stunt motor-cyclist, who had started fencing only at the age of 22, under Tom Norcross, and was now at Boston. He used his length with confident aggression, in contrast to Young (5v), who was equally tall but played a waiting game, drawing his opponent's blade to his wrist and gathering it in vigorous counter-attacks.

David Fairhall, sixth at Bristol, was the winner at *Nottingham*, ahead of Clark, of the local fencers Bob Sedols (3rd) and Robert Brooks and of his father John (5th) and Brian Henshall. At the *Kirklees Tournament*, in Huddersfield, Brian Matless, ex-Army, was the winner, followed by Julian Tyson and John Warburn (RAF). *Leicester* was much stronger, with Llewellyn the runner-up, followed by Lavington (third equal with Stanbury at Ashton), Hall (fifth in the Welsh Open) and John Tomlinson of Sheffield (5th). (West scratched in protest at the final being delayed for the benefit of the other weapons.)

West was runner-up in the still more strongly-contested *Martini Qualifying*, with sixteen wins in the final pool of 24, but Roose was the decisive winner with nineteen wins. They were followed by Lavington, still at Liverpool University (15v), Graham Paul (15v), Mallett (14v) and Bell (6v). A notable feature of the event was the welcome invasion of a galaxy of Scottish talent: Hugh Kernohan (Meadowbank; 7th), Brian McMiken (Glasgow; 9th), Mike Peat (Edinburgh Univ.; 11th), Ewan Ferguson (Edinburgh Univ.; 13th), George Liston (Meadowbank; 18th) and Tim Wilson (Ecosse; 23rd). There had been promising young Scots epeeists before, but never in such numbers (particularly bearing in mind that several equally gifted Scots were absent, such as Gregor Henderson, second at Ashton). The question was, would these pupils of Prof. Bert Bracewell (the National Coach) and his deputy Derek Titheradge have more staying power than previous generations of promise?

Others who qualified were Stanbury (8th), Pearman (10th), Hill (14th) and Higginson (15th). None of these survived the first round of the Martini itself, however, amongst the star-studded entries from every leading country but Russia. This was achieved only by Davenport, Brooks, Bourne, Hall, Hoskyns and Bell – and two others who went further. Stanbury was in the first fight-off for the bottom four of the match plan of the last 32. He lost to Muck, 1972 winner, on the last hit. Graham Paul, having gained a very good tenth seeding, had two successive needle bouts. Against Duchene of France he showed how he was unequalled in Britain for determination when fighting for the last hit and for the conviction with which he could carry out the boldest move in this situation if he judged it right. In this case he got his tenth and victorious hit en fleche.

His next fight, in the last sixteen, was equally exciting. This was against the Swiss Suchanecki, a fencer of black locks and snakelike, darting thrusts from a very low blade position. This time, sadly, it went 10–9 the wrong way. Harmenberg, reigning World Champion, went out at the same stage.

The eight in the gala final included no less than three Swiss and of these Gaille and Kauter reached the last four. There they were defeated in close, rousing bouts respectively by Boisse and Pusch, who held first and second seedings – which held to the very end: Pusch's cat-spring fleches and crouching, floor-level stop-hits failing by two hits to stem the ever-resilient aggression of Boisse.

The other senior London events confirmed both the rising trend of certain newcomers and the durability of those who had already been at the top for many years, though it was not always easy to see which were the young and which the aging epeeists. Ted Bourne, second in the *Championship* as far back as 1965, celebrated his victory this season by jumping in the air for all the world as though still an exuberant teenager. He had cause to celebrate, since he thus broke all records, being the victor, in spite of his retirement, not only for the third time running, but also for the sixth time in all, surpassing the five victories gained by Robert Montgomerie in the ten years up to 1914, when fencing was a smaller and more middle-aged sport. Runner-up was the equally established Johnson, who dominated his opponents (including Bourne by 5–3) until he pursued a winning rein of prises de fers too rashly against a physically determined Belson (3v; 3rd). Bourne beat Johnson 5–2 in the barrage. Third was Graham Paul, another veteran, in his sixth final since coming second in 1966. Fifth and sixth places, however, went to newcomers, though neither was especially young: for Bell this was the climax of his incursion; for Roose, confirmation of his promise.

Just short of the final was another future team possible, Liston, who dispatched Partridge in the last sixteen with both spirit and skill, lost 10–7 to Roose and came back through the repechage to miss the final only on the last hit to Graham Paul (in a fight not without rule problems). Equally close was David Brooks, who beat Belson 10–7 in the last sixteen and was then doubly unlucky: to confront Johnson and to lose 10–9.

John Llewellyn was absent from the Championship, working, training and improving in Switzerland. In the *Miller–Hallett* he showed his dominance. He lost to West in the final, which put him in a barrage with Bourne, who had only been hit three times by all the others in the pool, in spite of no training since the Championship three weeks before. As he had already done in the direct elimination and the final, Llewellyn now beat him on the last hit, putting more depth into his strokes and thus ridding himself of his bogyman. This was the eighth time Bourne had been in the first three, a record only equalled by Jay and surpassed by de Beaumont's ten times and Hoskyns' nine times. (Jacobs had made it seven times.)

West, in third place, was a finalist for the second year running. As in the Epee Club Cup, Steven Paul was fourth; he had also narrowly missed the Championship final; in all a very solid home run. Following him on hits was Johnson. On the Saturday there had been *matches* against Norway and Luxembourg (both won) and Austria (lost). Their representatives had been outshone by the British in the competition. Koppang went out early. In the match-plan Hoskyns gave the coup de grace to both Scharle (Lux.) and Vonen (Norway), but himself lost to West (twice). Eichinger, the Austrian World Youth finalist, was disposed of by Belson, who also ousted Roose, only in turn to go down to Bourne. Kernohan eliminated Bell, but was himself another of West's victims. Lindner of Austria was the only foreigner to reach the final, but scratched to catch his plane.

Only nine teams took part in the *Savage*. In the quarter-finals Boston 'B' (Mallett, Steventon, Tarran and Young) beat London–Thames 'B' (Jacobs, Halsted, Fare and Carpenter); Ecosse (Liston, Henderson, Post and Tyson) took six fights off London–Thames 'A' (for whom West was undefeated) before going under; Cardiff took five off second-seeded Pauls (Gray 2, Lewis 1, Turner 1, Colin Wickens 1); Boston 'A' beat Poly 9–2 (Jaron 2; Edwards, Forward, Bird 0).

In the semi-finals London–Thames led Pauls 8–7 but needed the last fight. Graham Paul beat Hoskyns 5–0 to take the match by seven hits. Boston 'B' almost managed the same feat against their own 'A' team, who had to win both last fights, so poor were their hits at 7–all. In the final, Boston 'A' continued to falter at first, going 3–1 down, but a smart last hit flick to the wrist gave Bruniges a 5–4 win over Barry Paul and initiated an unbroken run to 9–3 – the breaking point probably being Davenport's 5–4 defeat of Steven Paul (Bourne 3, Johnson 2, Bruniges 2, Davenport 2; G. Paul 1, S. Paul 1, B. Paul 0). The victory was the hat-trick for Boston.

In events abroad Hoskyns began well with second place in *Oslo*, but thereafter had a disappointing season, by contrast with Llewellyn (third at Oslo) and Steven Paul (who reached the last sixteen), both of whom went on to excellent seasons. Llewellyn reached the last twelve at *Zurich* and then scored a major triumph at *Carroccio*, the replacement for the Milan Spreafico, if not quite so strong. After several tough rounds he successively beat Suchanecki and Ivanoff in the direct elimination to go straight into the final. Here he fenced to such effect, including yet a third Swiss, Evequoz, among his victims, that he obtained second place, a splendid result, rivalled in the event only by Hoskyns reaching the last eight in 1957 and 1959.

In the less formidable event at *Innsbruck* Llewellyn came third, with Belson in the last eight. Here Steven Paul came into his own as the winner. Earlier he had come sixth at *Duren*, only a little less strong than heretofore. Roose affirmed his class by gaining fifth place. Johnson was third after barraging for first place with Begard and Guittet of France. At the *Monal*, which, unusually, attracted the Russians, Johnson reached the last twelve, defeating Zablowsky (Poland) and Väggo (Sweden) before missing the final by 10–8 to Behr (W. Germany), the eventual runner-up, and losing in the repechage to Lukomsky 10–7. Roose reached the last 32. Hall, having barely survived the first round, accelerated into the last 48, his best foreign performance. Johnson again reached the last twelve at *Bern*. In the last 24 was Belson, who had done very well to come fourth in *E. Berlin* amongst all the good Germans, Swiss and Swedes back in October, but was thereafter on duty in N. Ireland till March.

Steven Paul got his best results yet when he reached the last twelve of the enormous and supremely tough *Heidenheim* event, and went on to reach the last eight at *Poitiers*. Stanbury was in the last sixteen, his best performance since being fourth in the 1971 World Youth Games. Brooks was eighth this year at *Rennes*.

The team picked itself: Llewellyn, Johnson, Paul and Belson, plus Roose in Hoskyns' place. Of other potential candidates, Graham Paul's commitment to epee had been wavering and he had been plagued by injury; Mallett had a disappointing season and was abroad for much of the latter part and Steventon's training was interrupted by studies. Stanbury was the reserve.

## *SABRE*

This was an encouraging season. The pattern was set with the *Cole Cup*. A host of foreigners took part but the British came out on top. Five Britons survived the first two rounds to join two Germans, two Dutchmen, two Iranians and a Canadian. Four of the British won through to the final and among those eliminated were Fitting and Hamm, as well as Hutt.

Styles in the final varied from the economy of Lavoie (3rd) to the aggression of Convents (4th). Deanfield (6th) fenced with flair but lacked conviction, giving up early on. Etherton relied heavily on counter-attacks, but his timing justified him. Philbin fenced well, holding a closed line and keeping distance, but perhaps not changing his attacks enough; he got to a cliff-hanging 4–all with Convents, with the priority against him. He coolly found his opponent's blade and scored to force a barrage with Cohen. This Cohen won 5–3, deservedly after gaining the best two hits of the day: successively from 3–4 down to Convents he had produced a third counter-riposte and a brilliant point stop-hit, catching Convents full-flow, his first victory over the German.

In the *Championship* Philbin was back on top, achieving the hat-trick (equalling C. A. Wilson, Roger Tredgold, Mike Amberg and Sandy Leckie and only bettered by David Acfield since the start of the event in 1898). Added to the strength of his footwork and his determination was a much improved technique. There were 41 participants. Notable eliminations in the second round were Kovanda, Bryan Lewis and Scott. The semi-finals (3rd round) were as follows. A: Etherton 5, Cohen 4, Deanfield 3, Gryf-Lowczowski 2, J. Lewis 1, Dauppe 0; B: Philbin 4, Zarno 3, Slade 3, Magill 3, Hutt 1, Roberts 0. There followed the 'interpolated' final of the Ladies Championship. In the sabre final Cohen lost 5–2 to Philbin, but also lost 5–3 to Etherton and had to accept second place for the fourth year running. Etherton himself missed the chance of a barrage by losing his last fight to Philbin, by a crushing 5–0. Earlier he had lost 5–4 to Deanfield after the latter successfully argued the president out of awarding a final hit against him, although Etherton had shaken hands and left the piste. *The Sword* commented that Etherton's return to the piste to continue fencing rather than engaging in counter-arguments showed 'a certain naivety in modern sport' – a sad reflection of the erosion of the amateur spirit. He eventually secured third place on hits given. Zarno (1v; 5th) showed his lack of recent lessons by fencing speedily but with inadequate control at crucial moments. Slade got four hits each on Philbin, Etherton and Deanfield but no wins: he established some kind of record by coming sixth for the third year running.

The *Corble*, with its foreign element, saw Cohen top of the British squad again, in second place, after a three-way barrage with Strattmann of W. Germany (who beat him 5–4) and Deanfield (third on hits). Slade (2v) moved up to fourth place, having beaten Cohen 5–0 and Philbin 5–4. The last, in unaccustomed sixth place, beat only Cohen and Dehmer of W. Germany (5th), both on the last hit. Once more, however, he ruled the provincial tournaments. After claiming *Ashton* and the *Welsh Open*, he won *Leicester*, ahead of Cohen (4v), Hutt (3v), Milligan (2v), Richard Berry (Leicester YMCA; 1v) and Price (0v). At *Birmingham* he took the trophy by successive (hotly argued) wins in the direct elimination over Bartecki of Poland (fifth in the Touzard this year) and – on the last hit – Kiermasz (who had come second in the Touzard and had beaten Philbin 10-0 in that event). Roberts and Kay reached the last eight and last four respectively (both victims of Kiermasz). Kay was winner at *Liverpool*, followed by Glaister, Magill, Ian McConaghy (Boston) and Glenn Jones.

Philbin got four of Poly's nine wins in the final of the *Team Championship* against Salle Boston. Deanfield and Zarno got two each, the latter with one to go. Surprisingly, Cohen had no wins, though one fight to go. Boston mustered five wins (Etherton 2, Slade 2, Magill/J. Lewis 1, G. Li 0).

Jonathan Lewis of Boston won the *Junior Championship*, defeated only by his club-mate Magill (3v; 2nd). Milligan was a couple of hits behind and only one hit ahead of Gary Li, who was increasingly showing the ability to go far if he persisted. Martin Hall, the *Under-18 Champion* of Birmingham FC (2v) was well clear of Martin Hunt (Boston) (0v).

Slade recaptured the *Under-20 Championship* from Hunt. Indeed his main rival was the untidy but talented Hall, against whom he came from behind to win 5–4 in the first fight of the final. Thereafter neither was beaten. Hunt (3v) was third, followed predictably by Kenric Li (2v) and Gary Li (1v); but the last place – which might have gone to Patrick West (Ganchev), Steven Campbell or Gordon Drummond (both at Brentwood) or Andrew Cashen (now at Boston) – was actually captured by Paul Klenerman (0v), a 14-year-old taught by Paul Romang at City of London School and Salle Ganchev, who beat the last two 10–9 to reach the final. He was a natural, if not especially orthodox, sabreur, tending to rely on instinct, but with the ability to correct mistakes during a fight. Over half the rather low entry of 36 were taught by only two masters: Steve Boston and Paul Romang.

The *Public Schools Championship* was won by Hunt for Bristol GS, ahead of Campbell (3v), K. Li (3v), Mark Wright (George Heriot's; 2v) – who was also *Under-16 Champion* – Drummond (1v) and Foss (Eton; 1v).

Abroad, the under-twenties scored a number of successes. Slade came an outstanding second at *Dormagen* (W. Germany) behind the German Nolte and ahead of the Polish Baron, but this year only reached the last twelve at *Dourdan*, where K. Li and West were in the last 24. Hall reached the same stage at Dormagen.

The really good news was at senior level. At *Katowice* Philbin reached the last sixteen and Hutt the last 32. In *E. Berlin* Hutt got to the last 48. In the *Touzard* Deanfield and Cohen excelled to come third and fourth respectively. The only Frenchman to reach the final – Granger-Veyron – had to be content with last place. Karfanty was the winner. As already noted, Kiermasz and Bartecki took the other places. Cohen had eliminated Quivrin and Trottein in very good fights on the way to the final. Philbin was in the last sixteen. This was the best British showing so far in the event. At *Hamburg* Etherton and Philbin reached the last 32. In the *New York Martini* Philbin got to the last twelve,

Cohen to the last 24 and Hutt to the last 48. In *Munich* Cohen reached the last twelve, Etherton the last sixteen, Deanfield, Hutt and Slade the last 48. Finally at *Luxardo* Deanfield was in the last 24, Cohen in the last 32 and Philbin and Slade in the last 48.

In the *Seven Nations* team event Cohen beat all four W. Germans and three of the Italians. Deanfield hit top form in his three wins against the Russians and two against the Rumanians. Philbin now had a good tally of international results, but still tended to tense up on the big occasion, particularly in matches.

For the *World Championships*, Slade took the place of Oldcorn, who had retired at the end of the previous season (suffering from back injury) after fencing in eleven World Championships and three Olympics since his debut in 1964, only missing Cuba (to which no sabreurs went) and the Montreal Olympics.

## COMBINED EVENTS

The *World Youth Championships* were staged in Madrid again, after alternative venues had proved abortive. Alan Loveland was the captain. Troiano went out with two wins in the first round of the 72-strong men's foil. Gosbee, recovering from flu and insufficiently positive, was eliminated from the second round with one win. Seaman fenced well in the first rounds, but went off the boil during the subsequent siesta. In a tough quarter-final he got only one win, losing his last vital fight to the 1977 Bronze Medallist, Gey of W. Germany.

In the sabre, Slade, Hall and Gary Li all reached the second round, where Li found the going a little too tough, securing only one win. In the quarter-final Slade was disappointing, with a single win 5–0 over the Canadian Beaudry. Hall could also only manage one win, 5–4 against the Hungarian Balatoni.

Both Kim Cecil and Ann Brannon suffered uncharacteristically from nerves and went out in the first round. Liz Wood, however, practiced brinkmanship successfully in the second and third rounds to reach the last sixteen. There she met the uninhibitedly temperamental Vaccaroni (aged 14) of Italy (who eventually came fifth). She lost 8–2. In the repechage her over-use of stop-hits got her 7–1 down to Dubrawska of Poland. She changed tactics, but too late, though she reached 8–5. The final was notable for bad presiding and the second place, behind Latrille, of Luan Jujie of China, secured in spite of her sword-arm being speared by a broken blade in her first fight.

An off-form Fairhall went out of the first round of the epee. Steventon was promoted second, but got a second round with no less than three eventual finalists – Jablkowski (3rd), Koppang (1st) and Eichinger (6th). He was unable to raise his game to go up fourth. Young, undefeated in the first round, showed excellent mental attitude and control in the second round. (His pool was

Scottish team returning from victory in Quadrangular. *Back:* G. Henderson, G. Mackay, M. Mayo, M. Peat. *Front:* R. Elliott, F. McIntosh, L. Smith, J. Cooksey, A. Mitchell, C. Robertson, D. Paterson, F. Riddell (Manager).

reduced to five by the boycott on the part of a Kuwaiti objecting to an Israeli as an opponent – harbinger of the more widespread boycott of Moscow in 1980.) He topped the pool, conceding only a double defeat, to Katychev of the USSR. After the siesta-break he too lost his edge, and he went out narrowly in the last 24.

The *Quadrangular* this year ventured back to Northern Ireland, albeit to the seclusion of Coleraine University. The England team, now selected by the Sections Committee, was under the management of Colin Tyson and for the first time had track suits for the event. Nevertheless attention focused on the Scots. They beat N. Ireland 25–11. Against Wales they had a good 7–2 win in the ladies (Fiona McIntosh 3, Janet Cooksey 2, Cath Robertson 2; Audrey Bennett 1, Lindy Prys-Roberts 1, Linda Norrie 0); the men's foil they narrowly lost 5–4 (Lewis Smith 2, Duncan Paterson 1, Mike Mayo 1; Gareth Evans 3, Tony Garrington 2, Ian Edwards 0); in the epee they slumped 6–3, though four losses were on the last hit (Graham Mackay 1, Mike Peat 1, Gregor Henderson 1; Bob Turner 3, Lyndon Martin 2, Bob Lawson 1). To win the match, they needed to take the sabre 5–4. In the event they made it 6–3 (Tony Mitchell 3, Bob Elliott 2, Lewis Smith 1; Bryan Lewis 2, Marvin Evans 0, Ian Edwards 1).

Meanwhile they had gained twelve wins to England's fifteen. So they had the formidable task in the ladies' match of winning 7–2. It was soon 1–all and victory seemed unlikely; but with remarkable tenacity they snatched one win after another until they achieved a magnificent 8-1 and thus achieved their fourth win of the whole event since its inception in 1950.

The N. Irish, coached by Mike Westgate, put in a stronger challenge than usual and lost to Wales only 19-17. Their ladies won 5-4 (Clare Montgomery 2, Christine Convill 2, Kate Elvin 1) and the sabreurs 6-3 (Magill 3, Carson 2, Ian McConaghy 1).

The English were uneven: their ladies, for instance, did well enough against Wales (Maggie Browning 3, Jane Law 3, Lynne Taylor 2); likewise their epeeists (Davenport 3, Osbaldeston 2 and Lavington only hit twice). The Welsh, with almost the same team as the triumphant one from the year before, could not put it together this time.

The *London versus the Rest Match* was close. In the ladies' the Rest won 9-7 (A. Brannon 4, J. Jones 2, J. Erwteman 2, J. Lambert 1; C. Montgomery 3, K. Cecil 2, S. Hoad 2, S. Uff 0); the result at epee was the same (J. Tyson 3, S. Lavington 3, D. Brooks 2, B. Turner 1; R. Davenport 3, S. Lennox 2, H. West 1, J. Stanbury 1). At men's foil London won by six hits received (Harper 3, Gosbee 2, Waldman 2, Fox 1), and at sabre they managed to make up the deficit by an 11-5 win and thus take the match 33-31 (A. Roberts 4, M. Slade 3, S. Wasilewski 2, J. Lewis 2; R. Berry 2, M. Hunt 1, R. Jaine 1, B. Lewis 1). Richard Jaine of Boston (ex-Loughborough) was a rising newcomer.

In the *Commonwealth Championships*, a second time excluded from the Commonwealth Games, the Scots also secured some good team results, though nothing outstanding on the individual front. They certainly earned the gratitude of participants for their efficient organisation in Glasgow.

Benko was favourite for the foil title, even more clearly than in 1974, since he had been sixth in the World at Montreal. But in his first fight of the final he lost to his fellow-Australian and fellow-25-year-old, Ernie Simon, a student at Detroit, who beat him 5-4 with flair and athleticism, exemplified by a parry of prime coupé-riposte delivered with a leap, on his opponent's back. Simon went on to win all his other fights on the last hit – except against the 21-year-old Harper, who matched him in nerve and from 3-all got his last two hits by derobing with an extended arm, making Simon's fast attacks out of time.

Benko meanwhile kept losing – an ankle injury didn't help – until in his last fight he had the chance of giving Simon a barrage by beating Harper. In a bout notable for variation of pace, he won 5-2. In the barrage Simon too twisted an ankle, at 2-1 down. He continued after treatment, but lost 5-2. Harper thus added the Commonwealth Gold Medal to his Championship and Coronation trophies, a major achievement for himself and Roy Goodall his coach, who was present in support. Dessureault, a student at Ottawa, won the Bronze Medal with 5-1 wins over Benko and the 22-year-old Kay (2v; 4th) and 5-3 over Bartlett (also aged 22), who might have done better than fifth place (1v) if his good tactics had not so often ended off target.

# Competitions chronicle 1977–8

From the home countries, Gareth Evans (aged 24) and Elliott (27) reached the semi-finals. In the quarter finals (second round) was the 17-year-old John Davis, *Public Schools* Champion from Royal Belfast School, along with Robin Pearson (22) and Steven Carson (23) of N. Ireland, Tom Beattie (21), Duncan Paterson (21), Lewis Smith (29) and Mike Mayo (25) of Scotland, Marvin Evans (21) and Ian Edwards (30), captain of Wales, and Stephen Fox (28) of England.

The team events were by poule unique. The foil began with a shock 5–4 defeat of the England team by Canada, who then faded. This opened the door to Australia, who were undefeated till they met England. If Simon had been uninjured their chances would have been good. As it was, they went down 5–1, and lost the Gold by 33 bouts to 38. In their first match Scotland beat Canada 5–2 to gain the Bronze. Wales came fourth, three bouts better than Canada. N. Ireland had to be content with victory over the Isle of Man, for whom Ian Rogerson scored the sole win against Elder of Canada. Top scorer in the matches between the other six countries was Glaister with 80 per cent of his bouts won, though he started with only one win against Canada. He was followed, from the home countries, by Harper 73 per cent, Marvin Evans 56 per cent, Gareth Evans and Beattie 53 per cent, Kay 50 per cent, Elliott 47 per cent, Smith 44 per cent, Pearson 33 per cent, Davis 27 per cent, Garrington 25 per cent, Carson 22 per cent, Bartlett 20 per cent, David Carlisle (N. Ireland) 17 per cent, and Edwards 0 per cent.

The individual ladies' final contained four English foilists, but it was the

Foil Gold Medallists, Glasgow 1978: A. Bartlett, G. Kay, S. Glaister, P. Harper.

24-year-old Australian Helen Smith, a teacher who had been sixth in Ottawa, who swept through her first four fights for the loss of only three hits and then from 4-1 down to the very controlled Linda Martin overcame her nerves, returned to her aggressive flowing style and took the Gold Medal with some brave ripostes. But for this last win she would have had to barrage with Chantal Payer of Canada. Liz Wood (2v) took third place on hits over Linda Martin, while in turn Sue Wrigglesworth (1v) was better on hits than Ann Brannon.

Janet Cooksey (37) missed the final, and the chance of repeating her 1970 Gold Medal, by three hits. Also eliminated from the semi-finals were Clare Montgomery (20) of N. Ireland and Hilary Cawthorne (26) of England. Ousted from round two were Audrey Bennett (32), Linda Norrie (née Brown, 34) and Olivia Pontefract (28) of Wales, Cath Smith (27), Fiona McIntosh (17), Moira Montgomery (née Dignan, 22) of Scotland and Christine Convill (24) of N. Ireland.

In the team event, England was undefeated, though they were run to 5-4 by both Canada (2nd) and Australia (3rd). Scotland (4th) lost their chance of a medal by collapsing 5-1 to Canada at the outset and 7-2 to Australia at the end, though they disposed of the other teams firmly enough. Wales had a very experienced team, but lacked training. Only a year before they had beaten the Scots, now they lost 9-0. And although they beat New Zealand and the Isle of Man, they also lost 6-3 to N. Ireland – who in turn lost to New Zealand. With two match wins each, the three were separated on bouts: N. Ireland (26; 5th), New Zealand (22; 6th), Wales (19; 7th).

For the Isle of Man, the 17-year-old Sally Roberts saved two fights: one from N. Ireland and one from Wales. Scoring by the home countries in the other matches was as follows: Cawthorne 12/14, Brannon 5/6, Robertson 9/12, Martin 9/12, Wood 7/10, Montgomery 10/18, Cooksey 9/18, Smith 6/12, McIntosh 5/12, Wrigglesworth 5/12, C. Convill 6/18, Bennett 5/18, Myers (née Riley) 3/15, Elvin 2/11, Pontefract 2/12, Norrie 1/9, O. Convill 0/7.

The epee was very open, with more than a possibility that the 47-year-old Hoskyns would collect his fifth individual Gold Medal; in the event it was the 25-year-old Roose whose calm concentration took him undefeated to the title (after losing 5-5 to both Benko and the 23-year-old Steven Paul in the semi-final). Benko (3v; 2nd) lost to him 5-4 and succumbed on the last hit to Paul (3v; 3rd), who looked the most complete epeeist but lacked aggression. Hoskyns (2v; 4th) beat Paul 5-2, but lost to the top two and 5-5 to the 27-year-old Stanbury (2v; 5th). Brooks (Wales, 23) did well to reach the final and there to take the winner to assault point.

Tyson (28) went out of the semi-finals by four hits. Peat (21), Martin (32), and Turner (37) were also semi-finalists. Davenport (26) of England, Lewis (25) of Wales, Liston (18), Henderson (17) and Mackay (21) of Scotland, and

Carlisle (25), Ferguson (26) and William Hamilton (20) of N. Ireland reached the second round.

On these results, England should have won the team event easily, with Wales firmly ahead of Scotland in second place. England indeed were never taken beyond three wins, even without using Hoskyns, but Wales lost their first vital match against Scotland 8–1 (Liston 3, Peat 3, Henderson 2; Brooks 1, Turner 0, Lewis 0). The Scots then lost to Australia (Tyson 3, Liston 1, Peat 0/1, Henderson 0/2); but their fights-total was sufficient to assure them of the Silver Medal before the last round. In this Wales had the formidable task of beating Australia 8–1 to get the Bronze Medal. Martin did well to win all his fights; Lewis won two; Brooks was one bout up before the last deciding fight, but could not win it. Australia was ahead by seven hits.

Fifth place was also decided in the last round when N. Ireland beat Canada by the good score of 6–3 (Hamilton 3, Ferguson 2, Carlisle 1). Isle of Man scratched through injury.

Top scorer was Tyson (7/8), but then, oddly, he was not included against England. There followed: Davenport 10/12, Paul 8/11, Stanbury 8/11, Martin 7/9, Roose 7/11, Peat 8/13, Lewis 9/15, Liston 8/15, Ferguson 7/15, Brooks 6/15, Henderson 2/15, Hamilton 5/15, Carlisle 4/15, Turner 1 + 1 d.d./6, Mackay 0/4).

At sabre England by no means had it all their own way. Deanfield (26) had to scratch through injury before the event and his two team-mates who reached the final had to contend with a four-way barrage. For Cohen had lost 5–1 to Sekunda of Canada (1v; 6th) as well as 5–4 to Philbin – who in turn had lost on the last hit to Benko and to Lavoie of Canada. Outright victory by Lavoie was only prevented by his having lost to the third Canadian, Ott (2v; 5th).

In the barrage, the 31-year-old Cohen slumped after losing a fine fight 5–4 to the 27-year-old Philbin – who had now reached top form and disposed 5–1 of both Lavoie (2v; 2nd) and Benko (1v; 3rd), the latter handicapped by knee injury.

Gareth Evans of Wales did well to reach the semi-final at the wrong weapon. The elimination of Etherton (27) of England and Elliott (27) and Wiles (38) of Scotland at this stage showed the toughness of competition. Magill (N. Ireland) was unlucky to go out of a second round pool containing Philbin and Lavoie. Along with him went his compatriots Carson, Davis and McConaghy (28), and Mitchell (39) and Smith of Scotland. Lewis had to scratch after injury.

In the team event there was a wide gap between the top two countries and the rest: England and Canada lost an average of less than one fight a match to the others. (Benko did not fence in the team event.) Canadian hopes when they met England in the last round were dashed: Philbin and Cohen each won two and Etherton one. N. Ireland came into its own to take the Bronze Medal, beating Wales and Australia 7–2 and Scotland 5–4, Magill excelling to win all his fights. Scotland beat Wales 7–2 and Australia 5–4 to take fourth place. Wales beat Australia too (6–3) and was thus fifth.

The 24-year-old Joey Crook gained the sole win for Isle of Man. In the matches between the other teams Etherton and Cohen scored 13/15 and Philbin 12/15. Magill was next best, with 10/15 (Carson 5/15, McConaghy 4/15). Mitchell was the leading Scot, with 8/15 (Wiles 4/9, Elliott 5/12, Smith 3/9). For Wales, Lewis had 5/14, Edwards 4/15, G. Evans 2/9, M. Evans 1/7.

The outstanding fencer of the Championships was Greg Benko, with two Silver Medals and two Bronze, and places in all three finals. Harper, Roose and Philbin each collected two Gold Medals.

Inevitably the country with the most medals was England: four team Golds, three individual Golds and two individual Bronzes. Scotland got team Silver and team Bronze and N. Ireland team Bronze. Wales got no medals, but Brooks was the only finalist outside the magic circle of the English (13), the Canadians (5) and the Australians (5).

Alex Rae listed the occupations of all participants in the Championships in the SAFU *Newsletter*. Among the 63 fencers from the home countries thirteen were students and the same number were school or university teachers. Six were in medical jobs, five in the building trades (three of whom were from the Isle of Man) and three were still at school. Otherwise occupations were varied: systems analyst (Davenport and Ferguson), navigation officer (Carlisle), welder (Martin), actor (Muir) . . .

A week later, many of those at Glasgow moved on to the *World Championships* in Hamburg. Accommodation was so expensive that each of the British teams flew out and returned separately. Coaching was provided by Profs Anderson, Norcross, Imregi, Emery and Goodall. Richard Oldcorn was the new overall captain, as he was the two following years.

All the British got through the first round of the foil. Harper went out in the second round, along with Bartlett, who beat Reichert of W. Germany, but missed his promotion by one hit when he lost to a lesser opponent 5–4, and Glaister, who beat Smirnov in a very tough pool which also included Koukal (ultimately 5th) and Bach. In the last 48 Eames hit a pool with Flament (eventual winner), Behr and Haerter; apart from 4–5 against Scuri of Italy, he never got more than two hits. Bruniges showed his star class when he pulled back from 2–4 to 4–all against Tiu (eventual 4th) with four seconds to go – but he then lost. If he had won this fight or taken the last hit off Dal Zotto he would have gone up.

In the team event Britain beat Kuwait 15–1 and could afford to lose 12–2 to Russia (Eames beating both Smirnov and Romankov 5–1!). In the last twelve direct elimination Poland won 9–4, before going on to the Gold Medal. Bruniges won two. An innovation was the inclusion of Bell in the team event only. Despite his previous team record this didn't work well.

The ladies flourished. The new colour, Ann Brannon, survived a nervous beginning to reach the third round (last 48). Liz Wood topped a difficult second round pool, though she couldn't keep it up in the third round. Sue Wrigglesworth also reached her limit in the third round. Hilary Cawthorne, however, went on to the last 24, her best World Championship performance. She lost 8–1 to Demaille, but came back with an attacking strategy to beat Luan Jujie 8–4 in spite of having lost to her 5–0 in the third round. She then went out 8–0 to Belova.

Linda Martin also reached the last 24. After losing 8–3 to Hanisch she had a long bout with Giliazova similar to one they had fought at Goppingen which the Russian had won. After a tense, cautious eight minutes the score was only 1–all. After a further four minutes Linda took a well-chosen initiative and won with a good remise. Sadly, against Szolnoki (Hungary) she lost mobility and went down 8–1. The event was won by Sidorova for the second year running.

The team was seeded seventh out of nineteen. In a pool of four they beat Ireland 14–2 and Finland 13–3, both Liz Wood and Linda Martin taking seven out of eight fights; but lost 11–5 to Rumania, with only Sue Wrigglesworth winning two. The knock-out match in the last twelve, against Poland, was an 'if only' affair. Sue Wrigglesworth fenced intelligently to win three, two on the last hit, but Linda Martin and Hilary Cawthorne could only manage one each, though the former took Skapska to assault point. Liz Wood was out of touch and was replaced after two bouts by Ann Brannon, who fought with a new-found ferocity and won one fight. 46–63 down on hits, defeat had to be conceded at 8–6. In the final the Poles were runners-up to Russia.

In the sabre only three out of six were promoted. Deanfield started well, beating Boch (W. Germany) 5–1, but losing to a Swede and 5–4 to Sekunda to go out. Slade was initiated with a pool containing Maffei, Quivrin and Lekach (USA). He got one win. With Mustata (Rumania) and Korfanty (Poland), Philbin had to beat the two outsiders and the French number five, Granger-Veyron, to whom he lost 5–4 (after being 4–1 up). The other two reached the second round (last 48), but got only one win apiece. Cohen went out with Nilca, winner of two Category A events this season, and Etherton in a pool from which Gedovari, Marin and Nikichin were promoted. The winner of the event was Krovopuskov in the fourth barrage of four or more in these Championships.

Seeded eleventh, Britain had to beat France as well as Denmark in the first round – not impossible, given the results in the Touzard. Etherton excelled to win three fights 5–3, 5–2, 5–3. Deanfield won two (5–3, 5–0), as did Cohen (5–0, 5–3). The luckless Philbin took both Lamour and Bena to 5–4, but could not get that eighth win. Against Italy, Cohen got three and Deanfield two, to make it 11–5. Denmark was defeated 9–1; but by then it was too late.

John Zarno, after presiding extensively at foil, did so right through the sabre individual to a half-share of the final, and was widely praised.

There were distinct hopes for the epeeists, since the top four had each done well in a Grade A event during the season and Roose had won the Commonwealth Championships. But things started badly when Belson was in too low a gear in the first round, lost to a sharp Carmi of Israel and went out with one win. Roose had to reckon on beating an Iranian, an Austrian and a Brazilian – but the last was fencing too furiously for him.

In the second round Llewellyn drew a pool with Harmenberg, Lukomsky and Koppang. He began like a lion against Menghi of Luxembourg and was soon 4–0. Then in a few nightmare moments, he found he'd lost 5–4. His confidence sapped, he could not win another fight. Steven Paul not only beat Carmi but also Poffet, four times World Under-20 Champion. Johnson sailed through, losing only to Jacobson on the last hit.

The third round (last 48) presented Paul with a pool comprising Harmenberg, Koppang, Bellone (Italy), Kolcsonay (Hungary) and Peszthy (USA). He was running short of ideas and was frustrated by difficulty in landing his point when he penetrated his opponents' defences. Johnson in a less demanding pool needed to put at least four hits on Poffet after losing to Fischer of W. Germany and to the versatile Benko. Showing his exceptional coolness under pressure, he won 5–3. Next morning, however, in the last 32, he couldn't produce the same sharpness and aggression against the awkward and much improved Ganeff of Belgium and was hustled to a 10–5 defeat. He now met Dunaev, as he had (successfully) in 1977. Very youthful, but already some six foot six and with a deceptively loose style, the Russian was kept under control for the first half of the fight, but suddenly scored six hits in succession. Johnson could not regain the initiative and lost 10–8. The event was won by Pusch in yet another barrage, after Riboud had been disallowed an outright win, as time had expired before his winning hit, although a halt had not been called. Pusch was thus the fourth person to win the event three times.

In the team event, after beating Kuwait 15–1, Britain met W. Germany. It was calculated that the convoluted seeding system would give Finland as opponents in the last sixteen if Britain won and Switzerland if not. So a big effort was made, spearheaded by Belson, who won three fights, including one against Pusch. It was spectacular to watch his large frame bounding up and down or crouched like a malevolent spider as he worked up to an attack. Paul, now fencing sharply and constructively, won two, including one over Jana, who was otherwise only hit four times. Llewellyn also gained two and might have done even better if he had added a little more intentness on hitting to his speed and great stylishness. Unfortunately Johnson had gone off the boil. He lost his first three fights and at 8–7 down, with a noisy crowd, he needed to beat Adrians 5–3. It was not to be.

Belson opened well against Switzerland with a win over Giger (sixth in the individual); but the next seven fights all went the wrong way. Belson, Paul and

Llewellyn each then got a win, but at 8–4 Roose, replacing Johnson, had no answer to the superior footwork of Gaille, 1977 Bronze Medallist.

# 1978–9

## MEN'S FOIL

Pierre Harper continued his successes of the previous season with an impressive string of foreign results and consistently good home performances including wins in the Emrys Lloyd and at Leicester, second place in the National and positions in the finals of the Leon Paul and at Birmingham.

In the Paris *Duval* with over 120 fencers including contingents from Holland, USA and Israel, he took fourth place when he beat de Nogaret of France in the first fight of the direct elimination final of eight. On the form he showed in this fight, it looked as though he could go on to win the competition. Unfortunately, Boscherie proved too strong. Also a finalist was Gosbee and likewise a victim of Boscherie, in his first fight. He thus came sixth in his first international senior final. Bruniges lost to Pezzini, another Frenchman, at the same stage and was placed seventh. Barry Paul was in the last sixteen.

Gosbee's home wins included both the *Under-20 Championship*, in which he beat John Troiano and Donny McKenzie (Meadowbank) into second and third places, and the *Millfield International*, in which Fischer of Switzerland was runner-up. This year's Under-20 Championship was John Troiano's first final, and his height and reach and difficult sense of timing easily took him to second place. However, he was no match for the much shorter Gosbee's years of experience and greater command of distance. Troiano was also runner-up to John Ford (now at Pauls) in the *Junior* final, which included two New Zealand fencers, Wayne Hudson (3rd) and David Cocker (5th), both training at London–Thames.

Ford triumphed again in the *Universities Championship* (for City), beating Mark Thompson (Cambridge) 5–1. Third was Mike McEwan (Edinburgh), followed by Mallett (London), William Coley (Cambridge) and Tim Wilson (Newcastle). Mark Wright of George Heriot's was third in the Millfield, runner-up to Duncan Paterson of Meadowbank in the *Scottish Championship* and winner of the *Wilkinson Invitation* event, over Edwin Pearson of Wellington, with the now 14-year-old Justin Pitman (Ringmer College) and Colin Goodwin (Hereford Phoenix, Grimsby) completing the last four.

*The Eden Cup* was the strongest under-20 event in Britain for six years, with a total of 33 entries from Belgium, France, Holland, Sweden, Switzerland, W. Germany and elsewhere. Britain was only fifth in the preliminary team event. McKenzie bowed out in the last 24 in a pool with three finalists. Wright did

Scottish National Age Group Champions 1977 and 1978: George Liston (U-18 epee), Stewart MacAslan (U-16 epee), Fiona McIntosh (U-18), Mark Wright (U-16 sabre), Donald McMenzie (U-18 foil).

very well to reach the last sixteen. Gosbee reached the final by the long route after losing to Baska of W. Germany. He beat Groc (France), Tackenstrom (Sweden) and Joos (Holland) and then won three bouts to come fourth, being the only fencer to beat the winner, Planet of France. Baska was second, Pezzini third, Omnes (France) fifth and Akerburg (Sweden) sixth.

Abroad, Troiano did well to claim third place in an under-20 event at *Cracow*, with Gosbee fifth and Ward in the last 24.

The *Championship* was won by Barry Paul, followed (in order) by clubmates Bartlett and Graham Paul, Gareth Evans from Wales and Gosbee, in his first home senior final. Once again, the title eluded Bruniges, who retired injured during the direct elimination.

The Coronation was this year renamed the *Leon Paul*, a new Trophy having been presented by Leon Paul Ltd to replace the cup earlier stolen from Graham Paul. It was dominated by Ziemovit Wojciechowski, the 1974 World Finalist who had come to Britain to work for Leon Paul Ltd and to give coaching to the National Foil Squad. The standard was high. Andy Eames and Graham Paul were eliminated along with the last of the Swedish entry. Bruniges had come unstuck even earlier. In the last eight Wojciechowski disposed of Gosbee 10–1. By 10–5 a devastating Barry Paul beat an insufficiently mobile Gareth Evans (who had returned to Bristol to work in local radio and was taught there by François Roeder). Bartlett too, in his bout with Harper, began too static and could not score until after Harper's sixth hit, which began with a long, composed attack, was followed by an exchange and ended with his closing the line of Bartlett's second counter-riposte and hitting him en-marchant. But then Bartlett fought back magnificently, to finish only three hits behind in a bout rising above his usually rather technical fights with Harper. Wedge lost to Soumagne (ninth in the 1978 World Championship).

In the last four, Barry Paul's lack of recent top-class opposition left him a bit breathless at 3–0 up and he then tried to overcome the flexible Wojciechowski by ever faster attacks when variation of speed would have served him better. Soumagne overcame Harper by a comfortable 10–5. In the last bout Wojciechowski gave a beautiful display of closing the line against Soumagne's attacks, and when the Belgian too tried putting greater speed into them to reach the target they were only impaled on fine counter-sixte-ripostes. The score was 10–3. Third place went to Barry Paul, who out-foxed and out-boxed Harper.

There followed exhibition bouts between Talvard, Pietruszka, Harper and Wojciechowski.

Salle Paul won the *Team Championship* yet again. In the final Barry and Graham Paul, Tony Bartlett and Ziemek Wojciechowski (the last undefeated from the quarter-finals onwards) outclassed by 9–2 the Boston team of Bruniges, Gosbee, Waldman and Alvin Leopold (Gosbee saving the two). For Poly, Cohen, Deanfield, Eden and Philbin fought their way into the semifinals.

The provincial circuit opened at *Bristol*, where Barry More regained his title of four years before when he beat Mark Thompson of Chester and Boston in a barrage. Gareth Evans (3rd) and Steven Paul (4th) both seemed jaded. Cohen took fifth place with exuberance and several performances of his little-boy-robbed act. Richard Hill of Salle Paul, who ended fifth in the Bonfil rankings, now based on eleven top British events, took sixth place. The stronger *Leicester Open* foreshadowed the national rankings of the end of the season, with Harper first (4v), Bruniges second (3v) and an improved Glaister third (3v). Wojciechowski (2v), who fenced beautifully but without the edge he had shown the previous year, was fourth, followed by Thompson (2v) and Wedge (1v).

*The Hereford and Worcester Open* was won by the stylish Simon Routh-Jones, originally a pupil of Prof. Sanders and latterly of Laurie Dodman of Salisbury and Frank Tanner of Reading, who showed very sure point control and was only hit six times in the final, three times by Mike Cullen of Boston, the runner-up. Third on hits over Peter Carson (Worcs) was Ray Swinnerton (Hydra). At *Liverpool* Kay won for the third time running, followed by Glaister (4v), Mark Thompson (3v), Swinnerton (3v), Carlisle (1v) and Mark's brother John Thompson (0v).

At *Birmingham*, in front of a crowd of three hundred, Soumagne won the title, beating Bruniges 10–7. For third place Bartlett beat Wedge (after overcoming Glaister 10–9 in a see-saw fight of great excitement). Equal fifth in the direct elimination were Seaman, Glaister, Harper and Thompson – who was knocked out by the winner after being the only fencer to beat him in the earlier rounds. The *Kirklees* tournament saw a notable win by McKenzie in a barrage with John Lawrence of Salle Paul (2nd) and Ward (3rd) and ahead of Hudson, Cocker and Brian Green, each with one win.

Abroad, there were other impressive results apart from the Duval. In the *Rommel*, Bruniges was in the last twelve and Harper in the last 24. At *Bad Durkheim*, a strong but predominantly German event, Bartlett narrowly missed the final of four. Harper reached the last twelve. Bruniges reached the last 48 in the *Paris Martini* and was third at *Amsterdam*. Spurred on by rivalry with Harper, he was concentrating on his fencing more than in the previous few seasons. Bell, still in France, clocked up a third at *Cormeilles* and a second at *Besançon*. In the *Antwerp Golden Foil*, Eames and Glaister were both in a final which included four Poles, four W. Germans and four Frenchmen. Martewicz of Poland was predictably the victor with four wins. Eames, who had been ill and out of competition for most of the season, was second, over Soumagne, who also had three wins. Crahay (Belgium) was fourth (2v), with Glaister fifth and Omnes sixth (1v).

In *Venice*, almost as strong as the Rommel and Bonn, Barry Paul showed himself still a force to be reckoned with when he reached the last 32. Harper too was in the thick of world-ranking fencers in the last 32 at *Bonn*.

Harper, Bruniges, Bartlett, Glaister and Eames were the chosen five for the World Championships. Gosbee was initially nominated as reserve, but discouraged the selectors by promptly ceasing to train.

*LADIES' FOIL*

Elizabeth Wood equalled Gillian Mallard's record of three *Under-20* wins, showing great patience in waiting for opponents to make mistakes she could exploit, often attacking into a preparation. She was followed by Clare Gobey of Brownhill and Penny Johnson of Salle Paul. In the *Perigal* Fiona McIntosh, fencing very coolly, with attacks preceded by much preparation, was undefeated in the final. In third place, after Stamanne of Belgium, was Katie Arup, a very good result for one who was still young enough also to win the *Under-16 Brussels Tournament*. The remaining places went to Nili Drori of Israel, Liz Wood and Kim Cecil. At *Kussnacht* Kim Cecil did very well to come second to Vaccaroni (and Katie Arup was in the last twelve). At *Dornbirn* she was the third placed, with Penny Johnson sixth and Fiona McIntosh eighth. Liz Wood won at *Etampes*.

The *Felix Cup* was won by the newcomer Janet Thornton of Sondes Place, ahead of Ann and Mary, two more of the Gobey sisters from Brownhill. The *Jubilee Bowl*, the senior equivalent, was won for the second time by Linda Martin, who was also all-conquering on the provincial circuit. At *Bristol*, after losing to Maureen Lloyd (4th), she met an undefeated Ann Brannon in the last fight of the final, won and triumphed again in the barrage. Clare Montgomery (Boston) was third, Penny Johnson fifth and Pam Grindley (London–Thames) sixth.

At *Leicester* too, Linda won for the third time in four years – undefeated, but three times 4–all. She was followed by Hilary Cawthorne (4v) and Sue Hoad (3v) – both of Allen FC – Maggie Browning (2v) and Ann Brannon (1v). Christine Lewis of Cardiff, sister of Bryan, breaking into the ranks of the established, was sixth (ov). Linda Martin won again at *Redbridge* after a three-way barrage with Hilary Cawthorne (2nd) and Nili Drori (3rd), and completed the tally when she beat Ann Brannon 8–0 at *Birmingham*, in another display of finishing power, despite injury, and having earlier overcome Sheila Gallagher only by a short head in the semi-final. Ann Brannon, by contrast, had won 8–3 over Maureen Lloyd and 8–5 over Sue Hoad – who gained third place on the last hit from Clare Montgomery.

Meanwhile at *Liverpool* Jane Law (Hydra) opened the final by beating Hazel Rogerson (Hydra/BAF), the holder, 5–4, conceded only three hits in the next three fights, but then lost 5–2 to Sarah Kellett (Stevenage) and only clinched the trophy when she beat Ann Fraser-Smith (Northumbria) in the barrage. Sue Hoad was winner of the *Kirklees* event, beating Judith Mendelenyi (daughter of the famous Tamas) 5–2. Other places went to Ann Fraser-Smith (2v), Lynne Taylor (2v), Penny Whitehead of Westfield school (2v) and Mrs Jane Whitney of Sale (1v).

The *Scottish* Champion was Cath Robertson of Ainslie Park who also won the *Scottish Open* after a barrage with Julia Bracewell of Currie High School, daughter of the National Coach, and still under sixteen. They were followed by Sheila Anderson (Bellahouston), Margaret Porter (Stirling), Ann Swinney (Aberdeen Univ.) and Lynn Allison (Meadowbank). Julia Bracewell did very well to be runner-up in the new *Wilkinson Under-20 Invitation* event. Kim Cecil won 8–3. Katie Arup fenced intelligently to beat Francesca Darnell of Grimsby for third place.

In the *British Team Championship* semi-finals Salle Paul beat Ashton (Janet Garside, her sister Hilary Jones, Brenda Hewitt and Louise Meeks) while Poly, comprising Linda Martin, Hilary Cawthorne, Sue Lewis and Katie Arup, only beat Boston on an 8–all cliffhanger. In the final Poly had another nail-biting match before beating Paul's (comprising Sue Wrigglesworth, Liz Wood, Penny Johnson and Sheila Gallagher) by 8–7, again on hits.

The *Toupie Lowther*, was won this year by the newcomer Pauline Monk of Espada. Jill Dudley's daughter Sarah was second. Debbie Hall beat Fiona Wilson and Sarah Kellett to take the *Parker Trophy*. The *Bertrand*, by contrast,

Wilkinson finalists. F. Darnell (4th), K. Arup (3rd), K. Cecil (1st), J. Bracewell (2nd).

was contested by the experienced Brenda Hewitt who won it for the second time. Sadly, in 1980 she became diabetic and ceased fencing. Julia Single and Jacky Erwteman were second and third. Ann Brannon, fencing for Cambridge University, won the *Desprez*, her first senior title, ahead of the two (unrelated) Woods, Liz (Paul) and Gillian (New Zealand and LTFC). Hilary Cawthorne, Linda Martin and Sue Wrigglesworth took the remaining three places in the final. In the *Championship*, Liz Wood won a cliff-hanging barrage with Hilary Cawthorne that went to time. The remaining team members, Martin, Brannon and Wrigglesworth, followed in that order. Gillian Wood was sixth. A great pity that she had to return to New Zealand!

The *de Beaumont* entry was rather weak. The final contained two British girls, two Dutch and two Swiss. After a lengthy four-way barrage, Linda Martin forged ahead and took first place over Helbling, formerly of LFC, Leenders of Holland and Sue Wrigglesworth.

Abroad, the season started well with Sue Wrigglesworth fourth and Hilary Cawthorne sixth in *East Berlin*, in the company of two Russians and two E. Germans. Sue Wrigglesworth was in the last eight in *Leipzig*. Linda Martin, who was in the last twelve in Berlin, reached the last eight in the A Grade *Goppingen* event. Sue Wrigglesworth was in the last sixteen and Hilary Cawthorne in the last 32. These two spent two months training in Poland, but to no very immediate effect, though at *Turin*, the crown of the season, Hilary reached the fourth round, narrowly missing the direct elimination, as did

Linda Martin. Fiona McIntosh, who narrowly missed the finals of the Desprez and the Championship, showed great improvement, reaching the last 48 of her first Grade A event here. At *Como* Linda Martin reached the last twelve. A team of four (with no newcomers) went to the World Championships: Linda Martin, Sue Wrigglesworth, Hilary Cawthorne and Ann Brannon. Julia Barkley was team manager.

*EPEE*

George Liston was favourite for the *Under-20 Championship* but slipped to fifth place. John Troiano of London–Thames, switching from foil (at which he came second) was the surprise winner, on a barrage from the Catford schoolboy Ahmed Shaban (of Turkish Cypriot parentage). Third was another promising young epeeist: Simon Baldry, a pupil of Andy Archibald at Whitgift and at Fiveways Club. Jervis Rhodes (Dulwich) was fifth, ahead of Andrew Brannon.

It was a lean year for Under-20 results abroad: Liston got to the direct elimination at *Katowice*; otherwise nothing.

The provincial circuit opened with *Bristol*, which was strong enough to lose Roose as well as Liston before the final. Steven Paul won, ahead of Lewis, Tyson, Melville, Shaban and Young. At *Ashton* it was Steve Paul's turn not to reach the final, losing to Melville (3rd) in the knock-out, while it was Roose's turn to win, by beating Liston in the last bout. Steve Henshall, of Worcester Technical College, younger brother of Brian and winner of the *Under-18*, did well to come fourth. Archibald and Kernohan were ranked fifth and sixth. A super-cool Roose won again at *Leicester*, with Tyson squeaking into second place over Lewis, followed by Steven Paul, Dave Brooks and Andy Brannon.

Steventon asserted his quality by winning the *Junior Championship*, after coming third in 1975. His rivals, Liston and Melville, both went out early. Ousted in the direct elimination from sixteen were Warburn, Brooks and the Gloucester pentathletes Robbie and Richard Phelps. Brannon, Fairhall, Tyson and Roger Greenhalgh (son of the 1954 British Champion) went in the first repechage, followed by Lavington and Tony Woodall of London–Thames, who did well to get so far. Mallett (Boston) was the runner-up, ahead of Lewis (in his third final), Brierley (in his fifth final), Shaban, still only sixteen, and a surprise sixth – Philbin.

The *Welsh Open* was another event tough enough for many of the well-known not to reach the final. West won in his inimitable quick-fire manner, losing only to Lewis (3rd). Brierley was runner-up; Hill and Melville dead-heated fourth; Tyson was sixth. *Tyneside* was won for the second time running by Bob Sedols of Leicester, while the *Hereford and Worcester* took on unusual glamour: Brian Henshall, for Worcester FC, excelled himself by beating

Steven Paul and Ralph Jonhson into second and third places undefeated and with only ten hits against him! David Cocker of New Zealand and London –Thames was fourth, ahead of John Whitworth of Stockport and John Littlehales of Ashton.

In the *Martini Qualifying* the tall Melville (16v), the most aggressive, confident exponent of relentless fleche attacks since Bourne, proved unstoppable. He was followed by Graham Paul (15v) and Tyson, Steventon, Kernohan and Stanbury, all on fourteen wins. Woodall reached another peak to come eighth a few hits behind Hoskyns. Davenport, tenth between Mallett and Hall, was unlucky to lose seven fights on the last hit. Mark Rance, aged only fourteen, a pupil of Frank Tanner (and winner of the *Under-16 Championship*), did very well to come fourteenth, following Ferguson (11v) and Hill (11v) and ahead of Beevers, who was on leave from the Persian Gulf and only seen to lunge once in 22 fights. Also making reappearances were Paul Tarran (17th) and Chris White (19th).

Melville also won the *Welsh Games* invitation poule unique of eighteen, ahead of Tyson, Kernohan, Wood (now at Cardiff Univ. Coll. and much improved), Hill, Hoskyns and Brooks. At *Birmingham* the only foreigner to reach the final was Driessen of Delft, who was third – beaten by Steven Paul, who won the title by 10–7 in the final bout against Lavington, the perpetual student now at Birmingham University, on his fourth course. David Rapley won the *Northern Ireland Open*, ahead of Jerome Hartigan (an itinerant ergonomist) and David Carlisle, while Roose won yet again at *Kirklees*, but only on a barrage with the aggressive Cocker. They were followed by Matless (2v), Davenport (3v), Warburn (1v) and Bill Payne of Sheffield (0v).

For the second time running the *Universities Championship* went to Mallett, now in his last year of Business Studies at the London School of Economics, after first a barrage with Gregor Henderson of Heriot–Watt and Mike Peat of Edinburgh and then a count of hits. The other finalists also tied, with two wins apiece: Liston (Edinburgh; 4th) and Rhodes (Cambridge; 5th) and Kernohan (Oxford; 6th).

For the more senior events we go back to October and the *Epee Club Cup*; for though fencers from all parts of Britain were invited, only two non-Londoners were in the final of this and these both had much London experience: Tyson (4v; 5th) and Lavington (1v; 7th). Fights already fought in the two preliminary poules uniques of eighteen were not repeated in the final of eight. This accounted for Bourne's only two losses and his second place, as well as the winner, Steven Paul's, sole loss – to Hill (4v; 5th). Remaining places went to Belson (5v; 3rd), Young (2v; 6th), who had done very well to top his poule unique, and Hoskyns (1v; 8th), who by contrast arrived in the final with a deficit of three losses. Just missing the final were Johnson, Stanbury, Brooks and Lyndon Martin from one poule; and Steventon, Liston, Brian Henshall and Davenport from the other.

The *Martini* boasted 99 entries from fourteen countries, together with 27 Britons, of whom twelve survived the first round. Hoskyns and Gaille (finalist of 1978) were amongst those who succumbed. Seven more British fell in the second round: Roose, White, Hall, Mallett, Hill, Steventon and Bourne (his old rival Muck and the 1974 winner Poffet being eliminated from the same pool).

There were some sad near-misses for the valiant remaining five. Davenport, having done well to come through a tough pool, faced the 1977 World Champion, Harmenberg, in the knockout for a place in the tableau of 32. He led 8–7, but was unable to get the last two hits. Melville had done extremely well in the second round, sailing through with four wins to the three of Kauter and Bernadotte, applying not only confident deep attacks, but explosive remises and good defences as well. He could not overcome Ciszek of Poland, however, losing 10–5.

Llewellyn faced Bormann of W. Germany. With forty seconds to go he was 7–6 up, then 9–7, then 9–all. The final hit, alas, brought defeat. Steven Paul's fate was similar. He got 6–2 up on Longlet of France, relaxed, was 9–7 down, recovered to 9–all, did a superb change-direction one-two fleche – which was flat! Only Belson went down straightforwardly, by 10–3, to Moe of Norway.

The final began with Edling, three times World Champion, losing to Riboud, current Champion. Strzalka and Swornowski of Poland and Cramer of Switzerland were the other victims of the last eight. As sometimes happens with fencers who train together, in the semi-final between Riboud and the tall, cadaverous Longlet, it was the lesser fencer who won (10–5). The other semi-final was one of baroque exaggeration. Both fencers held their epees by the pommel: Boisse, hunched and bouncing, his sword elbow almost behind his waist, Suchanecki with his guard close to his front knee, sometimes with his rear knee almost on the floor and sometimes jiggling rapidly to and fro on the edge of the piste. Suchanecki won 10–9. And in the final he rained stop-hits on Longlet, however much he varied his attacks, all the way to 10–2.

The *Championship* was notable for the collapse of the old guard. Hoskyns, Graham Paul, Johnson and Bourne all fell by the wayside, the last knocked out by Tyson, who after many years in which his excellent technical and athletic abilities had never quite earned their rewards, was enjoying a very good season. He came fifth, ahead of Lavington, another epeeist with good technique whose deep lunges and fast, balanced fleches brought him inconsistent results. Now he showed a new edge, presumably unrelated to his having exchanged his tattered and faded blue track suit for a neatly trimmed beard.

Roose was fourth, but ahead of him was not only Davenport (3rd), in his fourth final, but a more elastic and determined Mallett, runner-up in his first national final. The winner was Belson, enjoying a very strong season.

The pattern in the *Miller-Hallett* was very similar: none of the old guard in the final; instead Llewellyn (6th), Steven Paul (5th) and Mallett (4th), confirming his new status. Again Belson was the winner, ahead of Ganeff and Pesthy.

Salle Boston won the *Team Championship* for the fifth season running, this time by 9–5 against London–Thames (Davenport 4, Johnson 3, Bourne 1, Stanbury 1; Belson 2, West 2, Hill 1, Melville 0).

Results abroad were good. Johnson made up for his lapses at home by solid performances: reaching the last twelve not only at *Zurich* and *Catania* but, much more to the point, in the *Monal*. He was also in the last 24 at *Bern*. The same was true of Llewellyn, who was in the last 24 at *Zurich* and in the *Carroccio*, reached the last sixteen in the Monal and also the last 48 at Bern.

Steven Paul had a few high spots: sixth at *Catania* and then, at the other end of the season, in the last sixteen at *Innsbruck* and the last 32 at *Poitiers*. Stephen Roose started the season badly, but recovered to a very good last 24 at *Heidenheim*, missing selection for the World Championship by a whisker.

Of the more senior team contenders Graham Paul was active for only part of the season, Hoskyns reached the last 48 of the Monal but thereafter did not shine (and had elbow trouble towards the end of the season) and Davenport reached the last sixteen in *Vienna* and the last 96 at *Heidenheim*. There was little progress amongst most of the more junior contenders. Stanbury got to the last twelve at *Toulon* and Melville to the last sixteen. Liston was dogged by injuries and illnesses and Steventon's training was alas intermittent.

One young contender did leap ahead, however (abroad as he had at home): Neal Mallett, now faster and sharper, adding deep attacks to his previous game of cautious waiting. He was sixth at Toulon but also got to the last 32 at Bern. Lyndon Martin, a non-contender, was third at *Dieppe*.

But it was Belson who made the foreign season a rich one. He topped his home wins with a last sixteen in the Carroccio, last twelve at Bern, the last eight at Poitiers and, above all, came sixth at Heidenheim, the first Briton ever to reach the final of the 350-strong supreme marathon, which included everybody who was anybody – a superb season which eventually gave him tenth place in the World Cup ranking based on the six A Category events plus the World Championships, the highest British place since the scheme started.

For the World Championships Mallett joined Belson, Johnson, Llewellyn and Steven Paul in place of Roose.

*SABRE*

At the senior level Poly continued supreme, but hardly challenged the dominance of Salle Boston and Salle Ganchev at junior levels. It provided just one of the two new faces in the *Under-20 Championship*, that of the left-handed Jan Falkowksi (6th). Patrick West of Ganchev (5th) was the other. Gary Li of Boston was the winner, but only thanks to his brother Kenric's victory over

Hall of Birmingham FC, which gave him the chance to reverse his earlier loss to the willowly Hall on the last hit of the barrage. Kenric Li was third and Hunt fourth. Hunt was the winner of the *Public Schools* for the second year running. (The newly introduced junior division was won by Mark Wilson of Royal Belfast.) The significant Under-20 result abroad this season was Hall's place in the last 24 in *Budapest*.

The final of the *Junior* was expected to contain many of the same fencers, but in fact was dominated by an older generation. Wasilewski (6th) had first been a finalist in 1975. Jandula (5th) had been fourth in 1976. Zitcer (4th) was three years on from his Under-20 achievements. Lankshear (3rd) had made his mark as a member of the LFC team which won the *Magrini* back in 1972. The other two were hardly newcomers either, though both had been 1977 finalists. It was Norman Milligan who won, lasting the course better than Jack Magill, despite losing to him. He had fenced in four previous finals, from 1972 onwards, always showing great patience in waiting for his opponents to deliver attacks, scoring mostly with impressively strong parries or well-judged stop-cuts. He had acquired this most difficult of techniques, also possessed by Kovanda, the previous Birmingham Champion, largely without the benefit of a professional sabre master.

The winner of the *Scottish* Championship for the fourth time running, Bob Elliott, was also a seasoned campaigner, but the other finalists were of a later vintage: Shahin Sanjar (now at St Andrew's University), Norman Mortimer (Glasgow FC), Alan Shafar (Glasgow FC), Richard Gardner (Lothian) and Neil Melville (Craiglockhart). The *Kelt* Open, another Scottish event, was also claimed by a veteran, the Assistant National Coach, Derek Titheradge. He was followed by Robert Jamieson (Lothian), Andy Muir (Lothian), Melville, Sanjar, Mark Ellis (Aberdeen Univ.), Colin Young (Lothian) and Gardner.

The Scots did not figure much in the provincial tournaments. At *Bristol* Philbin beat Cohen to head the final ahead of Hutt, G. Li, K. Li and Magill. Zarno won the *Welsh Open*, saying 'I only came to sell some blades'. Slade won the *Bristol Phoenix* and *Birmingham*, perhaps throwing off his habit of coming second. Wiles maintained tradition by winning at *Nottingham*. At *Leicester* he was fourth, ahead of Kovanda (1v) and Jaine (2v). But the significant result here was Philbin's loss to Cohen, the winner, and Magill (2nd). This brought to an end his amazing run of 21 consecutive wins in the provincial events he had entered. Both Richard Oldcorn, the captain, and Prof. Imregi had anyhow been trying to divert him from such tournaments, which they feared blunted his international performance.

Magill achieved a remarkable success (or ill-luck, whichever way you look at it) to be runner-up in all five of these competitions, but he was also the winner of both *Liverpool* and *Inverclyde*. Slade finished a distinguished Cambridge career with a third *Universities* win – ahead of Gary Li, Steve Lavington

(Birmingham), Sanjar, Terry Wishart (Kent), who was making a fleeting re-appearance, and Ross Campion (London). West and Klenerman showed the strength of the Salle Ganchev challenge to the top clubs by carrying off the *Senior* and *Junior National Schoolboys Championships* respectively.

In February 1979 the outstanding Hungarian sabreur Dr Tamas Mendelenyi arrived in Britain. He had indicated a willingness to teach in Britain. As he had been Hungarian national sabre coach since 1972 and had been both second and third in the World Championship he was welcomed as British Sabre Coach and a contract was arranged to employ him for eighteen hours a week 46 weeks a year for two and a half years, funded by the Sports Council.

It was hoped by the Sabre Sub-Committee and Richard Oldcorn that Prof. Imregi, the existing coach, would be content for Dr Mendelenyi to act jointly with him. Apart from other considerations, however, Prof. Imregi had never believed in fencers receiving lessons from more than one master at a time; he could not accept the arrangement and resigned. In the upshot his pupils had to choose between masters. Deanfield and Philbin took lessons from Dr Mendelenyi. Cohen remained with Prof. Imregi. All three, however, plus Zarno, fenced for Poly in the *Team Championship*. In the final they met Boston, after somewhat acrimonious semi-finals against the 'B' teams of the two clubs. They won 9–6 (Slade, Etherton and Gary Li each gaining two for Boston, but Magill none).

It was Gary Li who broke his way into the circle of the established stars in the *Cole Cup*, after Cohen (1st) and Philbin (2nd), and showing more spirit and aggression than the other finalists. For Philbin this was an omen for the *Championship*. Here he lost his chance of emulating Acfield's four in a row. The new Champion was Slade, at twenty one of the youngest to reach the top. His clinching win came at 4–all with a stop-cut delivered at extreme range after a series of hotly disputed split decisions.

Philbin made a come-back to win the *Corble* after a barrage with Volkmann of W. Germany; but Slade was close behind in third place.

Abroad, as usual, Cohen was in the lead. He was in the last 24 in *Munich*, fifth in the *New York Martini* and was in the last 32 in *Hamburg*. In matches he scored seven out of nine fights against USA, three out of five against Hungary (who won 18–7) the same in the *Santelli* Cup against France (who won 13–12) and all five fights against a young Italian team (beaten 13–12).

Philbin was in the last 24 in Munich and fourth in New York and was now scoring well in matches, with three wins against France, for instance. Deanfield, kept from training by hospital work, nevertheless reached the last twelve in both Munich and New York. For his part, work at the bar pre-occupied Etherton; indeed he had to stop fencing for a period in mid-season. He was in the last 24 in Munich. Slade and Zarno reached the last 32. Zarno and Jaine reached the last 24 in New York.

The World Championship team was unchanged: Cohen, Philbin, Deanfield, Etherton and Slade.

## COMBINED EVENTS

Ladies were included in the three-weapon *Granville Cup* for the first time. Fourteen clubs entered, including four from outside London, but Boston managed to get a team promoted from each of the four quarters of the direct elimination, and their 'D' team there sprung a surprise on Poly 'A'. For Poly, Andy Martin beat Andy Alderman 7–5, Linda Martin beat Kim Cecil 7–2 and Jonathan Lewis drew with Richard Cohen 7–7. So at epee, taken last under the rules, George Jaron came on 21–14 up and needed only to score seven hits before Mallett could score fourteen. However, fencing staunchly and accurately, Mallett steadily pulled up to snatch an exciting 28–27 victory. A lesser surprise occurred between Excalibur and Boston 'B', whose strongest member, Slade, fought first and therefore least usefully. He duly beat Andrew Cashen 7–4. Leopold of Boston then lost 10–6 to Steve Higginson. Sue Hoad, however, beat Sue Roose 9–3. John Steventon thus confronted Sue's husband, Steve Roose, 21–17 in the lead. The Commonwealth Champion could not close the gap: 7–all made it a 28–24 win for Boston 'B'. Less surprisingly, Boston 'A' beat Poly 'B' 28–18 (A. Brannon v. K. Brown 7–0; T. Etherton v. J. Philbin 7–8; R. Bruniges v. George Ince 7–2; J. Stanbury v. R. Edwards 7–8). For a change, London–Thames overcame Boston 'C' 28–27, thanks to Howard West (Pat Casey v. Nili Drori 4–7; J. Lankshear v. J. Magill 5–7; M. Fare v. W. Gosbee 7–7; H. West v. P. Young 12–6).

The semi-finals were less eventful: Boston 'B' beat 'D' 28–22 and Boston 'A' beat London–Thames 28–20. But a surprise in the internecine final: Boston 'B' trumped the 'A' team 28–26 (Sue Hoad v. Ann Brannon 5–7; Slade v. Etherton 6–7; Leopold v. Bruniges 10–4; Steventon v. Stanbury 7–8).

England were back on top in the *Quadrangular*, losing only the sabre (6–3) to N. Ireland and the Ladies' foil (5–4) to Wales, who fielded Maggie Myers, Olivia Pontefract and Christine Lewis, and who took second place overall, with wins over Scotland of 7–2 by Garrington and the Evanses at men's foil and by 5–4 at epee. The ebullient Ian Edwards was absent for the first time for many years and Linda Norrie had retired after first appearing in the Quadrangular in 1964; but again, as in 1964, Bob Turner was captain, albeit non-playing.

Scotland had a mixed time. Their ladies beat Wales 7–2 and N. Ireland 7–2, and the sabreurs, including the evergreen Mitchell and Wiles, did likewise (Wales 6–3, N. Ireland 6–3) – indeed they led England on fights 16–13. But the male foilists lost all three matches and the epeeists, though they beat N. Ireland 6–3, lost 9–0 to England (admittedly a strong team). N. Ireland had to rest content with two good match wins.

The *Public School Championships* were notable for the performance of Mark Wilson of Royal Belfast, who won both junior foil and junior epee. Julian Burney won the senior foil, Eton's only title since 1953, apart from Beith's win of the sabre in 1968.

The *World Youth Championships* were held in Chicago. Joe Eden and Rosemary Castle were team managers; the coach was Prof. Boston, travelling with the team for the fifteenth and last time. David Eden and John Ford presided.

Fiona McIntosh and Kim Cecil went out in the first round of the ladies' foil. Liz Wood reached the third round, the one bright spot in the results. In the men's foil Gosbee and Troiano were eliminated in the first round, though it is fair to add that all six of those promoted from their pools reached the last sixteen. McKenzie faded in the second round. In the epee first round Brannon went out in a difficult pool with two wins; Shaban also succumbed. Liston scraped up but was ousted in the second round. At sabre the Li brothers came unstuck in the first round and Hall in the second.

The expense of going to Melbourne for the *World Championships* meant that teams again travelled separately to keep the staying time short. Nearly everyone broke the journey with a two-day stop in Singapore to ease jet lag and enjoy duty free shopping and Chinese cooking. Some stopped in Bali on the way back.

The men's foil event, 82 strong, began badly. Glaister was unlucky to go out with three wins. Eames was not back on form after his long illness (and had three opponents who were to reach the last sixteen). Bartlett also fell by the wayside. By contrast, Harper was undefeated in a pool including Kuki of Rumania; but he came down with a bump in round two. Bruniges also went out after a good first round. He'd been in bed with flu. Romankov was the winner, as he had been in 1975 and 1976, being runner-up in the two intervening years.

In the team event, Britain, although seeded tenth out of fifteen, drew Kuwait, Australia and France. Glaister promised four wins against Australia and duly delivered them with tremendous determination, making possible a 9–7 victory. Kuwait was defeated 11–5. Against France, Bruniges beat both Boscherie and Pietruszka; Eames and Bartlett gained one each.

In the last eight the team went under to Italy 9–1. Bruniges beat Cervi (the teenage Italian outsider who was fifth in the individual). There followed, to decide fifth to eighth places, a match with Hungary. After starting 4–1 down the team climbed back to 8–6. Bartlett now replaced Glaister and annihilated the previously undefeated Rozsavari 5–0 in under two minutes. Unfortunately Eames could not take the last fight in this tremendous match. Against Japan the spark had gone. An 8–5 loss meant eighth place.

# Competitions chronicle 1978-9

The reduced entry of 71 in the ladies' foil made it tough. The British didn't start in top gear and three of them went out. Hilary Cawthorne lost three bouts on the last hit and Susan Wrigglesworth two. Ann Brannon was unlucky to lose 5-4 to both Smith of Australia and Szocs of Hungary. Linda Martin got four efficient wins and a reasonable second round pool. Here she beat Ferguson of Australia and Waples of USA and had only to beat Turcan of Rumania, Rachel of Poland or Palm of Sweden – but her edge was missing.

Meanwhile, the first three in the 1978 World Championship plus the 1970 Gold Medallist all incredibly met in the same pool. Raczova was eliminated; the others went on to the top three places in this order: Hanisch, Sidorova, Schwarzenberger. Vaccaroni was a portentous sixth, after Belova (5th), the evergreen Mexico Gold Medallist, and Losert (4th).

In the team event, a whole week later, the British were seeded tenth out of thirteen. With some elan, they led Italy 4-3 before losing 11-5, conceding six fights on assault point. (Brannon 2, Martin 2, Cawthorne 1, Wrigglesworth 0). Against Poland (yet again) it was 2-all then 6-2 down; then, by a stupendous effort, 6-all, with supporters ever more excited and the team ever more positive. Ann Brannon lost to a cool Skapska, but Hilary Cawthorne fought back with a fine 5-1 over Rachel. A revitalised Sue Wrigglesworth made it 8-7 up with an attacking win over Wysoczanska. Hits being poor, the last fight had to be won. The Poles brought on their substitute against Linda Martin, who sustained an onslaught of fleches with stop-hits and ripostes until the score stood at 4-all. Then she counter-attacked out of time. So it was defeat by 59 to 57 hits. Eventually W. Germany beat Poland for third place. Russia predictably beat Hungary in the final.

Like the two foil teams under Ziemovit Wojciechowski, the sabreurs under Tamas Mendelenyi had probably never reached a World Championship as fit or as thoroughly coached. It was all the more disappointing that Slade and Philbin went out in the first round and Etherton, Cohen and Deanfield in the second (last 48). Only Deanfield won a fight, against Simon of Australia. The final comprised Maffei (4th), Gedovari (6th) and four Russians, Nazlimov beating Krovopuskov in a barrage, with Burtsev third and Alekhine fifth.

Seeded eighth out of thirteen, Britain won a nervous first match against a much improved China by only two hits, Slade substituting for Etherton at the halfway point and firmly winning two fights. The team then lost 9-1 to Russia, Cohen beating Nazlimov. In the last eight they lost 9-1 to Italy (Philbin 1v) and, after a 2-0 lead, 8-2 to Hungary (Philbin 1, Cohen 1). So to Cuba, who had held Italy to 8-all, for a splendid fight-off for seventh place. After fifteen ding-dong bouts Cohen had to win the last one 5-3 to win on hits. He won 5-4. At least the result was better than the previous 9-3 and 11-4 losses to Cuba. Etherton won two good victories, mainly by use of the point, while Deanfield and Cohen each won three, both losing 5-4 to Ortiz, aptly nick-named 'the truck'. Slade and Philbin were both tried but could not contribute.

Once again Zarno shared the presiding of both individual and team finals.

There were 103 epeeists, posing a test well met by the two hundred Australian scorers, timekeepers, interpreters and so forth (headed by Caryl Oliver, familiar from her London days), none of whom received even expenses. The FIE did less well, for instance failing to use eliminated competitors as judges for the last 48 of the sabre, instead of inexpert Australians.

Of the epeeists (coached by Prof. Emery) only Paul fell in the first round. In the second round Llewellyn was unlucky to go out with two wins, along with Johnson. Mallett did very well to reach the last 36 in his first World Championship. He fought coolly and with great determination. Belson beat Lukomsky and Jacobson (5-0) to go through the third round and take sixteenth seed in the direct elimination. Unfortunately, he then faced Riboud, the eventual winner, who beat him 10-3. Rather tired, he met Edling in the repechage and was unable to score.

The team was seeded eighth out of nineteen. They beat Luxemburg 10-5 (and lost to Sweden 8-5); then in the second round against the Chinese, after three good wins by Llewellyn, they had reached 8-7 and won on an unassailable hits lead. So to the last eight and Switzerland. Johnson retired from the match, his epees being rejected (albeit inconclusively and only for this match), because their handles were rotated in relation to the blade, as he had mounted them for years. And the result was a 9-1 loss (Mallett coming in and beating Gaille 5-0). For places five to eight the first opponents were the Italians. In a splendid match, the British won 8-2, for once all the assault points going the right way – no less than six of them. Every one won two fights. Next came the French and another excellent win, 9-7 (Johnson 3, Llewellyn 2, Belson 2, Paul 2). Thus fifth place was gained, the best epee performance since 1965.

In the final, Russia beat W. Germany 9-6 and thus secured a remarkable six Gold Medals, with W. Germany and France gaining one apiece. For Britain a fifth place, two eights and a last sixteen. Good enough to justify £20,000 of government money?

About half the entrants to the *World Student Games* had fenced in the World Championships, arriving in Mexico directly from Australia. The winners included Romankov, Gedovari, Trinquet. Knowing the standard, the BUSF selectors chose only Ann Brannon and Sue Wrigglesworth at ladies' foil, Mallett at epee and Slade at sabre. For financial reasons neither a coach nor a team manager accompanied the team, arguably a false economy.

In the sabre, Slade reached the second round. In the ladies' foil Ann Brannon and Sue Wrigglesworth avoided being among the few eliminations in the first round. In the second round Sue never got going, losing all her fights

# Competitions chronicle 1978-9

and only taking one opponent to the last hit. Ann also started badly, losing 5-4 to Senser (USA) and 5-3 to Bugajska (Poland), but recovered well to beat Fujimaki (Japan) and Tsagareva (Russia), and had then beat Mochi (Italy) to ensure her promotion. Unfortunately at 3-all she twice ran on to good derobements from the Italian, and was eliminated. By the end of her pool Ann was fencing very well, and deserved better than her final 25th place, even though the event was, if anything, harder than the World Championships, the presence of the E. German team more than making up for the absence of Vaccaroni and Belova.

In the epee, Mallett put up a particularly fine performance. In fighting his way to the last eight he displayed great tenacity and maturity under pressure. He was thus enabled to get through a nightmare quarter-final pool, in which Kolczonay (Hungary) won all his bouts, and Väggo (Sweden), Parietti (Italy), Zidaru (Rumania), Picot (France) and Mallett won two each, almost all on the last hit. The key factor was how badly each had lost to Kolczonay, and with a 5-4 loss Mallett passed safely to the last sixteen.

In the direct elimination he again met Zidaru, and for the first time seemed nervous, eventually losing 10-6. In the repechage he was drawn against Pezza (Italy) whose slow style, in contrast to Neal's habitual bouncing, he allowed to set the pace at first and so found himself trailing by two hits. Vociferous encouragement from his team-mates inspired an increase in the tempo, and he began to dominate. At 9-8 to Pezza, the Italian made a seemingly good riposte for corps-a-corps to win, only to have the hit disallowed by the president as arriving after the halt; and Mallett mercifully scored a quick two hits to win 10-9.

His second lucky break, in the last eight of the repechage, was to draw Shelley (USA), arguably the weakest fencer left in the competition. He took an early lead of 4-2, but a hit from Shelley was followed immediately by an equipment penalty hit. This only channelled his anger into a series of all-out fleche attacks, never giving his opponent a chance to settle down, and gave him victory by ten hits to seven.

This victory meant a fight for the final with the short, left-handed Khondogo of Russia. Mallett now looked drained after fencing for twelve hours in the thin air of Mexico City. He launched a succession of half-hearted attacks into the Russian's excellent parries, and after ten minutes fencing was losing by four hits, though in the final minute he caught up to 10-8. His eighth place boded excellently for the future.

# 1979-80

## MEN'S FOIL

This year a points scheme based on Leicester, the Welsh Open, the Leon Paul International, Birmingham and the National Championship was introduced. This encouraged top fencers to compete in the three main provincial tournaments, and thus help to develop foil throughout the country, because international A Grade travel grants were made dependent on these results.

At *Leicester*, in a particularly tense final, Harper and Bruniges were beaten into third and fifth place by Glaister, fencing with his usual determined, aggressive manner. Gosbee was second and Eames fourth. The limitation on the size of teams in the Olympic Games meant some doubling between weapons might be required. Steven Paul was perhaps spurred on by this consideration in reaching the final, although, despite great fitness and mobility, he ended sixth.

In the *Welsh Open*, Harper (1st) and Bruniges (2nd) revenged themselves on Glaister (3rd). In another pre-Christmas tournament – the *Emrys Lloyd* – the experience and technical skills of Wojciechowski – now the Foil Squad coach – made up for his lack of lessons and combat training, when, with fourteen victories and only one defeat – to the 48-year-old Derrick Cawthorne – he took the trophy three fights clear of Harper (11v) and Bruniges (10v). Later in the season at *Birmingham* he repeated the performance, again leaving Harper in second place. Gosbee continued to dominate the Under-20s scene with wins in the *Under-20 Championship* and in the *Millfield*. Donny McKenzie, probably Britain's fastest and fittest junior, was third in the former and second in the latter, ahead of Valentin of France. Routh-Jones was again the winner of the *Hereford and Worcester Open*, this time ahead of More, Willy Bell of Portsmouth, Chris Ward of Birmingham, Richard Hill and René Paul.

A series of *international matches* were fought at the Leon Paul Cup; and although the 'A' team, consisting of Harper, Glaister, Gosbee and Bruniges beat the touring Japanese team 9–5 and Paris Racing Club (Royer, Teisseire, Dutripon and the Paris-based Bell) 9–5, the 'B' team (Seaman, Eames, Bartlett, G. Paul and Ford) only managed to tie 8–all against Sweden (Tachenstrom, Ekstedt, Akerberg and Rohlin). With hits also equal at 59–all, Eames faced Ekstedt in a barrage, but could not match him, lacking his usual point control, although his long absence-of-blade attacks were beating the parries.

In the *Leon Paul* itself, Graham Paul, Ford and Gosbee reached the last 24 and Seaman the last twelve. In the last eight Bruniges crushed the diminutive Dutripon of France 10–1 and Bell beat Akerberg 10–6, mostly with his very fast stop-hits, while Harper had an easy 10–3 victory over Royer. Glaister, in

Leon Paul Cup 1980: R. Bruniges
v N. Bell.

spite of his aggressiveness and superior, small-paced mobility, lost 10–9 to Eyal of Israel. In the last four, Bruniges beat Bell, fleching from a standing start more scorchingly than ever, and returning a few stop hits as well. Harper beat Eyal 10–4, nine of his hits being attacks, as again and again he drew his opponent forward with a couple of steps back, prepared with a couple of steps forward and a couple of feints, then hit with a lunge.

The final was the now usual, fascinating encounter between Harper and Bruniges – who tried everthing: fleche attacks, beautifully timed stop hits, mazy ripostes, jumping in the air. Harper hit him with seven attacks and two composed ripostes and reached 9–6 looking comfortable and composed. Another attack from Bruniges brought the score to 9–7, but there was an air of desperation about it. Then came one of his fleche attacks, unleashed faster than any that afternoon, drawing gasps from the audience at the suddenness of its speed from a perfectly relaxed stance. But Harper dismissed even this last effort with a neat stop-hit and completed a workmanlike performance in which he never seemed troubled. Bruniges showed once again his outstanding natural talent for the sport – greater than any other British fencer at any weapon at this date. He also showed that natural ability needed a background of hard work to realise its full potential. If he got himself fully fit, he could beat anybody in the world.

Although partially retired from fencing and concentrating on being a father, Barry Paul won the *Championship* – for the fifth time, a record only surpassed by Emrys Lloyd's remarkable seven wins. (René Paul won five times, Raymond Paul and Robert Montgomerie four times. Oddly, Allan Jay, Britain's supreme foilist, only won once). Harper was again second; Graham Paul was third.

In one of the closest finals ever in the *Team Championship*, Barry and Graham, Ford and Bartlett, fencing for Salle Paul, defeated Salle Boston (Bruniges, Fox, Eames and Gosbee) on hits, after tying 8–all on fights – Bruniges retiring injured with a gashed leg, to be replaced by Thompson. This was the 23rd time Salle Paul had won the event, only conceding the trophy to another club eleven time since the inception of the event in 1948.

The *Junior Foil*, was won by Julian Tyson, runner-up four years before. His classic style and elastic rhythm was too much for the unorthodox counter-attacks of Gabor Scott (S. Paul; 2nd) and the generous prime parries and beats of Robin Pearson (Leeds Univ.; 3rd).

Still only eighteen, Gosbee showed in the *Under-20* that he had no rivals. Lack of point control was a weakness of all the other finalists. There was increased mobility, but it was to little purpose. Like Gosbee, the fifteen-year-old Pitman was able to gain hits by simple evasion. He was fifth. Dale of Brentwood, also now aged fifteen, only missed the final when he lost 10–9 to the exiled Ulsterman, Johnnie Davis. Chris Ward of Birmingham was the runner-up, followed by McKenzie, who was now studying psychology at Edinburgh University.

The *Millfield Tournament* attracted only 41 entries, including five W. Germans, two French and two Swiss, of whom only Valentin of France reached the final, coming third. This was otherwise almost a repeat of the Under-20 Championship, though McKenzie forced Gosbee to a barrage, Ward sank from second (3v) to fifth (1v); Wright rose from sixth (1v) to fourth (2v), and Pitman slipped from fifth (5v) to sixth (1v). By contrast, all three top places went to foreigners in the *Eden Under-20 Cup*: Omnes, de Lagerie and Baska.

Abroad there were encouraging results at *Burgsteinfort*, to which a party went in the now veteran under-20 minibus. McKenzie reached the last twelve, where he lost to Omnes, and Wright did well to get to the last 24, where he lost only 10–9 to Masiero (France). At *Kussnacht*, Gosbee was in the last eight, being eliminated by Baska.

Britain's only finalist in a senior event abroad was Harper, who reached the final of the *Duval* for the second year running, beating Bell 10–1 in the last 32 and Magne (France) 10–4 in the last sixteen. In the final, however, he let Benko pull steadily ahead to 10–6, leaving him equal fifth. Bruniges reached the last sixteen, beating Soumagne 10–9, but was unlucky to lose to Bardini, a hard-edge French junior, 10–9.

In the *Martini* the best British place was Harper's in the last 48. At *Venice* Bell and Bruniges reached the last 32, and in the B Grade *Bad Durkheim*,

Glaister, achieving his only foreign result of the season, was in the last twelve, with Eames and Bartlett in the last 24. In the *Rommel* Bell and Bruniges were again in the last 32. In the direct elimination stage Bruniges beat Robak 10–9 in his first fight, only to lose 10–0 to Smirnov (Russia). In the repechage he lost 10–9 to Kuki of Rumania. Bell was beaten 10–6 by Scuri of Italy and 10–7 by Somodi, of Hungary. At *Budapest* Bruniges reached the last 24.

The four-year Olympic cycle ended with Bruniges scoring 61½ Olympic points, Harper 37, and Bell 27. These three were thus selected, though Bell joined the boycott of Moscow. Eames (18) and Glaister (17) failed to reach the 24-point qualifying standard.

At the end of the season, Steve Fox took over from Nick Halsted as Captain.

## *LADIES' FOIL*

On the *Under-20* front, Penny Johnson, after a 5–2 barrage with Clare Gobey, became the Champion, ahead, surprisingly, of both Fiona McIntosh and Katie Arup. Her strong, solidly defensive style was given edge by her fast quarte riposte. Another expert in counter-ripostes, Michelle Rose (LTFC), was fifth and Fiona Wilson sixth.

It was Fiona McIntosh, however, who came third in the *Perigal*, behind Schaeffner and Besser of W. Germany. Judith Mendelenyi did well to come sixth, after Faul (W. Germany) and Salle (France). For her part, Kim Cecil excelled to win at *Dornbirn*. Penny Johnson came sixth here.

Kim Cecil won the *Felix Cup*, followed by Clare Gobey and Katie Arup. The *Jubilee Bowl* was won for the first time by Wendy Grant, making a surprise return to serious training after two years off. Fiona McIntosh, now training in London between school and university, was second. Sue Wrigglesworth, ahead of Hilary Cawthorne on indicators, was third.

Wendy Grant also won at *Leicester*, after a deciding bout with Linda Martin, who, however, was the *Welsh Open* Champion and runner-up to Rodriguez of Cuba at perhaps the strongest ever *Birmingham*. In the associated *quadrangular match* here Sue Wrigglesworth, Linda Martin and Hilary Cawthorne had three clear wins over Belgium, USA and GB 'B'. At the end of the season Sue Hoad retained her *Kirklees* title, but only after a four-way barrage with the London–Thames pair Lesley Calver (2nd) and Sue Uff (3rd) and with Sheila Anderson, now fencing for Mary Hawdon FC (4th). Maggie Browning (*Nottingham* winner) was fifth, Michelle Rose sixth.

In the *Team Championship* an exceptionally strong Salle Paul beat a rather off-form Boston 9–6 (L. Martin 2, F. McIntosh 4, S. Wrigglesworth 2, P. Johnson/K. Arup 1; A. Brannon 2, C. Montgomery 2, S. Hoad 1, H. Cawthorne/K. Cecil 1).

The LAFU category competitions began with Jane Whitney of Sale F.C.

winning the *Toupie Lowther* ahead of Jane Roberts (Chester F.C., a pupil of Rosemary Castle) and Cathy Peppercorn (S. Roeder, daughter of Elizabeth). Debbie Hall, now at Leicester University, beat Fiona Wilson to take first place in the *Parker*. Sarah Kellett, the *Under-18 Champion*, beat Pauline Stonehouse of Brownhill for third place; the other finalists were Pauline Monk, Marcia Stretch of Surrey, Jane Whitney and Janet Hall. The *Bertrand* had a strong entry and consequently an exciting final. Debbie Hall was the winner, ahead of Hilary Jones, Katie Arup, Cath Robertson, Brenda Hewitt and Pat Casey (LTFC). The *Desprez Cup* was won by Linda Martin (4v), but Kim Cecil (3v) was runner-up. Along with Fiona McIntosh (2v), whom she just beat 5–4, she was making her first senior final. The other finalists were Wendy Grant (3v; 3rd), Hilary Cawthorne (3v; 4th) and Ann Brannon (2v; 6th). In the *Championship* (at Leicester) Wendy Grant recovered her title of 1974 after a barrage with Liz Wood. Sue Wrigglesworth and Hilary Cawthorne were third and fourth on indicators. An injured Linda Martin had to be satisfied with fifth place over Sue Hoad, who did well to reach her first senior final after several years in the middle ranks.

The *de Beaumont* included the French junior team, an Italian team and various Spaniards, Canadians, Israelis, Americans and an Argentinian, a Dane and an Irish girl. Ann Brannon was the only British finalist. She began shakily but recovered to come second equal, with Bougnol (France), to Leenders. Modaine of France (3v) was fourth, Max-Madsen of Denmark (2v) fifth and Hatuel of Israel (0v) sixth. Kim Cecil, Clare Gobey and Clare Montgomery fought their way to the last twelve. Linda Martin was absent.

The high point abroad was Linda Martin's excellent fourth place at *Como*, after she had eliminated Sidorova. It was her best result so far. She also reached the last eight in *Leipzig* and narrowly missed the final in *E. Berlin*. Earlier she had led Sue Wrigglesworth and Hilary Cawthorne to a team win at *Amsterdam*, where they also took first, second and fifth places respectively. Sue Wrigglesworth achieved nothing outstanding but reached the last twelve in Leipzig and also the last 24 in *Turin* and *Bucharest*, as did Hilary Cawthorne. A fit and determined Wendy Grant reached the last twelve in *Offenbach* and the last sixteen in *Bucharest*, while Fiona McIntosh, still improving, reached the last 32 in *Turin*. Salle Paul reached the last eight of the *Coupe d'Europe*, the fate of every British entry in the previous five years. Ann Brannon did well to reach the last twelve of the A Grade *Jeanty*. She also reached the last sixteen in *Bucharest* thereby qualifying for the Olympic team (with 38 points), along with Linda Martin (85), Wendy Grant (25), Sue Wrigglesworth (46½) and Hilary Cawthorne (29½) – who travelled as Captain but also fenced in the team.

# Competitions chronicle 1979–80

## EPEE

After being second in 1977 and fifth in 1978, George Liston finally won the *Under-20 Championship*. His main obstacle was the unorthodox and confidently aggressive Mark Nelson-Griffiths, who beat him in the direct elimination and again (5–2) in the final, but who was unable to beat any other finalist. Liston thus had to barrage with Steve Meredith, now in the Royal Navy, whose quick quarte-riposte he outreached with his penetrating lunges. Baldry, fourth with two 5–4 wins, was down a place on the previous year and Brannon, now at Kent University, was up one. Fifth was Christopher Shaw of London –Thames, who, in spite of tuition from the age of nine from Brian Pitman calculated to produce classic technique, found success with unorthodox bent-arm, almost straight-legged attacks.

Of those who reached the direct elimination, Gregor Henderson of Heriot-Watt set a hot early pace, as did the fast, fierce fleches of Greerson McMullen of Millfield, winner of the *Under-18 Championship*; they were defeated more by their own temperaments than by the skill of others. The pentathletes Richard Keers (Millfield) and Peter Tayler (pupil of Frank Tanner at Reading) fenced well, as did Peter Eames (Boston; 8th), another of the early leaders.

Runner-up to Hagen of Norway in the *British Under-20 International*, Steven Henshall was beginning to use his length with aggression as effectively as Liston, who was third. Abroad, Liston was third and Henshall fifth in the *Brussels Under-20* event. Liston also reached the last eight at *Tourcoing*, where Eames was in the last 24.

As in the previous season, Liston did not do himself justice in the *Junior*, but this time Jerry Melville got going from the start and in the final he lost only to Roger Greenhalgh (3v, 2nd), whose somewhat static classical technique contrasted with his own mobile aggression. Danny Nightingale took third place, combining patient care with decisive action in the best one-hit style of a pentathlete. David Brooks (2v; 4th) was a finalist for the fourth time, followed by two newcomers, Tayler (2v; 5th), who all but forced a four-way barrage when he lost 6–5 to Melville in the last fight of the pool, and Kernohan (1v; 6th), whose fast and tricky counter-time and unlikely continuations deprived Greenhalgh of his chance of the title.

The senior season had begun with the *Epee Club Cup*, which was won by Llewellyn (3v), ahead of Mallett (4v), Hoskyns (4v), Young (4v), Edwards (3v), Martin (3v), Melville (2v) and Steventon (1v). Tyson, Liston and John Troiano of London–Thames (who won the *Universities Championship*) just missed promotion from one preliminary pool of eighteen and Wood, Stanbury and Lewis from the other.

Stanbury won at *Bristol*, gaining every fight on the last hit. Steven Paul was the winner at *Ashton*, beating Roose in the final bout of the knock-out. Graham

Mackay of Bellahouston won at *Tyneside* (where he also won the foil). David Brooks won the *Welsh Open* for the third time and the second time running. The *Martini Qualifying* also went to the holder (and winner at *Leicester*) – Melville. Graham Paul was second (as he had been in 1966 and 1977), followed by Hoskyns (one hit behind) and Davenport.

The *Martini* itself was 126 strong. Eleven of the 24 British were promoted from the first round, not a bad proportion, though it was a pity several notable epeeists failed to get into top gear from the start – so necessary in this class of event. Young did well with five wins, as did Lewis with four wins in a tough pool from which Gaille was eliminated. This round was marred by an injury to Igor Bormann, whose chest was pierced by a broken epee.

The second round inevitably ousted many outstanding fencers: Hoskyns, Edling and Kauter all went out of the same pool, for instance. Steven Paul went out with Longlet, and Graham Paul with Riboud, each with two wins. Also eliminated were Belson, Hill, Greenhalgh, Lavington, Lewis and Young.

Johnson did very well to head a pool which shed Parietti. In the last 32, however, he met Hjerpe of Sweden, who beat him 10–5 before going on to give the winner a hard bout in the last eight. Llewellyn seeded 34, had to fight-off with Verbrackel of France for a place in the last 32. He lost 10–9.

Bellone of Italy, and Giger and Carrard of Switzerland, were the other losers in the last eight. In the last four, Bernadotte of Sweden went out to the tall, strongly-built, moustachioed Petho of Hungary, while Fischer of W. Germany lost 10–9 to Picot of France, who delighted the audience with his long, composed attacks, often en fleche, his renewals from the lunge and his elastic movements in the low line. His unfashionably classic stance contrasted with Petho's nearly straight-legged, bent-arm position. Both were super-fit and super-sharp as befitted men who were professionals in all but name. But it was Petho who had the subtlety of counter-time and greater ability to adjust. He won the final bout 10–7, the sixth Hungarian victor since the event started in 1960. (The French had won five times, the W. Germans three times.)

In the repechage from the last sixteen of the *Championship* every win was on the last hit: Roose beat Hoskyns, Melville beat Lewis, Johnson beat Davenport, and Mallett beat Brannon. In the last round of knock-out Roose beat Melville and Johnson beat Mallett, both by 10–7.

Steven Paul was the winner, sustaining not a single outright defeat in the entire competition, though he had a double defeat with Roose in the final. Now aged 25, he had developed excellent bladework and a sizzling turn of speed. He also trained hard, for instance running eight miles a week. Roose was unlucky to end fifth, as he successfully withstood a tremendous onslaught from Bourne and only missed two further wins on the last hit. Bourne (3v; 2nd) lost to Paul on assault point and thus forfeited the chance of a barrage. This was the thirteenth time he had been in the first three of the Championship (Hoskyns 10, Jay 9, C. B. Notley 9, J. Pelling 8, A. Pelling 7, de

Beaumont 7). Neither Johnson (3v; 3rd) nor Belson (2v; 4th) was on top form. The first-timer of the final was Stanbury (1v; 6th).

Steven Paul made a double of it by winning the *Miller-Hallett*, after beating Belson 5-4 in a barrage and against strong Norwegian opposition. Koppang (3v) was third, followed by Vonen (2v), Krogh (1v) and Llewellyn (0v). Rance did very well to reach the last sixteen along with Mallett, Roose, Melville, Liston and Stanbury and three Luxembourg team members. Shaw could also be pleased to be in the last 24, which eliminated Johnson, Jacobs, Partridge, Lavington and Ian Dunlop (an unorthodox latecomer to fencing, from London-Thames) – and the two Luxembourgers.

The semi-finals of the *Team Championship* were one-sided. The Pentathletes seemed to accept their doom from Boston on advance and duly lost 9-1. And yet again Thames (or rather London-Thames) allowed themselves to be put off by Salle Paul gamesmanship: they lost 9-3. The enjoyable final proved very close. Pauls won by two hits, and thus won for the sixth time since first doing so in 1950 (G. Paul 2, B. Paul 2, S. Paul 2, J. Llewellyn 1; Johnson 2, Mallett 2, Davenport 2, Stanbury 1).

At the end of the season the *Inter-Services Championship*, part of the Royal Tournament as usual, was almost a nostalgic occasion. The winner was Ian Campbell, who had been absent from national events since he came fourth in the Junior in 1972, the year Lawrence Burr, the runner-up and little seen in intervening years, came third in the Inter-Services. Brierley was third this time, having gained the same place in the Junior back in 1970.

Abroad, Johnson was a good second to Edling at *Catania*. At *Zurich* Belson was sixth, Mallett in the last eight and Johnson in the last twelve. In *Budapest* Steven Paul was in the last 24 and Belson and Roose in the last 32. In the *Carroccio* Johnson did well to reach the last eight. Paul was in the last 32. Thereafter results were a bit thin, a falling-off attributed to doubts and misgivings over the coming Olympics. Nothing good was achieved in the *Monal*. At *Bern* Llewellyn reached the last 32. At *Heidenheim*, however, Paul did well in getting to the last sixteen, as did Belson in getting to the last eight at *Poitiers* for the third time, beating Bormann by aggressive tactics after being well down and going out 10-7 to Mojaev of the Soviet Union, who overcame his blade-taking tactics by sheer strength.

The team selected for Moscow was the same as for the previous year: Belson, Johnson, Paul, Llewellyn and Mallett – but the first two declined, responding to the call to boycott the Games.

*SABRE*

Training for the national squad was now more intensive than ever. With the introduction of sessions at Albany Street Barracks supplementing the normal training at Salle Boston, it extended to four evenings a week. On top of that, there were no less than 26 Saturday morning sessions at St Paul's School. This affected entries to provincial and even national competitions, though it could hardly explain the very small entry to the *Junior*. Jack Magill, Cary Zitcer and Nigel Carr claimed the first three places for Boston here. From Salle Ganchev, coached by Paul Romang and Tamas Mendelenyi, came Klenerman (4th) and West (5th). Falkowski bore the Poly flag in sixth place (and was heard to say that in future he would stick to squash, a remark which no-one took seriously).

The National Age Group Championships were dominated by Paul Romang's pupils at City of London. The bouncy and aggressive West beat Klenerman 5–2 for the *Under-18* title – he was hit only six times in the final. The 'calm giant' Gary Fletcher of Ashton was third and J. Fellerman of Merchant Taylor's fourth. Malcolm Comrie and Ross Mack of Scotland took the remaining places. There were only 22 entries. In the *Under-16* event Chris Booton won, although taken to the last hit by his Ganchev team-mate Paul Branscombe (2nd) and by Pat Pearson's pupil Chris Brockbanks of Darlington (3rd), who showed considerable potential.

In the *Under-20 Championship* Boston triumphed again. With his ability to make opponents misjudge his considerable reach, Hall lost only to Klenerman (5–2), though West took him to 4–all; by 5–2 he won the ensuing barrage with Kenric Li, who was studying hard at Salford University and therefore scarcely training (though he did win the *Universities* title). West was ahead of Klenerman again, while the former champion Hunt, in the throes of medical studies, was only fifth. Sixth place went to the promisingly mobile Stan Stoodley of Meadowbank. Narrowly ousted in the direct elimination and repechage were Fletcher, Mark Bryant (Ganchev) and Gordon Drummond (now at Birmingham).

In the provincials, foilists put the sabreurs to shame. Graham Kay won the *Welsh Open* and his hat trick at *Liverpool*, McKenzie won *Inverclyde*. But, Magill was victor at *Nottingham* and Slade at *Bristol*. In *Birmingham* Manuel Ortiz collected the trophy, he and four other leading Cuban sabreurs calling in en route to other European tournaments and Moscow. In the team final they easily beat Mercia (G. Wiles, J. Magill, R. Berry). The individual event included the participants in the match between Britain, USA and Belgium which had attracted both sponsorship and television; but only one of them got to the finals, which comprised five Cubans, and the elegant technician Peter Westbrook of USA (2nd). Two of the Americans reached the semi-finals, together with Slade, Etherton, Philbin and Zarno, all of whom went out on indicators. Security guards were astonished to find fencing still in progress at 1.00 a.m.

At the end of the season, *Kirklees* was won by Fletcher, undefeated, three times snatching victory from 4–all. He was followed by Nino Moscardini

(LTFC; 4v) and two schoolboys – Chris Booton of Salle Ganchev (1v) and J. Smith of Guisborough FC, Co. Durham (ov).

The *Cole Cup* was won by Cohen for the third successive time and the fourth time in five years. Philbin was second for the third time running. He lost only to Cohen and only on the last hit. Etherton was third, his best performance in the event in his last season before retirement. Slade was a disappointing fourth. Zarno was fifth, apparently unsure whether he was in contention for Moscow. Richard Jaine, now master-in-charge of fencing at St Paul's, was sixth, his best national performance so far.

Coached and led by Convents and Wischeidt, 32 W. German senior and junior fencers entered the *Corble Cup* in the course of a training tour. Only seventeen British entered and they were out-numbered two to four in the final, but the standard of the two nations was seen to be close, eight out of the fifteen bouts being decided on the last hit. Boch (1st) was only beaten by Cohen (4th). Slade performed with conviction to capture second place ahead of Delberg.

Five of the *Championship* finalists were predictable. Cohen won, for only the second time in his long career. Slade was second, Philbin fourth, Etherton fifth and Deanfield sixth. The surprise was Dennis Hutt of London–Thames in third place, returning on a brief foray from British Airways duties.

In the *Team Championship* Deanfield, Cohen, Zarno and Philbin for Poly yet again beat Boston (Etherton, Slade, Jaine and Gary Li).

The hunt for international results was intense in this Olympic season and began early. Philbin, Cohen and Deanfield were all close to the total qualifying points for selection. Etherton and Slade were unlikely to qualify but were after the final places that might be available, under the rules, to complete the team. In the small but distinguished event in *Vienna* Zarno only missed the final when he lost to Bartecki (Poland) in the last round of elimination, after beating Platzer, losing to Bujdogo (World Youth Champion) and beating Slade. Cohen, Philbin and Slade had each lost by only 10–8 to noted opponents: Wodke (Poland), Aliokhin and Sidiak (USSR). Philbin and Slade had both won their repechages, but Cohen lost 11–10 to Hammung of Hungary. In the last twelve, Philbin, as well as Slade, was eliminated – by only 10–9 – to A. Kovacs. It has always to be remembered what a margin of superiority has to be shown over a Hungarian, given the advantage of reputation in the subjective judging of sabre.

With points under their belts, the contenders were off to the *Touzard*, which was replete with Bulgarians, Spaniards, Poles and over forty Germans. Both Deanfield and Cohen reached the last sixteen and thus qualified alongside Philbin (who was in the last 24). Nobody got beyond round two in *New York* and only Etherton got to the third round at *Hanover* (where the team stayed for a week's training); but at *Brasov* in Rumania, a very strong event, with large numbers of aggressive Rumanians, as well as Russians, Hungarians, Poles, E.

Germans and Cubans, Slade, so far behind at the beginning of the year, justified his decision to take a year off serious jobs after graduating, by qualifying for Moscow. After losing to Pop, eventual winner, he won three repechage bouts including one against Nilca (often an A Category winner) before going out to Jablonowski (Poland) who came second. Sadly, for the fifth time this season Etherton was eliminated in the round before he could gain the four points he needed. The star performance came in *Munich*, where Deanfield was sixth, despite his gruelling commitments as a junior doctor at Great Ormond Street. The final points tally over the three pre-Olympic seasons was: Cohen 43, Deanfield 39½, Philbin 34½, Slade 32, Zarno 17½, Etherton 13, Hutt 3½, Jaine 2. But all those selected except Slade joined the boycott. Deanfield denied himself his farewell appearance for Britain, and Cohen and Etherton (the reserve) withdrew, as well as Philbin, for whom it was a particular sacrifice, since he had missed Montreal.

*COMBINED EVENTS*

The British performance in the *World Youth Championships* in Venice was a decided improvement on the previous year. In the ladies' foil, although Penny Johnson went out in the first round, having earlier injured her foot, Kim Cecil and Fiona McIntosh both battled on to the third round (last 24). In the men's foil Ward and McKenzie reached the second round. Ward was unlucky to be eliminated by a few hits after tying with three others on three wins. Gosbee, still with another Under-20 season ahead of him, achieved a very encouraging fourteenth place, losing to Howe of E. Germany, a left-hander who eventually came second.

Only two epeeists were entered. Better things might have been hoped from the relatively experienced Liston, who reached the second round (last 48). On the other hand, Henshall, now making good use of his strongly built six foot four inches, just survived the first three rounds to be seeded number sixteen against the number one, Latychev of Russia, who finally asserted his class won 10–6, but only after Henshall had made all the going in the first half of the bout. In the repechage he lost.

In the sabre, Klenerman reached the second round, where he won his first two fights and might well have gone further if his composure had held after losing the third bout. Hall and West did as much as could be expected in reaching the third round (last 24).

The team coach was Zsolt Vadaszffy; the Ladies' Manager was Rosemary Castle; Joe Eden was overall Manager.

On its thirtieth anniversary the *Winton Cup* was won for the first time by Wales, who put in a co-ordinated effort under the captaincy of Bryan Lewis and the coaching and organisation of Prof. Peter Stewart, with Alf Pearce, as

Deborah Hall and Julian Tyson

so often, the ever-helpful armourer. They won *seven* matches 5–4! They beat Central Scotland 26–10, the NW 23–13, the SE 20–16 and E. Midlands 19–17; and they drew with W. Midlands (each weapon being 5–4). Top scorers were Bryan Lewis at sabre and epee (20/24) and his sister Christine (12/15), followed by Wood and Warburn at epee (11/15) and, at foil, Phil Davies (9/15), Sarah Melvin (8/13), Marvin Evans (9/15) and Tony Garrington (7/13). The best performer of any team, however, was Debbie Hall, who was undefeated throughout her fifteen bouts for the E. Midlands. Behind Wales by only two points was the SE. London at their first appearance in the event won the second division, in which Routh-Jones for the South only lost a single foil bout, and also fenced sabre.

The *Quadrangular* (now also known as the Home International), although held in Cardiff, was a different matter. England swept to victory, and Wales, after beating Scotland at men's foil and sabre, lost the crucial epee match 7–2 (Mackay 3, Kernohan 3, Henderson 1) and had to be content with beating N. Ireland by a greater margin than the other two countries. Their best scorers were Lewis again (7/9 at sabre) and Lindy Prys-Roberts, who had been a surprise omission from the team in 1978 (7/9). The high point of the event was the dinner in the neo-Arthurian splendours of Cardiff Castle.

The British team at the Moscow *Olympic Games* was overshadowed by the boycott controversy and short by six members who had decided to stay away on grounds of principle. It was captained by Richard Oldcorn, Hilary Cawthorne being the ladies' Captain (and potential reserve), Derrick Cawthorne the president and Profs Boston and Emery the coaches. John Zarno and Peter Jacobs were presidents, as guests of the FIE.

The events started all the tougher for being smaller than usual. In the 33-strong ladies' foil Sue Wrigglesworth, in her third Olympics, began well with a win over Madsen, but lost to Maros of Hungary (eventual Silver Medallist), Sparaciari of Italy and Niklaus (E. Germany). So she needed to beat Trinquet of France, eventual Gold Medallist, 5–1. She lost 5–4. Not an easy pool! A nervous Linda Martin lost to Brouquier (France) and Ferguson (Australia), but then had a good win over Stefanek (Hungary). After losing to the ex-World Champion Stahl, she had to beat Janke (E. Germany) 5–0. Again it was a 5–4 loss.

Ann Brannon went up from the first round, on hits, on a single win – 5–0 over Sidorova, who was suspected of fight-throwing. In the second round she showed she deserved to be there by beating the famous Schwarzenberger as well as Haertrampf of E. Germany. She was unlucky that her remaining fights were against the eventual first, fourth and sixth in the final. She was placed eighteenth, a very creditable achievement. The boycott meant that Hanisch and Losert were absent from the final, but there were no Russians either.

In the team event Britain were seeded ninth out of nine. Pitted against Hungary, they were soon 6–3 down. Then Wendy Grant beat Schwarzenber-

England team 1980. *Back:* Prof. V. Cassapi (Coach), M. Hunt, J. Troiano, M. Hall, P. Wedge, G. Kay, S. Roose, S. Hoad. *Front:* C. Tyson (Manager), K. Cecil, A. Fraser-Smith, D. Seaman, J. Stanbury, D. Hall, R. Davenport.

ger and Hilary Cawthorne (substituting for Ann Brannon with the encouragement of the overall captain) beat Stefanek. But the Hungarians took the next two fights and the end seemed in sight. Not so. Hilary, Wendy and Linda each won their last fight and it was an amazing victory on hits – the first *ever* against Hungary (Grant 4, Cawthorne 2/2, Martin 2, Wrigglesworth 0, Brannon 0).

The Polish top seeds should now have assured British promotion by beating Hungary, but instead the Hungarians rallied to a dramatic 10–6 victory. So the British had at least to repeat their 8–all of 1979 against the Poles. A revived Ann Brannon won three fights, but the only other victory came from Linda Martin. Seventh place, therefore.

In the men's foil (also with 33 entries) Bruniges beat Romankov in the first round, but could not get going in the second, scoring only one hit in his first three fights. His subsequent two good wins were too late for his hits to be adequate. The standard was such that Tiu, Papp and Koukal were eliminated in the first round, Flament and Cervi in the second. Harper, however, fenced steadily through the second round to reach the last sixteen. There he lost to Kuki, who was eventually sixth, and to Kotzmann of E. Germany (12th), finishing in thirteenth place, no mean achievement.

Romankov was favourite for the Gold Medal, with a record of dominance unrivalled since d'Oriola (1974 1st; 1976 2nd; 1977 1st; 1978 2nd; 1979 1st). But he was forced into third place in a barrage with Jolyot (2nd) and Smirnov (1st). All the finalists were left-handed.

For the team event the two British foilists were augmented by Llewellyn and Steven Paul. Bruniges excelled against the full Rumanian side with three wins. But of the others only Paul won one. The match with Russia was similar (Bruniges 2, Paul 1). Russia went on to lose 8–all to France in the final, Lapitski having been speared by a broken foil in the semi-final match with Poland and only the epeeist Karagian being available as substitute.

The boycott thinned out only the weaker end of the sabre entry, so the first round of thirty was especially harsh. The lone British entry, Slade, fenced excellently, ousting R. Muller of E. Germany and beating Lamour (incidentally, the only French fencer not to win a Gold Medal). He was one of only five westerners in the second round, in the last 24. In his first fight he led Krovopuskov 4–3, three of his hits being exquisitely timed stop cuts to wrist. To his astonishment, Krovopuskov, 1976 and 1978 Gold Medallist, again attacked with an exposed forearm. Hardly believing his luck, he fractionally hesitated. But for this, the fight would have been his. Lacking the boost of victory, he lost the other four fights. Krovopuskov went on to another Gold Medal.

In the 42-strong epee first round Mallett, looking a shadow of himself at Melbourne, picked away nervously for one win – not enough for promotion. Paul and Llewellyn, however, got two and three wins respectively to reach the last 24. Here Llewellyn had a formidable pool with two finalists, plus

Jacobson, Bellone and Pongracz. He could not get a victory. Paul did very well to beat Ganeff, Abushakhmetov and Picot and gain twelfth seed in the final tableau of sixteen. He was unlucky to meet Kolczonay, eventual Silver Medallist, to whom he lost 10–4 and then to lose 10–8 in a very tough fight to Mojaev, who went on to eliminate Jacobson, the top seed, and in the final to beat Riboud (3rd) and Harmenberg (1st) before coming sixth. Edling (4th) just missed another medal in his large collection.

The Italians scratched from the team event, leaving the British ready and waiting for three hours before they lost 8–3 to Sweden (Paul 2, Llewellyn 1, Mallett 0 and the co-opted Bruniges 0). The second round confronted them with Russia, who beat them 9–2, Paul and Llewellyn picking up one each. In the matches for the lower places, the team lost 9–4 to the Czechs, everybody winning one; they then got a walkover from the disheartened Hungarians to obtain seventh place.

The British team results were much affected by the withdrawals and the individual results were undoubtedly affected as well, especially by the uncertainties and pressures of the run-up period. To gain an eighteenth, a thirteenth and a twelfth place was far from discreditable.

As soon as the French had beaten the Poles in the epee team final the British were flown home, missing the last of the athletics and the closing ceremony, to ease the overstretched BOA finances. A damp end to a disturbed 'celebration'.

# 1980–1

## MEN'S FOIL

At the junior end of the scale there was little change among the fencers heading the different age groups. In the *Under-18 Championship* the Scots were to the fore: Mark Donaldson of Denny HS, Central Section, was fifth and Champion for the second year running was Stan Stoodley of Ainsley Park School, E. Section, who was also runner-up to his fellow Scot Ross Mack in the *Ashton Under-20* event and who went on to win the large Under-20 event at *the Hague*. The other *Under-18* places went to Rance (2nd), Andrew Moore of Stanborough School (3rd), Gerry Gajadharsingh, of Trinidad and Tobago and Burlington Danes School (4th) and Martin Murgatroyd of Warrington FC (6th). The *Under-16* Champion was also the holder, Pitman, followed by Dale, Paul Stanley of Brentwood, Simon Triptree of Beverley School, Richard Arthur of Winchester College, and Stephen Friendship of Downside. Peter Kay of York FC was the *Under-14* Champion.

Gosbee was the *Under-20* Champion after a barrage with Stoodley, winning

# Competitions chronicle 1980-1 451

the title for an amazing fourth successive time. Previously, only Wedge had ever won it even on *two* successive occasions. Gajadharsingh was third. Gosbee was also runner-up in the *Millfield*, between Caflisch and Keller of Switzerland. The *Wilkinson* invitation title was retained by Pitman when he beat Rance 10-5. Donaldson and Michael Guenigault of Crawley FC, a brother of Graham and pupil of Keith Griffin and Prof. Pitman, were the semi-finalists.

Robin Pearson of Hydra (third the previous year) won the *Junior Championship* in a barrage with Tony Garrington of Cardiff, a Quadrangular veteran (2nd), and Richard Sage of Lancaster University, followed by Pitman, London-Thames, John Bourne of Salle Paul and David Hiam of London -Thames (ex-Oxford). The *Universities* title was carried off by Ward (London), ahead of McKenzie (Edinburgh), M. Thompson (London), Troiano (Oxford), and Rhodes (Cambridge).

The travel grant points system again ensured that team members travelled the provincial circuit. Bruniges collected three wins – Leicester, the Welsh Open, and Birmingham – finding the new FIE system of direct elimination from the last eight helped him to concentrate. In the *Welsh Open* Richard Hill of Salle Paul was runner-up – his best result thus far, ahead of Harper (3rd), Ward (4th), McKenzie (5th), Troiano (6th), G. Evans (7th), and Glaister (8th). The technically excellent Ward, also now at Salle Paul, came to the top at *Nottingham*, followed by his club-mate John Franck, Richard Sage of Ashton, Pearson and Tim Smith (Goodall). Carson (Instonians) scratched. The same weekend the *York Open* was won by Swinnerton, followed by Mark Chetwood (2nd) and Jan Bulinski (3rd) – both of York FC – and by Trevor Thomas of Hull FC and René Paul, still campaigning at the age of 59. Graham Mackay was winner of the *Tyneside*, while the order at *Portsmouth* was: Graham Guenigault, Tony Garrington, Simon Routh-Jones, John Woods, Tim Smith and Adrian Collins (another Goodall fencer).

Harper was runner-up at *Birmingham*, which this year lacked the sponsorship to attract foreign teams and also dispensed with gala finals, but followed the prevailing international system of direct elimination from the last eight. Top of the preceding match-plan of 32 was Thompson, who went straight to the final, disposing of Wedge, Gareth Evans and Seaman (fencing elastically). Similarly, Bruniges beat the 19-year old John Smith (from the NE, now in the police and at Boston), Shepherd and Harper. Cocker first beat Kay, then René Paul (seeded no. 30, but victor over Tyson, no. 3) and finally McKenzie. Glaister beat Mike Medhurst (S. Paul), the Dutchman Kerkhoff and Bartlett. Out of the repechage emerged Harper (beating Hoskyns), the Frenchman Carniel (beating Bartlett), Seaman (beating Marvin Evans) and McKenzie (beating Ward). In the last eight, Carniel beat Thompson, but then lost to Harper (who had beaten Cocker), and McKenzie beat Glaister, but lost to Bruniges (who had beaten Seaman). In the final bout Bruniges snatched a close victory from Harper, as he had at *Leicester*. McKenzie, who had also been in the last four at Leicester, beat Carniel for third place.

The finalists at *Kirklees* were Graham Kay (1st), Hill (2nd), Lawrence (3rd), Chetwood (4th), Swinnerton (5th) and Tyson (6th). The evergreen Cawthorne was the winner in the *Norfolk Open*, over Colin Goodwin of Phoenix. In the *Royal Tournament* fencers mostly little seen elsewhere still held sway. John Ford (now a cadet in the RAF) was Champion, followed by Lt Julian Ferguson, Ft Lt C. Waldman, Midshipman S. Meredith, S. S. I. Brierley and Capt I. Campbell. The new *South London Open* was won by Wojciechowski, ahead of Harper, Lawrence and Bruniges.

Lawrence had also done well when he came third in the *Emrys Lloyd*, which was won by Bruniges in a barrage with McKenzie.

The last eight of the *Leon Paul* included four of the previous year's finalists but none of the thirteen Frenchmen and only three of the other 38 foreigners competing. In the first fight Gosbee lost to Eyal 12–11 after staying within the two-hit margin needed for a win at ten hits under this system. He had continually tried time-thrusts but he succeeded only in the low line, as Eyal cleared everything in the high line with large, looping attacks. Harper then beat Graham Paul, who held his foil by the pommel and went for stop-hits. Bruniges looked uncomfortable against Carmi, the second, relatively immobile Israeli, but eventually nailed him 10–6. Okazaki of Japan, fast on his feet, quickly destroyed Wedge, who was out-of-touch.

In the semi-finals against Okazaki Bruniges had the right idea to keep close to his mobile opponent and open up his defence with those long winding ripostes his admirers so enjoyed – but he kept missing, so he was 6–8 down at one minute. With two seconds to go, he levelled. But then it was Okazaki's turn to show courage. Driving Bruniges onto his back line, he snatched victory with a beat-attack. For third place (and a clock-radio presented by Leon Paul Ltd) Bruniges beat Eyal, while the television from his native land went to Okazaki when he beat Harper 10–7. Tony Bartlett rewarded the audience for the vigour of their cheering with free wine.

The *Championship* was held in London after its two years at Leicester. Neither McKenzie nor Bell reached the last sixteen. In the last eight the four who had come straight through beat the four from the repechage. Harper beat Kay; Bruniges beat Seaman (the only newcomer to a Championship final and beginning to fulfil his early promise); Gosbee beat G. Paul (in his thirteenth Foil Championship final) and B. Paul beat Glaister. This last fight was a hard struggle, however. From the abyss of 6–1 down, Barry, with a sixth title in his sights, staged a magnificent 10–8 recovery. He now faced a Gosbee who was on the crest of a wave – he had only been hit seven times in his previous three fights and was now determined to force the pace. With his stamina depleted, Paul was overcome before he could find an effective reply. In the other semi-final, Bruniges in his turn found himself 6–1 down, in his third climactic

Competitions chronicle 1980–1    453

battle of the season with Harper, who was reading his attacks and using a straight arm to derobe or block the line. When a now confident Harper in his turn began to attack, the situation was reversed and Bruniges won 10–8.

So to a final of two left-handed Bostonians. Gosbee attacked; Bruniges was content to defend. At 7–all a nippy attack to Bruniges' back was flat and he had an easy counter. He then seized the initiative, got to 9–7 with almost his first attack and at 9–8 won with one of his spectacular beat-fleches. In spite of all his talents and achievements, this was Bruniges' first national title of any kind since he had been under-16 Champion. For third place, Harper beat a not over-keenly interested Barry Paul 10–5.

Salle Boston won the *Team Championship* for the third time, revenging themselves on Salle Paul with the same team as the previous year (Bruniges, Gosbee, Eames and Fox). In the team event in *Amsterdam* Troiano, Hill and Ward came third.

A conspectus of foreign individual results is given in the following table.

|             | Amsterdam | Bordeaux | Martini | Duval | Rommel | Venice | B/Durkheim | Bonn | Charenton |
|---|---|---|---|---|---|---|---|---|---|
| A. Bartlett | – | – | R2  | L8  | –   | R1  | L32 | R2  | L32 |
| N. Bell     | – | – | L32 | R2  | L32 | R2  | –   | R2  | L32 |
| R. Bruniges | – | – | L48 | 1st | L24 | R2  | –   | R2  | –   |
| J. Davis    | – | – | R3  | R2  | R1  | –   | –   | –   | –   |
| M. Evans    | – | – | –   | –   | –   | –   | –   | –   | L48 |
| J. Ford     | R2 | – | –  | –   | –   | –   | –   | –   | –   |
| J. Franck   | L28 | – | – | –   | R1  | –   | –   | –   | –   |
| S. Glaister | – | – | –   | –   | –   | –   | R1  | –   | –   |
| W. Gosbee   | – | – | –   | L12 | L48 | L48 | L8  | R1  | –   |
| P. Harper   | – | – | L48 | L8  | R2  | L24 | R2  | L32 | –   |
| R. Hill     | L28 | – | R1 | L48 | –   | R1  | L48 | –   | L48 |
| J. Lawrence | – | – | R2  | L48 | R1  | –   | –   | –   | –   |
| D. McKenzie | – | – | R3  | 4th | R2  | R2  | L48 | R2  | L48 |
| G. Paul     | – | – | –   | R1  | L48 | –   | –   | –   | –   |
| R. Pearson  | – | – | –   | –   | –   | –   | R1  | R1  | R1  |
| D. Seaman   | – | – | R3  | R1  | R2  | –   | –   | R2  | –   |
| M. Thompson | – | – | R3  | L48 | R2  | L48 | L32 | –   | L32 |
| J. Troiano  | L24 | L8 | L48 | L24 | R2  | –   | R2  | –   | R1  |
| C. Ward     | – | – | R2  | R1  | R1  | –   | R2  | R1  | –   |
| P. Wedge    | – | – | –   | L48 | –   | –   | –   | –   | –   |

Notable among these results were the excellent last-eight place of Harper at *Bonn*, the last-24 places of Bruniges in the *Rommel* and Harper at *Venice* and Gosbee's last-eight at *Bad Durkheim*. But it was in the *Duval* that a real impact was made. There were fifteen British entrants and ten of them reached the third round. This proved the limit for Thompson, Lawrence, Wedge and Hill.

The others went on to victory in the tableau from 32. Troiano looked set to improve on the already impressive form he had shown in reaching the last 48 of the *Martini*, but after beating Montagne 10-5 luck deserted him and he lost 10-9 to Joos (Belgium) and 10-8 to Lemanage. In the last 24 Harper beat Esperanza (Spain), and Bruniges beat Koch, Montreal Team Gold Medallist from W. Germany, while McKenzie, having had the impudence as 31st seed to overwhelm Omnes with sheer aggression, beat M. Delagerie on the last hit. Bartlett drew on all his experience and craft to pull back six hits and beat Gosbee 10-9. In the repechage Gosbee beat Benoit but lost to Omnes – 10-9.

In the last twelve, Harper beat Brouquier 10-9 and Bruniges thwarted McKenzie 10-8. Bartlett lost to Pietruszka 10-3, but was not to be dismissed, outfoxing Koch in the last repechage. McKenzie too came back, with another 10-9 win, over Soumagne, winner at this season's Bonn. So to the final in the mirrored splendour of the Grand Hotel. Here McKenzie – still 'bouillant et fougeux' (dashing and mettlesome) – amazed the spectators by beating Flament, the 1978 World Champion (10-8). Omnes beat Harper and Pietruszka beat P. Delagerie. Bruniges beat Bartlett in a close but uninspiring fight. McKenzie found Omnes sharper than the day before and couldn't find a way round his counter attacks. Pietruszska then fell foul of Bruniges' sweeping ripostes (10-5). Now hungry for victory, Bruniges faced Omnes, yet another French left-hander specialising in cutting the distance and then closing the available lines with both blade and elbow – tactics less effective against a fellow left-hander. Bruniges' direct attacks thus took him to 9-7. Omnes then landed two classic attacks; but Bruniges grabbed the tenth hit with a quick remise. Finally a superb direct fleche took him to victory (and a music centre). Pietruszka beat McKenzie 10-4 for third place.

This was Bruniges' tenth major foreign result. Only one other British fencer had ever won the Duval – Jay, in his prime, in 1962.

McKenzie's fourth place in the Duval put him in the World Championship team, as did Gosbee's result in the World Youth Championship. Bruniges, Harper and Bell were the fixtures.

*LADIES' FOIL*

The under-20s collected some very good results abroad this season. Kim Cecil won at *Dornbirn* for the second year running. Runner-up was Weder, followed by three more Swiss – Starzynski, Wild and Nussbaum – an Austrian, Sarah Kellett (7th) and Katie Arup (8th). Three weeks later Clare Gobey gained second place at *Kussnacht*, behind Wojtczak of Poland. Weder and Nussbaum were third and fourth, Kim Cecil fifth and Katie Arup was in the last sixteen. These three Britons went on to win the *Millfield* team event in the face of stiff competition from Switzerland and Sweden. It was a measure of their prowess that it was the first time Britain had won.

In *Waldkirch* it was Katie Arup's turn. She came fifth, with Clare Gobey in the last twelve and Sarah Kellett in the last 24. At *Etampes* Katie Arup came sixth and Kim Cecil was in the last twelve. Two more last-eight places were Clare Gobey's at *Gelsenkirchen* and Katie Arup's in the very strong *Budapest* event. Modaine of France and Szocs of Hungary were within the top three in each of these three competitions, the last of which also had Russian, E. German, Italian and Rumanian finalists.

The Swiss had their revenge in the *Perigal*. The order of finalists was: Nussbaum, Gobey, Weder, Starzynski, Cecil, Oltner (Switzerland), Lange (Sweden) and Arup. In the *Under-20 Championship* the same three Britons took the top three places, but in the reverse order. Katie Arup also carried off the *Felix Cup* and *Wilkinson Sword* invitation events, in the latter beating Penny Whitehead of Westfield School, Newcastle in the semi-final bout and Pat Hunt of Sondes Place in the final (8–3). Penny Whitehead (second over Kantela Woodhouse of Salle Paul in the *Felix*) was the *Under-18* champion. She was also runner-up to Penny Johnson in the *Bertrand*. Third place here went to Lesley Calver. Mary Gobey of Brownhill was the *Under-16* Champion.

The juniors were also making an impact in the senior world and even bidding for the places in the team left vacant by the retirement of Hilary Cawthorne, Ann Brannon and (for the second time) Wendy Grant. In the *Desprez* Penny Johnson was third, Kim Cecil second and Clare Gobey was in the last eight. Linda Martin was the winner, and Sue Hoad fourth. Maureen Lloyd, Fiona McIntosh and Sue Wrigglesworth were the others in the last eight. The Under-20s combined with the re-appearance of several seniors from hibernation to make the *Championship* tough from the start. Katie Arup, Kim Cecil and Clare Gobey were eliminated in the last sixteen along with Fiona McIntosh. All were beset with exams. Hilary Cawthorne, Sue Hoad, Penny Johnson and Lesley Calver made it to the last eight. In the last four Mrs Thurley (erstwhile Liz Wood) beat Linda Martin, and Sue Wrigglesworth beat Clare Montgomery. Third place went to Linda Martin. In the final Liz Thurley regained, by 8–6, the title she had won in 1978 and 1979. In the *de Beaumont* Kim Cecil (7th) was one of only three Britons in the last eight. Linda Martin was the winner and Sue Wrigglesworth fourth. In between were Leblanc (Canada) and Max-Madsen.

The *Team Championship* was carried off for the third time by Salle Paul. Linda Martin, Liz Thurley, Sue Wrigglesworth and Fiona McIntosh – practically the national team – overwhelmed Boston 9–1.

Elizabeth Whitfield of London–Thames won the *Parker*. Janet Garside, going for her hat-trick in the event, sadly suffered a knee injury (originating in a skiing accident) and unwillingly had to scratch from the final bout although in the lead. She did not fence again. Nicky Walker from Newcastle Poly was third.

In the provincial events, Fiona McIntosh had a good season. She was the winner of the *Welsh Open*, where the runner-up was Maureen Lloyd of London-Thames, notching another high, ahead of Sue Hoad (Boston), Debbie Hall (Cassapi), Linda Martin (Paul), Penny Johnson (Paul), Catherine Fray (Roeder) and Lesley Calver (London-Thames). At *Birmingham*, Fiona McIntosh was runner-up, in a somewhat physical final bout, to Leenders of Holland. Brinkman of W. Germany wrested third place from Sue Hoad. In the last eight were Linda Strachan (a pupil of Frank Charnock at LTFC), Christine Lewis (Cardiff), Linda Martin and Lesley Calver. The team event was won by Behmber (Ceri Davies, J. Erwteman, L. Prys-Roberts) from Salle Ecosse (Lynne Mackay, wife of Graham, Margaret Porter of Stirling and the somewhat extraneous Maureen Lloyd). Linda Martin won the *South London Open*, ahead of Penny Johnson.

Maggie Browning was winner of the *Essex Open*, ahead of Sue Hoad, Sandy Maggs (formerly of Bristol Phoenix, now at London-Thames) and Maureen Lloyd. Maggie also won at *Nottingham*, in a barrage with Hilary Jones and Ann Fraser-Smith, now at London-Thames. Marilyn Wheelband (née Worster) was fourth, Elizabeth Pearson of Northumbria fifth and Susan Aldrich of Bath sixth. There was another barrage at *Portsmouth*, in which Maureen Lloyd was beaten by Marilyn Wheelband, a powerful left-hander who liked to lure opponents with her wide sixte. They were followed by the very fit Linda Strachan, who specialised in fast coupé attacks, and by Mary Gobey, Liz Whitfield and Pauline Stonehouse. In the team event Brownhill (A. Gobey, M. Gobey, P. Stonehouse) beat London-Thames (Michelle Rose, Linda Strachan and Karina Hoskyns, daughter of Bill) by 5-2.

Many of the same names appeared in other events: *Ilford* (1. K. Cecil, 2. L. Strachan, 3. P. Stonehouse, 4. C. Lewis, 5. L. Prys-Roberts, 6. Janet Huggins, wife of Peter, the epeeist); *Kirklees* (1. A. Fraser-Smith, 2. S. Hoad, 3. P. Grindley, 4. P. Whitehead, 5. H. Jones, 6. H. Rogerson); *Norfolk Open* (1. S. Hoad, 2. P. Casey, 3. Jo Blackmore of Welwyn, 4. L. Strachan, 5. M. Johnson of Allen, 6. Teresa Sewell of Cyrano). The *York Open*, however, had a different cast. It was won by Elizabeth Wallace of York FC over Christine Courtenay of Hydra (daughter of Rikki) and Sheila Anderson of Mary Hawdon, who also trained at Ashton. Sheila Anderson was the winner of the Edinburgh *Ford Cup*, ahead of Cath Robertson and Julia Bracewell.

At the senior level abroad the gap resulting from so many retirements made itself felt, although Sue Wrigglesworth regained her form. She reached the last twelve at *Como*, the last 24 of the *Jeanty* and the last 32 at *Goppingen* (with Kim Cecil). Liz Thurley did not fence abroad. Linda Martin was in the last 32 at Goppingen and the last 48 at *Turin* (along with Katie Arup), but otherwise achieved nothing notable.

Competitions chronicle 1980-1

The table below shows how the young Fiona McIntosh and the less young Sue Hoad were both making an impact.

|  | Amsterdam | Basle | East Berlin | St Maur | Goppingen | Turin | Paris | Offenbach | Jeanty | Como |
|---|---|---|---|---|---|---|---|---|---|---|
| K. Arup | – | L8 | – | – | – | L48 | – | – | – | – |
| K. Cecil | – | – | R2 | – | L32 | R1 | – | – | R1 | – |
| A. Fraser-Smith | R2 | – | – | – | R2 | – | R2 | R3 | L48 | – |
| C. Gobey | – | – | R2 | L16 | R2 | R2 | – | – | – | – |
| P. Johnson | – | – | – | – | R3 | R2 | – | R2 | R1 | – |
| S. Hoad | L8 | – | – | – | L48 | R1 | L16 | R2 | R1 | L48 |
| S. Kellett | – | – | – | L32 | – | – | – | R3 | R1 | – |
| M. Lloyd | R1 | L24 | – | – | R3 | R2 | – | R2 | R1 | – |
| C. Montgomery | – | L16 | – | L8 | R1 | R2 | – | L32 | R1 | – |
| L. Martin | – | – | – | – | L32 | L48 | – | – | L48 | – |
| F. McIntosh | – | 2nd | R2 | – | R2 | R2 | – | L12 | R1 | L24 |
| S. Wrigglesworth | – | – | – | – | L32 | R1 | – | R2 | L24 | L12 |

In the team event in *E. Berlin* the British came third, beating both the Italians and the Berliners on hits. At Turin in the *Coupe d'Europe* Salle Paul beat the Austrians 10–6 and the Portuguese 16–0 before losing to the Russians 9–2 and the Hungarians 9–4. In the *Amsterdam capital cities team event* Sue Hoad, Ann Fraser-Smith and Maureen Lloyd came second.

A team of four was selected for the World Championships – two seasoned campaigners in Sue Wrigglesworth and Linda Martin and two newcomers in Fiona McIntosh and Kim Cecil. (There was some dissension over the omission of Sue Hoad, due evidently to her lack of youth, which was no doubt also the ground for her not receiving travel grants to key foreign events in spite of her domestic results.)

*EPEE*

Overshadowing all else this season was a great British triumph in the Martini. The *Qualifying* event saw a return to form of Steve Roose, who won the pool of 24 with nineteen victories, two fights ahead of the field. Unfortunately, a hernia shortly afterwards removed him from the scene for the rest of the season. Liston, who had teetered on the brink of team-level fencing for a couple of years, got one of his best results in coming second with seventeen wins. If only John Stevenson of Boston, who was third (16v), had been able to train continuously, his talents would by now have made him a useful member of the British team. He was followed by Howard West (15v), Carpenter (14v),

Stanbury (14v), Young (13v), G. Paul (13v), Kernohan (13v), Edwards (11v), Hoskyns (11v), Lewis (11v), Chell (11v), R. Brooks (11v). Jeremy Hunt reached the final while still at St Paul's.

Come the *Martini* itself and, of the 35 Britons entered, thirteen fought their way out of first round pools strong enough to dispose of Malkar of Sweden and Normann of Norway from a foreign entry of 89 from seventeen countries. In the absence of Alexander Pusch and of the French team except for Picot, this was not the most star-studded of years, but it was, for instance, strong enough for both the 1980 winner and runner-up to get eliminated in the last 32. Johnson and Graham Paul, both of whom had topped their first round pools, went out in the second round with two wins apiece, as did Hoskyns and Mallett (who virtually stopped fencing this season to concentrate on accountancy exams); likewise Rance, Lavington, Robert Gore of Brownhill, Steventon and Rob Brooks, along with Swornowski, Chronowski, Fischer, Kolczonay and Poffet.

Four Britons remained to fight in the direct elimination. Llewellyn was the undefeated fourth seed. Steven Paul, with two defeats, was seeded 25th. Belson, with the same score, was 27th seed. Melville was seeded 35 and had to fight off for a place in the last 32. He lost 10–4 to Borrmann of W. Germany, who specialised in duck-hits. The Italian Andreoli also practised an awkward type of mobility, too much for Belson's defensive moves, rock-hard though they might be. 5–3 become 10–5. Steven Paul met the best of the Japanese, Nakamura, seeded eight. This was a close-run thing. Almost at the end of the last minute they stood at 4–2, in Paul's favour. Then Nakamura scored a third hit and with only one second to go he fleched for the equaliser – but Paul got the hit. Finally, it was Borrmann again, against Llewellyn, who showed his tremendous form by storming to a 10–2 victory, crouching and vibrant with alertness and speed of stroke and delivering more than one beautiful fleche.

In the second round of direct elimination (the last sixteen) Llewellyn faced Ganeff, the Belgian who held his epee in a highly retracted position – often above his head. Llewellyn was soon 3–0 up; though he lost the next five hits, mostly scored by Ganeff's attacks, several en fleche, he reasserted himself, largely by stop-hits, to win 10–7. Steven Paul was pitted against the Italian Parietti, sixth seed. He started well and from 2–0 he kept his margin and emerged 10–8.

So to the Seymour Hall, with two Britons in the last eight for only the third time since the start of the event in 1960 – together with two Swedes, two Swiss, a Pole and a Norwegian.

The first fight was between Paul and Strzalka, the Pole who opened the bout with a successful fleche against the pressure of the blade. Then it was Paul's turn to attack. He missed, almost fell over his opponent, but managed to snatch a hit. He got another hit to make it 2–1 in his favour. Strzalka was warned for back-turning, then equalised with a pressure-pressure-disengage.

Competitions chronicle 1980-1   459

A double hit brought them to 3-all. Then Strzalka reclaimed the lead with a stop-hit on Paul's long attack. Strzalka's strategy was to draw Paul's blade to work on, taking wide sixties and powerful octaves, and hooking round his ripostes. For his part, Paul was nervous and consequently missing, as he confessed later. Nevertheless he was holding his own. He made it 4-all when he nipped in a hit as Strzalka bounced provocatively. It became 5-4 in Paul's favour, but 5-all when he failed to evade Strzalka's point. Now it was Paul's turn to use angulation on a direct lunge, and 6-5 to him. A one-two and for the first time he was two ahead. He was hit on the raised forearm and it was 7-6. He attacked, and then scored by leaving his point in line: 8-6. He attacked with a one-two fleche, but Strzalka had spoilt his distance and it was 8-7. So close to victory, but could he do it? On the next attack, Strzalka stepped in to take the blade and it was a double: 9-8. The tension was nearly intolerable. It seemed either might find the right attack or the right counter-movement. But Paul lunged, and the fight was his. He'd nailed the top seed.

On to another nerve-racking fight: Llewellyn against the Swede Hjerpe, a 1980 finalist who had a penchant for taking the blade very strongly and for using his considerable strength to resist his opponent's blade. Thus Llewellyn's attempts at counter-time tended to be thwarted and on occasion he was made to look as if he was pausing in mid-attack. Fortunately Hjerpe's heaviness also meant that he tended to miss. The score went from 1-0 against Llewellyn to 3-1; but he recovered to 4-all and then collected Hjerpe's fleche to make it 5-4. A direct fleche and it was 6-4. Hopes rose. Hjerpe successfully took the blade, 6-5. A double. A long wrangle and another double. Hjerpe stepped back and stop-hitted, one of his favourite moves, so it was 8-all. Then, agonisingly, 9-8 against Llewellyn. Now, to evade Hjerpe's forcefulness, he did a beat-feint-disengage without trying to take the blade. 9-all! They engaged; they closed; anything could happen, the audience breathed mingled relief and disappointment when no hit occurred. Finally, Llewellyn landed a stop-hit over the guard. 10-9. Tremendous applause.

In the other quarter-final bouts Barvestad of Sweden lost 10-8 to Jean-Blaise Evequoz of Switzerland, a younger brother of Guy in a fight of very fast lunges and stop-hits; and Koppang of Norway produced some excellent fleches to beat Giger 10-8.

A short interval ensued – just long enough for a dash to the bar and back. Then Llewellyn versus Paul: Paul was now fencing with real confidence and authority, whereas John Llewellyn gave the impression of being just that fatal degree divided in his attitude. This did not mean he didn't fence hard; on the contrary, it was Paul who was the cool one of the pair – whipping in stop-hits, occasionally stretching in an attack. It ended 10-2.

In the other semi-final, Evequoz got everything right, especially putting in effective stop-hits, to beat Koppang 10-5.

So to the final, with the audience on the edges of their seats from the start.

Martini 1981: John Llewellyn v Steven Paul.

Evequoz had won the Monal only weeks before; he had also just defeated Petho, the holder, in the last 32. But those few who knew that Paul had beaten him in the 1979 Heidenheim nursed secret hopes.

Paul began with a typical long lunge, which Evequoz shrewdly stop-hit. The mobile Swiss made swinging beats at his opponent's blade in an attempt to provoke an attack, but Paul succeeded in his turn in provoking counter-attacks which he could stop-hit or parry-riposte from. So from 1–all he went to 2–1 and 3–1 with the crowd roaring encouragement. A time-thrust took him to 4–1. At this point he seemed to get a shade over-confident and Evequoz collected a hit off an over-eager attack. But he quickly resumed an admirable balance between care and aggression, coolness and fire. He followed no set strategy but was probably all the more effective for playing the instinctive game which can be so devastating when it is the outcome of intense and prolonged training. His fifth hit was a very sharp flick over the wrist against a half-lunge. Then, with the tide behind him, he did a direct fleche. 7–2 came as he got another wrist-hit at the end of the series of meetings of the blade. Nothing could stop him now. He fleched, missed, came to close-quarters, but still got the hit. The excitement grew yet more intense as he neared his goal, not least among the Paul family. As the Mayor of Westminster remarked in presenting the prizes, Steven's father Raymond almost did a handstand with exultation as each hit registered. Evequoz must have been despairing by this point of succeeding with anything, but he did not give up. He probed – only to receive another stop-hit. 9–2! Then – the coup de grace; a lunge, again to the top of the wrist. The hall erupted with cheers, the Paul family flew across the floor to their hero and the National Anthem was played for the first British winner since Hoskyns in 1962.

This was a signal triumph for Paul, only the fourth Briton to win a top-ranking international event at any weapon, since 1963. It was a triumph of talent, but also a triumph of dedication. Since joining the British team in 1977 his training had become progressively harder. For instance, four miles a week running had become sixteen. Latterly his lessons, apart from those from Prof. Emery in squad training, had been in foil from Ziemowit Wojciechowski. Employed in the catering trade (working for his mother) he trained as professionally as international fencing champions now had to, while remaining a true amateur with a full-time job.

Llewellyn's achievement in reaching the last four would be subject enough for rejoicing in any other year. Only five other Britons had ever got this far in the Martini. Now 23, he had resumed training with Frank Tanner after his return from Switzerland. He worked for a boat-building firm in Buckinghamshire and hoped to return to Switzerland to fence and to work.

In the very different world of junior British epee, it was Steve Henshall of Birmingham FC who was dominant, though he did not commit himself, as was hoped, to full participation in the national training squad, to the residence in the London area that this almost inevitably entailed or to a full competitive season. He won both the *Under-20* and the *Junior Championships*. In the former, the runner-up was Richard Phelps from Gloucester Modern Pentathlon, who was taught by his uncle, Robbie Phelps, and went on to win at *Nottingham*. Dominic Mahony, a pupil of Bryan Lewis at Millfield and wispish by contrast with Henshall or Phelps, was third. He was followed by Peter Tayler, Nigel Fancourt (at LTFC from Winchester) and Paul Cruthers (Whitgift).

The Junior final included no newcomers. In the last eight Brannon beat Kernohan 10–7, Henshall beat Rob Brooks 10–7, Liston beat Edwards 13–12 and Rance beat Gray 10–8. In the semi-finals Henshall beat Brannon 10–8 and Liston beat Rance 10–6. In a final of two equally tall, strongly-built contenders, it was Henshall who used his length the more confidently and effectively.

*The Epee Club Cup* finalists were also familiar figures. Melville was the undefeated winner of the final (7v), followed by Stanbury (4v), Roose (4v) Kernohan (4v), Edwards (4v), Llewellyn (3v), Greenhalgh (3v) and David Brooks (0v).

The provincial season opened with Carpenter's win of the *Essex Open* on September 7, ahead of Peter Eames and Ian Margan (Army). Liston won the *Welsh Open*, which was also a success for John Warburn (RAF and Wales), who specialised in high-speed preparatory sawing movements followed by equally fast fleches. He was second, followed by Rob Brooks, Eames, Edwards and David Brooks. The new *South London Open* was won, on a count of hits after a barrage of four, by Gray (who at the age of 41 had discovered the parry of quarte). Runner-up was Colin Sigrist, Prof. Fairhall's pupil, making a re-appearance after a long interval, followed by Mark Nelson-Griffiths and Steve Lavington. The invitation *Welsh Games* was won by Belson, ahead of Melville, D. Brooks, Lewis, Gray and Roose. At *Leicester* Kernohan beat David Brooks 5–3 in a barrage. Tony Finn of Edinburgh University was third, followed by Warburn, Carpenter and Philip (Bill) Noak, of Sheffield. Scottish domination was greatly furthered by Mackay, who was the winner at *Ashton* and *Inverclyde* and, for the second year running at *Tyneside*, where he beat Kernohan in the final bout, Greenhalgh and Andrew Pinder of York being the others in the last four.

*Birmingham*, foregoing its gala final for the first time and adhering to the protracted 32-strong version of the current FIE repechage system, was almost bereft of spectators to witness the triumph of Dave Cocker, a master of surprise and of sudden movement from immobility (who had already come 5th in the foil). He successively beat Hoskyns, Rob Brooks and Greenhalgh. Mackay beat Brooks for third place. Tyson, Driessen of Holland and Corish of Birmingham were the others in the last eight.

Nearly as strong this season was the *Universities Championship*. Nightingale (now training in PE at Loughborough), Woods (Leicester; taught by Prof. Cassapi), Wood (Cardiff) and Henderson (Aberdeen) perished before the final, which was won by Jervis Rhodes of Cambridge, undefeated but with four of his wins gained on the last hit. By contrast, Chell (5th, Cambridge) lost all four of his defeats 5–4. Brannon was second, ahead of Liston and Troiano. Kernohan, winner of the *Scottish Open* (by 11–9 over Mackay, with Liston in third place), could only salvage sixth place on this occasion.

Cocker and Liston were the two first-time finalists in the *Championship*. Also in the last eight, Davenport lost 10–4 to Johnson and Steven Paul 10–7 to Belson, who slowed the tempo to his advantage. Belson went on to beat Johnson 10–8 in one semi-final; Llewellyn beat Mallett 10–8 in the other. In the final bout, Belson lost his edge and went down 10–5 to Llewellyn, who had so narrowly missed the title in 1977 and 1978. Third place went to Johnson over his club-mate Mallett by the same score. Especially unlucky not to reach the final was Lewis, who beat both Llewellyn and Mallett in the last 24.

There were only ten teams in the *Savage*, and Salle Paul was absent after being a top contender for the trophy almost continuously for over thirty years. Carpenter won four fights for London–Thames 'B' in the quarter-finals, but couldn't prevent a 9–6 win for Boston 'B' – who were then smashed by Reading in the semi-finals while Boston 'A' were beating London–Thames 'A' 9–4.

Competitions chronicle 1980-1    463

Now that Bourne really had retired and Davenport had transferred from Boston to Reading, after moving home to Wokingham, Reading were the favourites to win. But Young rose to the occasion for Boston and both he and Johnson were undefeated with three wins each, while Reading could only muster three wins between them. (Scores over the whole competition were, for Boston, Young 9/9, Johnson 8/9, Bruniges 10/12, Steventon 7/11 and, for Reading, Greenhalgh 6/8, Davenport 7/11, Llewellyn 4/5, Rance 4/12).

Boston thus gained its eighth victory in the event, just ahead of McPherson's and LFC (7) but still behind Lansdowne (10) and Grosvenor (13).

The Norwegian team gave the *Miller–Hallett* a much tougher final. Belson (1st) and Johnson (2nd) did well to push Normann into third place. Graham Paul recaptured some of his old formidability to take fourth place, while Llewellyn and Steven Paul shared places in the last eight with Hagen and Vonen.

Abroad, joint top performer was – Hoskyns! Although he reached the finals of neither of the two main British events, he was in the last sixteen at *Heidenheim*, still supreme in the calendar both for size and for quality. After three decades of competition and at the age of fifty he still had the stamina and

|  | Catania | Oslo | Zurich | Carrocio | Monal | Berne | Heidenheim | Zurich | Poitiers |
|---|---|---|---|---|---|---|---|---|---|
| T. Belson | – | – | – | L32 | L32 | R1 | L32 | – | – |
| R. Davenport | – | L8 | – | – | – | – | – | L12 | R1 |
| R. Greenhalgh | – | R3 | L24 | – | – | – | – | L24 | – |
| W. Hoskyns | – | – | – | – | L48 | – | L16 | – | – |
| R. Johnson | L12 | – | 2nd | – | R2 | R1 | R1 | – | L32 |
| G. Liston | – | – | – | L96 | R2 | R1 | R2 | L8 | – |
| J. Llewellyn | – | – | – | L96 | L72 | L72 | L96 | – | – |
| N. Mallett | – | – | – | – | – | – | R2 | – | – |
| J. Melville | L16 | L16 | L16 | L96 | R1 | L72 | – | L32 | R2 |
| S. Paul | – | – | – | L96 | L24 | L48 | L64 | – | L8 |
| R. Rance | – | – | – | – | R2 | – | – | – | – |
| S. Roose | – | – | L16 | L96 | R1 | – | – | – | – |
| J. Stanbury | – | – | L12 | L96 | R1 | L48 | L64 | – | R1 |

the motivation, as well as the skill, to fight his way through battalions of eager young internationals and hardened, still young world-class epeeists. He also reached the last 48 of the *Monal*, with only Steven Paul (last 24) and Belson (last 32) ahead of him. Also doing very well abroad, as might be hoped, was Steven Paul, who got to the last eight at *Poitiers*. The full spread of results is shown in the table.

Paul, Llewellyn and Belson were obvious certainties for the team, but with Mallett and Roose out of contention the fourth and fifth team places were more than usually open. Early in the season several potential team members were tested in *Matches in Oslo*. Against Poland (Chronowski, Janikowski, Piasecki and Rinbem), the British got a good 8–4 (Greenhalgh 3, Lavington 2 + d.d., Roose 2, Davenport 1 + d.d.). They lost to a full Norwegian team (Koppang, Norman, Schjott, Hagen) by only 8–7 (Roose 3, Davenport 2, Greenhalgh 1, Melville 1). And they beat Norway 'B' even more narrowly 8–all (Roose 3, Greenhalgh 2, Melville 2, Lavington 1). Other possibles were tried in 'B' team *post-Martini matches*. Against Switzerland 'B' they went down 10–6 (Rance 3, Stanbury 2, Liston 1, Lavington 0). Against a mixed Norwegian team they got a creditable 11–5 (Stanbury 3, Liston 3, Lavington 3, Rance 2). Against French juniors, however, they slumped 12–3 (Stanbury 1, Liston 1, Rance 1, Lavington 0). Meanwhile Greenhalgh scored well in matches with Switzerland 'C' (4/4), Finland (1/3) and Japan (4/4). The British 'A' team beat Poland 9–7 on the same Sunday (Belson 3, Paul 2, Johnson 2, Melville 2). They lost 10–5 to Sweden (Johnson 3, Belson 1, Llewellyn 1, Paul 0). And they lost 12–4 to Switzerland (Belson 2, Johnson 1, Melville 1, Llewellyn 0).

Melville, who only reached the last sixteen of the Championship and went out early in the Miller-Hallett, was pipped in the points league for a team place by both Johnson and Stanbury, the latter transforming himself from non-playing captain to active contender as the season advanced.

*SABRE*

It was a triumph for the rest of Britain in the *Under-18 Championship*. Fellerman was the winner (technically, at least, E. Section) followed by Mark Donaldson (Denny HS, Scotland), Chris Brockbanks (Darlington SC), Smith (Guisborough FC, Co. Durham), Macdonald Patterson (George Heriot's) and Nick Barstow (Royal Belfast). London had its comeback in the *Under-16 Championship*, in which the top three were all from Brentwood: Paul Stanley, Simon Haynes and Duggie Dale. Fourth, between James Hudson of Edinburgh Academy and David Hair of Denny High School, Scotland, was the aggressive and promising Tarik Yassir of Haileybury, who also won the Junior *Public Schools* title. The Senior title went, as it should have done, to Klenerman. He was also the *Under-20* winner, though only after a barrage with Bryant, a much-liked and effective sabreur with an instinctive rather than calculating game. As West (3rd), Booton (4th) and David Bovill (5th) were also all from Salle Ganchev, here was a formidable show of strength. Klenerman was unable to repeat his success in the *Junior*. His rival West was the runner-up; the winner, sixth in 1977, but not even a finalist since then, was

Hunt, who had developed into a sabreur of complete technical training, compact and tidy, with every action in its place.

The *Universities* result was possibly a commentary on the standard of sabre, since it was won by the foilist Donny McKenzie, who never received more than two hits in the final. When he had priority, he attacked and when he didn't he left the point in line to make a derobement or foil attack. He was followed by the fellow London medical students and friends Hall and Hunt, and by John Chipman (Oxford), Chell (Cambridge) and Kernohan (Oxford).

The provincial tournaments saw a cross between the seasoned and the newly-arrived. In early September, for instance, the *Essex Open* was won by Magill, ahead of the two Ganchev sabreurs, Moscardini and West. Patrick West was the victor of the *Welsh Open* two months later. He was followed by Bryant, Andy Bornemisza (Bath), Moscardini, Booton and John Crouch (RAF). West also won the *Meadowbank Open*, ahead of Booton and McKenzie. Moscardini had a good season. He was winner at *Nottingham*, followed by Brockbanks, Wiles, Kovanda, Steve Carson (Instonians) and Gregory Kay (York). And in July he won the *Norfolk Open*, above his club-mates Booton, J. Wade, Nick Mildwater and C. Jobling. At *Birmingham* Magill won again (undefeated), ahead of Morris, Hunt, Wiles, Graham Kay and Bovill, who at his best was formidable. In the team event there, Magill, Hall and Carr of Boston defeated Booton, Bovill and Bryant of Ganchev.

None of these events were patronised by British team members. On the other hand, some of the new provincial finalists forced their way into Senior finals to an extent not simply accounted for by the retirement of Deanfield and Etherton. Not in the *Cole Cup*, it is true. Slade won this for the first time. Jaine also reached a new level in coming second. Philbin was third, followed by Magill, Banos (Canada), Cohen and Lavoie (Canada). But in the *Corble Cup* Philbin, and Slade were followed by Hunt, who was ahead of Cohen and Jaine. The lower places went to Morris, West and Zitcer, who looked formidably Russian in his stance.

Philbin and Slade consolidated their positions when they took the first two places in the *Championship* and Hunt confirmed his newly-won standing by coming third. But the striking results were the fourth and fifth places of Bovill and Bryant. Fifth and sixth were Eden and Magill, as if to reassure a shaken world.

There was nothing new about the *Team Championship*, however. Philbin (4v), Cohen (2v), Eden (2v) and Zarno (1v) performed the now habitual defeat of Boston, represented this year by Magill (3v), Etherton/Hunt (1v) and Jaine (1v). Salle Ganchev had to wait for this prize, which Poly were taking for the fourth successive time and for the ninth time since 1962 (against LFC's 20 times, stretching back to 1931, or the four each of Salle Paul and Boston, this quartet having monopolised the trophy since the war with only two interruptions, both by the Army).

Abroad, there was also no breakthrough yet by the new men, to set beside one glorious result by a member of the old guard. This was Cohen's victory in the *Touzard* in the Stade Coubertin in Paris in February. He became the first Englishman to win an international sabre event of any significance since Oldcorn won at *Ystad* almost twenty years before. The main foreign entry was that of 47 W. Germans.

Having twice been promoted on indicator through the preceding rounds Cohen continued to live dangerously through the direct elimination from sixteen and survived to the final of eight only after an exciting 10–9 win over Delrieu of France. He now met Petit (France), whom he only beat 12–11 after a tremendous battle. Next he faced Schneider, a tall, mobile W. German. He was down successively 7–3, 8–4 and 9–6, before rallying heroically to win five hits in a row. Finally, for the title, he fought another, shorter German, Jurg Nolte. This time he kept a firm psychological hold and from 3–all to his victory at 10–6 he always had the better of his opponent.

The table below shows that the next best result was reaching the last 24 at *Hanover* by Zarno, whose marriage prevented him going to New York. A strike prevented a fuller entry to *Munich*.

|  | Touzard | Hanover | New York | Brasov | Padua | Munich |
|---|---|---|---|---|---|---|
| R. Cohen | 1st | L48 | L48 | – | L48 | – |
| J. Gryf-Lowczowski | L36 | L98 | – | – | – | L32 |
| R. Jaine | L24 | L48 | L48 | R1 | L48 | – |
| P. Klenerman | – | – | L48 | – | – | – |
| W. Magill | L36 | – | – | R1 | L96 | – |
| J. Philbin | L24 | L48 | – | – | L48 | – |
| M. Slade | L36 | L48 | L48 | – | L48 | – |
| P. West | L82 | – | – | – | – | L72 |
| J. Zarno | – | L24 | – | – | – | – |

There were some good match results, especially an excellent win over W. Germany (Slade 4, Cohen 3, Philbin 1, Zarno 1), but also against E. Germany (Slade 3, Cohen 3, Philbin 1, Zarno 1) and Bulgaria (Slade 3, Cohen 3, Philbin 2, Jaine 1). Against Rumania, Britain lost 8–all (Slade 3, Cohen 3, Philbin 1, Jaine 1). Jaine showed his potential against Hungary (Cohen 2, Jaine 2, Slade 0, Klenerman 0); as did Klenerman against Italy (Klenerman 2, Cohen 1, Slade 1, Jaine 1). The leaders sometimes slipped: against USA (Cohen 1, Slade 2, Jaine 2, Klenerman 1) and against France (Slade 1, Cohen 2, Philbin 2, Zarno 2). Cohen, Slade, Zarno and Magill had a thumping 16–0 win over Switzerland. There was also a 9–6 loss to Cuba (Cohen 3, Slade 2,

Philbin 1, Jaine 0) and a 9–4 win over Legia (Philbin 3, Jaine 3, Cohen 2, Slade 1).

Slade was now at the strong end of the team. Philbin performed solidly, even if he still did not do himself full justice internationally. Jaine was forging ahead. His excellent technique promised more impact abroad when he had more experience and confidence – certainly possessed by Zarno, the fifth member of the team. Magill was reserve, having fenced tenaciously but sometimes too put out by the presiding and judging. Klenerman was clearly on the way to the team, though he was yet another sabreur threatening a medical career, which was already leaving Hunt with little time for training or competition.

## COMBINED EVENTS

The *World Youth Championships* were at Lausanne. Joe Eden was overall team manager, having accompanied the team every year since 1965 (except 1976, when he was ill), an impressive record of devoted effort, from a non-fencer. Kristin Payne was Ladies' Manager. Zoltan Vadaszffy, Ziemek Wojciechowski and Paul Romang were the coaches. Jim Philbin was the Captain. In the men's foil Dale and Pitman went up from the first round with three wins each and Gosbee with only seven hits received and a fine 5–2 win over Aptsiaouri (USSR), which gave him second seed for round two. Dale now made his exit from a tough pool which included Nemeth (Hungary) and Delagerie (France), discouraged from the outset by such opposition. Pitman made up for lack of technique by tremendous determination and went up with three wins, a promising performance. Gosbee lost only to Schenkel (E. Germany) in his pool.

In the last 24 Pitman reached his ceiling with no wins in a pool including Aptsiaouri, Masiero of France and Numa of Italy, the eventual winner. Gosbee only managed fourth place this time, behind Kliuchin (USSR), Caflisch (Switzerland) and Borella (Italy); but in the direct elimination he had an excellent fight against Koretski (USSR), attacking and defending with equal skill, remaining composed despite gamesmanship on the part of Russian officials and winning 10–9. In the next round he met the top seed and eventual runner-up, Schreck of W. Germany. He lost 10–6, probably still mentally as well as physically tired from the previous fight. In the repechage he faced on the centre piste the local Caflisch, who had beaten him in their three previous encounters. He recaptured his concentration and won through to the final by 10–6. Unfortunately he there drew Numa, who was in devastating form, and lost 10–1.

Gosbee was thus the first British finalist since Bruniges won in 1976 and

Bill Gosbee reaches the final of the
1981 World Youth Championships.

only the eighth since the age of twenty was adopted as the ceiling for the Championships in 1961.

Clare Gobey got furthest of the girls, just reaching the last 24. Kim Cecil was in the last 36 (placed 32nd). Katie Arup went out in the first round.

In the first round of the epee Rance went out on indicators and Phelps after leading 4-2 in a barrage with Felislak of Poland, who went on to win the event. Both were handicapped by nerves.

In the sabre, West and Klenerman were promoted despite nerves. West had no wins in round two, but Klenerman scraped promotion on indicators with two wins. This put him in the last 24, where, by luck, he had a fairly easy pool. Now he showed his true form, gaining three wins and putting himself in the last sixteen, in second place behind Malanotte of Italy (eventual fourth). In the direct elimination he drew Gardos of Hungary, who had just beaten him 5-1, but after a hesitant start he fenced well and was only overcome 10-8. In the repechage the Russian Grigorian's technique and concentration were too much for him and he lost 10-5; but his fourteenth place was the best Britain had obtained at sabre since Mather came fifth in 1973.

In the *Public Schools* Brentwood won the overall Graham Bartlett Cup for the twelfth time since its donation in 1939 (St Paul's being the nearest rival, with eight wins). Dale won both the foil and the epee, having won both at junior level the year before, giving Brentwood its nineteenth senior title. This

Competitions chronicle 1980-1 469

tally was surpassed only by Eton, with 24. (Next were St Paul's, 18, and Westminster, 16.)

The South won the *Winton Cup* for the seventh time, still one short of the record of eight times jointly held by the SW and the E. Midlands.

England won the *Quadrangular* for the 27th time – Scotland having won it four times and Wales once. It was held in Edinburgh, where the teams enjoyed memorable hospitality, including a civic reception and dinner and a superb buffet given in Bob Elliott's new restaurant. The English team was weak in sabreurs because of a clash with the Corble, and McKenzie, Liston and Fiona McIntosh were unavailable for Scotland. Nevertheless the order was as usual. England beat Scotland 22–13, and both Wales and N. Ireland 21–15. The nearest to an upset was the N. Irish 17 wins to the Welsh 19. Once again, Wiles won eight out of nine sabre bouts and Scotland also benefited from an undefeated epee team (Kernohan, Mackay, Rollo and Colin Scott).

Back in November, an Edinburgh team comprising a junior and a senior at each weapon visited the twin city of *Munich* to compete in a *triangular* against the home club and Bordeaux. They lost to the former 9–6 but beat the latter by the same score. McKenzie and Julia Bracewell won individual foil competitions and at epee Liston was second and Kernohan third.

Salle Boston won the *Granville Cup* for the ninth time. No other club except the hardly distinguishable Salle Emery had interrupted its monopoly of both top places since 1976, though by then Salle Paul had already won fourteen times. The only other winners since the event started were LFC (5) and Poly (2). The inter-county *Jackett Trophy* was won for the ninth time by Surrey who were thus one short of Somerset's record.

167 fencers from 27 universities competed in the *BUSF Championships*. The men's overall trophy was won by Edinburgh by 34 points to London's 32, Cambridge's 28 and Oxford's 17. This was a personal triumph for McKenzie, who contributed 17 points. At foil he only came second (to Ward of London), but he won the sabre – without conceding more than two hits to anyone in the final. For Cambridge, Rhodes won the epee and Fiona McIntosh cruised to first place in the ladies' foil, ahead of Debbie Hall (Leicester) and Anne Swinney (Aberdeen).

Fiona McIntosh and Donnie McKenzie were also the best performers for Britain at the *Student Games* in Bucharest. Both were 23rd.

The *World Championships* were at Clermont Ferrand. Bill Hoskyns was Captain and Sally Kenealy (née Littlejohns) was Ladies' Manager; Ray Emery, Tamas Mendelenyi and Ziemowit Wojciechowski were coaches. Andrew Cornford was one of the British presidents, as he had been at Lausanne and indeed many of the chief epee events in Europe since moving to Geneva in 1977.

In the men's foil the notable performance was that of the now veteran Bell. He went up top from his first round pool (beating Dal Zotto), got through a very tough second round pool with two wins and in the third round was promoted after victories over Ruziev (USSR), Sabart (Czechoslovakia) and Orosz (Hungary). (He lost to Soumagne and Robak.) Seeded 31st in the tableau, he met Smirnov and lost 10-6, but in the repechage had an impressive 10-4 victory over Montano, scoring with the fast, well-timed counter-attacks at which he excelled, interspersed with equally fast direct fleches. In the last 24 he was unlucky to lose 10-8 in a very close fight with Kotzmann.

All the others reached the last 48 – including the new colours – and obtained some handsome wins in the process. McKenzie beat Borella (Italy) in the first round and Harper gained 5-3 wins over both Romankov and Bonnin (France) in the third round. Bruniges beat Robak in his first round and included three world finalists in his four second round wins (Reichert 5-1, Omnes 5-3, Borella 5-4); unfortunately in the third round he went out on hits with two wins, losing to Omnes, Dal Zotto and Smirnov (5-4). Gosbee went up from the second round with three wins, but had no joy in a tough third round pool, in which, moreover, his foot was injured, so that Bartlett, the reserve, had to travel out to replace him.

Romankov and Jolyot both failed to reach the last eight, but Smirnov repeated his Moscow win. The Italians were runners-up in the team event even though their Bronze Medallist, Dal Zotto, had returned to Italy in disgust, leaving a team of four to fight without him. The British were promoted from the first round when they beat Australia 13-2 (McKenzie 4, Bartlett 4, Harper 3, Bruniges 3) and Argentina 13-3 (Harper 3, Bruniges 3, Bell 3, Bartlett 2). In the direct elimination they lost to the strong Japanese team 9-6 (Harper 3, McKenzie 2, Bruniges 1, Bell 0).

In the ladies' foil Fiona McIntosh had a disappointing debut, suffering from nerves and being eliminated in a barrage in the first round; but Kim Cecil, the other new colour, had her best result of the season, fencing confidently and aggressively and reaching the third round (last 48). Linda Martin was also handicapped by nerves and went out in the second round. Sue Wrigglesworth too was unsettled at first, but battled on to the last 32. Seeded 31st, she nevertheless gave a hard (5-8) fight to Hanisch, before being eliminated by Brouquier. Hanisch went on to win, re-asserting her supremacy after her absence from Moscow. The most remarkable result was Luan Jujie's second place.

The team was seeded ninth and did not manage to improve on that. They won a gruelling match against aggressive Spaniards 10-6, but lost to Poland 9-4 and, disappointingly, to Sweden, also 9-4.

The best result at epee was by Steven Paul, who reached the last 24 and was knocked out by Karagian. Llewellyn, Johnson and Belson reached respectable places in the last 48 (where Belson's energy somewhat flagged). Stanbury was ousted in the last 72 (but had to contend with Szekely, eventual Champion, Dunaev, 3rd, and two last-24s).

Competitions chronicle 1980-1

In the team event the British were seeded seventh. Only after they had beaten Iraq and New Zealand (for whom Cocker won three) was a misseeding in the first round discovered. They now beat Korea (Stanbury 3, Llewellyn 2, Belson 2, Johnson 1/Paul 2) and gained promotion, though they lost to the USA (Paul 3, Belson 2, Llewellyn 1, Stanbury 1). Against France, in the direct elimination, they gained an excellent 4-1 lead, but lost all the subsequent fights (Paul 2, Johnson 1, Belson 0, Llewellyn 0/Stanbury 1). Eighth place, therefore.

A striking feature of the epee was that the Swedes failed to reach either the last eight of the individual or the last four of the team.

After the good results early in the season it was disappointing for the sabreurs not to make a broader impact at Clermont Ferrand. The new colour, Jaine, went out in the first round, although he beat Schneider, the W. German number one. Slade had the psychological disadvantage in the first round of losing to his club-mate Magill, fencing for Ireland as usual, though this year also reserve for Britain. Neither, sadly, was promoted, although Slade beat Aliokhin. Zarno reached the last 48. There he beat Nolte of W. Germany but no-one else. Philbin, at the same stage, went one better and defeated Burtsev, no less, but likewise no-one else. Cohen also went no further, but gained two wins in a pool containing Bierkowski and Gerevich and was ranked 32nd.

The surprise Champion was Wodke, a 23-year-old Pole, the youngest fencer ever to win the title. (As in the ladies' foil, none of the three top Russians got a medal, though they were all in the last eight.)

In the seventeen-strong team event the British had to contend with Japan and Poland. They began shakily against Japan, who should have been no problem, but ended 10-6 up (Jaine 3, Slade 3, Cohen 2, Philbin 2). They succumbed to Poland 12-4 (Philbin 2, Jaine 1, Slade 1, Cohen 0). This meant they missed the last eight and were drawn against the USA for one of the two remaining quarter-final places. Westbrook, always good, was undefeated. An off-form House won nil. Unfortunately, Lekach and Reilly got five wins between them; so it was 9-6 (Philbin 2, Slade 2, Cohen 1, Jaine 1). It was unwonted for Cohen not to be scoring at the top end of the team, and a pity advantage could not be taken of the absence of Cuba, E. Germany and Rumania to get further than usual.

Overall, for depth of strength the Russians still had no rivals (3 Gold, 2 Silver, 0 Bronze, 2 fourth places; 28 per cent of all individual finalists). The Hungarians, however, were impressive in range, with finalists at all weapons and plenty of medals (2 Gold, 1 Silver, 2 Bronze, 1 fourth place). W. Germany was strong in all weapons except sabre (1 Gold, 1 Silver, 2 Bronze, 1 fourth place). Italy was strong in everything except their traditional epee! (2 Silver, 3 Bronze, 1 fourth place). France was unlucky – the lack of top places was even more misleading than the plethora of the previous year.

Russian predominance is only a phenomenon of the past generation. Their arrival at the top was very sudden. Their first medal at any weapon was gained in 1955 (team sabre). Yet in 1958 they were already able to seize three Gold Medals, four Silver and one Bronze. In the 27 years from 1955 to 1981 they took an amazing 41 per cent of all Gold Medals. Most strikingly, in the 26 years from 1956–81 they never got less than a Silver Medal in the ladies' team event, and at sabre, having first reached Gold in 1964, they also never got less than Silver.

Before 1955 the French, the Italians and, to a lesser extent, the Hungarians ruled the field between them. From the start of 1896 till 1956, for instance, only four people intruded on the Franco-Italian duopoly of the top two places at men's individual foil (two Hungarians, two Germans and an American, discounting, as I have throughout these statistics, the 1904 Olympics, which did not attract a representative entry). At epee, since the beginning in 1906 down to 1958 only the Belgians in 1912 and 1930 broke this duopoly on the top position in the team event. Epee, however, has always been easier than foil or sabre for outsiders to break into, and the position is less clear-cut even in the team event if all medal positions are taken into account. Britain, for instance, figures six times by this measure up to 1965, and an interloping country with an especially strong and continuing tradition, Sweden, gained team medals 24 times between 1931 and 1978.

Sabre, by contrast, has always been a tight world. Hungary failed to win the individual event only four times between 1924 and 1956 (three times to Italy, once to France). And in the team event from 1924 only Belgium (once) and France (twice) ever intruded on the Hungarian and Italian stranglehold of *both* top positions – and that occurred only because the Hungarians were absent in 1947, 1949 and 1950. Between 1954 and 1970 Poland intruded to an impressive extent, with four team Golds and four team Silvers (and seven Bronzes from 1953 to 1981). Otherwise, all *three* top positions have been shared between just three countries: Hungary, Italy and USSR – with only seven exceptions (France, third in 1954 and 1965–7, and Rumania, second in 1977 and third in 1975 and 1976).

The situation since 1957 in ladies' foil has not been so very different. The team and individual medals positions have been shared between six countries: USSR (48), Hungary (39), Rumania (19), W. Germany (14), Italy (9) and France (6 – including 2 Gold), with only three exceptions.

Before the mid-fifties a somewhat different range of countries figured in the ladies' events: no Russians and no Rumanians but Denmark (8) and Austria (8). Britain had five different ladies in medal positions between the start of the event in 1924 and Gwen Neligan's win of 1933. Like sabreurs, top ladies have long careers. Ilona Elek of Hungary stands supreme with eight individual medals, five of them wins – over 21 years. Also impressive are Preiss (Austria, 7), Gorokhova (USSR, 6), Rejto (Hungary, 6), Meyer (Germany, 5), Lachmann (Denmark, 5). The equivalent figures for men's foil are d'Oriola 8,

Gaudini 7, J. Kamuti 5, Romankov, 5; at epee G. Buchard 5; and at sabre Pawlowski 10, Nazlimov 7, R. Karpati 7, A. Gerevich 5, A. Petschauer 6, A. Kabos 5, Krovopuskov 5, Sidiak 5.

The fencer who stands at the head of all others, however, must be Eduardo Mangiarotti, who was in the first three at foil six times and at epee seven times. (The best British total is that of Jay, four times in the top three.) In terms of *first* places d'Oriola is supreme, with six, followed by Elek, with five. Both achieved the hat trick, unlike Pawlowski or Karpati, both of whom won four times. Of the ten other fencers who have won three times, only Piller of Hungary has done so in successive years, but Lucien Gaudin of France won both foil and epee in the same year (1928), the only person ever to do so, though Mangiorotti was twice runner-up to d'Oriola at foil when he was winner at epee, and in 1959 Jay missed the feat by just one hit. Jay was not only the last person to gain a medal at two weapons in the same year, but, with Hoskyns (who did so in 1964), the last to appear in two individual finals in one year.

The country with most first places, both team and individual, up to 1981 was Hungary, with 92, an amazing achievement for a population (in 1964) of only ten millions. Close behind was USSR (89), then Italy (75), France (69), Germany – including E. and W. Germany and Austria – (22), Poland (15), Sweden (9), Denmark (6), Rumania (5), Belgium (5) and Britain (4).

# AFA officers, honours and statistics

## OFFICERS

*Presidents*
1902–10 Capt Alfred Hutton, FSA
1911–26 Lord Desborough, KG
1926–46 Lord Howard de Walden
1946–53 Vice-Adm Earl Granville, KG
1953–6 L. V. Fildes
1956–72 C-L. de Beaumont, OBE
1972–3 J. Emrys Lloyd, OBE
1973– Mrs M. A. Glen Haig, CBE

*Hon. President*
1953–65 Sir Winston Churchill, KG, OM

*Associate Vice-Presidents*
1947–58 The Maharaja of Dhrangadhra
1948–65 Edward W. Hunter
1959–61 E. R. B. Graham
1963– Viscount Runciman, OBE, AFC
1963– J. Eaton Griffiths, CMG, OBE
1965–6 J. D. Aylward

*Vice-Presidents*
1904–26 Lord Howard de Walden
1909–10 Lord Desborough, KG
1911–31 Sir Cosmo Duff Gordon, Bart.
1919–27 A. G. Ross
1923–8 Sir Theodore Cook
1923–30 Edgar Seligman
1929–47 C. F. Clay
1929–39 R. Montgomerie
1930–53 A. Miller-Hallett
1936–48 C. H. Biscoe
1936–53 L. V. Fildes
1938–59 P. G. Doyne
1938–54 Major R. M. P. Willoughby
1948–52 Col R. E. Cole
1949–56 Brig T. H. Wand-Tetley
1951– Miss E. Carnegy Arbuthnott, OBE
1954–6 C-L. de Beaumont
1954– Sir R. E. Brook, CMG, OBE
1954–72 J. Emrys Lloyd, OBE
1954–80 A. G. Pilbrow
1957– Lady Simmons
1960– Dr R. Parfitt
1960–75 Dr R. F. Tredgold
1960–75 Dr P. M. Turquet
1965–73 Mrs M. A. Glen Haig
1965–76 Capt E. A. Mount Haes, RN
1965– R. C. Winton
1976– Miss J. L. M. Pearce
1976– Miss M. Somerville
1979– Dr A. A. Banks
1979– P. J. Pilbrow
1981– Mrs E. Davies

*Hon. Secretaries*
1902–6 C. F. Clay
1907–27 R. Montgomerie
1928–35 C. H. Biscoe
1936–56 C-L. de Beaumont
1956–65 Mrs M. A. Glen Haig

*Hon. Treasurers*
1902–26 J. Norbury, Jnr
1926–7 C. H. Biscoe
1928–36 Major R. M. P. Willoughby
1937–43 C. Campbell Dick
1943–5 Major R. M. P. Willoughby
1946–8 Lt Col A. Ridley Martin, OBE
1949–61 R. E. Brook, CMG, OBE
1961–6 Dr P. M. Turquet
1966– Miss J. L. M. Pearce, MBE

# AFA officers, honours and statistics

*Secretaries*
1907–11 C. Montgomerie
1965–7 Lt Cdr R. T. Forsdick, RN
1967–9 Major O. C. Weeks, MBE
1969–70 J. Creek

1970–72 L. A. Mowlam
1973–80 Cdr F. A. Booth, RN
1981– Mrs J. Pienne

*Secretaries to the Committee*
1933–63 E. J. Morten

1963–5 Mrs M. Goddard

*Assistant Hon. Secretaries for Ladies' Fencing*
1951–4 Miss M. Somerville
1954 Mrs Meyrick Browne
1955–61 Mrs J. G. Allwork
1961 Miss B. N. Solly

1962–8 Miss M. Somerville
1968–70 Mrs H. Davies-Cooke
1970–80 Mrs C. R. Payne
1980– Mrs P. Casey

*Assistant Hon. Treasurers*
1949 J. Creek
1950–51 M. J. Parker
1952–5 Miss S. W. Breese

1955–6 Mrs M. A. Glen Haig
1956–8 Miss D. L. Rose
1959–66 Miss J. L. M. Pearce

## *CHAIRMAN OF STANDING SUB-COMMITTEES 1964–81*

*Finance and General Purposes*
Dr P. M. Turquet 1961–5
Miss J. L. M. Pearce, MBE, 1966–

*Ladies' Foil (President, LAFU)*
Mrs M. A. Glen Haig 1964–73
Mrs E. Davies 1973–6
Mrs H. Davies-Cooke 1977–

*Epee*
C-L. de Beaumont 1962–72
S. Higginson 1972–3
D. Parham 1974–7
E. L. Gray 1977–80
P. Greenhalgh 1980–

*Under-20 Men's Championships*
J. W. Eden 1963–

*Colours (renamed Honours, 1969)*
L. V. Fildes 1962–70
C-L. de Beaumont 1970–72
J. Emrys Lloyd 1972
Mrs M. A. Glen Haig 1973–

*National Training
(renamed Coaching Scheme, 1973)*
C-L. de Beaumont 1952–72
Dr A. A. Banks 1972–

*Sections* (estab. 1973)
L. E. Veale 1973
C. D. Tyson 1974–

*Rules and International
(Rules and Presidents, from 1976)*
C-L. de Beaumont 1964–72
S. Higginson 1974–9
P. Jacobs 1980–

*Joint Weapon* (formally estab. 1972)
Mrs M. A. Glen Haig 1972
P. J. Hobson 1973–

*Men's Foil*
R. C. Winton 1961–77
N. Halsted 1978–

*Sabre*
P. M. Turquet 1963–4
M. J. Amberg 1965–9
J. A. Seymour 1970
P. J. Hobson 1971–

*Schools Fencing Union* (estab. 1969)
T. Norcross 1969
J. Ramsay 1970–77
J. R. Hall 1978
N. Carr 1979–

*Public Schools Championship*
Capt E. A. Mount Haes, RN 1954–76
B. W. Howes 1976–

*Technical*
Dr R. Parfitt 1957–68
René Paul 1969–

## CLUB REPRESENTATIVES ON COMMITTEE, 1964-73

*All England FC*
Mrs M. A. Glen Haig 1950-66
E. J. Morten 1967-73

*Grosvenor FC*
J. A. Pelling 1964-71
G. R. Potten 1972-3

*Leaders Club* (renamed *Coaches Club, 1968)*
Prof. E. B. Pearson 1957-67
Dr A. A. Banks 1968-9
R. C. Parsons 1970-71
Miss V. Matheson 1972
Miss P. Brooks 1973

*Sabre Club*
Dr R. F. Tredgold 1959-72
R. Oldcorn 1973

*Mercia FC*
Mrs P. Courtney-Lewis 1955-67

*Salle Boston*
E. L. Gray 1970-73

*Salle Paul*
René Paul 1951-73

*Polytechnic FC*
Dr E. B. Knott 1950-70
G. Birks 1971-3

*London FC*
A. M. Leckie 1963-72
B. D. Hill 1973

*Thames FC*
P. Jacobs 1964-73

*Wanstead FC*
C. R. Williams 1964-73

*Epee Club*
J. Creek 1965-72
D. A. Partridge 1973

*York Fencing Association*
A. G. Power 1969-73


## REPRESENTATIVE MEMBERS OF THE COMMITTEE, 1964-1981

*British Academy of Fencing*
Prof. R. J. G. Anderson 1960-68, 1970-79
Prof. R. H. Behmber 1960-69
Prof. S. C. Boston 1969
Prof. S. Ridley 1970-71
Prof. G. W. R. Emery 1972-3
Prof. R. Goodall 1974-

*British Universities Sports Fed.*
H. Maslin 1962-72
B. Paul 1973-

*Royal Navy Amateur Fencing Union*
Lt Cdr D. D. Howson 1960-65
Lt Cdr P. A. Baily 1966-9
Lt Cdr A. R. V. Thompson 1970-

*Army Fencing Union*
Capt S. Blacknell 1963-5
Major L. Lambert 1966-75
Major G. W. Gelder 1976-

*Scottish Amateur Fencing Union*
Col R. A. Hay 1964-78
Miss C. J. Tolland 1979
J. P. Ross 1980-

*Modern Pentathlon Assoc. of GB*
J. Majendie 1963-6
Major E. R. Freeman 1967-8
S. P. S. R. J. Moore 1969-71
R. E. Pontefract 1972-3
M. A. Proudfoot 1974-

*RAF Fencing Union*
Sq Leader R. J. Steele 1964-7
Ft Lt W. Manning 1968-73, 1979-
J. Stephton 1974-8

# AFA officers, honours and statistics 477

## ELECTED COMMITTEE MEMBERS 1964-81

| | | | |
|---|---|---|---|
| 1935-72 | A. E. Pelling | 1974- | D. Cawthorne |
| 1952-72 | Dr A. G. Signy | 1974- | E. L. Gray |
| 1953-65, 1979- | R. C. Winton | 1974-9 | P. Jacobs |
| 1954- | Miss M. Somerville | 1974- | R. Oldcorn |
| 1957-80 | A. L. N. Jay, MBE | 1974-8 | D. Partridge |
| 1958-68 | J. H. Critch | 1976-8 | J. Grimmett |
| 1961-72 | E. M. C. Fuller | 1978- | N. Halsted |
| 1962- | P. J. Hobson | 1981- | R. C. Dye |
| 1965-78 | P. J. Kirby | 1981- | Prof. B. Pitman |
| 1965-79 | D. H. Parham | 1981- | Mrs S. Kenealy |
| 1969-74 | M. Kallipetis | 1981- | C. Hillier |
| 1972- | L. E. Veale | 1981- | J. Philbin |
| 1973-6, 1978- | E. O. Bourne | 1981- | Miss J. Erwteman |
| 1973-5 | A. M. Leckie | | |

## HONOURS

*Gold Medal*
1954 E. J. Morten
1957 C-L. de Beaumont
     Miss G. M. Sheen
     Prof. Cav. Leon Bertrand
1958 H. W. F. Hoskyns
1959 A. L. N. Jay
1961 R. E. Brook
1966 Lady Simmons
1968 Miss M. Somerville
1970 Dr L. G. Morrison
     J. L. Hope
1973 Miss J. L. M. Pearce

*Silver Medal*
1957 A. L. N. Jay
1973 Dr A. G. Signy
     (posthumously)
     Col R. A. Hay
     René Paul
     A. E. Pelling
1976 Capt E. A. Mount Haes, RN
     L. E. Veale
1978 Miss M. Pollock-Smith
     R. Bruniges
     H. Cooke
1981 Miss M. Durne

*Bronze Medal*
1973 P. J. Hobson
1976 R. J. Wood
     W. M. Mann

*Award of Merit*
1970 Miss C. J. Tolland
     Mrs D. Allwork
     E. M. C. Fuller
     Dr A. A. Banks
     C. D. Tyson
     L. Johnson
     D. Holt
     R. C. Parsons
     A. A. Kaye
1973 W. C. Burgess
     R. E. Southcombe
     President, Chairman and
       Members of Men's Under-20
       Sub-Committee
1976 B. Cole
     P. Turner
1978 B. Piddington
     J. J. Lewis
     Mrs L. Hamments
     Mrs J. Scrivenor
     Mrs J. Tyson

*Award of Merit*
     G. L. Wiles
1979 J. W. Eden
     Mrs A. van Beukelen
     D. Littlejohn
     Miss S. Briggs
     Dr G. Thorne
     Mrs J. Mason
     J. Ramsay
     Mrs K. Hurford
     Miss D. Mellor
     N. Watkins
1981 G. Earl
     W. van Beukelen
     Miss W. Pass
     J. Fetherstone
     Mrs B. Hillier
     C. Hillier
     P. Bird
     Miss H. Hammond
     D. Cawthorne

## MEMBERSHIP AND FINANCES

| | Membership | | Income | | | | | Expenditure | | | |
|---|---|---|---|---|---|---|---|---|---|---|---|
| | Associated Bodies and Clubs | Individuals | Subscriptions | Other (badges, dividends etc.) | Government grant for coaching and admin. | Total | | Government grant to national squad | Administration (incl. Trg Scheme) | Premises | Total |
| 1901 | 16 | 0 | 21 | 4 | | 25 | | | 14 | -2 | 12 |
| 1905 | 27 | 87 | 37 | 10 | | 47 | | | 36 | 7 | 43 |
| 1909 | 28 | 149 | 56 | 4 | | 60 | | | 61 | -18 | 43 |
| 1913 | 25 | 129 | 63 | 6 | | 69 | | | 192 | 27 | 219 |
| 1924 | 9 | 77 | 31 | 7 | | 38 | | | 78 | 18 | 96 |
| 1928 | 43 | 486 | 150 | 23 | | 173 | | | 27 | 1 | 28 |
| 1930 | 56 | 568 | 165 | 269 | | 434 | | | 153 | 27 | 180 |
| 1934 | 66 | 479 | 208 | 42 | | 250 | | | 232 | 49 | 281 |
| 1938 | 100 | 514 | 232 | 32 | | 264 | | | 211 | 47 | 258 |
| 1948 | 155 | 589 | 358 | 139 | | 497 | | | 657 | 190 | 847 |
| 1952 | 322 | 1,012 | 820 | 161 | 850 | 1,831 | | | 816 | 171 | 987 |
| 1956 | 385 | 1,618 | 1,157 | 166 | 850 | 2,173 | | | 993 | 194 | 1,187 |
| 1960 | 417 | 2,263 | 1,319 | -84 | 850 | 2,085 | | | 1,217 | 332 | 1,549 |
| 1964 | 447 | 3,408 | 1,348 | 81 | 3,250 | 4,679 | | | 4,219 | 268 | 4,487 |
| 1965 | 507 | 2,020 | 1,408 | 129 | 3,600 | 6,137 | | 1,000 | 4,805 | 518 | 6,323 |
| 1966 | 509 | 2,033 | 1,333 | 533 | 4,075 | 6,972 | | 1,031 | 5,700 | 1,158 | 7,889 |
| 1967 | 577 | 2,068 | 3,228 | 783 | 4,275 | 9,984 | | 1,698 | 6,779 | 1,055 | 9,532 |
| 1968 | 635 | 2,216 | 3,280 | 979 | 5,525 | 11,544 | | 1,760 | 9,141 | 937 | 11,838 |
| 1969 | 646 | 2,651 | 3,850 | 873 | 5,636 | 11,294 | | 935 | 8,782 | 1,278 | 10,995 |
| 1970 | 770 | 2,371 | 4,111 | 1,198 | 5,664 | 14,842 | | 3,869 | 10,129 | 1,258 | 15,256 |

# AFA officers, honours and statistics

| | | | | | | | |
|---|---|---|---|---|---|---|---|
| 1971 | 533 | 2,315 | 3,945 | 626 | 17,260 | 5,969 | 10,477 | 1,288 | 17,734 |
| 1972 | 537 | 1,850 | 6,174 | 424 | 22,248 | 8,653 | 13,766 | 1,985 | 24,404 |
| 1973 | 589 | 1,980 | 6,104 | 709 | 24,328 | 8,011 | 13,950 | 2,441 | 24,402 |
| 1974 | 709 | 1,937 | 5,708 | 1,582 | 28,153 | 10,753 | 15,149 | 280 | 26,182 |
| 1975 | 680 | 2,164 | 6,743 | 1,269 | 51,208 | 21,307 | 23,740 | 4,407 | 49,454 |
| 1976 | 613 | 2,535 | 6,847 | 1,592 | 57,526 | 23,288 | 27,500 | 2,543 | 53,331 |
| 1977 | 623 | 2,642 | 6,743 | 2,349 | 76,856 | 39,678 | 36,169 | 2,834 | 78,681 |
| 1978 | 573 | 2,195 | 11,763 | 2,081 | 82,316 | 33,393 | 40,002 | 3,998 | 77,393 |
| 1979 | 646 | 2,356 | 11,415 | 2,342 | 114,131 | 62,237 | 41,840 | 8,044 | 112,121 |
| 1980 | 522 | 2,446 | 11,023 | 1,967 | 91,027 | 42,617 | 41,497 | 9,040 | 93,154 |
| 1981 | 512 | 2,762 | 11,708 | 1,564 | 118,809 | 56,057 | 41,274 | 17,198 | 114,529 |

LAFU allocation is included in both income and expenditure (excluded from both sides in Annual Reports). Cost of premises is given net of competition receipts (Annual Reports vary); cost of 'territorial medals' included for 1934 and 1938. Some items are given net of receipts in Annual Reports, others not; consistency between one year and another has been sought here. Government grant to the national squad, although shown only on the expenditure side, is also included in the figures of total income. The figure for coaching grant in 1952 is not given in the annual accounts (and those for 1956 and 1960 are estimates); the corresponding expenditure is also omitted and is thus not included above.

PROFICIENCY AWARDS (G = Gold, S = Silver, B = Bronze)

| | Foil | | | Epee | | | Sabre | | | Total |
|---|---|---|---|---|---|---|---|---|---|---|
| | G | S | B | G | S | B | G | S | B | |
| 1966 | 73 | 482 | 2,352 | 0 | 7 | 31 | 6 | 26 | 93 | 2,907 |
| 1967 | 87 | 613 | 2,891 | 3 | 18 | 73 | 4 | 43 | 215 | 3,591 |
| 1969 | 74 | 747 | 2,897 | 2 | 5 | 44 | 7 | 36 | 188 | 2,641 |
| 1971 | 47 | 372 | 2,195 | 3 | 16 | 52 | 4 | 40 | 187 | 2,777 |
| 1973 | 67 | 566 | 2,909 | 5 | 14 | 43 | 3 | 21 | 132 | 3,898 |
| 1975 | 57 | 481 | 3,207 | 1 | 6 | 41 | 7 | 17 | 248 | 4,027 |
| 1977 | 60 | 497 | 3,729 | 3 | 15 | 37 | 8 | 21 | 71 | 4,590 |
| 1979 | 48 | 363 | 2,659 | | | | | | | 3,284 |
| 1980 | 3 | 352 | 3,462 | | | | | | | 4,139 |
| 1981 | 29 | 308 | 1,919 | | | | | | | 2,410 |

MEMBERSHIP BY TYPE

|  | Associated Bodies and Clubs | | Individual Members | | | Associate Members |
|---|---|---|---|---|---|---|
|  |  |  | Adults | Schoolchildren | |  |
| 1972 | 537 | | 1,455 | 395 | |  |
| 1973 | 589 | | 1,520 | 460 | |  |
| 1974 | 709 | | 1,518 | 419 | |  |
| 1975 | 680 | | 1,654 | 511 | |  |
| 1976 | 613 | | 1,643 | 594 | | 298 |
| 1977 | 623 | | 1,708 | 658 | | 276 |

|  | Adult Clubs | School Clubs |  | Under-20s | Under-18s |  |
|---|---|---|---|---|---|---|
| 1978 | 277 | 288 | 1,079 | 117 | 657 | 342 |
| 1979 | 285 | 253 | 1,070 | 200 | 594 | 492 |
| 1980 | 271 | 243 | 982 | 183 | 949 | 332 |
| 1981 | 282 | 222 | 1,059 | 171 | 1,057 | 475 |

COACHING AWARDS (till 1966, Leaders' Certificates)

|  | Foil | Epee | Sabre | Advanced | School-teachers' | Total |
|---|---|---|---|---|---|---|
| 1965 | 764 | 73 | 102 | 18 |  | 957 |
| 1967 | 866 | 85 | 128 | 18 |  | 1,097 |
| 1969 | 988 | 106 | 140 | 20 | 51 | 1,305 |
| 1971 | 1,093 | 130 | 171 | 22 | 107 | 1,523 |
| 1973 | 1,181 | 136 | 187 | 24 | 136 | 1,664 |
| 1975 | 71 | 15 | 12 | 2 | 15 | 115 |
| 1977 | 42 | 33 | 25 | 0 | 23 | 123 |
| 1979 | 72 | 18 | 33 | 0 | 11 | 134 |
| 1980 | 35 | 16 | 22 | 0 | 0 | 73 |
| 1981 | 39 | 15 | 25 | 2 | 0 | 81 |

# Competition results

\* indicates barrage
† indicates competition always or usually held in the pre-New Year part of the season

## OUTSTANDING INTERNATIONAL RESULTS

All final and semi-final World Championship places are included, and a selection of results in other major tournaments. (Excluded are British international events and Commonwealth Games, listed separately.) Olympic Games and World Championships (and the pre-1935, equivalent, European Championships) are indicated in capitals.

M = Men's foil   L = Ladies' foil   E = Epee   S = Sabre   T = Team

| 1904 | London (Crystal Palace) | E | E. Seligman | 7th* |
|---|---|---|---|---|
| 1906 | ATHENS | ET | Sir C. Duff Gordon, Lord Desborough, E. Seligman, C. Newton Robinson | 2nd |
| 1908 | LONDON | E | R. Montgomerie | 3rd* |
|  |  | E | C. Haig | 5th† |
|  |  | E | M. Holt | 8th |
|  |  | ET | E. Castle, E. Amphlett, C. Daniell, C. Haig, M. Holt, S. Martineau, R. Montgomerie, E. Seligman | 2nd |
|  |  | S | C. Barry Notley | Semi-f. |
| 1909 | Brussels (Exhibition) | E | E. Amphlett | 9th |
| 1911 | Stockholm | L | J. Johnstone | 1st |
|  |  | L | M. Hall | 2nd |
|  |  | L | D. Cheetham | 3rd |
|  | Ostend | S | A. Ridley Martin | 3rd |
| 1912 | STOCKHOLM | M | E. Seligman | 6th |
|  |  | M | R. Montgomerie | 8th |
|  |  | M | E. Amphlett | Semi-f, |
|  |  | E | E. Seligman | 6th |
|  |  | E | M. Holt | 8th |
|  |  | E | G. Ames | Semi-f. |
|  |  | E | E. Amphlett | Semi-f. |
|  |  | E | R. Montgomerie | Semi-f. |
|  |  | ET | E. Seligman, E. Amphlett, J. Blake, P. Davson, A. Everitt, M. Holt, S. Martineau, R. Montgomerie | 2nd |
|  |  | S | C. van der Byl | Semi-f. |

| 1913 | London | E | R. Montgomerie | 6th |
|---|---|---|---|---|
| | (Earl's Court) | E | G. Ames | 7th |
| | | S | E. Brookfield | 1st |
| | | S | W. Marsh | 8th |
| | Ghent | L | Mrs C. Martin Edmunds | 1st |
| | | L | Mrs Edwardes | 2nd |
| | Le Touquet | E | R. Montgomerie | 1st |
| 1914 | Ostend | E | R. Montgomerie | 2nd |
| 1920 | ANTWERP | S | R. Dalglish | 6th |
| | | S | C. Kershaw | Semi-f. |
| 1921 | Ostend | L | J. Johnstone | 1st |
| 1922 | Ostend | L | G. M. Davis | 1st |
| | | E | G. Burt | 6th= |
| 1923 | Ostend | L | G. M. Davis | 1st |
| | | L | M. Pollock-Smith | 5th |
| | | L | W. Davis | 6th |
| | | E | R. Montgomerie | 4th |
| | | E | C. Biscoe | 5th= |
| | | E | G. Burt | 5th= |
| | THE HAGUE | E | R. A. Hay | 10th= |
| 1924 | Ostend | L | G. M. Davis | 1st |
| | PARIS | M | E. Seligman | Final (ret. inj.) |
| | | L | G. M. Davis | 2nd |
| | | L | Mrs M. Freeman | 4th |
| | | E | C. Biscoe | Semi-f. |
| | | S | R. Dalglish | Semi-f. |
| 1925 | Ostend | L | G. M. Davis | 1st |
| | | E | C. Biscoe | 4th |
| | | E | R. A. Hay | 9th |
| 1926 | New York | M | P. G. Doyne | 2nd |
| | (US Champs) | E | I. Campbell-Gray | 2nd |
| | | E | C. Biscoe | 5th |
| | | S | G. Dyer | 5th |
| 1927 | Paris | L | G. Daniell | 4th |
| | (Grande Semaine) | | | |
| 1928 | AMSTERDAM | L | Mrs M. Freeman | 2nd |
| | | L | G. Daniell | 5th |
| | | E | C. Biscoe | Semi-f. |
| | | E | B. Childs | Semi-f. |
| | | E | M. Holt | Semi-f. |
| 1929 | Le Touquet | E | C-L. de Beaumont | 2nd= |
| | Lisbon | L | G. Daniell | 2nd |
| 1930 | LIEGE | M | J. E. Lloyd | Semi-f. |
| | | L | M. Venables | 3rd |
| | | L | M. Butler | 4th |
| | | L | G. Daniell | 6th |
| | | L | J. Guinness | 8th |
| 1931 | Geneva | E | C-L. de Beaumont | 2nd |
| | (1st electric international) | | | |
| | VIENNA | M | J. E. Lloyd | 3rd |
| | | L | J. Guinness | 5th |
| 1932 | Ostend | E | D. Dexter | 4th |
| | | S | O. Trinder | 4th |
| | LOS ANGELES | M | J. E. Lloyd | 5th= |
| | | L | M. Butler | 10th |

|      |                  |    |                                    |             |
|------|------------------|----|------------------------------------|-------------|
| 1933 | BUDAPEST         | L  | J. Guinness                        | Silver Medal* |
|      |                  | M  | J. E. Lloyd                        | 3rd         |
|      |                  | L  | G. Neligan                         | 1st         |
|      |                  | L  | J. Guinness                        | 9th         |
|      |                  | LT | J. Guinness,                       | 2nd         |
|      |                  |    | E. C. Arbuthnott,                  |             |
|      |                  |    | M. Geddes, G. Neligan              |             |
|      |                  | E  | C-L. de Beaumont                   | Semi-f.     |
|      |                  | E  | T. Beddard                         | Semi-f.     |
|      |                  | E  | D. Dexter                          | Semi-f.     |
|      |                  | ST | R. E. Brook,                       | 3rd         |
|      |                  |    | C-L. de Beaumont,                  |             |
|      |                  |    | C. Hohler, J. E. Lloyd,            |             |
|      |                  |    | A. Pilbrow, O. Trinder             |             |
| 1934 | New York         | E  | D. Dexter                          | 1st         |
|      | (US Champs)      |    | C-L. de Beaumont                   | 3rd         |
|      | Dieppe           | E  | A. Pelling                         | 1st         |
|      | Biarritz         | E  | A. Pelling                         | 3rd         |
|      | WARSAW           | M  | J. E. Lloyd                        | 5th         |
|      |                  | L  | G. Neligan                         | 4th*        |
|      |                  | L  | J. Guinness                        | 7th         |
|      |                  | LT | G. Nelligan, J. Guinness,          | 2nd=        |
|      |                  |    | M. Geddes, K. Stanbury             |             |
|      |                  | E  | A. Craig                           | Semi-f.     |
|      |                  | S  | J. E. Lloyd                        | Semi-f.     |
| 1935 | LAUSANNE         | M  | J. E. Lloyd                        | 10th        |
|      |                  | L  | J. Guinness                        | 5th         |
|      |                  |    | G. Neligan                         | 7th         |
| 1936 | BERLIN           | M  | J. E. Lloyd                        | Semi-f.     |
|      |                  | L  | Mrs C. Penn-Hughes                 | Semi-f.     |
|      |                  | E  | I. Campbell-Gray                   | 8th         |
|      |                  | S  | O. Trinder                         | Semi-f.     |
| 1937 | Paris (Bachelard)| L  | E. Slingsby-Bethell                | 1st         |
|      | PARIS            | M  | J. E. Lloyd                        | Semi-f.     |
|      |                  | L  | G. Neligan                         | Semi-f.     |
|      |                  | E  | A. Pienne                          | Semi-f.     |
| 1939 | Ostend           | L  | C. Christie                        | 6th         |
|      | Monte Carlo      | M  | P. Turquet                         | 3rd         |
|      | (Student Games)  |    |                                    |             |
| 1947 | LISBON           | M  | J. E. Lloyd                        | Semi-f.     |
|      | Antwerp          | L  | Mrs M. Glen Haig                   | 1st         |
|      |                  | S  | P. Turquet                         | 2nd         |
|      | Mondorf          | E  | C-L. de Beaumont                   | 6th         |
|      | Copenhagen       | L  | E. Carnegy Arbuthnott              | 2nd         |
|      |                  |    | J. Majendie                        | 3rd         |
|      |                  | E  | A. Craig                           | 3rd         |
| 1948 | Le Touquet       | E  | R. Parfitt                         | Last 4      |
|      | LONDON           | M  | J. E. Lloyd                        | 4th         |
|      |                  | L  | Mrs M. Glen Haig                   | 8th         |
|      |                  | L  | Mrs G. Minton                      | Semi-f.     |
|      |                  | E  | R. Parfitt                         | 10th        |
| 1949 | Antwerp          | S  | D. Shalit                          | 5th         |
|      | Le Touquet       | E  | C-L. de Beaumont                   | 3rd         |
| 1950 | MONACO           | M  | Raymond Paul                       | Semi-f.     |
|      |                  | L  | Mrs M. Glen Haig                   | 4th         |
|      |                  | LT | Mrs M. Glen Haig,                  | 3rd         |
|      |                  |    | E. Carnegy Arbuthnott,             |             |

|      |                    |    |                               |            |
|------|--------------------|----|-------------------------------|------------|
|      |                    |    | C. Drew, G. Sheen,            |            |
|      |                    |    | M. Somerville                 |            |
|      |                    | E  | T. Beddard                    | Semi-f.    |
| 1951 | STOCKHOLM          | L  | Mrs M. Glen Haig              | 6th        |
|      |                    |    |                               | (injured)  |
|      | Luxembourg         | M  | A. Jay                        | 2nd*       |
|      | (Student Games)    | L  | G. Sheen                      | 1st        |
|      |                    | S  | A. J. Cotton                  | 1st        |
|      | Mondorf            | L  | G. Sheen                      | 1st        |
| 1952 | HELSINKI           | M  | René Paul                     | Semi-f.    |
|      |                    | L  | Mrs M. Glen Haig              | Semi-f.    |
|      |                    | E  | A. Jay                        | Semi-f.    |
| 1953 | The Hague          | S  | O. Porebski                   | 2nd        |
|      |                    | S  | R. Cooperman                  | 3rd        |
|      | Brussels           | S  | O. Porebski                   | 2nd        |
|      | Antwerp            | L  | B. Screech                    | 1st        |
|      |                    | L  | M. Somerville                 | 5th        |
|      | Noordwyck          | L  | E. Berry                      | 4th        |
|      | Dortmund           | L  | G. Sheen                      | 5th        |
|      | (Student Games)    | E  | A. Jay                        | 2nd        |
| 1953–4 | Copenhagen       | L  | G. Sheen                      | 1st        |
|      |                    | L  | Mrs M. Glen Haig              | 3rd        |
|      | Bremen             | S  | P. Turquet                    | 1st        |
| 1954–5 | Paris (Bachelard) | L | Mrs M. Glen Haig              | 2nd        |
|      |                    | L  | E. Berry                      | Last 4     |
|      |                    | L  | G. Sheen                      | Last 8     |
|      | Ostend             | E  | A. Jay                        | 3rd        |
|      |                    | S  | R. Sproul-Bolton              | 4th        |
|      |                    | S  | R. Cooperman                  | 1st        |
|      | San Sebastian      | L  | G. Sheen                      | 4th        |
|      | (Student Games)    | E  | A. Jay                        | 2nd        |
|      | ROME               | MT | H. Cooke, H. W. Hoskyns,      | 3rd        |
|      |                    |    | A. Jay, René Paul,            |            |
|      |                    |    | O. Reynolds                   |            |
| 1955–6 | Budapest         | M  | A. Jay                        | 2nd        |
|      | Noordwyck          | E  | A. Jay                        | 1st        |
|      | Paris (Jeanty)     | L  | G. Sheen                      | 5th        |
|      |                    | L  | E. Berry                      | 8th        |
|      | MELBOURNE          | M  | A. Jay                        | 4th        |
|      |                    | M  | Raymond Paul                  | 8th        |
|      |                    | M  | René Paul                     | Semi-f.    |
|      |                    | L  | G. Sheen                      | Gold Medal |
| 1956–7 | Paris (Duval)    | M  | Raymond Paul                  | 2nd        |
|      | Milan (Spreafico)  | E  | H. W. Hoskyns                 | Last 8     |
|      | Ghent              | M  | A. Jay                        | 1st        |
|      | Amsterdam          | L  | E. Berry                      | 2nd        |
|      | Paris (Martini)    | M  | A. Jay                        | 2nd        |
|      |                    | M  | Raymond Paul                  | Last 8     |
|      | Copenhagen         | L  | G. Sheen                      | 1st        |
|      |                    | L  | Mrs M. Glen Haig              | 2nd        |
|      |                    | L  | M. Stafford                   | 5th        |
|      | Como               | L  | G. Sheen                      | 7th        |
|      | Noordwyck          | E  | A. Jay                        | 1st        |
|      |                    | E  | H. W. Hoskyns                 | 4th        |
|      | Ostend             | E  | H. W. Hoskyns                 | 2nd        |
|      | PARIS              | M  | A. Jay                        | 3rd        |
|      |                    | M  | René Paul                     | 7th        |

|  |  |  | M | Raymond Paul | Semi-f. |
|---|---|---|---|---|---|
|  |  |  | L | G. Sheen | Semi-f. |
|  |  |  | E | A. Jay | 5th |
|  |  |  | ET | R. Harrison, H. W. Hoskyns, M. Howard, A. Jay, J. Pelling, R. Sproul-Bolton | 3rd |
|  |  |  | S | R. Cooperman | Semi-f. |
| 1957–8 |  | Paris (Duval) | M | A. Jay | 2nd |
|  |  | Huy | E | M. Howard | 1st |
|  |  | Amsterdam | L | M. Durne | 1st |
|  |  | Ghent | L | G. Sheen | 3rd |
|  |  | Noordwyck | L | G. Sheen | 2nd |
|  |  |  | L | T. Offredy | 3rd |
|  |  |  | S | R. Cooperman | 3rd |
|  |  |  | S | M. Straus | 5th |
|  |  | Luxembourg | E | H. W. Hoskyns | 1st |
|  |  | PHILADELPHIA | L | G. Sheen | 7th |
|  |  |  | E | H. W. Hoskyns | 1st |
|  |  |  | S | H. W. Hoskyns | Semi-f. |
| 1958–9 |  | Paris (Monal) | E | H. W. Hoskyns | 1st |
|  |  | Paris (Martini) | M | A. Jay | 2nd |
|  |  |  | M | H. W. Hoskyns | 3rd= |
|  |  | Paris (Duval) | M | H. W. Hoskyns | 3rd= |
|  |  | Milan (Spreafico) | E | H. W. Hoskyns | Last 8 |
|  |  | Paris (Ferrodo) | E | H. W. Hoskyns | Last 8 |
|  |  | Amsterdam | M | H. W. Hoskyns | 2nd |
|  |  |  | E | A. Jay | 1st |
|  |  |  | A | R. Cooperman | 1st |
|  |  | Brussels (Coup des Trentes) | E | H. W. Hoskyns | 1st |
|  |  | Lugano | E | J. Pelling | 1st |
|  |  | Bologna (Giovannini) | M | H. W. Hoskyns | 1st |
|  |  | Brussels | L | M. Durne | 3rd |
|  |  | Dieppe | L | M. Durne | 1st |
|  |  | Ostend | L | G. Sheen | 1st |
|  |  |  | S | R. Cooperman | 2nd |
|  |  | BUDAPEST | M | A. Jay | 1st |
|  |  |  | E | A. Jay | 2nd* |
|  |  | Turin (Student Games) | L | M. Stafford | 4th |
| 1959–60 |  | Paris (Monal) | E | H. W. Hoskyns | 2nd |
|  |  | Paris (Martini) | M | H. W. Hoskyns | Last 8 |
|  |  |  | M | A. Jay | Last 8 |
|  |  | Paris (Duval) | M | H. W. Hoskyns | 2nd |
|  |  |  | M | A. Jay | 3rd= |
|  |  | Paris (Ferrodo) | E | E. Knott | Last 8 |
|  |  |  | E | J. Pelling | Last 8 |
|  |  | London (Martini) | E | H. W. Hoskyns | 3rd= |
|  |  |  |  | A. Jay | 3rd= |
|  |  | Amsterdam | L | G. Sheen | 1st |
|  |  |  | E | J. Pelling | 1st |
|  |  | Brussels (Coup des Trentes) | E | H. W. Hoskyns | 1st |
|  |  | Ghent | M | H. W. Hoskyns | 2nd |
|  |  |  | L | G. Sheen | 3rd |

|  |  |  |  |  |
|---|---|---|---|---|
|  | Evreux | M | A. Jay | 1st |
|  | Warsaw | M | H. W. Hoskyns | 3rd |
|  |  | L | G. Sheen | 4th |
|  |  | E | H. W. Hoskyns | 5th |
|  | Paris (Touzard) | S | R. Cooperman | 3rd= |
|  | Brussels | L | G. Sheen | 1st |
|  | ROME | M | H. W. Hoskyns | 7th |
|  |  | E | A. Jay | Silver Medal |
|  |  | ET | M. Alexander, R. Harrison, H. W. Hoskyns, M. Howard, A. Jay, J. Pelling | Silver Medal |
| 1960–61 | Paris (Martini) | M | A. Jay | 3rd= |
|  | Paris (Duval top scorers) | M | J. Fethers | 1st |
|  | Paris (Picon) | E | H. W. Hoskyns | 1st |
|  | Les Andelys | E | J. Glasswell | 1st |
|  | Brussels | E | S. Higginson | 1st |
|  | TURIN | M | H. W. Hoskyns | 6th |
|  |  | E | H. W. Hoskyns | 8th |
|  | Sofia (Student Games) | E | P. Jacobs | 4th |
| 1961–2 | Hamburg | S | A. Leckie | 6th |
|  | Paris (Duval) | M | A. Jay | 1st |
|  | Paris (Picon) | E | H. W. Hoskyns | 2nd |
|  | New York (Athletic Club) | E | H. W. Hoskyns | 1st |
|  | London (Martini) | E | H. W. Hoskyns | 1st |
|  | Amsterdam | L | J. Bailey | 3rd |
|  | Budapest | M | A. Jay | 2nd |
|  | Copenhagen | L | Mrs P. Courtney-Lewis | 3rd |
|  | Paris (Touzard) | S | A. Leckie | 7th |
|  |  | S | R. Cooperman | 8th |
|  | Ystad | S | R. Oldcorn | 1st |
| 1962–3 | Dunkirk | L | J. Bailey | 1st |
|  | Paris (Martini top scorers) | M | H. W. Hoskyns | 1st |
|  |  | M | A. Jay | 4th |
|  | Melun (Borin) | M | A. Leckie | 3rd |
|  | Paris (Picon) | E | P. Jacobs | 1st |
|  | New York (Athletics Club) | E | H. W. Hoskyns | 1st |
|  | Paris (Touzard) | S | A. Leckie | 4th |
|  |  | S | R. Oldcorn | 7th |
|  | Brussels | L | M. Durne | 2nd |
|  | GDANSK | M | H. W. Hoskyns | 7th |
|  | Porto Alegre (Student Games) | E | P. Jacobs | 1st |
| 1963–4 | Rotterdam | L | M. Durne | 3rd |
|  | Amsterdam | L | J. Bewley-Cathie | 1st |
|  | Goppingen | L | Mrs M. Watts-Tobin | 3rd |
|  |  | L | J. Bewley-Cathie | 5th |
|  | Paris (Duval) | M | J. Fethers | Last 8 |
|  |  | M | A. Jay | Last 8 |
|  | Paris (Touzard) | S | J. Rayden | 5th |
|  |  | S | R. Oldcorn | 4th |
|  | Dieppe | L | Mrs S. Wilson | 1st |

|  |  |  |  |  |
|---|---|---|---|---|
|  | Mondorf | E | A. Jay | 1st |
|  | Tokyo | M | H. W. Hoskyns | 7th= |
|  |  | E | H. W. Hoskyns | Silver Medal |
| 1964–5 | Hamburg | S | R. Oldcorn | 4th |
|  | Rotterdam (World Youth) | M | M. Breckin | 5th= |
|  | New York (Athletic Club) | M | P. Jacobs | 6th |
|  | London (Martini) | E | A. Jay | 2nd |
|  |  |  | H. W. Hoskyns | Last 8 |
|  | Paris | E | P. Jacobs | 6th |
|  | Paris | E | H. W. Hoskyns | 2nd |
|  |  | ET | N. Halsted, H. W. Hoskyns, A. Jay, P. Jacobs, J. Pelling | 2nd |
| 1965–6 | Louviers | E | P. Jacobs | 1st |
|  | Paris (Monal) | E | P. Jacobs | 6th |
|  | Paris (Martini) | M | H. W. Hoskyns | Last 8 |
|  | Paris (Picon) | E | P. Jacobs | 3rd |
|  | Melun | L | M. Durne | 3rd= |
|  | New York (Athletic Club) | E | P. Jacobs | 6th |
|  | Poitiers | E | S. Higginson | 6th |
|  | Paris (Rommel) | M | A. Jay | 5th |
|  | Munich | S | A. Leckie | 6th |
|  | Paris (Jeanty) | L | J. Bailey | 3rd= |
| 1966–7 | Hamburg | S | R. Oldcorn | 6th |
|  | Chaux des Fonds | M&E | M. Breckin (U-20 M) & N. Halsted (E) | 1st |
|  | Cologne |  | M. Breckin | 3rd |
|  | Melun | M | M. Breckin | Last 8 |
|  | Duren | L | J. Davis | 1st |
|  | London (Martini) | E | A. Jay | Last 8 |
|  |  |  | N. Halsted | 3rd= |
|  | Amsterdam | L | Mrs J. Wardell-Yerburgh | 3rd |
|  | Tehran (World Youth) | M | G. Paul | 4th |
|  | New York (Martini) | E | N. Halsted | 5th |
|  | Tokyo (Student Games) | M | M. Breckin | 5th |
|  |  |  | W. R. Johnson | 6th |
|  | Montreal | L | Mrs J. Wardell-Yerburgh | Last 8 |
| 1967–8 | Chaux des Fonds | M&E | G. Paul (U-20 M) & N. Halsted (E) | 1st |
|  | Hamburg | S | R. Oldcorn | 5th |
|  | Paris (Schmetz) | U-20 E | E. Bourne | 1st |
|  |  |  | W. R. Johnson | 4th |
|  | Montpelier | M | G. Paul | 2nd |
|  | Paris (Martini) | M | M. Breckin | 8th |
|  | London (Martini) | E | G. Paul | Last 8 |
|  |  |  | K. Pearman | 3rd= |
|  | Heidenheim | E | E. Bourne | 6th= |
|  | Poitiers | E | N. Halsted | 8th |
|  | Hamburg | S | R. Craig | 8th |
|  | Mexico City | E | W. R. Johnson | 13th= |
| 1968–9 | Bad Durkheim | E | W. R. Johnson | 1st |
|  | Hamburg | S | R. Cohen | 4th |
|  |  |  | R. Oldcorn | 6th |

|         |                    |        |                        |          |
|---------|--------------------|--------|------------------------|----------|
|         | HAVANA             | M      | A. Power               | Semi-f.  |
| 1969–70 | Antwerp            | M      | A. Jay                 | 2nd      |
|         | Hamburg            | S      | R. Craig               | 3rd      |
|         | Bad Durkheim       | M      | G. Paul                | 1st      |
|         |                    |        | N. Halsted             | 3rd      |
|         | London (Martini)   | E      | H. W. Hoskyns          | 3rd=     |
|         | Amsterdam          | S      | R. Cohen               | 2nd      |
|         | Poitiers           | E      | S. Higginson           | Last 8   |
|         | Brussels           | L      | C. Henley              | 3rd      |
|         |                    | E      | S. Higginson           | 3rd      |
|         |                    | S      | J. Deanfield           | 3rd      |
| 1970–71 | Duren              | E      | W. R. Johnson          | 2nd      |
|         | Bad Durkheim       | M      | G. Paul                | 2nd      |
|         | Eupen              | L      | Mrs H. Rogerson        | 3rd      |
|         | London (Martini)   | E      | N. Halsted             | Last 8   |
|         |                    |        | H. W. Hoskyns          | Last 8   |
|         |                    |        | W. R. Johnson          | Last 8   |
|         | Munich (Invitation) | M     | G. Paul                | 6th      |
|         | South Bend (World Youth) | L | S. Wrigglesworth       | 5th      |
|         |                    | E      | J. Stanbury            | 4th      |
|         | VIENNA             | E      | E. Bourne              | Last 12  |
| 1971–2  | Duisberg           | U-20 L | S. Wrigglesworth       | 1st      |
|         | Bad Durkheim       | E      | E. Bourne              | 1st      |
|         | Warsaw             | M      | B. Paul                | 1st      |
|         | Paris (Debeur)     | L      | Mrs J. Wardell-Yerburgh | 3rd     |
|         | Gelsenkirchen      | U-20 M | R. Bruniges            | 1st      |
|         | Duren              | E      | H. W. Hoskyns          | 2nd      |
|         | London (Martini)   | E      | W. R. Johnson          | 3rd=     |
|         | Basel              | U-20 M | R. Bruniges            | 1st      |
|         | Madrid (World Youth) | S    | J. Deanfield           | 6th      |
|         | Paris (Touzard)    | S      | J. Deanfield           | 6th      |
|         | Paris (Duval)      | M      | B. Paul                | 6th      |
|         | Heidenheim         | E      | E. Bourne              | 5th      |
|         | Bad Durkheim       | M      | A. Jay                 | 6th      |
|         | Goppingen          | L      | Mrs J. Wardell-Yerburgh | 6th     |
|         | Eupen              | L      | S. Littlejohns         | 3rd      |
|         | Berlin             | E      | E. Bourne              | 3rd      |
| 1972–3  | Beirut             | L      | S. Littlejohns         | 1st      |
|         | Duren              | E      | H. W. Hoskyns          | 1st      |
|         | Genoa              | U-20 M | R. Bruniges            | 1st      |
|         | New York (Martini) | L      | S. Green               | 6th      |
|         | Buenos Aires (World Youth) | M | R. Bruniges        | 3rd      |
|         | London (Martini)   | E      | G. Paul                | Last 8   |
|         | Poitiers           | E      | R. Bruniges            | Last 8   |
|         | Brussels           | L      | H. Cawthorne           | 3rd      |
|         | Dieppe             | E      | M. Fare                | 1st      |
| 1973–4  | Budapest           | U-20 E | R. Bruniges            | 1st      |
|         | Duren              | E      | H. W. Hoskyns          | 1st      |
|         | Paris (Monal)      | E      | E. Bourne              | 4th      |
|         | Bern               | E      | E. Bourne              | 5th      |
|         | Heidenheim         | E      | T. Belson              | Last 8   |
|         | Goppingen          | L      | S. Wrigglesworth       | 6th      |

|  |  |  |  |  |
|---|---|---|---|---|
| | Innsbruck | E | T. Belson | 1st |
| | Dieppe | S | S. Fox | 1st |
| 1974–5 | Paris (Rommel) | M | B. Paul | 5th |
| | Bern | E | G. Paul | 6th |
| | London (Martini) | E | J. Noel | Last 8 |
| | Antwerp | M | N. Bell | 2nd |
| | Zofingen | U-20 E | R. Bruniges | 1st |
| | New York (Martini) | M | B. Paul | 6th |
| | Wattenscheid | U-20 E | P. Emberson | 1st |
| | Poitiers | E | T. Belson | 1st |
| | | | W. R. Johnson | 3rd |
| | Brussels | E | E. Bourne | 1st |
| | | L | W. Ager | 1st |
| | Moulins | E | G. Paul | 1st |
| 1975–6 | Duren | E | W. R. Johnson | 1st |
| | Heilbronn | U-20 M | R. Bruniges | 1st |
| | Le Havre | U-20 M | W. Gosbee | 1st |
| | Paris (Duval) | E | G. Paul | Last 8 |
| | Bern | E | E. Bourne | Last 8 |
| | | | T. Belson | Last 8 |
| | Magdeburg | L | H. Cawthorne | Last 8 |
| | | M | B. Paul | Last 8 |
| | | M | N. Bell | Last 8 |
| | Poznan (World Youth) | M | R. Bruniges | 1st |
| | Salzburg | L | C. Halsted | 1st |
| | Dieppe | E | M. Fare | 1st |
| | MONTREAL | L | S. Wrigglesworth | 13th= |
| | | E | W. R. Johnson | 13th= |
| 1976–7 | Rennes | E | D. Brooks | 2nd |
| | BUENOS AIRES | L | L. Martin | 13th |
| | | E | W. R. Johnson | 7th |
| | Bad Durkheim | E | J. Llewellyn | 2nd |
| 1977–8 | Amsterdam | L | L. Martin | 1st |
| | Oslo | E | H. W. Hoskyns | 2nd |
| | | | J. Llewellyn | 3rd |
| | E. Berlin | L | S. Wrigglesworth | 3rd |
| | | E | T. Belson | 3rd |
| | Turin | L | S. Wrigglesworth | 7th |
| | Duren | E | W. R. Johnson | 3rd |
| | Paris (Monal) | E | W. R. Johnson | Last 8 |
| | Paris (Touzard) | S | J. Deanfield | 3rd |
| | Legnano (Carroccio) | E | J. Llewellyn | 2nd |
| | Innsbruck | E | S. Paul | 1st |
| | Bern | E | W. R. Johnson | Last 8 |
| | Poitiers | E | S. Paul | Last 8 |
| 1978–9 | E. Berlin | L | S. Wrigglesworth | 4th |
| | | | H. Cawthorne | 6th |
| | Goppingen | L | L. Martin | Last 8 |
| | Paris (Duval) | M | P. Harper | 4th |
| | | M | W. Gosbee | 6th |
| | | M | R. Bruniges | 7th |
| | Heidenheim | E | T. Belson | 6th |
| | New York | S | J. Philbin | 4th |
| | | | R. Cohen | 5th |

|  |  |  |  |  |
|---|---|---|---|---|
|  | Poitiers | E | T. Belson | Last 8 |
|  | Flims | E | W. R. Johnson | 1st |
|  | Mexico City (Student Games) | E | N. Mallett | 8th |
| 1979–80 | E. Berlin | L | L. Martin | Last 8 |
|  | Catania | E | W. R. Johnson | 2nd |
|  | Legnano (Carroccio) | E | W. R. Johnson | Last 8 |
|  | Munich | S | J. Deanfield | 6th |
|  | Como | L | L. Martin | 5th |
|  | Paris (Duval) | M | P. Harper | 5th |
| 1980–81 | Zurich | E | W. R. Johnson | 2nd |
|  | Basel | L | F. McIntosh | 2nd |
|  | Paris (Duval) | M | R. Bruniges | 1st |
|  |  | M | D. McKenzie | 4th |
|  |  | M | P. Harper | Last 8 |
|  |  | M | A. Bartlett | Last 8 |
|  | Paris (Touzard) | S | R. Cohen | 1st |
|  | London (Martini) | E | S. Paul | 1st |
|  |  | E | J. Llewellyn | 3rd |
|  | Bad Durkheim | M | W. Gosbee | Last 8 |
|  | Bonn | M | P. Harper | Last 8 |
|  | Poitiers | E | S. Paul | Last 8 |

## MEN'S FOIL (HEADQUARTERS EVENTS)

### THE AMATEUR CHAMPIONSHIP

1898–1901, fought by knock-out; 1902–62, by pools; thereafter generally by prevailing FIE system. In 1912 a bronze shield bearing a portrait of Capt Alfred Hutton was presented by subscribers in his memory.

|  | 1 | 2 | 3 |
|---|---|---|---|
| 1898 | H. Turner | T. P. Hobbins |  |
| 1899 | B. C. Praed | T. P. Hobbins |  |
| 1900 | T. P. Hobbins | H. Evan James |  |
| 1901 | H. Evan James | R. Montgomerie |  |
| 1902 | J. Jenkinson* | H. Evan James* | A. Rawlinson, T. P. Hobbins, H. Balfour eq. |
| 1903 | J. Jenkinson* | H. Evan James* | R. Montgomerie |
| 1904 | J. Jenkinson | R. Montgomerie | H. Evan James, G. L. Jacobs eq. |
| 1905 | R. Montgomerie* | E. Seligman* | A. Rawlinson |
| 1906 | E. Seligman | P. M. Davson | R. Montgomerie |
| 1907 | E. Seligman | R. Montgomerie | E. M. Amphlett, P. M. Davson eq. |
| 1908 | R. Montgomerie | E. M. Amphlett, P. M. Davson, G. R. Alexander eq. |  |
| 1909 | R. Montgomerie | P. M. Davson | E. M. Amphlett |
| 1910 | R. Montgomerie* | P. M. Davson* | E. Seligman, R. Willoughby |
| 1911 | E. M. Amphlett | R. Willoughby | A. Rawlinson |
| 1912 | P. G. Doyne* | P. M. Davson* | R. Willoughby* |
| 1913 | G. R. Alexander | R. Sutton | P. G. Doyne |
| 1914 | R. Willoughby | G. R. Alexander | A. Rawlinson |
| 1915–19 | No competition |  |  |

491

|      | 1 | 2 | 3 |
|---|---|---|---|
| 1920 | P. G. Doyne | S. Martineau | R. Sutton, R. Willoughby |
| 1921 | R. Sutton | P. G. Doyne | E. Stenson Cooke, R. Willoughby eq. |
| 1922 | R. Sutton* | E. Stenson Cooke* | F. Sherriff |
| 1923 | E. Stenson Cooke | T. E. Ryves | F. G. Davis, R. Haig |
| 1924 | F. G. Sherriff* | R. S. S. Meade* | E. Stenson Cooke |
| 1925 | F. G. Sherriff | R. S. S. Meade* | M. Babington Smith* |
| 1926 | S. R. Bousfield* | J. A. Obdam* | M. Babington Smith* |
| 1927 | A. D. Pearce | J. E. Lloyd | J. Winder |
| 1928 | J. E. Lloyd* | F. Sherriff* | G. T. M. Gibson |
| 1929 | H. Evan James | C. A. Simey | A. D. Pearce |
| 1930 | J. E. Lloyd | T. E. Ryves | M. Babington Smith |
| 1931 | J. E. Lloyd | M. Babington Smith | F. E. Lloyd |
| 1932 | J. E. Lloyd | M. Babington Smith | J. Winder |
| 1933 | J. E. Lloyd | H. D. H. Bartlett | A. D. Pearce |
| 1934 | H. D. H. Bartlett | G. V. Hett | B. P. Cazaly |
| 1935 | H. D. H. Bartlett | A. D. Pearce | J. Winder |
| 1936 | C. R. Hammersley | A. D. Pearce | G. V. Hett |
| 1937 | J. E. Lloyd | G. V. Hett | R. Tredgold |
| 1938 | J. E. Lloyd* | G. V. Hett* | A. R. Smith* |
| 1939 | H. Cooke* | P. M. Turquet* | René Paul |
| 1940-46 | No competition | | |
| 1947 | René Paul* | R. Tredgold* | H. Cooke |
| 1948 | A. R. Smith* | René Paul* | U. L. Wendon* |
| 1949 | René Paul | A. R. Smith | Raymond Paul |
| 1950 | René Paul | U. L. Wendon | P. M. Turquet |
| 1951 | H. Cooke | Raymond Paul | René Paul |
| 1952 | U. L. Wendon | Raymond Paul | H. Cooke |
| 1953 | Raymond Paul | R. Cooperman | U. L. Wendon |
| 1954 | J. Fethers | Raymond Paul | René Paul |
| 1955 | Raymond Paul | E. O. Reynolds | René Paul |
| 1956 | René Paul | Raymond Paul | A. Jay |
| 1957 | Raymond Paul | A. Jay | H. W. Hoskyns |
| 1958 | Raymond Paul | H. W. Hoskyns | A. Jay |
| 1959 | H. W. Hoskyns | Raymond Paul | René Paul |
| 1960 | D. Cawthorne* | A. Jay* | L. C. Cook* |
| 1961 | A. Leckie | René Paul | R. A. McKenzie |
| 1962 | René Paul | A. Leckie | A. R. Cooperman |
| 1963 | A. Jay | R. A. McKenzie | M. Price |
| 1964 | H. W. Hoskyns* | A. Jay* | A. Leckie* |

|      | | | | | | |
|---|---|---|---|---|---|---|
| 1965 | 1 | A. Leckie | 2 | A. Jay | 3 | P. Kirby |
|      | 4 | D. Cawthorne | 5 | R. Peters | 6 | M. Breckin |
| 1966 | 1 | G. Paul* | 2 | A. Leckie* | 3 | H. W. Hoskyns |
|      | 4 | A. Ben-Nathan | 5 | A. Jay | 6 | M. Breckin |
| 1967 | 1 | A. Leckie | 2 | A. Jay | 3 | V. Bonfil |
|      | 4 | I. Single | 5 | G. Paul | 6 | H. W. Hoskyns |
| 1968 | 1 | G. Paul | 2 | H. W. Hoskyns | 3 | N. Halsted |
|      | 4 | B. Paul | 5 | A. Jay | 6 | V. Bonfil |
| 1969 | 1 | M. Breckin | 2 | H. W. Hoskyns | 3 | B. Paul |
|      | 4 | René Paul | 5 | G. Sandor | 6 | I. Single |
| 1970 | 1 | H. W. Hoskyns* | 2 | B. Paul* | 3 | M. Breckin |
|      | 4 | B. Waddelow | 5 | G. Grimmett | 6 | D. Cawthorne |
| 1971 | 1 | G. Paul* | 2 | B. Paul* | 3 | M. Breckin |

|      |              |                                |                              |
|------|--------------|--------------------------------|------------------------------|
|      | 4 S. Wooding | 5 A. Jay                       | 6 A. Power                   |
| 1972 | 1 A. Power   | 2 G. Grimmett                  | 3 M. Breckin                 |
|      | 4 A. Jay     | 5 A. Barrs                     | 6 I. Single                  |
| 1973 | 1 G. Paul    | 2 M. Breckin                   | 3 G. Grimmett                |
|      | 4 N. Bell    | 5 R. Cohen                     | 6 A. Loveland                |
| 1974 | 1 B. Paul    | 2 E. Bourne                    | 3 G. Paul                    |
|      | 4 R. Bruniges| 5 N. Bell                      | 6 H. W. Hoskyns              |
| 1975 | 1 B. Paul    | 2 G. Paul                      | 3 A. Eames                   |
|      | 4 N. Bell    | 5 I. Single                    | 6 G. Evans                   |
| 1976 | 1 B. Paul    | 2 R. Bruniges                  | 3 G. Paul                    |
|      | 4 D. Cawthorne | 5 S. Fox, S. Glaister, G. Grimmett, N. Bell eq. |         |
| 1977 | 1 N. Bell    | 2 B. Paul                      | 3 G. Paul                    |
|      | 4 G. Evans   | 5 S. Fox                       | 6 P. Harper                  |
| 1978 | 1 P. Harper  | 2 G. R. Paul                   | 3 N. Bell                    |
|      | 4 G. Kay     | 5 R. Bruniges                  | 6 A. Bartlett                |
| 1979 | 1 B. Paul    | 2 P. Harper                    | 3 A. Bartlett                |
|      | 4 G. Paul    | 5 G. Evans                     | 6 W. Gosbee                  |
| 1980 | 1 B. Paul    | 2 P. Harper                    | 3 G. Paul                    |
|      | 4 W. Gosbee  | 5 G. Kay                       | 6 R. Bruniges                |
| 1981 | 1 R. Bruniges| 2 W. Gosbee                    | 3 P. Harper                  |
|      | 4 B. Paul    | 5–8 S. Glaister, G. Kay, G. Paul, D. Seaman |                 |

CORONATION CUP – LEON PAUL CUP (INTERNATIONAL)
Presented in 1937 to commemorate the Coronation and in memory of F. C. Reynolds by his widow. Renamed Leon Paul Cup in 1979 after theft of cup and donation of replacement by Leon Paul Ltd.

|         | 1               | 2                | 3                |
|---------|-----------------|------------------|------------------|
| 1937    | J. E. Lloyd     | R. Bondoux       | H. Cooke         |
| 1938    | F. Stark*       | H. de Besche*    | C. Whitney-Smith*|
| 1939    | T. Praem        | F. Stark         | René Paul        |
| 1940–46 | No competition  |                  |                  |
| 1947    | H. Cooke*       | A. Liedersdorff* | René Paul        |
| 1948    | A. R. Smith*    | E. B. Christie*  | U. L. Wendon     |
| 1949    | H. Cooke*       | René Paul*       | U. L. Wendon     |
| 1950    | René Paul*      | U. L. Wendon*    | P. Turquet       |
| 1951    | René Paul       | U. L. Wendon     | H. Cooke         |
| 1952    | René Paul*      | P. van Houdt*    | A. Verhalle      |
| 1953    | R. Crosnier     | René Paul        | A. Verhalle      |
| 1954    | René Paul       | A. Jay           | J. Fethers       |
| 1955    | Raymond Paul*   | J. Fethers*      | René Paul*       |
| 1956    | J-P. Bancilhon  | A. Jay           | P. Casaban       |
| 1957    | A. Jay          | René Paul        | Raymond Paul     |
| 1958    | Raymond Paul    | A. R. Cooperman  | R. A. McKenzie   |
| 1959    | H. W. Hoskyns   | A. Jay           | Raymond Paul     |
| 1960    | Raymond Paul*   | H. W. Hoskyns*   | A. Jay           |
| 1961    | L. Kamuti       | A. Jay           | J. Kamuti        |
| 1962    | A. Jay          | B. Papp          | J. Fethers       |
| 1963    | R. Parulski     | W. Woyda         | E. Franke        |
| 1964    | A. Jay          | H. W. Hoskyns    | J. Gyuricza      |

|      |                  |              |              |
|------|------------------|--------------|--------------|
| 1965 | 1 A. Jay         | 2 P. Kirby   | 3 A. Power   |
|      | 4 J. Fethers     | 5 G. Paul    | 6 N. Halsted |
| 1966 | 1 N. Granieri    | 2 A. Leckie  | 3 M. Vaselli |
|      | 4 H. W. Hoskyns  | 5 A. Jay     | 6 G. Paul    |
| 1967 | 1 M. Breckin     | 2 G. Paul    | 3 N. Halsted |

|      |                      |                  |                 |
|------|----------------------|------------------|-----------------|
|      | 4 H. W. Hoskyns      | 5 V. Bonfil      | 6 A. Jay        |
| 1968 | 1 H. Hein            | 2 W. Wolfgarten  | 3 T. Gerresheim |
|      | 4 N. Halsted         | 5 D. Cawthorne   | 6 V. Bonfil     |
| 1969 | 1 H. Hein            | 2 V. P. Bonfil   | 3 A. Jay        |
|      | 4 A. Power           | 5 G. Paul        | 6 R. G. Peters  |
| 1970 | 1 M. Breckin         | 2 G. Paul        | 3 S. Wooding    |
|      | 4 A. Power           | 5 M. Vardi       | 6 R. Cohen      |
| 1971 | 1 M. Breckin         | 2 I. Single      | 3 G. Paul       |
|      | 4 B. Paul            | 5 B. Wasley      | 6 A. Barrs      |
| 1972 | 1 M. Breckin*        | 2 G. Paul*       | 3 I. Single     |
|      | 4 R. Bruniges        | 5 A. Power       | 6 J. Nonna      |
| 1973 | 1 B. Paul            | 2 G. Grimmett    | 3 M. Breckin    |
|      | 4 I. Single          | 5 A. Bartlett    | 6 D. Cawthorne  |
| 1974 | 1 G. Paul*           | 2 R. Bruniges*   | 3 B. Paul       |
|      | 4 M. Siffels         | 5 I. Single      | 6 A. Barrs      |
| 1975 | 1 P. Pfeiffer        | 2 K. Haertter    | 3 G. Paul       |
|      | 4 H. Lossius         | 5 R. Engelbracht | 6 A. Loveland   |
| 1976 | 1 G. Paul            | 2 R. Bruniges    | 3 T. Soumagne   |
|      | 4 G. Grimmett        | 5 P. Ashley      | 6 B. Paul       |
| 1977 | 1 R. Bruniges        | 2 G. Paul        | 3 T. Soumagne   |
|      | 4 I. Single          |                  |                 |
| 1978 | 1 P. Harper          | 2 A. Eames       | 3 S. Toshiman   |
|      | 4 N. Sato            |                  |                 |
| 1979 | 1 Z. Wojciechowski   | 2 T. Soumagne    | 3 B. Paul       |
|      | 4 P. Harper          |                  |                 |
| 1980 | 1 P. Harper          | 2 R. Bruniges    | 3 N. Bell       |
|      | 4 S. Eyal            |                  |                 |
| 1981 | 1 T. Okazaki         | 2 P. Harper      | 3 R. Bruniges   |
|      | 4 S. Eyal            |                  |                 |

EMRYS LLOYD CUP

|        | 1                | 2              | 3              |
|--------|------------------|----------------|----------------|
| 1949   | R. Crosnier      | René Paul      | Raymond Paul   |
| 1950   | R. Crosnier      | U. L. Wendon   |                |
| 1951   | Raymond Paul     | René Paul      |                |
| 1952   | Raymond Paul     | J. Fethers     |                |
| 1953   | M. A. Riaz       | J. Fethers     | Raymond Paul   |
| 1954   | Raymond Paul     | W. M. Beatley  | J. Fethers     |
| 1955   | René Paul        | Raymond Paul   | J. Fethers     |
| 1956   | A. Verhalle      | A. Jay         | Raymond Paul   |
| 1957   | René Paul        | A. Jay         | H. W. Hoskyns  |
| 1958   | René Paul        | L. C. Cook     | Raymond Paul   |
| 1959   | René Paul        | H. W. Hoskyns  |                |
| 1960   | Raymond Paul     | A. Jay         | René Paul      |
| 1961   | H. W. Hoskyns    | A. Jay         | A. R. Cooperman|
| 1962   | A. R. Cooperman  | A. Leckie      | René Paul      |
| 1963   | Raymond Paul*    | H. W. Hoskyns* | A. R. Cooperman|
| 1964   | H. W. Hoskyns    | A. Power       | Raymond Paul   |
| 1965   | A. Jay*          | M. Breckin*    | A. Power       |
| 1966   |                  |                |                |
| 1967   | H. W. Hoskyns*   | S. Higginson*  | A. Jay         |
| 1968   | H. W. Hoskyns    | V. Bonfil      | A. Jay         |
| 1969   | No competition   |                |                |
| 1970   | M. Breckin*      | S. Wooding*    | B. Paul        |
| 1971–3 | No competition   |                |                |

|      | 1 | 2 | 3 |
|---|---|---|---|
| 1974 | G. Paul | G. Grimmett | I. Hodges |
| 1975 | N. Bell | E. Bourne | G. Paul |
| 1976 | A. Eames | R. Bruniges | B. Paul |
| 1977 | A. Bartlett | A. Eames | P. Harper |
| 1978 | P. Harper | Z. Wojciechowski | |
| 1979 | Z. Wojciechowski | P. Harper | R. Bruniges |
| 1980 | Z. Wojciechowski | P. Harper | S. Glaister |
| 1980 | R. Bruniges* | D. McKenzie* | J. Lawrence |

JUNIOR AMATEUR CHAMPIONSHIP – Doyne Memorial Cup
Silver cup presented in 1921 by Oxford FC in memory of R. W. Doyne to be contested by British foilists who had not fenced in the final of the Championship or been foil internationals. Recognised as Junior Championship in 1937. From 1977 the FIE format of direct elimination from eight was employed, as became general with national events.

|      | 1 | 2 | 3 |
|---|---|---|---|
| 1922 | J. A. Franklin | T. E. Ryves | R. S. S. Meade, J. Perowne eq. |
| 1923 | R. S. S. Meade | F. G. Davis | A. D. Pearce |
| 1924 | C. Hammersley | S. Bousfield, F. Chalmers, J. Ditmas eq. | |
| 1925 | S. R. Bousfield | R. Crosnier | F. C. Chalmers |
| 1926 | J. E. Lloyd | Sub Lt Cowin | I. Campbell-Gray |
| 1927 | J. Winder | C. A. Simey | C. B. Notley |
| 1928 | H. R. Foss* | M. King-Hamilton* | G. V. Hett |
| 1929 | B. P. Cazaly* | R. C. Dicker* | O. G. Trinder |
| 1930 | C. Wellington | G. S. Cormack | C. R. Scott |
| 1931 | R. Alibert* | H. Bartlett* | G. S. Cormack |
| 1932 | H. Bartlett | F. S. Hoppé | R. Alibert |
| 1933 | A. G. Pilbrow* | L. Mowlam | F. S. Hoppé |
| 1934 | D. M. Paterson | C. A. Whitney-Smith | L. Mowlam |
| 1935 | P. Turquet* | A. R. Smith* | E. S. Boniface* |
| 1936 | E. S. Boniface* | René Paul* | A. R. Smith |
| 1937 | C. Whitney-Smith | R. Marriott | R. Balkwill |
| 1938 | René Paul | A. Pienne | T. W. Bradley |
| 1939–45 | No competition | | |
| 1946 | C. Trumper | P. C. Dix | Raymond Paul |
| 1947 | No competition | | |
| 1948 | D. A. Hopkin | U. L. Wendon | P. G. Williams |
| 1949 | C. Grose-Hodge* | Raymond Paul* | F. G. Rentoul* |
| 1950 | R. Cooperman | A. Goldstein | R. W. Fearnhead |
| 1951 | M. Amberg | E. O. Reynolds | R. W. Fearnhead |
| 1952 | H. W. Hoskyns* | A. J. Cotton* | A. Jay |
| 1953 | E. O. Reynolds* | N. E. Neter* | B. J. Whitehead |
| 1954 | C. Fisher* | P. C. Amberg* | P. Greenhalgh* |
| 1955 | J. A. G. MacGibbon | D. Cawthorne | A. Goldstein |
| 1956 | D. Cawthorne | C. Tienth | T. G. Cross |
| 1957 | B. W. Howes | C. Tienth | R. A. McKenzie |
| 1958 | M. Price* | R. McNeil* | J. J. Evans |
| 1959 | G. Leckie | G. T. Birks | M. O'D. Alexander |
| 1960 | M. O'D. Alexander | P. A. Redhead | G. B. Wilson |
| 1961 | P. A. Redhead | V. C. Cawthorne | P. J. Hobson |
| 1962 | S. Higginson | K. Staines | P. T. Finn |
| 1963 | N. Halsted | G. L. Wiles | A. Howell |
| 1964 | K. Pearson | M. J. Breckin | G. L. Wiles |

| | | | | | |
|---|---|---|---|---|---|
| 1965 | 1 D. Eden | 2 B. Paul | 3 M. Breckin |
| | 4 R. G. Peters | 5 R. D. Pederson | 6 A. Power |
| 1966 | 1 V. Bonfil | 2 I. Single | 3 G. Wiles |
| | 4 P. D. Russell | 5 E. A. Ben-Nathan | 6 R. Richardson |
| 1967 | 1 C. F. Green* | 2 S. Wooding* | 3 I. Single |
| | 4 R. J. Hamments | 5 G. Wiles | 6 W. R. Johnson |
| 1968 | 1 B. Paul | 2 G. Wiles | 3 E. O. Bourne |
| | 4 T. Burch | 5 R. Cohen | 6 W. R. Johnson |
| 1969 | 1 G. L. Wiles | 2 E. Bourne | 3 D. Scott |
| | 4 S. Routh-Jones | 5 A. Loveland | 6 R. Cohen |
| 1970 | 1 M. Fare | 2 B. Waddelow | 3 S. Wooding |
| | 4 S. Routh-Jones | 5 L. Edmunds | 6 G. Elder |
| 1971 | 1 W. R. Johnson | 2 T. Barrs | 3 E. O. Bourne |
| | 4 A. Loveland | 5 B. Wasley | 6 L. Edmonds |
| 1972 | 1 J. Grimmett* | 2 A. Loveland* | 3 J. Philbin |
| | 4 M. Beevers | 5 C. Waldman | 6 R. J. Hamments |
| 1973 | 1 N. Bell | 2 M. Beevers | 3 S. Fox |
| | 4 A. Loveland | 5 R. J. Hamments | 6 J. Higgins |
| 1974 | 1 P. Wedge | 2 G. Evans | 3 D. Harris |
| | 4 S. Fox | 5 R. J. Hamments | 6 I. Hodges |
| 1975 | 1 S. Glaister | 2 G. Evans | 3 J. Ford |
| | 4 F. Hindle | 5 I. Hodges | 6 P. Harper |
| 1976 | 1 P. Harper | 2 J. Tyson | 3 S. Fox |
| | 4 F. Hindle | 5 M. Thompson | 6 C. Waldman |
| 1977 | 1 J. Lawrence | 2 M. Thompson | 3 G. Guenigault |
| | 4 W. Gosbee | 5 G. Thompson | 6 J. Tyson |
| 1978 | 1 A. Martin | 2 C. Ward | 3 M. Thompson |
| | 4 M. Thornton | 5 J. Hamments | 6 J. Woods |
| 1979 | 1 J. Ford | 2 J. Troiano | 3 W. Hudson |
| | 4 M. Evans | 5 D. Cocker | 6 J. Bourne |
| 1980 | 1 J. Tyson | 2 G. Scott | 3 R. Pearson |
| | 4 M. Evans | 5 M. Rance | 6 T. Smith |
| 1981 | 1 R. Pearson | 2 R. Sage | 3 A. Garrington |
| | 4 J. Pitman | 5 J. Bourne | 6 D. Hiam |

NOVICES COMPETITION

Three fencers are promoted to a final series from competitions in each Section

| | 1 | 2 | 3 |
|---|---|---|---|
| 1951 | W. C. Burgess | R. Mattocks | D. Wiggins |
| 1952 | A. M. Smith | T. A. Bentley | D. Cawthorne |
| 1953 | L. C. Cook | L. Jones | T. G. Cross |
| 1954 | F. H. Hope | D. Cawthorne | B. C. Mortimer |
| 1955 | G. Rider | A. Ovington | F. Tanner |
| 1956 | V. C. Cawthorne* | G. T. Birks* | K. Paddle |
| 1957 | A. Cheyney | E. R. Bayley | W. H. M. Bradley |
| 1958 | R. Willslade | E. Goodall | J. Payne |
| 1959 | | | |
| 1960 | | | |
| 1961 | A. J. Berry | M. C. Priestley | J. Bishop |
| 1962 | F. Hindle | A. G. Power | R. Reynolds |
| 1963 | B. W. Krimke | B. Grimmett | J. Drayton |
| 1964 | L. Eden | R. Humphreys | F. M. T. Eveleigh |
| 1965 | D. Acfield | R. Cohen | R. P. Berry |
| 1966 | J. Robinson | | |
| 1967 | L. Wall | | |
| 1968 | S. Routh-Jones | | |
| 1969 | J. Philbin | R. Whittle | R. Ogley |

|  | 1 | 2 | 3 |
|---|---|---|---|
| 1970 | M. West | | |
| 1971 | A. Eames | C. Clark | I. Hodges |
| 1972 | M. Thompson | L. Taylor | J. Kojder |
| 1973 | C. Francis* | N. Thorn* | V. Giaroli |
| 1974 | G. Kay | | |
| 1975 | G. Quincey | | |
| 1976 | D. Barnes | D. Brooks | S. Winrow-Campbell |
| 1977 | H. Bailey | | |
| 1978 | R. Swinnerton | A. Garrington | E. Lee |
| 1979 | P. Davies | D. Eames | D. Stevenson |
| 1980 | B. Rooney | P. Lowen | A. Pollard |

UNDER-TWENTY CHAMPIONSHIP – 'WANDSWORTH BOROUGH NEWS' CUP†

| 1964 | 1 M. Breckin | 2 D. M. Eden | 3 R. Reynolds |
|---|---|---|---|
| | 4 D. Wherrett | | |
| 1965 | 1 A. Power | 2 M. Breckin | 3 B. Paul |
| Jan. | 4 D. Acfield | 5 B. Waddelow | 6 V. Bonfil |
| 1965 | 1 M. Breckin* | 2 G. R. Paul* | 3 V. Bonfil |
| Dec. | 4 I. Single | 5 E. Ben Nathan | 6 D. Such |
| 1966 | 1 G. R. Paul | 2 R. A. Cohen | 3 B. Paul |
| | 4 D. Acfield | 5 I. Single | 6 G. Clark |
| 1967 | 1 W. R. Johnson | 2 B. Paul | 3 M. West |
| | 4 E. Bourne | 5 E. Olympitis | 6 S. Frith |
| 1968 | 1 N. Bell* | 2 J. Noel* | 3 T. Etherton |
| | 4 S. Routh-Jones | 5 J. Deanfield | 6 S. Frith |
| 1969 | 1 G. Grimmett | 2 J. Stanbury | 3 C. Ackle |
| | 4 J. Deanfield | 5 J. Hall | 6 P. Michaeledes |
| 1970 | 1 C. Waldman | 2 R. Bruniges | 3 C. Ackle |
| | 4 J. Stanbury | 5 T. Wishart | 6 G. Brown |
| 1971 | 1 M. Knell* | 2 R. Bruniges* | 3 G. Thompson |
| | 4 D. Wade | 5 P. Murray | 6 I. Campbell |
| 1972 | 1 A. Eames | 2 R. Bruniges | 3 I. Campbell |
| | 4 M. Knell | 5 P. Wedge | 6 A. Bartlett |
| 1973 | 1 P. Wedge* | 2 J. Ford* | 3 A. Bartlett |
| | 4 M. Thompson | 5 G. Evans | 6 G. Thompson |
| 1974 | 1 P. Wedge* | 2 T. Beattie* | 3 M. Chetwood* |
| | 4 S. Glaister | 5 P. Harper | 6 M. Reynolds |
| 1975 | 1 S. Glaister | 2 R. Bruniges | 3 P. Harper |
| | 4 D. Patterson | 5 T. Smith | 6 J. Ford |
| 1976 | 1 P. Harper* | 2 A. Martin* | 3 M. Peat* |
| | 4 D. Seaman* | 5 J. Ford | 6 M. Evans |
| 1977 | 1 W. Gosbee | 2 D. Seaman | 3 J. Troiano |
| | 4 G. Jones | 5 M. Visholm | 6 D. McKenzie |
| 1978 | 1 W. Gosbee | 2 J. Troiano | 3 D. McKenzie |
| | 4 G. Gajadharsingh | 5 P. Mitchell | 6 G. Tait |
| 1979 | 1 W. Gosbee | 2 C. Ward | 3 D. McKenzie |
| | 4 J. Davis | 5 J. Pitman | 6 M. Wright |
| 1980 | 1 W. Gosbee* | 2 S. Stoodley* | 3 G. Gajadharsingh |
| | 4 J. Pitman | 5 D. Dale | 6 M. Rance |

MILLFIELD INTERNATIONAL UNDER-TWENTY COMPETITION†

|  | 1 | 2 | 3 |
|---|---|---|---|
| 1967 | A. Loveland | S. Frith | M. Allen |
| 1968 | S. Routh-Jones | M. Allen | P. Blake |

|      | 1            | 2            | 3             |
|------|--------------|--------------|---------------|
| 1969 | B. Boscherie | J. Vatter    | T. Bach       |
| 1970 | B. Boscherie | J. Dutripon  | T. Bach       |
| 1971 | T. Bach      | R. Bruniges  | M. Behr       |
| 1972 | R. Bruniges  | T. Bach      | P. Gaille     |
| 1973 | R. Bruniges  | P. Gaille    | M. Stemmerick |
| 1974 | R. Bruniges* | M. Siffels*  | W. Tonges     |
| 1975 | A. Robak     | R. Bruniges  | M. Siffels    |
| 1976 | W. Tonges    | P. Harper    | G. Guthauser  |
| 1977 | D. Seaman    | W. Gosbee    | M. Driessen   |
| 1978 | W. Gosbee    | O. Fischer   | M. Wright     |
| 1979 | W. Gosbee    | D. McKenzie  | O. Valentin   |
| 1980 | A. Caflisch  | W. Gosbee    | T. Keller     |

SCHOOLBOYS' CHAMPIONSHIP – NATIONAL AGE GROUP CHAMPIONSHIPS (from 1976)
Contested between finalists from each Section

|      | Senior          | Junior        |           |
|------|-----------------|---------------|-----------|
| 1961 | I. A. Hill      | D. Wherrett   |           |
| 1962 | C. A. Layton    | L. Eden       |           |
| 1963 | L. Eden         | B. Paul       |           |
| 1964 | B. Waddelow     | D. Cull       |           |
| 1965 | L. Eden         | M. Atkinson   |           |
| 1966 | J. R. Crouch    | M. J. West    |           |
| 1967 | K. M. Wilson    | J. Hallifax   |           |
| 1968 | S. Routh-Jones  | S. Price      |           |
| 1969 | D. Hill         | G. Brown      |           |
| 1970 | C. Brown        | R. Bruniges   |           |
| 1971 | A. Eames        | R. Bruniges   |           |
| 1972 | G. Evans        | G. Llewellyn  |           |
| 1973 | D. Maynard      | J. Cooper     |           |
|      | Under-19        | Under-16      | Under-14  |
| 1974 | S. Glaister     | N. Anderson   | K. Li     |
| 1975 | E. M. R. Reynolds | M. Visholm  | W. Gosbee |
|      | Under-18        | Under-16      | Under-14  |
| 1976 | R. Hill         | A. Thompson   | L. Skelton |
| 1977 | D. McKenzie     | J. Browne     | P. Mitchell |
| 1978 | J. Woods        | R. Wheeler    | J. Pitman |
| 1979 | L. O'Shea       | S. Pearce     | J. Pitman |
| 1980 | S. Stoodley     | J. Pitman     | S. Adeyinko |
| 1981 | S. Stoodley     | J. Pitman     | P. Kay    |

AMATEUR TEAM CHAMPIONSHIP – 'SPORTING RECORD' CUP†
Presented by the directors of the *Sporting Record*

|      |      | 1          | 2                        |
|------|------|------------|--------------------------|
| 1948 | Mar. | S. Paul    | London FC (10–6)         |
|      | Nov. | London FC  | S. Paul (8–8, 63–65 hits) |
| 1949 |      | S. Paul    | Polytechnic FC (9–4)     |
| 1950 |      | London FC  | Bertrand's FC (9–6)      |
| 1951 |      | S. Paul    | London FC (9–6)          |
| 1952 |      | S. Paul    | London FC (9–3)          |
| 1953 |      | S. Paul    | London FC (9–2)          |
| 1954 |      | S. Paul    | London FC (9–4)          |
| 1955 |      | S. Paul    | London FC (9–4)          |
| 1956 |      | S. Paul    | London FC (9–2)          |

|  | 1 | 2 |
|---|---|---|
| 1957 | S. Paul | London FC (8–8, 63–64 hits) |
| 1958 | S. Paul | Polytechnic FC |
| 1959 | Polytechnic FC | S. Nicklen |
| 1960 | S. Paul | Polytechnic FC (9–2) |
| 1961 | S. Paul | Polytechnic FC (9–5) |
| 1962 | Polytechnic FC | Thames FC (8–8, 3 hits) |
| 1963 | S. Paul | London FC (9–4) |
| 1964 | S. Paul | London FC |
| 1965 | S. Paul | London FC (9–1) |
| 1966 | London Univ. | S. Paul (8–8, 59–61 hits) |
| 1967 | London Univ. | S. Paul (9–6) |
| 1968 | London Univ. | S. Paul (9–3) |
| 1969 | S. Paul | S. Boston (9–1) |
| 1970 | S. Paul | Thames FC (9–4) |
| 1971 | S. Paul | Thames FC (9–4) |
| 1972 | S. Paul | S. Boston (9–3) |
| 1973 Dec. | Thames FC | S. Paul (9–6) |
| 1975 Jan. | S. Paul | Thames FC (9–4) |
| 1976 Jun. | S. Paul | Thames FC (9–4) |
| Dec. | S. Boston | S. Paul (9–4) |
| 1977 | S. Boston | Hydra Under-20 (9–5) |
| 1978 | S. Paul | S. Boston (9–2) |
| 1979 | S. Paul | S. Boston (8–8, 10 hits) |
| 1980 | S. Boston | S. Paul (8–6) |

## *LADIES' FOIL (HEADQUARTERS EVENTS)*

### THE AMATEUR CHAMPIONSHIP

In 1931 a silver cup was presented by Mrs J. L. Spong, President of the LAFU, who, as Miss Millicent Hall, was the original Champion.

|  | 1 | 2 | 3 |
|---|---|---|---|
| 1907 | M. Hall | D. Milman | Mrs Edwardes |
| 1908 | M. Hall | F. E. Carter, Mrs Edwardes, J. Johnstone eq. |  |
| 1909 | C. E. Martin Edmunds* | J. Johnstone* | M. Hall, A. B. Walker |
| 1910 | J. Johnstone | G. Daniell, F. E. Carter eq. |  |
| 1911 | G. Daniell | J. Johnstone | Mrs Edwardes, A. B. Walker |
| 1912 | G. Daniell* | C. A. Walker* | A. B. Walker* |
| 1913 | A. B. Walker | C. A. Walker | Mrs Martin Edmunds |
| 1914 | A. B. Walker* | C. A. Walker* | D. Cheetham |
| 1915-19 | No competition |  |  |
| 1920 | C. A. Walker | G. Daniell | A. B. Walker |
| 1921 | G. Daniell* | M. Hall* | G. M. Davis, J. Johnstone eq. |
| 1922 | M. Hall* | G. M. Davis* | J. Johnstone |
| 1923 | G. M. Davis | G. Daniell | J. Johnstone |
| 1924 | G. Daniell | Mrs M. Freeman | O. B. Pearce |
| 1925 | G. M. Davis | Mrs M. Freeman | F. Bibby |
| 1926 | G. M. Davis | G. Daniell | Mrs M. Freeman |
| 1927 | Mrs M. Freeman | G. Daniell | M. M. Butler, G. M. Davis eq. |
| 1928 | M. M. Butler* | Mrs M. Freeman* | G. Daniell |
| 1929 | Mrs M. Freeman* | W. Davis* | Mrs G. Minton |
| 1930 | M. M. Butler | G. Daniell | E. C. Arbuthnott |

|      | 1 | 2 | 3 |
|------|---|---|---|
| 1931 | M. M. Butler* | G. Neligan* | E. C. Arbuthnott |
| 1932 | M. M. Butler* | J. Guinness* | G. Neligan* |
| 1933 | J. Guinness* | E. C. Arbuthnott* | G. Neligan* |
| 1934 | G. Neligan* | J. Guinness* | M. M. Butler |
| 1935 | G. Neligan* | J. Guinness* | M. M. Butler |
| 1936 | G. Neligan | Mrs Penn Hughes | E. C. Arbuthnott |
| 1937 | G. Neligan | Mrs G. Minton | Mrs K. Bartlett |
| 1938 | Mrs Penn-Hughes | P. Etheridge | B. Puddefoot |
| 1939 | E. C. Arbuthnott | P. Etheridge | B. Puddefoot |
| 1940–46 | No competition | | |
| 1947 | E. C. Arbuthnott | L. M. Boyd | Mrs M. Glen Haig |
| 1948 | Mrs Glen Haig | E. C. Arbuthnott | Mrs G. Minton |
| 1949 | G. Sheen | E. C. Arbuthnott | M. Somerville |
| 1950 | Mrs M. Glen Haig | E. C. Arbuthnott | G. Sheen |
| 1951 | G. Sheen | Mrs M. Glen Haig | P. Buller |
| 1952 | G. Sheen | Mrs M. Glen Haig | C. Drew |
| 1953 | G. Sheen | Mrs M. Glen Haig | B. M. Screech |
| 1954 | G. Sheen | Mrs M. Glen Haig | J. Witchell |
| 1955 | G. Sheen* | Mrs M. Glen Haig* | B. M. Screech |
| 1956 | G. Sheen* | Mrs M. Glen Haig* | Mrs P. Ashmore |
| 1957 | G. Sheen | E. Berry | M. Durne |
| 1958 | G. Sheen | E. Berry | Mrs M. Glen Haig |
| 1959 | M. Stafford | Mrs M. Glen Haig | J. Bailey |
| 1960 | G. Sheen | Mrs M. Glen Haig | M. Stafford |
| 1961 | T. M. Offredy | J. Pearce | S. Netherway |
| 1962 | T. M. Offredy* | J. Bewley-Cathie* | Mrs Courtney-Lewis* |
| 1963 | M. A. Pritchard | J. Bewley-Cathie | J. Bailey |
| 1964 | S. Netherway | J. Bewley-Cathie | R. Rayner |
| 1965 | 1 J. Bewley-Cathie | 2 S. Netherway | 3 J. M. Davis |
|      | 4 M. Durne | 5 T. M. Offredy | 6 Mrs E. Davies |
| 1966 | 1 Mrs S. Parker | 2 J. Bewley-Cathie | 3 J. M. Davis |
|      | 4 J. Herriot | 5 M. Paul | 6 J. Pearce |
| 1967 | 1 Mrs Wardell-Yerburgh | 2 J. Herriot | 3 M. Holmes |
|      | 4 M. Durne | 5 J. M. Davis | 6 C. Henley |
| 1968 | 1 S. Green | 2 Mrs Bain | 3 J. M. Davis |
|      | 4 C. Henley | 5 J. Bailey | 6 M. Holmes |
| 1969 | 1 Mrs Wardell-Yerburgh | 2 M. Holmes | 3 Mrs Barkley |
|      | 4 J. Bailey | 5 M. Durne | 6 S. Youngs |
| 1970 | 1 Mrs Wardell-Yerburgh | 2 Mrs Rogerson | 3 K. Storry |
|      | 4 C. Henley | 5 H. Twomey | 6 M. Holmes |
| 1971 | 1 Mrs Wardell-Yerburgh | 2 B. Williams | 3 C. Henley |
|      | 4 S. Green | 5 J. Yates | 6 S. Wrigglesworth |
| 1972 | 1 Mrs Wardell-Yerburgh | 2 C. Henley, S. Wrigglesworth eq. | |
|      | 4 Mrs Davenport | 5 S. Green | 6 J. Bullmore |
| 1973 | 1 Mrs C. Halsted | 2 W. Ager | 3 S. Green |
|      | 4 S. Wrigglesworth | 5 Mrs A. Bowen | 6 S. Olley |
| 1974 | 1 W. Ager* | 2 S. Wrigglesworth* | 3 Mrs C. Halsted |
|      | 4 S. Green | 5 Mrs Hurford | 6 S. Rochard |
| 1975 | 1 S. Wrigglesworth | 2 H. Cawthorne | 3 S. Green |
|      | 4 Mrs S. Lewis | 5 L. Martin | 6 V. Windram |
| 1976 | 1 L. Martin* | 2 E. Wood* | 3 Mrs C. Halsted |
|      | 4 W. Ager | 5 H. Cawthorne | 6 S. Wrigglesworth |
| 1977 | 1 H. Cawthorne | 2 S. Wrigglesworth | 3 Mrs W. Grant |
|      | 4 L. Martin | 5 A. Brannon | 6 E. Wood |
| 1978 | 1 E. Wood | 2 Mrs W. Grant | 3 A. Brannon |
|      | 4 H. Cawthorne | 5 S. Wrigglesworth | 6 B. Hewitt |

| | | | |
|---|---|---|---|
| 1979 | 1 E. Wood | 2 H. Cawthorne | 3 L. Martin |
| | 4 A. Brannon | 5 S. Wrigglesworth | 6 G. Wood |
| 1980 | 1 Mrs W. Grant | 2 Mrs E. Thurley | 3 S. Wrigglesworth |
| | 4 H. Cawthorne | 5 L. Martin | 6 S. Hoad |
| 1981 | 1 Mrs E. Thurley | 2 S. Wrigglesworth | 3 L. Martin |
| | 4 C. Montgomery | 5–8 H. Cawthorne, S. Hoad, P. Johnson, L. Calver | |

ALFRED HUTTON MEMORIAL CUP – C-L. DE BEAUMONT CUP (INTERNATIONAL)
The Hutton Cup, lost during the Second World War, was replaced in 1947 by C-L. de Beaumont.

| | 1 | 2 | 3 |
|---|---|---|---|
| 1913 | A. B. Walker* | J. Colmer* | D. Cheetham |
| 1914–19 | No competition | | |
| 1920 | J. Johnstone | M. Hall | J. Colmer |
| 1921 | G. Daniell | S. Williams | G. M. Davis |
| 1922 | G. M. Davis | M. Smalley | S. Hurter |
| 1923 | G. M. Davis | G. Daniell | Frere |
| 1924 | Mrs M. Freeman | G. M. Davis | W. Davis |
| 1925 | G. Daniell | G. M. Davis | van Holhema |
| 1926 | G. Daniell | G. M. Davis | Mrs M. Freeman |
| 1927 | H. Mayer | Mrs M. Freeman | J. Addams |
| 1928 | Mrs M. Holst | M. M. Butler | O. Pearce |
| 1929 | M. M. Butler | G. Neligan | M. A. B. Venables |
| 1930 | H. Mayer* | M. M. Butler* | G. Daniell |
| 1931 | M. M. Butler | H. Mayer | G. Neligan |
| 1932 | G. Neligan | J. Guinness | Mrs G. Minton |
| 1933 | J. Guinness | G. Neligan | Mrs G. Olsen |
| 1934 | G. Neligan* | J. Guinness* | Mrs K. Lachmann |
| 1935 | E. Preiss* | J. Addams | Mrs K. Lachmann |
| 1936 | J. Addams | Mrs K. Lachmann | Mrs C. Penn-Hughes |
| 1937 | Mrs G. Olsen* | Mrs K. Lachmann* | J. Addams* |
| 1938 | J. Addams | E. C. Arbuthnott | Mrs G. Olsen |
| 1939–46 | No competition | | |
| 1947 | Mrs K. Lachmann* | Mrs G. Olsen* | E. Arbuthnott |
| 1948 | Mrs K. Lachmann | Mrs K. Mahaut | Mrs G. Olsen |
| 1949 | Mrs K. Lachmann | G. Sheen | Mrs M. Glen Haig |
| 1950 | G. Sheen | L. Guyonneau | Mrs M. Glen Haig |
| 1951 | Mrs K. Lachmann | Mrs M. Glen Haig | G. Sheen |
| 1952 | Mrs K. Lachmann | G. Sheen | P. Buller |
| 1953 | Mrs M. Glen Haig | G. Sheen | E. Williams |
| 1954 | G. Sheen | Mrs M. Glen Haig | I. Meyer |
| 1955 | Mrs K. Lachmann | G. M. Sheen | Mrs M. Glen Haig |
| 1956 | Mrs M. Glen Haig | G. Sheen | M. Stafford |
| 1957 | G. Sheen | M. Stafford | Mrs M. Glen Haig |
| 1958 | I. Keydel | Mrs M. Glen Haig | G. Sheen |
| 1959 | G. Sheen | N. Kleyweg | M. Stafford |
| 1960 | G. Sheen | M. Stafford | S. Netherway |
| 1961 | S. Netherway | C. Wallet | R. Noels |
| 1962 | G. Sheen | R. Noels | S. Netherway |
| 1963 | E. Botbijl | B. Gapais | Mrs Kokkes |
| 1964 | K. Juhasz-Nagy | L. Domolki-Sakovits | I. Rejto-Ujlaky |
| 1965 | 1 B. Gapais | 2 Mrs P. Marosi | 3 J. Mendelenyi-Agoston |
| | 4 C. Duront | 5 L. Domolki-Sakovits | 6 I. Rejto-Ujlaky |
| 1966 | 1 G. Masciotta | 2 H. Mees | 3 B. Gapais |

| | | | |
|---|---|---|---|
| 1967 | 4 Mrs Wardell-Yerburgh<br>1 Mrs Wardell-Yerburgh<br>4 J. Beauchamp | 5 C. Flesch<br>2 J. Herriot<br>5 M. Hoyau | 6 Mrs S. Parker<br>3 C. Herbster<br>6 G. van Oosten |
| 1968 | 1 I. Rejto-Ujlaky<br>4 Mrs Wardell-Yerburgh | 2 H. Mees<br>5 H. Bobis | 3 H. Schmid<br>6 L. Domolki-Sakovits |
| 1969 | 1 B. Giesselmann<br>4 G. Lotter | 2 Y. Thiry<br>5 B. Oertel | 3 K. Giesselmann<br>6 C. Olhoft |
| 1970 | 1 C. Lecomte<br>4 Mrs J. Bain | 2 Mrs Wardell-Yerburgh<br>5 C. Nicolet | 3 C. Henley<br>6 M. Pulch |
| 1971 | 1 Mrs Wardell-Yerburgh<br>4 S. Littlejohns | 2 C. Muzio<br>5 G. McDermit | 3 M. Hoyau<br>6 M. Holmes |
| 1972 | 1 Mrs Wardell Yerburgh<br>4 S. Wrigglesworth | 2 S. Littlejohns<br>5 C. Hall | 3 S. Green<br>6 Mrs Rogerson |
| 1973 | 1 S. Green<br>4 Mrs Halsted | 2 S. Littlejohns<br>5 H. Cawthorne | 3. W. Ager<br>6 S. Wrigglesworth |
| 1974 | 1 S. Green<br>4 Mrs Urbanska | 2 C. Hanisch<br>5 Mrs Single | 3 Mrs Krzykalska<br>5 S. Rochard |
| 1975 | 1 A. Max Madsen<br>4 M. Dick | 2 U. Eltz<br>5 S. Green | 3 Mrs Skladanowska<br>6 Mrs C. Halsted |
| 1976 | 1 G. Weniger<br>4 Mrs C. Halsted | 2 Mrs Palm<br>5 A. Max Madsen | 3 M. Dick<br>6 I. Gosch |
| 1977 | 1 T. Wolthuis<br>4 Mrs W. Grant | 2. J. Appert<br>5 D. Skapska | 3 H. Cawthorne<br>6 L. Martin |
| 1978 | 1 S. Wrigglesworth<br>4 B. Schubert | 2 G. Janke<br>5 L. Martin | 3 C. Hanisch<br>6 M. Schulze |
| 1979 | 1 L. Martin<br>4 S. Wrigglesworth | 2 F. Helbling<br>5 M. Starzinski | 3 J. Leenders<br>6 M. Rensink |
| 1980 | 1 J. Leenders<br>4 L. Mondaine | 2 A. Brannon, F. Bougnol eq. | |
| 1981 | 1 L. Martin<br>4 S. Wrigglesworth | 2 L. M. le Blanc<br>5–8 A. Meyer, N. Pallet, K. Cecil, M. Rensink | 3 A. Max Madsen |

INVITATION COMPETITION – THE SILVER JUBILEE BOWL
Presented by Mrs Henry Guinness to commemorate George V's Jubilee

| | 1 | 2 | 3 |
|---|---|---|---|
| 1935 | E. C. Arbuthnott | M. M. Butler | J. Guinness |
| 1936 | Mrs C. Penn-Hughes | E. C. Arbuthnott | M. Geddes |
| 1937 | Mrs G. Minton | E. C. Arbuthnott | M. L. Moore |
| 1938 | E. C. Arbuthnott* | Mrs G. Minton* | B. M. Puddefoot |
| 1939 | E. C. Arbuthnott | L. Teasdale | M. L. Moore |
| 1940–50 | No competition | | |
| 1951 | Mrs M. Glen Haig | E. C. Arbuthnott | G. Sheen |
| 1952 | Mrs M. Glen Haig | P. M. Buller | E. Williams |
| 1953 | G. Sheen | J. Witchell (direct elimination) | |
| 1954 | Mrs M. Glen Haig | G. M. Sheen | M. Somerville |
| 1955 | G. Sheen | Mrs M. Glen Haig | M. Stafford |
| 1956 | G. Sheen | Mrs M. Glen Haig | M. Stafford |
| 1957 | No competition | | |
| 1958 | G. Sheen | Mrs M. Glen Haig | M. Stafford |
| 1959 | G. Sheen* | Mrs E. Davies* | M. Durne* |
| 1960 | S. Netherway* | Mrs M. Glen Haig* | M. Durne* |
| 1961 | M. Kovacs-Nyari* | S. Netherway* | J. Mendelenyi-Agoston |
| 1962 | S. Netherway | T. M. Offredy | G. Sheen |

|  | 1 | 2 | 3 |
|---|---|---|---|
| 1963 | J. Bailey | M. Durne | Mrs E. Davies |
| 1964 | J. Bewley-Cathie | M. Durne | J. Bailey |
| 1965 | J. Bewley-Cathie | Mrs E. Davies | J. L. M. Pearce |
| 1966 | Mrs Wardell-Yerburgh | M. Durne | Mrs S. Parker |
| 1967 | Mrs Wardell-Yerburgh* | M. Durne* | A. Savva |
| 1968 | Mrs J. Bain* | Mrs Wardell-Yerburgh* | J. M. Davis* |
| 1969 | S. Green* | P. Patient* | H. Twomey |
| 1970 | Mrs Wardell-Yerburgh | Mrs Davenport | S. Green |
| 1971 | Mrs Wardell-Yerburgh | S. Green | S. Littlejohns |
| 1972 | Mrs Wardell-Yerburgh* | S. Littlejohns* | S. Green |
| 1973 | S. Wrigglesworth* | S. Green* | S. Littlejohns* |
| 1974 | S. Wrigglesworth* | W. Ager* | L. Martin |
| 1975 | S. Green* | C. Henley* | H. Cawthorne |
| 1976 | W. Ager* | L. Martin* | S. Wrigglesworth |
| 1977 | L. Martin | Mrs W. Grant | S. Wrigglesworth |
| 1978 | S. Hoad | C. Montgomery | A. Brannon |
| 1979 | L. Martin | E. Wood | A. Brannon |
| 1980 | Mrs W. Grant* | F. McIntosh* | S. Wrigglesworth |
| 1981 | No competition | | |

THE DESPREZ CUP
Presented by Ernest Desprez. Held in 1925 as the Bristol or West of England Championship, in 1926 at Bedells Dancing Academy, London, and later at London FC. Transferred to LAFU in 1945.

|  | 1 | 2 | 3 |
|---|---|---|---|
| 1925 | G. M. Davis | | |
| 1926 | G. Daniell | | |
| 1927 | G. Daniell | | |
| 1928 | M. M. Butler | | |
| 1929 | M. M. Butler | | |
| 1930 | M. A. Venables | | |
| 1931 | G. Neligan | | |
| 1932 | J. Guinness | G. Neligan | |
| 1933 | J. Guinness | M. A. Venables | |
| 1934 | B. Harris* | M. Geddes* | |
| 1935 | E. C. Arbuthnott | P. Etheridge | K. Stanbury |
| 1936 | E. C. Arbuthnott | P. Etheridge | Mrs G. Minton |
| 1937 | P. Etheridge | E. C. Arbuthnott | Mrs K. Bartlett |
| 1938 | Mrs G. Minton | M. L. Moore | P. Etheridge |
| 1939 | P. Etheridge | E. C. Arbuthnott | B. M. Puddefoot |
| 1940–45 | No competition | | |
| 1946 | Mrs M. Glen Haig | G. Sheen | S. Fleming |
| 1947 | Mrs M. Glen Haig | J. Majendie | D. L. Breese |
| 1948 | No competition | | |
| 1949 | Mrs M. Glen Haig | G. Sheen | E. Williams |
| 1950 | G. Sheen | S. Fleming | P. Buller |
| 1951 | G. Sheen | P. Buller | C. Drew |
| 1952 | Mrs M. Glen Haig | G. Sheen | |
| 1953 | G. Sheen | Mrs J. Pienne | M. Somerville |
| 1954 | G. Sheen | J. Witchell | E. Berry |
| 1955 | E. Berry* | M. Stafford* | M. Hart |
| 1956 | G. Sheen | M. Stafford | B. M. Screech |
| 1957 | M. Stafford* | E. Berry* | S. Netherway |
| 1958 | E. Berry | J. Bailey | S. Netherway |
| 1959 | M. Stafford* | J. Bailey* | E. Berry |

|   | 1 | 2 | 3 |
|---|---|---|---|
| 1960 | S. Netherway | M. Durne | Mrs V. Jones |
| 1961 | M. Durne | T. M. Offredy | P. Patient |
| 1962 | M. A. Pritchard | T. M. Offredy | J. Read |
| 1963 | M. A. Pritchard | J. Bewley Cathie | Mrs S. Fisher |
| 1964 | J. Bewley Cathie | J. Bailey | Mrs M. A. Watts-Tobin |
| 1965 | J. Bewley Cathie | J. Pearce | Mrs S. Parker |
| 1966 | J. Bewley Cathie | J. Pearce | Mrs S. Parker |
| 1967 | Mrs Wardell-Yerburgh* | M. Holmes* | J. Dorling |
| 1968 | Mrs J. Bain* | Mrs Beauchamp* | C. Henley |
| 1969 Jan. | Mrs Wardell-Yerburgh* | J. Bailey* | M. Holmes |
| 1969 Nov. | S. Green | M. Durne | J. Bailey |
| 1970 | S. Littlejohns | C. Henley | S. Green |
| 1971 | No competition | | |
| 1972 | Mrs Wardell-Yerburgh* | C. Henley* | W. Ager |
| 1973 | S. Green* | H. Cawthorne* | S. Wrigglesworth |
| 1974 | S. Wrigglesworth* | W. Ager* | S. Green |
| 1975 | S. Green | Mrs C. Halsted | H. Cawthorne |
| 1976 | S. Wrigglesworth | H. Cawthorne | W. Ager |
| 1977 | H. Cawthorne | Mrs W. Grant | S. Wrigglesworth |
| 1978 | L. Martin | Mrs W. Grant | H. Cawthorne |
| 1979 | A. Brannon | E. Wood | G. Wood |
| 1980 | L. Martin | K. Cecil | Mrs W. Grant |
| 1981 | L. Martin | K. Cecil | P. Johnson |

BAPTISTE BERTRAND MEMORIAL CUP
Presented by Alexander Miller-Hallett in memory of Prof. Bertrand and open to British ladies who were not internationals and who had not fenced in the final of the Championship or Hutton Cup. Recognised in 1938 as Junior Championship. In 1967 confined to fencers in Categories 'B' and 'C'.

|   | 1 | 2 | 3 |
|---|---|---|---|
| 1928 | G. Neligan | M. Venables | E. Braine |
| 1929 | B. Puddefoot | M. Venables | G. G. Redwood |
| 1930 | M. Venables | J. Guinness | B. Solly |
| 1931 | E. Braine | M. Angus | P. Etheridge |
| 1932 | M. Geddes | M. Angus | P. Etheridge |
| 1933 | I. Weekes | P. Etheridge | K. Stanbury |
| 1934 | No competition | | |
| 1935 | P. Etheridge | M. Angus, N. Muspratt eq. | |
| 1936 | Mrs Godfrey Adams | P. Godsell | M. Angus |
| 1937 | M. Angus | M. James | N. Morris |
| 1938 | M. Anderson | L. Teasdale | D. L. Breese |
| 1939–45 | No competition | | |
| 1946 | Mrs M. Glen Haig | M. Somerville | J. Majendie |
| 1947 | G. Sheen | M. Somerville | C. Drew |
| 1948 | P. Buller | C. Drew | E. Parkinson |
| 1949 | P. Sitwell | C. Drew | Mrs E. Copping |
| 1950 | J. Witchell | Mrs P. Taylor | Mrs J. Hutton |
| 1951 | J. Maskell | A. Harding | M. Evans, Mrs J. Thomas eq. |
| 1952 | E. Berry | G. B. Harvey | M. Stafford |
| 1953 | G. B. Harvey | Mrs J. Pengelly | A. Harding |
| 1954 | C. Rayner | P. Webber | Mrs A. Barton |
| 1955 | J. Bailey | Mrs A. Barton | M. Durne |

|   | 1 | 2 | 3 |
|---|---|---|---|
| 1956 | Mrs V. Jones | S. Netherway* | M. Durne |
| 1957 | M. Hunt* | H. Vickerage* | J. Cathie, |
|  |  |  | J. Read eq. |
| 1958 | S. Preston* | T. M. Offredy* | B. McCreath |
| 1959 | M. Brown | Mrs A. Barton | Mrs M. Hawksworth |
| 1960 | J. Read* | Mrs F. Simmonds* | G. Elliott* |
| 1961 | M. A. Pritchard* | A. Farndon* | R. Rayner* |
| 1962 | R. Rayner* | Mrs J. Mulshaw* | M. Paul* |
| 1963 | Mrs S. Fisher | J. M. Davis | Mrs M. Hawksworth |
| 1964 | Mrs G. Harding | A. Julian | Mrs M. Hawdon |
| 1965 | 1 A. Julian | 2 S. Brick | 3 L. Cuppage |
|  | 4 J. Herriot | 5 Mrs S. Ward | 6 Mrs M. Hawdon |
| 1966 | 1 J. Dorling | 2 C. Henley | 3 Mrs S. Ward |
|  | 4 V. Lengyel-Reinfuss | 5 Mrs H. Rogerson | 6 E. Earle |
| 1967 | 1 A. Savva | 2 S. Toller | 3 J. Yates |
|  | 4 J. Varley | 5 S. Littlejohns | 6 S. Green |
| 1968 | 1 S. Littlejohns | 2 Mrs L. Hamments | 3 D. Knowles |
|  | 4 K. Storry | 5 J. Bullmore | 6 Mrs Hawksworth |
| 1969 | 1 Mrs Rogerson | 2 B. Williams | 3 H. Towmey |
|  | 4 C. Wotherspoon | 5 Mrs I. Foulkes | 6 Mrs J. Dudley |
| 1970 | 1 B. Goodall* | 2 S. Wrigglesworth* | 3 J. Young* |
|  | 4 J. Swanson* | 5 C. Whitehurst | 6 S. Toller |
| 1971 | No competition (date altered from Nov. to Mar.) |  |  |
| 1972 | 1 W. Ager | 2 C. Hall | 3 J. Bullmore |
|  | 4 P. Patient | 5 V. Windram | 6 Mrs H. Whitcher |
| 1973 | 1 C. Whitehurst | 2 Mrs I. Foulkes | 3 C. Arup |
|  | 4 G. Ritchie | 5 L. Taylor | 6 Y. Grammer |
| 1974 | 1 Mrs Davenport | 2 Mrs Single | 3 L. Taylor |
|  | 4 S. Rochard | 5 J. Popland | 6 L. Andrews |
| 1975 | 1 A. Herbert* | 2 A. Brannon* | 3 J. Jones |
|  | 4 C. Oliver | 5 C. Holland | 6 S. Toller |
| 1976 | 1 B. Hewitt* | 2 L. Andrews* | 3 S. Harris |
|  | 4 Mrs P. Casey | 5 J. Law | 6 M. Riley |
| 1977 | 1 Mrs J. Law | 2 S. Hoad | 3 Mrs S. Lewis |
|  | 4 A. Fraser-Smith | 5 Mrs M. Hillier | 6 C. Arup |
| 1978 | 1 J. Erwteman | 2 F. McIntosh | 3 J. Jones |
|  | 4 M. Lloyd | 5 P. Johnson | 6 Mrs Pontefract |
| 1979 | 1 B. Hewitt | 2 Mrs Single | 3 J. Erwteman |
|  | 4 P. Johnson | 5 L. Calver | 6 L. Prys-Roberts |
| 1980 | 1 D. Hall | 2 H. Jones | 3 K. Arup |
|  | 4 C. Robertson | 5 B. Hewitt | 6 Mrs P. Casey |

PARKER TROPHY†
Presented by Mrs Shirley Parker

|   | 1 | 2 | 3 |
|---|---|---|---|
| 1968 | H. Gardner | Mrs M. Hawksworth | P. Robinson |
| 1969 | Mrs E. Cook | L. Brown | A. Milner-Barry |
| 1970 | C. Whitehurst | E. Simpson | S. Littlejohns |
| 1971 | J. Jones | Mrs A. Parker | L. Brown |
| 1972 | L. Bleasdale | C. Whitehurst | S. O'Connell |
| 1973 | Mrs H. Davenport* | L. Andrews* | C. Ord* |
| 1974 | B. Hewitt | P. Patient | A. Brannon |
| 1975 | Mrs L. Hamments | S. Holman | M. Bragg |

|      | 1              | 2              | 3                |
| ---- | -------------- | -------------- | ---------------- |
| 1976 | K. Cecil*      | Mrs P. Tovey*  | A. Charles*      |
| 1977 | J. Jones       | P. Johnson     | Mrs O. Pontefract |
| 1978 | G. Wood        | C. Fray        | S. Benney        |
| 1979 | D. Hall        | F. Wilson      | S. Kellett       |
| 1980 | E. Whitfield   | Mrs J. Garside | N. Walker        |

TOUPIE LOWTHER CUP†

|      | 1               | 2               | 3               |
| ---- | --------------- | --------------- | --------------- |
| 1968 | Mrs J. Tyson    | M. Hawksworth   | Mrs R. Castle   |
| 1969 | Mrs H. Rogerson | O. Drummond     | Mrs R. Castle   |
| 1970 | J. Young        | J. Plowright    | Mrs M. Davis    |
| 1971 | J. Court        | Mrs D. Robinson | M. Riley        |
| 1972 | L. Bleasdale    | Mrs Isherwood   | I. Marshall     |
| 1973 | M. Worster      | M. Browning     | S. Grieve       |
| 1974 | A. Brannon      | A. Herbert      | Y. Grammar      |
| 1975 | A. Tetlow       | S. Bailey       | S. Gallagher    |
| 1976 | P. Bell*        | H. Griffiths*   | P. Johnson      |
| 1977 | J. Millott      | J. Hall         | D. Freeman      |
| 1978 | P. Monk         | S. Dudley       | Mrs F. Mitchell |
| 1979 | J. Whitney      | J. Roberts      | C. Peppercorn   |
| 1980 | J. Thornton     | P. Hunt         | J. Montgomery   |

JUNIOR INVITATION COMPETITION – FELIX CUP
Presented by Gwendoline Neligan and named after her masters, Felix Bertrand and Felix Gravé.

|         | 1                   | 2                  | 3                |
| ------- | ------------------- | ------------------ | ---------------- |
| 1939    | L. Teasdale         |                    |                  |
| 1940–52 | No competition      |                    |                  |
| 1953    | Mrs V. Jones        | H. Boswell         | A. Moller        |
| 1954    | J. Bailey           | Mrs V. Jones       | Mrs A. Barton    |
| 1955    | Mrs Page            | J. Fitzmaurice     | M. Waters        |
| 1956    | Mrs P. Courtney-Lewis | B. Wyatt         | J. Manders       |
| 1957    | J. Cook             | Mrs Sellick        | T. M. Offredy    |
| 1958    | Mrs V. Ellis        | P. Patient         | M. Brown         |
| 1959    | J. Read             | Mrs V. Jones       | C. J. Tolland    |
| 1960    | G. Mallard          | P. Darnley         | J. Leckie        |
| 1961    | M. A. Pritchard     | R. Rayner          | Mrs J. Cartwright |
| 1962    | Mrs J. Mulshaw      | R. Rayner          | S. Pilot         |
| 1963    | E. M. Jones         | K. Howkins         | Mrs S. Fisher    |
| 1964    | S. Ward*            | M. Cobb*           | M. Paul          |
| 1965    | Mrs G. Harding      | G. Mallard         | L. Brown         |
| 1966    | M. Holmes           | J. Herriot         | G. Netherwood    |
| 1967    | J. Varley           | V. Lengyel-Rheinfuss | Mrs G. Harding |
| 1968    | H. Twomey           | Mrs G. Harding     | J. Bullmore      |
| 1969    | S. Olley            | C. Bailey          | L. Wheeler       |
| 1970    | S. Blanchard*       | S. McTurk*         | E. Simpson       |
| 1971    | S. Wrigglesworth*   | L. Andrews*        | J. Hurst*        |
| 1972    | S. Wrigglesworth    | C. Hall            | J. Jones         |
| 1973    | L. Martin           | S. Rochard         | V. Windram       |
| 1974    | B. Hewitt           | A. Tulloch         | K. Keuls         |
| 1975    | No competition      |                    |                  |
| 1976    | A. Brannon          | F. McIntosh        | A. Charles       |
| 1977    | C. Fray             | A. Charles         | J. Verne         |
| 1978    | K. Cecil            | C. Gobey           | J. Verne         |
| 1979    | J. Thornton         | A. Gobey           | M. Gobey         |

|   | 1 | 2 | 3 |
|---|---|---|---|
| 1980 | K. Cecil* | C. Gobey* | K. Arup |
| 1981 | K. Arup | P. Whitehead | K. Woodhouse |

UNDER-TWENTY CHAMPIONSHIP – SILVO TROPHY
Until 1960 an open competition for girls aged under twenty-one

|   | 1 | 2 | 3 |
|---|---|---|---|
| 1956 | M. Waters | S. Netherway | J. Breese |
| 1957 | M. Waters | J. Breese | S. Netherway |
| 1958 | J. Bewley-Cathie | S. Netherway | J. King |
| 1959 | M. Brown | J. Bewley-Cathie | B. McCreath |
| 1960 | G. Mallard | P. Chapman | P. M. Birt |
| 1961 | P. M. Birt | M. Cobb | A. B. Wilson |
| 1962 | G. Mallard | A. B. Wilson | P. Richter |
| 1963 | G. Mallard | J. Mullinger | J. Dorling |
| 1964 | 1 L. Brown | 2 L. Concannon | 3 C. Lucas |
|  | 4 F. Davison | 5 M. Holmes | 6 P. Roberts |
| 1965 | 1 M. Holmes* | 2 S. Brick* | 3 F. Davison |
|  | 2 E. Earle | 5 F. Reynolds | 6 S. O'Connell |
| 1966 | 1 A. Savva* | 2 M. Holmes* | 3 C. Henley |
|  | 4 F. Reynolds | 5 F. Davison | 6 G. Netherwood |
| 1967 | 1 M. Holmes | 2 C. Henley | 3 A. Hill |
|  | 4 A. Herbert | 5 J. Yates | 6 G. Netherwood |
| 1968 | 1 S. Green | 2 S. Littlejohns | 3 M. Holmes |
|  | 4 C. Henley | 5 J. Yates | 6 S. Youngs |
| 1969 | 1 H. Twomey | 2 S. Olley | 3 J. Yates |
|  | 4 M. Holmes | 5 S. Youngs | 6 S. Green |
| 1970 | 1 S. Green | 2 J. Raine | 3 J. Yates |
|  | 4 S. Wrigglesworth | 3 C. Whitehurst | 6 C. Bailey |
| 1971 | 1 S. Wrigglesworth* | 2 L. Andrews* | 3 J. Raine* |
|  | 4 E. Simpson | 5 S. Blanchard | 6 J. Yates |
| 1972 | 1 C. Hall | 2 W. Ager | 3 S. Wrigglesworth |
|  | 4 L. Andrews | 5 L. O'Keefe | 6 V. Windram |
| 1973 | 1 C. Hall* | 2 W. Ager* | 3 J. Popland |
|  | 4 A. Tulloch | 5 J. Jones | 6 S. Mitton |
| 1974 | 1 S. Wrigglesworth | 2 S. Rochard | 3 A. Tulloch |
|  | 4 L. Martin | 5 B. East | 6 C. Hall |
| 1975 | 1 E. Wood* | 2 J. Jones* | 3 D. Devlin |
|  | 4 A. Tulloch | 5 B. Hewitt | 6 L. Taylor |
| 1976 | 1 J. Jones | 2 B. Hewitt | 3 E. Wood |
|  | 4 A. Brannon | 5 M. Dignan | 6 K. Keuls |
| 1977 | 1 E. Wood | 2 B. Hewitt | 3 F. McIntosh |
|  | 4 A. Brannon | 5 K. Cecil | 6 D. Hall |
| 1978 | 1 C. Montgomery | 2 A. Brannon | 3 F. McIntosh |
|  | 4 C. Gobey | 5 S. Gallagher | 6 E. Wood |
| 1979 | 1 E. Wood | 2 C. Gobey | 3 P. Johnson |
|  | 4 H. Jones | 5 C. Fray | 6 F. Wilson |
| 1980 | 1 P. Johnson | 2 C. Gobey | 3 F. McIntosh |
|  | 4 K. Arup | 5 F. Wilson | 6 M. Rose |
| 1981 | 1 K. Arup | 2 C. Gobey | 3 K. Cecil |
|  | 4 P. Whitehead | 5–8 S. Kellett, L. Strachan, N. Jacobsen, M. Roberts | |

UNDER-20 INTERNATIONAL COMPETITION – SYBIL PERIGAL CUP †

|   | 1 | 2 | 3 |
|---|---|---|---|
| 1965 | C. Duront | J. Knapp | I. Bock |
| 1966 | M. Holmes | M. Pulch | K. Giesselmann |

|      | 1              | 2              | 3              |
| ---- | -------------- | -------------- | -------------- |
| 1967 | C. Muzio       | B. Barraud     | M. Holmes      |
| 1968 | M. Hoyau       | B. Giesselmann | R. Armbrust    |
| 1969 | M. P. van Eyck | S. Picard      | A. Eckert      |
| 1970 | E. Villing     | J. Yates       | J. Deakin      |
| 1971 | S. Wrigglesworth* | W. Ager*    | J. Hurst       |
| 1972 | S. Wrigglesworth | A. Tulloch   | J. Jones       |
| 1973 | S. Wrigglesworth | C. Hall      | J. Jones       |
| 1974 | E. Wood        | C. Hall        | J. Jones       |
| 1975 | N. Drori       | B. Hewitt      | A. Tulloch     |
| 1976 | A. Brannon     | F. McIntosh    | C. Montgomery  |
| 1977 | E. Wood        | K. Cecil       | F. McIntosh    |
| 1978 | F. McIntosh    | F. Stamanne    | K. Arup        |
| 1979 | E. Schaffner   | B. Besser      | F. McIntosh    |
| 1980 | I. Nussbaum    | C. Gobey       | U. Weder       |

MILLFIELD INTERNATIONAL UNDER-TWENTY COMPETITION

|      | 1               | 2            | 3           |
| ---- | --------------- | ------------ | ----------- |
| 1973 | S. Wrigglesworth | U. Kircheis | B. Oertel   |
| 1974 | E. Villing      | I. Hoffbauer | F. Helbing  |
| 1975 | B. Hewitt       | A. Astalosch | C. Beagrie  |
| 1976 | I. Losert       | D. Viret     | A. Brannon  |
| 1977 | F. Stammane     | I. Losert    | J. Leenders |

From October 1978 the Cup was awarded to winners of an international 3-a-side team competition.

|      |                   |              |                      |
| ---- | ----------------- | ------------ | -------------------- |
| 1978 | Belgium           | Great Britain | Salle Boston        |
| 1979 | W. Germany        | France       | England, Scotland eq. |
| 1980 | Great Britain 'A' | Switzerland  | Great Britain 'C'    |

SCHOOLGIRLS' CHAMPIONSHIP

| 1937    | K. Begg        | 1947 | C. Drew         |
| ------- | -------------- | ---- | --------------- |
| 1938    | J. Majendie    | 1948 | C. Drew         |
| 1939-44 | No competition | 1949 | A. G. M. Harding |
| 1945    | G. Sheen       | 1950 | H. Hoos         |
| 1946    | No competition | 1951 | C. Hoare        |

|      | Seniors (16–18) | Juniors (Under-16) |
| ---- | --------------- | ------------------ |
| 1952 | A. Moller       | S. Simpson         |
| 1953 | E. M. Grant     | S. Simpson         |
| 1954 | S. Simpson      | M. Waters          |
| 1955 | J. Fitzmaurice  | J. Cathie          |
| 1956 | M. Waters       | J. Cathie          |
| 1957 | J. Cathie       | C. Dunn            |
| 1958 | M. Edwards      | B. Davies          |
| 1959 | J. Davis        | G. Mallard         |
| 1960 | A. Wilson       | L. Brown           |
| 1961 | G. Mallard      | A. Dent            |
| 1962 | G. Mallard      | F. Reynolds        |
| 1963 | L. Concannon    | F. Davison         |
| 1964 | F. Davison      | M. Holmes          |
| 1965 | M. Holmes       | M. Holmes          |
| 1966 | A. Savva        | A. Hill            |
| 1967 | S. Green        | A. Hill            |
| 1968 | A. Hill         | C. Bailey          |
| 1969 | R. Staples      | J. Deakin          |

|  | 1 | 2 |  |
|---|---|---|---|
| 1970 | E. Simpson | S. Blanchard |  |
| 1971 | S. Wrigglesworth | J. Jones |  |
| 1972 | S. Rochard | A. Tulloch |  |
| 1973 | S. Rochard | J. Popland |  |
|  | *Under-19* | *Under-16* | *Under-14* |
| 1974 | A. Simpson | E. Wood | J. Hurst |
| 1975 | J. Jones | F. McIntosh | S. Arup |
|  | *Under-18* | *Under-16* | *Under-14* |
| 1976 | D. Hall | F. McIntosh | L. Dale |
| 1977 | F. McIntosh | K. Cecil | K. Arup |
| 1978 | J. Verne | K. Arup | P. Whitehead |
| 1979 | K. Cecil | P. Whitehead | M. Gobey |
| 1980 | S. Kellett | P. Whitehead | L. Matthews |
| 1981 | P. Whitehead | M. Gobey | C. Brown |

AMATEUR TEAM CHAMPIONSHIP – MARTIN EDMUNDS CUP†
Presented by Mrs Martin Edmunds

| 1909 | Bertrand's Academy | 1924 | Stempel's Sch. of Arms |
| 1910 | Bertrand's Academy | 1925 | Stempel's Sch. of Arms |
| 1911 | Bertrand's Academy | 1926 | Stempel's Sch. of Arms |
| 1912 | Tassart's Sch. of Arms | 1927 | Grave's Academy |
| 1913 | Bertrand's Academy | 1928 | Bertrand's Academy |
| 1914–21 | No competition | 1929 | Bertrand's Academy |
| 1922 | – Feb. Ladies' C. d'Escr. | 1930 | Bertrand's Academy |
|  | – Nov. Ladies' C. d'Escr. | 1931 | Bertrand's Academy |
| 1923 | Ladies' Cercle d'Escrime |  |  |

|  | 1 | 2 |
|---|---|---|
| 1932 | Tassart-Parkins Fencing Sch. | Bertrand's Academy |
| 1933 | Bertrand's Academy | Tassart-Parkins F. Sch. |
| 1934 | Gauthier's Penguins | Bertrand's Academy |
| 1935 | Bertrand's Academy | Gauthier's Penguins |
| 1936 | Bertrand's Academy | Gauthier's Penguins |
| 1937 | Gauthier's Penguins | Bertrand's Academy |
| 1938 | Gauthier's Penguins | Bertrand's Academy |
| 1939–45 | No competition |  |
| 1946 | Ladies' C. d'Escr. | Poly. Ladies' FC (9–7) |
| 1947 | Poly. Ladies' FC | London FC (9–7) |
| 1948 | Ladies' C. d'Escr. | London FC (9–7) |
| 1949 | London FC | Bertrand's FC (11–5) |
| 1950 | Poly. Ladies' FC | Lansdowne (9–7) |
| 1951 | London FC | Bertrand's FC (9–7) |
| 1952 | Poly. Ladies' FC | Bertrand's FC (10–6) |
| 1953 | London FC | Pauleons Ladies' FC (10–6) |
| 1954 | London FC | Pauleons Ladies' FC (13–3) |
| 1955 | London FC | Poly. Ladies' FC (13–3) |
| 1956 | London FC | Poly. Ladies' FC (9–3) |
| 1957 | London FC | Poly. Ladies' FC (9–4) |
| 1958 | London FC | Poly. Ladies' FC (9–7) |
| 1959 | London FC | Poly. Ladies' FC (9–5) |
| 1960 | Poly. Ladies' FC | London FC (9–6) |
| 1961 | London FC | Poly. Ladies' FC (9–4) |
| 1962 | London FC | Poly. Ladies' FC (9–6) |
| 1963 | Poly. Ladies' FC | London FC (9–7) |
| 1964 | Poly. Ladies' FC | London FC (9–3) |

|      | 1 | 2 |
|------|---|---|
| 1965 | Thames FC | Pauleons Ladies' FC (9–5) |
| 1966 | Poly. Ladies' FC | Pauleons Ladies' FC (8–8, 42–50 hits) |
| 1967 | Poly. Ladies' FC | Pauleons Ladies' FC (9–5) |
| 1968 | No competition as date changed from Autumn to Spring | |
| 1969 | Poly. Ladies' FC | S. Pearson (9–5) |
| 1970 | Ashton FC | Thames FC (9–7) |
| 1971 | London FC | Ashton FC (9–6) |
| 1972 | London FC | S. Boston (11–5) |
| 1973 | Ashton FC | London FC (9–4) |
| 1974 | Thames FC | S. Boston (8–8, 46–39 hits) |
| 1975 | London FC | S. Paul (9–7) |
| 1976 | Poly. FC | S. Paul (9–7) |
| 1977 | S. Paul | London-Thames FC (9–4) |
| 1979 | Poly. FC | S. Paul (8–7, 44–53 hits) |
| 1980 | S. Paul | S. Boston (9–6) |
| 1981 | S. Paul | S. Boston (9–1) |

## EPEE (HEADQUARTERS EVENTS)

THE AMATEUR CHAMPIONSHIP

Until 1908 the British fencer placed highest in the Epee Club's International Competition was regarded as national Champion. Bouts were for one hit until 1932, for the best of three hits until 1956 and thereafter for the best of nine hits. The 'Les Armes de France Challenge Shield' was presented by the Marquis de Chasseloup Laubat, Georges Berger, Georges Breittmeyer and Jean Stern.

|      | 1 | 2 | 3 |
|------|---|---|---|
| 1904 | E. Seligman | | |
| 1905 | R. Montgomerie | | |
| 1906 | E. Seligman | | |
| 1907 | R. Montgomerie | | |
| 1908 | C. L. Daniell | M. D. V. Holt | R. Montgomerie |
| 1909 | R. Montgomerie | C. L. Daniell | A. G. Everitt, S. Martineau eq. |
| 1910 | E. M. Amphlett | S. Martineau, E. Seligman eq. | |
| 1911 | J. P. Blake | L. V. Fildes, R. Montgomerie eq. | |
| 1912 | R. Montgomerie | S. Beale, W. Conduit, R. Leverson eq. | |
| 1913 | G. Vereker | L. V. Fildes | G. Ames, C. de Goldschmidt, M. Holt eq. |
| 1914 | R. Montgomerie | G. Cornet | A. G. Everitt |
| 1915–19 | No competition | | |
| 1920 | M. Holt | J. P. Blake | C. B. Notley |
| 1921 | H. Huntington | H. E. Blaiberg, J. P. Blake, R. Frater, C. B. Notley eq. | |
| 1922 | G. Burt | J. P. Blake, R. Frater, M. Holt, F. Sherriff eq. | |
| 1923 | M. Holt | G. Burt, C. Drake, C. B. Notley eq. | |
| 1924 | C. Biscoe | M. Holt | I. Campbell-Gray, C. B. Notley eq. |
| 1925 | C. B. Notley | C. Biscoe | T. Beddard, H. Blaiberg, G. Burt, A. Pelling eq. |

|  | 1 | 2 | 3 |
|---|---|---|---|
| 1926 | I. Campbell-Gray | R. E. Cole | L. V. Fildes, C. B. Notley, A. Whitehouse, R. Willoughby eq. |
| 1927 | C. B. Notley* | B. Childs* | D. D. Drury |
| 1928 | B. Childs* | A. E. Pelling* | C. C. A. Monro |
| 1929 | L. V. Fildes | I. Campbell-Gray, D. Dexter, C. Monro eq. | |
| 1930 | I. Campbell-Gray | J. B. Armstrong | B. Childs |
| 1931 | B. Childs | O. Mosley, C. B. Notley eq. | |
| 1932 | I. Campbell-Gray | C. B. Notley | O. Mosley |
| 1933 | A. Pelling* | D. Dexter* | L. V. Fildes |
| 1934 | A. Pelling | J. C. Bampfylde | D. Dexter |
| 1935 | I. Campbell-Gray | B. Childs | C-L. de Beaumont |
| 1936 | C-L. de Beaumont | T. Beddard | A. Pelling |
| 1937 | C-L. de Beaumont | B. Childs | A. Pienne |
| 1938 | C. L. de Beaumont* | René Paul* | A. Pelling |
| 1939 | T. Beddard* | M. D. McCready* | R. C. Winton |
| 1940–46 | No competition | | |
| 1947 | P. C. Dix | C-L. de Beaumont | René Paul |
| 1948 | R. Parfitt* | U. L. Windon* | C-L. de Beaumont* |
| 1949 | P. C. Dix | René Paul | C. Grose-Hodge |
| 1950 | R. Parfitt | René Paul | A. J. Payne |
| 1951 | A. Pelling | R. Parfitt | A. G. Signy |
| 1952 | A. Jay | R. Parfitt | R. A. Harrison |
| 1953 | C-L. de Beaumont* | E. B. Knott* | A. L. N. Jay |
| 1954 | P. Greenhalgh | A. Jay | R. Sproul-Bolton |
| 1955 | R. A. Harrison | A. Jay | J. A. Pelling |
| 1956 | H. W. Hoskyns | A. Jay | R. Sproul-Bolton |
| 1957 | H. W. Hoskyns* | A. Jay* | M. Howard |
| 1958 | H. W. Hoskyns | A. Jay | J. Pelling |
| 1959 | A. Jay | J. Pelling | H. W. Hoskyns |
| 1960 | A. Jay | M. Howard | I. Spofforth |
| 1961 | J. Pelling | R. A. Mackenzie | P. Jacobs |
| 1962 | P. Jacobs* | M. Howard* | J. Pelling |
| 1963 | J. Glasswell | P. Jacobs | J. Pelling |
| 1964 | P. Jacobs* | H. W. Hoskyns* | J. Pelling |
| 1965 | 1 J. Pelling | 2 E. Bourne | 3 N. Halsted |
|  | 4 P. Jacobs | 5 J. Shaw | 6 S. Higginson |
| 1966 | 1 E. Bourne | 2 G. Paul | 3 C. Purchase |
|  | 4 H. W. Hoskyns | 5 J. Pelling | 6 M. Howard |
| 1967 | 1 H. W. Hoskyns | 2 E. Bourne | 3 G. Paul |
|  | 4 S. Higginson | 5 N. Halsted | 6 P. Jacobs |
| 1968 | 1 W. R. Johnson | 2 H. W. Hoskyns | 3 J. Fox |
|  | 4 E. Bourne | 5 N. Halsted | 6 J. Pelling |
| 1969 | 1 G. Paul | 2 W. R. Johnson | 3 E. Bourne |
|  | 4 J. Noel | 5 C. Green | 6 J. Darby |
| 1970 | 1 P. Jacobs | 2 G. Paul | 3 H. W. Hoskyns |
|  | 4 W. R. Johnson | 5 E. Bourne | 6 J. Fox |
| 1971 | 1 G. Paul* | 2 E. Bourne* | 3 P. Jacobs |
|  | 4 W. R. Johnson | 5 R. Davenport | 6 E. Hudson |
| 1972 | 1 E. Bourne* | 2 H. W. Hoskyns* | 3 R. Davenport |
|  | 4 W. R. Johnson | 5 N. Halsted | 6 E. Hudson |
| 1973 | 1 E. P. K. Hudson | 2 E. Bourne | 3 W. R. Johnson |
|  | 4 H. W. Hoskyns | 5 D. Partridge | 6 R. Bruniges |
| 1974 | 1 E. Bourne | 2 E. Hudson | 3 R. Bruniges |
|  | 4 M. Murch | 5 H. W. Hoskyns | 6 G. Paul |

|      | 1              | 2                | 3                |
|------|----------------|------------------|------------------|
| 1975 | 1 T. Belson    | 2 H. W. Hoskyns  | 3 E. Bourne      |
|      | 4 M. Beevers   | 5 W. Osbaldeston | 6 R. Evans       |
| 1976 | 1 E. Bourne    | 2 M. Beevers     | 3 J. Noel        |
|      | 4 W. R. Johnson | 5 G. R. Paul    | 6 B. Hill        |
| 1977 | 1 E. Bourne    | 2 J. Llewellyn   | 3 T. Belson      |
|      | 4 H. West      | 5 W. R. Johnson  | 6 R. Davenport   |
| 1978 | 1 E. Bourne*   | 2 W. R. Johnson* | 3 T. Belson      |
|      | 4 G. Paul      | 5 N. Bell        | 6 S. Roose       |
| 1979 | 1 T. Belson    | 2 N. Mallett     | 3 R. Davenport   |
|      | 4 S. Roose     | 5 J. Tyson       | 6 S. Lavington   |
| 1980 | 1 S. Paul      | 2 E. Bourne      | 3 W. R. Johnson  |
|      | 4 T. Belson    | 5 S. Roose       | 6 J. Stanbury    |
| 1981 | 1 J. Llewellyn | 2 T. Belson      | 3 W. R. Johnson  |
|      | 4 N. Mallett   | 5–8 S. Paul, R. Davenport, G. Liston, D. Cocker | |

MILLER-HALLETT CUP (INTERNATIONAL)
Presented by Alexander Miller-Hallett

|         | 1                        | 2                    | 3                  |
|---------|--------------------------|----------------------|--------------------|
| 1928    | V. Clayton Morris*       | B. Cederin*          | K. Ennell*         |
| 1929    | L. V. Fildes             | C-L. de Beaumont     | I. Campbell-Gray   |
| 1930    | C-L. de Beaumont         | T. Praem             | L. V. Fildes       |
| 1931    | C-L. de Beaumont         | V. Clayton Morris    | E. Clausetti       |
| 1932    | C-L. de Beaumont         | T. Praem             | J. Mirabaud        |
| 1933    | T. E. Beddard            | A. Pelling           | C-L. de Beaumont   |
| 1934    | C-L. de Beaumont         | O. G. Trinder        | C. B. Notley       |
| 1935    | C-L. de Beaumont         | D. Dexter            | V. Clayton Morris  |
| 1936    | F. Soille                | C-L. de Beaumont     | T. Beddard         |
| 1937    | E. S. Bruneau            | H. Cooke             | S. Lerdon          |
| 1938    | C-L. de Beaumont         | A. Pienne            | René Paul          |
| 1939–46 | No competition           |                      |                    |
| 1947    | T. Beddard               | J. Reed              | F. Fattori         |
| 1948    | Dr M. D. McCready*       | D. Dagallier*        | Dr R. Parfitt      |
| 1949    | P. C. Dix*               | R. E. Amstad*        | Raymond Paul*      |
| 1950    | C. Grose-Hodge           | O. Zappelli          | J. von Kos         |
| 1951    | René Paul*               | E. B. Knott*         | J. C. Ellis        |
| 1952    | C. Nigon                 | A. Jay               | C-L. de Beaumont   |
| 1953    | A. Jay*                  | A. J. Cotton*        | Dr R. Parfitt*     |
| 1954    | H. W. Hoskyns            | P. Gnaier            | A. Jay             |
| 1955    | A. Jay                   | H. W. Hoskyns        | René Paul          |
| 1956    | A. Jay                   | H. W. Hoskyns        | I. R. Cameron      |
| 1957    | A. Jay                   | E. B. Knott          | A. Pienne          |
| 1958    | H. W. Hoskyns*           | A. Jay*              | I. R. Cameron      |
| 1959    | J. D. Simpson            | A. Jay               | H. W. Hoskyns      |
| 1960    | P. Jacobs*               | E. B. Knott*         | S. Higginson*      |
| 1961    | P. Jacobs                | J. Pelling           | J. Glasswell       |
| 1962    | No competition because date altered from Autumn to Spring |  |  |
| 1963    | S. Higginson             | P. Jacobs            | M. O'D. Alexander  |
| 1964    | M. Howard                | J. Pelling           | N. Halsted         |
| 1965    | 1 H. Lagerwall*          | 2 N. Halsted*        | 3 P. Jacobs        |
|         | 4 R. Zampini             | 5 K. Czarnecki       | 6 R. Rhodes        |
| 1966    | 1 S. Netburn*            | 2 H. W. Hoskyns*     | 3 J. Glasswell     |
|         | 4 J. Pelling             | 5 P. Jacobs          | 6 W. R. Johnson    |
| 1967    | 1 N. Halsted             | 2 P. Jacobs          | 3 J. Pelling       |
|         | 4 H. W. Hoskyns          | 5 I. Single          | 6 I. Spofforth     |

| | | | |
|---|---|---|---|
| 1968 | 1 E. Bourne | 2 H. W. Hoskyns | 3 N. Halsted |
| | 4 S. Higginson | 5 D. Partridge | 6 P. Jacobs |
| 1969 | 1 H. W. Hoskyns | 2 P. Jacobs | 3 R. Blomquist |
| | 4 G. Ganchev | 5 D. Partridge | 6 R. Davenport |
| 1970 | 1 D. Jung | 2 J. Noel | 3 H. Kilbert |
| | 4 H. W. Hoskyns | 5 M. Geuter | 6 R. Hauk |
| 1971 | 1 J. Muller | 2 E. Bourne | 3 R. Trost |
| | 4 J. Norman | 5 N. Halsted | 6 A. Cramer |
| 1972 | 1 J. Noel | 2 E. Bourne | 3 E. Hudson |
| | 4 H. W. Hoskyns | 5 H. West | 6 W. Osbaldeston |
| 1973 | 1 W. R. Johnson | 2 T. Belson | 3 P. Jacobs |
| | 4 M. Beevers | 5 E. Hudson | 6 R. Bruniges |
| 1974 | 1 E. Bourne | 2 J. Noel | 3 K. Morch |
| | 4 R. Davenport | 5 S. Higginson | 6 S. Netburn |
| 1975 | 1 K. Mueller* | 2 E. Bourne* | 3 N. Koppang |
| | 4 H. W. Hoskyns | 5 M. Beevers | 6 E. Hudson |
| 1976 | 1 P. Riboud | 2 H. W. Hoskyns | 3 E. Bourne |
| | 4 J. Norman | 5 O. Morch | 6 K. Muller |
| 1977 | 1 E. O. Bourne* | 2 W. R. Johnson* | 3 M. Beevers |
| | 4 H. W. Hoskyns | 5 K. Pearman | 6 J. Stanbury |
| 1978 | 1 J. Llewellyn | 2 E. Bourne | 3 H. West |
| | 4 W. R. Johnson | | |
| 1979 | 1 T. Belson | 2 S. Ganeff | 3 P. Pesthy |
| | 4 N. Mallett | 5 S. Paul | 6 J. Llewellyn |
| 1980 | 1 S. Paul* | 2 T. Belson | 3 N. Koppang |
| | 4 Vonen | 5 Krogh | 6 J. Llewellyn |
| 1981 | 1 T. Belson | 2 W. R. Johnson | 3 J. Norman |
| | 4 G. Paul | 5–8 J. Llewellyn, S. Paul, T. Hagen, B. Vonen | |

MARTINI QUALIFYING COMPETITION

| | 1 | 2 | 3 |
|---|---|---|---|
| 1960 | M. O'D. Alexander | M. Vickery | P. Jolly |
| 1961 | I. Spofforth | P. Jacobs | T. Berman |
| 1962 | S. Higginson | J. Payne | N. Grose-Hodge |
| 1963 | M. O'D. Alexander | S. Higginson | J. Glasswell |
| 1964 | R. Bright | N. Halsted | G. Coombs |
| 1965 | C. Green | A. Loetscher | G. Paul |
| 1966 | S. Netburn | G. Paul | J. Glasswell |
| 1967 | N. Halsted | J. Glasswell | P. D. Russell |
| 1968 | W. R. Johnson | E. Gray, J. Fox eq. | |
| 1969 | D. Russell | R. Deighton | R. Reynolds |
| 1970 | E. Hudson | D. Partridge | K. Pearman |
| 1971 | N. Halsted | B. More | J. Stanbury |
| 1972 | D. Partridge | R. Davenport | J. Stanbury |
| 1973 | M. Beevers | D. Partridge | J. Hall |
| 1974 | K. Pearman | T. Belson | R. Davenport |
| 1975 | W. R. Johnson | M. Beevers | J. Llewellyn |
| 1976 | J. Llewellyn | J. Hall | S. Higginson |
| 1977 | R. Davenport | G. Paul | H. West |
| 1978 | S. Roose | H. West | S. Lavington |
| 1979 | J. Melville | G. R. Paul | J. Steventon |
| 1980 | J. Melville | G. Paul | H. W. Hoskyns |
| 1981 | S. Roose | G. Liston | J. Steventon |

CHALLENGE MARTINI INTERNATIONAL EPEE COMPETITION
Sponsored by Messrs Martini & Rossi Ltd. The final of eight held en gala by direct elimination.

|      | 1 | 2 | 3 equal |
|------|---|---|---------|
| 1960 | G. Delfino (It.) | V. Chernikov (USSR) | A. Jay (GB) |
|      |                  |                     | H. W. Hoskyns (GB) |
| 1961 | J. Guittet (Fr.) | V. Chernikov (USSR) | D. Dagallier (Fr.) |
|      |                  |                     | M. Dordé (Fr.) |
| 1962 | H. W. Hoskyns (GB) | G. Lefranc (Fr.) | R. Chiari (It.) |
|      |                    |                  | Y. Dreyfus (Fr.) |
| 1963 | R. Queroux (Fr.) | B. Gonsior (Pol.) | R. Chiari (It.) |
|      |                  |                   | G. Breda (It.) |
| 1964 | Z. Nemere (Hu.) | G. Delfino (It.) | B. Andrezjewski (Pol.) |
|      |                 |                  | B. Gonsior (Pol.) |
| 1965 | P. Nagy (Hu.) | A. Jay (GB) | H. Nielaba (Pol.) |
|      |               |             | T. Gabor (Hu.) |
| 1966 | D. Jung (W. Ger.) | H. Kilbert (W. Ger.) | H. Lagerwall (Swe.) |
|      |                   |                      | G. Engdahl (Swe.) |
| 1967 | G. Kulcsar (Hu.) | A. Barany (Hu.) | N. Halsted (GB) |
|      |                  |                 | S. Netburn (US) |
| 1968 | Z. Nemere (Hu.) | C. Francesconi (It.) | K. Pearman (GB) |
|      |                 |                      | U. Birnbaum (Aus.) |
| 1969 | A. Varille (Fr.) | F. Reant (Fr.) | B. Gonsior (Pol.) |
|      |                  |                | H. Nielaba (Pol.) |
| 1970 | A. Varille (Fr.) | S. Netburn (US) | H. W. Hoskyns (GB) |
|      |                  |                 | J. Melcher (US) |
| 1971 | B. Gonsior (Pol.) | B. Andrjewski (Pol.) | A. Bretholz (Swi.) |
|      |                   |                      | F. Jeanne (Fr.) |
| 1972 | O. Muck (W. Ger.) | J-C. Sennecka (Monaco) | W. R. Johnson (GB) |
|      |                   |                         | G. Muzio (It.) |
| 1973 | S. Paramanov (USSR) | B. Lukomsky (USSR) | I. Valetov (USSR) |
|      |                     |                    | D. Giger (Swi.) |
| 1974 | M. Poffet (Swi.) | P. Schmitt (Hu.) | 3rd G. Kulscar (Hu.) |
|      |                  |                  | 4th J. Janikowski (Pol.) |
| 1975 | G. Flodstrom (Swe.) | R. Edling (Swe.) | H. Jacobson (Swe.) |
|      |                     |                  | M. Wiech (Pol.) |
| 1976 | A. Pusch (W. Ger.) | D. Giger (Swi.) | P. Boisse (Fr.) |
|      |                    |                 | S. Vino (It.) |
| 1977 | C. Fenyvesi (Hu.) | C. Kauter (Swi.) | H. Behr (W. Ger.) |
|      |                   |                  | H. Jana (W. Ger.) |
| 1978 | P. Boisse (Fr.) | A. Pusch (W. Ger.) | P. Gaille (Swi.) |
|      |                 |                    | C. Kauter (Swi.) |
| 1979 | F. Suchanecki (Swi.) | O. Lenglet (Fr.) | P. Riboud (Fr.) |
|      |                      |                  | P. Boisse (Fr.) |
| 1980 | L. Petho (Hu.) | P. Picot (Fr.) | C. Bernadotte (Swe.) |
|      |                |                | V. Fischer (W. Ger.) |
| 1981 | S. Paul (GB) | J-B. Evoquoz (Swi.) | J. Llewellyn (GB) |
|      |              |                     | N. Koppang (Nor.) |

EPEE CLUB CUP†
Presented by L. V. Fildes for a professional championship. From 1953 to 1958 awarded to the winner of an amateur-professors competition, organised by the Epee Club, who thereafter sanctioned its use for a training competition for the British team from time to time, to which Section representatives have been invited each year since 1974.

| | 1 | 2 | 3 |
|---|---|---|---|
| 1953 | J. C. Ellis | A. Pelling | R. Parfitt |
| 1954 | R. A. Harrison | E. B. Knott | René Paul |
| 1955 | René Paul | R. Sproul-Bolton | A. Jay |
| 1956 | A. Jay | H. W. Hoskyns | B. W. Howes |
| 1957 | M. Howard | H. W. Hoskyns | J. Pelling |
| 1958 | H. W. Hoskyns | J. A. Parkins | R. A. Harrison |
| 1959 | A. Jay | Y. Dreyfus | M. Jeanneau |
| 1960 | A. Jay | I. R. Spofforth | M. O'D. Alexander |
| 1962 | T. Berman | S. Higginson | J. Pelling |
| 1964 | H. W. Hoskyns | P. Jacobs | A. Jay |
| 1967 | H. W. Hoskyns | P. Jacobs | N. Halsted |
| 1974 | M. Beevers | G. Paul | T. Belson |
| 1975 | E. Bourne | M. Beevers | J. Noel |
| 1976 | E. Bourne | H. W. Hoskyns | T. Belson |
| 1977 | M. Beevers | E. O. Bourne | J. Llewellyn |
| 1978 | S. Paul | E. O. Bourne | T. Belson |
| 1979 | J. Llewellyn | N. Mallett | H. W. Hoskyns |
| 1980 | J. Melville | J. Stanbury | S. Roose |

JUNIOR AMATEUR EPEE CHAMPIONSHIP – L. V. FILDES CUP†

| | 1 | 2 | 3 |
|---|---|---|---|
| 1910 | F. G. Davis | E. Biedermann, E. Schwarz eq. | |
| 1911 | D. D. Drury | G. W. Tupper | M. Tom |
| 1912 | L. de Baeza | M. Poncet | J. A. Franklin |
| 1913 | C. Biscoe | L. de Baeza | G. Burt |
| 1914–19 | No competition | | |
| 1920 | C. B. Notley* | P. d'Aury* | R. L. Brown* |
| 1921 | M. Anglade | S. C. Dickson | H. T. H. Bond |
| 1922 | L. Cox | H. S. Riant* | J. Greenwood, Jnr* |
| 1923 | I. Campbell-Gray | L. Bernacchi | A. E. Pelling |
| 1924 | B. A. Harwood | J. F. Duff | L. R. Jackson |
| 1925 | J. F. Duff | T. E. Ryves | C. C. A. Monro |
| 1926 | J. C. Ellis | B. Childs | B. A. Harwood, C. Monro eq. |
| 1927 | C. P. Collins | J. Evan James | R. M. Dowdeswell |
| 1928 | C-L. de Beaumont | C. P. Collins | F. S. Hoppé |
| 1929 | A. G. Pilbrow* | E. L. Monkhouse | F. E. Charlton |
| 1930 | B. P. Cazaly | L. A. Mowlam | W. Rippon |
| 1931 | F. Kent | O. G. Trinder | G. Salmon |
| 1932 | F. Kent* | W. O'H. Giles* | R. Claringbull |
| 1933 | J. Fitzmaurice* | F. Kent* | D. L. A. Gibbs |
| 1934 | R. Teague | R. Ratman | J. John |
| 1935 | M. D. McCready* | H. Cooke* | L. E. Cording |
| 1936 | C. Whitney-Smith | M. D. McCready | D. S. Martin |
| 1937 | G. J. Gorrie* | R. C. Wertheim* | R. Ratman |
| 1938 | E. B. Christie | L. E. Cording | L. McLennan |
| 1939 | R. C. Winton | J. Reed | A. N. C. Weir |
| 1940–46 | No competition | | |

|  | 1 | 2 | 3 |
|---|---|---|---|
| 1947 | C. Grose-Hodge | A. H. Stenholm | U. L. Wendon |
| 1948 | R. C. Sproul-Bolton | P. G. Williams | U. L. Wendon |
| 1949 | Raymond Paul* | E. Knott* | R. A. Harrison |
| 1950 | C. A. Gentili* | R. W. Fearnhead* | J. Horley |
| 1951 | A. Jay | N. J. Mallett | N. E. Neter |
| 1952 | H. W. Hoskyns | D. Parham | D. Giles |
| 1953 | M. Howard | W. Romp | E. J. Saunders |
| 1954 | E. O. Reynolds | W. Romp | R. Lock |
| 1955 | B. W. Howes | R. S. Watkins | E. Newton |
| 1956 | R. A. McKenzie | P. Wilmot-Sitwell | F. Creagh Osborne |
| 1957 | J. A. King | A. M. Leckie | D. Giles |
| 1958 | A. Leckie* | H. Wicks* | T. Hudson |
| 1959 | G. B. Filmer | R. Lynn | B. Ortt |
| 1960 | P. A. Redhead* | P. Jacobs* | G. Ayliffe |
| 1961 | J. F. Kelly | J. Payne | T. Berman |
| 1962 (Spring) | J. M. McKenzie* | N. Grose-Hodge* | J. Payne* |
| 1962 (Aut.) | C. F. Green | J. Payne | C. Turner |
| 1963 | J. Anderson | O. N. P. Mylne | J. Fairhall |
| 1964 | C. Layton | C. Purchase | G. Tomlinson |
| 1965 | 1 F. Finnis | 2 R. G. Wilson | 3 A. H. Jones |
|  | 4 B. J. More | 5 J. Payne | 6 W. R. Johnson |
| 1966 | 1 K. Pearman* | 2 B. Paul* | 3 M. Steele |
|  | 4 A. Floyer | 5 M. Roberts | 6 I. Single |
| 1967 | 1 J. Fox* | 2 M. Murch* | 3 D. Johnson* |
|  | 4 J. Ogley* | 5 J. Henniker-Heaton | 6 T. Burch |
| 1968 | 1 J. Henniker-Heaton* | 2 J. Noel* | 3 R. Peters |
|  | 4 T. Burch | 5 R. Davenport | 6 S. Wooding |
| 1969 | 1 E. Hudson | 2 E. Gray | 3 N. Rouxel |
|  | 4 B. Hill | 5 T. Belson | 6 D. Russell |
| 1970 | 1 T. Belson | 2 W. Osbaldeson | 3 P. Brierley |
|  | 4 B. Hill | 5 C. Hallett | 6 C. White |
| 1971 | 1 B. Hill | 2 C. White | 3 R. Bird |
|  | 4 J. Hall | 5 A. Silvey | 6 D. Turner |
| 1972 | 1 M. West | 2 M. Murch | 3 P. Emberson |
|  | 4 I. Campbell | 5 J. Hall | 6 A. Silvey |
| 1973 | 1 M. Fare | 2 J. Hall | 3 J. Stanbury |
|  | 4 I. Worthington | 5 D. Brooks | 6 J. Higgins |
| 1974 | 1 J. Hall | 2 J. Llewellyn | 3 J. Stanbury |
|  | 4 R. Phelps | 5 D. Brooks | 6 F. Brierley |
| 1975 | 1 J. Llewellyn | 2 R. Edwards | 3 J. Steventon |
|  | 4 S. Lavington | 5 M. Gilbert | 6 P. Twine |
| 1976 | 1 S. Paul | 2 R. Edwards | 3 J. Tyson |
|  | 4 P. Brierley | 5 G. Jaron | 6 D. Turner |
| 1977 | 1 S. Roose | 2 D. Brooks | 3 R. Edwards |
|  | 4 N. Bell | 5 N. Clark | 6 B. Lewis |
| 1978 | 1 J. Steventon | 2 N. Mallett | 3 B. Lewis |
|  | 4 P. Brierley | 5 A. Shaban | 6 J. Philbin |
| 1979 | 1 J. Melville | 2 R. Greenhalgh | 3 R. Nightingale |
|  | 4 D. Brooks | 5 P. Tayler | 6 H. Kernohan |
| 1980 | 1 S. Henshall | 2 G. Liston | 3 M. Rance |
|  | 4 A. Brannon | 5–8 R. Brooks, R. Edwards, H. Kernohan, E. Gray |  |

UNDER-TWENTY CHAMPIONSHIP – WANDSWORTH P. T. A. TROPHY †

| | | | |
|---|---|---|---|
| 1964 | 1 J. W. G. Tomlinson | 2 G. Paul | 3 R. Reynolds |
| | 4 D. Wherrett | | |
| 1965 | 1 B. More | 2 R. Rhodes | 3 E. Bourne |
| | 4 D. Floyer | 5 I. Single | 6 A. Alexander |
| 1966 Jan. | 1 G. Paul | 2 E. Bourne | 3 P. D. Russell |
| | 4 I. Single | 5 S. Frick | 6 K. Pearman |
| 1966 Dec. | 1 P. D. Russell | 2 E. Bourne | 3 K. Pearman |
| | 4 G. Paul | 5 W. R. Johnson | 6 D. Exeter |
| 1967 | 1 E. Bourne | 2 W. R. Johnson | 3 J. Noel |
| | 4 E. Olympitis | 5 B. Hill | 6 B. Paul |
| 1968 | 1 R. Deighton | 2 J. Noel | 3 M. West |
| | 4 J. Tyson | 5 S. Frith | 6 J. Hall |
| 1969 | 1 M. West | 2 J. Deanfield | 3 R. Bird |
| | 4 J. Noel | 5 J. Stanbury | 6 R. Jamieson |
| 1970 | 1 J. Stanbury | 2 T. Belson | 3 C. White |
| | 4 P. Keuls | 5 R. Bruniges | 6 B. Lewis |
| 1971 | 1 P. Emberson* | 2 P. Keuls* | 3 P. Tarran |
| | 4 C. White | 5 D. Brooks | 6 M. Allton |
| 1972 | 1 R. Bruniges | 2 I. Campbell | 3 P. Tarran |
| | 4 A. Wickham | 5 J. Kenney | 6 P. Emberson |
| 1973 | 1 R. Bruniges* | 2 P. Tarran* | 3 K. Lovejoy |
| | 4 K. P. Maynard | 5 P. J. Ayliffe | 6 G. Alofouzo |
| 1974 | 1 P. Tarran* | 2 H. Kernohan* | 3 M. Gilbert |
| | 4 D. Fairhall | 5 P. Emberson | 6 P. Young |
| 1975 | 1 J. Llewellyn | 2 D. Fairhall | 3 J. Steventon |
| | 4 G. Jones | 5 P. Young | 6 D. Karlin |
| 1976 | 1 J. Steventon | 2 J. Llewellyn | 3 J. Rhodes |
| | 4 M. Bernard | 5 D. Fairhall | 6 P. Young |
| 1977 | 1 J. Steventon | 2 G. Liston | 3 D. Fairhall |
| | 4 M. Thornton | 5 M. Chell | 6 P. Young |
| 1978 | 1 J. Troiano | 2 A. Shaban | 3 S. Baldry |
| | 4 J. Rhodes | 5 G. Liston | 6 A. Brannon |
| 1979 | 1 G. Liston* | 2 S. Meredith* | 3 A. Brannon |
| | 4 S. Baldry | 5 C. Shaw | 6 M. Nelson-Griffiths |
| 1980 | 1 S. Henshall | 2 R. Phelps | 3 D. Mahony |
| | 4 P. Tayler | 5 N. Fancourt | 6 P. Cruther |

SCHOOLBOYS CHAMPIONSHIP – NATIONAL AGE GROUP CHAMPIONSHIPS (from 1976)

| | | | |
|---|---|---|---|
| 1968 | T. Belson | 1972 | R. Bruniges |
| 1969 | R. Allen | 1973 | G. Stafford-Bull |
| 1970 | P. Keuls | 1974 | J. Llewellyn |
| 1971 | P. Emberson | | |
| | Under-19 | | Under-16 |
| 1975 | N. Mallett | | P. Brushett |
| | Under-18 | | Under-16 |
| 1976 | J. Steventon | | A. Brannon |
| 1977 | M. Bernard | | A. Carnie |
| 1978 | G. Liston | | S. McAslan |
| 1979 | S. Henshall | | M. Rance |
| 1980 | G. McMullen | | D. Dale |
| 1981 | G. Green | | R. Arthur |

AMATEUR EPEE TEAM CHAMPIONSHIP – SAVAGE SHIELD
Presented by Dr G. H. (later Sir George) Savage

| | 1 | 2 |
|---|---|---|
| 1905 | Inns of Court RV Sch. of A. | Morel's Sch. of Arms (15–13) |
| 1906 | F. G. McPherson's Sch. of A. | W. McPherson's Sch. of A. (11–6) |
| 1907 | F. G. McPherson's Sch. of A. | Morel's Sch. of A. (9–6) |
| 1908 | F. G. McPherson's Sch. of A. | Sword Club (10–6) |
| 1909 | F. G. McPherson's Sch. of A. | Bertrand's Sch. of A. (9–1) |
| 1910 | F. G. McPherson's Sch. of A. | Inns of Court Sch. of A. (11–6) |
| 1911 | F. G. McPherson's Sch. of A. | Grave's Sch. of A. (9–2) |
| 1912 | F. G. McPherson's Sch. of A. | Bertrand's Sch. of A. (9–4) |
| 1913 | S. Bertrand | Gravé's Sch. of A. (9–1) |
| 1914 | Sword Club | Gravé's Sch. of A. (9–7) |
| 1915–19 | No competition | |
| 1920 | S. Bertrand | Army Fencing Union (13–3) |
| 1921 | London FC | Royal Automobile Club (9–5) |
| 1922 | Royal Automobile Club | Army Fencing Union (10–4) |
| 1923 | London FC | S. Tassart (10–5) |
| 1924 | London FC | S. Bertrand (11–4) |
| 1925 | Royal Automobile Club | S. Bertrand (9–5) |
| 1926 | S. Bertrand | Royal Automobile Club (9–6) |
| 1927 | Grosvenor FC | S. Bertrand (10–8) |
| 1928 | Grosvenor FC | S. Tassart (9–5) |
| 1929 | Lensbury FC | Royal Automobile Club (9–6) |
| 1930 | London FC | S. Tassart-Parkins (9–6) |
| 1931 | Grosvenor FC | S. Bertrand (10–7) |
| 1932 | Royal Automobile Club | London FC (10–6) |
| 1933 | Grosvenor FC | Lensbury FC (9–5) |
| 1934 | Grosvenor FC | London FC (18–8 pts) |
| 1935 | Grosvenor FC | Royal Automobile Club (18–10 pts) |
| 1936 | Grosvenor FC | S. Bertrand (19–13 pts) |
| 1937 | Grosvenor FC | Lansdowne (18–24 pts) |
| 1938 | London FC | Lansdowne (14–12 pts) |
| 1939 | London FC | Grosvenor FC (8–7) |
| 1940–46 | No competition | |
| 1947 | London FC and Lansdowne (tie 8–8) | |
| 1948 | Grosvenor FC | London FC (7–6) |
| 1949 | Lansdowne | Polytechnic FC (8–6) |
| 1950 | S. Paul | Grosvenor FC (8–6) |
| 1951 | Lansdowne | S. Paul (10–5) |
| 1952 | Lansdowne | S. Paul (9–7) |
| 1953 | Grosvenor | Lansdowne (8–8, 35–36 hits) |
| 1954 | Lansdowne | S. Paul (9–4) |
| 1955 | Lansdowne | S. Paul (11–5) |
| 1956 | Lansdowne | S. Paul (9–1) |
| 1957 | Lansdowne | London FC (9–1) |
| 1958 | Lansdowne | Grosvenor FC (10–6) |
| 1959 | Lansdowne | Army FU (9–3) |
| 1960 | Grosvenor | Polytechnic FC (9–4) |
| 1961 | Lansdowne | Grosvenor FC (9–3) |
| 1962 | Grosvenor FC | Oxford Univ. FC (8–5) |
| 1963 | Grosvenor FC | Oxford Univ. FC (9–2) |
| 1964 | London FC | Grosvenor FC (8–5) |
| 1965 | S. Paul | Grosvenor FC (9–3) |
| 1966 | London FC | S. Paul (8–7, 50–64 hits) |
| 1967 | S. Boston | Thames FC (8–2) |
| 1968 | London Univ. FC | Thames FC (9–6) |

|   | 1 | 2 |
|---|---|---|
| 1969 | Thames FC | London Univ. FC (8–8, 63–63 hits, fight-off 5–4) |
| 1970 | S. Paul | Army FU (9–3) |
| 1971 | S. Paul | S. Boston (9–6) |
| 1972 | S. Boston | Thames FC (8–8, 57–61 hits) |
| 1973 | S. Paul | S. Boston (9–6) |
| 1974 | Polytechnic | Excalibur (9–4) |
| 1975 | S. Boston | Thames (8–8, 59–58 hits) |
| 1976 | S. Boston | S. Paul (9–4) |
| 1977 | S. Boston | Thames (9–5) |
| 1978 | S. Boston | S. Paul (9–3) |
| 1979 | S. Boston | London-Thames FC (9–5) |
| 1980 | S. Paul | S. Boston (8–8, won on hits) |
| 1981 | S. Boston | Reading FC (9–3) |

## SABRE (HEADQUARTERS EVENTS)

### THE AMATEUR CHAMPIONSHIP

In 1898, 1900 and 1901 fought by knock-out; otherwise by pools till 1962. From 1963 generally by prevailing FIE system. In 1920 C. Holt-White presented a silver cup in memory of Capt John Jenkinson.

|   | 1 | 2 | 3 |
|---|---|---|---|
| 1898 | W. Edgworth-Johnstone | W. P. Gate |   |
| 1899 | T. P. Hobbins | R. A. Poore | W. R. Gate |
| 1900 | W. Edgworth-Johnstone | A. D. Bell |   |
| 1901 | T. P. Hobbins | A. C. Murray |   |
| 1902 | T. P. Hobbins | A. D. Bell, J. C. Newman eq. |   |
| 1903 | H. Evan James | J. C. Newman, C. A. Wilson eq. |   |
| 1904 | C. A. Wilson | W. W. Marsh | E. R. McClure |
| 1905 | C. A. Wilson | J. Jenkinson | W. W. Marsh |
| 1906 | C. A. Wilson | J. Jenkinson, W. W. Marsh, A. Ridley Martin eq. |   |
| 1907 | F. Fielmann | W. W. Marsh | A. G. Everitt |
| 1908 | W. W. Marsh | C. A. Wilson | A. V. Keene, L. Leith, A. C. Murray eq. |
| 1909 | W. W. Marsh | A. C. Murray | E. Brookfield |
| 1910 | A. Ridley Martin | F. Fielmann | D. W. Godfree |
| 1911 | W. Hammond | W. W. Marsh | F. Feilmann |
| 1912 | C. van der Byl | C. FitzClarence | A. Ridley Martin |
| 1913 | A. Ridley Martin | C. van der Byl | C. FitzClarence |
| 1914 | W. Hammond | A. H. Corble | H. Butterworth |
| 1915–19 | No competition |   |   |
| 1920 | C. Kershaw | R. Dalglish, R. Campbell, E. Seligman eq. |   |
| 1921 | W. Hammond | H. Huntington, C. Kershaw eq. |   |
| 1922 | A. H. Corble | C. Kershaw | E. Seligman |
| 1923 | E. Seligman | C. Kershaw | R. Willoughby |
| 1924 | E. Seligman | R. Daglish | E. Brookfield |
| 1925 | C. Kershaw | E. Brookfield, G. N. Dyer, D. Neilson eq. |   |
| 1926 | C. Kershaw* | J. A. Obdam* | R. Campbell |
| 1927 | A. H. Corble | G. L. G. Harry | C. B. Notley |
| 1928 | G. L. G. Harry | H. A. Forrest* | C. G. Hohler |
| 1929 | R. Campbell | O. G. Trinder | C. B. Notley |
| 1930 | O. G. Trinder* | G. L. G. Harry* | A. G. Pilbrow |
| 1931 | O. G. Trinder | G. L. G. Harry | A. G. Pilbrow |
| 1932 | A. G. Pilbrow | O. G. Trinder | C. G. Hohler |

|  | 1 | 2 | 3 |
|---|---|---|---|
| 1933 | O. G. Trinder | A. G. Pilbrow | C. G. Hohler |
| 1934 | O. G. Trinder | R. E. Brook | A. G. Pilbrow |
| 1935 | A. G. Pilbrow | O. G. Trinder | R. Tredgold |
| 1936 | R. E. Brook | G. L. G. Harry | A. G. Pilbrow |
| 1937 | R. Tredgold | P. Turquet | O. G. Trinder |
| 1938 | A. G. Pilbrow | C-L. de Beaumont | R. Tredgold |
| 1939 | R. Tredgold | P. Turquet | O. G. Trinder |
| 1940–46 | No competition | | |
| 1947 | R. Tredgold | A. G. Pilbrow | O. G. Trinder |
| 1948 | R. Tredgold* | A. G. Pilbrow* | R. E. Brook* |
| 1949 | R. Tredgold | D. Shalit | A. G. Pilbrow |
| 1950 | A. G. Pilbrow* | P. Turquet* | R. Tredgold |
| 1951 | P. Turquet | A. G. Pilbrow | W. M. Beatley |
| 1952 | O. B. Porebski | R. Anderson | R. Tredgold |
| 1953 | O. B. Porebski | M. Amberg* | U. L. Wendon* |
| 1954 | R. Cooperman* | H. W. Hoskyns* | W. M. Beatley* |
| 1955 | R. Tredgold | O. B. Porebski | R. Cooperman |
| 1956 | O. B. Porebski | R. F. Tredgold | R. Cooperman |
| 1957 | M. Amberg* | B. W. Howes | W. M. Beatley |
| 1958 | M. Amberg | A. R. Cooperman | E. M. Verebes |
| 1959 | M. Amberg | A. R. Cooperman | R. Tredgold |
| 1960 | A. R. Cooperman | A. Leckie | B. S. McCarthy |
| 1961 | A. R. Cooperman* | A. Leckie* | G. T. Birks |
| 1962 | C. Fisher | A. R. Cooperman | G. T. Birks |
| 1963 | A. Leckie | M. Amberg | A. R. Cooperman |
| 1964 | A. Leckie | A. R. Cooperman | W. J. Rayden |
| 1965 | 1 A. Leckie* | 2 W. J. Rayden* | 3 R. Oldcorn |
|  | 4 G. B. Wilson | 5 P. O. K. Wilson | 6 G. T. Birks |
| 1966 | 1 H. W. Hoskyns* | 2 R. Oldcorn* | 3 A. R. Cooperman |
|  | 4 A. Leckie | 5 D. C. Martin | 6 W. J. Rayden |
| 1967 | 1 A. Leckie | 2 W. J. Rayden | 3 D. Acfield |
|  | 4 D. Eden | 5 M. Breckin | 6 D. C. Martin |
| 1968 | 1 A. Leckie | 2 R. Craig | 3 W. J. Rayden |
|  | 4 R. Oldcorn | 5 H. W. Hoskyns | 6 D. Acfield |
| 1969 | 1 D. Acfield | 2 R. Craig | 3 H. W. Hoskyns |
|  | 4 M. Breckin | 5 W. J. Rayden | 6 A. Leckie |
| 1970 | 1 D. Acfield | 2 R. Craig | 3 R. Cohen |
|  | 4 D. C. Martin | 5 R. Oldcorn | 6 C. Purchase |
| 1971 | 1 D. Acfield | 2 R. Craig | 3 J. Deanfield |
|  | 4 T. Wishart | 5 R. Cohen | 6 D. Eden |
| 1972 | 1 D. Acfield | 2 J. Deanfield | 3 P. Mather |
|  | 4 R. Cohen | 5 R. Oldcorn | 6 D. Eden |
| 1973 | 1 P. Mather* | 2 R. Cohen* | 3 J. Deanfield |
|  | 4 J. Philbin, J. Zarno eq. | | 6 R. Oldcorn |
| 1974 | 1 R. Cohen* | 2 J. Philbin* | 3 D. Eden |
|  | 4 D. Scott | 5 A. Taylor | 6 J. Zarno |
| 1975 | 1 J. Deanfield | 2 R. Cohen | 3 A. Taylor |
|  | 4 B. Lewis | 5 D. Hutt | 6 D. Scott |
| 1976 | 1 J. Philbin | 2 R. Cohen | 3 J. Zarno |
|  | 4 T. Etherton | 5 D. Hutt | 6 M. Slade |
| 1977 | 1 J. Philbin | 2 J. Deanfield | 3 R. Cohen |
|  | 4 T. Etherton | 5 R. Oldcorn | 6 M. Slade |
| 1978 | 1 J. Philbin | 2 R. Cohen | 3 T. Etherton |
|  | 4 J. Deanfield | 5 J. Zarno | 6 M. Slade |
| 1979 | 1 M. Slade* | 2 J. Philbin* | 3 T. Etherton |
|  | 4 J. Deanfield | 5 J. Zarno | 6 R. Cohen |

| | | | |
|---|---|---|---|
| 1980 | 1 R. Cohen | 2 M. Slade | 3 D. Hutt |
| | 4 J. Philbin | 5 T. Etherton | 6 J. Deanfield |
| 1981 | 1 J. Philbin | 2 M. Slade | 3 R. Cohen |
| | 4 M. Hunt | 5–8 D. Bovill, M. Bryant, D. Eden, W. J. Magill | |

CORBLE MEMORIAL CUP (INTERNATIONAL)
Archibald Corble made a bequest for a cup and medals

| | 1 | 2 | 3 |
|---|---|---|---|
| 1947 | R. F. Tredgold | O. G. Trinder | W. H. Turner |
| 1948 | J. Erdelyi | P. Kovacs | R. Karpati |
| 1949 | O. B. Porebski | K. Miszewski | R. Tredgold |
| 1950 | Dr R. F. Tredgold | A. G. Pilbrow | E. Kanitz |
| 1951 | R. J. G. Anderson | Dr R. F. Tredgold | A. G. Pilbrow |
| 1952 | R. J. G. Anderson | M. J. Amberg | R. Cooperman |
| 1953 | M. J. Amberg | O. B. Porebski | J. Los |
| 1954 | O. B. Porebski | H. J. van de Meer | J. Los |
| 1955 | A. Gerevich* | R. Karpati* | R. Cooperman |
| 1956 | E. M. Verebes | M. J. Amberg | R. Cooperman |
| 1957 | E. M. Verebes* | Dr W. M. Beatley* | R. Tredgold* |
| 1958 | M. Amberg | J. van Baelen | H. W. F. Hoskyns |
| 1959 | D. D. Stringer* | M. Straus* | A. M. Leckie |
| 1960 | M. Straus | B. W. Howes | A. M. Leckie |
| 1961 | H. W. Hoskyns* | G. T. Birks* | P. Hobson* |
| 1962 | A. Leckie | P. Borucki | W. Woehler |
| 1963 | A. R. Cooperman | G. T. Birks | P. Kirby |
| 1964 | B. W. Howes | A. Leckie | R. Oldcorn |
| 1965 | 1 P. Borucki | 2 A. Leckie | 3 R. Oldcorn |
| | 4 J. Theuerkauff | 5 A. R. Cooperman | 6 D. C. Martin |
| 1966 | 1 P. Borucki | 2 A. Leckie | 3 W. J. Rayden |
| | 4 A. R. Cooperman | 5 B. Gral | 6 F. Luxardo |
| 1967 | 1 W. J. Rayden | 2 R. Oldcorn | 3 H. W. Hoskyns |
| | 4 A. Leckie | 5 R. Craig | 6 P. Borucki |
| 1968 | 1 Y. Brasseur | 2 H. W. Hoskyns | 3 R. Craig |
| | 4 A. Leckie | 5 R. Oldcorn | 6 D. Acfield |
| 1969 | 1 G. Ganchev | 2 Y. Brasseur | 3 R. Cohen |
| | 4 R. Oldcorn | 5 R. Craig | 6 W. J. Rayden |
| 1970 | 1 G. Ganchev | 2 R. Craig | 3 G. Dellocque |
| | 4 R. Cohen | 5 W. J. Rayden | 6 R. Oldcorn |
| 1971 | 1 G. Ganchev | 2 P. Hobson | 3 W. J. Rayden |
| | 4 D. Scott | 5 A. Leckie | 6 J. Lawday |
| 1972 | 1 J. Kalmar | 2 P. Mather | 3 E. Hamm |
| | 4 R. Oldcorn | 5 D. Eden | 6 R. Craig |
| 1973 | 1 J. Pawlowski | 2 K. Grzegorek | 3 Z. Kawecki |
| | 4 M. Czernicki | 5 J. Majewski | 6 D. Eden |
| 1974 | 1 D. Eden | 2 P. Storme | 3 R. Oldcorn |
| | 4 R. Cohen | 5 F. de Wisscher | 6 P. Gomez |
| 1975 | 1 R. Cohen | 2 S. Storme | 3 J. Philbin |
| | 4 G. Kaufman | 5 Y. Brasseur | 6 R. Gomez-Vaillard |
| 1976 | 1 R. Cohen | 2 W. Marik | 3 H. Brandstatter |
| | 4 J. Philbin | 5 F. Fitting | 6 E. Sekunda |
| 1977 | 1 J. Philbin | 2 R. A. Cohen | 3 M. Lavoie |
| | 4 T. Etherton | 5 J. Deanfield | 6 J. Zarno |
| 1978 | 1 J. Stratmann | 2 R. A. Cohen | 3 J. Deanfield |
| | 4 M. Slade | 5 M. Delberg | 6 J. Philbin |
| 1979 | 1 J. Philbin* | 2 J. Volkmann* | 3 M. Slade |
| | 4 V. Paraiso | 5 R. A. Cohen | 6 T. Etherton |

1980   1 G. Boch          2 M. Slade          3. Delberg
       4 R. Cohen         5 D. Schneider      6 W. Mazodko
1981   1 J. Philbin*      2 M. Slade*         3 M. Hunt
       4 R. Cohen         5-8 R. Jaine, C. Zitcer, C. Morris, P. West

R. E. COLE MEMORIAL CUP

|      | 1 | 2 | 3 |
|---|---|---|---|
| 1949 | J. Erdelyi | R. Tredgold | U. L. Wendon |
| 1951 | R. F. Tredgold | J. Erdelyi | A. G. Pilbrow |
| 1952 | R. Anderson | W. M. Beatley | Cottard, O. B. Porebski eq. |
| 1953 | O. B. Porebski | W. M. Beatley | R. Tredgold |
| 1954 | M. J. Amberg | O. B. Porebski | R. Tredgold |
| 1955 | H. W. Hoskyns | M. J. Amberg | W. M. Beatley |
| 1956 | W. M. Beatley | A. R. Cooperman | M. J. Amberg |
| 1957 | W. M. Beatley | E. M. Verebes | W. Nicklin |
| 1958 | A. R. Cooperman | M. Howard | E. M. Verebes |
| 1959 | A. R. Cooperman* | M. Straus* | K. Kardolus |
| 1960 | A. R. Cooperman* | A. Leckie* | B. S. McCarthy* |
| 1961 | A. Leckie* | M. J. Amberg* | M. Price |
| 1962 | A. Leckie | A. R. Cooperman | M. J. Amberg |
| 1963 | M. Price | J. F. Kelly | W. J. Rayden |
| 1964 | A. Leckie | A. R. Cooperman | H. W. Hoskyns |
| 1965 | Y. Brasseur | R. Oldcorn | A. Leckie |
| 1966 | A. R. Cooperman | R. Oldcorn | H. W. Hoskyns |
| 1967 | H. W. Hoskyns* | R. Oldcorn* | A. Leckie |
| 1968 | K. Allisaat | W. Duschner | A. Leckie |
| 1969 | M. Witczak | G. Ganchev | P. Stroka |
| 1970 | M. Czernicki | D. Acfield | W. Convents |
| 1971 | J. Pawlowski | M. Zakrewski | F. Sobszac |
| 1972 | W. Convents | P. Wischeidt | P. Stroka |
| 1973 | W. Convents | R. Cohen | G. Ganchev |
| 1974 | W. Convents | F. Prause | H. Brandstaetter |
| 1975 | J. Deanfield | R. Cohen | D. Eden |
| 1976 | R. Cohen | T. Barband | J. Philbin |
| 1977 | F. Fitting* | D. Eden* | R. Cohen* |
| 1978 | R. Cohen | J. Philbin | M. Lavoie |
| 1979 | R. Cohen | J. Philbin | G. Li |
| 1980 | R. Cohen | J. Philbin | T. Etherton |
| 1981 | M. Slade | R. Jaine | J. Philbin |

JUNIOR CHAMPIONSHIP †
Organised by the Association in 1923. Reinstated 1930 for a cup presented by Lt-Col A. Ridley Martin. Organised by the Sabre Club till 1937.

|      | 1 | 2 | 3 |
|---|---|---|---|
| 1923 | F. Sherriff | R. S. S. Meade | C-L. de Beaumont, G. L. C. Harry, C. Heys-Hallett eq. |
| 1930 | R. D. S. Anderson | P. G. Wardle | C. Heys-Hallett, G. Chatterton, J. Smallwood eq. |
| 1931 | R. J. P. Stewart | R. E. Brook | J. Willoughby |
| 1932 | B. P. Cazaly | R. J. P. Stewart | J. Willoughby |
| 1933 | R. Tredgold | G. F. Wright | B. P. Cazaly |
| 1934 | W. J. Turney | D. Shepherd | L. E. Cording |
| 1935 | J. B. Armstrong | G. Moore | P. M. Turquet |

|  | 1 | 2 | 3 |
|---|---|---|---|
| 1936 | G. Moore | P. Turquet | A. E. Pienne |
| 1937 | K. G. C. Campbell | C. Hankinson | L. Lambert |
| 1938 | L. Laxton | D. McLoughlin | L. Lambert, H. C. Tomlin eq. |
| 1939 | A. G. Lehmann | H. C. Tomlin | H. Cooke |
| 1946 | J. F. Field | L. Lambert | Lord Leveson |
| 1947 | G. Gelder | U. L. Wendon | D. E. Wright |
| 1948 | E. B. Christie | D. Shalit | A. Ellison |
| 1949 | A. J. Cotton | P. W. Johnson | R. W. Fearnhead |
| 1950 | R. W. Fearnhead | W. M. Beatley | R. Cooperman |
| 1951 | R. Cooperman | A. Ellison | P. C. Amberg |
| 1952 | P. C. Amberg | D. Parham | H. W. F. Hoskyns |
| 1953 | A. Jay | H. W. Hoskyns | B. S. McCarthy |
| 1954 | N. J. Mallett | R. S. Watkins | E. Mount Haes |
| 1955 | R. S. Watkins | B. W. Howes | C. Tienth |
| 1956 | B. W. Howes | H. MacLaughlin Smith | C. Hillier |
| 1957 | A. Leckie | M. Price | D. D. Stringer |
| 1958 | A. G. Mackeown | G. Leckie | C. Courtney-Lewis |
| 1959 | G. Talkington | H. J. Maslin | R. McNeil |
| 1960 | G. Leckie | J. F. Kelly | C. Courtney-Lewis |
| 1961 | C. Trent | W. J. Rayden | J. J. Evans |
| 1962 | K. Pearson | K. Staines | G. B. Wilson |
| 1963 | D. C. Martin | D. Titheradge | D. Parham |
| 1964 | D. Eden* | D. Titheradge* | R. Brearley |
| 1965 | 1 R. P. Ford | 2 R. Barsby | 3 D. Acfield |
|  | 4 D. J. Hunt | 5 P. Lennon | 6 R. Brearley |
| 1966 | 1 B. Fisher | 2 P. Lennon | 3 J. Eiser |
|  | 4 D. Titheradge | 5 E. Nyiri | 6 R. Cohen |
| 1967 | 1 R. Cohen* | 2 D. Scott* | 3 P. Rizzuto |
|  | 4 B. Waddelow | 5 C. Kovanda | 6 E. Nyiri |
| 1968 | 1 D. Scott | 2 T. Wishart | 3 C. Kovanda |
|  | 4 B. Waddelow | 5 L. Buffery | 6 M. Mazowiecki |
| 1969 | 1 J. Deanfield | 2 D. Hughes | 3 T. Etherton |
|  | 4 P. Lennon | 5 T. Wishart | 6 P. Mather |
| 1970 | 1 M. Eden | 2 P. Mather | 3 J. Lawday |
|  | 4 T. Wishart | 5 R. Fairburn | 6 D. Hughes |
| 1971 | 1 C. Kovanda | 2 P. Mather | 3 J. Philbin |
|  | 4 T. Norcross | 5 R. Fairburn | 6 M. D. Price |
| 1972 | 1 A. Taylor | 2 J. Philbin | 3 M. D. Price |
|  | 4 J. Magill | 5 N. Milligan | 6 J. Gryf-Lowczowski |
| 1973 | 1 B. Lewis | 2 M. D. Price | 3 T. Etherton |
|  | 4 J. Gryf-Lowczowski | 5 N. Milligan | 6 M. Streater |
| 1975 (Feb.) | 1 M. D. Price* | 2 M. Slade* | 3 D. Hutt |
|  | 4 S. Wasilewski | 5 R. Neal | 6 J. Gryf-Lowczowski |
| 1975 (Nov.) | 1 T. Etherton | 2 N. Milligan | 3 M. Slade |
|  | 4 A. Roberts | 5 S. Fox | 6 S. Wasilewski |
| 1976 | 1 A. Roberts* | 2 J. Gryf-Lowczowski* | 3 W. J. Magill |
|  | 4 R. Jandula | 5 C. N. Morris | 6 J. Lewis |
| 1977 | 1 J. Lewis | 2 M. J. Magill | 3 N. Milligan |
|  | 4 G. Li | 5 M. Hall | 6 M. Hunt |
| 1978 | 1 N. Milligan | 2 J. Magill | 3 J. Lankshear |
|  | 4 C. Zitcer | 5 R. Jandula | 6 S. Wasilewski |
| 1979 | 1 J. Magill | 2 C. Zitcer | 3 N. Carr |
|  | 4 P. Klenerman | 5 P. West | 6 J. Falkowski |
| 1980 | 1 M. Hunt | 2 P. West | 3 C. Zitcer |
|  | 4 M. Hall | 5 N. Carr | 6 C. Booton |

## UNDER-TWENTY CHAMPIONSHIP – TYZACK CHALLENGE BOWL

| | | | |
|---|---|---|---|
| 1964 | 1 R. Craig | 2 D. Acfield | 3 D. Eden |
| | 4 M. Breckin | | |
| 1965 | 1 R. Craig* | 2 D. Acfield* | 3 E. Ben-Nathan |
| | 4 D. Eden | 5 R. Brearley | 6 R. Forte |
| 1966 | 1 D. Acfield* | 2 E. Ben Nathan* | 3 M. Breckin |
| | 4 R. Cohen | 5 D. Wherrett | 6 A. Preiskel |
| 1967 | 1 D. Acfield | 2 B. Fisher | 3 B. Waddelow |
| | 4 R. Cohen | 5 G. H. Parsons | 6 L. Eden |
| 1968 | 1 J. Lawday | 2 M. Eden | 3 B. Fisher |
| | 4 K. Gordon | 5 T. Etherton | 6 M. Mazowiecki |
| 1969 | 1 T. Wishart | 2 S. Frith | 3 T. Etherton |
| | 4 M. Allen | 5 D. Hughes | 6 H. T. Tizard |
| 1970 | 1 J. Deanfield* | 2 M. Eden* | 3 T. Wishart |
| | 4 T. Etherton | 5 P. Mather | 6 J. Zarno |
| 1971 | 1 T. Wishart | 2 M. Eden | 3 J. Deanfield |
| | 4 P. Mather | 5 T. Etherton | 6 S. Lavington |
| 1972 | 1 B. Lewis* | 2 P. Mather* | 3 M. Price* |
| | 4 S. Pankhurst | 5 D. Hutt | 6 C. Grezesik |
| 1973 | 1 P. Mather | 2 M. Price | 3 J. Lewis |
| | 4 S. Pankhurst | 5 J. Lankshear | 6 A. Bartlett |
| 1974 (Jan.) | 1 J. Lewis | 2 M. Slade | 3 H. C. R. Campion |
| | 4 P. Bruce | 5 C. Grzesik | 6 E. Poole |
| 1974 (Nov.) | 1 H. C. R. Campion | 2 M. Streater | 3 M. Slade |
| | 4 D. Fairhall | 5 P. Emberson | 6 P. Young |
| 1975 | 1 M. Slade | 2 C. Zitcer | 3 S. Glaister |
| | 4 G. Li | 5 G. Kay | 6 P. Martin |
| 1976 | 1 M. Hunt | 2 M. Slade | 3 M. Hall |
| | 4 G. Li | 5 K. Li | 6 S. Muir |
| 1977 | 1 M. Slade | 2 M. Hall | 3 M. Hunt |
| | 4 K. Li | 5 G. Li | 6 P. Klenerman |
| 1978 | 1 G. Li | 2 M. Hall | 3 K. Li |
| | 4 M. Hunt | 5 P. West | 6 J. Falkowski |
| 1979 | 1 M. Hall* | 2 K. Li* | 3 P. West |
| | 4 P. Klenerman | 5 M. Hunt | 6 S. Stoodley |
| 1980 | 1 P. Klenerman* | 2 M. Bryant* | 3 P. West |
| | 4 C. Booton | 5 D. Bovill | 6 T. Yassir |

## SCHOOLBOYS CHAMPIONSHIP – NATIONAL AGE GROUP CHAMPIONSHIP (from 1976)

| | | |
|---|---|---|
| 1968 | T. Wishart | |
| 1969 | T. Wishart | |
| 1970 | M. J. Price | |
| 1971 | D. Keal | |
| | *Under-19* | *Under-16* |
| 1972 | F. Gardiner | J. Bailey |
| 1973 | J. Lewis | J. Bailey |
| 1974 | C. Howgego | M. Slade |
| 1975 | M. Slade | C. Tourmentin |
| | *Under-18* | *Under-16* |
| 1976 | A. Cashen | M. Hall |
| 1977 | G. Li | K. Kubiena |
| 1978 | M. Hall | M. Wright |
| 1979 | P. West | P. Klenerman |
| 1980 | P. West | C. Booton |
| 1981 | J. Fellerman | P. Stanley |

AMATEUR TEAM CHAMPIONSHIP – MAGRINI MEMORIAL CUP
Organised by the Sabre Club, whose members gave the silver cup in memory of Prof. Magrini. Held in 1913 and 1921 as an individual event. Reinstituted in 1927 as a four-a-side team competition. Recognised in 1947 as Team Championship.

|  | 1 | 2 |
|---|---|---|
| 1927 | Sabre Club |  |
| 1928 | Royal Automobile Club | S. Bertrand |
| 1929 | Royal Automobile Club | London FC |
| 1930 | S. Bertrand | London FC |
| 1931 | London FC | S. Bertrand |
| 1932 | London FC | Royal Automobile Club |
| 1933 | London FC | S. Bertrand |
| 1934 | S. Bertrand | London FC |
| 1935 | Royal Automobile Club | Birmingham FC |
| 1936 | S. Bertrand | London FC |
| 1937–38 | No competition |  |
| 1939 | London FC | Bertrand's FC |
| 1940–46 | No competition |  |
| 1947 | London FC | Bertrand's FC (13–3) |
| 1948 | London FC | Bertrand's FC (9–5) |
| 1949 | London FC | Bertrand's FC (9–1) |
| 1950 | S. Paul | London FC (8–8, 58–61 hits) |
| 1951 | London FC | Bertrand's FC (9–2) |
| 1952 | London FC 'A' | London FC 'B' (9–7) |
| 1953 | London FC | Not decided owing to foreign entry |
| 1954 | London FC 'A' | London FC 'B' (No match owing to foreign entry) |
| 1955 | S. Paul | Not decided owing to foreign entry |
| 1956 | S. Paul | London FC (9–7) |
| 1957 | London FC | S. Paul (8–8, 56–67 hits) |
| 1958 | London FC | S. Paul (9–3) |
| 1959 | Army FU | London FC (9–7) |
| 1960 | London FC | Polytechnic FC (11–5) |
| 1961 | Army FU | Polytechnic FC (8–8, 57–62 hits) |
| 1962 | Polytechnic FC | S. Paul ⎰ decided on final pool |
| 1963 | Polytechnic FC | S. Paul ⎱ of four teams |
| 1964 | London FC 'A' | London FC 'B' (9–3) |
| 1965 | London FC | Combined Services (9–0) |
| 1966 | London FC | S. Paul (9–7) |
| 1967 | S. Paul | London FC (9–2) |
| 1968 | London FC | S. Boston (8–8, 55–63 hits) |
| 1969 | S. Boston | London FC (9–7) |
| 1970 | London FC | S. Boston (9–5) |
| 1971 | S. Boston | S. Paul (9–4) |
| 1972 | London FC | Hydra FC (9–2) |
| 1973 | S. Boston 'A' | S. Boston 'B' (9–1) |
| 1974 | Polytechnic FC | S. Boston (8–8, 61–63 hits) |
| 1975 | Polytechnic FC | S. Boston (8–8, 62–62 hits, fight off 5–4) |
| 1976 | S. Boston | Polytechnic FC (9–7) |
| 1977 | Polytechnic FC | S. Boston (9–6) |
| 1978 | Polytechnic FC | S. Boston (9–4) |
| 1979 | Polytechnic FC | S. Boston (9–6) |
| 1980 | Polytechnic FC | S. Boston (9–6) |
| 1981 | Polytechnic FC | S. Boston (9–7) |

## UNIVERSITY CHAMPIONSHIPS

The championships of the British Universities Sports Federation have been recognised since their inception in 1963. Previously those of the Women's Inter-Varsity Athletic Board and of the Universities Athletic Union were recognised.

LADIES' FOIL – MARGARET SOMERVILLE CUP

| | | | |
|---|---|---|---|
| 1934 | M. Wood (Birm.) | 1962 | M. A. Pritchard (Lon.) |
| 1935 | M. Wood (Birm.) | 1963 | M. A. Pritchard (Lon.) |
| 1936 | D. Snelling (Lon.) | 1964 | M. Cobb (Lon.) |
| 1937 | E. Robinson (Manch.) | 1965 | M. Cobb (Lon.) |
| 1938 | B. Thurlow (Lon.) | 1966 | E. Earle (Lon.) |
| 1939 | M. Evans (Lon.) | 1967 | E. Earle (Lon.) |
| 1940–47 | No competition | 1968 | M. Holmes (Read.) |
| 1948 | E. Parkinson (Lon.) | 1969 | M. Ecob (Bris.) |
| 1949 | G. Sheen (Lon.) | 1970 | C. Wotherspoon (Edin.) |
| 1950 | G. Sheen (Lon.) | 1971 | C. Henley (Lon.) |
| 1951 | G. Sheen (Lon.) | 1972 | C. Henley (Lon.) |
| 1952 | G. Sheen (Lon.) | 1973 | G. Ritchie (Oxf.) |
| 1953 | G. Sheen (Lon.) | 1974 | S. Ross (Edin.) |
| 1954 | A. Moller Cam.) | 1975 | S. Wrigglesworth (Lon.) |
| 1955 | E. Grant (Cam.) | 1976 | S. Wrigglesworth (Lon.) |
| 1956 | M. Stafford (Lon.) | 1977 | S. Rochard (Lon.) |
| 1957 | M. Stafford (Lon.) | 1978 | A. Brannon (Cam.) |
| 1958 | M. Stafford (Lon.) | 1979 | A. Brannon (Cam.) |
| 1959 | M. Stafford (Lon.) | 1980 | S. Smith (Edin.) |
| 1960 | M. Stafford (Lon.) | 1981 | F. McIntosh (Cam.) |
| 1961 | M. A. Pritchard (Lon.) | | |

| | MEN'S FOIL | EPEE | SABRE |
|---|---|---|---|
| | WEBB MEMORIAL CUP | C-L. DE BEAUMONT CUP | CRAVEN HOHLER CUP |
| 1931 | D. V. Morse (Cam.) | | E. Monkhouse (Lon.) |
| 1932 | D. M. Paterson (Lon.) | W. H. A. Webb (Lon.) | G. F. Wright (Cam.) |
| 1933 | G. Kerlin (Cam.) | R. Tredgold (Lon.) | P. M. Turquet (Cam.) |
| 1934 | C. Whitney-Smith (Oxf.) | E. B. Pearson (Lon.) | G. Williams (Lon.) |
| 1935 | C. B. Nickalls (Shef.) | M. D. McReady (Oxf.) | C. Nickalls (Shef.) |
| 1936 | M. A. L. Cripps (Oxf.) | F. Platou (Oxf.) | M. A. L. Cripps (Oxf.) |
| 1937 | N. McClintock (Cam.) | F. L. Bell (Shef.) | K. G. C. Campbell (Cam.) |
| 1938 | N. McClintock (Cam.) | P. J. Orde (Oxf.) | S. Cressall (Lon.) |
| 1939 | E. B. Christie (Oxf.) | D. J. McLaren (Cam.) | O. Chan (Cam.) |
| 1940–45 | No competition | No competition | No competition |
| 1946 | U. L. Wendon (Lon.) | U. L. Wendon (Lon.) | J. Haase (Lon.) |
| 1947 | C. Grose-Hodge (Cam.) | U. L. Wendon (Cam.) | O. Porebski (Lon.) |
| 1948 | C. Grose-Hodge (Cam.) | C. Grose-Hodge (Cam.) | K. Miszewski (Cam.) |
| 1949 | P. Webb (Oxf.) | A. J. Cotton (Lon.) | O. Porebski (Lon.) |
| 1950 | H. J. Griffiths (Birm.) | P. Greenhalgh (Lon.) | A. J. Cotton (Oxf.) |
| 1951 | E. Gallico (Lon.) | J. von Kos (Lon.) | A. Ellison (Cam.) |
| 1952 | W. M. Beatley (Lon.) | A. Jay (Oxf.) | W. M. Beatley (Lon.) |
| 1953 | A. Jay (Oxf.) | C. Gentili (Leeds) | C. Fisher (Lon.) |
| 1954 | E. O. Reynolds (Lon.) | M. A. Riaz (Lon.) | C. Fisher (Lon.) |
| 1955 | P. Spahr (Cam.) | P. Spahr (Cam.) | C. Fisher (Lon.) |
| 1956 | C. Fisher (Lon.) | B. S. McCarthy (Lon.) | C. Fisher (Lon.) |
| 1957 | B. W. Howes (Oxf.) | B. W. Howes (Oxf.) | B. S. McCarthy (Lon.) |
| 1958 | M. O'D. Alexander (Cam.) | I. Cameron (Oxf.) | A. Leckie (Oxf.) |
| 1959 | A. Leckie (Oxf.) | A. Leckie (Oxf.) | A. Leckie (Oxf.) |
| 1960 | C. M. Warner (Birm.) | I. Higginbotham (Liv.) | J. Kelly (Lon.) |

| | MEN'S FOIL<br>WEBB MEMORIAL CUP | EPEE<br>C-L. DE BEAUMONT CUP | SABRE<br>CRAVEN HOHLER CUP |
|---|---|---|---|
| 1961 | I. Atkinson (Lon.) | P. Jacobs (Cam.) | C. M. Warner (Birm.) |
| 1962 | G. Wiles (Lough.) | G. Wiles (Lough.) | G. Wiles (Lough.) |
| 1963 | N. Halsted (Oxf.) | N. Halsted (Oxf.) | C. M. Warner (Birm.) |
| 1964 | A. J. R. Berry (Cam.) | N. Halsted (Oxf.) | P. W. Malim (Cam.) |
| 1965 | C. Rentoul (Oxf.) | G. Sandor (Edin.) | E. Ben-Nathan (Cam.) |
| 1966 | M. Breckin (Lon.) | R. Rhodes (Oxf.) | D. Acfield (Cam.) |
| 1967 | G. Paul (Lon.) | G. Paul (Lon.) | D. Acfield (Cam.) |
| 1968 | G. Paul (Lon.) | G. Paul (Lon.) | D. Acfield (Cam.) |
| 1969 | B. Paul (Lon.) | E. Bourne (Lon.) | B. Fisher (Cam.) |
| 1970 | G. Paul (Lon.) | D. Partridge (Lough.) | J. Deanfield (Cam.) |
| 1971 | G. Paul (Lon.) | J. Noel (Lon.) | T. Etherton (Cam.) |
| 1972 | G. Paul (Lon.) | G. Paul (Lon.) | W. J. Magill (Cam.) |
| 1973 | N. Bell (Lon.) | B. Lewis (Oxf.) | M. Breckin (Lon.) |
| 1974 | N. Bell (Lon.) | J. Stanbury (Lon.) | J. Deanfield (Lon.) |
| 1975 | G. Evans (Bris.) | J. Noel (Oxf.) | J. Deanfield (Lon.) |
| 1976 | P. Wedge (Manch.) | J. Noel Oxf.) | W. J. Magill (Cam.) |
| 1977 | S. Wooding (Cam.) | S. Lavington (Liv.) | M. Slade (Cam.) |
| 1978 | M. Chetwood (Cam.) | N. Mallett (Lon.) | M. Slade (Cam.) |
| 1979 | J. Ford (City) | N. Mallett (Lon.) | M. Slade (Cam.) |
| 1980 | R. Pearson (Leeds) | J. Troiano (Oxf.) | G. Li (Salf.) |
| 1981 | C. Ward (Lon.) | J. Rhodes (Cam.) | D. McKenzie (Edin.) |

LADIES' TEAM CHAMPIONSHIP – GILLIAN SHEEN CUP

| 1950 | London | 1961 | London | 1972 | London |
|---|---|---|---|---|---|
| 1951 | Manchester | 1962 | Glasgow | 1973 | Edinburgh and |
| 1952 | London | 1963 | Glasgow | | Glasgow |
| 1953 | London and Manchester | 1964 | London | 1974 | Edinburgh |
| 1954 | London | 1965 | Glasgow | 1975 | London |
| 1955 | Cambridge | 1966 | London | 1976 | Edinburgh |
| 1956 | Oxford | 1967 | London | 1977 | London |
| 1957 | London | 1968 | London | 1978 | London |
| 1958 | London | 1969 | Bristol | 1979 | London |
| 1959 | London | 1970 | Newcastle | 1980 | Edinburgh |
| 1960 | London | 1971 | Newcastle | 1981 | Loughborough |

MEN'S TEAM CHAMPIONSHIP – EDINBURGH TROPHY
Presented by Colonel R. A. Hay

| 1939 | Oxford | 1957 | Liverpool | 1970 | London |
|---|---|---|---|---|---|
| 1940–45 | No competition | 1958 | Durham | 1971 | London |
| 1946 | London | 1959 | Durham | 1972 | London |
| 1947 | Cambridge | 1960 | Durham | 1973 | London |
| 1948 | Cambridge | 1961 | Loughborough | 1974 | London |
| 1949 | Oxford | 1962 | Loughborough | 1975 | London |
| 1950 | London | 1963 | Loughborough | 1976 | London |
| 1951 | London | 1964 | Sheffield | 1977 | Cambridge |
| 1952 | Durham | 1965 | Birmingham | 1978 | Cambridge |
| 1953 | Durham | 1966 | Cambridge | 1979 | Cambridge |
| 1954 | Leeds | 1967 | London | 1980 | Oxford |
| 1955 | Sheffield | 1968 | London | 1981 | Edinburgh |
| 1956 | Manchester | 1969 | London | | |

## PUBLIC SCHOOLS CHAMPIONSHIPS
Organised by the Army from 1890. Organised by Oxford and Cambridge Blues 1924-45 and by the AFA from 1946. The Senior Foil cup was presented in 1924 by Count Charles Zanardi-Landi, that for the Junior Foil in 1939 by A. E. Cressall, the Sabre Cup in 1932 by the Oxford and Cambridge Fencing Clubs, and the Epee cup in 1933 by Julio de Amodio.

| | Foil | Sabre |
|---|---|---|
| 1890 | J. Openshaw (Harrow) | |
| 1891 | E. B. Milnes (Haileybury) | |
| 1892 | W. S. Churchill (Harrow) | |
| 1893 | A. F. Butler (Haileybury) | |
| 1894 | A. F. Butler (Haileybury) | |
| 1895 | H. M. Fleming (Dulwich) | |
| 1896 | D. H. Blunt (Charterhouse) | |
| 1897 | N. P. R. Freeston (Felstead) | G. T. Lee (Radley) |
| 1898 | G. T. Lee (Radley) | G. T. Lee (Radley) |
| 1899 | A. E. Bucknill (Charterhouse) | W. H. Turner (Cranleigh) |
| 1900 | K. Fisher (Charterhouse) | J. C. Boys (Epsom) |
| 1901 | H. MacMichael (Bedford) | R. Scriven (Tonbridge) |
| 1902 | R. J. Weeks (Charterhouse) | A. Currie (Bedford) |
| 1903 | D. C. Wakeford (Merchant Taylors') | J. H. P. Barcroft (RN School) |
| 1904 | M. B. U. Dewar (Rugby) | G. E. R. Slade (Cranleigh) |
| 1905 | R. Bernard (Bedford) | F. Watson (Bedford) |
| 1906 | R. Bernard (Bedford) | M. H. Mackintosh (Bromsgrove) |
| 1907 | C. Ogilvie (Bedford) | W. S. S. Bond (Epsom) |
| 1908 | B. C. Newton (Wellington) | F. W. W. Baynes (Harrow) |
| 1909 | C. Ogilvie (Bedford) | C. Sanderson (Bedford) |
| 1910 | E. M. Burrell (Merchant Taylors') | C. Sanderson (Bedford) |
| 1911 | K. A. Stewart (Harrow) | R. J. M. Bebb (Winchester) |
| 1912 | O. Mosley (Winchester) | O. Mosley (Winchester) |
| 1913 | R. C. Gavin (Westminster) | |
| 1914 | Blacker (Eton) | |
| 1924 | J. E. Lloyd (Winchester) | |
| 1925 | B. L. Seton (Edinburgh Acad.) | |
| 1926 | B. L. Seton (Edinburgh Acad.) | E. D. A. Shepherd (Glenalmond) |
| 1927 | R. Wood (Winchester) | |
| 1928 | P. M. S. Gedge (Loretto) | J. P. Halpin (Dulwich) |
| 1929 | F. S. Hoppé (Westminster) | C. J. Chatterton (Pangbourne) |
| 1930 | H. D. H. Bartlett (Stowe) | J. Smallwood (Pangbourne) |
| 1931 | G. A. L. Cheatle (Stowe) | M. S. Balmain (Eton) |
| 1932 | C. Bampfylde (Eton) | R. D. Hearne (Cheltenham) |
| 1933 | J. L. W. Cheyne (Stowe) | J. L. W. Cheyne (Stowe) |
| 1934 | C. T. J. Cripps (Eton) | C. T. J. Cripps (Eton) |
| 1935 | P. V. A. Oldak (Westminster) | M. W. Waddington (Eton) |
| 1936 | M. W. Waddington (Eton) | F. P. Crowder (Eton) |
| 1937 | F. P. Crowder (Eton) | G. J. Leveson-Gower (Eton) |
| 1938 | A. J. A. Weir (Winchester) | A. G. Lehmann (Dulwich) |
| 1939 | N. E. Neter (Bradfield) | A. G. Lehmann (Dulwich) |
| 1940 | J. Corsellis (Westminster) | G. R. d'A. Hoskins (Cheltenham) |
| 1941 | L. A. Wilson (Westminster) | C. Grose-Hodge (Eton) |
| 1942 | R. A. W. Holland (Dulwich) | C. Grose-Hodge (Eton) |
| 1943 | U. L. Wendon (Cheltenham) | U. L. Wendon (Cheltenham) |
| 1944 | M. J. Amberg (Charterhouse) | M. J. Amberg (Charterhouse) |
| 1945 | D. Hawkins (Merchant Taylors) | A. H. King (Dulwich) |
| 1946 | A. Ellison (Cheltenham) | A. Ellison (Cheltenham) |
| 1947 | M. McCreery (Eton) | J. Goldsmith (Dulwich) |

|  | *Foil* | *Sabre* |
|---|---|---|
| 1948 | P. Webb (Westminster) | N. Elliot Baxter (Eton) |
| 1949 | P. Petrie (Westminster) | P. Warnford-Davis (Bradfield) |
| 1950 | P. Petrie (Westminster) | P. Petrie (Westminster) |
| 1951 | E. O. Reynolds (St Paul's) | D. Wright (Pangbourne) |
| 1952 | T. W. G. Brook (Winchester) | B. W. Howes (Dulwich) |
| 1953 | R. A. McKenzie (St Paul's) | B. W. Howes (Dulwich) |
| 1954 | A. Vickers-Miles (Winchester) | C. Croft (Westminster) |
| 1955 | M. O'D. Alexander (St Paul's) | M. Gifford-Gifford (St Paul's) |
| 1956 | D. A. Young (Dulwich) | C. Redgrave (Westminster) |
| 1957 | A. Leckie (Merchant Taylors') | A. Leckie (Merchant Taylors') |
| 1958 | R. Lynn (Sutton Valence) | G. Leckie (Merchant Taylors') |
| 1959 | I. Atkinson (Dulwich) | I. Atkinson (Dulwich) |
| 1960 | I. F. Duthie (Merchant Taylors') | J. W. F. Harris (Merchant Taylors') |
| 1961 | D. Shapland (Dulwich) | R. P. Ford (St Paul's) |
| 1962 | C. F. Green (Brentwood) | C. A. Layton (City of London) |
| 1963 | R. Brearley (St Paul's) | R. Craig (Merchant Taylors') |
| 1964 | E. Ben-Nathan (St Paul's) | E. Ben-Nathan (St Paul's) |
| 1965 | D. Acfield (Brentwood) | D. Acfield (Brentwood) |
| 1966 | J. Pawson (St Peter's, York) | B. H. Fisher (St Paul's) |
| 1967 | J. Brydon (St Dunstans) | N. W. Lambourn (Forrest) |
| 1968 | G. Grimmett (King Edward's) | I. M. Beith (Eton) |
| 1969 | J. A. McGregor (Merchiston) | P. Mather (Brentwood) |
| 1970 | G. Jones (Royal Belfast) | B. Lewis (King's, Rochester) |
| 1971 | I. Paretti (King's, Taunton) | P. Mather (Brentwood) |
| 1972 | G. Thompson (Dover College) | J. M. Lewis (St Paul's) |
| 1973 | M. Thompson (Kings, Chester) | J. M. Lewis (St Paul's) |
| 1974 | S. Carson (Royal Belfast) | S. Carson (Royal Belfast) |
| 1975 | E. M. R. Reynolds (St Paul's) | C. F. Webb (Brentwood) |
| 1976 | R. Hill (Whitgift) | C. F. Webb (Brentwood) |
| 1977 | J. Ferguson (Worth) | G. Li (Brentwood) |
| 1978 | J. S. Davis (Royal Belfast) | M. J. Hunt (Bristol GS) |
| 1979 | J. Burney (Eton) | M. J. Hunt (Bristol GS) |
| 1980 | K. A. Smith (Brentwood) | S. Baldry (Whitgift) |
| 1981 | D. Dale (Brentwood) | P. Klenerman (City of London) |

|  | *Epee* |  |  |
|---|---|---|---|
| 1933 | T. E. Mansfield (Stowe) | 1953 | P. Wilmot-Sitwell (Eton) |
| 1934 | C. T. J. Cripps (Eton) | 1954 | I. Cameron (Westminster) |
| 1935 | C. T. J. Cripps (Eton) | 1955 | B. J. M. Green (St Paul's) |
| 1936 | M. W. Waddington (Eton) | 1956 | V. H. Wells (City of London) |
| 1937 | R. P. Warre (Eton) | 1957 | R. Lynn (Sutton Valence) |
| 1938 | M. A. Pears (Westminster) | 1958 | J. Morland (St Paul's) |
| 1939 | N. E. Neter (Bradfield) | 1959 | S. Higginson (Merchant Taylors') |
| 1940 | P. R. V. Meyers (Bradfield) |  |  |
| 1941 | L. A. Wilson (Westminster) | 1960 | M. L. R. Davies (Dulwich) |
| 1942 | H. S. Ball (ISC) | 1961 | A. E. Boyd (Westminster) |
| 1943 | H. S. Ball (ISC) | 1962 | C. F. Green (Brentwood) |
| 1944 | G. Vane (Eton) | 1963 | J. S. Underwood (Brentwood) |
| 1945 | L. W. Prescott (Eton) | 1964 | D. Floyer (Brentwood) |
| 1946 | N. Elliot-Baxter (Eton) | 1965 | D. Floyer (Brentwood) |
| 1947 | A. J. Cotton (Cheltenham) | 1966 | E. Bourne (Brentwood) |
| 1948 | S. L. H. Clarke (Westminster) | 1967 | M. West (Brentwood) |
| 1949 | P. F. Hartshorn (St Paul's) | 1968 | J. M. Fordham (Dulwich) |
| 1950 | D. T. Fabian (St Paul's) | 1969 | A. N. Downing (St Dunstan's) |
| 1951 | C. A. Gentili (St Paul's) | 1970 | B. Lewis (King's, Rochester) |
| 1952 | J. Lee (Westminster) | 1971 | R. Maurer (Brentwood) |

|  |  |  |  |
|---|---|---|---|
|  | *Epee* |  |  |
| 1972 | S. Compson (King's, Rochester) | 1977 | A. Brannon (King's, Chester) |
| 1973 | K. M. O'Shea (Downside) | 1978 | G. D. Liston (George Heriot's) |
| 1974 | N. Mallett (Dover College) | 1979 | M. Wright (George Heriot's) |
| 1975 | S. J. S. Webb (St Paul's) | 1980 | M. R. Wilson (Royal Belfast) |
| 1976 | J. Steventon (Brentwood) | 1981 | D. Dale (Brentwood) |
|  | *Junior Foil (under-16)* |  |  |
| 1939 | J. Corsellis (Westminster) | 1961 | R. Brearley (St Paul's) |
| 1940 | J. Corsellis (Westminster) | 1962 | D. Acfield (Brentwood) |
| 1941 | R. Uffindell (Cranleigh) | 1963 | M. A. T. Ward (Whitgift) |
| 1942 | H. S. Ball (IS College) | 1964 | L. F. Took (Brentwood) |
| 1943 | D. S. Leese (Bedford) | 1965 | M. West (Brentwood) |
| 1944 | A. Ellison (Cheltenham) | 1966 | J. Noel (Downside) |
| 1945 | A. M. MacEwan (Wellington) | 1967 | T. Etherton (St Paul's) |
| 1946 | H. T. Kirwan-Taylor (Eton) | 1968 | J. Deanfield (Westminster) |
| 1947 | J. M. Stubbs (Cheltenham) | 1969 | G. Jones (Royal Belfast) |
| 1948 | P. Petrie (Westminster) | 1970 | G. M. Brown (Dover College) |
| 1949 | E. O. Reynolds (St Paul's) | 1971 | H. C. R. Campion (Merchant Taylors') |
| 1950 | M. B. Connock (Marlborough) |  |  |
| 1951 | R. A. McKenzie (St Paul's) | 1972 | A. G. Horne (Royal Belfast) |
| 1952 | R. J. A. Harmer (Eton) | 1973 | N. Mallett (Dover) |
| 1953 | B. J. L. Greene (St Paul's) | 1974 | J. Steventon (Brentwood) |
| 1954 | D. A. Young (Dulwich) | 1975 | A. J. Webb (St Paul's) |
| 1955 | D. A. Young (Dulwich) | 1976 | G. W. Tait (St Peter's, York) |
| 1956 | R. Peters (St Paul's) | 1977 | M. S. Andrew (St Dunstan's) |
| 1957 | C. M. M. Stern (Marlborough) | 1978 | M. Whitcombe (City of London) |
| 1958 | C. C. Walker (Pangbourne) | 1979 | M. Wilson (Royal Belfast) |
| 1959 | S. C. Peck (Clifton) | 1980 | D. Dale (Brentwood) |
| 1960 | R. M. Slater (Pangbourne) | 1981 | P. Stanley (Brentwood) |
|  | *Junior sabre* |  | *Junior epee* |
| 1979 | P. Klenerman (City of London) |  | M. Wilson (Royal Belfast) |
| 1980 | D. Dale (Brentwood) |  | D. Dale (Brentwood) |
| 1981 | T. Yassir (Haileybury) |  | J. Hudson (Edinburgh Acad.) |

GRAHAM-BARTLETT CUP
Presented in 1939 by E. R. B. Graham. Awarded on a points system in the senior events.

| | | | | | |
|---|---|---|---|---|---|
| 1939 | Dulwich | 1954 | Westminster | 1969 | Brentwood |
| 1940 | Cheltenham | 1955 | St Paul's | 1970 | King's, Rochester |
| 1941 | Eton | 1956 | Westminster | 1971 | Royal Belfast |
| 1942 | Eton | 1957 | Merchant Taylors' | 1972 | Brentwood |
| 1943 | Cheltenham | 1958 | St Paul's | 1973 | Brentwood |
| 1944 | Dulwich | 1959 | Merchant Taylors' | 1974 | Brentwood |
| 1945 | Cheltenham | 1960 | Merchant Taylors' | 1975 | St Paul's |
| 1946 | Cheltenham | 1961 | Dulwich | 1976 | Brentwood |
| 1947 | Eton | 1962 | Brentwood | 1977 | Brentwood |
| 1948 | Westminster | 1963 | Brentwood | 1978 | Brentwood |
| 1949 | St Paul's | 1964 | Brentwood | 1979 | Brentwood |
| 1950 | St Paul's | 1965 | Brentwood | 1980 | Brentwood |
| 1951 | St Paul's | 1966 | Brentwood | 1981 | Brentwood |
| 1952 | St Paul's | 1967 | St Dunstan's | | |
| 1953 | St Paul's | 1968 | Brentwood | | |

## INTER-SERVICES CHAMPIONSHIPS

Compiled from the files of the Royal Tournament. Competitions, confined to the Army till 1905, were held from 1888, but no results recorded till 1896. The winners given from 1905 onwards are those of the combined Royal Navy and Regular Army Championships, which became the Inter-Services Championships in 1912. (These are preceded by the winners of the Gold Medal Championships of 1904, evidently more broadly based than the two Army events of that year.) Epee was introduced in 1904, but though the Navy was included from 1905 it was confined to officers till 1921, there being a separate championship for other ranks from 1912 to 1920. A ladies' foil event was introduced in 1947. (Service is only stated if it is not the Army and is not indicated by rank.)

| | *Men's Foil* Other Ranks | Officers |
|---|---|---|
| 1896 | SSgt B. Foerster (AGS) | Capt J. McCall Maxwell (RA) |
| 1897 | Fencing Inst. W. Elliott (2nd Life Grds) | Capt J. McCall Maxwell (RA) |
| 1898 | SSgt J. Betts (AGS) | Capt J. McCall Maxwell (RA) |
| 1899 | SSgt J. Betts (AGS) | Lt Col J. S. S. Barker (RA) |
| 1900 | Sgt E. Adams (AGS) | Capt H. Pollock (14th Middx RV) |
| 1901 | Sgt Maj J. Betts (AGS) | 2nd Lt T. Hobbins (12th Middx VR) |
| 1902 | Sgt Maj J. Betts (AGS) | Capt E. G. S. Cooke (Lond. Rifle Brig.) |
| 1903 | Sgt Inst. W. Palmer (AGS) | Maj H. Bethune (Gordon Hdrs.) |
| 1904 | St Sgt D. Hunter (AGS) | Sub Lt F. Feilmann (RN) |
| | *Sabre* Other Ranks | Officers |
| 1896 | SSgt B. Foerster (AGS) | Capt W. Edgworth-Johnstone (Roy. Irish Regt) |
| 1897 | Fencing Inst. W. Elliott (2nd Life Gds) | Lt E. G. S. Cooke (Lond. Rifle Brig.) |
| 1898 | Fencing Inst. W. Elliott (2nd Life Gds) | Capt W. Edgworth-Johnstone (Roy. Irish Regt) |
| 1899 | SSgt J. Woolfoot (AGS) | Lt R. Poore (Roy. Wilts. Yeo.) |
| 1900 | Sgt Inst. J. Betts (AGS) | Capt W. Edgworth-Johnstone (Roy. Irish Regt) |
| 1901 | Sgt Maj J. Betts (AGS) | Lt W. Hulke (2nd Lincoln Regt) |
| 1902 | Sgt Maj J. Betts (AGS) | 2nd Lt T. Hobbins (12th Middx VR) |
| 1903 | Fencing Inst. W. Elliott (2nd Life Gds) | Maj F. Higgins Bernard (18th Middx VR) |
| 1904 | Fencing Inst. F. Eggleton (Roy. Horse Gds) | Maj H. Bethune (Gordon Hdrs) |

| | *Men's Foil* | *Sabre* |
|---|---|---|
| 1904 | Sgt Maj J. Betts (AGS) | Sgt Maj J. Betts (AGS) |
| 1905 | Cpl H. E. James (2nd Co. of Lond. Yeo.) | SCM W. Elliott (2nd Life Gds) |
| 1906 | Sgt Maj J. Betts (AGS) | Sgt Maj J. Betts (AGS) |
| 1907 | Lt J. Betts (AGS) | Lt J. Betts (AGS) |
| 1908 | Lt J. Betts (AGS) | Lt J. Betts (AGS) |
| 1909 | Lt J. Betts (AGS) | Lt J. Betts (AGS) |
| 1910 | Lt J. Betts (AGS) | CSM A. Langley (AGS) |
| 1911 | Lt J. Betts (AGS) | Lt J. Betts (AGS) |
| 1912 | Lt J. Betts (AGS) | Lt J. Betts |
| 1913 | SCM H. Grainger | SCM H. Grainger |

|      | Men's Foil | Sabre |
| --- | --- | --- |
| 1914 | Sgt Maj W. Palmer | Lt E. W. H. Brookfield (RN) |
| 1919 | Capt W. Palmer | Col R. B. Campbell |
| 1920 | Maj R. Willoughby | Capt W. Palmer |
| 1921 | Sgt Maj H. Grainger (RAF) | Sgt Maj H. Grainger (RAF) |
| 1922 | CSMI G. Wyatt | Lt C. Kershaw (RN) |
| 1923 | Flt Lt F. Sherriff | Lt C. Kershaw (RN) |
| 1924 | Lt C. Kershaw (RN) | Lt C. Kershaw (RN) |
| 1925 | Flt Lt F. Sherriff (RAF) | Lt Cdr C. Kershaw (RN) |
| 1926 | Lt Cdr C. Kershaw | QMSI G. Wyatt |
| 1927 | SSMI J. T. Reid | QMSI G. Wyatt |
| 1928 | CSMI J. T. Reid | SMI G. Wyatt |
| 1929 | CSMI J. T. Reid | CSMI J. T. Reid |
| 1930 | SMI G. Wyatt | QMSI H. Parsons |
| 1931 | QMSI H. Parsons | SMI G. Wyatt |
| 1932 | SMI J. T. Reid | SMI G. Wyatt |
| 1933 | SMI H. Parsons | SMI H. Parsons |
| 1934 | Sgt W. Hancock (RAF) | Sgt L. V. Clarke (RM) |
| 1935 | 2nd Lt J. Armstrong | Sgt L. V. Clarke (RM) |
| 1936 | Lt Cdr E. Mount Haes | Lt C. J. Bampfylde |
| 1937 | Sgt J. F. Field (RM) | Sgt Inst. G. Moore |
| 1938 | CSMI G. Moore | CSMI G. Moore |
| 1939 | CSMI G. Moore | Cpl J. Fitzmaurice (RAF) |
| 1947 | Maj A. Hatfield | Maj C. Hankinson |
| 1948 | Maj G. Moore (Army) | Cpl R. Anderson (RM) |
| 1949 | Sgt R. Anderson (RM) | Sgt R. Anderson (RM) |
| 1950 | Sgt J. Holland (RM) | Sgt R. Anderson (RM) |
| 1951 | Sgt R. Anderson (RM) | Col Sgt T. St L. Hirst (RM) |
| 1952 | Sgt R. Anderson (RM) | Sgt R. Anderson (RM) |
| 1953 | Col Sgt R. Anderson (RM) | Col Sgt R. Anderson (RM) |
| 1954 | Col Sgt R. Anderson (RM) | Col Sgt R. Anderson (RM) |
| 1955 | Sgt R. Thompson (RM) | Sgt R. Thompson (RM) |
| 1956 | Sgt R. Thompson (RM) | Sgt R. Thompson (RM) |
| 1957 | Sgt R. Thompson (RM) | Sgt R. Thompson (RM) |
| 1958 | SSI M. Howard | Col Sgt D. McKenzie (RM) |
| 1959 | Flt Lt J. J. Evans | Sgt R. Thompson (RM) |
| 1960 | Sgt R. Thompson (RM) | Lt M. Howard |
| 1961 | CSMI G. Gelder | Lt M. Howard |
| 1962 | Lt M. Howard | Cpl Tec R. Maunder (RAF) |
| 1963 | SI R. E. Bright | PO K. Pearson |
| 1964 | Maj H. W. Hoskyns | Maj H. W. Hoskyns |

*Epee*
Officers
| | | |
| --- | --- | --- |
| 1904 | Maj W. H. Grenfell, MP (1st Bucks VRC) | |
| 1905 | Lt F. Feilmann (RN) | |
| 1906 | Maj Lord Desborough (1st Bucks VRC) | |
| 1907 | Capt S. B. B. Dyer, DSO (2nd Life Gds) | |
| 1908 | Lt J. Betts (AGS) | |
| 1909 | Lt F. Feilmann (RN) | |
| 1910 | A Paymt. C. Drake (RN) | |
| 1911 | Lt J. Betts (AGS) | Other Ranks |
| 1912 | Lt J. Betts (AGS) | SCM H. Grainger (2nd Life Gds) |
| 1913 | Lt G. Dunsterville (1st Devon Regt) | SCM H. Grainger (2nd Life Gds) |
| 1914 | 2nd Lt B. J. M. Bebb (RE) | QMS A. Langley (AGS) |
| 1919 | Capt G. Brunton (NZ Rifle Brig.) | Sgt Maj F. Eggleton (AGS) |
| 1920 | Capt P. Dalglish (RN) | Sgt Maj H. Grainger |

*Epee*
All Ranks
1921    Flt Lt F. Sherriff
1922    Flt Lt F. Sherriff
1923    CSMI G. Wyatt
1924    Flt Lt F. Sherriff
1925    QMSI T. James
1926    QMSI G. Wyatt
1927    QMSI G. E. Ware
1928    CSMI J. T. Reid
1929    Flt Sgt L. Bishop
1930    SMI G. Wyatt
1931    Sgt F. Stubberfield (RAF)
1932    Sgt W. R. Hancock (RAF)
1933    LAC J. Fitzmaurice (RAF)
1934    Rfn R. Stanley
1935    Lt Cdr E. A. Mount Haes
1936    Lt Cdr E. A. Mount Haes
1937    Sgt J. F. Field (RM)
1938    CSMI L. Lambert (Army)
1939    Cpl J. Fitzmaurice (RAF)    *Ladies' Foil*
1947    Flt Lt W. H. Turner         SO Z. Taylor (WAAF)
1948    Maj G. Moore                Wren A. Heaton
1949    Surg Cdr C. P. Collins      WOII M. Humphrey
1950    Offr Cadet P. Hartshorn     WOII J. Marmont
1951    QMSI W. Teague              WOII J. Marmont
1952    Sgt R. Anderson (RM)        WOII J. Marmont
1953    Capt T. A. Bentley          Lt I. Milne
1954    Lt R. A. King               3rd Off B. J. G. Allen
1955    Lt Cdr R. Sproul-Bolton     Cpl B. Colclough (WRAF)
1956    Jnr Tech R. Maunder (RAF)   Capt J. Tappin
1957    FO R. Harrison              Capt J. Tappin
1958    FO R. Harrison              Ldg Wren S. M. Brooks
1959    Flt Lt R. Harrison          Capt J. Tappin
1960    CSMI G. Gelder              Lt P. Binny
1961    Lt M. Howard                Cpl D. R. Watkinson (RAF)
1962    Lt Cdr J. Dougan            3rd Off J. Damrel (WRNS)
1963    Flt Lt R. Harrison          Cpl A. Swancott
1964    Maj H. W. Hoskyns           Flt Off R. Lynn

*Men's Foil*
        1                           2                           3
1965    Flt Lt R. Peters            FO A. Painter               WOII G. Gelder
1966    Sq Ldr R. Peters            Maj D. Simpson              Flt Lt
                                                                W. H. M. Bradley
1967    Flt Off A. Painter          Sgt W. F. Cooper (RAF)      Sgt G. E. West
                                                                (RAF)
1968    Lt C. C. Walker (RN)        Lt L. C. Llewellyn          QMSI P. Lennon
                                    (RN)
1969    Flt Lt A. Painter           Sq Ldr R. Peters            Sgt T. Harrison
                                                                (RM)
1970    Lt C. C. Walker (RN)        Flt Off A. Painter          Capt A. Graham
                                    (RAF)
1971    Flt Lt A. Painter           Capt G. Alfred              Flt Lt L. Wall
1972    Flt Lt A. Painter           Sq Ldr R. G. Peters         Lt Cdr J. H. McGrath
1973    Maj J. Moore                Flt Lt A. Painter           Sgt T. Harrison
                                                                (RM)

|  | 1 | 2 | 3 |
|---|---|---|---|
| 1974 | PO C. Waldman (RAF) | Cpl S. A. Graham | Lt Cdr C. Walker |
| 1975 | PO C. Waldman (RAF) | Lt Col J. Moore | Sq Ldr R. Peters |
| 1976 | Lt M. Chetwood | Lt Col J. Moore | Lt Cdr C. Walker |
| 1977 | SSI P. J. Brierley | Cpl S. Graham | Lt M. Chetwood |
| 1978 | Flt Lt C. Waldman | SSI P. Brierley | Flt Lt J. Crouch |
| 1979 | Lt I. Campbell | Lt Lt J. Crouch | SSI P. Brierley |
| 1980 | Flt Lt C. Waldman | Lt J. Ferguson | Lt J. Gay |
| 1981 | Flt Off J. Ford | Lt J. Ferguson | Flt Lt C. Waldman |

*Sabre*

|  | 1 | 2 | 3 |
|---|---|---|---|
| 1965 | PO K. Pearson | Capt J. Moore | WOII G. Gelder |
| 1966 | Capt J. Moore | Col Sgt M. Joyce (RM) | Lt R. Craig |
| 1967 | Lt R. Craig | Maj J. Moore | Capt M. Howard |
| 1968 | Lt R. Craig | Maj J. Moore | QMSI P. Lennon |
| 1969 | Lt R. Craig | CTech R. Maunder (RAF) | Maj J. Moore |
| 1970 | Maj J. Moore | CTech R. Maunder (RAF) | PO R. Tiller |
| 1971 | Flt Off R. Maunder | Capt R. Craig | Maj J. Moore |
| 1972 | Maj J. Moore | Flt Off R. Maunder | Flt Lt Wall |
| 1973 | Capt R. Craig | Flt Lt A. Painter | Maj J. Moore |
| 1974 | Lt Cdr C. Walker | Lt Col J. Moore | Flt Lt A. Painter |
| 1975 | Lt Cdr C. Walker | Lt Col J. Moore | Flt Lt L. Wall |
| 1976 | Lt Col J. Moore | Flt Off R. Simpson | SSI J. Larkham |
| 1977 | Lt Col J. Moore | WOI D. Hughes | Sqd Ldr L. Wall |
| 1978 | WOI D. Hughes | WOII J. Larkham | Sqd Ldr A. Painter |
| 1979 | Lt Cdr C. Walker | Lt J. Gay (RN) | Maj A. Bell |
| 1980 | Sqd Ldr L. Wall | Cdr C. Walker | WOII J. Larkham |
| 1981 | Sqd Ldr L. Wall | Capt I. Campbell | Flt Lt R. Simpson |

*Epee*

|  | 1 | 2 | 3 |
|---|---|---|---|
| 1964 | Maj H. Hoskyns | CSMI G. Gelder | PO K. Pearson |
| 1965 | Sgt F. Finnis | Flt Off D. Parkinson | Sgt C. Edridge |
| 1966 | Lt L. Llewellyn (RN) | Capt M. Howard | Sgt J. Fox |
| 1967 | Sgt J. Darby | Capt M. Howard | Sgt J. Fox |
| 1968 | Sgt J. Fox | L Cpl B. Lillywhite | SSI A. Flood |
| 1969 | Sq Ldr R. Peters | CSMI A. Flood | Lt P. Johnstone (RN) |
| 1970 | Sgt J. Fox | Lt L. Llewellyn (RN) | Sq Ldr R. Peters |
| 1971 | 2nd Lt T. Belson | Sgt J. Fox | SI B. Lillywhite |
| 1972 | 2nd Lt T. Belson | Sgt T. Harrison (RM) | 2nd Lt L. Burr |
| 1973 | 2nd Lt T. Belson | Maj J. Moore | SI P. Brierley |
| 1974 | SI P. Brierley | Lt Col J. Moore | Sgt H. Baker (RAF) |
| 1975 | Sgt J. Fox | SI P. Brierley | Lt Col J. Moore |
| 1976 | SI P. Brierley | CSM B. Matlass | Flt Lt J. Crouch |
| 1977 | SSI P. Brierley | Jnr Tech J. Melville (RAF) | Lt Cdr J. McGrath |
| 1978 | SSI P. Brierley | Fg Off J. Warburn | Flt Lt J. Crouch |
| 1979 | SSI P. Brierley | Jnr Tech J. Melville (RAF) | Lt I. Campbell |
| 1980 | Lt I. Campbell | Capt L. Burr | St Sgt P. Brierley |
| 1981 | Sub Lt T. Kenealy | Capt I. Campbell | QMSI P. Brierley |

*Ladies' Foil*

|  | 1 | 2 | 3 |
|---|---|---|---|
| 1965 | SACW M. Merry (RAF) | SACW F. Igoe (RAF) | Wren C. Horseman (WRNS) |
| 1966 | JT M. Watterson | Sgt C. Bolland (WRAC) | SACW E. Igoe (RAF) |

|      | 1 | 2 | 3 |
|---|---|---|---|
| 1967 | L Cpl E. Harding | Sgt(w) M. Ryan (RAF) | LACW P. Blakemore (RAF) |
| 1968 | Cpl E. Harding | Flt Off M. Watterson | Flt Off M. Ryan |
| 1969 | Cpl E. Harding | Flt Off M. Ryan | PO Wren R. McHugh |
| 1970 | L Wren A. Bennett | PO Wren R. McHugh | Cpl (W) A. Beasley (RAF) |
| 1971 | PO M. Holmes (RAF) | L Wren A. Bennett | Sgt A. Wake (RAF) |
| 1972 | OC D. Forster-Smith (TAVR) | 3rd Off B. Williams | Pte R. Wilson |
| 1973 | 3rd Off B. Williams | LCpl R. Wilson | Wren S. Kay |
| 1974 | 3rd Off B. Williams | Wren M. Riley | Wren K. Eyton-Jones |
| 1975 | Flt Lt C. Ryan | Wren M. Aston | Cpl(W) L. Gordon (RAF) |
| 1976 | 2nd Off B. Williams | (Cpl (W) L. Gordon (RAF) | Capt R. Wheelock |
| 1977 | Wren M. Riley | 2nd Off B. Williams | S Aircr. W. L. Ward |
| 1978 | 2nd Off B. Williams | 3rd Off M. Myers | S Aircr W. L. Ward |
| 1979 | 2nd Off B. Williams | 3rd Off M. Myers | S Aircr W. L. Ward |
| 1980 | Flt Lt J. Kirk | 3rd Off M. Myers | PO Wren E. Kaczor |
| 1981 | 3rd Off M. Myers | Flt Lt J. Kirk | Cpl L. Ward (RAF) |

## *SCOTTISH CHAMPIONSHIPS*

*Ladies' Foil*

| | | | |
|---|---|---|---|
| 1923 | D. Aitken | 1956 | P. Robinson |
| 1924 | D. Aitken | 1957 | Mrs M. Garrow |
| 1925 | L. Findlay | 1958 | P. Cormack |
| 1926 | A. H. Robertson | 1959 | C. Tolland |
| 1927 | A. H. Robertson | 1960 | C. Tolland |
| 1928 | Mrs F. M. Russell | 1961 | C. Tolland |
| 1929 | H. J. Gunn | 1962 | C. Tolland |
| 1930 | Mrs F. M. Russell | 1963 | P. Cormack |
| 1931 | E. C. Arbuthnott | 1964 | A. B. Wilson |
| 1932 | E. C. Arbuthnott | 1965 | F. Shields |
| 1933 | M. E. Angus | 1966 | J. Little |
| 1934 | Hanbury | 1967 | F. Shields |
| 1935 | J. Guinness | 1968 | S. Youngs |
| 1936 | M. E. Angus | 1969 | J. Stewart |
| 1937 | M. E. Angus | 1970 | B. Williams |
| 1938 | M. A. James | 1971 | G. Ritchie |
| 1939 | M. A. James | 1972 | G. Ritchie |
| 1940–47 | No Competition | 1973 | G. Ritchie |
| 1948 | J. Armstrong | 1974 | Mrs G. Horne |
| 1949 | H. J. Gunn | 1975 | A. Simpson |
| 1950 | D. Dermody | 1976 | F. McIntosh |
| 1951 | Mrs A. Padden | 1977 | Mrs J. Cooksey |
| 1952 | Mrs E. Paton | 1978 | Mrs J. Cooksey |
| 1953 | I. Milne | 1979 | C. Robertson |
| 1954 | E. Berry | 1980 | F. McIntosh |
| 1955 | Mrs M. Garrow | 1981 | Mrs C. Smith |

|  | Men's Foil | Epee | Sabre |
|---|---|---|---|
| 1922 | | H. C. Myers | |
| 1923 | | H. C. Myers | |
| 1924 | | R. S. S. Meade | |
| 1925 | R. S. S. Meade | R. S. S. Meade | R. Crosnier |
| 1926 | R. Crosnier | W. R. Gray Muir | R. Crosnier |
| 1927 | A. H. C. Hope | C-L. de Beaumont | C-L. de Beaumont |
| 1928 | A. H. C. Hope | C-L. de Beaumont | A. H. C. Hope |
| 1929 | A. H. C. Hope | A. M. Anstruther | T. P. Saunders |
| 1930 | A. H. C. Hope | J. L. Hope | A. W. Brooks |
| 1931 | A. H. C. Hope | T. A. Wright | A. H. C. Hope |
| 1932 | T. A. Wright | W. C. A. Milligan | W. Leveson-Gower |
| 1933 | W. C. A. Milligan | P. M. S. Gedge | E. J. Keeling |
| 1934 | P. M. S. Gedge | C. R. Cammell | J. L. Hope |
| 1935 | L. G. Morrison | A. H. C. Hope | J. B. Armstrong |
| 1936 | W. C. A. Milligan | A. H. C. Hope | J. L. Hope |
| 1937 | W. C. A. Milligan | P. A. Fletcher | C-L. de Beaumont |
| 1938 | W. P. G. Maclachlan | W. C. A. Milligan | E. Mount Haes |
| 1939 | W. C. A. Milligan | J. L. Hope | C. D. Walker |
| 1940–47 | No competition | | |
| 1948 | Z. Czajkowski | W. F. Coulson | G. Gelder |
| 1949 | J. W. A. Peck | A. H. Stenning | R. Rosenberger |
| 1950 | L. G. Morrison | L. Morrison | No competition |
| 1951 | D. R. B. Mends | R. A. Hay | R. Rosenberger |
| 1952 | D. R. B. Mends | L. Morrison | J. L. Hope |
| 1953 | L. Morrison | D. R. B. Mends | R. Rosenberger |
| 1954 | L. Morrison | No competition | P. Snell |
| 1955 | L. Morrison | J. A. King | R. A. Napier |
| 1956 | L. Morrison | J. A. King | F. C. Churchman |
| 1957 | T. Broadhurst | L. Morrison | L. Morrison |
| 1958 | L. Morrison | R. T. Richardson | T. Broadhurst |
| 1959 | D. C. Martin | J. A. King | E. Mount Haes |
| 1960 | D. C. Martin | D. C. Hunter | W. F. Coulson |
| 1961 | D. C. Martin | J. A. King | A. H. Mitchell |
| 1962 | D. C. Martin | R. A. Hay | A. H. Mitchell |
| 1963 | J. Rorke | G. Sandor | A. H. Mitchell |
| 1964 | J. A. King | I. Duthie | A. H. Mitchell |
| 1965 | G. Sandor | J. A. King | J. Harris |
| 1966 | J. Rorke | J. Rorke | |
| 1967 | G. Sandor | No competition | No competition |
| 1968 | R. G. Wilson | R. G. Wilson | A. H. Mitchell |
| 1969 | P. D. Russell | P. D. Russell | A. H. Mitchell |
| 1970 | A. H. Mitchell | P. D. Russell | G. Wiles |
| 1971 | N. Millar | P. D. Russell | G. Wiles |
| 1972 | L. Smith | P. D. Russell | A. H. Mitchell |
| 1973 | P. D. Russell | P. D. Russell | L. M. Smith |
| 1974 | I. S. Campbell | J. McKenzie | R. S. Elliott |
| 1975 | N. Johnstone | J. Duthie | R. Jamieson |
| 1976 | J. Tyson | J. Tyson | R. S. Elliott |
| 1977 | T. Beattie | M. Mayo | R. S. Elliott |
| 1978 | D. Paterson | M. Peat | R. S. Elliott |
| 1979 | D. Paterson | D. McKenzie | R. S. Elliott |
| 1980 | J. Tyson | G. Mackay | R. S. Elliott |
| 1981 | D. McKenzie | G. Liston | R. S. Elliott |

## PROVINCIAL TOURNAMENTS
ASHTON†

*Ladies' Foil* – Richard Sorby Cup

| | | | |
|---|---|---|---|
| 1953 | P. North | 1967 | Mrs G. Harding |
| 1954 | B. M. Screech | 1968 | Mrs G. Harding |
| 1955 | J. Bailey | 1969 | M. Durne |
| 1956 | M. Durne | 1970 | Mrs M. A. Watts-Tobin |
| 1957 | C. Rayner | 1971 | S. Green |
| 1958 | T. M. Offredy | 1972 | S. Green |
| 1959 | F. Shields | 1973 | S. Green |
| 1960 | S. A. Netherway | 1974 | A. Knockaert |
| 1961 | P. Patient | 1975 | S. Green |
| 1962 | M. Durne | 1976 | L. Martin |
| 1963 | M. Durne | 1977 | L. Martin |
| 1964 | Mrs G. Harding | 1978 | L. Martin |
| 1965 | M. Durne | 1979 | E. Wood |
| 1966 | Mrs G. Harding | 1980 | Mrs E. Thurley |

| | *Men's Foil* | *Epee* | *Sabre* |
|---|---|---|---|
| | J. W. Hall Cup | S. H. Jackson Cup | Ashton Coronation Cup |
| 1953 | U. L. Wendon | | R. S. Watkins |
| 1954 | L. Jones | | R. S. Hogg |
| 1955 | R. S. Watkins | | R. S. Watkins |
| 1956 | L. Jones | | R. S. Watkins |
| 1957 | D. Cawthorne | J. Payne | P. A. Potter |
| 1958 | L. Jones | J. A. King | T. Broadhurst |
| 1959 | G. Hawksworth | J. Payne | L. Jones |
| 1960 | L. Jones | J. Payne | L. Jones |
| 1961 | K. Staines | G. Wiles | K. Staines |
| 1962 | K. Staines | M. Kallipetis | K. Staines |
| 1963 | H. W. Hoskyns | H. W. Hoskyns | G. Wiles |
| 1964 | A. Power | C. Purchase | D. Titheradge |
| 1965 | C. Purchase | J. Payne | G. Wiles |
| 1966 | G. Paul | V. Bonfil | R. Oldcorn |
| 1967 | A. Power | C. Purchase | G. Wiles |
| 1968 | D. Eden | G. Grimmett | G. Ganchev |
| 1969 | I. Single | A. Flood | G. Ganchev |
| 1970 | B. Paul | B. Wasley | G. Ganchev |
| 1971 | B. Paul | R. Bruniges | G. Ganchev |
| 1972 | A. Loveland | J. Fairhall | J. Philbin |
| 1973 | D. Flament | K. Lovejoy | P. Quivrin |
| 1974 | D. Flament | E. Teintenier | P. Quivrin |
| 1975 | S. Glaister | W. Osbaldeston | J. Philbin |
| 1976 | A. Eames | W. Osbaldeston | J. Philbin |
| 1977 | Z. Wojciechowski | S. Paul | J. Philbin |
| 1978 | P. Harper | S. Roose | J. Philbin |
| 1979 | S. Glaister | S. Paul | R. Cohen |
| 1980 | J. Troiano | G. Mackay | G. Li |

LEICESTER OPEN†

*Ladies' Foil* – Levesley Cup

| | | | |
|---|---|---|---|
| 1957 | C. Rayner | 1961 | G. Elliot |
| 1958 | S. Preston | 1962 | G. Sheen |
| 1959 | T. M. Offredy | 1963 | C. Rayner |
| 1960 | S. Netherway | 1964 | Mrs P. Courtney-Lewis |

| | | | | |
|---|---|---|---|---|
| 1965 | E. M. Jones | | 1973 | W. Ager |
| 1966 | E. Earle | | 1974 | S. Green |
| 1967 | P. Patient | | 1975 | L. Martin |
| 1968 | Mrs G. Harding | | 1976 | L. Martin |
| 1969 | Mrs G. Harding | | 1977 | H. Cawthorne |
| 1970 | Mrs H. Rogerson | | 1978 | L. Taylor |
| 1961 | S. Green | | 1979 | Mrs W. Grant |
| 1972 | S. Green | | 1980 | L. Martin |

| | *Men's Foil* | *Epee* | *Sabre* |
|---|---|---|---|
| | Martin Baker Cup | YMCA Cup | Oliver Cup |
| 1957 | H. W. Hoskyns | | P. C. Amberg |
| 1958 | René Paul | | G. T. Birks |
| 1959 | H. W. Hoskyns | | H. W. Hoskyns |
| 1960 | G. Wiles | | C. T. Courtney-Lewis |
| 1961 | M. Kallipetis | | W. J. Rayden |
| 1962 | A. Jay | | A. R. Cooperman |
| 1963 | G. Wiles | | A. R. Cooperman |
| 1964 | J. Tomlinson | | W. J. Rayden |
| 1965 | A. Painter | | C. Purchase |
| 1966 | A. Painter | | R. Oldcorn |
| 1967 | P. Jacobs | C. Purchase | G. Wiles |
| 1968 | J. Tomlinson | C. Purchase | G. Ganchev |
| 1969 | René Paul | E. Hudson | G. Ganchev |
| 1970 | G. Paul | D. Partridge | G. Ganchev |
| 1971 | B. Paul | D. Partridge | R. Cohen |
| 1972 | A. Eames | M. Beevers | A. J. Taylor |
| 1973 | R. Bruniges | B. Paul | G. Wiles |
| 1974 | D. Cawthorne | H. West | R. Cohen |
| 1975 | R. Bruniges | W. Osbaldeston | R. Cohen |
| 1976 | A. Eames | W. R. Johnson | J. Philbin |
| 1977 | A. Eames | J. Tomlinson | J. Philbin |
| 1978 | R. Bruniges | S. Paul | C. Kovanda |
| 1979 | S. Glaister | J. Melville | J. Philbin |
| 1980 | R. Bruniges | H. Kernohan | M. Slade |

WELSH OPEN†

*Ladies' Foil* – Welsh Games Cup

| | | | | |
|---|---|---|---|---|
| 1971 | M. Edwards | | 1976 | B. Williams |
| 1972 | C. Whitehurst | | 1977 | K. Cecil |
| 1973 | L. Brown | | 1978 | P. Grindley |
| 1974 | S. Harris | | 1979 | L. Martin |
| 1975 | L. Martin | | 1980 | F. McIntosh |

| | *Men's Foil* | *Epee* | *Sabre* |
|---|---|---|---|
| | Glyn Reynolds Cup | Kelvin Challenge Cup | John McCombe Cup |
| 1971 | B. Wasley | E. Gray | |
| 1972 | M. Fare | W. Osbaldeston | I. Edwards |
| 1973 | D. Russell | W. Osbaldeston | I. Edwards |
| 1974 | R. Bruniges | R. Bruniges | I. Edwards |
| 1975 | M. Fare | J. Llewellyn | R. Berry |
| 1976 | S. Glaister | S. Roose | J. Philbin |
| 1977 | P. Harper | S. Paul | T. Wishart |
| 1978 | G. Evans | H. West | J. Zarno |
| 1979 | P. Harper | H. W. Hoskyns | G. Kay |
| 1980 | R. Bruniges | G. Liston | P. West |

CLARA RAYNER MEMORIAL TOURNAMENT, NOTTINGHAM
Trophies presented by the Friends of Clara Rayner

| | Ladies' Foil | Men's Foil |
|---|---|---|
| 1959 | Mrs P. Courtney Lewis | H. MacLaughlan Smith |
| 1960 | R. Rayner | B. R. Wilson |
| 1961 | Mrs M. Hawdon | A. J. R. Berry |
| 1962 | No competition | No competition |
| 1963 | J. Plowright | R. D. Cornhill |
| 1964 | Mrs M. Hawksworth | G. Hanselman |
| 1965 | J. Bewley-Cathie | G. Hanselman |
| 1966 | A. Fodor | R. H. Turner |
| 1967 | E. M. Earle | G. Wiles |
| 1968 | Mrs G. Harding | G. Wiles |
| 1969 | J. Varley | G. Wiles |
| 1970 | J. Yates | S. Wooding |
| 1971 | Mrs H. Rogerson | G. Wiles |
| 1972 | Mrs M. Hawksworth | C. F. Brown |
| 1973 | J. Yates | B. A. Eames |
| 1974 | L. Martin | C. Waldmann |
| 1975 | C. Beagrie | M. Chetwood |
| 1976 | M. Worster | J. Ford |
| 1977 | Mrs M. Hawksworth | G. Wiles |
| 1978 | Mrs E. Emms | M. W. Thompson |
| 1979 | Mrs P. Tovey | A. C. W. Hudson |
| 1980 | M. Browning | M. Chetwood |
| 1981 | M. Browning | C. Ward |

| | Epee<br>Trophy presented by the<br>Carlton Forum FC | Sabre<br>Trophy presented by the Notts and<br>Derby Coaching Panel |
|---|---|---|
| 1964 | | C. Purchase |
| 1965 | | R. Oldcorn |
| 1966 | | R. Oldcorn |
| 1967 | | R. Oldcorn |
| 1968 | | G. Wiles |
| 1969 | | G. Wiles |
| 1970 | | G. Wiles |
| 1971 | | G. Wiles |
| 1972 | R. Evans | C. Kovanda |
| 1973 | B. Lewis | C. Kovanda |
| 1974 | M. West | C. Kovanda |
| 1975 | D. Brooks | R. Berry |
| 1976 | J. Tyson | R. S. Elliott |
| 1977 | W. Osbaldeston | R. Berry |
| 1978 | D. Fairhall | G. Wiles |
| 1979 | H. West | G. Wiles |
| 1980 | H. West | J. Magill |
| 1981 | R. Phelps | N. Moscardini |

## LEAMINGTON EASTER TOURNAMENT – BIRMINGHAM OPEN TOURNAMENT

Organised by Birmingham Fencing Club at Leamington Spa till 1974, then at Birmingham University.

*Ladies' Foil* – Sapcote Cup
presented by Mrs W. W. Sapcote

| | | | |
|---|---|---|---|
| 1934 | G. Neligan | 1961 | T. Offredy |
| 1935 | B. Puddefoot | 1962 | J. Bailey |
| 1936 | D. L. Breese | 1963 | J. Bewley-Cathie |
| 1937 | E. Richards | 1964 | U. Steinfort |
| 1938 | C. Willis | 1965 | P. Patient |
| 1939 | K. Swanton | 1966 | C. Maenich |
| 1940–46 | No competition | 1967 | Mrs Wardell-Yerburgh |
| 1947 | Mrs M. Glen Haig | 1968 | No competition |
| 1948 | D. Knowles | 1969 | P. Patient |
| 1949 | B. Screech | 1970 | S. Youngs |
| 1950 | B. Screech | 1971 | Mrs G. Harding |
| 1951 | G. Sheen | 1972 | S. Green |
| 1952 | B. Screech | 1973 | S. Olley |
| 1953 | M. Stafford | 1974 | S. Green |
| 1954 | P. Webber | 1975 | Mrs S. Lewis |
| 1955 | V. Jorgensen | 1976 | L. Martin |
| 1956 | S. Preston | 1977 | H. Cawthorne |
| 1957 | C. Rayner | 1978 | H. Cawthorne |
| 1958 | P. Reynolds | 1979 | L. Martin |
| 1959 | M. Durne | 1980 | M. Rodrigues |
| 1960 | Mrs P. Courtney-Lewis | 1981 | J. Leenders |

| | Men's Foil<br>Edgbaston Cup<br>presented by<br>Thomas Foden Flint | Epee<br>De Escofet Cup<br>presented by<br>Dr De Escofet | Sabre<br>Leamington Spa Cup<br>presented by<br>Birmingham FC |
|---|---|---|---|
| 1934 | | A. Pelling | |
| 1935 | | A. D. Pearce | V. Clayton-Morris |
| 1936 | | V. Clayton-Morris | V. Clayton-Morris |
| 1937 | | H. Cooke | R. E. Cole |
| 1938 | | M. Marley | G. Moore |
| 1939 | | J. Fitzmaurice | G. Moore |
| 1940–46 | No competition | | |
| 1947 | | C-L. de Beaumont | O. Porebski |
| 1948 | U. L. Wendon | René Paul | O. Porebski |
| 1949 | René Paul | B. W. Sapcote | E. R. Watts |
| 1950 | Raymond Paul | P. Meister | E. D. Dagallier |
| 1951 | René Paul | D. Parham | J. Frought |
| 1952 | René Paul | J. Cottar | M. J. Amberg |
| 1953 | René Paul | P. Whitta | P. C. Amberg |
| 1954 | René Paul | M. Howard | R. S. Watkins |
| 1955 | René Paul | D. Parham | H. W. Hoskyns |
| 1956 | A. Jay | H. W. Hoskyns | A. Jay |
| 1957 | D. Cawthorne | C. Piedfer | G. Piedfer |
| 1958 | H. W. Hoskyns | J. Pelling | H. W. Hoskyns |
| 1959 | René Paul | H. W. Hoskyns | G. Birks |
| 1960 | H. W. Hoskyns | H. W. Hoskyns | B. Heydennyk |
| 1961 | René Paul | René Paul | A. R. Cooperman |
| 1962 | P. Kirby | P. Jacobs | A. R. Cooperman |
| 1963 | René Paul | J. Glasswell | R. Fraisse |

|  | Men's Foil | Epee | Sabre |
|---|---|---|---|
| 1964 | H. W. Hoskyns | J. Glasswell | A. Orban |
| 1965 | A. Leckie | P. Jacobs | A. Leckie |
| 1966 | G. Sandor | S. Netburn | R. Oldcorn |
| 1967 | A. Leckie | G. Ayliffe | P. Wischeidt |
| 1968 | No competition | No competition | No competition |
| 1969 | P. D. Russell | P. D. Russell | P. Wischeidt |
| 1970 | G. Paul | E. Hudson | P. Wischeidt |
| 1971 | I. Single | G. Paul | P. Wischeidt |
| 1972 | G. Grimmett | G. Bohnen | P. Wischeidt |
| 1973 | N. Bell | D. Partridge | P. Wischeidt |
| 1974 | D. Cawthorne | H. West | G. Gomez |
| 1975 | T. Soumagne | R. Evans | R. Gomez |
| 1976 | C. Noel | J. Noel | S. Wasilewski |
| 1977 | Z. Wojciechowski | C. Frohwein | J. Philbin |
| 1978 | N. Bell | P. Weglinski | J. Philbin |
| 1979 | T. Soumagne | S. Paul | M. Slade |
| 1980 | Z. Wojciechowski | Losey | M. Ortiz |
| 1981 | R. Bruniges | D. Cocker | W. J. Magill |

|  | Ladies' Foil Team<br>Harrison Slade Cup<br>presented by<br>Mrs W. W. Sapcote | Epee Team Event<br>Darge Cup<br>presented by Mr Darge | Sabre Team Event<br>Birmingham Cup |
|---|---|---|---|
| 1934 | Bertrand's FC | | |
| 1935 | Ladies' C. d' Escrime | | |
| 1936 | Poly. Ladies' FC | | |
| 1937 | Poly. Ladies' FC | | |
| 1938 | Poly. Ladies' FC | | |
| 1939 | Birmingham FC | | |
| 1940–46 | No competition | | |
| 1947 | Poly. Ladies' FC | | |
| 1948 | S. Grave | Birmingham FC | S. Paul |
| 1949 | Poly. Ladies' FC | S. Paul | S. Paul |
| 1950 | Poly. Ladies' FC | S. Paul | S. Paul |
| 1951 | Poly. Ladies' FC | S. Paul | S. Paul |
| 1952 | Poly. Ladies' FC | S. Paul | S. Paul |
| 1953 | Poly. Ladies' FC | Birmingham FC | Northampton FC |
| 1954 | Poly. Ladies FC | Grosvenor | S. Paul |
| 1955 | S. Behmber | S. Behmber | S. Nicklen |
| 1956 | AFA Leaders | Birmingham FC | No competition |
| 1957 | AFA Leaders | Birmingham FC | S. Nicklen |
| 1958 | Poly. Ladies' FC | Grosvenor FC | Northampton FC |
| 1959 | Northampton FC | Grosvenor FC | Northampton FC |
| 1960 | Northampton FC | Grosvenor FC | Dutch Team |
| 1961 | Poly. Ladies' FC | Grosvenor FC | The Hague |
| 1962 | Poly. Ladies' FC | Grosvenor FC | Birmingham FC |
| 1963 | Poly. Ladies' FC | Grosvenor FC | Racing C. de France |
| 1964 | Rhineland | Grosvenor FC | US Army |
| 1965 | Poly. Ladies' FC | Grosvenor FC | Rhineland |
| 1966 | Poly. Ladies' FC | Grosvenor FC | Rhineland |
| 1967 | Rhein-Fechterbund | Rhein Fechterbund | Rhineland |
| 1968 | No competition | No competition | No competition |
| 1969 | Caledonian FC | Thames | London FC |
| 1970 | Caledonian FC | Thames | Rhineland |
| 1971 | Hydra FC | S. Paul | Rhineland |

|  | Ladies' Foil Team | Epee Team Event | Sabre Team Event |
|---|---|---|---|
| 1972 | Hydra FC | S. Boston | Rhineland |
| 1973 | Ashton FC | S. Boston | Hydra FC |
| 1974 | Hydra FC | Mod. Pentathlon Ass. | Hydra FC |
| 1975 | S. Boston | Mod. Pentathlon Ass. | Birmingham FC |
| 1976 | The BOTS | Grosvenor FC | Birmingham FC |
| 1977 | Allen FC | Ex-Under-20 | Birmingham FC |
| 1978 | Katowice FC | Katowice FC | Katowice FC |
| 1979 | London-Thames FC | London-Thames FC | Birmingham FC |
| 1980 | Cuba | USA | Cuba |
| 1981 | S. Behmber | RAF | S. Boston |

**INVERCLYDE TOURNAMENT**

*Ladies' Foil* – Barker Quaich

| 1959 | C. Tolland | 1971 | Mrs B. Goodall |
|---|---|---|---|
| 1960 | D. Plews | 1972 | B. Rae |
| 1961 | P. Cormack | 1973 | S. Youngs |
| 1963 | P. Cormack | 1974 | D. Devlin |
| 1964 | Mrs M. Hawdon | 1975 | L. Ramage |
| 1965 | M. Durne | 1976 | E. Wood |
| 1966 | J. Herriot | 1977 | Mrs J. Cooksey |
| 1967 | J. Herriot | 1978 | C. Robertson |
| 1968 | Mrs R. Castle | 1979 | A. Fraser-Smith |
| 1969 | Mrs G. McGechan | 1980 | J. Bracewell |
| 1970 | Mrs J. Bain | 1981 | D. Paterson |

|  | *Men's Foil*<br>Glasgow Cup | *Epee*<br>SFC Bowl | *Sabre*<br>Clyde Trophy |
|---|---|---|---|
| 1959 | L. Morrison |  | T. B. Broadhurst |
| 1960 | J. Fethers | J. Payne | D. C. Martin |
| 1961 | J. Fethers | J. Fethers | J. Fethers |
| 1962 | J. Fethers | S. Berndt | C. Fisher |
| 1963 | J. Fethers | J. Fethers | J. Fethers |
| 1964 | J. Fethers | G. Sandor | J. Roulot |
| 1965 | J. Bougnoux | A. H. Mitchell | G. Vauchelle |
| 1966 | J. Rorke | R. Wilson | G. Wiles |
| 1967 | M. Rainbow | A. H. Mitchell | G. Wiles |
| 1968 | R. T. Richardson | N. Rouxel | G. Wiles |
| 1969 | G. Sandor | R. Blomquist | G. Wiles |
| 1970 | H. Bracewell | I. A. Hunter | M. Joyce |
| 1971 | M. Breckin | I. A. Hunter | T. Wishart |
| 1972 | I. S. Campbell | R. Bruniges | G. Wiles |
| 1973 | B. Green | M. Alton | G. Wiles |
| 1974 | S. Glaister | M. Mayo | G. Wiles |
| 1975 | B. Green | W. Osbaldeston | G. Wiles |
| 1976 | J. Tyson | J. Llewellyn | R. S. Elliott |
| 1977 | R. S. Elliott | G. Toland | R. S. Elliott |
| 1978 | R. S. Elliott | E. Ferguson | J. Magill |
| 1979 | J. Tyson | R. Davenport | J. Magill |
| 1980 | D. McKenzie | J. Tyson | D. McKenzie |
| 1981 | D. Paterson | G. Mackay | D. Paterson |

PORTSMOUTH TOURNAMENT

| | Ladies' Foil | Men's Foil |
|---|---|---|
| 1962 | J. O'Connell | K. Pearson |
| 1963-4 | No competition | No competition |
| 1965 | P. Patient | B. Paul |
| 1966 | No competition | No competition |
| 1967 | P. Patient | A. Bongianni |
| 1968 | P. Patient | K. Pearson |
| 1969 | Mrs G. Harding | L. Edmonds |
| 1970 | Mrs J. Barkley | S. Routh-Jones |
| 1971 | M. Durne | J. Grimmett |
| 1972 | Mrs R. Castle | M. Fare |
| 1973 | W. Ager | A. Loveland |
| 1974 | E. Joyce | A. Loveland |
| 1975 | M. Browning | A. Loveland |
| 1976 | N. Drori | T. Harrison |
| 1977 | N. Drori | P. Harper |
| 1978 | B. Williams | G. Scott |
| 1979 | K. Cecil | R. Hill |
| 1980 | S. Hoad | G. Guenigault |
| 1981 | M. Wheelband | G. Guenigault |

## *GRANVILLE CUP*
Presented by the 4th Earl Granville

| | | Foil | Epee | Sabre |
|---|---|---|---|---|
| 1948 | 1 London FC<br>2 S. Paul | A. R. Smith | C-L. de Beaumont | R. Tredgold |
| 1949 | 1 S. Paul<br>2 London FC | René Paul | R. Parfitt | U. L. Wendon |
| 1950 | 1 S. Paul<br>2 London FC | Raymond Paul | R. Parfitt | U. L. Wendon |
| 1951 | 1 S. Paul<br>2 London FC | René Paul | R. Parfitt | U. L. Wendon |
| 1952 | 1 S. Paul<br>2 London FC | Raymond Paul | René Paul | U. L. Wendon |
| 1953 | 1 S. Paul<br>2 London FC | Raymond Paul | R. Parfitt | A. R. Cooperman |
| 1954 | 1 London FC<br>2 S. Paul | J. Fethers | C-L. de Beaumont | O. B. Porebski |
| 1955 | 1 S. Paul<br>2 London FC 'E' | Raymond Paul | René Paul | A. R. Cooperman |
| 1956 | 1 S. Paul 'A'<br>2 S. Paul 'B' | Raymond Paul | René Paul | A. R. Cooperman |
| 1957 | 1 S. Paul<br>2 London FC | Raymond Paul | René Paul | A. R. Cooperman |
| 1958 | 1 S. Paul<br>2 Poly | Raymond Paul | René Paul | A. R. Cooperman |
| 1959 | 1 S. Paul<br>2 London FC | Raymond Paul | René Paul | A. R. Cooperman |
| 1960 | 1 London FC<br>2 Poly | H. W. Hoskyns | J. Pelling | M. Straus |
| 1961 | 1 London FC<br>2 Poly. FC | M. Price | J. Pelling | A. Leckie |
| 1962 | 1 S. Paul<br>2 Poly. FC | A. Jay | René Paul | A. R. Cooperman |

|      |                      | Foil              | Epee                   | Sabre         |
| ---- | -------------------- | ----------------- | ---------------------- | ------------- |
| 1963 | 1 Poly. FC           | M. Price          | E. B. Knott            | G. T. Birks   |
|      | 2 Oxford Univ.       |                   |                        |               |
| 1964 | 1 London FC 'A'      | A. Leckie         | A. Seeman              | W. J. Rayden  |
|      | 2 London FC 'B'      |                   |                        |               |
| 1965 | 1 S. Paul            | A. Jay            | R. Zampini             | G. Paul       |
|      | 2 London FC          |                   |                        |               |
| 1966 | 1 London FC          | C. Rentoul        | R. Rhodes              | D. C. Martin  |
|      | 2 S. Boston          |                   |                        |               |
| 1967 | 1 Poly. FC           | G. Kestler        | S. Netburn             | E. Mills      |
|      | 2 London Univ.       |                   |                        |               |
| 1968 | 1 London Univ.       | G. Paul           | E. Bourne              | M. Breckin    |
|      | 2 S. Paul            |                   |                        |               |
| 1969 | 1 London Univ.       | G. Paul           | E. Bourne              | M. Mazowiecki |
|      | 2 S. Boston          |                   |                        |               |
| 1970 | 1 S. Boston          | E. Bourne         | W. R. Johnson          | R. Cohen      |
|      | 2 S. Paul            |                   |                        |               |
| 1971 | 1 S. Boston 'A'      | B. Wasley         | E. Bourne              | R. Cohen      |
|      | 2 S. Boston 'B'      |                   |                        |               |
| 1972 Jun. | 1 S. Boston     | W. R. Johnson     | E. Bourne              | R. Cohen      |
|      | 2 London FC          |                   |                        |               |
| 1972 Oct | 1 S. Boston      | E. Bourne         | W. R. Johnson          | R. Cohen      |
|      | 2 London FC          |                   |                        |               |
| 1973 | 1 S. Boston          | E. Bourne         | W. R. Johnson          | R. Cohen      |
|      | 2 London FC          |                   |                        |               |
| 1974 | 1 S. Paul            | B. Paul           | G. Paul                | D. Scott      |
|      | 2 S. Boston          |                   |                        |               |
| 1975 | 1 S. Paul            | B. Paul           | R. Gomez-Vaillard      | I. Single     |
|      | 2 London FC          |                   |                        |               |
| 1976 | 1 S. Boston          | R. Bruniges       | R. Davenport           | R. Cohen      |
|      | 2 S. Emery           |                   |                        |               |
| 1977 | 1 S. Emery           | S. Fox            | J. Stanbury            | W. J. Magill  |
|      | 2 S. Boston          |                   |                        |               |
| 1978 | 1 S. Boston 'A'      | A. Eames          | W. R. Johnson          | T. Etherton   |
|      | 2 S. Boston 'B'      |                   |                        |               |
| 1979 | 1 S. Emery           |                   |                        |               |
|      | 2 S. Boston          |                   |                        |               |
| 1980 | 1 S. Boston 'A'      | R. Bruniges       | W. R. Johnson          | M. Slade      |
|      |                      | A. Brannon (Ladies' Foil) |                |               |
|      | 2 S. Boston 'B'      |                   |                        |               |
| 1981 | 1 S. Boston 'A'      | R. Bruniges       | W. R. Johnson          | M. Slade      |
|      |                      | A. Brannon (Ladies' Foil) |                |               |
|      | 2 S. Boston 'B'      |                   |                        |               |

## LONDON v REST-OF-BRITAIN MATCH

The Rest-of-Britain team is selected from fencers who are not full members of a London Club or British Internationals. A silver Rose Bowl trophy was presented by R. E. Southcombe. The teams were of three-a-side at each weapon till 1971, when they were increased to four, though the men's foil teams were of four in 1962 and 1964.

| 1959 | Lon. 20–16   | 1965 | Lon. 20–16   | 1971 | RoB 40–24    | 1977 | Lon. 35–28 |
| ---- | ------------ | ---- | ------------ | ---- | ------------ | ---- | ---------- |
| 1960 | Lon. 18–18   | 1966 | Lon. 19–17   | 1972 | Lon. 35–29   | 1978 | Lon. 33–31 |
|      | (130–141)    | 1967 | Match aband. | 1973 | RoB 34–30    | 1979 | Lon. 34–30 |
| 1961 | Lon. 21–15   | 1968 | Lon. 20–16   | 1974 | Lon. 35–29   | 1980 | Lon. 34–30 |
| 1962 | Lon. 27–16   | 1969 | RoB 20–16    | 1975 | RoB 33–31    | 1981 | Lon. 44–20 |
| 1963 | RoB 19–17    | 1970 | RoB 19–17    | 1976 | Lon. 39–25   |      |            |
| 1964 | RoB 25–17    |      |              |      |              |      |            |

## INTER-SECTION TEAM COMPETITION – WINTON CUP

Presented to the AFA by N. G. and R. C. Winton. From 1953 the final series for six teams was fenced at a central venue, as was the entire competition from 1974, it being then divided into two divisions.

|      | 1      | 2       |      | 1      | 2             |
|------|--------|---------|------|--------|---------------|
| 1950 | North  | Wales   | 1967 | E Mids | SE            |
| 1951 | E Mids | North   | 1968 | SW     | E Mids        |
| 1952 | South  | W Mids  | 1969 | E Mids | SW            |
| 1953 | SW     |         | 1970 | W Mids | SE            |
| 1954 | SW     |         | 1971 | NW     | SE            |
| 1955 | SW     |         | 1972 | E Mids | NW            |
| 1956 | E Mids | SW      | 1973 | SW     | NW            |
| 1957 | South  | SE      | 1974 | NW     | SW            |
| 1958 | South  | E Mids  | 1975 | SE     | E Mids        |
| 1959 | South  | E Mids  | 1976 | E Mids | W Mids        |
| 1960 | South  | E Mids  | 1977 | NW     | E Mids        |
| 1961 | South  | E Mids  | 1978 | E Mids | NW, W Mids eq.|
| 1962 | W Mids | South   | 1979 | NW     | SE            |
| 1963 | E Mids | SW      | 1980 | Wales  | SE            |
| 1964 | SW     | E Mids  | 1981 | South  | E Mids        |
| 1965 | SW     | NW      |      |        |               |
| 1966 | SW     | E Mids  |      |        |               |

## QUADRANGULAR MATCH

(also known as the Home International from 1979)
An antique dagger, presented by C-L. de Beaumont, is awarded to the winning team. The Edward VII Trophy is awarded for the England–Scotland match incorporated in this event. Places are by number of match wins (but fight wins are also given here).

|       | 1           | 2    |    | 3     |    | 4       |    |
|-------|-------------|------|----|-------|----|---------|----|
| 1950  | Edinburgh   | Eng. | 82 | Ire.  | 58 | Wales   | 46 | Scot.   | 56 |
| 1951  | Cardiff     | Eng. | 88 | Wales | 53 | Scot.   | 56 | Ire.    | 43 |
| 1952  | Athlone     | Eng. | 80 | Wales | 52 | Scot.   | 55 | Ire.    | 49 |
| 1953  | London      | Eng. | 91 | Wales | 54 | Scot.   | 58 | Ire.    | 41 |
| 1954  | Edinburgh   | Eng. | 96 | Scot. | 77 | Wales   | 55 | Ire.    | 16 |
| 1955  | Newport     | Eng. | 97 | Wales | 54 | Scot.   | 65 | Ire.    | 28 |
| 1956  | Dublin      | Eng. | 63 | Ire.  | 54 | Wales   | 58 | Scot.   | 41 |
| 1957  | London      | Eng. | 74 | Scot. | 60 | Wales   | 56 | Ire.    | 26 |
| 1958  | Edinburgh   | Eng. | 61 | Wales | 62 | Scot.   | 54 | Ire.    | 29 |
| 1959  | Cardiff     | Eng. | 42 | Scot. | 36 | Wales   | 22 | Ireland absent |
| 1960  | Dublin      | Eng. | 66 | Wales | 53 | Scot.   | 45 | Ire.    | 52 |
| 1961  | London      | Eng. | 82 | Scot. | 59 | Wales   | 47 | Ire.    | 28 |
| 1962  | Aberdeen    | Eng. | 77 | Scot. | 61 | Wales   | 55 | Ire.    | 22 |
| 1963  | Cardiff     | Eng. | 81 | Wales | 61 | Scot.   | 48 | Ire.    | 25 |
| 1964  | Dublin      | Eng. | 81 | Scot. | 48 | Ire.    | 44 | Wales   | 43 |
| 1965  | London      | Eng. | 75 | Scot. | 62 | Ire.    | 35 | Wales   | 43 |
| 1966  | Largs       | Scot.| 44 | Eng.  | 41 | Wales   | 23 | Ireland absent |
| 1967* | Cardiff     | Scot.| 79 | Eng.  | 74 | Wales   | 44 | N. Ire. | 16 |
| 1968  | Belfast     | Eng. | 83 | Scot. | 62 | Wales   | 40 | N. Ire. | 31 |
| 1969  | London      | Eng. | 78 | Scot. | 70 | Wales   | 46 | N. Ire. | 22 |
| 1970  | Largs       | Eng. | 78 | Scot. | 61 | Wales   | 56 | N. Ire. | 20 |
| 1971  | Belfast     | Eng. | 81 | Scot. | 58 | Wales   | 49 | N. Ire. | 25 |
| 1972  | Cardiff     | Eng. | 84 | Scot. | 58 | N. Ire. | 41 | Wales   | 39 |
| 1973  | Sandhurst   | Eng. | 67 | Scot. | 55 | Wales   | 52 | N. Ire. | 42 |
| 1974  | Aberdeen    | Eng. | 62 | Wales | 55 | Scot.   | 57 | N. Ire. | 40 |
| 1975  | Cardiff     | Eng. | 71 | Scot. | 59 | Wales   | 56 | N. Ire. | 30 |
| 1976  | Huddersfield| Scot.| 62 | Eng.  | 65 | Wales   | 51 | N. Ire. | 38 |

|      |           | 1     |    | 2    |    | 3     |    | 4       |    |
|------|-----------|-------|----|------|----|-------|----|---------|----|
| 1977 | Glasgow   | Wales | 66 | Eng. | 59 | Scot. | 51 | N. Ire. | 40 |
| 1978 | Coleraine | Scot. | 65 | Eng. | 71 | Wales | 43 | N. Ire. | 37 |
| 1979 | Salford   | Eng.  | 71 | Scot.| 59 | Wales | 56 | N. Ire. | 30 |
| 1980 | Cardiff   | Eng.  | 72 | Scot.| 55 | Wales | 53 | N. Ire. | 36 |
| 1981 | Edinburgh | Eng.  | 68 | Scot.| 55 | Wales | 47 | N. Ire. | 45 |

*N. Ireland replaced Ireland from this year.

## COMMONWEALTH GAMES AND CHAMPIONSHIPS

The Games have had various titles (initially 'British Empire Games'). When fencing was excluded from the Games in 1974 and 1978, Commonwealth Championships were held instead.

### 1950 AUCKLAND
(Fencing included for first time)

|    | 1 | 2 | 3 |
|----|---|---|---|
| LF | Mrs Glen Haig (Eng.) | P. Woodroff (NZ) | P. Pym (Aus.) |
| MF | René Paul (Eng.) | J. Fethers (Aus.) | G. Pouliot (Can.) |
| E  | C-L. de Beaumont (Eng.) | R. Anderson (Eng.) | I. Lund (Aus.) |
| S  | A. G. Pilbrow (Eng.) | R. Anderson (Eng.) | G. Pouliot (Can.) |
| Team | | | |
| MF | England | New Zealand | Canada |
| E  | Australia | England | Canada |
| S  | England | Canada | Australia |

### 1954 VANCOUVER
| LF | Mrs Glen Haig (Eng.) | G. Sheen (Eng.) | A. Harding (Wales) |
|----|---|---|---|
| MF | René Paul (Eng.) | J. Fethers (Aus.) | A. Jay (Eng.) |
| E  | I. Lund (Aus.) | René Paul (Eng.) | C. Schwende (Can.) |
| S  | M. Amberg (Eng.) | A. R. Cooperman (Eng.) | J. Fethers (Aus.) |
| Team | | | |
| MF | England | Australia | Canada |
| E  | England | Canada | Australia |
| S  | Canada | England | Australia |

### 1958 CARDIFF
| LF | G. Sheen (Eng.) | B. McCreath (Aus.) | Mrs Glen Haig (Eng.) |
|----|---|---|---|
| MF | Raymond Paul (Eng.) | I. Lund (Aus.) | René Paul (Eng.) |
| E  | H. W. Hoskyns (Eng.) | M. J. P. Howard (Eng.) | A. Jay (Eng.) |
| S  | H. W. Hoskyns (Eng.) | A. R. Cooperman (Eng.) | M. Amberg (Eng.) |
| Team | | | |
| MF | England | Australia | Wales |
| E  | England | Canada | Australia |
| S  | England | Australia | Wales |

### 1962 PERTH
| LF | M. Coleman (NZ) | J. Winter (Aus.) | J. Hopner (Aus.) |
|----|---|---|---|
| MF | A. Leckie (Scot.) | A. Jay (Eng.) | A. Cooperman (Eng.) |
| E  | I. Lund (Aus.) | J. Pelling (Eng.) | P. Jacobs (Eng.) |
| S  | A. R. Cooperman (Eng.) | B. Simo (Can.) | J. Andru (Can.) |
| Team | | | |
| MF | England | Australia | Canada |
| E  | England | Australia | Canada |
| S  | England | Canada | New Zealand |

### 1966 KINGSTON (Ladies' team event included for first time.)
| LF | Mrs Wardell-Yerburgh (Eng.) | Mrs S. Parker (Eng.) | G. McDermitt (NZ) |
|----|---|---|---|
| MF | A. Jay (Eng.) | H. W. Hoskyns (Eng.) | G. Paul (Eng.) |
| E  | H. W. Hoskyns (Eng.) | J. Pelling (Eng.) | R. Reynolds (Wal.) |
| S  | A. R. Cooperman (Eng.) | A. Leckie (Scot.) | G. Arato (Aus.) |

|  | 1 | 2 | 3 |
|---|---|---|---|
| *Team* | | | |
| LF | England | Australia | New Zealand |
| MF | England | Australia | Scotland |
| E | England | Canada | Australia |
| S | England | Australia | Canada |

1970 EDINBURGH

| | | | |
|---|---|---|---|
| LF | Mrs Wardell-Yerburgh (Eng.) | M. Exelby (Aus.) | S. Youngs (Scot.) |
| MF | M. Breckin (Eng.) | B. Paul (Eng.) | G. Paul (Eng.) |
| E | H. W. Hoskyns (Eng.) | L. Wong (Can.) | P. Jacobs (Eng.) |
| S | A. Leckie (Scot.) | R. Craig (Eng.) | R. Cohen (Eng.) |
| *Team* | | | |
| LF | England | Scotland | Canada |
| MF | England | Australia | Canada |
| E | England | Scotland | Canada |
| S | England | Scotland | Australia |

1974 (COMMONWEALTH CHAMPIONSHIPS) OTTAWA
(Canada, as host nation, entered two teams)

| | | | |
|---|---|---|---|
| LF | S. Wrigglesworth (Eng.) | Mrs M. Gray (NI) | S. Youngs (Scot.) |
| MF | A. Eames (NI) | G. Benko (Aus.) | N. Bell (Eng.) |
| E | G. Benko (Aus.) | D. Partridge (Eng.) | J. Noel (Eng.) |
| S | D. Eden (Eng.) | A. Taylor (Eng.) | J. Philbin (Eng.) |
| *Team* | | | |
| LF | Australia | England | Scotland |
| MF | England | Australia | N. Ireland |
| E | England | Wales | Australia |
| S | England | Canada 'B' | Canada 'A' |

1978 (COMMONWEALTH CHAMPIONSHIPS) GLASGOW

| | | | |
|---|---|---|---|
| LF | H. Smith (Aus.) | C. Payer (Can.) | E. Wood (Eng.) |
| MF | P. Harper (Eng.) | E. Simon (Aus.) | M. Dessureault (Can.) |
| E | S. Roose (Eng.) | G. Benko (Aus.) | S. Paul (Eng.) |
| S | J. Philbin (Eng.) | M. Lavoie (Can.) | G. Benko (Aus.) |
| *Team* | | | |
| LF | England | Canada | Australia |
| MF | England | Australia | Scotland |
| E | England | Scotland | Australia |
| S | England | Canada | N. Ireland |

# WORLD AND OLYMPIC CHAMPIONSHIPS

Venues in Olympic years are in capital letters. The European Championships up to 1935 were the equivalent of World Championships and are therefore included. (R. = USSR)

## MEN'S FOIL

| | | 1 | 2 | 3 |
|---|---|---|---|---|
| 1896 | ATHENS | E. Gravelotte (Fr.) | H. Callot (Fr.) | P. Dankla (Gr.) |
| 1900 | PARIS | C. Costa (Fr.) | H. Masson (Fr.) | J. Boulanger (Fr.) |
| 1904 | ST LOUIS | R. Fonst (Cuba) | A. Post (Cuba) | C. Tatham (Cuba) |
| 1906 | ATHENS | M. Dillon-Cavanagh (Fr.) | G. Casmir (Ger.) | Comte d'Huges (Fr.) |
| 1912 | STOCKHOLM | N. Nadi (It.) | P. Speciale (It.) | R. Verderber (Ger.) |
| 1920 | ANTWERP | N. Nadi (It.) | P. Cattiau (Fr.) | R. Ducret (Fr.) |
| 1924 | PARIS | R. Ducret (Fr.) | P. Cattiau (Fr.) | M. van Damme (Bel.) |
| 1926 | Budapest | G. Chiavacci (It.) | L. Berti (Hu.) | U. Pignotti (It.) |
| 1927 | Vichy | O. Puliti (It.) | P. Cattiau (Fr.) | G. Guaragna (It.) |
| 1928 | AMSTERDAM | L. Gaudin (Fr.) | E. Casmir (Ger.) | G. Gaudini (It.) |
| 1929 | Naples | O. Puliti (It.) | P. Cattiau (Fr.) | G. Gaudini (It.) |
| 1930 | Liège | G. Gaudini (It.) | G. Marzi (It.) | G. Guaragna (It.) |
| 1931 | Vienna | R. Lemoine (Fr.) | G. Marzi (It.) | J. E. Lloyd (GB) |
| 1932 | LOS ANGELES | G. Marzi (It.) | E. Lewis (US) | G. Gaudini (It.) |
| 1933 | Budapest | G. Guaragna (It.) | G. Gaudini (It.) | J. E. Lloyd (GB) |
| 1934 | Warsaw | G. Gaudini (It.) | G. Marzi (It.) | G. Bocchino (It.) |
| 1935 | Lausanne | G. Marzi (It.), G. Bocchino (It.), R. Lemoine (Fr.), E. Gardère (Fr.) eq. | | |
| 1936 | BERLIN | G. Gaudini (It.) | E. Gardère (Fr.) | G. Bocchino (It.) |
| 1937 | Paris | G. Marzi (It.) | E. Gardère (Fr.) | R. Lemoine (Fr.) |
| 1938 | Piestany | G. Guaragna (It.) | G. Bocchino (It.) | E. Gardère (Fr.) |
| 1947 | Lisbon | C. d'Oriola (Fr.) | M. di Rosa (It.) | E. Mangiarotti (It.) |
| 1948 | LONDON | J. Buhan (Fr.) | C. d'Oriola (Fr.) | L. Maszlay (Hu.) |
| 1949 | Cairo | C. d'Oriola (Fr.) | R. Nostini (It.) | G. Nostini (It.), E. Mangiarotti (It.) eq. |
| 1950 | Monte-Carlo | R. Nostini (It.) | J. Buhan (Fr.) | J. Lataste (Fr.) |
| 1951 | Stockholm | M. di Rosa (It.) | E. Mangiarotti (It.) | J. Buhan (Fr.) |
| 1952 | HELSINKI | C. d'Oriola (Fr.) | E. Mangiarotti (It.) | M. di Rosa (It.) |
| 1953 | Brussels | C. d'Oriola (Fr.) | E. Mangiarotti (It.) | M. di Rosa (It.) |
| 1954 | Luxembourg | C. d'Oriola (Fr.) | E. Mangiarotti (It.) | G. Bergamini (It.) |
| 1955 | Rome | J. Gyuricza (Hu.) | C. d'Oriola (Fr.) | J. Lataste (Fr.) |
| 1956 | MELBOURNE | C. d'Oriola (Fr.) | G. Bergamini (It.) | A. Spallino (It.) |
| 1957 | Paris | M. Fulop (Hu.) | M. Midler (R.) | A. Jay (GB) |
| 1958 | Philadelphia | G. Bergamini (It.) | F. Czvikovsky (Hu.) | B. Baudoux (Fr.) |
| 1959 | Budapest | A. Jay (GB) | C. Netter (Fr.) | M. Midler (R.) |
| 1960 | ROME | V. Jdanovich (R.) | Y. Sissikin (R.) | A. Axelrod (US) |
| 1961 | Turin | R. Parulski (Pol.) | J. Kamuti (Hu.) | M. Midler (R.) |
| 1962 | Buenos Aires | G. Sveshnikov (R.) | W. Woyda (Pol.) | J. Brecht (W. Ger.) |
| 1963 | Gdansk | J-C. Magnan (Fr.) | R. Parulski (Pol.) | E. Franke (Pol.) |
| 1964 | TOKYO | E. Franke (Pol.) | J-C. Magnan (Fr.) | D. Revenu (Fr.) |
| 1965 | Paris | J-C. Magnan (Fr.) | D. Revenu (Fr.) | G. Sveshnikov (R.) |
| 1966 | Moscow | G. Sveshnikov (R.) | J-C. Magnan (Fr.) | V. Putiatin (R.) |
| 1967 | Montreal | V. Putiatin (R.) | J. Kamuti (Hu.) | B. Talvard (Fr.) |
| 1968 | MEXICO CITY | I. Drimba (Rum.) | J. Kamuti (Hu.) | D. Revenu (Fr.) |
| 1969 | Cuba | F. Wessel (W. Ger.) | V. Stankovich (R.) | R. Parulski (Pol.) |
| 1970 | Ankara | F. Wessel (W. Ger.) | L. Romanov (R.) | M. Dabrowski (Pol.) |
| 1971 | Vienna | V. Stankovich (R.) | M. Dabrowski (Pol.) | L. Romanov (R.) |
| 1972 | MUNICH | W. Woyda (Pol.) | J. Kamuti (Hu.) | C. Noel (Fr.) |

|  |  | 1 | 2 | 3 |
|---|---|---|---|---|
| 1973 | Gothenburg | C. Noel (Fr.) | Y. Tchij (R.) | J. Kamuti (Hu.) |
| 1974 | Grenoble | A. Romankov (R.) | C. Montano (It.) | F. Pietruszka (Fr.) |
| 1975 | Budapest | C. Noel (Fr.) | B. Talvard (Fr.) | V. Dennisov (R.) |
| 1976 | MONTREAL | F. Dal Zotto (It.) | A. Romankov (R.) | B. Talvard (Fr.) |
| 1977 | Buenos Aires | A. Romankov (R.) | H. Hein (W. Ger.) | C. Montano (It.) |
| 1978 | Hamburg | D. Flament (Fr.) | A. Romankov (R.) | H. Hein (W. Ger.) |
| 1979 | Melbourne | A. Romankov (R.) | P. Jolyot (Fr.) | F. Dal Zotto (It.) |
| 1980 | MOSCOW | V. Smirnov (R.) | P. Jolyot (Fr.) | A. Romankov (R.) |
| 1981 | Clermont Ferrand | V. Smirnov (R.) | A. Kuki (Rum.) | A. Scuri (It.) |

MEN'S FOIL TEAMS

|  |  | 1 | 2 | 3 |
|---|---|---|---|---|
| 1904 | ST. LOUIS | Cuba | Int. Team |  |
| 1920 | ANTWERP | Italy | France | USA |
| 1924 | PARIS | France | Belgium | Hungary |
| 1928 | AMSTERDAM | Italy | France | Argentine |
| 1929 | Naples | Italy | Belgium | Hungary |
| 1930 | Liège | Italy | France | Belgium |
| 1931 | Vienna | Italy | Hungary | Austria |
| 1932 | LOS ANGELES | France | Italy | USA |
| 1933 | Budapest | Italy | Hungary and Austria eq. |  |
| 1934 | Warsaw | Italy | France | Germany |
| 1935 | Lausanne | Italy | France | Hungary |
| 1936 | BERLIN | Italy | France | Germany |
| 1937 | Paris | Italy | France | Austria |
| 1938 | Piestany | Italy | France | Czechoslovakia |
| 1947 | Lisbon | France | Italy | Belgium |
| 1948 | LONDON | France | Italy | Belgium |
| 1949 | Cairo | Italy | France | Egypt |
| 1950 | Monte-Carlo | Italy | France | Egypt |
| 1951 | Stockholm | France | Italy | Egypt |
| 1952 | HELSINKI | France | Italy | Hungary |
| 1953 | Brussels | France | Italy | Hungary |
| 1954 | Luxembourg | Italy | France | Hungary |
| 1955 | Rome | Italy | Hungary | Great Britain |
| 1956 | MELBOURNE | Italy | France | Hungary |
| 1957 | Paris | Hungary | France | Italy |
| 1958 | Philadelphia | France | USSR | Italy |
| 1959 | Budapest | USSR | W. Germany | Hungary |
| 1960 | ROME | USSR | Italy | W. Germany |
| 1961 | Turin | USSR | Hungary | Poland |
| 1962 | Buenos Aires | USSR | Hungary | Poland |
| 1963 | Gdansk | USSR | Poland | France |
| 1964 | TOKYO | USSR | Poland | France |
| 1965 | Paris | USSR | Poland | France |
| 1966 | Moscow | USSR | Hungary | Poland |
| 1967 | Montreal | Rumania | USSR | Poland |
| 1968 | MEXICO CITY | France | USSR | Poland |
| 1969 | Cuba | USSR | Poland | Rumania |
| 1970 | Ankara | USSR | Hungary | Rumania |
| 1971 | Vienna | France | Poland | USSR |
| 1972 | MUNICH | Poland | USSR | France |
| 1973 | Gothenburg | USSR | W. Germany | Poland |
| 1974 | Grenoble | USSR | Poland | France |
| 1975 | Budapest | France | USSR | Italy |

|      |                 | 1              | 2       | 3            |
|------|-----------------|----------------|---------|--------------|
| 1976 | Montreal        | W. Germany     | Italy   | France       |
| 1977 | Buenos Aires    | W. Germany     | Italy   | USSR         |
| 1978 | Hamburg         | Poland         | France  | USSR         |
| 1979 | Melbourne       | USSR           | Italy   | W. Germany   |
| 1980 | Moscow          | France         | USSR    | Poland       |
| 1981 | Clermont Ferrand| USSR           | Italy   | W. Germany   |

## LADIES' FOIL

|      |                | 1                            | 2                           | 3                              |
|------|----------------|------------------------------|-----------------------------|--------------------------------|
| 1924 | Paris          | E. Osiier (Den.)             | G. M. Davis (GB)            | B. Heckscher (Den.)            |
| 1928 | Amsterdam      | H. Mayer (Ger.)              | M. Freeman (GB)             | Oelkers (Ger.)                 |
| 1929 | Naples         | H. Mayer (Ger.)              | J. de Boer (Hol.)           | M. Dany (Hu.)                  |
| 1930 | Liège          | J. Addams (Bel.)             | G. Schwaiger (It.)          | M-A. Venables (GB)             |
| 1931 | Vienna         | H. Mayer (Ger.)              | E. Bogathy (Hu.)            | E. Preiss (Aus.)               |
| 1932 | Los Angeles    | E. Preiss (Aus.)             | J. Guinness (GB)            | E. Bogathy (Hu.)               |
| 1933 | Budapest       | G. Neligan (GB)              | E. Bogathy (Hu.)            | M. With (Den.)                 |
| 1934 | Warsaw         | I. Elek (Hu.)                | M. Elek (Hu.)               | H. Hass (Ger.)                 |
| 1935 | Lausanne       | I. Elek (Hu.)                | E. Preiss (Aus.)            | J. Addams (Bel.)               |
| 1936 | Berlin         | I. Elek (Hu.)                | H. Mayer (Ger.)             | E. Preiss (Aus.)               |
| 1937 | Paris          | H. Mayer (Ger.)              | I. Elek (Hu.)               | E. Preiss (Aus.)               |
| 1938 | Piestany       | M. Sediva (Cz.)              | C. Slabochova (Cz.)         | J. Addams (Bel.)               |
| 1947 | Lisbon         | E. Muller-Preiss (Aus.)      | S. Strukel (It.)            | I. Malherbaud (Fr.)            |
| 1948 | London         | I. Elek (Hu.)                | K. Lachmann (Den.)          | E. Muller-Preiss (Aus.)        |
| 1949 | Cairo          | E. Muller-Preiss (Aus.)      | K. Lachmann (Den.)          | R. Garilhe (Fr.)               |
| 1950 | Monte-Carlo    | R. Garilhe (Fr.), E. Muller-Preiss (Aus.) eq. |         | F. Filz (Aus.)                 |
| 1951 | Stockholm      | I. Elek (Hu.)                | K. Lachmann (Den.)          | M. Nyari (Hu.)                 |
| 1952 | Helsinki       | I. Camber (It.)              | I. Elek (Hu.)               | K. Lachmann (Den.)             |
| 1953 | Brussels       | I. Camber (It.)              | R. Garilhe (Fr.)            | I. Keydel (Ger.)               |
| 1954 | Luxembourg     | K. Lachmann (Den.)           | I. Elek (Hu.)               | R. Garilhe (Fr.)               |
| 1955 | Rome           | L. Domolki (Hu.)             | B. Colombetti (It.)         | I. Elek (Hu.)                  |
| 1956 | Melbourne      | G. M. Sheen (GB)             | O. Orban (Hu.)              | R. Garilhe (Fr.)               |
| 1957 | Paris          | A. Zabelina (R.)             | H. Schmid (W. Ger.)         | I. Camber (It.)                |
| 1958 | Philadelphia   | V. Kisseleva (R.)            | E. Gitnikova (R.)           | I. Rejto (Hu.)                 |
| 1959 | Budapest       | E. Efimova (R.)              | G. Gorokhova (R.)           | T. Petrenko (R.)               |
| 1960 | Rome           | H. Schmid (W. Ger.)          | V. Rastvorova (R.)          | M. Vicol (Rum.)                |
| 1961 | Turin          | H. Schmid (W. Ger.)          | A. Zabelina (R.)            | V. Rastvorova (R.)             |
| 1962 | Buenos Aires   | O. Orban-Szabo (Rum.)        | G. Gorokhova (R.)           | K. Juhasz (Hu.)                |
| 1963 | Gdansk         | I. Rejto (Hu.)               | L. Domolki-Sakovitz (Hu.)   | K. Juhasz (Hu.)                |
| 1964 | Tokyo          | I. Rejto-Ujlaki (Hu.)        | H. Mees (W. Ger.)           | A. Ragno (It.)                 |
| 1965 | Paris          | G. Gorokhova (R.)            | O. Orban-Szabo (Rum.)       | V. Prudskova (R.)              |
| 1966 | Moscow         | T. Samusenko (R.)            | A. Zabelina (R.)            | I. Bobis (Hu.), E. Iencic (Rum.), G. Gorokhova (R.) eq. |
| 1967 | Montreal       | A. Zabelina (R.)             | A. Ragno (It.)              | I. Bobis (Hu.)                 |
| 1968 | Mexico City    | E. Novikova (R.)             | P. Roldan (Mex.)            | I. Rejto-Ujlaki (Hu.)          |
| 1969 | Cuba           | E. Novikova (R.)             | I. Drimba (Rum.)            | S. Cirkova (R.)                |
| 1970 | Ankara         | G. Gorokhova (R.)            | E. Belova-Novikova (R.)     | O. Orban-Szabo (Rum.)          |
| 1971 | Vienna         | M-C. Demaille (Fr.)          | I. Rejto-Ujlaki (Hu.)       | A. Pascu (Rum.)                |
| 1972 | Munich         | A. R. Lonzi (It.)            | I. Bobis (Hu.)              | G. Gorokhova (R.)              |
| 1973 | Gothenburg     | V. Nikonova (R.)             | I. Schwarzenberger (Hu.)    | I. Rejto-Ujlaki (Hu.)          |
| 1974 | Grenoble       | I. Bobis (Hu.)               | I. Schwarzenberger (Hu.)    | N. Giliazova (R.)              |

|  | | 1 | 2 | 3 |
|---|---|---|---|---|
| 1975 | Budapest | C. Stahl (Rum.) | O. Kniazeva (R.) | I. Bobis (Hu.) |
| 1976 | MONTREAL | I. Schwarzenberger (Hu.) | M. C. Collino (It.) | E. Belova (R.) |
| 1977 | Buenos Aires | V. Sidorova (R.) | E. Belova (R.) | I. Schwarzenberger (Hu.) |
| 1978 | Hamburg | V. Sidorova (R.) | K. Raczova (Cze.) | C. Hanisch (W. Ger.) |
| 1979 | Melbourne | C. Hanisch (W. Ger.) | V. Sidorova (R.) | I. Schwarzenberger (Hu.) |
| 1980 | MOSCOW | P. Trinquet (Fr.) | M. Maros (Hung.) | B. Wysoczanska (Pol.) |
| 1981 | Clermont Ferrand | C. Hanisch (W. Ger.) | Luan Jujie (China) | D. Vaccaroni (It.) |

LADIES' FOIL TEAMS

|  | | 1 | 2 | 3 |
|---|---|---|---|---|
| 1932 | Copenhagen | Denmark | Austria | Germany |
| 1933 | Budapest | Hungary | GB | Austria |
| 1934 | Warsaw | Hungary | Germany, GB eq. | Italy |
| 1935 | Lausanne | Hungary | Austria | Germany |
| 1936 | San Remo | Germany | Hungary | Italy |
| 1937 | Paris | Hungary | Germany | Denmark |
| 1947 | Lisbon | Denmark | France | Italy |
| 1948 | The Hague | Denmark | Hungary | France |
| 1950 | Monte Carlo | France | Denmark | GB |
| 1951 | Stockholm | France | Hungary | Denmark |
| 1952 | Copenhagen | Hungary | France | Italy |
| 1953 | Brussels | Hungary | France | Italy |
| 1954 | Luxembourg | Hungary | Italy | France |
| 1955 | Rome | Hungary | France | Italy |
| 1956 | London | USSR | France | Hungary |
| 1957 | Paris | Italy | W. Germany | Austria |
| 1958 | Philadelphia | USSR | W. Germany | France |
| 1959 | Budapest | Hungary | USSR | W. Germany |
| 1960 | ROME | USSR | Hungary | Italy |
| 1961 | Turin | USSR | Hungary | Rumania |
| 1962 | Buenos Aires | Hungary | USSR | Italy |
| 1963 | Gdansk | USSR | Hungary | Italy |
| 1964 | TOKYO | Hungary | USSR | W. Germany |
| 1965 | Paris | USSR | Rumania | Italy |
| 1966 | Moscow | USSR | Hungary | France |
| 1967 | Montreal | Hungary | USSR | Rumania |
| 1968 | MEXICO CITY | USSR | Hungary | Rumania |
| 1969 | Cuba | Rumania | USSR | Hungary |
| 1970 | Ankara | USSR | Rumania | France |
| 1971 | Vienna | USSR | Hungary | Poland |
| 1972 | MUNICH | USSR | Hungary | Rumania |
| 1973 | Gothenburg | Hungary | USSR | Rumania |
| 1974 | Grenoble | USSR | Hungary | Rumania |
| 1975 | Budapest | USSR | Hungary | Rumania |
| 1976 | MONTREAL | USSR | France | Hungary |
| 1977 | Buenos Aires | USSR | W. Germany | Rumania |
| 1978 | Hamburg | USSR | Poland | Rumania |
| 1979 | Melbourne | USSR | Hungary | W. Germany |
| 1980 | MOSCOW | France | USSR | Hungary |
| 1981 | Clermont Ferrand | USSR | W. Germany | Hungary |

EPEE

| | | 1 | 2 | 3 |
|---|---|---|---|---|
| 1900 | Paris | R. Fonst (Cuba) | L. Perrée (Fr.) | L. Sée (Fr.) |
| 1904 | St. Louis | R. Fonst (Cuba) | C. Tatham (Cuba) | A. Post (Cuba) |
| 1906 | Athens | G. de la Falaise (Fr.) | M. Dillon-Cavanagh (Fr.) | V. Blyenburgh (Hol.) |
| 1908 | London | G. Alibert (Fr.) | A. Lippmann (Fr.) | P. Anspach (Bel.) |
| 1912 | Stockholm | P. Anspach (Bel.) | I. Ossiier (Den.) | Le Hardy de Beaulieu (Bel.) |
| 1920 | Antwerp | A. Massard (Fr.) | A. Lippmann (Fr.) | E. Gevers (Bel.) |
| 1921 | Paris | L. Gaudin (Fr.) | E. Cornereau (Fr.) | W. Daniels (Hol.) |
| 1922 | Paris | R. Heide (Nor.) | R. Liottel (Fr.) | E. Cornereau (Fr.) |
| 1923 | The Hague | W. Brouwer (Hol.) | A. de Jong (Hol.) | P. Ducret (Fr.) |
| 1924 | Paris | C. Delporte (Bel.) | R. Ducret (Fr.) | N. Hellsten (Swe.) |
| 1926 | Ostend | G. Tainturier (Fr.) | F. de Montigny (Bel.) | L. Tom (Bel.) |
| 1927 | Vichy | G. Buchard (Fr.) | F. Jourdant (Fr.) | X. de Beukelaer (Bel.) |
| 1928 | Amsterdam | L. Gaudin (Fr.) | G. Buchard (Fr.) | L. Tom (Bel.) |
| 1929 | Naples | P. Cattiau (Fr.) | F. Riccardi (It.) | M. Bertinetti (It.) |
| 1930 | Liège | P. Cattiau (Fr.) | A. Pezzana (It.) | A. Rossignol (Fr.) |
| 1931 | Vienna | G. Buchard (Fr.) | B. Schmetz (Fr.) | L. Rousset (Fr.) |
| 1932 | Los Angeles | G-C. Cornaggia (It.) | G. Buchard (Fr.) | C. Agostoni (It.) |
| 1933 | Budapest | G. Buchard (Fr.) | S. Ragno (It.) | B. Schmetz (Fr.) |
| 1934 | Warsaw | P. Dunay (Hu.) | G. Dyrssen (Swe.) | H. Drakenberg (Swe.), S. Ragno (It.) eq. |
| 1935 | Lausanne | H. Drakenberg (Swe.) | P. Dydier (Fr.) | S. Ragno (It.) |
| 1936 | Berlin | F. Riccardi (It.) | S. Ragno (It.) | G-C. Cornaggia (It.) |
| 1937 | Paris | B. Schmetz (Fr.) | J. Coutrot (Fr.) | R. Stasse (Bel.) |
| 1938 | Piestany | M. Pécheux (Fr.) | E. Mangiarotti (It.) | B. Schmetz (Fr.) |
| 1947 | Lisbon | E. Artigas (Fr.) | B. Ljungquist (Swe.) | R. Henkart (Bel.) |
| 1948 | London | L. Cantone (It.) | A. Zapelli (Swe.) | E. Mangiarotti (It.) |
| 1949 | Cairo | D. Mangiarotti (It.) | R. Bougnol (Fr.) | P. Carleson (Swe.) |
| 1950 | Monte-Carlo | M. Luchow (Den.) | C. Forssell (Swe.), D. Mangiarotti (It.) eq. | |
| 1951 | Stockholm | E. Mangiarotti (It.) | C. Pavesi (It.) | S. Fahlman (Swe.) |
| 1952 | Helsinki | E. Mangiarotti (It.) | D. Mangiarotti (It.) | A. Zapelli (Swi.) |
| 1953 | Brussels | J. Sakovits (Hu.) | B. Berczenyi (Hu.) | F. Marini (It.) |
| 1954 | Luxembourg | E. Mangiarotti (It.) | C. Pavesi (It.) | F. Bertinetti (It.) |
| 1955 | Rome | G. Anglesio (It.) | F. Bertinetti (It.) | C. Pavesi (It.) |
| 1956 | Melbourne | C. Pavesi (It.) | G. Delfino (It.) | E. Mangiarotti (It.) |
| 1957 | Paris | A. Mouyal (Fr.) | G. Baranyi (Hu.) | F. Bertinetti (It.) |
| 1958 | Philadelphia | H. W. Hoskyns (GB) | E. Mangiarotti (It.) | A. Chernuchevich (R.) |
| 1959 | Budapest | B. Khabarov (R.) | A. Jay (GB) | G. Delfino (It.) |
| 1960 | Rome | G. Delfino (It.) | A. Jay (GB) | B. Khabarov (R.) |
| 1961 | Turin | J. Guittet (Fr.) | H. Lagerwall (Swe.) | T. Gabor (Hu.) |
| 1962 | Buenos Aires | I. Kausz (Hu.) | T. Gabor (Hu.) | Y. Dreyfus (Fr.) |
| 1963 | Gdansk | R. Losert (Aus.) | Y. Dreyfus (Fr.) | G. Kostava (R.) |
| 1964 | Tokyo | G. Kriss (R.) | H. W. Hoskyns (GB) | G. Kostava (R.) |
| 1965 | Paris | Z. Nemere (Hu.) | H. W. Hoskyns (GB) | G. Kostava (R.) |
| 1966 | Moscow | A. Nikanchikov (R.) | C. Bourquard (Fr.) | B. Gonsior (Pol.) |
| 1967 | Montreal | A. Nikanchikov (R.) | G. Kriss (R.) | R. Trost (Aus.) |
| 1968 | Mexico City | G. Kulcsar (Hu.) | G. Kriss (R.) | G. Saccaro (It.) |
| 1969 | Cuba | B. Andrzejewski (Pol.) | A. Nikanchikov (R.) | C. von Essen (Swe.) |
| 1970 | Ankara | A. Nikanchikov (R.) | S. Paramanov (R.) | C. Fenyvesi (Hu.) |
| 1971 | Vienna | G. Kriss (R.) | N. Granieri (It.) | R. Edling (Swe.) |
| 1972 | Munich | C. Fenyvesi (Hu.) | J. Ladegaillerie (Fr.) | G. Kulcsar (Hu.) |
| 1973 | Gothenburg | R. Edling (Swe.) | H. Jacobson (Swe.) | J. Pezza (It.) |

|      |           | 1 | 2 | 3 |
|------|-----------|---|---|---|
| 1974 | Grenoble | R. Edling (Swe.) | J. Brodin (Fr.) | B. Lukomsky (R.) |
| 1975 | Budapest | A. Pusch (W. Ger.) | B. Lukomsky (R.) | I. Osztrics (Hu.) |
| 1976 | MONTREAL | A. Pusch (W. Ger.) | J. Hehn (W. Ger.) | G. Kulscar (Hu.) |
| 1977 | Buenos Aires | J. Harmenberg (Swe.) | R. Edling (Swe.) | P. Gaille (Swi.) |
| 1978 | Hamburg | A. Pusch (W. Ger.) | P. Riboud (Fr.) | H. Jacobson (Swe.) |
| 1979 | Melbourne | P. Riboud (Fr.) | E. Kolczonay (Hu.) | L. Swornowski (Pol.) |
| 1980 | MOSCOW | J. Harmenberg (Swe.) | E. Kolczonay (Hu.) | P. Riboud (Fr.) |
| 1981 | Clermont Ferrand | Z. Szekely (Hu.) | Mojaev (USSR) | E. Bormann (W. Ger.) |

EPEE TEAMS

|      |            | 1 | 2 | 3 |
|------|------------|---|---|---|
| 1906 | ATHENS | France | GB | Germany |
| 1908 | LONDON | France | GB | Belgium |
| 1912 | STOCKHOLM | Belgium | GB | Holland |
| 1920 | ANTWERP | Italy | Belgium | France |
| 1924 | PARIS | France | Belgium | Italy |
| 1928 | AMSTERDAM | Italy | France | Portugal |
| 1930 | Liège | Belgium | Italy | France |
| 1931 | Vienna | Italy | France | Sweden |
| 1932 | LOS ANGELES | France | Italy | USA |
| 1933 | Budapest | Italy | France | Sweden |
| 1934 | Warsaw | France | Italy | Sweden |
| 1935 | Lausanne | France | Sweden | Germany |
| 1936 | BERLIN | Italy | Sweden | France |
| 1937 | Paris | Italy | France | Sweden |
| 1938 | Piestany | France | Sweden | Italy |
| 1947 | Lisbon | France | Sweden | Italy |
| 1948 | LONDON | France | Italy | Sweden |
| 1949 | Cairo | Italy | Sweden | Egypt |
| 1950 | Monte-Carlo | Italy | France | Sweden |
| 1951 | Stockholm | France | Italy | Sweden |
| 1952 | HELSINKI | Italy | Sweden | Switzerland |
| 1953 | Brussels | Italy | France | Switzerland |
| 1954 | Luxembourg | Italy | Sweden | France |
| 1955 | Rome | Italy | France | Hungary |
| 1956 | MELBOURNE | Italy | Hungary | France |
| 1957 | Paris | Italy | Hungary | GB |
| 1958 | Philadelphia | Italy | Hungary | France |
| 1959 | Budapest | Hungary | USSR | France |
| 1960 | ROME | Italy | GB | USSR |
| 1961 | Turin | USSR | France | Sweden |
| 1962 | Buenos Aires | France | Sweden | USSR |
| 1963 | Gdansk | Poland | France | Hungary |
| 1964 | TOKYO | Hungary | Italy | France |
| 1965 | Paris | France | GB | USSR |
| 1966 | Moscow | France | USSR | Sweden |
| 1967 | Montreal | USSR | France | Hungary |
| 1968 | MEXICO CITY | Hungary | USSR | Poland |
| 1969 | Cuba | USSR | Hungary | Sweden |
| 1970 | Ankara | Hungary | Poland | Switzerland |
| 1971 | Vienna | Hungary | USSR | Sweden |
| 1972 | MUNICH | Hungary | Switzerland | USSR |
| 1973 | Gothenburg | W. Germany | Hungary | USSR |
| 1974 | Grenoble | Sweden | W. Germany | Hungary |

|      |             | 1                 | 2                  | 3                   |
|------|-------------|-------------------|--------------------|---------------------|
| 1975 | Budapest    | Sweden            | W. Germany         | Hungary             |
| 1976 | MONTREAL    | Sweden            | W. Germany         | Switzerland         |
| 1977 | Buenos Aires| Sweden            | Switzerland        | USSR                |
| 1978 | Hamburg     | Hungary           | USSR               | Sweden              |
| 1979 | Melbourne   | USSR              | W. Germany         | Switzerland         |
| 1980 | MOSCOW      | France            | Poland             | USSR                |
| 1981 | Clermont Ferrand | USSR         | Switzerland        | Hungary             |

SABRE

|      |             | 1                      | 2                     | 3                       |
|------|-------------|------------------------|-----------------------|-------------------------|
| 1896 | ATHENS      | J. Giorgiadis (Gr.)    | T. Karakalos (Gr.)    | H. Nielsen (Den.)       |
| 1900 | PARIS       | G. de la Falaise (Fr.) | L. Thiebaut (Fr.)     | S. Flesch (Aus.)        |
| 1904 | ST. LOUIS   | M. de Diaz (Cuba)      | W. Grebe (US)         | A. Post (Cuba)          |
| 1906 | ATHENS      | J. Giorgiadis (Gr.)    | G. Casmir (Ger.)      | Cesarano (It.)          |
| 1908 | LONDON      | J. Fuchs (Hu.)         | B. Zulawski (Hu.)     | V. Goppold (Bohemia)    |
| 1912 | STOCKHOLM   | J. Fuchs (Hu.)         | B. Bekessy (Hu.)      | E. Maszaros (Hu.)       |
| 1920 | ANTWERP     | N. Nadi (It.)          | A. Nadi (It.)         | A. de Jong (Hol.)       |
| 1922 | Ostend      | A. de Jong (Hol.)      | M. Taillandier (Fr.)  | L. Tom (Bel.)           |
| 1923 | The Hague   | A. de Jong (Hol.)      | M. Perrodon (Fr.)     | W. Daniels (Hol.)       |
| 1924 | PARIS       | A. Posta (Hu.)         | R. Ducret (Fr.)       | J. Garay (Hu.)          |
| 1925 | Ostend      | J. Garay (Hu.)         | E. Uhlyarick (Hu.)    | A. Petschauer (Hu.)     |
| 1926 | Budapest    | A. Gombos (Hu.)        | A. Petschauer (Hu.)   | B. Bini (It.)           |
| 1927 | Vichy       | A. Gombos (Hu.)        | E. Tersztyanszky (Hu.)| J. Glycais (Hu.)        |
| 1928 | AMSTERDAM   | E. Tersztyanszky (Hu.) | A. Petschauer (Hu.)   | B. Bini (It.)           |
| 1929 | Naples      | J. Glycais (Hu.)       | G. Marzi (It.)        | A. Petschauer (Hu.)     |
| 1930 | Liège       | G. Piller (Hu.)        | A. Petschauer (Hu.)   | G. Doros (Hu.)          |
| 1931 | Vienna      | G. Piller (Hu.)        | A. Kabos (Hu.)        | A. Petschauer (Hu.)     |
| 1932 | LOS ANGELES | G. Piller (Hu.)        | G. Gaudini (It.)      | A. Kabos (Hu.)          |
| 1933 | Budapest    | A. Kabos (Hu.)         | G. Marzi (It.)        | G. Gaudini (It.)        |
| 1934 | Warsaw      | A. Kobos (Hu.)         | G. Gaudini (It.)      | L. Rajcsanyi (Hu.)      |
| 1935 | Lausanne    | A. Gerevich (Hu.)      | E. Rajczy (Hu.)       | L. Rajcsanyi (Hu.)      |
| 1936 | BERLIN      | A. Kabos (Hu.)         | G. Marzi (It.)        | A. Gerevich (Hu.)       |
| 1937 | Paris       | P. Kovacs (Hu.)        | T. Berczelly (Hu.)    | L. Rajcsanyi (Hu.)      |
| 1938 | Piestany    | A. Montano (It.)       | A. Masciotta (It.)    | G. Perenno (It.)        |
| 1947 | Lisbon      | A. Montano (It.)       | G. de Bourguignon (Bel.) | G. Daré (It.)        |
| 1948 | LONDON      | A. Gerevich (Hu.)      | V. Pinton (It.)       | P. Kovacs (Hu.)         |
| 1949 | Cairo       | G. Daré (It.)          | G. Pellini (It.)      | V. Stagni (It.)         |
| 1950 | Monte-Carlo | J. Levavasseur (Fr.)   | E. Pinton (It.)       | G. Daré (It.)           |
| 1951 | Stockholm   | A. Gerevich (Hu.)      | P. Kovacs (Hu.)       | G. Daré (It.)           |
| 1952 | HELSINKI    | P. Kovacs (Hu.)        | A. Gerevich (Hu.)     | T. Berczelly (Hu.)      |
| 1953 | Brussels    | P. Kovacs (Hu.)        | A. Gerevich (Hu.)     | R. Karpati (Hu.)        |
| 1954 | Luxembourg  | R. Karpati (Hu.)       | P. Kovacs (Hu.)       | T. Berczelly (Hu.)      |
| 1955 | Rome        | A. Gerevich (Hu.)      | R. Karpati (Hu.)      | R. Nostini (It.)        |
| 1956 | MELBOURNE   | R. Karpati (Hu.)       | J. Pawlowski (Pol.)   | L. Kuznetsov (R.)       |
| 1957 | Paris       | J. Pawlowski (Pol.)    | R. Karpati (Hu.)      | T. Mendelenyi (Hu.)     |
| 1958 | Philadelphia| Y. Rylski (R.)         | D. Tychler (R.)       | J. Twardokens (Pol.)    |
| 1959 | Budapest    | R. Karpati (Hu.)       | T. Mendelenyi (Hu.)   | J. Pawlowski (Pol.)     |
| 1960 | ROME        | R. Karpati (Hu.)       | Z. Horvath (Hu.)      | W. Calarese (It.)       |
| 1961 | Turin       | Y. Rylski (R.)         | E. Ochyra (Pol.)      | W. Zablocki (Pol.)      |
| 1962 | Buenos Aires| Z. Horvath (Hu.)       | J. Pawlowski (Pol.)   | C. Arabo (Fr.)          |
| 1963 | Gdansk      | Y. Rylski (R.)         | J. Pawlowski (Pol.)   | W. Calarese (It.)       |
| 1964 | TOKYO       | T. Pezsa (Hu.)         | C. Arabo (Fr.)        | U. Mavlikhanov (R.)     |

|  |  | 1 | 2 | 3 |
|---|---|---|---|---|
| 1965 | Paris | J. Pawlowski (Pol.) | M. Meszena (Hu.) | Z. Horvath (Hu.) |
| 1966 | Moscow | J. Pawlowski (Pol.) | T. Pezsa (Hu.) | Z. Horvath (Hu.) |
| 1967 | Montreal | M. Rakita (R.) | J. Pawlowski (Pol.) | T. Pezsa (Hu.) |
| 1968 | MEXICO CITY | J. Pawlowski (Pol.) | M. Rakita (R.) | T. Pezsa (Hu.) |
| 1969 | Cuba | V. Sidiak (R.) | J. Kalmar (Hu.) | P. Balonyi (Hu.) |
| 1970 | Ankara | T. Pezsa (Hu.) | M. Rakita (R.) | V. Nazlimov (R.) |
| 1971 | Vienna | M. Maffei (It.) | J. Pawlowski (Pol.) | V. Sidiak (R.) |
| 1972 | MUNICH | V. Sidiak (R.) | P. Maroth (Hu.) | V. Nazlimov (R.) |
| 1973 | Gothenburg | M. Montano (It.) | V. Sidiak (R.) | V. Nazlimov (R.) |
| 1974 | Grenoble | M. Montano (It.) | V. Krovopuskov (R.) | V. Sidiak (R.) |
| 1975 | Budapest | V. Nazlimov (R.) | J. Bierkowski (Pol.) | P. Marot (Hu.) |
| 1976 | MONTREAL | V. Krovopuskov (R.) | V. Nazlimov (R.) | V. Sidiak (R.) |
| 1977 | Buenos Aires | P. Gerevich (Hu.) | V. Nazlimov (R.) | A. Arcidiacono (It.) |
| 1978 | Hamburg | V. Krovopuskov (R.) | M. Burtsev (R.) | M. Maffei (It.) |
| 1979 | Melbourne | N. Nazlimov (R.) | V. Krovopuskov (R.) | M. Burtsev (R.) |
| 1980 | MOSCOW | V. Krovopuskov (R.) | M. Burtsev (R.) | I. Gedovari (Hu.) |
| 1981 | Clermont Ferrand | T. Wodke (Pol.) | I. Gedovari (Hu.) | M. Maffei (It.) |

SABRE TEAMS

|  |  | 1 | 2 | 3 |
|---|---|---|---|---|
| 1904 | ST. LOUIS | Cuba | USA |  |
| 1906 | ATHENS | Germany | Greece | Holland |
| 1908 | LONDON | Hungary | Italy | Bohemia |
| 1912 | STOCKHOLM | Hungary | Austria | Holland |
| 1920 | ANTWERP | Italy | France | Holland |
| 1924 | PARIS | Italy | Hungary | Holland |
| 1928 | AMSTERDAM | Hungary | Italy | Poland |
| 1930 | Liège | Hungary | Italy | Poland |
| 1931 | Vienna | Hungary | Italy | Germany |
| 1932 | LOS ANGELES | Hungary | Italy | Poland |
| 1933 | Budapest | Hungary | Italy | GB |
| 1934 | Warsaw | Hungary | Italy | Poland |
| 1935 | Lausanne | Hungary | Italy | Germany |
| 1936 | BERLIN | Hungary | Italy | Germany |
| 1937 | Paris | Hungary | Italy | Germany |
| 1938 | Piestany | Italy | France | Holland |
| 1947 | Lisbon | Italy | Belgium | Egypt |
| 1948 | LONDON | Hungary | Italy | USA |
| 1949 | Cairo | Italy | France | Egypt |
| 1950 | Monte-Carlo | Italy | France | Egypt |
| 1951 | Stockholm | Hungary | Italy | Belgium |
| 1952 | HELSINKI | Hungary | Italy | France |
| 1953 | Brussels | Hungary | Italy | Poland |
| 1954 | Luxembourg | Hungary | Poland | France |
| 1955 | Rome | Hungary | Italy | USSR |
| 1956 | MELBOURNE | Hungary | Poland | USSR |
| 1957 | Paris | Hungary | USSR | Poland |
| 1958 | Philadelphia | Hungary | USSR | Poland |
| 1959 | Budapest | Poland | Hungary | USSR |
| 1960 | ROME | Hungary | Poland | Italy |
| 1961 | Turin | Poland | USSR | Hungary |
| 1962 | Buenos Aires | Poland | Hungary | USSR |
| 1963 | Gdansk | Poland | USSR | Hungary |
| 1964 | TOKYO | USSR | Italy | Poland |
| 1965 | Paris | USSR | Italy | France |

|      |                 | 1       | 2       | 3       |
|------|-----------------|---------|---------|---------|
| 1966 | Moscow          | Hungary | USSR    | France  |
| 1967 | Montreal        | USSR    | Hungary | France  |
| 1968 | MEXICO CITY     | USSR    | Italy   | Hungary |
| 1969 | Cuba            | USSR    | Poland  | Hungary |
| 1970 | Ankara          | USSR    | Hungary | Poland  |
| 1971 | Vienna          | USSR    | Hungary | Italy   |
| 1972 | MUNICH          | Italy   | USSR    | Hungary |
| 1973 | Gothenburg      | Hungary | USSR    | Italy   |
| 1974 | Grenoble        | USSR    | Italy   | Hungary |
| 1975 | Budapest        | USSR    | Hungary | Rumania |
| 1976 | MONTREAL        | USSR    | Italy   | Rumania |
| 1977 | Buenos Aires    | USSR    | Rumania | Hungary |
| 1978 | Hamburg         | Hungary | USSR    | Italy   |
| 1979 | Melbourne       | USSR    | Italy   | Poland  |
| 1980 | MOSCOW          | USSR    | Italy   | Hungary |
| 1981 | Clermont Ferrand| Hungary | USSR    | Poland  |

## WORLD YOUTH CHAMPIONSHIPS
The age limit was 21 till 1960, when it was changed to twenty.

### LADIES' FOIL

| | | 1 | 2 | 3 |
|---|---|---|---|---|
| 1955 | Budapest | V. Kelemen (Hu.) | B. Colombetti (It.) | L. Domolki (Hu.) |
| 1956 | Luxembourg | I. Rejto (Hu.) | Taitis (Rum.) | H. Mees (W. Ger.) |
| 1957 | Warsaw | I. Rejto (Hu.) | B. Colombetti (It.) | Omerborn (W. Ger.) |
| 1958 | Bucharest | A. Zabelina (R.) | N. Kleyweg (Hol.) | C. Flesch (Lux.) |
| 1959 | Paris | V. Proudskova (R.) | O. Orban (Rum.) | N. Kleyweg (Hol.) |
| 1960 | Leningrad | A. Chepeleva (R.) | A. Ragno (It.) | Szalontay (Hu.) |
| 1961 | Duisberg | C. Rousselet (Fr.) | I. Heidenrijk (Hol.) | V. Masciotta (It.) |
| 1962 | Cairo | C. Mirzoeva (R.) | V. Masciotta (It.) | C. Rousselet (Fr.) |
| 1963 | Ghent | A. Ene (Rum.) | B. Berger (S. Afr.) | C. Rousselet (Fr.) |
| 1964 | Budapest | B. Gapais (Fr.) | I. Giulai (Rum.) | K. Palm (Swe.) |
| 1965 | Rotterdam | E. Iencic (Rum.) | I. Giulai (Rum.) | K. Palm (Swe.) |
| 1966 | Vienna | K. Palm (Swe.) | H. Balon (Pol.) | C. Herbster (Fr.) |
| 1967 | Teheran | N. Kondratjeva (R.) | E. Novikova (R.) | E. Szolnoki (Hu.) |
| 1968 | London | N. Kozlenko (R.) | O. Seregi (Hu.) | M. Pulch (W. Ger.) |
| 1969 | Genoa | T. Kanurkina (R.) | N. Kozlenko (R.) | S. Picard (Fr.) |
| 1970 | Minsk | V. Nikonova (R.) | V. Bourochkina (R.) | J. Popken (W. Ger.) |
| 1971 | Chicago | I. Schwarzenberger (Hu.) | S. Picard (Fr.) | R. White (US) |
| 1972 | Madrid | Z. Filatova (R.) | G. Makowska (Pol.) | V. Burochkina (R.) |
| 1973 | Buenos Aires | V. Burochkina (R.) | Z. Filotova (R.) | V. Brouquier (Fr.) |
| 1974 | Istanbul | V. Sidorova (R.) | O. Kniazeva (R.) | O. Pavlenko (R.) |
| 1975 | Mexico City | M. Trinquet (Fr.) | S. Batazzi (It.) | I. Losert (Aus.) |
| 1976 | Poznan | I. Dolguick (R.) | B. Latrille (Fr.) | E. Kulinenko (R.) |
| 1977 | Vienna | C. Fekete (Fr.) | Dmitrenko (R.) | B. Latrille (Fr.) |
| 1978 | Madrid | B. Latrille (Fr.) | Luan Jujie (China) | Tsgaraeva (R.) |
| 1979 | Chicago | A. R. Sparaciari (It.) | D. Vaccaroni (It.) | Z. Szocs (Hu.) |
| 1980 | Venice | Boeri (Fr.) | Radecke (W. Ger.) | Vorschakina (R.) |

### MEN'S FOIL

| | | 1 | 2 | 3 |
|---|---|---|---|---|
| 1950 | Nice | Favia (It.) | | |
| 1951 | Paris | Favia (It.) | | |
| 1952 | Cremona | Cintrat (Fr.) | | |
| 1953 | Paris | P. Closset (Fr.) | Montorsi (It.) | |
| 1954 | Cremona | P. Closset (Fr.) | | |
| 1955 | Budapest | J. Guyricza (Hu.) | Lebard (Fr.) | |
| 1956 | Luxembourg | M. Fulop (Hu.) | | |
| 1957 | Warsaw | M. Fulop (Hu.) | | |
| 1958 | Bucharest | J. Link (Lux.) | J. Kamuti (Hu.) | T. Meresano (Rum.) |
| 1959 | Paris | J. Link (Lux.) | Gerresheim (W. Ger.) | J. Kamuti (Hu.) |
| 1960 | Leningrad | J. Kamuti (Hu.) | | |
| 1961 | Duisburg | J. C. Magnan (Fr.) | J. Courtillat (Fr.) | F. Wessel (W. Ger.) |
| 1962 | Cairo | J. Courtillat (Fr.) | | |
| 1963 | Ghent | N. Andriadze (R.) | I. Drimba (Rum.) | J. Courtillat (Fr.) |
| 1964 | Budapest | R. Losert (Aus.) | P. Simonov (R.) | C. Noel (Fr.) |
| 1965 | Rotterdam | R. Losert (Aus.) | J. Dimont (Fr.) | T. Olexa (Czech.) |
| 1966 | Vienna | S. Weisbach (Rum.) | M. Berkovits (Hu.) | M. Tiu (Rum.) |
| 1967 | Teheran | L. Romanov (R.) | B. Talvard (Fr.) | M. Dabrowski (Pol.) |
| 1968 | London | J. Kaczmarek (Pol.) | S. Yunichenko (R.) | E. Beierstettel (W. Ger.) |

|      |              | 1                       | 2                      | 3                   |
|------|--------------|-------------------------|------------------------|---------------------|
| 1969 | Genoa        | L. Koziejowski (Pol.)   | M. Dabrowski (Pol.)    | E. Bernkopf (It.)   |
| 1970 | Minsk        | H. Hein (W. Ger.)       | A. Volochin (R.)       | A. Kalinski (Pol.)  |
| 1971 | Chicago      | B. Boscherie (Fr.)      | E. Bernkopff (It.)     | T. Bach (W. Ger.)   |
| 1972 | Madrid       | A. Godel (Pol.)         | V. Rodionov (R.)       | F. Pietruska (Fr.)  |
| 1973 | Buenos Aires | F. Pietruszka (Fr.)     | M. Behr (W. Ger.)      | R. Bruniges (GB)    |
| 1974 | Istanbul     | P. Kuki (Rum.)          | M. Behr (W. Ger.)      | F. Pietruska (Fr.)  |
| 1975 | Mexico City  | P. Kuki (Rum.)          | M. Behr (W. Ger.)      | S. Kosenko (R.)     |
| 1976 | Poznan       | R. Bruniges (GB)        | P. Jolyot (Fr.)        | F. Dal Zotto (It.)  |
| 1977 | Vienna       | B. Lapitski (R.)        | A. Borella (It.)       | M. Gey (W. Ger.)    |
| 1978 | Madrid       | M. Numa (It.)           | A. Borella (It.)       | B. Lapitski (R.)    |
| 1979 | Chicago      | A. Borella* (It.)       | M. Gey* (W. Ger.)      | M. Numa (It.)       |
| 1980 | Venice       | F. Cervi (It.)          | J. Howe (E. Ger.)      | M. Numa (It.)       |

EPEE

|      |              | 1                            | 2                         | 3                     |
|------|--------------|------------------------------|---------------------------|-----------------------|
| 1956 | Luxembourg   | Bulleri (It.)                |                           |                       |
| 1957 | Warsaw       | J. Wojciechowski (Pol.)      |                           |                       |
| 1958 | Bucharest    | V. Chernikov (R.)            | Jeanneau (Fr.)            | G-C. Saccaro (It.)    |
| 1959 | Paris        | B. Khabarov (R.)             | G-C. Saccaro (It.)        | Muresano (Rum.)       |
| 1960 | Leningrad    | Hurat (Rum.)                 |                           |                       |
| 1961 | Duisburg     | H. Lagerwall (Swe.)          | A. Whalberg (Swe.)        | O. Lindwall (Swe.)    |
| 1962 | Cairo        | J. Brodin (Fr.)              |                           |                       |
| 1963 | Ghent        | R. Losert (Aus.)             | J. Brodin (Fr.)           | G. Pavese (It.)       |
| 1964 | Budapest     | J. Brodin (Fr.)              | M. Becher (Aus.)          | L-E. Larsson (Swe.)   |
| 1965 | Rotterdam    | J. Brodin (Fr.), H. Jacobson (Swe.) eq. |                | V. Donin (R.)         |
| 1966 | Vienna       | J. Brodin (Fr.)              | I. Samochkin (R.)         | Zajitsky (R.)         |
| 1967 | Teheran      | A. Pongracz (Hu.)            | C. Kauter (Swi.)          | S. Erdos (Hu.)        |
| 1968 | London       | I. Samochkin (R.)            | V. Rossar (R.)            | Z. Matwiejew (Pol.)   |
| 1969 | Genoa        | D. Giger (Swi.)              | H. Hein (W. Ger.)         | B. Ioffe (R.)         |
| 1970 | Minsk        | B. Lukomsky (R.)             | J. Normann (Nor.)         | A. Karagian (R.)      |
| 1971 | Chicago      | A. Karagian (R.)             | A. Abushakmetov (R.)      | B. Lofficiel (Fr.)    |
| 1972 | Madrid       | G. Evequoz (Swi.)            | J. Janikowski (Pol.)      | P. Szabo (Rum.)       |
| 1973 | Buenos Aires | G. Mochi (It.)               | Romanelli (It.)           | M. Wiech (Pol.)       |
| 1974 | Istanbul     | M. Poffet (Swi.)             | A. Pusch (W. Ger.)        | M. Wiech (Pol.)       |
| 1975 | Mexico City  | M. Poffet (Swi.)             | P. Boisse (Fr.)           | T. Glass (US)         |
| 1976 | Poznan       | M. Poffet (Swi.)             | J-C. Krebs (Fr.)          | P. Gaille (Swi.)      |
| 1977 | Vienna       | N. Koppang (Nor.)            | M. Beckman (W. Ger.)      | Mojaev (R.)           |
| 1978 | Madrid       | N. Koppang (Nor.)            | Mojaev (R.)               | Jablkowski (Pol.)     |
| 1979 | Chicago      | Kucheriani (R.)              | Lis (Pol.)                | Latichev (R.)         |
| 1980 | Venice       | Kubista (Cze.)               | Khint (R.)                | Zerbib (Fr.)          |

SABRE

|      |              | 1                      | 2                      | 3                       |
|------|--------------|------------------------|------------------------|-------------------------|
| 1952 | Cremona      | L. Narduzzi (It.)      |                        |                         |
| 1953 | Paris        | V. Zablocki (Pol.)     | P. Narduzzi (It.)      |                         |
| 1954 | Cremona      | Z. Orley (Hu.)         |                        |                         |
| 1955 | Budapest     | J. Szerences (Hu.)     | M. Parent (Fr.)        | Orley (Hu.)             |
| 1956 | Luxembourg   | T. Mendelenyi (Hu.)    | Z. Horvath (Hu.)       |                         |
| 1957 | Warsaw       | P. Chicca (It.)        | Z. Horvath (Hu.)       |                         |
| 1958 | Bucharest    | Z. Horvath (Hu.)       | C. Arabo (Fr.)         | Vecchioni (It.)         |
| 1959 | Paris        | R. Parulski (Pol.)     | P. Bakonyi (Hu.)       | B. Heidenryk (Hol.)     |
| 1960 | Leningrad    | M. Meszena (Hu.)       |                        |                         |
| 1961 | Duisburg     | C. Salvadori (It.)     | S. Panizza (Fr.)       | W. Ragossnig (Aus.)     |

|      |             | 1                    | 2                    | 3                    |
|------|-------------|----------------------|----------------------|----------------------|
| 1962 | Cairo       | J. Kalmar (Hu.)      |                      |                      |
| 1963 | Ghent       | G. Lordkipanidze (R.)| Y. Brasseur (Bel.)   | P. La Ragione (It.)  |
| 1964 | Budapest    | Z. Nagy (Hu.)        | V. Nazlymov (R.)     | J. Novara (Pol.)     |
| 1965 | Rotterdam   | P. Maroth (Hu.)      | S. Kommissarov (R.)  | Z. Nagy (Hu.)        |
| 1966 | Vienna      | Z. Nagy (Hu.)        | E. Gos (Pol.)        | G. Gerevich (Hu.)    |
| 1967 | Teheran     | I. Kocsis (Hu.)      | A. Parakhin (R.)     | R. Bonnissent (Fr.)  |
| 1968 | London      | V. Krovopuskov (R.)  | G. Tocqueboeuf (Fr.) | P. Rensky (R.)       |
| 1969 | Genoa       | P. Renski (R.)       | D. Irimiciuc (Rum.)  | D. Charachenidze (R.)|
| 1970 | Minsk       | P. Renski (R.)       | K. Varga (Hu.)       | A. Komar (R.)        |
| 1971 | Chicago     | A. Komar (R.)        | I. Gedovari (Hu.)    | E. Zakharian (R.)    |
| 1972 | Madrid      | V. Pavlenko (R.)     | P. Quivrin (Fr.)     | T. Montano (It.)     |
| 1973 | Buenos Aires| T. Montano (It.)     | Romano (It.)         | F. Gulacsi (Hu.)     |
| 1974 | Istanbul    | I. Pop (Rum.)        | M. Gellert (Hu.)     | A. Kiknadze (R.)     |
| 1975 | Mexico City | A. Arcidiacono (It.) | M. Burtsev (R.)      | D. Baria (It.)       |
| 1976 | Poznan      | J. Nebald (Hu.)      | Todorov (R.)         | Dalla Barba (It.)    |
| 1977 | Vienna      | Ismailov (R.)        | Baianov (R.)         | Shamshutdinov (R.)   |
| 1978 | Madrid      | Baianov (R.)         | Kostarzewa (Pol.)    | Shamshutdinov (R.)   |
| 1979 | Chicago     | Bujdosa (Hu.)        | A. Alchan (R.)       | Koriagkin (R.)       |
| 1980 | Venice      | Pogosov (R.)         | A. Alchan (R.)       | Abay (Hu.)           |

# Indexes

*Compiled by Julian Tyson*

B: references in biography; A: all other non-competitive references; M: men's foil; L: ladies' foil; E: epee; S: sabre; C: combined weapons; R: tables of results. Photographs are indicated in **heavy type**.

## SUBJECT INDEX

Amateur Fencing Association
amateurs and professionals, A 81–3, 95, 104, 112
Annual Report, A 91
Articles and non-competition rules, A 87, 93, 94, 96, 112, 119–20
BAF links, A 104, 119, 120
Coaching, B 55, 65, 69; A 7–8, 81–2, 83, 89, 98, 100–102, 103, 116, 117, 118, 124, 128
Committee, composition of the, 89, 94, 95, 119–20
Conference, 77, 88–9, 93, 104, 112
development plans, 78, 95, 102–3, 112, 116, 118, 124–5, 325
FIE links, A 93, 98
finance, A 9, 76, 77, 78, 88, 89, 95, 98, 99, 100, 109
honours and awards, A 78, 84, 86, 97, 107, 110, 114, 115, 123, 124, 125, 126
Joint Weapon Sub-Committee, B 68, 69; A 7, 83, 84, 101–2
membership and subscriptions, A 40, 77, 89, 95, 99, 100, 112, 118–19, 124, 125
national squad training, A 83, 100, 102, 103, 116, 117, 132, 313, 352, 368, 433, 436, 443–4
national team selection, A 7, 83–4, 93, 101, 109, 115, 351
officers, B 40; A 76, 78, 93, 95, 107, 114, 115, 122, 123

origins, B 40
premises, B 63; A 9, 76, 78, 88, 99, 110
presidents, A 103–4
press coverage, B 63; A 105
rules for competitors, A 82, 96, 97, 102, 109, 112; see also *FIE rules*
see also *Under-20s*
Army, the, A 118, 239

British Academy of Fencing, A 8, 120, 169–70
British Empire Fencing Federation, A 9
see also *Commonwealth Fencing Federation*
British Olympic Association and Committee, B 65; A 101, 114, 122, 123, 450
British Universities Sports Federation, A 434

Category System, Ladies, A 82, 231, 243–4
Central Council of Physical Recreation, A 7, 8, 81, 84, 86–7, 119, 131, 154; B 41
Centres of Excellence, A 118
East Midlands, A 139
N.E., A 129
S.W., A 155
West Midlands, A 138
Circuses, 8, 14, 56–8, 225
Combined Services Fencing Union, A 171

Commonwealth Fencing Federation, A
9, 97, 211

Department of Education and Science, A
77, 85, 103

Fédération Internationale d'Escrime
(FIE)
Congresses, B 39, 54; A 9
headquarters, B 54, 61
management of, B 54, 61–2; A 332,
376, 390, 434
rules and statues, B 36, 39, 59, 60; A 9,
96, 97–8, 104, 105, 109–10,
112–3, 119, 120, 128
Fencing, previously The Fencing Master, A
10, 12, 169

Government grant aid
general, B 73; A 8, 76, 77, 83, 88, 99,
100–101, 103, 109, 110, 117, 118,
352
travel, A 77, 79, 84, 100, 108, 110,
115, 207, 209, 223, 253, 256, 351,
352, 436

International Fencing Academy (AAI), A
104, 169–70
Irish Amateur Fencing Union, B 40; C
207

Junior Administrator's Award, A 104

Ladies' Amateur Fencing Union, 7, 39,
76, 78, 81, 85, 86, 97, 107, 110, 123,
205, 353
Ladies' epee and sabre, A 97; E 154, 172;
S 310
Leaders, B 65; A 8, 80, 81, 157; C 222

Martini-Rossi see Sponsorship; also index
of names
Modern British Fencing, B 58, 60, 73; A
10, 11
Modern Pentathlon Association of Great
Britain, A 171–2; E 339; C 378–9
Moscow Olympics boycott, A 122–3,
448, 450

National Coaching Scheme; see AFA,
coaching

Newsletter (Scottish), A 10, 161, 167
New Zealand Amateur Fencing
Association, A 9; L 424; E 426
N. Ireland Amateur Fencing Union, A
159, 160, 207

Obituaries, A 78–9, 87–8, 91–2, 105–6,
107–8, 111, 114–15, 120–22, 126,
133–4, 142–3, 163, 166–7, 167–8

Paraplegic fencing, A 126–7
The Point, A 167
Proficiency Scheme, A 479

Record competition performances, M
153, 173, 214, 243, 298, 349, 365,
437, 438, 450–51; L 135, 137, 301,
302, 369, 455; E 115, 199, 340, 405,
406, 442, 463; S 105, 168, 203, 236,
290, 329, 389, 429, 465; C 139, 143,
148, 149, 150, 154, 164, 171, 179,
203, 211, 242, 270, 468, 469, 471–3
Rest of Britain Match, A 140
Rules, see AFA and FIE

Schools Fencing Union, A 80, 84, 102,
103, 115, 116, 119, 125
Scottish Amateur Fencing Union, A 85,
86, 161–8; E 306
Sections and Sections Sub-Committee,
B 56; A 8, 77, 89–90, 94, 95, 100,
102–3, 104, 112, 120, 124, 411
E. Midlands, A 103, 110, 139–40, 155
Eastern, A 86, 115, 140–42
London, A 142–51
North East, A 103, 113, 129–30
North West, A 84, 133–7
South East, A 110, 115, 123, 151–2
South West, A 84, 86, 100, 102, 123,
154–7
Southern, A 115, 153–4
W. Midlands, A 86, 103, 113, 123–4,
137–9
Yorkshire and Humberside, A 89,
131–3, 325–6
Sponsorship
Alka Seltzer, A 113
Allen, Irving, A 85, 320, 349
Avon Rubber, A 155
Bowater, A 80, 96

Brook, Sir Robin, A 84
Brown and Poulson, A 80
British Steel Corporation, A 326
Churchill Fellowships, A 109
Clarkes, of Street, A 229
Coaches' Club, A 134
Egg Marketing Board, A 96, 336
Ellis Pearson, A 326
Leon Paul Ltd, A 80, 109, 271, 420
Mars Health Education Fund, A 114
Martini-Rossi, A 106, 181, 219, 246, 248, 251, 291–2
Nescafé, A 85
Old Bushmills Distillery, A 160
Omega, A 80
Robinson's Barley Water, A 84
Sports Aid Foundation, A 109, 113
State Express, A 113
Usher-Vaux, A 162
Vaux Breweries, A 130
Wilkinson Sword, A 108, 109, 113, 171

Sports Council, A 77, 98, 100, 103, 110, 116, 117, 119
N. Ireland, A 160
Scotland, A 167
Wales, A 158
*The Sword*, B 14, 28; A 10, 12, 77, 78, 88, 89, 91, 99, 105, 110, 124, 128, 133

Trophies
Feyerick, B 60
Gauthier, A 168, 170
Seton, B 31
Torch, A 84, 134
Vincent Bonfil, A 88; M 317–8, 421

Under-20s, A 76, 79, 85, 101, 102, 103, 136, 186, 205, 400

Welsh Amateur Fencing Union, A 124, 157–9; E 372; C 330
Wilkinson Sword, see *Sponsorship*; also index of names

*INDEX OF NAMES*

To avoid excessive numbers of page references, the relevant seasons are sometimes given instead. *Clubs, Competitions* and *Schools etc.* are to be found under those headings. References in these cases are selective. (Results given in the lists are not indexed; nor are mentions of club-members who have been included in the club narratives.)

Abashidze, C 390
Abay, R 557
Abrahams, H., B 40
Abrahamson, C 311
Abushakhmetov, C 293, 378, 390, 450; R 557
Abunza, C 239
Acfield, D., 88, **241**, 314; A 144; M 175, 213; S *1964–73*, 408; C *1964–72*; R 495–6, 519–23, 526, 528–9
Ackle, C., M 280; R 496
Adams, Sgt E., R 530
Adams, Mrs G., R 503
Addams, J., R 500, 549
Addison, Mrs I., A 126
Adeyinko, S., R 497
Adrian, E. D., Baron, A 108
Adrians, C 418
Ager, W., **393**; A 146, 151; L *1971–7*; C 313, 333, 348, 377–8, 392; R 489, 499, 501–4, 506–7, 537, 542; *see also* Grant, Mrs
Agostoni, C., R 551
Ainley, D., A 141
Aitken, D., R 534
Akerburg, M 420, 436
Albanese, E 202
Alchan, A., R 557
Alderman, A., M 399, 431; C 431
Aldrich, S., L 456
Alexander, A., C 188, 204; R 516
Alexander, F., C 269; R 154, 156
Alexander, G. R., R 490
Alexander, M. O'D., A 148, 151; R 486, 494, 511, 512, 514, 525, 528
Alexandre, A., S 236
Alfred, Capt. G., R 532
Alibert, G., R 551

Alibert, R., R 494
Aliokhin, S 445; C 433, 471
Allemand, J.-P., E 200, 218, 233, 248, 286
Allen, 3rd Off., B. J. G., R 532
Allen, D., A 229
Allen, I., A 85, 320, 349
Allen, M., M 229; S 250; R 139, 496, 516, 523
Allen, Nigel, E 355
Allen, W., A 152
Allen-Williams, D., R 154
Allisaat, K., S 237; R 521
Allison, L., L 423
Allton, Mrs J., A 140
Allton, M., R 140; E 305, 324; R 516
Allwork, Mrs D. (J.G.), A 86, 114, 475, 477
Alofouzo, G., R 516
Alton, M., R 541
Amberg, M. J., A 140, 147, 475; S 184, 185, 408; R 494, 519–22, 527, 545
Amberg, P. C., A 147; R 537, 539
Ames, Gerald, R 481, 482, 509
Amphlett, E. M., A 11; R 481, 490, 509
Amstad, R. E., R 511
Anderson, C., 82
Anderson, D., M 228
Anderson, J. F., E 181, 183, 234; C 222; R 515
Anderson, N., R 497
Anderson, R. D. S., R 521
Anderson, S., L 423, 439, 456
Anderson, Prof. (Col-Sgt) R. J. G., 82, 211, 240, 272, 314; B 58, 65; A 8, 79, 81, 83, 100, 102, 104, 112, 116, 131, 134, 136, 170, 186, 190, 209, 224, 255, 295, 313, 329, 416, 476; S 389; R 170, 519–21, 531–2, 545
Anderson, Sam, E 371
Andreoli, E 458
Andrew, M. S., R 529
Andrews, L., L 1969–72, 337, 366, 368; C 331; R 504–6
Andriadge, N., R 556
Andru, J., C 211; R 545
Anglade, M., R 514
Anglesio, G., R 551
Andrzejewski, B., E 182, 234, 248, 286; C 296; R 513, 551

Angus, M. E., R 503, 534
Annavedder, Mrs M., C 222; R 141
Anspach, Paul, B 54; R 551
Anstruther, A. M., R 535
Antropova, C 224
Appert, J., L 300, 319, 384; R 501
Aptsiaouri, C 467
Arabo, C., S 237; R 554, 557
Arato, G., S 266, 269; C 211; R 545
Arbuthnott, Elizabeth Carnegy, A 474; R 483, 498, 499, 500, 501, 502, 534
Archibald, A., **379**; A 172, 425; E 386, 425; R 152
Arcidiacono, A., C 395; R 554, 557
Aredondo, C 224
Armbrust, L 259, 283, 300; C 293; R 507
Armstrong, 2nd Lt J. B., R 521, 531, 534, 535
Aron, C 187
Arthur, R., M 450; R 516
Artigas, E., R 551
Arup, C., L *1974–7*; R 141, 504
Arup, K., **424**; L *1977–81*; C 468; R 504, 506–8
Arup, Mrs Sheila, A 11, 400
Arup, Sophie, L 354; R 508
Asfar, **55**
Ashley, P., M 365; R 493
Ashmore, Mrs P. M., R 499; *see also* Buller, P. M.
Askew, A., A 111
Astolosch, A., L 354; R 507
Aston, Wren M., R 534
Atholl, Duke of, A 161
Atkinson, I., R 526, 528
Atkinson, M., R 497
Atkinson, R., M 399
Austin, Prof. D., **169**; A 143, 150, 170, 392
Austin, Diane, L 232, 244–5
Avis, J., A 152
Axelrod, A., R 547
Ayliffe, G., A 11, 138; E 218; R 515, 540
Ayliffe, P. J., E 338; R 516
Aylward, J. D., A 133–4, 479

Babington-Smith, M. J., B 36; R 491
Bach, T., M 299; C 416; R 497, 556
Baden-Powell, Agnes, B 24
Baden-Powell, Sir Robert, B 23–4
Baionov, C 391; R 557

# Index

Bailey, C., **262**; A 135; L 216, 231, 260–2; R 505–7
Bailey, H., M 364; S 389; R 496
Bailey, J., S 308
Bailey, J., A 150; L *1964–70*; C 191, 208, 226; R 485–7, 499, 502–3, 505, 523, 536, 539
Bailey, Lt Cdr P. A., A 476
Bailey, S., L 366; R 505
Bain, Mrs J., **240, 274**; A 149; L 230–1, 260–1; C 238; R 499, 501–3, 541; *see also* Herriot, J.
Baker, Sgt H., R 533
Bakonyi, P., C 210, 274; R 557
Balatoni, S 410
Baldry, S., A 172; M 363; E 425, 441; R 516, 528
Bales, R., A 141
Balfour, H., R 490
Balkwill, R. G., R 494
Ball, H. S., R 528, 529
Balmain, M. S., R 527
Balnave, B., R 160
Balon, H., L 384; R 555
Balonyi, P., R 554
Bampfylde, Lt C. J., R 527, 531
Bancilhon, J.-P., R 492
Baudoux, B., R 547
Banos, S 465
Banks, Dr A. A., **82**; A 11, 79, 85, 86, 104, 116, 134, 137, 474–7; R 137
Banks, Mrs B., **82**; A 134
Baranyi, A., E 200, 219; C 191; R 513, 551
Barbaud, S 373; R 521
Barburski, K., E 198, 248; C 334
Barcroft, J. H. P., R 527
Bardini, M 438
Baria, D., R 557
Barker, F., A 162, 165
Barker, Lt Col J. S. S., R 530
Barkley, Mrs J., A 142, 425; L 244–6, 261, 262; C 269, 274, 276; R 159, 499, 542;; *see also* Davis, J.
Barnes, D., M 336; R 496
Baroni, S 409
Barratt, Mrs S., A 12
Barraud, B., R 506
Barrey, L 300, 319
Barrie, Mrs M., A 162
Barrow, I., A 141

Barrs, A., M 279, 280, 297, 298, 334, 335, 336; C 270, 311; R 492–3, 495
Barsby, R., A 144; S 203; R 522
Barstow, N., S 464
Bartecki, E 307
Bartecki, S 408, 409, 445
Bartlett, A., **413**; A 452; M 298–9, 318, *1974–81*; S 325; C 330, 412–3, 416, 432, 470; R 490, 492–4, 496, 523
Bartlett, H. D. H., R 491, 494, 527
Bartlett, Mrs K., R 499, 502
Barton, Mrs A., R 503, 504–5
Bartos, C 348
Baska, M 420, 438
Batazzi, S., L 320; C 344; R 555
Bauer, S 373
Bayley, E. R., R 495
Bayliss, K., C 255
Baynes, F. W. W., R 527
Beagrie, C., L 352, 354; R 132, 507, 538
Beale, S., R 509
Beamish, G., A 160; R 160
Beard, P., A 138
Beasley, Cpl (W) A., R 534
Beatley, Dr W. M., B 57; A 147; R 493, 519–22, 525
Beattie, T., M 349–50, 364, 380; S 389; C 345, 346, 347, 361, 397, 413; R 496, 535
Beauchamp, J., L 231; C 210; R 501, 503
Beaudry, S 410
Bebb, 2nd Lt B. J. M., R 527, 531
Bebel, C 378
Becher, M., R 556
Beck, L 300
Beckmann, M., C 391; R 557
Beddard, T. E., B 40, 53, 63; A 9, 79; R 483, 485, 509–11
Beeker, C 191
Beevers, M., **332, 367**; A 150; M 298, 316, 317, 365; E *1972–9*; C 312, 331, 334, *1975–6*; R 132, 495, 511–2, 514, 537
Begard, E 407
Begg, K., R 507
Behmber, Prof R. H., **143**; A 142–3, 144, 150, 170, 176, 194, 216, 476
Behr, M., M 336; C 312, 330, 331, 344, 416; R 497, 556
Behr, R., E 235, 307, 386, 407; R 513
Beierstettel, E., R 556

Beith, I. M., C 432; R 528
Bekesay, B., R 553
Bell, Maj. A., R 533
Bell, A. D., R 518
Bell, F. L., R 525
Bell, N., **256, 332, 393, 437**; A 123, 150–1, 439; M 243, *1972–80*; E 232, 404–6; C 255, 313, *1973–80*, 469–70; R 152, 489, 492–6, 511, 515, 526, 540, 546
Bell, P., L 366, 383; R 505
Bell, R., C 431
Bell, W., M 436
Bellamy, M., A 156
Bellone, E 442; C 330, 344, 418, 450
Belova(-Novikova), E., C 295, 417, 433, 435; R 549–50
Belson, T., **293, 356, 393**; A 123, 151, 171, 443; E *1969–81*; C 293, *1973–9*; R 488–9, 511–2, 514–6, 553
Bena, J.-J., E 255
Bena, P., S 267, 308; C 417
Benko, G., M 438; C 273, 312, 344, 346, 412, 414–6, 418; R 546
Ben-Nathan, E., A 151; M 194, 195, 200, 214, 228, 229; S 185, 186, 203; C 187–8, 204, 206; R 491, 495–6, 523, 526, 528
Bennett, A., **391**; A 157; C 330, 346, 361, 392, 411, 414; R 159, 534
Benney, S., R 156, 505
Benoit, M 454
Bentham, P., E 386
Bentley, Capt. T. A., R 494, 532
Berczelly, T., R 553
Berczenyi, B., R 551
Bergamini, G., R 547
Berger, B., R 555
Bergouzelli, C 224
Berkovits, M., C 205; R 556
Berlioux, M., B 54
Berman, T., R 512, 514, 515
Bernacchi, L., R 514
Bernadotte, E 427, 442; R 513
Bernard, Maj. F. Higgins, R 530
Bernard, M., E 385; R 516
Bernard, R., R 527
Berndt, S., R 541
Bernkopf, E., M 258; R 556
Berolatti, G., M 212, 248, 364; C 227, 254, 257, 314

Berry, A. J. R., R 495, 526, 538
Berry, E., A 149; R 484, 499, 502–3, 534; *see also* Davies, Mrs
Berry, J., **256**; A 12, 85, 205, 271
Berry, R. P., M 334; S 408, 444; C 412; R 140, 495, 537–8
Berti, L., R 547
Bertinetti, M., E 340; R 551
Bertrand, B., R 142
Bertrand, Prof. Baptiste, A 120
Bertrand, Prof. Felix, B 33; A 120
Bertrand, Prof. L. ('Punch'), **121**; B 32, 38; A 8, 92, 120, 146, 147, 148, 149, 304, 477
Bessemans, F., A 171
Besser, B., L 439; R 507
Bethune, Maj. H., R 530
Betts, Lt J., A 171; R 530, 531
Beverley, E., A 289
Beverley, S., A 132; R 132
Bewley-Cathie, J., A 150; L 175–8, 196; C 191; R 499, 502–4, 506–7, 538–9; *see also* Cooksey, Mrs *and* Wardell-Yerborough, Mrs
Bialosky, W., R 130
Bibby, F., R 498
Bicher, C 391
Biedermann, E., R 514
Bierkowski, C 394, 471; R 554
Bini, B., R 553
Binning, R., C 211
Binny, Lt P., R 532
Birch, H. L., A 157
Bird, E., C 254
Bird, E., R 132
Bird, P., A 123, 477
Bird, R., A 150; E 247, 304, 406; C 271; R 152, 515–6
Birks, G. T., A 150, 476; S 185, 269, 310; R 494–5, 519–20, 537, 539, 543
Birnbaum, U., M 239; E 233–4; R 513
Birt, P. M., A 506
Biscoe, Charles H., B 40; A 122, 274; R 482, 509, 514
Bishop, A., A 154
Bishop, C., R 130
Bishop, J., R 495
Bishop, Flt Sgt L., R 532
Bissitt, I., C 255
Blacker, R 527

# Index

Blackmore, F., S 310
Blackmore, J., L 456
Blacknell, Capt S., A 476
Blaiberg, H. E., R 509
Blake, J. P., R 481, 509
Blake, P., R 496
Blakemore, LACW P., R 534
Blanchard, S., A 135; L 259, 261, 283, 284; R 505–7
Bleasdale, L., **332**; A 132; L 319; R 504–5
Bligh, N., C 188
Blomquist, R., A 151; E 248; R 512, 541
Bloor, G., R 132
Blumenthal, W., A 12
Blunt, D. H., R 527
Blyenburgh, V., R 551
Bobis, I., L 231; C 377; R 501, 550
Bocchino, G., R 547
Boch, S 445; C 417; R 521
Bock, I., R 506
Boeri, R 556
Bogathy, E., R 549
Bohnen, G., E 307; R 540
Bois, C 227
Boisse, P., E 370, 405, 427; C 344, 361, 395; R 513, 557
Boissier, E 198; C 226
Bolland, Sgt C., R 533
Bollobas, B., E 263
Bond, H. T. H., R 514
Bond, V., L 232
Bond, W. S. S., R 527
Bondoux, René, R 492
Bonfil, V., **88**; A 87–8, 151; M 194, 196, 213–5, 228, 229, 241–3, 281; E 249; C 205, 207, 222, 223, 227, 257; R 491, 493, 495–6, 536
Bongianni, A., R 542
Boniface, E. S., R 494
Bonissent, R., S 343; R 557
Bonnin, C 470
Booth, Cdr F. A., **113**; A 12, 95, 110, 123, 475
Booth, J., A 112
Booton, C., A 145; S 444–5, 464–5; R 523
Borella, A., C 375–6, 394, 467, 470; R 556
Bormann, E., R 552

Borrmann, I., E 443
Borucki, P., S 185–6, 203, 221, 237; R 520
Boscherie, B., M 351, 419; C 432; R 497, 556
Boston, Prof. S., **256, 293**; A 81, 101, 141, 143, 144, 146, 160, 170, 175, 181, 189, 202, 205, 224, 255, 271, 289, 292, 295, 312, 313, 327, 329, 330, 344, 375, 409, 432, **448**, 476
Boswell, H., R 505
Botbijl, E., R 500
Bouchier-Hayes, J., A 160
Bougnol, L 440; R 501, 551
Bougnoux, J., R 541
Boulanger, J., R 547
Boulot, A., E 198
Bourne, E. O., **240, 311, 314, 356**; A 11, 12, 85, 122, 144, 477; M 229, 241, 243, 280, 316, 334, 335, 365, 382, 400; E *1964–81*; C *1964–76*; R 487–9, 492, 494–6, 510–12, 514, 516, 526, 528, 543
Bourne, J., M 451; R 495
Bournemisza, A., S 465
Bourquard, C., E 198; C 191; R 551
Bousfield, S. R., R 491, 494
Bovill, D., A 145; S 464–5, 520, 523
Bowen, Mrs A., C 270; R 499
Boyd, A. E., R 528
Boyd, L. M., R 499
Boys, J. C., R 527
Bracewell, Prof. H. T., A 162, 163, 168, 170, 175, 366, 380, 405, 423; L 423; R 541
Bracewell, J., **424**; L 423, 456; C 469; R 541
Bradbury, E., **233**; A 136; S 289, 327; C 331; R 137
Bradley, T. W., R 494
Bradley, Flt Lt W. H. M., R 495, 532
Bragg, M., L 368, 401; R 505; *see also* Thornton, Mrs
Braine, E., R 503
Brandstaetter, S 373; R 520–1
Brannon, Ann, A 111, 136, 144; L *1973–80*; C *1976–80*; R 499, 500–7, 543
Brannon, Andrew, A 136; M 363; E *1975–81*; S 389; C 431, 432; R 137, 515–6, 525, 529

Branscombe, P., A 145; S 444
Brasseur, Y., S 185, 236, 252, 359; R 520-1, 557
Brearley, R. E., A 144; S 186, 203; R 522, 523, 528-9
Brecht, J., M 212; R 547
Breckin, M. J., **88, 240, 314**; A 151; M *1964-74*, 220; S *1965-9*, 327; C *1964-73*; R 487, 491-6, 519, 523, 526, 541, 543, 545
Breda, G.-B., E 202; C 191-2; R 513
Breese, D. L., L 147; R 502-3, 539
Breese, J., R 506
Breese, S. W., A 475
Bretholz, A., E 286, 287; R 513
Brick, S., **88**; L 176, 187, 216; R 504, 506; *see also* Yeomans, Mrs
Brierley, CPO P., A 171-2; M 452; E 285, 338, 339, 355, 356, 385, 386, 425, 443; R 515, 533
Briggs, S., A 115, 477; R 132
Bright, R., **188, 379**; A 171; E 181, 234; R 512, 531
Brinkman, L 456
Briscoe, T., R 137
Brittain, P., R 142
Broadhurst, Brig. R., A 160, 238
Broadhurst, T., **165, 206**; A 187; R 535, 536, 541
Broadley, I., M 381
Brocherie, C 227
Brockbanks, C., A 129, 130; S 444, 464-5
Brodie, A 172
Brodin, J., E 340; C 187, 191-2, 206, 316, 349; R 552, 556
Broms, E 219
Brook, Sir R. E., **113**; B 61; A 12, 76, 78, 84, 86, 97, 107, 120, 474, 477; R 483, 519, 521
Brook, Lady, **113**
Brook, T. W. G., R 528
Brookfield, Cdr E. W. H., R 482, 518, 531
Brooks, A. W., R 535
Brooks, D., **388, 391**; A 147; E *1971-5, 1976-81*; C 392, 412, 414, 415-6; R 140, 489, 496, 515-6, 538
Brooks, P., A 476
Brooks, R., E 403, 404, 458, 462; R 515

Brooks, Ldg Wren S. M., R 532
Brouquier, M 454
Brouquier, V., C 448, 470; R 555
Brouwer, W., R 551
Brown, Miss C., R 508
Brown, Chris, **280, 293**; A 145; M 280; C 292; R 497, 538
Brown, D., M 363
Brown, G. M., A 152; M 258; S 308; R 496-7, 529
Brown, Linda, **391**; A 157; L 301, 319, 337, 353; C 223, 275, 313, 330, 346, 361; R 159, 504, 505-7, 537
Brown, M., R 504-6
Brown, P., R 140
Brown, R. L., R 514
Brown, S., C 431
Browne, J., R 497
Browne, Mrs Meyrick, A 475
Browning, M., A 138; L 337, 353, 368, 423, 439, 456; C 412; R 138, 140, 505, 538, 542
Bruce, P., A 137; R 523
Bruneau, E. S., R 511
Bruniges, R., **280, 375, 437**; A 106, 109-10, 128, 144, 145, 150, 477; M *1969-81*; E *1970-75, 1976-8*; C *1971-81*; R 488-90, 492-4, 496-7, 510, 512, 516, 536-7, 540-1, 543, 556
Brunton, Capt. G., R 531
Brushett, P., R 516
Bryant, C., **127**
Bryant, M., A 145; S 444, 464-5; R 520, 523
Brydon, J., R 528
Buchard, G., C 473; R 551
Buckmill, A. E., R 527
Budahazy, S 290
Buffery, J., **233**; A 155; S 250, R 522
Bugajska, C 435
Buhan, J., R 547
Bujdoso, S 445; R 557
Bulinski, J., M 451
Buller, P. M., R 499, 500, 501, 503; *see also* Ashmore, Mrs
Bulleri, R 556
Bullmore, J., **332, 345**; A 144; L 230, 232, 261, 282, 301, 302, 320; C 270; R 499, 504-5; *see also* Single, Mrs

# Index

Burch, T., M 299; E 220, 232, 234, 247; R 170, 495, 515
Burgess, W. C., A 97, 111, 150, 477; R 495
Burney, J., C 432; R 528
Burochkina, V., L 292; R 555
Burr, Capt. L., A 144, 152; E 266, 443; R 553
Burt, Sir G. M., A 146; R 482, 509, 514
Burt, R., S 204, C 188
Burtsev, M., C 471; R 554, 557
Butler, A. F., R 527
Butler, Mrs M., A 138
Butler, M. M., R 482, 498, 499, 500, 501, 502
Butler, Peggy, B 36
Butterworth, H. R., R 518
Byl, Capt. C. van der, R 481, 518
Byrne, V., R 160

Caflisch, M 451; C 467; R 497
Calarese, W., C 193; R 554
Calder, N., A 146
Callot, H., R 547
Calver, L., A 148; L 383, 439, 455, 456; R 500, 504
Calvert, J., R 152
Calvert, W., R 141
Camber, I., R 549
Cambridge, D., R 156
Cameron, I. R., R 511, 525, 528
Campbell, I., (N.E. Section), R 130
Campbell, Ian S., M 298, 318, 452; E 321, 324, 443; C 313, 331, 345–7, 361; R 496, 515–6, 533, 535, 541
Campbell, K. G. C., R 522, 525
Campbell, Col R. V., A 138, 161; R 518, 531
Campbell, Steven, S 389, 409
Campbell-Gray, Hon. I. D., B 41, 46; R 482, 483, 494, 509, 510, 511, 514
Cammell, C. R., R 535
Campion, H. C. R., A 149; S 308, 359, 430; C 330; R 523, 529
Cantone, L., R 551
Capek, C 375
Caraes, E 263
Carleson, P., R 551
Carlisle, D., M 399, 421; E 426; C 413, 415–6; R 137, 160
Carmi, M 452; C 418

Carnie, A., E 385; R 516
Carniel, M 451–2
Carpenter, M., A 148; E 386, 403, 406, 457, 461, 462
Carr, N., A 144, 475; S 465; R 142, 522
Carrard, E 442
Carruthers, D., S 249, 299
Carson, P., A 139; M 421
Carson, S., M 335, 364, 451; S 341, 389, 465; C 313, 330, 345, 347, 412–3, 415–6; R 160, 528
Carter, F. E., R 498
Carter, P., A 155
Cartwright, Mrs J., R 505
Casaban, P., R 492
Casey, Mrs P., A 124, 148, 475; L 366, 440, 456; C 431; R 504
Casey, P., A 148; C 331
Cashen, A., M 350; S 359, 372, 409 R 523
Casmir, E., R 547
Casmir, G., R 547, 553
Cassapi, Prof. V., **448**; A 139, 170; E 462
Castle, Egerton, R 481
Castle, Prof. R., **233**; A 136, 170, 432, 440, 446; L 260, 301, 383; C 253, 254, 311; R 505, 541–2
Cathie, *see* Bewley-Cathie
Cattiau, Philippe, B 38; C 349; R 547, 551
Cavin, C 189
Cawthorne, D., **393**; A 124, 300, 392, 448, 477; M 174, 195, 229, 317, 334, 350, 365, 436, 452; R 491–5, 536–7, 539–40
Cawthorne, H., **332**, **393**; A 11, 144; L *1971–80*; C *1973–80*; R 488, 499, 500–3, 537, 539
Cawthorne, V. C., A 142; R 494, 495
Cawton, M., R 140
Cazaban, S 184
Cazaly, B. P., E 179; R 491, 494, 514, 521
Cecil, F., R 506
Cecil, K., **424**, **448**; A 141, 144; L *1975–81*; C *1977–81*; R 141, 501, 503–8, 537, 542
Cederin, B., R 511
Celentano, M 195; C 205
Ceretti, L 262; C 254
Cervi, F., C 432, 499; R 556

Cesarano, R 553
Cessac, E 357
Chalmers, F. C., R 494
Chalwyn, V., 165
Chan, O., R 525
Chanchet, Renée, B 29; *see also* Henry, Mrs R.
Chapella, S 329
Chapman, P., R 506
Charachenidze, D., R 557
Charles, A., L 366, 383; R 505
Charlton, F. E., R 514
Charney, J., A 129
Charnock, F., A 148, 151, 456
Charov, C 225
Chatterton, C. J., R 527
Chatterton, G., R 521
Cheetham, D., R 481, 498, 500
Cheatle, G. A. L., R 527
Chell, M., M 363; E 386, 403, 458, 462; S 389, 465; R 516
Chepeleva, A., R 555
Chernikov, V., R 513, 556
Chernuchevich, A., R 551
Chesney, M., A 138
Chetwood, Lt M., A 132, 146; M 316, 349, 350, 364, 380, 451–2; C 330; R 132, 496, 526, 533, 538
Chetwood, P., A 146
Cheyne, J. L. W., R 527
Cheyney, A., R 495
Cheyney, P., B 47
Chiari, R., R 513
Chiavacci, G., R 547
Chicca, P., R 557
Childs, B., A 147; R 482, 510, 514
Chipola, A 146
Chipman, J., S 465
Chirkova, C 295
Christie, C. H., R 483
Christie, E. B., A 121; R 492, 514, 522, 527
Chronowski, E 458, 464
Church, V., L 384
Churchill, Winston S., B 47; A 474; R 527
Churchman, F. C., R 535
Cipriani, E 201, 286
Cirkova, S., R 549
Cintrat, R 556
Ciszek, E 427

Claringbull, R., R 514
Clark, C., R 496
Clark, G., R 496
Clark, J., R 130, 154
Clark, Nigel, E 404; R 515
Clarke, A., L 366
Clarke, Sgt L. V., R 531
Clarke, M., E 248, 263, 264; C 253
Clarke, S. L. H., R 528
Clauselti, E., R 511
Clay, C. F., A 474
Clayton-Morris, V., A 138; R 511, 539
Closset, P., R 556
Clubs etc.
  All England, B 39, 56; A 8
  AFA Coaches' (Leaders'), C 238; R 540
  Allen, M 229; L 401, 423, 456; R 541
  Annan, A 168
  Army FU, A 118, 171; E 288, 306, 322, 358, 461; S 269, 291, 465; R 517–8, 524
  Artists' Rifles, B 33
  Ashton Tameside, A 134; M 352; L 215, 216, 238, 244, 261, 320, 354, 423, 456; E 426; C 444, 238; R 509, 540
  Avalon, L 368
  Bath Sword, A 154, 155; L 456; S 465
  S. Behmber, A 142–3; L 366, 456; R 540–1
  Bellahouston, A 168; L 423; E 442
  Benfleet Blades, M 335, 350
  S. Bertrand (Sch. of A.), B 33, 66; A 9, 120, 147; L 369; R 497, 508, 517, 524, 540
  Birmingham, A 138, 155; M 380; E 371, 461–2; S 310, 388, 444; R 540–1
  Birmingham School of Arms, L 178
  Bon Accord, Aberdeen, A 162, 168
  S. Boston, A 143, 144, 146; M 281, 352, 451; L 244, 254, 303, 354, 369, 423; E 184, 200, 220, 235, 249, 265, 306, 441; S 185, 203, 237, 310, 327, 388, 409, 428, 444, 465; C 412, 431, 469; R 498, 507, 509, 517–8, 524, 540, 543
  Bristol, A 156
  Brownhill, A 144, 145; M 316; L 368, 440, 456; E 458

# Index

Caledonian, A 162; L 217, 246, 254, 301, 310; C 270; R 540
Cardiff, M 451; L 327, 353, 423; E 385, 404, 406
S. Cassapi *see* Leicester YMCA
Chase, A 141; L 401
Chester, A 136; L 366, 440
Coaches' Club, A 134
Combined Circles, A 146
Combined Services, S 185; R 524
Corby, E 305
Craiglockhart, A 168; S 429
Cyrano, A 162; L 456
Darlington, S 444
S. Darnell, L 301
Ecosse, M 399; L 456; E 406
Elmbridge, L 401
Edmonton, A 146; L 218, 337
S. Emery, C 469; R 543
Espada, A 108, 153; L 423, 456
Excalibur, L 244; E 341; C 431; R 518
Exeter, A 156; L 246
Fiveways, E 425
Fleet, A 146
Folkestone, FC, A 152; M 299
Froeschlen, Salle, M 174, 229
S. Ganchev, A 145, 146; M 379; S 409, 428, 430, 444, 464–5
Gauthier's Penguins, R 508
Glasgow, A 162; E 404; S 429
Gloucester Mod. Penth., E 425, 461
S. Goodall, A 146; M 381, 451; L 303
S. Gravé (Academy, Sch. of A.), R 508, 517, 540
Grosvenor, A 145, 146, 147; E 184, 198, 200, 220, 265, 463; R 517, 540–1
Guisborough, S 445
Halifax, L 178
Hanwell, E 234
Hawick, A 168
Huddersfield, C 222
Hull, M 451
Hydra (and Hydra U-20), A 134, 136; M 381, 399–9, 451; L 423, 456; S 291, 310, 327; R 498, 524, 540–1
Ilford, A 141, 144, 145
Inns of Court Sch. of A., B 33; R 517
Instonians, M 399
Jard, A 167, 168; L 230; E 386
Kings Cross, S 359

Ladies' C. d'Escr., R 508, 540
Lansdowne, A 87, 150, 179; E 265; R 508, 517
Latista, A 162, 165; M 104, 175, 194; L 353; E 403
Leicester YMCA FC (Salle Cassapi), A 139; M 380; L 243; E 385, 403; S 408
Lensbury, R 517
Leyton, A 144
Lilia, S 236
Lloyds Bank, A 145, 149
Londack, A 151
London FC, B 33, 53, 66; A 7, 9, 147, 148; M 175, 194, 212; L 216, 244, 354, 369; E 184, 200, 220, 463; S 185, 237, 291, 327, 465; C 469; R 497–8, 508–9, 517, 524, 540, 542–3
London-Thames, M 419, 451; L 401, 423, 424, 439, 456; E 404, 406, 425–6, 441, 443, 462; C 431; R 509, 518, 540
Lothian, A 163, 168; M 380; L 366, 368; E 323, 386; S 429
Loughton, L 336

F. G. McPherson's Sch. of A., E 463
W. MacPherson's Sch. of A., R 517
S. Mangiarotti, B 26–7
Mary Hawdon, L 439
Mayfield FC, M 335
Meadowbank, A 168; M 363; L 366, 368, 423; E 404; S 444
MEL Club, A 151
Mercia, S 444
MPAGB, E 354, 443; R 540
Morel's Sch. of A., R 517
Neasden, E 339
Nemo, M 379
Newcastle FS, *see* S. van Oeveren
S. Nicklen, R 498, 540
Northampton, C 207; R 540
Northumbria, A 130; L 423, 456

Park Lane, A 145
Paladin Sword, L 368
S. Paul, A 148–50, 173, 399, 438, 451; M 175, 194, 228, 281, 399, 438, 451; E 184, 200, 220, 249, 306, 341, 358, 462; S 221, 252,

Clubs: S. Paul – *cont.*
  269, 327, 343, 465; C 331, 469; R
  59, 497–8, 517–8, 524, 540,
  542–3
Pauleons Ladies', A 149; L 176; R
  508–9
S. Pearson, M 325; L 244, 303, 320,
  318; R 509
Phoenix (Bristol; S. Roeder), A 156; M
  379; L 440, 456
Plymouth, A 154, 156
Plymstock, A 152, 156
Polytechnic (inc. Ladies'), A 144, 150;
  M 175, 381, 399, 421; L 175–6,
  197, 261, 303, 401; E 322; S 185,
  252, 269, 327, 389, 428, 465; C
  431, 469; R 497–8, 508–9, 517–8,
  524, 540, 542–3
Portland FC, A 137
Portsmouth and Southsea, A 153; M
  436
Ranmore, M 381
Racing Club de France, M 364, 436; R
  540
Reading, A 153; E 354, 355, 403,
  462–3; S 185; R 518
REME, E 370
S. Reynolds, L 178
S. Roeder *see* Phoenix
Royal Air Force, E 404; S 465;
  R 540
Royal Automobile Club, R 517, 524
Royal Navy, E 441; S 465
Sabre Club, R 524
Sale, L 423
Scottish FC, A 161, 168; E 235
Scottish Coaches' Assoc., E 386
Sheffield, E 426, 462
Somerset, C 469
Sondes Place, L 401, 455; E 403
Southside, L 197
Spartan, L 337
Stempel's Sch. of Arms, R 508
Stratford-on-Avon, 137
Streatham, A 145
Stanhope, S 327
S. Stempel, B 32
Stevenage, L 423
Stirling, A 168; L 423
Stockport, E 426
Surrey, L 440; C 469

Sword Club, R 517
S. Tassart(-Parkins), R 508, 517
Taunton, A 156
Thames, A 148, 150, 151; M 194, 228,
  316, 381; L 176, 197, 216, 244,
  303, 369; E 184, 220, 235, 265,
  288, 306, 322, 341; R 498, 509,
  517–8, 540
US Army, R 540
S. van Oeveren, A 130; L 259–60, 303
Vasas, Budapèst, S 342
Wanstead, A 145
Wellesbourne, A 153
Wells, M 350
Welwyn, M 380; L 456
Worcester, E 425
Yeovil, A 156, 179
York (Fencing Association), A 131,
  132; M 450, 451; L 456; E 462; S 465
Cob, L 300
Cobb, M., A 151; L 178; C 189; R 505–6,
  525
Cocker, D., A 148; M 419, 451; E 426,
  462; C 471; R 495, 511, 540
Cofield, Sgt, A 111
Cohen, L., A 154
Cohen, R. A., **233, 314, 328, 393**; A 11,
  12, 91, 93, 110, 123, 128, 144, 150,
  154, 446; M 175, 214, 229, 243, 297,
  317, 421; S *1965–81*; C 190, 204, 224,
  *1969–80*, 471; R 487–90, 492–3,
  495–6, 519–23, 536–7, 543, 546
Coke, The Hon. Richard, B 45
Colclough, Cpl B., R 532
Cole, B., A 477
Cole, Col R. E., **27**; B 26; A 137–8, 474;
  R 510, 539
Coleman, M., C 210; R 545
Coletti, C 394
Coley, W., M 419
Collino, M. C., R 550
Collins, A., A 146; M 451
Collins, Surg Cdr C. P., R 514, 532
Collins, R., M 334, 364
Colmer, J., R 500
Colombetti, B., 549, 555
Commander, D., E 403
Competitions – British
  Ashton, A 136; R 536; U-20, M 317,
  450; L 281, 284, 300
  Aviemore Tournament, A 163

# Index

BAF, C 391–2
Baptiste Bertrand Memorial Cup, R 503
Birmingham FC's Invitation, S 237
Birmingham, A 123, 138; R 539
Brighton, E 403; S 389
Bristol Phoenix, M 421; L 423; E 404, 425, 441; S 389, 429, 444
British U-20 International, E 441
British Universities Championship, A 163; R 525
Clara Rayner (Notts.), A 139; R 538
R. E. Cole Memorial, R 521
Corble Cup, A 131; S 326–7; R 520
Coronation Cup (Leon Paul), R 492
Cyrano, A 141; E 324
C.-L. de Beaumont, R 500
Desprez, R 502
Doyne, R 494
Eden International U-20, M 399, 419, 438
Emrys Lloyd, R 493
Epee Championship, R 509
Epee Club Cup, R 514
Essex Open, L 456; E 461; S 465
Excalibur Inter-County, A 154
Fanfare for Europe (Edinburgh), E 323
L. V. Fildes Cup, R 514
Ford Cup, Edinburgh, L 230, 456
Granville Cup, A 97; R 542
Halifax, A 131; C 253
Harrogate, A 131
Hereford and Worcester Open, M 421, 436; E 425–6
Highland Open, A 163
Hutton, B 35, 56; A 92, R 500
Ilford, A 141; L 384; E 339, 386; C 331
Invicta, L 300
Inter-Services, M 452; E 443; S 389; R 530–4
Inverclyde, A 162; R 541
Jackett Trophy, C 469
King Edward VII Cup, A 161
Kelt, S 429
Kirklees, A 131; M 422, 452; L 423, 439; E 404, 426; S 444–5
Ladies' Open Sabre, A 154
Ladies' Foil National Championship, R 498

Leamington, A 123, 137; R 539
Leicester, A 139, 140; R 536
Leon Paul, *see* Coronation
Liverpool, A 134; M 398–9, 421; L 383, 423; S 409, 429, 444; C 204, 223; U-20, L 401
Magrini, R 524
Martin Edmunds, R 508
Martini International Epee, B 63, 69; R 513; *see also* Sponsorship
Martini Qualifying, A 115; R 512
Mayflower Cup Tournament, A 154
Meadowbank, L 368; S 465
Men's Foil National Championship, R 490
Miller-Hallett, B 35, 59; A 474; R 511
Millfield Ladies U-20 International, A 154, 366; L 400; R 507
Millfield Men's Under-20 International, A 154; R 496
National U-20 Team, M 363; L 151, 354
National Age Group Championships, A 102, 119; R 497, 516, 523
Nescafé U-20, M 258; L 260, 300, 320; E 263, 285, 305, 324; S 267, 289, 308, 325
Norfolk Tournament, A 141; M 452; L 456; S 465
N. Ireland Open, E 426
Novices, R 495
Olympic Championships, R 547
One-hit, Chelsea, E 371
Oxford and Cambridge Match, C 204
Parker, R 504
Polytechnic Championships, A 134
Portsmouth, A 153; R 542
Public Schools, B 46; A 108, 113; R 527–9
Quadrangular Match (Home International), A 75, 113, 157, 160–1, 166, 207
Redbridge Tournament, A 141; L 319, 338, 353, 368, 384, 423
Rest of Britain Match, R 543
Ridley Martin, R 521
Royal Tournament, *see* Inter-Services
Sandhurst, E 323, 338
Savage, R 517
Schoolboys', *see* National Age Group Championships

Competitions – British – *cont.*
  Schoolgirls', R 507
  Schools Quadrangular, C 376
  Scottish, B 32; R 534–5
  Scottish Open, L 423; E 462
  Silver Jubilee, R 501
  S. London Open, M 452; L 456; E 462
  Spartan, M 365; L 368; E 371; S 373
  Sporting Record, R 497
  Sybil Perigal, R 506
  Team Championships, A 82
  Toupie Lowther, R 505
  Tyneside, A 129, 130, 246, 268; M 365, 451; L 401; E 425, 442, 462
  Under-20 Epee, R 516
  Under-20 Ladies' Foil, R 506
  Under-20 Men's Foil, R 496
  Under-20 Sabre, R 523
  University Championships, A 163; R 525–6
  University Athletic Union (UAU), A 134, 525; M 242
  Wanstead, C 223
  Welsh Games, A 157; E 371, 462
  Welsh Open, A 158; R 537
  Wickford, A 141
  Wilkinson Sword, M 350, 363, 379, 399, 419, 451; L 423, 455
  Winton Cup, A 90; C 294; R 544
  York Open, M 451; L 456
  Yorkshire Mixed Pairs, A 131
  – foreign
  Aarhus, L 352
  Alassio, C 291, 311
  Amsterdam Inter-Cities, M 453; L 197, 217, 232, 282, 303, 457
  Amsterdam, M 243, 422, 453; L 178, 217, 457; E 235, 249; S 186, 253, 269, 402
  Ankara, M 351
  Antwerp, M 382, 400
  Arlon Under-20, L 299, 320, 337
  Arnhem U-20, L 401
  Arnsberg, S 373
  Bad Durkheim, M 229, 278, 298, 364, 398, 400, 422, 438–9, 453
    Champions pool, E 235, 249, 265, 307
  Balaton, L 320
  Basel, M 299, 364; L 457
  Beirut, M 351; L 320; E 200

Bergamo team, E 235
Berlin, L 320, 402, 424, 457; E 307, 325, 340, 358, 372, 407; S 409
Bern, E 307, 340, 357, 372, 387, 407, 428, 443, 463
Besançon, M 400, 422
Bologna, M 175, 278, 336, 352, 364
Bonn, M 336, 351, 364, 382, 422, 453
Bordeaux, M 453
Brasov, Rumania, S 445, 466
Brussels, M 298, 335, 351, 364, 382, 400; L 178, 197, 303; E 183, 387; S 360; U-16, M 364, 399; U-16, L 422; U-14, L 401; U-20, E 441; *see also* Martini
Bucharest, L 440
Budapest, M 335, 351, 364, 439; E 443; S 343, 390; U-20, M 350, 364; U-20, L 455; U-20, E 338, 372; U-20, S 360, 389, 429
Burgsteinfurt U-20, M 399, 438
Carroccio, Legnano, E 407, 428, 443, 463
Catania, E 324, 358, 428, 463; Under-20, E 249
Chabine, Paris, L 402
Chalons, M 336
Charenton, M 453
Chaux des Fonds, M 215, 229; E 200, 235
Cologne, M 212, 259
Common Market Cup, E 358
Cormeilles, M 422
Como, L 178, 197, 217, 230, 281, 282, 320, 338, 368, 384, 402, 425, 440, 456–7
Coupe des Trentes, Brussels, E 183, 202
Coupe d'Europe, M 175, 259, 336; L 197, 244, 261, 284, 303, 320, 440, 457; E 183, 235, 265, 288, 325
Cracow, S 310; U-20, M 420
Decade Sportive, Brussels, L 262; E 266; S 269
Dieppe, L 178, 197, 218, 262; E 249, 325, 340, 372, 428; S 204, 343
Differdange, E 387, 403
Dormagen U-20, S 409
Dornbirn, L 320, 352, 383, 400–1, 422, 439, 454
Dourdan, S 388, 409

# Index

Duisburg U-20, M 350, 364; L 218, & *passim*
Duren, L 217, 230, 262, 281, 303, 320, 338, 366, 368, 402; E 182, 288, 307, 324, 340, 357, 372, 387, 407; S 204, 269
Duval, Paris, M 298, 336, 351, 364, 382, 400, 419, 438, 453–4
Etampes, L 383, 400–1, 422, 455
Eupen, L 262, 282, 303, 320; E 220
Fencing Masters World Championships, C 271
Flanders Golden Foil, M 259, 336, 351, 364, 422
Ferranio, E 200
Gelsenkirchen U-20, M 299, 317, 350, 364; L 230, 281, 283, 300, 320, 337, 366, 400, 455
Genoa U-20, E 324, 338, 355; team, E 358
Ghent, S 253
Giovanini, M 317
Golub Castle, S 290
Goppingen, L 217, 282, 303, 320, 337, 352, 368, 384, 402, 424, 456–7; E 305; S 269, 308; U-20, S 253, 359
Gothenberg, E 288
Graz, S 360, 373
Groningen, M 278
The Hague U-20, M 450
Hamburg, S 221 & *passim*
Hanover, S 445, 466
Heidenheim, E 183, 265, 307, 324, 340, 357–8, 372, 387, 407, 428, 443, 463
Heilbronn, M 364
Huy, E 202, 324; U-20, M 280; U-20 team, M 243
Innsbruck, E 340, 358, 407, 428
Iran, L 352
Irish Open, L 352
Istanbul, M 351
Jeanty, Paris, L 197 & *passim*
Katowice, L 402; E 425; S 374, 409
Koblenz U-20, S 289, 308, 359
Kussnacht U-20, M 379, 399, 438; L 400–1, 422, 454
Lauphheim U-20, E 265, 403
Le Havre, M 364; E 308
Leipzig, L 424, 440

Louviers, E 200
Luxembourg, E 325; U-20, M 259, 299
Lyons, E 200
Maccabiah Games 1969, S 253
Magdeburg, M 351, 364; L 368
Martini,
  Paris, M 196, 229, 243, 259, 279, 298, 317, 351, 364, 382, 400, 422, 438, 453
  Turin, L 230, 262, 281, 352, 368, 385, 402, 424, 440, 456–7
  Brussels, S 186, 237, 251, 269, 290, 308, 329
  New York, S 409–10, 430, 445, 466
Melun, M 215, 229; L 197, 217, 230
Minsk, L 303, 384
Moers U-16, M 399
Monal, Paris, E 182 & *passim*
Montpelier, M 229
Montreal, L 352
Moulins, E 358
Montreuil, S 237, 309, 343
Munich, S 204, 269, 310, 329, 343, 374, 390, 410, 430, 446, 466
New York, M 215
NYC Athletic Club, E 202
Noordwijk, L 178
Offenbach, L 352, 368, 402, 440, 457
Oslo, E 407, 463
Padua, S 186, 237, 329, 374, 466
Papendal, M 379, 399
Paris, L 457
Picon, Paris, E 180, 200
Poitiers, E 202, 266, 307, 324, 340, 358, 372, 407, 428, 443, 463
Remich, L 230; U-20, L 247
Rennes, E 387, 407
Rheims, E 340
Rommel, Paris, M 175, 196, 229, 258, 336, 351, 364, 400, 422, 439, 453
St Maur, L 457
Salzburg, L 368
Santelli Cup, S 430
Schmetz U-20, E 249, 305, 355
Seven-Nations team, L 402; S 410
Soest, E 235
Spitzer U-18, M 317; L 320, 352, 366
Spreafico, Milan, E 324, 372

Competitions – foreign – *cont.*
Steinfurter Schloss, M 379
Stolberg U-20, E 235
Taillendier, Paris, S 374, 390
Tauberbischofsheim U-20, E 235, 305; team, M 383; E 358, 387
Toronto Exhibition, M 196; L 197; E 202
Toronto, M 215; E 220
Toulon, E 358, 428
Tourcoing, E 441
Touzard, Paris, S 308, 373, 409, 445, 466
Turin, *see* Coupe d'Europe *and* Martini
Universiade, C 189, 227, 277, 397, 434–5, 469
Venice, M 400, 422, 438, 453
Vienna, E 428, S 390, 445
Waldkirch, L 455
Warsaw, M 175, 297, 400; L 178; S 390
Wattenscheid U-20, E 355
Weinheim U-20, M 229, 243; L 230
Wentdorf, M 350
Ystad, S 185
Zofingen U-20, E 355
Zurich U-20, L 401; E 407, 428, 443, 463
Compson, S., R 529
Comrie, M., S 444
Condoumi, E 263
Conduit, W. A., R 509
Connock, M. B., R 529
Convents, W., A 445; S 268, 309, 327, 342, 408; R 521
Convill, C., L 319; C 313, 346, 412, 414; R 160
Convill, O., C 313, 414
Conyd, M., C 273
Cook, Mrs E., L 260; R 504
Cooke, Capt. E. G. S., R 530
Cooke, Sir E. Stenson, R 491
Cook, J., R 505
Cook, L. C., R 491, 493, 495
Cook, Sir Theodore, A 474
Cooke, Harry, A 12, 77, 110, 148–9, 477; R 484, 491, 492, 511, 514, 522, 539
Cooke, R., C 188
Cooksey, Mrs J., 411; L 401, 411, 414; R 534, 541; *see also* Bewley-Cathie, Mrs *and* Wardell-Yerburgh, Mrs
Concannon, L., R 506–7
Coombs, G., R 512
Cooper, Sgt W. F., R 532
Cooper, J., A 145; E 323, 338; R 497
Cooperman, A. R., **211**; A 148; M 175; S 184–6, 203–4, 221, 253; C 193–4, 208, 211; R 484–6, 491, 493–4, 519–22, 537, 539, 542, 545
Copping, Mrs E., R 503
Corble, A. H., A 520; R 518
Cording, L. E., R 514, 521
Corish, M., E 462
Cormack, P., A 162; R 534, 541
Cormack, G. S., R 494
Cornaggia, G.-C., R 551
Cornereau, E., R 551
Cornet, G., R 509
Cornford, A., A 11, 91, 469; E 307
Cornhill, R. D., R 538
Corsellis, J., R 527, 529
Costa, C., R 547
Cottar, J., R 539
Cottard, Prof. P., B 56; A 146; S 184; R 520
Cotton, A. J., R 484, 494, 522, 525, 528
Cotton, J., A 11, 140
Cotton, L., A 139
Coulson, W. F., C 190; R 535
Coutard, E 266
Court, J., L 320; R 505
Courtenay, R., A 137, 456
Courtenay, C., L 456
Courtillat, J., R 556
Courtney-Lewis, C. T., A 140; R 522, 537
Courtney-Lewis, Mrs P., A 476; L 178; R 140, 486, 505, 536, 538–9
Cousins, T., A 149
Coutrot, J., R 551
Coventon, Maj. J., A 106
Coverdale, D., A 141
Cowin, Sub. Lt, R 494
Cox, L., R 514
Crahay, M 365, 381, 422
Craig, Capt. A. D. E., R 483
Craig, R., **188**, **213**, **240**, **314**; A 149; S 185–6, 203–4, 236–7, 250–2, 267–9, 289–91, 310; C 187, 207, 240,

# Index

275, 296, 313, 315; R 487–8, 519–20, 523, 528, 533, 546
Cramer, A., E 287; R 512
Creagh Osborne, F., R 515
Creagh-Snell, N., E 200
Creek, J., A 84, 475–6
Cressall, A. E., A 527
Cressall, S., R 525
Cripp, C. T. J., C 270; R 527, 528
Cripps, M. A. L., R 525
Critch, J. H., A 477
Croft, C., R 528
Croft, L., 215
Cromarty-Dickson, Prof., A 179
Crook, J., C 416
Crosnier, Prof. L., A 161, 163
Crosnier, Prof. R., B 31, 55, 60, 65; A 8, 81, 135, 150, 161; R 492, 493, 494, 535
Cross, T. G., R 494
Crouch, J., A 130; S 465; R 130, 497, 533
Crowder, F. P., R 527
Cruthers, P., E 461; R 516
Cull, D., R 497
Cullen, M., M 350, 421
Cuppage, L., L 176, 216, 217; R 504
Currie, A., R 527
Cymermann, C 189, 191
Czaikowski, Dr Z., A 83, 134, 161, 169; R 535
Czakkel, M 351; C 224
Czarnecki, K., E 181, 184; R 511
Czernicki, M., S 268; R 520–1
Czipler, C 190
Czvikovsky, F., R 547

Dabrowski, M., R 547, 556
Dagallier, E. D., R 511, 513, 539
Daglish, A., A 326; R 132–3
Dains, E., A 141
Dale, D., A 144; M 399, 438, 450; S 464; C 467–8; R 141, 496, 516, 528–9
Dale, L., A 141; L 401; R 508
Dalglish, Capt. R., RN, R 482, 518, 531
Dalla Barba, R 557
Dal Zotto, F., M 364; C 344, 375, 376, 394, 416, 469–70; R 548, 556
Damrel, 3rd Off J., R 532
Daniell, C. Leaf, R 481, 509

Daniell, Gladys, R 482, 498, 500
Daniels, W., R 551, 553
Dankla, P., R 547
Danosi, C 330
Dany, M., R 549
Dap, Prof., B 31
Darby, Sgt J., A 172; E 265; R 510, 533
Daré, G., R 553
Darge, Mr, A 540
Darnell, F., **424**; L 423
Darnley, P., R 505
Dauppe, S 408
d'Aury, R 514
Davenport, Mrs H., L 261, 282, 284, 302, 304, 337, 338; C 295; R 152, 499, 502, 504; *see also* Twomey, H.
Davenport, R., **323**, **448**; A 144, 153; E 1967–75, 1976–81; C 253, 254, 412, 414–6; R 152, 510–12, 515, 541, 543
Davies, B., R 507
Davies, C., A 159
Davies, Ceri, L 456
Davies, Mrs E. M., **240**, **314**; A 11, 107, 123, 303, 474–5; L 176, 178, 196, 197, 231; C 191, 205; R 141, 499, 502; *see also* Berry, E. M.
Davis, G. M., R 549
Davies, Mrs Maxwell, A 87
Davies, Mrs May, **256**; A 80, 255
Davies, M. L. R., R 528
Davies-Cooke, D., A 83
Davies-Cooke, Mrs H., **107**; A 78, 83, 107, 475; L 176, 232; *see also* Hoos, H.
Davis, F. G., R 491, 494, 514
Davis, Gladys M., R 482, 498, 500, 502
Davis, J. M., **158**, **240**; A 150, 157; L 1964–9; C 1965–8; R 159, 487, 499, 502, 504, 507; *see also* Barkley, Mrs
Davis, John, M 438, 453; C 413, 415, 438; R 160, 496, 528
Davis, Mrs M., R 505
Davies, P., C 447; R 496
Davis, S., R 156
Davis, W., R 498, 500
Davison, F., L 129; C 187; R 160, 506–7
Davson, P. M., R 481, 490
Deakin, J., **262**; A 135; L 259, 261, 283, 284, 303; R 507
de Amodio, J., A 527

Deanfield, J., **256, 293, 314, 393**; A 123, 150, 446; M 243, 381, 421; E 263; S 253, 266–9, 289–91, 309, 310; C 271, 277, 294, 296–7, 312, 315, 415, 417, 433; R 488–90, 496, 516, 519–23, 526, 529
de Baeza, L., R 514
de Beaumont, C.-L., **frontis, 19, 27, 32, 34, 49, 54, 57, 64, 68, 88, 211, 240, 293**
  and parents, 15–20, 45
  sisters, 18–20, 24–5, 38, 46, 50, 73
  education, 20, 23
  scouting, 23–4
  rowing, 24
  boxing, 24, 25, 39
  early employment, 26, 30, 31
  homes and marriages, 29–30, 45, 52
  children, 30, 43–4, 52
  Scotland, 29, 31–2, 41, 48
  FIE, 13, 35, 36, 39, 41, 60–2, 74; A 97
  RAF, 42, 50–2
  Sir O. Mosley, 46–50
  circuses, 14, 56–8; A 8, 225
  publications, 13, 58, 60, 73; A 7, 10, 11
  Commonwealth, 13, 58; A 9, 97, 211
  honours, 59–60, 65, 73
  as fencer, 13, 25, 26–9, 31–9, 40, 41, 42, 54, 58–9; A 120, 147; R 482, 483, 510–1, 514, 521, 535, 539, 542, 545
  wine merchant, 29
  British Captain, 36–7, 54, 74; A 93, 175, 190
  AFA official, 13, 36, 40–1, 53–60, 63–9, 73–5; A 7–9, 76, 78, 79, 80, 83, 85, 89, 91, 93, 96, 97, 122, 131, 135, 140, 474–5, 477, 500, 544
  antique dealer, 13–14, 30, 45, 52, 53, 67, 70–3
  property dealer, 51
  broadcaster, 58
  critic of fencers, A 205, 293, 296
  character of, 14, 24, 33, 38, 39, 50, 66, 69, 75; A 8–9
de Beaumont, Carolyn, **68**; B 52
de Beaumont, Dominic, **68**
de Beaumont, Elizabeth (Elouise), **19**; B 23, 45

de Beaumont, Mrs Joy, **68**
de Beaumont, Kathleen, B 17, 21, 23
de Beaumont, Lys, **68**
de Beaumont, Marguerite, **44**; B 25–6, 38, 45–6, 50, 70; A 12
de Beaumont, Mrs G., B 30; *see also* Grove-Crofts, G.
de Beaumont, Mrs P., **68**; *see also* Holdsworth, P.
de Beaumont, Robin, **68**; B 30, 43, 46; A 12
de Besche, H., R 492
de Beukelaer, R 551
de Beur, Charles, B 62
Debiard, E 263
de Boer, J., R 549
de Bourguignon, G., R 553
de Capriles, Miguel A., B 62
de Diaz, M., R 553
Dee, M., S 253
De Escofet, Dr, A 539
Dehmer, S 408
Deighton, R., **256**; A 144, 152; E 247; C 255; R 516
de Jong, A., R 551, 553
de la Falaise, G., R 551
Delagerie, M 438, 454
Delagerie P./M., M 454; C 467
de Lavradio, Count, A 78
Delfino, G., R 513, 551
Del Francia, M 195
Delberg, M., S 445; R 520–1
Delfino, E 179
Delhem, F., E 304
Dellocque, S 268; R 520
Delporte, C., R 551
Delrieu, S 466
Delukin, C 238
Delvaque, C 204
Delzi, Prof. F., B 53; A 121, 145, 147
Demaille, M., L 282; C 315, 348, 417; R 549
de Montigny, F., R 551
Dennett, J., A 141
Dennis, R., **233**; R 137
Dennisov, V., R 548
de Nogaret, M 419
Dent, A., R 507
Dermody, D., R 534
Desborough, Lord, A 474; R 481, 531; *see also* Grenfell, W. H.

# Index

Dessureault, M., C 412; R 546
Devlin, D., C 346; R 506, 541
de Walden, Lord Howard, B 40; A 474
Dewar, M. B. U., R 527
Dexter, Douglas, **49**; R 482, 483, 510, 511
Dhrangadhra, Maharaja of, A 474
d'Hughes, Comte, R 547
Diamond, Mrs P., A 159
Diaz, B., E 57, 371; R 130
Dick, C. Campbell, A 474
Dick, M., L 353, 368; R 501
Dicker, R. C., R 494
Dickson, S. C., R 514
Dignan, M., L 366, 368; R 506; *see also* Montgomery, Mrs M.
Dilkes, K., A 139
Dillon-Cavanagh, M., R 547, 551
Dimont, J., M 212; C 187, 256; R 556
Dinsdale, Prof. M., A 129
di Rosa, M., R 547
Ditmas, J. M. R., R 494
Dix, P. C., R 494, 511
Dmitrenko, R 555
Dobson, M., S 188
Dodds, C., R 130
Dodman, L., A 421
Domolki(-Sakovits), L., R 500-1, 549, 555
Donaldson, M., M 450-1; S 464
Donin, V., C 187; R 556
Dolquick, I., R 555
Dordé, M., R 513
d'Oriola, M 173; C 472-3; R 547
Dorling, J., A 150; L 197, 216, 217, 232; C 223; R 503-4, 506
Doros, G., R 553
Dougan, Lt Cdr J., R 532
Dove, D., R 140
Dowdeswell, R. M., R 514
Downing, A. N., R 142, 528
Doyle, D., **165**
Doyne, P. G., A 474; R 482, 490, 491
Drake, Paymt C., R 531
Drake, C., R 509
Drakenberg, C 333; R 551
Drayton, J., R 495
Drew, C., R 484, 499, 502, 503, 507; *see also* Miszewska, Mrs
Dreyfus, Y., C 191, 193, 208; R 513-4, 551

Driessen, M., M 399; E 426, 462; R 497
Drimba, I., L 246, 282; C 189, 227, 241, 257; R 547, 549, 556
Drori, N., L 383, 422-3; C 431; R 507, 542
Drozdzowski, E 404
Drummond, G., S 389, 409, 444
Drummond, O., L 260, 384; R 505
Drury, D. D., R 514
Dubrawska, C 410
Ducamp, L 300
Duchene, M., E 266, 285, 358, 405
Ducret, R., R 547, 551, 553
Dudley, Mrs J., A 151, 423; L 232, 261, 318, 320, 337, 338, 353, 354; C 270; R 504
Dudley, S., L 423; R 505
Duff, J. F., R 514
Duffy, Vincent, C 2
Dumigan, I., C 346; R 160
Dumke, C 241
Dunaev, C 395, 418, 470
Dunay, P., R 551
Dunlop, I., E 443
Dunn, C., R 507
Dunn, F., R 132
Dunsterville, Lt G., R 531
Durne, M., **302**; A 11, 78, 121, 123, 147; L *1964-70 passim*; C 254, 313; R 485, 486, 499, 501-4, 536, 539, 541, 542
Duront, C., L 176; R 500, 506
Duschner, S 237, 250, 343; R 521
Duthie, I. F., A 162; R 528, 535
Duthie, J., R 535
Duthie, Mrs M., A 162; L 217, 230, 244
Dutripon, J., M 258, 436; R 497
Duvallon-Lonan, D., R 152
Dydier, P., R 551
Dye, R., A 94, 124, 141, 477; R 141
Dyer, Eric, **280**
Dyer, Lt-Col G. N., R 482, 518
Dyer, Capt S. B. B., R 531
Dyrssen, G., R 551

Eames, A., **381, 393**; A 140, 144, 151, 160; M *1970-81*; C 254, 311, 312, 330, 345, 394, 416, 432; R 140, 492-4, 496-7, 536-8, 543, 546
Eames, D., R 140, 496
Eames, P., E 441, 461-2

Earl, G., A 123, 477
Earle, E., A 151; L 197, 216, 217, 230, 231; C 222, 223; R 504, 506, 525, 537–8
East, B., L 337, 353, 354; R 506
Eckert, A., L 259; R 507
Ecob, M., R 156, 525
Eden, D., **188, 213, 367**; A 149–50, 326, 361, 363, 432; M 175, 195, 213, 228, 297, 316, 421; S *1964–9, 1970–76*, 465; C 207, 222, 238, 253; R 495–6, 519–22, 536, 546
Eden, J., **293**; A 11, 76, 79, 85, 101, 102, 115, 271, 312, 330, 344, 432, 446, 475, 477, 467
Eden, L., **213**; M 175; S 221; R 495, 497, 523
Eden, M., **213**, S 236, 253, 267, 289, 329; C 239, 271, 522–3
Edgworth-Johnstone, Capt. W., R 518, 530
Edling, R., **356**; E 321, 324, 340, 357, 403, 427, 442; C 291, 311, 333, 349, 362–3, 370, 378, 387, 395, 434, 450; R 513, 552
Edmunds, Mrs C. Martin, R 482, 498
Edridge, Sgt C., R 533
Edmunds, L., A 495; M 280; R 154, 542
Edward, Prince, **379**
Edwardes, Mrs, R 482, 498
Edwards, Ian, **391**; A 157; S 342; C 275, 313, 330, 346, 347, 392, 411, 413, 416, 431; R 159, 537
Edwards, M., **158**; A 157; R 507, 537
Edwards, R., **388**; A 150; E *1975–81*; C 392, 431; R 515
Efimova, E., R 549
Eggleton, Sgt Maj. F., R 530, 531
Eichinger, E 406; C 410
Eiser, J. R., S 221; C 204; R 522
Eiserfey, M., R 132
Elder, G., C 270; R 495
Elek, I., B 54; A 147; C 472–3; R 549
Elek, M., A 147; R 549
Elizabeth II, **379**
Elliot, N., R 528
Elliot-Baxter, N., R 528
Elliott, G., R 504, 536
Elliott, R. S., **411**; A 168, 469; S 373; C 313, 361, 380, 411, 413, 415–6, 429; R 535, 538, 541

Elliott, Fencing Inst. W., R 530
Ellis, C., A 147
Ellis, J. C., A 147; R 511, 514
Ellis, M., S 429
Ellis, Mrs V., A 159; R 505
Ellison, A., R 522, 525, 527, 529
Eltz, U., L 353; R 501
Ekstedt, M 436
Elvin, K., L 383; C 412, 414
Emberson, P., **281**; A 145; E *1970–75*; C 312, 331, 361; R 489, 515–6, 523
Emery, Prof. R., **302**; A 144, 160, 170, 387, 416, 434, 448, 461, 469, 476
Emly, Lord, B 16
Emms, Mrs E., R 538
Ene, A., R 555
Engdahl, E 199, 219; R 513
Engelbracht, R., M 350; R 493
Ennell, K., R 511
Erdelyi, Prof. J., B 56; A 146, 150; R 520–1
Erdos, S., E 325, 340, 357; C 349, 395, 556
Erwteman, J., A 104, 107, 143, 344, 477; L 401, 424, 456; C 331, 412, 424; R 152, 504
Esperanza, M 454
Etchells, T., A 135–6, 325; R 137
Etheridge, P., **49**; R 499, 502, 503
Etherton, T., **256, 393**; A 123, 144, 446; M 243, 258; S 236, 250, 267, 289, *1973–81*; C 255, 376, 394–5, 415–6, 417, 431, 433; R 496, 519–23, 526, 529, 543
Evans, G., **391**; A 158; M 334, 350–1, 364, 380–1, 398, 420–1, 451; C 330, 344–6, 361, 411, 413, 415, 431, 416; R 156, 159, 492, 495–7, 526, 537
Evans, Flt-Lt John J., A 157; R 494, 522, 531
Evans, M., **391**; A 158–9; M 379, 451, 453; C 411, 413, 416, 431, 447; R 156, 495–6, 503, 525
Evans, R., A 12, 138, 150; E 306, *1974–8*; R 139, 511, 538, 540
Eveleigh, F. M. T., R 495
Evequoz, G., A 459; E 285–6, 407; C 312; R 557

# Index

Evequoz, J. B., M 299; E 263; R 513
Evered, D., A 12
Everitt, A. G., R 481, 509, 518
Evill, W., B 71
Ewing, J., A 160
Exeter, D., E 218; R 516
Exelby, M., C 273-4; R 546; see also Gray, Mrs
Eyal, C., M 436, 452; R 493
Eyton, K., L 353
Eyton-Jones, Wren K., R 534

Fabian, D. T., R 528
Fagan, A. W., A 108
Fahlman, S., R 551
Fairburn, R., A 144; S 236, 249, 269, 289, 290, 308, 325; C 295; R 522
Fairhall, D., A 145, 147; E *1974-9*; C 331, 410, 516, 523, 528
Fairhall, Prof. J., **169**, **280**; A 144, 146, 170, 258, 285, 312, 317, 375, 404; E 285, 323, 355, 404, 462; C 330, 359, 392; R 141, 170, 515, 536
Falkowski, J., S 428, 444; R 522, 523
Fancourt, N., A 148; E 461; R 516
Fare, M., **233**; A 11, 151; E *1971-6*, 406; M 258, 298, 317, 366; C 270, 295, 431; R 488-9, 495, 515, 537, 542
Farndon, A., R 504
Fattori, F., R 511
Faul, L 439
Faux, C., A 138
Favia, R 556
Fearnhead, R. W., R 494, 515, 522
Featherstone, J., A 123, 144, 242, 477
Feilmann, Lt F. E. B., R 518, 530-1
Feith, J., E 219
Fekete, C., C 390; R 555
Felislak, C 468
Fellerman, Julian, S 444, 464; R 523
Fenyvesi, C., E 233, 263-4, 266, 325, 340, 355, 386; C 296; R 513, 552
Ferguson, E., E 386, 403, 404, 426, 541
Ferguson, James, A 160; C 313, 415-6; R 160
Ferguson, Julian, M 380, 452; E 385; R 528, 533
Ferguson, M., C 433, 448
Fernandez, S., E 286

Ferris, Mrs J., A 159
Fethers, Prof. J., **82**; A 161, 162, 207; M 174; R 170, 486, 491, 492, 493, 541, 545
Field, Prof. J., A 156; R 522, 531-2
Filatova, C 312; R 555
Fildes, L. V., B 53, 54, 59, 60, 67; A 87, 474-5, 514; R 509, 510, 511
Filipkowski, C 205
Filmer, G. B., R 515
Filz, F., R 549
Finch, T., A 153; R 154
Findlay, L., R 534
Finn, P. Timothy, R 494
Finn, Tony, E 462
Finnis, Sgt M., A 172; E 198; R 515, 533
Fischer, O., M 299, 419; R 497
Fischer, V., E 355, 442, 458; C 418; R 513
Fisher, B. H., A 144; S 202, 221, 236, 251-2; R 522, 523, 526, 528
Fisher, Clive R., A 149; R 494, 519, 525, 541
Fisher, K., R 527
Fisher, Mrs S., A 149; L 176, 231; R 503, 504-5
Fitch, J., A 144
Fitting, F., S 373, 389, 407; R 520
FitzClarence, C., R 518
Fitzmaurice, Miss J., R 505, 507
Fitzmaurice, J. R., A 141, 242; R 514, 531, 532, 539
Flament, D., M 258, 454; C 416, 449; R 536, 548
Fleck, J., A 11, 161, 166, 167, 168
Fleming, D. M., R 527
Fleming, S., A 149; R 502
Flesch, C., L 197; R 501, 555
Flesch, S., R 553
Fletcher, G., A 136; S 444; R 137
Fletcher, P. A., A 138; R 535
Flint, Thomas Foden, A 539
Flodstrom, E 356, 370; R 513
Flood, CSMI A., A 172; E 265; R 152, 533, 536
Floquet, 311; C 296, 311
Floyer, D., A 144; E 183, 218; C 190; R 515, 516, 528
Flynn, L., A 96, 282
Fodor, A., R 538

Foerster, S Sgt B., R 530
Fonst, R., R 547, 551
Ford, Flt Off. John, A 145, 432; M *1972–8*, 436, 452–3; C 390; R 152, 495–6, 526, 533, 538
Ford, R. P., **88**; A 144; S 203; C 207; R 522, 528
Fordham, J. M., R 528
Fordham, Prof., B 25, 31
Foreman, K., A 141
Forgacs, C 344
Forrest, H. A., R 518
Forssell, C., R 551
Forsdick, Lt Cdr R. T., A 76, 78, 475
Forster-Smith, OC D., R 534
Forte, R., S 269; C 188, 204; R 523
Forward, W., A 150; E *1973–5 passim*, 406
Foss, Alexander, E 403; S 409
Foss, Hugh R., R 494
Foster, D., R 152, 154
Foster-Smith, D., R 130
Fouere, J., C 188
Foulkes, Mrs I., L 232, 319; C 254; R 504
Foulon, S 184
Fox, Sgt J., **379**; A 97, 172; E 220, 235, 265, 286, 323, 339, 355, 371; C 238, 378; R 154, 510, 512, 514, 533
Fox, S., **367**; A 11, 142, 144, 439; M *1972–8*, 438, 453; S 343, 373; C 331, 345, 346, 412, 413; R 489, 492, 495, 522, 543
Foxcroft, R., C 211, 275
Fraisse, R., R 539
Francesconi, E 202, 234; C 187; R 513
Francis, C., R 496
Franck, J., A 128, 150; M 350, 451, 453
Franke, E., R 492, 547
Franklin, J. A., R 494, 514
Fraser-Smith, A., **448**; A 130, 148; L 383, 423, 456–7; R 504, 541
Frater, R., R 509
Fray, C., L 456; R 156, 505–6
Freedman, C., A 152
Freeman, D., A 146; L 401; R 505
Freeman, Maj E. R., A 476
Freeman, Mrs Muriel, R 482, 498, 500, 549

Freeman, S., A 146; L 383
Freeston, N. P. R., R 527
Frere, Miss, R 500
Friendship, S., M 450
Friis, E 324; C 205
Frith, S., **256**; M 213, 229; E 247; S 250; C 255; R 496, 516, 523
Frohwein, C., E 386; R 540
Frolich, P., C 224
Frought, J., R 539
Fuchs, J., R 553
Fujimaki, C 435
Fuller, E. M. C., A 86, 477
Fulop, M., R 547, 556

Gabor, T., E 182; R 513, 551
Gaille, P., M 335, 349; E 405, 426, 442; C 395–6, 419, 434; R 497, 513, 552, 557
Gajadharsingh, G., M 450–1; R 496
Gal, B., R 520
Galacsy, C 189
Gallagher, S., L 366, 401, 423; R 505–6
Gallico, E., R 525
Gallico, Paul, A 107
Ganchev, Prof. G., **272**; B 56; A 83, 145, 148, 169, 170; M 242; R 170, 512, 520–1, 536–7
Ganeff, E 429, 458; C 418, 450; R 512
Ganser, L 337
Gapais, B., L 176, 197; C 189, 226, 311, 315; R 500–1, 555
Garay, J., R 553
Gardère, E., R 547
Gardiner, F., S 308
Gardner, H., L 244; R 504
Gardner, R., S 429
Gardos, C 468
Garilhe, R., R 549
Garner, C., R 130
Garrow, Mrs M., R 534
Garside, Mrs J., L 423, 455–6; R 505
Garrington, A., A 158; M 379, 451; C 411, 413, 431, 447; R 495–6
Gate, W. P., R 518
Gaudin, Lucien, A 120; C 473; R 547, 551
Gaudini, G., C 473; R 547, 553
Gault, C., A 159, 160
Gauthier, Prof. André, B 33; A 7

# Index

Gavin, R. C., R 527
Gay, Lt J., M 399; R 533
Geddes, M., R 483, 501, 502, 503
Gedge, P. M. S., R 527, 535
Gedovari, I., C 417, 433, 434; R 554, 557
Gelder, Col G., A 171
Gelder, Maj. G. W., A 171, 477; M 175; S 269; R 522, 531–3, 535
Gellert, M., R 557
Gentili, C., A 142; R 515, 525, 528
Georgiou, Peter, C 330
George, S., C 207
George, T., A 141
Gerevich, A., B 59; C 473; R 520, 553
Gerevich, G., A 147; C 187, 394; R 557
Gerevich, P., C 471; R 554
Gerresheim, T., M 229; C 190; R 493, 556
Geuter, M., E 264; R 512
Gevers, E., R 551
Gey, C 410; R 556
Ghezzi, E 235
Giaroli, V., R 496
Gibbs, D. L. A., R 514
Gibson, G. T. M., R 491
Gibson, J., R 130
Giesselman, B., R 501, 507
Giesselmann, K., L 215, 246; C 224; R 501, 506
Gifford-Gifford, M., R 528
Giger, D., E 286, 321–2, 324, 357, 370, 442, 459; C 187, 205, 418; R 513, 557
Gil, C 256
Gilbert, A., R 141
Gilbert, M., E 355, 370; R 154, 515–6
Giles, D., A 147; E 181, 198; R 515
Giles, G., R 139
Giles, W. O'H., R 514
Giliazova, N., C 417; R 549
Gille, E 307
Gillett, D., R 159
Gillon, J., A 105
Gitnikova, E., R 549
Giulai, I., R 555
Glaister, S., **413**; A 134, 136; M 334, *1974–81*; S 373, 409; C 360, 361, 376, 413, 416, 432; R 137, 492, 494, 496–7, 523, 536–7, 541
Glass, T., R 557

Glasswell, J. D., **201**; A 147, 151; E 181, 184, 198, 199, 200–2, 234, 235; R 486, 511–2, 539–40
Glen Haig, Mrs M. A., **88**, **211**, **332**; B 54, 57–8, 69, 74; A 76, 79, 85–6, 89, 93, 95–8, 104, 108, 112, 114, 119, 122, 124, 147, 150, 155, 186, 205, 239; R 483–4, 499–503, 539, 545; *see also* James, M. A.
Glover, S., R 140
Glycais, J., R 553
Gnaier, L 215; C 224
Gobey, A., A 145; L 423, 456; R 506
Gobey, C., A 145; L *1979–81*; C 468; R 504–7
Gobey, M., A 145; L 423, 455, 456; R 506, 508
Goddard, Mrs M., A 76, 474
Godel, A., C 312; R 556
Godfree, D. W., R 518
Godhelp, F., E 199, 219
Godsell, P., R 503
Golding, N., A 123, 155
Goldschmidt, C. de, R 509
Goldsmith, J., R 527
Goldstein, A., R 494
Gombos, A., R 553
Gomez, P., R 520
Gomez-Vaillard, R., R 520, 543
Gomez, R., S 329, 343, 359; R 540
Gonsior, B., E 198, 234, 248, 286, 304; C 241; R 513, 551
Goodall, Prof. A., **169**; A 146, 170
Goodall, Mrs R., L 282, 283; C 313; R 504, 541; *see also* Rae, B.
Goodall, Prof. R., **169**; A 12, 143–4, 146, 170, 300, 365, 392, 398, 412, 416, 476
Goodwin, C., M 419, 452
Goose, E 286
Goppold, V., R 553
Gordon, J., **206**; S 236; C 188
Gordon, Sir Cosmo Duff, A 474; R 481
Gordon, K., R 130, 523
Gordon, Cpl(W) L., R 534
Gore, R., E 458
Gorokhova, G., L 245, 262; C 472; R 549
Gorrie, G. J., R 514
Gos, E., C 206; R 557
Gosch, I., L 368; R 501

Gosbee, W., **468**; A 144; M *1974–81*; C 390, 410, 412, 431–2, 446, 467–8, 470; R 489–90, 492, 495–7
Gough, C., E 371
Graham, Capt A., R 532
Graham, E. R. B., A 474, 529
Graham, S., R 132
Graham, Cpl S. A., R 553
Grainger, F., R 130
Graham, E. R. B., A 529
Grainger, SCM H., R 530, 531
Grajczyk, C 344
Gral, S 203
Grammar, Mrs Y., L 319, 353, 368; R 152, 504–5
Grande, L 320
Granger-Veyron, S 409; C 417
Granieri, N., C 227, 276, 292, 311, 378; R 492, 552
Grant, E. M., R 507, 525; *see also* Peppercorn, Mrs
Grant, H., L 231
Grant, Mrs W., A 12, 143; L *1976–81*; C 448, 449; R 499, 500–3, 537; *see also* Ager, W.
Granville, 4th Earl, B 53; A 474, 542; R 522, 535; *see also* Leveson, Lord
Gravé, F., A 142
Gravelotte, E., R 547
Gray, E. L., **391**; A 12, 91, 97, 122, 124, 144, 158, 475–7; E *1966–70, 1971–7*, 406, 462; C 313, 330, 347, 392; R 159, 512, 515
Gray, Mrs M., C 346; R 546; *see also* Exelby, M.
Gray, R., A 346; C 275, 345, 347
Gray, J., E 200
Greaves, W., E 200
Grebe, W., R 553
Green, Brian, M 380, 422; R 137, 541
Green, B. J. M., R 528
Green, C. F., A 144, 305; M 214, 331; E 181, 220, 263, 304; C 189, 223; R 495, 510, 512, 515, 528
Green, D., A 139
Green, F., A 168
Green, G., R 516
Green, Mrs M., L 246; R 156
Green, S., **240**, **262**, **314**; A 134, 135; L *1965–77*; C *1966–75*, 378; R 137, 488, 499, 501–4, 506–7, 536–7, 539

Greene, B. J. L., R 529
Greenfield, R., R 140
Greenhalgh, R., A 148, 153; E 403, 425, 441, 442, 461–4; R 154, 515, 525
Greenhalgh, P. A., A 148, 475; R 494, 510
Greenwood, J. jnr, R 514
Gregory, B., R 160
Grey, C., A 160
Grey, R., R 160
Grieve, S., R 505
Griffin, K., A 451
Griffin, R., E 181; R 130
Griffiths, H., L 366, 383; R 505, 525
Griffiths, J. Eaton, A 474
Grigorian, C 205, 468
Grimmett, G., **367 393**; A 138, 150; M *1967–78*; C *1968–72*, 334, 361, 376, 394; R 491–4, 496, 528, 536, 540.
Grimmett, J. B., A 150, 477; M 279, 298, 335, 336; C 313; R 495, 542
Grindley, P., L 423, 456; R 537
Groc, M 420
Grose-Hodge, C. D., A 418; R 494, 511, 515, 525, 527
Grose-Hodge, N., R 512, 515
Grosser, S 289, 308
Grove-Crofts, Guinevere, B 29; *see also* de Beaumont, Mrs G.
Gryf-Lowczowski, J., **332**; A 150; S 289, 290, 325, 327, 329, 342, 359, 389, 408, 466, 522; R 152
Grzegorek, K., R 520
Grzesik, C., **332**; S 308, 329, 341; C 331; R 523
Guaragna, G., R 547
Gubbins, B., R 160
Gubbins, L., R 160
Guenigault, G., A 451; M 365, 380, 451; R 495
Guenigault, M., M 451
Guercia, L 320
Guinness, Mrs H., A 501
Guinness, Judy, B 36; R 482, 483, 499, 500, 501, 502, 503, 534, 549
Guittet, J., R 513, 551
Guittet, L., E 407
Gulacsi, F., L 557
Gulacsi, M., C 312, 330
Gundle, A., **233**; A 139; R 140

# Index

Gunn, H. J., A 163; R 534
Guthauser, G., R 497
Guyonneau, L., R 500
Gyuricza, J., R 492, 547, 556

Haase, J., R 525
Haekart, R., R 551
Haerter, K., M 297, 350; C 416; R 493
Hage, C 254
Hagen, E 441, 463–4; R 512
Haig, Cecil H., R 481
Haig, Brig-Gen Roland, R 491
Haigh, P., A 132
Haile, J., 233; E 232
Hair, D., S 464
Hall, C., 345; A 132, 135; L *1968–71*, 336–8, 352–3; C 312, 330, 344; R 501, 504–7
Hall, D., 447, 448; L 366, 368, 383, 423, 440, 456; C 447, 469; R 140, 504–6, 508
Hall, I., A 137
Hall, Mrs Janet, L 401, 440; R 152, 505
Hall, J. R., A 96, 119, 475; M 258, 334, 350; E 247, 263, 304, 321, 322, 323, 354–6, 357, 386, 387, 404, 426; R 152, 154, 496, 512, 515–6, 512
Hall, M., 448; A 138, 144, 498; S *1975–81*; C 410, 432, 446, 465; R 139, 522–3
Hall, Millicent, R 481, 498, 500; *see also* Mrs Spong
Hallam, B., A 135, 137; M 298; R 137
Hallett, C., E 285, 304; R 515
Hallifax, J., R 497
Halpin, J. P., R 527
Halsted, Mrs C., 369; A 11, 105; L *1972–7*; C 333, *1974–6*; R 489, 499, 501, 503; *see also* Henley, C.
Halsted, N., 240, 367, 393; A 11, 12, 112, 122, 148, 150, 336, 381, 392, 400, 439, 475, 477; M *1964–71*, *1974–8*; E *1964–73*, 406; C 189, 191–3, *1966–9*, 295, 296; R 477–8, 491–4, 510–4, 526
Hamilton, Mrs C., A 141
Hamilton, W., C 414–5; R 160
Hamm, E., A 134

Hamm, S 267, 310, 343, 407; R 520
Hammang, C 394
Hamments, J., A 94, 110; M 214, 299, 316, 335, 350, 399; R 152, 495
Hamments, Mrs L., A 99, 110, 112, 152, 477; L 232, 368; R 504–5
Hammersley, C. R., R 491, 494
Hammond, H., A 124, 477
Hammond, W., A 138; R 518
Hanbury, R 534
Hancock, Sgt W. R., R 531, 532
Hanisch, C., L 337, 402, 417; C 433, 448, 470; R 501, 550
Hankinson, Maj. C., R 522, 531
Hannah, S., R 130
Hanselman, G., M 175; R 538
Harden, P., 213
Harding, A. G. M., R 503, 507, 545
Harding, LCpl E., R 534
Harding, Mrs G., 188; A 137; L 178, 197, 217, 232, 246, 284; C 204, 222, 223, 238, 253, 254, 270, 294; R 138, 504–5, 536–9, 542
Hardwick, F., R 133
Harmenberg, E 405, 427; C 397, 418, 450; R 552
Harmer, R. J. A., R 529
Harmer-Brown, Prof. W., 143; A 81, 83, 148, 151, 170, 175, 180, 194, 195, 197, 203, 230, 243, 284, 335
Harper, P., 367, 413; A 146, 150; M *1974–81*; C *1976–81*; R 489–90, 492–7, 536–7, 542, 546
Harris, B., R 502
Harris, D., M 334; R 495
Harris, Mrs J., R 140
Harris, J. W. F., 206; R 528, 535
Harris, M., M 379; R 141
Harris, S., L 337, 352, 366; R 504, 537; *see also* Uff, Mrs S.
Harrison, J., R 156
Harrison, R. A., R 486, 514–5, 532
Harrison, T., E 323, 338; C 331; R 154, 532–3, 542
Harry, Maj. G. L. G., A 114; R 518–9, 521
Hart, E., R 140
Hart, M., R 502
Hartigan, J., E 426
Hartshorn, P. F., R 528, 532
Harvey, G. B., R 503

Harwood, B. A., R 514
Hass, H., R 549
Hatael, L 440
Hatfield, Maj A., R 531
Hauk, R., E 264, 285; R 512
Haukler, C 241
Hawdon, Mrs M., L 178; C 222, 255; R 504, 538, 541
Hawkins, D., R 527
Hawkins, K., A 151; R 130
Hawksworth, Prof. G., **272**; A 136, 137, 170; C 271, 272, 289; R 536
Hawksworth, Mrs M., **233**; A 11, 136, 137; R 137, 504–5, 538
Hawcroft, J., L 383
Hay, Col R. A., **165**; B 53; A 11, 93, 97, 163, 476, 477, 526; E 237; R 482, 535
Haynes, S., S 464
Hazel, A., R 132
Heads, N., **82**; R 154
Hearne, R. D., R 527
Heaton, Wren A., R 532
Heckscher, B., R 549
Heder, B., R 159
Hehn, J., E 307, 340, 357, 358, 386; C 294, 378; R 552
Heide, R., R 551
Heidenryk, B., R 557
Heidenrijk, I., R 555
Hein, H., M 212, 229, 242, 351; C 394; R 493, 548, 556–7
Helbling, F., L 369, 424; R 501, 507
Hellsten, N., R 551
Henderson, M., C 209
Henderson, G., **411**; E 385, 404, 426, 441; C 411, 414, 415, 447
Henley, C., **314**; A 151; L *1965–8*, *1969–72*; C *1965–8*, *1969–72*; R 488, 499, 501–4, 506, 525; *see also* Halsted, Mrs
Henniker-Heaton, E., R 156
Henniker-Heaton, J., E 232, 247; R 515
Henshall, B., A 138; E 371, 404, 425–6; R 139
Henshall, S., A 138; E 425, 441, 461; C 446; R 515–6
Henry, R., B 29; A 12
Henry, Mrs R., A 12; *see also* Chanchet, R.

Herbert, A., A 144; L *1966–8, 1969–72, 1974–6*; C 294; R 504–6
Herbster, C., L 217; C 270; R 501, 555
Herriot, J., **206**; A 162; L 196–7, 216–7; C 223; R 499, 501, 504–5, 541; *see also* Bain, Mrs
Herron, B., R 160
Hertrampf, L 402; C 448
Hett, G. V., R 491, 494
Hewitt, B., A 134, 135; L *1973–80*; C 361, 376; R 499, 504–7
Hewitt, M., M 213; R 156
Heydennyk, B., R 539
Heys-Hallett, C., R 521
Hiam, D., A 148, 150; M 451; R 495
Hickenbusch, L 320
Higginbotham, I., R 525
Higgins, J., M 316; E 324, 338; R 495, 515
Higginson, S., **201**; A 98, 128, 148, 151, 334, 347, 475; E *1964–78*; C 209, 276, 277, 347, 431; R 139, 486–8, 494, 510–12, 514, 528
Hilbert, H., R 513
Hill, A., L 197, 215, 216, 232; C 238; R 506–7
Hill, B. D., **323, 388**; A 12, 148, 476; E *1967–73, 1974–8*; C 313, 331; R 511, 515–6
Hill, D., R 156, 497
Hill, I. A., R 497
Hill, Prof. L., **113, 272**; A 81, 83, 102, 104, 136, 137, 170, 334; C 271–2; R 137
Hill, R., A 128, 150; M 363, 421, 436, 451–3; R 497, 528, 542
Hillier, Mrs B., A 123, 155, 156, 477
Hillier, C., **233**; A 123, 155, 156, 477; R 156, 522
Hillier, Mrs M., L 383, 402; R 504
Hindle, F., **233**; A 136–7; M 317, 336, 364; C 254; R 137, 495
Hirst, Col Sgt T. St L., R 531
Hitler, A., B 41
Hjerpe, E 442, 459
Hoad, S., A 144; L 383, 384, *1977–81*, 439–40, 455–7; C 412, 431; R 500, 502, 504, 542
Hoare, C., R 507
Hobbins, Lt T. P., R 490, 518, 530

# Index

Hobby, R., C 209
Hobson, P. J., **314, 332**; A 77, 84–5, 93–5, 98, 101–4, 115, 150, 289, 325, 475, 477; S 290; C 312–3; R 494, 520
Hobson, Dr Peter (Aberdeen), A 162, 163, 167
Hodson, P., A 156; R 156
Hoffbauer, I., R 507
Hogg, R. S., R 536
Hogstrom, C 378, 395
Hohler, C. G., R 483, 518, 519
Hohne, S 309
Holdsworth, Paula, **68**; B 52; *see also* de Beaumont, Mrs
Hodges, I., M 335, 350; R 142, 152, 494–6
Holland, C., A 434; L 320, 353; R 504
Holland, R. A. W., R 527
Holman, S., L 368; R 156, 505
Holmes, M., **188**; A 135, 153; L 176, 197, 215–8, 230, 231, 261, 281; C 187, 205, 222, 224, 226, 238; R 137, 499, 501, 503, 505–7, 525, 534
Holmes, Mrs, C 186
Holt, M. D. V., R 481–2, 509
Holt, D., **233**; A 86, 154, 156, 477
Hoos, H., R 507
Hope, A. H. C., **32**; A 164; R 535
Hope, F. H., R 495
Hope, J. L. (Tommy), **86**; A 161, 163–4, 168, 477; R 535
Hope, M., **158**
Hope, Sir W., A 161
Hopkin, D. A., A 121; R 494
Hopkin, E. B., A 121
Hopner, J., R 545
Hoppé, F. S., R 494, 514, 527
Hopson, J., R 142
Horley, Flt-Lt J., R 515
Horne, A., R 160
Horne, A. G., R 529
Horne, Mrs G., R 534
Horton, A., A 153
Horseman, Wren C., R 533
Horvath, Z., R 554, 557
Hoskins, G. R. d'A., R 527
Hoskyns, H. W. F., **61, 201, 211, 233, 240, 314, 339, 393**; B 60; A 63, 80, 84, 110, 155–6, 395, 456, 469, 477; M *1964–9*, 335, 451; E *1964–81*; S *1964–9*, 377; C *1964–78*; R 156–7, 484–9, 491–4, 510–5, 519–22, 531–3, 536–7, 539–40, 542, 545–6, 551
Hoskyns, K., L 456
Hossack, W., A 166
Houkes, A., A 156
Houkes, Mrs T., A 155
House, C 471
Howard, Mrs E., A 130
Howard, Maj. M. J. P., A 171; E 180–2, 200; S 186, 269; R 485–6, 510–11, 514–5, 521, 531–3, 539, 545
Howard, R., A 130; R 130
Howe, J., C 446; R 556
Howe, M., A 172; E 235, 247
Howell, A., R 496
Howell, D., A 85, 224
Howes, B. W., A 150, 475; R 494, 514, 515, 519, 520, 522, 525, 528
Howgego, C. J., S 341; R 523
Howkins, K., R 505
Howson, Lt Cdr D. D., A 476
Hoyau, M., L 281; R 501, 507
Hudson, A. C. W., R 538
Hudson, C., A 132
Hudson, E., **233, 314**; A 148, 151, 155; E *1967–75*; C *1969–73*; R 156, 157, 510, 512, 515, 537, 540
Hudson, J., E 464; R 529
Hudson, T., R 515
Hudson, W., M 419; R 495
Huggins, Mrs J., L 456
Huggins, P., A 456; E 324; R 152
Hughes, Alan, **233**; C 204, 223, 253, 294; R 137
Hughes, Alyth, A 144
Hughes, D., **256**; S 250, 267, 289; C 255; R 522–3
Hulin, M 336
Hulke, Lt W. B., R 530
Humphrey, WOII M., R 532
Humphreys, J., C 210
Humphries, R., M 195; R 495
Hunt, Mrs A., A 156; L 178; R 156
Hunt, D., **233**; A 156; S 203, 252; C 207, 312, 331, 391; R 522
Hunt, J., E 458
Hunt, M. J., **449**; S *1976–81*; C 391, 412; R 157, 520–3, 528

Hunt, M., **449**; S *1976–81*; C 391, 412; R 157
Hunt, P., L 455; R 505
Hunter, D., E 183, 263; C 223
Hunter, S. Sgt D., R 530
Hunter, D. C., R 535
Hunter, E. W., A 474
Hunter, Ian, E 263; C 275; R 541
Huntington, Capt. H. F. S., R 509, 518
Hurat, R 556
Hurford, Mrs K., **107**; A 116, 121, 477; R 499; *see also* Storry, K.
Hurst, J., L 300; R 505, 507
Hurst, J. (younger), R 508
Hurter, S., R 500
Hutt, D., A 148; S 308, 310, 327, 359, 373–4, 389–90, 407–10, 429, 445–6; R 519–20, 522–3
Hutton, Capt. A., A 474
Hyndman, C., **391**; A 157; C 313, 346; R 159

Iencic, E., R 549, 555
Igoe, SACW F., R 533
Imregi, Prof. B., **323**; B 56; A 81, 139, 146–8, 150, 174, 180, 198, 230, 263, 267, 298, 319, 343, 360, 389, 416, 429–30
Ince, G., C 431
Ingleson, L., A 145; M 363
Ioffe, B., C 271, 557
Ip, D., R 142
Irimiciuc, D., R 557
Isherwood, Mrs S., A 132; R 132, 505
Isiakov, M 351; C 361
Ismailov, C 391; R 557
Istrate, C 315
Ivanoff, W., E 263, 407

Jablonowski, S 446
Jablkowski, C 410; R 557
Jackett, I., A 156
Jacks, Brian, A 119
Jackson, L. R., R 514
Jackson, R., C 211, 272–3
Jacobs, G. L., R 490
Jacobs, P., **211**, **240**, **314**; B 75; A 11, 12, 93–4, 98, 106, 128, 147, 151, 287, 296, 313, 334, 376, 448, 475, 476, 477; M 228, 229, 281, 298; E *1964–78*, 443; C *1964–8, 1969–73*, 374; R 486, 487, 510–2, 514–5, 526–7, 539–40, 545–6
Jacobson, H., E 219, 340, 356; C 187, 205, 276, 348, 378, 418, 434, 450; R 513, 552, 556
Jacobsen, N., L 401; R 152, 506
Jahna, C 333, 344
Jaine, R., S 429–30, 445–6, 465–7; C 412, 471; R 521
James, H. Evan, R 490, 514, 518, 530
James, J., A 147
James, M. A., R 503, 534; *see also* Glen Haig, Mrs
James, QMSI T., R 532
James, Capt. W. C., A 150
Jamieson, Mrs J., L 368
Jamieson, R., S 429; R 516, 535
Jana, H., E 307, 386; C 418; R 513
Jandula, R., S 389, 429; R 522
Janikowski, J., E 464; C 312, 378; R 513, 557
Janke, L 402; C 448; R 501
Jansen, C 205
Jasco, A 155
Jantsen, S 185
Jaretzky, C 255
Jaron, G., A 150; E 355, 385, 406; C 431; R 515
Jalanovich, V., R 547
Jay, A. L. N., **61**, **211**, **240**; B 58–9, 63; A 93, 96, 104, 112, 148–9, 477; M *1964–72*, 398, 438, 454; E *1964–74*, 406, 438, 442; S 327; C *1964–9*, 473; R 484–8, 491–4, 510–1, 513–5, 522, 525, 537, 539, 542–3, 545, 547, 551
Jeanne, F., E 233, 286, 324, 370; C 316; R 513
Jeanneau, M., R 514, 556
Jebb, Dom P., A 154
Jenkinson, Capt John, M 365; R 490, 518
Jerry, D., A 163
Jobling, C., S 465
Jocelyn, R., Viscount, S 236, 249
John, J., R 514
Johnson, D., E 198, 232; R 154, 515

# Index

Johnson, J., R 139
Johnson, L., A 86, 138, 477
Johnson, M., L 456
Johnson, P., A 149; L *1976–81*; C 446; R 152, 500, 503–6
Johnson, P. W., R 522
Johnson, W. R., **240, 314, 393, 398**; A 12, 109, 123, 144, 443; M 214, 229, 280; E *1964–81*; C *1965–73, 1974–9*, 470–1; R 487–90, 495–6, 510–3, 515–6, 537, 543
Johnston, Brian, B 58
Johnstone, Julia, R 481, 482, 498, 500
Johnstone, N., R 535
Johnstone, Lt P., R 533
Jolly, P., A 150; R 512
Jolyot, P., C 375–6, 390, 449, 470; R 548, 556
Jones, A. H., E 198; R 515
Jones, Mrs E., R 152
Jones, Eileen M., **88**; A 78, 149; R 505, 537
Jones, G. (N.I.), R 160, 528–9
Jones, Glenn, A 136; M 363, 399–400; E 370; R 137, 496, 516
Jones, Gregory, A 136
Jones, H., A 136; L 423, 440, 456; R 504
Jones, J., A 136; L *1971–8*; C 222, 311, 313, 376, 412; R 504–8
Jones, Leslie, **262, 293**; A 11, 12, 135, 136, 197, 282, 300, 312, 375; R 495, 536
Jones, P., A 167
Jones, Richard, C 331; R 141
Jones, Mrs V., R 503, 504–5
Jones, Mrs W., A 135
Jonsson, C 239
Joos, M 420, 454
Jorgensen, V., R 539
Joseph, Prof. M., **169**; A 170
Josland, C., C 254, 315, 377
Jourdant, F., R 551
Joyce, D., A 97; L 216, 259, 260, 319; R 141, 156
Joyce, E., L 319; R 141, 156, 542
Joyce, M., **206**; A 98, 207, 219, 222, 302; S 268; C 223; R 533, 541
Juhasz(-Nagy), K., R 500, 549
Julian, A., **158**; L 178; C 210, 223; R 159, 504

Jung, D., E 199, 219, 264; C 294; R 512–3

Kabos, A., C 473; R 553
Kaczmarek, J., R 556
Kaczor, PO Wren E., R 534
Kalinski, A., R 556
Kallipetis, M., A 92, 228, 260, 300, 381, 477; R 536, 537
Kalmar, J., S 251, 310; C 311; R 520, 554, 557
Kamuti, J., C 189, 225, 256, 473; R 492, 547–8, 556
Kamuti, L., R 492
Kanitz, E., R 520
Kanurkina, T., R 555
Karagian, A., C 293, 449, 470; R 557
Karakalos, T., R 553
Kardolus, K., R 521
Karlin, D., E 370; R 516
Karpati, R., C 473; R 520, 553–4
Katychev, C 411
Kaub, S 204
Kaufman, S 360
Kausy, I., R 551
Kausz, E 182
Kauter, B., C 227–8
Kauter, C., E 355, 386, 406, 427, 442; R 513, 556
Kawecki, Z., S 251; R 520
Kay, Graham, **413, 448**; A 136; M 363, 364, 398–400, 421, 451–2; S 409, 444, 465; C 376, 412–3; R 137, 492, 496, 523, 537
Kay, Gregory, A 132; S 465
Kay, P., M 132, 450; R 497
Kay, Wren S., R 534
Kaye, A. A., A 86, 93, 477
Keal, D., S 289; C 312; R 523
Keddie, I., R 141
Keeling, E. J., R 535
Keene, A. V., R 518
Keers, R., E 441
Kelemen, V., R 555
Keller, T., M 451; R 497
Kellett, S., L 423, 439, 440, 454–5, 457; R 505–6, 508
Kelly, J. F., A 151; R 515, 521–2, 525
Kelman, Eric, C 392
Kemnitz, E 330

Kendrick, C., L 232
Kenealy, Sub. Lt T., A 171; R 533
Kenealy, Mrs S., A 107, 469, 477; L 401; see also Littlejohns, S.
Kennedy, M., A 244
Kenney, J., R 516
Kent, F., A 147; R 514
Kenyon, B., A 159
Keresu, E 234
Kerkhoff, M 451
Kerlin, G., R 525
Kernohan, H., A 11, 166, 167; E 355, *1976–81*; S 465; C 447, 469, 515–6; R 537
Kernohan, Mrs K., A 167
Kershaw, Lt C. A., R 482, 518, 531
Kerr, D., A 130
Kershaw, Capt. Cecil, A 87
Kestler, J., M 214; C 222–3; R 543
Keuls, K., L 354; R 505–6
Keuls, P., E 285, 305; R 516
Keydel, I., R 500, 549
Khabarov, E 179; C 191; R 551, 556
Khiazeva, C 392
Khint, R 557
Khondogo, C 435
Kibbly, M., A 137
Kiermasz, S 409
Kiknadze, A., R 557
Kilbert, H., E 199, 264; R 512
Kilvert, Bob, C 223, 255, 270
Kim, C 227
King, A. H., R 527
King, C., L 336
King, G., A 77
King, J. A., **165**; A 162; E 183; R 515, 535–6
King, Jenny, A 157; L 506
King, Lt R. A., R 532
King-Hamilton, M. A. B., R 494
Kirby, P., **188, 213**; A 89, 92, 93, 102, 149, 477; M 174, 175, 194–6, 228; C 187; R 491–2, 520, 539
Kirby, R., R 130
Kircheis, U., L 300, 320; R 507
Kirchoffer, Prof. G., A 87
Kirk, Flt Lt, J., R 534
Kirkpatrick, L., C 414
Kirwan-Taylor, H. T., R 529
Kisseleva, V., R 549

Klein, M., B 18; *see also* de Beaumont, Marguerite
Klein, Elizabeth, B 18; *see also* de Beaumont, Elizabeth
Klein, L. M., B 15
Klein, Mme, M.-A., B 15
Klenerman, P., A 145; S 409, 430, 444, 464, 466–7; C 446, 468; R 522–3, 528–9
Klette, M 214
Kleyweg, N. R 500, 555
Kliuchin, C 467
Knapp, J., R 506
Knell, M., **280**; A 145; M 258, 280, 292, 299, 316–8; R 496
Kniazeva, O., R 550, 555
Knockaert, A., R 536
Knott, Dr E. B., B 59; A 114, 115, 147, 150, 476; E 200; R 485, 511, 514–5, 543
Knowles, Dr D., **133**; A 131, 134, 147, 401; L 232; C 204; R 504, 539
Koch, M 214, 454
Kocsis, I., R 557
Kokkes, Mrs, R 500
Kosenko, S., R 556
Kohler, S 325
Kojder, J., R 496
Kolczonay, E 458; C 418, 435, 450; R 552
Kommissarov, S., R 557
Komnar, A., C 294, 312; R 557
Kondratjeva, N., R 555
Koppang, N., E 357, 370, 371, 372, 443, 459, 464; C 378, 391, 406, 410, 418; R 512–3, 557
Korfanty, S 409; C 417
Koretsky, C 467
Koriagkin, R 557
Koscielniakowski, S 268
Kostarzewa, R 557
Kostava, C 191–3; R 551
Kostrakova, C 292
Kotzmann, C 449, 470
Koukal, C 416, 449
Koutcher, C 330
Kovacs, M 351
Kovacs, A., S 251, 290, 445
Kovacs(-Nyari), M., R 501
Kovacs, P., B 59; R 520, 553
Kovacs, T., S 342, 394

# Index

Kovanda, C., **309**; A 138; S 236, 250, 266, 289, 290, 308, 327, 342, 408, 429, 465; C 312, 313, 522, 537–8; R 139
Koziejowski, L., C 224, 351, 395; R 556
Kozlenko, C 238; R 555
Krebs, J.-C., E 371; C 344; R 557
Krimke, Mrs Anne-Marie, L 312
Krimke, B. W., R 495
Kriss, G., E 266; C 191, 276, 296; R 552
Krogh, E 306, 443; R 512
Krovopuskov, C 417, 433, 449, 473; R 554, 557
Krzykalska, Mrs, R 501
Kubiena, K., A 150; S 388–9; R 523
Kubbeler, S 221
Kubista, R 557
Kucheriani, R 557
Kucziewicz, S 290
Kuki, P., M 439; C 344, 360, 432, 449; R 548, 556
Kulinenko, E., R 555
Kulcsar, G., E 182, 200, 218–9, 355, 386; C 192, 241, 296, 378; R 513, 551–2
Kuperus, E 404
Kurczab, E 182
Kuzma, **375**; C 375–6
Kuznetsov, L., R 553

Lachmann, K., C 472; R 500, 549
Ladegaillerie, J., E 233, 263, 286, 307, 339, 358, 370; C 227; R 552
Lagerwall, H., E 180, 182, 199; R 511, 513, 551, 556
Lagnado, Prof. V., **213**, **302**; A 11, 83, 149, 150, 173, 195, 214, 218, 259, 278, 283
Lakey, M 363
Lambert, Mrs J., L 368, 384; C 412; R 140
Lambert, Maj. L., A 476
Lambert, L., R 522, 532
Lambourn, N. W., A 144; R 528
L'Amie, N. St.-C., A 11, 161, 163, 164, 166, 167, 168
Lamon, M 349; C 344
Lamour, C 417, 449
Lamothe, D., R 142
Lange, L 455

Langeweg, A., E 219
Langley, CSM A., R 530, 531
Lankester, R., L 366
Lankshear, J., A 148; S 310, 325, 329, 331, 429; C 431; R 522–3
Lapitski, B., C 390, 449; R 556
La Ragione, P., M 195; C 256; R 557
Larkham, WOII J., A 171; R 553
Larner, J., A 141
Larsson, L.-E., E 182, 263–4; R 556
Lataste, J., R 547
Latrille, B., C 410; R 555
Latter, C., S 327
Latychev, C 446; R 557
Lavington, S., A 134, 148; E *1974–81*; S 389, 429; C 397, 412; R 137, 511–2, 515, 523, 526
Lavoie, M., S 389, 408, 465; C 347, 415; R 520–1, 546
Law, J., A 136; L 366, 383, 423; C 412; R 137, 504
Law, Prof. M., A 170
Lawday, J., E 183; S 236, 289, 290; C 239; R 520, 522–3
Lawrence, J., A 150; M 380, 422, 452, 453; R 494–5
Lawson, R., **391**; A 159; E 372, 386; C 376, 392, 411
Laxton, Capt. L., A 179; R 522
Layton, C. A., **188**; E 181, 183; C 188, 189; R 497, 515, 528
Lebard, R 556
le Blanc, L. M., R 501
Leblanc, M., L 455
Leckie, A., **206**, **213**, **240**; A 93, 94, 148, 149, 227, 476; M *1964–9*; E 179, 200, 324; S *1964–71*, 327, 408; C *1964–71*, 331; R 486–7, 491–3, 515, 519–22, 525–6, 540, 542–3, 545–6
Leckie, George B., R 494, 522, 528
Leckie, J., R 505
Lecomte, C., L 261, 318; R 501
Lee, E., R 496
Lee, G. T., R 527
Lee, J., R 528
Leece, A., R 130
Leenders, J., L 424, 440, 456; R 501, 507, 539
Lees, P., C 255; R 137
Leese, D. S., R 529

Lefranc, G., R 513
Lehmann, A. G., R 522, 527, 528
Leigh, M., A 130
Le Hardy de Beaulieu, R 551
Leith, L., R 518
LeKach, C 417, 471
Lemenage, M 453; C 375–6
Lemoine, R., R 547
Lenglet, O., E 427; R 513
Lengyel-Rheinfuss, V., L 176, 217; R 504–5
Lennon, QMSI P. M., A 159, 323; S 203, 221, 236, 267; C 532–3
Lennox, S., A 144; M 334; E 247, 355, C 330, 412; R 170
Leon Paul Ltd, B 53; A 80
Leopold, A., A 144; M 421; C 431
Lerdon, S., R 511
Leseur, M 365; C 311
Levasseur, E 304
Levavasseur, J., S 373; C 330; R 553
Level, A., C 189, 254
Leverhulme, Viscount, A 137
Leverson, B., R 509
Leveson-Gower, G. J., R 527
Leveson-Gower, W., R 535; *see also* Granville, Earl
Leveson, Lord, A 147; *see also* Granville, Earl
Lewis, B., **391**; A 150, 158, 446, 461; M 299; E 285, *1973–81*; S 308, 342, 374; C 270, *1973–8*, 447; R 156, 159, 515–6, 519, 522–3, 526, 528, 538
Lewis, C., A 158; L 423, 456; C 431, 447; R 159
Lewis, E., R 547
Lewis, Edward ('Kid'), B 47, 48
Lewis, J. J., A 110, 477
Lewis, Jonathan, A 144; S 308, 325, 359, 389, 408, 409; C 330, 361, 412, 431; R 522–3, 528
Lewis, P., **233**
Lewis, Pamela, C 313
Lewis, Mrs S., A 150; L 353, 354, 383, 423; R 156, 499, 504, 539; *see also* Youngs, S.
Li, Gary, A 144; S 373, 388–9, 391, 409, 428–30, 445; C 410, 432, 521–3, 526, 528, 536
Li, Kenric, A 144; S 359, 388, 391, 409, 428–9, 444; C 432; R 497, 523

Liedersdorff, A., R 492
Lightowler, F., R 132
Lillywhite, B., A 172; E 198, 233, 234; C 238; R 533
Lindner, H., E 370, 406
Lindwall, O., E 182; R 556
Linger, L., A 142
Link, J., R 556
Liottel, R., R 551
Lippmann, A., R 551
Lis, R 557
Lisewski, A., M 279; C 190, 225
Liston, G. D., **420**; E *1976–81*; C 414–5, 432, 446, 469; R 511–12, 515–6, 529, 535, 537
Little, J., **206**; A 162; L 197; C 187; R 534
Littlehales, J., A 137; E 426
Littlejohn, D., A 115, 152, 477
Littlejohns, S., **302, 314**; A 121, 148; L 230, 232, *1970–76*; C *1971–4*; R 488, 501–4, 506; *see also* Kenealy, Mrs S.
Livak, E 266
Ljungquist, B., R 551
Llewellyn, G., R 497
Llewellyn, J., **393, 460**; A 108, 145, 153; M 316; E *1973–81*; C *1973–81*; R 154, 489–90, 511–6, 537, 541
Llewellyn, Lt L. C., E 181, 183; R 532, 533
Lloyd, J. Emrys, **49, 113**; B 36–7, 39, 54, 65; A 12, 91–2, 96–7, 104, 114, 147, 159, 170, 474–5; M 365, 438; R 482–3, 491–2, 494, 527, 547
Lloyd, Mrs J. E., **113**
Lloyd, M., L 384, 401, 423, 455–7; R 504
Lock, M., R 139
Lock, R. A., R 515
Lockyer, J., L 232
Loetscher, A., **339**; E 181, 355–6; C 241; R 512
Lofficiel, B., C 293; R 557
Lomax, S., A 149
Longlet, E 427, 442
Lonzi, A. R., R 549
Lord, F., **233**; A 135
Lorenzoni, L 196, 197, 246; C 226
Lordkipanidze, G., R 557
Los, J., R 570
Losert, I., L 366; C 433, 448; R 507, 555
Losert, R., E 219, 287; C 187, 228; R 551, 556

# Index

Losey, R 540
Losonczy, C 331
Lossius, M 350, 364; C 374, 390; R 493
Lotter, G., L 320; R 501
Lovejoy, K., A 145; E 323, 338; R 516, 536
Loveland, A., 233, 332; A 144, 410; M 228, 243, 280, 298, 317, 336, 350, 365, 380, 399; C 270, 331, 376; R 154, 492–3, 495–6, 536, 542
Lowen, P., R 496
Loyd, J., 82
Luan, Jujïe, C 410, 417, 470; R 550, 555
Lucas, C., R 506
Lucas, D., A 157; C 275, 313; R 159
Lucas, E., A 157
Luchow, M., R 551
Luckman, F., A 131
Lukomsky, B., E 321–2, 407; C 349, 362, 378, 418, 434; R 513, 552, 557
Lukovitch, A 118, 169
Lund, I., 165; B 56; R 545
Lunt, J., A 137
Luxardo, F., S 203; R 520
Lynn, R., C 204; R 515, 528, 532

Mabey, D., A 153; R 152, 154, 170
McAslan, S., 420; R 516
McCarthy, B. S., R 519, 521, 522, 525
McClintock, N., R 525
McCollum, K., M 213
McCombe, J., A 157
McCombe, Y., C 313
McCombie, Mrs J., A 149
McConaghy, I., A 160; S 409; C 412, 415–6; R 160
McClure, E. R., R 518
McCowage, B., C 209
McCready, Dr M. D., R 511, 514, 525
McCreery, M., R 527
McCreath, B., R 504, 506, 545
McDermitt, G., L 281–2; C 210, 273; R 501
McDonald, M., A 326
McDougall, C., C 346
McDougall, S., A 164
MacEwan, A. M., R 529
McGechan, Mrs G., L 282; C 346; R 541
MacGibbon, J. A. G., R 494
MacGlochlan, G., A 153
MacGowan, J., A 141; R 141

McGrath, Lt Cdr J. H., 158; A 157; R 159, 532, 533
McGregor, J. A., R 528
McHugh, PO Wren R., R 534
McIntosh, F., 411, 420; A 168; L 1975–81; C 1977–81; R 490, 502, 504–8, 525, 534, 537
Mack, R., M 450; S 444
Mackay, B., R 160
Mackay, G., 411; A 12, 166, 456; M 451; E 371, 441–2, 447, 462; C 411, 414, 415, 469, 535–6, 541
Mackay, Mrs L., L 456
McKechnie, Mrs A., R 141
MacKenna, E., L 218
McKenzie, Col Sgt D., R 531
McKenzie, D., 420; A 168; M 364, 380, 399, 419, 420, 436, 438, 451–4; S 444, 464; C 432, 446, 469–70; R 490, 494, 496–7, 526, 535, 541
McKenzie, J., C 347; R 535
McKenzie, J. M., R 515
McKenzie, R. Angus, A 142; R 491, 492, 494, 515, 528–9
Mackeown, A. G., R 522
McEwan, M., M 419
MacKinnon, A., A 161, 165
Mackintosh, M. H., R 527
Maclachlan, W. P. G., R 535
Maclagan, M., A 163
McLaren, D. J., R 525
McLaren, L., C 346
MacLaughlin Smith, H., R 522, 538
McLennan, L., R 514
MacLeod, J., A 142
McLoughlin, D., R 522
MacMichael, M., R 527
McMiken, B., E 263, 404
McMullen, G., E 441; R 516
Macnair, Mrs J., A 162
Macnair, J. I., A 162
McNeil, R., C 254; R 494, 522
McPherson, Prof. F. G., A 108, 146
Macrae, D., A 148
McTurk, S., R 505
Madeley, Mrs J., L 319; R 152
Madsen, see Max-Madsen
Maenich, R., R 539
Maestri, C 272
Maffei, M., S 237, 309; C 292, 296, 417, 433; R 554

Maggs, S., A 148; L 215, 456
Magill, W. J., A 11, 110, 144; S 325, 327, 389, 408, 409, 429, 444, 465–7; C 275, 313, 345, 347, 391, 397, 412, 431, 471; R 141, 160, 520, 522, 526, 538, 540–1, 543
Magnan, J.-C., M 184, 196, 229, 248, 279; C 314; R 547, 556
Magne, M 438
Magrini, Prof., A 524
Maguire, A., **82**; C 222; R 130
Mahony, D., E 461; R 516
Maier, E 307
Majendie, J., R 476; R 483, 502, 503, 507
Majewski, J., S 237; R 520
Makler, C 377
Makowski, C 312; R 555
Malanotte, C 468
Malherbaud, I., R 549
Malim, P. W., R 526
Malkar, E 458
Mallard, Prof. A., **272**; A 152, 170, 258, 308, 313, 329
Mallard, G., **188**; A 152; L 178; R 152, 505–7
Mallard, Mrs I., A 152
Mallett, N., A 152; M 335, 350, 601; E *1973–81*; C 329–30, 361, 391, 431, 434–5, 449–50; R 490, 511–2, 514–6, 522, 526, 529
Mallett, N. J., R 515
Malmurowicz, S 309
Manders, J., R 505
Mangiarotti, D., R 551
Mangiarotti, E., A 245; C 349, 473; R 543, 551
Mangiarotti, Prof. Giuseppe, B 26
Manley, I., E 403
Mann, K. S., A 150
Mann, S., R 160
Mann, W. M., A 140, 477
Manners, W., R 140
Manning, Ft Lt W., A 476
Mansfield, T. E., R 528
Mardzoko, S 268
Marchand, E 304; C 316
Margan, I., E 461
Marik, S 373; R 520
Marin, C 417
Marini, F., R 551
Marley, M., R 539

Marmont, WOII J., R 532
Marriott, R. F. S., R 494
Maros, C 448; R 550
Marosi, P., L 176; R 500
Maroth, P., C 187; R 557
Marsh, W. W., R 482, 518
Marshall, I., R 505
Martewicz, M 422; C 344
Martin, A., **345**; A 150; M 379, 399, 431; C 431; R 495–6
Martin, Lt-Col A. Ridley, A 87, 474, 521; R 481, 518
Martin, D. C., A 80, 144; S 185, 186, 203, 204, 221, 236, 250, 252, 268, 269; C 193, 194, 206, 208; R 519–20, 522, 535, 541, 543
Martin, D. S., R 514
Martin, Linda, **345**, **393**; A 109, 141, 150; L *1972–81*; C 331, *1976–81*; R 141, 489–90, 499, 500–3, 505–6, 536–9
Martin, Lionel, A 151
Martin, Lyndon, A 158; E 355, 404, 426, 428, 441; C 330, 347, 411, 414–6, 426
Martin, P., R 523
Martin, R., A 319
Martin, S., A 160
Martineau, S., R 481, 491, 509
Martonffy, A., **165**
Marzi, G., R 547
Masciotta, G., L 197, 262; C 311; R 500, 555
Masiero, M 438; C 467
Maskell, J., R 503
Maslin, H. J., **213**; A 476; R 522
Mason, Doris, B 46
Mason, Mrs J., A 115, 153, 477
Massard, A., R 551
Masson, H., R 547
Master, D., C 204
Maszlay, L., R 547
Mater, Prof. H., A 160, 163
Mather, P., **293**; A 144; S 267, 289, 290, 291, 308–10, 325, 329, 330, 343, 359; C 294, 312, 325, 327, 330–1, 332–3, 377; R 519–20, 522–3, 528
Matheson, V., **82**; A 476; L 232, 244
Matless, CSM B., A 132; E 404, 426; R 533
Matthews, C., L 232

# Index

Matthews, L., R 508
Mattocks, R., R 495
Matwiejew, Z., E 355; C 333; R 556
Maunder, Flt Off. R., A 157; R 531, 532, 533
Maurer, R., R 528
Mavlikhanov, O., C 194
Max-Madsen, M., L 352–3, 368, 402, 440, 455; C 448; R 501
Maxwell, Capt. J. McCall, R 530
Mayer, A., L 366
Maynard, D., R 497
Maynard, K. P., R 516
Mayo, M., **411**; E 358; C 345–7, 361, 380, 411, 413, 535, 541
Mazowiecki, M., S 236, 250, 251, 266; R 522–3, 543
Meade, R. S. S., R 491, 494, 521, 535
Mealing, Mrs C., A 142
Meares, J., R 141
Medhurst, M., M 451
Meeks, L., A 136; L 423; R 137
Mees, H., L 197, 231; R 500–1, 549, 555
Meister, P., R 539
Melcher, J., E 263–4; R 513
Mellor, D., A 477; L 232
Melville, J., A 148; E *1977–81*; R 512, 514–5
Melville, N., A 163, 380; S 429; R 533, 537
Melvin, Mrs N.,
Melvin, S., C 447
Melzig, C 296
Mendelenyi(-Agoston), J., R 500–1
Mendelenyi, J., L 423, 439
Mendelenyi, Prof. T., **117**; A 117, 146, 423, 430, 433, 444, 469; R 557
Mends, Dr D. R. B., A 167, 168; R 535
Menon, M 365
Menghi, C 418
Meredith, S., M 380, 452; E 441; R 516
Meresano, T., R 556
Merrill, Mrs S., R 140
Merry, SACW M., R 533
Merry, R., A 137
Meszena, S 269, 290; R 557
Meyer, A., R 501
Meyer, H., B 41; C 472; R 500, 549
Meyrick, O., L 320; C 331; *see also* Pontefract, Mrs

Michaeledes, P., M 258, 299; R 156, 496
Midler, C 225; R 547
Midling, C 205
Miesse, E 265
Mikhailov, C 377
Mildwater, N., S 465
Millar, N., A 132, 168; R 535
Miller, Dr T., A 126
Milligan, N., A 138; S *1970–79*, R 139, 522
Milligan, W. C. A., R 535
Millott, J., L 401; R 505
Mills, E., R 543
Mills, F., R 152
Milne, Lt I., R 532, 534
Milner-Barry, A., A 151; L 301, 319, 353, 354, 401; C 270; R 504
Milnes, E. B., R 527
Minnen, S 237
Minton, Mrs Gytte, A 147; R 483, 498, 499, 500, 501, 502
Mirabaud, J., A 511
Mirzoeva, C., R 555
Miszewska, Mrs., A 170, 299
Miszewski, K., R 520, 525
Mitchell, A., **206**, **411**; A 162, 164, 166; E 218; C 223, 275, 295, 313, 347, 410, 415–6, 431; R 535, 541
Mitchell, B., R 154
Mitchell, Mrs F., R 505
Mitchell, P., M 399; R 496–7
Mitton, S., L 300, 319; C 331; R 506
Mocchi, L 300; C 331, 344, 435
Mochi, G., R 557
Modzolevsky, E 321–2, 358; C 333
Modaine, L 440, 455
Moe, E 427
Mohoss, S 250
Moir, J., L 232; C 223
Mojaev, E 443, 450; C 391; R 552, 557
Moldovanyi, A., **113**, **272**; B 56; A 86, 95, 104, 145, 149–50, 169–70, 218, 235, 289, 359
Moller, A., R 505, 507, 525
Molloy, A., A 156
Moncet, M., R 514
Monkhouse, E. L., R 514
Monk, P., L 423, 440; R 154, 505
Monkhouse, E., R 525
Monro, C. C. A., R 514
Monshouwer, C 272

Montagne, M 454
Montano, A., C 332–3, 394; R 553
Montano, C., C 470; R 548
Montano, M., R 554
Montano, M. T., M 258; C 311, 348
Montano, T., C 276, 312, 315, 330; R 557
Montgomerie, R., B 36; A 87, 474; M 220, 365, 438; E 287; R 481–2, 490, 509
Montgomery, C., A 144; L 336, 354, 385, 400, 423, 439, 440, 455, 457; C 390, 412, 414; R 500, 502, 506–7
Montgomery, J., R 505
Montgomery, Mrs M., C 414; *see also* Dignan, M.
Montorsi, R 556
Moody, C 344
Mooney, F., 82
Moore, A., M 450
Moore, Maj. G., A 171; R 521–2, 531, 532, 539
Moore, Lt Col J., 88, **332**; A 171, 476; S 185, 236, 252, 269, 389; C 313; R 531, 532–3
Moore, M. L., R 501, 502
Morch, C., E 306, 340, 355, 358; R 512
Morch, O., E 306, 357, 371; R 512
More, B. J., A 148, 151, 369; M 351, 398, 421, 436; E 183, 198, 263, 264, 286, 338; C 294; R 512, 515–6
Morel, Prof. J., A 108, 146, 150
Morgan, A., A 146; C 223
Morland, J., R 528
Morris, C., S 341–2, 389, 465; R 521, 522
Morris, J., R 138
Morrish, A., R 138, 139
Morrison, Dr L. G., A 86, 161, 163–4, 168, 477; R 535, 541
Morse, D. V., R 525
Mort, D., A 159
Morten, E. J., **49**; A 7, 76, 120, 475–7
Mortimer, B. C., R 495
Mortimer, Maj. M., A 172
Mortimer, N., S 429
Moscardini, N., A 145, 148; S 444, 465; R 538
Mosley, Sir O., **49**; B 14, 46–50, 55; A 12, 138; R 527
Mottel, J., A 137

Mount Haes, Capt. E. A., A 89, 107, 108, 140, 474, 477; R 522, 531–2, 535
Mouyal, A., E 182; R 551
Mowlam, L. A., **49**; A 84, 122, 145, 475; R 494, 514
Muck, O., E 266, 305, 355, 405, 427; R 513
Muir, A., S 429; C 416
Muir, S., S 388; R 523
Muir, W. R. Gray, R 535
Muller, K., E 287–8, 357, 371; C 333; R 512
Muller, R., C 449
Mullinger, J., R 506
Mulshaw, Mrs J., R 504–5
Munster, E 330, 355–6
Munro, Gen. Sir C., B 16
Murch, M., **332**; A 149; M 214; E 220, 321, 338, 339, 341, 356; R 510, 515
Murdoch, W. G. Burn, B 31
Muresan, C 239
Murgatroyd, M., M 450
Murphy, H., C 188
Murray, A. C., R 518
Murray, J., S 291
Murray, P., M 299, 364; R 496
Muspratt, N., R 503
Mustata, C 417
Muzio, C., L 260, 281, 283; R 501, 506
Muzio, G., R 513
Myers, H. C., R 535
Myers, Mrs M., C 414, 431; R 534; *see also* Riley, M.,
Myers, P., R 133
Mylne, O. N. P., E 234; R 515

Nadi, A., R 553
Nadi, Prof. Nedo, A 120; R 547, 553
Nagy, P., E 182; C 192, 206; R 513
Nagy, Z., R 557
Nakamura, E 458
Napier, R. A., R 535
Narduzzi, L., R 557
Narduzzi, P., R 557
Nash, D., R 142
Nathanson, D., C 204
Nazlimov, V., C 225, 333, 362, 394, 435, 473; R 557
Neal, R., S 308, 359; R 522
Nebald, J., R 557

# Index

Neilson, D. W., R 518
Neligan, G., **49**; B 36–7, 67, 75; A 92; L 301; C 472; R 483, 539, 549
Nelson, C., C 313
Nelson-Griffiths, M., E 441, 462; R 516
Nemere, Z., E 182–3, 233–4; C 191–2, 226, 276; R 513, 551
Nemeth, C 224, 467
Nesbitt, B., R 130
Netburn, S., A 148, 150; E 199, 200, 219, 263–4, 340; R 511–3, 540, 543
Neter, N. E., R 494, 515, 528
Netherway, S. A., R 536; *see also* Parker, Mrs
Netherwood, G., L 197, 215, 232; R 505–6
Netter, C., R 547
Newman, J. C., R 518
Newman, Cardinal, B 18
Newton, B. C., R 527
Newton, E., R 515
Nicholls, D., A 326; R 132–3
Nicholls, E., A 118
Nicholson, P., R 156
Nickalls, C. B., R 525
Nicklen, Prof. W., A 143, 150, 176, 180, 184; R 521
Nicolet, C., L 261; R 501
Niedermuller, E 357
Nielaba, H., E 182, 234, 248, 263, 308, 324; R 513
Nightingale, D., **379**; A 172; E 441, 462; C 379; R 515
Nigon, C., R 511
Nikichin, C 417
Niklaus, C 448
Nikanchikov, A., E 265, 266; C 193, 276, 349; R 552
Nikonova, C 271; R 549, 555
Nilca, S 446; C 394, 417
Nixon, P., R 130
Noak, P. (Bill), E 462
Noel, C., M 212, 335, 336, 351, 364, 365; C 332, 348, 361; R 540, 548, 556
Noel, J., **233**, **256**; A 12, 98, 105, 128, 144, 151, 154, 392; M 229, 243, 258; E *1967–77*; C 239, 255, 271, 294, 331, 346–7, 397; R 489, 496, 510–2, 514–6, 526, 529, 540, 546
Noels, R.,
Noguchi, C 333

Nolte, S 409, 466; C 471
Nonna, J., M 298
Norbury, J. Jnr., A 474
Norcliffe, Mrs J., A 142
Norcliffe, N., A 124, 142; R 132
Norcross, Prof. T., **169**, **309**; A 80, 82, 103, 116, 138, 139, 170, 330, 385, 404, 416, 475; C 330, 347; R 522
Norden, C., **169**
Norman, W., A 172
Normann, J., E 288, 306, 321, 371–2, 378, 458, 463–4; R 512, 557
Norrie, J., C 330, 347, 361
Norrie, Mrs L., C 391, 411, 414, 431; *see also* Brown, Linda
North, P., R 536
Northam, Prof. P., A 138, 170
Nostini, G., R 547
Nostini, R., R 547
Notley, Maj. C. Barry, B 46; E 442; R 481, 494, 509, 510, 511, 514
Novikova, E., L 262; R 549
Nowara, J., C 332; R 557
Numa, C 467; R 556
Nussbaum, I., L 454–5; R 507
Nyari, M., R 549
Nyiry, E., S 221, 236, 249; R 522

Obdam, J. A., R 491, 518
O'Brien, C., C 188; R 160
Obst, C 345
O'Connell, J., R 542
O'Connell, Sheila, L 319
O'Connell, Susan, L 231, 232
Oelkers, R 549
Oertel, B., L 260, 283, 300, 320; C 292; R 501, 507
Offlager, M 317
Offredy, T. M., A 78, 142, 150; L 176, 178, 197; C 191; R 499, 501, 503, 504–5, 536, 539
Oggero, C 224
Ogilvie, C., R 527
Oldak, P. V. A., R 527
Ogley, J., A 152, E 220, 232; R 515
Ogley, R., R 495
O'Hagan, K., B 16
O'Hagan, M. C., B 16
O'Hagan, Lord, B 16, 18
O'Keefe, L., L 301; R 506
Okawa, C 208

Okazaki, T., A 493; C 452
Oldcorn, R., **211, 240, 314, 393**; A 148, 150, 344, 416, 429–30, 447, 449, 476–7; S *1964–77*, 410, 466; C *1964–8, 1969–75*, 394; R 137, 486–7, 519–21, 536–8, 540
Olexa, C 205; R 556
Olhof, K., L 176; R 501
Oliver, C., A 434; L 353, 354, 368; R 504
Olley, S., **256**; A 121, 144; L *1967–76*; C 255, 346; R 141, 499, 505–6, 539
Olsen, Mrs G., R 500
Oltner, L 455
Olympitis, E., A 152; E 233; R 496, 516
Omerborn, R 555
Omnes, M 420, 422, 438, 454; C 470
Openshaw, J., R 527
Opgenorth, G., E 263
Orban(-Szabo), O., R 540, 549, 555
Ord, C., L 337; R 504
Orde, P. J., R 525
Oreste, L 300
Orley, Z., R 557
Orosz, C 470
Ortiz, M., S 444; C 433; R 540
Ortt, B., A 149; E 263; R 515
Osbaldeston, W., **233, 332**; A 144; E *1967–9, 1970–77*; C 253, 294, 312, 331, 412; R 511–2, 515, 536–8, 541
Osborne, F., E 355
Osiier, E., R 549
Ossiier, I., R 551
O'Shea, L., R 497
O'Shea, K. M., R 529
O'Shea, M., C 330
Osztrics, I., E 339, 386; C 349, 362, 378; R 552
Ott, P., C 415
Ovington, A., R 495

Padden, Mrs A., R 534
Paddle, K., A 141; R 495
Page, Mrs, R 505
Painter, Sqd. Ldr A., A 140; M 175, 243, 280, 298, 380; S 237, 253; C 223; R 532–3, 537
Palker, Mrs A., R 140
Pallet, N., R 501
Palm, K., L 246, 262, 368; C 189, 208, 311, 433; R 501, 555

Palmer, Capt. W., R 530, 531
Panella, S 251
Panizza, S., R 557
Pankhurst, S., S 308, 325; R 523
Paolucci, C 191
Papp, B., E 325; C 449; R 492
Paraiso, V., R 520
Parakhin, A., R 557
Paramanov, S., E 307, 321–2; R 513, 552
Parent, M., R 557
Paretti, I., M 299; R 528
Parfitt, Dr R., B 54; A 98, 148, 474–5; R 483, 510–11, 514, 542
Parham, Caroline, A 111
Parham, Mrs C., A 138
Parham, D., **328**; A 89, 102, 138, 475, 477; E 181, 199; S 237; R 139, 515, 522, 539
Parietti, E 442, 458; C 435
Park, W., A 154, 156
Parker, Mrs A., R 132
Parker, Adrian, **379**; A 172; C 379
Parker, Mrs Alex, L 301; C 312; R 141, 504
Parker, M. J., A 475
Parker, Sarah, A 172
Parker, N., C 188; R 160
Parker, Sarah, A 172
Parker, Mrs Shirley, **211**; A 142, 170, 243; L 196; C 191, 208, 210; R 501, 502, 503; *see also* Netherway, S.
Parkin, R., A 127
Parkins, Prof. A., A 87, 107, 122, 150, 179
Parkins, Prof. J. A., R 514
Parkinson, Flt Off. D., R 533
Parkinson, E., R 503
Parkinson, E., R 524
Parry, D., A 153
Parsons, G. H., S 221; R 523
Parsons, SMI H., R 531
Parsons, R. C., A 86, 141, 476–7
Partridge, D., **233**; A 149; E *1967–75*, 406, 443; C 312, 331, 334, 346–9; R 140, 510, 512, 526, 537, 540, 546
Parulski, R., C 239, 256; R 492, 547, 557
Pascu, A., R 549
Pass, W., A 123, 138, 477
Paterson, Dawn, R 541

# Index

Paterson, D. M., **49**; A 106; R 494, 525
Paterson, Duncan, **411**; M 363–4, 419; C 411, 413; R 496, 535, 541
Patient, P., **233**; A 152; L 178, 197, 216, 231, 253, 301; C 207, 222, 254, 294; R 154, 502, 504–5, 536–7, 539, 542
Patman, B., A 153; E 233, 234, 338; C 222; R 154
Paton, Mrs E., R 534
Patterson, J., E 247
Patterson, M., S 464
Paul B., **190, 213, 314, 323, 393**; A 149, 150, 476; M *1964–81*; E *1966–68, 1970–73*, 406, 443; C *1966–77*; R 488–9, 491–7, 515–6, 526, 536–7, 542–3, 546
Paul, G., **188, 211, 213, 240, 314, 381, 393**; A 11, 149, 150, 420; M *1964–81*; E *1964–81*; C *1965–81*; R 487–9, 491–4, 496, 510–12, 514, 515, 526, 536–7, 540, 543, 545–6
Paul, Prof. L., A 8, 78, 122, 173, 214, 148, 149, 173, 184, 214
Paul, Margaret, **88**; L 176, 217; R 154, 499, 504–5; *see also* Fentum, Mrs
Paul, René, **88, 213, 302, 314**; A 97, 98, 148, 149, 313; M *1964–9*; 298, 436, 438, 451; E 200; C 208, 254; R 484, 491–4, 511, 514, 537, 539, 542, 545
Paul, Raymond, B 57; A 79, 93, 94, 105, 460; M 148, 172, 195, 214, 228, 438; C 294; R 483–5, 491–4, 515, 539, 542, 545
Paul, S., **393, 460**; A 128; M 436; E *1976–81*; C *1976–81*; R 489–90, 511–5, 537, 540, 546
Pavese, G., R 556
Pavesi, C., R 551
Pavlenko, O., C 312; R 555, 557
Pawlowski, J., A 326; S 237, 251, 269, 290, 326; C 194, 209, 241, 333, 473; R 520–1, 553–4
Pawson, J., R 528
Payer, C., C 414; R 546
Payne, A., A 150
Payne, John, A 144, 153; E 181, 183, 234, 247, 263, 403; C 222; R 152, 154, 495, 512, 515, 536, 541
Payne, Mrs K., **293, 302**; A 107, 292, 312, 467, 475; L 246
Payne, W. (Bill), E 426; R 132

Pearce, A., **391**; A 446–7
Pearce, Maj. A. D., **49**; A 138; R 491, 494, 539
Pearce, J. L. M., **211**; A 11, 78–9, 88, 93, 96–7, 100, 107, 109, 112, 123, 147, 152, 155–6, 239, 474–5, 477; L 176, 178, 196, 216–7, 231; C 208, 210; R 499, 502, 503
Pearce, M., A 326; S 327; R 132
Pearce, O. B., R 498, 500
Pearce, S., R 497
Pearman, K., **356**; A 149; E 183, *1965–74*, 387, 405; C 223, 224, 312; R 130, 487, 512–3, 515–6
Pears, M. A., R 528
Pearton, B., R 130
Pearson, E., L 456
Pearson, Edwin, M 419
Pearson, Prof. E. B., A 476; R 525
Pearson, J., A 160
Pearson, Prof. K., **256, 272**; A 83, 103, 112, 124, 129, 137, 150, 153, 170, 255, 271; C 271, 272; R 154, 494, 531, 533, 542
Pearson, Prof. P., **82, 169, 272**; A 81, 103, 129, 132, 143, 146, 150, 181, 205, 221, 444; C 271–2
Pearson, R., M 438, 451, 453; C 413; R 160, 495, 526
Peat, M., **411**; M 364, 379; E 371, 387, 404, 406, 426; C 411, 414, 415; R 496, 535
Pécheux, M., R 551
Pedder, D., A 156
Pederson, R. D., R 495
Peeters, S 373
Peck, J. W. A., R 535
Peck, S. C., R 529
Pellegrino, E 202
Pelling, A. E., **49**; B 68; A 97, 122, 146, 147, 150, 168, 477; L 180, 442; R 509, 510–1, 539
Pelling, J. A., **188, 201, 211**; B 59, 68; A 147, 476; E 180–4, 199–202, 219–20, 234–5, 249, 442; C 191–2, 208–9, 210, 226
Pengelly, Mrs J., R 503
Penn-Hughes, Mrs C., R 483, 499
Peppercorn, C., L 440; R 505
Peppercorn, E., A 440; L 232
Periera, C., R 152

Perigal, Mme, A 142, 176, 299
Perone, Maestro A., **169**; A 118, 170, 196
Perrée, L., R 551
Perowne, J. T. W., R 494
Perry, Mrs L., A 159
Pesthy, E 264, 286, 428; R 512
Peszthy, C 418
Peter, E 307
Peters, Sq Ldr R., M 175, 195, 241, 242; E 220, 247; C 223; R 491, 493, 495, 515, 529, 532–3
Petho, E 442, 460; R 513
Petit, S 466
Petrenko, T., R 549
Petrie, P., R 528–9
Petrus, L 318
Petschauer, A., C 473
Pezsa, T., R 554
Pezza, J., M 258; C 333, 344, 435; R 552
Peyzana, A., R 551
Pezzini, M 419, 420
Pfeiffer, M 350; R 493
Phelps, Richard, A 172; E 425, 461; C 468; R 516, 538
Phelps, Robert, A 172, 461; E 339, 354, 425; R 156, 515
Philbin, J., **326**, **393**; A 123, 134, 136, 343, 447, 467, 477; M 298, 317, 421; E 425; S *1970–81*; C 311, 313, *1971–5, 1976–81*; R 137, 489, 495, 515, 519–22, 536–7, 540, 546
Phillips, P., L 232, R 132
Piasecki, E 464
Picard, S., L 259, 283; R 507, 555
Pickworth, B., C 209, 211, 273
Picot, E 442, 458; C 435, 450; R 513
Piddington, B., A 110, 151, 152, 480
Piedfer, C., R 539
Pienne, A. E., A 114, 147; R 483, 494, 510–1, 511, 522
Pienne, Mrs J., A 114, 123, 475; R 502; *see also* Shipston, J.
Pietruszka, F., M 312, 421, 454; C 330, 344, 432; R 548, 556
Pignotti, U., R 547
Pilbrow, A. G., B 33, 39, 41, 47, 57; A 474; R 483, 494, 518–21, 545
Pilbrow, P. J., A 474
Pilkington, J., A 94, 100, 154, 156

Piller, G., C 473; R 553
Pilot, S., R 505
Pinder, E 462; R 132
Pinelli, A., C 225, 227, 239
Pinto, C 361
Pirone, C 189
Pitman, Benny, **188**; L 178
Pitman, Prof. B., **113**, **169**; A 117, 151, 170, 363, 386, 441, 451
Pitman, Mrs E., L 178
Pitman, J., M 363, 399, 419, 438, 450–51; C 467; R 152, 495–7
Pitts, Dr T., A 156
Planet, M 420
Platzer, S 445
Plews, D., **165**; R 591
Plowright, J., R 505, 538
Poffet, M., E 339, 355, 427, 458; C 330, 361, 376, 391, 418; R 513, 557
Pogosov, L 557
Pollard, A., R 496
Pollock, Capt. H., R 530
Pollock, J., L 231; C 346
Pollock-Smith, M., A 105, 110, 477; R 482
Polzuber, H., E 287
Pomeroy, D., A 147; E 181
Pongratz, A., C 205, 333, 450; R 556
Pontefract, Mrs O., A 148; L 401; C 414, 431; R 504–5; *see also* Meyrick, O.
Pontefract, R. E., A 476
Poole, E., A 148; S 327; R 523
Poore, Lt R. A., R 518, 530
Poote, G., C 313
Pop, I., S 446; R 557
Popescu, C 224, 255
Popken, J., L 282–3; C 292; R 555
Popland, J., A 135; L *1971–4*, 384; R 504, 506–7
Porebski, O. B., A 121, 147; S 310; R 484, 519, 520, 521, 525, 539, 592
Porter, Prof. H., A 108, 170.
Porter, Mrs H., A 390
Porter, M., L 423, 456
Post, A., R 547, 551
Posta, A., R 553
Potten, G. R., A 476
Potter, P. A., R 536
Pouliot, G., R 545
Poutiatin, C 225, 257

# Index

Powell, Mrs D., R 141
Power, A. G., **188, 314**; A 79, 111, 476; M 174, 175, 242, 243, 259, 297, 298, 317; E 249; C 187, 188, 189–91, 222, 227, 238, 256, 257, 276, 314; R 132, 488, 492–3, 495–6, 536
Power, Prof. P., A 111, 132, 259, 319
Praed, B. C., R 490
Praem, T., R 492, 511
Prat, C 187
Pratt, S., C 346
Prause, F., C 270; R 521
Pregowski, S 250
Preiskel, A., S 203, 523
Preiss, E., C 472; R 500, 549
Prentice, J., A 160
Prescott, L. W., R 528
Preston, S., R 504, 536, 539
Prezza, E 321
Price, M. D. (the younger), **326, 332**; A 144; S 308, 325, 329, 342, 359, 360, 408; C 312, 331; R 522, 523
Price, M. J. (elder), A 144; S 251, 253, 269; R 491, 494, 521–2, 542–3
Price, S., R 497
Price-Thomas, B., C 254
Priestley, M. C., C 223; R 495
Prikhodko, C 206
Primeau, J., C 346
Pringle, A 148
Pritchard, M. A., R 499, 503, 504–5, 525; *see also* Watts-Tobin, Mrs
Prochotta, E 386
Proudfoot, H. A., **379**; A 172, 476
Prudskova, V., R 549, 555
Prys-Roberts, L., A 143, 157; L 366, 456; C 411, 447; R 159, 504
Puddefoot, B. M., A 79; R 499, 502, 503, 539
Puff, C 239
Puissesseau, J., E 181
Pulch, M., L 215, 261; C 238, 276; R 501, 506, 555
Puliti, O., R 547
Purchase, C., **88, 188, 201**; A 137, 138; E 181, 183, 199, 200–2, 219, 220, 233, 234, 235; S 237, 252, 268; C 207, 222, 238, 253; R 138–9, 510, 515, 519, 536–8
Purkiss, Dr J., A 124, 138
Pusch, A., E 355, 357, 370, 386, 458; C 344, 362, 370, 378, 395, 405, 418; R 513, 552, 557
Pusch, M., E 357
Puschel, M 299
Putiatin, V., R 547
Putz, J., A 155, 156
Pye, R., R 152
Pym, P., R 545

Queroux, R., R 513
Quincey, G., R 496
Quivrin, S 267, 308, 409; C 255, 311, 312, 417; R 536, 557

Rabe, S 203
Rachel, C 433
Raczova, C 433; R 550
Radecke, R 556
Rae, A., A 11, 161, 163, 416
Rae, B., R 541
Ragno, A., C 226; R 549, 555
Ragno, S., R 551
Ragossnig, W., R 557
Rainbow, M., **233**; R 541
Raine, J., **293**; A 130; L 260, 283; C 271, 292; R 507
Rakita, M., S 269; C 297, 315
Ramage, L., C 346; R 541
Ramsay, J., A 80, 115, 475, 477
Rance, M., M 450–1; E 426, 443, 458, 461, 463, 464; C 468; R 495–6, 515–6
Rand, R., A 141; R 141
Randle, Mrs A., R 140
Rapley, D., E 355, 403, 426
Rastvorova, V., R 549
Ratcliffe, J., R 152
Rathbone, Mrs J., A 99
Ratman, R., R 514
Rawlinson, A., R 490
Rayden, W. J., **57, 188, 211**; A 148; S 1964–72; C 193, 210, 223, 225; R 486, 519, 520–2, 537, 543
Rayner, C., R 536, 539
Rayner, R., R 499, 504–5, 538
Read, J., A 144; R 503–5
Readman, A., A 152
Reant, A., E 248; R 513
Redgrave, C., R 528
Redhead, D., A 130; C 273; R 130
Redhead, P., **233**; A 156; R 156, 494, 515

Reed, Flt Lt J., R 511, 514
Regulski, J., R 156
Reichert, M 279, 297; C 205, 394, 416, 470
Reid, SMI J. T., R 531, 532
Reid, M., C 188
Reilly, C 471
Rejto(-Ujlaky), I., L 231, 262; C 348, 362, 472; R 500–1, 549, 555
Rensink, M., R 501
Renski, P., R 557
Rentoul, C., **188**; A 77, 89; M 175, 195, 187–9, 206, 223; R 526, 543
Rentoul, F. G., A 77, 121, 147; R 494
Revenu, D., A 118, 169, 352; M 174; C 189, 191; R 547
Reynolds, A., **158**; A 157; R 159
Reynolds, E. M. R., M 349–50; C 361; R 496–7, 528
Reynolds, E. O. R., B 56; A 142; M 349, 361; C 361; R 484, 491, 494, 515, 525, 528–9
Reynolds, F., A 157; C 209, 223, 275; R 506–7
Reynolds, Prof. G., **158**; A 156, 157, 176, 209, 275
Reynolds, Mrs J., **158**; A 157, 159, 209
Reynolds, P., R 539
Reynolds, R., **158**; A 157; E 198, 199, 247; C 207, 209, 210, 255, 275; R 159, 495–6, 512, 516, 545
Rhodes, Jervis, A 146; M 363, 451; E 385, 425, 426, 462; S 389; C 469; R 516, 526
Rhodes, R., E 181, 183, 198; C 188, 189, 204, 206; R 511, 516, 526, 543
Riant, H. S., R 514
Riaz, M. A., R 493, 525
Riboud, P., E 371, 386, 427, 442; C 391, 395, 418, 434, 450; R 512–3, 552
Riccardi, F., R 551
Riccardo, L 320
Richards, C 271
Richards, E., R 539
Richardson, R., **165**, **206**; M 194; R 495, 535, 541
Richardson, W., C 347
Richter, P., R 506
Riddle, D., R 142, 152
Riddell, Dr F., **411**; A 166
Rider, G., R 495

Ridley, Prof. S., A 142, 143, 150, 170, 246, 476
Riley, M., **391**; A 157; L 353, 366; C 330, 346, 361, 391–2; R 159, 504–5, 534
Rinbem, E 464
Rippon, W., R 514
Ritchie, G., A 162; L 319; C 313; R 504, 525, 534
Rix, B., C 204
Rizzuto, P., S 236, 237, 252; R 522
Robak, M 364, 439; C 374, 470; R 497
Robert the Bruce, C 345
Roberts, A., A 150; S 373, 389, 408, 409; C 412; R 522
Roberts, J., L 440; R 137, 505
Roberts, M., E 181, 218; C 204; R 504, 515
Roberts, P., **206**; L 217; R 506
Roberts, S., C 414
Robertson, A. H., R 534
Robertson, C., **411**; L 368, 383, 423, 440, 456; C 391, 411, 414; R 504, 534, 541
Robertson, S., A 162; L 217, 301
Robinson, B., A 160; R 160
Robinson, C. Newton, R 481
Robinson, Mrs D., R 505
Robinson, E., R 525
Robinson, J., R 495
Robinson, P., **274**; L 217, 244; C 274; R 504, 534
Rochard, S., A 148; L *1972–5*, 384–5, 401; R 525
Rodionov, V., C 312; R 556
Rodocanachi, E., C 190, 227
Rodriguez, L 439; R 539
Roeder, F., A 156, 420
Roeth, S 185
Rogers, P., A 115
Rogerson, Mrs H., **82**; A 136, 423; L 216, 217, 282, 284, 301, 456; C 204, 222, 223, 238, 255; R 488, 499, 501, 504–5, 537–8
Rohlin, M 436; E 266
Roldan, P., R 549
Rollo, D., E 386; C 347, 469
Romanelli, R 557
Romang, P., A 145, 146, 409, 444, 467
Romankov, A., M 351; C 348, 394, 416, 432, 434, 449, 470, 473; R 548
Romano, M., S 308; C 331; R 557

# Index

Romanov, L., M 297; C 224–5, 256–7; R 547, 556
Romp, W., A 147; E 181, 184, 220; R 515
Romza, E 200
Ronleau, Profs Georges and Adolphus, A 120
Rooney, B., R 496
Roose, S., 388; E *1975–81*; C 331, *1977–9*, 414–6, 418–9, 431; R 511–2, 514, 515, 536–7, 546
Roose, Mrs S., C 431
Rorke, J., 206; A 162; E 183; C 207; R 535, 541
Rose, D. L., A 475
Rose, M., L 439, 456; R 506
Rosenberger, R., R 535
Rosner, E 198
Ross, A. G., A 474
Ross, Dr J. P., A 167, 168, 476
Ross, S., R 525
Ross, W., E 386
Rossar, V., R 556
Rossignol, A., R 551
Rotchell, Mrs B., A 132
Rotchell, W. E., A 132
Roulot, J., R 541
Rousselet, C., R 555
Rousset, L., R 551
Routh-Jones, S., 256; A 153; M 229, 243, 258, 421, 436, 451; C 255, 270, 447; R 154, 495–7, 542
Rouxel, N., A 144; E 263, 285, 386; C 254; R 515, 541
Rowlands, K., 82
Royall, D., C 190; R 142
Royer, M 436
Rozsavari, C 432
Rudge, G., A 140
Ruffe, L., L 232
Runciman, Viscount, A 474
Russ, A., E 386
Russell, A., 233; A 134
Russell, Hon. C., B 14
Russell, Mrs F. M., R 534
Russell, J., A 166
Russell, Prof. K., A 108, 152, 170
Russell, P. D., A 144, 164; E 129, 183, 198, 218, 247, 263, 324; M 194, 241; C *1964–70*, 313; R 495, 535, 537, 540
Rutecki, E 321
Ruziev, C 312, 469

Ryan, Flt Lt C., R 534
Ryan, Sgt(W) M., R 534
Ryden, L., C 414
Rylski, Y., R 554
Ryves, T. E., R 491, 494, 514

Sabort, C 470
Saccaro, G., E 198, 202, 219, 248, 288; C 241; R 551, 556
Saffra, M 336
Sage, R., A 136; M 451; R 137, 495
Sakovits, J., R 551
Sakovits, L., L 231; C 192, 226
Salamon, L., A 135, 136
Salle, L 439
Salmon, G., R 514
Salvadori, C., C 315; R 557
Samek, P., C 275, 347
Samochkin, I., C 239; R 556
Samussenko, T., L 245; C 191; R 549
Sanders, Prof. J., 155; A 151, 154, 156, 170, 179, 233, 236
Sanders, R., R 139
Sanderson, C., R 527
Sanderson, J., R 140
Sandor, G., 206; A 162; M 175, 241; E 183; C 187, 188, 207, 223, 270, 273, 275; R 491, 526, 535, 540–1
Sanjar, S., S 308, 429, 430; C 330
San Miguel, L 319
Sapcote, B. W., A 138; R 539
Sapcote, Mrs W. W., A 539–40
Sato, N., R 493
Saunders, E. J., R 515
Saunders, T. P., R 535
Savage, Sir George, A 517
Savill, Prof. J., A 153
Savra, A., A 151; L 197, 217, 232; C 205; R 502, 504, 506–7
Schaffner, E., L 283, 439; R 507
Scharle, E 406
Schenkel, C 467
Schjott, E 464
Schlettweiss, L 368
Schmetz, B., R 551
Schmid, H., L 231; C 189, 226; R 501, 549
Schmidt, P., E 181, 266
Schmitt, Pal, E 339; R 513
Schneider, S 466; C 471
Schools, colleges etc.
  Aberdeen Academy, A 162

Schools – *cont.*
Aberdeen Univ., A 168; L 423; E 462; S 429
Ainslie Park, M 450; L 368, 423
Alleyn's, A 149
Beaufoy, Lambeth, M 299
Beverley, M 212, 450
Birmingham Univ., E 426; S 327
Brentwood, A 144; M 363, 450, 175; E 370, 386; S 341, 389, 464; C 189, 330, 468
Bristol Grammar, S 388
Brooke House, S 289, 291, 308
Burlington Danes, M 450
Cambridge Univ., B 25, 31; A 151; M 380, 381, 399, 419, 451; L 401, 423; E 403, 426, 462; S 389; C 204, 469
Carshalton High, A 146
Cardiff Univ. Coll., E 426, 462
Catford, A 144–5; M 258, 363; E 425
Cheltenham College, M 173; C 330
Cheltenham Ladies College, L 175
Christopher Wren, A 148
City of London, A 145, 146; S 409, 444
City of London Girls', A 146
City Univ., M 380
Coopers Coburn, L 401
Crawley, M 451
Croydon High, L 197
Currie High, L 423
Denny High, M 450; S 464
Dingwall Academy, A 166, 168; E 385
Dover College, M 335; C 329–30
Dover College Junior, A 152
Downside, A 154; M 175, 450; C 330
Dulwich, A 143; E 385; C 330
Durham Univ., E 371
Edinburgh Academy, S 464
Edinburgh Univ., A 161; M 364, 419, 438; E 371, 386, 404, 426, 462; S 327; C 469
Eton, A 179; S 403; C 469
Fettes, L 399
Flixton, G. S., L 197
Forest, A 144
Glasgow H.S. for Girls, A 162, 166
Glasgow Univ., A 161; E 371
George Heriot's, E 385, 403; S 464; C 363

Godolphin and Latymer, L 354
George Watson's, E 385
Haileybury, A 145; S 464
Hereford Sch., Grimsby, M 419; S 359
Heriot-Watt Univ., M 380; E 426
Highgate, A 149
Hull Univ., S 389
Imperial College FC, A 149
James Allen's, A 146
Kent Univ., E 441; S 430
Kenwall Manor, A 145
King's, Canterbury, A 152
King's, Chester, M 335; E 385, 403; C 330
King's, Taunton, M 299
King's College School, A 145
King's College FC, A 149
Kingussie High, A 166
Lancaster Univ., M 451
Lansdowne Ho., L 366
Leeds Univ., M 438
Leicester Univ., L 440; E 462; C 469
Liverpool Poly, A 134
Liverpool Univ., A 134; M 335–6; E 370
London Univ., A 151; M 194, 419, 451; E 371, 386; S 389, 430; C 469; R 498, 517–8
Loughborough Univ., E 462; C 412
Lycée Française, A 143
Manchester G.S., L 197
Manchester Univ., A 134; M 364, 380; S 359
Maria Fidelis, L 366
Merchant Taylors', A 149; S 444; C 330, 355
Merchiston Castle, A 162, 167
Millfield, A 154, 404; L 366; E 370, 441, 461; C 375
Moray Ho. Coll., A 168
Morley College, A 146
Newcastle Poly, L 456
Newcastle Univ., M 419
Oxford Univ., A 148, 179; M 451; E 322, 386, 426; S 465; C 204, 469; R 517
Ringmer, M 419
Royal Belfast Academical Inst., A 159, 160; M 335; S 429, 464; C 238, 413, 432
Sacred Heart Coll., Droitwich

# Index

St Andrew's Univ., S 429
St Dunstans, A 144
St Clement Danes, M 350
St Paul's, A 115, 143, 145, 354, 445; E 458; S 444, C 361, 468–9
St Paul's Girls', L 401
St Peter's, York, M 363
Sheffield Univ., 327
Stanborough, M 450
Surrey Univ., E 386
Tottenham Technical College, L 197
Trinity, Edinburgh, M 364, 380
Wandsworth, A 165; M 363, 399
Warrington, M 450
Wellington, M 419
Westfield, Newcastle, L 423
Westminster, A 106, 148–9, 151; C 469
Whitgift, A 149; M 363, 381; E 425, 461
Winchester, M 450; E 461
Worcester Technical College, E 425
Worth, A 151; M 380; E 385
Schreck, C 467
Schubert, B., L 402; R 501
Schulze, M., R 501
Schwaiger, G., R 549
Schwarz, E., R 514
Schwarzenberger, I., C 293, 433, 448–9; R 549–50, 555
Schwende, C., R 545
Scotland, B., A 144; C 272
Scott, C., A 168; C 469; R 494
Scott, D., A 149; M 243; S 236, 249, 250, 268, 269, 290, 308, 342, 359, 408; C 238, 253, 312, 327, 331; R 495, 519–20, 522, 543
Scott, G., M 350, 365, 398, 438; E 339; R 495, 542
Scott, I.., A 112, 141
Screech, B. M., L 150; R 484, 499, 502, 536, 539
Scriven, R., R 527
Scrivenor, Mrs J., A 110, 477
Scuri, M 439; C 416; R 548
Seaman, D., **448**; A 108, 146; M *1975–81*; C 410; R 492, 496–7
Seager, S., A 197
Sediva, M., R 549
Sedols, R., E 404; R 140
Sée, L., R 551

Seeman, A., R 543
Segda, Maj. W., A 161
Sekunda, E., S 373; C 415, 417
Seligman, E., A 474; S 203; R 481–2, 490, 509
Sellick, Mrs, R 505
Sennecka, E 305; C 315; R 513
Senser, C 435
Sepsin, C 208–9
Seregi, O., R 555
Seruya, A 148
Seton, B. L., R 527
Sewell, T., L 456
Seymour, J. A., A 475; S 250
Seymour, W., A 286
Shaban, A., A 145; E 425; C 432; R 515–6
Shackwell, J., R 152
Shafar, A., S 429
Shalit, D. M., R 483, 519, 522
Shamshutdinov, R 557
Shapland, D., E 199; R 528
Sharp, Mrs G., R 152
Sharp, R., E 247
Shaw, C., E 441, 443; R 516
Shaw, J., 88; E 181; C 207; R 510
Sheen, G. M., B 57, 60, 62–3; A 120, 147, 476; L 178, 301, 303, 377; C 377; R 484, 485, 486, 500, 501, 502, 503, 507, 525, 537, 539, 545, 549
Shelley, C 435
Shepherd, J., A 148; M 451
Shepherd, E. D. A., R 527
Shepherd, D., R 521
Shewring, J., M 195; S 185
Sherriff, Sq-Ldr F. G., R 491, 509, 521, 531–2
Shields, F., L 217; C 223; R 534, 536
Shimizu, C 190
Shipston, J., *see* Pienne, Mrs J.
Siddall, J., A 135
Sidiak, V., S 269, 445; C 315, 333, 473; R 554
Sidorova, V., L 440; C 344, 393, 417, 433, 448; R 550, 555
Siffels, M 335, 349, 364; R 493, 497
Signy, Dr A. G., **240**; A 91, 97, 121, 175, 281, 385, 477
Sigrist, C., A 145; E 305, 339, 462; C 331
Silvey, A., E 304, 321, 323; R 515

Simey, C. S. A., R 491, 494
Simmonds, Prof. A., A 81, 148, 162, 165, 175, 186, 250
Simmonds, Mrs F., R 504
Simmons, Lady, A 76, 215, 474, 477
Simo, B., R 545
Simon, E., C 412, 433; R 546
Simoncelli, C 311
Simonov, P., R 556
Simpson, A., L 336; R 508, 534
Simpson, Maj. D., R 154, 532
Simpson, E., L 282–4, 300; R 504–7
Simpson, J., A 148, 318; E 249
Simpson, Flt Lt R., R 533
Simpson, S., R 507
Single, I., 88, 213, 314; A 149, 150, 400; M *1965–78*; E *1965–8*, 265, 323, 357; C *1965–8*, *1969–75*; R 491–3, 495–6, 511, 515–6, 536, 540, 543
Single, Mrs J., L *1972–5*, 424; R 501, 504; *see also* Bullmore, J.
Sissikin, Y., R 547
Skapska, D., L 384; C 417, 433; R 501
Skelton, L., M 363; R 497
Skladanowska, Mrs, L 353; R 501
Skogh, J., E 219
Slabochova, C., R 549
Slade, G. E. R., R 527
Slade, M., A 12, 108, 111, 144; S *1973–81*; C *1974–81*; R 519, 520–6, 537, 540, 543
Slingsby-Bethel, Eve, R 483
Smalley, M., R 500
Smallwood, J., R 521, 527
Smirnov, M 439; C 344, 416, 449, 470; R 548
Smith, Alistair, 280; A 145; M 280; E 305
Smith, A. M., R 495
Smith, Arthur R., A 77, 120; C 147; R 491, 492, 494, 542
Smith, Mrs C., L 401; C 414; R 534; *see also* Wotherspoon, C.
Smith, G. H., A 140; R 140
Smith, Helen, C 246, 414, 433; R 546
Smith, John A., M 451; S 445, 464
Smith, J. E. S., A 401; C 392
Smith, Mrs K., R 140
Smith, K. A., R 528
Smith, Lewis, 411; A 401; M 380; S 253, 327; C 411, 413, 415–6, 535
Smith, S., R 130, 525

Smith, T., A 146; M 363, 364, 451; R 495–6
Smoliakov, E 265
Snell, P., R 535
Snelling, D., R 525
Sobszac, F., R 521
Soille, F., R 511
Solly, B. N., A 474; R 503
Somerville, M., A 7, 78, 107, 150, 474–5, 477; R 484, 499, 501, 503
Somodi, M 439
Somos, Prof., A 267
Soumagne, T., M 350, 365, 381, 421, 438, 454; C 470; R 493, 540
Southcombe, R., 233; A 11, 90, 154, 156, 477, 543
Southern, Y., A 138
Spahr, P., R 525
Spallino, A., R 547
Sparaciari, C 448; R 556
Speciale, P., R 547
Spiers, T., M 363
Spink, Mrs P., A 156
Spires, E., L 353
Spofforth, I., A 11, 88; E 200, 219; R 511–2
Spong, Mrs J. L., A 498; *see also* Hall, M.
Sproul-Bolton, Lt Cdr R. St C., R 484, 485, 514–5, 532
Squires, G., A 152
Stafford, M., B 56; A 149; R 484, 485, 499, 500, 501, 502, 503, 525, 539
Stafford, P., M 242; S 308
Stafford-Bull, G., S 341; R 516
Stahl, C., C 448; R 550
Staines, K., A 149–50; C 223; R 494, 522, 536
Stamanne, F., L 422; R 507
Stanbury, J., 293, 448; A 144, 464; M 280, 299; E *1969–73*, *1974–81*; C 271, 292, *1976–9*, 470, 471; R 152, 488, 496, 511–2, 514–6, 526, 543
Stanbury, K., R 483, 502, 503
Stangroom, J., A 132; R 132
Stankovich, V., M 279; C 394; R 547
Stanley, G., A 141
Stanley, P., M 450; S 464; R 523
Stanley, Rfn R., R 532
Stansfield, J., A 130; R 130
Staples, R., L 216; R 507

# Index

Stark, F., R 492
Starzynski, M., L 454–5; R 501
Stasse, R., R 551
Steele, M., 82; A 151; E 199, 200, 202, 218, 219; R 515
Steele, Sq Ldr R. J., A 476
Steen, I., A 137
Stefanek, C 448
Steiner, H., E 285
Steinfort, U., R 539
Stemmerick, M 349; R 497
Stenholm, A. H., R 515
Stenholm, C., A 150
Stenning, A. H., R 535
Stephton, J., A 476
Stern, C. M. M., R 529
Stern, J., A 509
Stevenson, D., R 496
Steventon, J., A 144; E *1975–81*; S 341; C *1975–81*; R 512, 515–6, 529
Stewart, J., R 534
Stewart, K. A., R 527
Stewart, Mrs Jennifer, C 330
Stewart, P., **391**; A 158, 170; C 313, 346, 446
Stewart, R. J. P., R 521
Stobbs, D., A 130
Stonehouse, P., L 401, 440, 456; R 160
Stoodley, S., M 450; S 444; R 496–7, 523
Storey, I., R 142
Storme, P., S 343, 359; R 520
Storry, K., L 232, 245–7, 261, 262, 282; C 276; R 499, 504
Strachan, L., A 148; L 456; R 506
Strattmann, S 408; R 520
Straus, M., A 148; S 186, 203, 252; R 485, 520–1, 542
Streater, M., S 308, 342, 359; R 522–3
Stretch, M., L 440
Stricker, C 238
Stringer, D. D., A 150; R 520, 522
Stroka, P., S 268; R 521
Strukel, S., R 549
Strzalka, E 427, 458–9
Stubberfield, Sgt F., R 532
Stubbs, J. M., R 529
Such, D., R 496
Suchanecki, F., E 355–6, 405, 407, 427; R 513
Sullivan, C 361

Sullivan, Prof. D., **272**; A 143, 150
Sundfelt, E 219
Sutton, R., R 490, 491
Sveshnikov, G., M 317; R 547
Swancott, Cpl A., R 532
Swanson, J., A 129; L 259, 283; C 271; R 130, 504
Swanton, K., R 539
Swinnerton, R., M 399, 421, 451–2; R 496
Swinney, A., L 423; C 469
Swornowski, L., E 427, 458; R 552
Szalontay, R 555
Szerences, J., R 557
Szolnoki, E., R 555
Szabo, M 336; R 557
Szeja, C 295
Szekely, C 470; R 552
Szepesi, E 324; C 333
Szlichcinsky, K., E 321
Szocs, L 455; C 433; R 556
Szolnoki, C 417

Tackenstrom, M 420, 436
Tainturier, G., R 551
Tait, A., M 363, 380; R 132, 496
Tait, G. W., R 529
Tait, J. W. U., **49**
Taitis, R 555
Talkington, G., R 522
Talvard, B., C 224, 314, 332, 361; R 547–8, 556
Tanner, F., A 153, 421, 426, 441, 461; R 154, 495
Tapley, J., 165
Tappin, Capt J., R 532
Tapprogge, G., E 198–9
Tarran, P., E 305, 324, 338, 355, 406, 426; C 344; R 516
Tarzoni, L 197
Tassart, Prof. E., A 87, 133
Tassinari, E 201
Tatham, C., R 547, 551
Tatrallyay, G., A 150; E 322, 356–7
Tayler, C., A 172
Tayler, P., A 153, 172; E 441, 461; R 515–6
Taylor, A., **233, 326**; A 134, 136; S *1970–76*; C 255, 331, 362; R 137, 519, 522, 537, 546
Taylor, L., R 496

Taylor, Lynne, A 134, 136, 137; L 354, 368, 423; C 344, 360, 412; R 137, 504, 506, 537
Taylor, Mrs P., A 12; R 503
Taylor, SO Z., R 532
Tchij, Y., R 548
Teague, Corpl R., R 514
Teague, QMSI W., R 532
Teasdale, L., R 501, 503, 505
Teintenier, C 361; R 536
Teisseire, M 436
Telm, M 299
Teranek, C 376
Terqueux, C 205
Tersytyansyky, E., R 553
Testoni, P., E 264, 321; C 292
Tetlow, A., A 107; L 366; R 505
Theseira, R., C 272
Theuerkauff, J., S 185–6; C 225; R 520
Thiry, Y., R 501
Thomas, C., S 127
Thomas, Mrs J., R 503
Thomas, T., M 451
Thompson, A., M 363; R 497
Thompson, Lt Cdr A. R. V., A 476
Thompson, B., A 136
Thompson, G., A 152; M 299, 350, 380; S 308; C 313, 330; R 495–6, 528
Thompson, J., A 136; M 421
Thompson, K., C 313; R 160
Thompson, M. W., A 136; M *1973–81*; C 391, 330, 392; R 495–6, 528, 538
Thompson, Sgt R. A. C., **165**; R 531
Thompson, Mrs R., A 80, 84
Thompson, T., R 152
Thompson, W., A 80, 137
Thorn, J., A 138; S 325
Thorn, N., R 496
Thorne, Dr G., A 115, 119, 141, 477; R 138, 141
Thornton, J., L 422–3; R 505–6
Thornton, M., M 399; E 403; R 495, 516
Thurley, Mrs E., L 455–6; R 500, 536; *see also* Wood, E.
Thurlow, B., R 525
Tienth, C., R 522; *see also* Trent, C.
Tiller, Prof. R., **82**; A 170; C 392; R 154, 533
Tilles, David, M 299; R 139
Tilling, M., A 137
Titchmarsh, J., A 146

Titheradge, D., A 165, 168, 405; S 253, 429; C 376; R 522, 536
Tiu, M., C 187, 205, 416, 449; R 556
Tizard, H., S 250; R 523
Tocqueboeuf, G., R 557
Todorov, R 557
Toland, G., E 386; R 541
Tolland, C., **165**; A 86, 161, 163–4, 166, 168, 272, 476–7; R 505, 534, 541
Toller, S., A 151; L 178, 217, 231, 283, 353; C 223; R 504
Tom, L., R 551
Tom, M., R 514
Tomlin, H. C., R 522
Tomlinson, J., E 404; R 132, 537
Tomlinson, J. W. G., A 151; M 175; E 183, 198; R 152, 515–6
Tomlinson, W., A 127
Tonges, W., M 349, 379; R 497
Tonks, G., M 350; L 366
Tooley, M., R 130
Took, L. F., R 529
Torday, J., A 130
Torok, E 357
'Total Abstainer', B 62; A 79
Torre, de la, C 332
Toshiman, S., R 493
Touche, D. la, A 138
Tourmentin, C., A 145; S 359; R 523
Tovey, Mrs. P., A 136; L 383; R 505, 538
Townsend, A 153; E 220
Trachez, T., L 283
Tredgold, Dr R., A 77, 105, 121, 147, 474, 476; S 185, 236, 408; R 491, 519, 520, 521, 525, 542
Trent, C. (*formerly* Tienth, *q.v.*), A 150; R 494, 522
Trevis, Mr, B 25
Trinder, O. G., **49**; A 126, 147; R 482, 483, 494, 511, 514, 518, 519, 520
Trinquet, P., C 361, 392, 434, 448; R 550, 555
Triptree, S., M 450
Troiano, J., **448**; A 148; M 379, 380, 399, 419, 451, 453–4; E 425, 441, 462; C 410, 432; R 495–6, 516, 526, 536
Trost, R., E 248, 263–4, 288; C 315; R 512, 551
Trottein, S 409
Trumper, C., R 494
Tsagareva, C 435; R 555

# Index

Tshij, C 332
Tsuruta, K., C 227
Tulloch, A., L 319, 320, 337; R 505–8
Turcan, C 433
Tuck, S., A 132
Tupper, G. W., R 514
Turner, C., R 515
Turner, Desmond, A 150; E 304, 385; R 515
Turner, D. R. (Bob), **158**; A 12, 157; E 183, 200, 235, 307, 323, 340, *1975–8*; S 237; C 188, *1967–72*, 330, 347, 361, 376, 411–2, 431
Turner, H., R 490
Turner, P., A 85, 154, 156, 212, 213, 229, 477
Turner, R. H., **233**; A 381; R 140–1, 538
Turner, S., **158**
Turner, Flt Lt W. H., R 520, 527, 532
Turney, W. J., R 521
Turquet, Dr P. M., B 61; A 76, 78, 106, 147, 474–5; R 483–4, 491–2, 494, 519, 521–2, 525
Turton, J., A 326
Twine, P., E 370; R 515
Twomey, H., **256**; A 115, 144; L 244, 246, 247, 260, 261; C 255; R 152, 499, 502, 504, 505, 506; *see also* Davenport, Mrs
Tyson, C. D., **448**; A 86, 139, 140, 411, 475, 477
Tyson, Mrs J., A 110, 139; L 243; C 253; R 140, 505
Tyson, J. F., **447**; A 10, 139, 144; M 243, 298, 316, 318, *1974–7*, 438, 451–2; E 247, 263, *1974–81*; C 313, 376, 412, 414, 415; R 140, 152, 495, 511, 515–6, 535, 538, 541
Tyson, P., A 140

Uffindell, R., R 529
Uff, S., L 384, 401, 439; C 412; *see also* Harris, Mrs
Underwood, John, A 144; R 528
Upton, P., A 80, 152
Urbanska, Mrs, C 224; R 501
Urquhart, A., A 166
Usher, Col C. M., A 161, 163, 167, 168

Vaccaroni, D., L 422; C 410, 433, 435; R 550, 556

Vadaszffy, Z., A 144, 446, 467; R 170
Väggo, E 407; C 435
Valentin, O., M 436, 438; R 497
Valetov, E 321–2; R 513
van Aspern, S 327
van Baelen, J., R 520
van Beukelen, W., A 123, 477; R 152
van Beukelen, Mrs A., A 115, 477
Van Damme, M., R 547
van Holhema, Miss, R 500
van Hollebecke, C 187
van Houdt, P., R 492
Van der Meer, H. J., R 520
van der Ostende, S 359
Van der Voodt, J.-P., E 285; C 293
Vane, G., R 528
van Eyck, M.-P., L 259–60; R 507
van Hilten, M 349
van Oeveren, Prof. R., **293**; A 130, 260, 292
van Oosten, G., R 501
van Strydonck de Burkel, Gen., **51**
Vardi, M., R 493
Varga, K., R 557
Varille, A., E 248, 264, 304; C 254; R 513
Varley, Jackie, C 253
Varley, Janet, **233**; A 316; L 217, 230, 231, 246; C 204, 254; R 137, 504–5, 538
Vaselli, M 195; R 492
Vatter, J., M 299; R 497
Vauchelle, G., R 541
Veale, L., **90**; A 11, 89, 94, 96, 107, 122, 126–8, 132, 325–6, 475, 477
Veanes, C 224
Vecchioni, R 557
Venables, M. A. B., R 482, 500, 502, 503, 549
Verbrackel, E 442
Verbrugge, C 205
Verderber, R., R 547
Verebes, Dr E. M., R 519, 520, 521
Vereker, G., R 509
Verhalle, A., R 492
Verne, J., L 401; R 505, 508
Verschraegen, C 344
Verseli, A 147
Vickerage, R 504
Vickers-Miles, A., R 528
Vickery, M., E 181; R 512
Vicol, M., R 549
Villing, E., L 283–4; R 507

Vino, S., E 370
Vinokurov, C 315
Viret, D., L 383; R 507
Visholm, M., M 380, 399; S 359; R 496-7
Volkmann, J., S 430; R 520
Volland, Prof. E. G., A 87
Volochin, A., R 556
Vonen, E 406, 443, 463; R 512
von Essen, C., R 552 E 182, 248, 304, 322, 340; C 227, 315, 333, 378
von Kos, J., R 511, 525
von Kriegstein, M 212
Vorschakina, R 556
Vuille, M 399

Waddington, M. W., R 527, 528
Waddelow, B., 213; M 258, 279; S 204, 221, 236, 250, 269; C 224; R 491, 495-7, 522-3
Waddleton, N., A 142, 150
Wade, D., M 299, 317; R 496
Wade, J., A 145; S 465
Wake, Sgt A., R 534
Wakeford, D. C., R 527
Waldman, C., 293; A 144; M *1969-73, 1974-9*, 452; C 292, 331, 412; R 495-6, 533, 538
Walker, Alice B., R 498, 500
Walker, C. A., R 498
Walker, C., R 130
Walker, Lt C. C., R 529, 532, 533
Walker, C. D., R 535
Walker, D., A 138
Walker, M., R 141, 156
Walker, N., L 456; R 505
Walker, S., R 140
Wall, A., S 249
Wall, Sqd Ldr L., C 222, 238, 255; R 532, 533
Wallace, B., R 132
Wallett, C., L 284; R 500
Walsh, T., R 154
Walters, M., A 157
Wand-Tetley, Brig T. H., A 474
Waples, C 433
Warburn, Flg Off J., E 356, 404, 425, 426, 461-2; C 447; R 533
Ward, C., A 138; M *1976-81*; C 446, 469; R 495-6, 526, 538
Ward, E., L 384

Ward, M. A. T., R 152, 529
Ward, Shiela, 88; L 197, 217, 232; R 504-5
Ward, Cpl W. L., R 534
Wardell-Yerburgh, Mrs J., **177, 211,** 240, 302; A 121; L 197, 216-8, 230-1, 244-6, 260-2, 301-4; C 208, 210, 226, 240, 273-4, 276, 291, 295, 311, 314-5; R 487-8, 499, 501-3, 539, 546; *see also* Cathie, J. *and* Cooksey, Mrs
Wardle, P. G., R 521
Ware, QMSI G. E., R 532
Warnford-Davis, P., R 528
Warner, C. M., S 237; R 526
Warre, R. P., R 528
Wasilewski, S., A 148, 150; S 310, 359, 373, 429; C 313, 412, 522, 540
Wasley, B., A 144; M 280, 298; R 152, 493, 495, 536-7, 543
Waters, M., R 505-7
Watkins, N., A 116, 138, 477; R 139
Watkins, R. S., R 515, 522, 536
Watkinson, Cpl D. R., R 532
Watson, A. G., **165**
Watson, F., R 527
Watterson, Flt Off. M., R 533, 534
Watts, E. R., A 150; R 539
Watts, G., A 128, 142, 146; M 363
Watts-Tobin, Mrs M.-A., A 134; L 151, 176, 178, 232; R 503, 536; *see also* Pritchard, M. A.
Webb, A. J., M 363, 380, 399; C 361; R 529
Webb, Chris, S 359, 372; C 365; R 528
Webb, P., R 525, 528
Webb, S. J. S., C 361; R 529
Webb, W. H. A., R 525
Webber, P., R 503, 539
Webster, Prof. M., A 102, 154, 170, 370; R 170
Weder, U., L 454-5; R 507
Wedge, P., **448**; A 134, 136; M *1972-9*, 451-3; C 344-6, 360, 397; R 495-6, 526
Weeks, R. J., R 527
Weglinski, P., E 404; R 540
Weir, A. J. A., R 527
Weir, A. N. C., R 514
Weissgerber, S 289, 308
Weekes, I., R 503
Weeks, Maj. O. C., A 78, 84, 475

Weisbach, S., R 556
Wellington, C. T., R 494
Whitney-Smith, C. A., R 492
Wellman, C 239
Wells, V. H., R 528
Wendon, U. L., A 148; R 491, 492, 493, 494, 515, 519, 521, 522, 525, 527, 542, 536, 539
Weniger, G., **369**; L 368; R 501
Wertheim, R. C., R 514
Wessel, F., C 239, 257, 276, 314; R 547, 556
West, H., A 147, 148, 157; E *1970–9*, 457; C 392, 412, 431; R 152, 511–2, 537–8, 540
West, M., **256**, **332**; A 144; M 229; E 218, 247, 263, *1972–6*; C 190, 238, 255, 271; R 515–6, 528–9, 538
West, P., A 145; S 409, 430, 444, 464–6; C 446, 468; R 437, 521–3
Westbrook, P., S 444; C 471
Western, Mrs B., A 126, 129, 130
Western, B., A 126, 129, 130
Westgate, M., A 160, 401, 412
Whalberg, A., R 556
Wheelband, Mrs M., L 456; R 542; see also Worster, M.
Wheeler, L., L 260; R 505
Wheeler, R., R 497
Wheelhouse, B. P., A 112, 142
Wheelock, Capt. R., R 534
Wherrett, D., S 203; R 496–7, 516, 523
Whitaker, J., A 132
Whitcombe, K., L 215; R 529
Whitcher, Mrs H., L 301; R 504
White, C., **293**; A 145; E 285, 304, 305, 321, 426–7; C 312; R 515–6
White, R., R 555
Whitehead, B. J., R 494
Whitehead, G., A 130
Whitehead, P., L 129, 423, 455–6; R 130, 504, 506, 508
Whitehouse, Maj. A. L., R 510
Whitehouse, J., R 138
Whitehurst, C., A 129, 130, 135; L 260, 283, 319, 338, 369; C 254; R 130, 504, 506, 537
Whitehurst, P., E 355
Whitfield, E., A 148; L 440, 455–6; R 505
Whitney, J., L 423, 439–40; R 505

Whitney-Smith, C. A., R 494, 514, 525
Whitta, P., R 539
Whittle, R., R 495
Whitworth, J., E 426; R 137
Whyte, Mrs N., A 159
Wicks, H., R 515
Wickens, C., E 406
Wickham, A., R 516
Widera, C 330
Wiech, E 356, 358; C 331, 334, 344; R 513, 557
Wiedmaier, C 210
Wierzbicki, S 268
Wiggins, D., R 495
Wigzell, B., A 186, 239; E 234
Wilcox, E., A 78
Wild, L 454
Wiles, G., **90**, **233**; A 90, 110, 139–40, 166, 477; M 194, 214, 229, 242, 243, 280, 298, 380; E 285; S 203, 236–7, 253, 268, 289, 308, 342, 359, 429, 444, 465; C *1965–70*, 313, 345–7, 392, 415–6, 431, 469; R 494–5, 526, 535–8, 541
Williams, B., **274**, **302**; A 162, 163, 171; L 217, 260, 282, 284, 304; C 274, 295; R 154, 499, 504, 534, 537, 542
Williams, C. R., A 476
Williams, E., R 500, 501, 502
Williams, G., R 525
Williams, Prof. Gomer, **272**; A 151, 169–70, 271–2
Williams, Julian, E 385
Williams, P. G., R 494, 515
Williams, S., R 500
Williams, Sharon, A 157; L 260; C 313; R 156
Willett, T., S 127
Willis, C., R 539
Willoughby, J., R 521
Willoughby, Maj. R. M. P., B 53; A 87, 474; R 490–1, 518, 531
Willslade, R., R 495
Wilmot-Sitwell, P., R 515, 528
Wilson, A. B., A 162; L 178, 196, 197; C 187; R 506–7, 534
Wilson, B. R., R 538
Wilson, C., R 132
Wilson, C. A., S 185, 408; R 518
Wilson, E., E 198; C 205, 223
Wilson, F., A 141; L 384, 423, 439–40; R 505–6

Wilson, G. B., A 148; S 185, 204, 237; R 494, 519, 522
Wilson, L. A., R 527–8
Wilson, K. M., R 497
Wilson, P. O. K., R 519
Wilson, Mr and Mrs J., A 168
Wilson, Mark R., A 160; S 429; C 432; R 529
Wilson, Muriel, L 401, C 223
Wilson, R. G., **206**; E 183, 198, 219; S 203; C 207, 209, 223; R 515, 535, 541
Wilson, LCpl R., R 534
Wilson, Mrs S., R 486
Wilson, T., M 419; E 404
Wilson, W., A 299
Winder, J., R 491, 494
Windram, V., A 145; L 301, 319, 353; R 152, 499, 504–6
Winrow-Campbell, S., R 496
Winter, J., R 545
Winton, N., A 153, 544
Winton, R. C., **86**; B 62, 66, 67; A 11, 12, 79, 92, 94, 97, 104, 112, 120, 142, 239, 474–5, 477, 544; R 514
Wischeidt, P., A 445; S 221, 250, 267–8, 309, 327, 343; C 254, 270, 294; R 521, 540
Wishart, T., **256**; A 144; M 280; S 250, 252, 253, 267, 289, 291, 430; C 255, 271, 294; R 496, 519, 522–3, 537, 541
Wisscher, F. de, S 343; R 520
Witchell, J., R 499, 501, 502
With, M., R 549
Wither, B., C 347
Witzak, M., S 250–1, 268; R 521
Wodke, S 445; C 391, 471
Woehler, W., S 185; R 520
Wojciechowski, J., R 556
Wojciechowski, Z., **117**; A 117, 433, 461, 467, 469; M 351, 398, 420–21, 436, 452; R 493–4, 536, 540
Wojtczak, L 454
Wolfgarten, W., M 229; R 493
Wolinetz, E 340
Wolthius, T., L 384; R 501
Wong, L., C 274; R 546
Wood, E., **393**; A 108, 141, 150; L *1973–80*; C *1974–9*; R 499, 500, 502–3, 506–8, 536, 541, 546; *see also* Thurley, Mrs

Wood, G., A 148; L 424; R 500, 503, 505
Wood, L., A 131
Wood, Matthew, E 385, 403, 426, 441, 462; C 447; R 159, 525
Wood, R., R 527
Wood, R. J., A 477
Wood, T., A 141
Woodall, A., A 148; E 425–6
Woodfine, Mrs D., A 152
Woodhouse, K., L 455; R 506
Wooding, S., A 151; M 214, *1969–75*, 380; E 247; C 222; R 492–3, 495, 515, 526, 538
Woodroff, P., R 545
Woods, J., M 399, 451; E 462; R 495, 497
Woolfoot, S Sgt J., R 530
Worster, M., L 337, 368; R 505, 538; *see also* Wheelband, Mrs
Worthington, I., E 324, 338; R 515
Wotherspoon, C., A 162; L 259–60, 301, 401; R 504, 525; *see also* Smith, Mrs C.
Woyda, W., M 336; C 208, 276; R 492, 548
Wren, Prof. K., **272**; A 108, 170, 244, 272
Wrigglesworth, S., **293, 302, 314, 393**; A 12, 111, 132, 150; L *1969–81*; C *1970–81*; R 132, 488–9, 499, 500–8, 525, 546
Wright, C., A 12
Wright, D., D 528
Wright, D. E., R 522
Wright, Mrs E., A 166
Wright, G. F., R 521, 525
Wright, M., **420**; M 363, 419, 438; E 403; S 409; R 496–7, 523, 529
Wrigley, Mrs B., **82**; A 134
Wrzesien, C. G., A 141
Wurz, E 265
Wyatt, B., R 505
Wyatt, SMI G. A. F., A 171; S 389; R 531–2
Wysoczanska, B., C 362, 433; R 550

Yassir, T., A 145; S 464; R 142, 523, 529
Yates, B., R 139
Yates, J., **256, 262, 293**; A 135; L 215–6, 230–1, 244, 247, 259–62, 282–3, 300, 303, 318, 320; C 238, 253, 255,

271, 292, 331; R 499, 504, 506–7, 538
Yeomans, Mrs S., L 217, 232; *see also* Brick, S.
Yogi, C 227
Young, C., S 429
Young, D. A., R 529
Young, J., L 216, 283; R 504–5
Young, P., E *1974–81*; C 410–1, 431; R 516, 523
Younghusband, Sir Francis, B 18, 45
Youngs, S., **274**; A 144, 162; L 217, 230, 232, 246, 247, 301, 319, 320; C 270, 273–4, 313, 346; R 499, 506, 534, 539, 541, 546; *see also* Lewis, Mrs
Yunichenko, S., R 556

Zaaloff, Prof., **133**; A 133–4, 204
Zabellina, A., L 245; R 549, 555
Zabielski, Prof. G., A 117, 149
Zablocki, V., R 557
Zablowsky, E 407
Zajitsky, E 266, 322; C 187, 205; R 556

Zakharian, E., R 557
Zakreszewski, E., R 130
Zakrewski, M., R 521
Zampini, R., M 194; E 181, 184, 249; R 543
Zanardi-Landi, Count Charles, A 527
Zapasnik, J., R 130
Zappelli, O., R 511, 551
Zarno, J., **393**; A 144, 150, 391, 392, 394, 417, 434; S 267, 289, 309, 310, 325, 327, 329, 334, 342, 343, 359, 360, 429, 430, 444–6, 448, 464; C 294, 395–6, 471; R 142, 519–20, 523, 537
Zawadzki, E 304
Zawalynski, C., A 166
Zerbib, R 557
Zeh, M., L 259
Zidaru, C 435
Zimmermann, F., E 285
Zitcer, C., A 144; S 359, 372, 376, 429, 444, 465, 521–3
Zolnowski, C 333